Cash Box
Pop Singles Charts,
1950-1993

Also by Pat Downey

Top 40 Music on Compact Disc, 1955-1981
Libraries Unlimited, 1994
P.O. Box 6633
Englewood, CO 80155-6633
1-800-237-6124

Pop Singles Charts
1950-1993

PAT DOWNEY

GEORGE ALBERT   FRANK HOFFMANN

1994

Libraries Unlimited, Inc.
Englewood, Colorado

LIBRARIES UNLIMITED, INC.
P.O. Box 6633
Englewood, CO 80155-6633

Project Editor: Stephen Haenel
Design and Layout: Alan Livingston

Library of Congress Cataloging-in-Publication Data

Downey, Pat.
    Cash box pop singles charts, 1950-1993 / Pat Downey, George Albert, Frank Hoffmann.
    x, 526 p. 17x25 cm.
    ISBN 1-56308-316-7 (cloth)
    1. Popular music--United States--Discography.   I. Albert, George.
II. Hoffmann, Frank W., 1949-   . III. Title.
ML156.4.P6D68   1994
016.78164'0973--dc20   94-30806
                                                       CIP
                                                       MN

Contents

Introduction

Cash Box has undergone three distinct phases of development since it began publication in 1941. During World War II it existed as a mimeographed tip sheet of two or three pages catering to distributors of coin-operated music and game machines. The publication's primary purpose was to inform and advise route owners and operators about trends relating to jukeboxes, pinball games, slot machines, and pool halls.

Following World War II, *Cash Box* played a pioneering role in the integration of the hardware end of the music business with sound recordings. Jukebox operators accounted for over 90 percent of all record purchases throughout the 1930s and 1940s; *Cash Box* endeavored to reflect this state of affairs in its record reviews and sales charts. News about nonmusic vending machines, however, continued to occupy a prominent position in the magazine.

The third phase of *Cash Box*'s history coincided with the substantial impact made by consumer buying habits upon the record industry, beginning in the early 1950s. In response, *Cash Box* redirected the bulk of its energies and news space to private sector impact points such as retail outlets and the mass media (radio, television, and motion pictures).

Today, *Cash Box*'s main audience is record company executives, booking agents, artists and musicians, talent agents and managers, music publishers, and music industry unions and organizations. It employs a standard trade weekly format, incorporating feature stories (devoted to major names and events in the music business), news briefs divided by genre headings (such as mainstream pop, country, rhythm and blues, jazz, inspirational/gospel), and record and concert reviews. George Albert, president and publisher of *Cash Box* (213-464-8241), considers the magazine's primary purpose to be one of "serving the music business at large by offering a commercial gauge of noteworthy contemporary trends."

To this day, charts hold a prominent place in each issue and *Cash Box* has long been regarded as having the best defined and most accurate charts in the business. *Cash Box*'s leadership role in chart publishing should render this authorized publication an invaluable source for students, scholars, educators, librarians, retailers, radio and television programmers, record collectors, and hobbyists concerned with popular music.

Though *Cash Box* has charted records as far back as 1942, its early years were determined to be inappropriate to the scope of this volume. During the 1940s the charts were organized around the song rather than the artist in much the same manner as the long-running radio and television program *Your Hit Parade*, such that all versions of a song were given equal billing. It was not until March 25, 1950, that the performer or performers of a given song were designated in the *Cash Box* charts. This date, therefore, was chosen as the logical starting point for this compilation, which extends to songs that entered the *Cash Box* pop charts through the end of 1993. For purposes of completeness, all songs on the *Cash Box* pop chart at the end of 1993 were tracked into 1994 to clearly establish the total number of weeks charted.

The *Cash Box* singles charts have evolved considerably over the period covered in this compilation to reflect the state of the industry at various times. As an example, the *Cash Box* charts in the '50s and '60s awarded equal chart positions to multiple artists who recorded the same song. This was valid at the time because, in that era, the emphasis in the industry was on the popularity of a given song rather than the artist involved. Further evidence of evolution can be seen by examining the number of positions charted over the years. In 1950 there were only 10 positions on the pop charts whereas today there are 100.

For historical purposes, here is a listing of the *Cash Box* chart titles used in this publication:

March 25, 1950-July 28, 1956	Nation's Top 10 Juke Box Tunes
August 4, 1956-April 6, 1957	Top 50 Best Selling Records
April 13, 1957-June 14, 1958	Top 60
June 21, 1958-September 6, 1958	Top 75
September 13, 1958-October 14, 1972	Top 100
October 21, 1972-July 6, 1991	Top 100 Singles
July 31, 1991-current	Top 100 Pop Singles

In closing, it should be noted that while the *Cash Box* singles charts present a fascinating and fairly accurate barometer of the popularity of a song at a given point in time, such a source falls short as a means of comparing songs from different time periods. The market conditions for popular music tend to fluctuate almost as greatly as the public's taste. For example, Boston's "More Than A Feeling," which reached only number four on the singles charts, was largely responsible for selling some 10 million record albums and remains an FM radio staple to this day. Many other songs, like "Brandy" by Looking Glass, reached number one but generated far less sales and radio play. So, as you can see, one must exercise caution in drawing too many conclusions from this form of measurement.

Frank Hoffmann

Key to Listings

Record company name and individual record number

Artist

Debut Date	Peak Pos	Wks Chr	ARTIST/Song Title	Label & Number
			PETER GABRIEL	
5/07/77	#81	6	Solsbury Hill	Atco 7079
8/02/80	#60	12	Games Without Frontiers	Mercury 76063
10/30/82	#33	18	Shock The Monkey	Geffen 29883
5/10/86	#1	22	Sledgehammer	Geffen 28718
8/30/86	#24	14	In Your Eyes	Geffen 28622
11/29/86	#8	24	Big Time	Geffen 28503
4/04/87	#69	6	Don't Give Up*	Geffen 28463
6/03/89	#39	13	In Your Eyes	WTG 68936
10/10/92	#46	15	Digging In The Dirt	Geffen 19136
12/26/92	#32	17	Steam	Geffen 19145
			*released as by PETER GABRIEL/KATE BUSH	
			GABRIEL and THE ANGELS	
10/27/62	#44	14	That's Life (That's Tough)	Swan 4118
			GABRIELLE	
10/30/93	#27	32	Dreams	Go! Discs 857141
			MEL GADSON	
5/14/60	#50	9	Comin' Down With Love	Big Top 3034
			GAINORS	
10/11/58	#39	3	The Secret	Cameo 151
			SUNNY GALE	
3/08/52	#2	3	Wheel Of Fortune	Derby 787
7/31/54	#5	7	Goodnight Sweetheart, Goodnight	RCA 5746
10/23/54	#9	4	Smile	RCA 5836
			MARVIN GAYE	
5/02/64	#27	9	Once Upon A Time/	Motown 1057
5/09/64	#25	12	What's The Matter With You Baby	Motown 1057

Additional information

/ indicates flip side of single also charted

Song title

Number of weeks song remained on Cash Box charts

Highest position reached on Cash Box charts

Date song entered Cash Box charts

A

Debut Date	Peak Pos	Wks Chr	**ARTIST**/Song Title	Label & Number
			ABACO DREAM	
9/06/69	#58	7	Life And Death In G & A	A&M 1081
			ABBA	
5/25/74	#10	14	Waterloo	Atlantic 3035
9/14/74	#37	9	Honey, Honey	Atlantic 3209
8/16/75	#12	18	SOS	Atlantic 3265
2/21/76	#19	16	I Do, I Do, I Do, I Do, I Do	Atlantic 3310
5/29/76	#36	15	Mamma Mia	Atlantic 3315
8/28/76	#10	19	Fernando	Atlantic 3346
12/11/76	#1	24	Dancing Queen	Atlantic 3372
5/14/77	#11	17	Knowing Me, Knowing You	Atlantic 3387
10/15/77	#63	8	Money, Money, Money	Atlantic 3434
12/24/77	#16	18	The Name Of The Game	Atlantic 3449
4/22/78	#5	19	Take A Chance On Me	Atlantic 3457
5/19/79	#16	15	Does Your Mother Know	Atlantic 3574
9/01/79	#85	3	Voulez-Vous/	Atlantic 3609
9/15/79	#76	6	Angel Eyes	Atlantic 3609
11/10/79	#36	14	Chiquitita	Atlantic 3629
11/22/80	#11	11	The Winner Takes It All	Atlantic 3776
4/04/81	#64	8	Super Trouper	Atlantic 3806
1/16/82	#1	18	When All Is Said And Done	Atlantic 3889
5/08/82	#81	4	The Visitors	Atlantic 4031
			ABBEY TAVERN SINGERS	
9/10/66	#68	5	Off To Dublin In The Green	HBR 498
			BILLY ABBOTT and THE JEWELS	
7/13/63	#66	9	Groovy Baby	Parkway 874
			GREGORY ABBOTT	
10/18/86	#1	25	Shake You Down	Columbia 06191
2/21/87	#55	10	I Got The Feelin' (It's Over)	Columbia 06632
			ABC	
9/11/82	#9	24	The Look Of Love (Part 1)	Mercury 76168
1/29/83	#24	16	Poison Arrow	Mercury 810340
8/24/85	#10	24	Be Near Me	Mercury 880626
1/18/86	#23	17	(How To Be A) Millionaire	Mercury 884382
5/17/86	#85	5	Vanity Kills	Mercury 884714
7/04/87	#8	21	When Smokey Sings	Mercury 888604
			PAULA ABDUL	
6/25/88	#43	16	Knocked Out	Virgin 99329
10/22/88	#75	7	(It's Just) The Way That You Love Me	Virgin 99282
12/03/88	#1	22	Straight Up	Virgin 99256
3/11/89	#2	23	Forever Your Girl	Virgin 99230
6/24/89	#1	23	Coldhearted	Virgin 99196
9/23/89	#1	22	(It's Just) The Way That You Love Me	Virgin 99282
12/23/89	#1	19	Opposites Attract	Virgin 99168
5/11/91	#1	22	Rush Rush	Virgin 98828
7/20/91	#1	19	The Promise Of A New Day	Virgin 98752
10/19/91	#3	27	Blowing Kisses In The Wind	Captive 98683
1/18/92	#7	21	Vibeology	Captive 98737
4/04/92	#12	21	Will You Marry Me?	Captive 98584
			AB LOGIC	
8/08/92	#52	11	The Hitman	Interscope 98506
			ABRAHAM'S CHILDREN	
3/03/73	#78	3	Gypsy	Buddah 340
			ACCENTS	
1/03/59	#62	8	Wiggle, Wiggle	Brunswick 55100

Debut Date	Peak Pos	Wks Chr	ARTIST/Song Title	Label & Number
			AC/DC	
10/20/79	#57	8	Highway To Hell	Atlantic 3617
9/13/80	#42	18	You Shook Me All Night Long	Atlantic 3761
12/13/80	#39	18	Back In Black	Atlantic 3787
1/16/81	#61	9	Let's Get It Up	Atlantic 3894
12/08/90	#28	19	Money Talks	Atco 98881
7/17/93	#59	7	Big Gun	East West 98406
			ACE	
3/15/75	#1	15	How Long	Anchor 21000
8/02/75	#63	4	Rock & Roll Runaway	Anchor 21002
			JOHNNY ACE	
4/02/55	#7	5	Pledging My Love	Duke 136
			ACE OF BASE	
10/02/93	#3	38	All That She Wants	Arista 2614
			ACE SPECTRUM	
10/05/74	#84	4	Don't Send Nobody Else	Atlantic 3012
			BARBARA ACKLIN	
6/29/68	#16	15	Love Makes A Woman	Brunswick 55379
10/19/68	#40	6	From The Teacher To The Preacher*	Brunswick 55387
11/23/68	#55	5	Just Ain't No Love	Brunswick 55388
2/15/69	#52	5	Am I The Same Girl	Brunswick 55399
			*released as by GENE CHANDLER and BARBARA ACKLIN	
			ACT 1	
3/31/73	#99	1	Friends Or Lovers	Spring 132
			BRYAN ADAMS	
3/20/82	#79	5	Lonely Nights	A&M 2359
3/12/83	#18	18	Straight From The Heart	A&M 2536
6/11/83	#27	14	Cuts Like A Knife	A&M 2553
9/03/83	#29	14	This Time	A&M 2574
11/03/84	#4	21	Run To You	A&M 2686
2/02/85	#9	17	Somebody	A&M 2701
4/20/85	#1	20	Heaven	A&M 2729
6/29/85	#7	18	Summer Of '69	A&M 2739
9/14/85	#17	18	One Night Love Affair	A&M 2770
11/23/85	#14	17	It's Only Love*	A&M 2791
3/28/87	#6	17	Heat Of The Night	A&M 2921
6/13/87	#27	14	Hearts On Fire	A&M 2948
8/22/87	#32	12	Victims Of Love	A&M 2964
6/29/91	#1	25	(Everything I Do) I Do It For You	A&M 1567
9/14/91	#1	29	Can't Stop This Thing We Started	A&M 1576
12/21/91	#8	23	There Will Never Be Another Tonight	A&M 1588
3/14/92	#7	21	Thought I'd Died And Gone To Heaven	A&M 1592
8/01/92	#8	19	Do I Have To Say The Words	A&M 1611
10/30/93	#3	32	Please Forgive Me	A&M 0422
12/18/93	#1	24	All For Love**	A&M 0476
			*released as by BRYAN ADAMS/TINA TURNER	
			**released as by BRYAN ADAMS/ROD STEWART/STING	
			JOHNNY ADAMS	
6/28/69	#18	9	Reconsider Me	SSS International 770
10/11/69	#88	2	I Can't Be All Bad	SSS International 780
			OLETA ADAMS	
12/15/90	#10	27	Get Here	Fontana 878476
			CANNONBALL ADDERLY	
4/08/61	#41	8	African Waltz	Riverside 45457
2/02/63	#77	10	Jive Samba	Riverside 4541
12/31/66	#18	14	Mercy, Mercy, Mercy	Capitol 5798
4/08/67	#76	5	Why? (Am I Treated So Bad)	Capitol 5877
1/31/70	#93	2	Country Preacher	Capitol 2698
			ADDRISI BROTHERS	
6/20/59	#73	8	Cherry Stone	Del-Fi 4116
1/15/72	#15	14	We've Got To Get It On Again	Columbia 45521
6/10/72	#90	5	I Can Feel You	Columbia 45610
3/27/77	#18	18	Slow Dancin' Don't Turn Me On	Buddah 566
8/27/77	#85	5	Does She Do It Like She Dances	Buddah 579
11/26/77	#69	9	Never My Love	Buddah 587
8/11/79	#65	7	Ghost Dancer	Scotti Brothers 500

Debut Date	Peak Pos	Wks Chr	ARTIST/Song Title	Label & Number
			AD LIBS	
1/16/65	#10	11	Boy From New York City	Blue Cat 102
			ADVENTURES	
5/14/88	#83	3	Broken Land	Elektra 69414
			ADVENTURES OF STEVIE V	
7/28/90	#23	18	Dirty Cash (Money Talks)	Mercury 875802
			AEROSMITH	
10/06/73	#43	11	Dream On	Columbia 45894
6/07/75	#36	10	Sweet Emotion	Columbia 10155
1/03/76	#6	22	Dream On	Columbia 10278
6/05/76	#21	16	Last Child	Columbia 10359
10/16/76	#89	4	Home Tonight	Columbia 10407
11/20/76	#7	20	Walk This Way	Columbia 10449
4/23/77	#67	6	Back In The Saddle	Columbia 10516
10/15/77	#37	9	Draw The Line	Columbia 10637
3/18/78	#80	5	Kings And Queens	Columbia 10699
8/12/78	#20	13	Come Together	Columbia 10802
12/29/79	#91	5	Remember (Walking In The Sand)	Columbia 11181
10/03/87	#15	22	Dude (Looks Like A Lady)	Geffen 28240
1/30/88	#3	26	Angel	Geffen 28249
6/04/88	#23	19	Rag Doll	Geffen 27915
12/31/88	#82	6	Chip Away The Stone	Columbia 10880
9/02/89	#6	21	Love In An Elevator	Geffen 22845
11/25/89	#3	21	Janie's Got A Gun	Geffen 22727
3/17/90	#8	19	What It Takes	Geffen 19944
6/23/90	#19	15	The Other Side	Geffen 19927
4/10/93	#3	24	Livin' On The Edge	Geffen 19149
8/14/93	#11	32	Cryin'	Geffen 19256
12/18/93	#20	24	Amazing	Geffen 19264
			AFRIQUE	
6/16/73	#41	10	Soul Makossa	Mainstream 5542
			AFTERNOON DELIGHTS	
7/25/81	#31	18	General Hospi-Tale	MCA 51148
			AFTER 7	
4/07/90	#4	23	Ready Or Not	Virgin 98995
8/04/90	#7	24	Can't Stop	Virgin 98961
12/01/90	#15	20	Heat Of The Moment	Virgin 96553
6/22/91	#57	14	Nights Like This	Virgin 98798
8/22/92	#44	13	Kickin' It	Virgin 12594
11/14/92	#50	13	Baby I'm For Real/Natural High	Virgin 12623
			AFTER SHOCK	
5/11/91	#89	3	Going Through The Motions	Virgin 98868
			AFTER THE FIRE	
2/12/83	#5	22	Der Kommissar	Epic 03559
			A-HA	
7/27/85	#1	26	Take On Me	Warner Brothers 29011
11/30/85	#24	20	The Sun Always Shines On T.V.	Warner Brothers 28846
1/24/87	#51	10	Cry Wolf	Warner Brothers 28500
			AIR SUPPLY	
2/09/80	#2	25	Lost In Love	Arista 0479
6/07/80	#2	25	All Out Of Love	Arista 0520
10/25/80	#9	22	Every Woman In The World	Arista 0564
5/16/81	#1	20	The One That You Love	Arista 0604
9/19/81	#5	20	Here I Am (Just When I Thought I Was Over You)	Arista 0626
12/12/81	#8	20	Sweet Dreams	Arista 0655
6/12/82	#8	19	Even The Nights Are Better	Arista 0692
9/18/82	#47	9	Young Love	Arista 1005
11/13/82	#33	17	Two Less Lonely People In The World	Arista 1004
7/30/83	#2	27	Making Love Out Of Nothing At All	Arista 9056
5/25/83	#16	15	Just As I Am	Arista 9353
8/10/85	#80	4	The Power Of Love	Arista 9391
8/09/86	#67	9	Lonely Is The Night	Arista 9521
			AIRWAVES	
6/10/78	#82	3	So Hard Livin' Without You	A&M 2032

Debut Date	Peak Pos	Wks Chr	ARTIST/Song Title	Label & Number
			JEWEL AKENS	
1/23/65	#2	15	The Birds And The Bees	Era 3141
5/01/65	#65	5	Georgie Porgie	Era 3142
			ALABAMA	
6/13/81	#23	23	Feels So Right	RCA 12236
11/28/81	#20	21	Love In The First Degree	RCA 12288
5/22/82	#17	14	Take Me Down	RCA 13210
9/04/82	#69	6	Close Enough To Perfect	RCA 13294
5/07/83	#39	12	The Closer You Get	RCA 13524
1/24/87	#86	3	Deep River Woman*	Motown 1873
			released as by LIONEL RICHIE with ALABAMA	
			CHUCK ALAIMO QUARTET	
4/13/57	#56	3	Leap Frog	MGM 12449
			STEVE ALAIMO	
1/12/63	#45	11	Every Day I Have To Cry	Checker 1032
11/30/63	#94	5	Gotta Have Love	Imperial 66003
1/30/65	#86	6	Real Live Girl	ABC Paramount 10620
5/07/66	#72	5	So Much Love	ABC Paramount 10805
4/15/72	#98	4	Amerikan Music	Entrance 7507
			ALARM	
1/18/86	#80	5	Strength	I.R.S. 52736
12/26/87	#85	7	Rain In The Summertime	I.R.S. 53219
4/02/88	#79	5	Presence Of Love	I.R.S. 53259
10/28/89	#58	8	Sold Me Down The River	I.R.S. 73002
			MORRIS ALBERT	
6/14/75	#10	32	Feelings	RCA 10279
12/20/75	#85	5	Sweet Loving Man	RCA 10437
			WILLY ALBERTI	
11/07/59	#12	12	Marina	London 1888
			AL B. SURE!	
4/09/88	#8	24	Nite And Day	Warner Brothers 28192
8/06/88	#52	11	Off On Your Own (Girl)	Warner Brothers 27870
11/19/88	#83	4	Killing Me Softly	Warner Brothers 27772
3/17/90	#30	12	The Secret Garden*	Qwest 19992
10/20/90	#41	10	Missunderstanding	Warner Brothers 19590
9/05/92	#49	12	Right Now	Warner Brothers 18819
			released as by QUINCY JONES/AL B. SURE!/JAMES INGRAM/EL DeBARGE/BARRY WHITE	
			AKI ALEONG	
11/25/61	#93	3	Trade Winds	Reprise 20003
			ALESSI	
9/10/77	#84	3	Oh Lori	A&M 1955
5/01/82	#79	4	Put Away Your Love	Qwest 50055
			ARTHUR ALEXANDER	
3/10/62	#27	10	You Better Move On	Dot 16309
6/30/62	#97	1	Where Have You Been (All My Life)	Dot 16357
11/03/62	#67	6	Anna (Go To Him)	Dot 16387
8/30/75	#51	10	Every Day I Have To Cry Some	Buddah 492
5/29/76	#94	3	Sharing The Night Together	Buddah 522
			ALIAS	
9/15/90	#2	24	More Than Words Can Say	EMI 50324
1/19/91	#10	18	Waiting For Love	EMI 50337
6/29/91	#79	6	Perfect World	Giant 19249
			ALICE WONDER LAND	
8/24/63	#65	8	He's Mine	Bardell 774
			ALISHA	
12/28/85	#81	8	Baby Talk	Vanguard 35262
6/02/90	#55	10	Bounce Back	MCA 79021
			ALIVE AND KICKING	
5/30/70	#5	16	Tighter, Tighter	Roulette 7078
9/12/70	#49	6	Just Let It Come	Roulette 7087
			DAVIE ALLAN and THE ARROWS	
2/27/65	#85	5	Apache '65	Tower 116
4/22/67	#33	23	Blue's Theme	Tower 295

Debut Date	Peak Pos	Wks Chr	ARTIST/Song Title	Label & Number
			DEBORAH ALLEN	
11/12/83	#23	21	Baby I Lied	RCA 13600
			DONNA ALLEN	
2/14/87	#20	22	Serious	21 Records 99497
			LEE ALLEN and HIS BAND	
1/11/58	#46	4	Walkin' With Mr. Lee	Ember 1027
10/11/58	#97	2	Tic Toc	Ember 1039
			PETER ALLEN	
1/24/81	#74	6	Fly Away	A&M 2288
			REX ALLEN	
9/12/53	#1	10	Crying In The Chapel	Decca 28758
9/15/62	#25	9	Don't Go Near The Indians	Mercury 71997
			STEVE ALLEN	
5/11/63	#74	6	Gravy Waltz	Dot 16457
			ALLEY CATS	
1/19/63	#49	7	Puddin N' Tain	Philles 108
			ALLISONS	
4/08/61	#85	5	Are You Sure	London 1197
			GREGG ALLMAN	
12/22/73	#16	11	Midnight Rider	Capricorn 0035
4/20/74	#91	2	Don't Mess Up A Good Thing	Capricorn 0042
4/11/87	#62	9	I'm No Angel*	Epic 06998
			***released as by THE GREGG ALLMAN BAND**	
			ALLMAN BROTHERS BAND	
5/06/72	#72	3	Ain't Wastin' Time No More	Capricorn 0003
8/18/73	#1	14	Ramblin' Man	Capricorn 0027
12/29/73	#33	10	Jessica	Capricorn 0036
3/24/79	#41	9	Crazy Love	Capricorn 0320
9/02/80	#68	7	Angeline	Arista 0555
8/08/81	#40	12	Straight From The Heart	Arista 0618
			MARC ALMOND	
12/31/88	#70	10	Tears Run Rings	Capitol 44240
			HERB ALPERT & THE TIJUANA BRASS	
10/20/62	#6	16	The Lonely Bull*	A&M 703
3/23/63	#90	2	Marching Thru Madrid	A&M 706
8/01/64	#98	1	The Mexican Shuffle	A&M 742
3/27/65	#85	3	Whipped Cream	A&M 760
8/28/65	#1	19	A Taste Of Honey/	A&M 775
8/28/65	#57	7	3rd Man Theme	A&M 775
12/25/65	#8	11	Zorba The Greek/	A&M 787
12/25/65	#42	7	Tijuana Taxi	A&M 787
3/12/66	#27	8	What Now My Love/	A&M 792
3/12/66	#21	9	Spanish Flea	A&M 792
7/02/66	#20	8	The Work Song	A&M 805
9/03/66	#24	7	Flamingo	A&M 813
11/12/66	#17	10	Mame	A&M 823
3/11/67	#60	4	Wade In The Water	A&M 840
4/08/67	#22	11	Casino Royale	A&M 850
7/08/67	#36	6	The Happening	A&M 860
9/09/67	#32	7	A Banda	A&M 870
1/06/68	#51	8	Carmen	A&M 890
4/27/68	#96	2	Cabaret	A&M 925
5/11/68	#1	14	This Guy's In Love With You**	A&M 929
8/31/68	#39	5	To Wait For Love**	A&M 964
12/14/68	#35	5	My Favorite Things	A&M 1001
3/22/69	#74	6	Zazueira	A&M 1043
5/24/69	#38	8	Without Her**	A&M 1065
11/22/69	#88	3	You Are My Life	A&M 1143
10/17/70	#74	3	Jerusalem	A&M 1225
3/10/73	#70	6	Last Tango In Paris	A&M 1420
5/25/74	#70	6	Fox Hunt	A&M 1526
7/28/79	#1	25	Rise**	A&M 2151
12/08/79	#47	10	Rotation**	A&M 2202
6/28/80	#58	9	Beyond**	A&M 2246
6/26/82	#30	12	Route 101**	A&M 2422
2/28/87	#56	10	Keep Your Eye On Me**	A&M 2915

Debut Date	Peak Pos	Wks Chr	**ARTIST**/Song Title	Label & Number
			HERB ALPERT & THE TIJUANA BRASS—*continued*	
4/11/87	#8	20	Diamonds**.	A&M 2929
7/18/87	#40	12	Making Love In The Rain**.	A&M 2949
			*released as by **THE TIJUANA BRASS featuring HERB ALPERT**	
			released as by **HERB ALPERT	
			ALPHA TEAM	
2/06/93	#84	5	Speed	Strictly Hype 106
			ALPHAVILLE	
12/01/84	#68	9	Big In Japan.	Atlantic 89665
11/05/88	#81	11	Forever Young	Atlantic 89013
			AMAZING RHYTHM ACES	
6/28/75	#17	14	Third Rate Romance	ABC 12078
1/03/76	#77	5	Amazing Grace	ABC 12142
9/11/76	#56	12	The End Is Not In Sight	ABC 12202
			AMAZULU	
8/01/87	#88	4	Montego Bay	Mango 121
			AMBOY DUKES	
3/23/68	#100	1	Baby Please Don't Go	Mainstream 576
6/22/68	#20	13	Journey To The Center Of The Mind	Mainstream 684
10/26/68	#97	2	You Talk Sunshine, I Breathe Fire	Mainstream 693
			AMBROSIA	
6/21/75	#18	13	Holdin' On To Yesterday	20th Century 2207
10/25/75	#78	7	Nice, Nice, Very Nice	20th Century 2244
12/04/76	#88	5	Can't Let A Woman	20th Century 2310
2/26/77	#41	9	Magical Mystery Tour	20th Century 2327
9/02/78	#2	21	How Much I Feel	Warner Brothers 8640
4/05/80	#2	21	The Biggest Part Of Me	Warner Brothers 49225
7/12/80	#17	17	You're The Only Woman (You & I)	Warner Brothers 49508
			AMERICA	
2/19/72	#1	13	Horse With No Name	Warner Brothers 7555
5/13/72	#8	11	I Need You	Warner Brothers 7580
10/14/72	#8	13	Ventura Highway	Warner Brothers 7641
1/27/73	#20	9	Don't Cross The River	Warner Brothers 7670
4/21/73	#58	7	Only In Your Heart	Warner Brothers 7694
8/11/73	#33	9	Muskrat Love	Warner Brothers 7725
8/17/74	#6	18	Tin Man	Warner Brothers 7839
12/21/74	#10	14	Lonely People	Warner Brothers 8048
4/12/75	#2	15	Sister Golden Hair	Warner Brothers 8086
7/26/75	#27	12	Daisy Jane	Warner Brothers 8118
11/22/75	#42	9	Woman Tonight	Warner Brothers 8157
5/15/76	#24	24	Today's The Day	Warner Brothers 8212
9/11/76	#99	2	Amber Cascades	Warner Brothers 8238
3/24/79	#62	7	California Dreamin'	American Int. 700
7/31/82	#7	21	You Can Do Magic	Capitol 5142
11/27/82	#49	13	Right Before Your Eyes	Capitol 5177
6/25/83	#34	12	The Border	Capitol 5236
			AMERICAN BREED	
6/10/67	#29	9	Step Out Of Your Mind	Acta 804
8/19/67	#91	3	Don't Forget About Me	Acta 808
11/25/67	#3	3	Bend Me, Shape Me	Acta 811
3/02/68	#30	7	Green Light	Acta 821
5/11/68	#77	5	Ready, Willing And Able.	Acta 824
7/27/68	#77	3	Anyway That You Want Me	Acta 827
			AMERICAN COMEDY NETWORK	
2/04/84	#71	6	Breaking Up Is Hard On You	Critique 704
			ED AMES	
1/16/65	#83	4	Try To Remember	RCA 8483
1/14/67	#8	15	My Cup Runneth Over	RCA 9002
5/06/67	#66	5	Time Time.	RCA 9178
10/07/67	#97	3	When The Snow Is On The Roses	RCA 9319
12/16/67	#14	8	Who Will Answer	RCA 9400
5/04/68	#66	8	Apologize	RCA 9517
10/19/68	#77	5	Kiss Her Now	RCA 9647
6/07/69	#94	1	Son Of A Travelin' Man	RCA 0156

Debut Date	Peak Pos	Wks Chr	ARTIST/Song Title	Label & Number
			NANCY AMES	
10/15/66	#98	2	Cry Softly	Epic 10056
			AMES BROTHERS	
3/25/50	#2	4	Rag Mop	Coral 60140
5/06/50	#3	15	Sentimental Me	Coral 60173
9/16/50	#2	15	Can Anyone Explain	Coral 60254
11/17/51	#3	13	Undecided*	Coral 60566
8/15/53	#1	24	You, You, You	RCA 5325
4/17/54	#4	8	Man With The Banjo	RCA 5644
12/25/54	#2	10	The Naughty Lady Of Shady Lane	RCA 5897
8/04/56	#22	7	It Only Hurts For A Little While	RCA 6481
12/22/56	#49	1	I Saw Esau	RCA 6720
7/06/57	#10	5	Tammy/	RCA 6930
7/13/57	#41	3	Rockin' Shoes	RCA 6930
9/21/57	#7	18	Melodie D'Amour	RCA 7046
3/22/58	#53	1	A Very Precious Love	RCA 7167
6/28/58	#45	8	Little Serenade	RCA 7268
9/20/58	#36	14	Pussy Cat/	RCA 7315
9/20/58	#34	12	No One But You (In My Heart)	RCA 7315
12/27/58	#33	10	Red River Rose	RCA 7413
5/30/59	#84	4	Someone To Come Home To	RCA 7526
2/20/60	#69	8	China Doll	RCA 7655
			*released as by THE AMES BROTHERS with LES BROWN	
			BILL AMESBURY	
2/09/74	#38	12	Virginia (Touch Me Like You Do)	Casablanca 0001
			TORI AMOS	
7/04/92	#52	16	Crucify	Atlantic 82399
			ANA	
5/26/90	#64	9	Got To Tell Me Something	Parc 73317
			ANACOSTIA	
12/09/72	#76	7	On And Off (Part 1)	Columbia 45685
			BILL ANDERSON	
10/20/62	#31	8	Mama Sang A Song	Decca 31404
4/13/63	#7	15	Still	Decca 31458
8/24/63	#67	5	8 x 10	Decca 31521
			JOHN ANDERSON	
3/05/83	#30	18	Swingin'	Warner Brothers 29788
			LEROY ANDERSON	
3/29/52	#1	20	Blue Tango	Decca 27875
8/31/57	#43	4	Forgotten Dreams	Decca 30403
			LYNN ANDERSON	
11/28/70	#1	18	Rose Garden	Columbia 45252
5/01/71	#56	6	You're My Man	Columbia 45356
8/21/71	#60	6	How Can I Unlove You	Columbia 45429
1/29/72	#81	4	Cry	Columbia 45529
2/24/73	#91	2	Keep Me In Mind	Columbia 45768
6/23/73	#81	6	Top Of The World	Columbia 45857
1/11/75	#99	3	What A Man, My Man Is	Columbia 10041
			CHRIS ANDREWS	
12/25/65	#85	5	Yesterday Man	Atco 6385
			JULIE ANDREWS/DICK VAN DYKE and THE PEARLIES	
5/01/65	#80	3	Super-cali-fragil-istic-expi-ali-docious	Vista 434
			LEE ANDREWS and THE HEARTS	
7/27/57	#33	9	Long Lonely Nights	Chess 1665
12/07/57	#25	11	Tear Drops	Chess 1675
5/10/58	#38	9	Try The Impossible	United Artists 123
8/23/58	#72	2	Why Do I	United Artists 137
			RUBY ANDREWS	
8/26/67	#52	9	Casanova (Your Playing Days Are Over)	Zodiac 1004
7/05/69	#94	4	You Made A Believer (Out Of Me)	Zodiac 1015
			ANDREWS SISTERS	
6/10/50	#1	16	I Wanna Be Loved	Decca 27007

Debut Date	Peak Pos	Wks Chr	ARTIST/Song Title	Label & Number
			ANGEL	
4/02/77	#74	9	That Magic Touch	Casablanca 878
4/08/78	#56	7	Ain't Gonna Eat Out My Heart Anymore	Casablanca 914
			ANGELICA	
11/02/91	#49	16	Angel Baby	Quality 15171
			ANGELS	
9/23/61	#16	20	'Til	Caprice 107
2/17/62	#35	11	Cry Baby Cry	Caprice 112
7/27/63	#1	15	My Boyfriend's Back	Smash 1834
10/19/63	#23	9	I Adore Him/	Smash 1854
12/14/63	#99	1	Thank You And Goodnight	Smash 1854
1/25/64	#40	6	Wow Wow Wee (He's The Boy For Me)	Smash 1870
			ANIMALS	
8/08/64	#1	12	The House Of The Rising Sun	MGM 13264
9/12/64	#84	3	Gonna Send You Back To Walker	MGM 13242
10/03/64	#17	9	I'm Crying	MGM 13274
12/05/64	#35	7	Boom Boom	MGM 13298
2/13/65	#17	10	Don't Let Me Be Misunderstood	MGM 13311
5/15/65	#32	6	Bring It On Home To Me	MGM 13339
8/14/65	#14	11	We Gotta Get Out Of This Place	MGM 13382
11/06/65	#20	13	It's My Life	MGM 13414
2/26/66	#34	7	Inside-Looking Out	MGM 13468
5/14/66	#11	12	Don't Bring Me Down	MGM 13514
9/10/66	#12	11	See See Rider*	MGM 13582
11/26/66	#33	10	Help Me Girl*	MGM 13636
4/08/67	#19	9	When I Was Young*	MGM 13721
8/05/67	#8	11	San Franciscan Nights*	MGM 13769
12/16/67	#10	9	Monterey*	MGM 13868
4/06/68	#54	6	Anything*	MGM 13917
5/18/68	#16	16	Sky Pilot (Parts 1 & 2)*	MGM 13939
11/23/68	#55	6	White Houses*	MGM 14013
8/20/83	#48	10	The Night	I.R.S. 9920
			***released as by ERIC BURDON & THE ANIMALS**	
			ANIMOTION	
1/26/85	#6	25	Obsession	Mercury 880266
6/01/85	#35	14	Let Him Go	Mercury 880737
5/10/86	#74	5	I Want You	Casablanca 884729
2/25/89	#12	12	Room To Move	Polydor 871418
6/17/89	#54	10	Calling It Love	Polydor 889054
			PAUL ANKA	
7/13/57	#2	22	Diana	ABC Paramount 9831
10/19/57	#48	3	I Love You, Baby	ABC Paramount 9855
1/18/58	#9	12	You Are My Destiny	ABC Paramount 9880
4/05/58	#60	1	Midnight	ABC Paramount 9937
4/12/58	#36	5	Crazy Love/	ABC Paramount 9907
4/26/58	#24	8	Let The Bells Keep Ringing	ABC Paramount 9907
10/04/58	#28	5	Just Young	ABC Paramount 9956
11/22/58	#46	9	Teen Commandments*	ABC Paramount 9974
12/27/58	#12	17	(All Of A Sudden) My Heart Sings	ABC Paramount 9987
3/28/59	#29	8	I Miss You So	ABC Paramount 10011
5/23/59	#1	17	Lonely Boy/	ABC Paramount 10022
5/23/59	#83	2	Your Love	ABC Paramount 10022
9/05/59	#2	17	Put Your Head On My Shoulder/	ABC Paramount 10040
9/05/59	#96	1	Don't Ever Leave Me	ABC Paramount 10040
11/21/59	#6	14	It's Time To Cry	ABC Paramount 10064
2/20/60	#2	14	Puppy Love	ABC Paramount 10082
5/14/60	#8	15	My Home Town/	ABC Paramount 10106
5/28/60	#51	8	Something Happened	ABC Paramount 10106
8/06/60	#24	9	Hello Young Lovers/	ABC Paramount 10132
8/13/60	#86	7	I Love You In The Same Old Way	ABC Paramount 10132
10/01/60	#23	11	Summer's Gone	ABC Paramount 10147
12/24/60	#54	2	Rudolph The Red-Nosed Reindeer	ABC Paramount 10163
1/14/61	#23	10	The Story Of My Love	ABC Paramount 10168
3/18/61	#11	12	Tonight My Love, Tonight	ABC Paramount 10194
5/27/61	#12	11	Dance On Little Girl	ABC Paramount 10220
8/26/61	#32	8	Kissin' On The Phone/	ABC Paramount 10239
8/26/61	#73	4	Cinderella	ABC Paramount 10239
12/16/61	#98	1	The Bells At My Wedding	ABC Paramount 10279
2/24/62	#12	13	Love Me Warm And Tender	RCA 7977

Debut Date	Peak Pos	Wks Chr	ARTIST/Song Title	Label & Number
5/26/62	#22	10	A Steel Guitar And A Glass Of Wine	RCA 8030
8/18/62	#52	7	Every Night	RCA 8068
10/27/62	#24	10	Eso Beso (That Kiss!)	RCA 8097
1/19/63	#30	8	Love (Makes The World Go 'Round)	RCA 8115
4/20/63	#35	6	Remember Diana	RCA 8170
6/22/63	#90	3	Hello Jim	RCA 8195
10/19/63	#97	1	Hurry Up & Tell Me	RCA 8237
12/28/68	#26	11	Goodnight My Love	RCA 9648
3/22/69	#64	6	In The Still Of The Night	RCA 0126
5/24/69	#78	5	Sincerely	RCA 0164
11/15/69	#80	5	Happy	RCA 9767
9/25/71	#38	11	Do I Love You	Buddah 252
3/25/72	#58	9	Jubilation	Buddah 294
12/15/73	#54	11	Let Me Get To Know You	Fame 345
7/06/74	#1	16	(You're) Having My Baby**	United Artists 454
11/09/74	#7	15	One Man Woman/One Woman Man**	United Artists 569
3/15/75	#5	14	I Don't Like To Sleep Alone**	United Artists 615
7/19/75	#14	13	(I Believe) There's Nothing Stronger Than Our Love**	United Artists 685
11/15/75	#17	16	Times Of Your Life	United Artists 737
4/03/76	#50	8	Anytime	United Artists 789
1/01/77	#97	3	Happier	United Artists 911
4/23/77	#74	5	My Best Friend's Wife	United Artists 972
7/09/77	#83	3	Everybody Ought To Be In Love	United Artists 1018
10/07/78	#70	6	This Is Love	RCA 11395
4/25/81	#63	5	I've Been Waiting For You All My Life	RCA 12225
7/02/83	#38	14	Hold Me 'Til The Mornin' Comes	Columbia 03897

*released as by PAUL ANKA/GEORGE HAMILTON IV/JOHNNY NASH
**released as by PAUL ANKA with ODIA COATES

			ANNETTE (Annette Funicello)	
6/14/58	#55	5	How Will I Know My Love	Disneyland 102
1/03/59	#18	16	Tall Paul	Disneyland 118
4/11/59	#59	6	Jo-Jo The Dog-Faced Boy	Vista 336
6/27/59	#51	9	Lonely Guitar	Vista 339
11/07/59	#16	16	First Name Initial	Vista 349
2/20/60	#13	12	O Dio Mio	Vista 354
5/28/60	#47	8	Train Of Love	Vista 359
8/20/60	#15	14	Pineapple Princess	Vista 362
12/17/60	#98	2	Talk To Me Baby	Vista 369

			ANN-MARGRET	
7/29/61	#15	12	I Just Don't Understand	RCA 7894
11/25/61	#90	3	It Do Me So Good	RCA 7952
4/07/62	#89	2	What Am I Supposed To Do	RCA 7986

			ANOTHER BAD CREATION	
2/09/91	#25	20	Iesha	Motown 2070

			ADAM ANT	
11/20/82	#12	21	Goody Two Shoes	Epic 03367
3/12/83	#67	7	Desperate But Not Serious	Epic 03688
2/11/84	#41	12	Strip	Epic 04337
3/10/90	#18	17	Room At The Top	MCA 53679

			PETE ANTELL	
11/17/62	#85	7	Night Time	Cameo 234

			RAY ANTHONY	
9/26/53	#2	9	Dragnet	Capitol 2562
1/17/59	#7	17	Peter Gunn	Capitol 4041
6/30/62	#74	8	Worried Mind	Capitol 4742

			ANYTHING BOX	
2/24/90	#65	9	Living In Oblivion	Epic 73231

			APACHE	
2/06/93	#68	12	Gangsta Bitch	Tommy Boy 541

			APOLLO 100	
1/01/72	#6	14	Joy	Mega 0050
4/22/72	#93	1	Mendelssohn's 4th (Second Movement)	Mega 0069

			APPALACHIANS	
4/13/63	#78	6	Bony Moronie	ABC Paramount 10419

Debut Date	Peak Pos	Wks Chr	ARTIST/Song Title	Label & Number
			DAVE APPELL	
1/20/62	#53	6	Happy Jose	Cameo 207
			APPLE & APPLEBERRY	
4/06/74	#97	3	What Do You Know About Love	ABC 11415
			APPLEJACKS	
9/27/58	#26	13	Mexican Hat Rock	Cameo 149
12/20/58	#31	10	Rocka-Conga	Cameo 155
3/07/59	#83	4	Bunny Hop	Cameo 158
			APRIL (April Stevens)	
6/15/74	#81	4	Wake Up And Love Me	A&M 1528
			APRIL WINE	
3/18/72	#27	11	You Could Have Been A Lady	Big Tree 133
7/29/72	#90	3	Bad Side Of The Moon	Big Tree 142
3/03/79	#47	11	Roller	Capitol 4660
2/09/80	#92	3	I Like To Rock	Capitol 4828
2/07/81	#20	18	Just Between You And Me	Capitol 4975
5/23/81	#56	11	Sign Of The Gypsy Queen	Capitol 5001
7/10/82	#64	6	Enough Is Enough	Capitol 5133
2/18/84	#78	5	This Could Be The Right One	Capitol 5319
			AQUATONES	
4/26/58	#24	7	You	Fargo 1001
			ARBORS	
10/15/66	#49	11	A Symphony For Susan	Date 1529
6/03/67	#71	6	Graduation Day	Date 1561
2/15/69	#24	11	The Letter	Date 1638
5/24/69	#72	7	I Can't Quit Her	Date 1645
			ARCADIA	
10/26/85	#7	19	Election Day	Capitol 5501
2/01/86	#29	13	Goodbye Is Forever	Capitol 5542
			TASMIN ARCHER	
4/10/93	#24	18	Sleeping Satellite	SBK 50426
			ARCHIBALD PLAYERS	
12/20/58	#100	1	Mr. Grillon	Arch 1606
			ARCHIES	
9/14/68	#9	16	Bang-Shang-A-Lang	Calendar 1006
12/21/68	#30	9	Feelin' So Good (S.k.o.o.b.y-D.o.o)	Calendar 1007
7/19/69	#1	22	Sugar Sugar	Calendar 1008
11/29/69	#8	13	Jingle Jangle	Kirshner 5002
2/28/70	#29	7	Who's Your Baby?	Kirshner 5003
6/27/70	#30	8	Sunshine	Kirshner 1009
			ARDELLS	
9/28/63	#85	3	Eefananny	Epic 9621
			TONI ARDEN	
5/03/58	#12	16	Padre	Decca 30628
			ARGENT	
6/03/72	#5	17	Hold Your Head Up	Epic 10852
11/11/72	#81	4	Tragedy	Epic 10119
			ARKADE	
2/06/71	#67	6	The Morning Of Our Lives	Dunhill 4268
			JOAN ARMATRADING	
6/18/83	#82	5	Drop The Pilot	A&M 2538
			ARMENIAN JAZZ SEXTET	
4/27/57	#28	8	Harem Dance	Kapp 181
			RUSSELL ARMS	
12/22/56	#17	14	Cinco Robles (Five Oaks)	Era 1026
			LOUIS ARMSTRONG	
2/22/64	#1	22	Hello Dolly!	Kapp 573
6/13/64	#33	6	I Still Get Jealous*	Kapp 597
9/26/64	#42	7	So Long Dearie	Mercury 72338
5/07/66	#60	5	Mame	Mercury 72574
2/20/88	#39	12	What A Wonderful World	A&M 3010
			***released as by LOUIS ARMSTRONG and THE ALL STARS**	

10

Debut Date	Peak Pos	Wks Chr	ARTIST/Song Title	Label & Number
			GINNY ARNELL	
12/14/63	#60	9	Dumb Head	MGM 13177
			CALVIN ARNOLD	
2/03/68	#97	3	Funky Way	Venture 605
			EDDY ARNOLD	
11/24/56	#24	5	Mutual Admiration Society*	RCA 6708
7/04/59	#53	11	Tennessee Stud	RCA 7542
5/29/65	#80	5	What's He Doing In My World	RCA 8516
10/25/65	#12	14	Make The World Go Away	RCA 8679
2/05/66	#36	10	I Want To Go With You	RCA 8749
5/07/66	#37	7	The Last Word In Lonesome Is Me	RCA 8818
7/16/66	#38	8	The Tip Of My Fingers	RCA 8869
10/08/66	#41	7	Somebody Like Me	RCA 8965
3/25/67	#90	3	Lonely Again	RCA 9080
5/06/67	#50	9	Misty Blue	RCA 9182
8/12/67	#61	10	Turn The World Around	RCA 9265
11/18/67	#79	4	Here Comes Heaven	RCA 9368
2/03/68	#56	6	Here Comes The Rain, Baby	RCA 9437
5/18/68	#71	7	It's Over	RCA 9525
8/24/68	#69	6	Then You Can Tell Me Goodbye	RCA 9606
11/30/68	#73	4	They Don't Make Love Like They Used To	RCA 9667
			released as by EDDY ARNOLD and JAYE P. MORGAN	
			AROUND THE WAY	
11/14/92	#92	3	Really Into You	Atlantic 87427
			ARPEGGIO	
3/24/79	#91	3	Love And Desire (Part 1)	Polydor 14535
			ARRESTED DEVELOPMENT	
5/23/92	#5	21	Tennessee	Chrysalis 23829
8/22/92	#8	23	People Everyday	Chrysalis 50397
12/19/92	#93	6	Revolution	Chrysalis 24812
12/26/92	#5	26	Mr. Wendall	Chrysalis 24810
			STEVE ARRINGTON	
8/24/85	#83	5	Dancin' In The Key Of Life	Atlantic 89535
			ARTHUR, HURLEY & GOTTLIEB	
7/21/73	#96	3	Sunshine Ship	Columbia 45881
			ARTISTICS	
12/10/66	#58	12	I'm Gonna Miss You	Brunswick 55301
4/08/67	#100	1	Girl I Need You	Brunswick 55315
5/27/67	#77	2	Love Song	Brunswick 55326
			ARTISTS UNITED AGAINST APARTHEID	
11/02/85	#42	16	Sun City	Manhattan 50017
			ART OF NOISE	
5/24/86	#49	10	Peter Gunn*	China 42986
8/16/86	#32	14	Paranoimia**	China 43002
11/26/88	#37	12	Kiss***	China 871038
			released as by THE ART OF NOISE featuring DUANE EDDY	
			**released as by THE ART OF NOISE with MAX HEADROOM*	
			***released as by THE ART OF NOISE featuring TOM JONES*	
			BOBBY ARVON	
12/10/77	#59	14	Until Now	First Artists 41000
			ASHFORD & SIMPSON	
3/18/78	#66	7	Don't Cost You Nothing	Warner Brothers 8514
8/18/79	#35	14	Found A Cure	Warner Brothers 8870
6/26/82	#73	6	Street Corner	Capitol 5109
11/17/84	#14	22	Solid	Capitol 5397
			ASHTON, GARDNER & DYKE	
6/26/71	#37	9	Resurrection Shuffle	Capitol 3060
			ASIA	
4/17/82	#6	18	Heat Of The Moment	Geffen 50040
7/24/82	#16	15	Only Time Will Tell	Geffen 29970
7/30/83	#9	15	Don't Cry	Geffen 29571
10/15/83	#38	14	The Smile Has Left Your Eyes	Geffen 29475
12/07/85	#45	13	Go	Geffen 28872
9/22/90	#55	9	Days Like These	Geffen 19677

Debut Date	Peak Pos	Wks Chr	ARTIST/Song Title	Label & Number
			ASSEMBLED MULTITUDE	
6/13/70	#16	15	Overture From Tommy (A Rock Opera)	Atlantic 2737
10/10/70	#78	4	Woodstock	Atlantic 2764
			ASSOCIATION	
5/28/66	#9	12	Along Comes Mary	Valiant 741
8/27/66	#1	13	Cherish	Valiant 747
11/26/66	#26	7	Pandora's Golden Heebie Jeebies	Valiant 755
2/04/67	#53	7	No Fair At All	Valiant 758
5/27/67	#1	15	Windy	Warner Brothers 7041
9/02/67	#1	12	Never My Love	Warner Brothers 7074
1/27/68	#11	11	Everything That Touches You	Warner Brothers 7163
5/11/68	#23	9	Time For Livin'	Warner Brothers 7195
8/24/68	#29	6	Six Man Band	Warner Brothers 7229
3/01/69	#78	6	Goodbye Columbus	Warner Brothers 7267
11/02/69	#84	3	Dubuque Blues	Warner Brothers 7349
3/07/70	#91	2	Just About The Same	Warner Brothers 7372
5/27/72	#90	2	Darling Be Home Soon	Columbia 45602
2/17/73	#85	4	Names, Tags, Numbers & Labels	Mums 6016
1/31/81	#78	5	Dreamer	Elektra 47094
			JON ASTLEY	
7/18/87	#90	6	Jane's Getting Serious	Atlantic 89258
10/22/88	#70	8	Put This Love To The Test	Atlantic 89027
			RICK ASTLEY	
12/19/87	#1	26	Never Gonna Give You Up	RCA 5347
4/16/88	#1	19	Together Forever	RCA 8319
7/16/88	#12	16	It Would Take A Strong Strong Man	RCA 8663
12/17/88	#6	19	She Wants To Dance With Me	RCA 8838
4/22/89	#34	11	Giving Up On Love	RCA 8872
2/16/91	#7	23	Cry For Help	RCA 2774
6/15/91	#75	8	Move Right Out	RCA 2839
9/25/93	#22	19	Hopelessly	RCA 62597
			ASTORS	
7/17/65	#68	4	Candy	Stax 170
			ASYLUM CHOIR	
2/05/72	#98	2	Tryin' To Stay Alive	Shelter 7313
			CHET ATKINS	
9/26/59	#45	7	Boo Boo Stick Beat	RCA 7589
1/30/60	#68	7	Teensville	RCA 7684
7/10/65	#85	3	Yakety Axe	RCA 8590
			CHRISTOPHER ATKINS	
8/07/82	#69	4	How Can I Live Without Her	Polydor 2210
			ATLANTA DISCO BAND	
1/31/76	#99	2	Bad Luck	Ariola 7611
			ATLANTA RHYTHM SECTION	
9/21/74	#57	10	Doraville	Polydor 14248
2/02/75	#74	5	Angel	Polydor 14262
5/22/76	#75	7	Jukin	Polydor 14323
9/04/76	#76	10	Free Spirit	Polydor 14339
1/22/77	#5	20	So Into You	Polydor 14373
6/04/77	#65	8	Neon Nites	Polydor 14397
8/20/77	#63	7	Dog Days	Polydor 14411
10/15/77	#77	6	Georgia Rhythm	Polydor 14432
3/04/78	#9	18	Imaginary Lover	Polydor 14459
6/10/78	#16	16	I'm Not Gonna Let It Bother Me Tonight	Polydor 14484
9/30/78	#66	5	Champagne Jam	Polydor 14504
5/26/79	#21	15	Do It Or Die	Polydor 14568
8/18/79	#15	14	Spooky	Polydor 2001
9/20/80	#80	5	I Ain't Much	Polydor 2125
8/29/81	#27	27	Alien	Columbia 02471
			ATLANTIC STARR	
4/03/82	#48	12	Circles	A&M 2392
12/28/85	#3	23	Secret Lovers	A&M 2788
5/03/86	#72	6	If Your Heart Isn't In It	A&M 2822
3/28/87	#1	23	Always	Warner Brothers 28455
8/15/87	#60	9	One Love At A Time	Warner Brothers 28327
2/01/92	#3	25	Masterpiece	Reprise 19076

Debut Date	Peak Pos	Wks Chr	ARTIST/Song Title	Label & Number
			AUDIENCE	
7/24/71	#76	5	Indian Summer	Elektra 45732
			AURRA	
3/20/82	#81	4	Make Up Your Mind	Salsoul 7017
			DONALD AUSTIN	
2/17/73	#87	4	Crazy Legs	Eastbound 603
			PATTI AUSTIN	
12/19/81	#72	8	Every Home Should Have One	Qwest 49854
4/24/82	#78	5	Baby, Come To Me*	Qwest 50036
10/02/82	#2	32	Baby, Come To Me*	Qwest 50036
3/19/83	#51	9	Every Home Should Have One	Qwest 29727
5/07/83	#45	21	How Do You Keep The Music Playing**	Qwest 29618
5/03/86	#57	10	The Heat Of Heat	Qwest 28788
			*released as by PATTI AUSTIN with JAMES INGRAM	
			**released as by JAMES INGRAM and PATTI AUSTIN	
			SIL AUSTIN	
11/17/56	#12	11	Slow Walk	Mercury 70963
5/30/59	#54	9	Danny Boy	Mercury 71442
			AUTOGRAPH	
12/22/84	#25	20	Turn Up The Radio	RCA 13953
			AUTOMATIC MAN	
12/25/76	#88	6	My Pearl	Island 063
			GENE AUTRY	
4/15/50	#8	2	Peter Cottontail	Columbia 38750
			FRANKIE AVALON	
1/11/58	#11	12	Dede Dinah	Chancellor 1011
4/12/58	#44	5	You Excite Me	Chancellor 1016
7/12/58	#17	15	Ginger Bread	Chancellor 1021
10/25/58	#25	15	I'll Wait For You	Chancellor 1026
2/14/59	#1	17	Venus	Chancellor 1031
5/30/59	#7	13	Bobby Sox To Stockings/	Chancellor 1036
5/30/59	#17	12	A Boy Without A Girl	Chancellor 1036
9/05/59	#10	14	Just Ask Your Heart/	Chancellor 1040
9/05/59	#51	3	Two Fools	Chancellor 1040
11/21/59	#1	17	Why/	Chancellor 1045
1/09/60	#87	2	Swinging On A Rainbow	Chancellor 1045
3/12/60	#19	10	Don't Throw Away All Those Teardrops	Chancellor 1048
6/25/60	#25	12	Where Are You/	Chancellor 1052
6/25/60	#73	4	Tuxedo Junction	Chancellor 1052
9/24/60	#26	14	Togetherness	Chancellor 1056
12/17/60	#68	7	A Perfect Love/	Chancellor 1065
12/24/60	#72	4	The Puppet Song	Chancellor 1065
2/25/61	#77	4	All Of Everything	Chancellor 1071
5/20/61	#76	5	Who Else But You	Chancellor 1077
3/31/62	#36	10	You Are Mine	Chancellor 1107
7/21/62	#99	2	A Miracle	Chancellor 1115
1/24/76	#32	11	Venus	De-Lite 1578
			AVANT-GARDE	
8/24/68	#35	11	Naturally Stoned	Columbia 44590
12/21/68	#80	4	Fly With Me	Columbia 44701
			JOHNNY AVERAGE BAND	
2/28/81	#66	7	Ch Ch Cherie	Bearsville 49671
			AVERAGE WHITE BAND	
11/23/74	#1	20	Pick Up The Pieces	Atlantic 3229
4/05/75	#12	16	Cut The Cake	Atlantic 3261
8/09/75	#44	10	If I Ever Lose This Heaven	Atlantic 3285
11/15/75	#31	11	School Boy Crush*	Atlantic 3304
9/04/76	#67	10	Queen Of My Soul	Atlantic 3354
6/14/80	#57	10	Let's Go 'Round Again	Arista 0515
			*released as by AWB	
			BOBBY ROSS AVILA	
5/15/93	#83	4	La La Love	Perspective 7422
			AXE	
7/17/82	#56	7	Now Or Never	Atco 7408

Debut Date	Peak Pos	Wks Chr	ARTIST/Song Title	Label & Number
			HOYT AXTON	
6/22/74	#72	5	When The Morning Comes	A&M 1497

B

Debut Date	Peak Pos	Wks Chr	ARTIST/Song Title	Label & Number
			BABYFACE	
8/19/89	#12	19	It's No Crime	Solar 68966
11/25/89	#15	20	Tender Lover	Solar 74003
3/03/90	#5	20	Whip Appeal	Solar 74007
6/16/90	#32	15	My Kinda Girl	Solar 74515
7/04/92	#24	19	Give U My Heart*	Laface 4026
10/30/93	#16	27	Never Keeping Secrets	Epic 77264
			released as by BABYFACE featuring TONI BRAXTON	
			BABY JANE & THE ROCKABYES	
1/12/63	#88	3	How Much Is That Doggie In The Window	United Artists 560
			BABY RAY	
12/03/66	#92	4	There's Something On Your Mind	Imperial 66216
			BABYS	
2/26/77	#95	3	If You've Got The Time	Chrysalis 2132
10/01/77	#8	19	Isn't It Time	Chrysalis 2173
1/28/78	#48	9	Silver Dreams	Chrysalis 2201
12/30/78	#8	21	Every Time I Think Of You	Chrysalis 2279
6/02/79	#71	4	Head First	Chrysalis 2323
1/19/80	#29	14	Back On My Feet Again	Chrysalis 2398
5/03/80	#81	3	Midnight Rendezvous	Chrysalis 2425
11/15/80	#53	12	Turn And Walk Away	Chrysalis 2467
			BURT BACHARACH	
8/03/63	#95	3	Saturday's Sunshine	Kapp 532
			BACHELORS	
4/04/64	#10	15	Diane	London 9639
6/27/64	#34	9	I Believe	London 9672
9/19/64	#67	6	I Wouldn't Trade You For The World	London 9693
1/02/65	#27	11	No Arms Can Ever Hold You	London 9724
6/05/65	#16	11	Marie	London 9762
10/09/65	#40	8	Chapel In The Moonlight	London 9793
4/09/66	#47	8	Love Me With All Your Heart	London 9828
6/25/66	#37	7	Can I Trust You?	London 20010
12/31/66	#95	5	Walk With Faith In Your Heart	London 20018
7/15/67	#98	2	Marta	London 20027
			BACHMAN-TURNER OVERDRIVE	
12/01/73	#68	7	Blue Collar	Mercury 73417
3/02/74	#14	13	Let It Ride	Mercury 73457
5/25/74	#6	18	Takin' Care Of Business	Mercury 73487
9/14/74	#1	16	You Ain't Seen Nothing Yet	Mercury 73622
1/25/75	#8	9	Roll On Down The Highway	Mercury 73656
5/17/75	#16	11	Hey You	Mercury 73683
11/22/75	#38	9	Down To The Line	Mercury 73724
2/07/76	#63	8	Take It Like A Man	Mercury 73766
4/24/76	#79	5	Lookin' Out For #1	Mercury 73784
9/25/76	#86	6	Gimme Your Money Please	Mercury 73843
4/30/77	#84	6	My Wheels Won't Turn	Mercury 73903
4/01/78	#92	3	Down The Road	Mercury 73987
3/03/79	#57	7	Heartaches*	Mercury 74046
			released as by BTO	
			JIM BACKUS and FRIEND*	
7/12/58	#36	8	Delicious	Jubilee 5330
			Jim's name was mistakenly spelled BAKUS on the record label	
			BAD COMPANY	
8/03/74	#1	16	Can't Get Enough	Swan Song 70015
1/18/75	#23	10	Movin' On	Swan Song 70101
4/19/75	#32	9	Good Lovin' Gone Bad	Swan Song 70103
6/21/75	#10	16	Feel Like Makin' Love	Swan Song 70106
3/13/76	#22	15	Young Blood	Swan Song 70108
7/24/76	#86	3	Honey Child	Swan Song 70109
5/21/77	#83	3	Burnin' Sky	Swan Song 70112
3/17/79	#11	21	Rock 'N' Roll Fantasy	Swan Song 70119
7/28/79	#63	8	Gone, Gone, Gone	Swan Song 71000

Debut Date	Peak Pos	Wks Chr	ARTIST/Song Title	Label & Number
10/09/82	#92	4	Electricland	Swan Song 99966
10/18/86	#82	5	This Love	Atlantic 89355
11/10/90	#15	26	If You Needed Somebody	Atco 98944
8/24/91	#18	21	Walk Through Fire	Atco 98748
9/05/92	#31	22	How About That	Atco East West 98509
11/28/92	#75	7	This Could Be The One	Atco East West 98463
			BAD ENGLISH	
7/29/89	#38	12	Forget Me Not	Epic 68946
9/23/89	#1	22	When I See You Smile	Epic 69082
12/23/89	#4	20	Price Of Love	Epic 73094
4/07/90	#60	10	Heaven Is A Four Letter Word	Epic 73307
6/09/90	#20	18	Possession	Epic 73398
8/31/91	#34	15	Straight To Your Heart	Epic 73982
2/01/92	#70	6	Time Alone With You	Epic 74091
			BADFINGER	
2/08/69	#51	6	Maybe Tomorrow*	Apple 1803
2/07/70	#6	15	Come And Get It	Apple 1815
10/17/70	#6	14	No Matter What	Apple 1822
12/04/71	#3	13	Day After Day	Apple 1841
3/18/72	#9	10	Baby Blue	Apple 1844
1/26/74	#88	3	Apple Of My Eye	Apple 1864
4/07/79	#79	4	Love Is Gonna Come At Last	Elektra 46025
2/28/81	#67	8	Hold On	Radio 3793
			*released as by THE IVEYS, who later became BADFINGER	
			JOAN BAEZ	
9/04/65	#31	9	There But For Fortune	Vanguard 35031
4/26/69	#75	4	Love Is Just A Four-Letter Word	Vanguard 35088
8/07/71	#3	15	The Night They Drove Old Dixie Down	Vanguard 35138
11/13/71	#47	9	Let It Be	Vanguard 35145
7/22/72	#64	8	In The Quiet Morning	A&M 1362
7/19/75	#68	4	Blue Sky	A&M 1703
9/25/75	#48	9	Diamonds And Rust	A&M 1737
			DOC BAGBY	
9/07/57	#47	3	Dumplin's	Okeh 7089
			PEARL BAILEY	
11/22/52	#5	11	Takes Two To Tango	Coral 60817
			PHILIP BAILEY	
11/24/84	#1	24	Easy Lover*	Columbia 04679
4/06/85	#49	10	Walking On The Chinese Wall	Columbia 04826
			*released as by PHILIP BAILEY with PHIL COLLINS	
			DAN BAIRD	
12/12/92	#25	16	I Love You Period	Def American 18724
			BAJA MARIMBA BAND	
1/04/64	#58	6	Comin' In The Back Door	Almo 201
10/08/66	#98	2	Portuguese Washerwoman	A&M 816
11/26/66	#57	6	Ghost Riders In The Sky	A&M 824
8/05/67	#100	1	Along Comes Mary	A&M 862
6/15/68	#93	1	Yes Sir, That's My Baby	A&M 937
			ANITA BAKER	
8/16/86	#12	22	Sweet Love	Elektra 69557
12/13/86	#42	15	Caught Up In The Rapture	Elektra 69511
3/28/87	#43	12	Same Ole Love (365 Days A Year)	Elektra 69484
9/26/87	#59	12	No One In The World	Elektra 69456
9/24/88	#2	24	Giving You The Best That I Got	Elektra 69371
1/21/89	#17	17	Just Because	Elektra 69327
6/30/90	#39	11	Talk To Me	Elektra 64964
9/15/90	#64	9	Soul Inspiration	Elektra 64935
			GEORGE BAKER SELECTION	
3/14/70	#16	13	Little Green Bag	Colossus 112
6/13/70	#85	3	Dear Ann	Colossus 117
11/29/75	#22	14	Paloma Blanca	Warner Brothers 8115
			GINGER BAKER'S AIR FORCE	
5/30/70	#79	2	Man Of Constant Sorrow	Atco 6750
			LAVERN BAKER	
2/19/55	#3	7	Tweedlee Dee	Atlantic 1047
10/06/56	#37	3	I Can't Love You Enough	Atlantic 1104

15

Debut Date	Peak Pos	Wks Chr	ARTIST/Song Title	Label & Number
			LAVERN BAKER—continued	
12/22/56	#15	17	Jim Dandy*	Atlantic 1116
8/31/57	#53	3	Humpty Dumpty Heart	Atlantic 1150
12/20/58	#10	18	I Cried A Tear	Atlantic 2007
4/25/59	#41	10	I Waited Too Long	Atlantic 2021
8/08/59	#68	6	So High, So Low/	Atlantic 2033
8/15/59	#100	1	If You Love Me	Atlantic 2033
11/14/59	#82	5	Tiny Tim	Atlantic 2041
1/30/60	#96	1	Shake A Hand	Atlantic 2048
11/26/60	#36	10	Bumble Bee	Atlantic 2077
2/04/61	#82	4	You're The Boss**	Atlantic 2090
4/22/61	#54	6	Saved	Atlantic 2099
12/08/62	#37	11	See See Rider	Atlantic 2167
1/22/66	#94	2	Think Twice***	Brunswick 55287
			***released as by LAVERN BAKER and THE GLIDERS**	
			****released as by LAVERN BAKER & JIMMY RICKS**	
			*****released as by JACKIE WILSON and LAVERN BAKER**	
			TEDDY BAKER	
9/26/81	#81	6	It's Over	Casablanca 2340
			BALANCE	
7/11/81	#23	19	Breaking Away	Portrait 02177
11/28/81	#53	11	Falling In Love	Portrait 02608
			BALCONES FAULT	
7/30/77	#93	4	Take Me Home	Cream 7714
			LONG JOHN BALDRY	
1/20/68	#100	1	Let The Heartaches Begin	Warner Brothers 7098
8/28/71	#89	4	Don't Try To Lay No Boogie-Woogie On The King Of	
			Rock And Roll	Warner Brothers 7506
			MARTY BALIN	
5/23/81	#9	19	Hearts	EMI America 8084
9/12/81	#26	14	Atlanta Lady	EMI America 8093
2/19/83	#73	4	What Love Is	EMI America 8153
			KENNY BALL	
1/20/62	#2	17	Midnight In Moskow	Kapp 442
4/21/62	#98	1	March Of The Siamese Children	Kapp 451
5/26/62	#68	8	Green Leaves Of Summer	Kapp 460
			BALLADS	
7/20/68	#48	7	God Bless Our Love	Venture 615
			HANK BALLARD and THE MIDNIGHTERS	
7/25/59	#64	4	Sugaree	King 5215
6/04/60	#6	21	Finger Poppin' Time	King 5341
7/23/60	#42	2	The Twist	King 5171
10/01/60	#7	17	Let's Go, Let's Go, Let's Go	King 5400
12/17/60	#14	11	The Hoochi Coochi Coo	King 5430
2/25/61	#52	6	Let's Go Again	King 5459
4/15/61	#24	8	The Continental Walk	King 5491
6/24/61	#45	8	The Switch-A-Roo	King 5510
9/09/61	#92	2	Keep On Dancing	King 5535
			RUSS BALLARD	
6/21/80	#84	7	On The Rebound	Epic 50883
			BALLOON FARM	
2/03/68	#77	9	A Question Of Temperature	Laurie 3405
			BALTIMORA	
10/19/85	#18	28	Tarzan Boy	Manhattan 50018
4/10/93	#54	11	Tarzan Boy	SBK 50424
			BAMA	
10/06/79	#93	3	Touch Me When We're Dancing	Free Flight 11629
			AFRICA BAMBAATAA & THE SOUL SONIC FORCE	
8/07/82	#89	6	Planet Rock	Tommy Boy 823
			BANANARAMA	
6/25/83	#74	7	Shy Boy (Don't It Make You Feel Good)	London 810112
7/21/84	#10	19	Cruel Summer	London 810127
11/24/84	#77	8	The Wild Life	London 882019
6/28/86	#3	19	Venus	London 886056
10/25/86	#72	5	More Than Physical	London 886080

16

Debut Date	Peak Pos	Wks Chr	ARTIST/Song Title	Label & Number
12/13/86	#71	9	A Trick Of The Night	London 886119
7/11/87	#4	23	I Heard A Rumour	London 886165
11/21/87	#55	13	I Can't Help It	London 886212
3/23/88	#48	11	Love In The First Degree	London 886255
11/12/88	#72	7	Love, Truth & Honesty	London 886362
			BAND	
9/07/68	#52	6	The Weight	Capitol 2269
10/18/69	#26	13	Up On Cripple Creek	Capitol 2635
2/21/70	#50	5	Rag Mama Rag	Capitol 2705
10/10/70	#88	4	Time To Kill	Capitol 2870
10/16/71	#80	6	Life Is A Carnival	Capitol 3199
9/16/72	#23	12	Don't Do It	Capitol 3433
11/24/73	#53	7	Ain't Got No Home	Capitol 3758
7/27/74	#47	8	Most Likely You Go Your Way*	Asylum 11043
3/20/76	#66	4	Ophelia	Capitol 4230
			*released as by THE BOB DYLAN/BAND	
			BAND AID	
12/22/84	#7	12	Do They Know It's Christmas	Columbia 04749
			BAND OF GOLD	
10/20/84	#70	8	Love Songs Are Back Again	RCA 13866
			BAND OF THE BLACK WATCH	
2/07/76	#77	7	Scotch On The Rocks	Private Stock 45055
			BANDWAGON	
8/17/68	#100	1	Breaking Down The Walls Of Heartache	Epic 10352
			BANG (Florida group)	
5/13/72	#94	1	Questions	Capitol 3304
			BANG (London duo)	
8/18/90	#76	7	Holding My Heart	Vendetta 1504
			BANGLES	
1/25/86	#3	21	Manic Monday	Columbia 05757
5/10/86	#28	14	If She Knew What She Wants	Columbia 05886
9/27/86	#1	25	Walk Like An Egyptian	Columbia 06257
2/14/87	#9	19	Walking Down Your Street	Columbia 06674
11/14/87	#3	23	Hazy Shade Of Winter	Def Jam 07630
10/15/88	#10	21	In Your Room	Columbia 08090
2/04/89	#1	20	Eternal Flame	Columbia 68533
5/06/89	#19	16	Be With You	Columbia 68744
			DARRELL BANKS	
7/16/66	#24	12	Open The Door To Your Heart	Revilot 201
10/22/66	#61	6	Somebody (Somewhere) Needs You	Revilot 203
			BARBARA and THE UNIQUES	
1/09/71	#88	3	There It Goes Again	Arden 3001
			BARBARIANS	
9/18/65	#62	7	Are You A Boy Or Are You A Girl	Laurie 3308
3/05/66	#97	1	Moulty	Laurie 3326
			CHRIS BARBER'S JAZZ BAND	
1/10/59	#4	16	Petite Fleur (Little Flower)	Laurie 3022
			KEITH BARBOUR	
9/20/69	#33	9	Echo Park	Epic 10486
			BARBUSTERS (see JOAN JETT)	
			BARDEUX	
2/20/88	#78	7	Magic Carpet Ride	Synthicide 75016
4/09/88	#36	14	When We Kiss	Synthicide 75018
9/23/89	#64	10	I Love The Bass	Enigma 75047
			BOBBY BARE	
12/13/58	#10	16	All American Boy*	Fraternity 835
5/02/59	#91	3	Carefree Wanderer*	Fraternity 838
7/21/62	#29	13	Shame On Me	RCA 8032
11/10/62	#99	1	I Don't Believe I'll Fall In Love Today	RCA 8083
6/08/63	#13	14	Detroit City	RCA 8183
10/05/63	#15	12	500 Miles Away From Home	RCA 8238
2/08/64	#45	7	Miller's Cave	RCA 8294
10/31/64	#88	8	Four Strong Winds	RCA 8443

Debut Date	Peak Pos	Wks Chr	ARTIST/Song Title	Label & Number
			BOBBY BARE—*continued*	
1/05/74	#50	9	Daddy What If	RCA 0197
			released mistakenly under the name BILL PARSONS	
			BAR-KAYS	
6/03/67	#17	14	Soul Finger/	Volt 148
8/19/67	#100	1	Knucklehead	Volt 148
10/14/67	#74	3	Give Everybody Some	Volt 154
12/25/71	#55	9	Son Of Shaft	Volt 4073
10/21/72	#90	3	Memphis At Sunrise	Volt 4081
11/13/76	#53	15	Shake Your Rump To The Funk	Mercury 73833
2/18/78	#91	4	Let's Have Some Fun	Mercury 73971
12/01/79	#64	10	Move Your Boogie Body	Mercury 76015
3/15/80	#60	7	Today Is The Day	Mercury 76036
6/02/84	#80	5	Freakshow On The Dance Floor	Mercury 818631
			CHERYL BARNES	
5/12/79	#89	5	Easy To Be Hard	RCA 11548
			J.J. BARNES	
3/26/66	#89	5	A Real Humdinger	Ric-Tic 110
5/27/67	#50	8	Baby Please Come Back Home	Groovesville 1006
			H.B. BARNUM	
1/21/61	#68	5	Lost Love	Eldo 111
			BARRACUDA	
12/07/68	#89	2	The Dance At St. Francis	RCA 9660
			HUGH BARRETT and THE VICTORS	
7/15/61	#98	2	There Was A Fungus Among Us	Madison 164
			RAY BARRETTO	
4/20/63	#18	11	El Watusi	Tico 419
			BARRON KNIGHTS	
8/25/79	#76	4	The Topical Song	Epic 50755
			CLAUDJA BARRY	
4/07/79	#65	9	Boogie Woogie Dancin' Shoes	Chrysalis 2313
			JOE BARRY	
4/29/61	#19	12	I'm A Fool To Care	Smash 1702
8/12/61	#89	3	Teardrops In My Heart	Smash 1710
			JOHN BARRY	
2/13/65	#50	1	Goldfinger	United Artists 791
			LEN BARRY	
6/19/65	#94	2	Lip Sync	Decca 31788
9/18/65	#1	16	1-2-3	Decca 31827
12/25/65	#13	10	Like A Baby	Decca 31889
3/19/66	#17	9	Somewhere	Decca 31923
6/11/66	#82	3	It's That Time Of The Year	Decca 31969
			BARRY and THE TAMERLANES	
10/26/63	#25	11	I Wonder What She's Doing Tonight	Valiant 6034
2/01/64	#76	4	Roberta	Valiant 6040
			CHRIS BARTLEY	
7/15/67	#35	9	The Sweetest Thing This Side Of Heaven	Vando 101
			EILEEN BARTON	
3/25/50	#1	13	If I Knew You Were Coming I'd've Baked You A Cake . . .	Mercury 5392
			BASIA	
8/06/88	#32	17	Time And Tide	Epic 07730
11/19/88	#73	6	New Day For You	Epic 08112
4/22/89	#86	3	Promises	Epic 68608
4/14/90	#27	15	Cruising For Bruising	Epic 73239
			COUNT BASIE	
6/29/63	#88	3	I Can't Stop Loving You	Reprise 20170
2/17/68	#60	6	For Your Precious Love*	Brunswick 55365
4/20/68	#80	5	Chain Gang*	Brunswick 55373
			released as by JACKIE WILSON and COUNT BASIE	
			TONI BASIL	
9/11/82	#2	29	Mickey	Chrysalis 2638
2/26/83	#81	4	Shoppin' From A To Z	Chrysalis 03537
1/21/84	#77	4	Over My Head	Chrysalis 42753

18

Debut Date	Peak Pos	Wks Chr	ARTIST/Song Title	Label & Number
			BASKERVILLE HOUNDS	
9/13/69	#68	7	Hold Me	Avco Embassy 4504
			FONTELLA BASS	
2/06/65	#29	12	Don't Mess Up A Good Thing*	Checker 1097
6/12/65	#99	1	You'll Miss Me (When I'm Gone)*	Checker 1111
9/18/65	#3	15	Rescue Me	Checker 1120
1/01/66	#38	7	Recovery	Checker 1131
3/26/66	#82	4	I Surrender	Checker 1137
			*released as by FONTELLA BASS & BOBBY McCLURE	
			SHIRLEY BASSEY	
1/30/65	#7	13	Goldfinger	United Artists 790
10/03/70	#81	6	Something	United Artists 50698
1/15/72	#54	8	Diamonds Are Forever	United Artists 50845
5/05/73	#58	14	Never, Never, Never	United Artists 211
			BATDORF & RODNEY	
8/16/75	#80	5	You Are A Song	Arista 0132
11/29/75	#74	7	Somewhere In The Night	Arista 0159
			DUKE BAXTER	
7/12/69	#69	7	Everybody Knows Matilda	VMC 740
			LES BAXTER	
5/02/53	#2	17	April In Portugal	Capitol 2374
8/28/54	#3	9	The High And The Mighty	Capitol 2845
4/30/55	#1	19	Unchained Melody	Capitol 3055
9/10/55	#7	5	Wake The Town And Tell The People	Capitol 3120
3/10/56	#1	14	The Poor People Of Paris	Capitol 3336
			BAY BOPS	
5/17/58	#58	1	Joanie	Coral 61975
			BAY CITY ROLLERS	
10/04/75	#1	20	Saturday Night	Arista 0149
2/07/76	#7	16	Money Honey	Arista 0170
4/24/76	#30	13	Rock And Roll Love Letter	Arista 0185
9/04/76	#8	15	I Only Want To Be With You	Arista 0205
11/27/76	#49	9	Yesterday's Hero	Arista 0216
2/12/77	#70	5	Dedication	Arista 0233
6/04/77	#7	18	You Made Me Believe In Magic	Arista 0256
10/08/77	#19	18	The Way I Feel Tonight	Arista 0272
			BAZUKA	
4/26/75	#12	18	Dynomite (Part 1)	A&M 1666
			B. BUMBLE & THE STINGERS	
3/04/61	#21	15	Bumble Boogie	Rendezvous 140
2/24/62	#25	13	Nut Rocker	Rendezvous 166
			BEACH BOYS	
2/10/62	#85	5	Surfin'	Candix 331
7/14/62	#10	21	Surfin' Safari	Capitol 4777
12/01/62	#50	8	Ten Little Indians	Capitol 4880
3/30/63	#1	12	Surfin' U.S.A./	Capitol 4932
4/06/63	#25	18	Shut Down	Capitol 4932
8/03/63	#5	15	Surfer Girl/	Capitol 5009
8/03/63	#19	13	Little Deuce Coupe	Capitol 5009
11/02/63	#8	13	Be True To Your School/	Capitol 5069
11/09/63	#34	11	In My Room	Capitol 5069
12/21/63	#69	2	Little Saint Nick	Capitol 5096
2/15/64	#6	12	Fun Fun Fun/	Capitol 5118
2/22/64	#94	1	Why Do Fools Fall In Love	Capitol 5118
5/23/64	#1	17	I Get Around/	Capitol 5174
5/23/64	#26	11	Don't Worry Baby	Capitol 5174
9/12/64	#7	10	When I Grow Up To Be A Man	Capitol 5245
10/10/64	#59	7	Four By The Beach Boys*	Capitol 5267
11/14/64	#10	11	Dance Dance Dance	Capitol 5306
3/06/65	#13	8	Do You Wanna Dance?/	Capitol 5372
3/06/65	#85	2	Please Let Me Wonder	Capitol 5372
4/24/65	#1	13	Help Me Rhonda	Capitol 5395
7/24/65	#3	11	California Girls	Capitol 5464
11/27/65	#15	7	The Little Girl I Once Knew	Capitol 5540
12/25/65	#1	12	Barbara Ann	Capitol 5561
4/02/66	#5	11	Sloop John B	Capitol 5602

Debut Date	Peak Pos	Wks Chr	ARTIST/Song Title	Label & Number
			BEACH BOYS—*continued*	
8/06/66	#7	10	Wouldn't It Be Nice/	Capitol 5706
8/06/66	#38	7	God Only Knows	Capitol 5706
10/22/66	#1	14	Good Vibrations	Capitol 5676
8/05/67	#8	8	Heroes And Villains	Brother 1001
11/04/67	#22	7	Wild Honey	Capitol 2028
12/23/67	#10	10	Darlin'	Capitol 2068
4/27/68	#37	7	Friends	Capitol 2160
7/20/68	#8	12	Do It Again	Capitol 2239
11/30/68	#56	7	Bluebirds Over The Mountain	Capitol 2360
3/08/69	#20	10	I Can Hear Music	Capitol 2432
6/28/69	#38	7	Break Away	Capitol 2530
3/07/70	#49	5	Add Some Music To Your Day	Reprise 0894
11/06/71	#79	4	Long Promised Road	Brother 1047
3/03/73	#96	3	Sail On Sailor	Brother 1138
8/10/74	#51	8	Surfin' U.S.A.	Capitol 3924
4/19/75	#62	10	Sail On Sailor	Brother 1325
6/05/76	#11	22	Rock And Roll Music	Brother 1354
8/28/76	#39	10	It's O.K.	Brother 1368
9/02/78	#66	6	Peggy Sue	Brother 1394
3/03/79	#52	7	Here Comes The Night	Caribou 9026
4/28/79	#33	10	Good Timin'	Caribou 9029
7/25/81	#8	17	The Beach Boys Medley	Capitol 5030
11/21/81	#20	16	Come Go With Me	Caribou 02633
5/25/85	#25	13	Getcha Back	Caribou 04913
8/03/85	#78	4	It's Gettin' Late	Caribou 05433
6/28/86	#68	6	Rock 'N' Roll To The Rescue	Capitol 5595
9/20/86	#49	10	California Dreamin'	Capitol 5630
7/11/87	#28	19	Wipeout**	Tin Pan Apple 885960
9/10/88	#1	20	Kokomo	Elektra 69385
			***four song EP**	
			****released as by THE FAT BOYS and THE BEACH BOYS**	
			BEACH NUTS	
7/31/65	#91	3	Out In The Sun	Bang 504
			BEASTIE BOYS	
12/20/86	#3	20	(You Gotta) Fight For Your Right (To Party!)	Def Jam 06595
3/21/87	#50	10	Brass Monkey	Def Jam 07020
8/05/89	#40	11	Hey Ladies	Capitol 44454
7/11/92	#87	3	So What'cha Want	Capitol 15847
			BEATLES	
1/11/64	#1	18	I Want To Hold Your Hand	Capitol 5112
1/25/64	#1	16	She Loves You	Swan 4152
2/01/64	#3	14	Please Please Me/	Vee-Jay 581
2/08/64	#41	9	From Me To You	Vee-Jay 581
2/08/64	#29	8	My Bonnie*	MGM 13213
2/08/64	#100	1	I Saw Her Standing There	Capitol 5112
3/07/64	#1	13	Twist And Shout	Tollie 9001
3/21/64	#30	7	Roll Over Beethoven	Capitol 72133
3/28/64	#31	8	All My Loving	Capitol 72144
3/28/64	#1	11	Can't Buy Me Love/	Capitol 5150
3/28/64	#3	12	Do You Want To Know A Secret/	Vee-Jay 587
3/28/64	#38	9	Thank You Girl	Vee-Jay 587
4/04/64	#77	3	You Can't Do That	Capitol 5150
4/04/64	#1	16	Love Me Do/	Tollie 9008
5/02/64	#10	10	P.S. I Love You	Tollie 9008
5/30/64	#86	3	Four By The Beatles**	Capitol 2121
7/11/64	#1	14	A Hard Day's Night/	Capitol 5222
7/18/64	#43	5	I Should Have Known Better	Capitol 5222
7/18/64	#14	9	Ain't She Sweet	Atco 6308
7/25/64	#22	9	I'll Cry Instead/	Capitol 5234
8/01/64	#14	9	And I Love Her/	Capitol 5235
8/08/64	#91	2	I'm Happy Just To Dance With You	Capitol 5234
8/08/64	#64	5	If I Fell	Capitol 5235
9/05/64	#17	8	Matchbox/	Capitol 5255
9/05/64	#34	7	Slow Down	Capitol 5255
12/05/64	#1	12	I Feel Fine/	Capitol 5327
12/05/64	#8	10	She's A Woman	Capitol 5327
2/20/65	#1	10	Eight Days A Week/	Capitol 5371
2/27/65	#83	2	I Don't Want To Spoil The Party	Capitol 5371
3/06/65	#68	4	4 By The Beatles**	Capitol 5365

Debut Date	Peak Pos	Wks Chr	ARTIST/Song Title	Label & Number
4/17/65	#1	12	Ticket To Ride	Capitol 5407
7/31/65	#1	14	Help	Capitol 5476
9/18/65	#1	13	Yesterday/	Capitol 5498
9/18/65	#28	7	Act Naturally	Capitol 5498
10/23/65	#73	3	Boys/	Capitol 6066
10/23/65	#75	2	Kansas City	Capitol 6066
12/18/65	#1	12	We Can Work It Out/	Capitol 5555
12/18/65	#10	10	Day Tripper	Capitol 5555
3/05/66	#2	9	Nowhere Man	Capitol 5587
6/11/66	#1	10	Paperback Writer/	Capitol 5651
6/11/66	#31	5	Rain	Capitol 5651
8/20/66	#1	10	Yellow Submarine/	Capitol 5715
8/20/66	#12	8	Eleanor Rigby	Capitol 5715
2/25/67	#1	10	Penny Lane/	Capitol 5810
2/25/67	#10	9	Strawberry Fields Forever	Capitol 5810
7/29/67	#1	9	All You Need Is Love/	Capitol 5964
7/29/67	#60	4	Baby You're A Rich Man	Capitol 5964
12/02/67	#1	12	Hello Goodbye/	Capitol 2056
12/02/67	#46	6	I Am The Walrus	Capitol 2056
3/23/68	#2	11	Lady Madonna	Capitol 2138
9/14/68	#1	19	Hey Jude/	Apple 2276
9/14/68	#11	10	Revolution	Apple 2276
5/03/69	#1	12	Get Back/	Apple 2490
5/03/69	#57	3	Don't Let Me Down	Apple 2490
6/14/69	#10	9	Ballad Of John And Yoko	Apple 2531
10/18/69	#1	14	Come Together/	Apple 2654
10/18/69	#2	13	Something	Apple 2654
3/14/70	#1	13	Let It Be	Apple 2764
5/16/70	#1	11	The Long And Winding Road/	Apple 2832
5/16/70	#71	2	For You Blue	Apple 2832
6/05/76	#3	17	Got To Get You Into My Life	Capitol 4274
11/13/76	#47	7	Ob-La-Di, Ob-La-Da	Capitol 4347
9/09/78	#92	4	Sgt. Pepper's Lonely Hearts Club Band/With A Little Help From My Friends	Capitol 4612
3/27/82	#14	13	Movie Medley	Capitol 5107
8/16/86	#32	14	Twist And Shout	Capitol 5624

*released as by THE BEATLES with TONY SHERIDAN
**four song EP

BEATS INTERNATIONAL

4/21/90	#69	6	Dub Be Good To Me	Elektra 64970
9/01/90	#75	5	Won't Talk About It	Elektra 64948

E.C. BEATTY

9/19/59	#40	8	Ski King	Colonial 7003

BEAU BRUMMELS

1/02/65	#17	13	Laugh Laugh	Autumn 8
4/07/65	#7	12	Just A Little	Autumn 10
7/17/65	#36	8	You Tell Me Why	Autumn 16
10/16/65	#53	6	Don't Talk To Strangers	Autumn 20
1/01/66	#93	2	Good Time Music	Autumn 24
6/18/66	#98	1	One Too Many Mornings	Warner Brothers 5813

BEAU-MARKS

5/21/60	#40	15	Clap Your Hands	Shad 5017

JEAN BEAUVOIR

6/07/86	#66	7	Feel The Heat	Columbia 05904

JEFF BECK

7/26/69	#28	8	Goo Goo Barabajagal (Love Is Hot)*	Epic 10510
6/15/85	#44	12	People Get Ready**	Epic 05416

*released as by DONOVAN with THE JEFF BECK GROUP
**released as by JEFF BECK and ROD STEWART

BOB BECKHAM

8/22/59	#41	22	Just As Much As Ever	Decca 30861
1/16/60	#38	10	Crazy Arms	Decca 31029

BECKMEIER BROTHERS

7/21/79	#57	6	Rock And Roll Dancin'	Casablanca 1000

JOHNNY BEECHER

3/16/63	#82	5	Sax Fifth Avenue	Warner Brothers 5341

Debut Date	Peak Pos	Wks Chr	ARTIST/Song Title	Label & Number
			BEE GEES	
5/27/67	#17	8	New York Mining Disaster 1941 (Have You Seen My Wife, Mr. Jones)	Atco 6487
7/08/67	#24	11	To Love Somebody	Atco 6503
9/30/67	#12	9	Holiday	Atco 6521
11/11/67	#14	10	(The Lights Went Out In) Massachusetts	Atco 6532
1/20/68	#19	12	Words	Atco 6548
4/06/68	#40	7	Jumbo	Atco 6570
8/10/68	#3	15	I've Gotta Get A Message To You	Atco 6603
12/14/68	#6	13	I Started A Joke	Atco 6639
3/22/69	#18	7	First Of May	Atco 6657
5/24/69	#32	7	Tomorrow Tomorrow	Atco 6682
8/30/69	#63	3	Don't Forget To Remember	Atco 6702
3/14/70	#76	4	If I Only Had My Mind On Something Else	Atco 6741
11/28/70	#1	16	Lonely Days	Atco 6795
6/19/71	#1	15	How Can You Mend A Broken Heart	Atco 6824
10/16/71	#39	7	Don't Wanna Live Inside Myself	Atco 6847
1/22/72	#15	10	My World	Atco 6871
7/22/72	#11	13	Run To Me	Atco 6896
11/04/72	#26	9	Alive	Atco 6909
3/10/73	#78	5	Saw A New Morning	RSO 401
3/02/74	#87	4	Mr. Natural	RSO 408
5/24/75	#1	19	Jive Talkin'	RSO 510
10/04/75	#4	17	Nights On Broadway	RSO 515
12/20/75	#9	18	Fanny (Be Tender With My Love)	RSO 519
7/03/76	#1	20	You Should Be Dancing	RSO 853
9/18/76	#3	24	Love So Right	RSO 859
1/15/77	#14	14	Boogie Child	RSO 867
7/23/77	#26	11	Edge Of The Universe	RSO 880
9/24/77	#1	28	How Deep Is Your Love	RSO 882
12/10/77	#1	27	Stayin' Alive	RSO 885
2/04/78	#1	21	Night Fever	RSO 889
11/18/78	#2	20	Too Much Heaven	RSO 913
2/10/79	#1	16	Tragedy	RSO 918
4/21/79	#2	14	Love You Inside And Out	RSO 925
9/26/81	#29	9	He's A Liar	RSO 1066
11/07/81	#40	12	Living Eyes	RSO 1067
5/21/83	#21	14	The Woman In You	RSO 813173
8/20/83	#49	9	Someone Belonging To Someone	RSO 815235
9/19/87	#80	4	You Win Again	Warner Brothers 28351
7/29/89	#9	16	One	Warner Brothers 22899
5/25/91	#86	4	He's Gone	Warner Brothers 19369
10/30/93	#71	14	Paying The Price Of Love	Polydor 859164
			BEGINNING OF THE END	
5/01/71	#10	15	Funky Nassau (Part 1)	Alston 4595
			HARRY BELAFONTE	
11/24/56	#17	18	Jamaica Farewell	RCA 6663
12/29/56	#25	3	Mary's Boy Child	RCA 6735
1/12/57	#4	17	Banana Boat (Day-O)	RCA 6771
3/09/57	#44	1	Hold 'Em Joe	RCA 0322
3/16/57	#9	13	Mama Look At Bubu	RCA 6830
5/25/57	#35	5	Cocoanut Woman/	RCA 6885
6/08/57	#32	9	Island In The Sun	RCA 6885
3/22/58	#57	1	The Marching Saints	RCA 7176
7/19/58	#57	11	The Waiting Game/	RCA 7289
7/26/58	#70	1	Ain't That Love	RCA 7289
			ADRIAN BELEW	
8/12/89	#70	8	Oh Daddy	Atlantic 88904
			CARL BELEW	
10/06/62	#85	4	Hello Out There	RCA 8050
			ARCHIE BELL & THE DRELLS	
4/06/68	#1	15	Tighten Up	Atlantic 2478
7/20/68	#15	9	I Can't Stop Dancing	Atlantic 2534
9/28/68	#46	6	Do The Choo Choo	Atlantic 2559
12/14/68	#20	11	There's Gonna Be A Showdown	Atlantic 2583
3/29/69	#80	3	I Love My Baby	Atlantic 2612
6/21/69	#58	7	Girl You're Too Young	Atlantic 2644
9/13/69	#98	2	My Balloon's Going Up	Atlantic 2663

Debut Date	Peak Pos	Wks Chr	ARTIST/Song Title	Label & Number
3/17/73	#78	7	Dancing To Your Music	Glades 1707
3/06/76	#77	6	Let's Groove	TSOP 4775
			BENNY BELL	
3/01/75	#34	11	Shaving Cream	Vanguard 35183
			MADELINE BELL	
2/10/68	#36	10	I'm Gonna Make You Love Me	Philips 40517
			MAGGIE BELL	
4/27/74	#76	4	After Midnight	Atlantic 3018
			VINCENT BELL	
3/28/70	#27	10	Airport Love Theme (Gwen And Vern)	Decca 32659
			WILLIAM BELL	
5/06/67	#78	3	Everybody Loves A Winner	Stax 212
3/30/68	#83	2	Every Man Ought To Have A Woman/	Stax 248
5/04/68	#79	5	A Tribute To A King	Stax 248
8/31/68	#84	3	Private Number*	Stax 0005
1/11/69	#36	9	I Forgot To Be Your Lover	Stax 0015
11/22/69	#100	1	Born Under A Bad Sign	Stax 0054
2/19/77	#8	17	Tryin' To Love Two	Mercury 73839
			*released as by **JUDY CLAY & WILLIAM BELL**	
			DAVID BELLAMY	
10/11/75	#98	1	Nothin' Heavy	Warner Brothers 8123
			BELLAMY BROTHERS	
2/07/76	#1	21	Let Your Love Flow	Warner Brothers 8169
7/10/76	#93	3	Hell Cat	Warner Brothers 8220
9/04/76	#77	3	Satin Sheets	Warner Brothers 8248
5/26/79	#58	9	If I Said You Had A Beautiful Body Would You Hold It Against Me	Warner Brothers 8790
			BELL & JAMES	
1/27/79	#16	18	Livin' It Up (Friday Night)	A&M 2069
			BELL BIV DeVOE	
4/14/90	#2	22	Poison	MCA 53772
7/07/90	#5	23	Do Me!	MCA 79045
10/20/90	#23	15	B.B.D. (I Thought It Was Me)?	MCA 53897
11/21/92	#18	16	Gangsta	MCA 54555
9/04/93	#39	22	Something In Your Eyes	MCA 54725
			REGINA BELLE	
7/18/87	#62	8	Show Me The Way	Columbia 07080
10/14/89	#62	10	Baby Come To Me	Columbia 68969
3/03/90	#45	11	Make It Like It Was	Columbia 73022
1/23/93	#2	22	A Whole New World (Alladin's Theme)*	Columbia 74751
4/24/93	#46	16	If I Could	Columbia 74864
			*released as by **PEABO BRYSON** and **REGINA BELLE**	
			BELLE STARS	
5/07/83	#86	4	Sign Of The Times	Warner Brothers 29672
3/11/89	#16	20	Iko Iko	Capitol 44343
			BELL NOTES	
1/03/59	#8	18	I've Had It	Time 1004
5/09/59	#48	8	Old Spanish Town	Time 1010
9/03/60	#88	1	Shortnin' Bread	Madison 136
			BELLS	
12/26/70	#86	6	Fly Little White Dove Fly	Polydor 15016
3/06/71	#4	14	Stay Awhile	Polydor 15023
6/12/71	#52	7	I Love You Lady Dawn	Polydor 15027
			BELL SISTERS	
3/08/52	#8	5	Bermuda	RCA 4422
			TONY BELLUS	
5/30/59	#42	17	Robbin' The Cradle	NRC 023
			BELMONTS	
6/03/61	#22	11	Tell Me Why	Sabrina 500
9/16/61	#75	5	Don't Get Around Much Anymore	Sabrina 501
12/02/61	#57	9	I Need Someone	Sabina 502
7/21/62	#26	15	Come On Little Angel	Sabina 505
11/10/62	#51	6	Diddle-De-Dum	Sabina 507
4/13/63	#81	6	Ann-Marie	Sabina 509

23

Debut Date	Peak Pos	Wks Chr	ARTIST/Song Title	Label & Number
			BELMONTS—continued	
9/26/81	#77	6	Let's Put The Fun Back In Rock N Roll*	MiaSound 1002
			*released as by FREDDY CANNON & THE BELMONTS	
			JOHN BELUSHI	
10/07/78	#91	4	Louie, Louie	MCA 40950
			JESSE BELVIN	
12/08/56	#23	8	Goodnight My Love	Modern 1005
3/28/59	#28	13	Guess Who	RCA 7469
6/20/59	#58	7	It Could've Been Worse	RCA 7543
			PAT BENATAR	
12/22/79	#19	21	Heartbreaker	Chrysalis 2395
4/05/80	#28	15	We Live For Love	Chrysalis 2419
7/26/80	#44	12	You Better Run	Chrysalis 2450
10/04/80	#7	25	Hit Me With Your Best Shot	Chrysalis 2464
1/17/81	#10	18	Treat Me Right	Chrysalis 2487
7/18/81	#15	13	Fire And Ice	Chrysalis 2529
10/03/81	#35	12	Promises In The Dark	Chrysalis 2555
10/23/82	#13	17	Shadows Of The Night	Chrysalis 2647
2/05/83	#41	11	Little Too Late	Chrysalis 03536
4/23/83	#41	10	Looking For A Stranger	Chrysalis 42688
9/24/83	#4	24	Love Is A Battlefield	Chrysalis 42732
10/27/84	#6	20	We Belong	Chrysalis 42826
1/19/85	#35	11	Ooh Ooh Song	Chrysalis 42843
7/06/85	#9	18	Invincible (Theme From The Legend Of Billie Jean) . . .	Chrysalis 43877
11/23/85	#27	15	Sex As A Weapon	Chrysalis 42927
2/15/86	#54	10	Le Bel Age	Chrysalis 42968
7/02/88	#25	17	All Fired Up	Chrysalis 43268
			BOYD BENNETT and HIS ROCKETS	
9/10/55	#3	10	Seventeen	King 1470
9/05/59	#63	9	Boogie Bear*	Mercury 71479
			*released as by Boyd Bennett	
			JOE BENNETT and THE SPARKLETONES	
8/31/57	#19	12	Black Slacks	ABC Paramount 9837
12/14/57	#41	6	Penny Loafers And Bobby Socks	ABC Paramount 9867
10/31/59	#95	1	Boys Do Cry	Paris 537
			PETE BENNETT	
12/30/61	#93	3	Fever	Sun 1002
			TONY BENNETT	
8/18/51	#1	23	Because Of You	Columbia 39362
9/15/51	#1	22	Cold, Cold Heart	Columbia 39449
3/14/53	#10	2	Congratulations To Someone	Columbia 39910
10/24/53	#1	19	Rags To Riches	Columbia 40048
12/26/53	#1	19	Stranger In Paradise	Columbia 40121
8/11/56	#30	10	Happiness Street/	Columbia 40726
9/01/56	#34	4	From The Candy Store On The Corner To The Chapel On The Hill	Columbia 40726
11/17/56	#38	7	Just In Time	Columbia 40770
5/11/57	#32	7	One For My Baby	Columbia 40907
7/27/57	#8	17	In The Middle Of An Island/	Columbia 40965
7/27/57	#35	7	I Am	Columbia 40965
11/02/57	#52	3	Ca, C'est L'Amour/	Columbia 41032
11/16/57	#49	5	I Never Felt More Like Falling In Love	Columbia 41032
6/07/58	#31	11	Young And Warm And Wonderful	Columbia 41172
9/13/58	#20	14	Firefly	Columbia 41237
12/13/58	#83	3	Love Look Away	Columbia 41298
3/28/59	#56	7	Being True To One Another	Columbia 41341
8/08/59	#43	10	Smile	Columbia 41434
1/02/60	#85	4	Climb Ev'ry Mountain	Columbia 41520
4/14/62	#22	26	I Left My Heart In San Francisco	Columbia 42332
1/19/63	#15	16	I Wanna Be Around/	Columbia 42634
1/19/63	#86	5	I Will Live My Life For You	Columbia 42634
5/11/63	#25	11	The Good Life/	Columbia 42779
5/11/63	#94	3	Spring In Manhattan	Columbia 42779
7/20/63	#55	8	This Is All I Ask	Columbia 42820
10/12/63	#49	8	Don't Wait Too Long	Columbia 42886
12/28/63	#54	7	The Little Boy	Columbia 42931
3/21/64	#70	6	When Joanna Loved Me	Columbia 42996
7/18/64	#81	2	It's A Sin To Tell A Lie/	Columbia 43073

Debut Date	Peak Pos	Wks Chr	ARTIST/Song Title	Label & Number
7/18/64	#82	8	A Taste Of Honey	Columbia 43073
10/03/64	#38	11	Who Can I Turn To	Columbia 43141
2/20/65	#48	7	If I Ruled The World	Columbia 43220
7/10/65	#60	7	Fly Me To The Moon	Columbia 43331
7/30/66	#97	4	Georgia Rose	Columbia 43715
10/14/67	#94	6	For Once In My Life	Columbia 44258
3/09/68	#95	2	Fool Of Fools	Columbia 44443
			GEORGE BENSON	
6/05/76	#12	22	This Masquerade	Warner Brothers 8209
7/30/77	#29	14	The Greatest Love Of All	Arista 0251
3/18/78	#11	20	On Broadway	Warner Brothers 8542
7/15/78	#94	3	Lady Blue	Warner Brothers 8604
2/24/79	#14	15	Love Ballad	Warner Brothers 8759
7/05/80	#6	25	Give Me The Night	Warner Brothers 49505
10/18/80	#77	6	Love X Love	Warner Brothers 49570
8/29/81	#44	10	Love All The Hurt Away*	Arista 0624
10/24/81	#5	22	Turn Your Love Around	Warner Brothers 49846
2/27/82	#55	9	Never Give Up On A Good Thing	Warner Brothers 50005
5/14/83	#40	12	Inside Love (So Personal)	Warner Brothers 29649
7/30/83	#37	12	Lady Love Me (One More Time)	Warner Brothers 29563
12/15/84	#46	12	20/20	Warner Brothers 29120
			***released as by ARETHA FRANKLIN and GEORGE BENSON**	
			BROOK BENTON	
1/24/59	#2	19	It's Just A Matter Of Time	Mercury 71394
4/18/59	#11	13	Endlessly/	Mercury 71443
5/02/59	#60	4	So Close	Mercury 71443
7/18/59	#10	14	Thank You Pretty Baby/	Mercury 71478
7/18/59	#42	8	With All My Heart	Mercury 71478
10/10/59	#3	17	So Many Ways	Mercury 71512
12/26/59	#65	5	This Time Of The Year	Mercury 71554
1/30/60	#2	16	Baby (You've Got What It Takes)*	Mercury 71565
4/09/60	#23	11	The Ties That Bind/	Mercury 71566
4/09/60	#49	9	Hither And Thither And Yon	Mercury 71566
5/21/60	#5	14	A Rockin' Good Way (To Mess Around And Fall In Love)*	Mercury 71629
8/13/60	#3	18	Kiddio/	Mercury 71652
8/13/60	#16	14	The Same One	Mercury 71652
11/19/60	#15	11	Fools Rush In	Mercury 71722
2/11/61	#7	14	Think Twice/	Mercury 71774
2/18/61	#24	9	For My Baby	Mercury 71774
5/20/61	#2	16	The Boll Weevil Song	Mercury 71820
9/02/61	#16	8	Frankie And Johnny/	Mercury 71859
10/14/61	#71	6	It's Just A House Without You	Mercury 71859
11/25/61	#16	11	Revenge	Mercury 71903
1/13/62	#29	9	Shadrack/	Mercury 71912
1/20/62	#94	2	The Lost Penny	Mercury 71912
2/17/62	#42	8	Walk On The Wild Side	Mercury 71925
5/05/62	#36	9	Hit Record/	Mercury 71962
5/19/62	#86	3	Thanks To The Fool	Mercury 71962
8/18/62	#10	12	Lie To Me	Mercury 72024
11/24/62	#6	14	Hotel Happiness/	Mercury 72055
11/24/62	#81	2	Still Waters Run Deep	Mercury 72055
3/09/63	#22	10	I Got What I Wanted/	Mercury 72099
3/09/63	#72	6	Dearer Than Life	Mercury 72099
6/15/63	#29	10	My True Confession/	Mercury 72135
6/22/63	#87	2	Tender Years	Mercury 72135
9/14/63	#30	8	Two Tickets To Paradise	Mercury 72177
12/14/63	#59	3	You're All I Want For Christmas	Mercury 72214
1/25/64	#30	7	Going Going Gone	Mercury 72230
5/16/64	#40	7	Another Cup Of Coffee/	Mercury 72266
5/16/64	#38	8	Too Late To Turn Back Now	Mercury 72266
7/25/64	#50	7	A House Is Not A Home	Mercury 72303
9/26/64	#47	6	Lumberjack	Mercury 72333
12/12/64	#58	6	Do It Right	Mercury 72365
7/24/65	#97	2	Love Me Now	Mercury 72446
11/13/65	#43	6	Mother Nature, Father Time	RCA 8693
8/26/67	#88	2	Laura (Tell Me What He's Got That I Ain't Got)	Reprise 0611
6/28/69	#67	7	Nothing Can Take The Place Of You	Cotillion 44034
1/03/70	#2	15	Rainy Night In Georgia	Cotillion 44057
4/18/70	#48	5	My Way	Cotillion 44072
5/23/70	#48	7	Don't It Make You Wanna Go Home	Cotillion 44078

Debut Date	Peak Pos	Wks Chr	ARTIST/Song Title	Label & Number
			BROOK BENTON—*continued*	
12/19/70	#52	9	Shoes	Cotillion 44093
			released as by DINAH WASHINGTON & BROOK BENTON	
			POLLY BERGEN	
11/15/58	#24	12	Come Prima	Columbia 41275
			BERLIN	
3/05/83	#57	9	Sex (I'm A....)	Geffen 29747
6/04/83	#50	11	The Metro	Geffen 29638
10/01/83	#79	4	Masquerade	Geffen 29504
3/17/84	#16	19	No More Words	Geffen 29360
6/21/86	#1	22	Take My Breath Away	Columbia 05903
10/25/86	#83	4	Like Flames	Geffen 28563
			BERMUDAS	
4/18/64	#75	11	Donnie	Era 3125
			ROD BERNARD	
3/07/59	#17	13	This Should Go On Forever	Argo 5327
4/07/62	#92	6	Colinda	Hall Way 1902
			CHUCK BERRY	
9/24/55	#5	5	Maybellene	Chess 1604
4/06/57	#3	17	School Day	Chess 1653
7/20/57	#45	5	Oh Baby Doll	Chess 1664
11/09/57	#14	12	Rock & Roll Music	Chess 1671
2/15/58	#2	12	Sweet Little Sixteen	Chess 1683
4/26/58	#11	12	Johnny B. Goode	Chess 1691
8/30/58	#31	10	Carol	Chess 1700
11/15/58	#52	9	Sweet Little Rock And Roller/	Chess 1709
11/15/58	#74	7	Jo Jo Gunne	Chess 1709
12/27/58	#97	1	Merry Christmas Baby	Chess 1714
2/07/59	#76	5	Anthony Boy	Chess 1716
4/04/59	#31	10	Almost Grown/	Chess 1722
4/04/59	#91	2	Little Queenie	Chess 1722
6/20/59	#49	5	Back In The U.S.A./	Chess 1729
7/25/59	#87	5	Memphis Tennessee	Chess 1729
2/06/60	#56	7	Too Pooped To Pop/	Chess 1747
2/13/60	#60	5	Let It Rock	Chess 1747
6/04/60	#64	4	Bye Bye Johnny	Chess 1754
11/26/60	#93	3	Jaguar And Thunderbird	Chess 1767
2/29/64	#32	14	Nadine (Is It You?)	Chess 1883
5/30/64	#9	10	No Particular Place To Go	Chess 1898
8/08/64	#15	8	You Never Can Tell	Chess 1906
10/24/64	#51	6	Little Marie	Chess 1912
12/12/64	#35	8	Promised Land	Chess 1916
7/29/72	#1	18	My Ding-A-Ling	Chess 2131
11/25/72	#30	13	Reelin' & Rockin'	Chess 2136
			PLASTIC BERTRAND	
5/06/78	#57	8	Ca Plane Pour Moi	Sire 1020
			HAROLD BETTERS	
11/28/64	#88	3	Do Anything You Wanna	Gateway 747
			BETTY BOO	
11/10/90	#82	3	Doin' The Do	Sire 19570
			BEVERLY SISTERS	
12/22/56	#31	7	Greensleeves	London 1703
			B-52'S	
4/19/80	#74	6	Rock Lobster	Warner Brothers 49173
10/18/80	#78	5	Private Idaho	Warner Brothers 49537
7/16/83	#81	5	Legal Tender	Warner Brothers 29579
8/26/89	#4	28	Love Shack	Reprise 22817
12/23/89	#3	22	Roam	Reprise 22667
4/21/90	#27	16	Dead Beat Club	Reprise 19938
6/20/92	#19	16	Good Stuff	Reprise 18895
			BIDDU ORCHESTRA	
9/13/75	#54	10	Summer Of '42	Epic 50139
			BIG AUDIO DYNAMITE II	
9/28/91	#37	19	Rush	Columbia 73844
2/01/92	#51	12	The Globe	Columbia 74149

Debut Date	Peak Pos	Wks Chr	ARTIST/Song Title	Label & Number
			BIG BOPPER	
8/16/58	#4	23	Chantilly Lace	Mercury 71343
11/29/58	#39	8	Big Bopper's Wedding/	Mercury 71375
11/29/58	#63	6	Little Red Riding Hood	Mercury 71375
			BIG BROTHER and THE HOLDING COMPANY	
9/07/68	#14	12	Piece Of My Heart	Columbia 44626
9/07/68	#48	7	Down On Me	Mainstream 662
			BIG COUNTRY	
10/22/83	#11	16	In A Big Country	Mercury 814467
2/11/84	#62	7	Fields Of Fire	Mercury 811450
7/26/86	#82	5	Look Away	Mercury 884645
			BIG DADDY KANE	
7/17/93	#44	19	Very Special*	Cold Chillin' 18437
			***released as by BIG DADDY KANE featuring SPINDERELLA**	
			BIG MAYBELLE	
1/21/67	#99	1	96 Tears	Rojac 112
			BIG MOUNTAIN	
5/01/93	#45	18	Touch My Light	Quality 19120
			BIG PIG	
3/26/88	#55	11	Breakaway	A&M 3014
			BIG RIC	
9/03/83	#77	4	Take Away	Scotti Brothers 04084
			BIG SAMBO and THE HOUSE WRECKERS	
3/10/62	#72	7	The Rains Came	Epic 7003
			BIG TROUBLE	
10/17/87	#71	9	Crazy World	Epic 07432
			BIKINIS	
5/31/58	#57	2	Bikini	Roulette 4072
			MR. ACKER BILK	
3/15/60	#85	1	Summer Set	Atco 6160
3/17/62	#1	22	Stranger On The Shore	Atco 6217
7/14/62	#48	7	Above The Stars	Atco 6230
11/10/62	#88	3	Limelight	Atco 6238
			BILLY & LILLIE	
8/01/59	#4	12	La Dee Dah	Swan 4002
12/20/58	#27	13	Lucky Ladybug	Swan 4020
8/01/59	#88	3	Bells, Bells, Bells	Swan 4036
			BILLY & THE BEATERS (see BILLY VERA)	
			BILLY & THE ESSENTIALS	
12/15/62	#90	5	Maybe You'll Be There	Jamie 1239
			BILLY JOE & THE CHECKMATES	
1/20/62	#20	12	Percolator (Twist)	Dore 620
			BIMBO JET	
6/21/75	#74	6	El Bimbo	Scepter 12406
			BINGO BOYS	
2/16/91	#32	19	How To Dance	Atlantic 87756
			BIRDLEGS & PAULINE and THEIR VERSATILITY BIRDS	
5/18/63	#96	4	Spring	Vee-Jay 510
			JANE BIRKIN & SERGE GAINSBOURG	
2/07/70	#92	2	Je T'Aime...Moi Non Plus	Fontana 1665
			BISCUIT	
11/03/90	#75	3	Biscuit's In The House	Columbia 73585
			ELVIN BISHOP	
9/14/74	#70	10	Travelin' Shoes	Capricorn 0202
7/05/75	#76	5	Sure Feels Good	Capricorn 0237
3/06/76	#3	19	Fooled Around And Fell In Love	Capricorn 0252
			STEPHEN BISHOP	
12/04/76	#21	17	Save It For A Rainy Day	ABC 12232
6/11/77	#5	24	On And On	ABC 12260
9/09/78	#29	14	Everybody Needs Love	ABC 12406

Debut Date	Peak Pos	Wks Chr	ARTIST/Song Title	Label & Number
			STEPHEN BISHOP—*continued*	
12/16/78	#57	8	Animal House	ABC 12435
1/29/83	#19	22	It Might Be You	Warner Brothers 29791
			BIZARRE INC.	
1/30/93	#46	29	I'm Gonna Get You*	Columbia 74814
			*released as by BIZARRE INC. featuring ANGIE BROWN	
			BIZ MARKIE	
1/27/90	#9	16	Just A Friend	Cold Chillin' 22764
			BILL BLACK'S COMBO	
11/14/59	#13	16	Smokie (Part 2)	Hi 2018
2/27/60	#4	19	White Silver Sands	Hi 2021
6/18/60	#9	13	Josephine	Hi 2022
9/10/60	#7	15	Don't Be Cruel	Hi 2026
12/03/60	#17	11	Blue Tango/	Hi 2027
12/31/60	#82	3	Willie	Hi 2027
2/18/61	#17	9	Hearts Of Stone	Hi 2028
6/10/61	#23	8	Ole Buttermilk Sky	Hi 2036
9/16/61	#39	9	Movin'	Hi 2038
12/16/61	#37	10	Twist Her	Hi 2042
4/28/62	#86	5	Twistin' -- White Silver Sands	Hi 2052
8/18/62	#65	7	So What	Hi 2055
4/20/63	#44	8	Do It -- Rat Now	Hi 2064
9/21/63	#77	7	Monkey Shine	Hi 2069
1/25/64	#75	6	Comin' On	Hi 2072
6/29/68	#78	6	Turn On Your Love Light	Hi 2145
			CILLA BLACK	
6/13/64	#38	10	You're My World	Capitol 5196
9/19/64	#91	1	He Won't Ask Me	Capitol 5258
6/29/68	#97	1	Step Inside Love	Bell 726
			CLINT BLACK	
7/03/93	#45	12	A Bad Goodbye*	RCA 62503
			*released as by CLINT BLACK with WYNONNA	
			JEANNE BLACK	
4/30/60	#5	12	He'll Have To Stay	Capitol 4368
8/06/60	#47	7	Lisa	Capitol 4396
12/31/60	#74	6	Oh How I Miss You Tonight	Capitol 4492
			MARION BLACK	
2/20/71	#93	4	Go On Fool	Avco Embassy 4559
			TERRY BLACK	
11/14/64	#85	4	Unless You Care	Tollie 9026
2/05/72	#59	7	Goin' Down (On The Road To L.A.)*	Kama Sutra 540
			*released as by TERRY BLACK and LAUREL WARD	
			BLACK BOX	
8/11/90	#7	19	Everybody Everybody	RCA 2628
12/15/90	#49	13	I Don't Know Anybody else	RCA 2751
4/20/91	#14	22	Strike It Up	RCA 2794
			BLACKBYRDS	
9/14/74	#82	5	Do It Fluid	Fantasy 729
2/08/75	#7	17	Walking In Rhythm	Fantasy 736
7/26/75	#72	6	Flyin' High	Fantasy 747
3/06/76	#42	11	Happy Music	Fantasy 762
			BLACK CROWES	
5/19/90	#73	10	Jealous Again	Def American 19697
11/03/90	#49	13	Hard To Handle	Def American 19668
3/16/91	#31	20	She Talks To Angels	Def American 19403
6/22/91	#21	19	Hard To Handle	Def American 19245
6/20/92	#35	16	Remedy	Def American 18877
9/12/92	#77	6	Thorn In My Pride	Def American 18803
			BLACKFOOT	
6/23/79	#32	14	Highway Song	Atco 7104
10/20/79	#36	14	Train, Train	Atco 7207
6/27/81	#57	11	Fly Away	Atco 7331
			BLACK IVORY	
4/29/72	#95	3	You And I	Today 1508

Debut Date	Peak Pos	Wks Chr	**ARTIST**/Song Title	Label & Number
			BLACKJACK	
7/14/79	#69	6	Love Me Tonight	Polydor 14572
			BLACK OAK ARKANSAS	
12/08/73	#12	13	Jim Dandy	Atco 6948
			BLACK SABBATH	
12/05/70	#79	6	Paranoid	Warner Brothers 7437
2/05/72	#67	5	Iron Man	Warner Brothers 7530
			BLACKWELL	
10/25/69	#73	3	Wonderful	Astro 1000
			CHARLIE BLACKWELL	
2/07/59	#53	9	Midnight Oil	Warner Brothers 5031
			BLACKWELLS	
7/02/60	#83	4	Unchained Melody	Jamie 1157
4/15/61	#87	4	Love Or Money	Jamie 1179
			BLADES OF GRASS	
7/22/67	#64	4	Happy	Jubilee 5582
			JACK BLANCHARD & MISTY MORGAN	
3/14/70	#14	11	Tennessee Bird Walk	Wayside 010
6/27/70	#81	3	Humphrey The Camel	Wayside 013
			BILLY BLAND	
3/19/60	#10	17	Let The Little Girl Dance	Old Town 1076
7/16/60	#81	4	Pardon Me	Old Town 1082
			BOBBY BLAND	
2/06/60	#94	4	I'll Take Care Of You	Duke 314
4/16/60	#95	3	Hold Me Tenderly	Duke 318
10/15/60	#53	14	Cry, Cry, Cry	Duke 327
2/11/61	#45	10	I Pity The Fool	Duke 332
7/22/61	#49	15	Don't Cry No More	Duke 340
12/09/61	#27	11	Turn On Your Love Light	Duke 344
4/07/62	#90	2	Ain't That Loving You	Duke 338
8/11/62	#50	7	Yield Not To Temptation	Duke 352
9/15/62	#48	13	Stormy Monday Blues	Duke 355
1/05/63	#29	15	Call On Me/	Duke 360
1/19/63	#30	12	That's The Way Love Is	Duke 360
7/13/63	#78	5	Sometimes You Gotta Cry A Little	Duke 366
1/04/64	#98	1	I Can't Stop Singing	Duke 370
3/07/64	#16	10	Ain't Nothing You Can Do	Duke 375
6/20/64	#55	9	Share Your Love With Me	Duke 377
10/10/64	#30	10	Ain't Doing Too Bad (Part 1)	Duke 383
12/26/64	#47	8	Blind Man	Duke 386
5/01/65	#99	1	Dust In Daddy's Eyes	Duke 390
8/28/65	#53	10	These Hands (Small But Mighty)	Duke 385
1/08/66	#53	7	I'm Too Far Gone (To Turn Around)	Duke 393
5/21/66	#51	6	Good Time Charlie	Duke 402
9/24/66	#95	2	Poverty	Duke 407
4/29/67	#95	2	You're All I Need	Duke 416
8/05/67	#95	2	That Did It	Duke 421
11/02/68	#58	10	Rockin' In The Same Old Boat	Duke 440
6/28/69	#91	2	Gotta Get To Know You	Duke 447
9/20/69	#51	7	Chains Of Love	Duke 449
1/31/70	#74	5	If You've Got A Heart	Duke 458
5/23/70	#93	3	If Love Ruled The World	Duke 460
12/12/70	#73	2	Keep On Loving Me	Duke 464
2/19/72	#58	7	Do What You Set Out To Do	Duke 472
11/17/73	#44	11	This Time I'm Gone For Good	Dunhill 4369
3/30/74	#81	5	Goin' Down Slow	Dunhill 4379
8/17/74	#90	5	Ain't No Love In The Heart Of The City	Dunhill 15003
12/21/74	#82	5	I Wouldn't Treat A Dog (The Way You Treated Me)	Dunhill 15015
			MARCIE BLANE	
10/13/62	#2	19	Bobby's Girl	Seville 120
2/09/63	#68	6	What Does A Girl Do	Seville 123
			BLAZE	
12/11/76	#88	3	Silver Heels	Epic 50292
			BLENDELLS	
9/05/64	#74	8	La La La La La	Reprise 0291

Debut Date	Peak Pos	Wks Chr	ARTIST/Song Title	Label & Number
			BLENDERS	
7/13/63	#55	9	Daughter	Witch 114
			ARCHIE BLEYER	
6/19/54	#1	13	Hernando's Hideaway	Cadence 1241
			MARY J. BLIGE	
6/27/92	#17	21	You Remind Me	Uptown 54327
9/05/92	#9	36	Real Love	Uptown 54455
12/26/92	#58	14	Reminisce	Uptown 54526
2/20/93	#19	21	Sweet Thing	Uptown 54586
5/29/93	#43	12	Love No Limit	Uptown 54639
			BLIND MELON	
9/04/93	#17	30	No Rain	Capitol 15994
			BLINKY	
8/30/69	#93	1	Oh How Happy	Gordy 7090
			BLONDIE	
2/10/79	#1	23	Heart Of Glass	Chrysalis 2295
6/02/79	#22	14	One Way Or Another	Chrysalis 2336
9/27/79	#20	16	Dreaming	Chrysalis 2379
1/26/80	#72	6	The Hardest Part	Chrysalis 2408
2/16/80	#1	28	Call Me	Chrysalis 2414
5/17/80	#49	9	Atomic	Chrysalis 2410
11/15/80	#1	27	The Tide Is High	Chrysalis 2465
1/31/81	#1	21	Rapture	Chrysalis 2485
6/05/82	#41	8	Island Of Lost Souls	Chrysalis 2603
			BLOODROCK	
12/26/70	#36	13	D.O.A.	Capitol 3009
			BLOODSTONE	
4/07/73	#5	20	Natural High	London 1046
9/01/73	#35	14	Never Let You Go	London 1051
2/02/74	#31	14	Outside Woman	London 1052
7/27/74	#50	7	That's Not How It Goes	London 1055
3/08/75	#41	10	My Little Lady	London 1061
			BLOOD, SWEAT & TEARS	
3/01/69	#2	13	You've Made Me So Very Happy	Columbia 44776
5/31/69	#3	13	Spinning Wheel	Columbia 44781
10/18/69	#1	12	And When I Die	Columbia 45008
8/01/70	#9	9	Hi-De-Ho	Columbia 45204
9/26/70	#17	9	Lucretia Mac Evil	Columbia 45235
7/31/71	#21	8	Go Down Gamblin'	Columbia 45427
10/23/71	#66	4	Lisa, Listen To Me	Columbia 45477
9/30/72	#62	10	So Long Dixie	Columbia 45661
12/30/72	#78	3	I Can't Move No Mountains	Columbia 45755
10/27/73	#90	2	Roller Coaster	Columbia 45937
6/07/75	#62	7	Got To Get You Into My Life	Columbia 10151
			BOBBY BLOOM	
9/19/70	#6	15	Montego Bay	L&R/MGM 157
1/23/71	#78	4	Make Me Happy	MGM 14212
1/30/71	#97	2	Where Are We Going	Roulette 7095
2/03/73	#100	1	Sha La Boom Boom	MGM 14437
			BLOSSOMS	
5/27/61	#98	1	Son-In-Law	Challenge 9109
			KURTIS BLOW	
8/30/80	#93	4	The Breaks (Part 1)	Mercury 76075
4/13/85	#80	5	Basketball	Polydor 881529
			BLOW MONKEES	
5/10/86	#18	19	Digging Your Scene	RCA 14325
			BLUE	
5/07/77	#93	5	Capture Your Heart	Rocket 40706
			DAVID BLUE	
4/21/73	#73	9	Outlaw Man	Asylum 11015
			BLUE-BELLES (same group as THE STARLETS)	
6/03/61	#57	9	Better Tell Him No*	PAM 1003
4/14/62	#16	13	I Sold My Heart To The Junkman	Newtown 5000

Debut Date	Peak Pos	Wks Chr	ARTIST/Song Title	Label & Number
7/28/62	#90	4	Tear After Tear	Newtown 5007
			*released as by THE STARLETS	
			BLUE CHEER	
2/10/68	#9	16	Summertime Blues	Philips 40516
7/20/68	#97	2	Just A Little Bit	Philips 40541
			BLUE DIAMONDS	
12/10/60	#79	6	Ramona	London 1954
			BLUE HAZE	
11/04/72	#21	14	Smoke Gets In Your Eyes	A&M 1357
6/02/73	#93	4	You'll Never Walk Alone	A&M 1426
			BLUE JAYS	
7/29/61	#26	13	Lover's Island	Milestone 2008
			BLUE MAGIC	
1/19/74	#56	9	Stop To Start	Atco 6949
5/04/74	#5	19	Sideshow	Atco 6961
10/12/74	#44	9	Three Ring Circus	Atco 7004
12/06/75	#97	2	What's Come Over Me*	Atco 7030
			*released as by MARGIE JOSEPH and BLUE MAGIC	
			BLUE MERCEDES	
3/05/88	#70	7	I Want To Be Your Property	MCA 53262
			BLUE MINK	
2/14/70	#82	3	Melting Pot	Philips 40658
9/19/70	#66	8	Our World	Philips 40686
			BLUENOTES	
12/26/59	#61	9	I Don't Know What It Is	Brooke 111
			BLUE OYSTER CULT	
7/31/76	#7	21	(Don't Fear) The Reaper	Columbia 10384
9/01/79	#92	3	In Thee	Columbia 11055
8/15/81	#34	17	Burnin' For You	Columbia 02415
			BLUE RIDGE RANGERS	
12/09/72	#10	14	Jambalaya (On The Bayou)	Fantasy 689
3/31/73	#33	10	Hearts Of Stone	Fantasy 700
10/13/73	#93	1	You Don't Owe Me	Fantasy 710
			BLUES BROTHERS	
12/09/78	#9	17	Soul Man	Atlantic 3545
3/03/79	#42	8	Rubber Biscuit	Atlantic 3564
5/31/80	#18	14	Gimme Some Lovin'	Atlantic 3666
12/20/80	#46	12	Who's Making Love	Atlantic 3785
			BLUES IMAGE	
5/02/70	#4	16	Ride Captain Ride	Atco 6746
10/03/70	#95	3	Gas Lamps And Clay	Atco 6777
			BLUES MAGOOS	
11/26/66	#6	17	(We Ain't Got) Nothin' Yet	Mercury 72622
3/11/67	#92	3	There's A Chance We Can Make It/	Mercury 72660
3/25/67	#47	6	Pipe Dream	Mercury 72660
6/17/67	#91	3	One By One	Mercury 72692
			BLUES PROJECT	
4/08/67	#66	3	No Time Like The Right Time	Verve Folkways 5040
			BLUE SWEDE	
2/09/74	#1	16	Hooked On A Feeling	EMI 3627
6/01/74	#56	7	Silly Milly	EMI 3893
8/24/74	#10	12	Never My Love	EMI 3938
3/22/75	#58	5	Hush-I'm Alive	EMI 4029
			BLUE TRAIN	
10/05/91	#47	16	All I Need Is You	Zoo 14018
			BLUE ZONE U.K.	
8/13/88	#58	10	Jackie	Arista 9725
			BLUR	
12/28/91	#61	10	There's No Other Way	SBK 07374
			EDDIE BO	
8/30/69	#74	3	Hook And Sling (Part 1)	Scram 117

Debut Date	Peak Pos	Wks Chr	**ARTIST**/Song Title	Label & Number
			BOB & EARL	
12/28/63	#36	10	Harlem Shuffle	Marc 104
			BOBBETTES	
8/03/57	#6	16	Mr. Lee	Atlantic 1144
7/16/60	#55	9	I Shot Mr. Lee	Triple-X 104
11/05/60	#86	6	Have Mercy Baby	Triple-X 106
			BOB B. SOXX and THE BLUE JEANS	
11/17/62	#9	14	Zip-A-Dee-Doo-Dah	Philles 107
2/16/63	#30	10	Why Do Lovers Break Each Other's Heart	Philles 110
6/01/63	#61	8	Not Too Young To Get Married	Philles 113
			WILLIE BOBO	
11/26/66	#98	1	Sunshine Superman	Verve 10448
			MICHAEL BOLTON	
8/29/87	#22	26	That's What Love Is All About	Columbia 07322
1/23/88	#12	19	(Sittin' On) The Dock Of The Bay	Columbia 07680
6/04/88	#85	5	Wait On Love	Columbia 07794
7/01/89	#21	20	Soul Provider	Columbia 68909
10/28/89	#2	24	How Am I Supposed To Live Without You	Columbia 73017
3/03/90	#4	21	How Can We Be Lovers	Columbia 73318
5/26/90	#8	19	When I'm Back On My Feet Again	Columbia 73342
8/25/90	#33	13	Georgia On My Mind	Columbia 73490
4/20/91	#3	22	Love Is A Wonderful Thing	Columbia 73719
7/13/91	#3	23	Time, Love And Tenderness	Columbia 73889
10/12/91	#1	24	When A Man Loves A Woman	Columbia 74020
1/25/92	#2	22	Missing You Now	Columbia 74184
5/09/92	#29	16	Steel Bars	Columbia 74294
10/24/92	#9	24	To Love Somebody	Columbia 74733
11/27/93	#5	25	Said I Loved You....But I Lied	Columbia 77260
			JOANN BON & THE COQUETTES	
9/16/67	#89	4	I'll Release You	MTA 129
			JOHNNY BOND	
8/13/60	#25	11	Hot Rod Lincoln	Republic 2005
2/27/65	#34	10	10 Little Bottles	Starday 704
			GARY U.S. BONDS	
10/22/60	#5	15	New Orleans	Legrand 1003
5/27/61	#1	16	Quarter To Three	Legrand 1008
7/22/61	#2	12	School Is Out	Legrand 1009
10/21/61	#32	6	School Is In	Legrand 1012
12/16/61	#6	17	Dear Lady Twist	Legrand 1015
3/24/62	#12	12	Twist, Twist Senora	Legrand 1018
6/16/62	#51	8	Seven Day Weekend	Legrand 1019
4/25/81	#7	18	This Little Girl	EMI America 8079
7/18/81	#69	6	Jole Blon	EMI America 8089
6/12/82	#25	17	Out Of Work	EMI America 8117
			BONES	
10/21/72	#85	3	Roberta	Signpost 70008
			BONEY M	
12/25/76	#90	8	Daddy Cool	Atco 7063
6/10/78	#54	11	Rivers Of Babylon	Sire 1027
			BONHAM	
1/20/89	#58	5	Wait For You	WTG 73034
			BON JOVI	
3/03/84	#37	16	Runaway	Mercury 818309
6/09/84	#46	11	She Don't Know Me	Mercury 818958
4/27/85	#67	9	Only Lonely	Mercury 880736
8/03/85	#71	7	In And Out Of Love	Mercury 880951
9/06/86	#1	26	You Give Love A Bad Name	Mercury 884953
12/13/86	#1	23	Livin' On A Prayer	Mercury 888184
4/11/87	#7	19	Wanted Dead Or Alive	Mercury 888467
9/24/88	#1	21	Bad Medicine	Mercury 870657
11/26/88	#2	22	Born To Be My Baby	Mercury 872156
3/11/89	#1	22	I'll Be There For You	Mercury 872564
6/03/89	#5	21	Lay Your Hands On Me	Mercury 874452
10/07/89	#9	19	Living In Sin	Mercury 876070
10/31/92	#21	16	Keep The Faith	Jambco 864432

Debut Date	Peak Pos	Wks Chr	ARTIST/Song Title	Label & Number
1/30/93	#4	23	Bed Of Roses	Jambco 864852
5/01/93	#24	21	In These Arms	Jambco 862088
			JON BON JOVI	
7/21/90	#1	20	Blaze Of Glory	Mercury 875896
10/13/90	#12	23	Miracle	Mercury 878392
			GARY BONNER	
12/28/74	#85	5	Should Anybody Ask	Atlantic 3234
			BONNIE and THE TREASURES	
9/04/65	#83	3	Home Of The Brave	Phi-Dan 5005
			BONNIE LOU	
1/07/56	#10	1	Daddy-O	King 4835
			KARLA BONOFF	
1/28/78	#69	8	I Can't Hold On	Columbia 10618
4/08/78	#85	6	Isn't It Always Love	Columbia 10710
3/01/80	#82	6	Baby Don't Go	Columbia 11206
5/01/82	#12	20	Personally	Columbia 02805
10/02/82	#66	6	Please Be The One	Columbia 03172
			CHUCKII BOOKER	
7/15/89	#47	11	Turned Away	Atlantic 88917
11/28/92	#63	11	Games	Atlantic 87448
			JAMES BOOKER	
10/22/60	#27	15	Gonzo	Peacock 1697
			BOOKER T & THE MG'S	
8/11/62	#3	16	Green Onions	Stax 127
1/12/63	#89	3	Jelly Bread	Stax 131
8/24/63	#88	6	Chinese Checkers	Stax 137
5/29/65	#50	10	Boot-Leg	Stax 169
8/27/66	#76	5	My Sweet Potato	Stax 196
3/25/67	#36	14	Hip Hug-Her	Stax 211
8/05/67	#24	12	Groovin'	Stax 224
7/06/68	#9	12	Soul Limbo	Stax 0001
11/09/68	#14	16	Hang 'Em High	Stax 0013
3/22/69	#8	11	Time Is Tight	Stax 0028
6/07/69	#26	6	Mrs. Robinson	Stax 0037
9/06/69	#79	5	Slum Baby	Stax 0049
8/01/70	#93	2	Something	Stax 0073
3/13/71	#53	11	Melting Pot	Stax 0082
			BOOK OF LOVE	
3/09/91	#85	5	Alice Everyday	Sire 19550
			TAKA BOOM	
4/28/79	#74	5	Night Dancin'	Ariola 7748
			BOOM CRASH OPERA	
2/23/91	#85	5	Talk About It	Giant 19476
			BOOMTOWN RATS	
1/26/80	#84	7	I Don't Like Mondays	Columbia 11117
			DANIEL BOONE	
6/03/72	#16	20	Beautiful Sunday	Mercury 73281
11/18/72	#81	4	Annabelle	Mercury 73339
			DEBBY BOONE	
8/27/77	#1	27	You Light Up My Life	Warner Brothers 8455
2/11/78	#57	7	California	Warner Brothers 8511
			PAT BOONE	
8/13/55	#1	16	Ain't That A Shame	Dot 15377
12/03/55	#8	3	At My Front Door (Crazy Little Mama)	Dot 15422
3/17/56	#5	9	I'll Be Home	Dot 15443
7/07/56	#2	14	I Almost Lost My Mind	Dot 15472
9/15/56	#10	19	Friendly Persuasion (Thee I Love)/	Dot 15490
9/15/56	#16	11	Chains Of Love	Dot 15490
12/15/56	#25	9	Anastasia/	Dot 15521
12/22/56	#3	20	Don't Forbid Me	Dot 15521
3/09/57	#9	14	Why Baby Why/	Dot 15545
3/09/57	#24	8	I'm Waiting Just For You	Dot 15545
5/18/57	#1	21	Love Letters In The Sand/	Dot 15570
5/18/57	#20	7	Bernadine	Dot 15570

Debut Date	Peak Pos	Wks Chr	ARTIST/Song Title	Label & Number
			PAT BOONE—*continued*	
8/10/57	#10	15	Remember You're Mine/	Dot 15602
8/10/57	#15	11	There's A Goldmine In The Sky	Dot 15602
10/29/57	#3	19	April Love/	Dot 15660
11/02/57	#50	2	When The Swallows Come Back To Capistrano	Dot 15660
2/15/58	#6	14	A Wonderful Time Up There/	Dot 15690
2/15/58	#6	12	It's Too Soon To Know	Dot 15690
5/03/58	#9	12	Sugar Moon/	Dot 15750
5/03/58	#41	5	Cherie, I Love You	Dot 15750
7/05/58	#11	14	If Dreams Came True/	Dot 15785
7/05/58	#61	4	That's How Much I Love You	Dot 15785
9/20/58	#44	10	For My Good Fortune/	Dot 15825
9/27/58	#25	8	Gee, But It's Lonely	Dot 15825
10/25/58	#33	13	I'll Remember Tonight	Dot 15840
1/10/59	#17	12	With The Wind And Rain In Your Hair/	Dot 15888
1/17/59	#58	6	Good Rockin' Tonight	Dot 15888
3/28/59	#61	6	Wang Dang Taffy Apple Tango/	Dot 15914
3/28/59	#21	11	For A Penny	Dot 15914
6/20/59	#23	11	Twixt Twelve And Twenty	Dot 15955
9/12/59	#25	10	Fools Hall Of Fame	Dot 15982
11/28/59	#51	8	Beyond The Sunset	Dot 16006
2/13/60	#23	12	(Welcome) New Lovers/	Dot 16048
2/13/60	#94	1	Words	Dot 16048
5/14/60	#36	10	Walking The Floor Over You/	Dot 16073
5/28/60	#49	9	Spring Rain	Dot 16073
8/13/60	#60	6	Candy Sweet/	Dot 16122
9/03/60	#86	2	Delia Gone	Dot 16122
11/05/60	#60	7	Dear John/	Dot 16152
11/12/60	#70	5	Alabam	Dot 16152
1/28/61	#71	5	The Exodus Song (This Land Is Mine)	Dot 16176
5/06/61	#2	15	Moody River	Dot 16209
8/19/61	#28	10	Big Cold Wind	Dot 16244
11/18/61	#36	9	Johnny Will	Dot 16284
1/20/62	#35	9	I'll See You In My Dreams/	Dot 16312
1/20/62	#63	7	Pictures In The Fire	Dot 16312
4/28/62	#89	2	Willing And Eager	Dot 16349
6/12/62	#6	13	Speedy Gonzales	Dot 16368
9/29/62	#58	5	Ten Lonely Guys	Dot 16391
2/16/63	#70	6	Meditation	Dot 16439
10/03/64	#88	4	Beach Girl	Dot 16658
10/15/66	#51	8	Wish You Were Here Buddy	Dot 16933
4/05/69	#91	3	July, You're A Woman	Tetragrammaton 1516
			BOOTSY'S RUBBER BAND	
3/04/78	#59	6	Bootzilla	Warner Brothers 8512
			BOSS	
5/22/93	#68	9	Deeper	DJ West 74853
			BOSTON	
9/11/76	#4	23	More Than A Feeling	Epic 50266
1/22/77	#12	15	Long Time	Epic 50329
5/14/77	#33	12	Peace Of Mind	Epic 50381
8/19/78	#7	14	Don't Look Back	Epic 50590
11/11/78	#51	7	A Man I'll Never Be	Epic 50628
3/24/79	#51	7	Feelin' Satisfied	Epic 50677
9/27/86	#1	18	Amanda	MCA 52576
12/06/86	#12	17	We're Ready	MCA 52985
3/07/87	#27	12	Can'tcha Say (You Believe In Me)/Still Love	MCA 53029
			BOSTON POPS ORCHESTRA	
7/04/64	#80	3	I Want To Hold Your Hand	RCA 8378
			PERRY BOTKIN JR.	
9/04/76	#5	24	Nadia's Theme	A&M 1856
			BRENT BOURGEOIS	
5/05/90	#25	16	Dare To Fall In Love	Charisma 98971
			BOURGEOIS TAGG	
4/26/86	#67	7	Mutual Surrender (What A Wonderful World)	Island 99558
10/17/87	#41	17	I Don't Mind At All	Island 99409
			JIMMY BOWEN with THE RHYTHM ORCHIDS	
2/16/57	#12	15	I'm Stickin' With You	Roulette 4001

Debut Date	Peak Pos	Wks Chr	**ARTIST**/Song Title	Label & Number
5/11/57	#56	1	I Trusted You/	Roulette 4010
5/18/57	#33	7	Warm Up To Me Baby	Roulette 4010
7/12/58	#46	10	By The Light Of The Silvery Moon	Roulette 4083
10/11/58	#92	4	Blue Moon	Roulette 4102
			DAVID BOWIE	
4/08/72	#59	7	Changes	RCA 0605
6/17/72	#64	8	Starman	RCA 0719
12/09/72	#87	4	Jean Genie	RCA 0838
1/27/73	#17	13	Space Oddity	RCA 0876
8/04/73	#97	2	Let's Spend The Night Together	RCA 0028
11/17/73	#69	7	Sorrow	RCA 0160
6/01/74	#53	8	Rebel Rebel	RCA 0287
8/31/74	#96	2	1984	RCA 10026
11/03/74	#38	11	Changes	RCA 0605
3/15/75	#20	10	Young Americans	RCA 10152
6/28/75	#1	21	Fame	RCA 10320
12/13/75	#12	23	Golden Years	RCA 10441
4/16/77	#88	4	Sound And Vision	RCA 10905
10/04/80	#79	5	Ashes To Ashes	RCA 12078
12/06/80	#79	8	Fashion	RCA 12134
11/07/81	#22	18	Under Pressure*	Elektra 47235
4/17/82	#61	9	Cat People (Putting Out Fire)	Backstreet 52024
3/26/83	#1	22	Let's Dance	EMI America 8158
6/04/83	#9	20	China Girl	EMI America 8165
9/17/83	#15	17	Modern Love	EMI America 8177
9/15/84	#5	18	Blue Jean	EMI America 8231
12/01/84	#51	11	Tonight	EMI America 8246
2/02/85	#24	15	This Is Not America**	EMI America 8251
8/31/85	#8	16	Dancing In The Street***	EMI America 8288
3/29/86	#61	9	Absolute Beginners	EMI America 8308
4/04/87	#29	14	Day-In Day-Out	EMI America 8380
8/08/87	#30	14	Never Let Me Down	EMI America 43031
			*released as by QUEEN & DAVID BOWIE	
			**released as by DAVID BOWIE/PAT METHENY GROUP	
			***released as by MICK JAGGER/DAVID BOWIE	
			RICK BOWLES	
7/03/82	#75	5	Too Good To Turn Back Now	Polydor 2209
			ALAN BOWN	
1/28/68	#94	2	Toyland	Music Factory 402
			BOW WOW WOW	
5/29/82	#61	9	I Want Candy	RCA 13204
4/23/83	#66	5	Do You Wanna Hold Me?	RCA 13467
			BOX TOPS	
8/12/67	#1	17	The Letter	Mala 565
11/11/67	#24	10	Neon Rainbow	Mala 580
3/02/68	#2	14	Cry Like A Baby	Mala 593
5/25/68	#17	8	Choo Choo Train	Mala 12005
9/14/68	#41	7	I Met Her In Church	Mala 12017
12/28/68	#29	15	Sweet Cream Ladies, Forward March	Mala 12035
4/26/69	#72	4	I Shall Be Released	Mala 12038
7/05/69	#13	13	Soul Deep	Mala 12040
10/11/69	#35	8	Turn On A Dream	Mala 12042
3/14/70	#74	4	You Keep Tightening Up On Me	Bell 865
			TOMMY BOYCE	
10/13/62	#78	4	I'll Remember Carol	RCA 8074
			TOMMY BOYCE & BOBBY HART	
7/01/67	#34	10	Out & About	A&M 858
9/23/67	#90	3	Sometime's She's A Little Girl	A&M 874
12/23/67	#7	14	I Wonder What She's Doing Tonight	A&M 893
3/30/68	#52	8	Goodbye Baby	A&M 919
7/06/68	#16	10	Alice Long (You're Still My Favorite Girlfriend)	A&M 948
			JIMMY BOYD	
12/27/52	#4	4	I Saw Mommy Kissing Santa Claus	Columbia 39871
4/04/53	#5	6	Tell Me A Story*	Columbia 39945
			*released as by FRANKIE LAINE with JIMMY BOYD	
			BONNIE BOYER	
7/28/79	#56	7	Got To Give In To Love	Columbia 11028

Debut Date	Peak Pos	Wks Chr	**ARTIST**/Song Title	Label & Number
			BOY GEORGE	
12/26/87	#47	14	Live My Life	Virgin 99390
4/08/89	#86	4	Don't Take My Mind On A Trip	Virgin 99272
3/20/93	#10	18	The Crying Game	SBK 50437
			BOY KRAZY	
1/30/93	#9	24	That's What Love Can Do	Next Plateau 857024
6/12/93	#45	12	Good Times With Bad Boys	Next Plateau 857136
			BOY MEETS GIRL	
4/06/85	#32	15	Oh Girl	A&M 2713
9/03/88	#4	28	Waiting For A Star To Fall	RCA 8691
2/04/89	#59	4	Bring Down The Moon	RCA 8807
			BOYS	
12/10/88	#16	18	Dial My Heart	Motown 53301
9/01/90	#30	10	Crazy	Motown 2053
			BOYS BAND	
3/20/82	#73	6	Don't Stop Me Baby (I'm On Fire)	Elektra 47406
			BOYS CLUB	
10/22/88	#4	21	I Remember Holding You	MCA 53430
			BOYS DON'T CRY	
4/19/86	#13	17	I Wanna Be A Cowboy	Profile 5084
			BOYS IN THE BAND	
5/23/70	#41	11	(How Bout A Little Hand For) The Boys In The Band . . .	Spring 103
			BOYZ II MEN	
7/27/91	#3	26	Motownphilly	Motown 2090
10/12/91	#1	27	It's So Hard To Say Goodbye To Yesterday	Motown 2136
2/01/92	#30	18	Uhh Ahh	Motown 2141
4/11/92	#38	13	Please Don't Go	Motown 2155
7/25/92	#1	35	End Of The Road	Motown 2178
12/05/92	#3	24	In The Still Of The Night	Motown 2193
12/18/93	#45	7	Let It Snow	Motown 2218
			JAN BRADLEY	
1/12/63	#14	14	Mama Didn't Lie	Chess 1845
1/30/65	#61	8	I'm Over You	Chess 1919
			OWEN BRADLEY QUINTET	
2/08/58	#32	9	Big Guitar	Decca 30564
			DARYL BRAITHWAITE	
5/25/91	#44	13	Higher Than Hope	CBS Associated 73788
			LAURA BRANIGAN	
7/03/82	#1	34	Gloria	Atlantic 4048
3/19/83	#8	19	Solitaire	Atlantic 89868
7/02/83	#13	21	How Am I Supposed To Live Without You	Atlantic 89805
4/14/84	#5	25	Self Control	Atlantic 89676
8/04/84	#22	15	The Lucky One	Atlantic 89636
11/17/84	#54	12	Ti Amo	Atlantic 89608
7/27/85	#37	13	Spanish Eddie	Atlantic 89531
10/19/85	#79	5	Hold Me	Atlantic 89496
2/22/86	#81	5	I Found Someone	Atlantic 89451
7/04/87	#51	11	Shattered Glass	Atlantic 89245
11/07/87	#29	16	Power Of Love	Atlantic 89191
4/07/90	#58	9	Moonlight On Water	Atlantic 87969
			BRASS CONSTRUCTION	
3/20/76	#14	18	Movin'	United Artists 775
			BRASS RING	
3/19/66	#39	8	Phoenix Love Theme	Dunhill 4023
2/04/67	#50	7	The Dis-Advantages Of You	Dunhill 4065
			BRAT PACK	
2/10/90	#55	11	You're The Only Woman	Vendetta 1447
7/07/90	#77	7	I'm Never Gonna Give You Up	A&M 8037
			BOB BRAUN	
7/07/62	#26	12	Till Death Do Us Part	Decca 31355
			TONI BRAXTON	
7/04/92	#24	19	Give U My Heart*	Laface 4026
11/21/92	#30	22	Love Shoulda Brought You Home	Laface 4035
7/17/93	#4	32	Another Sad Love Song	Laface 4047

36

Debut Date	Peak Pos	Wks Chr	ARTIST/Song Title	Label & Number
10/23/93	#2	38	Breathe Again	Laface 4054
			*released as by BABYFACE featuring TONI BRAXTON	
			BREAD	
6/13/70	#1	16	Make It With You	Elektra 45686
9/26/70	#7	11	It Don't Matter To Me	Elektra 45701
12/26/70	#20	10	Let Your Love Go	Elektra 45711
3/20/71	#6	13	If	Elektra 45720
7/10/71	#45	9	Mother Freedom	Elektra 45740
10/16/71	#3	14	Baby I'm A Want You	Elektra 45751
1/22/72	#6	13	Everything I Own	Elektra 45765
4/22/72	#15	11	Diary	Elektra 45784
7/22/72	#10	11	The Guitar Man	Elektra 45803
11/04/72	#11	11	Sweet Surrender	Elektra 45818
2/03/73	#11	11	Aubrey	Elektra 45832
11/20/76	#12	20	Lost Without Your Love	Elektra 45365
4/23/77	#72	6	Hooked On You	Elektra 45389
			BREAKFAST CLUB	
3/14/87	#11	24	Right On Track	MCA 52954
7/11/87	#55	10	Kiss And Tell	MCA 53128
			BREATHE	
5/07/88	#2	25	Hands To Heaven	A&M 2991
9/10/88	#2	25	How Can I Fall?	A&M 1224
1/21/89	#12	18	Don't Tell Me Lies	A&M 1267
4/22/89	#76	5	All This I Should Have Known	A&M 1401
8/25/90	#16	15	Say A Prayer	A&M 1519
11/10/90	#33	18	Does She Love That Man?	A&M 1535
			BREATHLESS	
12/15/79	#94	5	Takin' It Back	EMI America 8020
			BRECKER BROTHERS	
6/14/75	#47	8	Sneakin' Up Behind You	Arista 0122
			BEVERLY BREMERS	
5/29/71	#77	4	Don't Say You Don't Remember	Scepter 12315
12/11/71	#16	16	Don't Say You Don't Remember	Scepter 12315
4/22/72	#45	15	We're Free	Scepter 12348
9/16/72	#54	8	I'll Make You Music	Scepter 12363
			BRENDA & THE TABULATIONS	
3/04/67	#22	11	Dry Your Eyes	Dionn 500
6/03/67	#64	7	Who's Loving You	Dionn 501
11/11/67	#59	5	When You're Gone	Dionn 504
3/30/68	#96	1	Baby You're So Right	Dionn 507
1/17/70	#54	8	The Touch Of You	Top & Bottom 401
5/02/70	#58	8	And My Heart Sang (Tra La La)	Top & Bottom 403
8/29/70	#76	2	Don't Make Me Over	Top & Bottom 404
4/03/71	#14	12	Right On The Tip Of My Tongue	Top & Bottom 407
9/04/71	#84	4	A Part Of You	Top & Bottom 408
			BUDDY BRENNAN QUARTET	
1/23/60	#88	2	Big River	Warwick 517
			WALTER BRENNAN	
4/30/60	#36	11	Dutchman's Gold	Dot 16066
4/07/62	#8	13	Old Rivers	Liberty 55436
10/20/60	#31	8	Mama Sang A Song	Liberty 55508
			TERESA BREWER	
3/25/50	#1	8	Music! Music! Music!	London 604
1/10/53	#1	20	Till I Waltz Again With You	Coral 60873
11/14/53	#1	14	Ricochet	Coral 61043
5/15/54	#9	3	Jilted	Coral 61152
4/02/55	#7	5	Pledging My Love	Coral 61362
4/14/56	#6	8	A Tear Fell	Coral 61590
7/28/56	#10	9	A Sweet Old Fashioned Girl	Coral 61636
9/15/56	#50	1	I Love Mickey*	Coral 61700
11/03/56	#24	11	Mutual Admiration Society	Coral 61737
3/02/57	#40	2	I'm Drowning My Sorrows/	Coral 61776
3/02/57	#49	1	How Lonely Can One Be	Coral 61776
3/30/57	#17	12	Empty Arms	Coral 61805
6/29/57	#40	5	Teardrops In My Heart	Coral 61850
12/07/57	#1	2	You Send Me	Coral 61898
10/04/58	#37	8	The Hula Hoop Song	Coral 62033

Debut Date	Peak Pos	Wks Chr	ARTIST/Song Title	Label & Number
			TERESA BREWER—*continued*	
12/20/58	#67	9	The One Rose	Coral 62057
3/07/59	#44	8	Heavenly Lover	Coral 62084
7/25/59	#99	2	Bye Bye Baby, Goodbye	Coral 62126
2/20/60	#81	3	Peace Of Mind	Coral 62167
8/06/60	#24	18	Anymore	Coral 62219
			*released as by TERESA BREWER and MICKEY MANTLE	
			BREWER & SHIPLEY	
2/06/71	#8	15	One Toke Over The Line	Kama Sutra 516
5/15/71	#39	8	Tarkio Road	Kama Sutra 524
7/22/72	#90	2	Yankee Lady	Kama Sutra 547
			BRICK	
10/23/76	#5	22	Dazz	Bang 727
9/03/77	#30	15	Dusic	Bang 734
12/31/77	#76	7	Ain't Gonna Hurt Nobody	Bang 735
6/07/80	#93	3	All The Way	Bang 4810
			EDIE BRICKELL & NEW BOHEMIANS	
12/03/88	#6	21	What I Am	Geffen 27696
4/08/89	#32	15	Circle	Geffen 27580
			ALICIA BRIDGES	
7/01/78	#6	35	I Love The Nightlife (Disco 'Round)	Polydor 14483
			LARRY BRIGHT	
6/04/60	#96	5	Mojo Workout	Tide 006
			BRIGHTER SIDE OF DARKNESS	
11/25/72	#10	14	Love Jones	20th Century 2002
			MARTIN BRILEY	
6/04/83	#38	13	The Salt In My Tears	Mercury 812165
			CHARLES BRIMMER	
7/19/75	#95	2	God Bless Our Love	Chelsea 3017
			JOHNNY BRISTOL	
6/29/74	#8	16	Hang On In There Baby	MGM 14715
11/09/74	#51	6	You And I	MGM 14762
11/27/76	#68	12	Do It To My Mind	Atlantic 3360
8/30/80	#62	10	My Guy/My Girl*	Handshake 5300
			*released as by AMII STEWART & JOHNNY BRISTOL	
			BRITISH WALKERS	
4/15/67	#89	4	Shake	Cameo 446
			BRONSKI BEAT	
12/29/84	#32	17	Smalltown Boy	MCA 52494
			HERMAN BROOD	
7/14/79	#44	13	Saturday Night	Ariola 7754
			BROOKLYN BRIDGE	
12/07/68	#4	14	Worst That Could Happen	Buddah 75
3/08/69	#40	7	Blessed Is The Rain/	Buddah 95
5/10/69	#47	8	Welcome Me Love	Buddah 95
7/12/69	#41	8	Your Husband - My Wife	Buddah 126
9/27/69	#37	7	You'll Never Walk Alone	Buddah 139
3/07/70	#67	3	Free As The Wind	Buddah 162
10/03/70	#89	3	Day Is Done	Buddah 193
			BROOKLYN DREAMS	
11/12/77	#66	6	Sad Eyes	Millennium 606
3/25/78	#80	6	Music, Harmony And Rhythm	Millennium 610
1/13/79	#4	16	Heaven Knows*	Casablanca 959
3/03/79	#73	4	Make It Last	Casablanca 962
			*released as by DONNA SUMMER with BROOKLYN DREAMS	
			DONNIE BROOKS	
6/18/60	#13	21	Mission Bell	Era 3018
11/26/60	#34	12	Doll House	Era 3028
3/25/61	#87	3	Memphis	Era 3042
			NANCY BROOKS	
2/17/79	#62	7	I'm Not Gonna Cry Anymore	Arista 0385
			BROTHER BEYOND	
6/30/90	#23	17	The Girl I Used To Know	EMI 50287

Debut Date	Peak Pos	Wks Chr	ARTIST/Song Title	Label & Number
			BROTHERHOOD CREED	
2/15/92	#78	6	Helluva	MCA 54350
			BROTHERHOOD OF MAN	
4/18/70	#13	15	United We Stand	Deram 85059
8/15/70	#54	9	Where Are You Going To My Love	Deram 85065
4/21/71	#73	5	Reach Out Your Hand	Deram 85073
5/08/76	#48	11	Save Your Kisses For Me	Pye 71066
			BROTHERS FOUR	
2/27/60	#2	20	Greenfields	Columbia 41571
6/08/60	#68	10	My Tani	Columbia 41692
11/12/60	#58	7	Green Leaves Of Summer	Columbia 41808
4/08/61	#61	7	Frogg	Columbia 41958
1/20/62	#56	8	Blue Water Line	Columbia 42256
			BROTHERS JOHNSON	
5/01/76	#7	21	I'll Be Good To You	A&M 1806
8/14/76	#34	14	Get The Funk Out Ma Face	A&M 1851
7/16/77	#8	18	Strawberry Letter 23	A&M 1949
3/15/80	#8	18	Stomp!	A&M 2216
6/20/81	#69	6	The Real Thing	A&M 2343
			BROTHER TO BROTHER	
9/14/74	#64	10	In The Bottle	Turbo 039
			AL BROWN'S TUNETOPPERS	
4/02/60	#14	12	The Madison	Amy 804
			ALEX BROWN	
5/11/85	#77	5	(Come On) Shout	Mercury 880694
			ARTHUR BROWN (see CRAZY WORLD OF ARTHUR BROWN)	
			BOBBY BROWN	
12/20/86	#61	10	Girlfriend	MCA 52866
8/06/88	#7	20	Don't Be Cruel	MCA 53327
11/05/88	#2	18	My Prerogative	MCA 53383
12/10/88	#3	23	Roni	MCA 53463
4/01/89	#2	23	Every Little Step	MCA 53618
6/10/89	#2	21	On Our Own	MCA 53662
8/26/89	#7	22	Rock Wit'cha	MCA 53652
5/19/90	#1	20	She Ain't Worth It*	MCA 79047
8/08/92	#3	26	Humpin' Around	MCA 54342
10/17/92	#7	25	Good Enough	MCA 54517
1/23/93	#13	20	Get Away	MCA 54511
5/01/93	#54	9	That's The Way Love Is	MCA 54618
			***released as by GLENN MEDEIROS featuring BOBBY BROWN**	
			BOOTS BROWN and HIS BLOCKBUSTERS	
8/23/58	#53	9	Cervesa	RCA 7269
			BUSTER BROWN	
2/20/60	#34	14	Fannie Mae	Fire 1008
9/17/60	#88	5	Is You Is Or Is You Ain't My Baby	Fire 1023
			CHARLES BROWN	
12/31/60	#90	2	Please Come Home For Christmas	King 5405
1/06/62	#96	1	Please Come Home For Christmas	King 5405
			CHUCK BROWN & THE SOUL SEARCHERS	
2/03/79	#29	12	Bustin' Loose (Part 1)	Source 40967
			DON BROWN	
3/11/78	#64	6	Sitting In Limbo	1st American 102
			JAMES BROWN	
1/31/59	#60	5	Try Me	Federal 12337
5/21/60	#55	8	Think/	Federal 12370
6/11/60	#72	3	You've Got The Power	Federal 12370
9/24/60	#97	2	This Old Heart	Federal 12378
11/26/60	#71	6	The Bells	King 5423
2/18/61	#85	5	Bewildered	King 5442
6/10/61	#90	3	I Don't Mind	King 5466
12/30/61	#40	11	Lost Someone	King 5573
4/28/62	#35	11	Night Train	King 5614
7/21/62	#88	3	Shout And Shimmy	King 5657
4/27/63	#16	11	Prisoner Of Love	King 5739
7/27/63	#67	6	These Foolish Things	King 5767

Debut Date	Peak Pos	Wks Chr	ARTIST/Song Title	Label & Number
			JAMES BROWN—*continued*	
10/19/63	#83	5	Signed, Sealed And Delivered	King 5803
1/25/64	#26	11	Oh Baby Don't You Weep (Part 1)	King 5842
6/20/64	#92	2	The Things That I Used To Do	Smash 1908
8/08/64	#21	11	Out Of Sight	Smash 1919
7/15/65	#8	13	Papa's Got A Brand New Bag (Part 1)	King 5999
11/06/65	#2	13	I Got You (I Feel Good)	King 6015
11/13/65	#53	5	Try Me	Smash 2008
2/12/66	#98	1	I'll Go Crazy	King 6020
3/05/66	#48	8	Ain't That A Groove (Part 1)	King 6025
4/16/66	#100	1	New Breed	Smash 2028
4/30/66	#4	9	It's A Man's Man's Man's World	King 6035
7/30/66	#41	8	Money Won't Change You (Part 1)	King 6048
10/15/66	#39	7	Don't Be A Dropout	King 6056
1/07/67	#34	7	Bring It Up	King 6071
3/11/67	#53	5	Kansas City	King 6086
5/06/67	#41	8	Let Yourself Go	King 6100
7/22/67	#10	12	Cold Sweat (Part 1)	King 6110
10/28/67	#29	6	Get It Together (Part 1)	King 6122
12/09/67	#32	8	I Can't Stand Myself/	King 6144
1/20/68	#31	8	There Was A Time	King 6144
3/16/68	#9	11	I Got The Feelin'	King 6155
5/18/68	#16	10	Licking Stick - Licking Stick (Part 1)	King 6166
6/15/68	#74	3	America Is My Home (Part 1)	King 6112
7/20/68	#43	5	I Guess I'll Have To Cry, Cry, Cry	King 6141
9/07/68	#17	10	Say It Loud - I'm Black And I'm Proud	King 6187
11/09/68	#36	8	Goodbye My Love	King 6198
12/28/68	#50	4	Tit For Tat (Ain't No Taking Back)	King 6204
1/25/69	#24	9	Give It Up Or Turn It A Loose	King 6213
3/02/69	#99	2	Soul Pride (Part 1)	King 6222
3/29/69	#34	9	I Don't Want Nobody To Give Me Nothing (Open Up	
			The Door, I'll Get It Myself)	King 6224
5/31/69	#43	5	The Popcorn	King 6240
6/14/69	#11	11	Mother Popcorn (You Got To Have A Mother	
			For Me) (Part 1)	King 6245
8/23/69	#48	5	Lowdown Popcorn	King 6250
9/06/69	#34	7	World (Part 1)	King 6258
10/18/69	#31	5	Let A Man Come In And Do The Popcorn (Part 1)	King 6255
11/15/69	#40	11	Ain't It Funky Now (Part 1)	King 6280
1/10/70	#57	5	Let A Man Come In And Do The Popcorn (Part 2)	King 6275
2/14/70	#26	7	It's A New Day (Parts 1 & 2)	King 6292
3/21/70	#37	5	Funky Drummer (Part 1)	King 6290
5/02/70	#30	6	Brother Rapp (Parts 1 & 2)	King 6310
7/18/70	#17	9	Get Up I Feel Like Being A Sex Machine	King 6318
10/03/70	#15	10	Super Bad (Parts 1 & 2)	King 6329
12/26/70	#35	7	Get Up, Get Into It, Get Involved	King 6347
2/13/71	#78	2	Spinning Wheel (Part 1)	King 6366
2/20/71	#32	10	Soul Power (Part 1)	King 6368
5/01/71	#43	6	I Cried	King 6363
6/05/71	#40	8	Escape-Ism (Part 1)	People 2500
7/03/71	#10	10	Hot Pants (She Got To Use What She Got, To Get	
			What She Wants) (Part 1)	People 2501
8/21/71	#20	10	Make It Funky (Part 1)	Polydor 14088
10/30/71	#75	5	My Part/Make It Funky (Part 3)	Polydor 14098
11/06/71	#29	8	I'm A Greedy Man (Part 1)	Polydor 14100
1/29/72	#30	6	Talking Loud And Saying Nothing	Polydor 14109
2/26/72	#32	9	King Heroin	Polydor 14116
4/29/72	#38	8	There It Is (Part 1)	Polydor 14125
6/17/72	#38	8	Honky Tonk (Part 1)	Polydor 14129
7/29/72	#10	14	Get On The Good Foot (Part 1)	Polydor 14139
11/11/72	#32	8	I Got A Bag Of My Own	Polydor 14153
12/16/72	#51	8	What My Baby Needs Now Is A Little More Lovin'*	Polydor 14157
1/20/73	#33	7	I Got Ants In My Pants (Part 1)	Polydor 14162
3/17/73	#61	4	Down And Out In New York City	Polydor 14168
8/25/73	#46	7	Sexy, Sexy, Sexy	Polydor 14194
11/17/73	#46	11	Stoned To The Bone (Part 1)	Polydor 14210
3/09/74	#23	13	The Payback (Part 1)	Polydor 14223
6/08/74	#30	11	My Thang	Polydor 14244
8/24/74	#27	9	Papa Don't Take No Mess (Part 1)	Polydor 14255
11/02/74	#87	3	Funky President (People It's Bad)/	Polydor 14258
11/23/74	#78	7	Cold Blooded	Polydor 14258

Debut Date	Peak Pos	Wks Chr	ARTIST/Song Title	Label & Number
3/01/75	#73	4	Reality	Polydor 14268
7/26/75	#95	2	Hustle!!!	Polydor 14281
7/31/76	#72	9	Get Up Offa That Thing	Polydor 14326
12/07/85	#5	22	Living In America	Scotti Brothers 05682
			*released as by JAMES BROWN/LYN COLLINS	
			JIM ED BROWN	
12/05/70	#59	8	Morning	RCA 9909
			LOUISE BROWN	
5/27/61	#98	1	Son-In-Law	Witch 101
			MAXINE BROWN	
12/31/60	#15	14	All In My Mind	Nomar 103
3/25/61	#15	13	Funny	Nomar 106
7/08/61	#82	3	Think Of Me	ABC Paramount 10235
3/30/63	#92	7	Ask Me	Wand 135
10/31/64	#22	13	Oh No Not My Baby	Wand 162
2/27/65	#73	6	It's Gonna Be Alright	Wand 173
4/24/65	#45	9	Something You Got*	Wand 181
7/03/65	#53	8	One Step At A Time	Wand 185
8/28/65	#85	3	Can't Let You Out Of My Sight*	Wand 191
12/04/65	#63	7	If You Gotta Make A Fool Of Somebody	Wand 1104
2/18/67	#78	5	Hold On I'm Coming*	Wand 1148
4/29/67	#87	5	Daddy's Home*	Wand 1155
10/04/69	#80	6	We'll Cry Together	Comm. United 3001
			*released as by CHUCK JACKSON & MAXINE BROWN	
			MIGUEL BROWN	
9/24/83	#94	5	So Many Men, So Little Time	TSR 828
			NAPPY BROWN	
6/04/55	#9	2	Don't Be Angry	Savoy 1155
1/19/57	#22	8	Little By Little	Savoy 1506
10/18/58	#80	6	It Don't Hurt No More	Savoy 1551
			OSCAR BROWN JR.	
5/11/74	#71	5	The Lone Ranger	Atlantic 3001
			PETER BROWN	
9/10/77	#41	11	Do Ya Wanna Get Funky With Me	Drive 6258
3/18/78	#8	24	Dance With Me*	Drive 6269
9/30/78	#91	2	You Should Do It*	Drive 6272
9/08/79	#90	4	Crank It Up (Funky Town) Part 1	Drive 6278
			*released as by PETER BROWN with BETTY WRIGHT	
			POLLY BROWN	
12/28/74	#16	14	Up In A Puff Of Smoke	GTO 1002
			RANDY BROWN	
4/07/79	#69	5	You Says It All	Parachute 523
			ROY BROWN	
7/13/57	#48	5	Let The Four Winds Blow	Imperial 5439
			RUTH BROWN	
2/16/57	#26	9	Lucky Lips	Atlantic 1125
9/13/58	#59	11	This Little Girl's Gone Rockin'	Atlantic 1197
5/23/59	#77	4	Jack O'Diamonds	Atlantic 2026
9/26/59	#55	12	I Don't Know	Atlantic 2035
3/19/60	#58	8	Don't Deceive Me	Atlantic 2052
6/30/62	#99	2	Shake A Hand	Philips 40028
			SAM BROWN	
4/22/89	#70	7	Stop	A&M 1234
			SHIRLEY BROWN	
10/12/74	#26	13	Woman To Woman	Truth 3206
			JACKSON BROWNE	
3/11/72	#12	13	Doctor My Eyes	Asylum 11004
8/05/72	#45	7	Rock Me On The Water	Asylum 11006
10/06/73	#72	9	Redneck Friend	Asylum 11023
1/29/77	#18	16	Here Come Those Tears Again	Asylum 45379
5/21/77	#58	5	The Pretender	Asylum 45399
2/11/78	#6	17	Running On Empty	Asylum 45460
6/10/78	#22	15	Stay/	Asylum 45485
6/10/78	#22	15	The Load Out	Asylum 45485
7/05/80	#13	17	Boulevard	Asylum 47003

Debut Date	Peak Pos	Wks Chr	ARTIST/Song Title	Label & Number
			JACKSON BROWNE—*continued*	
9/20/80	#23	17	That Girl Could Sing	Asylum 47036
12/27/80	#87	4	Hold On, Hold Out	Asylum 11477
7/31/82	#5	21	Somebody's Baby	Asylum 69982
7/09/83	#13	15	Lawyers In Love	Asylum 69826
10/01/83	#26	17	Tender Is The Night	Asylum 69791
1/21/84	#47	10	For A Rocker	Asylum 69764
10/26/85	#20	20	You're A Friend Of Mine*	Columbia 05660
3/01/86	#27	13	For America	Asylum 69566
6/14/86	#77	6	In The Shape Of A Heart	Asylum 69543
			*released as by CLARENCE CLEMONS and JACKSON BROWNE	
			TOM BROWNE	
10/04/80	#95	3	Funkin' For Jamaica	GRP 2506
			BROWNS	
7/25/59	#1	17	The Three Bells	RCA 7555
11/07/59	#17	15	Scarlet Ribbons (For Her Hair)	RCA 7614
3/12/60	#8	15	The Old Lamplighter	RCA 7700
7/09/60	#78	6	Lonely Little Robin/	RCA 7755
7/23/60	#89	1	Margo	RCA 7755
11/13/60	#50	9	Send Me The Pillow You Dream On	RCA 7804
			BROWN SUGAR	
2/21/76	#76	5	The Game Is Over	Capitol 4198
			BROWNSVILLE STATION	
12/09/72	#85	2	The Red Back Spider	Big Tree 156
2/24/73	#60	10	Let Your Yeah Be Yeah	Big Tree 161
10/27/73	#2	18	Smokin' In The Boys Room	Big Tree 16011
5/25/74	#26	8	I'm The Leader Of The Gang	Big Tree 15005
8/17/74	#31	10	Kings Of The Party	Big Tree 16001
12/07/74	#74	6	Mama Don't Allow No Parkin'	Big Tree 16029
5/28/77	#44	12	Lady (Put The Light On Me)	Private Stock 45149
8/27/77	#45	9	The Martian Boogie	Private Stock 45167
			DAVE BRUBECK QUARTET	
7/29/61	#23	16	Take Five	Columbia 41479
12/09/61	#93	3	Unsquare Dance	Columbia 42228
1/12/63	#86	8	Bossa Nova U.S.A.	Columbia 42651
			ANITA BRYANT	
6/27/59	#14	14	Till There Was You	Carlton 512
10/03/59	#68	5	Six Boys And Seven Girls	Carlton 518
1/02/60	#48	6	Do-Re-Mi	Carlton 523
4/16/60	#7	16	Paper Roses	Carlton 528
7/23/60	#20	14	In My Little Corner Of The World	Carlton 530
10/29/60	#81	5	One Of The Lucky Ones	Carlton 535
12/24/60	#2	2	Wonderland By Night	Carlton 537
2/11/61	#72	5	A Texan And A Girl From Mexico	Carlton 538
5/30/64	#69	6	The World Of Lonely People	Columbia 43037
			RAY BRYANT COMBO	
2/27/60	#81	6	Little Susie	Columbia 41553
4/02/60	#25	12	Madison Time (Part 1)	Columbia 41628
			SHARON BRYANT	
8/19/86	#37	17	Let Go	Wing 871722
12/23/89	#90	6	Foolish Heart	Wing 889878
			PEABO BRYSON	
3/04/78	#60	6	Reaching For The Sky	Capitol 4522
3/07/81	#74	7	Lovers After All*	Arista 0587
12/26/81	#47	13	Let The Feeling Flow	Capitol 5065
7/09/83	#14	30	Tonight, I Celebrate My Love**	Capitol 5242
12/24/83	#67	15	You're Looking Like Love To Me**	Capitol 5307
5/19/84	#12	23	If Ever You're In My Arms Again	Elektra 69728
7/13/85	#78	5	Take No Prisoners (In The Game Of Love)	Elektra 69632
6/22/91	#54	14	Can You Stop The Rain	Columbia 73745
2/22/92	#9	24	Beauty And The Beast***	Epic 74090
1/23/93	#2	22	A Whole New World (Alladin's Theme)****	Columbia 74751
5/22/93	#26	20	By The Time This Night Is Over*****	Arista 2565
			*released as by MELISSA MANCHESTER and PEABO BRYSON	
			**released as by PEABO BRYSON/ROBERTA FLACK	
			***released as by CELINE DION and PEABO BRYSON	

Debut Date	Peak Pos	Wks Chr	ARTIST/Song Title	Label & Number
			****released as by PEABO BRYSON and REGINA BELLE	
			*****released as by KENNY G with PEABO BRYSON	
			B.T. EXPRESS	
9/21/74	#6	19	Do It ('Til You're Satisfied)	Scepter 12395
2/01/75	#9	14	Express	Roadshow 7001
8/16/75	#46	7	Give It What You Got/	Roadshow 7003
9/20/75	#40	10	Peace pipe	Roadshow 7003
1/31/76	#86	3	Close To You	Roadshow 7005
6/05/76	#74	4	Can't Stop Groovin' Now, Wanna Do It Some More	Columbia 10346
2/11/78	#89	4	Shout It	Columbia 10649
			BUBBLE PUPPY	
2/08/69	#16	12	Hot Smoke & Sasafrass	International Artists 128
			BUCHANAN and GOODMAN	
8/04/56	#3	10	The Flying Saucer (Parts 1 & 2)	Luniverse 101
10/27/56	#42	4	Buchanan And Goodman On Trial	Luniverse 102
7/22/57	#37	7	Flying Saucer The 2nd	Luniverse 105
12/14/57	#51	3	Santa And The Satellite (Parts 1 & 2)	Luniverse 107
2/14/59	#71	4	Frankenstein Of '59	Novelty 301
			BUCHANAN BROTHERS	
4/19/69	#21	13	Medicine Man (Part 1)	Event 3302
9/06/69	#51	6	Son Of A Lovin' Man	Event 3305
12/06/69	#90	4	The Last Time	Event 3307
			BUCKEYE	
8/18/79	#66	8	Where Will Your Heart Take You	Polydor 14578
			LINDSEY BUCKINGHAM	
10/24/81	#8	21	Trouble	Asylum 47223
7/28/84	#24	16	Go Insane	Elektra 69714
9/05/92	#84	6	Countdown	Reprise 18860
			BUCKINGHAMS	
12/24/66	#3	15	Kind Of A Drag	U.S.A. 860
3/11/67	#39	7	Laudy Miss Claudy	U.S.A. 869
3/18/67	#6	14	Don't You Care	Columbia 44053
6/17/67	#5	13	Mercy, Mercy, Mercy	Columbia 44182
9/09/67	#5	10	Hey Baby (They're Playing Our Song)	Columbia 44254
12/09/67	#7	13	Susan	Columbia 44378
6/01/68	#53	5	Back In Love Again	Columbia 44533
			BUCKNER & GARCIA	
12/26/81	#7	23	Pac-Man Fever	Columbia 02673
			BUCKWHEAT	
3/25/72	#69	7	Simple Song Of Freedom	London 176
5/19/73	#100	1	I Just Can't Turn My Habit Into Love	London 189
			BUD and TRAVIS	
10/29/60	#35	10	Ballad Of The Alamo	Liberty 55284
			JULIE BUDD	
8/10/68	#87	3	All's Quiet On West 23rd	MGM 13925
			BUENA VISTAS	
6/25/66	#82	6	Hot Shot	Swan 4255
6/01/68	#85	3	Here Come Da Judge	Marquee 443
			BUFFALO SPRINGFIELD	
1/14/67	#7	17	For What It's Worth	Atco 6459
7/08/67	#68	6	Bluebird	Atco 6499
9/23/67	#52	7	Rock 'N' Roll Woman	Atco 6519
12/23/67	#99	1	Expecting To Fly	Atco 6545
11/02/68	#90	2	On The Way Home	Atco 6615
			JIMMY BUFFETT	
4/27/74	#26	14	Come Monday	Dunhill 4385
4/12/75	#97	2	A Pirate Looks At Forty	Dunhill 15029
3/26/77	#7	24	Margaritaville	ABC 12254
9/17/77	#34	8	Changes In Latitudes, Changes In Attitudes	ABC 12305
4/22/78	#29	12	Cheeseburger In Paradise	ABC 12358
8/12/78	#73	6	Livingston Saturday Night	ABC 12391
9/01/79	#25	13	Fins	MCA 41109
12/15/79	#61	8	Volcano	MCA 41161
3/15/80	#71	5	Survive	MCA 41199
2/14/81	#62	9	It's My Job	MCA 51061

43

Debut Date	Peak Pos	Wks Chr	ARTIST/Song Title	Label & Number
			BUGGLES	
11/10/79	#40	11	Video Killed The Radio Star	Island 49114
			BULAWAYO BAND	
9/18/54	#4	11	Skokiaan	London 1491
			BULL & THE MATADORS	
8/31/68	#59	10	The Funky Judge	Toddlin' Town 108
			BULLDOG	
10/21/72	#51	11	No	Decca 32996
			CINDY BULLENS	
2/03/79	#57	8	Survivor	United Artists 1261
12/29/79	#94	5	Trust Me	Casablanca 2217
			BULLET	
10/23/71	#25	15	White Lies, Blue Eyes	Big Tree 123
2/19/72	#68	5	Willpower Weak, Temptation Strong	Big Tree 131
6/10/72	#80	4	A Little Bit Of Soul	Big Tree 140
			BUOYS	
3/13/71	#13	12	Timothy	Scepter 12275
6/12/71	#81	4	Give Up Your Guns	Scepter 12318
			GARY BURBANK	
6/28/80	#77	5	Who Shot J.R.?	Ovation 1150
			DOC BURCH	
3/07/59	#75	2	Catch A Little Moonbeam	Challenge 59038
			ERIC BURDON & THE ANIMALS (see ANIMALS)	
			ERIC BURDON & JIMMY WITHERSPOON	
10/30/71	#91	2	Soledad	MGM 14296
			ERIC BURDON and WAR	
5/30/70	#1	19	Spill The Wine	MGM 14118
12/19/70	#37	7	They Can't Take Away Our Music	MGM 14196
			SOLOMON BURKE	
9/30/61	#21	17	Just Out Of Reach (Of My Two Open Arms)	Atlantic 2114
2/03/62	#38	11	Cry To Me	Atlantic 2131
6/09/62	#87	6	Down In The Valley	Atlantic 2147
4/20/63	#22	12	If You Need Me	Atlantic 2185
8/03/63	#96	2	Can't Nobody Love You	Atlantic 2196
11/02/63	#37	9	You're Good For Me	Atlantic 2205
2/15/64	#60	7	He'll Have To Go	Atlantic 2218
4/25/64	#32	9	Goodbye Baby (Baby Goodbye)	Atlantic 2226
7/18/64	#62	7	Everybody Needs Somebody To Love	Atlantic 2241
11/21/64	#56	7	The Price	Atlantic 2259
3/06/65	#22	11	Got To Get You Off My Mind	Atlantic 2276
5/29/65	#23	10	Tonight's The Night	Atlantic 2288
9/18/65	#94	2	Someone Is Watching	Atlantic 2299
11/13/65	#81	2	Only Love	Atlantic 2308
1/15/66	#91	2	Baby Come On Home	Atlantic 2314
8/20/66	#93	3	Keep Looking	Atlantic 2349
1/28/67	#79	4	Keep A Light In The Window Till I Come Home	Atlantic 2378
7/01/67	#50	5	Take Me	Atlantic 2416
12/02/67	#86	3	Detroit City	Atlantic 2459
4/27/68	#79	4	I Wish I Knew	Atlantic 2507
5/03/69	#49	6	Proud Mary	Bell 783
3/13/71	#95	1	Electronic Magnetism	MGM 14221
4/15/72	#82	4	Love's Street And Fool's Road	MGM 14353
			BILLY BURNETTE	
11/22/80	#85	3	Don't Say No	Columbia 11380
			DORSEY BURNETTE	
2/13/60	#19	12	(There Was A) Tall Oak Tree	ERA 3012
6/11/60	#40	12	Hey Little One	ERA 3019
1/25/69	#56	5	The Greatest Love	Liberty 56087
			JOHNNY BURNETTE	
7/09/60	#8	19	Dreamin'	Liberty 55258
11/12/60	#7	15	You're Sixteen	Liberty 55285
2/04/61	#19	11	Little Boy Sad	Liberty 55298
4/22/61	#49	10	Big Big World	Liberty 55318

Debut Date	Peak Pos	Wks Chr	**ARTIST**/Song Title	Label & Number
10/21/61	#31	9	God, Country And My Baby	Liberty 55379
3/03/62	#92	4	Clown Shoes	Liberty 55416
			ROCKY BURNETTE	
5/10/80	#6	22	Tired Of Toein' The Line	EMI America 8043
			GEORGE BURNS	
1/19/80	#56	11	I Wish I Was Eighteen Again	Mercury 57011
			TONY BURROWS	
6/20/70	#95	3	Melanie Makes Me Smile	Bell 884
			GLEN BURTNICK	
10/03/87	#74	7	Follow You	A&M 2968
			JENNY BURTON & PATRICK JUDE	
6/09/84	#59	10	Strangers In A Strange World	Atlantic 89660
			RICHARD BURTON	
1/23/65	#56	6	Married Man	MGM 13307
			BUS BOYS	
8/04/84	#76	5	Cleanin' Up The Town	Arista 9229
			KATE BUSH	
9/07/85	#28	22	Running Up That Hill	EMI America 8285
4/04/87	#69	6	Don't Give Up*	Geffen 28463
			*released as by **PETER GABRIEL/KATE BUSH**	
			BUSTERS	
9/14/63	#29	8	Bust Out	Arlen 735
			BILLY BUTLER & THE CHANTERS	
7/03/65	#58	6	I Can't Work No Longer	Okeh 7221
			CARL BUTLER	
3/23/63	#92	3	Don't Let Me Cross Over	Columbia 42593
			CHAMP BUTLER	
10/27/51	#8	1	Down Yonder	Columbia 39533
			JERRY BUTLER	
6/21/58	#22	11	For Your Precious Love*	Falcon 1013
10/11/58	#94	3	Come Back My Love*	Abner 1017
2/14/59	#83	4	Lost	Abner 1024
5/21/60	#100	2	A Lonely Soldier	Abner 1035
10/15/60	#3	19	He Will Break Your Heart	Vee-Jay 354
3/04/61	#21	12	Find Another Girl	Vee-Jay 375
7/22/61	#35	8	I'm A Telling You	Vee-Jay 390
9/30/61	#5	17	Moon River	Vee-Jay 405
7/07/62	#24	12	Make It Easy On Yourself	Vee-Jay 451
10/20/62	#83	3	You Can Run	Vee-Jay 463
11/16/63	#28	13	Need To Belong	Vee-Jay 567
3/28/64	#59	7	Giving Up On Love	Vee-Jay 588
8/08/64	#58	8	I Stand Accused	Vee-Jay 598
9/05/64	#91	1	Ain't That Loving You Baby**/	Vee-Jay 613
9/12/64	#9	13	Let It Be Me**	Vee-Jay 613
12/05/64	#52	7	Smile**	Vee-Jay 633
2/20/65	#69	6	Good Times	Vee-Jay 651
1/28/67	#60	9	I Dig You Baby	Mercury 72648
10/21/67	#46	7	Mr. Dream Merchant	Mercury 72721
12/23/67	#52	6	Lost	Mercury 72764
5/11/68	#18	14	Never Give You Up	Mercury 72798
8/31/68	#24	13	Hey, Western Union Man	Mercury 72850
12/14/68	#33	8	Are You Happy	Mercury 72876
3/01/69	#5	12	Only The Strong Survive	Mercury 72898
5/31/69	#22	10	Moody Woman	Mercury 72929
8/23/69	#23	10	What's The Use Of Breaking Up	Mercury 72960
11/22/69	#49	6	Don't Let Love Hang You Up	Mercury 72991
1/17/70	#57	4	Got To See If I Can't Get Mommy (To Come Back Home) .	Mercury 73015
3/14/70	#50	6	I Could Write A Book	Mercury 73045
8/15/70	#74	4	Where Are You Going	Mercury 73101
10/24/70	#96	3	Special Memory	Mercury 73131
2/27/71	#89	5	If It's Real What I Feel	Mercury 73169
7/17/71	#97	2	How Did We Lose It Baby	Mercury 73210
10/30/71	#93	2	Walk Easy My Son	Mercury 73241
12/25/71	#24	16	Ain't Understanding Mellow***	Mercury 73255
5/13/72	#67	5	I Only Have Eyes For You	Mercury 73290

45

Debut Date	Peak Pos	Wks Chr	ARTIST/Song Title	Label & Number
			JERRY BUTLER—continued	
7/22/72	#66	7	(They Long To Be) Close To You***	Mercury 73301
11/11/72	#57	6	One Night Affair	Mercury 73335
3/12/77	#64	11	I Wanna Do It To You	Motown 1414
			*released as by JERRY BUTLER and THE IMPRESSIONS	
			**released as by BETTY EVERETT & JERRY BUTLER	
			***released as by JERRY BUTLER and BRENDA LEE EAGER	
			JONATHAN BUTLER	
6/27/86	#30	16	Lies	Jive 1038
			BUTTERFLYS	
9/12/64	#44	7	Goodnight Baby	Red Bird 009
1/30/65	#91	2	I Wonder	Red Bird 016
			RED BUTTONS	
6/13/53	#7	4	The Ho Ho Song	Coral 39981
			MAX BYGRAVES	
8/16/58	#43	6	You Gotta Have Rain	London 1813
			BOBBY BYRD	
3/28/64	#63	8	Baby, Baby, Baby*	Smash 1884
10/10/70	#61	6	I Need Help	King 6323
10/02/71	#72	4	Hot Pants - I'm Coming, I'm Coming, I'm Coming	Brown Stone 4203
3/04/72	#81	3	Keep On Doin' What You're Doin'	Brown Stone 4205
			*released as by ANNA KING/BOBBY BYRD	
			CHARLIE BYRD	
9/22/62	#11	18	Desafinado*	Verve 10323
2/02/63	#70	8	Meditation	Riverside 4544
			*released as by STAN GETZ/CHARLIE BYRD	
			DONALD BYRD	
6/02/73	#71	11	Black Byrd	Blue Note 212
			JERRY BYRD	
7/16/60	#80	6	Theme From Adventures In Paradise	Monument 419
3/24/62	#63	7	Memories Of Maria	Monument 449
			BYRDS	
5/08/65	#1	14	Mr. Tambourine Man	Columbia 43271
7/03/65	#9	8	All I Really Want To Do	Columbia 43332
10/23/65	#1	14	Turn! Turn! Turn! (To Everything There Is A Season)	Columbia 43424
2/05/66	#39	7	It Won't Be Wrong/	Columbia 43501
2/12/66	#83	1	Set You Free This Time	Columbia 43501
4/02/66	#2	10	Eight Miles High	Columbia 43578
7/09/66	#39	5	5 D (Fifth Dimension)	Columbia 43702
9/17/66	#34	8	Mr. Spaceman	Columbia 43766
1/28/67	#28	7	So You Want To Be A Rock 'N' Roll Star	Columbia 43987
4/01/67	#26	8	My Back Pages	Columbia 44054
6/03/67	#73	2	Have You Seen Her Face	Columbia 44157
8/12/67	#83	4	Lady Friend	Columbia 44230
11/11/67	#58	3	Goin' Back	Columbia 44362
4/27/68	#81	6	You Ain't Going Nowhere	Columbia 44499
11/15/69	#87	2	Ballad Of Easy Rider	Columbia 44990
11/28/70	#95	3	Chestnut Mare	Columbia 45259
9/18/71	#65	2	Glory, Glory	Columbia 45444
5/05/73	#87	2	Full Circle	Asylum 11016
			ROBERT BYRNE	
6/09/79	#93	3	Baby Fat	Mercury 74070
			EDWARD BYRNES	
4/25/59	#3	13	Kookie, Kookie (Lend Me Your Comb)*	Warner Brothers 5047
8/08/59	#80	2	Kookie's Mad Pad/	Warner Brothers 5087
8/15/59	#41	8	Like I Love You	Warner Brothers 5087
			*released as by EDWARD BYRNES and CONNIE STEVENS	

C

			C + C MUSIC FACTORY	
11/24/90	#1	25	Gonna Make You Sweat	Columbia 73604
3/09/91	#1	25	Here We Go*	Columbia 73690
7/20/91	#5	20	Things That Make You Go Hmmmm...**	Columbia 73687
11/16/91	#65	11	Just A Touch Of Love	Columbia 74033
8/22/92	#86	3	Keep It Comin'	Columbia 74432

Debut Date	Peak Pos	Wks Chr	ARTIST/Song Title	Label & Number
			*released as by C + C MUSIC FACTORY featuring FREEDOM WILLIAMS & ZELMA DAVIS	
			**released as by C + C MUSIC FACTORY featuring FREEDOM WILLIAMS	
			CABOOSE	
7/18/70	#79	5	Black Hands White Cotton	Enterprise 9015
			CADETS	
8/04/56	#10	5	Stranded In The Jungle	Modern 994
			CADILLACS	
11/29/58	#33	11	Peek-A-Boo	Josie 846
			SHIRLEY CAESAR	
5/24/75	#97	2	No Charge	Scepter 12402
			JOHN CAFFERTY and THE BEAVER BROWN BAND	
2/04/84	#75	4	Tender Years	Scotti Brothers 04327
8/25/84	#12	21	On The Dark Side	Scotti Brothers 04594
11/17/84	#29	15	Tender Years	Scotti Brothers 04682
5/11/85	#20	15	Tough All Over	Scotti Brothers 04891
8/10/85	#20	14	C-I-T-Y	Scotti Brothers 05452
11/09/85	#56	10	Small Town Girl	Scotti Brothers 05668
2/22/86	#69	7	Heart's On Fire	Scotti Brothers 05774
6/14/86	#52	8	Voice Of America's Sons	Scotti Brothers 06048
8/12/89	#69	6	Pride & Passion	Scotti Brothers 68999
			JONATHAN CAIN	
1/10/76	#48	9	'Til It's Time To Say Goodbye	October 1001
			TANE CAIN	
8/14/82	#36	12	Holdin' On	RCA 13287
			AL CAIOLA	
12/03/60	#24	15	The Magnificent Seven	United Artists 261
4/01/61	#27	12	Bonanza	United Artists 302
			BOBBY CALDWELL	
12/16/78	#10	19	What You Won't Do For Love	Clouds 11
4/19/80	#94	4	Coming Down From Love	Clouds 21
9/18/82	#70	6	All Of My Love	Polydor 2212
			J.J. CALE	
2/19/72	#35	10	Crazy Mama	Shelter 7314
5/27/72	#49	8	After Midnight	Shelter 7321
11/04/72	#62	6	Lies	Shelter 7326
			CALL	
5/07/83	#75	7	The Walls Came Down	Mercury 811487
8/19/86	#74	6	Let The Day Begin	MCA 53658
			CALLOWAY	
2/10/90	#2	24	I Wanna Be Rich	Solar 74005
7/28/90	#59	8	All The Way	Solar 74516
			CAB CALLOWAY	
4/02/66	#82	5	History Repeats Itself	Boom 60006
			EDDIE CALVERT	
12/26/53	#1	8	Oh, Mein Papa	Essex 336
			CAMBRIDGE STRINGS and SINGERS	
2/25/61	#65	6	Tunes Of Glory	London 1960
			CAMEO	
9/15/79	#90	5	I Just Want To Be	Chocolate City 19
4/07/84	#43	13	She's Strange	Atlanta Artists 818384
9/13/86	#7	22	Word Up	Atlanta Artists 884933
1/17/87	#28	15	Candy	Atlanta Artists 888193
4/25/87	#58	9	Back And Forth	Atlanta Artists 888385
11/12/88	#86	4	You Make Me Work	Atlanta Artists 870587
			CAMOUFLAGE	
12/31/88	#67	6	The Great Commandment	Atlantic 89031
			HAMILTON CAMP	
4/13/68	#75	8	Here's To You	Warner Brothers 7165
			GLEN CAMPBELL	
11/11/61	#49	10	Turn Around, Look At Me	Crest 1087
8/11/62	#81	6	Too Late To Worry - Too Blue To Cry	Capitol 4783

Debut Date	Peak Pos	Wks Chr	ARTIST/Song Title	Label & Number
			GLEN CAMPBELL—*continued*	
9/18/65	#61	8	Universal Soldier	Capitol 5504
7/15/67	#85	3	Gentle On My Mind	Capitol 5939
10/21/67	#26	13	By The Time I Get To Phoenix	Capitol 2015
1/20/68	#54	8	Hey Little One	Capitol 2076
4/06/68	#38	12	I Wanna Live	Capitol 2146
6/09/68	#38	8	Dreams Of The Everyday Housewife	Capitol 2224
11/02/68	#2	15	Wichita Lineman	Capitol 2302
11/23/68	#94	1	Morning Glory*	Capitol 2314
2/08/69	#96	3	Let It Be Me*	Capitol 2387
3/01/69	#4	11	Galveston	Capitol 2428
5/03/69	#13	7	Where's The Playground Susie	Capitol 2494
7/26/69	#34	6	True Grit	Capitol 2573
10/11/69	#15	11	Try A Little Kindness	Capitol 2659
1/17/70	#11	10	Honey Come Back	Capitol 2718
2/14/70	#31	9	All I Have To Do Is Dream*	Capitol 2745
4/11/70	#34	8	Oh Happy Day	Capitol 2787
7/04/70	#45	6	Everything A Man Could Ever Need	Capitol 2843
9/05/70	#9	13	It's Only Make Believe	Capitol 2905
3/06/71	#24	8	Dream Baby (How Long Must I Dream)	Capitol 3062
6/26/71	#57	6	The Last Time I Saw Her	Capitol 3123
10/30/71	#72	3	I Say A Little Prayer/By The Time I Get To Phoenix** . . .	Capitol 3200
9/02/72	#65	6	I Will Never Pass This Way Again	Capitol 3411
12/16/72	#78	6	One Last Time	Capitol 3483
3/24/73	#46	10	I Knew Jesus (Before He Was A Star)	Capitol 3548
2/02/74	#54	7	Houston	Capitol 3808
5/03/75	#1	23	Rhinestone Cowboy	Capitol 4095
11/08/75	#17	14	Country Boy (You Got Your Feet In L.A.)	Capitol 4155
3/27/76	#41	10	Don't Pull Your Love/Then You Can Tell Me Goodbye . . .	Capitol 4245
2/19/77	#1	22	Southern Nights	Capitol 4376
7/02/77	#39	13	Sunflower	Capitol 4445
10/21/78	#38	12	Can You Fool	Capitol 4584
5/24/80	#53	10	Somethin' 'Bout You Baby I Like***	Capitol 4865
1/24/81	#71	7	I Don't Want To Know Your Name	Capitol 4959
			*released as by **BOBBIE GENTRY & GLEN CAMPBELL**	
			released as by **GLEN CAMPBELL/ANNE MURRAY	
			***released as by **GLEN CAMPBELL and RITA COOLIDGE**	
			JO ANN CAMPBELL	
9/03/60	#59	6	A Kookie Little Paradise	ABC Paramount 10134
8/18/62	#37	7	(I'm The Girl On) Wolverton Mountain	Cameo 223
4/20/63	#92	2	Mother Please!	Cameo 249
			TEVIN CAMPBELL	
6/02/90	#70	5	Tomorrow (A Better You, Better Me)*	Qwest 19881
12/15/90	#10	27	Round And Round	Paisley Park 19748
8/31/91	#87	5	Just Ask Me To	Qwest 19275
11/16/91	#12	30	Tell Me What You Want Me To Do	Qwest 19131
4/18/92	#62	12	Goodbye	Qwest 19008
6/13/92	#36	13	Strawberry Letter 23	Qwest 18919
10/24/92	#66	5	Alone With You	Qwest 18874
10/23/93	#7	31	Can We Talk	Qwest 18346
			*released as by **QUINCY JONES featuring TEVIN CAMPBELL**	
			CANDI	
10/15/88	#61	10	Dancing Under A Latin Moon	I.R.S. 53436
			PENNY CANDY	
8/29/59	#96	5	Rockin' Lady	Flash 201
			CANDY and THE KISSES	
11/14/64	#39	9	The 81	Cameo 336
			CANDYMAN	
9/08/90	#10	26	Knockin' Boots	Epic 73450
12/22/90	#82	10	Melt In Your Mouth	Epic 73639
			CANDYMEN	
11/04/67	#54	6	Georgia Pines	ABC 10995
			GARY CANE	
6/18/60	#93	3	The Yen Yet Song	Shell 719
			CANE'S COUSINS	
7/05/69	#97	2	Take Your Love And Shove It	Shove Love 500

Debut Date	Peak Pos	Wks Chr	ARTIST/Song Title	Label & Number
			CANNED HEAT	
8/03/68	#9	13	On The Road Again	Liberty 56038
11/30/68	#9	12	Going Up The Country	Liberty 56077
3/08/69	#47	6	Time Was	Liberty 56097
8/09/69	#95	3	Poor Man	Liberty 56127
10/03/70	#17	12	Let's Work Together	Liberty 56151
			CANNIBAL & THE HEADHUNTERS	
3/20/65	#30	13	Land Of 1000 Dances	Rampart 642
			ACE CANNON	
12/09/61	#15	20	Tuff	Hi 2040
4/07/62	#46	9	Blues (Stay Away From Me)	Hi 2051
4/21/62	#100	1	Sugar Blues	Santo 503
11/10/62	#90	3	Volare	Hi 2057
6/29/63	#83	5	Cottonfields	Hi 2065
3/14/64	#79	4	Searchin'	Hi 2074
			FREDDY CANNON	
5/09/59	#6	15	Tallahassee Lassie	Swan 4031
8/29/59	#41	8	Okefenokee	Swan 4038
11/28/59	#3	15	Way Down Yonder In New Orleans	Swan 4043
2/13/60	#27	9	Chattanooga Shoe Shine Boy	Swan 4050
4/30/60	#76	5	The Urge/	Swan 4053
5/07/60	#24	11	Jump Over	Swan 4053
7/12/60	#54	6	Happy Shades Of Blue	Swan 4057
10/15/60	#63	5	Humdinger	Swan 4061
1/14/61	#48	8	Muskrat Ramble	Swan 4066
4/29/61	#35	10	Buzz Buzz A Diddle It	Swan 4071
8/12/61	#31	8	Transistor Sister	Swan 4078
10/21/61	#56	6	For Me And My Gal	Swan 4083
1/27/62	#64	6	Teen Queen Of The Week	Swan 4096
5/12/62	#3	15	Palisades Park	Swan 4106
8/25/62	#72	7	What's Gonna Happen When Summer's	Done/Swan 4117
9/01/62	#100	1	Broadway	Swan 4117
11/10/62	#75	4	If You Were A Rock And Roll Record	Swan 4122
5/04/63	#62	6	Patty Baby	Swan 4139
7/27/63	#56	7	Everybody Monkey	Swan 4149
2/01/64	#24	9	Abigail Beecher	Warner Brothers 5409
8/14/65	#13	10	Action	Warner Brothers 5645
2/26/66	#50	6	The Dedication Song	Warner Brothers 5693
9/26/81	#77	6	Let's Put The Fun Back In Rock N Roll*	MiaSound 1002
			*released as by FREDDY CANNON & THE BELMONTS	
			LANA CANTRELL	
3/01/75	#90	4	Like A Sunday Morning	Polydor 14261
			CANYON	
6/14/75	#98	3	Top Of The World (Make My Reservation)	Magna-Glide 323
			JIM CAPALDI	
1/11/75	#53	8	It's All Right	Island 003
12/27/75	#95	3	Love Hurts	Island 045
10/02/76	#81	6	Good Night And Good Morning	Island 067
4/23/83	#27	15	That's Love	Atlantic 89849
8/27/83	#68	7	Living On The Edge	Atlantic 89799
11/19/88	#88	5	Some Come Running	Island 91024
			CAPITOLS	
4/23/66	#5	15	Cool Jerk	Karen 1524
11/12/66	#79	4	We Got A Thing That's In The Groove	Karen 1526
			AL CAPPS BAND	
10/10/70	#97	1	Odyssey Rock Park	Columbia 45219
			CAPREES	
10/15/66	#92	1	Rosanna	Sound 126
			CAPRIS	
12/31/60	#7	16	There's A Moon Out Tonight	Old Town 1094
4/15/61	#86	2	Where I Fell In Love	Old Town 1099
			CAPTAIN & TENNILLE	
4/26/75	#1	21	Love Will Keep Us Together	A&M 1672
8/09/75	#57	6	Por Amor Viviremos	A&M 1715
9/20/75	#3	18	The Way I Want To Touch You	A&M 1725
1/24/76	#1	19	Lonely Night (Angel Face)	A&M 1782

49

Debut Date	Peak Pos	Wks Chr	ARTIST/Song Title	Label & Number
			CAPTAIN & TENNILLE—*continued*	
4/24/76	#6	20	Shop Around	A&M 1817
9/25/76	#2	22	Muskrat Love	A&M 1870
3/19/77	#17	13	Can't Stop Dancin'	A&M 1912
4/29/78	#86	5	I'm On My Way	A&M 2027
7/29/78	#10	21	You Never Done It Like That	A&M 2063
12/02/78	#36	12	You Need A Woman Tonight	A&M 2106
10/20/79	#1	25	Do That To Me One More Time	Casablanca 2215
3/08/80	#63	7	Love On A Shoestring	Casablanca 2243
5/10/80	#67	5	Happy Together (A Fantasy)	Casablanca 2264
			CAPTAIN HOLLYWOOD PROJECT	
5/15/93	#14	20	More And More	Imago 25029
			IRENE CARA	
6/28/80	#5	23	Fame	RSO 1034
8/16/80	#25	18	Out Here On My Own	RSO 1048
11/28/81	#41	21	Anyone Can See	Network 47950
4/02/83	#1	31	Flashdance....What A Feeling	Casablanca 811440
10/22/83	#15	16	Why Me?	Geffen 29464
12/10/83	#38	14	The Dream (Hold On To Your Dream)	Network 29396
3/24/84	#10	20	Breakdance	Network 29328
			CARAVELLES	
11/02/63	#6	14	You Don't Have To Be A Baby To Cry	Smash 1852
2/08/64	#82	4	Have You Ever Been Lonely	Smash 1869
			LUIS CARDENAS	
9/13/86	#68	8	Runaway	Allied Artists 72500
			CARDIGANS	
3/01/58	#52	5	Your Graduation Means Goodbye	Mercury 71251
			CAREFREES	
3/14/64	#36	6	We Love You Beatles	London Int'l. 10614
			MARIAH CAREY	
6/02/90	#1	22	Vision Of Love	Columbia 73348
9/15/90	#1	25	Love Takes Time	Columbia 73455
1/19/91	#1	22	Someday	Columbia 73561
4/06/91	#1	24	I Don't Wanna Cry	Columbia 73743
8/31/91	#1	26	Emotions	Columbia 73977
11/16/91	#1	28	Can't Let Go	Columbia 74088
2/29/92	#3	24	Make It Happen	Columbia 74239
6/06/92	#1	22	I'll Be There	Columbia 74330
8/14/93	#1	33	Dream Lover	Columbia 77080
10/30/93	#2	32	Hero	Columbia 77224
			TONY CAREY	
3/19/83	#92	6	I Won't Be Home Tonight	Rocshire 95030
7/16/83	#67	7	West Coast Summer Nights	Rocshire 95037
3/03/84	#25	17	A Fine Fine Day	MCA 52343
6/16/84	#35	12	The First Day Of Summer	MCA 52388
			HENSON CARGILL	
12/23/67	#22	13	Skip A Rope	Monument 1041
			CARGOE	
8/19/72	#91	7	Feel Alright	Ardent 2901
			BELINDA CARLISLE	
5/17/86	#4	22	Mad About You	I.R.S. 52815
9/27/86	#77	5	I Feel The Magic	I.R.S. 52889
9/26/87	#1	23	Heaven Is A Place On Earth	MCA 53181
1/16/88	#3	17	I Get Weak	MCA 53242
4/16/88	#7	18	Circle In The Sand	MCA 53308
7/30/88	#81	5	I Feel Free	MCA 53377
9/30/89	#12	19	Leave A Light On	MCA 53706
1/20/90	#36	12	Summer Rain	MCA 53783
10/19/91	#60	13	Do You Feel Like I Feel?	MCA 54183
			STEVE CARLISLE	
11/21/81	#66	12	WKRP In Cincinnati	MCA 51205
			CARLOS BROTHERS	
9/10/60	#81	3	La Bamba	Del-Fi 4145
			CARL CARLTON	
6/08/68	#60	10	Competition Ain't Nothin'*	Back Beat 588

Debut Date	Peak Pos	Wks Chr	ARTIST/Song Title	Label & Number
7/18/70	#77	6	Drop By My Place*	Back Beat 613
9/21/74	#9	14	Everlasting Love	Back Beat 27001
8/22/81	#23	22	She's A Bad Mama Jama (She's Built, She's Stacked)	20th Century 2488
			*released as by LITTLE CARL CARLTON	
			LARRY CARLTON	
3/20/82	#74	5	Sleepwalk	Warner Brothers 50019
			RUSS CARLYLE	
2/02/57	#36	6	Stashu Pandowski	ABC Paramount 9772
			ERIC CARMEN	
12/13/75	#1	22	All By Myself	Arista 0165
5/01/76	#9	15	Never Gonna Fall In Love Again	Arista 0184
8/21/76	#38	11	Sunrise	Arista 0200
8/27/77	#15	14	She Did It	Arista 0266
1/14/78	#92	5	Boats Against The Current	Arista 0295
9/16/78	#19	18	Change Of Heart	Arista 0354
1/27/79	#60	7	Baby, I Need Your Lovin'	Arista 0384
6/28/80	#83	5	It Hurts Too Much	Arista 0506
1/19/85	#37	13	I Wanna Hear It From Your Lips	Geffen 29118
4/27/85	#79	4	I'm Through With Love	Geffen 29032
11/07/87	#3	26	Hungry Eyes	RCA 5315
5/21/88	#4	23	Make Me Lose Control	Arista 9686
			KIM CARNES	
6/10/78	#35	13	You're A Part Of Me*	Ariola 7704
2/17/79	#54	8	It Hurts So Bad	EMI America 8011
3/29/80	#4	18	Don't Fall In Love With A Dreamer**	United Artists 1345
5/31/80	#9	21	More Love	EMI America 8045
10/04/80	#51	10	Cry Like A Baby	EMI America 8058
3/28/81	#1	27	Bette Davis Eyes	EMI America 8077
8/08/81	#25	13	Draw Of The Cards	EMI America 8087
10/24/81	#63	7	Mistaken Identity	EMI America 8098
8/21/82	#25	11	Voyeur	EMI America 8127
11/06/82	#38	14	Does It Make You Remember	EMI America 8147
10/15/83	#34	14	Invisible Hands	EMI America 8181
2/04/84	#63	7	You Make My Heart Beat Faster	EMI America 8191
9/15/84	#21	18	What About Me***	RCA 13899
12/15/84	#42	11	Make No Mistake, He's Mine****	Columbia 04695
1/19/85	#62	8	Invitation To Dance	EMI America 8250
5/11/85	#22	16	Crazy In The Night (Barking At Airplanes)	EMI America 8267
8/03/85	#70	6	Abadabadango	EMI America 8281
5/24/86	#72	5	Divided Hearts	EMI America 8322
			*released as by GENE COTTON with KIM CARNES	
			**released as by KENNY ROGERS with KIM CARNES	
			***released as by KENNY ROGERS with KIM CARNES and JAMES INGRAM	
			****released as by BARBRA STREISAND with KIM CARNES	
			RENATO CAROSONE	
4/26/58	#26	13	Torero	Capitol 71080
			CARLETON CARPENTER & DEBBIE REYNOLDS	
3/10/51	#5	10	Aba Daba Honeymoon	MGM 30282
			MARY-CHAPIN CARPENTER	
2/20/93	#53	13	Passionate Kisses	Columbia 74795
			THELMA CARPENTER	
1/14/61	#68	4	Yes, I'm Lonesome Tonight	Coral 62241
			CARPENTERS	
2/21/70	#78	4	Ticket To Ride	A&M 1142
6/13/70	#1	14	(They Long To Be) Close To You	A&M 1183
9/12/70	#1	15	We've Only Just Begun	A&M 1217
12/12/70	#41	3	Merry Christmas Darling	A&M 1236
2/06/71	#6	13	For All We Know	A&M 1243
5/08/71	#2	12	Rainy Days And Mondays	A&M 1260
8/28/71	#2	15	Superstar	A&M 1289
1/15/72	#2	13	Hurting Each Other	A&M 1322
4/29/72	#17	9	It's Going To Take Some Time	A&M 1351
7/08/72	#7	12	Goodbye To Love	A&M 1367
2/17/73	#5	15	Sing	A&M 1413
6/02/73	#1	14	Yesterday Once More	A&M 1446
9/29/73	#1	19	Top Of The World	A&M 1468

Debut Date	Peak Pos	Wks Chr	ARTIST/Song Title	Label & Number
			CARPENTERS—*continued*	
4/06/74	#9	12	I Won't Last A Day Without You	A&M 1521
11/23/74	#1	15	Please Mr. Postman	A&M 1646
3/29/75	#8	12	Only Yesterday	A&M 1677
8/02/75	#15	9	Solitaire	A&M 1721
2/28/76	#12	14	There's A Kind Of Hush (All Over The World)	A&M 1800
6/05/76	#31	14	I Need To Be In Love	A&M 1828
9/25/76	#87	3	Goofus	A&M 1859
5/21/77	#43	11	All You Get From Love Is A Love Song	A&M 1940
9/24/77	#24	18	Calling Occupants Of Interplanetary Craft	A&M 1978
2/04/78	#42	13	Sweet, Sweet Smile	A&M 2008
11/25/78	#70	8	I Believe You	A&M 2097
6/20/81	#17	14	Touch Me When We're Dancing	A&M 2344
10/03/81	#75	7	(Want You) Back In My Life Again	A&M 2370
12/19/81	#78	6	Those Good Old Dreams	A&M 2386
5/08/82	#88	2	Beechwood 4-5789	A&M 2405
			BILLY CARR	
12/04/65	#100	1	What's Come Over This World	Colpix 791
			CATHY CARR	
5/19/56	#2	11	Ivory Tower	Fraternity 734
8/11/56	#48	3	Heart Hideaway	Fraternity 743
1/17/59	#31	11	First Anniversary	Roulette 4125
6/13/59	#70	4	I'm Gonna Change Him	Roulette 4152
			JAMES CARR	
4/02/66	#52	7	You've Got My Mind Messed Up	Goldwax 302
8/06/66	#99	2	Love Attack	Goldwax 309
2/18/67	#91	4	Dark End Of The Street	Goldwax 317
1/13/68	#63	9	A Man Needs A Woman	Goldwax 332
1/18/69	#96	1	Freedom Train	Goldwax 338
			JOE "FINGERS" CARR	
8/04/56	#46	1	Portuguese Washerwoman	Capitol 3418
			VALERIE CARR	
4/26/58	#36	8	When The Boys Talk About The Girls	Roulette 4066
			VIKKI CARR	
8/26/67	#5	16	It Must Be Him	Liberty 55986
12/23/67	#35	8	The Lesson	Liberty 56012
3/23/68	#92	2	She'll Be There	Liberty 56026
3/29/69	#42	13	With Pen In Hand	Liberty 56092
9/20/69	#69	5	Eternity	Liberty 56132
			PAUL CARRACK	
9/04/82	#26	13	I Need You	Epic 03146
11/14/87	#9	25	Don't Shed A Tear	Chrysalis 43164
3/19/88	#33	14	One Good Reason	Chrysalis 43204
6/11/88	#91	4	When You Walk In The Room	Chrysalis 43252
10/21/89	#27	16	I Live By The Groove	Chrysalis 23427
			KEITH CARRADINE	
5/08/76	#10	22	I'm Easy	ABC 12117
			ANDREA CARROLL	
7/20/63	#60	9	It Hurts To Be Sixteen	Big Top 3156
			BERNADETTE CARROLL	
5/23/64	#55	8	Party Girl	Laurie 3238
			CATHY CARROLL	
6/24/61	#79	6	Jimmy Love	Tri-O-Dex 110
			DAVID CARROLL	
1/15/55	#1	19	Melody Of Love	Mercury 70516
3/16/57	#41	4	The Ship That Never Sailed	Mercury 71069
10/29/60	#89	2	Midnight Lace	Mercury 71703
2/24/62	#57	10	The White Rose Of Athens	Mercury 71917
			DINA CARROLL	
4/03/93	#79	5	So Close	A&M 0206
			RONNIE CARROLL	
6/15/63	#82	5	Say Wonderful Things	Philips 40110
			CARROLL BROTHERS	
9/01/62	#100	1	Sweet Georgia Brown	Cameo 221

Debut Date	Peak Pos	Wks Chr	ARTIST/Song Title	Label & Number
			CARS	
6/17/78	#24	17	Just What I Needed	Elektra 45491
10/28/78	#44	14	My Best Friend's Girl	Elektra 45537
3/24/79	#60	8	Good Times Roll	Elektra 46014
6/30/79	#14	16	Let's Go	Elektra 46063
10/13/79	#40	9	It's All I Can Do	Elektra 46546
9/06/80	#38	13	Touch And Go	Elektra 47039
11/21/81	#3	24	Shake It Up	Elektra 47250
3/27/82	#51	8	Since You're Gone	Elektra 47433
3/10/84	#7	18	You Might Think	Elektra 69744
5/19/84	#16	19	Magic	Elektra 69724
8/04/84	#4	19	Drive	Elektra 69706
10/27/84	#19	16	Hello Again	Elektra 69681
1/26/85	#34	14	Why Can't I Have You	Elektra 69657
11/02/85	#10	20	Tonight She Comes	Elektra 69589
2/01/86	#34	14	I'm Not The One	Elektra 69569
8/29/87	#17	16	You Are The Girl	Elektra 69446
11/14/87	#84	5	Strap Me In	Elektra 69427
1/30/88	#83	4	Coming Up You	Elektra 69432
			MINDY CARSON	
4/09/50	#9	1	Candy And Cake	RCA 3681
9/10/55	#7	7	Wake The Town And Tell The People	Columbia 40537
			CLARENCE CARTER	
2/24/68	#91	1	Looking For A Fox	Atlantic 2461
6/01/68	#96	2	Funky Fever/	Atlantic 2508
7/20/68	#11	16	Slip Away	Atlantic 2508
11/02/68	#13	14	Too Weak To Fight	Atlantic 2569
2/22/69	#17	10	Snatching It Back	Atlantic 2605
6/14/69	#39	8	The Feeling Is Right	Atlantic 2642
9/27/69	#52	8	Doin' Our Thing	Atlantic 2660
1/24/70	#95	1	Take It Off Him And Put It On Me	Atlantic 2702
4/18/70	#49	10	I Can't Leave Your Love Alone	Atlantic 2726
7/18/70	#1	14	Patches	Atlantic 2748
11/07/70	#39	7	It's All In Your Mind	Atlantic 2774
5/08/71	#49	6	The Court Room	Atlantic 2801
7/31/71	#50	4	Slipped, Tripped And Fell In Love	Atlantic 2818
12/18/71	#97	1	Scratch My Back	Atlantic 2842
2/17/73	#83	4	Put On Your Shoes And Walk	Fame 179
6/02/73	#66	4	Mother-In-Law/	Fame 250
7/07/73	#51	9	Sixty Minute Man	Fame 250
12/08/73	#87	3	I'm The Midnight Special	Fame 330
			MEL CARTER	
6/29/63	#38	12	When A Boy Falls In Love	Derby 1003
6/19/65	#12	15	Hold Me, Thrill Me, Kiss Me	Imperial 66113
10/30/65	#35	7	(All Of A Sudden) My Heart Sings	Imperial 66138
1/22/66	#54	7	Love Is All We Need	Imperial 66148
4/09/66	#37	9	Band Of Gold	Imperial 66165
7/16/66	#57	7	You You You	Imperial 66183
9/24/66	#91	4	Take Good Care Of Her	Imperial 66208
			CARTOUCHE	
4/13/91	#66	9	Feel The Groove	Scotti Brothers 5281
			FLIP CARTRIDGE	
8/06/66	#91	4	Dear Mrs. Applebee	Parrot 306
			DICK CARUSO	
6/11/60	#95	4	Two Long Years	MGM 12900
			CASCADES	
1/12/63	#2	17	Rhythm Of The Rain	Valiant 6026
4/27/63	#97	2	Shy Girl/	Valiant 6028
5/04/63	#42	7	The Last Leaf	Valiant 6028
8/09/69	#50	8	Maybe The Rain Will Fall	Uni 55152
			AL CASEY	
7/28/62	#73	6	Jivin' Around*	Stacy 936
7/20/63	#39	8	Surfin' Hootenany	Stacy 962
			*released as by AL CASEY COMBO	
			ALVIN CASH	
1/09/65	#9	11	Twine Time*	Mar-V-Lus 6002
4/10/65	#87	4	The Barracuda*	Mar-V-Lus 6005

Debut Date	Peak Pos	Wks Chr	ARTIST/Song Title	Label & Number
			ALVIN CASH—*continued*	
7/23/66	#44	10	Philly Freeze**	Mar-V-Lus 6012
12/03/66	#79	3	Alvin's Boo-Ga-Loo**	Mar-V-Lus 6014
11/30/68	#81	4	Keep On Dancing	Toddlin' Town 111
			*released as by ALVIN CASH & THE CRAWLERS	
			**released as by ALVIN CASH & THE REGISTERS	
			JOHNNY CASH	
9/29/56	#23	13	I Walk The Line	Sun 241
12/29/56	#45	2	There You Go	Sun 258
2/01/58	#28	11	Ballad Of A Teenage Queen	Sun 283
6/14/58	#24	13	Guess Things Happen That Way	Sun 295
9/06/58	#40	6	The Ways Of A Woman In Love/	Sun 302
9/20/58	#82	1	You're The Nearest Thing To Heaven	Sun 302
10/11/58	#81	5	What Do I Care/	Columbia 41251
10/18/58	#86	5	All Over Again	Columbia 41251
12/13/58	#90	3	It's Just About Time	Sun 309
1/17/59	#19	10	Don't Take Your Guns To Town	Columbia 41313
4/18/59	#62	4	Frankie's Man Johnny	Columbia 41371
7/11/59	#77	3	Katy Too	Sun 321
8/01/59	#45	10	I Got Stripes/	Columbia 41427
8/15/59	#90	2	Five Feet High And Rising	Columbia 41427
11/14/59	#26	10	The Little Drummer Boy	Columbia 41481
7/23/60	#99	1	Second Honeymoon	Columbia 41707
11/25/61	#88	5	Tennessee Flat-Top Box	Columbia 42147
6/08/63	#14	14	Ring Of Fire	Columbia 42788
10/19/63	#49	9	The Matador	Columbia 42880
2/15/64	#45	9	Understand Your Man	Columbia 42964
11/07/64	#49	8	It Ain't Me Babe	Columbia 43145
2/06/65	#94	3	Orange Blossom Special	Columbia 43206
2/19/66	#56	8	The One On The Right Is On The Left	Columbia 43496
6/18/66	#67	5	Everybody Loves A Nut	Columbia 43673
6/08/68	#36	10	Folsom Prison Blues	Columbia 44513
1/04/69	#56	8	Daddy Sang Bass	Columbia 44689
7/26/69	#2	12	A Boy Named Sue	Columbia 44944
10/11/69	#62	9	Get Rhythm	Sun 1103
11/08/69	#40	7	See Ruby Fall/	Columbia 45020
11/08/69	#58	7	Blistered	Columbia 45020
1/17/70	#26	7	If I Were A Carpenter*	Columbia 45064
4/11/70	#11	9	What Is Truth	Columbia 45134
8/29/70	#41	8	Sunday Morning Coming Down	Columbia 45211
12/19/70	#49	6	Flesh And Blood	Columbia 45269
3/13/71	#56	6	Man In Black	Columbia 45339
5/27/72	#85	3	Kate	Columbia 45590
4/10/76	#41	10	One Piece At A Time	Columbia 10321
			*released as by JOHNNY CASH & JUNE CARTER	
			ROSANNE CASH	
4/11/81	#22	20	Seven Year Ache	Columbia 11426
			TOMMY CASH	
12/13/69	#81	6	Six White Horses	Epic 10540
			TERRY CASHMAN	
11/13/76	#81	4	Baby, Baby I Love You	Lifesong 45015
			CASHMAN & WEST	
9/16/72	#28	11	American City Suite	Dunhill 4324
12/16/72	#54	7	Songman	Dunhill 4333
8/18/73	#98	2	The King Of Rock 'N' Roll	Dunhill 4349
			CASHMERES	
10/29/60	#64	8	Satisfied (Part 2)	Lake 705
			CASINOS	
1/21/67	#5	13	Then You Can Tell Me Goodbye	Fraternity 977
5/06/67	#68	3	It's All Over Now	Fraternity 985
			CASLONS	
9/09/61	#95	5	Anniversary Of Love	Seeco 6078
			DAVID CASSIDY	
10/30/71	#3	15	Cherish	Bell 45150
2/12/71	#15	11	Could It Be Forever	Bell 45187
5/13/72	#15	10	How Can I Be Sure	Bell 45220
9/09/72	#26	8	Rock Me Baby	Bell 45260

Debut Date	Peak Pos	Wks Chr	ARTIST/Song Title	Label & Number
8/18/73	#91	2	Daydream	Bell 45386
9/22/90	#27	12	Lyin' To Myself	Enigma 75084
			SHAUN CASSIDY	
5/14/77	#1	19	Da Doo Ron Ron	Warner Brothers 8365
7/30/77	#4	20	That's Rock 'N' Roll	Warner Brothers 8423
11/12/77	#21	16	Hey Deanie	Warner Brothers 8488
3/25/78	#37	9	Do You Believe In Magic	Warner Brothers 8533
			CASTAWAYS	
8/28/65	#12	14	Liar Liar	Soma 1433
12/04/65	#90	2	Goodbye Babe	Soma 1442
			CASTELLS	
6/10/61	#21	12	Sacred	Era 3048
4/21/62	#34	13	So This Is Love	Era 3073
			DAVID CASTLE	
10/01/77	#79	7	Ten To Eight	Parachute 501
12/31/77	#74	5	The Loneliest Man On The Moon	Parachute 505
			BOOMER CASTLEMAN	
5/03/75	#29	9	Judy Mae	Mums 6038
			CASTLE SISTERS	
6/23/62	#66	7	Goodbye Dad	Terrace 7506
			JIMMY CASTOR	
12/31/66	#35	9	Hey, Leroy, Your Mama's Callin' You	Smash 2069
5/06/72	#2	14	Troglodyte (Cave Man)*	RCA 1029
2/08/75	#21	14	Bertha Butt Boogie*	Atlantic 3232
10/04/75	#81	7	King Kong (Parts 1 & 2)*	Atlantic 3295
4/26/80	#98	3	Can't Help Falling In Love With You	Long Distance 702
			*released as by the **JIMMY CASTOR BUNCH**	
			CATE BROTHERS	
2/21/76	#32	19	Union Man	Asylum 45294
7/17/76	#73	6	Can't Change My Heart	Asylum 45326
			GEORGE CATES	
5/19/56	#1	18	Moonglow And Theme From "Picnic"	Coral 61618
			CATHY and JOE	
10/03/64	#82	5	I See You	Smash 1929
			CATHY JEAN and THE ROOMMATES	
2/11/61	#12	15	Please Love Me Forever	Valmor 007
			CAT MOTHER and THE ALL NIGHT NEWS BOYS	
6/21/69	#16	10	Good Old Rock 'N Roll	Polydor 14002
9/27/69	#93	2	Can You Dance To It	Polydor 14007
			CAUSE & EFFECT	
2/01/92	#29	24	You Think You Know Her	SRC 14025
7/25/92	#70	7	Another Minute	SRC 14036
			FELIX CAVALIERE	
3/01/80	#40	12	Only A Lonely Heart Sees	Epic 50829
			CAZZ	
3/04/78	#96	2	Let's Live Together	Number 1 210
			C COMPANY featuring TERRY NELSON	
4/17/71	#26	5	Battle Hymn Of Lt. Calley	Plantation 73
			C.C.S.	
1/30/71	#58	5	Whole Lotta Love	Rak 4501
			CECILIA & KAPONO	
1/10/76	#95	3	Goodnight And Good Morning	Columbia 10223
			CELEBRATION	
4/29/78	#35	13	Almost Summer	MCA 40891
			CELI BEE & THE BUZZY BUNCH	
6/11/77	#77	8	Superman	APA 17001
			CELLARFUL OF NOISE	
3/05/88	#76	6	Samantha (What You Gonna Do?)	CBS Associated 07731
			CELLOS	
5/18/57	#46	7	Rang Tang Ding Dong	Apollo 510

Debut Date	Peak Pos	Wks Chr	ARTIST/Song Title	Label & Number
			CERRONE	
3/19/77	#80	4	Love In 'C' Minor (Part 1)	Cotillion 44215
			PETER CETERA	
6/07/86	#1	20	Glory Of Love	Full Moon 28662
9/20/86	#3	23	The Next Time I Fall*	Full Moon 28597
1/24/87	#55	7	Big Mistake	Full Moon 28507
7/23/88	#6	18	One Good Woman	Full Moon 27824
11/05/88	#50	8	Best Of Times	Full Moon 27712
3/11/89	#7	22	After All**	Geffen 27529
1/30/93	#68	8	Feels Like Heaven***	Warner Brothers 18651
6/12/93	#67	3	Even A Fool Can See	Warner Bros. album cut
7/24/93	#61	13	Even A Fool Can See	Warner Brothers 18561
			*released as by PETER CETERA with AMY GRANT	
			**released as by CHER and PETER CETERA	
			***released as by PETER CETERA with CHAKA KHAN	
			FRANK CHACKSFIELD ORCHESTRA	
6/20/53	#3	11	Terry's Theme From "Limelight"	London 1342
10/17/53	#3	11	Ebb Tide	London 1358
2/06/60	#71	8	On The Beach	London 1901
			CHAD & JEREMY	
5/09/64	#28	12	Yesterday's Gone	World Artists 1021
8/22/64	#8	14	A Summer Song	World Artists 1027
11/21/64	#22	12	Willow Weep For Me	World Artists 1034
2/20/65	#20	9	If I Loved You	World Artists 1041
4/17/65	#48	8	What Do You Want With Me	World Artists 1052
5/15/65	#15	11	Before And After	Columbia 43277
6/26/65	#93	4	From A Window	World Artists 1056
8/07/65	#43	6	I Don't Wanna Lose You Baby	Columbia 43339
10/16/65	#97	1	I Have Dreamed/	Columbia 43414
10/30/65	#100	1	Should I	Columbia 43414
7/23/66	#48	6	Distant Shores	Columbia 43682
			CHAIRMEN OF THE BOARD	
1/24/70	#9	12	Give Me Just A Little More Time	Invictus 9074
5/02/70	#30	9	(You've Got Me) Dangling On A String	Invictus 9078
8/08/70	#39	8	Everything's Tuesday	Invictus 9079
11/07/70	#10	13	Pay To The Piper	Invictus 9081
2/13/71	#37	7	Chairman Of The Board	Invictus 9086
11/27/71	#68	3	Men Are Getting Scarce	Invictus 9103
6/02/73	#69	6	Finder's Keepers	Invictus 1251
			CHAKACHAS	
12/25/71	#6	19	Jungle Fever	Polydor 15030
8/25/72	#99	2	Stories?	Avco 4596
			RICHARD CHAMBERLAIN	
6/09/62	#13	13	Theme From Dr. Kildare (Three Stars Will Shine Tonight) .	MGM 13075
10/13/62	#24	9	Love Me Tender	MGM 13097
2/16/63	#20	12	All I Have To Do Is Dream/	MGM 13121
2/23/63	#60	5	Hi-Lili, Hi-Lo	MGM 13121
6/29/63	#68	7	I Will Love You	MGM 13148
10/05/63	#41	8	Blue Guitar	MGM 13170
			CHAMBERS BROTHERS	
8/24/68	#11	13	Time Has Come Today	Columbia 44414
11/16/68	#39	10	I Can't Turn You Loose	Columbia 44679
2/27/71	#96	1	Funky	Columbia 45277
			CHAMPAGNE	
3/12/77	#68	4	Rock And Roll Star	Ariola America 7658
			CHAMPAIGN	
2/14/81	#10	23	How 'Bout Us	Columbia 11433
4/02/83	#18	21	Try Again	Columbia 03563
			BILL CHAMPLIN	
12/26/81	#69	9	Tonight Tonight	Elektra 47240
7/31/82	#68	6	Sara	Elektra 47456
			CHAMPS	
2/22/58	#1	16	Tequila	Challenge 1016
5/10/58	#21	9	El Rancho Rock	Challenge 59007
8/23/58	#74	1	Chariot Rock	Challenge 59018
4/18/59	#100	1	Caramba	Challenge 59043

Debut Date	Peak Pos	Wks Chr	ARTIST/Song Title	Label & Number
1/30/60	#21	11	Too Much Tequila	Challenge 59063
5/19/62	#33	15	Limbo Rock	Challenge 9131
			GENE CHANDLER	
1/06/62	#1	17	Duke Of Earl	Vee-Jay 416
4/21/62	#74	4	Walk On With The Duke	Vee-Jay 440
11/24/62	#60	5	You Threw A Lucky Punch/	Vee-Jay 468
3/02/63	#65	11	Rainbow	Vee-Jay 468
8/03/63	#49	8	A Man's Temptation	Vee-Jay 536
4/25/64	#90	3	Soul Hootenany	Constellation 114
7/04/64	#21	12	Just Be True	Constellation 130
10/03/64	#44	8	Bless Our Love	Constellation 136
11/28/64	#41	10	What Now	Constellation 141
3/08/65	#92	2	You Can't Hurt Me No More	Constellation 146
4/10/65	#18	13	Nothing Can Stop Me	Constellation 149
11/13/65	#87	8	Rainbow '65 (Part 1)	Constellation 158
3/12/66	#96	2	(I'm Just A) Fool For You	Constellation 167
12/03/66	#45	9	I Fooled You This Time	Checker 1155
2/18/67	#64	7	Girl Don't Care	Brunswick 55312
5/27/67	#88	3	To Be A Lover	Checker 1165
10/05/68	#63	3	There Was A Time	Brunswick 55383
10/19/68	#40	6	From The Teacher To The Preacher*	Brunswick 55387
6/27/70	#11	18	Groovy Situation	Mercury 73083
10/24/70	#62	8	Simply Call It Love	Mercury 73121
1/02/71	#76	3	You Just Can't Win**	Mercury 73163
7/03/71	#93	1	You're A Lady	Mercury 73206
12/09/78	#50	14	Get Down	Chi-Sound 2386
			*released as by GENE CHANDLER and BARBARA ACKLIN	
			**released as by GENE & JERRY (Gene Chandler & Jerry Butler)	
			KAREN CHANDLER	
1/17/53	#5	8	Hold Me, Thrill Me, Kiss Me	Coral 60831
			KENNY CHANDLER	
3/30/63	#52	9	Heart	Laurie 3158
			CHANGE	
5/31/80	#47	10	A Lover's Holiday	RFC 49208
5/23/81	#92	5	Paradise	Atlantic 3809
			CHANGIN' TIMES	
10/16/65	#92	5	Pied Piper	Philips 40320
			BRUCE CHANNEL	
1/20/62	#1	17	Hey! Baby	Smash 1731
4/14/62	#38	9	Number One Man	Smash 1752
2/22/64	#96	3	Going Back To Louisiana	Le Cam 122
12/30/67	#100	2	Mr. Bus Driver	Mala 579
			CHANSON	
11/04/78	#20	19	Don't Hold Back	Ariola 7717
			CHANTAYS	
3/02/63	#5	17	Pipeline	Dot 16440
			CHANTELS	
1/25/58	#19	12	Maybe	End 1005
3/29/58	#32	3	Every Night (I Pray)	End 1015
6/21/58	#72	2	I Love You So	End 1020
9/02/61	#14	12	Look In My Eyes	Carlton 555
11/25/61	#28	8	Well, I Told You	Carlton 564
3/30/63	#100	1	Eternally	Ludix 101
			CHANTERS	
7/15/61	#84	3	No, No, No	DeLuxe 6191
			HARRY CHAPIN	
3/04/72	#20	16	Taxi	Elektra 45770
7/29/72	#81	4	Could You Put Your Light On Please	Elektra 45792
10/28/72	#77	5	Sunday Morning Sunshine	Elektra 45811
12/29/73	#26	15	WOLD	Elektra 45874
7/06/74	#87	2	What Made America Famous	Elektra 45893
9/21/74	#1	20	Cat's In The Cradle	Elektra 45203
2/22/75	#40	8	I Wanna Learn A Love Song	Elektra 45236
6/12/76	#76	4	Better Place To Be (Parts 1 & 2)	Elektra 45327
11/01/80	#34	13	Sequel	Boardwalk 5700

Debut Date	Peak Pos	Wks Chr	ARTIST/Song Title	Label & Number
			PAUL CHAPLAIN and HIS EMERALDS	
9/30/60	#55	7	Shortnin' Bread	Harper 100
			TRACY CHAPMAN	
6/18/88	#4	20	Fast Car	Elektra 69412
9/24/88	#67	6	Talkin' Bout A Revolution	Elektra 69383
11/05/88	#39	16	Baby Can I Hold You	Elektra 69356
11/04/89	#88	4	Crossroads	Elektra 69273
			CHARGERS	
9/13/58	#96	1	Old MacDonald	RCA 7301
			CHARLATANS U.K.	
12/22/90	#80	8	The Only One I Know	Beggars Banquet 2451
			CHARLENE	
3/06/82	#3	21	I've Never Been To Me	Motown 1611
10/30/82	#48	13	Used To Be*	Motown 1650
			released as by CHARLENE & STEVIE WONDER	
			JIMMY CHARLES	
8/06/60	#6	19	A Million To One	Promo 1002
12/10/60	#42	14	The Age For Love	Promo 1003
			RAY CHARLES	
10/19/57	#51	1	Swanee River Rock	Atlantic 1154
7/04/59	#6	16	What'd I Say (Part 1)	Atlantic 2031
11/07/59	#45	10	I'm Movin' On	Atlantic 2043
1/30/60	#94	2	Let The Good Times Roll	Atlantic 2047
2/20/60	#92	3	Who Are You Gonna Love	ABC Paramount 10081
6/25/60	#27	10	Sticks And Stones/	ABC Paramount 10118
7/09/60	#88	2	Worried Life Blues	ABC Paramount 10118
7/30/60	#72	5	Tell The Truth	Atlantic 2068
9/17/60	#3	17	Georgia On My Mind	ABC Paramount 10135
11/26/60	#54	4	Come Rain Or Come Shine	Atlantic 2084
11/26/60	#60	5	Hard Hearted Hannah/	ABC Paramount 10164
12/03/60	#21	9	Ruby	ABC Paramount 10164
1/21/61	#38	9	Them That Got	ABC Paramount 10141
3/18/61	#9	13	One Mint Julep	Impulse 200
3/18/61	#98	2	Early In The Mornin'	Atlantic 2094
7/01/61	#58	3	I've Got News For You	Impulse 202
9/09/61	#1	14	Hit The Road Jack	ABC Paramount 10244
12/02/61	#9	13	Unchain My Heart/	ABC Paramount 10266
12/23/61	#82	5	But On The Other Hand Baby	ABC Paramount 10266
3/31/62	#26	8	Hide 'Nor Hair/	ABC Paramount 10314
3/31/62	#40	9	At The Club	ABC Paramount 10314
5/12/62	#1	18	I Can't Stop Loving You/	ABC Paramount 10330
5/12/62	#39	11	Born To Lose	ABC Paramount 10330
7/28/62	#5	12	You Don't Know Me/	ABC Paramount 10345
7/28/62	#55	5	Careless Love	ABC Paramount 10345
11/17/62	#9	13	You Are My Sunshine/	ABC Paramount 10375
11/24/62	#56	8	Your Cheatin' Heart	ABC Paramount 10375
2/23/63	#25	8	Don't Set Me Free	ABC Paramount 10405
4/23/63	#11	11	Take These Chains From My Heart	ABC Paramount 10435
6/22/63	#22	9	No One/	ABC Paramount 10453
6/22/63	#35	8	Without Love (There Is Nothing)	ABC Paramount 10453
9/07/63	#2	14	Busted/	ABC Paramount 10481
9/28/63	#99	1	Makin' Believe	ABC Paramount 10481
12/07/63	#20	9	That Lucky Old Sun	ABC Paramount 10509
2/22/64	#45	6	Baby, Don't You Cry/	ABC Paramount 10530
2/22/64	#41	6	My Heart Cries For You	ABC Paramount 10530
6/06/64	#50	5	My Baby Don't Dig Me	ABC Paramount 10557
7/18/64	#57	8	A Tear Fell/	ABC Paramount 10571
7/25/64	#53	4	No One To Cry To	ABC Paramount 10571
10/03/64	#58	5	Smack Dab In The Middle	ABC Paramount 10588
12/12/64	#39	9	Makin' Whoopee	ABC Paramount 10609
2/13/65	#77	5	Cry	ABC Paramount 10615
4/17/65	#87	2	I Got A Woman	ABC Paramount 10649
7/17/65	#81	2	I'm A Fool To Care	ABC Paramount 10700
12/18/65	#6	15	Crying Time	ABC Paramount 10739
3/26/66	#22	8	Together Again/	ABC Paramount 10785
3/26/66	#91	2	You're Just About To Lose Your Clown	ABC Paramount 10785
5/28/66	#23	10	Let's Go Get Stoned	ABC 10808
8/27/66	#42	8	I Chose To Sing The Blues	ABC 10840

58

Debut Date	Peak Pos	Wks Chr	ARTIST/Song Title	Label & Number
11/05/66	#77	4	Please Say You're Fooling	ABC 10865
5/06/67	#18	14	Here We Go Again	ABC 10938
8/26/67	#45	8	In The Heat Of The Night	ABC 10970
11/04/67	#28	8	Yesterday	ABC 11009
2/24/68	#46	6	That's A Lie	ABC 11045
6/15/68	#39	9	Eleanor Rigby	ABC 11090
9/21/68	#57	4	Sweet Young Thing Like You	ABC 11133
12/28/68	#76	6	If It Wasn't For Bad Luck*	ABC 11170
3/01/69	#69	3	I Didn't Know What Time It Was	ABC 11193
5/17/69	#89	4	Let Me Love You	ABC 11213
9/06/69	#92	3	We Can Make It	ABC 11239
4/18/70	#90	3	Laughin And Clownin	ABC 11259
9/19/70	#50	16	If You Were Mine	ABC 11271
3/06/71	#28	12	Don't Change On Me	ABC 11291
3/20/71	#24	12	Booty Butt**	Tangerine 1015
8/21/71	#67	4	Feel So Bad	ABC 11308
12/25/71	#61	7	What Am I Living For	ABC 11317
7/01/72	#49	6	Look What They've Done To My Song, Ma	ABC 11329
6/02/73	#79	6	I Can Make It Through The Days	ABC 11351
11/10/73	#52	7	Come Live With Me	Crossover 973
9/06/75	#87	5	Living For The City	Crossover 981
4/18/87	#87	3	Baby Grand***	Columbia 06994
11/18/89	#19	18	I'll Be Good To You****	Qwest 22697
5/08/93	#48	7	A Song For You	Warner Brothers 18611

*released as by RAY CHARLES & JIMMY LEWIS
**released as by RAY CHARLES ORCHESTRA
***released as by BILLY JOEL featuring RAY CHARLES
****released as by QUINCY JONES featuring RAY CHARLES and CHAKA KHAN

Debut Date	Peak Pos	Wks Chr	ARTIST/Song Title	Label & Number
			RAY CHARLES SINGERS	
4/18/64	#4	15	Love Me With All Your Heart	Command 4046
7/11/64	#32	7	Al-Di-La	Command 4049
11/21/64	#33	10	One More Time	Command 4057
2/27/65	#82	5	This Is My Prayer	Command 4059
5/30/70	#91	3	Move Me, O Wondrous Music	Command 4135
			SONNY CHARLES	
11/27/82	#54	11	Put It In A Magazine	Highrise 2001
			CHARLES & EDDIE	
8/29/92	#11	24	Would I Lie To You?	Capitol 44809
			CHARLIE	
7/30/77	#88	4	Turning To You	Janus 270
7/29/78	#61	9	She Loves To Be In Love	Janus 276
9/01/79	#70	6	Killer Cut	Arista 0449
6/25/83	#43	11	It's Inevitable	Mirage 99862
			CHARMETTES	
10/05/73	#62	7	Please Don't Kiss Me Again	Kapp 547
			CHARTBUSTERS	
7/04/64	#39	10	She's The One	Mutual 502
11/07/64	#96	3	Why	Mutual 508
			CHASE	
5/29/71	#22	11	Get It On	Epic 10738
9/11/71	#74	3	Handbags And Gladrags	Epic 10775
12/11/71	#93	5	So Many People	Epic 10806
			CAROL CHASE	
12/27/75	#92	4	One Woman Band	Janus 256
			ELLISON CHASE	
8/28/76	#82	7	Let's Rock	Big Tree 16072
			KERRY CHATER	
2/26/77	#80	5	Part Time Love	Warner Brothers 8310
			CHEAP TRICK	
7/22/78	#83	5	Surrender	Epic 50570
4/21/79	#3	23	I Want You To Want Me	Epic 50680
8/04/79	#35	11	Ain't That A Shame	Epic 50743
10/06/79	#27	12	Dream Police	Epic 50774
12/01/79	#30	12	Voices	Epic 50814
5/24/80	#51	10	Everything Works If You Let It	Epic 50887

59

Debut Date	Peak Pos	Wks Chr	ARTIST/Song Title	Label & Number
			CHEAP TRICK—*continued*	
11/08/80	#44	13	Stop This Game	Epic 50942
6/05/82	#42	11	If You Want My Love	Epic 02968
8/03/85	#45	16	Tonight It's You	Epic 05431
4/09/88	#1	26	The Flame	Epic 07745
7/30/88	#3	19	Don't Be Cruel	Epic 07965
11/05/88	#20	14	Ghost Town	Epic 08097
2/18/89	#54	7	Never Had A Lot To Lose	Epic 68563
7/21/90	#7	18	Can't Stop Fallin' Into Love	Epic 73444
10/27/90	#44	9	Wherever Would I Be	Epic 73580
			CHUBBY CHECKER	
5/23/59	#37	7	The Class	Parkway 804
7/23/60	#1	21	The Twist	Parkway 811
10/22/60	#13	13	The Hucklebuck/	Parkway 813
10/22/60	#48	8	Whole Lotta Shakin' Goin' On	Parkway 813
1/28/61	#1	17	Pony Time	Parkway 818
4/22/61	#16	9	Dance The Mess Around	Parkway 822
6/24/61	#3	14	Let's Twist Again	Parkway 824
9/30/61	#7	16	The Fly	Parkway 830
11/18/61	#1	22	The Twist	Parkway 811
12/02/61	#31	11	Let's Twist Again	Parkway 824
12/16/61	#38	4	Jingle Bell Rock*	Cameo 205
3/03/62	#1	15	Slow Twistin'	Parkway 835
4/28/62	#76	3	Teach Me How To Twist*	Cameo 214
6/23/62	#14	11	Dancin' Party	Parkway 842
9/08/62	#8	17	Popeye The Hitchhiker/	Parkway 849
9/15/62	#1	24	Limbo Rock	Parkway 849
12/15/62	#59	4	Jingle Bell Rock*	Cameo 205
2/16/63	#15	10	Let's Limbo Some More/	Parkway 862
3/02/63	#28	11	Twenty Miles	Parkway 862
5/18/63	#14	9	Birdland/	Parkway 873
6/01/63	#89	3	Black Cloud	Parkway 873
7/13/63	#48	5	Surf Party/	Parkway 879
7/20/63	#23	8	Twist It Up	Parkway 879
11/02/63	#15	13	Loddy Lo/	Parkway 890
12/14/63	#16	13	Hooka Tooka	Parkway 890
3/14/64	#18	10	Hey, Bobba Needle	Parkway 907
6/06/64	#39	8	Lazy Elsie Molly/	Parkway 920
6/20/64	#89	2	Rosie	Parkway 920
8/29/64	#52	6	She Wants T' Swim	Parkway 922
12/19/64	#92	3	Lovely, Lovely (Loverly, Loverly)	Parkway 936
4/03/65	#40	8	Let's Do The Freddie	Parkway 949
6/25/66	#60	5	Hey You! Little Boo-Ga-Loo	Parkway 989
4/05/69	#90	4	Back In The U.S.S.R.	Buddah 100
2/13/82	#87	7	Running	MCA 51233
6/18/88	#20	16	The Twist (Yo, Twist!)**	Tin Pan Apple 887571
			*released as by BOBBY RYDELL/CHUBBY CHECKER	
			**released as by THE FAT BOYS with CHUBBY CHECKER	
			CHECKMATES LTD.	
4/05/69	#53	5	Love Is All I Have To Give	A&M 1039
4/26/69	#10	16	Black Pearl*	A&M 1053
10/18/69	#78	3	Proud Mary**	A&M 1127
			*released as by SONNY CHARLES and THE CHECKMATES LTD.	
			**released as by THE CHECKMATES LTD. featuring SONNY CHARLES	
			CHEECH & CHONG	
9/01/73	#13	12	Basketball Jones	Ode 66038
11/17/73	#36	13	Sister Mary Elephant (Shudd-Up!)	Ode 66041
8/10/74	#4	12	Earache My Eye	Ode 66102
11/02/74	#47	7	Black Lassie	Ode 66104
10/18/75	#53	4	(How I Spent My Summer Vacation) Or A Day At The Beach With Pedro & Man	Ode 66115
6/05/76	#46	9	Framed	Ode 66124
11/12/77	#47	10	Bloat On	Epic 50471
9/21/85	#54	9	Born In East L.A.	MCA 52655
			CHEE-CHEE and PEPPY	
5/22/71	#35	11	I Know I'm In Love	Buddah 225

Debut Date	Peak Pos	Wks Chr	**ARTIST**/Song Title	Label & Number
			CHEEKS	
7/12/80	#95	2	Bony Moronie	Capitol 4883
			JOE CHEMAY BAND	
2/07/81	#91	4	Proud	Unicorn 95001
			CHER	
7/03/65	#9	11	All I Really Want To Do	Imperial 66114
10/16/65	#32	7	Where Do You Go	Imperial 66136
3/05/66	#2	12	Bang Bang (My Baby Shot Me Down)	Imperial 66160
7/30/66	#32	7	Alfie	Imperial 66192
11/26/66	#76	2	Behind The Door	Imperial 66217
12/17/66	#70	3	Mama	Imperial 66223
8/26/67	#95	2	Hey Joe	Imperial 66252
10/28/67	#8	13	You Better Sit Down Kids	Imperial 66261
2/10/68	#78	2	The Click Song Number One	Imperial 66282
9/18/71	#1	15	Gypsys, Tramps & Thieves	Kapp 2146
1/22/72	#9	14	The Way Of Love	Kapp 2158
5/13/72	#21	10	Living In A House Divided	Kapp 2171
9/09/72	#50	7	Don't Hide Your Love	Kapp 2184
4/28/73	#79	2	Am I Blue	MCA 40039
7/21/73	#1	19	Half-Breed	MCA 40102
1/12/74	#2	15	Dark Lady	MCA 40161
5/18/74	#18	10	Train Of Thought	MCA 40245
8/03/74	#33	10	I Saw A Man And He Danced With His Wife	MCA 40273
12/14/74	#66	5	A Woman's Story	Warner/Spector 0400
3/29/75	#84	4	Rescue Me	MCA 40375
2/10/79	#10	19	Take Me Home	Casablanca 965
6/02/79	#69	6	Wasn't It Good	Casablanca 987
9/15/79	#64	7	Hell On Wheels	Casablanca 2208
4/17/82	#37	14	Murphy's Law	Venture 5019
11/21/87	#14	25	I Found Someone	Geffen 28191
4/09/88	#12	17	We All Sleep Alone	Geffen 27986
7/30/88	#78	6	Skin Deep	Geffen 27894
3/11/89	#7	22	After All*	Geffen 27529
7/15/89	#3	25	If I Could Turn Back Time	Geffen 22886
10/21/89	#4	20	Just Like Jesse James	Geffen 22844
2/17/90	#19	17	Heart Of Stone	Geffen 19953
11/17/90	#43	16	The Shoop Shoop Song (It's In His Kiss)	Geffen 19659
6/15/91	#12	19	Love And Understanding	Geffen 19023
10/19/91	#27	21	Save Up All Your Tears	Geffen 19105
			*released as by CHER and PETER CETERA	
			CHERRELLE	
7/28/84	#71	6	I Didn't Mean To Turn You On	Tabu 04406
2/15/86	#33	16	Saturday Love*	Tabu 05767
1/30/88	#34	14	Never Knew Love Like This*	Tabu 07646
			*released as by CHERRELLE with ALEXANDER O'NEAL	
			DON CHERRY	
11/25/50	#3	11	Thinking Of You	Decca 27128
1/14/56	#5	9	Band Of Gold	Columbia 40597
8/04/56	#35	6	Ghost Town	Columbia 40705
8/31/57	#60	1	14 Karat Gold	Columbia 40958
			NENEH CHERRY	
4/08/89	#3	21	Buffalo Stance	Virgin 99231
7/22/89	#11	17	Kisses On The Wind	Virgin 99183
12/16/89	#54	9	Heart	Virgin 99153
2/20/93	#38	16	Buddy X	Virgin 12648
			CHERRY PEOPLE	
7/06/68	#43	11	And Suddenly	Heritage 801
			CHESTER	
9/01/73	#100	1	Make My Life A Little Bit Brighter	Bell 379
			CHEVRONS	
1/23/60	#87	2	Lullabye	Brent 7007
			CHIC	
10/22/77	#6	24	Dance, Dance, Dance (Yowsah, Yowsah, Yowsah)	Atlantic 3435
5/06/78	#49	8	Everybody Dance	Atlantic 3469
10/28/78	#1	26	Le Freak	Atlantic 3519
2/10/79	#10	18	I Want Your Love	Atlantic 3557

Debut Date	Peak Pos	Wks Chr	ARTIST/Song Title	Label & Number
			CHIC—*continued*	
6/16/79	#1	21	Good Times	Atlantic 3584
8/16/80	#77	7	Rebels Are We	Atlantic 3665
			CHICAGO	
8/23/69	#82	2	Questions 67 & 68	Columbia 44909
3/28/70	#11	16	Make Me Smile	Columbia 45127
7/18/70	#6	13	25 Or 6 To 4	Columbia 45194
11/07/70	#5	12	Does Anybody Really Know What Time It Is?	Columbia 45264
2/20/71	#19	8	Free	Columbia 45331
5/08/71	#25	7	Lowdown	Columbia 45370
6/26/71	#11	13	Beginnings/	Columbia 45417
7/10/71	#75	6	Colour My World	Columbia 45417
10/02/71	#13	11	Questions 67 & 68/	Columbia 45467
10/09/71	#67	4	I'm A Man	Columbia 45467
7/29/72	#3	12	Saturday In The Park	Columbia 45657
10/28/72	#17	10	Dialogue (Parts 1 & 2)	Columbia 45717
6/23/73	#8	13	Feelin' Stronger Every Day	Columbia 45880
9/22/73	#1	17	Just You 'N' Me	Columbia 45933
3/23/74	#7	14	(I've Been) Searchin' So Long	Columbia 46020
6/22/74	#10	12	Call On Me	Columbia 46062
10/12/74	#9	12	Wishing You Were Here	Columbia 10049
2/15/75	#19	9	Harry Truman	Columbia 10092
4/26/75	#6	11	Old Days	Columbia 10131
8/30/75	#43	6	Brand New Love Affair	Columbia 10200
6/26/76	#33	13	Another Rainy Day In New York City	Columbia 10360
8/07/76	#1	19	If You Leave Me Now	Columbia 10390
4/16/77	#56	6	You Are On My Mind	Columbia 10523
9/24/77	#4	17	Baby, What A Big Surprise	Columbia 10620
2/18/78	#59	9	Little One	Columbia 10683
5/13/78	#62	6	Take Me Back To Chicago	Columbia 10737
10/21/78	#13	13	Alive Again	Columbia 10845
12/23/78	#14	15	No Tell Lover	Columbia 10879
4/14/79	#75	5	Gone Long Gone	Columbia 10935
8/25/79	#84	4	Must Have Been Crazy	Columbia 11061
8/30/80	#67	8	Thunder And Lightning	Columbia 11345
6/05/82	#2	25	Hard To Say I'm Sorry	Full Moon 29979
9/25/82	#22	17	Love Me Tomorrow	Full Moon 29911
5/05/84	#15	18	Stay The Night	Full Moon 29306
8/04/84	#2	22	Hard Habit To Break	Full Moon 29214
11/17/84	#4	22	You're The Inspiration	Full Moon 29126
2/23/85	#19	17	Along Comes A Woman	Full Moon 29082
9/06/86	#46	9	25 Or 6 To 4	Full Moon 28628
11/15/86	#4	25	Will You Still Love Me	Full Moon 28512
3/21/87	#16	19	If She Would Have Been Faithful...	Full Moon 28424
6/04/88	#5	21	I Don't Wanna Live Without Your Love	Reprise 27855
9/24/88	#1	24	Look Away	Reprise 27766
1/21/89	#9	19	You're Not Alone	Reprise 27757
5/06/89	#53	13	We Can Last Forever	Reprise 22985
12/02/89	#5	20	What Kind Of Man Would I Be	Reprise 22741
7/28/90	#57	6	Hearts In Trouble	DGC 19679
1/19/91	#31	15	Chasin' The Wind	Reprise 19466
			CHICAGO BEARS SHUFFLIN' CREW	
2/01/86	#75	5	Superbowl Shuffle	Red Label 71012
			CHICAGO LOOP	
11/05/66	#44	8	She Comes To Me	DynoVoice 226
			CHICORY	
2/26/72	#82	4	Son Of My Father	Epic 10837
			CHIFFONS (same group as THE FOUR PENNIES)	
2/23/63	#1	15	He's So Fine	Laurie 3152
6/01/63	#7	10	One Fine Day	Laurie 3179
6/29/63	#76	4	My Block*	Rust 5071
9/14/63	#38	8	A Love So Fine	Laurie 3195
11/16/63	#37	10	I Have A Boyfriend	Laurie 3212
7/11/64	#75	6	Sailor Boy	Laurie 3262
6/26/65	#76	5	Nobody Knows What's Goin' On	Laurie 3301
5/07/66	#10	11	Sweet Talkin' Guy	Laurie 3340
8/13/66	#81	2	Out Of This World	Laurie 3350
			*released as by THE FOUR PENNIES	

Debut Date	Peak Pos	Wks Chr	**ARTIST**/Song Title	Label & Number
			DESMOND CHILD	
2/24/79	#60	6	Our Love Is Insane*	Capitol 4669
6/29/91	#34	17	Love On A Rooftop	Elektra 64883
9/28/91	#55	11	You're The Story Of My Life	Elektra 64850
			*released as by DESMOND CHILD and ROUGE	
			JANE CHILD	
2/10/90	#2	23	Don't Wanna Fall In Love	Warner Brothers 19933
6/02/90	#46	11	Welcome To The Real World	Warner Brothers 19834
			TONI CHILDS	
8/06/88	#80	8	Don't Walk Away	A&M 1237
			CHI-LITES	
3/08/69	#74	5	Give It Away	Brunswick 55398
7/18/70	#88	4	I Like Your Lovin' (Do You Like Mine)	Brunswick 55438
4/10/71	#29	8	(For God's Sake) Give More Power To The People	Brunswick 55450
8/07/71	#87	5	We Are Neighbors	Brunswick 55455
9/25/71	#97	2	I Want To Pay You Back	Brunswick 55458
10/23/71	#5	13	Have You Seen Her	Brunswick 55462
4/08/72	#1	14	Oh Girl	Brunswick 55471
7/22/72	#52	5	The Coldest Days Of My Life (Part 1)	Brunswick 55478
9/30/72	#69	4	A Lonely Man	Brunswick 55483
12/09/72	#74	5	We Need Order	Brunswick 55489
2/03/73	#41	10	A Letter To Myself	Brunswick 55491
8/18/73	#53	9	Stoned Out Of My Head	Brunswick 55500
11/17/73	#80	6	I Found Sunshine	Brunswick 55503
2/16/74	#77	6	Homely Girl	Brunswick 55505
9/07/74	#75	4	You Got To Be The One	Brunswick 55514
			CHILLIWACK	
1/22/72	#77	5	Lonesome Mary	A&M 1310
12/28/74	#90	3	Crazy Talk	Sire 716
4/16/77	#57	8	Fly At Night	Mushroom 7024
9/03/77	#92	3	Something Better	Mushroom 7025
8/12/78	#92	4	Arms Of Mary	Mushroom 7033
9/26/81	#19	20	My Girl (Gone, Gone, Gone)	Millennium 11813
1/16/82	#29	14	I Believe	Millennium 13102
10/16/82	#32	15	Whatcha Gonna Do	Millennium 13110
			CHIMES (Brooklyn group)	
12/17/60	#11	13	Once In A While	Tag 444
4/01/61	#40	9	I'm In The Mood For Love	Tag 445
			CHIMES (Scottish group)	
2/10/90	#82	4	1-2-3	Columbia 73087
			CHIPMUNKS	
12/06/58	#1	13	The Chipmunk Song*	Liberty 55168
2/14/59	#3	12	Alvin's Harmonica**	Liberty 55179
7/04/59	#14	10	Ragtime Cowboy Joe**	Liberty 55200
12/19/59	#37	4	The Chipmunk Song*	Liberty 55250
2/13/60	#32	8	Alvin's Orchestra**	Liberty 55233
5/07/60	#96	2	(She'll Be) Coming Round The Mountain**	Liberty 55246
9/10/60	#71	6	Alvin For President**	Liberty 55277
12/24/60	#51	3	Rudolph The Red Nosed Reindeer**	Liberty 55289
12/30/61	#89	2	The Chipmunk Song*	Liberty 55250
12/30/61	#83	2	Rudolph The Red Nosed Reindeer**	Liberty 55289
3/10/62	#54	5	The Alvin Twist**	Liberty 55424
12/15/62	#84	4	The Chipmunk Song*	Liberty 55250
			*released as by THE CHIPMUNKS with DAVID SEVILLE	
			**released as by DAVID SEVILLE and THE CHIPMUNKS	
			CHOCOLATE MILK	
7/12/75	#74	5	Action Speaks Louder Than Words	RCA 10290
			CHOIR	
5/20/67	#55	9	It's Cold Outside	Roulette 4738
			CHOIRBOYS	
3/18/89	#81	5	Run To Paradise	WTG 68564
			CHORDETTES	
12/04/54	#1	16	Mr. Sandman	Cadence 1247
7/14/56	#8	10	Born To Be With You	Cadence 1291
9/29/56	#18	11	Lay Down Your Arms	Cadence 1299
8/03/57	#12	16	Just Between You And Me/	Cadence 1330

Debut Date	Peak Pos	Wks Chr	ARTIST/Song Title	Label & Number
			CHORDETTES—*continued*	
8/17/57	#56	3	Soft Sands	Cadence 1330
3/08/58	#2	12	Lollipop	Cadence 1345
5/17/58	#21	6	Zorro	Cadence 1349
2/28/59	#28	11	No Other Arms, No Other Lips	Cadence 1361
8/29/59	#92	4	No Wheels	Cadence 1366
6/24/61	#14	13	Never On Sunday	Cadence 1402
			CHORDS	
8/28/54	#1	12	Sh-Boom	Cat 104
			CHRIS CHRISTIAN	
10/03/81	#36	15	I Want You, I Need You	Boardwalk 126
			CHRISTIE	
7/04/70	#16	25	Yellow River	Epic 10626
1/30/71	#86	4	San Bernadino	Epic 10695
			DEAN CHRISTIE	
11/03/62	#77	5	Heart Breaker	Select 715
			LOU CHRISTIE	
1/12/63	#18	13	The Gypsy Cried	Roulette 4457
4/06/63	#3	15	Two Faces Have I	Roulette 4481
7/06/63	#41	7	How Many Teardrops	Roulette 4504
12/25/65	#1	15	Lightnin' Strikes	MGM 13412
3/12/66	#59	5	Outside The Gates Of Heaven	Co & Ce 235
3/26/66	#20	8	Rhapsody In The Rain	MGM 13473
6/18/66	#77	5	Painter	MGM 13533
8/16/69	#7	14	I'm Gonna Make You Mine	Buddah 116
12/20/69	#84	5	Are You Getting Any Sunshine	Buddah 149
10/17/70	#75	4	Indian Lady	Buddah 192
2/23/74	#72	9	Beyond The Blue Horizon	Three Brothers 402
6/11/77	#95	2	Spanish Wine	Midsong 10959
			SUSAN CHRISTIE	
6/04/66	#65	6	I Love Onions	Columbia 43595
			GAVIN CHRISTOPHER	
5/24/86	#25	18	One Step Closer To You	Manhattan 50028
			CHURCH	
4/09/88	#33	17	Under The Milky Way	Arista 9673
			EUGENE CHURCH	
12/27/58	#65	13	Pretty Girls Everywhere	Class 235
8/15/59	#69	4	Miami	Class 254
11/12/60	#96	4	Good News	Rendezvous 132
			CINDERELLA	
11/15/86	#23	23	Nobody's Fool	Mercury 884851
5/02/87	#68	6	Somebody Save Me	Mercury 888483
8/27/88	#17	23	Don't Know What You Got (Till It's Gone)	Mercury 870644
1/21/89	#36	12	The Last Mile	Mercury 872148
4/08/89	#22	20	Coming Home	Mercury 872982
12/08/90	#31	16	Shelter Me	Mercury 878700
3/23/91	#49	10	Heartbreak Station	Mercury 878796
			CIRCUS	
1/27/73	#81	5	Stop, Wait & Listen	Metromedia 265
			CITY BOY	
7/15/78	#52	16	5.7.0.5.	Mercury 73999
			C.J. & CO.	
7/16/77	#65	15	Devil's Gun	Westbound 55400
			IKE CLANTON	
6/30/62	#88	4	Sugar Plum	Mercury 71975
			JIMMY CLANTON	
7/05/58	#5	20	Just A Dream	Ace 546
10/18/58	#33	14	A Letter To An Angel/	Ace 551
10/25/58	#56	13	A Part Of Me	Ace 551
7/25/59	#28	13	My Own True Love	Ace 567
12/05/59	#7	16	Go, Jimmy, Go	Ace 575
4/23/60	#17	15	Another Sleepless Night	Ace 585
9/03/60	#75	8	Come Back	Ace 600
1/07/61	#58	7	What Am I Gonna Do	Ace 607

64

Debut Date	Peak Pos	Wks Chr	ARTIST/Song Title	Label & Number
8/18/62	#10	14	Venus In Blue Jeans	Ace 8001
12/22/62	#88	4	Darkest Street In Town	Ace 8005
			ERIC CLAPTON	
2/14/70	#74	4	Comin' Home*	Atco 6725
10/10/70	#13	14	After Midnight	Atco 6784
2/13/71	#96	2	Bell Bottom Blues**	Atco 6803
3/20/71	#52	10	Layla**	Atco 6809
5/27/72	#14	13	Layla**	Atco 6809
9/16/72	#57	7	Let It Rain	Polydor 15049
2/17/73	#95	4	Bell Bottom Blues	Polydor 15056
7/13/74	#1	14	I Shot The Sheriff	RSO 409
10/26/74	#40	9	Willie And The Hand Jive	RSO 503
10/30/76	#28	13	Hello Old Friend	RSO 861
12/13/77	#3	23	Lay Down Sally	RSO 886
5/13/78	#24	13	Wonderful Tonight	RSO 895
10/14/78	#11	20	Promises***/	RSO 910
2/17/79	#45	8	Watch Out For Lucy***	RSO 910
6/14/80	#36	14	Tulsa Time***	RSO 1039
2/28/81	#13	15	I Can't Stand It***	RSO 1060
6/13/81	#80	5	Another Ticket***	RSO 1064
1/29/83	#19	16	I've Got A Rock N' Roll Heart	Duck 29780
3/09/85	#24	13	Forever Man	Duck 29081
11/11/89	#50	13	Pretending	Duck 22732
3/17/90	#73	4	Bad Love	Duck 19980
2/08/92	#1	30	Tears In Heaven	Duck 19038
9/26/92	#7	26	Layla	Duck 18787
			*released as by **DELANEY & BONNIE AND FRIENDS** featuring **ERIC CLAPTON**	
			released as by **DEREK and THE DOMINOS	
			***released as by **ERIC CLAPTON and HIS BAND**	
			CLAUDINE CLARK	
7/07/62	#6	15	Party Lights	Chancellor 1113
			DAVE CLARK FIVE	
2/15/64	#5	16	Glad All Over	Epic 9656
4/04/64	#4	11	Bits And Pieces	Epic 9671
5/02/64	#73	3	I Knew It All The Time	Congress 212
5/02/64	#8	10	Do You Love Me	Epic 9678
6/13/64	#4	11	Can't You See That She's Mine	Epic 9692
8/01/64	#7	11	Because	Epic 9704
10/03/64	#22	8	Everybody Knows (I Still Love You)	Epic 9722
11/21/64	#9	12	Any Way You Want It	Epic 9739
2/13/65	#13	8	Come Home	Epic 9763
4/24/65	#15	7	Reelin' And Rockin'	Epic 9786
6/26/65	#6	10	I Like It Like That	Epic 9811
8/21/65	#6	11	Catch Us If You Can	Epic 9833
11/06/65	#1	12	Over And Over	Epic 9863
1/29/66	#13	9	At The Scene	Epic 9882
4/02/66	#10	8	Try Too Hard	Epic 10004
6/04/66	#18	8	Please Tell Me Why	Epic 10031
8/13/66	#51	7	Satisfied With You	Epic 10053
10/15/66	#45	8	Nineteen Days	Epic 10076
1/07/67	#55	6	I've Got To Have A Reason	Epic 10114
4/01/67	#8	9	You Got What It Takes	Epic 10144
6/03/67	#35	7	You Must Have Been A Beautiful Baby	Epic 10179
8/05/67	#52	5	A Little Bit Now	Epic 10209
11/04/67	#69	5	Red And Blue	Epic 10244
12/09/67	#41	9	Everybody Knows	Epic 10265
5/25/68	#96	3	Please Stay	Epic 10325
			DEE CLARK	
11/29/58	#34	16	Nobody But You	Abner 1019
5/09/59	#17	13	Just Keep It Up	Abner 1026
8/22/59	#20	15	Hey Little Girl	Abner 1029
12/12/59	#31	12	How About That	Abner 1032
3/19/60	#56	7	At My Front Door	Abner 1037
8/20/60	#40	11	You're Looking Good	Vee-Jay 355
1/28/61	#49	11	Your Friends	Vee-Jay 372
5/06/61	#2	17	Raindrops	Vee-Jay 383
10/13/62	#65	6	I'm Going Back To School	Vee-Jay 462
11/09/63	#89	3	Crossfire Time	Constellation 108

Debut Date	Peak Pos	Wks Chr	**ARTIST**/Song Title	Label & Number
			PETULA CLARK	
12/19/64	#1	16	Downtown	Warner Brothers 5494
3/20/65	#2	12	I Know A Place	Warner Brothers 5612
7/10/65	#25	8	You'd Better Come Home	Warner Brothers 5643
10/09/65	#23	9	Round Every Corner	Warner Brothers 5661
12/25/65	#2	13	My Love	Warner Brothers 5684
3/19/66	#15	9	A Sign Of The Times	Warner Brothers 5802
7/16/66	#8	10	I Couldn't Live Without Your Love	Warner Brothers 5835
10/22/66	#22	8	Who Am I	Warner Brothers 5863
12/24/66	#18	8	Color My World	Warner Brothers 5882
3/04/67	#5	12	This Is My Song	Warner Brothers 7002
6/03/67	#6	11	Don't Sleep In The Subway	Warner Brothers 7049
9/02/67	#27	8	The Cat In The Window	Warner Brothers 7073
12/02/67	#28	8	The Other Man's Grass Is Always Greener	Warner Brothers 7097
2/17/68	#12	11	Kiss Me Goodbye	Warner Brothers 7170
7/20/68	#27	7	Don't Give Up	Warner Brothers 7216
11/23/68	#49	4	American Boys	Warner Brothers 7244
4/05/69	#71	4	Happy Heart	Warner Brothers 7275
8/02/69	#62	5	Look At Mine	Warner Brothers 7310
11/15/69	#91	2	No One Better Than You	Warner Brothers 7343
7/08/72	#89	6	My Guy	MGM 14392
10/07/72	#77	5	Wedding Song (There Is Love)	MGM 14431
			ROY CLARK	
6/08/63	#42	12	Tips Of My Fingers	Capitol 4956
5/31/69	#19	12	Yesterday, When I Was Young	Dot 17246
9/20/69	#65	3	September song	Dot 17299
12/13/69	#96	3	Right Or Left At Oak Street	Dot 17324
1/31/70	#83	2	Then She's A Lover	Dot 17335
11/28/70	#99	2	Thank God And Greyhound	Dot 17355
5/12/73	#79	6	Come Live With Me	Dot 17449
12/22/73	#94	5	Somewhere Between Love And Tomorrow	Dot 17480
			SANFORD CLARK	
8/04/56	#8	17	The Fool	Dot 15481
3/02/57	#48	1	Nine Pound Hammer	Dot 15534
9/13/58	#80	1	Still As The Night	Jamie 1107
			ALLAN CLARKE	
3/25/78	#47	10	(I Will Be Your) Shadow In The Street	Atlantic 3459
4/26/80	#87	7	Slipstream	Elektra 46617
			STANLEY CLARKE	
5/02/81	#21	21	Sweet Baby*	Epic 01052
			*released as by STANLEY CLARKE/GEORGE DUKE	
			TONY CLARKE	
2/15/64	#83	6	(The Story Of) Woman, Love, And A Man	Chess 1880
3/27/65	#28	9	The Entertainer	Chess 1924
			CLASH	
3/22/80	#24	15	Train In Vain (Stand By Me)	Epic 50851
7/31/82	#75	7	Should I Stay Or Should I Go	Epic 03006
10/09/82	#13	24	Rock The Casbah	Epic 03245
2/19/83	#63	8	Should I Stay Or Should I Go	Epic 03547
			CLASSIC EXAMPLE	
11/21/92	#65	14	It's Alright	Hollywood Basic 64690
			CLASSICS	
6/01/63	#21	14	Till Then	Musicnote 1116
			CLASSICS IV	
9/24/66	#85	3	Pollyana	Capitol 5710
12/09/67	#2	17	Spooky	Imperial 66259
4/20/68	#72	6	Soul Train	Imperial 66293
10/19/68	#2	16	Stormy	Imperial 66328
2/01/69	#3	13	Traces	Imperial 66352
5/03/69	#15	10	Everyday With You Girl	Imperial 66378
8/02/69	#53	5	Change Of Heart	Imperial 66393
11/08/69	#38	9	Midnight*	Imperial 66424
3/14/70	#50	7	The Funniest Thing	Imperial 66439
10/24/70	#67	8	Where Did All The Good Times Go	Liberty 56200
10/14/72	#31	11	What Am I Crying For?*	MGM South 7002
3/03/73	#90	3	Rosanna	MGM South 7012
			*released as by DENNIS YOST and THE CLASSICS IV	

Debut Date	Peak Pos	Wks Chr	ARTIST/Song Title	Label & Number
			CASSIUS CLAY	
3/28/64	#94	2	Stand By Me	Columbia 43007
			JUDY CLAY	
12/02/67	#58	8	Storybook Children*	Atlantic 2445
2/17/68	#49	6	Country Girl - City Man*	Atlantic 2480
8/31/68	#84	3	Private Number**	Stax 0005
4/18/70	#86	2	His Greatest Love	Atlantic 2697
			*released as by BILLY VERA & JUDY CLAY	
			**released as by JUDY CLAY & WILLIAM BELL	
			OTIS CLAY	
4/16/66	#95	1	I'm Satisfied	One-derful! 4841
8/17/68	#96	1	She's About A Mover	Cotillion 44001
12/16/72	#70	7	Trying To Live My Life Without You	Hi 2226
			TOM CLAY	
7/10/71	#7	10	What The World Needs Now Is Love/Abraham, Martin And John (medley)	Mowest 5002
			MERRY CLAYTON	
6/06/70	#82	6	Gimme Shelter	Ode 66003
12/11/71	#71	6	After All This Time	Ode 66018
12/30/72	#61	8	Oh No, Not My Baby	Ode 66030
7/26/75	#58	9	Keep Your Eye On The Sparrow	Ode 66110
3/05/88	#42	12	Yes	RCA 6989
			DAVID CLAYTON-THOMAS	
4/01/72	#85	3	Sing A Song	Columbia 45569
			CLEAN LIVING	
10/28/72	#34	11	In Heaven There Is No Beer	Vanguard 35162
			CLEFS OF LAVENDER HILL	
7/02/66	#72	6	Stop! Get A Ticket	Date 1510
			CLEFTONES	
8/04/56	#50	1	Can't We Be Sweethearts	Gee 1016
5/20/61	#16	10	Heart And Soul	Gee 1064
9/30/61	#76	3	For Sentimental Reasons	Gee 1067
11/24/62	#88	3	Lover Come Back To Me	Gee 1079
			CLARENCE CLEMONS	
10/26/85	#20	20	You're A Friend Of Mine*	Columbia 05660
			*released as by CLARENCE CLEMONS and JACKSON BROWNE	
			JAMES CLEVELAND	
7/23/66	#81	2	Without A Song	Savoy 4269
			CLICK-CLACKS	
10/04/58	#96	2	Little Pearly	Apt 25010
			JIMMY CLIFF	
11/29/69	#18	12	Wonderful World, Beautiful People	A&M 1146
3/21/70	#99	2	Come Into My Life	A&M 1167
11/27/93	#25	25	I Can See Clearly Now	Chaos 77207
			BUZZ CLIFFORD	
1/07/61	#10	15	Baby Sittin' Boogie	Columbia 41876
4/22/61	#98	2	Three Little Fishes	Columbia 41979
			LINDA CLIFFORD	
7/01/78	#69	6	Runaway Love	Curtom 0138
3/24/79	#59	5	Bridge Over Troubled Water	RSO 921
8/09/80	#53	11	Red Light	RSO 1041
			MIKE CLIFFORD	
9/15/62	#13	13	Close To Cathy	United Artists 489
1/05/63	#78	5	What To Do With Laurie	United Artists 557
5/18/63	#98	3	One Boy Too Late	United Artists 588
			CLIMAX	
12/25/71	#1	17	Precious And Few	Rocky Road 30055
4/29/72	#42	13	Life And Breath	Rocky Road 30061
			CLIMAX BLUES BAND	
2/12/77	#7	22	Couldn't Get It Right	Sire 736
11/08/80	#60	12	Gotta Have More Love	Warner Brothers 49605
2/14/81	#9	29	I Love You	Warner Brothers 49669

Debut Date	Peak Pos	Wks Chr	ARTIST/Song Title	Label & Number
			CLIMIE FISHER	
5/14/88	#27	20	Love Changes (Everything)	Capitol 44137
			PATSY CLINE	
2/16/57	#14	13	Walkin' After Midnight	Decca 30221
6/03/61	#15	20	I Fall To Pieces	Decca 31205
10/21/61	#13	14	Crazy	Decca 31317
1/27/62	#11	13	She's Got You	Decca 31354
5/05/62	#78	4	Imagine That/	Decca 31377
5/12/62	#43	7	When I Get Thru With You	Decca 31377
7/14/62	#66	5	So Wrong/	Decca 31406
7/21/62	#95	2	You're Stronger Than Me	Decca 31406
10/13/62	#65	6	Heartaches	Decca 31429
2/09/63	#100	1	Leavin' On Your Mind	Decca 31455
4/27/63	#57	8	Sweet Dreams	Decca 31483
			CLIQUE	
8/16/69	#20	12	Sugar On Sunday	White Whale 323
11/15/69	#34	7	I'll Hold Out My Hand	White Whale 333
2/21/70	#70	3	Sparkle And Shine	White Whale 338
			CLOCKS	
8/28/82	#77	5	She Looks A Lot Like You	Boulevard 03075
			ROSEMARY CLOONEY	
4/14/51	#7	8	Beautiful Brown Eyes	Columbia 39212
7/28/51	#1	15	Come On-A My House	Columbia 39467
7/19/52	#1	18	Half As Much	Columbia 39710
8/02/52	#3	10	Botch-A-Me	Columbia 39767
8/21/54	#1	18	Hey There/	Columbia 40266
10/09/54	#3	10	This Ole House	Columbia 40266
12/04/54	#6	6	Mambo Italiano	Columbia 40361
8/04/56	#47	1	I Could Have Danced All Night	Columbia 40676
3/30/57	#23	10	Mangos	Columbia 40835
			CLOUT	
9/02/78	#52	11	Substitute	Epic 50591
			CLOVERS	
8/04/56	#34	3	Love, Love, Love	Atlantic 1094
9/05/59	#21	19	Love Potion No. 9	United Artists 180
			CLUB HOUSE	
8/06/93	#76	8	Do It Again/Billie Jean (medley)	Atlantic 89795
			CLUB NOUVEAU	
2/14/87	#1	17	Lean On Me	Warner Brothers 28430
6/06/87	#45	14	Why Do You Treat Me So Bad	Warner Brothers 28360
			COASTERS	
5/25/57	#7	19	Searchin'/	Atco 6087
5/11/57	#15	16	Young Blood	Atco 6087
5/31/58	#1	16	Yakety Yak	Atco 6116
2/07/59	#2	15	Charlie Brown	Atco 6132
5/23/59	#11	11	Along Came Jones	Atco 6141
8/22/59	#9	16	Poison Ivy/	Atco 6146
8/29/59	#95	2	I'm A Hog For You	Atco 6146
12/12/59	#33	8	What About Us/	Atco 6153
12/12/59	#51	9	Run Red Run	Atco 6153
4/09/60	#53	8	Besame Mucho	Atco 6163
6/25/60	#34	9	Wake Me, Shake Me	Atco 6168
10/08/60	#57	6	Shoppin' For Clothes	Atco 6178
1/28/61	#42	9	Wait A Minute	Atco 6186
4/29/61	#30	12	Little Egypt	Atco 6192
8/12/61	#98	3	Girls, Girls, Girls	Atco 6204
3/07/64	#73	8	T'ain't Nothin' To Me	Atco 6287
12/25/71	#96	3	Love Potion No. 9	King 6385
			ODIA COATES	
7/06/74	#1	16	(You're) Having My Baby*	United Artists 454
11/09/74	#7	15	One Man Woman/One Woman Man*	United Artists 569
2/22/75	#62	7	Showdown	United Artists 601
3/15/75	#5	14	I Don't Like To Sleep Alone*	United Artists 615
4/19/75	#80	4	Don't Leave Me In The Morning	United Artists 601
7/19/75	#14	13	(I Believe) There's Nothing Stronger Than Our Love* . . .	United Artists 685
			*released as by PAUL ANKA with ODIA COATES	

Debut Date	Peak Pos	Wks Chr	**ARTIST**/Song Title	Label & Number
			JOYCE COBB	
12/08/79	#75	10	Dig The Gold	Cream 7939
			RICHARD COCCIANTE	
4/03/76	#62	5	When Love Has Gone Away	20th Century 2275
			COCHISE	
5/01/71	#90	5	Love's Made A Fool Of You	United Artists 50756
			EDDIE COCHRAN	
3/09/57	#15	11	Sittin' In The Balcony	Liberty 55056
8/09/58	#11	15	Summertime Blues	Liberty 55144
11/15/58	#42	14	C'mon Everybody	Liberty 55166
8/29/59	#56	8	Somethin' Else	Liberty 55203
12/12/59	#98	2	Hallelujah	Liberty 55217
5/28/60	#99	1	Three Steps To Heaven	Liberty 55242
			TOM COCHRAN	
5/23/92	#6	31	Life Is A Highway	Capitol 44815
11/21/92	#85	5	Washed Away	Capitol 44879
			BRUCE COCKBURN	
3/22/80	#27	15	Wondering Where The Lions Are	Millenium 11786
2/02/85	#71	7	If I Had A Rocket Launcher	Gold Mountain 82013
			JOE COCKER	
11/09/68	#54	6	With A Little Help From My Friends	A&M 991
6/21/69	#72	6	Feeling Alright	A&M 1063
10/04/69	#91	3	Delta Lady	A&M 1112
12/13/69	#36	10	She Came In Through The Bathroom Window	A&M 1147
4/18/70	#5	13	The Letter	A&M 1174
10/03/70	#16	10	Cry Me A River	A&M 1200
5/15/71	#29	11	High Time We Went/	A&M 1258
7/17/71	#100	1	Black-Eyed Blues	A&M 1258
1/01/72	#36	9	Feeling Alright	A&M 1063
9/16/72	#31	8	Midnight Rider*/	A&M 1370
12/02/72	#52	8	Woman To Woman*	A&M 1370
2/17/73	#49	7	Pardon Me Sir	A&M 1407
6/15/74	#38	10	Put Out The Light	A&M 1539
10/26/74	#91	2	I Can Stand A Little Rain	A&M 1626
1/18/75	#4	15	You Are So Beautiful	A&M 1641
10/14/78	#45	9	Fun Time	Asylum 45540
8/28/82	#1	25	Up Where We Belong**	Island 99996
10/27/82	#63	7	Edge Of A Dream	Capitol 5412
3/01/86	#80	6	Shelter Me	Capitol 5557
11/04/89	#11	21	When The Night Comes	Capitol 44437
6/16/90	#69	7	What Are You Doing With A Fool Like Me	Capitol 44543
			*released as by JOE COCKER and THE CHRIS STAINTON BAND	
			**released as by JOE COCKER and JENNIFER WARNES	
			COCK ROBIN	
6/22/85	#33	17	When Your Heart Is Weak	Columbia 04875
			C.O.D.'s	
12/04/65	#42	12	Michael	Kellmac 1003
			DENNIS COFFEY and THE DETROIT GUITAR BAND	
10/31/71	#4	16	Scorpio	Sussex 226
2/12/72	#13	13	Taurus	Sussex 233
5/27/72	#55	5	Ride Sally Ride	Sussex 237
			MARC COHN	
4/06/91	#11	25	Walking In Memphis	Atlantic 87747
8/03/91	#44	14	Silver Thunderbird	Atlantic 87678
10/19/91	#60	15	True Companion	Atlantic 87583
			COLD BLOOD	
1/03/70	#64	9	You Got Me Hummin'	San Francisco 60
			BEN COLDER (see SHEB WOOLEY)	
			BOBBY COLE	
7/13/68	#75	6	Mr. Bojangles	Date 1613
			COZY COLE	
9/06/58	#1	21	Topsy II	Love 5004
11/29/58	#25	8	Turvy II	Love 5013
11/29/58	#97	1	Caravan II	Grand Award 1023

69

Debut Date	Peak Pos	Wks Chr	ARTIST/Song Title	Label & Number
			GARDNER COLE	
10/15/88	#84	3	Live It Up	Warner Brothers 27793
			JUDE COLE	
4/14/90	#11	20	Baby, It's Tonight	Reprise 19869
7/28/90	#36	15	Time For Letting Go	Reprise 19743
12/08/90	#59	10	House Full Of Reasons	Reprise 19530
9/19/92	#67	7	Start The Car	Reprise 18793
1/30/93	#54	16	Tell The Truth	Reprise 18673
			NATALIE COLE	
8/30/75	#9	16	This Will Be	Capitol 4109
12/20/75	#33	16	Inseparable	Capitol 4193
5/29/76	#40	17	Sophisticated Lady (She's A Different Lady)	Capitol 4259
9/18/76	#54	11	Mr. Melody	Capitol 4328
2/05/77	#3	23	I've Got Love On My Mind	Capitol 4360
1/14/78	#16	18	Our Love	Capitol 4509
6/28/80	#29	18	Someone That I Used To Love	Capitol 4869
5/04/85	#55	12	Dangerous	Modern 99648
7/25/87	#18	22	Jump Start	Manhattan 50073
11/07/87	#19	23	I Live For Your Love	Manhattan 50094
3/05/88	#5	19	Pink Cadillac	EMI-Manhattan 50117
4/15/89	#8	21	Miss You Like Crazy	EMI 50185
2/17/90	#36	13	Wild Women Do	EMI 50275
7/27/91	#23	16	Unforgettable	Elektra 64875
			NAT KING COLE	
7/08/50	#1	23	Mona Lisa	Capitol 1010
11/18/50	#6	7	Orange Colored Sky*	Capitol 1184
5/19/51	#1	23	Too Young	Capitol 1449
9/13/52	#8	5	Somewhere Along The Way	Capitol 2069
3/14/53	#2	13	Pretend	Capitol 2346
4/24/54	#6	8	Answer Me, My Love	Capitol 2687
10/23/54	#9	4	Smile	Capitol 2897
5/07/55	#7	4	Darling Je Vous Aime Beaucoup	Capitol 3027
6/04/55	#3	16	A Blossom Fell/	Capitol 3095
8/06/55	#10	11	If I May	Capitol 3095
8/04/56	#17	12	That's All There Is To That	Capitol 3456
10/20/56	#25	7	To The Ends Of The Earth/	Capitol 3551
10/27/56	#17	11	Night Lights	Capitol 3551
2/09/57	#29	6	Ballerina/	Capitol 3619
2/09/57	#34	4	You Are My First Love	Capitol 3619
4/20/57	#44	7	When Rock And Roll Came To Trinidad	Capitol 3702
6/22/57	#7	20	Send For Me/	Capitol 3737
6/22/57	#26	12	My Personal Possession	Capitol 3737
9/14/57	#22	13	With You On My Mind/	Capitol 3782
9/14/57	#53	1	The Song Of Raintree County	Capitol 3782
1/18/58	#28	10	Angel Smile/	Capitol 3860
1/18/58	#60	1	Back In My Arms	Capitol 3860
4/05/58	#10	16	Looking Back	Capitol 3939
7/26/58	#25	10	Come Closer To Me/	Capitol 4004
7/26/58	#51	2	Nothing In The World	Capitol 4004
10/11/58	#22	14	Non Dimenticar (Don't Forget)	Capitol 4056
1/31/59	#75	5	Give Me Your Love/	Capitol 4125
2/07/59	#65	6	Madrid	Capitol 4125
5/09/59	#39	8	You Made Me Love You/	Capitol 4184
5/09/59	#54	5	I Must Be Dreaming	Capitol 4184
8/08/59	#32	11	Midnight Flyer/	Capitol 4248
8/22/59	#100	1	Sweet Bird Of Youth	Capitol 4248
1/16/60	#46	9	Time And The River/	Capitol 4325
2/13/60	#100	1	What'cha Gonna Do	Capitol 4325
7/16/60	#43	11	My Love*	Capitol 4393
7/01/61	#67	6	Take A Fool's Advice	Capitol 4582
8/04/62	#2	17	Ramblin' Rose	Capitol 4804
11/10/62	#14	11	Dear Lonely Hearts	Capitol 4870
3/02/63	#81	2	Nothing Goes Up (Without Coming Down)/	Capitol 4919
3/09/63	#43	9	All Over The World	Capitol 4919
5/11/63	#7	12	Those Lazy Hazy Crazy Days Of Summer	Capitol 4965
8/31/63	#15	14	That Sunday, That Summer/	Capitol 5027
9/07/63	#66	3	Mr. Wishing Well	Capitol 5027
2/15/64	#42	7	My True Carrie, Love	Capitol 5125
4/11/64	#19	12	I Don't Want To Be Hurt Anymore	Capitol 5155

Debut Date	Peak Pos	Wks Chr	ARTIST/Song Title	Label & Number
8/01/64	#97	1	More And More Of Your Amor	Capitol 5219
9/19/64	#34	9	I Don't Want To See Tomorrow	Capitol 5261
8/20/66	#100	1	Let Me Tell You	Capitol 5683
			*released as by NAT KING COLE-STAN KENTON	
			TONY COLE	
11/11/72	#95	2	Suite: Man And Woman	20th Century 2001
			COLLAGE	
12/18/93	#52	13	I'll Be Loving You	Viper 1002
			KEITH COLLEY	
9/07/63	#68	7	Enamorado	Unical 3006
			MITTY COLLIER	
10/03/64	#43	11	I Had A Talk With My Man	Chess 1907
1/16/65	#74	6	No Faith, No Love	Chess 1918
3/26/66	#80	4	Sharing You	Chess 1953
			DAVE and ANSIL COLLINS	
6/05/71	#27	11	Double Barrel	Big Tree 115
			DOROTHY COLLINS	
12/26/59	#51	9	Baciare Baciare (Kissing Kissing)	Top Rank 2024
6/18/60	#62	7	Banjo Boy	Top Rank 2052
			JUDY COLLINS	
11/02/68	#8	12	Both Sides Now	Elektra 45639
1/25/69	#40	6	Someday Soon	Elektra 45649
8/02/69	#93	5	Chelsea Morning	Elektra 45657
11/22/69	#58	7	Turn! Turn! Turn!	Elektra 45680
12/19/70	#13	14	Amazing Grace	Elektra 45709
1/01/72	#82	5	Open The Door (Song For Judith)	Elektra 45755
2/10/73	#29	11	Cook With Honey	Elektra 45831
6/28/75	#53	9	Send In The Clowns	Elektra 45253
9/24/77	#17	17	Send In The Clowns	Elektra 45253
3/10/79	#63	9	Hard Times For Lovers	Elektra 46020
			LYN COLLINS	
8/12/72	#55	11	Think (About It)	People 608
12/16/72	#51	8	What My Baby Needs Now Is A Little More Lovin'*	Polydor 14157
			*released as by JAMES BROWN/LYN COLLINS	
			PHIL COLLINS	
3/14/81	#19	17	I Missed Again	Atlantic 3790
5/30/81	#19	17	In The Air Tonight	Atlantic 3824
11/06/82	#10	20	You Can't Hurry Love	Atlantic 89933
2/12/83	#47	10	I Don't Care Anymore	Atlantic 89877
5/07/83	#80	5	I Cannot Believe It's True	Atlantic 89864
2/25/84	#1	23	Against All Odds	Atlantic 89700
11/24/84	#1	24	Easy Lover*	Columbia 04679
2/09/85	#1	20	One More Night	Atlantic 89588
5/11/85	#1	18	Sussudio	Atlantic 89560
7/20/85	#5	18	Don't Lose My Number	Atlantic 89536
10/05/85	#1	24	Separate Lives (Love Theme From White Nights)**	Atlantic 89498
3/15/86	#7	18	Take Me Home	Atlantic 89472
9/03/88	#1	17	Groovy Kind Of Love	Atlantic 89017
11/19/88	#1	18	Two Hearts	Atlantic 88980
11/04/89	#1	21	Another Day In Paradise	Atlantic 88774
2/10/90	#3	17	I Wish It Would Rain Down	Atlantic 88738
4/28/90	#3	21	Do You Remember?	Atlantic 87955
8/04/90	#3	19	Something Happened On The Way To Heaven	Atlantic 87885
11/10/90	#11	19	Hang In Long Enough	Atlantic 87800
1/26/91	#67	9	Who Said I Would	Atlantic 87754
4/24/93	#35	24	Hero***	Atlantic 87360
10/30/93	#20	22	Both Sides Of The Story	Atlantic 87299
			*released as by PHILIP BAILEY with PHIL COLLINS	
			**released as by PHIL COLLINS and MARYLIN MARTIN	
			***released as by DAVID CROSBY & PHIL COLLINS	
			RODGER COLLINS	
3/11/67	#74	5	She's Looking Good	Galaxy 750
			TYLER COLLINS	
5/05/90	#7	24	Girls Nite Out	RCA 2630
9/01/90	#47	10	Second Chance	RCA 2639
9/05/92	#73	9	It Doesn't Matter	RCA 62325

Debut Date	Peak Pos	Wks Chr	ARTIST/Song Title	Label & Number
			COLORHAUS	
6/06/92	#45	10	Innocent Child	Interscope 98613
			COLOR ME BADD	
4/20/91	#2	24	I Wanna Sex You Up	Giant 19382
7/27/91	#1	27	I Adore Mi Amor	Giant 19204
11/02/91	#2	30	All-4 Love	Giant 19236
2/01/92	#7	22	Thinkin' Back	Giant 19074
5/09/92	#10	20	Slow Motion	Giant 18908
9/05/92	#14	22	Forever Love	Giant 18727
11/27/93	#23	18	Time And Chance	Giant 18339
			COLOURS	
8/24/68	#70	7	Love Heals	Dot 17132
			JESSI COLTER	
3/29/75	#5	19	I'm Not Lisa	Capitol 4009
9/06/75	#56	5	You Ain't Never Been Loved/	Capitol 4087
10/11/75	#78	5	What's Happened To Blue Eyes	Capitol 4087
			CHI COLTRANE	
9/02/72	#15	14	Thunder And Lightning	Columbia 45640
			CHRIS COLUMBO QUINTET	
7/06/63	#92	3	Summertime	Strand 25056
			COMMANDER CODY and HIS LOST PLANET AIRMEN	
3/25/72	#7	13	Hot Rod Lincoln	Paramount 0146
8/12/72	#90	5	Beat Me Daddy Eight To The Bar	Paramount 0169
6/23/73	#71	5	Smoke! Smoke! Smoke! (That Cigarette)	Paramount 0216
3/01/75	#53	6	Don't Let Go	Warner Brothers 8073
			COMMITMENTS	
10/05/91	#56	11	Try A Little Tenderness	MCA 54260
			COMMODORES	
6/15/74	#13	12	Machine Gun	Motown 1307
11/23/74	#78	5	I Feel Sanctified	Motown 1319
5/17/75	#29	14	Slippery When Wet	Motown 1338
11/01/75	#77	4	This Is Your Life	Motown 1361
12/20/75	#9	24	Sweet Love	Motown 1381
9/11/76	#11	19	Just To Be Close To You	Motown 1402
12/25/76	#63	12	Fancy Dancer	Motown 1408
5/28/77	#4	21	Easy	Motown 1418
8/27/77	#6	16	Brick House	Motown 1425
12/17/77	#37	13	Too Hot Ta Trot	Motown 1432
6/24/78	#1	21	Three Times A Lady	Motown 1443
9/30/78	#52	9	Flying High	Motown 1452
8/11/79	#1	20	Sail On	Motown 1466
9/29/79	#1	19	Still	Motown 1474
12/29/79	#54	11	Wonderland	Motown 1479
6/21/80	#17	17	Old-Fashion Love	Motown 1489
9/20/80	#50	9	Heroes	Motown 1495
6/20/81	#8	21	Lady (You Bring Me Up)	Motown 1514
9/19/81	#4	22	Oh No	Motown 1527
2/06/82	#69	7	Why You Wanna Try Me	Motown 1604
12/11/82	#76	7	Painted Picture	Motown 1651
9/24/83	#60	18	Only You	Motown 1694
1/26/85	#4	23	Nightshift	Motown 1773
5/25/85	#50	9	Animal Instinct	Motown 1788
11/01/86	#68	12	Goin' To The Bank	Polydor 885358
			COMMUNARDS	
1/31/87	#55	7	Don't Leave Me This Way	MCA 52928
1/30/88	#58	9	Never Can Say Goodbye	MCA 53224
			NICKY COMO	
7/09/60	#13	12	Look For A Star	Laurie 3061
			PERRY COMO	
5/27/50	#4	14	Hoop-De-Doo	RCA 3747
12/02/50	#10	10	A Bushel And A Peck*	RCA 3930
1/21/51	#3	13	You're Just In Love**	RCA 3945
2/10/51	#1	20	If/	RCA 3997
3/03/51	#8	2	Zing, Zing -- Zoom, Zoom	RCA 3997
7/19/52	#5	8	Maybe***	RCA 4744
12/20/52	#1	16	Don't Let The Stars Get In Your Eyes	RCA 5064

Debut Date	Peak Pos	Wks Chr	ARTIST/Song Title	Label & Number
3/21/53	#7	7	Wild Horses	RCA 5152
5/30/53	#4	9	Say You're Mine Again/	RCA 5277
7/11/53	#10	1	My One And Only Heart	RCA 5277
7/18/53	#1	17	No Other Love	RCA 5317
11/28/53	#7	9	You Alone	RCA 5447
4/03/54	#1	18	Wanted	RCA 5647
10/30/54	#2	14	Papa Loves Mambo	RCA 5857
2/26/55	#3	9	Ko Ko Mo (I Love You So)	RCA 5994
6/24/55	#6	7	Tina Marie	RCA 6192
3/01/56	#7	5	Juke Box Baby/	RCA 6427
4/07/56	#1	12	Hot Diggity (Dog Ziggity Boom)	RCA 6427
7/21/56	#9	10	More/	RCA 6554
8/04/56	#18	3	Glendora	RCA 6554
8/04/56	#29	7	Somebody Up There Likes Me	RCA 6590
10/27/56	#33	8	Moonlight Love/	RCA 6670
11/10/56	#44	4	Chincherinchee	RCA 6670
2/23/57	#2	19	Round And Round/	RCA 6815
3/09/57	#50	1	Mi Casa, Su Casa	RCA 6815
5/18/57	#22	10	The Girl With The Golden Braids/	RCA 6904
5/18/57	#23	8	My Little Baby	RCA 6904
8/17/57	#51	3	Dancin'/	RCA 6991
8/17/57	#42	4	Marching Along To The Blues	RCA 6991
10/12/57	#14	14	Just Born (To Be Your Baby)/	RCA 7050
10/12/57	#36	9	Ivy Rose	RCA 7050
1/18/58	#2	17	Catch A Falling Star/	RCA 7128
2/01/58	#21	10	Magic Moments	RCA 7128
4/12/58	#9	13	Kewpie Doll	RCA 7202
7/26/58	#24	11	Moon Talk/	RCA 7274
8/02/58	#44	7	Beats There A Heart So True	RCA 7274
10/18/58	#46	10	Love Makes The World Go 'Round/	RCA 7353
10/18/58	#53	10	Mandolins In The Moonlight	RCA 7353
2/21/59	#26	11	Tomboy	RCA 7464
6/13/59	#37	10	I Know	RCA 7541
1/30/60	#17	12	Deleware/	RCA 7670
2/06/60	#93	1	I Know What God Is	RCA 7670
12/03/60	#86	4	Make Someone Happy	RCA 7812
12/02/61	#99	2	You're Following Me	RCA 7962
3/31/62	#22	12	Caterina	RCA 8004
6/01/63	#54	8	(I Love You) Don't You Forget It	RCA 8186
4/10/65	#29	10	Dream On Little Dreamer	RCA 8533
8/07/65	#68	4	Oowee, Oowee	RCA 8636
5/20/67	#95	2	Stop! And Think It Over	RCA 9165
4/12/69	#42	9	Seattle	RCA 9722
10/31/70	#10	17	It's Impossible	RCA 0387
3/13/71	#45	9	I Think Of You	RCA 0444
4/07/73	#18	16	And I Love You So	RCA 0906
1/04/75	#88	2	Christmas Dream	RCA 10122

*released as by PERRY COMO and BETTY HUTTON
**released as by PERRY COMO and THE FONTANE SISTERS
***released as by PERRY COMO and EDDIE FISHER

COMPANY B

3/28/87	#25	18	Fascinated	Atlantic 89294

BOBBY COMSTOCK

10/17/59	#42	9	Tennessee Waltz	Blaze 349
2/02/63	#61	8	Let's Stomp	Lawn 202

CONCRETE BLONDE

8/25/90	#20	21	Joey	I.R.S. 73014
12/29/90	#84	7	Caroline	I.R.S. 67029

CONDUCTOR

1/30/82	#68	7	Voice On The Radio	Montage 1210

CON FUNK SHUN

12/10/77	#18	15	Ffun	Mercury 73959
7/29/78	#59	10	Shake And Dance With Me	Mercury 74008
7/21/79	#94	3	Chase Me	Mercury 74059
1/24/81	#37	13	Too Tight	Mercury 76089

ARTHUR CONLEY

3/11/67	#4	15	Sweet Soul Music	Atco 6463
6/10/67	#47	6	Shake, Rattle And Roll	Atco 6494

Debut Date	Peak Pos	Wks Chr	ARTIST/Song Title	Label & Number
			ARTHUR CONLEY—*continued*	
11/04/67	#92	2	Whole Lotta Woman	Atco 6529
3/16/68	#19	12	Funky Street	Atco 6563
6/15/68	#41	5	People Sure Act Funny	Atco 6588
10/19/68	#75	4	Aunt Dora's Love Soul Shack	Atco 6622
1/11/69	#74	4	Ob-La-Di, Ob-La-Da	Atco 6640
4/25/70	#91	3	God Bless	Atco 6747
			RAY CONNIFF and THE SINGERS	
10/29/60	#89	2	Midnight Lace (Part 1)*	Columbia 41800
7/25/64	#50	10	Invisible Tears	Columbia 43061
6/11/66	#11	15	Somewhere My Love	Columbia 43626
			***released as by RAY CONNIFF**	
			CHRIS CONNOR	
12/22/56	#45	4	I Miss You So	Atlantic 1105
			NORMAN CONNORS	
11/29/75	#81	5	Valentine Love	Buddah 499
8/21/76	#98	2	We Both Need Each Other	Buddah 534
9/18/76	#26	14	You Are My Starship	Buddah 542
			CONSUMER RAPPORT	
4/12/75	#42	9	Ease On Down The Road	Wing And A Prayer 101
			BILL CONTI	
4/16/77	#1	19	Gonna Fly Now	United Artists 940
11/20/82	#65	9	Theme From Dynasty	Arista 1021
			CONTINENTAL 4	
6/26/71	#83	3	Day By Day (Every Minute Of The Hour)	Jay Walking 011
			CONTINENTAL MINIATURES	
5/13/78	#74	4	Stay Awhile	London 266
			DICK CONTINO	
4/20/57	#15	1	Pledge Of Love	Mercury 71079
			CONTOURS	
8/18/62	#2	18	Do You Love Me	Gordy 7005
12/22/62	#45	10	Shake Sherry	Gordy 7012
4/13/63	#82	4	Don't Let Her Be Your Baby	Gordy 7016
4/04/64	#59	7	Can You Do It	Gordy 7029
12/12/64	#77	7	Can You Jerk Like Me	Gordy 7037
8/21/65	#55	7	First I Look At The Purse	Gordy 7044
5/14/66	#92	2	Just A Little Misunderstanding	Gordy 7052
4/08/67	#66	5	It's So Hard Being A Loser	Gordy 7059
6/11/88	#13	16	Do You Love Me	Motown 448
			CONTROLLERS	
12/24/77	#84	5	Somebody's Gotta Win, Somebody's Gotta Lose	Juana 3414
			TOMMY CONWELL and THE YOUNG RUMBLERS	
9/24/88	#81	7	I'm Not Your Man	Columbia 07980
12/10/88	#57	12	If We Never Meet Again	Columbia 08505
			LAWRENCE COOKE	
5/20/50	#7	5	Old Piano Roll Blues	Abbey 15003
			SAM COOKE	
10/19/57	#1	17	You Send Me	Keen 34013
12/14/57	#20	8	I'll Come Running Back To You	Specialty 619
12/21/57	#33	7	(I Love You) For Sentimental Reasons/	Keen 4002
12/21/57	#53	4	Desire Me	Keen 4002
3/15/58	#39	5	Lonely Island	Keen 4009
9/13/58	#71	11	Win Your Love For Me	Keen 2006
11/29/58	#37	12	Love You Most Of All	Keen 2008
3/07/59	#29	13	Everybody Likes To Cha Cha Cha	Keen 2018
6/20/59	#32	8	Only Sixteen	Keen 2022
10/24/59	#64	8	There I've Said It Again	Keen 2105
3/12/60	#40	7	Teenage Sonata	RCA 7701
5/07/60	#10	16	Wonderful World	Keen 2112
8/20/60	#3	17	Chain Gang	RCA 7783
12/03/60	#28	9	Sad Mood	RCA 7816
3/11/61	#28	9	That's It-I Quit-I'm Movin' On	RCA 7853
6/10/61	#16	13	Cupid	RCA 7883
9/23/61	#57	6	Feel It	RCA 7927
2/03/62	#6	16	Twistin' The Night Away	RCA 7983

Debut Date	Peak Pos	Wks Chr	ARTIST/Song Title	Label & Number
5/26/62	#16	14	Having A Party/	RCA 8036
6/30/62	#9	15	Bring It On Home To Me	RCA 8036
10/06/62	#21	11	Nothing Can Change This Love/	RCA 8088
10/27/62	#74	6	Somebody Have Mercy	RCA 8088
1/19/63	#20	11	Send Me Some Lovin'/	RCA 8129
1/26/63	#79	7	Baby, Baby, Baby	RCA 8129
4/20/63	#14	12	Another Saturday Night	RCA 8164
7/27/63	#15	11	Frankie And Johnny	RCA 8215
10/26/63	#11	12	Little Red Rooster	RCA 8247
2/01/64	#9	11	Good News	RCA 8299
6/06/64	#16	11	Good Times/	RCA 8368
6/06/64	#38	9	Tennessee Waltz	RCA 8368
9/26/64	#24	8	Cousin Of Mine/	RCA 8426
9/26/64	#55	6	That's Where It's At	RCA 8426
1/09/65	#6	12	Shake/	RCA 8486
1/30/65	#46	8	A Change Is Gonna Come	RCA 8486
4/10/65	#36	7	It's Got The Whole World Shakin'	RCA 8539
6/05/65	#73	3	When A Boy Falls In Love	RCA 8586
7/24/65	#30	8	Sugar Dumpling	RCA 8631
			COOKER	
2/09/74	#67	5	Try (Try To Fall In Love)	Scepter 12388
			COOKIE and HIS CUPCAKES	
5/25/63	#96	2	Got You On My Mind	Chess 1848
			COOKIES	
11/10/62	#21	13	Chains	Dimension 1002
3/09/63	#8	12	Don't Say Nothin' Bad (About My Baby)	Dimension 1008
7/06/63	#82	4	Will Power	Dimension 1012
11/30/63	#38	10	Girls Grow Up Faster Than Boys	Dimension 1020
			COOL HEAT	
9/05/70	#98	1	Groovin' With Mr. Bloe	Forward 152
			EDDIE COOLEY and THE DIMPLES	
11/03/56	#25	10	Priscilla	Royal Roost 621
			RITA COOLIDGE	
1/06/73	#87	2	My Crew/	A&M 1398
1/20/73	#90	2	Fever	A&M 1398
11/10/73	#33	10	A Song I'd Like To Sing*	A&M 1475
3/30/74	#97	2	Loving Arms	A&M 1498
5/07/77	#1	24	(Your Love Has Lifted Me) Higher And Higher	A&M 1922
9/10/77	#5	19	We're All Alone	A&M 1965
1/21/78	#18	12	The Way You Do The Things You Do	A&M 2004
6/24/78	#17	15	You	A&M 2058
11/04/78	#71	5	Love Me Again	A&M 2090
9/01/79	#84	6	One Fine Day	A&M 2169
11/17/79	#39	13	I'd Rather Leave While I'm In Love	A&M 2199
5/24/80	#53	10	Somethin' 'Bout You Baby I Like**	Capitol 4865
12/13/80	#55	13	Fool That I Am	A&M 2281
7/02/83	#33	13	All Time High	A&M 2551
			*released as by KRIS KRISTOFFERSON and RITA COOLIDGE	
			**released as by GLEN CAMPBELL and RITA COOLIDGE	
			ALICE COOPER	
2/20/71	#21	12	Eighteen	Warner Brothers 7449
6/12/71	#86	4	Caught In A Dream	Warner Brothers 7490
1/01/72	#74	5	Under My Wheels	Warner Brothers 7529
3/18/72	#36	8	Be My Lover	Warner Brothers 7568
5/27/72	#6	15	School's Out	Warner Brothers 7596
10/07/72	#18	9	Elected	Warner Brothers 7631
2/03/73	#25	9	Hello Hurray	Warner Brothers 7673
4/07/73	#26	14	No More Mr. Nice Guy	Warner Brothers 7691
8/11/73	#36	6	Billion Dollar Babies	Warner Brothers 7724
12/22/73	#24	10	Teenage Lament '74	Warner Brothers 7762
4/05/75	#10	16	Only Women	Atlantic 3254
8/09/75	#58	6	Department Of Youth	Atlantic 3280
10/25/75	#40	6	Welcome To My Nightmare	Atlantic 3298
7/25/76	#9	22	I Never Cry	Warner Brothers 8228
4/23/77	#8	23	You And Me	Warner Brothers 8349
10/21/78	#16	16	How You Gonna See Me Now	Warner Brothers 8695
5/10/80	#49	13	Clones (We're All)	Warner Brothers 49204

Debut Date	Peak Pos	Wks Chr	ARTIST/Song Title	Label & Number
			ALICE COOPER—*continued*	
9/09/89	#8	22	Poison	Epic 68958
1/27/90	#50	10	House Of Fire	Epic 73085
5/05/90	#85	4	Only My Heart Talkin'	Epic 73268
8/03/91	#81	6	Hey Stoopid	Epic 73845
			CHRISTINE COOPER	
2/05/66	#99	3	S.O.S.	Parkway 971
			LES COOPER and THE SOUL ROCKERS	
10/13/62	#21	17	Wiggle Wobble	Everlast 5019
			MICHAEL COOPER	
3/27/93	#67	7	Shoop Shoop (Never Stop Givin' You Love)	Reprise 18649
			COOPER BROTHERS	
10/14/78	#44	16	The Dream Never Dies	Capricorn 0308
6/23/79	#75	5	I'll Know Her When I See Her	Capricorn 0325
			COWBOY COPAS	
10/15/60	#73	9	Alabam	Starday 501
			JULIAN COPE	
3/14/87	#83	6	World Shut Your Mouth	Island 99479
			KEN COPELAND	
4/06/57	#14	11	Pledge Of Love	Imperial 5432
			JILL COREY	
1/12/57	#46	6	I Love My Baby (My Baby Loves Me)	Columbia 40794
4/20/57	#54	2	Let It Be Me	Columbia 40878
8/03/57	#19	9	Love Me To Pieces	Columbia 40955
9/20/58	#83	2	Big Daddy	Columbia 41202
			CORINA	
6/08/91	#5	21	Temptation/	Cutting 98775
10/05/91	#59	11	Whispers	Cutting 98775
			AL CORLEY	
5/18/85	#84	3	Square Rooms	Mercury 822241
			CORNELIUS BROTHERS & SISTER ROSE	
3/13/71	#2	23	Treat Her Like A Lady	United Artists 50721
5/20/72	#1	15	Too Late To Turn Back Now	United Artists 50910
9/02/72	#23	11	Don't Ever Be Lonely (A Poor Little Fool Like Me)	United Artists 50954
12/23/72	#31	9	I'm Never Gonna Be Alone Anymore	United Artists 50996
4/07/73	#72	7	Let Me Down Easy	United Artists 208
11/10/73	#89	3	I Just Can't Stop Loving You	United Artists 313
			DON CORNELL	
5/03/52	#3	11	I'll Walk Alone	Coral 60659
5/31/52	#2	14	I'm Yours	Coral 60690
12/13/52	#10	1	I	Coral 60860
1/09/54	#3	10	Heart Of My Heart*	Coral 61079
10/16/54	#6	10	Hold My Hand	Coral 61206
10/15/55	#10	2	The Bible Tells Me So	Coral 61467
4/13/57	#57	1	My Faith, My Hope, My Love	Coral 61811
5/11/57	#57	1	Mama Guitar	Coral 61819
11/01/58	#95	2	Play Some Music For Broken Hearts	Dot 15829
			***released as by DON CORNELL and JOHNNY and DALE DESMOND**	
			CORNERSTONE	
3/28/70	#92	3	Holly Go Softly	Liberty 56149
			CORSAIRS	
1/06/62	#12	15	Smoky Places*	Tuff 1808
4/21/62	#70	7	I'll Take You Home*	Tuff 1818
			***released as by THE CORSAIRS featuring the voice of JAY "BIRD" UZZELL**	
			DAVE "BABY" CORTEZ	
3/14/59	#1	18	The Happy Organ	Clock 1009
6/20/59	#57	6	The Whistling Organ	Clock 1012
10/31/59	#99	1	Piano Shuffle	Clock 1014
6/18/60	#75	9	Cat Nip	Clock 1024
7/14/62	#11	15	Rinky Dink	Chess 1829
8/13/62	#73	5	Happy Weekend	Chess 1834

Debut Date	Peak Pos	Wks Chr	ARTIST/Song Title	Label & Number
8/31/63	#87	3	Organ Shout	Chess 1861
5/21/66	#92	4	Count Down	Roulette 4679
			CORY	
1/22/77	#77	8	Fire Sign	Phantom 10856
			BILL COSBY	
9/02/67	#5	11	Little Ole Man (Uptight - Everything's Alright)	Warner Brothers 7072
12/02/67	#73	3	Hooray For The Salvation Army Band	Warner Brothers 7096
12/20/69	#92	2	Hikky Burr (Part 1)	Uni 55184
4/18/70	#70	5	Grover Henson Feels Forgotten	Uni 55223
5/15/76	#63	9	Yes, Yes, Yes	Capitol 4258
			DON COSTA	
11/07/59	#61	8	I Walk The Line	United Artists 190
5/07/60	#18	16	Theme From "The Unforgiven"	United Artists 221
7/30/60	#12	19	Never On Sunday	United Artists 234
2/11/61	#98	2	The Misfits	United Artists 286
			ELVIS COSTELLO	
3/11/78	#61	7	Watching The Detectives/	Columbia 10705
3/11/78	#61	7	Alison	Columbia 10705
8/27/83	#41	13	Everyday I Write The Book*	Columbia 04045
8/04/84	#59	10	The Only Flame In Town*	Columbia 04502
4/15/89	#20	20	Veronica	Warner Brothers 22981
			*released as by ELVIS COSTELLO & THE ATTRACTIONS	
			GENE COTTON	
11/16/74	#63	6	Sunshine Roses	Myrrh 137
5/17/75	#97	1	Damn It All	ABC 12087
12/04/76	#49	13	You've Got Me Runnin'	ABC 12227
1/21/78	#16	16	Before My Heart Finds Out	Ariola 7675
6/10/78	#35	13	You're A Part Of Me*	Ariola 7704
9/30/78	#37	11	Like A Sunday In Salem (The Amos & Andy Song)	Ariola 7723
10/10/81	#93	3	Bein' Here With You Tonight	Knoll 5001
3/27/82	#88	6	If I Could Get You (Into My Life)	Knoll 5002
			*released as by GENE COTTON with KIM CARNES	
			JOSIE COTTON	
8/21/82	#67	7	He Could Be The One	Elektra 47481
			COTTON, LLOYD and CHRISTIAN	
10/18/75	#95	2	I Go To Pieces	20th Century 2217
			COUCHOIS	
3/24/79	#83	5	Walkin' The Fence	Warner Brothers 8749
			JOHN COUGAR (see JOHN COUGAR MELLENCAMP)	
			COUNT FIVE	
9/10/66	#4	11	Psychotic Reaction	Double Shot 104
			COUNT VICTORS	
9/15/62	#91	6	Peepin' N' Hidin'	Coral 62324
			COUNTRY COALITION	
3/14/70	#80	4	Time To Get It Together	BluesWay 61034
			COUNTS	
3/11/72	#89	3	Why Not Start All Over Again	Westbound 191
			COUPLINGS	
2/15/58	#58	2	Young Dove's Calling	Josie 834
			LOU COURTNEY	
1/21/67	#81	3	Skate Now	Riverside 4588
4/22/67	#96	2	Do The Thing	Riverside 4589
			COURTSHIP	
5/27/72	#96	2	It's The Same Old Love	Tamla 54217
			COUSINS	
8/19/61	#98	2	St. Louis Blues	Parkway 823
			DON COVAY	
4/22/61	#20	2	Pony Time*	Arnold 1002
1/05/63	#67	8	The Popeye Waddle	Cameo 239
9/12/64	#26	10	Mercy, Mercy**	Rosemart 801
10/23/65	#48	11	See Saw**	Atlantic 2301
6/23/73	#28	12	I Was Checkin' Out, She Was Checkin' In	Mercury 73385

Debut Date	Peak Pos	Wks Chr	ARTIST/Song Title	Label & Number
			DON COVAY—*continued*	
7/20/74	#95	1	It's Better To Have (And Don't Need)	Mercury 73469
			***released as by THE GOODTIMERS**	
			****released as by DON COVAY & THE GOODTIMERS**	
			COVEN	
9/11/71	#18	15	One Tin Soldier, The Legend Of Billy Jack	Warner Brothers 7509
7/07/73	#68	7	One Tin Soldier (The Legend Of Billy Jack)	MGM 14308
1/05/74	#73	7	One Tin Soldier, The Legend Of Billy Jack	Warner Brothers 0101
			COVER GIRLS	
3/21/87	#45	14	Show Me	Fever 1911
12/12/87	#31	19	Because Of You	Fever 1914
4/02/88	#52	14	Promise Me	Fever 1917
7/23/88	#76	11	Inside Outside	Fever 1916
9/16/89	#49	14	My Heart Skips A Beat	Capitol 44436
12/09/89	#5	21	We Can't Go Wrong	Capitol 44498
4/14/90	#47	10	All That Glitters Isn't Gold	Capitol 44545
2/16/91	#62	10	Funk Boutique	Epic 73698
6/06/92	#2	24	Wishing On A Star	Epic 74343
9/05/92	#64	9	Thank You	Epic 74438
			COWBOY JUNKIES	
4/22/89	#87	6	Sweet Jane	RCA 8872
			COWSILLS	
9/30/67	#1	16	The Rain, The Park & Other Things	MGM 13810
1/13/68	#17	9	We Can Fly	MGM 13886
3/16/68	#50	6	In Need Of A Friend	MGM 13909
5/25/68	#6	13	Indian Lake	MGM 13944
9/07/68	#33	7	Poor Baby	MGM 13981
3/22/69	#1	14	Hair	MGM 14026
6/14/69	#56	4	The Prophecy Of Daniel And John The Divine (Six-Six-Six)	MGM 14063
10/04/69	#57	8	Silver Threads And Golden Needles	MGM 14084
			COYOTE SISTERS	
8/18/84	#72	8	Straight From The Heart	Morocco 1742
			CRABBY APPLETON	
5/02/70	#30	14	Go Back	Elektra 45687
			BILLY "CRASH" CRADDOCK	
10/17/59	#77	4	Don't Destroy Me	Columbia 41470
7/06/74	#22	12	Rub It In	ABC 12013
11/23/74	#50	8	Ruby Baby	ABC 12036
12/20/75	#52	6	Easy As Pie	ABC/Dot 17584
			FLOYD CRAMER	
10/15/60	#2	21	Last Date	RCA 7775
3/04/61	#7	15	On The Rebound	RCA 7840
6/17/61	#15	11	San Antonio Rose	RCA 7893
9/30/61	#66	6	Your Last Goodbye/	RCA 7907
9/30/61	#73	7	Hang On	RCA 7907
1/20/62	#45	9	Chattanooga Choo Choo	RCA 7978
7/07/62	#83	2	Hot Pepper	RCA 8051
12/29/62	#44	11	Java	RCA 8116
5/04/63	#100	1	(These Are) The Young Years	RCA 8171
			CRAMPTON SISTERS	
2/08/64	#87	3	I Didn't Know What Time It Was	DCP 1001
			CRANBERRIES	
11/06/93	#11	28	Linger	Island 862800
			LES CRANE	
10/16/71	#11	11	Desiderata	Warner Brothers 7520
			JOHNNY CRAWFORD	
6/24/61	#89	3	Daydreams	Del-Fi 4162
2/24/62	#40	10	Patti Ann	Del-Fi 4172
5/12/62	#13	14	Cindy's Birthday	Del-Fi 4178
8/04/62	#27	10	Your Nose Is Gonna Grow	Del-Fi 4181
11/03/62	#20	11	Rumors	Del-Fi 4188
12/29/62	#34	9	Proud	Del-Fi 4193
4/27/63	#100	1	Cry On My Shoulder	Del-Fi 4203
9/14/63	#91	4	Cindy's Gonna Cry	Del-Fi 4221

Debut Date	Peak Pos	Wks Chr	ARTIST/Song Title	Label & Number
			CRAWLER	
10/01/77	#62	15	Stone Cold Sober	Epic 50442
			ROBERT CRAY BAND	
2/21/87	#34	13	Smoking Gun	Mercury 888343
5/30/87	#82	5	Right Next Door (Because Of Me)	Mercury 888327
10/01/88	#85	5	Don't Be Afraid Of The Dark	Mercury 870569
			CRAZY ELEPHANT	
2/22/69	#6	15	Gimme Gimme Good Lovin'	Bell 763
7/05/69	#91	2	Sunshine Red Wine	Bell 804
			CRAZY WORLD OF ARTHUR BROWN	
9/07/68	#2	12	Fire	Atlantic 2556
11/30/68	#74	2	Nightmare/	Track 2582
12/07/68	#99	1	I Put A Spell On You	Track 2582
			CREAM	
1/06/68	#48	11	Sunshine Of Your Love	Atco 6544
5/25/68	#83	3	Anyone For Tennis	Atco 6575
7/06/68	#6	13	Sunshine Of Your Love	Atco 6544
9/28/68	#5	5	White Room	Atco 6617
1/25/69	#17	8	Crossroads	Atco 6646
4/05/69	#65	5	Badge	Atco 6668
			CREATIVE SOURCE	
3/16/74	#60	10	Who Is He And What Is He To You	Sussex 509
			CREEDENCE CLEARWATER REVIVAL	
9/21/68	#9	10	Suzie Q (Part 1)	Fantasy 616
11/23/68	#65	8	I Put A Spell On You	Fantasy 617
1/25/69	#2	13	Proud Mary	Fantasy 619
5/03/69	#2	13	Bad Moon Rising/	Fantasy 622
5/03/69	#58	3	Lodi	Fantasy 622
7/26/69	#3	14	Green River/	Fantasy 625
7/26/69	#40	7	Commotion	Fantasy 625
10/25/69	#6	11	Fortunate Son/	Fantasy 634
10/25/69	#10	14	Down On The Corner	Fantasy 634
1/24/70	#5	11	Travelin' Band/	Fantasy 637
1/24/70	#13	8	Who'll Stop The Rain	Fantasy 637
4/18/70	#2	12	Up Around The Bend/	Fantasy 641
4/18/70	#48	3	Run Through The Jungle	Fantasy 641
8/08/70	#1	12	Lookin' Out My Back Door/	Fantasy 645
8/08/70	#57	3	Long As I Can See The Light	Fantasy 645
1/30/71	#3	10	Have You Ever Seen The Rain	Fantasy 655
7/17/71	#5	10	Sweet Hitch Hiker	Fantasy 665
4/29/72	#25	9	Someday Never Comes	Fantasy 676
1/24/76	#47	8	I Heard It Through The Grapevine	Fantasy 759
			MARSHALL CRENSHAW	
7/10/82	#31	13	Someday, Someway	Warner Brothers 29974
			CRESCENDOS	
12/28/57	#6	17	Oh Julie	Nasco 6005
			CRESCENTS	
2/15/64	#89	2	Pink Dominoes	Era 3116
			CRESTS	
12/06/58	#3	18	16 Candles	Coed 506
3/28/59	#29	11	Six Nights A Week	Coed 509
6/20/59	#72	4	Flower Of Love	Coed 511
8/15/59	#15	15	The Angels Listened In	Coed 515
12/12/59	#41	10	A Year Ago Tonight	Coed 521
3/05/60	#13	16	Step By Step	Coed 525
6/25/60	#20	13	Trouble In Paradise	Coed 531
11/05/60	#89	4	Isn't It Amazing	Coed 537
			CRETONES	
5/17/80	#79	4	Real Love	Planet 45911
			CREW-CUTS	
7/17/54	#6	5	Crazy 'Bout You Baby	Mercury 70341
8/07/54	#1	15	Sh-Boom	Mercury 70404
2/19/55	#3	9	Earth Angel/	Mercury 70529
2/26/55	#3	9	Ko Ko Mo (I Love You So)	Mercury 70529
6/04/55	#9	2	Don't Be Angry	Mercury 70597
9/13/58	#82	3	Hey, Stella	RCA 7320

Debut Date	Peak Pos	Wks Chr	**ARTIST**/Song Title	Label & Number
			BOB CREWE GENERATION	
12/31/66	#9	11	Music To Watch Girls By	DynoVoice 229
3/13/76	#86	4	Street Talk*	20th Century 2271
			*released as by B.C.G.	
			CRICKETS (see BUDDY HOLLY)	
			CRITTERS	
5/14/66	#21	11	Younger Girl	Kapp 752
8/06/66	#14	12	Mr. Dieingly Sad	Kapp 769
11/26/66	#60	7	Bad Misunderstanding	Kapp 793
7/08/67	#47	10	Don't Let The Rain Fall Down On Me	Kapp 838
			JIM CROCE	
6/24/72	#7	15	You Don't Mess Around With Jim	ABC 11328
10/14/72	#7	15	Operator (That's Not The Way It Feels)	ABC 11335
2/03/73	#30	10	One Less Set Of Footsteps	ABC 11346
4/21/73	#1	22	Bad, Bad Leroy Brown	ABC 11359
9/29/73	#3	16	I Got A Name	ABC 11389
11/17/73	#1	14	Time In A Bottle	ABC 11405
1/05/74	#47	6	It Doesn't Have To Be	ABC 11413
3/02/74	#7	13	I'll Have To Say I Love You In A Song	ABC 11424
6/08/74	#20	10	Workin' At The Car Wash Blues	ABC 11447
1/10/76	#56	9	Chain Gang Medley	Lifesong 45001
			G.L. CROCKETT	
8/14/65	#73	4	It's A Man Down There	4 Brothers 445
			BING CROSBY	
3/25/50	#3	6	Chattanoogie Shoeshine Boy	Decca 24863
8/12/50	#3	15	Sam's Song*/	Decca 27112
8/19/50	#4	13	Play A Simple Melody*	Decca 27112
6/02/51	#7	4	When You And I Were Young Maggie Blues	Decca 27577
9/08/56	#4	26	True Love**	Capitol 3507
11/09/57	#50	3	Never Be Afraid	Kapp 195
12/30/61	#77	2	White Christmas	Decca 23778
12/15/62	#90	4	White Christmas	Decca 23778
2/21/63	#66	2	Do You Hear What I Hear?	Capitol 5088
			*released as by BING and GARY CROSBY	
			**released as by BING CROSBY and GRACE KELLY	
			CHRIS CROSBY	
2/15/64	#50	8	Young And In Love	MGM 13191
			DAVID CROSBY	
4/24/71	#96	1	Music Is Love	Atlantic 2792
5/06/72	#31	8	Immigration Man*	Atlantic 2873
11/08/75	#44	8	Carry Me*	ABC 12140
7/24/76	#77	5	Out Of The Darkness*	ABC 12199
4/24/93	#35	24	Hero**	Atlantic 87360
			*released as by GRAHAM NASH & DAVID CROSBY	
			**released as by DAVID CROSBY & PHIL COLLINS	
			CROSBY, STILLS & NASH	
7/12/69	#19	9	Marrakesh Express	Atlantic 2652
10/04/69	#15	12	Suite: Judy Blue Eyes	Atlantic 2676
3/21/70	#13	12	Woodstock*	Atlantic 2723
6/06/70	#16	11	Teach Your Children*	Atlantic 2735
6/20/70	#14	10	Ohio*	Atlantic 2740
9/19/70	#20	10	Our House*	Atlantic 2760
5/28/77	#8	20	Just A Song Before I Go	Atlantic 3401
10/08/77	#47	9	Fair Game	Atlantic 3432
6/26/82	#8	17	Wasted On The Way	Atlantic 4058
9/18/82	#18	19	Southern Cross	Atlantic 89969
2/05/83	#81	4	Too Much Love To Hide	Atlantic 89888
6/25/83	#53	10	War Games	Atlantic 89812
11/12/88	#59	11	American Dream*	Atlantic 89003
1/28/89	#58	10	Got It Made*	Atlantic 88966
			*released as by CROSBY, STILLS, NASH & YOUNG	
			CHRISTOPHER CROSS	
2/09/80	#3	23	Ride Like The Wind	Warner Brothers 49184
6/07/80	#1	24	Sailing	Warner Brothers 49507
10/11/80	#15	18	Never Be The Same	Warner Brothers 49580
3/28/81	#27	14	Say You'll Be Mine	Warner Brothers 49705
8/15/81	#1	25	Arthur's Theme (Best That You Can Do)	Warner Brothers 49787

Debut Date	Peak Pos	Wks Chr	ARTIST/Song Title	Label & Number
1/22/83	#9	14	All Right	Warner Brothers 29843
4/30/83	#43	11	No Time For Talk	Warner Brothers 29662
12/10/83	#6	18	Think Of Laura	Warner Brothers 29658
6/23/84	#79	6	A Chance For Heaven	Columbia 04492
10/26/85	#68	7	Charm The Snake	Warner Brothers 28864
			JIMMY CROSS	
1/23/65	#81	4	I Want My Baby Back	Tollie 9039
			CROSS COUNTRY	
8/11/73	#18	12	In The Midnight Hour	Atco 6934
			CROW	
10/25/69	#16	14	Evil Woman Don't Play Your Games With Me	Amaret 112
3/28/70	#94	3	Slow Down/	Amaret 119
5/23/70	#66	14	Cottage Cheese	Amaret 119
10/17/70	#40	9	Don't Try To Lay No Boogie Woogie On The "King Of Rock & Roll"	Amaret 125
			CROWDED HOUSE	
1/17/87	#3	26	Don't Dream It's Over	Capitol 5614
5/02/87	#8	21	Something So Strong	Capitol 5695
8/22/87	#70	8	World Where You Live	Capitol 44033
7/09/88	#56	11	Better Be Home Soon	Capitol 44164
			RODNEY CROWELL	
5/03/80	#36	15	Ashes By Now	Warner Brothers 49224
			CROWN HEIGHTS AFFAIR	
8/09/75	#46	13	Dreaming A Dream	De-Lite 1570
1/03/76	#97	2	Every Beat Of My Heart	De-Lite 1575
6/05/76	#64	9	Foxy Lady	De-Lite 1581
4/09/77	#65	6	Dancin'	De-Lite 1588
			CRUSADERS	
12/19/70	#73	6	Way Back Home*	Chisa 8010
5/13/72	#40	10	Put It Where You Want It	Blue Thumb 208
6/02/73	#90	3	Don't Let It Get You Down	Blue Thumb 225
5/11/74	#77	6	Scratch	Blue Thumb 249
8/18/79	#29	17	Street Life	MCA 41054
			***released as by THE JAZZ CRUSADERS**	
			CRYAN' SHAMES	
8/06/66	#52	7	Sugar And Spice	Destination 624
10/29/66	#65	9	I Wanna Meet You	Columbia 43836
7/29/67	#70	11	It Could Be We're In Love	Columbia 44191
3/16/68	#70	6	Up On The Roof	Columbia 44457
6/22/68	#86	2	Young Birds Fly	Columbia 44545
10/05/68	#73	4	Greenberg, Glickstein, Charles, David Smith & Jones . . .	Columbia 44638
			BILLY CRYSTAL	
7/27/85	#60	12	You Look Marvelous	A&M 2764
			CRYSTAL MANSION	
12/28/68	#94	3	The Thought Of Loving You	Capitol 2275
10/17/70	#61	9	Carolina In My Mind	Colossus 128
			CRYSTALS	
11/04/61	#19	14	There's No Other Like My Baby	Philles 100
3/31/62	#10	14	Uptown	Philles 102
9/15/62	#2	18	He's A Rebel	Philles 106
1/05/63	#14	12	He's Sure The Boy I Love	Philles 109
4/20/63	#4	15	Da Doo Ron Ron (Then He Walked Me Home) . . .	Philles 112
8/17/63	#6	13	Then He Kissed Me	Philles 115
1/25/64	#94	4	Little Boy	Philles 119
7/11/64	#85	3	All Grown Up	Philles 122
			JOE CUBA SEXTET	
7/30/66	#98	2	El Pito	Tico 470
10/22/66	#60	8	Bang Bang	Tico 475
12/31/66	#91	3	Oh Yeah!	Tico 490
			CHRIS CUEVAS	
2/01/92	#47	16	You Are The One	Atlantic 87563
			CUFF LINKS	
8/30/69	#5	15	Tracy	Decca 32533
11/29/69	#31	11	When Julie Comes Around	Decca 32592
2/28/70	#40	7	Run Sally Run	Decca 32639

Debut Date	Peak Pos	Wks Chr	**ARTIST**/Song Title	Label & Number
			CULT	
5/20/89	#48	14	Fire Woman	Sire 27543
			CULTURE BEAT	
11/27/93	#15	21	Mr. Vain	550 Music 77214
			CULTURE CLUB	
12/04/82	#1	30	Do You Really Want To Hurt Me	Epic 03368
4/16/83	#3	20	Time (Clock Of The Heart)	Epic 03796
7/02/83	#8	18	I'll Tumble 4 Ya	Epic 03912
10/22/83	#10	17	Church Of The Poison Mind	Epic 04144
12/03/83	#1	24	Karma Chameleon	Virgin 04221
3/03/84	#5	18	Miss Me Blind	Virgin 04388
5/12/84	#15	13	It's A Miracle	Virgin 04457
10/06/84	#14	15	The War Song	Virgin 04638
12/15/84	#43	13	Mistake No. 3	Virgin 04727
4/05/86	#14	15	Move Away	Virgin 05847
			BURTON CUMMINGS	
10/02/76	#5	22	Stand Tall	Portrait 70001
2/26/77	#90	3	I'm Scared	Portrait 70002
7/08/78	#82	4	Break It To Them Gently	Portrait 70016
9/12/81	#32	15	You Saved My Soul	Alfa 7008
			RICK CUNHA	
4/20/74	#47	9	(I'm A) Yo Yo Man	GRC 2016
			GINO CUNICO	
12/20/75	#91	4	Fanny	Arista 0162
			CUPIDS	
6/22/63	#45	9	Brenda	KC 115
			MIKE CURB CONGREGATION	
12/12/70	#34	16	Burning Bridges	MGM 14151
9/01/73	#79	6	It's A Small, Small World	MGM 14494
			CURE	
6/27/87	#47	11	Why Can't I Be You?	Elektra 69474
10/17/87	#42	18	Just Like Heaven	Elektra 69443
3/19/88	#82	4	Hot Hot Hot!!!	Elektra 69424
5/27/89	#74	7	Fascination Street	Elektra 69300
8/05/89	#2	25	Love Song	Elektra 69280
11/25/89	#57	10	Lullaby	Elektra 69249
4/28/90	#67	7	Pictures Of You	Elektra 64974
11/10/90	#72	6	Never Enough	Elektra 64928
12/22/90	#64	11	Close To Me	Elektra 64911
4/11/92	#33	14	High	Fiction 64666
6/13/92	#18	19	Friday I'm In Love	Fiction 64742
			CURIOSITY KILLED THE CAT	
8/01/87	#47	14	Misfit	Mercury 888674
			CHERIE & MARIE CURRIE	
10/13/79	#91	4	Since You've Been Gone	Capitol 4754
			CLIFFORD CURRY	
5/06/67	#99	1	She Shot A Hole In My Soul	Elf 90002
			TIM CURRY	
11/24/79	#85	3	I Do The Rock	A&M 2166
			CURTIE and THE BOOMBOX	
7/27/85	#81	5	Black Kisses (Never Make You Bluc)	RCA 14103
			BOBBY CURTOLA	
5/26/62	#52	10	Fortune Teller	Del-Fi 4177
11/03/62	#93	2	Aladdin	Del-Fi 4185
			CUTTING CREW	
3/07/87	#1	21	(I Just) Died In Your Arms	Virgin 99481
6/06/87	#32	12	One For The Mockingbird	Virgin 99464
9/05/87	#11	23	I've Been In Love Before	Virgin 99425
5/13/89	#75	7	(Between A) Rock And A Hard Place	Virgin 99215
			CYMANDE	
1/06/73	#39	10	The Message	Janus 203
6/02/73	#93	2	Bra	Janus 215

Debut Date	Peak Pos	Wks Chr	ARTIST/Song Title	Label & Number
			CYMARRON	
6/05/71	#17	14	Rings	Entrance 7500
10/09/71	#98	2	Valerie	Entrance 7502
			JOHNNY CYMBAL	
2/16/63	#17	13	Mr. Bass Man	Kapp 503
5/11/63	#59	5	Teenage Heaven	Kapp 524
7/27/63	#81	6	Dum Dum Dee Dum	Kapp 539
			CYPRESS HILL	
7/17/93	#23	29	Insane In The Brain	Ruffhouse 77135
			CYRKLE	
5/21/66	#3	14	Red Rubber Ball	Columbia 43589
8/13/66	#18	9	Turn Down Day	Columbia 43729
11/26/66	#52	5	Please Don't Ever Leave Me	Columbia 43871
1/14/67	#57	7	I Wish You Could Be Here	Columbia 43965
5/13/67	#65	9	We Had A Good Thing Goin'	Columbia 44108
8/05/67	#61	5	Penny Arcade	Columbia 44224
			BILLY RAY CYRUS	
5/16/92	#4	29	Achy Breaky Heart	Mercury 866522
10/17/92	#70	6	Could've Been Me	Mercury 866988

D

Debut Date	Peak Pos	Wks Chr	ARTIST/Song Title	Label & Number
			DADDY DEWDROP	
3/06/71	#5	16	Chick-A-Boom (Don't Ya Jes' Love It)	Sunflower 105
7/17/71	#87	3	Fox Huntin'	Sunflower 111
2/10/79	#95	3	Nanu, Nanu (I Wanna Get Funky Wich You)	Inphasion 7201
			DADDY-O'S	
6/21/58	#31	6	Got A Match	Cabot 122
			STEVE DAHL and TEENAGE RADIATION	
9/15/79	#61	9	Do You Think I'm Disco	Ovation 1132
			PATTI DAHLSTROM	
10/12/74	#100	1	He Did Me Wrong	20th Century 2113
			E.G. DAILY	
5/10/86	#86	4	Say It, Say It	A&M 2825
			ALAN DALE	
7/23/55	#7	6	Sweet And Gentle	Coral 61435
			DICK DALE and THE DEL-TONES	
12/02/61	#70	9	Let's Go Trippin'	Deltone 5017
1/12/63	#91	5	Peppermint Man	Deltone 5020
10/26/63	#94	2	The Scavenger	Capitol 5048
			DALE & GRACE	
10/05/63	#1	17	I'm Leaving It Up To You	Montel 921
2/01/64	#8	9	Stop And Think It Over	Montel 922
5/09/64	#83	6	The Loneliest Night	Montel 928
7/18/64	#91	1	What's Happening To Me/	Montel 930
7/25/64	#91	3	Darling It's Wonderful	Montel 930
			TONY DALLARA	
11/15/58	#24	12	Come Prima	Mercury 71327
			KATHY DALTON	
8/24/74	#61	8	Boogie Bands And One Night Stands	DiscReet 1210
			ROGER DALTRY	
5/26/73	#60	9	Giving It All Away	Track 40053
9/13/75	#63	8	Come And Get Your Love	MCA 40453
10/01/77	#87	6	Avenging Annie	MCA 40800
7/05/80	#44	11	Free Me	Polydor 2105
9/20/80	#23	19	Without Your Love	Polydor 2121
3/03/84	#73	6	Walking In My Sleep	Atlantic 89704
9/21/85	#59	11	After The Fire	Atlantic 89491
			MICHAEL DAMIAN	
6/13/81	#95	4	She Did It	LEG 007
3/25/89	#1	21	Rock On	Cypress 1420
6/24/89	#30	16	Cover Of Love	Cypress 1430
11/25/89	#23	17	Was It Nothing At All	Cypress 1451
6/08/91	#57	14	What A Price To Pay	A&M 1559

Debut Date	Peak Pos	Wks Chr	ARTIST/Song Title	Label & Number
			JOE DAMIANO	
9/12/59	#90	2	I Cried	Chancellor 1039
			DAMNATION OF ADAM BLESSING	
12/19/70	#85	5	Back To The River	United Artists 50726
			DAMN YANKEES	
4/28/90	#50	9	Coming Of Age	Warner Brothers 19838
9/22/90	#2	29	High Enough	Warner Brothers 19570
4/13/91	#41	14	Come Again	Warner Brothers 19408
10/10/92	#14	23	Where You Goin' Now	Warner Brothers 18728
4/17/93	#46	12	Silence Is Broken	Warner Brothers 18612
			LIZ DAMON'S ORIENT EXPRESS	
12/19/70	#29	11	1900 Yesterday	White Whale 368
			VIC DAMONE	
7/07/51	#3	14	My Truly, Truly Fair	Mercury 5646
7/07/56	#5	11	On The Street Where You Live	Columbia 40654
7/20/57	#25	16	An Affair To Remember (Our Love Affair)	Columbia 40945
3/08/58	#48	4	Gigi	Columbia 41122
5/01/65	#28	9	You Were Only Fooling (While I Was Falling In Love) . . .	Warner Brothers 5616
7/10/65	#90	3	Why Don't You Believe Me	Warner Brothers 5644
			VIC DANA	
12/02/61	#42	9	Little Altar Boy	Dolton 48
3/24/62	#42	10	I Will	Dolton 51
5/18/63	#76	5	Danger	Dolton 73
9/14/63	#18	7	More	Dolton 81
4/18/64	#9	10	Shangri-La	Dolton 92
6/27/64	#63	6	Love Is All We Need	Dolton 95
10/10/64	#90	2	Garden In The Rain	Dolton 99
2/13/65	#11	11	Red Roses For A Blue Lady	Dolton 304
5/29/65	#68	6	Bring A Little Sunshine	Dolton 305
8/07/65	#54	8	Moonlight And Roses	Dolton 309
11/27/65	#53	8	Crystal Chandelier	Dolton 313
4/30/66	#42	9	I Love You Drops	Dolton 319
7/23/66	#69	4	A Million And One	Dolton 322
10/29/66	#92	2	Distant Drums	Dolton 324
1/17/70	#39	11	If I Never Knew Your Name	Liberty 56150
5/16/70	#94	2	Red Red Wine	Liberty 56163
			DANCER, PRANCER & NERVOUS	
12/05/59	#31	6	The Happy Reindeer	Capitol 4300
			DANGER DANGER	
6/09/90	#47	13	Bang Bang	Epic 73380
			RODNEY DANGERFIELD	
12/10/83	#59	10	Rappin' Rodney	RCA 13656
			CHARLIE DANIELS BAND	
6/02/73	#10	16	Uneasy Rider*	Kama Sutra 576
1/18/75	#26	12	The South's Gonna Do It Again	Kama Sutra 598
5/10/75	#50	7	Long Haired Country Boy	Kama Sutra 601
11/29/75	#79	3	Birmingham Blues	Kama Sutra 606
2/21/76	#92	3	Texas	Kama Sutra 607
6/23/79	#4	20	The Devil Went Down To Georgia	Epic 50700
5/31/80	#10	17	In America	Epic 50888
8/23/80	#31	15	The Legend Of Wooley Swamp	Epic 50921
3/27/82	#24	14	Still In Saigon	Epic 02828
			*released as by CHARLIE DANIELS	
			JOHNNY DANKWORTH	
4/15/61	#41	7	African Waltz	Roulette 4353
			DANLEERS	
5/31/58	#9	19	One Summer Night	Mercury 71322
10/04/58	#58	5	I Really Love You	Mercury 71356
			DANNY & THE JUNIORS	
11/30/57	#1	18	At The Hop	ABC Paramount 9871
2/22/58	#22	9	Rock And Roll Is Here To Stay	ABC Paramount 9888
6/14/58	#56	5	Dottie	ABC Paramount 9926
9/24/60	#47	10	Twistin' U.S.A.	Swan 4060
3/04/61	#55	7	Pony Express	Swan 4068
9/16/61	#84	9	Back At The Hop	Swan 4082
1/19/63	#83	2	Oo-La-La-Limbo	Guyden 2076

Debut Date	Peak Pos	Wks Chr	ARTIST/Song Title	Label & Number
			DANNY WILSON	
6/13/87	#26	19	Mary's Prayer	Virgin 99465
			RON DANTE	
3/01/75	#94	2	Midnight Show	Arista 0111
			DANTE and THE EVERGREENS	
6/04/60	#1	15	Alley-Oop	Madison 130
9/17/60	#81	7	Time Machine	Madison 135
			TERENCE TRENT D'ARBY	
10/31/87	#77	8	If You Let Me Stay	Columbia 07398
1/16/88	#1	28	Wishing Well	Columbia 07675
5/28/88	#3	21	Sign Your Name	Columbia 07911
9/10/88	#28	12	Dance Little Sister (Part 1)	Columbia 08023
1/27/90	#80	5	To Know Someone Deeply Is To Love Someone Softly . . .	Columbia 73217
9/04/93	#65	8	Delicate	Columbia 77128
			JOE DARENSBOURG and HIS DIXIE FLYERS	
1/18/58	#30	8	Yellow Dog Blues	Lark 452
			FRED DARIEN	
8/05/61	#79	6	Johnny Willow	JAF 2023
			BOBBY DARIN	
6/21/58	#2	15	Splish Splash	Atco 6117
7/26/58	#25	10	Early In The Morning*	Atco 6121
10/04/58	#12	18	Queen Of The Hop	Atco 6127
1/31/59	#30	10	Plain Jane	Atco 6133
4/18/59	#3	17	Dream Lover	Atco 6140
8/29/59	#1	15	Mack The Knife	Atco 6147
1/23/60	#7	13	Beyond The Sea	Atco 6158
3/26/60	#13	9	Clementine	Atco 6161
5/28/60	#16	11	Won't You Come Home Bill Bailey	Atco 6167
9/03/60	#50	7	Beachcomber	Atco 6173
10/08/60	#19	12	Artificial Flowers/	Atco 6179
10/08/60	#58	8	Somebody To Love	Atco 6179
12/03/60	#95	2	Child Of God/	Atco 6183
12/24/60	#50	3	Christmas Auld Lang Syne	Atco 6183
2/11/61	#18	11	Lazy River	Atco 6188
6/10/61	#31	9	Nature Boy	Atco 6196
9/02/61	#7	12	You Must Have Been A Beautiful Baby	Atco 6206
10/28/61	#55	5	Theme From Come September	Atco 6200
12/23/61	#16	11	Irresistable You/	Atco 6214
12/23/61	#26	12	Multiplication	Atco 6214
3/31/62	#26	8	What'd I Say (Part 1)	Atco 6221
7/07/62	#10	12	Things	Atco 6229
9/29/62	#28	7	If A Man Answers	Capitol 4837
9/29/62	#38	6	Baby Face	Atco 6236
1/19/63	#5	15	You're The Reason I'm Living	Capitol 4897
5/11/63	#12	11	18 Yellow Roses	Capitol 4970
8/24/63	#38	8	Treat My Baby Good	Capitol 5019
11/30/63	#74	6	Be Mad Little Girl	Capitol 5079
2/29/64	#83	4	I Wonder Who's Kissing Her Now	Capitol 5126
5/16/64	#39	9	Milord	Atco 6297
9/19/64	#89	2	The Things In This House	Capitol 5257
4/10/65	#94	3	Venice Blue	Capitol 5399
4/30/66	#63	6	Mame	Atlantic 2329
9/24/66	#9	11	If I Were A Carpenter	Atlantic 2350
12/10/66	#65	4	The Girl That Stood Beside Me	Atlantic 2367
1/21/67	#43	7	Lovin' You	Atlantic 2376
4/08/67	#73	4	The Lady Came From Baltimore	Atlantic 2395
1/04/69	#66	7	Long Line Rider	Direction 350
12/23/72	#59	11	Happy	Motown 1217
			*released as by THE RINKY-DINKS	
			FLORRAINE DARLIN	
9/01/62	#73	4	Long As The Rose Is Red	Epic 9529
			JAMES DARREN	
5/02/59	#32	10	Gidget	Colpix 113
7/18/59	#43	10	Angel Face	Colpix 119
10/28/61	#2	16	Goodbye Cruel World	Colpix 609
2/03/62	#9	11	Her Royal Majesty	Colpix 622
4/14/62	#24	11	Conscience	Colpix 630

Debut Date	Peak Pos	Wks Chr	ARTIST/Song Title	Label & Number
			JAMES DARREN—*continued*	
7/07/62	#52	6	Mary's Little Lamb	Colpix 644
2/09/63	#51	6	Pin A Medal On Joey	Colpix 672
1/21/67	#38	7	All	Warner Brothers 5874
10/16/71	#77	5	Mammy Blue	Kirshner 5015
4/09/77	#95	3	You Take My Heart Away	Private Stock 45136
			DARTELLS	
4/13/63	#13	11	Hot Pastrami	Dot 16453
			DAS EFX	
8/14/93	#13	18	Check Yo Self*	Priority 53830
11/27/93	#38	16	Freakit	East West 98341
			***released as by ICE CUBE featuring DAS EFX**	
			SARAH DASH	
2/17/79	#72	5	Sinner Man	Kirshner 4278
			F.R. DAVID	
8/06/83	#59	7	Words	Carrere 101
			DAVID & DAVID	
9/27/86	#41	18	Welcome To The Boomtown	A&M 2857
1/31/87	#56	10	Ain't So Easy	A&M 2905
			DAVID & JONATHAN	
1/15/66	#18	9	Michelle	Capitol 5563
			HUTCH DAVIE and HIS HONKY TONKERS	
6/21/58	#53	4	Woodchopper's Ball	Atco 6110
			DANNY DAVIS	
11/15/58	#90	3	Trumpet Cha Cha	Cabot 126
			JIMMY DAVIS & JUNCTION	
11/07/87	#79	7	Kick The Wall	QMI Music 53107
			MAC DAVIS	
5/02/70	#69	8	Whoever Finds This, I Love You	Columbia 45117
7/01/72	#1	19	Baby Don't Get Hooked On Me	Columbia 45618
11/18/72	#41	8	Everybody Loves A Love Song	Columbia 45727
2/10/73	#66	5	Dream Me A Home	Columbia 45773
4/28/73	#83	5	Your Side Of The Bed	Columbia 45839
3/30/74	#14	20	One Hell Of A Woman	Columbia 46004
8/17/74	#7	15	Stop And Smell The Roses	Columbia 10018
12/07/74	#16	11	Rock N' Roll (I Gave You The Best Years Of My Life)	Columbia 10070
3/22/75	#62	6	(If You Add) All The Love In The World	Columbia 10111
6/07/75	#52	7	Burnin' Thing	Columbia 10148
3/29/80	#35	13	It's Hard To Be Humble	Casablanca 2244
10/18/80	#55	10	Texas In My Rearview Mirror	Casablanca 2305
8/01/81	#88	4	Secrets	Casablanca 2336
			PAUL DAVIS	
6/06/70	#56	8	A Little Bit Of Soap	Bang 576
9/05/70	#42	10	I Just Wanna Keep It Together	Bang 579
1/13/73	#79	4	Boogie Woogie Man	Bang 599
10/05/74	#27	17	Ride 'Em Cowboy	Bang 712
7/12/75	#90	3	Keep Our Love Alive	Bang 718
4/17/76	#75	9	Thinking Of You	Bang 724
8/07/76	#41	9	Superstar	Bang 726
8/27/77	#7	36	I Go Crazy	Bang 733
5/13/78	#45	9	Darlin'	Bang 736
8/12/78	#15	24	Sweet Life	Bang 738
3/08/80	#23	15	Do Right	Bang 4808
11/07/81	#16	21	Cool Night	Arista 0645
2/27/82	#10	19	'65 Love Affair	Arista 0661
7/17/82	#41	12	Love Or Let Me Be Lonely	Arista 0697
			SAMMY DAVIS JR.	
9/04/54	#1	5	Hey There	Decca 29199
8/18/56	#31	12	Earthbound	Decca 30035
8/25/62	#14	18	What Kind Of Fool Am I	Reprise 20048
12/08/62	#79	5	Me And My Shadow*	Reprise 20128
1/26/63	#73	8	As Long As She Needs Me	Reprise 20138
12/14/63	#19	18	The Shelter Of Your Arms	Reprise 20216
6/03/67	#79	9	Don't Blame The Children	Reprise 0566
12/07/68	#14	17	I've Gotta Be Me	Reprise 0779
3/18/72	#1	20	Candy Man	MGM 14320

Debut Date	Peak Pos	Wks Chr	ARTIST/Song Title	Label & Number
10/28/72	#87	4	The People Tree	MGM 14426
			released as by FRANK SINATRA and SAMY DAVIS JR.	
			SKEETER DAVIS	
8/27/60	#35	7	(I Can't Help You) I'm Falling Too	RCA 7767
12/24/60	#54	7	My Last Date	RCA 7825
1/19/63	#2	18	The End Of The World	RCA 8098
5/04/63	#39	7	I'm Saving My Love	RCA 8176
9/07/63	#6	15	I Can't Stay Mad At You	RCA 8219
1/11/64	#58	8	He Says The Same Things To Me	RCA 8288
4/18/64	#35	10	Gonna Get Along Without You Now	RCA 8357
			SPENCER DAVIS GROUP	
2/26/66	#94	4	Keep On Running	Atco 6400
1/07/67	#5	11	Gimme Some Lovin'	United Artists 50108
3/25/67	#10	10	I'm A Man	United Artists 50144
6/24/67	#46	6	Somebody Help Me	United Artists 50162
9/23/67	#98	2	Time Seller	United Artists 50202
			TIM DAVIS	
9/02/72	#80	5	Buzzy Brown	Metromedia 253
			TYRONE DAVIS	
12/28/68	#5	12	Can I Change My Mind	Dakar 602
3/22/69	#22	8	Is It Something You've Got	Dakar 605
8/02/69	#91	2	All The Waiting Is Not In Vain	Dakar 609
3/07/70	#4	15	Turn Back The Hands Of Time	Dakar 616
6/20/70	#33	10	I'll Be Right Here	Dakar 618
9/26/70	#53	7	Let Me Back In	Dakar 621
3/06/71	#58	9	Could I Forget You	Dakar 623
6/26/71	#68	8	One-Way Ticket	Dakar 624
10/09/71	#80	5	You Keep Me Holding On	Dakar 626
3/25/72	#54	6	I Had It All The Time	Dakar 4501
4/14/73	#51	10	Without You In My Life	Dakar 4519
8/04/73	#39	8	There It Is	Dakar 4523
10/20/73	#84	4	Wrapped Up In Your Warm And Tender Love	Dakar 4526
2/09/74	#78	8	I Wish It Was Me	Dakar 4529
1/17/76	#78	6	Turning Point	Dakar 4550
8/28/76	#36	17	Give It Up (Turn It Loose)	Columbia 10388
6/25/77	#88	7	This I Swear	Columbia 10528
			DAWN	
8/01/70	#1	16	Candida	Bell 903
11/14/70	#1	17	Knock Three Times	Bell 938
3/20/71	#22	8	I Play And Sing	Bell 970
6/12/71	#19	10	Summer Sand	Bell 45107
9/25/71	#26	11	What Are You Doing Sunday*	Bell 45141
6/17/72	#60	6	Vaya Con Dios*	Bell 45225
11/11/72	#68	9	You're A Lady*	Bell 45285
2/03/73	#1	23	Tie A Yellow Ribbon Round The Old Oak Tree*	Bell 45318
7/14/73	#4	15	Say, Has Anybody Seen My Sweet Gypsy Rose*	Bell 45374
11/10/73	#13	11	Who's In The Strawberry Patch With Sally**	Bell 45424
3/30/74	#56	7	It Only Hurts When I Try To Smile**	Bell 45450
8/17/74	#14	14	Steppin' Out (Gonna Boogie Tonight)**	Bell 45601
12/14/74	#20	12	Look In My Eyes Pretty Woman**	Bell 45620
3/08/75	#1	14	He Don't Love You (Like I Love You)**	Elektra 45240
6/21/75	#15	10	Mornin' Beautiful**	Elektra 45260
8/30/75	#38	6	You're All I Need To Get By**	Elektra 45275
10/18/75	#52	8	Skybird**	Arista 0156
2/07/76	#21	12	Cupid**	Elektra 45302
5/15/76	#93	3	Midnight Love Affair**	Elektra 45319
3/12/77	#62	6	Sing**	Elektra 45387
			released as by DAWN featuring TONY ORLANDO **released as by TONY ORLANDO & DAWN*	
			ARLAN DAY	
10/10/81	#61	8	I Surrender	Pasha 02480
			BING DAY	
6/06/59	#98	2	Mama's Place	Mercury 71446
			BOBBY DAY	
10/19/57	#9	14	Little Bitty Pretty One*	Class 211
7/26/58	#4	23	Rock-In Robin/	Class 229
8/30/58	#51	7	Over And Over	Class 229

Debut Date	Peak Pos	Wks Chr	ARTIST/Song Title	Label & Number
			BOBBY DAY—*continued*	
12/20/58	#87	3	The Bluebird, The Buzzard & The Oriole	Class 241
6/06/59	#79	5	Gotta New Girl	Class 252
1/23/60	#86	2	My Blue Heaven	Class 263
12/03/60	#37	5	Gee Whiz	Rendezvous 136
			***released as by BOBBY DAY and THE SATELLITES**	
			DORIS DAY	
8/25/51	#7	4	Shanghai	Columbia 39423
4/19/52	#1	11	A Guy Is A Guy	Columbia 39673
2/13/54	#1	13	Secret Love	Columbia 40108
10/02/54	#1	14	If I Give My Heart To You	Columbia 40300
8/04/56	#3	18	Whatever Will Be, Will Be (Que Sera, Sera)	Columbia 40704
10/20/56	#40	3	Julie	Columbia 40758
2/02/57	#47	1	Party's Over	Columbia 40798
4/05/58	#36	5	Teacher's Pet	Columbia 41123
7/12/58	#6	18	Everybody Loves A Lover	Columbia 41195
10/25/58	#53	9	Tunnel Of Love	Columbia 41252
4/11/59	#51	7	Leave Me In The Daytime	Columbia 41354
			MORRIS DAY	
10/12/85	#66	8	The Old Oak Tree	Warner Brothers 28899
2/20/88	#41	13	Fishnet	Warner Brothers 28201
			DAYBREAK	
6/20/70	#83	4	Good Morning Freedom	Uni 55234
			TAYLOR DAYNE	
10/17/87	#9	25	Tell It To My Heart	Arista 9612
2/20/88	#7	18	Prove Your Love	Arista 9676
6/11/88	#4	24	I'll Always Love You	Arista 9700
11/05/88	#1	21	Don't Rush Me	Arista 9722
10/21/89	#5	21	With Every Beat Of My Heart	Arista 9895
1/27/90	#1	21	Love Will Lead You Back	Arista 9938
5/05/90	#5	21	I'll Be Your Shelter	Arista 2005
8/04/90	#10	16	Heart Of Stone	Arista 2057
6/12/93	#14	20	Can't Get Enough Of Your Love	Arista 2582
10/09/93	#44	17	Send Me A Lover	Arista 2603
			DAYTON	
7/24/82	#75	5	Hot Fun In The Summertime	Liberty 1468
			DAZZ BAND	
5/01/82	#13	22	Let It Whip	Motown 1609
2/11/84	#59	11	Joystick	Motown 1701
			DEADLY NIGHTSHADE	
7/03/76	#65	9	Mary Hartman, Mary Hartman	Phantom 10709
			DEAD OR ALIVE	
6/01/85	#13	20	You Spin Me Around (Like A Record)	Epic 04894
9/21/85	#72	5	Love Come Back To Me	Epic 05607
12/20/86	#17	20	Brand New Lover	Epic 06374
5/09/87	#85	4	Something In My House	Epic 07022
7/08/89	#64	7	Come Home With Me Baby	Epic 68885
			BILL DEAL & THE RHONDELS	
12/28/68	#35	13	May I	Heritage 803
4/19/69	#29	10	I've Been Hurt	Heritage 812
8/09/69	#22	11	What Kind Of Fool Do You Think I Am	Heritage 817
11/08/69	#52	6	Swingin' Tight	Heritage 818
3/14/70	#62	7	Nothing Succeeds Like Success	Heritage 821
8/19/72	#100	1	It's Too Late	Buddah 318
			JIMMY DEAN	
10/05/57	#57	4	Deep Blue Sea	Columbia 40995
6/06/59	#59	10	Sing Along	Columbia 41395
10/07/61	#1	18	Big Bad John	Columbia 42175
1/06/62	#21	8	Dear Ivan	Columbia 42259
1/20/62	#58	8	To A Sleeping Beauty/	Columbia 42282
1/27/62	#23	9	The Cajun Queen	Columbia 42282
3/31/62	#7	12	P.T. 109	Columbia 42338
6/16/62	#59	8	Steel Men	Columbia 42483
9/08/62	#31	11	Little Black Book	Columbia 42529
5/15/76	#33	5	I.O.U.	Casino 052

Debut Date	Peak Pos	Wks Chr	ARTIST/Song Title	Label & Number
			TERRI DEAN	
5/30/59	#89	3	I'm Confessin'	Laurel 1003
8/22/59	#79	3	Adonis	Laurie 3032
			DEAN and JEAN	
11/16/63	#36	12	Tra La La La Suzy	Rust 5067
3/07/64	#62	6	Hey Jean, Hey Dean	Rust 5075
6/06/64	#89	3	I Wanna Be Loved	Rust 5081
			DEARDORFF & JOSEPH	
4/16/77	#99	2	Never Have To Say Goodbye Again	Arista 0230
			DEARLY BELOVEDS	
10/29/66	#98	1	Peep Peep Pop Pop	Columbia 43797
			DeBARGE	
2/05/83	#24	17	I Like It	Gordy 1645
4/16/83	#9	21	All This Love	Gordy 1660
10/22/83	#22	22	Time Will Reveal	Gordy 1705
3/24/84	#50	11	Love Me In A Special Way	Gordy 1723
2/16/85	#3	23	Rhythm Of The Night	Gordy 1770
6/01/85	#12	18	Who's Holding Donna Now	Gordy 1793
			CHICO DeBARGE	
11/22/86	#22	20	Talk To Me	Motown 1858
			EL DeBARGE	
8/31/85	#47	11	You Wear It Well*	Gordy 1804
12/14/85	#73	8	The Heart Is Not So Smart*	Gordy 1822
4/26/86	#7	18	Who's Johnny	Gordy 1842
8/09/86	#48	11	Love Always	Gordy 1857
3/17/90	#30	12	The Secret Garden**	Qwest 19992
			*released as EL DeBARGE with DeBARGE	
			**released as by QUINCY JONES/AL B. SURE!/JAMES INGRAM/EL DeBARGE/ BARRY WHITE	
			DEB-TONES	
6/21/58	#73	3	Cuddly Baby	RCA 7472
			CHRIS DeBURGH	
4/30/83	#32	16	Don't Pay The Ferryman	A&M 2511
8/20/83	#81	6	Ship To Shore	A&M 2565
7/07/84	#44	14	High On Emotion	A&M 2643
2/21/87	#2	24	The Lady In Red	A&M 2848
			NICK DeCARO	
12/21/68	#71	5	If I Only Had Time	A&M 1000
			DeCASTRO SISTERS	
11/20/54	#2	13	Teach Me Tonight	Abbott 3001
12/20/58	#84	6	Teach Me Tonight Cha Cha	ABC Paramount 9988
			DECEMBER'S CHILDREN	
6/01/68	#80	2	Backwards And Forwards	World Pacific 77887
			DAVE DEE, DOZY, BEAKY, MICK and TICH	
1/07/67	#100	1	Bend It	Fontana 1559
12/30/67	#46	7	Zabadak	Imperial 66270
			JIMMY DEE and THE OFFBEATS	
1/25/58	#49	2	Henrietta	Dot 15664
			JOEY DEE & THE STARLITERS	
11/18/61	#2	20	Peppermint Twist (Part 1)	Roulette 4401
2/10/62	#37	8	Hey, Let's Twist/	Roulette 4408
2/24/62	#100	1	Roly Poly	Roulette 4408
3/24/62	#9	12	Shout (Part 1)	Roulette 4416
6/16/62	#80	3	Everytime	Roulette 4431
8/18/62	#17	12	What Kind Of Love Is This	Roulette 4438
11/10/62	#61	6	I Lost My Baby*	Roulette 4456
4/20/63	#40	9	Hot Pastrami With Mashed Potatoes (Part 1)	Roulette 4488
7/13/63	#90	3	Dance, Dance, Dance*	Roulette 4503
			*released as by JOEY DEE	
			JOHNNY DEE (see also JOHN D. LOUDERMILK)	
3/09/57	#15	11	Sittin' In The Balcony	Colonial 430
			KIKI DEE	
4/03/71	#95	2	Love Makes The World Go Round	Rare Earth 5025
9/14/74	#18	16	I've Got The Music In Me*	Rocket 40293

Debut Date	Peak Pos	Wks Chr	ARTIST/Song Title	Label & Number
			KIKI DEE *—continued*	
3/01/75	#85	3	Step By Step	Rocket 40355
5/17/75	#75	6	How Glad I Am	Rocket 40401
3/13/76	#85	6	Once A Fool	Rocket 40506
7/03/76	#1	20	Don't Go Breaking My Heart**	Rocket 40585
12/04/93	#58	15	True Love**	MCA 54762
			*released as by the **KIKI DEE BAND**	
			released as by **ELTON JOHN and KIKI DEE	
			TOMMY DEE	
4/04/59	#16	11	Three Stars	Crest 1057
			DEEE-LITE	
9/22/90	#3	24	Groove Is In The Heart/	Elektra 64934
12/22/90	#47	17	Power Of Love	Elektra 64934
			DEE JAY and THE RUNAWAYS	
5/14/66	#56	8	Peter Rabbit	Smash 2034
			DEELE	
1/28/84	#63	10	Body Talk	Solar 69785
3/05/88	#12	22	Two Occasions	Solar 70015
			DEEP PURPLE	
8/10/68	#4	12	Hush	Tetragrammaton 1503
11/02/68	#28	10	Kentucky Woman	Tetragrammaton 1508
1/25/69	#52	6	River Deep-Mountain High	Tetragrammaton 1514
3/22/69	#99	1	The Bird Has Flown/	Tetragrammaton 1519
3/29/69	#97	1	Emmaretta	Tetragrammaton 1519
12/26/70	#96	3	Black Night	Warner Brothers 7405
2/17/73	#90	3	Woman From Tokyo	Warner Brothers 7672
5/26/73	#3	14	Smoke On The Water	Warner Brothers 7710
9/29/73	#59	6	Woman From Tokyo	Warner Brothers 7737
3/23/74	#87	4	Might Just Take Your Life	Warner Brothers 7784
12/28/74	#93	2	You Can't Do It Right	Warner Brothers 8049
12/29/84	#65	8	Knocking At Your Back Door	Mercury 880477
			RICK DEES	
8/14/76	#1	20	Disco Duck (Part 1)*	RSO 857
1/22/77	#81	5	Dis-Gorilla (Part 1)*	RSO 866
12/01/84	#66	9	Eat My Shorts	Atlantic 89601
			*released as by **RICK DEES and HIS CAST OF IDIOTS**	
			DEF LEPPARD	
7/05/80	#97	2	Rock Brigade	Mercury 76064
3/19/83	#13	20	Photograph	Mercury 811215
6/11/83	#19	18	Rock Of Ages	Mercury 812604
9/10/83	#27	14	Foolin'	Mercury 814178
6/16/84	#70	8	Bringin' On The Heartbreak	Mercury 818779
10/10/87	#28	19	Animal	Mercury 888832
1/23/88	#11	17	Hysteria	Mercury 870004
4/30/88	#1	25	Pour Some Sugar On Me	Mercury 870298
8/13/88	#1	15	Love Bites	Mercury 870402
11/19/88	#2	20	Armageddon It	Mercury 870692
3/04/89	#11	17	Rocket	Mercury 872614
4/04/92	#7	22	Let's Get Rocked	Mercury 866568
6/13/92	#28	15	Make Love Like A Man	Mercury 864038
8/29/92	#11	24	Have You Ever Needed Someone So Bad	Mercury 864136
12/19/92	#35	17	Stand Up (Kick Love Into Motion)	Mercury 864604
4/10/93	#59	9	Tonight	Mercury 862016
9/25/93	#10	25	Two Steps Behind	Columbia 77116
12/18/93	#37	22	Miss You In A Heartbeat	Mercury 858080
			DeFRANCO FAMILY featuring TONY DeFRANCO	
8/25/73	#1	17	Heartbeat - It's A Lovebeat	20th Century 2030
12/29/73	#23	10	Abra-Ca-Dabra	20th Century 2070
4/27/74	#16	12	Save The Last Dance For Me	20th Century 2088
			DEJA	
11/28/87	#56	12	You And Me Tonight	Virgin 99422
			DeJOHN SISTERS	
2/05/55	#6	5	(My Baby Don't Love Me) No More	Epic 9085
			DESMOND DEKKER & THE ACES	
5/10/69	#8	11	Israelites	Uni 55129

90

Debut Date	Peak Pos	Wks Chr	ARTIST/Song Title	Label & Number
			DELACARDOS	
7/15/61	#97	1	Hold Back The Tears	United Artists 310
			del AMITRI	
5/19/90	#35	14	Kiss This Thing Goodbye	A&M 1485
8/08/92	#25	20	Always The Last To Know	A&M 1604
			DELANEY & BONNIE	
2/14/70	#74	4	Comin' Home*	Atco 6725
8/22/70	#43	7	Soul Shake**	Atco 6756
5/29/71	#9	16	Never Ending Song Of Love**	Atco 6804
9/25/71	#18	9	Only You Know And I Know	Atco 6838
1/15/72	#68	6	Move 'Em Out	Atco 6866
			***released as by DELANEY & BONNIE and FRIENDS featuring ERIC CLAPTON**	
			****released as by DELANEY & BONNIE and FRIENDS**	
			DE LA SOUL	
6/10/89	#59	9	Me, Myself And I	Tommy Boy 7926
10/02/93	#73	4	Breakadawn	Tommy Boy 586
			DELBERT & GLEN	
11/18/72	#80	4	I Received A Letter	Clean 60003
			DELEGATES	
10/21/72	#9	7	Convention '72	Mainstream 5525
			DELEGATION	
1/27/79	#60	13	Oh Honey	Shady Brook 1048
			DELFONICS	
2/10/68	#4	13	La-La Means I Love You	Philly Groove 150
5/04/68	#50	6	I'm Sorry	Philly Groove 151
8/24/68	#46	10	Break Your Promise	Philly Groove 152
12/07/68	#31	9	Ready Or Not Here I Come/	Philly Groove 154
2/08/69	#92	4	Somebody Loves You	Philly Groove 154
5/31/69	#96	3	Funny Feeling	Philly Groove 156
8/09/69	#40	9	You Got Yours And I'll Get Mine	Philly Groove 157
1/10/70	#13	14	Didn't I (Blow Your Mind This Time)	Philly Groove 161
5/30/70	#41	8	Trying To Make A Fool Out Of Me	Philly Groove 162
9/05/70	#41	9	When You Get Right Down To It	Philly Groove 163
6/05/71	#61	9	Over And Over	Philly Groove 166
10/09/71	#62	10	Walk Right Up To The Sun	Philly Groove 169
5/27/72	#73	8	Tell Me This Is A Dream	Philly Groove 172
1/13/73	#75	5	Think It Over	Philly Groove 174
4/28/73	#86	4	I Don't Want To Make Sweet Music	Philly Groove 176
			DEL FUEGOS	
6/07/86	#81	5	I Still Want You	Slash 28822
			DELIVERANCE	
9/06/80	#81	5	Leaving L.A.	Columbia 11320
			DELLS	
11/11/67	#50	8	O-O, I Love You	Cadet 5574
1/20/68	#24	10	There Is	Cadet 5590
4/13/68	#41	9	Wear It On Our Face	Cadet 5599
7/06/68	#16	12	Stay In My Corner	Cadet 5612
10/19/68	#35	8	Always Together	Cadet 5621
12/28/68	#46	7	Does Anybody Know I'm Here	Cadet 5631
3/01/69	#82	3	Hallways Of My Mind/	Cadet 5636
4/19/69	#93	2	I Can't Do Enough	Cadet 5636
5/17/69	#18	12	I Can Sing A Rainbow/Love Is Blue	Cadet 5641
8/09/69	#14	12	Oh, What A Night	Cadet 5649
11/01/69	#51	7	On The Dock Of The Bay	Cadet 5658
1/17/70	#36	8	Oh What A Day	Cadet 5663
4/04/70	#51	9	Open Up My Heart	Cadet 5667
7/11/70	#64	7	Long Lonely Nights	Cadet 5672
1/16/71	#91	5	The Glory Of Love	Cadet 5679
8/21/71	#33	10	The Love We Had (Stays On My Mind)	Cadet 5683
2/26/72	#76	3	It's All Up To You	Cadet 5689
4/14/73	#20	15	Give Your Baby A Standing Ovation	Cadet 5696
9/29/73	#60	6	My Pretending Days Are Over	Cadet 5698
11/24/73	#56	10	I Miss You	Cadet 5700
6/01/74	#78	5	I Wish It Was Me You Loved	Cadet 5702

Debut Date	Peak Pos	Wks Chr	**ARTIST**/Song Title	Label & Number
			DELL-VIKINGS	
2/23/57	#3	20	Come Go With Me	Dot 15538
6/29/57	#9	14	Whispering Bells	Dot 15592
7/13/57	#43	12	Cool Shake	Mercury 71132
8/09/58	#61	3	You Cheated	Mercury 71345
5/27/61	#66	6	Bring Back Your Heart	ABC-Paramount 10208
			AL DeLORY	
7/11/70	#93	2	Song From M*A*S*H	Capitol 2811
			JIMMY DELPS	
5/18/68	#94	2	Don't Sign The Paper	Karen 1538
			DEL RAYS	
8/03/57	#56	3	Bermuda Shorts	Apollo 514
			RALPH DeMARCO	
11/14/59	#56	7	Old Shep	Guaranteed 202
			NICKEY DeMATTEO	
2/27/60	#74	7	Suddenly	Guyden 2024
			DEMENSIONS	
7/23/60	#19	15	Over The Rainbow	Mohawk 116
2/23/63	#87	5	My Foolish Heart	Coral 62344
			CATHY DENNIS	
4/28/90	#55	9	That's The Way Of The World*	FFRR 886980
11/03/90	#10	24	Just Another Dream	Polydor 877962
3/02/91	#5	27	Touch Me (All Night Long)	Polydor 879466
6/29/91	#11	23	Too Many Walls	Polydor 879466
9/12/92	#27	18	You Lied To Me	Polydor 863452
			*released as by D-MOB featuring CATHY DENNIS	
			MARTIN DENNY	
4/11/59	#3	17	Quiet Village	Liberty 55162
7/11/59	#78	6	Martinique	Liberty 55199
10/03/59	#39	3	The Enchanted Sea	Liberty 55212
8/11/62	#70	10	A Taste Of Honey	Liberty 55470
11/28/64	#81	3	Hawaii Tattoo	Liberty 55754
			JOHN DENVER	
5/08/71	#1	22	Take Me Home, Country Roads	RCA 0445
11/06/71	#27	11	Friends With You	RCA 0567
3/11/72	#83	3	Everyday	RCA 0647
8/05/72	#87	2	Goodbye Again	RCA 0737
12/02/72	#7	18	Rocky Mountain High	RCA 0829
5/26/73	#27	12	I'd Rather Be A Cowboy	RCA 0955
9/01/73	#59	6	Farewell Andromeda	RCA 0067
11/24/73	#51	10	Please, Daddy	RCA 0182
1/19/74	#1	18	Sunshine On My Shoulders	RCA 0213
5/25/74	#1	16	Annie's Song	RCA 0295
9/21/74	#5	14	Back Home Again	RCA 10065
12/28/74	#14	11	Sweet Surrender	RCA 10148
3/22/75	#1	17	Thank God I'm A Country Boy	RCA 10239
8/09/75	#1	17	I'm Sorry/	RCA 10353
10/11/75	#26	9	Calypso	RCA 10353
12/06/75	#6	11	Fly Away	RCA 10517
12/20/75	#59	2	Christmas For Cowboys	RCA 10464
2/28/76	#18	11	Looking For Space	RCA 10586
5/15/76	#66	5	It Makes Me Giggle	RCA 10687
9/11/76	#60	6	Like A Sad Song	RCA 10774
1/01/77	#85	6	Baby, You Look Good To Me Tonight	RCA 10854
4/02/77	#44	7	My Sweet Lady	RCA 10911
11/19/77	#38	11	How Can I Leave You Again	RCA 11036
2/25/78	#81	5	It Amazes Me	RCA 11214
4/22/78	#76	3	I Want To Live	RCA 11267
3/08/80	#91	4	Autograph	RCA 11915
7/25/81	#45	12	Some Days Are Diamonds	RCA 12246
10/31/81	#66	8	The Cowboy And The Lady	RCA 12345
1/16/82	#81	4	Perhaps Love*	Columbia 02679
3/06/82	#25	15	Shanghai Breezes	RCA 13071
			*released as by PLACIDO DOMINGO and JOHN DENVER	
			DEODATO	
2/03/73	#4	12	Also Sprach Zarathustra (2001)	CTI 12

Debut Date	Peak Pos	Wks Chr	ARTIST/Song Title	Label & Number
8/18/73	#55	9	Rhapsody In Blue	CTI 16
11/13/76	#100	1	Peter Gunn	MCA 40631
			DEPECHE MODE	
5/18/85	#16	19	People Are People	Sire 29221
1/30/88	#75	4	Never Let Me Down Again	Sire 28189
5/14/88	#81	6	Route 66/Behind The Wheel	Sire 27991
9/10/88	#41	10	Strangelove	Sire 27777
5/27/89	#76	8	Everything Counts	Sire 22993
12/16/89	#31	17	Personal Jesus	Sire 19941
4/14/90	#2	24	Enjoy The Silence	Sire 19885
8/18/90	#17	15	Policy Of Truth	Sire 19842
11/24/90	#48	12	World In My Eyes	Sire 19580
3/13/93	#37	13	I Feel For You	Sire 18600
6/12/93	#66	10	Walking In My Shoes	Mute 40852
			DEREK	
9/14/68	#10	21	Cinnamon	Bang 558
2/22/69	#48	6	Back Door Man	Bang 566
			DEREK and THE DOMINOS (see also ERIC CLAPTON)	
2/13/71	#96	2	Bell Bottom Blues	Atco 6803
3/20/71	#52	10	Layla	Atco 6809
5/27/72	#14	13	Layla	Atco 6809
			RICK DERRINGER	
1/19/74	#15	12	Rock And Roll, Hoochie Koo	Blue Sky 2751
4/27/74	#70	6	Teenage Love Affair	Blue Sky 2752
3/29/75	#67	6	Hang On Sloopy	Blue Sky 2755
			SUGAR PIE DeSANTO	
10/01/60	#80	6	I Want To Know	Check 103
4/11/64	#55	6	Slip-In-Mules (No High Heel Sneakers)	Checker 1073
12/04/65	#94	2	Do I Make Myself Clear*	Cadet 5519
7/23/66	#93	1	In The Basement (Part I)*	Cadet 5539
			*released as by **ETTA JAMES & SUGAR PIE DeSANTO**	
			TERI DeSARIO with K.C.	
7/08/78	#59	9	Ain't Nothing Gonna Keep Me From You*	Casablanca 929
11/17/79	#3	25	Yes, I'm Ready	Casablanca 2227
6/28/80	#70	4	Dancin' In The Streets	Casablanca 2278
			*released as by **TERI DeSARIO**	
			JACKIE DeSHANNON	
5/11/63	#58	8	Needles And Pins	Liberty 55563
1/04/64	#81	6	When You Walk In The Room	Liberty 55645
5/22/65	#8	14	What The World Needs Now Is Love	Imperial 66110
10/02/65	#72	4	A Lifetime Of Loneliness	Imperial 66132
6/04/66	#99	1	Come And Get Me	Imperial 66171
9/17/66	#87	2	I Can Make It With You	Imperial 66202
8/17/68	#35	10	The Weight	Imperial 66313
6/14/69	#4	16	Put A Little Love In Your Heart	Imperial 66385
10/25/69	#33	8	Love Will Find A Way	Imperial 66419
2/21/70	#52	7	Brighton Hill	Imperial 66438
8/15/70	#92	3	It's So Nice	Liberty 56187
6/10/72	#95	2	Vanilla Olay/	Atlantic 2871
8/26/72	#96	2	Only Love Can Break A Heart	Atlantic 2871
10/29/77	#70	11	Don't Let The Flame Burn Out	Amherst 725
			JOHNNY DESMOND	
5/06/50	#7	3	C'est Si Bon	MGM 10613
1/23/54	#5	7	Woman	Coral 61069
8/28/54	#3	6	The High And The Mighty	Coral 61232
9/03/55	#1	15	The Yellow Rose Of Texas	Coral 61476
			DETERGENTS	
12/05/64	#11	9	Leader Of The Laundromat	Roulette 4590
3/27/65	#74	3	Double-O-Seven	Roulette 4603
			DETROIT featuring MITCH RYDER	
1/22/72	#95	2	Rock 'N' Roll	Paramount 0133
			DETROIT EMERALDS	
2/24/68	#91	2	Show Time	Ric-Tic 135
1/23/71	#42	15	Do Me Right	Westbound 172
8/21/71	#78	4	Wear This Ring	Westbound 181
1/15/72	#35	11	You Want It, You Got It	Westbound 192

Debut Date	Peak Pos	Wks Chr	ARTIST/Song Title	Label & Number
			DETROIT EMERALDS—*continued*	
5/27/72	#19	16	Baby Let Me Take You (In My Arms)	Westbound 203
12/02/72	#88	6	Feel The Need In Me	Westbound 209
6/30/73	#82	5	You're Gettin' A Little Too Smart	Westbound 213
			WILLIAM DeVAUGHN	
4/13/74	#3	16	Be Thankful For What You Got	Roxbury 0236
9/07/74	#55	8	Blood Is Thicker Than Water	Roxbury 2001
			DEVICE	
6/14/86	#27	15	Hanging On A Heart Attack	Chrysalis 42996
9/27/86	#73	7	Who Says	Chrysalis 43063
			DEVO	
8/30/80	#13	29	Whip It	Warner Brothers 49550
9/05/81	#36	15	Working In The Coal Mine	Full Moon 47204
5/21/83	#67	10	Theme From Doctor Detroit	Backstreet 52215
			FRANK DeVOL and HIS RAINBOW STRINGS	
5/28/60	#62	6	La Montana (If She Should Come To You)	Columbia 41620
			DEVONSQUARE	
4/25/92	#95	4	If You Could See Me Now	Atlantic 87564
			DEVOTIONS	
2/08/64	#30	11	Rip Van Winkle	Roulette 4541
			DEXY'S MIDNIGHT RUNNERS	
1/22/83	#1	24	Come On Eileen	Mercury 76189
			TRACEY DEY	
9/21/63	#73	4	Teenage Cleopatra	Liberty 55604
2/01/64	#92	3	Here Comes The Boy	Amy 894
4/18/64	#35	10	Gonna' Get Along Without You Now	Amy 901
			CLIFF DeYOUNG	
12/22/73	#23	16	My Sweet Lady	MCA 40156
			DENNIS DeYOUNG	
9/08/84	#10	20	Desert Moon	A&M 2666
12/08/84	#81	7	Don't Wait For Heroes	A&M 2692
3/22/86	#60	10	Call Me	A&M 2816
7/05/86	#84	4	This Is The Time	A&M 2839
			JOEL DIAMOND	
2/14/81	#90	3	Theme From Raging Bull	Motown 1504
			NEIL DIAMOND	
5/14/66	#57	11	Solitary Man	Bang 519
8/20/66	#6	13	Cherry Cherry (studio version)	Bang 528
10/29/66	#23	11	I Got The Feelin' (Oh No No)	Bang 536
1/28/67	#22	9	You Got To Me	Bang 540
4/08/67	#9	11	Girl, You'll Be A Woman Soon	Bang 542
7/15/67	#13	41	Thank The Lord For The Night Time	Bang 547
10/14/67	#12	9	Kentucky Woman	Bang 551
1/06/68	#38	7	New Orleans	Bang 554
3/23/68	#69	7	Red Red Wine	Bang 556
5/04/68	#51	7	Brooklyn Roads	Uni 55065
7/06/68	#51	7	Two-Bit Manchild	Uni 55075
9/28/68	#42	10	Sunday Sun	Uni 55084
2/22/69	#13	12	Brother Love's Travelling Salvation Show	Uni 55109
6/14/69	#3	15	Sweet Caroline	Uni 55136
10/25/69	#4	14	Holly Holy	Uni 55175
2/21/70	#23	11	Shilo	Bang 575
2/21/70	#44	6	Until It's Time For You To Go	Uni 55204
4/25/70	#24	9	Soolaimon (African Trilogy II)	Uni 55224
7/18/70	#20	11	Solitary Man	Bang 578
8/15/70	#1	15	Cracklin' Rosie	Uni 55250
11/07/70	#17	10	He Ain't Heavy...He's My Brother	Uni 55264
11/07/70	#36	8	Do It	Bang 580
3/20/71	#4	11	I Am I Said/	Uni 55278
5/22/71	#69	4	Done Too Soon	Uni 55278
6/19/71	#52	8	I'm A Believer	Bang 586
11/06/71	#13	11	Stones	Uni 55310
4/29/72	#1	14	Song Sung Blue	Uni 55326
8/12/72	#16	11	Play Me	Uni 55346
11/04/72	#16	12	Walk On Water	Uni 55352
3/10/73	#24	11	Cherry Cherry from "Hot August Night" (live version) . . .	MCA 40017

Debut Date	Peak Pos	Wks Chr	ARTIST/Song Title	Label & Number
7/21/73	#67	7	The Long Way Home	Bang 703
8/18/73	#42	8	The Last Thing On My Mind	MCA 40092
10/20/73	#19	10	Be	Columbia 45942
3/02/74	#48	7	Skybird	Columbia 45998
10/06/74	#4	14	Longfellow Serenade	Columbia 10043
2/01/75	#43	7	I've Been This Way Before	Columbia 10084
6/12/76	#16	15	If You Know What I Mean	Columbia 10366
9/25/76	#77	7	Don't Think....Feel	Columbia 10405
11/26/77	#9	16	Desiree	Columbia 10657
10/28/78	#1	18	You Don't Bring Me Flowers*	Columbia 10840
1/27/79	#20	15	Forever In Blue Jeans	Columbia 10897
5/19/79	#63	6	Say Maybe	Columbia 10945
12/22/79	#14	18	September Morn	Columbia 11175
5/03/80	#97	2	The Good Lord Loves You	Columbia 11232
11/01/80	#4	23	Love On The Rocks	Capitol 4939
1/31/81	#8	16	Hello Again	Capitol 4960
4/25/81	#10	16	America	Capitol 4994
11/07/81	#12	16	Yesterday's Songs	Columbia 02604
2/13/82	#31	13	On The Way To The Sky	Columbia 02712
5/22/82	#36	11	Be Mine Tonight	Columbia 02928
9/11/82	#10	20	Heartlight	Columbia 03219
1/15/83	#30	11	I'm Alive	Columbia 03503
4/23/83	#65	8	Front Page Story	Columbia 03801
8/25/84	#75	5	Turn Around	Columbia 04541
5/24/86	#46	10	Headed For The Future	Columbia 05889
			*released as by BARBRA & NEIL (Barbra Streisand & Neil Diamond)	
			DIAMOND HEAD	
5/26/73	#95	1	If That's The Way You Want It	Dunhill 4342
			DIAMOND REO	
12/28/74	#36	9	Ain't That Peculiar	Big Tree 16030
			DIAMONDS	
8/11/56	#17	11	Ka-Ding-Dong	Mercury 70934
3/16/57	#2	19	Little Darlin'	Mercury 71060
6/22/57	#47	5	Words Of Love	Mercury 71128
9/07/57	#36	5	Zip Zip	Mercury 71165
12/28/57	#1	15	The Stroll	Mercury 71242
4/05/58	#21	10	High Sign	Mercury 71291
7/05/58	#37	12	Kathy-O	Mercury 71330
10/11/58	#19	13	Walking Along	Mercury 71366
1/24/59	#12	13	She Say (Oom Dooby Doom)	Mercury 71404
4/25/59	#95	1	Gretchen	Mercury 71449
9/26/59	#80	6	Young In Years	Mercury 71505
7/01/61	#43	10	One Summer Night	Mercury 718371
			MANU DIBANGO	
6/16/73	#22	11	Soul Makossa	Atlantic 2971
			DICK and DEEDEE	
8/12/61	#3	14	The Mountain's High	Liberty 55350
3/17/62	#23	15	Tell Me	Liberty 55412
3/09/63	#24	12	Young And In Love	Warner Brothers 5342
11/23/63	#22	10	Turn Around	Warner Brothers 5396
11/28/64	#16	13	Thou Shalt Not Steal	Warner Brothers 5482
3/06/65	#93	3	Be My Baby	Warner Brothers 5608
			"LITTLE" JIMMY DICKENS	
10/23/65	#28	8	May The Bird Of Paradise Fly Up Your Nose	Columbia 43388
2/12/66	#83	2	When The Ship Hits The Sand	Columbia 43514
			DICKY DOO and THE DON'TS	
2/01/58	#29	9	Click Clack	Swan 4001
5/03/58	#60	1	Nee Nee Na Na Na Na Nu Nu	Swan 4006
10/11/58	#47	8	Leave Me Alone	Swan 4014
2/07/59	#91	2	Teardrops Will Fall	Swan 4025
			BO DIDDLEY	
7/18/59	#71	4	Crackin' Up	Checker 924
9/12/59	#21	13	Say Man	Checker 931
12/05/59	#87	3	Say Man, Back Again	Checker 936
4/02/60	#100	1	Road Runner	Checker 942
9/15/62	#68	4	You Can't Judge A Book By It's Cover	Checker 1019

Debut Date	Peak Pos	Wks Chr	**ARTIST**/Song Title	Label & Number
			DIESEL	
9/12/81	#26	18	Sausalito Summernight	Regency 7339
			DIGABLE PLANETS	
1/23/93	#14	21	Rebirth Of Slick (Cool Like Dat)	Pendulum 64674
			DIGITAL UNDERGROUND	
3/24/90	#13	23	Humpty Dance	Tommy Boy 7944
			DILLARDS	
8/07/71	#99	2	It's About Time	Anthem 101
			DILLMAN BAND	
5/16/81	#59	8	Lovin' The Night Away	RCA 12206
			MARK DINNING	
12/26/59	#1	16	Teen Angel	MGM 12845
4/16/60	#58	8	A Star Is Born	MGM 12888
9/03/60	#64	7	The Lovin' Touch	MGM 12929
2/25/61	#59	6	Top Forty, News, Weather And Sports	MGM 12980
			DINO	
7/23/88	#51	12	Summergirls	4th & B'way 7468
2/18/89	#44	9	24/7	4th & B'way 7471
5/13/89	#4	25	I Like It	4th & B'way 7483
9/16/89	#27	19	Sunshine	4th & B'way 7489
1/20/90	#58	7	Never 2 Much Of U	4th & B'way 7495
8/11/90	#7	20	Romeo	Island 878012
11/10/90	#30	16	Gentle	Island 878472
7/17/93	#30	22	Ooh Child	East West 98398
			KENNY DINO	
10/14/61	#39	16	Your Ma Said You Cried In Your Sleep Last Night	Musicor 1013
			PAUL DINO	
2/04/61	#56	9	Ginnie Bell	Promo 2180
			DINO, DESI & BILLY	
7/03/65	#19	11	I'm A Fool	Reprise 0367
9/25/65	#32	8	Not The Lovin' Kind	Reprise 0401
12/11/65	#82	5	Please Don't Fight It	Reprise 0426
2/26/66	#94	3	Superman	Reprise 0444
6/03/67	#100	1	Two In The Afternoon	Reprise 0579
9/23/67	#98	2	Kitty Doyle	Reprise 0619
8/03/68	#69	5	Tell Someone You Love Them	Reprise 0698
			DION	
5/10/58	#20	13	I Wonder Why*	Laurie 3013
8/23/58	#25	15	No One Knows*	Laurie 3015
12/13/58	#37	12	Don't Pity Me*	Laurie 3021
4/18/59	#6	15	A Teenager In Love*	Laurie 3027
9/19/59	#48	8	Every Little Thing You Do*/	Laurie 3035
9/19/59	#61	6	A Lover's Prayer*	Laurie 3035
12/26/59	#4	15	Where Or When*	Laurie 3044
4/23/60	#25	9	When You Wish Upon A Star*	Laurie 3052
7/16/60	#35	9	In The Still Of The Night*	Laurie 3059
10/22/60	#12	17	Lonely Teenager	Laurie 3070
2/18/61	#51	6	Havin' Fun	Laurie 3081
4/29/61	#71	5	Kissin' Game	Laurie 3090
7/08/61	#73	3	Somebody Nobody Wants	Laurie 3101
9/23/61	#1	17	Runaround Sue	Laurie 3110
12/02/61	#43	8	The Majestic/	Laurie 3115
12/16/61	#3	18	The Wanderer	Laurie 3115
4/21/62	#5	13	Lovers Who Wander/	Laurie 3123
4/21/62	#40	8	(I Was) Born To Cry	Laurie 3123
7/07/62	#14	12	Little Diane	Laurie 3134
11/10/62	#17	12	Love Came To Me	Laurie 3145
1/19/63	#3	14	Ruby Baby	Columbia 42662
3/09/63	#23	11	Sandy	Laurie 3153
4/20/63	#19	9	This Little Girl	Columbia 42776
6/15/63	#56	6	Come Go With Me	Laurie 3171
6/29/63	#30	9	Be Careful Of Stones That You Throw	Columbia 42810
9/14/63	#6	11	Donna The Prima Donna	Columbia 42852
11/16/63	#5	12	Drip Drop	Columbia 42917
2/29/64	#72	3	I'm Your Hoochie Coochie Man	Columbia 42977
8/22/64	#66	5	Johnny B. Goode	Columbia 43096
10/19/68	#2	14	Abraham, Martin And John	Laurie 3464

Debut Date	Peak Pos	Wks Chr	ARTIST/Song Title	Label & Number
2/01/69	#80	2	Purple Haze	Laurie 3478
7/04/70	#69	3	Your Own Back Yard	Warner Brothers 7401
8/12/89	#87	3	And The Night Stood Still	Arista 9787
			*released as by DION and THE BELMONTS	
			CELINE DION	
12/08/90	#4	24	Where Does My Heart Beat Now	Epic 73536
4/06/91	#32	17	(If There Was) Any Other Way	Epic 73665
2/22/92	#9	24	Beauty And The Beast*	Epic 74090
5/02/92	#5	29	If You Asked Me To	Epic 74277
8/01/92	#22	18	Nothing Broken But My Heart	Epic 74336
11/28/92	#48	18	Love Can Move Mountains	Epic 74337
7/24/93	#20	28	When I Fall In Love**	Epic 77021
12/04/93	#1	38	The Power Of Love	550 Music 77230
			*released as by CELINE DION and PEABO BRYSON	
			**released as by CELINE DION & CLIVE GRIFFIN	
			DIRE STRAITS	
2/03/79	#5	16	Sultans Of Swing	Warner Brothers 8736
7/28/79	#63	7	Lady Writer	Warner Brothers 49006
7/13/85	#1	28	Money For Nothing	Warner Brothers 28950
11/02/85	#10	22	Walk Of Life	Warner Brothers 28878
3/01/86	#15	15	So Far Away	Warner Brothers 28789
			SENATOR EVERETT McKINLEY DIRKSEN	
12/17/66	#43	6	Gallant Men	Capitol 5085
			DIRT BAND (see NITTY GRITTY DIRT BAND)	
			DISCO TEX & THE SEX-O-LETTES	
11/30/74	#10	14	Get Dancin'	Chelsea 3004
4/12/75	#34	11	I Wanna Dance Wit' Choo (Part 1)	Chelsea 3015
9/06/75	#89	3	Jam Band	Chelsea 3026
7/10/76	#69	5	Dancin' Kid	Chelsea 3045
			DISTANT COUSINS	
9/10/66	#90	5	She Ain't Lovin' You	Date 1514
			DIVINYLS	
1/25/86	#80	5	Pleasure And Pain	Chrysalis 42916
3/09/91	#6	23	I Touch Myself	Virgin 91397
7/06/91	#87	5	Make Out Alright	Virgin 98780
			DIXIEBELLES	
10/05/63	#13	13	(Down At) Papa Joe's	Sound Stage 2507
1/11/64	#20	9	Southtown U.S.A.	Sound Stage 2517
			DIXIE CUPS	
5/02/64	#1	14	Chapel Of Love	Red Bird 001
7/18/64	#10	9	People Say	Red Bird 006
10/31/64	#56	5	You Should Have Seen The Way He Looked At Me	Red Bird 012
12/26/64	#68	8	Little Bell	Red Bird 017
4/03/65	#19	10	Iko Iko	Red Bird 024
			DIXIE DREGS	
5/20/78	#92	6	Take It Off The Top	Capricorn 0291
			DIXIE DRIFTER	
8/28/65	#76	4	Soul Heaven	Roulette 4641
			D.J. JAZZY JEFF & THE FRESH PRINCE	
5/07/88	#17	22	Parents Just Don't Understand	Jive 1099
8/06/88	#20	14	A Nightmare On My Street	Jive 1124
10/29/88	#54	8	Girls Ain't Nothing But Trouble	Jive 1147
6/29/91	#14	18	Summertime	Jive 1465
10/12/91	#55	16	Ring My Bell	Jive 42024
8/14/93	#12	25	Boom! Shake The Room*	Jive 42108
			*released as by JAZZY JEFF & FRESH PRINCE	
			DJ QUIK	
8/01/92	#54	6	Jus Lyke Compton	Profile 5372
			D-MOB	
12/30/89	#7	20	C'mon And Get My Love	FFRR 886798
4/28/90	#55	9	That's The Way Of The World*	FFRR 886980
			*released as by D-MOB featuring CATHY DENNIS	

Debut Date	Peak Pos	Wks Chr	ARTIST/Song Title	Label & Number
			D.N.A.	
10/06/90	#4	24	Tom's Diner*	A&M 1529
			*released as by D.N.A. featuring SUZANNE VEGA	
			CARL DOBKINS JR.	
5/09/59	#3	21	My Heart Is An Open Book	Decca 30803
9/05/59	#75	9	If You Don't Want My Lovin'	Decca 30656
12/19/59	#32	14	Lucky Devil	Decca 31020
5/28/60	#86	4	Exclusively Yours	Decca 31088
			DOCTOR and THE MEDICS	
8/02/86	#62	12	Spirit In The Sky	I.R.S. 52880
			DR. BUZZARD'S ORIGINAL "SAVANNAH" BAND	
9/25/76	#83	5	I'll Play The Fool	RCA 10762
11/13/76	#23	17	Whispering/Cherchez La Femme/Se Si Bon	RCA 10827
			DR. DRE	
2/06/93	#2	28	Nuthin' But A "G" Thang	Death Row 53819
6/12/93	#8	24	Dre Day	Death Row 53827
10/02/93	#31	21	Let Me Ride	Death Row 57128
			DR. FEELGOOD and THE INTERNS	
4/07/62	#74	12	Doctor Feel-Good	Okeh 7144
			DR. HOOK	
3/18/72	#1	16	Sylvia's Mother*	Columbia 45562
9/23/72	#74	3	Carry Me, Carrie*	Columbia 45667
11/25/72	#5	21	The Cover Of The Rolling Stone*	Columbia 45732
6/30/73	#59	6	Roland The Roadie And Gertrude The Groupie*	Columbia 45878
9/22/73	#80	5	Life Ain't Easy*	Columbia 45925
9/27/75	#97	1	The Millionaire	Capitol 4104
1/03/76	#5	23	Only Sixteen	Capitol 4171
6/19/76	#9	25	A Little Bit More	Capitol 4280
11/27/76	#63	11	If Not You	Capitol 4364
6/18/77	#72	7	Walk Right In	Capitol 4423
9/16/78	#4	22	Sharing The Night Together	Capitol 4621
2/03/79	#62	7	All The Time In The World	Capitol 4677
4/14/79	#5	26	When You're In Love With A Beautiful Woman	Capitol 4705
10/13/79	#21	19	Better Love Next Time	Capitol 4785
2/16/80	#6	22	Sexy Eyes	Capitol 4831
7/05/80	#67	8	Years From Now	Capitol 4885
11/01/80	#34	18	Girls Can Get It	Casablanca 2314
4/04/81	#73	7	That Didn't Hurt Too Bad	Casablanca 2325
2/27/82	#27	13	Baby Makes Her Blue Jeans Talk	Casablanca 2347
6/12/82	#76	6	Loveline	Casablanca 2351
			*released as by DR. HOOK and THE MEDICINE SHOW	
			DR. JOHN	
4/01/72	#52	6	Iko Iko	Atco 6882
4/14/73	#11	16	Right Place Wrong time	Atco 6914
9/08/73	#45	9	Such A Night	Atco 6937
5/04/74	#72	6	(Everybody Wanna Get Rich) Rite Away	Atco 6957
			DR. WEST'S MEDICINE SHOW and JUNK BAND	
11/26/86	#69	5	The Eggplant That Ate Chicago	Go Go 100
			JOE DODO & THE GROOVERS	
4/19/58	#55	5	Groovy	RCA 7207
			BILL DOGGETT	
8/18/56	#2	24	Honky Tonk (Parts 1 & 2)	King 4950
11/24/56	#12	11	Slow Walk	King 5000
12/06/58	#97	1	Hold It	King 5149
1/14/61	#97	2	Hully Gully Twist	Warner Brothers 5181
			DOKKEN	
5/18/85	#72	8	Alone Again	Elektra 69650
3/01/86	#82	6	In My Dreams	Elektra 69563
12/26/87	#87	7	Burning Like A Flame	Elektra 69435
			THOMAS DOLBY	
2/19/83	#4	24	She Blinded Me With Science	Capitol 5204
6/18/83	#65	8	Europa And The Pirate Twins	Capitol 5238
3/10/84	#59	10	Hyperactive	Capitol 5321
			JOE DOLCE	
4/25/81	#43	17	Shaddup Your Face	MCA 51053

Debut Date	Peak Pos	Wks Chr	ARTIST/Song Title	Label & Number
			MICKEY DOLENZ	
3/11/67	#88	3	Don't Do It	Challenge 59353
7/05/86	#24	14	That Was Then, This Is Now*	Arista 8505
			*released as by MICKEY DOLENZ and PETER TORK of THE MONKEES	
			DOLLAR	
12/15/79	#92	5	Shooting Star	Carrere 7208
			DOLPHINS	
12/12/64	#69	8	Hey-Da-Da-Dow	Fraternity 937
			PLACIDO DOMINGO	
1/16/82	#81	4	Perhaps Love*	Columbia 02679
			*released as by PLACIDO DOMINGO and JOHN DENVER	
			DOMINO	
12/04/93	#11	22	Getto Jam	Outburst 77298
			FATS DOMINO	
8/13/55	#1	7	Ain't That A Shame	Imperial 5348
6/23/56	#4	11	I'm In Love Again	Imperial 5386
8/04/56	#21	10	When My Dreamboat Comes Home/	Imperial 5396
8/04/56	#44	4	So-Long	Imperial 5396
10/06/56	#4	22	Blueberry Hill	Imperial 5407
12/29/56	#8	15	Blue Monday/	Imperial 5417
1/05/57	#22	7	What's The Reason I'm Not Pleasing You	Imperial 5417
3/09/57	#5	15	I'm Walkin'	Imperial 5428
5/18/57	#20	12	Valley Of Tears/	Imperial 5442
5/18/57	#19	6	It's You That I Love	Imperial 5442
8/03/57	#29	7	When I See You/	Imperial 5454
8/03/57	#41	4	What Will I Tell My Heart	Imperial 5454
10/12/57	#34	7	Wait And See/	Imperial 5467
10/12/57	#60	1	I Still Love You	Imperial 5467
12/21/57	#37	6	I Want You To Know/	Imperial 5477
12/21/57	#43	4	The Big Beat	Imperial 5477
3/01/58	#53	1	Yes, My Darling/	Imperial 5492
3/08/58	#54	1	Don't Know I Love You	Imperial 5492
4/26/58	#41	5	Sick And Tired	Imperial 5515
11/15/58	#9	16	Whole Lotta Loving/	Imperial 5553
11/22/58	#61	5	Coquette	Imperial 5553
2/14/59	#40	8	When The Saints Go Marching In/	Imperial 5569
2/21/59	#55	6	Telling Lies	Imperial 5569
5/09/59	#16	11	I'm Ready	Imperial 5585
5/16/59	#32	6	Margie	Imperial 5585
8/01/59	#9	13	I Want To Walk You Home/	Imperial 5606
8/01/59	#26	11	I'm Gonna Be A Wheel Some Day	Imperial 5606
10/31/59	#8	13	Be My Guest/	Imperial 5629
11/14/59	#54	6	I've Been Around	Imperial 5629
1/30/60	#29	10	Country Boy	Imperial 5645
4/23/60	#56	8	Tell Me That You Love Me/	Imperial 5660
4/23/60	#74	6	Before I Grow Too Old	Imperial 5660
6/25/60	#30	12	Don't Come Knockin'/	Imperial 5675
7/02/60	#10	13	Walking To New Orleans	Imperial 5675
9/03/60	#18	13	Three Nights A Week/	Imperial 5687
9/17/60	#90	3	Put Your Arms Around Me Honey	Imperial 5687
11/05/60	#16	14	My Girl Josephine/	Imperial 5704
11/05/60	#46	8	Natural Born Lover	Imperial 5704
1/28/61	#26	9	Ain't That Just Like A Woman/	Imperial 5723
1/28/61	#30	9	What A Price	Imperial 5723
3/25/61	#34	8	Shu Rah/	Imperial 5734
4/01/61	#53	4	Fell In Love On Monday	Imperial 5734
5/20/61	#34	10	It Keeps Rainin'	Imperial 5753
7/22/61	#17	11	Let The Four Winds Blow	Imperial 5764
10/07/61	#38	8	What A Party/	Imperial 5779
10/28/61	#93	1	Rockin' Bicycle	Imperial 5779
12/09/61	#38	8	Jambalaya (On The Bayou)	Imperial 5796
2/24/62	#30	9	You Win Again	Imperial 5816
5/19/62	#59	5	My Real Name/	Imperial 5833
5/26/62	#99	2	My Heart Is Bleeding	Imperial 5833
10/06/62	#94	4	Did You Ever See A Dream Walking	Imperial 5875
12/15/62	#94	1	Won't You Come On Back	Imperial 5895
5/25/63	#64	6	There Goes (My Heart Again)	ABC-Paramount 10444

Debut Date	Peak Pos	Wks Chr	**ARTIST**/Song Title	Label & Number
			FATS DOMINO—*continued*	
9/21/63	#43	9	Red Sails In The Sunset	ABC-Paramount 10484
1/11/64	#82	3	Who Cares	ABC-Paramount 10512
8/17/68	#87	3	Lady Madonna	Reprise 0763
			BO DONALDSON and THE HEYWOODS	
10/07/72	#51	10	Special Someone*	Family 0911
4/13/74	#1	16	Billy, Don't Be A Hero	ABC 11435
8/03/74	#13	12	Who Do You Think You Are	ABC 12006
11/16/74	#51	6	The Heartbreak Kid	ABC 12039
4/12/75	#89	2	The House On Telegraph Hill	ABC 12072
7/12/75	#98	3	Our Last Song Together	ABC 12108
			***released as by THE HEYWOODS**	
			LOU DONALDSON	
10/28/67	#98	1	Alligator Boogaloo	Blue Note 1934
			DON & JUAN	
2/03/62	#5	14	What's Your Name	Big Top 3079
			DON and THE GOODTIMES	
5/06/67	#76	6	I Could Be So Good To You	Epic 10145
			LONNIE DONEGAN and HIS SKIFFLE GROUP	
5/05/56	#9	3	Rock Island Line	London 1650
8/05/61	#6	13	Does Your Chewing Gum Lose It's Flavor (On The Bedpost Overnight)	Dot 15911
			RAL DONNER	
4/15/61	#27	13	Girl Of My Best Friend	Gone 5102
7/22/61	#10	11	You Don't Know What You've Got (Until You Lose It)	Gone 5108
10/07/61	#30	9	Please Don't Go/	Gone 5114
10/07/61	#97	2	I Didn't Figure On Him	Gone 5114
12/16/61	#10	13	She's Everything (I Wanted You To Be)	Gone 5121
3/31/62	#79	6	(What A Sad Way) To Love Someone	Gone 5125
			DONNIE and THE DREAMERS	
5/20/61	#55	8	Count Every Star	Whale 500
			DONOVAN	
5/08/65	#28	11	Catch The Wind	Hickory 1309
8/07/65	#40	8	Colours	Hickory 1324
9/18/65	#45	8	Universal Soldier	Hickory 1338
7/23/66	#1	13	Sunshine Superman	Epic 10045
11/12/66	#3	12	Mellow Yellow	Epic 10098
2/04/67	#10	9	Epistle To Dippy	Epic 10127
8/12/67	#9	10	There Is A Mountain	Epic 10212
12/02/67	#26	8	Wear Your Love Like Heaven	Epic 10253
3/09/68	#18	10	Jennifer Juniper	Epic 10300
6/15/68	#3	12	Hurdy Gurdy Man	Epic 10345
9/28/68	#31	8	Lalena	Epic 10393
2/01/69	#31	8	To Susan On The West Coast Waiting/	Epic 10434
4/12/69	#9	12	Atlantis	Epic 10434
7/26/69	#28	8	Goo Goo Barabajagal (Love Is Hot)*	Epic 10510
8/15/70	#40	8	Riki Tiki Tavi	Epic 10649
3/06/71	#93	2	Celia Of The Seals	Epic 10694
4/28/73	#57	7	I Like You	Epic 10983
			***released as by DONOVAN with THE JEFF BECK GROUP**	
			DOOBIE BROTHERS	
9/02/72	#9	13	Listen To The Music	Warner Brothers 7619
12/23/72	#33	10	Jcsus Is Just Alright	Warner Brothers 7661
4/21/73	#9	16	Long Train Runnin'	Warner Brothers 7698
8/18/73	#8	12	China Grove	Warner Brothers 7728
4/06/74	#38	14	Another Park, Another Sunday	Warner Brothers 7795
7/20/74	#43	10	Eyes Of Silver	Warner Brothers 7832
10/26/74	#51	6	Nobody	Warner Brothers 8041
12/21/74	#3	17	Black Water	Warner Brothers 8062
5/03/75	#10	12	Take Me In Your Arms (Rock Me)	Warner Brothers 8092
8/09/75	#44	6	Sweet Maxine	Warner Brothers 8126
11/29/75	#76	6	I Cheat The Hangman	Warner Brothers 8161
4/24/76	#15	17	Takin' It To The Streets	Warner Brothers 8196
11/20/76	#52	14	It Keeps You Runnin'	Warner Brothers 8282
7/23/77	#39	12	Little Darling (I Need You)	Warner Brothers 8408
10/15/77	#78	7	Echoes Of Love	Warner Brothers 8471
1/27/79	#1	21	What A Fool Believes	Warner Brothers 8725

Debut Date	Peak Pos	Wks Chr	**ARTIST**/Song Title	Label & Number
5/05/79	#13	14	Minute By Minute	Warner Brothers 8828
8/11/79	#30	12	Dependin' On You	Warner Brothers 49029
9/06/80	#7	14	Real Love	Warner Brothers 49503
11/22/80	#24	15	One Step Closer	Warner Brothers 49622
1/17/81	#77	5	Wynken, Blynken And Nod	Warner Brothers 49642
2/21/81	#72	6	Keep This Train A-Rollin'	Warner Brothers 49670
2/06/82	#72	5	Here To Love You	Warner Brothers 50001
5/20/89	#13	17	The Doctor	Capitol 44376
8/12/89	#38	12	Need A Little Taste Of Love	Capitol 44441
5/25/91	#75	6	Dangerous	Capitol 44700
			DOOLITTLE BAND	
10/11/80	#66	9	Who Were You Thinkin' Of	Columbia 11355
			DOORS	
5/27/67	#1	18	Light My Fire	Elektra 45615
9/23/67	#10	9	People Are Strange	Elektra 45621
12/02/67	#25	9	Love Me Two Times	Elektra 45624
3/23/68	#22	10	The Unknown Soldier	Elektra 45628
6/29/68	#1	14	Hello, I Love You/	Elektra 45635
6/29/68	#81	1	Love Street	Elektra 45635
12/28/68	#1	12	Touch Me	Elektra 45646
3/29/69	#28	7	Wishful Sinful	Elektra 45656
6/14/69	#33	8	Tell All The People	Elektra 45663
8/30/69	#40	7	Runnin' Blue	Elektra 45675
4/04/70	#40	7	You Make Me Real/	Elektra 45685
4/25/70	#76	4	Road House Blues	Elektra 45685
4/03/71	#7	12	Love Her Madly	Elektra 45726
7/03/71	#12	12	Riders On The Storm	Elektra 45738
12/04/71	#64	6	Tightrope Ride	Elektra 45757
10/21/72	#94	1	The Mosquito	Elektra 45807
			CHARLIE DORE	
2/16/80	#12	19	Pilot Of The Airwaves	Island 49166
			HAROLD DORMAN	
3/12/60	#17	17	Mountain Of Love	Rita 1003
			JIMMY DORSEY	
4/06/57	#2	25	So Rare	Fraternity 755
8/03/57	#25	10	June Night	Fraternity 777
			LEE DORSEY	
9/02/61	#7	15	Ya Ya	Fury 1053
12/23/61	#33	9	Do-Re-Mi	Fury 1056
6/19/65	#29	11	Ride Your Pony	Amy 927
10/02/65	#100	1	Work, Work, Work	Amy 939
1/08/66	#38	9	Get Out Of My Life, Woman	Amy 945
7/23/66	#10	13	Working In The Coal Mine	Amy 958
10/22/66	#29	10	Holy Cow	Amy 965
5/20/67	#96	1	My Old Car	Amy 987
10/28/67	#90	3	Go-Go Girl	Amy 998
7/05/69	#91	3	Everything I Do Gohn Be Funky	Amy 11055
			TOMMY DORSEY ORCHESTRA starring WARREN COVINGTON	
8/23/58	#2	23	Tea For Two Cha Cha Cha	Decca 30704
11/15/58	#30	10	I Want To Be Happy Cha Cha	Decca 30790
			DOTTIE and RAY	
1/23/65	#86	4	I Love You Baby	Le Sage 701
			DOUBLE	
6/28/86	#20	19	The Captain Of Her Heart	A&M 2838
			DOUCETTE	
4/01/78	#69	9	Mama Let Him Play	Mushroom 7030
10/14/78	#97	3	All I Wanna Do	Mushroom 7036
7/14/79	#91	6	Nobody	Mushroom 7042
			CARL DOUGLAS	
10/19/74	#1	18	Kung Fu Fighting	20th Century 2140
2/08/75	#46	7	Dance The Kung Fu	2oth Century 2168
			CAROL DOUGLAS	
11/23/74	#10	16	Doctor's Orders	Midland Int'l. 10113
4/05/75	#85	3	A Hurricane Is Coming Tonite	Midland Int'l. 10229
12/25/76	#96	5	Midnight Love Affair	Midland Int'l. 10753

Debut Date	Peak Pos	Wks Chr	ARTIST/Song Title	Label & Number
			MIKE DOUGLAS	
3/06/65	#86	3	Pass Me By	Epic 9760
12/18/65	#7	10	The Men In My Little Girl's Life	Epic 9876
			DEBBIE DOVALE	
11/02/63	#75	6	Hey Lover	Roulette 4521
			RONNIE DOVE	
7/25/64	#31	11	Say You	Diamond 167
10/31/64	#21	9	Right Or Wrong	Diamond 173
1/16/65	#50	5	Hello Pretty Girl	Diamond 176
3/20/65	#9	11	One Kiss For Old Times Sake	Diamond 179
6/05/65	#15	11	A Little Bit Of Heaven	Diamond 184
9/04/65	#25	7	I'll Make All Your Dreams Come True	Diamond 188
10/30/65	#27	9	Kiss Away	Diamond 191
1/22/66	#17	9	When Liking Turns To Loving	Diamond 195
4/09/66	#25	8	Let's Start All Over Again	Diamond 198
6/18/66	#30	8	Happy Summer Days	Diamond 205
9/03/66	#29	9	I Really Don't Want To Know	Diamond 208
11/19/66	#17	10	Cry	Diamond 214
2/18/67	#47	7	One More Mountain To Climb	Diamond 217
4/15/67	#40	7	My Babe	Diamond 221
8/05/67	#65	5	I Want To Love You For What You Are	Diamond 227
12/09/67	#64	6	Dancing Out Of My Heart	Diamond 233
3/23/68	#95	2	In Some Time	Diamond 240
6/01/68	#62	6	Mountain Of Love	Diamond 244
9/14/68	#76	9	Tomboy	Diamond 249
5/24/69	#97	3	I Need You Now	Diamond 260
			DOVELLS	
9/16/61	#3	17	Bristol Stomp	Parkway 827
2/03/62	#32	10	Do The New Continental	Parkway 833
5/12/62	#34	11	Bristol Twistin' Annie	Parkway 838
8/18/62	#21	12	Hully Gully Baby	Parkway 845
11/17/62	#70	4	The Jitterbug	Parkway 855
4/20/63	#3	15	You Can't Sit Down	Parkway 867
8/24/63	#50	8	Betty In Bermudas	Parkway 882
8/10/74	#100	1	Dancing In The Street	Event 216
			DOVES	
2/29/92	#81	3	Beatin Up In Love Again	Elektra 64839
			JOE DOWELL	
7/08/61	#3	17	Wooden Heart	Smash 1708
10/14/61	#49	8	Bridge Of Love	Smash 1717
6/30/62	#36	8	Little Red Rented Rowboat	Smash 1759
			AL DOWNING	
2/15/75	#71	8	I'll Be Holding On	Chess 2158
			LAMONT DOZIER	
12/29/73	#14	15	Trying To Hold On To My Woman	ABC 11407
6/29/74	#26	8	Fish Ain't Bitin'	ABC 11438
1/04/75	#72	5	Let Me Start Tonight	ABC 12044
			DRAFI	
4/30/66	#60	5	Marble Breaks And Iron Bends	London 10825
			CHARLIE DRAKE	
1/20/62	#22	12	My Boomerang Won't Come Back	United Artists 398
			GUY DRAKE	
2/14/70	#63	10	Welfare Cadillac	Royal American 1
			PETE DRAKE	
3/21/64	#22	10	Forever	Smash 1867
			DRAMATICS	
7/10/71	#14	14	Whatcha See Is Whatcha Get	Volt 4058
1/01/72	#69	7	Get Up And Get Down	Volt 4071
2/19/72	#3	14	In The Rain	Volt 4075
8/05/72	#52	13	Toast To The Fool	Volt 4082
4/21/73	#51	10	Hey You! Get Off My Mountain	Volt 4090
10/27/73	#50	8	Fell For You	Volt 4099
8/03/74	#55	10	Door To Your Heart	Cadet 5704
4/26/75	#46	10	Me And Mrs. Jones	ABC 12090
12/25/76	#62	12	Be My Girl	ABC 12235
6/11/77	#84	4	I Can't Get Over You	ABC 12256

Debut Date	Peak Pos	Wks Chr	**ARTIST**/Song Title	Label & Number
10/08/77	#86	7	Shake It Well	ABC 12299
4/15/78	#89	3	Ocean Of Thoughts And Dreams	ABC 12331
			RUSTY DRAPER	
8/25/53	#9	5	Gambler's Guitar	Mercury 70167
10/29/55	#5	8	The Shifting, Whispering Sands	Mercury 70696
8/25/56	#22	10	In The Middle Of The House	Mercury 70921
5/18/57	#18	12	Freight Train	Mercury 71102
7/09/58	#65	3	June, July And August	Mercury 71336
6/11/60	#80	1	Mule Skinner Blues	Mercury 71634
10/12/63	#81	4	Night Life	Monument 823
			DREAM ACADEMY	
11/30/85	#6	24	Life In A Northern Town	Warner Brothers 28841
4/26/86	#32	12	The Love Parade	Reprise 28750
			DREAMERS	
2/18/61	#100	1	Teenage Vows Of Love	Goldisc 3015
			DREAMLOVERS	
8/12/61	#19	11	When We Get Married	Heritage 102
7/07/62	#72	5	If I Should Lose You	End 1114
			DREAM WEAVERS	
12/24/55	#4	9	It's Almost Tomorrow	Decca 29683
			PATTI DREW	
2/22/64	#90	2	Tell Him*	Capitol 5505
9/30/67	#92	1	Tell Him	Capitol 5861
8/17/68	#82	8	Working On A Groovy Thing	Capitol 2197
			*released as by the **DREW-VELS**	
			DRIFTERS	
6/07/58	#53	4	Moonlight Bay	Atlantic 1187
6/06/59	#1	19	There Goes My Baby	Atlantic 2025
10/17/59	#10	15	Dance With Me/	Atlantic 2040
10/24/59	#23	13	(If You Cry) True Love, True Love	Atlantic 2040
2/13/60	#9	13	This Magic Moment	Atlantic 2050
6/04/60	#40	8	Lonely Winds	Atlantic 2062
9/10/60	#1	17	Save The Last Dance For Me	Atlantic 2071
12/24/60	#11	12	I Count The Tears	Atlantic 2087
3/25/61	#11	12	Some Kind Of Wonderful	Atlantic 2096
6/10/61	#13	12	Please Stay	Atlantic 2105
9/09/61	#16	12	Sweets For My Sweet	Atlantic 2117
3/03/62	#18	10	When My Little Girl Is Smiling	Atlantic 2134
11/10/62	#6	19	Up On The Roof	Atlantic 2162
3/16/63	#12	11	On Broadway	Atlantic 2182
6/08/63	#81	5	Rat Race	Atlantic 2191
9/07/63	#27	11	I'll Take You Home	Atlantic 2201
1/25/64	#42	9	Vaya Con Dios	Atlantic 2216
5/09/64	#83	6	One Way Love	Atlantic 2225
6/27/64	#5	15	Under The Boardwalk	Atlantic 2237
9/26/64	#31	7	I've Got Sand In My Shoes	Atlantic 2253
11/21/64	#24	8	Saturday Night At The Movies	Atlantic 2260
1/30/65	#43	6	At The Club	Atlantic 2268
4/24/65	#77	4	Come On Over To My Place	Atlantic 2285
8/21/65	#88	3	I'll Take You Where The Music's Playing	Atlantic 2298
3/26/66	#67	5	Memories Are Made Of This	Atlantic 2325
12/10/66	#84	6	Baby What I Mean	Atlantic 2366
			DRIVER	
8/06/77	#83	8	(I've Been Looking For) A New Way To Say I Love You . .	A&M 1966
			DRS	
10/30/93	#6	24	Gangsta Lean	Capitol 44958
			DRUPI	
10/20/73	#89	4	Vado Via	A&M 1460
			ROY DRUSKY	
6/10/61	#78	6	Three Hearts In A Tangle	Decca 31193
			DUALS	
9/02/61	#24	12	Stick Shift	Sue 745
			DUBS	
11/09/57	#25	10	Could This Be Magic	Gone 5011
9/05/59	#84	2	Chapel Of Dreams	Gone 5069

Debut Date	Peak Pos	Wks Chr	ARTIST/Song Title	Label & Number
			DAVE DUDLEY	
6/01/63	#39	12	Six Days On The Road	Golden Wing 3020
			DUICE	
1/16/93	#14	42	Dazzy Duks	TNR 3089
			DUKAYS	
7/22/61	#83	3	The Girl's A Devil	Nat 4001
1/27/62	#84	6	Nite Owl	Nat 4002
			DORIS DUKE	
2/21/70	#57	9	To The Other Woman	Canyon 28
5/23/70	#86	4	Feet Start Walkin'	Canyon 35
			GEORGE DUKE	
12/03/77	#61	12	Reach For It	Epic 50463
5/02/81	#21	21	Sweet Baby*	Epic 01052
2/27/82	#50	10	Shine On	Epic 0271
			*released as by STANLEY CLARKE/GEORGE DUKE	
			PATTY DUKE	
6/19/65	#6	12	Don't Just Stand There	United Artists 875
9/18/65	#51	6	Funny Little Butterflies/	United Artists 915
10/09/65	#31	8	Say Something Funny	United Artists 915
2/19/66	#63	7	Whenever She Holds You	United Artists 978
			DUKE & THE DRIVERS	
8/30/75	#96	3	What You Got	ABC 12110
			DUKE JUPITER	
3/20/82	#52	10	I'll Drink To You	Coast To Coast 02801
5/12/84	#66	8	Little Lady	Morocco 1736
			DUKES	
8/28/82	#96	4	Mystery Girl	Atlantic 89999
			CHARLENE DUNCAN	
3/26/77	#99	2	It Ain't Easy Coming Down	Prodigal 0663
			DAVID DUNDAS	
9/18/76	#14	28	Jeans On	Chrysalis 2094
			ROBBIE DUPREE	
4/12/80	#5	24	Steal Away	Elektra 46621
7/19/80	#15	19	Hot Rod Hearts	Elektra 47005
5/23/81	#55	8	Brooklyn Girls	Elektra 47145
			DUPREES	
7/21/62	#7	16	You Belong To Me	Coed 569
10/27/62	#16	10	My Own True Love	Coed 571
1/19/63	#70	5	I'd Rather Be Here In Your Arms	Coed 574
3/30/63	#77	3	Gone With The Wind	Coed 576
8/17/63	#28	9	Why Don't You Believe Me	Coed 584
11/02/63	#19	12	Have You Heard	Coed 585
1/18/64	#47	6	(It's No) Sin	Coed 587
4/11/64	#94	2	Where Are You	Coed 590
7/10/65	#83	3	Around The Corner	Columbia 43336
11/23/68	#91	3	Goodnight My Love	Heritage 805
			DURAN DURAN	
12/25/82	#4	23	Hungry Like The Wolf	Harvest 5195
3/26/83	#14	16	Rio	Capitol 5215
6/04/83	#7	19	Is There Something I Should Know	Capitol 5233
11/05/83	#1	20	Union Of The Snake	Capitol 5290
1/14/84	#10	17	New Moon On Sunday	Capitol 5309
4/21/84	#1	21	The Reflex	Capitol 5345
11/03/84	#1	19	The Wild Boys	Capitol 5417
2/02/85	#19	15	Save A Prayer	Capitol 5438
5/18/85	#1	18	A View To A Kill	Capitol 5475
11/01/86	#4	20	Notorious	Capitol 5648
1/31/87	#47	11	Skin Trade	Capitol 5670
5/02/87	#76	6	Meet El Presidente	Capitol 44001
10/15/88	#3	19	I Don't Want Your Love	Capitol 44237
12/24/88	#27	14	All She Wants Is	Capitol 44287
3/25/89	#63	6	Do You Believe In Shame?	Capitol 44337
8/25/90	#56	10	Violence Of Summer (Love's Taking Over)	Capitol 44608
1/16/93	#1	25	Ordinary World	Capitol 44908
4/24/93	#4	27	Come Undone	Capitol 44918

Debut Date	Peak Pos	Wks Chr	ARTIST/Song Title	Label & Number
9/25/93	#41	12	Too Much Information	Capitol 44955
			JIMMY DURANTE	
9/14/63	#50	7	September Song	Warner Brothers 5382
			DUSK	
1/23/71	#62	10	Angel Baby	Bell 961
5/29/71	#41	14	I Hear Those Church Bells Ringing	Bell 990
11/27/71	#71	4	Treat Me Like A Good Piece Of Candy	Bell 45148
			DYKE and THE BLAZERS	
4/22/67	#73	12	Funky Broadway (Part 1)	Original Sound 64
3/30/68	#71	7	Funky Walk (Part 1)	Original Sound 79
5/17/69	#50	10	We Got More Soul	Original Sound 86
9/13/69	#49	9	Let A Woman Be A Woman - Let A Man Be A Man	Original Sound 89
1/10/70	#96	2	You Are My Sunshine	Original Sound 90
4/18/70	#85	4	Uhh	Original Sound 89
			BOB DYLAN	
4/03/65	#52	8	Subterranean Homesick Blues	Columbia 43242
7/31/65	#1	12	Like A Rolling Stone	Columbia 43346
9/25/65	#9	10	Positively 4th Street	Columbia 43389
1/01/66	#58	6	Can You Please Crawl Out Your Window?	Columbia 43477
4/16/66	#2	10	Rainy Day Women #12 & 35	Columbia 43592
7/02/66	#25	7	I Want You	Columbia 43683
9/10/66	#28	7	Just Like A Woman	Columbia 43792
5/27/67	#97	1	Leopard-Skin Pill-Box Hat	Columbia 44069
5/24/69	#60	4	I Threw It All Away	Columbia 44826
7/12/69	#8	14	Lay Lady Lay	Columbia 44926
11/01/69	#45	5	Tonight I'll Be Staying Here With You	Columbia 45004
7/18/70	#28	9	Wigwam	Columbia 45199
6/26/71	#31	8	Watching The River Run	Columbia 45409
12/04/71	#30	9	George Jackson	Columbia 45516
9/01/73	#10	14	Knockin' On Heaven's Door	Columbia 45913
12/22/73	#47	6	A Fool Such As I	Columbia 45982
2/23/74	#30	8	On A Night Like This	Asylum 11033
5/04/74	#76	2	Something There Is About You	Asylum 11035
7/27/74	#47	8	Most Likely You Go Your Way*	Asylum 11043
3/08/75	#43	8	Tangled Up In Blue	Columbia 10106
11/22/75	#27	11	Hurricane (Part 1)	Columbia 10245
3/06/76	#49	7	Mozambique	Columbia 10298
9/15/79	#37	11	Gotta Serve Somebody	Columbia 11072
12/24/83	#60	9	Sweetheart Like You	Columbia 04301
			***released as by BOB DYLAN/THE BAND**	
			DYNAMICS	
10/19/63	#40	10	Misery	Big Top 3161
3/15/69	#58	8	Ice Cream Song	Cotillion 44021
			DYNAMIC SUPERIORS	
11/02/74	#72	8	Shoe Shoe Shine	Motown 1324
			DYNASTY	
9/06/80	#95	3	I've Just Begun To Love You	Solar 12021
			DYNATONES	
6/20/59	#95	2	Steel Guitar Rag	Bomarc 303
8/20/66	#74	9	The Fife Piper	HBR 494
			RONNIE DYSON	
6/13/70	#10	15	(If You Let Me Make Love To You) Why Can't I Touch You?	Columbia 45110
10/17/70	#35	8	I Don't Wanna Cry	Columbia 45240
7/03/71	#81	5	When You Get Right Down To It	Columbia 45387
2/10/73	#20	13	One Man Band (Plays All Alone)	Columbia 45776
8/11/73	#70	7	Just Don't Want To Be Lonely	Columbia 45867
7/17/76	#59	10	The More You Do It	Columbia 10356

E

			EAGLES	
5/20/72	#9	13	Take It Easy	Asylum 11005
8/26/72	#11	16	Witchy Woman	Asylum 11008
12/30/72	#20	12	Peaceful Easy Feeling	Asylum 11013
6/09/73	#40	9	Tequila Sunrise	Asylum 11017
9/01/73	#49	9	Outlaw Man	Asylum 11025

Debut Date	Peak Pos	Wks Chr	ARTIST/Song Title	Label & Number
			EAGLES—*continued*	
5/04/74	#17	12	Already Gone	Asylum 11036
9/07/74	#49	7	James Dean	Asylum 45202
11/30/74	#4	18	Best Of My Love	Asylum 45218
5/31/75	#1	16	One Of These Nights	Asylum 45257
9/20/75	#3	13	Lyin' Eyes	Asylum 45279
12/20/75	#5	22	Take It To The Limit	Asylum 45293
12/11/76	#2	20	New Kid In Town	Asylum 45373
3/05/77	#1	20	Hotel California	Asylum 45386
5/14/77	#11	13	Life In The Fast Lane	Asylum 45403
12/09/78	#29	8	Please Come Home For Christmas	Asylum 45555
10/06/79	#1	16	Heartache Tonight	Asylum 46545
12/01/79	#10	15	The Long Run	Asylum 46569
2/23/80	#9	16	I Can't Tell You Why	Asylum 46608
12/27/80	#27	14	Seven Bridges Road	Asylum 47100
			STACY EARL	
11/23/91	#26	20	Love Me All Up	RCA 62116
2/22/92	#15	20	Romeo And Juliet	RCA 62192
6/13/92	#31	20	Slowly	RCA 62271
			EARL-JEAN	
7/04/64	#42	8	I'm Into Somethin' Good	Colpix 729
			EARLS	
6/17/61	#81	6	Life Is But A Dream	Rome 101
12/08/62	#26	11	Remember Then	Old Town 1130
3/16/63	#82	7	Never	Old Town 1133
			EARTH, WIND & FIRE	
6/19/71	#83	7	Love Is Life	Warner Brothers 7492
8/25/73	#54	8	Evil	Columbia 45888
11/24/73	#34	10	Keep Your Head To The Sky	Columbia 45953
3/16/74	#35	13	Mighty Mighty	Columbia 46007
7/06/74	#55	9	Kalimba	Columbia 46070
9/28/74	#57	5	Devotion	Columbia 10026
12/28/74	#72	8	Hot Dawgit*	Columbia 10056
2/08/75	#1	21	Shining Star	Columbia 10090
3/15/75	#67	7	Sun Goddess*	Columbia 10103
7/05/75	#13	13	That's The Way Of The World	Columbia 10172
11/22/75	#7	17	Sing A Song	Columbia 10251
3/27/76	#45	9	Can't Hide Love	Columbia 10309
7/17/76	#10	20	Getaway	Columbia 10373
11/27/76	#21	16	Saturday Nite	Columbia 10439
11/05/77	#15	18	Serpentine Fire	Columbia 10625
2/25/78	#33	15	Fantasy	Columbia 10688
7/22/78	#11	14	Got To Get You Into My Life	Columbia 10796
11/18/78	#6	18	September	ARC 10854
5/12/79	#5	17	Boogie Wonderland**	ARC 10956
7/07/79	#3	17	After The Love Has Gone	ARC 11033
10/13/79	#66	7	In The Stone	ARC 11093
12/29/79	#68	6	Star	ARC 11165
9/20/80	#42	10	Let Me Talk	ARC 11366
11/22/80	#53	10	You	ARC 11407
2/07/81	#54	8	And Love Goes On	ARC 11434
10/03/81	#3	24	Let's Groove	ARC 02536
1/23/82	#60	8	Wanna Be With You	ARC 02668
1/22/83	#28	14	Fall In Love With Me	Columbia 03375
4/30/83	#75	5	Side By Side	Columbia 03814
11/12/83	#63	10	Magnetic	Columbia 04210
10/31/87	#68	13	System Of Survival	Columbia 07608
2/06/88	#73	9	Thinking Of You	Columbia 07695
9/04/83	#40	22	Sunday Morning	Reprise 18461
			***released as by RAMSEY LEWIS and EARTH, WIND & FIRE**	
			****released as by EARTH, WIND & FIRE with THE EMOTIONS**	
			EAST COAST FAMILY	
8/29/92	#75	7	1-4-All-4-1	BIV/Motown 2171
			EASTERHOUSE	
4/01/89	#69	6	Come Out Fighting	Columbia 68552
			SHEENA EASTON	
2/14/81	#1	22	Morning Train (Nine To Five)	EMI America 8071
5/09/81	#15	17	Modern Girl	EMI America 8080

106

Debut Date	Peak Pos	Wks Chr	ARTIST/Song Title	Label & Number
7/25/81	#3	25	For Your Eyes Only	Liberty 1418
11/28/81	#12	19	You Could Have Been With Me	EMI America 8101
4/03/82	#24	15	When He Shines	Emi America 8113
9/04/82	#61	8	Machinery	EMI America 8131
10/30/82	#66	11	I Wouldn't Beg For Water	EMI America 8142
1/29/83	#10	19	We've Got Tonight*	Liberty 1492
8/20/83	#8	23	Telefone (Long Distance Love Affair)	EMI America 8172
12/10/83	#23	21	Almost Over You	EMI America 8186
8/25/84	#4	25	Strut	EMI America 8227
12/22/84	#5	20	Sugar Walls	EMI America 8253
3/23/85	#65	8	Swear	EMI America 8263
10/27/85	#28	16	Do It For Love	EMI America 8295
2/08/86	#67	8	Jimmy Mack	EMI America 8309
7/26/86	#42	14	So Far So Good	EMI America 8332
10/29/88	#2	28	The Lover In Me	MCA 53416
10/28/89	#33	15	The Arms Of Orion**	Warner Brothers 22757
3/30/91	#18	18	What Comes Naturally	MCA 53957
			*released as by KENNY ROGERS and SHEENA EASTON	
			**released as by PRINCE with SHEENA EASTON	
			EASYBEATS	
3/18/67	#16	13	Friday On My Mind	United Artists 50106
7/15/67	#92	2	Heaven And Hell	United Artists 50187
11/08/69	#72	4	St. Louis	Rare Earth 5009
			EASY STREET	
7/10/76	#79	4	I've Been Lovin' You	Capricorn 0255
			EAZY-E	
11/27/93	#42	13	Real Muthaphuckhin G's	Ruthless 5508
			EBONYS	
6/19/71	#46	7	You're The Reason Why	Phil. Int'l. 3503
7/28/73	#90	2	It's Forever	Phil. Int'l. 3529
			ECHOES	
3/11/61	#15	13	Baby Blue	Seg-way 103
11/10/62	#86	2	Bluebirds Over The Mountain	Smash 1766
			BILLY ECKSTINE	
6/10/50	#1	12	My Foolish Heart	MGM 10623
5/05/51	#5	10	I Apologize	MGM 10903
3/08/58	#49	2	Gigi	Mercury 71250
			ECSTASY, PASSION & PAIN	
7/13/74	#68	8	Good Things Don't Last Forever	Roulette 7156
10/12/74	#57	8	Ask Me	Roulette 7159
3/22/75	#52	8	One Beautiful Day	Roulette 7163
			JOHN EDDIE	
6/14/86	#53	10	Jungle Boy	Columbia 05858
			EDDIE and BETTY	
7/04/59	#83	6	Sweet Someone	Warner Brothers 5054
			EDDIE & DUTCH	
4/04/70	#68	6	My Wife, The Dancer	Ivanhoe 502
			EDDIE and THE CRUISERS	
10/08/83	#64	9	On The Dark Side	Scotti Brothers 04107
			DUANE EDDY	
3/01/58	#54	1	Movin' N' Groovin'	Jamie 1101
6/21/58	#7	15	Rebel-'Rouser	Jamie 1104
8/23/58	#33	8	Ramrod	Jamie 1109
11/01/58	#16	13	Cannonball	Jamie 1111
1/24/59	#19	10	The Lonely One	Jamie 1117
4/04/59	#27	8	"Yep!"	Jamie 1122
6/13/59	#10	15	Forty Miles Of Bad Road/	Jamie 1126
6/20/59	#68	5	The Quiet Three	Jamie 1126
10/03/59	#28	9	Some Kind A-Earthquake/	Jamie 1130
10/10/59	#75	5	First Love, First Tears	Jamie 1130
12/19/59	#20	12	Bonnie Came Back	Jamie 1144
3/19/60	#41	8	Shazam!	Jamie 1151
5/14/60	#3	18	Because They're Young	Jamie 1156
8/27/60	#39	7	Kommotion	Jamie 1163
10/08/60	#26	11	Peter Gunn	Jamie 1168
12/24/60	#19	12	"Pepe"	Jamie 1175

Debut Date	Peak Pos	Wks Chr	ARTIST/Song Title	Label & Number
			DUANE EDDY—*continued*	
3/25/61	#37	8	Theme From Dixie	Jamie 1183
5/27/61	#57	5	Ring Of Fire	Jamie 1187
7/22/61	#69	3	Drivin' Home	Jamie 1195
9/09/61	#81	4	My Blue Heaven	Jamie 1200
1/27/62	#100	2	The Battle	Jamie 1209
4/28/62	#83	3	Deep In The Heart Of Texas	RCA 7999
7/14/62	#48	8	The Ballad Of Paladin	RCA 8047
9/29/62	#11	18	(Dance With The) Guitar Man	RCA 8087
2/09/63	#30	10	Boss Guitar	RCA 8131
5/18/63	#76	4	Lonely Boy, Lonely Guitar	RCA 8180
8/10/63	#82	6	Your Baby's Gone Surfin'	RCA 8214
1/04/64	#90	2	The Son Of Rebel Rouser	RCA 8276
1/17/70	#95	1	Freight Train	Congress 6010
5/24/86	#49	10	Peter Gunn*	China 42986
			*released as by THE ART OF NOISE featuring DUANE EDDY	
			RANDY EDELMAN	
3/15/75	#91	3	Everybody Wants To Find A Bluebird	20th Century 2155
10/22/77	#91	5	Can't It All Be Love	Arista 0268
			EDISON LIGHTHOUSE	
2/14/70	#4	13	Love Grows (Where My Rosemary Goes)	Bell 858
1/02/71	#69	8	It's Up To You Petula	Bell 960
			DAVE EDMUNDS	
12/19/70	#4	14	I Hear You Knocking	MAM 3601
5/01/71	#53	4	I'm Comin' Home	MAM 3608
8/25/79	#65	7	Girls Talk	Swan Song 71001
5/16/81	#65	6	Almost Saturday Night	Swan Song 72000
5/21/83	#32	15	Slipping Away	Columbia 03877
			EDSELS	
5/13/61	#21	10	Rama Lama Ding Dong	Twin 700
			EDWARD BEAR	
5/16/70	#78	6	You, Me And Mexico	Capitol 2801
12/23/72	#3	17	Last Song	Capitol 3452
4/14/73	#24	12	Close Your Eyes	Capitol 3581
8/25/73	#77	3	Walking On The Beach	Capitol 3683
			BOBBY EDWARDS	
8/19/61	#8	22	You're The Reason	Crest 1075
1/20/62	#83	4	What's The Reason	Capitol 4674
			JIMMY EDWARDS	
11/16/57	#35	9	Love Bug Crawl	Mercury 71209
			JOHN EDWARDS	
11/16/74	#86	3	Careful Man	Aware 043
			JONATHAN EDWARDS	
11/13/71	#5	16	Sunshine	Capricorn 8021
3/18/72	#69	2	Train Of Glory	Atco 6881
			TOMMY EDWARDS	
8/16/58	#1	23	It's All In The Game	MGM 12688
10/25/58	#14	14	Love Is All We Need	MGM 12722
2/21/59	#18	14	Please Mr. Sun/	MGM 12757
2/28/59	#40	12	The Morning Side Of The Mountain	MGM 12757
5/16/59	#21	10	My Melancholy Baby/	MGM 12794
6/13/59	#78	3	It's Only The Good Times	MGM 12794
8/08/59	#29	12	I've Been There	MGM 12814
11/28/59	#73	6	Honestly And Truly/	MGM 12837
11/28/59	#69	9	(New In) The Ways Of Love	MGM 12837
2/20/60	#57	9	Don't Fence Me In	MGM 12871
5/14/60	#21	14	I Really Don't Want To Know	MGM 12890
			VINCENT EDWARDS	
7/14/62	#95	2	Why Did You Leave Me?	Russ-Fi 7001
			WALTER EGAN	
6/11/77	#74	6	Only The Lucky	Columbia 10531
5/20/78	#9	23	Magnet And Steel	Columbia 10719
10/14/78	#57	8	Hot Summer Nights	Columbia 10824
3/10/79	#93	2	Unloved	Columbia 10916
4/09/83	#38	12	Fool Moon Fire	Backstreet 52200

Debut Date	Peak Pos	Wks Chr	ARTIST/Song Title	Label & Number
			8TH DAY	
5/08/71	#8	13	She's Not Just Another Woman	Invictus 9087
9/11/71	#34	11	You've Got To Crawl (Before You Walk)	Invictus 9098
1/01/72	#78	4	If I Could See The Light	Invictus 9107
			EIGHTH WONDER	
11/26/88	#52	10	Cross My Heart	WTG 08036
4/08/89	#81	4	Baby Baby	WTG 68610
			EIGHT SECONDS	
1/31/87	#62	10	Kiss You (When It's Dangerous)	Polydor 885352
			DONNIE ELBERT	
11/14/70	#91	4	Can't Get Over Losing You	Rare Bullet 101
10/09/71	#30	14	Where Did Our Love Go	All Platinum 2330
1/22/72	#19	10	I Can't Help Myself	Avco 4587
1/22/72	#79	4	Sweet Baby	All Platinum 2333
			EL CHICANO	
4/04/70	#27	11	Viva Tirado (Part 1)	Kapp 2085
6/17/72	#49	6	Brown Eyed Girl	Kapp 2173
11/17/73	#28	10	Tell Her She's Lovely	MCA 40104
			EL COCO	
12/24/77	#52	11	Cocomotion	AVI 147
			EL DORADOS	
12/03/55	#8	3	At My Front Door	Vee-Jay 147
			ELECTRIC EXPRESS	
7/10/71	#65	7	It's The Real Thing (Part 1)	Linco 1001
			ELECTRIC INDIAN	
8/02/69	#18	11	Keem-O-Sabe	United Artists 50563
12/06/69	#71	4	Land Of 1000 Dances	United Artists 50613
			ELECTRIC LIGHT ORCHESTRA	
5/19/73	#48	14	Roll Over Beethoven	United Artists 173
12/08/73	#51	11	Showdown	United Artists 337
4/20/74	#61	8	Daybreaker	United Artists 405
12/14/74	#14	17	Can't Get It Out Of My Head	United Artists 573
11/15/75	#9	20	Evil Woman	United Artists 729
3/06/76	#14	17	Strange Magic	United Artists 770
8/21/76	#75	4	Showdown	United Artists 842
10/30/76	#10	20	Livin' Thing	United Artists 888
2/05/77	#16	14	Do Ya	United Artists 939
6/18/77	#4	21	Telephone Line	United Artists 1000
11/19/77	#11	15	Turn To Stone	Jet 1099
2/18/78	#18	16	Sweet Talkin' Woman	Jet 1145
6/24/78	#27	12	Mr. Blue Sky	Jet 5050
5/19/79	#7	14	Shine A Little Love	Jet 5057
7/28/79	#4	17	Don't Bring Me Down	Jet 5060
10/13/79	#47	9	Confusion	Jet 5064
12/01/79	#36	12	Last Train To London	Jet 5067
5/24/80	#14	15	I'm Alive	MCA 41246
8/02/80	#14	16	All Over The World	MCA 41289
8/09/80	#9	20	Xanadu*	MCA 41285
7/25/81	#8	17	Hold On Tight**	Jet 02408
10/24/81	#38	13	Twilight**	Jet 02559
6/25/83	#22	13	Rock 'N' Roll Is King**	Jet 03964
2/01/86	#26	16	Calling America	CBS Associated 05766
			*released as by OLIVIA NEWTON-JOHN/ELECTRIC LIGHT ORCHESTRA	
			**released as by ELO	
			ELECTRIC PRUNES	
12/17/66	#12	15	I Had Too Much To Dream (Last Night)	Reprise 0532
4/01/67	#44	8	Get Me To The World On Time	Reprise 0564
			ELECTRONIC	
4/07/90	#31	15	Getting Away With It	Warner Brothers 19880
			ELEGANTS	
7/12/58	#2	19	Little Star	Apt 25005
11/01/58	#94	1	Please Believe Me/	Apt 25017
11/08/58	#77	4	Goodnight	Apt 25017

Debut Date	Peak Pos	Wks Chr	ARTIST/Song Title	Label & Number
			ELEPHANT'S MEMORY	
8/01/70	#49	16	Mongoose	Metromedia 182
			ELEVENTH HOUR	
9/20/75	#94	2	Hollywood Hot	20th Century 2215
			LARRY ELGART and HIS MANHATTAN SWING ORCHESTRA	
6/05/82	#36	13	Hooked On Swing	RCA 13219
			ELGINS	
2/12/66	#88	4	Put Yourself In My Place/	V.I.P. 25029
3/19/66	#55	8	Darling Baby	V.I.P. 25029
10/22/66	#65	5	Heaven Must Have Sent You	V.I.P. 25037
			JIMMY ELLEDGE	
12/02/61	#33	12	Funny How Time Slips Away	RCA 7946
			YVONNE ELLIMAN	
4/17/71	#30	11	I Don't Know How To Love Him	Decca 32785
10/02/71	#95	3	Everything's Alright	Decca 32870
10/02/76	#10	21	Love Me	RSO 858
3/19/77	#14	17	Hello Stranger	RSO 871
2/04/78	#1	21	If I Can't Have You	RSO 884
10/13/79	#53	13	Love Pains	RSO 1007
			JOEY B. ELLIS & TYNETTA HARE	
12/29/90	#63	8	Go For It! (Heart And Fire)	Bust It/Capitol 44667
			RAY ELLIS	
10/29/60	#89	2	Midnight Lace	MGM 12942
			SHIRLEY ELLIS	
11/09/63	#7	16	The Nitty Gritty	Congress 202
3/29/64	#70	4	(That's) What The Nitty Gritty Is	Congress 208
12/19/64	#3	14	The Name Game	Congress 230
3/20/65	#7	9	The Clapping Song (Clap Pat Clap Slap)	Congress 234
6/05/65	#69	4	The Puzzle Song	Congress 238
3/04/67	#67	5	Soul Time	Columbia 44021
			LORRAINE ELLISON	
2/05/66	#80	5	I Dig You Baby	Mercury 72472
10/01/66	#63	7	Stay With Me	Warner Brothers 5850
			ELOISE TRIO	
4/30/60	#87	4	Chi Chi Merengue	Decca 31047
			EMBERS	
7/29/61	#36	9	Solitaire	Empress 101
			EMERSON, LAKE & PALMER	
4/03/71	#65	6	Lucky Man	Cotillion 44106
9/11/71	#84	2	Stone Of Years	Cotillion 44131
4/01/72	#92	3	Nutrocker	Cotillion 44151
8/26/72	#40	11	From The Beginning	Cotillion 44158
1/13/73	#63	4	Lucky Man	Cotillion 44106
			EMERSON, LAKE & POWELL	
6/21/86	#71	6	Touch And Go	Polydor 885101
			RALPH EMERY	
9/02/61	#100	1	Hello Fool	Liberty 55352
			EMF	
4/20/91	#1	27	Unbelievable	EMI 50350
9/21/91	#27	21	Lies	EMI 50363
			LES EMMERSON	
12/30/72	#37	10	Control Of Me	Lion 141
			EMOTIONS (female trio)	
5/31/69	#40	9	So I Can Love You	Volt 4010
4/11/70	#100	1	Stealing Love	Volt 4031
11/13/71	#33	14	Show Me How	Volt 4066
3/11/72	#85	3	My Honey And Me	Volt 4077
8/05/72	#92	4	I Could Never Be Happy	Volt 4083
3/16/74	#72	7	Put A Little Love Away	Volt 4106
11/13/76	#55	15	I Don't Wanna Lose Your Love	Columbia 10347
6/18/77	#1	21	Best Of My Love	Columbia 10544
11/12/77	#73	7	Don't Ask My Neighbors	Columbia 10622

Debut Date	Peak Pos	Wks Chr	ARTIST/Song Title	Label & Number
5/12/79	#5	17	Boogie Wonderland*	ARC 10956
			*released as by EARTH, WIND & FIRE with THE EMOTIONS	
			EMOTIONS (male quintet)	
11/17/62	#64	10	Echo	Kapp 490
10/12/63	#82	5	A Story Untold	20th Century Fox 430
			EMPEROR'S	
12/10/66	#49	9	Karate	Mala 543
			LAURA ENEA	
4/25/92	#71	10	This Is The Last Time	Next Plateau 50172
			ENCHANTMENT	
1/22/77	#46	15	Gloria	United Artists 912
7/02/77	#93	7	Sunshine.	Roadshow 991
2/04/78	#36	11	It's You That I Need	Roadshow 1124
			ENGLAND DAN & JOHN FORD COLEY	
6/12/76	#4	24	I'd Really Love To See You Tonight	Big Tree 16069
10/09/76	#10	18	Nights Are Forever Without You	Big Tree 16079
5/07/77	#13	18	It's Sad To Belong	Big Tree 16088
10/01/77	#17	13	Gone Too Far	Big Tree 16102
3/25/78	#14	13	We'll Never Have To Say Goodbye Again	Big Tree 16110
6/10/78	#74	5	You Can't Dance	Big Tree 16117
3/10/79	#13	17	Love Is The Answer	Big Tree 16131
10/27/79	#64	7	What Can I Do With This Broken Heart	Big Tree 17000
			SCOTT ENGLISH	
2/15/64	#87	6	High On A Hill	Spokane 4003
3/18/72	#98	1	Brandy	Janus 171
			ENGLISH CONGREGATION	
1/15/72	#28	10	Softly Whispering I Love You	Atco 6865
7/01/72	#74	5	Jesahel	Signpost 70004
			ENIGMA	
2/16/91	#6	21	Sadeness (Part 1)	Charisma 98864
			ENTOUCH	
1/27/90	#65	8	All Nite*	Vintertainment 69260
			*released as by ENTOUCH featuring KEITH SWEAT	
			ENUFF Z'NUFF	
11/18/89	#74	5	New Thing	Atco 99207
2/03/90	#90	4	Fly High Michelle	Atco 99135
3/24/90	#90	1	Fly High Michelle	Atco 99135
5/25/91	#84	5	Mother's Eyes	Atco 98845
			EN VOGUE	
5/12/90	#3	23	Hold On	Atlantic 87984
9/01/90	#36	12	Lies	Atlantic 87893
3/28/92	#1	30	My Lovin' (You're Never Gonna Get It)	Atco East West 98586
6/13/92	#6	31	Giving Him Something He Can Feel	Atco East West 98560
9/19/92	#5	25	Free Your Mind	Atco East West 98487
12/12/92	#13	22	Give It Up, Turn It Loose	Atco East West 98455
4/03/93	#31	17	Love Don't Love You	East West 98432
10/23/93	#43	9	Runaway Love	East West 98354
			ENYA	
1/28/89	#25	18	Orinoco Flow (Sail Away)	Geffen 27633
3/07/92	#68	9	Carribean Blue	Reprise 19089
			EPIC SPLENDOR	
12/09/67	#77	10	A Little Rain Must Fall	Hot Biscuit 1450
			EPMD	
8/01/92	#28	14	Crossover	RAL 74173
			PRESTON EPPS	
5/16/59	#16	10	Bongo Rock.	Original Sound 4
7/02/60	#60	10	Bongo Bongo Bongo	Original Sound 9
			EQUALS	
8/17/68	#26	12	Baby, Come Back	RCA 9583
			ERASURE	
8/06/88	#13	20	Chains Of Love	Sire 27844
12/03/88	#16	20	A Little Respect	Sire 27738

111

Debut Date	Peak Pos	Wks Chr	ARTIST/Song Title	Label & Number
			ERNIE	
8/08/70	#13	10	Rubber Duckie	Columbia 45207
			ERUPTION	
4/01/78	#19	19	I Can't Stand The Rain	Ariola 7686
			ESCAPE CLUB	
8/20/88	#1	25	Wild, Wild West	Atlantic 89048
12/03/88	#26	15	Shake For The Sheik	Atlantic 88983
4/01/89	#71	5	Walking Through Walls	Atlantic 88951
2/23/91	#28	16	Call It Poison	Atlantic 87759
5/25/91	#9	22	I'll Be There	Atlantic 87683
			JOE "BEAN" ESPOSITO	
10/22/83	#82	4	Lady, Lady, Lady	Casablanca 814430
			ESQUIRES	
8/19/67	#20	14	Get On Up	Bunky 7750
11/25/67	#29	9	And Get Away	Bunky 7752
12/21/68	#100	1	You Got The Power	Wand 1193
			ESSEX	
6/01/63	#1	15	Easier Said Than Done	Roulette 4494
8/24/63	#10	11	A Walkin' Miracle	Roulette 4515
11/09/63	#75	5	She's Got Everything/	Roulette 4530
11/16/63	#97	1	Out Of Sight, Out Of Mind	Roulette 4530
			DAVID ESSEX	
11/24/73	#1	22	Rock On	Columbia 45940
5/25/74	#65	7	Lamplight	Columbia 46041
			GLORIA ESTEFAN (also MIAMI SOUND MACHINE)	
10/19/85	#17	27	Conga*	Epic 05457
3/08/86	#8	19	Bad Boy*	Epic 05805
6/21/86	#8	22	Words Get In The Way*	Epic 06120
11/08/86	#23	15	Falling In Love (Uh-Oh)*	Epic 06352
5/30/87	#5	19	Rhythm Is Gonna Get You**	Epic 07059
9/05/87	#38	13	Betcha Say That**	Epic 07371
11/21/87	#10	25	Can't Stay Away From You**	Epic 07641
3/12/88	#1	21	Anything For You**	Epic 07759
6/04/88	#3	20	1-2-3**	Epic 07921
7/08/89	#1	22	Don't Wanna Lose You	Epic 68959
9/30/89	#9	19	Get On Your Feet	Epic 69064
12/16/89	#9	20	Here We Are	Epic 73084
4/07/90	#45	10	Oye Mi Canto	Epic 73269
6/30/90	#48	11	Cuts Both Ways	Epic 73395
1/26/91	#1	23	Coming Out Of The Dark	Epic 73666
4/20/91	#40	10	Seal Our Fate	Epic 73769
6/08/91	#35	18	Can't Forget You	Epic 73864
10/12/91	#11	26	Live For Loving You	Epic 73962
11/07/92	#73	10	Always Tomorrow	Epic 74472
2/27/93	#34	15	I See Your Smile	Epic 74847
			*released as by MIAMI SOUND MACHINE	
			**released as by GLORIA ESTEFAN and MIAMI SOUND MACHINE	
			DEON ESTUS	
2/25/89	#4	21	Heaven Help Me*	Mika 871538
			*released as by DEON ESTUS with GEORGE MICHAEL	
			ETERNALS	
7/11/59	#84	6	Rockin' In The Jungle	Hollywood 68
			ETERNITY'S CHILDREN	
6/29/68	#54	8	Mrs. Bluebird	Tower 416
			ETTA and HARVEY (ETTA JAMES and HARVEY FUQUA)	
8/06/60	#32	13	If I Can't Have You	Chess 1760
1/07/61	#82	3	Spoonful	Chess 1771
			E.U.	
4/09/88	#40	14	Da'Butt	EMI-Manhattan 50115
			JACK EUBANKS	
12/02/61	#81	8	Searching	Monument 451
			EUCLID BEACH BAND	
3/31/79	#93	3	I Need You	Epic 50676

Debut Date	Peak Pos	Wks Chr	ARTIST/Song Title	Label & Number
			EUROGLIDERS	
11/10/84	#59	11	Heaven (Must Be There)	Columbia 04626
			EUROPE	
1/24/87	#10	18	The Final Countdown	Epic 06416
5/02/87	#35	15	Rock The Night	Epic 07091
8/01/87	#3	25	Carrie	Epic 07282
8/13/88	#41	13	Superstitious	Epic 07979
			EURYTHMICS	
5/21/83	#1	26	Sweet Dreams (Are Made Of This)	RCA 13533
9/24/83	#24	17	Love Is A Stranger	RCA 13618
1/28/84	#5	20	Here Comes The Rain	RCA 13725
5/05/84	#21	15	Who's That Girl?	RCA 13800
7/21/84	#30	13	Right By Your Side	RCA 13695
4/27/85	#6	20	Would I Lie To You?	RCA 14078
8/03/85	#23	13	There Must Be An Angel (Playing With My Heart)	RCA 14160
10/19/85	#22	15	Sisters Are Doin' It For Themselves*	RCA 14214
2/22/86	#79	5	It's Alright (Baby's Coming Back)	RCA 14284
7/19/86	#15	18	Missionary Man	RCA 14414
11/22/86	#56	9	Thorn In My Side	RCA 5058
12/19/87	#62	11	I Need A Man	RCA 5361
5/28/88	#62	9	You Have Placed A Chill In My Heart	RCA 7615
9/30/89	#37	17	Don't Ask Me Why	Arista 9880
			*released as by THE EURYTHMICS and ARETHA FRANKLIN	
			PAUL EVANS	
9/19/59	#5	18	Seven Little Girls Sitting In The Back Seat	Guaranteed 200
1/23/60	#16	13	Midnite Special	Guaranteed 205
5/07/60	#11	12	Happy-Go-Lucky Me	Guaranteed 208
8/06/60	#79	4	Brigade Of Broken Hearts	Guaranteed 210
2/18/61	#98	2	Show Folk	Carlton 539
			BETTY EVERETT	
11/02/63	#40	14	You're No Good	Vee-Jay 566
2/29/64	#6	14	The Shoop Shoop Song (It's In His Kiss)	Vee-Jay 585
7/04/64	#85	2	I Can't Hear You	Vee-Jay 599
9/05/64	#91	1	Ain't That Loving You Baby*/	Vee-Jay 613
9/12/64	#9	13	Let It Be Me*	Vee-Jay 613
11/28/64	#79	7	Getting Mighty Crowded	Vee-Jay 628
12/05/64	#52	7	Smile*	Vee-Jay 633
1/18/69	#41	9	There'll Come A Time	Uni 55100
5/03/69	#80	4	I Can't Say No To You	Uni 55122
1/16/71	#97	3	I Got To Tell Somebody	Fantasy 652
			*released as by BETTY EVERETT & JERRY BUTLER	
			DON EVERLY	
7/06/74	#92	3	Warmin' Up The Band	Ode 66046
			EVERLY BROTHERS	
5/25/57	#1	20	Bye Bye Love	Cadence 1315
9/21/57	#1	19	Wake Up Little Susie	Cadence 1337
2/01/58	#34	6	This Little Girl Of Mine	Cadence 1342
4/19/58	#1	17	All I Have To Do Is Dream/	Cadence 1348
4/19/58	#51	1	Claudette	Cadence 1348
8/09/58	#2	19	Bird Dog/	Cadence 1350
8/09/58	#11	16	Devoted To You	Cadence 1350
11/15/58	#7	14	Problems/	Cadence 1355
11/22/58	#47	8	Love Of My Life	Cadence 1355
4/04/59	#17	12	Take A Message To Mary/	Cadence 1364
4/11/59	#25	10	Poor Jenny	Cadence 1364
8/15/59	#5	18	('Til) I Kissed You/	Cadence 1369
8/22/59	#96	1	Oh What A Feeling	Cadence 1369
1/16/60	#8	14	Let It Be Me/	Cadence 1376
1/16/60	#93	2	Since You Broke My Heart	Cadence 1376
4/23/60	#1	17	Cathy's Clown/	Warner Brothers 5151
4/23/60	#83	1	Always With You	Warner Brothers 5151
6/11/60	#9	12	When Will I Be Loved/	Cadence 1380
7/02/60	#84	5	Be-Bop-A-Lula	Cadence 1380
9/03/60	#9	13	So Sad (To Watch Good Love Go Bad)/	Warner Brothers 5163
9/03/60	#41	9	Lucille	Warner Brothers 5163
11/05/60	#25	11	Like Strangers/	Cadence 1388
11/12/60	#84	3	Brand New Heartache	Cadence 1388
2/04/61	#11	15	Walk Right Back/	Warner Brothers 5199

113

Debut Date	Peak Pos	Wks Chr	**ARTIST**/Song Title	Label & Number
			EVERLY BROTHERS—*continued*	
2/04/61	#8	12	Ebony Eyes	Warner Brothers 5199
6/03/61	#20	9	Temptation/	Warner Brothers 5220
6/10/61	#55	6	Stick With Me Baby	Warner Brothers 5220
9/23/61	#31	9	Don't Blame Me/	Warner Brothers 5501
9/23/61	#95	2	Muskrat	Warner Brothers 5501
1/20/62	#7	13	Crying In The Rain	Warner Brothers 5250
5/12/62	#15	10	That's Old Fashioned/	Warner Brothers 5273
5/12/62	#69	4	How Can I Meet Her	Warner Brothers 5273
10/27/62	#64	5	Don't Ask Me To Be Friends	Warner Brothers 5297
10/27/62	#78	4	I'm Here To Get My Baby Out Of Jail	Cadence 1429
7/11/64	#95	1	Ferris Wheel	Warner Brothers 5441
10/31/64	#33	8	Gone, Gone, Gone	Warner Brothers 5478
3/27/65	#90	1	That'll Be The Day	Warner Brothers 5611
8/28/65	#96	2	Love Is Strange	Warner Brothers 5649
5/13/67	#60	9	Bowling Green	Warner Brothers 7020
9/08/84	#47	10	On The Wings Of A Nightingale	Mercury 880213
			EVERY MOTHERS' SON	
5/13/67	#5	15	Come On Down To My Boat	MGM 13733
8/26/67	#36	7	Put Your Mind At Ease	MGM 13788
11/04/67	#64	4	Pony With The Golden Mane	MGM 13844
			EVERYTHING IS EVERYTHING	
1/25/69	#61	7	Witchi Tai To	Vanguard 35082
			EXCELLENTS	
11/24/62	#63	9	Coney Island Baby	Blast 205
			EXCITERS	
11/24/62	#5	15	Tell Him	United Artists 544
3/02/63	#64	6	He's Got The Power	United Artists 572
1/22/66	#56	7	A Little Bit Of Soap	Bang 515
			EXILE	
7/08/78	#1	28	Kiss You All Over	Warner Brothers 8589
11/18/78	#43	13	You Thrill Me	Warner Brothers 8711
			EXPOSE	
1/24/87	#5	19	Come Go With Me	Arista 9555
5/09/87	#7	21	Point Of No Return	Arista 9579
8/15/87	#8	25	Let Me Be The One	Arista 9617
11/28/87	#4	22	Seasons Change	Arista 9640
5/20/89	#8	19	What You Don't Know	Arista 9836
8/19/89	#11	18	When I Looked At Him	Arista 9868
12/09/89	#6	19	Tell Me Why	Arista 9916
3/31/90	#16	17	Your Baby Never Looked Good In Blue	Arista 2011
11/07/92	#20	16	I Wish The Phone Would Ring	Arista 2466
4/03/93	#6	31	I'll Never Get Over You (Getting Over Me)	Arista 2518
10/23/93	#51	15	As Long As I Can Dream	Arista 2600
			EXTREME	
3/23/91	#1	27	More Than Words	A&M 1552
8/10/91	#4	28	Hole Hearted	A&M 1564
10/10/92	#66	10	Rest In Peace	A&M 0055
2/27/93	#82	6	Stop The World	A&M 0120
			EYE TO EYE	
5/22/82	#33	13	Nice Girls	Warner Brothers 50050

F

			SHELLEY FABARES	
3/03/62	#1	16	Johnny Angel	Colpix 621
6/09/62	#34	10	Johnny Loves Me	Colpix 636
9/22/62	#69	5	The Things We Did Last Summer	Colpix 654
5/04/63	#81	3	Ronnie, Call Me When You Get A Chance	Colpix 682
10/05/63	#100	1	Welcome Home	Colpix 705
			FABIAN	
1/03/59	#40	10	I'm A Man	Chancellor 1029
3/28/59	#8	14	Turn Me Loose	Chancellor 1033
6/13/59	#6	13	Tiger	Chancellor 1037
9/12/59	#34	8	Come On And Get Me/	Chancellor 1041
9/19/59	#46	6	Got The Feeling	Chancellor 1041
11/14/59	#11	15	Hound Dog Man/	Chancellor 1044

Debut Date	Peak Pos	Wks Chr	**ARTIST**/Song Title	Label & Number
11/14/59	#16	14	This Friendly World	Chancellor 1044
2/20/60	#32	10	About This Thing Called Love/	Chancellor 1047
2/27/60	#35	8	String Along	Chancellor 1047
5/28/60	#83	4	Strollin' In The Springtime/	Chancellor 1051
6/04/60	#85	2	I'm Gonna Sit Right Down	Chancellor 1051
8/13/60	#93	3	King Of Love	Chancellor 1055
11/05/60	#86	5	Kissin' And Twistin'	Chancellor 1061
			BENT FABRIC	
7/28/62	#6	20	Alley Cat	Atco 6226
12/22/62	#65	11	Chicken Feed	Atco 6245
8/10/63	#95	4	The Happy Puppy	Atco 6271
			FABULOUS COUNTS	
5/09/70	#86	2	Get Down People	Moira 108
			FABULOUS RHINESTONES	
7/01/72	#67	5	What A Wonderful Thing We Have	Just Sunshine 500
			FABULOUS THUNDERBIRDS	
4/26/86	#12	19	Tuff Enough	CBS Associated 05838
8/09/86	#41	12	Wrap It Up	CBS Associated 06270
7/11/87	#73	6	Stand Back	CBS Associated 07230
9/03/88	#68	8	Powerful Stuff	Elektra 69384
			TOMMY FACENDA	
10/31/59	#30	9	High School U.S.A.*	Atlantic 51 to 78
			*there were 28 different versions of this song each mentioning high schools in different cities	
			FACES	
11/20/71	#22	9	(I Know) I'm Losing You*	Mercury 73244
1/01/72	#10	11	Stay With Me	Warner Brothers 7545
3/17/73	#43	7	Cindy Incidentally	Warner Brothers 7681
			*released as by ROD STEWART with FACES	
			FACE TO FACE	
6/09/84	#40	14	10-9-8	Epic 04430
			ERIA FACHIN	
3/05/88	#76	9	Savin' Myself	Critique 99356
			FACTS OF LIFE	
2/19/77	#60	13	Sometimes	Kayvette 5128
			DONALD FAGEN	
10/09/82	#19	16	I.G.Y. (What A Beautiful World)	Warner Brothers 29900
1/29/83	#68	7	New Frontier	Warner Brothers 29792
4/09/88	#77	5	Century's End	Warner Brothers 27972
			YVONNE FAIR	
5/22/76	#100	1	It Should Have Been Me	Motown 1384
			BARBARA FAIRCHILD	
3/03/73	#32	16	Teddy Bear Song	Columbia 45743
			FAIRGROUND ATTRACTION	
12/24/88	#81	6	Perfect	RCA 8789
			ADAM FAITH	
1/16/65	#30	9	It's Alright	Amy 913
4/24/65	#97	2	Talk About Love	Amy 922
			PERCY FAITH	
6/14/52	#3	15	Delicado	Columbia 39708
5/02/53	#1	19	Song From Moulin Rouge	Columbia 39944
8/31/57	#48	2	Till	Columbia 40826
1/16/60	#1	23	The Theme From "A Summer Place"	Columbia 41490
5/14/60	#48	9	Theme For Young Lovers	Columbia 41655
10/22/60	#86	6	The Theme From "The Dark At The Top Of The Stairs" . .	Columbia 41796
			FAITH BAND	
12/16/78	#63	9	Dancin' Shoes	Mercury 74037
6/02/79	#67	8	You're My Weakness	Mercury 74068
			MARIANNE FAITHFULL	
10/31/64	#30	14	As Tears Go By	London 9697
3/13/65	#32	8	Come And Stay With Me	London 9731
6/05/65	#34	8	This Little Bird	London 9759

Debut Date	Peak Pos	Wks Chr	ARTIST/Song Title	Label & Number
			MARIANNE FAITHFULL—*continued*	
8/14/65	#38	8	Summer Nights	London 9780
12/11/65	#75	4	Go Away From My World	London 9802
			FAITH, HOPE & CHARITY	
5/23/70	#36	9	So Much Love	Maxwell 805
8/16/75	#42	14	To Each His Own	RCA 10343
			FAITH NO MORE	
6/09/90	#7	21	Epic	Slash 19813
11/17/90	#80	4	Falling To Pieces	Slash 19563
7/18/92	#63	12	Midlife Crisis	Slash 18832
3/20/93	#54	10	Easy	Slash 18569
			FALCO	
4/02/83	#74	7	Der Kommissar	A&M 2532
2/08/86	#1	20	Rock Me Amadeus	A&M 2821
4/26/86	#17	15	Vienna Calling	A&M 2832
			BILLY FALCON	
8/03/91	#31	21	Power Windows	Jambco 868672
			FALCONS	
5/02/59	#14	18	You're So Fine	Unart 2013
7/09/60	#84	5	The Teacher	United Artists 229
3/31/62	#51	10	I Found A Love	Lu Pine 1003
			HAROLD FALTERMEYER	
3/30/85	#3	19	Axel F	MCA 52536
			AGNETHA FALTSKOG	
8/27/83	#32	15	Can't Shake Loose	Polydor 815230
			GEORGIE FAME	
2/13/65	#17	8	Yeh, Yeh*	Imperial 66086
8/27/66	#58	7	Get Away*	Imperial 66189
2/10/68	#6	16	The Ballad Of Bonnie And Clyde	Epic 10283
			*released as by GEORGIE FAME with THE BLUE FLAMES	
			FAMILY	
9/28/85	#73	6	The Screams Of Passion	Paisley Park 28953
			FANCY	
6/01/74	#12	17	Wild Thing	Big Tree 15004
10/12/74	#37	9	Touch Me	Big Tree 16026
			FANNY	
9/25/71	#32	9	Charity Ball	Reprise 1033
5/13/72	#91	2	Ain't That Peculiar	Reprise 1080
6/01/74	#63	8	I've Had It	Casablanca 0009
2/01/75	#27	11	Butter Boy	Casablanca 814
			FANTASTIC FOUR	
4/01/67	#70	8	The Whole World Is A Stage	Ric-Tic 122
6/10/67	#67	5	You Gave Me Something	Ric-Tic 128
10/05/68	#44	6	I Love You Madly	Ric-Tic 144
8/02/75	#76	6	Alvin Stone	Westbound 5009
			FANTASTIC JOHNNY C	
10/14/67	#9	16	Boogaloo Down Broadway	Phil-L.A. Of Soul 305
2/10/68	#72	4	Got What You Need	Phil-L.A. Of Soul 309
7/06/68	#37	7	Hitch It To The Horse	Phil-L.A. Of Soul 315
			FANTASTICS	
2/26/72	#88	3	(Love Me) Love The Life I Lead	Bell 45157
			FANTASY	
9/26/70	#93	4	Stoned Cowboy	Liberty 56190
			FARAGHER BROTHERS	
2/24/79	#48	8	Stay The Night	Polydor 14533
			FAR CORPORATION	
10/11/86	#82	5	Stairway To Heaven	Atco 99509
			DON FARDON	
8/24/68	#19	11	Indian Reservation	GNP Crescendo 405
12/14/68	#95	1	Take A Heart	GNP Crescendo 418
3/24/73	#75	6	Delta Queen	Chelsea 0115
			DONNA FARGO	
6/03/72	#8	16	The Happiest Girl In The Whole U.S.A.	Dot 17409

Debut Date	Peak Pos	Wks Chr	ARTIST/Song Title	Label & Number
9/30/72	#9	18	Funny Face	Dot 17429
2/17/73	#31	10	Superman	Dot 17444
6/30/73	#76	6	You Were Always There	Dot 17460
10/13/73	#61	8	Little Girl Gone	Dot 17476
6/29/74	#48	12	You Can't Be A Beacon (If Your Light Don't Shine)	Dot 17506
3/18/78	#94	2	Do I Love You	Warner Brothers 8509
			FARM	
9/14/91	#25	21	Groovy Train	Sire 19209
1/18/92	#71	7	All Together Now	Sire 19269
			JOHN FARNHAM	
2/17/90	#72	6	You're The Voice	RCA 9086
			FASCINATIONS	
1/28/67	#80	6	Girls Are Out To Get You	Mayfield 7714
			FASTER PUSSYCAT	
3/03/90	#32	18	House Of Pain	Elektra 64995
			FATBACK BAND	
3/27/76	#60	8	Spanish Hustle	Event 229
			FAT BOYS	
7/04/87	#90	1	Falling In Love	Tin Pan Apple 885766
7/11/87	#28	19	Wipeout*	Tin Pan Apple 885960
6/18/88	#20	16	The Twist (Yo, Twist!)**	Tin Pan Apple 887571
			*released as by **THE FAT BOYS and THE BEACH BOYS**	
			released as by **THE FAT BOYS with CHUBBY CHECKER	
			FATHER M.C.	
2/16/91	#45	14	I'll Do 4 U	Uptown 53914
9/07/91	#49	10	Everyotherday*	EMI 50359
12/12/92	#38	20	Everything's Gonna Be Alright	Uptown 54523
			*released as by **OR-N-MORE featuring FATHER M.C.**	
			FAVORITE ANGEL	
8/25/90	#64	7	Only Women Bleed	Columbia 73476
			FEATHER	
5/16/70	#76	6	Friends	White Whale 353
			DON FELDER	
7/25/81	#42	19	Heavy Metal (Takin' A Ride)	Full Moon 47175
			JOSE FELICIANO	
7/20/68	#3	13	Light My Fire	RCA 9550
10/12/68	#13	8	Hi-Heel Sneakers	RCA 9641
11/02/68	#48	4	Star Spangled Banner	RCA 9665
1/25/69	#32	6	Hey! Baby/	RCA 9714
1/25/69	#61	2	My World Is Empty Without You	RCA 9714
4/26/69	#60	5	Marley Purt Drive	RCA 9739
8/30/69	#68	3	Rain	RCA 9757
6/27/70	#75	4	Destiny	RCA 0358
12/26/70	#71	1	Feliz Navidad	RCA 0404
			DICK FELLER	
6/15/74	#89	3	Makin' The Best Of A Bad Situation	Asylum 11037
			FELONY	
2/19/83	#56	10	The Fanatic	Rock 'n' Roll 03497
			NARVEL FELTS	
6/07/75	#86	4	Reconsider Me	ABC/Dot 17549
5/29/76	#85	4	Lonely Teardrops	ABC/Dot 17620
			FREDDY FENDER	
7/09/60	#82	5	Wasted Days And Wasted Nights	Imperial 5670
2/15/75	#1	19	Before The Next Teardrop Falls	ABC/Dot 17540
6/14/75	#6	19	Wasted Days And Wasted Nights	ABC/Dot 17558
10/18/75	#25	11	Secret Love	ABC/Dot 17585
10/18/75	#44	9	Since I Met You Baby	GRT 031
2/07/76	#36	10	You'll Lose A Good Thing	ABC/Dot 17607
5/29/76	#80	4	Vaya Con Dios	ABC/Dot 17627
11/13/76	#93	3	Living It Down	ABC/Dot 17652
			FENDERMEN	
6/04/60	#5	16	Mule Skinner Blues	Soma 1137
9/17/60	#85	3	Don't You Just Know It	Soma 1142

Debut Date	Peak Pos	Wks Chr	ARTIST/Song Title	Label & Number
			ZOOT FENSTER	
11/29/75	#91	3	The Man On Page 602	Antique 106
			HELENA FERGUSON	
11/18/67	#97	3	Where Is The Party	Compass 7009
			JAY FERGUSON	
12/17/77	#6	23	Thunder Island	Asylum 45444
5/05/79	#27	13	Shakedown Cruise	Asylum 46041
			JOHNNY FERGUSON	
2/06/60	#43	17	Angela Jones	MGM 12855
			MAYNARD FERGUSON	
4/16/77	#31	14	Gonna Fly Now (Theme From "Rocky")	Columbia 10468
			FERRANTE & TEICHER	
7/09/60	#9	24	Theme From The Apartment	United Artists 231
11/19/60	#1	20	Exodus	United Artists 274
3/18/61	#39	9	Love Theme From One Eyed Jacks	United Artists 300
6/24/61	#84	3	Theme From "Goodbye Again"	United Artists 319
10/28/61	#6	14	Tonight	United Artists 373
3/24/62	#93	2	Smile	United Artists 431
6/09/62	#81	4	Lisa	United Artists 470
11/01/69	#10	15	Midnight Cowboy	United Artists 50554
2/28/70	#71	3	Lay Lady Lay	United Artists 50646
			BRYAN FERRY	
2/27/88	#45	12	Kiss And Tell	Reprise 28117
			FESTIVAL	
4/05/80	#94	4	Don't Cry For Me Argentina	RSO 1020
			FESTIVALS	
9/26/70	#99	1	You're Gonna Make It	Colossus 122
			FEVER TREE	
5/18/68	#92	2	San Francisco Girls	Uni 55060
9/07/68	#65	6	San Francisco Girls	Uni 55060
			SALLY FIELD	
11/11/67	#91	6	Felicidad	Colgems 1008
			ERNIE FIELDS	
9/26/59	#7	20	In The Mood	Rendezvous 110
3/12/60	#72	6	Chattanooga Choo Choo	Rendezvous 117
7/01/61	#49	8	The Charleston	Rendezvous 150
			RICHARD "DIMPLES" FIELDS	
4/10/82	#41	12	If It Ain't One Thing....It's Another	Boardwalk 139
			FIESTAS	
4/04/59	#12	16	So Fine	Old Town 1062
8/18/62	#53	8	Broken Heart	Old Town 1122
			FIFTH DIMENSION	
1/21/67	#16	10	Go Where You Wanna Go	Soul City 753
4/29/67	#62	5	Another Day, Another Heartache	Soul City 755
6/03/67	#4	11	Up-Up And Away	Soul City 756
11/04/67	#38	7	Paper Cup	Soul City 760
1/28/68	#22	10	Carpet Man	Soul City 762
6/01/68	#6	14	Stoned Soul Picnic	Soul City 766
9/21/68	#11	12	Sweet Blindness	Soul City 768
12/28/68	#23	7	California Soul	Soul City 770
3/08/69	#1	16	Aquarius/Let The Sunshine In	Soul City 772
7/19/69	#23	9	Workin' On A Groovy Thing	Soul City 776
9/20/69	#1	15	Wedding Bell Blues	Soul City 779
1/03/70	#14	8	Blowing Away	Soul City 780
2/14/70	#66	3	The Declaration/	Bell 860
3/07/70	#84	2	A Change Is Gonna Come & People Gotta Be Free	Bell 860
3/28/70	#46	6	The Girl's Song	Soul City 781
4/11/70	#22	9	Puppet Man	Bell 880
6/06/70	#20	9	Save The Country	Bell 895
8/15/70	#41	7	On The Beach (In The Summertime)	Bell 913
10/17/70	#2	18	One Less Bell To Answer	Bell 940
2/20/71	#11	12	Love's Lines, Angles And Rhymes	Bell 965
5/15/71	#22	8	Light Sings	Bell 999
9/18/71	#14	12	Never My Love	Bell 45134
12/25/71	#24	11	Together Let's Find Love	Bell 45170

118

Debut Date	Peak Pos	Wks Chr	ARTIST/Song Title	Label & Number
3/25/72	#6	17	(Last Night) I Didn't Get To Sleep At All	Bell 45195
9/02/72	#10	16	If I Could Reach You	Bell 45261
1/06/73	#20	10	Living Together, Growing Together	Bell 45310
4/07/73	#55	6	Everything's Been Changed	Bell 45338
8/04/73	#71	12	Ashes To Ashes	Bell 45380
12/22/73	#92	4	Flashback	Bell 45425
11/23/74	#92	3	Harlem	Bell 45612
2/22/75	#99	1	No Love In The Room	Arista 0101
4/10/76	#82	4	Love Hangover	ABC 12181
			FIFTH ESTATE	
5/13/67	#12	11	Ding Dong! The Witch Is Dead	Jubilee 5573
10/21/67	#91	3	Heigh-Ho	Jubilee 5595
			FIGURES ON A BEACH	
4/15/89	#68	8	You Ain't Seen Nothing Yet	Sire 27628
			FINE YOUNG CANNIBALS	
4/12/86	#80	4	Johnny Come Home	I.R.S. 52760
1/28/89	#1	24	She Drives Me Crazy	I.R.S. 53483
5/06/89	#1	20	Good Thing	I.R.S. 53639
8/12/89	#10	18	Don't Look Back	I.R.S. 53695
10/28/89	#47	14	I'm Not The Man I Used To Be	I.R.S. 53686
2/17/90	#84	4	I'm Not Satisfied	I.R.S. 53789
			LARRY FINNEGAN	
3/03/62	#11	13	Dear One	Old Town 1113
			MIKE FINNEGAN	
7/01/78	#84	3	Just One Minute More	Columbia 10741
			FIONA	
4/20/85	#76	5	Talk To Me	Atlantic 89572
12/23/89	#56	9	Everything You Do (You're Sexing Me)*	Atlantic 88823
			*released as by FIONA with KIP WINGER	
			ELISA FIORILLO	
7/11/87	#16	17	Who Found Who*	Chrysalis 43120
1/23/88	#65	8	How Can I Forget You	Chrysalis 43189
5/14/88	#51	12	Forgive Me For Dreaming	Chrysalis 43237
9/29/90	#32	21	On The Way Up	Chrysalis 23497
			*released as by JELLYBEAN/ELISA FIORILLO	
			FIREBALLS	
9/19/59	#35	17	Torquay	Top Rank 2008
1/16/60	#23	11	Bulldog	Top Rank 2026
8/27/60	#100	1	Vaquero	Top Rank 2054
6/24/61	#57	10	Quite A Party	Warwick 644
9/21/63	#1	16	Sugar Shack*	Dot 16487
12/21/63	#15	10	Daisy Petal Pickin'*	Dot 16539
3/14/64	#62	7	Ain't Gonna Tell Nobody*	Dot 16583
1/06/68	#9	14	Bottle Of Wine	Atco 6491
4/06/68	#58	5	Goin' Away	Atco 6569
11/16/68	#69	6	Come On React!	Atco 6614
3/01/69	#43	6	Long Green	Atco 6651
			*released as by JIMMY GILMER and THE FIREBALLS	
			FIREFALL	
6/05/76	#41	12	Livin' Ain't Livin'	Atlantic 3333
8/14/76	#8	24	You Are The Woman	Atlantic 3335
3/26/77	#30	15	Cinderella	Atlantic 3392
8/13/77	#9	21	Just Remember I Love You	Atlantic 3420
1/21/78	#67	6	So Long	Atlantic 3452
9/30/78	#11	19	Strange Way	Atlantic 3518
1/20/79	#40	9	Goodbye, I Love You	Atlantic 3544
4/12/80	#36	11	Headed For A Fall	Atlantic 3657
6/28/80	#55	10	Love That Got Away	Atlantic 3670
1/24/81	#42	11	Staying With It	Atlantic 3791
1/15/83	#51	12	Always	Atlantic 89916
			FIREFLIES	
8/08/59	#10	20	You Were Mine	Ribbon 6901
12/26/59	#49	11	I Can't Say Goodbye	Ribbon 6904
4/09/60	#86	3	Because Of My Pride	Ribbon 6906
			FIREFLY	
11/08/75	#75	7	Hey There Little Firefly (Part 1)	A&M 1736

119

Debut Date	Peak Pos	Wks Chr	ARTIST/Song Title	Label & Number
			FIREHOUSE	
3/02/91	#20	24	Don't Treat Me Bad	Epic 73676
6/29/91	#7	29	Love Of A Lifetime	Epic 73771
11/16/91	#37	15	All She Wants	Epic 73984
6/27/92	#59	11	Reach For The Sky	Epic 74335
8/08/92	#7	27	When I Look Into Your Eyes	Epic 74440
			FIRM	
2/16/85	#28	14	Radioactive	Atlantic 89586
5/11/85	#78	4	Satisfaction Guaranteed	Atlantic 89561
3/01/86	#67	7	All The Kings Horses	Atlantic 89458
			FIRST CHOICE	
2/24/73	#19	16	Armed And Extremely Dangerous	Philly Groove 175
10/13/73	#38	13	Smarty Pants	Philly Groove 179
3/09/74	#93	3	Newsy Neighbors	Philly Groove 183
9/14/74	#73	6	The Player (Part 1)	Philly Groove 200
9/10/77	#79	6	Doctor Love	Gold Mind 4004
			FIRST CLASS	
7/27/74	#3	15	Beach Baby	UK 49022
11/09/74	#71	7	Dreams Are Ten A Penny	UK 49028
6/07/75	#90	4	Funny How Love Can Be	UK 49033
			FIRST EDITION (see KENNY ROGERS and THE FIRST EDITION)	
			LISA FISCHER	
5/04/91	#31	18	How Can I Ease The Pain	Elektra 64897
9/14/91	#72	7	Save Me	Elektra 64854
			GEORGE FISCHOFF	
5/25/74	#65	8	Georgia Porcupine	United Artists 410
			EDDIE FISHER	
11/25/50	#3	11	Thinking Of You	RCA 3901
11/10/51	#8	5	Turn Back The Hands Of Time	RCA 4257
2/09/52	#3	16	Anytime	RCA 4359
5/10/52	#7	6	Forgive Me	RCA 4574
5/31/52	#2	14	I'm Yours	RCA 4680
8/16/52	#2	16	Wish You Were Here	RCA 4830
11/01/52	#4	10	Lady Of Spain	RCA 4953
12/06/52	#10	1	Outside Of Heaven	RCA 4953
2/14/53	#7	5	Even Now	RCA 5106
5/30/53	#1	18	I'm Walking Behind You	RCA 5293
8/01/53	#6	8	With These Hands	RCA 5365
11/07/53	#5	7	Many Times	RCA 5453
12/26/53	#1	17	(Oh My Papa) Oh Mein Papa	RCA 5552
9/25/54	#1	19	I Need You Now	RCA 5830
12/18/54	#8	5	Count Your Blessings	RCA 5871
6/25/55	#10	4	Heart	RCA 6097
2/04/56	#9	2	Dungaree Doll	RCA 6337
10/06/56	#9	19	Cindy, Oh Cindy	RCA 6677
10/19/57	#55	3	That's The Way It Goes	RCA 7005
10/26/57	#56	2	Sayonara	RCA 7051
1/25/58	#43	4	What's The Use Of Crying	RCA 7135
10/29/66	#41	9	Games That Lovers Play	RCA 8956
2/11/67	#74	4	People Like You	RCA 9070
			MARY ANN FISHER	
9/02/61	#93	3	I Can't Take It	Seg-Way 1001
			MISS TONI FISHER	
11/21/59	#2	16	The Big Hurt	Signet 275
4/23/60	#90	2	How Deep Is The Ocean	Signet 276
5/26/62	#23	12	West Of The Wall	Big Top 3097
			TRICIA LEIGH FISHER	
9/01/90	#69	9	Empty Beach	Atco 98932
			ELLA FITZGERALD	
5/14/60	#31	12	Mack The Knife	Verve 10209
			FIVE AMERICANS	
1/08/66	#41	11	I See The Light	HBR 454
4/16/66	#68	6	Evol-Not Love	HBR 468
3/04/67	#7	11	Western Union	Abnak 118
5/20/67	#31	9	Sound Of Love	Abnak 120
8/12/67	#55	7	Zip Code	Abnak 123

Debut Date	Peak Pos	Wks Chr	ARTIST/Song Title	Label & Number
			FIVE BLOBS	
10/18/58	#39	8	The Blob	Columbia 41250
			FIVE BY FIVE	
10/05/68	#38	11	Fire	Paula 302
			FIVE DU-TONES	
5/25/63	#46	12	Shake A Tail Feather	One-derful! 4815
			FIVE EMPREES	
9/18/65	#85	4	Little Miss Sad	Freeport 1001
			FIVE FLIGHTS UP	
8/29/70	#29	10	Do What You Wanna Do	T-A 202
12/05/70	#84	6	After The Feeling Is Gone	T-A 207
			FIVE KEYS	
9/29/56	#19	12	Out Of Sight, Out Of Mind	Capitol 3502
12/08/56	#31	8	Wisdom Of A Fool	Capitol 3597
			FIVE MAN ELECTRICAL BAND	
5/15/71	#7	20	Signs	Lionel 3213
10/09/71	#20	9	Absolutely Right	Lionel 3220
3/04/72	#61	4	Julianna	Lionel 3224
9/02/72	#71	6	Money Back Guarantee	Lion 127
3/31/73	#65	9	I'm A Stranger Here	Lion 149
3/30/74	#44	8	Werewolf	Polydor 14221
			FIVE ROYALES	
6/11/60	#97	1	I'm With You	King 5329
			FIVE SATINS	
8/25/56	#32	9	In The Still Of The Nite	Ember 1005
7/13/57	#39	11	To The Aisle	Ember 1019
11/07/59	#90	7	Shadows	Ember 1056
3/20/82	#84	3	Memories Of Days Gone By*	Elektra 47411
			*released as by **FRED PARRIS & THE FIVE SATINS**	
			FIVE SPECIAL	
7/28/79	#86	5	Why Leave Us Alone	Elektra 46032
			FIVE STAIRSTEPS	
5/14/66	#67	5	You Waited Too Long	Windy City 601
7/23/66	#44	10	World Of Fantasy	Windy City 602
10/29/66	#62	6	Come Back	Windy City 603
1/14/67	#67	5	Danger, She's A Stranger	Windy City 604
4/01/67	#85	3	Ain't Gonna Rest (Till I Get You)	Windy City 605
6/03/67	#62	5	Ooh Baby Baby	Windy City 607
12/09/67	#95	6	Something's Missing	Buddah 20
2/03/68	#68	6	A Million To One*	Buddah 26
4/20/68	#95	2	The Shadow Of Your Love*	Buddah 35
9/07/68	#71	6	Don't Change Your Love*	Curtom 1931
2/15/69	#96	2	Baby You Make Me Feel So Good*	Curtom 1936
10/25/69	#81	3	We Must Be In Love*	Curtom 1945
3/14/70	#69	6	Dear Prudence/	Buddah 165
6/06/70	#4	13	O-o-h Child	Buddah 165
10/10/70	#71	3	America/Standing/Because I Love You . .	Buddah 188
2/13/71	#65	4	Didn't It Look So Easy	Buddah 213
			*released as by **THE FIVE STAIRSTEPS & CUBIE**	
			FIVE STAR	
9/14/85	#79	8	All Fall Down	RCA 14108
2/15/86	#66	8	Let Me Be The One	RCA 14229
9/13/86	#47	11	Can't Wait Another Minute	RCA 14421
1/17/87	#78	7	If I Say Yes	RCA 5083
			5000 VOLTS	
10/18/75	#24	10	I'm On Fire	Philips 40801
			FIVE WHISPERS	
10/20/62	#99	2	Midnight Sun	Dolton 61
			FIXX	
10/16/82	#91	6	Stand Or Fall	MCA 52106
5/28/83	#19	18	Saved By Zero	MCA 52213
8/27/83	#6	22	One Thing Leads To Another	MCA 52264
11/26/83	#32	13	The Sign Of Fire	MCA 52316
8/18/84	#20	15	Are We Ourselves?	MCA 52444
11/17/84	#68	9	Sunshine In The Shade	MCA 52498

Debut Date	Peak Pos	Wks Chr	ARTIST/Song Title	Label & Number
			FIXX—continued	
5/24/86	#25	15	Secret Separation	MCA 52832
2/18/89	#47	10	Driven Out	RCA 8837
3/23/91	#33	15	How Much Is Enough	Impact 54028
8/24/91	#85	5	No One Has To Cry	Impact 54106
			ROBERTA FLACK	
5/29/71	#28	13	You've Got A Friend*	Atlantic 2808
10/16/71	#57	6	You've Lost That Lovin' Feelin'*	Atlantic 2837
1/15/72	#66	4	Will You Love Me Tomorrow	Atlantic 2851
3/04/72	#1	16	The First Time Ever I Saw Your Face	Atlantic 2864
6/10/72	#7	13	Where Is The Love*	Atlantic 2879
1/20/73	#1	15	Killing Me Softly With His Song	Atlantic 2940
9/22/73	#12	9	Jesse	Atlantic 2982
6/15/74	#1	16	Feel Like Makin' Love	Atlantic 3025
12/17/77	#92	5	25th Of Last December	Atlantic 3441
2/11/78	#2	23	The Closer I Get To You*	Atlantic 3463
6/03/78	#38	10	If Ever I See You Again	Atlantic 3483
3/08/80	#78	6	You Are My Heaven*	Atlantic 3627
5/31/80	#91	5	Back Together Again*	Atlantic 3661
3/06/82	#14	21	Making Love	Atlantic 4005
7/31/82	#36	13	I'm The One	Atlantic 4068
7/09/83	#14	30	Tonight I Celebrate My Love**	Capitol 5242
12/24/83	#67	15	You're Looking Like Love To Me**	Capitol 5307
9/21/91	#5	27	Set The Night To Music***	Atlantic 87607
			*released as by ROBERTA FLACK & DONNY HATHAWAY	
			**released as by PEABO BRYSON/ROBERTA FLACK	
			***released as by ROBERTA FLACK with MAXI PRIEST	
			FLAME	
11/21/70	#96	1	See The Light	Brother 3500
			FLAMING EMBER	
10/04/69	#19	12	Mind, Body And Soul	Hot Wax 6902
1/24/70	#56	4	Shades Of Green	Hot Wax 6907
5/16/70	#23	16	Westbound #9	Hot Wax 7003
10/24/70	#22	12	I'm Not My Brothers Keeper	Hot Wax 7006
2/27/71	#98	1	Stop The World And Let Me Off	Hot Wax 7010
11/06/71	#91	3	If It's Good To You	Hot Wax 7109
			FLAMINGOS	
12/06/58	#70	12	Lovers Never Say Goodbye	End 1035
5/23/59	#10	14	I Only Have Eyes For You	End 1046
9/19/59	#54	11	Love Walked In	End 1055
2/06/60	#67	8	I Was Such A Fool	End 1062
4/09/60	#42	11	Nobody Loves Me Like You	End 1068
7/23/60	#45	8	Mio Amore	End 1073
12/17/60	#42	8	Your Other Love	End 1081
7/29/61	#88	4	Time Was	End 1092
3/26/66	#100	1	Boogaloo Party	Philips 40347
3/21/70	#56	5	Buffalo Soldier	Polydor 14019
			RALPH FLANAGAN ORCHESTRA	
12/09/50	#4	13	Nevertheless	RCA 3904
			FLARES	
9/02/61	#25	18	Foot Stomping (Part 1)	Felsted 8624
			FLASH	
6/10/72	#30	13	Small Beginnings	Capitol 3345
			FLASH and THE PAN	
7/21/79	#76	5	Hey, St. Peter	Epic 50715
			FLASH CADILLAC & THE CONTINENTAL KIDS	
6/08/74	#79	4	Dancin' (On A Saturday Night)	Epic 11102
1/18/75	#45	9	Good Times, Rock & Roll	Private Stock 45006
7/24/76	#25	19	Did You Boogie (With Your Baby)	Private Stock 45079
			FLATT & SCRUGGS	
12/01/62	#48	13	The Ballad Of Jed Clampett	Columbia 42606
5/04/68	#97	1	Foggy Mountain Breakdown	Columbia 44380
			FLAVOR	
7/06/68	#66	9	Sally Had A Party	Columbia 44521
			FLEETWOOD MAC	
3/15/69	#98	2	Albatross	Epic 10436

Debut Date	Peak Pos	Wks Chr	**ARTIST**/Song Title	Label & Number
2/07/70	#62	7	Oh Well (Part 1)	Rerpise 0883
11/08/75	#18	14	Over My Head	Reprise 1339
3/06/76	#9	20	Rhiannon (Will You Ever Win)	Reprise 1345
7/03/76	#12	21	Say You Love Me	Reprise 1356
1/08/77	#10	16	Go Your Own Way	Warner Brothers 8304
4/16/77	#1	20	Dreams	Warner Brothers 8371
7/09/77	#1	17	Don't Stop	Warner Brothers 8413
10/15/77	#7	15	You Make Loving Fun	Warner Brothers 8483
10/06/79	#8	16	Tusk	Warner Brothers 49077
12/15/79	#6	15	Sara	Warner Brothers 49150
3/08/80	#22	11	Think About Me	Warner Brothers 49196
2/07/81	#68	6	Fireflies	Warner Brothers 49660
6/19/82	#3	19	Hold Me	Warner Brothers 29966
9/04/82	#13	14	Gypsy	Warner Brothers 29918
11/27/82	#28	15	Love In Store	Warner Brothers 29848
3/28/87	#7	19	Big Love	Warner Brothers 28398
6/13/87	#24	16	Seven Wonders	Warner Brothers 28317
8/29/87	#9	23	Little Lies	Warner Brothers 28291
11/28/87	#13	20	Everywhere	Warner Brothers 28143
11/26/88	#40	14	As Long As You Follow	Warner Brothers 27644
4/07/90	#29	12	Save Me	Warner Brothers 19866
			FLEETWOODS	
3/07/59	#1	15	Come Softly To Me	Dolphin 1
5/23/59	#34	9	Graduation's Here	Dolton 3
9/12/59	#1	19	Mr. Blue	Dolton 5
2/06/60	#34	11	Outside My Window	Dolton 15
5/14/60	#22	15	Runaround	Dolton 22
10/01/60	#79	4	The Last One To Know	Dolton 27
4/22/61	#19	12	Tragedy	Dolton 40
9/02/61	#41	11	The Great Imposter	Dolton 45
9/15/62	#34	15	Lovers By Night, Strangers By Day	Dolton 62
6/08/63	#43	10	Goodnight My Love	Dolton 75
			WADE FLEMONS	
1/31/59	#58	5	Here I Stand	Vee-Jay 295
8/22/59	#91	2	Slow Motion	Vee-Jay 321
4/16/60	#72	10	Easy Lovin'	Vee-Jay 344
			DARROW FLETCHER	
2/05/66	#98	1	The Pain Gets A Little Deeper	Groovy 3001
			LOIS FLETCHER	
3/23/74	#53	9	I Am What I Am	Playboy 50049
			SHELBY FLINT	
1/14/61	#26	12	Angel On My Shoulder	Valiant 6001
8/13/66	#73	5	Cast Your Fate To The Wind	Valiant 743
			FLIRTATIONS	
3/08/69	#31	14	Nothing But A Heartache	Deram 85038
7/11/70	#96	1	Can't Stop Lovin' You	Deram 85062
			FLOATERS	
6/25/77	#3	19	Float On	ABC 12284
			FLOCK OF SEAGULLS	
7/10/82	#14	23	I Ran (So Far Away)	Jive 102
11/20/82	#35	15	Space Age Love Song	Jive 2003
5/14/83	#35	15	Wishing (If I Had A Photograph Of You)	Jive 2006
8/18/84	#58	9	The More You Live, The More You Love	Jive 9220
			PHIL FLOWERS and THE FLOWERSHOP	
10/11/69	#94	5	Like A Rolling Stone	A&M 1122
			EDDIE FLOYD	
8/27/66	#31	21	Knock On Wood	Stax 194
2/04/67	#70	5	Raise Your Hand	Stax 208
10/21/67	#95	2	On A Saturday Night	Stax 233
8/03/68	#47	8	I've Never Found A Girl (To Love Me Like You Do)	Stax 0002
10/26/68	#20	10	Bring It On Home To Me	Stax 0012
2/15/69	#68	4	I've Got To Have Your Love	Stax 0025
6/14/69	#90	3	Don't Tell Your Mama	Stax 0036
10/25/69	#80	3	Why Is Wine Sweeter	Stax 0051
2/28/70	#54	7	California Girl	Stax 0060
7/18/70	#69	4	My Girl	Stax 0072

Debut Date	Peak Pos	Wks Chr	ARTIST/Song Title	Label & Number
			KING FLOYD	
10/31/70	#4	20	Groove Me	Chimneyville 435
3/06/71	#19	11	Baby Let Me Kiss You	Chimneyville 437
7/24/71	#72	4	Got To Have Your Lovin'	Chimneyville 439
9/02/72	#35	11	Woman Don't Go Astray	Chimneyville 443
			FLYING LIZARDS	
12/08/79	#34	12	Money	Virgin 67003
			FLYING MACHINE	
9/20/69	#5	16	Smile A Little Smile For Me	Congress 6000
2/21/70	#97	3	Baby Make It Soon	Congress 6012
			FOCUS	
3/17/73	#4	17	Hocus Pocus	Sire 704
7/14/73	#58	7	Sylvia	Sire 708
			DAN FOGELBERG	
12/28/74	#24	14	Part Of The Plan	Epic 50055
7/16/77	#75	9	Love Gone By	Full Moon 50412
10/07/78	#23	14	The Power Of Gold*	Full Moon 50606
12/15/79	#1	22	Longer	Full Moon 50824
3/22/80	#23	13	Heart Hotels	Full Moon 50862
12/13/80	#7	19	Same Old Lang Syne	Full Moon 50961
8/29/81	#7	17	Hard To Say	Full Moon 02488
11/28/81	#9	20	Leader Of The Band	Full Moon 02647
4/03/82	#14	13	Run For The Roses	Full Moon 02821
10/09/82	#23	16	Missing You	Full Moon 03289
2/05/83	#26	13	Make Love Stay	Full Moon 03525
2/04/84	#15	15	Language Of Love	Full Moon 04314
4/28/84	#60	13	Believe In Me	Full Moon 04447
5/30/87	#76	6	She Don't Look Back	Full Moon 07044
			*released as by **DAN FOGELBERG/TIM WEISBERG**	
			JOHN FOGERTY (see also BLUE RIDGE RANGERS)	
8/30/75	#25	12	Rockin' All Over The World	Asylum 45274
12/20/75	#78	4	Almost Saturday Night	Asylum 45291
12/22/84	#10	18	The Old Man Down The Road	Warner Brothers 29100
3/16/85	#24	15	Rock And Roll Girls/	Warner Brothers 29053
5/25/85	#44	13	Centerfield	Warner Brothers 29053
			TOM FOGERTY	
8/07/71	#93	2	Goodbye Media Man	Fantasy 661
9/22/73	#84	3	Joyful Resurrection	Fantasy 702
			FOGHAT	
5/19/73	#92	2	What A Shame	Bearsville 0014
12/13/75	#20	19	Slow Ride	Bearsville 0306
5/22/76	#57	9	Fool For The City	Bearsville 0307
11/20/76	#37	14	Drivin' Wheel	Bearsville 0313
3/26/77	#90	3	I'll Be Standing By	Bearsville 0315
9/03/77	#31	11	I Just Want To Make Love To You (live)	Bearsville 0319
5/20/78	#47	8	Stone Blue	Bearsville 0325
11/10/79	#19	17	Third Time Lucky	Bearsville 49125
8/02/80	#84	3	Stranger In My Home Town	Bearsville 49510
			ELLEN FOLEY	
11/03/79	#93	4	What's A Matter Baby	Epic 50770
			RED FOLEY	
3/25/50	#3	6	Chattanoogie Shoe Shine Boy	Decca 46205
11/30/57	#52	4	If I Can Help Somebody	Decca 2609
			WAYNE FONTANA & THE MINDBENDERS (see MINDBENDERS)	
			FONTANE SISTERS	
1/08/55	#1	14	Hearts Of Stone	Dot 15265
3/26/55	#10	1	Rock Love	Dot 15333
9/10/55	#3	10	Seventeen	Dot 15386
1/07/56	#10	1	Daddy-O	Dot 15428
8/04/56	#39	2	Voices*	Dot 15480
10/13/56	#48	2	Please Don't Leave Me	Dot 15501
12/29/56	#15	1	The Banana Boat Song	Dot 15527
11/08/58	#71	3	Jealous Heart	Dot 15853
7/18/59	#96	1	A Lover's Hymn	Dot 15943
			*released as by **THE FONTANE SISTERS** with narration by **PAT BOONE**	

Debut Date	Peak Pos	Wks Chr	ARTIST/Song Title	Label & Number
			FOOLS	
4/12/80	#73	5	It's A Night For Beautiful Girls	EMI America 8036
3/07/81	#57	7	Running Scared	EMI America 8072
			FOOL'S GOLD	
5/15/76	#67	9	Rain, Oh Rain	Morning Sky 700
			CHUCK FOOTE	
12/09/61	#87	5	You're Running Out Of Kisses	Soncraft 401
			STEVE FORBERT	
12/01/79	#11	18	Romeo's Tune	Nemperor 7525
4/12/80	#82	4	Say Goodbye To Little Jo	Nemperor 7529
			FORCE	
7/23/77	#94	3	The Star Wars Stars	Lifesong 45031
			FORCE M.D.'S	
2/08/86	#10	18	Tender Love	Warner Brothers 28818
			FRANKIE FORD	
2/07/59	#12	18	Sea Cruise	Ace 554
7/11/59	#71	4	Alimony	Ace 566
1/16/60	#48	9	Time After Time	Ace 580
			JIM FORD	
9/20/69	#85	2	Harlan County	Sun Down 115
			LITA FORD	
4/02/88	#16	20	Kiss Me Deadly	RCA 6866
3/04/89	#13	23	Close My Eyes Forever*	RCA 8899
10/26/91	#26	21	Shot Of Poison	RCA 62074
			*released as by LITA FORD with OZZY OSBORNE	
			TENNESSEE ERNIE FORD	
10/21/50	#3	11	I'll Never Be Free*	Capitol 1124
12/03/55	#1	15	Sixteen Tons	Capitol 3262
10/27/56	#41	5	First Born	Capitol 3553
			*released as by KAY STARR with TENNESSEE ERNIE FORD	
			FOREIGNER	
3/26/77	#5	22	Feels Like The First Time	Atlantic 3394
7/23/77	#10	19	Cold As Ice	Atlantic 3410
12/10/77	#27	13	Long, Long Way From Home	Atlantic 3439
7/01/78	#4	19	Hot Blooded	Atlantic 3488
9/23/78	#5	18	Double Vision	Atlantic 3514
12/23/78	#19	14	Blue Morning, Blue Day	Atlantic 3543
9/08/79	#16	14	Dirty White Boy	Atlantic 3618
11/10/79	#12	14	Head Games	Atlantic 3633
2/16/80	#47	8	Women	Atlantic 3651
7/04/81	#5	21	Urgent	Atlantic 3831
10/10/81	#2	24	Waiting For A Girl Like You	Atlantic 3868
2/13/82	#34	11	Juke Box Hero	Atlantic 4017
5/15/82	#46	11	Break It Up	Atlantic 4044
12/08/84	#1	21	I Want To Know What Love Is	Atlantic 89596
3/16/85	#10	15	That Was Yesterday	Atlantic 89571
6/01/85	#49	9	Reaction To Action	Atlantic 89542
8/17/85	#59	9	Down On Love	Atlantic 89493
12/05/87	#8	20	Say You Will	Atlantic 89169
3/19/88	#8	19	I Don't Want To Live Without You	Atlantic 89101
7/16/88	#54	10	Heart Turns To Stone	Atlantic 89046
			FORMATIONS	
2/17/68	#64	7	At The Top Of The Stairs	MGM 13899
			FORTUNE TELLERS	
8/12/61	#91	5	The Song Of The Nairobi Trio	Music Makers 105
			FORTUNES	
8/28/65	#7	11	You've Got Your Troubles	Press 9773
11/06/65	#37	7	Here It Comes Again	Press 9798
2/05/66	#85	4	This Golden Ring	Press 9811
5/16/70	#59	9	That Same Old Feeling	World Pacific 77937
5/15/71	#8	15	Here Comes That Rainy Day Feeling Again	Capitol 3086
10/02/71	#80	4	Freedom Comes, Freedom Goes	Capitol 3179
			49ER'S	
6/23/90	#77	6	Don't You Love Me	4th & B'way 447506

Debut Date	Peak Pos	Wks Chr	ARTIST/Song Title	Label & Number
			FORUM	
7/01/67	#44	9	The River Is Wide	Mira 232
			BRUCE FOSTER	
6/25/77	#66	6	Platinum Heroes	Millennium 602
			DAVID FOSTER	
8/24/85	#20	22	Love Theme From St. Elmo's Fire	Atlantic 89528
6/07/86	#81	7	The Best Of Me*	Atlantic 89420
2/20/88	#78	6	Winter Games	Atlantic 89140
			*released as by DAVID FOSTER and OLIVIA NEWTON-JOHN	
			FOTOMAKER	
4/29/78	#88	5	Where Have You Been All My Life	Atlantic 3471
11/18/78	#70	8	Miles Away	Atlantic 3531
			FOUNDATIONS	
12/16/67	#8	15	Baby, Now That I've Found You	Uni 55038
3/09/68	#49	5	Back On My Feet Again	Uni 55058
12/28/68	#1	15	Build Me Up Buttercup	Uni 55101
3/29/69	#26	5	In The Bad Bad Old Days	Uni 55117
6/21/69	#81	2	My Little Chickadee	Uni 55137
			PETE FOUNTAIN	
3/03/62	#85	4	Yes Indeed	Coral 65549
6/20/64	#94	2	Licorice Stick	Coral 62413
			FOUR ACES	
10/13/51	#1	21	Sin	Victoria 101
1/19/52	#2	15	Tell Me Why	Decca 27860
4/12/52	#7	5	Perfidia	Decca 27987
12/26/53	#1	18	Stranger In Paradise/	Decca 28927
1/09/54	#3	10	Heart Of My Heart	Decca 28927
6/12/54	#1	14	Three Coins In The Fountain	Decca 29123
1/15/55	#1	19	Melody Of Love	Decca 29395
6/25/55	#10	4	Heart	Decca 29476
9/17/55	#1	16	Love Is A Many Splendored Thing	Decca 29625
8/04/56	#38	2	I Only Know I Love You	Decca 29989
9/15/56	#10	6	Friendly Persuasion (Thee I Love)	Decca 30041
12/08/56	#39	6	Written On The Wind	Decca 30123
3/23/57	#36	4	Bahama Mama/	Decca 30242
3/23/57	#45	2	You're Mine	Decca 30242
9/13/58	#89	2	Roses Of Rio	Decca 30721
11/08/58	#25	12	The World Outside	Decca 30764
2/28/59	#28	11	No Other Arms, No Other Lips	Decca 30822
			4 BY FOUR	
7/04/87	#83	5	Want You For My Girlfriend	Capitol 5690
			FOUR COINS	
6/01/57	#15	17	Shangri-La	Epic 9213
9/14/57	#25	13	My One Sin	Epic 9229
2/01/58	#48	3	A Broken Promise	Epic 9253
11/08/58	#25	12	The World Outside	Epic 9295
5/30/59	#69	5	One Love, One Heart	Epic 9314
			FOUR ESQUIRES	
1/12/57	#43	3	Follow Me	Pilgrim 717
11/09/57	#29	10	Love Me Forever	Paris 509
9/26/58	#19	15	Hideaway	Paris 520
1/03/59	#81	4	Land Of You And Me	Paris 526
			FOUR-EVERS	
5/30/64	#69	4	Be My Girl	Smash 1887
			FOUR FRESHMEN	
6/30/56	#6	3	Graduation Day	Capitol 3410
			FOUR JACKS and A JILL	
3/16/68	#10	17	Master Jack	RCA 9473
			FOUR KNIGHTS	
3/27/54	#3	16	I Get So Lonely	Capitol 2654
1/03/59	#76	5	O' Falling Star	Coral 62045
			FOUR LADS	
11/28/53	#4	7	Istanbul	Columbia 40082
9/18/54	#3	11	Skokiaan	Columbia 40306
10/22/55	#2	13	Moments To Remember	Columbia 40539

Debut Date	Peak Pos	Wks Chr	ARTIST/Song Title	Label & Number
2/18/56	#1	11	No, Not Much!	Columbia 40629
6/09/56	#3	12	Standing On The Corner	Columbia 40674
8/25/56	#18	10	The Bus Stop Song (A Paper Of Pins)/	Columbia 40736
9/01/56	#20	8	A House With Love In It	Columbia 40736
1/12/57	#9	17	Who Needs You	Columbia 40811
5/11/57	#28	12	I Just Don't Know	Columbia 40914
9/29/57	#49	7	Eyes Of God	Columbia 40974
11/30/57	#22	10	Put A Light In The Window	Columbia 41058
3/22/58	#13	15	There's Only One Of You	Columbia 41136
6/14/58	#12	15	Enchanted Island	Columbia 41194
11/01/58	#45	8	The Mocking Bird	Columbia 41266
1/03/59	#31	12	The Girl On Page 44	Columbia 41310
4/25/59	#76	5	The Fountain Of Youth	Columbia 41365
10/24/59	#34	14	Happy Anniversary	Columbia 41497

FOURMOST

Debut Date	Peak Pos	Wks Chr	ARTIST/Song Title	Label & Number
9/17/66	#97	2	Here, There And Everywhere	Capitol 5738

4 NON BLONDES

Debut Date	Peak Pos	Wks Chr	ARTIST/Song Title	Label & Number
4/24/93	#13	28	What's Up	Interscope 98430

4 OF US

Debut Date	Peak Pos	Wks Chr	ARTIST/Song Title	Label & Number
4/21/90	#55	5	Drag My Bad Name Down	Columbia 73243

FOUR PENNIES (same group as THE CHIFFONS)

Debut Date	Peak Pos	Wks Chr	ARTIST/Song Title	Label & Number
6/29/63	#76	4	My Block	Rust 5071

FOUR PREPS

Debut Date	Peak Pos	Wks Chr	ARTIST/Song Title	Label & Number
1/18/58	#4	15	26 Miles (Santa Catalina)	Capitol 3845
5/10/58	#5	14	Big Man	Capitol 3960
8/16/58	#39	10	Lazy Summer Night/	Capitol 4023
8/23/58	#71	1	Summertime Lies	Capitol 4023
12/26/59	#15	15	Down By The Station	Capitol 4312
4/23/60	#34	9	Got A Girl	Capitol 4362
8/19/61	#18	11	More Money For You And Me	Capitol 4599
3/17/62	#64	8	The Big Draft	Capitol 4716
3/28/64	#88	3	A Letter To The Beatles	Capitol 5143

FOUR SEASONS

Debut Date	Peak Pos	Wks Chr	ARTIST/Song Title	Label & Number
8/18/62	#1	16	Sherry	Vee-Jay 456
10/20/62	#1	17	Big Girls Don't Cry	Vee-Jay 465
12/15/62	#28	4	Santa Claus Is Coming To Town	Vee-Jay 478
1/19/63	#1	15	Walk Like A Man	Vee-Jay 485
4/20/63	#20	8	Ain't That A Shame/	Vee-Jay 512
4/27/63	#70	9	Soon	Vee-Jay 512
7/06/63	#4	14	Candy Girl	Vee-Jay 539
7/06/63	#35	8	Marlena	Vee-Jay 539
10/05/63	#30	7	New Mexican Rose/	Vee-Jay 562
10/05/63	#65	4	That's The Only Way	Vee-Jay 562
2/01/64	#3	14	Dawn (Go Away)	Philips 40166
2/15/64	#15	13	Stay	Vee-Jay 582
4/11/64	#6	9	Ronnie	Philips 40185
6/06/64	#74	3	Long, Lonely Nights/	Vee-Jay 597
6/13/64	#24	8	Alone	Vee-Jay 597
6/20/64	#1	13	Rag Doll	Philips 40211
8/22/64	#87	5	Sincerely	Vee-Jay 608
8/29/64	#9	9	Save It For Me	Philips 40225
11/07/64	#14	9	Big Man In Town	Philips 40238
1/25/65	#10	9	Bye, Bye, Baby (Baby Goodbye)	Philips 40260
4/03/65	#62	5	Toy Soldier/	Philips 40278
4/24/65	#91	1	Betrayed	Philips 40278
6/12/65	#27	8	Girl Come Running	Philips 40305
10/02/65	#1	17	Let's Hang On!	Philips 40317
11/06/65	#10	11	Don't Think Twice*	Philips 40324
1/01/66	#91	3	Little Boy (In Grown Up Clothes)	Vee-Jay 713
1/29/66	#10	9	Working My Way Back To You	Philips 40350
5/14/66	#9	10	Opus 17 (Don't You Worry 'Bout Me)	Philips 40370
6/25/66	#86	3	You're Nobody Till Somebody Loves You*	Philips 40380
9/03/66	#9	10	I've Got You Under My Skin	Philips 40393
12/10/66	#12	10	Tell It To The Rain	Philips 40412
3/04/67	#12	10	Beggin'	Philips 40433
6/10/67	#9	10	C'mon Marianne	Philips 40460
7/22/67	#62	4	Lonesome Road*	Philips 40471
10/28/67	#14	7	Watch The Flowers Grow	Philips 40490

Debut Date	Peak Pos	Wks Chr	**ARTIST**/Song Title	Label & Number
			FOUR SEASONS—*continued*	
2/24/68	#15	8	Will You Love Me Tomorrow	Philips 40523
6/22/68	#50	4	Saturday's Father	Philips 40542
12/14/68	#41	8	Electric Stories	Philips 40577
3/22/69	#64	4	Idaho	Philips 40597
9/06/69	#33	8	And That Reminds Me	Crewe 333
4/25/70	#53	6	Patch Of Blue	Philips 40662
5/25/74	#90	5	Hickory	Motown 1288
8/30/75	#7	17	Who Loves You	Warner Brothers 8122
12/27/75	#1	23	December, 1963 (Oh, What A Night)	Warner Brothers 8168
5/29/76	#68	5	Silver Star	Warner Brothers 8203
7/23/77	#77	5	Down The Hall	Warner Brothers 8407
			*released as by **THE WONDER WHO?**	
			FOUR SONICS	
2/10/68	#93	1	You Don't Have To Say You Love Me	Sport 110
			FOUR TOPS	
8/15/64	#15	13	Baby I Need Your Loving	Motown 1062
11/28/64	#58	5	Without The One You Love	Motown 1069
2/06/65	#26	9	Ask The Lonely	Motown 1073
5/15/65	#1	15	I Can't Help Myself	Motown 1076
7/24/65	#6	11	It's The Same Old Song	Motown 1081
11/06/65	#12	8	Something About You	Motown 1084
2/19/66	#15	10	Shake Me, Wake Me (When It's Over)	Motown 1090
5/28/66	#44	8	Loving You Is Sweeter Than Ever	Motown 1096
9/03/66	#1	14	Reach Out I'll Be There	Motown 1098
12/17/66	#7	10	Standing In The Shadows Of Love	Motown 1102
3/11/67	#8	10	Bernadette	Motown 1104
5/20/67	#9	9	7 Rooms Of Gloom/	Motown 1110
7/22/67	#91	1	I'll Turn To Stone	Motown 1110
9/16/67	#18	8	You Keep Running Away	Motown 1113
2/03/68	#8	9	Walk Away Renee	Motown 1119
4/20/68	#20	9	If I Were A Carpenter	Motown 1124
7/20/68	#31	6	Yesterday's Dreams	Motown 1127
10/05/68	#32	6	I'm In A Different World	Motown 1132
5/03/69	#52	4	What Is A Man	Motown 1147
11/29/69	#52	7	Don't Let Him Take Your Love From Me	Motown 1159
4/25/70	#14	12	It's All In The Game	Motown 1164
8/29/70	#12	13	Still Water (Love)	Motown 1170
11/21/70	#15	11	River Deep - Mountain High*	Motown 1173
1/16/71	#26	9	Just Seven Numbers	Motown 1175
6/05/71	#51	4	You Gotta Have Love In Your Heart*	Motown 1181
8/28/71	#38	9	MacArthur Park (Part 2)	Motown 1189
2/05/72	#80	3	A Simple Game	Motown 1196
8/26/72	#53	9	(It's The Way) Nature Planned It	Motown 1210
11/04/72	#9	13	Keeper Of The Castle	Dunhill 4330
2/03/73	#1	15	Ain't No Woman (Like The One I've Got)	Dunhill 4339
6/23/73	#14	14	Are You Man Enough	Dunhill 4354
10/13/73	#30	7	Sweet Understanding Love	Dunhill 4366
1/19/74	#41	10	I Just Can't Get You Out Of My Mind	Dunhill 4377
4/27/74	#36	9	One Chain Don't Make No Prison	Dunhill 4386
8/03/74	#76	9	Midnight Flower	Dunhill 15005
5/31/75	#79	5	Seven Lonely Nights	ABC 12096
11/08/75	#87	4	We Gotta All Stick Together	ABC 12123
10/23/76	#75	6	Catfish	ABC 12214
8/22/81	#10	21	When She Was My Girl	Casablanca 2338
9/04/82	#85	4	Sad Hearts	Casablanca 2353
11/05/83	#70	6	I Just Can't Walk Away	Motown 1706
8/20/88	#40	12	Indestructable	Arista 9706
12/24/88	#88	5	If Ever A Love There Was**	Arista 9751
			*released as by **THE SUPREMES & FOUR TOPS**	
			released as by **THE FOUR TOPS & ARETHA FRANKLIN	
			FOUR TUNES	
1/30/53	#10	1	Marie	Jubilee 5128
7/03/54	#4	9	I Understand Just How You Feel	Jubilee 5132
10/24/59	#90	2	Marie	Jubilee 6000
			FOUR VOICES	
1/25/58	#46	7	Dancing With My Shadow	Columbia 41076
			FOX	
8/23/75	#58	7	Only You Can	Ariola America 7601

Debut Date	Peak Pos	Wks Chr	**ARTIST**/Song Title	Label & Number
			CHARLES FOX	
12/27/80	#81	8	Seasons	Handshake 5307
			SAMANTHA FOX	
11/08/86	#7	23	Touch Me (I Want Your Body)	Jive 1006
3/21/87	#81	5	Do Ya Do Ya (Wanna Please Me)	Jive 1031
10/17/87	#84	5	Nothing's Gonna Stop Me Now	Jive 1072
2/27/88	#4	23	Naughty Girls (Need Love Too)	Jive 1089
11/05/88	#19	21	I Wanna Have Some Fun	Jive 1154
3/25/89	#38	14	I Only Wanna Be With You	Jive 1192
			INEZ FOXX	
6/22/63	#7	19	Mockingbird	Symbol 919
1/11/64	#78	4	Ask Me	Symbol 926
5/09/64	#71	7	Hurt By Love	Symbol 20-001
12/16/67	#73	11	(1-2-3-4-5-6-7) Count The Days	Dynamo 112
			FOXY	
7/29/78	#17	22	Get Off	Dash 5046
3/24/79	#29	15	Hot Number	Dash 5050
			PETER FRAMPTON	
7/12/75	#81	3	Show Me The Way (studio)	A&M 1693
2/28/76	#4	18	Show Me The Way (live)	A&M 1795
6/19/76	#16	22	Baby, I Love Your Way	A&M 1832
10/02/76	#13	13	Do You Feel Like We Do	A&M 1867
5/28/77	#1	17	I'm In You	A&M 1941
8/27/77	#13	13	Signed, Sealed, Delivered (I'm Yours)	A&M 1972
12/03/77	#57	9	Tried To Love	A&M 1988
5/26/79	#18	14	I Can't Stand It No More	A&M 2148
2/08/86	#78	7	Lying	Atlantic 89463
			CONNIE FRANCIS	
2/08/58	#3	17	Who's Sorry Now	MGM 12588
5/03/58	#31	8	I'm Sorry I Made You Cry	MGM 12647
8/02/58	#16	14	Stupid Cupid	MGM 12683
10/11/58	#39	11	Fallin'/	MGM 12713
10/11/58	#88	4	Happy Days And Lonely Nights	MGM 12713
12/06/58	#2	18	My Happiness/	MGM 12738
12/13/58	#99	1	Never Before	MGM 12738
3/07/59	#15	10	If I Didn't Care	MGM 12769
5/16/59	#3	17	Lipstick On Your Collar/	MGM 12793
5/16/59	#9	14	Frankie	MGM 12793
9/12/59	#32	9	You're Gonna Miss Me/	MGM 12824
9/12/59	#63	5	Plenty Good Lovin'	MGM 12824
11/21/59	#5	15	Among My Souvenirs/	MGM 12841
11/21/59	#36	10	God Bless America	MGM 12841
2/27/60	#7	14	Mama/	MGM 12878
2/27/60	#31	11	Teddy	MGM 12878
5/14/60	#1	18	Everybody's Somebody's Fool/	MGM 12899
5/14/60	#27	11	Jealous Of You	MGM 12899
8/27/60	#1	17	My Heart Has A Mind Of Its Own/	MGM 12923
8/27/60	#67	7	Malaguena	MGM 12923
11/12/60	#9	13	Many Tears Ago	MGM 12964
1/21/61	#4	14	Where The Boys Are	MGM 12971
1/21/61	#63	7	No One	MGM 12971
4/22/61	#5	11	Breakin' In A Brand New Broken Heart	MGM 12995
7/01/61	#7	12	Together/	MGM 13019
7/01/61	#64	6	Too Many Blues	MGM 13019
9/23/61	#22	10	(He's My) Dreamboat/	MGM 13039
9/23/61	#26	8	Hollywood	MGM 13039
11/25/61	#8	12	When The Boy In Your Arms (Is The Boy In Your Heart)/	MGM 13051
12/16/61	#52	4	Baby's First Christmas	MGM 13051
2/10/62	#2	13	Don't Break The Heart That Loves You	MGM 13059
5/12/62	#7	10	Second Hand Love	MGM 13074
7/28/62	#10	9	Vacation/	MGM 13087
8/11/62	#89	1	The Biggest Sin	MGM 13087
10/06/62	#18	10	I Was Such A Fool/	MGM 13096
10/13/62	#51	6	He Thinks I Still Care	MGM 13096
12/15/62	#18	11	I'm Gonna Be Warm This Winter	MGM 13116
1/12/63	#87	2	Al Di La	MGM 13116
3/02/63	#11	10	Follow The Boys	MGM 13127
5/18/63	#16	9	If My Pillow Could Talk	MGm 13143
8/03/63	#34	8	Drownin' My Sorrows	MGM 13160

Debut Date	Peak Pos	Wks Chr	ARTIST/Song Title	Label & Number
			CONNIE FRANCIS—*continued*	
10/12/63	#22	9	Your Other Love	MGM 13176
12/28/63	#31	6	In The Summer Of His Years	MGM 13203
2/15/64	#16	9	Blue Winter	MGM 13214
5/09/64	#23	8	Be Anything (But Be Mine)	MGM 13237
7/18/64	#34	6	Looking For Love	MGM 13256
10/24/64	#37	7	Don't Ever Leave Me	MGM 13287
1/16/65	#42	6	Whose Heart Are You Breaking Tonight	MGM 13303
2/27/65	#35	7	For Mama (La Mamma)	MGM 13325
5/01/65	#49	6	Wishing It Was You	MGM 13331
6/26/65	#58	5	Forget Domani	MGM 13363
8/28/65	#83	6	Roundabout	MGM 13389
11/27/65	#29	9	Jealous Heart	MGM 13420
3/12/66	#68	5	Love Is Me, Love Is You	MGM 13470
11/12/66	#81	4	Spanish Nights And You	MGM 13610
2/11/67	#98	2	Another Page	MGM 13665
7/29/67	#96	2	My Heart Cries For You	MGM 13773
3/15/69	#97	3	The Wedding Cake	MGM 14034
7/14/73	#99	1	The Answer (Should I Tie A Yellow Ribbon Around The Old Oak Tree)	GSF 6901
			FRANKE & THE KNOCKOUTS	
3/07/81	#13	20	Sweetheart	Millennium 11801
7/04/81	#29	13	You're My Girl	Millennium 11808
4/03/82	#22	15	Without You (Not Another Lonely Night)	Millennium 13105
			FRANKIE GOES TO HOLLYWOOD	
4/07/84	#61	7	Relax	Island 99805
10/20/84	#37	18	Two Tribes	Island 99695
1/19/85	#13	18	Relax	Island 99805
4/06/85	#48	9	Welcome To The Pleasuredome	Island 99653
			ARETHA FRANKLIN	
12/03/60	#72	5	Today I Sing The Blues	Columbia 41793
1/28/61	#87	6	Won't Be Long	Columbia 41923
10/07/61	#24	13	Rock-A-Bye Your Baby With A Dixie Melody	Columbia 42157
2/03/62	#91	3	I Surrender Dear	Columbia 42266
10/03/64	#61	10	Runnin' Out Of Fools	Columbia 43113
7/17/65	#100	1	(No, No) I'm Losing You	Columbia 43333
3/04/67	#10	11	I Never Loved A Man (The Way I Love You)	Atlantic 2386
4/29/67	#3	13	Respect	Atlantic 2403
7/22/67	#3	11	Baby I Love You	Atlantic 2427
9/02/67	#81	5	Take A Look	Columbia 44270
9/30/67	#12	7	A Natural Woman (You Make Me Feel Like)	Atlantic 2441
12/09/67	#1	12	Chain Of Fools	Atlantic 2464
12/30/67	#90	3	Mockingbird	Columbia 44381
3/02/68	#5	10	(Sweet Sweet Baby) Since You've Been Gone/	Atlantic 2486
4/06/68	#71	6	Ain't No Way	Atlantic 2486
5/18/68	#7	9	Think/	Atlantic 2518
6/22/68	#88	2	You Send Me	Atlantic 2518
8/10/68	#9	10	The House That Jack Built/	Atlantic 2546
8/17/68	#18	11	I Say A Little Prayer	Atlantic 2546
11/16/68	#12	10	See Saw	Atlantic 2574
2/22/69	#10	7	The Weight	Atlantic 2603
4/19/69	#21	8	I Can't See Myself Leaving You/	Atlantic 2619
5/17/69	#90	1	Gentle On My Mind	Atlantic 2619
7/26/69	#18	12	Share Your Love With Me	Atlantic 2650
11/08/69	#23	8	Eleanor Rigby	Atlantic 2683
2/14/70	#13	11	Call Me	Atlantic 2706
5/23/70	#25	8	Spirit In The Dark	Atlantic 2731
8/08/70	#10	11	Don't Play That Song	Atlantic 2751
11/14/70	#23	9	Border Song (Holy Moses)	Atlantic 2772
2/20/71	#15	8	You're All I Need To Get By	Atlantic 2787
4/17/71	#2	11	Bridge Over Troubled Water/	Atlantic 2796
6/05/71	#72	4	Brand New Me	Atlantic 2796
7/31/71	#1	12	Spanish Harlem	Atlantic 2817
10/30/71	#7	10	Rock Steady/	Atlantic 2838
1/08/72	#70	4	Oh Me, Oh My (I'm A Fool For You Baby)	Atlantic 2838
3/11/72	#5	11	Day Dreaming	Atlantic 2866
6/03/72	#20	8	All The King's Horses	Atlantic 2883
8/12/72	#54	3	Wholy Holy	Atlantic 2901
2/10/73	#36	9	Master Of Eyes	Atlantic 2941
6/30/73	#16	13	Angel	Atlantic 2969

Debut Date	Peak Pos	Wks Chr	ARTIST/Song Title	Label & Number
11/17/73	#7	17	Until You Come Back To Me	Atlantic 2995
4/06/74	#16	12	I'm In Love	Atlantic 2999
8/31/74	#44	7	Ain't Nothing Like The Real Thing	Atlantic 3200
11/16/74	#52	8	Without Love	Atlantic 3224
9/27/75	#50	5	Mr. D.J. (5 For The D.J.)	Atlantic 3289
1/17/76	#90	3	You	Atlantic 3311
6/05/76	#30	16	Something He Can Feel	Atlantic 3326
10/16/76	#77	4	Jump	Atlantic 3358
2/26/77	#75	4	Look Into Your Heart	Atlantic 3373
12/27/80	#74	8	United Together	Arista 0569
5/30/81	#88	4	Come To Me	Arista 0600
8/29/81	#44	10	Love All The Hurt Away*	Arista 0624
8/21/82	#28	15	Jump To It	Arista 0699
8/06/83	#65	7	Get It Right	Arista 9034
6/22/85	#3	20	Freeway Of Love	Arista 9354
9/28/85	#8	20	Who's Zoomin' Who	Arista 9410
10/19/85	#22	15	Sisters Are Doin It For Themselves**	RCA 14214
1/18/86	#25	16	Another Night	Arista 9453
9/27/86	#23	11	Jumpin' Jack Flash	Arista 9528
12/06/86	#36	13	Jimmy Lee	Arista 9546
2/21/87	#1	21	I Knew You Were Waiting (For Me)***	Arista 9559
6/20/87	#83	5	Rock-A-Lott	Arista 9574
12/24/88	#88	5	If Ever A Love There Was****	Arista 9751
4/15/89	#15	17	Through The Storm*****	Arista 9809
7/01/89	#37	12	It Isn't, It Wasn't, It Ain't Never Gonna Be******	Arista 9850

*released as by ARETHA FRANKLIN and GEORGE BENSON
**released as by THE EURYTHMICS and ARETHA FRANKLIN
***released as by ARETHA FRANKLIN and GEORGE MICHAEL
****released as by THE FOUR TOPS & ARETHA FRANKLIN
*****released as by ARETHA FRANKLIN and ELTON JOHN
******released as by ARETHA FRANKLIN and WHITNEY HOUSTON

			CAROLYN FRANKLIN	
9/13/69	#98	1	It's True I'm Gonna Miss You	RCA 0188
			DOUG FRANKLIN with THE BLUENOTES	
8/30/58	#72	9	My Lucky Love	Colonial 7777
			ERMA FRANKLIN	
11/11/67	#61	7	Piece Of My Heart	Shout 221
			MICHAEL FRANKS	
7/31/76	#65	10	Popsicle Toes	Reprise 1360
			ANDY FRASER	
3/10/84	#88	4	Do You Love Me	Island 99784
			DALLAS FRAZIER	
5/07/66	#100	1	Elvira	Capitol 5560
			STAN FREBERG	
11/21/53	#8	3	St. George And The Dragonet	Capitol 2596
4/20/57	#30	4	Banana Boat (Day-O)	Capitol 3687
10/26/57	#22	8	Wun'erful Wun'erful! (Parts 1 & 2)	Capitol 3815
12/27/58	#34	4	Green Chritma	Capitol 4097
			JOHN FRED & HIS PLAYBOY BAND	
3/21/59	#78	3	Shirley	Montel 1002
11/18/67	#1	18	Judy In Disguise (With Glasses)	Paula 282
2/24/68	#41	6	Hey Hey Bunny/	Paula 294
2/24/68	#87	1	Love Explosion	Paula 294
			FREDDIE and THE DREAMERS	
3/20/65	#1	11	I'm Telling You Now	Tower 125
3/20/65	#43	8	I Understand	Mercury 72377
5/01/65	#15	9	Do The Freddie	Mercury 72428
5/01/65	#17	8	You Were Made For Me	Tower 127
7/31/65	#41	6	A Little You	Mercury 72462
			FREE	
8/22/70	#3	16	All Right Now	A&M 1206
12/05/70	#46	6	Stealer	A&M 1230

Debut Date	Peak Pos	Wks Chr	ARTIST/Song Title	Label & Number
			BOBBY FREEMAN	
4/12/58	#5	17	Do You Want To Dance	Josie 835
8/02/58	#31	10	Betty Lou Got A New Pair Of Shoes	Josie 841
12/06/58	#56	5	Need Your Love	Josie 844
2/07/59	#87	3	When You're Smiling	Josie 855
6/13/59	#82	3	Mary Ann Thomas	Josie 863
11/21/59	#52	10	Ebb Tide	Josie 872
8/27/60	#55	12	(I Do The) Shimmy Shimmy	King 5373
7/04/64	#6	14	C'mon And Swim	Autumn 2
10/24/64	#74	5	S-W-I-M	Autumn 5
			ERNIE FREEMAN	
11/16/57	#1	16	Raunchy	Imperial 5474
10/22/60	#86	6	Theme From "The Dark At The Top Of The Stairs"	Imperial 5693
			FREE MOVEMENT	
5/29/71	#6	21	I've Found Someone Of My Own	Decca 32818
12/11/71	#43	10	The Harder I Try	Columbia 45512
			ACE FREHLEY	
10/14/78	#16	21	New York Groove	Casablanca 941
			DON FRENCH	
4/18/59	#61	10	Lonely Saturday Night	Lancer 104
10/24/59	#95	4	Little Blonde Girl	Lancer 105
			FRESH START	
8/10/74	#91	3	Free	Dunhill 15002
			GLENN FREY	
6/05/82	#23	13	I Found Somebody	Asylum 47466
8/21/82	#12	21	The One You Love	Asylum 69974
12/11/82	#37	12	All Those Lies	Asylum 69857
6/30/84	#23	17	Sexy Girl	MCA 52413
9/29/84	#53	8	The Allnighter	MCA 52461
12/08/84	#4	25	The Heat Is On	MCA 52512
4/06/85	#14	20	Smuggler's Blues	MCA 52546
9/14/85	#3	22	You Belong To The City	MCA 52651
8/20/88	#14	16	True Love	MCA 53363
5/11/91	#49	11	Part Of Me, Part Of You	MCA 54060
7/18/92	#81	7	I've Got Mine	MCA 54429
			FRIDA	
11/06/82	#14	28	I Know There's Something Going On	Atlantic 89984
			DEAN FRIEDMAN	
4/09/77	#17	24	Ariel	Lifesong 45022
			FRIEND AND LOVER	
5/04/68	#7	15	Reach Out Of The Darkness	Verve Forecast 5069
8/24/68	#58	4	If Love Is In Your Heart	Verve Forecast 5091
			FRIENDS OF DISTINCTION	
4/05/69	#6	15	Grazing In The Grass	RCA 0107
7/26/69	#59	5	Let Yourself Go	RCA 0204
8/16/69	#23	17	Going In Circles	RCA 0204
3/07/70	#8	13	Love Or Let Me Be Lonely	RCA 0319
10/03/70	#44	8	Time Waits For No One	RCA 0385
1/16/71	#79	5	I Need You	RCA 0416
			FRIJID PINK	
1/24/70	#6	16	House Of The Rising Sun	Parrot 341
7/25/70	#39	8	Sing A Song For Freedom	Parrot 349
12/05/70	#53	7	Heartbreak Hotel	Parrot 352
			DAVID FRIZZELL	
8/14/82	#85	6	I'm Gonna Hire A Wino To Decorate Our Home	Warner Brothers 50063
			LEFTY FRIZELL	
2/22/64	#95	2	Saginaw, Michigan	Columbia 42924
			FROGMEN	
4/15/61	#34	9	Underwater	Candix 314
			FRANK FROST	
7/16/66	#98	2	My Backscratcher	Jewel 765
			MAX FROST and THE TROOPERS	
8/31/68	#17	14	Shape Of Things To Come	Tower 419

Debut Date	Peak Pos	Wks Chr	ARTIST/Song Title	Label & Number
			THOMAS & RICHARD FROST	
10/11/69	#79	5	She's Got Love	Imperial 66405
			FROZEN GHOST	
4/18/87	#64	9	Should I See	Atlantic 89279
			BOBBY FULLER FOUR	
1/29/66	#9	11	I Fought The Law	Mustang 3014
4/23/66	#51	6	Love Makes A Fool Of You	Mustang 3016
			JERRY FULLER	
8/22/59	#91	5	Betty My Angel	Challenge 59052
10/24/59	#42	8	Tennessee Waltz	Challenge 59057
9/23/61	#95	3	Guilty Of Loving You	Challenge 9114
			LOWELL FULSOM	
1/01/66	#87	3	Black Knight	Kent 431
1/14/67	#53	7	The Tramp	Kent 456
			FUN AND GAMES	
1/18/69	#53	5	The Grooviest Girl In The World	Uni 55098
			FUNKADELIC	
10/18/69	#81	3	I'll Bet You	Westbound 150
3/14/70	#91	3	I Got A Thing, You Got A Thing, Everybody's Got A Thing	Westbound 158
8/29/70	#85	4	I Wanna Know If It's Good To You?	Westbound 167
4/03/71	#85	4	You And Your Folks, Me And My Folks	Westbound 175
9/04/71	#61	5	Can You Get To That	Westbound 185
9/16/78	#22	15	One Nation Under A Groove (Part 1)	Warner Brothers 8618
9/08/79	#45	13	(Not Just) Knee Deep (Part 1)	Warner Brothers 49040
			FUNKY COMMUNICATIONS COMMITTEE	
7/07/79	#59	10	Baby I Want You	Free Flight 11595
			FUNKY KINGS	
12/04/76	#66	6	Slow Dancing	Arista 0209
			RICHIE FURAY	
6/10/78	#92	4	This Magic Moment	Asylum 45487
10/27/79	#40	13	I Still Have Dreams	Asylum 46534
			FU-SCHNICKENS	
7/17/93	#36	15	What's Up Doc? (Can We Rock)*	Jive 42164
			*released as by FU-SCHNICKENS with SHAQUILLE O'NEAL	
			FUZZ	
1/30/71	#20	19	I Love You For All Seasons	Calla 174
6/19/71	#70	8	Like An Open Door	Calla 177
9/18/71	#90	5	I'm So Glad	Calla 179
			FUZZ BUNNIES	
9/07/68	#96	3	The Sun Ain't Gonna Shine Anymore	Decca 32364

G

Debut Date	Peak Pos	Wks Chr	ARTIST/Song Title	Label & Number
			GABRIEL	
10/07/78	#82	5	Martha	Epic 50594
			PETER GABRIEL	
5/07/77	#81	6	Solsbury Hill	Atco 7079
8/02/80	#60	12	Games Without Frontiers	Mercury 76063
10/30/82	#33	18	Shock The Monkey	Geffen 29883
5/10/86	#1	22	Sledgehammer	Geffen 28718
8/30/86	#24	14	In Your Eyes	Geffen 28622
11/29/86	#8	24	Big Time	Geffen 28503
4/04/87	#69	6	Don't Give Up*	Geffen 28463
6/03/89	#39	13	In Your Eyes	WTG 68936
10/10/92	#46	15	Digging In The Dirt	Geffen 19136
12/26/92	#32	17	Steam	Geffen 19145
			*released as by PETER GABRIEL/KATE BUSH	
			GABRIEL and THE ANGELS	
10/27/62	#44	14	That's Life (That's Tough)	Swan 4118
			GABRIELLE	
10/30/93	#27	32	Dreams	Go! Discs 857141
			MEL GADSON	
5/14/60	#50	9	Comin' Down With Love	Big Top 3034

Debut Date	Peak Pos	Wks Chr	ARTIST/Song Title	Label & Number
			GAINORS	
10/11/58	#39	3	The Secret	Cameo 151
			SUNNY GALE	
3/08/52	#2	3	Wheel Of Fortune	Derby 787
7/31/54	#5	7	Goodnight Sweetheart, Goodnight	RCA 5746
10/23/54	#9	4	Smile	RCA 5836
			GALENS	
11/09/63	#75	6	Baby I Do Love You	Challenge 9212
			GALLAGHER and LYLE	
5/15/76	#79	5	I Want To Stay With You	A&M 1778
10/09/76	#89	6	Heart On My Sleeve	A&M 1850
4/02/77	#92	1	Every Little Teardrop	A&M 1904
			GALLAHADS	
8/04/56	#8	10	The Fool	Jubilee 5252
			GALLERY	
3/04/72	#1	21	Nice To Be With You	Sussex 232
8/05/72	#13	17	I Believe In Music	Sussex 239
12/23/72	#12	16	Big City Miss Ruth Ann	Sussex 248
			FRANK GALLOP	
6/21/58	#31	6	Got A Match?	ABC-Paramount 9931
4/16/66	#46	6	Ballad Of Irving	Kapp 745
			GAMMA	
12/22/79	#58	8	I'm Alive	Elektra 46555
4/10/82	#77	4	Right The First Time	Elektra 47423
			GANTS	
9/25/65	#41	11	Road Runner	Liberty 55829
			GAP BAND	
2/21/81	#90	5	Burn Rubber	Mercury 76091
5/23/81	#75	6	Yearning For Your Love	Mercury 76101
5/22/82	#33	15	Early In The Morning	Total Experience 8201
8/14/82	#37	15	You Dropped A Bomb On Me	Total Experience 8203
3/05/83	#55	9	Outstanding	Total Experience 8205
			DAVE GARDNER	
6/29/57	#36	2	White Silver Sands	OJ 1002
			DON GARDNER and DEE DEE FORD	
6/09/62	#16	13	I Need Your Loving	Fire 508
8/18/62	#88	4	Glory Of Love	KC 106
9/01/62	#83	5	Don't You Worry	Fire 513
			ART GARFUNKEL	
9/08/73	#6	14	All I Know	Columbia 45926
12/22/73	#18	10	I Shall Sing*	Columbia 45983
4/06/74	#70	3	Traveling Boy	Columbia 46030
9/07/74	#44	10	Second Avenue*	Columbia 10020
8/23/75	#19	17	I Only Have Eyes For You	Columbia 10190
12/27/75	#38	11	Breakaway	Columbia 10273
1/21/78	#15	12	(What A) Wonderful World**	Columbia 10676
6/02/79	#52	9	Since I Don't Have You	Columbia 10999
8/08/81	#58	10	A Heart In New York	Columbia 02307
			*released as by GARFUNKEL	
			**released as by ART GARFUNKEL with JAMES TAYLOR & PAUL SIMON	
			FRANK GARI	
12/31/60	#36	14	Utopia	Crusade 1020
4/22/61	#40	10	Lullaby Of Love	Crusade 1021
7/22/61	#57	7	Princess	Crusade 1022
			GALE GARNETT	
8/22/64	#1	17	We'll Sing In The Sunshine	RCA 8388
12/05/64	#36	10	Lovin' Place	RCA 8472
			LEE GARRETT	
5/15/76	#67	8	You're My Everything	Chrysalis 2112
			LEIF GARRETT	
8/27/77	#29	12	Surfin' USA	Atlantic 3423
11/05/77	#18	14	Runaround Sue	Atlantic 3440
2/25/78	#66	5	Put Your Head On My Shoulder	Atlantic 3466

Debut Date	Peak Pos	Wks Chr	ARTIST/Song Title	Label & Number
4/29/78	#62	5	The Wanderer	Atlantic 3476
11/04/78	#15	19	I Was Made For Dancin'	Scotti Brothers 403
5/12/79	#63	6	Feel The Need	Scotti Brothers 407
			SCOTT GARRETT	
2/28/59	#87	4	A House Of Love	Laurie 3023
			GARY & DAVE	
11/17/73	#91	9	Could You Ever Love Me Again	London 200
			GARY and THE HORNETS	
11/19/66	#92	3	Hi Hi Hazel	Smash 2061
			GARY O'	
7/18/81	#76	5	Pay You Back With Interest	Capitol 5018
			GARY'S GANG	
2/17/79	#33	13	Keep On Dancin'	Columbia 10884
			DAVID GATES	
6/30/73	#36	10	Clouds	Elektra 45857
10/13/73	#49	9	Sail Around The World	Elektra 45868
12/28/74	#26	13	Never Let Her Go	Elektra 45223
12/10/77	#9	25	Goodbye Girl	Elektra 45450
8/26/78	#30	11	Took The Last Train	Elektra 45500
2/16/80	#63	7	Where Does The Lovin' Go	Elektra 46588
10/10/81	#80	4	Take Me Now	Arista 0615
			MARVIN GAYE	
9/15/62	#36	16	Stubborn Kind Of Fellow	Tamla 54068
1/26/63	#41	11	Hitch Hike	Tamla 54075
5/18/63	#10	16	Pride And Joy	Tamla 54079
10/19/63	#18	17	Can I Get A Witness	Tamla 54087
3/14/64	#18	12	You're A Wonderful One	Tamla 54093
5/02/64	#27	9	Once Upon A Time*/	Motown 1057
5/09/64	#25	12	What's The Matter With You Baby*	Motown 1057
6/13/64	#19	11	Try It Baby	Tamla 54095
9/19/64	#27	9	Baby Don't You Do It	Tamla 54101
10/24/64	#73	4	What Good Am I Without You**/	Tamla 54104
10/24/64	#98	1	I Want You 'Round**	Tamla 54104
11/21/64	#9	16	How Sweet It Is To Be Loved By You	Tamla 54107
3/20/65	#10	12	I'll Be Doggone	Tamla 54112
7/03/65	#20	8	Pretty Little Baby	Tamla 54117
10/02/65	#10	14	Ain't That Peculiar	Tamla 54122
2/19/66	#23	9	One More Heartache	Tamla 54129
5/21/66	#32	9	Take This Heart Of Mine	Tamla 54132
8/20/66	#52	6	Little Darling, I Need You	Tamla 54138
1/21/67	#43	11	It Takes Two**	Tamla 54141
5/20/67	#22	12	Ain't No Mountain High Enough***	Tamla 54149
7/01/67	#34	7	Your Unchanging Love	Tamla 54153
9/16/67	#6	12	Your Precious Love***	Tamla 54156
12/02/67	#18	12	If I Could Build My Whole World Around You***	Tamla 54161
1/06/68	#30	8	You	Tamla 54160
3/09/68	#70	3	If This World Were Mine***	Tamla 54161
4/13/68	#9	12	Ain't Nothing Like The Real Thing***	Tamla 54163
7/27/68	#7	11	You're All I Need To Get By***	Tamla 54169
9/21/68	#34	7	Chained	Tamla 54170
10/05/68	#25	8	Keep On Lovin' Me Honey***	Tamla 54173
11/16/68	#1	15	I Heard It Through The Grapevine	Tamla 54176
2/01/69	#45	6	Good Lovin' Ain't Easy To Come By***	Tamla 54179
4/19/69	#5	14	Too Busy Thinking About My Baby	Tamla 54181
8/23/69	#10	13	That's The Way Love Is	Tamla 54185
11/22/69	#47	8	What You Gave Me***	Tamla 54187
1/30/70	#27	7	How Can I Forget	Tamla 54190
4/18/70	#63	5	California Soul***	Tamla 54192
6/06/70	#28	8	The End Of Our Road	Tamla 54195
2/20/71	#1	14	What's Going On	Tamla 54201
6/26/71	#4	13	Mercy Mercy Me (The Ecology)	Tamla 54207
10/02/71	#6	11	Inner City Blues	Tamla 54209
5/13/72	#41	7	You're The Man	Tamla 54221
12/16/72	#8	11	Trouble Man	Tamla 54228
7/07/73	#1	18	Let's Get It On	Tamla 54234
9/29/73	#14	11	You're A Special Part Of Me****	Motown 1280
11/03/73	#18	10	Come Get To This	Tamla 54241
1/26/74	#40	7	You Sure Love To Ball	Tamla 54244

Debut Date	Peak Pos	Wks Chr	ARTIST/Song Title	Label & Number
			MARVIN GAYE—*continued*	
2/16/74	#20	14	My Mistake (Was To Love You)****	Motown 1269
7/20/74	#38	7	Don't Knock My Love****	Motown 1296
9/21/74	#33	9	Distant Lover	Tamla 54253
4/17/76	#20	17	I Want You	Tamla 54264
4/16/77	#1	19	Got To Give It Up (Part 1)	Tamla 54280
1/20/79	#65	6	Pops, We Love You*****	Motown 1455
10/30/82	#5	22	Sexual Healing	Columbia 03302
			*released as by MARVIN GAYE & MARY WELLS	
			**released as by MARVIN GAYE & KIM WESTON	
			***released as by MARVIN GAYE & TAMMI TERRELL	
			****released as by DIANA ROSS & MARVIN GAYE	
			*****released as by DIANA ROSS, MARVIN GAYE, SMOKEY ROBINSON & STEVIE WONDER	
			NONA GAYE	
10/17/92	#78	6	I'm Overjoyed	Third Stone 98486
			CRYSTAL GAYLE	
8/06/77	#1	27	Don't It Make My Brown Eyes Blue	United Artists 1016
2/18/78	#66	11	Ready For The Times To Get Better	United Artists 1136
7/08/78	#16	23	Talking In Your Sleep	United Artists 1214
9/22/79	#18	19	Half The Way	Columbia 11087
2/23/80	#71	5	It's Like We Never Said Goodbye	Columbia 11198
6/21/80	#93	4	The Blue Side	Columbia 11270
10/16/82	#20	26	You And I*	Elektra 69936
			*released as by EDDIE RABBITT with CRYSTAL GAYLE	
			GAYLORDS (Ronnie Gaylord and Burt Holiday)	
2/07/53	#2	12	Tell Me You're Mine	Mercury 70030
3/06/54	#3	7	From The Vine Came The Grape	Mercury 70296
7/10/54	#8	4	Isle Of Capri	Mercury 70350
8/07/54	#2	11	The Little Shoemaker	Mercury 70403
7/12/58	#43	7	Ma Ma Ma Marie	Mercury 71337
11/01/58	#59	9	Flamingo l'Amore	Mercury 71369
2/28/76	#79	6	Eh! Cumpari*	Prodigal 0622
			*released as by GAYLORD & HOLIDAY	
			GLORIA GAYNOR	
11/02/74	#8	16	Never Can Say Goodbye	MGM 14748
3/15/75	#60	6	Reach Out I'll Be There	MGM 14790
11/29/75	#83	6	How High The Moon	MGM 14838
12/23/78	#1	23	I Will Survive	Polydor 14508
6/30/79	#94	3	Anybody Wanna Party	Polydor 14558
9/22/79	#62	7	Let Me Know (I Have A Right)	Polydor 2021
			PAUL GAYTON	
10/31/59	#46	8	The Hunch	Anna 1106
			G-CLEFS	
8/11/56	#17	11	Ka-Ding Dong	Pilgrim 715
9/16/61	#16	18	I Understand (Just How You Feel)	Terrace 7500
3/03/62	#73	5	A Girl Has To Know	Terrace 7503
			DAVID GEDDES	
8/02/75	#1	13	Run Joey Run	Big Tree 16044
11/08/75	#22	9	The Last Game Of The Season	Big Tree 16052
			J. GEILS BAND	
11/27/71	#37	10	Looking For A Love	Atlantic 2844
3/31/73	#15	16	Give It To Me	Atlantic 2953
8/11/73	#76	3	Make Up Your Mind	Atlantic 2974
11/02/74	#17	13	Must Of Got Lost	Atlantic 3214
2/15/75	#86	3	Givin' It All Up	Atlantic 3251
3/27/76	#62	13	Where Did Our Love Go	Atlantic 3320
7/31/76	#77	5	(Ain't Nothin' But A) Houseparty	Atlantic 3350
11/18/78	#37	13	One Last Kiss	EMI America 8007
3/24/79	#80	4	Take It Back	EMI America 8012
2/02/80	#32	13	Come Back	EMI America 8032
4/12/80	#37	12	Love Stinks	EMI America 8039
7/19/80	#80	4	Just Can't Wait	EMI America 8047
11/07/81	#1	28	Centerfold	EMI America 8102
2/20/82	#4	19	Freeze-Frame/	EMI America 8108
2/20/82	#4	19	Flamethrower	EMI America 8108
5/22/82	#32	11	Angel In Blue	EMI America 8100

Debut Date	Peak Pos	Wks Chr	ARTIST/Song Title	Label & Number
11/20/82	#30	13	I Do	EMI America 8148
2/26/83	#62	6	Land Of A Thousand Dances	EMI America 8156
11/03/84	#63	7	Concealed Weapons	EMI America 8242
			BOB GELDOF	
12/20/86	#79	6	This Is The World Calling	Atlantic 89341
			GENE & DEBBE	
9/30/67	#84	5	Go With Me	TRX 5002
2/17/68	#14	15	Playboy	TRX 5006
6/15/68	#51	6	Lovin' Season	TRX 5010
			GENE & EUNICE	
9/05/59	#73	9	Poco Loco	Case 1001
			GENE & TOMMY	
10/14/67	#100	1	Richard & Me	ABC 10981
			GENE LOVES JEZEBEL	
8/25/90	#66	12	Jealous	Geffen 19688
			GENERAL PUBLIC	
11/17/84	#24	20	Tenderness	I.R.S. 9934
			GENESIS	
3/19/77	#87	3	Your Own Special Way	Atco 7076
4/22/78	#22	17	Follow You Follow Me	Atlantic 3474
5/24/80	#14	20	Misunderstanding	Atlantic 3662
8/30/80	#55	11	Turn It On Again	Atlantic 3751
9/26/81	#28	17	No Reply At All	Atlantic 3858
12/26/81	#40	12	Abacab	Atlantic 3891
3/27/82	#45	10	Man On The Corner	Atlantic 4025
6/05/82	#31	15	Paperlate	Atlantic 4053
10/15/83	#60	8	Mama	Atlantic 89770
11/26/83	#10	22	That's All	Atlantic 89724
3/17/84	#49	10	Illegal Alien	Atlantic 89698
6/16/84	#49	15	Taking It All Too Hard	Atlantic 89656
5/31/86	#1	18	Invisible Touch	Atlantic 89407
8/16/86	#3	18	Throwing It All Away	Atlantic 89372
11/01/86	#5	21	Land Of Confusion	Atlantic 89336
2/14/87	#3	16	Tonight, Tonight, Tonight	Atlantic 89290
4/25/87	#4	18	In Too Deep	Atlantic 89316
11/02/91	#6	26	No Son Of Mine	Atlantic 87571
2/01/92	#3	23	I Can't Dance	Atlantic 87532
5/23/92	#11	19	Hold On My Heart	Atlantic 87481
8/01/92	#16	18	Jesus He Knows Me	Atlantic 87454
11/14/92	#19	24	Never A Time	Atlantic 87411
			GENIES	
3/07/59	#33	10	Who's That Knocking	Shad 5002
			GENTLE PERSUASION	
2/26/83	#79	3	Please Mr. Postman	Capitol 5207
			BOBBIE GENTRY	
8/05/67	#1	14	Ode To Billie Joe	Capitol 5950
11/25/67	#41	5	Okolona River Bottom Band	Capitol 2044
4/13/68	#96	1	Louisiana Man	Capitol 2147
11/23/68	#94	1	Morning Glory*	Capitol 2314
2/08/69	#96	3	Let It Be Me*	Capitol 2387
11/15/69	#31	16	Fancy	Capitol 2675
2/14/70	#13	9	All I Have To Do Is Dream*	Capitol 2745
4/11/70	#74	5	He Made A Woman Out Of Me	Capitol 2788
7/04/70	#70	3	Apartment 21	Capitol 2849
7/17/76	#67	7	Ode To Billie Joe	Capitol 4294
			*released as by BOBBIE GENTRY & GLEN CAMPBELL	
			GENTRYS	
9/04/65	#5	14	Keep On Dancing	MGM 13379
12/25/65	#37	7	Spread It On Thick	MGM 13432
1/24/70	#50	6	Why Should I Cry	Sun 1108
4/04/70	#45	11	Cinnamon Girl	Sun 1114
2/13/71	#78	5	Wild World	Sun 1122
			BARBARA GEORGE	
11/25/61	#3	17	I Know (You Don't Love Me No More)	A.F.O. 302
3/24/62	#66	7	You Talk About Love	A.F.O. 304

Debut Date	Peak Pos	Wks Chr	ARTIST/Song Title	Label & Number
			GEORGIA SATELLITES	
11/22/86	#5	23	Keep Your Hands To Yourself	Elektra 69502
10/29/88	#51	13	Hippy Hippy Shake	Elektra 69366
			GEORGIO	
3/07/87	#70	9	Sexappeal	Motown 1882
12/19/87	#77	7	Lover's Lane	Motown 1906
			DANYEL GERARD	
7/01/72	#96	3	Butterfly	Verve 10670
			GERARDO	
2/16/91	#17	19	Rico Suave	Interscope 98871
5/04/91	#15	17	We Want The Funk	Interscope 98815
			DONNY GERRARD	
4/10/76	#95	5	Words	Greedy 101
			GERRY and THE PACEMAKERS	
5/23/64	#6	12	Don't Let The Sun Catch You Crying	Laurie 3251
7/18/64	#10	11	How Do You Do It?	Laurie 3261
9/26/64	#23	10	I Like It	Laurie 3271
12/12/64	#19	10	I'll Be There	Laurie 3279
2/06/65	#4	12	Ferry Across The Mersey	Laurie 3284
4/10/65	#20	8	It's Gonna Be Alright	Laurie 3293
6/12/65	#63	4	You'll Never Walk Alone	Laurie 3302
8/14/65	#69	4	Give All Your Love To Me/	Laurie 3313
8/28/65	#91	1	You're The Reason	Laurie 3313
4/02/66	#87	1	La La La	Laurie 3337
9/24/66	#45	7	Girl On A Swing	Laurie 3354
			GESTURES	
11/21/64	#47	9	Run, Run, Run	Soma 1417
			GETO BOYS	
5/15/93	#42	14	Six Feet Deep	Rap-A-Lot 53823
			GET WET	
4/25/81	#51	8	Just So Lonely	Boardwalk 02018
			STAN GETZ	
9/22/62	#11	11	Desafinado*	Verve 10260
6/06/64	#5	13	The Girl From Ipanema**	Verve 10322
			*released as by STAN GETZ/CHARLIE BYRD	
			**released as by STAN GETZ/ASTRUD GILBERTO	
			GIANT	
10/21/89	#64	9	I'm A Believer	A&M 1454
3/31/90	#18	19	I'll See You In My Dreams	A&M 1495
			GIANT STEPS	
8/20/88	#12	22	Another Lover	A&M 1226
2/04/89	#55	9	Into You	A&M 1256
			ANDY GIBB	
4/23/77	#1	29	I Just Want To Be Your Everything	RSO 872
11/05/77	#1	28	(Love Is) Thicker Than Water	RSO 883
4/15/78	#1	24	Shadow Dancing	RSO 893
7/15/78	#5	16	An Everlasting Love	RSO 904
10/14/78	#7	18	(Our Love) Don't Throw It All Away	RSO 911
1/26/80	#6	15	Desire	RSO 1019
3/29/80	#13	14	I Can't Help It*	RSO 1026
11/22/80	#19	18	Time Is Time	RSO 1059
3/14/81	#56	9	Me (Without You)	RSO 1056
8/15/81	#59	8	All I Have To Do Is Dream**	RSO 1065
			*released as by ANDY GIBB and OLIVIA NEWTON-JOHN	
			**released as by ANDY GIBB and VICTORIA PRINCIPAL	
			BARRY GIBB	
11/01/80	#8	22	Guilty*	Columbia 11390
1/31/81	#10	16	What Kind Of Fool*	Columbia 11430
9/01/84	#39	10	Shine Shine	MCA 52443
			*released as by BARBRA STREISAND & BARRY GIBB	
			ROBIN GIBB	
8/12/78	#24	11	Oh! Darling	RSO 907
11/15/80	#63	10	Help Me!*	RSO 1047
6/02/84	#50	12	Boys Do Fall In Love	Mirage 99743
			*released as by MARCY LEVY and ROBIN GIBB	

Debut Date	Peak Pos	Wks Chr	ARTIST/Song Title	Label & Number
			STEVE GIBBONS BAND	
6/05/76	#77	5	Johnny Cool	MCA 40551
			GEORGIA GIBBS	
5/17/52	#1	15	Kiss Of Fire	Mercury 5823
4/18/53	#8	6	Seven Lonely Days	Mercury 70095
2/19/55	#2	16	Tweedlee Dee	Mercury 70517
4/23/55	#3	15	Dance With Me Henry (Wallflower)	Mercury 70572
8/11/56	#30	10	Happiness Street	Mercury 70920
12/08/56	#36	5	Tra La La	Mercury 70998
3/16/57	#50	1	Silent Lips	Mercury 71058
10/04/58	#37	8	The Hula Hoop Song	Roulette 4106
5/22/65	#87	3	Let Me Cry On Your Shoulder	Bell 615
			TERRI GIBBS	
1/17/81	#10	24	Somebody's Knockin'	MCA 41309
6/20/81	#91	4	Rich Man	MCA 51119
			DEBBIE GIBSON	
5/23/87	#6	27	Only In My Dreams	Atlantic 89322
10/10/87	#5	22	Shake Your Love	Atlantic 89187
1/30/88	#5	20	Out Of The Blue	Atlantic 89129
4/23/88	#1	22	Foolish Beat	Atlantic 89109
8/06/88	#24	13	Staying Together	Atlantic 89034
1/21/89	#1	19	Lost In Your Eyes	Atlantic 88970
4/01/89	#9	18	Electric Youth	Atlantic 88919
6/17/89	#20	18	No More Rhyme	Atlantic 88885
9/30/89	#76	7	We Could Be Together	Atlantic 88896
11/17/90	#26	16	Anything Is Possible	Atlantic 87793
2/13/93	#84	6	Losin' Myself	Atlantic 87392
			DON GIBSON	
2/22/58	#10	20	Oh Lonesome Me	RCA 7133
6/14/58	#38	17	Blue Blue Day	RCA 7010
9/27/58	#64	7	Look Who's Blue	RCA 7330
1/24/59	#51	9	Who Cares	RCA 7437
8/29/59	#85	1	Don't Tell Me Your Troubles	RCA 7566
12/26/59	#50	3	I'm Movin' On	RCA 7629
2/27/60	#33	14	Just One Time	RCA 7690
8/06/60	#62	5	Far Far Away	RCA 7762
11/16/60	#89	4	Sweet Dreams	RCA 7805
6/24/61	#20	15	Sea Of Heartbreak	RCA 7890
12/16/61	#91	3	Lonesome Number One	RCA 7959
			GINNY GIBSON	
10/13/56	#50	1	Two Innocent Hearts/	ABC-Paramount 9739
11/10/56	#37	2	Miracle Of Love	ABC-Paramount 9739
			JOHNNY GIBSON	
1/27/62	#81	6	Midnight	Big Top 3088
			GIDEA PARK	
12/26/81	#82	7	Seasons Of Gold*	Profile 5003
			*released as by GIDEA PARK featuring ADRIAN BAKER	
			NICK GILDER	
6/17/78	#1	31	Hot Child In The City	Chrysalis 2226
11/04/78	#39	11	Here Comes The Night	Chrysalis 2264
5/26/79	#53	9	(You Really) Rock Me	Chrysalis 2332
			TERRY GILKYSON and THE EASY RIDERS	
2/02/57	#2	15	Marianne	Columbia 40817
			JOHNNY GILL	
4/14/84	#79	5	Perfect Combination*	Cotillion 99785
5/12/90	#15	23	Rub You The Right Way	Motown 1982
8/11/90	#9	19	My, My, My	Motown 2033
10/27/90	#31	16	Fairweather Friend	Motown 2049
3/30/91	#89	4	Wrap My Body Tight	Motown 2077
10/31/92	#37	21	Slow And Sexy**	Epic 74741
5/29/93	#53	11	The Floor	Motown 2202
			*released as by STACY LATTISAW & JOHNNY GILL	
			**released as by SHABBA RANKS featuring JOHNNY GILL	
			MICKEY GILLEY	
6/22/74	#61	6	Room Full Of Roses	Playboy 50056
5/17/80	#22	21	Stand By Me	Full Moon 46640

Debut Date	Peak Pos	Wks Chr	ARTIST/Song Title	Label & Number
			MICKEY GILLEY—*continued*	
9/13/80	#88	3	True Love Ways	Epic 50876
7/11/81	#48	15	You Don't Know Me	Epic 02172
			JIMMY GILMER & THE FIREBALLS (see FIREBALLS)	
			DAVID GILMOUR	
4/14/84	#75	7	Blue Light	Columbia 04378
			JAMES GILREATH	
3/23/63	#28	11	Little Band Of Gold	Joy 274
			GILMORE, GEOFF & THE SHEIKS	
8/29/59	#84	5	Tres Chic	Jamie 1132
			JIM GILSTRAP	
3/08/75	#57	9	Swing Your Daddy	Roxbury 2006
8/23/75	#97	2	House Of Strangers	Roxbury 2013
11/22/75	#99	3	I'm On Fire	Roxbury 2016
			GINA GO-GO	
3/04/89	#77	5	I Can't Face The Fact	Capitol 44233
			GIN BLOSSOMS	
7/31/93	#23	27	Hey Jealousy	A&M 0242
11/27/93	#30	36	Found Out About You	A&M 0418
			GINGER	
9/18/76	#89	6	Julie Ann	Shock 3
			GINO & GINA	
5/10/58	#28	12	(It's Been A Long Time) Pretty Baby	Mercury 71283
			GIORGIO (see GIORGIO MORODER)	
			CAESAR GIOVANNINI	
10/20/56	#29	2	Petticoats Of Portugal	Bally 1018
			GIRLFRIENDS	
1/04/64	#77	6	My One And Only, Jimmy Boy	Colpix 712
			GIUFFRIA	
11/10/84	#20	20	Call To The Heart	MCA 52497
3/30/85	#58	8	Lonely In Love	MCA 52558
5/03/86	#61	10	I Must Be Dreaming	MCA 52794
			GLADSTONE	
8/12/72	#38	11	A Piece Of Paper	ABC 11327
			WILL GLAHE	
11/02/57	#11	16	Liechtensteiner Polka	London 1755
3/01/58	#45	3	Sweet Elizabeth	London 1788
			GLASS BOTTLE	
7/10/71	#26	13	I Ain't Got Time Anymore	Avco Embassy 4575
11/13/71	#78	5	The Girl Who Loved Me When	Avco 4584
			GLASS HOUSE	
10/25/69	#57	6	Crumbs Off The Table	Invictus 9071
7/25/70	#90	3	I Can't Be You	Invictus 9076
12/12/70	#92	1	Stealing Moments	Invictus 9082
			GLASS MOON	
3/13/82	#65	10	On A Carousel	Atlantic 4022
			GLASS TIGER	
7/12/86	#3	21	Don't Forget Me (When I'm Gone)	Manhattan 50037
11/01/86	#8	21	Someday	Manhattan 50048
2/28/87	#33	11	I Will Be There	Manhattan 50066
4/09/88	#32	13	I'm Still Searching	EMI-Manhattan 50116
11/26/88	#71	8	My Song	EMI-Manhattan 50172
			TOM GLAZER and THE DO-RE-MI CHILDREN'S CHORUS	
6/01/63	#16	10	On Top Of Spaghetti	Kapp 526
			GLENCOVES	
6/22/63	#39	8	Hootenanny	Select 724
			DARRELL GLENN	
8/29/53	#1	12	Crying In The Chapel	Valley 101
			GARY GLITTER	
7/15/72	#3	13	Rock And Roll (Part 2)	Bell 45237
10/28/72	#30	9	I Didn't Know I Loved You	Bell 45276

Debut Date	Peak Pos	Wks Chr	ARTIST/Song Title	Label & Number
			GLORIES	
6/24/67	#95	1	I Stand Accused (Of Loving You)	Date 1553
			ARTHUR GODFREY	
2/25/52	#9	4	Dance Me Loose	Columbia 39632
			GODDESS	
12/19/92	#73	10	Sexual	Big Beat 98457
			GODLEY & CREME	
7/27/85	#16	17	Cry	Polydor 881786
			GODSPELL	
5/13/72	#9	16	Day By Day	Bell 45210
			LOUISE GOFFIN	
8/18/79	#44	10	Remember (Walking In The Sand)	Asylum 46521
			GO GO's	
8/29/81	#20	31	Our Lips Are Sealed	I.R.S. 9901
1/23/82	#2	24	We Got The Beat	I.R.S. 9903
7/03/82	#6	19	Vacation	I.R.S. 9907
9/25/82	#50	9	Get Up And Go	I.R.S. 9910
3/17/84	#10	19	Head Over Heels	I.R.S. 9926
6/23/84	#28	15	Turn To You	I.R.S. 9928
			ANDREW GOLD	
1/10/76	#69	4	That's Why I Love You	Asylum 45286
3/19/77	#3	23	Lonely Boy	Asylum 45384
2/11/78	#11	15	Thank You For Being A Friend	Asylum 45456
6/17/78	#70	8	Never Let Her Slip Away	Asylum 45489
			BARRY GOLDBERG	
9/21/68	#90	4	Hole In My Pocket	Buddah 59
			GOLDEN EARRING	
5/18/74	#10	15	Radar Love	Track 40202
10/05/74	#78	7	Candy's Going Bad	Track 40309
3/22/75	#90	3	Ce Soir	Track 40369
11/27/82	#16	26	Twilight Zone	21 Records 103
4/23/83	#80	5	The Devil Made Me Do It	21 Records 108
			BOBBY GOLDSBORO	
12/22/62	#60	8	Molly	Laurie 3148
1/18/64	#10	13	See The Funny Little Clown	United Artists 672
4/18/64	#41	8	Whenever He Holds You	United Artists 710
8/29/64	#83	2	Me Japanese Boy I Love You	United Artists 742
1/30/65	#12	12	Little Things	United Artists 810
5/01/65	#27	10	Voodoo Woman	United Artists 862
9/04/65	#97	1	If You Wait For Love/	United Artists 908
9/11/65	#58	9	If You've Got A Heart	United Artists 908
12/11/65	#52	9	Broomstick Cowboy	United Artists 952
2/12/66	#28	9	It's Too Late	United Artists 980
5/21/66	#77	3	I Know You Better	United Artists 50018
9/24/66	#100	1	It Hurts Me Too	United Artists 50056
11/26/66	#37	11	Blue Autumn	United Artists 50087
3/23/68	#1	15	Honey	United Artists 50283
6/29/68	#14	10	Autumn Of My Life	United Artists 50318
10/19/68	#29	9	The Straight Life	United Artists 50461
2/08/69	#45	5	Glad She's A Woman	United Artists 50497
4/19/69	#44	9	I'm A Drifter	United Artists 50525
8/09/69	#46	10	Muddy Mississippi Line	United Artists 50565
12/27/69	#78	7	Mornin' Mornin'	United Artists 50614
4/25/70	#98	2	Can You Feel It	United Artists 50650
12/19/70	#8	14	Watching Scotty Grow	United Artists 50727
5/15/71	#91	2	And I Love You So	United Artists 50776
7/17/71	#74	7	Come Back Home	United Artists 50807
9/09/72	#87	5	With Pen In Hand	United Artists 50938
8/18/73	#17	15	Summer (The First Time)	United Artists 251
			IAN GOMM	
9/01/79	#25	13	Hold On	Stiff 50747
			GONE ALL STARS	
2/08/58	#60	1	7-11	Gone 5016
			GONZALES	
1/20/79	#46	10	Haven't Stopped Dancing Yet	Capitol 4647

Debut Date	Peak Pos	Wks Chr	ARTIST/Song Title	Label & Number
			GOODEES	
12/21/68	#38	10	Condition Red	Hip 8005
			GOODIES	
5/17/75	#94	2	The Funky Gibbon	20th Century 2189
			DICKIE GOODMAN	
2/11/61	#32	10	The Touchables	Mark-X 8009
5/06/61	#57	6	The Touchables In Brooklyn	Mark-X 8010
7/14/62	#50	7	Ben Crazy	Diamond 119
5/21/66	#81	4	Batman & His Grandmother	Red Bird 058
7/05/69	#58	6	On Campus	Cotique 158
6/16/73	#66	6	Watergate	Rainy Wednesday 202
1/26/74	#37	9	Energy Crisis '74	Rainy Wednesday 206
6/08/74	#85	4	Mr. President	Rainy Wednesday 207
8/23/75	#1	13	Mr. Jaws	Cash 451
1/29/77	#50	8	Kong	Shock 6
6/30/79	#75	4	Energy Crisis '79	Hot Line 1017
9/11/82	#92	5	Hey, E.T.	Extran 601
			GOOD QUESTION	
10/29/88	#83	4	Got A New Love	Paisley Park 27861
			GOODTIMERS (see DON COVAY & THE GOODTIMERS)	
			DON GOODWIN	
12/22/73	#82	6	This Is Your Song	Silver Blue 806
			RON GOODWIN ORCHESTRA	
8/03/57	#30	8	Swinging Sweethearts	Capitol 3748
			GOOSE CREEK SYMPHONY	
2/26/72	#83	4	(Oh Lord Won't You Buy Me A) Mercedes Benz	Capitol 3246
			ROBERT GORDON	
9/17/77	#69	11	Red Hot	Private Stock 45156
6/27/81	#72	6	Someday, Someway	RCA 12239
			ROSCOE GORDON	
3/12/60	#79	6	Just A Little Bit	Vee-Jay 332
			LESLEY GORE	
5/04/63	#1	14	It's My Party	Mercury 72119
7/13/63	#4	11	Judy's Turn To Cry	Mercury 72143
9/28/63	#6	16	She's A Fool	Mercury 72180
12/28/63	#2	14	You Don't Own Me	Mercury 72206
3/28/64	#14	9	That's The Way Boys Are	Mercury 72259
5/23/64	#42	6	I Don't Wanna Be A Loser	Mercury 72270
7/25/64	#10	11	Maybe I Know	Mercury 72309
10/17/64	#54	6	Hey Now	Mercury 72353
12/26/64	#20	10	Look Of Love	Mercury 72372
4/03/65	#95	2	All Of My Life	Mercury 72412
6/19/65	#19	11	Sunshine, Lollipops And Rainbows	Mercury 72433
9/11/65	#39	7	My Town, My Guy And Me	Mercury 72475
11/27/65	#61	5	I Won't Love You Anymore	Mercury 72513
1/22/66	#69	5	We Know We're In Love	Mercury 72530
3/19/66	#57	7	Young Love	Mercury 72553
6/04/66	#98	2	Off And Running	Mercury 72580
2/11/67	#11	13	California Nights	Mercury 72649
6/03/67	#54	6	Summer And Sandy	Mercury 72683
10/07/67	#87	2	Brink Of Disaster	Mercury 72726
6/29/68	#91	3	He Gives Me Love	Mercury 72819
			MICHAEL GORE	
4/28/84	#80	4	Theme From "Terms Of Endearment"	Capitol 5334
			EYDIE GORME	
8/04/56	#31	9	Mama, Teach Me To Dance	ABC-Paramount 9722
11/30/57	#29	7	Love Me Forever	ABC-Paramount 9863
5/17/58	#21	11	You Need Hands	ABC-Paramount 9925
8/16/58	#43	6	Gotta Have Rain	ABC-Paramount 9944
11/22/58	#68	4	Voice In My Heart	ABC-Paramount 9971
1/19/63	#6	16	Blame It On The Bossa Nova	Columbia 42661
6/01/63	#57	6	Don't Try To Fight It Baby	Columbia 42790
7/27/63	#28	11	I Want To Stay Here*	Columbia 42815
9/28/63	#70	5	Everybody Go Home	Columbia 42854
12/21/63	#51	9	I Can't Stop Talking About You*	Columbia 42932
8/08/64	#65	6	I Want You To Meet My Baby	Columbia 43082

Debut Date	Peak Pos	Wks Chr	ARTIST/Song Title	Label & Number
12/06/69	#54	10	Tonight I'll Say A Prayer	RCA 0250
9/23/72	#64	7	We Can Make It Together**	MGM 14383
			*released as by STEVE & EYDIE (Steve Lawrence & Eydie Gorme)	
			**released as by STEVE & EYDIE featuring THE OSMONDS	
			ROBERT GOULET	
10/31/64	#15	16	My Love, Forgive Me (Amore, Scusami)	Columbia 43131
3/13/65	#79	2	Begin To Love	Columbia 43224
5/29/65	#43	8	Summer Sounds	Columbia 43301
			GO WEST	
3/02/85	#33	13	We Close Our Eyes	Chrysalis 42850
6/08/85	#48	12	Call Me	Chrysalis 42865
10/12/85	#83	4	Eye To Eye	Chrysalis 42903
8/15/87	#39	12	Don't Look Down - The Sequel	Chrysalis 43141
5/26/90	#8	23	King Of Wishful Thinking	EMI 50307
11/14/92	#12	22	Faithful	EMI 50411
3/27/93	#50	11	What You Won't Do For Love	EMI 50428
			GQ	
3/17/79	#10	19	Disco Nights (Rock-Freak)	Arista 0388
7/07/79	#27	18	I Do Love You	Arista 0426
6/07/80	#94	5	Sitting In The Park	Arista 0510
			GRACES	
8/26/89	#62	8	Lay Down In Your Arms	A&M 1440
			CHARLIE GRACIE	
2/16/57	#3	17	Butterfly	Cameo 105
5/11/57	#14	9	Fabulous	Cameo 107
			GRADUATES	
3/21/59	#74	6	Ballad Of A Girl And Boy	Shan-Todd 0055
			LARRY GRAHAM	
6/28/80	#15	20	One In A Million You	Warner Brothers 49221
8/08/81	#91	5	Just Be My Lady	Warner Brothers 49744
			GRAHAM CENTRAL STATION	
4/13/74	#49	11	Can You Handle It?	Warner Brothers 7782
8/02/75	#42	10	Your Love	Warner Brothers 8105
12/06/75	#95	2	It's Alright	Warner Brothers 8148
2/07/76	#79	6	The Jam	Warner Brothers 8175
			LOU GRAMM	
1/31/87	#8	18	Midnight Blue	Atlantic 89304
5/16/87	#58	10	Ready Or Not	Atlantic 89269
10/28/89	#6	22	Just Between You And Me	Atlantic 88781
2/24/90	#39	12	True Blue Love	Atlantic 88768
			BILLY GRAMMER	
11/08/58	#6	19	Gotta Travel On	Monument 400
4/04/59	#68	6	The Kissing Tree/	Monument 403
4/11/59	#58	7	Bonaparte's Retreat	Monument 403
			GERRY GRANAHAN	
6/07/58	#14	10	No Chemise, Please	Sunbeam 102
			ROCCO GRANATA	
11/07/59	#12	12	Marina	Laurie 3041
			GRAND CANYON	
10/19/74	#61	8	Evil Boll-Weevil	Bang 713
			GRAND FUNK RAILROAD	
9/27/69	#54	9	Time Machine	Capitol 2567
1/17/70	#99	1	Mr. Limousine Driver	Capitol 2691
2/07/70	#72	5	Heartbreaker	Capitol 2732
8/08/70	#27	12	Closer To Home	Capitol 2877
12/19/70	#44	7	Mean Mistreater	Capitol 2996
5/01/71	#45	7	Feelin' Alright	Capitol 3095
8/28/71	#57	5	Gimme Shelter	Capitol 3160
1/15/72	#40	9	Footstompin' Music	Capitol 3255
4/15/72	#82	6	Upsetter	Capitol 3316
9/16/72	#24	13	Rock 'N Roll Soul	Capitol 3363
7/21/73	#1	16	We're An American Band*	Capitol 3660
11/17/73	#17	12	Walk Like A Man*	Capitol 3760
3/09/74	#1	17	The Loco-Motion*	Capitol 3840

Debut Date	Peak Pos	Wks Chr	ARTIST/Song Title	Label & Number
			GRAND FUNK RAILROAD—*continued*	
7/06/74	#18	12	Shinin' On*	Capitol 3917
12/14/74	#7	13	Some Kind Of Wonderful*	Capitol 4002
4/05/75	#5	14	Bad Time*	Capitol 4046
1/24/76	#50	5	Take Me	Capitol 4199
3/27/76	#69	3	Sally	Capitol 4235
8/07/76	#70	9	Can You Do It	MCA 40590
			***released as by GRAND FUNK**	
			GRAND MASTER FLASH & THE FURIOUS FIVE	
10/30/82	#94	4	The Message	Sugar Hill 584
			GRAND PUBA	
10/24/92	#88	4	360 Degrees (What Goes Around)	Elektra 64708
			AMY GRANT	
5/18/85	#28	17	Find A Way	A&M 2734
8/31/85	#70	7	Wise Up	A&M 2762
9/20/86	#3	23	The Next Time I Fall*	Full Moon 28597
2/23/91	#1	27	Baby Baby	A&M 1549
6/15/91	#2	22	Every Heartbeat	A&M 1557
9/28/91	#2	30	That's What Love Is For	A&M 1566
1/18/92	#4	25	Good For Me	A&M 1573
5/02/92	#17	23	I Will Remember You	A&M 1600
			***released as by PETER CETERA with AMY GRANT**	
			EARL GRANT	
9/13/58	#10	19	The End	Decca 30719
1/24/59	#51	8	Evening Rain	Decca 30819
4/09/60	#93	2	House Of Bamboo	Decca 31044
6/02/62	#51	9	Swingin' Gently	Decca 25560
9/08/62	#61	8	Sweet Sixteen Bars	Decca 25574
10/09/65	#66	7	Stand By Me	Decca 25674
			EDDY GRANT	
4/23/83	#1	24	Electric Avenue	Portrait 03793
8/13/83	#54	8	I Don't Wanna Dance	Portrait 04039
5/26/84	#22	18	Romancing The Stone	Portrait 04433
			GOGI GRANT	
10/29/55	#8	4	Suddenly There's A Valley	Era 1003
6/09/56	#1	17	The Wayward Wind	Era 1013
9/22/56	#45	3	You're In Love	Era 1019
9/13/58	#85	2	Strange Are The Ways Of Love	RCA 7294
5/27/61	#78	6	Wayward Wind	Era 3046
			JANIE GRANT	
4/08/61	#23	15	Triangle	Caprice 104
6/02/62	#70	9	That Greasy Kid Stuff	Caprice 115
			GRASS ROOTS	
6/18/66	#33	9	Where Were You When I Needed You	Dunhill 4029
9/17/66	#77	2	Only When You're Lonely	Dunhill 4043
5/20/67	#5	12	Let's Live For Today	Dunhill 4084
8/12/67	#36	8	Things I Should Have Said	Dunhill 4094
10/21/67	#64	7	Wake Up, Wake Up	Dunhill 4105
8/24/68	#5	15	Midnight Confessions	Dunhill 4144
11/30/68	#20	9	Bella Linda	Dunhill 4162
2/15/69	#35	7	Lovin' Things	Dunhill 4180
4/05/69	#16	11	The River Is Wide	Dunhill 4187
6/21/69	#12	17	I'd Wait A Million Years	Dunhill 4198
11/01/69	#13	12	Heaven Knows	Dunhill 4217
2/14/70	#30	8	Walking Through The Country	Dunhill 4227
5/02/70	#25	10	Baby Hold On	Dunhill 4237
9/19/70	#39	6	Come On And Say It	Dunhill 4249
12/19/70	#16	19	Temptation Eyes	Dunhill 4263
5/29/71	#12	13	Sooner Or Later	Dunhill 4279
10/09/71	#8	11	Two Divided By Love	Dunhill 4289
2/12/72	#22	10	Glory Bound	Dunhill 4302
6/10/72	#29	10	The Runway	Dunhill 4316
2/03/73	#32	9	Love Is What You Make It	Dunhill 4335
6/30/73	#88	4	Where There's Smoke There's Fire	Dunhill 4345
12/15/73	#97	1	We Can't Dance To Your Music	Dunhill 4371
9/20/75	#84	4	Mamacita	Haven 7015

Debut Date	Peak Pos	Wks Chr	ARTIST/Song Title	Label & Number
			GRATEFUL DEAD	
8/22/70	#84	4	Uncle John's Band	Warner Brothers 7410
12/04/71	#64	7	Truckin'	Warner Brothers 7464
10/18/75	#78	5	The Music Never Stopped	Grateful Dead 718
12/16/78	#87	5	Good Lovin'	Arista 0383
6/14/80	#79	5	Alabama Getaway	Arista 0519
7/25/87	#17	16	Touch Of Grey	Arista 9606
			BILLY GRAVES	
1/24/59	#45	9	The Shag (Is Totally Cool)	Monument 401
			CARL GRAVES	
11/30/74	#62	9	Baby, Hang Up The Phone	A&M 1620
4/09/77	#68	8	Sad Girl	Ariola America 7660
			CLAUDE GRAY	
4/01/61	#78	5	I'll Just Have A Cup Of Coffee	Mercury 71732
			DOBIE GRAY	
1/02/65	#17	12	The "In" Crowd	Charger 105
4/10/65	#70	5	See You At The "Go-Go"	Charger 107
5/17/69	#98	1	Rose Garden	White Whale 300
2/17/73	#8	20	Drift Away	Decca 33057
7/28/73	#36	11	Loving Arms	MCA 40100
1/20/79	#54	7	You Can Do It	Infinity 50003
			DOLORES GRAY	
12/29/51	#10	2	Shrimp Boats	Decca 27832
			CHARLES RANDOLPH GREAN SOUNDE	
6/07/69	#8	12	Quentin's Theme	Ranwood 840
			GREAT WHITE	
8/29/87	#64	11	Rock Me	Capitol 44042
1/30/88	#78	10	Save Your Love	Capitol 44104
5/20/89	#5	25	Once Bitten Twice Shy	Capitol 44366
9/23/89	#33	19	The Angel Song	Capitol 44449
3/24/90	#78	6	House Of Broken Love	Capitol 44491
3/02/91	#49	12	Call It Rock N' Roll	Capitol 44676
			R.B. GREAVES	
10/04/69	#3	16	Take A Letter Maria	Atco 6714
1/24/70	#22	8	Always Something There To Remind Me	Atco 6726
4/11/70	#65	4	Fire & Rain	Atco 6745
9/05/70	#92	2	Georgia Took Her Back	Atco 6778
12/05/70	#80	2	Whiter Shade Of Pale	Atco 6789
			CYNDI GRECCO	
4/24/76	#21	16	Making Our Dreams Come True	Private Stock 45086
			BUDDY GRECO	
9/29/62	#63	8	Mr. Lonely	Epic 9536
			AL GREEN	
12/02/67	#46	13	Back Up Train*	Hot Line 15000
11/14/70	#70	6	I Can't Get Next To You	Hi 2182
7/31/71	#6	17	Tired Of Being Alone	Hi 2194
11/27/72	#1	17	Let's Stay Together	Hi 2202
3/25/72	#3	14	Look What You've Done For Me	Hi 2211
7/01/72	#1	14	I'm Still In Love With You	Hi 2216
9/16/72	#46	10	Guilty	Bell 45258
10/21/72	#2	14	You Ought To Be With Me	Hi 2227
1/27/73	#91	3	Hot Wire	Bell 45305
2/17/73	#9	11	Call Me (Come Back Home)	Hi 2235
6/30/73	#10	14	Here I Am (Come And Take Me)	Hi 2247
11/24/73	#14	12	Livin' For You	Hi 2257
3/16/74	#21	11	Let's Get Married	Hi 2262
9/28/74	#7	17	Sha-La-La (Make Me Happy)	Hi 2274
3/01/75	#10	12	L-O-V-E (Love)	Hi 2282
6/28/75	#40	7	Oh Me, Oh My (Dreams In My Arms)	Hi 2288
11/08/75	#30	11	Full Of Fire	Hi 2300
11/20/76	#63	10	Keep Me Cryin'	HI 2319
12/24/77	#81	6	Belle	Hi 77505
11/05/88	#5	20	Put A Little Love In Your Heart**	A&M 1255
			*released as by AL GREEN & THE SOUL MATES	
			**released as by ANNIE LENNOX & AL GREEN	

145

Debut Date	Peak Pos	Wks Chr	ARTIST/Song Title	Label & Number
			GARLAND GREEN	
9/13/69	#29	9	Jealous Kind Of Fella	Uni 55143
4/10/71	#90	3	Plain And Simple Girl	Cotillion 44098
			NORMAN GREENBAUM	
2/21/70	#1	17	Spirit In The Sky	Reprise 0885
6/06/70	#32	7	Canned Ham	Reprise 0919
			BARBARA GREENE	
6/22/68	#93	2	Young Boy	Renee 5001
			LORNE GREENE	
10/31/64	#1	13	Ringo	RCA 8444
2/06/65	#97	3	The Man	RCA 8490
2/26/66	#91	3	Five Card Stud	RCA 8757
			GREEN JELLO (group was later forced to change their name to GREEN JELLY)	
4/17/93	#16	23	Three Little Pigs	Zoo 14088
			LEE GREENLEE	
9/26/59	#100	1	Starlight	Brent 7003
			ELLIE GREENWICH	
5/13/67	#90	3	I Want You To Be My Baby	United Artists 50151
			LEE GREENWOOD	
5/28/83	#54	9	I.O.U.	MCA 52199
			GREENWOOD COUNTY SINGERS	
8/01/64	#81	5	(The New) Frankie And Johnny	Kapp 591
5/07/66	#86	4	Please Don't Sell My Daddy No More Wine*	Kapp 742
			*released as by THE GREENWOODS	
			BOBBY GREGG and HIS FRIENDS	
3/24/62	#34	8	The Jam (Part 1)	Cotton 1003
7/06/63	#100	1	Scarlett O'Hara	Epic 9601
			MERV GRIFFIN	
2/25/61	#80	5	Banned In Boston	Carlton 540
4/15/61	#79	4	The Charanga	Carlton 545
			MARCIA GRIFFITHS	
12/16/89	#47	11	Electric Boogie	Mango 126
			GRIN	
2/12/72	#69	5	White Lies	Spindizzy 4005
			LARRY GROCE	
1/03/76	#9	16	Junk Food Junkie	Warner Brothers 8165
			HENRY GROSS	
3/30/74	#94	3	Simone	A&M 1494
7/13/74	#79	3	Come On Say It	A&M 1534
4/26/75	#93	2	One More Tomorrow	A&M 1682
3/06/76	#5	21	Shannon	Lifesong 45002
7/10/76	#39	12	Springtime Mama	Lifesong 45008
			GTR	
5/10/86	#20	16	When The Heart Rules The Mind	Arista 9470
8/23/86	#80	5	The Hunter	Arista 9512
			VINCE GUARALDI TRIO	
12/15/62	#31	19	Cast Your Fate To The Wind	Fantasy 563
			GUESS WHO	
4/17/65	#19	14	Shakin' All Over	Scepter 1295
4/05/69	#4	15	These Eyes	RCA 0102
7/12/69	#8	12	Laughing/	RCA 0195
10/11/69	#26	9	Undun	RCA 0195
12/13/69	#4	16	No Time	RCA 0300
3/21/70	#1	14	American Woman/	RCA 0325
3/21/70	#39	5	No Sugar Tonight	RCA 0325
7/18/70	#13	12	Hand Me Down World	RCA 0367
10/17/70	#5	12	Share The Land	RCA 0388
1/30/71	#35	7	Hang On To Your Life	RCA 0414
4/10/71	#77	4	Broken/	RCA 0458
4/17/71	#35	13	Albert Flasher	RCA 0458
8/14/71	#15	11	Rain Dance	RCA 0522
11/27/71	#41	8	Sour Suite	RCA 0578
3/04/72	#26	8	Heartbroken Bopper	RCA 0659

Debut Date	Peak Pos	Wks Chr	ARTIST/Song Title	Label & Number
5/20/72	#66	4	Guns, Guns, Guns	RCA 0708
10/07/72	#74	4	Runnin' Back To Saskatoon	RCA 0803
2/10/73	#71	5	Follow Your Daughter Home	RCA 0880
7/14/73	#83	4	Glamour Boy	RCA 0977
3/02/74	#30	17	Star Baby	RCA 0217
7/13/74	#10	16	Clap For The Wolfman	RCA 0324
11/23/74	#24	10	Dancin' Fool	RCA 10075
5/10/75	#88	3	Seems Like I Can't Live With You, But I Can't Live Without You	RCA 10075
			GREGG GUIDRY	
2/20/82	#20	16	Goin' Down	Columbia 02691
			BONNIE GUITAR	
4/13/57	#5	19	Dark Moon	Dot 15550
9/28/57	#43	5	Mister Fire Eyes	Dot 15612
4/09/66	#97	2	I'm Living In Two Worlds	Dot 16811
			GUNHILL ROAD	
3/31/73	#25	15	Back When My Hair Was Short	Kama Sutra 569
			GUNS N' ROSES	
6/25/88	#1	22	Sweet Child O' Mine	Geffen 27963
10/22/88	#9	19	Welcome To The Jungle	Geffen 27759
1/21/89	#4	18	Paradise City	Geffen 27570
4/08/89	#4	18	Patience	Geffen 22996
9/21/91	#7	27	Don't Cry	Geffen 19027
12/21/91	#26	19	Live And Let Die	Geffen 19114
6/20/92	#1	32	November Rain	Geffen 19067
11/28/92	#58	9	Yesterdays	Geffen 19142
			ARLO GUTHRIE	
10/31/70	#84	4	Valley To Pray	Reprise 0951
8/05/72	#21	16	The City Of New Orleans	Reprise 1103
			GWEN GUTHRIE	
8/02/86	#66	12	Ain't Nothin' Goin' On But The Rent	Polydor 885106
			GUY	
11/17/90	#49	11	I Wanna Get With You	MCA 53928
			JASMINE GUY	
3/30/91	#81	6	Another Like My Lover	Warner Brothers 19486
8/10/91	#43	20	Just Want To Hold You	Warner Brothers 19330
			GUYS NEXT DOOR	
12/29/90	#50	15	I've Been Waiting For You	SBK 07340
			G-WIZ	
7/31/93	#80	8	Teddy Bear	Scotti Brothers 75360
			GYPSY	
12/12/70	#66	8	Gypsy Queen (Part 1)	Metromedia 202
10/21/78	#58	9	Cuz It's You*	RCA 11403
5/19/79	#91	3	Love Is For The Best In Us*	RCA 11480
			***released as by THE JAMES WALSH GYPSY BAND**	

H

Debut Date	Peak Pos	Wks Chr	ARTIST/Song Title	Label & Number
			HADDAWAY	
9/25/93	#9	27	What Is Love	Arista 2575
			SAMMY HAGAR	
12/03/77	#83	9	You Make Me Crazy	Capitol 4502
4/07/79	#66	6	(Sitin' On) The Dock Of The Bay	Capitol 4699
1/30/82	#43	10	I'll Fall In Love Again	Geffen 49881
12/04/82	#25	17	Your Love Is Driving Me Crazy	Geffen 29816
3/26/83	#49	9	Never Give Up	Geffen 29718
7/14/84	#38	13	Two Sides Of Love	Geffen 29246
9/29/84	#28	12	I Can't Drive 55	Geffen 29173
2/14/87	#56	10	Winner Takes It All	Columbia 06647
6/13/87	#28	19	Give To Live	Geffen 28314
10/24/87	#81	5	Eagles Fly	Geffen 28185
			HAGERS	
10/26/74	#84	4	(I Wanna) Love My Life Away	Elektra 45209

147

Debut Date	Peak Pos	Wks Chr	ARTIST/Song Title	Label & Number
			MERLE HAGGARD	
2/07/70	#99	1	The Fightin' Side Of Me	Capitol 2719
12/11/71	#77	5	Carolyn	Capitol 3222
9/15/73	#77	5	Everybody's Had The Blues	Capitol 3641
11/10/73	#29	12	If We Make It Through December	Capitol 3746
10/01/77	#58	10	From Graceland To The Promised Land	MCA 40804
			HAIRCUT ONE HUNDRED	
5/29/82	#49	12	Love Plus One	Arista 0672
			BILL HALEY and HIS COMETS	
6/27/53	#7	4	Crazy Man, Crazy	Essex 321
11/06/54	#5	10	Shake, Rattle And Roll	Decca 29204
7/09/55	#1	15	(We're Gonna) Rock Around The Clock	Decca 29124
2/11/56	#5	9	See You Later, Alligator	Decca 29791
8/11/56	#45	3	Teenager's Mother/	Decca 30028
9/01/56	#24	24	Rip It Up	Decca 30028
10/27/56	#38	4	Rudy's Rock	Decca 30085
3/30/57	#46	4	Forty Cups Of Coffee	Decca 30214
6/08/57	#54	4	Billy Goat	Decca 30314
4/05/58	#25	10	Skinny Minnie	Decca 30592
8/02/58	#54	3	Lean Jean	Decca 30681
9/12/59	#35	15	Joey's Song	Decca 30956
1/16/60	#83	5	Skokiaan (South African Song)	Decca 31030
2/20/60	#79	4	Tamiami	Warner Brothers 5145
3/30/74	#36	11	(We're Gonna) Rock Around The Clock	MCA 60025
			DARYL HALL	
8/02/86	#5	16	Dreamtime	RCA 14387
10/18/86	#29	14	Foolish Pride	RCA 5038
1/24/87	#58	7	Someone Like You	RCA 5105
10/09/93	#72	3	I'm In A Philly Mood	Epic 77139
			DARYL HALL & JOHN OATES	
2/02/74	#52	10	She's Gone	Atlantic 2993
2/14/76	#6	27	Sara Smile	RCA 10530
7/17/76	#6	24	She's Gone	Atlantic 3332
11/06/76	#55	11	Do What You Want, Be What You Are	RCA 10808
1/22/77	#1	18	Rich Girl	RCA 10860
5/07/77	#25	12	Back Together Again	RCA 10970
7/30/77	#84	4	It's Uncanny	Atlantic 3397
10/22/77	#87	5	Why Do Lovers (Break Each Other's Heart?)	RCA 11132
8/26/78	#21	15	It's A Laugh	RCA 11371
12/16/78	#44	10	I Don't Wanna Lose You	RCA 11424
10/27/79	#24	19	Wait For Me	RCA 11747
7/19/80	#37	16	How Does It Feel To Be Back	RCA 12048
9/27/80	#10	21	You've Lost That Lovin' Feeling	RCA 12103
1/24/81	#1	24	Kiss On My List	RCA 12142
5/02/81	#7	20	You Make My Dreams	RCA 12217
8/29/81	#1	25	Private Eyes	RCA 12296
11/14/81	#1	24	I Can't Go For That (No Can Do)	RCA 12357
3/20/82	#10	14	Did It In A Minute	RCA 13065
6/19/82	#27	12	Your Imagination	RCA 13252
10/16/82	#1	24	Maneater	RCA 13354
1/29/83	#5	21	One On One	RCA 13421
4/30/83	#10	17	Family Man	RCA 13507
10/29/83	#3	19	Say It Isn't So	RCA 13654
2/18/84	#12	15	Adult Education	RCA 13714
9/29/84	#3	21	Out Of Touch	RCA 13916
12/15/84	#9	18	Method Of Modern Love	RCA 13970
3/16/85	#15	14	Some Things Are Better Left Unsaid	RCA 14035
6/01/85	#29	12	Possession Obsession	RCA 14098
8/31/85	#22	13	The Way You Do The Things You Do/My Girl	RCA 14178
4/16/88	#5	17	Everything Your Heart Desires	Arista 9684
7/09/88	#34	13	Missed Opportunity	Arista 9727
10/01/88	#33	11	Downtown Life	Arista 9753
9/29/90	#12	16	So Close	Arista 2085
12/29/90	#33	15	Don't Hold Back Your Love	Arista 2157
			JIMMY HALL	
10/11/80	#24	14	I'm Happy That Love Has Found You	Epic 50931
5/01/82	#74	4	Fool For Your Love	Epic 02857

148

Debut Date	Peak Pos	Wks Chr	ARTIST/Song Title	Label & Number
			JOHN HALL BAND	
12/26/81	#42	13	Crazy (Keep On Falling)	EMI America 8096
4/03/82	#78	5	You Sure Fooled Me	EMI America 8112
1/29/83	#67	7	Love Me Again	EMI America 8151
			LANI HALL	
3/14/81	#97	3	Where's Your Angel?	A&M 2305
			LARRY HALL	
11/14/59	#19	16	Sandy	Strand 25007
			TOM T. HALL	
9/11/71	#58	8	The Year That Clayton Delaney Died	Mercury 73221
12/22/73	#17	14	I Love	Mercury 73436
6/29/74	#60	5	That Song Is Driving Me Crazy	Mercury 73488
3/01/75	#93	4	Sneaky Snake	Mercury 73641
			DAVID HALLYDAY	
8/22/87	#72	9	He's My Girl	Scotti Brothers 07299
5/04/91	#63	15	Ooh La La	Scotti Brothers 5282
			HALOS	
7/29/61	#34	11	"Nag"	7 Arts 709
			GEORGE HAMILTON IV	
11/03/56	#6	18	A Rose And A Baby Ruth	ABC-Paramount 9765
2/09/57	#23	12	Only One Love	ABC-Paramount 9782
11/30/57	#9	14	Why Don't They Understand	ABC-Paramount 9862
3/15/58	#35	6	Now And For Always	ABC-Paramount 9898
5/24/58	#43	9	I Know Where I'm Going	ABC-Paramount 9916
8/23/58	#53	2	Your Cheatin' Heart	ABC-Paramount 9946
11/22/58	#46	9	Teen Commandments*	ABC-Paramount 9974
8/01/59	#100	1	Gee	ABC-Paramount 10028
6/22/63	#21	15	Abilene	RCA 8184
			*released as by PAUL ANKA/GEORGE HAMILTON IV/JOHNNY NASH	
			ROY HAMILTON	
4/30/55	#1	19	Unchained Melody	Epic 9102
7/13/57	#47	2	To The Aisle	Epic 9224
12/28/57	#13	12	Don't Let Go	Epic 9257
11/22/58	#98	1	My One And Only Love/	Epic 9294
11/22/58	#51	9	Pledging My Love	Epic 9294
4/11/59	#46	10	I Need Your Loving	Epic 9307
7/25/59	#59	7	Time Marches On	Epic 9323
12/15/59	#52	7	Ebb Tide	Epic 9068
1/21/61	#12	13	You Can Have Her	Epic 9434
4/29/61	#67	7	You're Gonna Need Magic	Epic 9443
7/15/61	#81	2	No Substitute For Love	Epic 9449
			RUSS HAMILTON	
6/29/57	#6	22	Rainbow	Kapp 184
			HAMILTON, JOE FRANK & REYNOLDS	
5/15/71	#1	15	Don't Pull Your Love	Dunhill 4276
8/21/71	#42	8	Annabella	Dunhill 4287
11/27/71	#39	11	Daisy Mae	Dunhill 4296
6/21/75	#1	17	Fallin' In Love	Playboy 6024
11/08/75	#18	14	Winners And Losers	Playboy 6054
4/10/76	#82	5	Everyday Without You	Playboy 6068
			MARVIN HAMLISCH	
3/16/74	#1	16	The Entertainer	MCA 40174
12/27/80	#95	4	Theme From Ordinary People	Planet 47922
			KARL HAMMEL JR.	
8/05/61	#64	9	Summer Souvenirs	Arliss 1007
			HAMMER (see M.C. HAMMER)	
			JAN HAMMER	
9/07/85	#1	22	"Miami Vice" Theme	MCA 52666
			ALBERT HAMMOND	
7/22/72	#64	8	Down By The River	Mums 6009
10/14/72	#2	18	It Never Rains In Southern California	Mums 6011
2/24/73	#57	6	If You Gotta Break Another Heart	Mums 6015
5/05/73	#41	10	Free Electric Band	Mums 6018
8/04/73	#85	6	Peacemaker	Mums 6021

Debug Date	Peak Pos	Wks Chr	ARTIST/Song Title	Label & Number
			ALBERT HAMMOND—*continued*	
11/24/73	#72	5	Half A Million Miles From Home	Mums 6024
3/02/74	#31	12	I'm A Train	Mums 6026
7/06/74	#73	4	Air Disaster	Mums 6030
5/03/75	#78	5	99 Miles From L.A.	Mums 6037
			KEITH HAMPSHIRE	
12/16/72	#43	10	Daytime Night-Time	A&M 1403
4/14/73	#40	13	The First Cut Is The Deepest	A&M 1432
11/24/73	#58	8	Big Time Operator	A&M 1486
			HERBIE HANCOCK	
3/16/74	#41	13	Chameleon	Columbia 46002
9/24/83	#64	10	Rockit	Columbia 04054
			JOHN HANDY	
6/19/76	#48	18	Hard Work	ABC Impulse 31005
			HAPPENINGS	
7/09/66	#4	14	See You In September	B.T. Puppy 520
10/01/66	#13	9	Go Away Little Girl	B.T. Puppy 522
12/10/66	#53	6	Goodnight My Love	B.T. Puppy 523
4/08/67	#1	14	I Got Rhythm	B.T. Puppy 527
7/08/67	#16	9	My Mammy	B.T. Puppy 530
9/23/67	#43	6	Why Do Fools Fall In Love	B.T. Puppy 532
2/10/68	#84	4	Music, Music, Music	B.T. Puppy 538
5/18/68	#90	4	Randy	B.T. Puppy 540
7/13/68	#46	8	Breaking Up Is Hard To Do	B.T. Puppy 543
6/28/69	#38	8	Where Do I Go/Be-In/Hare Krishna	Jubilee 5666
1/17/70	#95	3	Answer Me My Love	Jubilee 5686
			HAPPY MONDAYS	
3/30/91	#55	11	Step On	Elektra 64899
			PAUL HARDCASTLE	
1/26/85	#43	15	Rain Forest	Profile 7059
6/01/85	#21	16	19	Chrysalis 42860
			HARDEN TRIO	
3/26/66	#59	6	Tippy Toeing	Columbia 43463
			TIM HARDEN	
7/26/69	#47	8	Simple Song Of Freedom	Columbia 44920
			HAGOOD HARDY	
12/06/75	#46	15	The Homecoming	Capitol 4156
			JOE HARNELL	
12/22/62	#17	15	Fly Me To The Moon Bossa Nova	Kapp 497
4/27/63	#90	1	Diane	Kapp 521
			JANICE HARPER	
8/03/57	#28	12	Bon Voyage	Prep 111
11/23/57	#41	5	That's Why I Was Born	Prep 123
8/09/58	#67	6	Devotion	Capitol 3984
1/30/60	#85	4	Cry Me A River	Capitol 4324
			HARPERS BIZARRE	
2/25/67	#14	11	The 59th Street Bridge Song	Warner Brothers 5890
5/27/67	#52	6	Come To The Sunshine	Warner Brothers 7028
8/26/67	#51	9	Anything Goes	Warner Brothers 7063
11/11/67	#49	7	Chattanooga Choo Choo	Warner Brothers 7090
			SLIM HARPO	
5/27/61	#24	12	Rainin' In My Heart	Excello 2194
1/22/66	#13	14	Baby Scratch My Back	Excello 2273
7/02/66	#91	4	Shake Your Hips	Excello 2278
12/17/66	#100	1	I'm Your Bread Maker	Excello 2282
7/22/67	#97	3	Tip On In	Excello 2285
			HARRIET	
3/09/91	#49	11	Temple Of Love	East West 98863
			BETTY HARRIS	
9/28/63	#27	12	Cry To Me	Jubilee 5456
1/11/64	#74	4	His Kiss	Jubilee 5465
7/22/67	#73	5	Nearer To You	Sansu 466
			BOBBY HARRIS	
9/24/66	#99	1	Sticky Sticky	Shout 203

150

Debut Date	Peak Pos	Wks Chr	ARTIST/Song Title	Label & Number
			EDDIE HARRIS	
4/22/61	#47	14	Exodus	Vee-Jay 378
7/27/68	#79	6	Listen Here	Atlantic 2487
10/26/68	#95	2	It's Crazy	Atlantic 2561
			EMMYLOU HARRIS	
8/23/75	#67	8	If I Could Only Win Your Love	Reprise 1332
3/13/76	#82	4	Here, There And Everywhere	Reprise 1346
6/21/80	#59	9	That Lovin' You Feelin' Again*	Warner Brothers 49262
3/07/81	#37	12	Mister Sandman	Warner Brothers 49684
			*released as by ROY ORBISON & EMMYLOU HARRIS	
			MAJOR HARRIS	
3/29/75	#3	18	Love Won't Let Me Wait	Atlantic 3248
1/10/76	#86	4	I Got Over Love	Atlantic 3303
4/10/76	#77	6	Jealousy	Atlantic 3321
			PHIL HARRIS	
12/16/50	#1	10	The Thing	RCA 3968
			RICHARD HARRIS	
5/04/68	#2	14	MacArthur Park	Dunhill 4134
11/02/68	#46	6	The Yard Went On Forever	Dunhill 4170
6/14/69	#80	3	Didn't We	Dunhill 4194
11/13/71	#46	12	My Boy	Dunhill 4293
3/08/75	#94	2	Theme From Prophet	Atlantic 3238
			ROLF HARRIS	
3/09/63	#44	9	Sun Arise	Epic 9567
6/08/63	#4	13	Tie Me Kangaroo Down, Sport	Epic 9596
			SAM HARRIS	
9/15/84	#35	13	Sugar Don't Bite	Motown 1743
2/01/86	#71	7	I'll Do It All Again	Motown 1829
			THURSTON HARRIS	
10/12/57	#9	14	Little Bitty Pretty One	Aladdin 3398
8/30/58	#51	7	Over And Over	Aladdin 3430
10/04/58	#82	5	Tears From My Heart	Aladdin 3435
			DON HARRISON BAND	
4/17/76	#65	9	Sixteen Tons	Atlantic 3323
			GEORGE HARRISON	
11/28/70	#1	14	My Sweet Lord/	Apple 2995
11/28/70	#46	4	Isn't It A Pity	Apple 2995
2/20/71	#7	11	What Is Life	Apple 1828
8/07/71	#20	7	Bangla-Desh	Apple 1836
5/12/73	#1	13	Give Me Love (Give Me Peace On Earth)	Apple 1862
11/23/74	#19	9	Dark Horse	Apple 1877
1/11/75	#36	6	Ding Dong; Ding Dong	Apple 1879
9/20/75	#19	10	You	Apple 1884
11/20/76	#28	16	This Song	Dark Horse 8294
1/29/77	#17	12	Crackerbox Palace	Dark Horse 8313
2/24/79	#12	16	Blow Away	Dark Horse 8763
5/23/81	#3	15	All Those Years Ago	Dark Horse 49725
8/08/81	#88	4	Teardrops	Dark Horse 49785
11/13/82	#67	9	Wake Up My Love	Dark Horse 29864
10/24/87	#1	24	Got My Mind Set On You	Dark Horse 28178
2/06/88	#36	12	When We Was Fab	Dark Horse 28131
			NOEL HARRISON	
11/27/65	#38	10	A Young Girl	London 9795
10/21/67	#72	6	Suzanne	Reprise 0615
			WILBERT HARRISON	
4/18/59	#1	15	Kansas City	Fury 1023
12/13/69	#30	11	Let's Work Together (Part 1)	Sue 11
			DEBBIE HARRY	
8/15/81	#39	11	Backfired	Chrysalis 2526
11/22/86	#51	12	French Kissin	Geffen 28546
7/04/87	#74	7	In Love With You	Geffen 28476
			COREY HART	
5/26/84	#7	24	Sunglasses At Night	EMI America 8203
9/29/84	#19	18	It Ain't Enough	EMI America 8236
6/08/85	#4	20	Never Surrender	EMI America 8268

Debut Date	Peak Pos	Wks Chr	ARTIST/Song Title	Label & Number
			COREY HART—*continued*	
9/14/85	#25	14	Boy In The Box	EMI America 8287
11/30/85	#30	16	Everything In My Heart	EMI America 8300
9/20/86	#19	13	I Am By Your Side	EMI America 8348
12/06/86	#35	15	Can't Help Falling In Love	EMI America 8368
6/11/88	#46	12	In Your Soul	EMI-Manhattan 50134
3/17/90	#54	7	Little Bit Of Love	EMI 50239
			FREDDIE HART	
8/28/71	#12	17	Easy Loving	Capitol 3115
			ROD HART	
12/11/76	#59	10	C.B. Savage	Plantation 144
			DAN HARTMAN	
10/14/78	#22	17	Instant Replay	Blue Sky 2772
6/27/81	#80	4	It Hurts To Be In Love	Blue Sky 02115
5/05/84	#6	25	I Can Dream About You	MCA 52378
10/06/84	#28	17	We Are The Young	MCA 52471
2/16/85	#38	12	Second Nature	MCA 52519
12/17/88	#75	7	The Love You Take*	A&M 1264
			*released as by **DAN HARTMAN and DENISE LOPEZ**	
			HARVEY and THE MOONGLOWS (see **MOONGLOWS**)	
			HASSLES	
11/04/67	#81	3	You've Got Me Hummin'	United Artists 50215
			BOBBY HATFIELD	
3/01/69	#91	3	Only You (And You Alone)	Verve 10634
			DONNY HATHAWAY	
2/14/70	#89	5	The Ghetto (Part 1)	Atco 6719
5/29/71	#28	13	You've Got A Friend*	Atlantic 2808
10/16/71	#57	6	You've Lost That Lovin' Feelin'*	Atlantic 2837
5/20/72	#87	2	Giving Up	Atco 6884
6/10/72	#7	13	Where Is The Love*	Atlantic 2879
10/28/72	#64	5	I Love You More Than You'll Ever Know	Atco 6903
7/14/73	#56	8	Love, Love, Love	Atco 6928
2/11/78	#2	23	The Closer I Get To You*	Atlantic 3463
3/08/80	#78	6	You Are My Heaven*	Atlantic 3627
5/31/80	#91	5	Back Together Again*	Atlantic 3661
			*released as by **ROBERTA FLACK & DONNY HATHAWAY**	
			RICHIE HAVENS	
10/11/69	#92	1	Rocky Raccoon	Stormy Forest 650
3/27/71	#15	12	Here Comes The Sun	Stormy Forest 656
			CHESNEY HAWKES	
8/10/91	#11	28	The One And Only	Chrysalis 23730
			DALE HAWKINS	
6/15/57	#47	8	Susie-Q	Checker 863
9/06/58	#35	11	La-Do-Dada	Checker 900
11/08/58	#57	9	A House, A Car And A Wedding Ring	Checker 906
3/14/59	#60	7	Class Cutter (Yeah Yeah)	Checker 916
			EDWIN HAWKINS SINGERS	
5/03/69	#3	9	Oh Happy Day	Pavillion 20001
4/18/70	#3	17	Lay Down (Candles In The Rain)*	Buddah 167
			*released as by **MELANIE with THE EDWIN HAWKINS SINGERS**	
			JENNELL HAWKINS	
2/10/62	#69	10	Moments	Amazon 1003
			RONNIE HAWKINS	
5/30/59	#54	9	Forty Days	Roulette 4154
8/29/59	#24	12	Mary Lou	Roulette 4177
1/16/60	#100	1	Southern Love	Roulette 4209
2/07/70	#78	3	Down In The Alley	Cotillion 44060
			SOPHIE B. HAWKINS	
4/25/92	#5	25	Damn I Wish I Was Your Lover	Columbia 74164
8/08/92	#79	6	California Here I Come	Columbia 74594
			HAWKS	
3/21/81	#68	6	Right Away	Columbia 60500

Debut Date	Peak Pos	Wks Chr	**ARTIST**/Song Title	Label & Number
			DEANE HAWLEY	
6/25/60	#13	14	Look For A Star	Dore 554
10/14/61	#98	3	Pocketful Of Rainbows	Liberty 55359
			BILL HAYES	
4/09/55	#1	15	The Ballad Of Davy Crockett	Cadence 1256
1/19/57	#12	13	Wringle, Wrangle	ABC-Paramount 9785
			ISAAC HAYES	
8/23/69	#59	5	By The Time I Get To Phoenix/	Enterprise 9003
9/20/69	#69	5	Walk On By	Enterprise 9003
8/29/70	#38	8	I Stand Accused	Enterprise 9017
2/20/71	#68	3	The Look Of Love	Enterprise 9028
5/08/71	#33	10	Never Can Say Goodbye	Enterprise 9031
10/16/71	#1	14	Theme From Shaft	Enterprise 9038
2/19/72	#23	11	Do Your Thing	Enterprise 9042
3/18/72	#45	6	Let's Stay Together/	Enterprise 9045
4/29/72	#94	2	Soulsville	Enterprise 9045
4/29/72	#67	5	Ain't That Loving You	Enterprise 9049
10/07/72	#36	12	Theme From The Men	Enterprise 9058
12/22/73	#31	9	Joy (Part 1)	Enterprise 9085
8/09/75	#65	5	Chocolate Chip	ABC 12118
10/27/79	#17	20	Don't Let Go	Polydor 2011
			RICHARD HAYMAN ORCHESTRA	
5/16/53	#3	13	Ruby	Mercury 70115
7/20/57	#10	3	Tammy	Mercury 71123
			JUSTIN HAYWARD	
9/30/78	#34	18	Forever Autumn	Columbia 10799
			JUSTIN HAYWARD & JOHN LODGE	
5/10/75	#45	8	I Dreamed Last Night	Threshold 67019
12/06/75	#82	5	Blue Guitar	Threshold 67021
			LEON HAYWARD	
10/23/65	#93	3	She's With Her Other Love	Imperial 66123
			LEON HAYWOOD	
9/02/67	#84	7	It's Got To Be Mellow	Decca 32164
3/09/74	#56	12	Keep It In The Family	20th Century 2066
7/27/74	#68	8	Sugar Lump	20th Century 2103
7/19/75	#82	3	Come An' Get Yourself Some	20th Century 2191
9/13/75	#20	15	I Want'a Do Something Freaky To You	20th Century 2228
4/12/80	#60	10	Don't Push It Don't Force It	20th Century 2443
			ROBERT HAZARD	
3/12/83	#52	9	Escalator Of Life	RCA 13449
			LEE HAZLEWOOD	
6/24/67	#13	10	Jackson*	Reprise 0595
10/21/67	#40	6	Lady Bird*	Reprise 0629
1/06/68	#37	9	Some Velvet Morning*	Reprise 0651
11/29/69	#91	2	Trouble Maker	LHI 20
			*released as by NANCY SINATRA & LEE HAZLEWOOD	
			MURRAY HEAD	
1/24/70	#67	7	Superstar	Decca 32603
1/09/71	#8	23	Superstar	Decca 32603
2/23/85	#4	22	One Night In Bangkok	RCA 13988
			ROY HEAD	
9/11/65	#3	12	Treat Her Right*	Back Beat 546
11/06/65	#38	6	Just A Little Bit	Scepter 12116
11/27/65	#50	8	Apple Of My Eye	Back Beat 555
			*released as by ROY HEAD and THE TRAITS	
			HEAD EAST	
10/25/75	#71	9	Never Been Any Reason	A&M 1718
2/21/76	#92	5	Love Me Tonight	A&M 1784
4/08/78	#65	8	Since You Been Gone	A&M 2026
			HEADPINS	
12/31/83	#68	9	Just One More Time	Solid Gold 90001
			JEFF HEALEY BAND	
6/03/89	#6	25	Angel Eyes	Arista 9808
4/10/93	#59	9	Lost In Your Eyes	Arista 2521

Debut Date	Peak Pos	Wks Chr	ARTIST/Song Title	Label & Number
			HEART	
4/24/76	#40	11	Crazy On You	Mushroom 7021
7/10/76	#7	24	Magic Man	Mushroom 7011
8/14/76	#83	3	Crazy On You	Mushroom 7021
12/11/76	#32	13	Dreamboat Annie	Mushroom 7023
5/28/77	#10	19	Barracuda	Portrait 70004
9/10/77	#48	7	Little Queen	Portrait 70008
11/12/77	#69	4	Kick It Out	Portrait 70010
12/31/77	#69	7	Crazy On You	Portrait 70021
4/08/78	#18	17	Heartless	Mushroom 7031
9/16/78	#18	19	Straight On	Portrait 70020
2/03/79	#31	12	Dog & Butterfly	Portrait 70025
2/09/80	#30	13	Even It Up	Epic 50847
11/22/80	#14	16	Tell It Like It Is	Epic 50950
5/15/82	#29	12	This Man Is Mine	Epic 02925
8/20/83	#56	8	How Can I Refuse	Epic 04047
6/01/85	#17	21	What About Love?	Capitol 5481
9/14/85	#6	23	Never	Capitol 5512
1/18/86	#1	20	These Dreams	Capitol 5541
4/19/86	#11	15	Nothin' At All	Capitol 5572
7/19/86	#60	9	If Looks Could Kill	Capitol 5605
5/16/87	#1	22	Alone	Capitol 44002
8/15/87	#6	19	Who Will You Run To	Capitol 44040
11/07/87	#19	19	There's The Girl	Capitol 44089
2/20/88	#55	9	I Want You So Bad	Capitol 44116
3/31/90	#1	21	All I Wanna Do Is Make Love To You	Capitol 44507
6/23/90	#21	15	I Didn't Want To Need You	Capitol 44553
9/22/90	#11	21	Stranded	Capitol 44621
1/26/91	#41	12	Secret	Capitol 44614
			HEARTBEATS	
12/15/56	#36	4	A Thousand Miles Away	Rama 216
4/19/58	#60	1	Down On My Knees	Roulette 4054
			HEARTS	
10/19/63	#94	3	Dear Abby	Tuff 370
			HEARTSFIELD	
3/16/74	#85	4	Music Eyes	Mercury 73449
			JOEY HEATHERTON	
5/20/72	#26	14	Gone	MGM 14687
12/02/72	#76	5	I'm Sorry	MGM 14434
			HEATWAVE	
7/09/77	#2	27	Boogie Nights	Epic 50370
12/24/77	#12	21	Always And Forever	Epic 50490
4/15/78	#10	21	The Groove Line	Epic 50524
			HEAVEN BOUND	
8/21/71	#80	7	He'd Rather Have The Rain	MGM 14284
11/27/71	#82	7	Five Hundred Miles	MGM 14314
			HEAVY D. & THE BOYZ	
8/10/91	#27	23	Now That We Found Love	Uptown 54090
			BOBBY HEBB	
6/11/66	#1	18	Sunny	Philips 40365
10/08/66	#40	7	A Satisfied Mind	Philips 40400
12/31/66	#83	3	Love Me	Philips 40421
			HEDGEHOPPERS ANONYMOUS	
12/04/65	#44	10	It's Good News Week	Parrot 9800
			NEAL HEFTI	
2/12/66	#32	7	Batman Theme	RCA 8755
			HEIGHTS	
10/10/92	#1	22	How Do You Talk To An Angel	Capitol 44890
			HELLO PEOPLE	
8/17/68	#98	1	(As I Went Down To) Jerusalem	Philips 40531
1/04/75	#70	8	Future Shock	ABC/Dunhill 15023
			BOBBY HELMS	
9/21/57	#8	20	My Special Angel	Decca 30423
9/21/57	#45	5	Fraulein	Decca 30194
12/14/57	#11	7	Jingle Bell Rock	Decca 30513

Debut Date	Peak Pos	Wks Chr	ARTIST/Song Title	Label & Number
2/22/58	#57	2	Just A Little Lonesome	Decca 30557
5/03/58	#45	3	Jacqueline	Decca 30619
12/15/62	#59	4	Jingle Bell Rock	Decca 30513
			BILLY HEMMANS & THE CLAYS COMPOSITE	
11/14/70	#97	2	Summertime	Blue Fox 102
			JOE HENDERSON	
5/12/62	#7	14	Snap Your Fingers	Todd 1072
9/08/62	#80	5	Big Love	Todd 1077
			WILLIE HENDERSON	
7/06/74	#69	6	Dance Master	Playboy 50057
			BOBBY HENDRICKS	
8/09/58	#42	12	Itchy Twitchy Feeling	Sue 706
10/29/60	#82	6	Psycho	Sue 732
			JIMI HENDRIX EXPERIENCE	
9/02/67	#64	9	Purple Haze	Reprise 0597
12/30/67	#83	3	Foxey Lady	Reprise 0641
9/14/68	#18	10	All Along The Watchtower	Reprise 0767
11/30/68	#36	8	Crosstown Traffic	Reprise 0792
3/02/71	#76	6	Freedom	Reprise 1000
10/30/71	#94	2	Dolly Dagger	Reprise 1044
			NONA HENDRYX	
5/23/87	#59	8	Why Should I Cry?	EMI America 8382
			HENHOUSE FIVE PLUS TOO	
12/25/76	#37	12	In The Mood	Warner Brothers 8301
			DON HENLEY	
10/24/81	#9	21	Leather And Lace*	Modern 7341
8/14/82	#33	13	Johnny Can't Read	Asylum 69971
10/30/82	#5	20	Dirty Laundry	Asylum 69894
1/15/83	#38	10	I Can't Stand Still	Asylum 69931
11/10/84	#6	24	The Boys Of Summer (After The Boys Of Summer Have Gone)	Geffen 29141
2/23/85	#9	20	All She Wants To Do Is Dance	Geffen 29065
5/25/85	#29	15	Not Enough Love In The World	Geffen 29012
8/31/85	#20	15	Sunset Grill	Geffen 28906
6/24/89	#5	21	The End Of The Innocence	Geffen 22925
10/07/89	#20	18	The Last Worthless Evening	Geffen 22771
2/24/90	#18	17	The Heart Of The Matter	Geffen 19898
7/21/90	#39	14	How Bad Do You Want It?	Geffen 19699
11/17/90	#43	13	New York Minute	Geffen 19660
			***released as by STEVIE NICKS with DON HENLEY**	
			CLARENCE HENRY	
12/29/56	#30	10	Ain't Got No Home	Argo 5259
3/04/61	#4	16	But I Do	Argo 5378
5/20/61	#12	11	You Always Hurt The One You Love	Argo 5388
8/12/61	#57	6	Lonely Street	Argo 5395
11/04/61	#78	6	On Bended Knees	Argo 5401
1/20/62	#74	4	A Little Too Much	Argo 5408
			KEITH HERMAN	
11/17/79	#96	3	She's Got A Whole Number	Radio 418
			HERMAN'S HERMITS	
10/10/64	#7	15	I'm Into Something Good	MGM 13280
2/06/65	#1	15	Can't You Hear My Heartbeat	MGM 13310
4/03/65	#5	13	Silhouettes	MGM 13332
4/17/65	#1	12	Mrs. Brown You've Got A Lovely Daughter	MGM 13341
5/22/65	#5	10	Wonderful World	MGM 13354
7/03/65	#1	10	I'm Henry VIII I Am	MGM 13367
9/18/65	#8	11	Just A Little Bit Better	MGM 13398
12/18/65	#6	9	A Must To Avoid	MGM 13437
2/12/66	#3	9	Listen People	MGM 13462
4/09/66	#8	8	Leaning On The Lamp Post	MGM 13500
7/09/66	#10	9	This Door Swings Both Ways	MGM 13548
10/01/66	#8	10	Dandy	MGM 13603
12/10/66	#15	8	East West	MGM 13639
2/11/67	#3	12	There's A Kind Of Hush/	MGM 13681
2/18/67	#33	9	No Milk Today	MGM 13681
6/24/67	#13	7	Don't Go Out Into The Rain	MGM 13761

Debut Date	Peak Pos	Wks Chr	ARTIST/Song Title	Label & Number
			HERMAN'S HERMITS—*continued*	
8/26/67	#21	7	Museum	MGM 13787
1/13/68	#21	10	I Can Take Or Leave Your Loving	MGM 13885
5/04/68	#54	7	Sleepy Joe	MGM 13934
8/10/68	#82	3	Sunshine Girl	MGM 13973
			PATRICK HERNANDEZ	
6/09/79	#17	23	Born To Be Alive	Columbia 10986
			HESITATIONS	
1/13/68	#36	8	Born Free	Kapp 878
3/16/68	#52	8	The Impossible Dream	Kapp 899
5/25/68	#86	3	Climb Every Mountain	Kapp 911
11/09/68	#88	3	A Whiter Shade Of Pale	Kapp 948
			HOWARD HEWETT	
6/02/90	#59	7	Show Me	Elektra 64978
			BEN HEWITT	
3/21/59	#84	3	I Ain't Giving Up Nothing	Mercury 71413
			HEYETTES	
4/10/76	#66	8	The Fonz Song	London 232
			EDDIE HEYWOOD	
8/04/56	#11	18	Soft Summer Breeze	Mercury 70863
8/04/56	#2	19	Canadian Sunset*	RCA 6537
7/11/59	#100	1	Soft Summer Breeze	Mercury 71462
			*released as by HUGO WINTERHALTER/EDDIE HEYWOOD	
			HEYWOODS (see BO DONALDSON and THE HEYWOODS)	
			AL HIBBLER	
4/30/55	#1	19	Unchained Melody	Decca 29441
11/12/55	#4	11	He	Decca 29660
8/04/56	#15	19	After The Lights Go Down Low	Decca 29982
11/17/56	#41	5	I'm Free	Decca 30100
			ERSEL HICKEY	
3/29/58	#39	5	Bluebirds Over The Mountain	Epic 9263
			BERTIE HIGGINS	
11/07/81	#7	32	Key Largo	Kat Family 02524
5/08/82	#42	9	Just Another Day In Paradise	Kat Family 02839
			MONK HIGGINS	
7/30/66	#69	5	Who-Dun-It?	Saint Lawrence 1013
6/03/72	#86	3	Gotta Be Funky	United Artists 50897
			HI-FIVE	
3/23/91	#8	24	I Like The Way (Kissing Game)	Jive 1424
7/06/91	#16	20	I Can't Wait Another Minute	Jive 1445
9/12/92	#5	22	She's Playing Hard To Get	Jive 42067
12/12/92	#34	18	Quality Time	Jive 42109
10/30/93	#29	22	Never Should've Let You Go	Jive 42178
			HIGH INERGY	
10/22/77	#12	17	You Can't Turn Me Off	Gordy 7155
			HIGH KEYS	
8/03/63	#48	9	Que Sera, Sera	Atco 6268
			HIGHLIGHTS	
11/03/56	#24	10	City Of Angels	Bally 1016
			HIGHWAYMEN	
6/24/61	#1	20	Michael	United Artists 258
11/04/61	#49	12	The Gypsy Rover/	United Artists 370
12/02/61	#13	17	Cotton Fields	United Artists 370
4/21/62	#95	2	I'm On My Way	United Artists 439
7/21/62	#82	4	The Bird Man*	United Artists 475
			*narration by BURT LANCASTER	
			BUNKER HILL	
9/08/62	#39	12	Hide & Go Seek (Part 1)	Mala 451
			DAN HILL	
1/31/76	#98	2	Growin' Up	20th Century 2254
11/26/77	#4	22	Sometimes When We Touch	20th Century 2355
8/12/78	#35	10	All I See Is Your Face	20th Century 2378
6/13/87	#6	24	Can't We Try*	Columbia 07050

156

Debut Date	Peak Pos	Wks Chr	ARTIST/Song Title	Label & Number
12/19/87	#57	16	Never Thought (That I Could Love)	Columbia 07618
			*released as by DAN HILL with VONDA SHEPPARD	
			DAVID HILL	
4/11/59	#89	5	Two Brothers	Kapp 266
9/12/59	#58	5	Living Doll	Kapp 293
			JESSE HILL	
3/26/60	#32	14	Ooh Poo Pah Doo (Part 2)	Minit 607
8/06/60	#100	1	Whip It On Me	Minit 611
			Z.Z. HILL	
3/28/64	#95	2	You Were Wrong	M.H. 200
3/06/71	#65	5	Don't Make Me Pay For His Mistakes	Hill 222
6/26/71	#88	3	I Need Someone To Love (To Love Me)	Kent 4547
7/10/71	#99	2	Faithful And True	Mankind 12003
10/09/71	#94	2	Chokin' Kind	Mankind 12007
			HILLSIDE SINGERS	
11/27/71	#16	11	I'd Like To Teach The World To Sing	Metromedia 231
2/12/72	#73	4	We're Together	Metromedia 241
			HILLTOPPERS	
10/11/52	#4	15	Trying	Dot 15018
7/25/53	#10	1	I'd Rather Die Young/	Dot 15085
8/08/53	#4	13	P.S. I Love You	Dot 15085
12/12/53	#7	2	Love Walked In	Dot 15105
2/20/54	#6	5	Till Then	Dot 15132
3/06/54	#3	7	From The Vine Came The Grape	Dot 15127
8/11/56	#17	11	Ka-Ding-Dong	Dot 15489
2/09/57	#2	14	Marianne	Dot 15537
4/27/57	#45	3	I Love My Girl	Dot 15560
6/29/57	#24	11	A Fallen Star	Dot 15594
11/16/57	#20	10	The Joker (That's What They Call Me)	Dot 15662
			ERIC HINE	
8/29/81	#88	4	Not Fade Away	Montage 1200
			JOE HINTON	
4/27/63	#92	5	You Know It Ain't Right	Back Beat 537
8/08/64	#12	14	Funny	Back Beat 541
11/14/64	#92	3	A Thousand Cups Of Happiness	Back Beat 532
			HIPPIES	
3/30/63	#57	8	Memory Lane	Parkway 863
			HIPSWAY	
1/24/87	#28	16	The Honeythief	Columbia 06579
			AL HIRT	
1/11/64	#4	17	Java	RCA 8280
4/11/64	#15	12	Cotton Candy	RCA 8346
7/11/64	#20	8	Sugar Lips	RCA 8391
10/17/64	#94	3	Up Above My Head	RCA 8439
1/16/65	#37	8	Fancy Pants	RCA 8487
1/25/69	#95	2	If	RCA 9717
			HI TEK 3	
4/21/90	#62	6	Spin That Wheel*	SBK 07320
			*released as by HI TEK 3 featuring YA KID K	
			DON HO and THE ALIIS	
1/07/67	#55	10	Tiny Bubbles	Reprise 0507
			CHRIS HODGE	
5/27/72	#36	8	We're On Our Way	Apple 1850
			EDDIE HODGES	
5/27/61	#13	19	I'm Gonna Knock On Your Door	Cadence 1397
1/20/62	#65	8	Bandit Of My Dreams	Cadence 1410
6/09/62	#20	14	(Girls, Girls, Girls) Made To Love	Cadence 1421
6/19/65	#36	11	New Orleans	Aurora 153
			HODGES, JAMES and SMITH	
8/20/77	#100	2	Since I Fell For You/I'm Falling In Love	London 256
			ROGER HODGSON	
10/20/84	#44	14	Had A Dream (Sleeping With The Enemy)	A&M 2678

157

Debut Date	Peak Pos	Wks Chr	**ARTIST**/Song Title	Label & Number
			SUSANNA HOFFS	
2/02/91	#26	15	My Side Of The Bed	Columbia 73529
			RON HOLDEN	
4/02/60	#5	19	Love You So	Donna 1315
8/13/60	#74	6	Gee, But I'm Lonesome	Donna 1324
			CHICO HOLIDAY	
4/25/59	#52	7	Young Ideas	RCA 7499
			JIMMY HOLIDAY	
3/09/63	#50	11	How Can I Forget	Everest 2022
			HOLIDAYS	
5/07/66	#50	8	I'll Love You Forever	Golden World 36
			DANNY HOLIEN	
9/16/72	#80	6	Colorado	Tumbleweed 1004
			AMY HOLLAND	
8/09/80	#26	18	How Do I Survive	Capitol 4884
			EDDIE HOLLAND	
1/27/62	#40	12	Jamie	Motown 1021
2/15/64	#71	3	Leaving Here	Motown 1052
5/30/64	#89	5	Just Ain't Enough Love	Motown 1058
9/05/64	#88	6	Candy To Me	Motown 1063
			HOLLAND-DOZIER	
9/23/72	#48	11	Why Can't We Be Lovers*	Invictus 9125
1/13/73	#49	6	Don't Leave Me Starvin' For Your Love (Part 1)**	Invictus 9133
			*released as by HOLLAND-DOZIER featuring LAMONT DOZIER	
			**released as by HOLLAND-DOZIER featuring BRIAN HOLLAND	
			JENNIFER HOLLIDAY	
7/03/82	#34	14	And I'm Telling You I'm Not Going	Geffen 29983
10/15/83	#42	14	I Am Love	Geffen 29525
10/05/85	#80	4	Hard Times For Lovers	Geffen 28958
			HOLLIES	
4/18/64	#84	2	Just One Look	Imperial 66026
7/17/65	#84	4	I'm Alive	Imperial 66119
11/27/65	#34	11	Look Through Any Window	Imperial 66134
3/19/66	#59	10	I Can't Let Go	Imperial 66158
7/23/66	#5	13	Bus Stop	Imperial 66186
10/22/66	#8	11	Stop Stop Stop	Imperial 66214
3/11/67	#7	13	On A Carousel	Imperial 66231
6/03/67	#29	7	Pay You Back With Interest	Imperial 66240
6/24/67	#10	12	Carrie-Anne	Epic 10180
9/30/67	#54	5	King Midas In Reverse	Epic 10234
10/07/67	#65	4	Just One Look	Imperial 66258
12/02/67	#53	8	Dear Eloise	Epic 10251
3/09/68	#54	8	Jennifer Eccles	Epic 10298
4/12/69	#58	10	Sorry Suzanne	Epic 10454
12/20/69	#8	16	He Ain't Heavy, He's My Brother	Epic 10532
5/23/70	#64	6	I Can't Tell The Bottom From The top	Epic 10613
6/17/72	#1	16	Long Cool Woman (In A Black Dress)	Epic 10871
11/04/72	#24	10	Long Dark Road	Epic 10920
2/17/73	#43	7	Magic Woman Touch	Epic 10951
11/03/73	#86	3	The Day That Curly Billy Shot Down Crazy Sam McGee	Epic 11051
4/20/74	#7	18	The Air That I Breathe	Epic 11100
4/19/75	#86	2	Sandy	Epic 50086
6/04/83	#29	14	Stop In The Name Of Love	Atlantic 89819
			BRENDA HOLLOWAY	
5/02/64	#18	11	Every Little Bit Hurts	Tamla 54094
3/13/65	#26	9	When I'm Gone	Tamla 54111
6/12/65	#85	3	Operator	Tamla 54115
5/06/67	#93	4	Just Look What You've Done	Tamla 54148
9/16/67	#58	9	You've Made Me So Very Happy	Tamla 54155
			LOLEATTA HOLLOWAY	
3/22/75	#66	6	Cry To Me	Aware 047

Debut Date	Peak Pos	Wks Chr	ARTIST/Song Title	Label & Number
7/27/91	#4	27	Good Vibrations*	Interscope 98764
			*released as by MARKY MARK & THE FUNKY BUNCH featuring LOLEATTA HOLLOWAY	
			BUDDY HOLLY (also CRICKETS)	
8/03/57	#3	20	That'll Be The Day*	Brunswick 55009
10/26/57	#2	20	Peggy Sue	Coral 61885
11/16/57	#13	14	Oh Boy!*	Brunswick 55035
11/30/57	#51	3	Everyday	Coral 61885
2/22/58	#11	11	Maybe Baby*	Brunswick 55053
3/15/58	#56	1	I'm Gonna Love You Too	Coral 61947
5/17/58	#54	2	Rave On	Coral 61985
7/05/58	#42	10	Think It Over*/	Brunswick 55072
7/05/58	#73	1	Fool's Paradise*	Brunswick 55072
7/26/58	#25	10	Early In The Morning	Coral 62006
2/21/59	#30	14	It Doesn't Matter Anymore/	Coral 62074
2/21/59	#88	2	Raining In My Heart	Coral 62074
5/03/69	#94	3	Love Is Strange	Coral 62558
			*released as by THE CRICKETS	
			HOLLYWOOD ARGYLES	
5/28/60	#1	16	Alley-Oop	Lute 5905
			HOLLYWOOD FLAMES	
11/23/57	#18	11	Buzz-Buzz-Buzz	Ebb 119
9/17/60	#18	1	Devil Or Angel	Atco 6171
			MICHAEL HOLM	
12/21/74	#38	7	When A Child Is Born	Mercury 73642
			EDDIE HOLMAN	
1/22/66	#47	10	This Can't Be True	Parkway 960
12/20/69	#2	16	Hey There Lonely Girl	ABC 11240
4/11/70	#43	6	Don't Stop Now	ABC 11261
7/29/72	#98	3	My Mind Keeps Telling Me	GSF 6873
			CLINT HOLMES	
3/17/73	#2	22	Playground In My Mind	Epic 10891
			JAKE HOLMES	
9/26/70	#29	12	So Close	Polydor 14041
			LeROY HOLMES	
8/28/54	#3	9	The High And The Mighty	MGM 11761
8/25/56	#16	7	When The White Lilacs Bloom Again	MGM 12317
			RICHARD "GROOVE" HOLMES	
6/25/66	#32	10	Misty	Prestige 401
			RUPERT HOLMES	
8/26/78	#64	6	Let's Get Crazy Tonight	Private Stock 45199
10/20/79	#1	21	Escape (The Pina Colada Song)	Infinity 50035
1/19/80	#6	17	Him	MCA 41173
5/10/80	#46	10	Answering Machine	MCA 41235
11/08/80	#79	6	Morning Man	MCA 51019
2/14/81	#92	3	Blackjack	MCA 51045
4/04/81	#56	8	I Don't Need You	MCA 51092
			HOMBRES	
9/09/67	#7	14	Let It Out (Let It All Hang Out)	Verve Forecast 5058
1/20/68	#98	1	It's A Gas	Verve Forecast 5076
			HOMER and JETHRO	
9/05/59	#16	10	The Battle Of Kookamonga	RCA 7585
			HONDELLS	
9/12/64	#10	13	Little Honda	Mercury 72324
12/19/64	#71	4	My Buddy Seat	Mercury 72366
5/28/66	#38	9	Younger Girl	Mercury 72563
			HONEYCOMBS	
9/12/64	#4	15	Have I The Right?	Interphon 7707
12/19/64	#45	7	I Can't Stop	Interphon 7713
			HONEYCONE	
6/21/69	#80	6	While You're Out Looking For Sugar	Hot Wax 6901
11/01/69	#74	5	Girls It Ain't Easy	Hot Wax 6903
5/09/70	#93	1	Take Me With You	Hot Wax 7001
4/10/71	#1	15	Want Ads	Hot Wax 7011

Debut Date	Peak Pos	Wks Chr	ARTIST/Song Title	Label & Number
			HONEYCONE—*continued*	
7/31/71	#7	14	Stick Up	Hot Wax 7106
11/20/71	#14	12	One Monkey Don't Stop No Show (Part 1)	Hot Wax 7110
2/19/72	#15	11	The Day I Found Myself	Hot Wax 7113
7/29/72	#75	2	Sittin' On A Time Bomb	Hot Wax 7205
			HONEYCONES	
7/12/58	#65	2	Op	Ember 1036
			HONEYDRIPPERS	
10/13/84	#3	22	Sea Of Love	Es Paranza 99701
1/19/85	#28	11	Rockin' At Midnight	Es Paranza 99686
			HONEYMOON SUITE	
9/22/84	#76	6	New Girl Now	Warner Brothers 29208
3/08/86	#32	15	Feel It Again	Warner Brothers 28779
7/19/86	#51	14	What Does It Take	Warner Brothers 28670
5/07/88	#89	3	Love Changes Everything	Warner Brothers 27935
			JOHN LEE HOOKER	
6/12/62	#83	5	Boom Boom	Vee-Jay 438
			HOOTERS	
5/25/85	#53	10	All You Zombies	Columbia 04854
8/10/85	#23	19	And We Danced	Columbia 05568
12/14/85	#25	19	Day By Day	Columbia 05730
4/05/86	#37	12	Where Do The Children Go	Columbia 05854
7/18/87	#64	10	Johnny B	Columbia 07241
10/03/87	#67	9	Satellite	Columbia 07607
2/17/90	#85	4	Brother Don't You Walk Away	Columbia 73235
			MARY HOPKIN	
9/21/68	#1	16	Those Were The Days	Apple 1801
4/19/69	#17	8	Goodbye	Apple 1806
2/21/70	#43	8	Temma Harbour	Apple 1816
6/27/70	#49	7	Que Sera Sera	Apple 1823
12/02/72	#86	5	Knock Knock (Who's There)	Apple 1855
			JIMMY "BO" HORNE	
4/01/78	#51	15	Dance Across The Floor	Sunshine Sound 1003
			LENA HORNE	
11/23/63	#90	4	Now!	20th Century 449
			BRUCE HORNSBY and THE RANGE	
8/02/86	#62	8	Every Little Kiss	RCA 14361
9/20/86	#1	25	The Way It Is	RCA 5023
1/17/87	#4	19	Mandolin Rain	RCA 5087
5/16/87	#16	15	Every Little Kiss	RCA 5165
4/30/88	#5	17	The Valley Road	RCA 7645
7/23/88	#41	12	Look Out Any Window	RCA 8678
6/23/90	#16	18	Across The River	RCA 2621
10/30/93	#65	14	Fields Of Gray	RCA 62618
			JAMIE HORTON	
1/23/60	#58	5	My Little Marine	Joy 234
			JOHNNY HORTON	
4/25/59	#1	21	The Battle Of New Orleans	Columbia 41339
8/15/59	#77	4	Johnny Reb	Columbia 41437
8/29/59	#65	4	Sal's Got A Sugar Lip	Columbia 41437
2/27/60	#5	18	Sink The Bismarck	Columbia 41568
6/25/60	#73	6	Johnny Freedom	Columbia 41685
10/01/60	#6	22	North To Alaska	Columbia 41782
4/08/61	#50	6	Sleepy-Eyed John	Columbia 41963
			HOT	
2/12/77	#6	30	Angel In Your Arms	Big Tree 16085
1/28/78	#83	6	You Brought The Woman Out Of Me	Big Tree 16108
			HOT BUTTER	
7/01/72	#11	19	Popcorn	Musicor 1458
4/21/73	#82	5	Percolator	Musicor 1473
			HOT CHOCOLATE	
2/01/75	#6	16	Emma	Big Tree 16031
5/24/75	#21	12	Disco Queen	Big Tree 16038
10/18/75	#2	25	You Sexy Thing	Big Tree 16047
4/03/76	#68	8	Don't Stop It Now	Big Tree 16060

Debut Date	Peak Pos	Wks Chr	**ARTIST**/Song Title	Label & Number
7/09/77	#48	10	So You Win Again	Big Tree 16096
11/11/78	#7	19	Every 1's A Winner	Infinity 50002
7/21/79	#71	5	Going Through The Motions	Infinity 50016
1/15/83	#86	3	Are You Getting Enough Happiness	EMI America 8143
			HOTEL	
3/04/78	#67	11	You'll Love Again	Mercury 73979
7/07/79	#63	8	You've Got Another Thing Coming	MCA 41050
9/22/79	#77	3	Hold On To The Night	MCA 41113
7/19/80	#93	2	Half Moon Silver	MCA 41277
			HOTLEGS	
8/15/70	#20	10	Neanderthal Man	Capitol 2886
			HOT TODDY'S	
4/04/59	#59	10	Rockin' Crickets	Shan-Todd 0056
			HOUSE OF LORDS	
12/17/88	#74	7	I Wanna Be Loved	RCA 8805
2/11/89	#68	5	I Wanna Be Loved	RCA 8805
12/15/90	#65	15	Remember My Name	RCA 2376
			HOUSE OF PAIN	
9/12/92	#3	26	Jump Around	Tommy Boy 526
12/19/92	#67	10	Shamrocks And Shenanigans	Tommy Boy 543
			CISSY HOUSTON	
4/24/71	#86	4	Be My Baby	Janus 145
			DAVID HOUSTON	
7/23/66	#27	14	Almost Persuaded	Epic 10025
7/22/67	#96	3	My Elusive Dreams*	Epic 10194
9/30/67	#67	8	You Mean The World To Me	Epic 10224
			*released as by **DAVID HOUSTON** and **TAMMY WYNETTE**	
			THELMA HOUSTON	
1/17/70	#83	5	Save The Country	Dunhill 4222
12/25/76	#3	24	Don't Leave Me This Way	Tamla 54278
6/18/77	#85	5	If It's The Last Thing I Do	Tamla 54283
3/24/79	#44	13	Saturday Night, Sunday Morning	Tamla 54297
			WHITNEY HOUSTON	
6/16/84	#46	16	Hold Me*	Asylum 69720
5/11/85	#3	22	You Give Good Love To Me	Arista 9274
8/17/85	#10	16	Saving All My Love For You	Arista 9381
12/07/85	#1	26	How Will I Know	Arista 9434
3/29/86	#1	19	Greatest Love Of All	Arista 9466
5/16/87	#1	21	I Wanna Dance With Somebody	Arista 9598
8/01/87	#1	26	Didn't We Almost Have It All	Arista 9616
10/31/87	#4	22	So Emotional	Arista 9642
2/27/88	#1	21	Where Do Broken Hearts Go	Arista 9674
7/02/88	#11	15	Love Will Save The Day	Arista 9720
9/10/88	#6	19	One Moment In Time	Arista 9743
7/01/89	#37	12	It Isn't, It Wasn't, It Ain't Never Gonna Be**	Arista 9850
10/20/90	#1	23	I'm Your Baby Tonight	Arista 2108
12/22/90	#1	24	All The Man I Need	Arista 2156
4/13/91	#14	22	Miracle	Arista 2222
7/27/91	#27	14	My Name Is Not Susan	Arista 2259
11/21/92	#1	30	I Will Always Love You	Arista 2490
1/16/93	#1	26	I'm Every Woman	Arista 2519
2/13/93	#1	29	I Have Nothing	Arista 2527
6/26/93	#25	22	Run To You	Arista 2570
			*released as by **TEDDY PENDERGRASS** with **WHITNEY HOUSTON**	
			released as by **ARETHA FRANKLIN and **WHITNEY HOUSTON**	
			DON HOWARD	
1/24/58	#4	5	Oh Happy Day	Essex 311
			EDDY HOWARD ORCHESTRA	
1/06/51	#7	7	To Think You've Chosen Me	Mercury 5517
10/20/51	#1	20	Sin	Mercury 5711
5/03/52	#7	9	Be Anything	Mercury 5815
			MIKI HOWARD	
11/28/92	#80	4	Ain't Nobody Like You	Giant 18849

Debut Date	Peak Pos	Wks Chr	ARTIST/Song Title	Label & Number
			REUBEN HOWELL	
7/27/74	#88	2	Ringo	Motown 1305
			H-TOWN	
4/24/93	#4	26	Knockin' Da Boots	Luke 161
8/21/93	#75	9	Lick U Up	Luke 163
			DAVID HUDSON	
6/28/80	#93	4	Honey, Honey	Alston 3750
			HUDSON and LANDRY	
6/05/71	#61	5	Ajax Liquor Store	Dore 855
12/25/71	#81	6	Ajax Airlines	Dore 868
			HUDSON BROTHERS	
9/07/74	#20	14	So You Are A Star	Casablanca 0108
6/28/75	#32	11	Rendezvous	Rocket 40417
11/01/75	#68	9	Lonely School Year	Rocket 40464
10/30/76	#70	6	Help Wanted	Arista 0208
			HUES CORPORATION	
7/21/73	#38	12	Freedom For The Stallion	RCA 0900
5/18/74	#1	18	Rock The Boat	RCA 0232
10/12/74	#28	10	Rockin' Soul	RCA 10066
2/08/75	#49	8	Love Corporation	RCA 10200
			GRAYSON HUGH	
7/01/89	#19	21	Talk It Over	RCA 8802
3/31/90	#59	7	How 'Bout Us	RCA 9163
			FRED HUGHES	
5/22/65	#25	11	Oo Wee Baby, I Love You	Vee-Jay 684
9/18/65	#93	3	You Can't Take It Away	Vee-Jay 703
7/20/68	#89	6	Send My Baby Back	Wand 1182
			JIMMY HUGHES	
6/20/64	#12	14	Steal Away	Fame 6401
10/03/64	#85	4	Try Me	Fame 6403
5/21/66	#54	7	Neighbor, Neighbor	Fame 1003
2/18/67	#82	7	Why Not Tonight	Fame 1011
			RHETTA HUGHES	
1/25/67	#100	1	Light My Fire	Tetragrammaton 1513
			HUGO & LUIGI	
6/22/57	#40	6	Shenandoah Rose	Roulette 4012
5/24/58	#18	9	Cha-Hua-Hua	Roulette 4070
5/23/59	#33	10	La Plume De Ma Tante	RCA 7518
12/12/59	#43	9	Just Come Home	RCA 7639
			HULLABALLOOS	
12/05/64	#50	7	I'm Gonna Love You Too	Roulette 4587
			HUMAN BEINZ	
11/04/67	#5	17	Nobody But Me	Capitol 5990
3/16/68	#83	3	Turn On Your Love Light	Capitol 2119
			HUMAN LEAGUE	
3/06/82	#1	30	Don't You Want Me	A&M 2397
8/14/82	#77	5	Love Action (I Believe In Love)	A&M 2425
5/21/83	#7	22	(Keep Feeling) Fascination	A&M 2547
10/08/83	#28	14	Mirror Man	A&M 2587
6/16/84	#76	5	The Lebanon	A&M 2641
9/13/86	#1	18	Human	A&M 2861
12/06/86	#40	11	I Need Your Loving	A&M 2893
9/22/90	#30	14	Heart Like A Wheel	Virgin/A&M 1520
			HUMBLE PIE	
10/02/71	#70	5	I Don't Need No Doctor	A&M 1282
4/29/72	#44	10	Hot 'N' Nasty	A&M 1349
4/26/80	#67	6	Fool For A Pretty Face (Hurt By Love)	Atco 7216
			ENGELBERT HUMPERDINCK	
4/08/67	#3	15	Release Me (And Let Me Love Again)	Parrot 40011
7/01/67	#24	7	There Goes My Everything	Parrot 40015
9/16/67	#21	11	The Last Waltz	Parrot 40019
12/16/67	#24	10	Am I That Easy To Forget	Parrot 40023
5/11/68	#18	10	A Man Without Love	Parrot 40027
10/12/68	#22	12	Les Bicyclettes De Belsize	Parrot 40032

Debut Date	Peak Pos	Wks Chr	ARTIST/Song Title	Label & Number
3/01/69	#26	11	The Way It Used To Be	Parrot 40036
8/16/69	#39	8	I'm A Better Man	Parrot 40040
11/29/69	#13	13	Winter World Of Love	Parrot 40044
6/27/70	#27	8	My Marie	Parrot 40049
9/26/70	#38	9	Sweetheart	Parrot 40054
3/06/71	#37	6	When There's No You	Parrot 40059
8/21/71	#40	8	Another Time, Another Place	Parrot 40065
4/01/72	#75	4	Too Beautiful To Last	Parrot 40069
8/12/72	#86	4	In Time	Parrot 40071
10/28/72	#70	10	I Never Said Goodbye	Parrot 40072
5/12/73	#90	3	I'm Leaving You	Parrot 40073
9/22/73	#95	3	Love Is All	Parrot 40076
11/15/75	#87	4	This Is What You Mean To Me	Parrot 40085
10/16/76	#5	21	After The Lovin'	Epic 50270
12/16/78	#88	6	This Moment In Time	Epic 50632
			PAUL HUMPHREY & HIS COOL AID CHEMISTS	
3/27/71	#22	14	Cool Aid............................	Lizard 21006
7/24/71	#97	2	Funky L.A.	Lizard 1009
			PEE WEE HUNT ORCHESTRA	
9/05/53	#3	11	Oh!	Capitol 2442
			TOMMY HUNT	
8/26/61	#45	13	Human..............................	Scepter 1219
1/13/62	#88	5	The Door Is Open	Scepter 1226
9/08/62	#93	4	I Just Don't Know What To Do With Myself	Scepter 1236
11/09/63	#65	6	I'm A Witness	Scepter 1261
			IAN HUNTER	
8/18/79	#75	4	Just Another Night	Chrysalis 2352
			IVORY JOE HUNTER	
11/24/56	#12	17	Since I Met You Baby	Atlantic 1111
3/30/57	#17	12	Empty Arms.........................	Atlantic 1128
			JOHN HUNTER	
12/08/84	#30	16	Tragedy	Private I 04643
			TAB HUNTER	
1/12/57	#1	18	Young Love	Dot 15533
3/23/57	#16	10	Ninety-Nine Ways/	Dot 15548
3/23/57	#48	1	Don't Get Around Much Anymore	Dot 15548
11/01/58	#60	9	Jealous Heart	Warner Brothers 5008
1/31/59	#22	11	(I'll Be With You In) Apple Blossom Time	Warner Brothers 5032
5/16/59	#76	3	There's No Fool Like A Young Fool	Warner Brothers 5051
			FERLIN HUSKY	
2/23/57	#6	20	Gone...............................	Capitol 3628
6/22/57	#24	10	A Fallen Star	Capitol 3742
12/24/60	#11	16	Wings Of A Dove	Capitol 4406
			WILLIE HUTCH	
4/28/73	#60	7	Brother's Gonna Work It Out	Motown 1222
9/01/73	#83	4	Slick	Motown 1252
10/04/75	#48	10	Love Power	Motown 1360
			DANNY HUTTON	
9/25/65	#68	9	Roses And Rainbows	HBR 447
			BRIAN HYLAND	
7/09/60	#1	16	Itsy Bitsy Teenie Weenie Yellow Polkadot Bikini	Kapp 342
10/15/60	#79	4	(The Clickity Clack Song) Four Little Heels/	Kapp 352
11/05/60	#98	1	That's How Much	Kapp 352
8/12/61	#23	11	Let Me Belong To You	ABC-Paramount 10236
3/10/62	#28	11	Ginny Come Lately....................	ABC-Paramount 10294
6/09/62	#3	15	Sealed With A Kiss	ABC-Paramount 10336
9/29/62	#24	8	Warmed Over Kisses (Left Over Love)	ABC-Paramount 10359
12/01/62	#70	6	I May Not Live To See Tomorrow	ABC-Paramount 10374
2/16/63	#63	6	If Mary's There	ABC-Paramount 10400
6/22/63	#59	10	I'm Afraid To Go Home	ABC-Paramount 10452
3/26/66	#83	3	3000 Miles	Philips 40354
7/09/66	#29	13	The Joker Went Wild	Philips 40377
10/22/66	#42	11	Run, Run, Look And See	Philips 40405
2/11/67	#71	7	Hung Up In Your Eyes	Philips 40424
5/20/67	#84	1	Holiday For Clowns	Philips 40444
12/14/68	#53	10	Tragedy	Dot 17176

163

Debut Date	Peak Pos	Wks Chr	ARTIST/Song Title	Label & Number
			BRIAN HYLAND—*continued*	
3/29/69	#76	7	A Million To One	Dot 17222
6/14/69	#77	6	Stay And Love Me All Summer	Dot 17258
8/29/70	#3	20	Gypsy Woman	Uni 55240
2/06/71	#48	9	Lonely Teardrops	Uni 55272
7/03/71	#93	2	So Long Marianne	Uni 55287
			DICK HYMAN	
3/03/56	#7	5	Moritat (A Theme From The "Three Penny Opera")*	MGM 12149
5/17/69	#34	10	The Minotaur**	Command 4126
9/13/69	#91	3	Green Onions**	Command 4129
			*released as by **THE DICK HYMAN TRIO**	
			released as by **DICK HYMAN & HIS ELECTRIC ECLECTICS	

I

Debut Date	Peak Pos	Wks Chr	ARTIST/Song Title	Label & Number
			JANIS IAN	
5/20/67	#13	16	Society's Child	Verve Forecast 5027
12/09/67	#82	3	Insanity Comes Quietly To The Structured Mind	Verve Forecast 5072
6/21/75	#1	19	At Seventeen	Columbia 10154
11/29/75	#97	3	In The Winter	Columbia 10228
7/11/81	#79	4	Under The Covers	Columbia 02176
			IAN & SYLVIA	
8/19/67	#96	1	Lovin' Sound	MGM 13686
			ICE CUBE	
11/28/92	#48	12	Wicked	Priority 53813
3/13/93	#16	25	It Was A Good Day	Priority 53817
8/14/93	#13	18	Check Yo Self*	Priority 53830
12/18/93	#35	14	Really Doe	Priority 53843
			*released as by **ICE CUBE featuring DAS EFX**	
			ICEHOUSE	
8/08/81	#75	7	We Can Get Together	Chrysalis 2530
7/05/86	#80	8	No Promises	Chrysalis 42978
10/24/87	#20	21	Crazy	Chrysalis 43156
2/13/88	#10	23	Electric Blue	Chrysalis 43201
7/09/88	#86	5	My Obsession	Chrysalis 43240
			ICICLE WORKS	
4/28/84	#34	12	Whisper To A Scream (Birds Fly)	Arista 9155
			ICY BLUE	
12/21/91	#76	6	I Wanna Be Your Girl	Giant 19170
			IDES OF MARCH	
6/11/66	#47	9	You Wouldn't Listen	Parrot 304
3/21/70	#6	13	Vehicle	Warner Brothers 7378
6/27/70	#50	5	Superman	Warner Brothers 7403
3/20/71	#72	8	L.A. Goodbye	Warner Brothers 7466
			BILLY IDOL	
9/19/81	#81	5	Mony Mony (studio version)	Chrysalis 2543
7/10/82	#27	13	Hot In The City	Chrysalis 2605
5/21/83	#36	13	White Wedding	Chrysalis 42697
1/28/84	#29	15	Rebel Yell	Chrysalis 42762
5/05/84	#4	22	Eyes Without A Face	Chrysalis 42786
8/25/84	#34	13	Flesh For Fantasy	Chrysalis 42809
11/03/84	#53	12	Catch My Fall	Chrysalis 42840
10/04/86	#9	18	To Be A Lover	Chrysalis 43024
1/24/87	#37	11	Don't Need A Gun	Chrysalis 43087
4/25/87	#32	15	Sweet Sixteen	Chrysalis 43114
9/05/87	#1	23	Mony Mony (live version)	Chrysalis 43161
12/12/87	#57	10	Hot In The City	Chrysalis 43203
5/05/90	#2	24	Cradle Of Love	Chrysalis 23509
9/08/90	#46	10	L.A. Woman	Chrysalis 23571
			FRANK IFIELD	
9/01/62	#9	12	I Remember You	Vee-Jay 457
12/22/62	#50	6	Lovesick Blues	Vee-Jay 477
9/14/63	#53	6	I'm Confessin' (That I Love You)	Capitol 5032
11/30/63	#73	7	Please	Capitol 5089

Debut Date	Peak Pos	Wks Chr	**ARTIST**/Song Title	Label & Number
			JULIO IGLESIAS	
3/03/84	#3	22	To All The Girls I've Loved Before*	Columbia 04217
7/07/84	#12	18	All Of You**	Columbia 04507
5/14/88	#82	7	My Love***	Columbia 07781
			*released as by JULIO IGLESIAS & WILLIE NELSON	
			**released as by JULIO IGLESIAS & DIANA ROSS	
			***released as by JULIO IGLESIAS featuring STEVIE WONDER	
			IKETTES	
12/30/61	#16	15	I'm Blue (The Gong Gong Song)	Atco 6212
3/20/65	#52	6	Peaches 'N' Cream	Modern 1005
10/09/65	#70	5	I'm So Thankful	Modern 1011
			ILLUSION	
7/12/69	#30	11	Did You See Her Eyes	Steed 718
12/13/69	#55	6	Together	Steed 722
			IMPALAS	
3/07/59	#2	18	Sorry (I Ran All The Way Home)	Cub 9022
6/27/59	#89	5	Oh What A Fool	Cub 9033
			IMPRESSIONS	
6/21/58	#22	11	For Your Precious Love*	Falcon 1013
10/28/61	#17	15	Gypsy Woman	ABC-Paramount 10241
10/05/63	#4	15	It's All Right	ABC-Paramount 10487
1/11/64	#13	10	Talking About My Baby	ABC-Paramount 10511
4/04/64	#16	12	I'm So Proud	ABC-Paramount 10544
6/13/64	#10	13	Keep On Pushing	ABC-Paramount 10554
9/05/64	#14	12	You Must Believe Me	ABC-Paramount 10581
11/21/64	#8	11	Amen	ABC-Paramount 10602
2/13/65	#15	8	People Get Ready/	ABC-Paramount 10622
2/20/65	#96	1	I've Been Trying	ABC-Paramount 10622
4/03/65	#29	8	Woman's Got Soul	ABC-Paramount 10647
6/12/65	#46	6	Meeting Over Yonder	ABC-Paramount 10670
8/21/65	#47	5	I Need You	ABC-Paramount 10710
10/09/65	#70	4	Just One Kiss From You	ABC-Paramount 10725
11/27/65	#36	9	You've Been Cheatin'	ABC-Paramount 10750
2/05/66	#73	4	Since I Lost The One I Love	ABC-Paramount 10761
4/09/66	#95	1	Too Slow	ABC-Paramount 10789
8/27/66	#59	7	Can't Satisfy	ABC 10831
3/11/67	#77	3	You Always Hurt Me	ABC 10900
8/19/67	#84	6	I Can't Stay Away From You	ABC 10964
12/23/67	#11	15	We're A Winner	ABC 11022
4/13/68	#49	7	We're Rolling On	ABC 11071
7/13/68	#49	9	I Loved And I Lost	ABC 11103
9/07/68	#18	12	Fool For You	Curtom 1932
11/23/68	#82	4	Don't Cry My Love	ABC 11135
11/30/68	#27	10	This Is My Country	Curtom 1934
2/22/69	#79	3	My Deceiving Heart	Curtom 1937
4/26/69	#85	2	Seven Years	Curtom 1940
6/21/69	#21	12	Choice Of Colors	Curtom 1943
10/18/69	#67	4	Say You Love Me	Curtom 1946
5/16/70	#21	13	Check Out Your Mind	Curtom 1951
9/05/70	#47	8	(Baby) Turn On To Me	Curtom 1954
2/27/71	#50	6	Ain't Got Time	Curtom 1957
3/17/73	#90	3	Preacher Man	Curtom 1982
5/04/74	#17	16	Finally Got Myself Together	Curtom 1997
5/31/75	#63	11	Sooner Or Later	Curtom 0103
10/04/75	#62	8	Same Thing It Took	Curtom 0106
1/17/76	#79	5	Loving Power	Curtom 0110
			*released as by JERRY BUTLER and THE IMPRESSIONS	
			INCREDIBLE BONGO BAND	
6/09/73	#57	12	Bongo Rock	Pride 1015
11/10/73	#93	2	Let There Be Drums	MGM 14635
			IN CROWD	
11/26/66	#93	3	Questions And Answers	Viva 604
			INDECENT OBSESSION	
8/04/90	#27	14	Tell Me Something	MCA 79029
			INDEEP	
3/05/83	#91	6	Last Night A D.J. Saved My Life	Sound Of New York 5102

165

Debut Date	Peak Pos	Wks Chr	ARTIST/Song Title	Label & Number
			INDEPENDENTS	
5/06/72	#77	5	Just As Long As You Need Me	Wand 11245
3/24/73	#18	14	Leaving Me	Wand 11252
7/14/73	#36	9	Baby I've Been Missing You	Wand 11258
11/10/73	#69	6	It's All Over	Wand 11263
10/05/74	#63	10	Let This Be A Lesson To You	Wand 11279
			INDIGO GIRLS	
8/12/89	#59	8	Closer To Fine	Epic 68912
8/15/92	#81	2	Galileo	Epic 74326
			INDUSTRY	
11/26/83	#79	8	State Of The Nation	Capitol 5268
			INFORMATION SOCIETY	
7/23/88	#3	22	What's On Your Mind (Pure Energy)	Tommy Boy 27826
11/26/88	#10	22	Walking Away	Tommy Boy 27736
4/08/89	#66	7	Repetition	Tommy Boy 27659
8/12/89	#61	7	Lay All Your Love On Me	Tommy Boy 27534
9/29/90	#24	16	Think	Tommy Boy 19591
			JORGEN INGMANN	
1/21/61	#4	19	Apache	Atco 6184
5/27/61	#73	4	Anna	Atco 6195
			JAMES INGRAM	
8/15/81	#13	23	Just Once*	A&M 2357
1/16/82	#20	18	One Hundred Ways*	A&M 2387
5/07/83	#45	21	How Do You Keep The Music Playing**	Qwest 29618
12/17/83	#25	18	Yah Mo B There***	Qwest 29394
4/28/84	#71	10	There's No Easy Way Out	Qwest 29316
9/15/84	#21	18	What About Me****	RCA 13899
12/20/86	#4	23	Somewhere Out There*****	MCA 52973
3/17/90	#30	12	The Secret Garden******	Qwest 19992
8/11/90	#1	23	I Don't Have The Heart	Warner Brothers 19911
			*released as by QUINCY JONES featuring JAMES INGRAM	
			**released as by JAMES INGRAM and PATTI AUSTIN	
			***released as by JAMES INGRAM with MICHAEL McDONALD	
			****released as by KENNY ROGERS with KIM CARNES and JAMES INGRAM	
			*****released as by LINDA RONSTADT and JAMES INGRAM	
			******released as by QUINCY JONES/AL B. SURE!/JAMES INGRAM/ EL DeBARGE/BARRY WHITE	
			LUTHER INGRAM	
1/03/70	#47	6	My Honey And Me	KoKo 2104
5/23/70	#45	9	Ain't That Lovin' You	KoKo 2105
10/17/70	#97	1	To The Other Man	KoKo 2106
5/15/71	#88	3	Be Good To My Baby	KoKo 2107
2/05/72	#72	4	Missing You/	KoKo 2110
3/04/72	#57	9	You Were Made For Me	KoKo 2110
5/20/72	#3	18	(If Loving You Is Wrong) I Don't Want To Be Right	KoKo 2111
11/25/72	#32	12	I'll Be Your Shelter (In Time Of Storm)	KoKo 2113
3/24/73	#64	8	Always	KoKo 2115
			AUTRY INMAN	
11/16/68	#51	5	Ballad Of Two Brothers	Epic 10389
			INMATES	
12/08/79	#52	10	Dirty Water	Polydor 2032
2/16/80	#95	3	The Walk	Polydor 2058
			INNER CIRCLE	
5/08/93	#8	25	Bad Boys	Big Beat 98426
8/14/93	#12	33	Sweat (A La La La La Song)	Big Beat 98429
			INNER CITY	
3/04/89	#64	6	Good Life	Virgin 99236
3/10/90	#77	6	Whatcha Gonna Do With My Lovin'	Virgin 98999
			INNOCENCE	
11/19/66	#47	11	There's Got To Be A Word!	Kama Sutra 214
2/25/67	#75	6	Mairzy Doats	Kama Sutra 222

Debut Date	Peak Pos	Wks Chr	ARTIST/Song Title	Label & Number
			INNOCENTS	
8/27/60	#37	11	Honest I Do	Indigo 105
12/03/60	#33	10	Gee Whiz	Indigo 111
			INSTANT FUNK	
2/24/79	#22	15	I Got My Mind Made Up	Salsoul 2078
			INSTRUMENTALS	
7/12/58	#64	4	Are You Nervous	Hanover 4502
			INTERPRETATIONS	
2/08/69	#92	1	Snap Out	Bell 757
			INTRIGUES	
7/26/69	#37	13	In A Moment	Yew 1001
11/29/69	#68	8	I'm Gonna Love You	Yew 1002
6/26/71	#82	3	The Language Of Love	Yew 1012
			INTRO	
9/25/93	#27	22	Come Inside	Atlantic 87317
			INTRUDERS (New Jersey instrumental group)	
2/14/59	#78	8	Fried Eggs	Fame 101
			INTRUDERS (Philadelphia vocal group)	
7/16/66	#91	4	United	Gamble 201
4/29/67	#57	10	Together	Gamble 205
9/23/67	#85	4	Baby I'm Lonely/	Gamble 209
12/09/67	#95	2	A Love That's Real	Gamble 209
3/23/68	#5	14	Cowboys To Girls	Gamble 214
7/06/68	#41	10	(Love Is Like) A Baseball Game	Gamble 217
11/09/68	#57	6	Slow Drag	Gamble 221
6/07/69	#96	2	Lollipop (I Like You)	Gamble 231
8/23/69	#52	9	Sad Girl	Gamble 235
6/20/70	#48	7	When We Get Married	Gamble 4004
10/24/70	#87	6	This Is My Love Song	Gamble 4007
3/27/71	#74	5	I'm Girl Scoutin'	Gamble 4009
7/10/71	#88	3	Pray For Me	Gamble 4014
10/23/71	#86	3	I Bet He Don't Love You	Gamble 4016
6/09/73	#25	10	I'll Always Love My Mama (Part 1)	Gamble 2506
11/24/73	#80	4	I Wanna Know Your Name	Gamble 2508
			INVISIBLE MAN'S BAND	
5/24/80	#59	9	All Night Thing	Mango 103
			INVITATIONS	
7/03/65	#98	1	Hallelujah	DynoVoice 206
			INXS	
3/26/83	#30	15	The One Thing	Atco 99905
5/05/84	#62	8	Original Sin	Atco 99766
11/23/85	#80	5	This Time	Atlantic 89497
1/18/86	#4	23	What You Need	Atlantic 89460
5/10/86	#54	11	Listen Like Thieves	Atlantic 89429
8/02/86	#87	3	Kiss The Dirt	Atlantic 89418
6/20/87	#48	14	Good Times*	Atlantic 89237
10/24/87	#1	27	Need You Tonight	Atlantic 89188
2/13/88	#2	20	Devil Inside	Atlantic 89144
5/14/88	#3	20	New Sensation	Atlantic 89080
8/13/88	#8	20	Never Tear Us Apart	Atlantic 89038
9/08/90	#5	14	Suicide Blonde	Atlantic 87860
11/24/90	#7	24	Disappear	Atlantic 87784
4/06/91	#36	13	Bitter Tears	Atlantic 87760
11/23/91	#84	5	Shining Star	Atlantic 87576
8/29/92	#23	16	Not Enough Time	Atlantic 87437
2/27/93	#45	15	Beautiful Girl	Atlantic 87383
			*released as by INXS and JIMMY BARNES	
			JOYCE "FENDERELLA" IRBY	
2/24/90	#70	5	I'll Be There	Motown 2032
			DONNIE IRIS	
12/13/80	#22	22	Ah! Leah!	MCA 51025
10/31/81	#65	7	Sweet Merilee	MCA 51198
12/19/81	#36	14	Love Is Like A Rock	MCA 51223
4/03/82	#27	14	My Girl	MCA 52031
10/23/82	#63	7	Tough World	MCA 52127
7/09/83	#78	5	Do You Compute	MCA 52230

Debut Date	Peak Pos	Wks Chr	ARTIST/Song Title	Label & Number
			IRISH ROVERS	
3/16/68	#6	14	The Unicorn	Decca 32254
6/15/68	#64	4	Whiskey On Sunday	Decca 32333
9/14/68	#78	6	Biplane Evermore	Decca 32371
2/21/81	#37	17	Wasn't That A Party*	Epic 51007
			*released as by THE ROVERS	
			IRON BUTTERFLY	
8/24/68	#56	9	In-A-Gadda-Da-Vida	Atco 6606
5/10/69	#94	1	In-A-Gadda-Da-Vida	Atco 6606
2/22/69	#68	5	Soul Experience	Atco 6647
7/19/69	#100	1	In The Time Of Our Lives	Atco 6676
10/31/70	#98	3	Easy Rider	Atco 6782
			IRONHORSE	
3/17/79	#42	9	Sweet Lui-Louise	Scotti Brothers 406
			BIG DEE IRWIN	
5/25/63	#21	11	Swinging On A Star*	Dimension 1010
			*released as by BIG DEE IRWIN with LITTLE EVA	
			RUSS IRWIN	
9/14/91	#38	19	My Heart Belongs To You	SBK 07363
			CHRIS ISAAK	
12/01/90	#16	24	Wicked Game	Reprise 19704
4/13/91	#79	6	Don't Make Me Dream About You	Reprise 19357
			ISLANDERS	
10/03/59	#16	14	The Enchanted Sea	Mayflower 16
			ISLEY BROTHERS	
9/19/59	#28	11	Shout (Part 1)	RCA 7588
6/02/62	#7	21	Twist And Shout	Wand 124
9/22/62	#54	7	Twistin' With Linda	Wand 127
2/19/66	#15	12	This Old Heart Of Mine	Tamla 54128
5/21/66	#72	4	Take Some Time Out For Love	Tamla 54133
7/23/66	#55	4	I Guess I'll Always Love You	Tamla 54135
4/29/67	#96	2	Got To Have You Back	Tamla 54146
4/20/68	#97	1	Take Me In Your Arms	Tamla 54164
3/15/69	#2	12	It's Your Thing	T-Neck 901
5/31/69	#17	10	I Turned You On	T-Neck 902
8/30/69	#43	4	Black Berries (Part 1)	T-Neck 906
9/27/69	#56	4	Was It Good To You	T-Neck 908
2/07/70	#55	6	Keep On Doin'	T-Neck 914
7/25/70	#69	4	Girls Will Be Girls, Boys Will Be Boys	T-Neck 921
10/24/70	#93	3	Get Into Something	T-Neck 924
1/02/71	#53	9	Freedom	T-Neck 927
3/27/71	#76	4	Warpath	T-Neck 929
6/19/71	#10	12	Love The One You're With	T-Neck 930
9/25/71	#39	7	Spill The Wine	T-Neck 932
11/27/71	#57	5	Lay Lady Lay	T-Neck 933
3/18/72	#36	10	Lay Away	T-Neck 934
7/01/72	#23	14	Pop That Thing	T-Neck 935
10/28/72	#43	8	Work To Do	T-Neck 936
7/28/73	#6	17	That Lady (Part 1)	T-Neck 2251
1/05/74	#63	6	What It Comes Down To	T-Neck 2252
3/30/74	#71	6	Summer Breeze	T-Neck 2253
8/17/74	#62	13	Live It Up (Part 1)	T-Neck 2254
1/11/75	#65	4	Midnight Sky	T-Neck 2255
6/14/75	#6	18	Fight The Power (Part 1)	T-Neck 2256
11/08/75	#26	13	For The Love Of You	T-Neck 2259
6/05/76	#62	5	Who Loves You Better	T-Neck 2260
8/28/76	#63	12	Harvest For The World	T-Neck 2261
5/21/77	#96	2	The Pride (Part 1)	T-Neck 2262
6/18/77	#60	8	Livin' In The Life	T-Neck 2264
5/06/78	#69	6	Take Me To The Next Phase	T-Neck 2278
5/05/79	#76	5	I Wanna Be With You (Part 1)	T-Neck 2279
3/29/80	#40	13	Don't Say Goodnight (Parts 1 & 2)	T-Neck 2290
4/18/81	#62	6	Hurry Up And Wait	T-Neck 02033
			ISLEY, JASPER, ISLEY	
2/16/85	#60	9	Kiss And Tell	CBS Associated 04741
12/21/85	#54	12	Caravan Of Love	CBS Associated 05611

Debut Date	Peak Pos	Wks Chr	ARTIST/Song Title	Label & Number
			BURL IVES	
12/16/61	#7	15	A Little Bitty Tear	Decca 31330
3/31/62	#11	13	Funny Way Of Laughin'	Decca 31371
7/07/62	#22	12	Call Me Mr. In-Between	Decca 31405
11/03/62	#39	8	Mary Ann Regrets	Decca 31433
7/20/63	#55	8	This Is All I Ask	Decca 31518
1/04/64	#91	4	True Love Goes On And On	Decca 31571
8/29/64	#62	8	Pearly Shells	Decca 31659
			CHET "POISON" IVEY and HIS FABULOUS AVENGERS	
1/01/69	#100	1	Shake A Poo Poo	Tangerine 989
			IVEYS (see BADFINGER)	
			IVY LEAGUE	
9/11/65	#58	6	Tossing & Turning	Cameo 377
			IVY THREE	
8/06/60	#10	13	Yogi	Shell 720

J

			SUSAN JACKS	
4/21/73	#70	5	You Don't Know What Love Is	London 183
3/15/75	#95	2	You're A Part Of Me	Mercury 73649
			TERRY JACKS	
1/12/74	#1	18	Seasons In The Sun	Bell 45432
6/01/74	#45	7	If You Go Away	Bell 45467
11/23/74	#92	4	Rock 'N' Roll (I Gave You The Best Years Of My Life) . .	Bell 45606
5/31/75	#83	5	Christina	Private Stock 45023
6/25/76	#74	5	In My Father's Footsteps	Private Stock 45094
			ALAN JACKSON	
7/17/93	#45	22	Chattahoochee	Arista 2573
			CHUCK JACKSON	
2/11/61	#24	12	I Don't Want To Cry	Wand 106
5/06/61	#85	4	In Real Life	Wand 108
8/05/61	#41	13	I Wake Up Crying	Wand 110
4/14/62	#12	17	Any Day Now (My Wild Beautiful Bird)	Wand 122
8/11/62	#48	10	I Keep Forgettin'	Wand 126
1/26/63	#43	12	Tell Him I'm Not Home	Wand 132
10/19/63	#60	9	Any Other Way	Wand 141
3/07/64	#72	6	Hand It Over	Wand 149
5/16/64	#50	10	Beg Me	Wand 154
11/14/64	#42	9	Since I Don't Have You	Wand 169
4/03/65	#88	4	I Need You	Wand 179
4/24/65	#45	9	Something You Got*	Wand 181
7/31/65	#50	8	If I Didn't Love You	Wand 188
8/28/65	#85	3	Can't Let You Out Of My Sight*	Wand 191
2/18/67	#78	5	Hold On I'm Coming*	Wand 1148
4/29/67	#87	5	Daddy's Home*	Wand 1155
11/04/67	#86	7	Shame On Me	Wand 1166
3/23/68	#92	3	(You Can't Let The Boy Overpower) The Man In You . . .	Motown 1118
			*released as by CHUCK JACKSON & MAXINE BROWN	
			DEON JACKSON	
1/29/66	#12	13	Love Makes The World Go Round	Carla 2526
5/07/66	#83	3	Love Takes A Long Time Growing	Carla 2527
			EARNEST JACKSON	
6/09/73	#80	5	Love And Happiness	Stone 200
			FREDDIE JACKSON	
6/08/85	#19	18	Rock Me Tonight (For Old Times Sake)	Capitol 5459
9/07/85	#14	21	You Are My Lady	Capitol 5495
12/14/85	#32	17	He'll Never Love You (Like I Do)	Capitol 5535
11/22/86	#74	11	Tasty Love	Capitol 5616
2/07/87	#77	9	Have You Ever Loved Somebody	Capitol 5661
6/27/87	#35	15	Jam Tonight	Capitol 44037
7/30/88	#67	11	Nice 'N' Slow	Capitol 44171
			JANET JACKSON	
12/18/82	#76	6	Young Love	A&M 2440
2/26/83	#73	4	Come Give Your Love To Me	A&M 2522
2/22/86	#5	21	What Have You Done For Me Lately	A&M 2812

Debut Date	Peak Pos	Wks Chr	ARTIST/Song Title	Label & Number
			JANET JACKSON—*continued*	
5/17/86	#3	17	Nasty	A&M 2830
8/09/86	#1	20	When I Think Of You	A&M 2855
11/01/86	#5	21	Control	A&M 2877
1/24/87	#3	19	Let's Wait A While	A&M 2906
5/23/87	#13	20	The Pleasure Principle	A&M 2927
9/02/89	#1	22	Miss You Much	A&M 1445
11/11/89	#3	18	Rhythm Nation	A&M 1455
1/20/90	#1	19	Escapade	A&M 1490
4/07/90	#4	20	Alright	A&M 1479
7/07/90	#1	18	Come Back To Me	A&M 1475
9/08/90	#2	16	Black Cat	A&M 1477
11/24/90	#1	22	Love Will Never Do (Without You)	A&M 1538
2/16/91	#8	7	State Of The World	A&M album cut
6/06/92	#9	22	The Best Things In Life Are Free*	Perspective 0010
5/01/93	#1	27	That's The Way Love Goes	Virgin 12650
7/24/93	#2	35	If	Virgin 12676
10/30/93	#1	29	Again	Virgin 38404
			***released as by LUTHER VANDROSS and JANET JACKSON**	
			JERMAINE JACKSON	
12/16/72	#7	17	Daddy's Home	Motown 1216
10/06/73	#89	2	You're In Good Hands	Motown 1244
11/06/76	#66	7	Let's Be Young Tonight	Motown 1401
3/22/80	#9	25	Let's Get Serious	Motown 1469
7/19/80	#46	12	You're Supposed To Keep Your Love For Me	Motown 1490
4/25/81	#55	10	You Like Me Don't You	Motown 1503
10/31/81	#68	11	I'm Just Too Shy	Motown 1525
7/24/82	#22	17	Let Me Tickle Your Fancy	Motown 1628
7/21/84	#20	16	Dynamite	Arista 9190
10/27/84	#12	20	Do What You Do	Arista 9279
2/16/85	#48	10	When The Rain Begins To Fall*	Curb 52521
6/08/85	#60	8	(Closest Thing To) Perfect	Arista 9356
2/22/86	#15	17	I Think It's Love	Arista 9444
7/12/86	#66	5	Do You Remember Me?	Arista 9502
11/18/89	#78	10	Don't Take It Personal	Arista 9875
			***released as by JERMAINE JACKSON/PIA ZADORA**	
			J.J. JACKSON	
10/01/66	#26	12	But It's Alright	Calla 119
12/31/66	#74	4	I Dig Girls	Calla 125
7/01/67	#82	4	Four Walls	Calla 133
5/31/69	#67	6	But It's Alright	Warner Brothers 7276
			JOE JACKSON	
5/12/79	#21	22	Is She Really Going Out With Him?	A&M 2132
8/21/82	#5	27	Steppin' Out	A&M 2428
1/15/83	#17	16	Breaking Us In Two	A&M 2510
4/21/84	#19	18	You Can't Get What You Want	A&M 2628
7/21/84	#61	9	Happy Ending	A&M 2635
			LA TOYA JACKSON	
5/05/84	#57	11	Heart Don't Lie	Private I 04439
			MICHAEL JACKSON (see also THE JACKSON FIVE)	
10/30/71	#1	14	Got To Be There	Motown 1191
3/04/72	#1	14	Rockin' Robin	Motown 1197
5/20/72	#7	12	I Wanna Be Where You Are	Motown 1202
8/05/72	#2	16	Ben	Motown 1207
5/05/73	#37	7	With A Child's Heart	Motown 1218
3/01/75	#57	7	We're Almost There	Motown 1341
5/17/75	#30	13	Just A Little Bit Of You	Motown 1349
9/02/78	#36	14	Ease On Down The Road*	MCA 40947
8/11/79	#1	20	Don't Stop 'Til You Get Enough	Epic 50742
11/03/79	#1	27	Rock With You	Epic 50797
2/16/80	#11	17	Off The Wall	Epic 50838
4/12/80	#14	20	She's Out Of My Life	Epic 50871
4/18/81	#72	8	One Day In Your LIfe	Motown 1512
11/06/82	#3	18	This Girl Is Mine**	Epic 03288
1/22/83	#1	27	Billie Jean	Epic 03509
2/26/83	#1	26	Beat It	Epic 03759
5/28/83	#6	17	Wanna Be Startin' Somethin'	Epic 03914
7/23/83	#10	16	Human Nature	Epic 04026
10/08/83	#15	17	P.Y.T. (Pretty Young Thing)	Epic 04165

Debut Date	Peak Pos	Wks Chr	ARTIST/Song Title	Label & Number
10/15/83	#1	27	Say, Say, Say***	Columbia 04168
2/04/84	#4	18	Thriller	Epic 04364
5/26/84	#34	12	Farewell My Summer Love	Motown 1739
8/08/87	#1	18	I Just Can't Stop Loving You	Epic 07253
9/19/87	#1	20	Bad	Epic 07418
11/21/87	#1	21	The Way You Make Me Feel	Epic 07645
2/06/88	#1	20	Man In The Mirror	Epic 07668
5/07/88	#1	18	Dirty Diana	Epic 07739
5/07/88	#84	5	Get It****	Motown 1930
7/23/88	#12	14	Another Part Of Me	Epic 07962
11/12/88	#7	18	Smooth Criminal	Epic 08044
11/23/91	#1	22	Black Or White	Epic 74100
1/25/92	#1	22	Remember The Time	Epic 74200
5/02/92	#6	16	In The Closet	Epic 74266
7/11/92	#21	14	Jam	Epic 74333
12/19/92	#26	25	Heal The World	Epic 74790
4/03/93	#5	16	Who Is It	Epic 74406
7/24/93	#6	28	Will You Be There	Epic 77060

*released as by MICHAEL JACKSON/DIANA ROSS
**released as by MICHAEL JACKSON/PAUL McCARTNEY
***released as by PAUL McCARTNEY and MICHAEL JACKSON
****released as by STEVIE WONDER & MICHAEL JACKSON

MICK JACKSON

Debut Date	Peak Pos	Wks Chr	ARTIST/Song Title	Label & Number
8/19/78	#64	6	Blame It On The Boogie	Atco 7091

MILLIE JACKSON

Debut Date	Peak Pos	Wks Chr	ARTIST/Song Title	Label & Number
3/25/72	#19	14	Ask Me What You Want	Spring 123
7/29/72	#34	11	My Man, A Sweet Man	Spring 127
12/02/72	#69	7	I Miss You Baby	Spring 131
4/07/73	#80	5	Breakaway	Spring 134
8/25/73	#18	13	Hurts So Good	Spring 139
6/15/74	#56	7	How Do You Feel The Morning After	Spring 147
1/25/75	#48	7	If Loving You Is Wrong I Don't Want To Be Right	Spring 155
9/27/75	#74	6	Leftovers	Spring 161
11/19/77	#35	10	If You're Not Back In Love By Monday	Spring 175
4/08/78	#88	4	All The Way Lover	Spring 179

REBBIE JACKSON

Debut Date	Peak Pos	Wks Chr	ARTIST/Song Title	Label & Number
10/06/84	#15	22	Centipede	Columbia 04547

STONEWALL JACKSON

Debut Date	Peak Pos	Wks Chr	ARTIST/Song Title	Label & Number
5/23/59	#3	17	Waterloo	Columbia 41393
10/17/59	#79	5	Igmoo (The Pride Of Central High)	Columbia 41488
1/09/60	#86	7	Mary Don't You Weep	Columbia 41533

WALTER JACKSON

Debut Date	Peak Pos	Wks Chr	ARTIST/Song Title	Label & Number
11/07/64	#60	9	It's All Over	Okeh 7204
1/30/65	#92	6	Suddenly I'm All Alone	Okeh 7215
6/05/65	#90	4	Welcome Home	Okeh 7219
5/21/66	#73	8	It's An Uphill Climb To The Bottom	Okeh 7247
10/29/66	#76	5	A Corner In The Sun	Okeh 7260
4/08/67	#88	4	Speak Her Name	Okeh 7272
7/01/67	#96	2	Deep In The Heart Of Harlem	Okeh 7285

WANDA JACKSON

Debut Date	Peak Pos	Wks Chr	ARTIST/Song Title	Label & Number
8/13/60	#37	14	Let's Have A Party	Capitol 4397
6/17/61	#43	12	Right Or Wrong	Capitol 4553
10/21/61	#29	12	In The Middle Of A Heartache	Capitol 4635
5/19/62	#70	5	If I Cried Every Time You Hurt Me	Capitol 4723

JACKSON FIVE

Debut Date	Peak Pos	Wks Chr	ARTIST/Song Title	Label & Number
11/15/69	#1	17	I Want You Back	Motown 1157
3/14/70	#1	13	ABC	Motown 1163
5/23/70	#1	14	The Love You Save	Motown 1166
9/19/70	#1	16	I'll Be There	Motown 1171
12/19/70	#51	2	Santa Claus Is Comin' To Town	Motown 1174
1/23/71	#1	11	Mama's Pearl	Motown 1177
4/03/71	#1	12	Never Can Say Goodbye	Motown 1179
7/10/71	#16	10	Maybe Tomorrow	Motown 1186
12/11/71	#6	12	Sugar Daddy	Motown 1194
4/22/72	#5	10	Little Bitty Pretty One	Motown 1199
7/08/72	#15	10	Lookin' Through The Windows	Motown 1205
10/28/72	#12	11	Corner Of The Sky	Motown 1214

Debut Date	Peak Pos	Wks Chr	ARTIST/Song Title	Label & Number
			JACKSON FIVE—*continued*	
3/17/73	#21	8	Hallelujah Day	Motown 1224
8/25/73	#24	11	Get It Together	Motown 1277
3/09/74	#1	17	Dancing Machine	Motown 1286
10/19/74	#30	10	Whatever You Got, I Want	Motown 1308
1/18/75	#18	13	I Am Love	Motown 1310
7/12/75	#55	8	Forever Came Today	Motown 1356
			JACKSONS	
11/13/76	#4	22	Enjoy Yourself	Epic 50289
4/09/77	#45	9	Show You The Way To Go	Epic 50350
10/08/77	#55	9	Goin' Places	Epic 50454
11/04/78	#63	7	Blame It On The Boogie	Epic 50595
2/17/79	#5	24	Shake Your Body (Down To The Ground)	Epic 50656
9/27/80	#10	20	Lovely One	Epic 50938
12/06/80	#21	17	Heartbreak Hotel	Epic 50959
4/25/81	#75	5	Can You Feel It	Epic 01032
6/27/81	#76	5	Walk Right Now	Epic 02132
6/30/84	#3	16	State Of Shock	Epic 04503
8/18/84	#16	13	Torture	Epic 04575
10/27/84	#46	8	Body	Epic 04673
6/03/89	#72	7	Nothin (That Compares 2 U)	Epic 68688
			DICK JACOBS	
10/20/56	#21	11	Petticoats Of Portugal	Coral 61724
8/10/57	#12	6	Fascination	Coral 61864
			HANK JACOBS	
2/08/64	#63	4	So Far Away	Sue 795
			JADE	
7/18/92	#16	28	I Wanna Love You	Giant 18950
12/26/92	#4	40	Don't Walk Away	Giant 18686
6/19/93	#19	23	One Woman	Giant 18606
11/27/93	#67	13	Looking For Mr. Do Right	Giant 18429
			MICK JAGGER	
2/09/85	#10	15	Just Another Night	Columbia 04743
4/27/85	#36	12	Lucky In Love	Columbia 04893
8/31/85	#8	16	Dancing In The Street*	EMI America 8288
8/02/86	#52	9	Ruthless People	Epic 06211
9/12/87	#37	11	Let's Work	Columbia 07306
11/28/87	#79	8	Throwaway	Columbia 07653
2/13/93	#57	10	Sweet Thing	Atlantic 87410
			***released as by MICK JAGGER/DAVID BOWIE**	
			JAGGERZ	
1/24/70	#2	14	The Rapper	Kama Sutra 502
5/09/70	#56	4	I Call My Baby Candy	Kama Sutra 509
			JAGS	
5/17/80	#81	4	Back Of My Hand (I've Got Your Number)	Island 49202
			ETTA JAMES	
4/23/60	#23	18	All I Could Do Was Cry	Argo 5359
8/06/60	#32	13	If I Can't Have You*	Chess 1760
9/17/60	#25	15	My Dearest Darling	Argo 5368
1/07/61	#82	3	Spoonful*	Chess 1771
1/21/61	#30	10	At Last	Argo 5380
3/18/61	#25	12	Trust In Me	Argo 5385
6/03/61	#51	9	Fool That I Am/	Argo 5390
6/03/61	#63	8	Dream	Argo 5390
8/26/61	#57	8	Don't Cry Baby	Argo 5393
11/04/61	#60	9	It's Too Soon To Know	Argo 5402
2/10/62	#20	15	Something's Got A Hold On Me	Argo 5409
7/28/62	#22	10	Stop The Wedding	Argo 5418
10/13/62	#67	8	Next Door To The Blues	Argo 5424
12/29/62	#68	8	Would It Make Any Difference To You	Argo 5430
4/13/63	#24	13	Pushover	Argo 5437
8/31/63	#91	2	Pay Back	Argo 5445
10/12/63	#90	2	Two Sides (To Every Story)	Argo 5452
4/11/64	#84	8	Loving You More Every Day	Argo 5465
12/04/65	#94	2	Do I Make Myself Clear**	Cadet 5519
7/23/66	#93	1	In The Basement (Part 1)**	Cadet 5539
11/18/67	#27	14	Tell Mama	Cadet 5578

Debut Date	Peak Pos	Wks Chr	ARTIST/Song Title	Label & Number
3/02/68	#37	9	Security	Cadet 5594
5/18/68	#52	6	I Got You Babe	Cadet 5606
1/25/69	#79	3	Almost Persuaded	Cadet 5630
10/03/70	#76	6	Losers Weepers (Part 1)	Cadet 5676
10/06/73	#70	6	All The Way Down	Chess 2144
			*released as by ETTA and HARVEY (Etta James and Harvey Fuqua)	
			**released as by ETTA JAMES & SUGAR PIE DeSANTO	
			JONI JAMES	
11/22/52	#1	17	Why Don't You Believe Me	MGM 5903
1/31/53	#3	9	Have You Heard	MGM 11390
3/14/53	#3	14	Your Cheatin' Heart	MGM 11426
3/12/55	#5	11	How Important Can It Be?	MGM 11919
11/19/55	#9	2	You Are My Love	MGM 12066
8/04/56	#30	3	Give Us This Day	MGM 12288
9/27/58	#21	16	There Goes My Heart	MGM 12706
1/24/59	#28	11	There Must Be A Way	MGM 12746
4/11/59	#45	7	I Still Get A Thrill (Thinking Of You)	MGM 12779
7/25/59	#66	6	I Still Get Jealous	MGM 12807
12/19/59	#54	10	Little Things Mean A Lot	MGM 12849
1/21/61	#54	3	My Last Date (With You)	MGM 12933
			RICK JAMES	
7/01/78	#15	19	You And I	Gordy 7156
11/11/78	#53	7	Mary Jane	Gordy 7162
5/19/79	#74	6	Bustin' Out	Gordy 7167
5/23/81	#34	18	Give It To Me Baby	Gordy 7197
8/08/81	#17	25	Super Freak (Part 1)	Gordy 7205
5/08/82	#67	6	Standing On The Top (Part 1)*	Gordy 1616
5/29/82	#56	9	Dance Wit' Me (Part 1)	Gordy 1619
7/23/83	#38	16	Cold Blooded	Gordy 1687
12/10/83	#45	12	Ebony Eyes**	Gordy 1714
7/14/84	#39	14	17	Gordy 1730
3/30/85	#53	8	Can't Stop	Gordy 1776
			*released as by THE TEMPTATIONS featuring RICK JAMES	
			**released as by RICK JAMES featuring SMOKEY ROBINSON	
			SONNY JAMES	
12/29/56	#1	19	Young Love	Capitol 3602
3/30/57	#31	7	First Date, First Kiss, First Love	Capitol 3674
7/06/57	#52	1	Lovesick Blues	Capitol 3734
12/28/57	#42	4	Uh-Huh--mm	Capitol 3840
4/03/60	#79	4	Jenny Lou	NRC 050
7/13/63	#90	8	The Minute You're Gone	Capitol 4969
1/02/65	#96	2	You're The Only World I Know	Capitol 5280
1/25/69	#97	2	Only The Lonely	Capitol 2370
5/17/69	#79	4	Running Bear	Capitol 2486
10/11/69	#83	2	Since I Met You	Capitol 2595
2/07/70	#93	2	It's Just A Matter Of Time	Capitol 2700
10/17/70	#91	2	Endlessly	Capitol 2914
8/14/71	#97	1	Bright Lights, Big City	Capitol 3114
			TOMMY JAMES and THE SHONDELLS	
5/28/66	#1	14	Hanky Panky	Roulette 4686
8/06/66	#15	9	Say I Am (What I Am)	Roulette 4695
11/05/66	#27	10	It's Only Love	Roulette 4710
2/11/67	#3	16	I Think We're Alone Now	Roulette 4720
4/29/67	#10	9	Mirage	Roulette 4736
7/08/67	#30	7	I Like The Way	Roulette 4756
8/26/67	#14	9	Gettin' Together	Roulette 4762
11/04/67	#37	5	Out Of The Blue	Roulette 4775
1/27/68	#38	6	Get Out Now	Roulette 7000
3/30/68	#3	16	Mony Mony	Roulette 7008
7/13/68	#38	8	Somebody Cares	Roulette 7016
10/19/68	#24	9	Do Something To Me	Roulette 7024
12/14/68	#1	14	Crimson And Clover	Roulette 7028
3/22/69	#10	11	Sweet Cherry Wine	Roulette 7039
6/07/69	#2	15	Crystal Blue Persuasion	Roulette 7050
10/04/69	#11	8	Ball Of Fire	Roulette 7060
12/13/69	#19	8	She	Roulette 7066
2/14/70	#28	9	Gotta Get Back To You	Roulette 7071
5/16/70	#36	8	Come To Me	Roulette 7076

Debut Date	Peak Pos	Wks Chr	ARTIST/Song Title	Label & Number
			TOMMY JAMES and THE SHONDELLS—*continued*	
8/01/70	#45	6	Ball And Chain*	Roulette 7084
12/26/70	#63	5	Church Street Soul Revival*	Roulette 7093
3/20/71	#90	2	Adrienne*	Roulette 7100
6/05/71	#2	15	Draggin' The Line*	Roulette 7103
9/18/71	#23	8	I'm Comin' Home*	Roulette 7110
11/20/71	#25	9	Nothing To Hide*	Roulette 7114
2/12/72	#58	4	Tell 'Em Willie Boy's A'Comin'*	Roulette 7119
5/12/72	#48	9	Cat's Eye In The Window*	Roulette 7126
7/29/72	#50	9	Love Song*	Roulette 7130
10/21/72	#75	4	Celebration*	Roulette 7135
2/10/73	#40	7	Boo, Boo, Don't 'Cha Be Blue*	Roulette 7140
10/20/73	#94	2	Calico*	Roulette 7147
1/19/80	#19	17	Three Times In Love*	Millennium 11785
5/02/81	#68	7	You're So Easy To Love*	Millennium 11802
			*released as by **TOMMY JAMES**	
			JAMES BOYS	
9/07/68	#97	5	The Mule	Phil-L.A. Of Soul 316
			JAMES GANG	
9/05/70	#60	8	Funk #49	ABC 11272
5/22/71	#29	9	Walk Away	ABC 11301
9/25/71	#51	6	Midnight Man	ABC 11312
1/19/74	#45	11	Must Be Love	Atco 6953
5/11/74	#82	5	Standing In The Rain	Atco 6966
			CODY JAMESON	
3/19/77	#71	5	Brooklyn	Atco 7073
			NICK JAMESON	
8/16/86	#81	5	Weatherman	Motown 1853
			JAMESTOWN MASSACRE	
7/29/72	#78	7	Summer Sun	Warner Brothers 7603
			JAMIES	
8/23/58	#26	10	Summertime, Summertime	Epic 9281
6/23/62	#58	9	Summertime, Summertime	Epic 9281
			JAN & ARNIE	
5/17/58	#3	13	Jennie Lee	Arwin 108
			JAN & DEAN	
7/11/59	#7	15	Baby Talk	Dore 522
10/24/59	#80	5	There's A Girl	Dore 531
2/13/60	#88	2	Clementine	Dore 539
7/30/60	#39	10	We Go Together	Dore 555
7/15/61	#16	6	Heart And Soul	Challenge 9111
6/02/62	#83	6	Tennessee	Liberty 55454
3/02/63	#26	13	Linda	Liberty 55531
6/08/63	#1	15	Surf City	Liberty 55580
9/07/63	#10	10	Honolulu Lulu	Liberty 55613
11/30/63	#10	12	Drag City	Liberty 55641
3/07/64	#9	14	Dead Man's Curve/	Liberty 55672
3/07/64	#26	10	The New Girl In School	Liberty 55672
6/27/64	#5	12	The Little Old Lady (From Pasadena)	Liberty 55704
9/19/64	#23	9	Ride The Wild Surf/	Liberty 55724
9/19/64	#50	5	The Anaheim, Azusa & Cucamonga Sewing Circle, Book Review And Timing Association	Liberty 55724
10/31/64	#28	8	Sidewalk Surfin'	Liberty 55727
2/27/65	#50	6	From All Over The World	Liberty 55766
5/29/65	#42	8	You Really Know How To Hurt A Guy	Liberty 55792
10/09/65	#39	9	I Found A Girl	Liberty 55833
2/12/66	#60	3	Batman	Liberty 55860
5/28/66	#24	10	Popsicle	Liberty 55886
9/03/66	#73	4	Fiddle Around	Liberty 55905
			JAN and KJELD	
6/18/60	#62	7	Banjo Boy	Kapp 335
			HORST JANKOWSKI	
5/01/65	#9	15	A Walk In The Black Forest	Mercury 72425
8/07/65	#66	6	Simple Gimple	Mercury 72465
			JARMELS	
7/22/61	#13	15	A Little Bit Of Soap	Laurie 3098

174

Debut Date	Peak Pos	Wks Chr	**ARTIST**/Song Title	Label & Number
			AL JARREAU	
8/01/81	#13	24	We're In This Love Together	Warner Brothers 49746
11/28/81	#44	14	Breakin' Away	Warner Brothers 49842
4/24/82	#77	4	Teach Me Tonight	Warner Brothers 50032
3/19/83	#25	14	Mornin'*	Warner Brothers 29720
7/09/83	#68	6	Boogie Down*	Warner Brothers 29624
9/17/83	#73	6	Trouble In Paradise*	Warner Brothers 29501
10/20/84	#84	4	After All	Warner Brothers 29262
6/06/87	#33	13	Moonlighting	MCA 53124
			*released as by JARREAU	
			CAROL JARVIS	
9/07/57	#44	4	Rebel	Dot 15586
			JAYA	
2/17/90	#90	3	If You Leave Me Now	LMR 77000
			JAY & THE AMERICANS	
3/17/62	#4	16	She Cried	United Artists 415
7/21/62	#83	3	This Is It	United Artists 479
8/17/63	#28	12	Only In America	United Artists 626
11/30/63	#82	7	Come Dance With Me	United Artists 669
9/19/64	#4	15	Come A Little Bit Closer	United Artists 759
12/26/64	#10	12	Let's Lock The Door	United Artists 805
4/03/65	#54	6	Think Of The Good Times	United Artists 845
5/29/65	#4	14	Cara Mia	United Artists 881
9/04/65	#15	10	Some Enchanted Evening	United Artists 919
11/13/65	#20	10	Sunday And Me	United Artists 948
2/19/66	#55	5	Why Can't You Bring Me Home	United Artists 992
5/28/66	#32	7	Crying	United Artists 50016
8/06/66	#78	3	Livin' Above Your Head	United Artists 50046
11/19/66	#62	5	(He's) Raining In My Sunshine	United Artists 50094
8/12/67	#93	3	Yellow Forest	United Artists 50196
12/14/68	#5	16	This Magic Moment	United Artists 50475
3/29/69	#41	6	When You Dance	United Artists 50510
5/24/69	#45	7	Hushabye	United Artists 50535
11/15/69	#14	16	Walkin' In The Rain	United Artists 50605
3/14/70	#45	7	Capture The Moment	United Artists 50654
			JAY and THE TECHNIQUES	
7/22/67	#4	15	Apples, Peaches, Pumpkin Pie	Smash 2086
10/21/67	#10	12	Keep The Ball Rollin'	Smash 2124
1/20/68	#29	7	Strawberry Shortcake	Smash 2142
4/13/68	#53	8	Baby Make Your Own Sweet Music	Smash 2154
8/10/68	#98	1	Single Games	Smash 2171
			JERRY JAYE	
4/08/67	#27	11	My Girl Josephine	Hi 2120
			JAYHAWKS	
8/04/56	#10	5	Stranded In The Jungle	Flash 109
			JAYNETTES	
8/24/63	#3	12	Sally Go 'Round The Roses	Tuff 369
			JAZZY JEFF & FRESH PRINCE (see D.J. JAZZY JEFF & THE FRESH PRINCE)	
			JB'S	
1/29/72	#55	7	Gimme Some More	People 602
5/13/72	#76	5	Pass The Peas	People 607
5/26/73	#21	12	Doing It To Death*	People 621
			*released as by FRED WESLEY & THE JB'S	
			JEFFERSON	
9/13/69	#65	9	Colour Of My Love	Decca 32501
12/06/69	#19	13	Baby Take Me In Your Arms	Janus 106
4/25/70	#96	3	You Know How It Is With A Woman	Janus 117
			JEFFERSON AIRPLANE	
2/04/67	#89	4	My Best Friend	RCA 9063
4/08/67	#5	15	Somebody To Love	RCA 9140
6/24/67	#6	11	White Rabbit	RCA 9248
9/02/67	#24	6	Ballad Of You & Me & Pooneil	RCA 9297
12/09/67	#37	6	Watch Her Ride	RCA 9389
4/06/68	#77	4	Greasy Heart	RCA 9496
11/08/69	#60	11	Volunteers	RCA 0245
11/13/71	#35	10	Pretty As You Feel	Grunt 0500

Debut Date	Peak Pos	Wks Chr	ARTIST/Song Title	Label & Number
			JEFFERSON STARSHIP	
11/30/74	#94	3	Ride The Tiger	Grunt 10080
8/23/75	#4	17	Miracles	Grunt 10367
12/06/75	#47	8	Play On Love	Grunt 10456
7/31/76	#13	17	With Your Love	Grunt 10746
3/11/78	#9	16	Count On Me	Grunt 11196
5/27/78	#13	15	Runaway	Grunt 11274
9/23/78	#73	5	Crazy Feeling	Grunt 11374
12/02/78	#65	7	Light The Sky	Grunt 11426
11/03/79	#6	17	Jane	Grunt 11750
3/01/80	#70	4	Girl With The Hungry Eyes	Grunt 11921
4/04/81	#29	14	Find Your Way Back	Grunt 12211
7/11/81	#55	8	Stranger	Grunt 12275
10/09/82	#26	17	Be My Lady	Grunt 13350
1/29/83	#37	11	Winds Of Change	Grunt 13439
5/12/84	#25	17	No Way Out	Grunt 13811
9/08/84	#66	7	Layin' It On The Line	Grunt 13872
9/07/85	#1	25	We Built This City*	Grunt 14170
12/28/85	#1	21	Sara*	Grunt 14253
4/05/86	#24	14	Tomorrow Doesn't Matter Tonight*	Grunt 14332
7/12/86	#61	7	Before I Go*	Grunt 14393
1/31/87	#1	21	Nothing's Gonna Stop Us Now*	Grunt 5109
6/27/87	#12	16	It's Not Over ('Til It's Over)*	Grunt 5225
9/26/87	#50	12	Beat Patrol*	Grunt 5308
12/17/88	#76	6	Wild Again*	Elektra 69349
8/05/89	#11	19	It's Not Enough*	RCA 9032
4/20/91	#73	8	Good Heart*	RCA 2796
			**released as by STARSHIP*	
			JOE JEFFREY GROUP	
5/31/69	#13	14	My Pledge Of Love	Wand 11200
			GARLAND JEFFREYS	
3/28/81	#89	4	96 Tears	Epic 51008
			JELLYBEAN	
11/16/85	#20	19	Sidewalk Talk	EMI America 8297
7/11/87	#16	17	Who Found Who*	Chrysalis 43120
			**released as by JELLYBEAN/ELISA FIORILLO*	
			JELLY BEANS	
6/27/64	#10	11	I Wanna Love Him So Bad	Red Bird 003
9/26/64	#49	6	Baby Be Mine	Red Bird 011
			JELLYFISH	
3/09/91	#46	11	Baby's Coming Back	Charisma 98837
			JELLYROLL	
9/12/70	#97	3	Strange	Kapp 2107
			DONALD JENKINS & THE DELIGHTERS	
9/14/63	#54	6	(Native Girl) Elephant Walk	Cortland 109
			GORDON JENKINS ORCHESTRA	
4/22/50	#1	19	My Foolish Heart	Decca 24830
8/12/50	#1	18	Goodnight Irene*	Decca 27077
7/29/50	#2	14	Tzena, Tzena, Tzena*	Decca 27077
2/17/51	#7	6	So Long*	Decca 27376
			**released as by THE GORDON JENKINS ORCHESTRA with THE WEAVERS*	
			WAYLON JENNINGS	
8/30/69	#96	2	MacArthur Park*	RCA 0210
10/24/70	#84	4	The Taker	RCA 9885
9/14/74	#82	5	I'm A Ramblin' Man	RCA 10020
9/27/75	#74	6	Are You Sure Hank Done It This Way	RCA 10379
2/14/76	#37	9	Good Hearted Woman**	RCA 10529
4/23/77	#23	19	Luckenbach, Texas	RCA 10924
2/11/78	#44	8	Mammas Don't Let Your Babies Grow Up To	
			Be Cowboys**	RCA 11198
6/09/79	#87	5	Amanda***	RCA 11596
9/13/80	#22	22	Theme From The Dukes Of Hazzard***	RCA 12067
4/03/82	#57	9	Just To Satisfy You**	RCA 13073
			**released as by WAYLON JENNINGS and THE KIMBERLYS*	

176

Debut Date	Peak Pos	Wks Chr	ARTIST/Song Title	Label & Number
			**released as by WAYLON & WILLIE (Waylon Jennings & Willie Nelson)	
			***released as by WAYLON	
			CURT JENSEN	
9/27/58	#71	3	If I Only Knew	Pet 806
			KRIS JENSEN	
9/08/62	#20	13	Torture	Hickory 1173
			JERRYO	
9/30/67	#57	8	Karate-Boo-Ga-Loo	Shout 217
			JESUS JONES	
5/18/91	#1	23	Right Here, Right Now	SBK 07345
8/24/91	#7	26	Real, Real, Real	SBK 07364
			JETHRO TULL	
7/24/71	#77	3	Hymn 43	Reprise 1024
11/11/72	#15	11	Living In The Past	Chrysalis 2006
5/26/73	#60	6	A Passion Play	Chrysalis 2012
10/26/74	#12	16	Bungle In The Jungle	Chrysalis 2101
3/08/75	#75	3	Skating Away	Chrysalis 2103
2/21/76	#74	6	Locomotive Breath	Chrysalis 2110
4/09/77	#52	6	The Whistler	Chrysalis 2135
			JOAN JETT & THE BLACKHEARTS	
2/06/82	#1	25	I Love Rock 'N Roll	Boardwalk 135
5/01/82	#6	15	Crimson And Clover	Boardwalk 144
7/31/82	#29	15	Do You Wanna Touch Me (Oh Yeah)	Boardwalk 150
7/09/83	#36	10	Fake Friends	Blackheart 52240
9/10/83	#47	10	Everyday People	Blackheart 52272
10/11/86	#71	7	Good Music	Blackheart 06336
2/21/87	#39	12	Light Of Day*	Blackheart 06692
6/25/88	#10	22	I Hate Myself For Loving You	Blackheart 07919
10/29/88	#20	19	Little Liar	Blackheart 08095
1/27/90	#42	10	Dirty Deeds	Blackheart 73267
			*released as by THE BARBUSTERS	
			JETS	
4/12/86	#5	19	Crush On You	MCA 52774
8/02/86	#45	11	Private Number	MCA 52846
11/15/86	#6	27	You Got It All	MCA 52968
6/06/87	#8	20	Cross My Broken Heart	MCA 53123
10/17/87	#21	18	I Do You	MCA 53193
1/23/88	#5	24	Rocket 2 U	MCA 53254
4/23/88	#4	20	Make It Real	MCA 53311
8/06/88	#80	7	Sendin' All My Love	MCA 53380
8/05/89	#50	10	You Better Dance	MCA 53673
			JEWELS	
10/17/64	#59	10	Opportunity	Dimension 1034
			JIGSAW	
9/06/75	#5	21	Sky High	Chelsea 3022
2/07/76	#34	11	Love Fire	Chelsea 3037
9/04/76	#72	10	Brand New Love Affair	Chelsea 3043
9/03/77	#89	3	If I Have To Go Away	20th Century 2347
			JIM & JEAN	
2/10/68	#85	3	People World	Verve Forecast 5073
			JOSE JIMENEZ	
7/29/61	#19	15	The Astronaut (Parts 1 & 2)	Kapp 409
			JIVE BOMBERS	
2/02/57	#24	12	Bad Boy	Savoy 1508
			JIVE BUNNY and THE MASTERMIXERS	
11/18/89	#13	18	Swing The Mood	Music Factory 99140
2/10/90	#67	6	That's The Way I Like It	Music Factory 99122
			JIVE FIVE	
7/15/61	#6	18	My True Story	Beltone 1006
11/25/61	#75	5	Never, Never	Beltone 1014
9/22/62	#75	5	What Time Is It?	Beltone 2024
7/24/65	#35	10	I'm A Happy Man	United Artists 853
7/29/67	#94	1	Crying Like A Baby	Musicor 1250

Debut Date	Peak Pos	Wks Chr	ARTIST/Song Title	Label & Number
			JIVIN' GENE and THE JOKERS	
9/05/59	#53	12	Breaking Up Is Hard To Do	Mercury 71485
10/15/60	#90	4	Release Me/	Mercury 71680
11/12/60	#94	2	Going Out With The Tide	Mercury 71680
			J.J. FAD	
4/30/88	#48	14	Supersonic	Ruthless 99328
10/01/88	#71	7	Way Out	Ruthless 99285
12/10/88	#71	6	Is It Love	Ruthless 99257
			DAMITA JO	
10/29/60	#17	11	I'll Save The Last Dance For You	Mercury 71690
1/28/61	#74	6	Keep Your Hands Off Him	Mercury 71760
7/15/61	#30	8	I'll Be There	Mercury 71840
3/20/65	#88	3	Tomorrow Night	Epic 9766
12/03/66	#84	8	If You Go Away	Epic 10061
			SAMI JO	
2/02/74	#21	13	Tell Me A Lie	MGM South 7029
7/06/74	#49	13	It Could Have Been Me	MGM South 7034
			JO ANN & TROY	
1/02/65	#86	5	I Found A Love Oh What A Love	Atlantic 2256
			JoBOXERS	
9/24/83	#40	14	Just Got Lucky	RCA 13601
			JODECI	
12/28/91	#66	9	Forever My Lady	Uptown 54197
2/29/92	#86	3	Stay	Uptown 54285
7/04/92	#9	18	Come & Talk To Me	Uptown 54175
11/07/92	#81	5	I'm Still Waiting	Uptown 54451
5/01/93	#72	8	Let's Go Through The Motions	Uptown 54602
6/19/93	#7	27	Lately	Uptown 54652
12/04/93	#19	24	Cry For You	Uptown 54723
			JOE	
9/25/93	#62	12	I'm In Luv	Mercury 862462
			JOE & ANN	
12/31/60	#97	3	Gee Baby	Ace 577
			BILLY JOEL	
2/09/74	#16	14	Piano Man	Columbia 45963
6/22/74	#70	6	Worse Comes To Worst	Columbia 46055
8/24/74	#59	6	Travelin' Prayer	Columbia 10015
11/30/74	#37	10	The Entertainer	Columbia 10064
11/12/77	#2	23	Just The Way You Are	Columbia 10646
3/18/78	#14	15	Movin' Out (Anthony's Song)	Columbia 10708
5/20/78	#25	13	Only The Good Die Young	Columbia 10750
8/05/78	#18	19	She's Always A Woman	Columbia 10788
11/04/78	#3	20	My Life	Columbia 10853
2/10/79	#13	11	Big Shot	Columbia 10913
4/21/79	#23	11	Honesty	Columbia 10959
3/15/80	#8	15	You May Be Right	Columbia 11231
5/24/80	#1	22	It's Still Rock And Roll To Me	Columbia 11276
8/02/80	#21	16	Don't Ask Me Why	Columbia 11331
10/11/80	#40	14	Sometimes A Fantasy	Columbia 11379
9/12/81	#20	15	Say Goodbye To Hollywood	Columbia 02518
11/21/81	#25	15	She's Got A Way	Columbia 02628
9/25/82	#21	12	Pressure	Columbia 03244
11/27/82	#14	19	Allentown	Columbia 03413
3/19/83	#75	5	Goodnight Saigon	Columbia 03780
7/30/83	#3	21	Tell Her About It	Columbia 04012
9/24/83	#3	23	Uptown Girl	Columbia 04149
12/17/83	#15	18	An Innocent Man	Columbia 04259
3/24/84	#10	19	The Longest Time	Columbia 04400
7/07/84	#32	15	Leave A Tender Moment Alone	Columbia 04514
1/26/85	#23	15	Keeping The Faith	Columbia 04681
7/13/85	#10	16	You're Only Human (Second Wind)	Columbia 05417
10/05/85	#34	12	The Night Is Still Young	Columbia 05657
6/07/86	#10	15	Modern Woman	Epic 06118
8/09/86	#15	17	A Matter Of Trust	Columbia 06108
11/15/86	#20	18	This Is The Time	Columbia 06526
4/18/87	#87	3	Baby Grand*	Columbia 06994
10/14/89	#1	22	We Didn't Start The Fire	Columbia 73021

Debut Date	Peak Pos	Wks Chr	ARTIST/Song Title	Label & Number
1/20/90	#5	18	I Go To Extremes	Columbia 73091
5/12/90	#61	7	The Downeaster "Alexa"	Columbia 73333
7/28/90	#52	8	That's Not Her Style	Columbia 73442
10/20/90	#37	10	And So It Goes	Columbia 73602
8/29/92	#88	5	All Shook Up	Epic 74422
8/14/93	#1	32	The River Of Dreams	Columbia 77086
11/27/93	#24	21	All About Soul	Columbia 77254
			*released as by BILLY JOEL featuring RAY CHARLES	
			JOE PUBLIC	
3/21/92	#5	24	Live And Learn	Columbia 74012
7/11/92	#60	6	I Miss You	Columbia 74321
10/24/92	#87	4	Do You Everynight	Columbia 74467
			ELTON JOHN	
8/22/70	#69	7	Border Song	Uni 55246
11/21/70	#8	16	Your Song	Uni 55265
3/20/71	#17	8	Friends	Uni 55277
12/18/71	#17	9	Levon	Uni 55314
3/04/72	#29	7	Tiny Dancer	Uni 55318
4/29/72	#11	14	Rocket Man	Uni 55328
8/12/72	#18	10	Honky Cat	Uni 55343
12/09/72	#1	17	Crocodile Rock	MCA 40000
4/07/73	#2	15	Daniel	MCA 40046
7/28/73	#9	12	Saturday Night's Alright For Fighting	MCA 40105
10/27/73	#1	15	Goodbye Yellow Brick Road	MCA 40148
12/15/73	#56	3	Step Into Christmas	MCA 65018
2/16/74	#1	16	Bennie And The Jets	MCA 40198
6/22/74	#1	13	Don't Let The Sun Go Down On Me	MCA 40259
9/14/74	#5	11	The Bitch Is Back	MCA 40297
11/30/74	#1	13	Lucy In The Sky With Diamonds	MCA 40344
3/08/75	#1	17	Philadelphia Freedom	MCA 40364
7/05/75	#1	12	Someone Saved My Life Tonight	MCA 40421
10/11/75	#1	15	Island Girl	MCA 40461
1/24/76	#9	9	Grow Some Funk Of Your Own/	MCA 40505
1/24/76	#18	9	I Feel Like A Bullet (In The Gun Of Robert Ford)	MCA 40505
7/03/76	#1	20	Don't Go Breaking My Heart*	Rocket 40585
11/06/76	#7	19	Sorry Seems To Be The Hardest Word	MCA 40645
2/12/77	#42	7	Bite Your Lip	MCA 40677
4/15/78	#22	8	Ego	MCA 40892
11/04/78	#13	14	Part-Time Love	MCA 40973
6/09/79	#10	18	Mama Can't Buy You Love	MCA 41042
9/29/79	#38	11	Victim Of Love	MCA 41126
5/03/80	#3	20	Little Jeannie	MCA 41236
8/16/80	#58	11	(Sartorial Eloquence) Don't Ya Wanna Play This Game No More?	MCA 41293
5/09/81	#24	13	Nobody Wins	Geffen 49722
7/25/81	#31	11	Chloe	Geffen 49788
3/20/82	#12	18	Empty Garden (Hey Hey Johnnie)	Geffen 50049
7/17/82	#10	18	Blue Eyes	Geffen 29954
5/07/83	#18	16	I'm Still Standing	Geffen 29639
8/06/83	#31	13	Kiss The Bride	Geffen 29568
10/29/83	#5	24	I Guess That's Why They Call It The Blues	Geffen 29460
6/09/84	#10	19	Sad Songs (Say So Much)	Geffen 29292
9/08/84	#23	14	Who Wears These Shoes?	Geffen 29189
12/01/84	#34	12	In Neon	Geffen 29111
10/26/85	#14	16	Wrap Her Up	Geffen 28873
11/09/85	#1	26	That's What Friends Are For**	Arista 9422
1/18/86	#9	19	Nikita	Geffen 28800
10/18/86	#48	8	Heartache All Over The World	Geffen 28578
5/16/87	#38	14	Flames Of Paradise***	Epic 07119
11/07/87	#7	22	Candle In The Wind	MCA 53196
6/18/88	#2	19	I Don't Wanna Go On With You Like That	MCA 53345
9/24/88	#18	17	A Word In Spanish	MCA 53408
4/15/89	#15	17	Through The Storm****	Arista 9809
8/26/89	#11	22	Healing Hands	MCA 53692
1/27/90	#19	17	Sacrifice	MCA 53750
5/05/90	#24	16	Club At The End Of The Street	MCA 79026
11/24/90	#37	15	You Gotta Love Someone	MCA 53953
12/07/91	#1	22	Don't Let The Sun Go Down On Me*****	Columbia 74086
6/27/92	#7	24	The One	MCA 54423
11/07/92	#20	24	The Last Song	MCA 54510

Debut Date	Peak Pos	Wks Chr	ARTIST/Song Title	Label & Number
			ELTON JOHN—*continued*	
3/13/93	#18	18	Simple Life	MCA 54581
12/04/93	#58	15	True Love*	MCA 54762
			*released as by ELTON JOHN and KIKI DEE	
			**released as by DIONNE and FRIENDS: ELTON JOHN, GLADYS KNIGHT,	
			STEVIE WONDER and DIONNE WARWICK	
			***released as by JENNIFER RUSH with ELTON JOHN	
			****released as by ARETHA FRANKLIN and ELTON JOHN	
			*****released as by GEORGE MICHAEL/ELTON JOHN	
			LITTLE WILLIE JOHN	
8/04/56	#24	6	Fever	King 4935
4/26/58	#43	5	Talk To Me, Talk To Me	King 5108
9/13/58	#99	1	You're A Sweetheart	King 5142
12/19/59	#96	1	Let Them Talk	King 5274
6/18/60	#27	12	Heartbreak (It's Hurtin' Me)	King 5356
9/17/60	#18	16	Sleep	King 5394
12/10/60	#50	8	Walk Slow	King 5428
			MABLE JOHN	
7/23/66	#68	4	Your Good Thing (Is About to End)	Stax 192
			ROBERT JOHN	
4/06/68	#34	12	If You Don't Want My Love	Columbia 44435
11/14/70	#69	6	When The Party Is Over	A&M 1210
12/25/71	#2	19	The Lion Sleeps Tonight	Atlantic 2846
6/10/72	#77	3	Hushabye	Atlantic 2884
4/29/78	#89	3	Give A Little More	Ariola America 7693
5/19/79	#1	30	Sad Eyes	EMI America 8015
12/01/79	#37	13	Lonely Eyes	EMI America 8030
7/19/80	#31	15	Hey There Lonely Girl	EMI America 8049
10/25/80	#70	5	Sherry	EMI America 8061
			JOHN & ERNEST	
4/07/73	#43	9	Super Fly Meets Shaft	Rainy Wednesday 201
			JOHNNIE & JOE	
5/11/57	#22	15	Over The Mountain; Across The Sea	Chess 1654
			JOHNNY and THE EXPRESSIONS	
1/15/66	#62	6	Something I Want To Tell You	Josie 946
			JOHNNY and THE HURRICANES	
5/02/59	#26	10	Crossfire	Warwick 502
8/01/59	#5	19	Red River Rock	Warwick 509
10/31/59	#22	13	Reveille Rock	Warwick 513
2/06/60	#10	13	Beatnik Fly	Warwick 520
6/04/60	#31	9	Down Yonder	Big Top 3036
9/03/60	#60	8	Rockin' Goose	Big Top 3051
2/04/61	#88	4	Ja-Da	Big Top 3063
			JOHNNY HATES JAZZ	
3/19/88	#3	21	Shattered Dreams	Virgin 99383
7/09/88	#30	15	I Don't Want To Be A Hero	Virgin 99304
			JOHNNY T. ANGEL	
6/01/74	#80	5	Tell Laura I Love Her	Bell 45472
			SAMMY JOHNS	
9/14/74	#49	13	Early Morning Love	GRC 2021
2/01/75	#5	17	Chevy Van	GRC 2046
6/07/75	#49	8	Rag Doll	GRC 2062
			BETTY JOHNSON	
11/24/56	#20	19	I Dreamed	Bally 1020
5/04/57	#55	3	Little White Lies	Bally 1033
2/15/58	#25	13	The Little Blue Man	Atlantic 1169
6/07/58	#48	4	Dream	Atlantic 1186
10/18/58	#75	2	Hoopa Hoola	Atlantic 2002
1/24/59	#99	1	You Can't Get To Heaven On Roller Skates	Atlantic 2009
4/18/59	#91	2	Does Your Heart Beat For Me	Atlantic 2019
			DON JOHNSON	
8/23/86	#4	17	Heartbeat	Epic 06285
11/22/86	#43	11	Heartache Away	Epic 06426

Debut Date	Peak Pos	Wks Chr	ARTIST/Song Title	Label & Number
10/22/88	#26	14	Till I Loved You*	Columbia 08062
			*released as by BARBRA STREISAND and DON JOHNSON	
			HOLLY JOHNSON	
6/24/89	#70	7	Love Train	Uni 50023
			JESSE JOHNSON	
3/30/85	#51	12	Be Your Man*	A&M 2702
8/10/85	#82	4	I Want My Girl*	A&M 2749
12/06/86	#56	10	Crazay**	A&M 2878
4/23/88	#75	7	Love Struck	A&M 3020
			*released as by JESSE JOHNSON'S REVUE	
			**released as by JESSE JOHNSON featuring SLY STONE	
			KEVIN JOHNSON	
11/10/73	#90	3	Rock 'N Roll (I Gave You The Best Years Of My Life) . . .	Mainstream 5548
			LOU JOHNSON	
9/23/63	#52	11	Reach Out For Me	Big Top 3153
8/08/64	#52	8	(There's) Always Something There To Remind Me	Big Hill 552
11/06/65	#56	8	A Time To Love - A Time To Cry	Big Top 101
			MARV JOHNSON	
3/14/59	#30	13	Come To Me	United Artists 160
6/27/59	#93	5	I'm Coming Home	United Artists 175
11/14/59	#5	20	You Got What It Takes	United Artists 185
2/27/60	#8	15	I Love The Way You Love	United Artists 208
5/28/60	#52	9	Ain't Gonna Be That Way/	United Artists 226
6/25/60	#58	7	All The Love I've Got	United Artists 226
8/27/60	#22	13	(You've Got To) Move Two Mountains	United Artists 241
12/03/60	#39	10	Happy Days	United Artists 273
3/11/61	#44	9	Merry-Go-Round	United Artists 294
7/01/61	#93	1	I've Got A Notion	United Artists 322
			MICHAEL JOHNSON	
4/22/78	#10	19	Bluer Than Blue	EMI America 8001
8/12/78	#37	13	Almost Like Being In Love	EMI America 8004
8/04/79	#18	21	This Night Won't Last Forever	EMI America 8019
9/06/80	#87	4	You Can Call Me Blue	EMI America 8054
			SYL JOHNSON	
8/12/67	#92	3	Come On Sock It To Me	Twilight 100
10/28/67	#96	2	Different Strokes	Twilight 103
2/03/73	#72	7	We Did It	Hi 2229
10/20/73	#74	6	Back For A Taste Of Your Love	Hi 2250
5/31/75	#59	9	Take Me To The River	Hi 2285
			TOM JOHNSTON	
11/10/79	#34	13	Savannah Nights	Warner Brothers 49096
			JOINER, ARKANSAS JUNIOR HIGH SCHOOL BAND	
5/21/60	#54	7	National City	Liberty 55244
			JO JO GUNNE	
3/18/72	#31	11	Run Run Run	Asylum 11003
			FRANCE JOLI	
9/15/79	#15	15	Come To Me	Prelude 8001
			JOMANDA	
8/03/91	#54	12	Got A Love For You	Big Beat 98731
7/17/93	#69	10	I Like It	Big Beat 98413
			JON & ROBIN and THE IN CROWD	
5/06/67	#21	11	Do It Again A Little Bit Slower	Abnak 119
2/17/68	#87	7	Dr. Jon (The Medicine Man)	Abnak 127
6/15/68	#85	6	You Got Style	Abnak 130
			JON & VANGELIS	
8/02/80	#63	7	I Hear You Now	Polydor 2098
5/22/82	#54	10	I'll Find My Way Home	Polydor 2205
			DAVY JONES	
8/07/65	#94	3	What Are We Going To Do?	Colpix 784
6/19/71	#32	10	Rainy Jane	Bell 45111
10/23/71	#96	2	I Really Love You	Bell 45136
			ETTA JONES	
10/15/60	#36	15	Don't Go To Strangers	Prestige 180
3/11/61	#98	2	Canadian Sunset	Prestige 191

Debut Date	Peak Pos	Wks Chr	ARTIST/Song Title	Label & Number
			GEORGE JONES	
5/23/59	#81	2	White Lightning	Mercury 71406
8/08/59	#83	3	Who Shot Sam	Mercury 71464
			GLENN JONES	
11/14/87	#84	10	We've Only Just Begun	Jive 1049
			GRACE JONES	
7/04/81	#95	3	Pull Up To The Bumper	Island 49697
11/29/86	#62	9	I'm Not Perfect (But I'm Perfect For You)	Manhattan 50052
			HOWARD JONES	
1/21/84	#29	16	New Song	Elektra 69766
4/28/84	#35	17	What Is Love?	Elektra 69737
3/23/85	#7	22	Things Can Only Get Better	Elektra 69651
7/06/85	#22	16	Life In One Day	Elektra 69631
9/28/85	#46	11	Like To Get To Know You Well	Elektra 69598
4/05/86	#3	21	No One Is To Blame	Elektra 69549
10/18/86	#15	18	You Know I Love You...Don't You?	Elektra 69512
1/17/87	#69	7	All I Want	Elektra 69494
3/18/89	#13	21	Everlasting Love	Elektra 69308
7/08/89	#22	18	The Prisoner	Elektra 69388
4/25/92	#25	16	Lift Me Up	Elektra 64779
			JACK JONES	
2/10/62	#42	10	Lollipops And Roses	Kapp 435
4/13/63	#62	8	Call Me Irresponsible	Kapp 516
11/02/63	#12	15	Wives And Lovers	Kapp 551
2/08/64	#59	9	Love With The Proper Stranger	Kapp 571
6/13/64	#62	7	The First Night Of The Full Moon	Kapp 589
8/22/64	#69	6	Where Love Has Gone	Kapp 608
11/28/64	#15	12	Dear Heart	Kapp 635
2/27/65	#12	12	The Race Is On	Kapp 651
6/05/65	#41	10	Seein' The Right Love Go Wrong	Kapp 672
10/02/65	#83	5	Just Yesterday	Kapp 699
11/27/65	#56	8	Love Bug	Kapp 722
2/19/66	#100	1	Weekend	Kapp 736
6/04/66	#32	11	The Impossible Dream	Kapp 755
10/22/66	#55	7	A Day In The Life Of A Fool	Kapp 781
1/21/67	#34	11	Lady	Kapp 800
4/22/67	#84	4	I'm Indestructable	Kapp 818
6/03/67	#74	7	Now I Know	Kapp 833
8/26/67	#76	5	Our Song	Kapp 847
			JIMMY JONES	
12/26/59	#2	19	Handy Man	Cub 9049
4/16/60	#3	16	Good Timin'	Cub 9067
7/16/60	#44	8	That's When I Cried/	Cub 9072
7/23/60	#88	2	I Just Go For You	Cub 9072
3/25/61	#83	4	I Told You So	Cub 9085
			JOE JONES	
9/10/60	#2	17	You Talk Too Much	Roulette 4304
4/01/61	#81	5	California Sun	Roulette 4344
			LINDA JONES	
6/24/67	#29	11	Hypnotized	Loma 2070
10/21/67	#89	2	What've I Done (To Make You Mad)	Loma 2077
3/11/72	#92	1	Your Precious Love	Turbo 021
			ORAN "JUICE" JONES	
9/20/86	#10	19	The Rain	Def Jam 06209
			QUINCY JONES	
4/25/70	#55	6	Killer Joe	A&M 1163
12/18/71	#96	1	What's Going On	A&M 1316
3/11/72	#84	5	Money Runner	Reprise 1062
9/01/73	#87	2	Summer In The City	A&M 1455
10/18/75	#66	5	Is It Love That We're Missin'*	A&M 1743
2/19/77	#62	8	"Roots" Medley	A&M 1909
5/20/78	#21	19	Stuff Like That	A&M 2043
4/11/81	#30	13	Ai No Corrida	A&M 2309
8/15/81	#13	23	Just Once**	A&M 2357
1/16/82	#20	18	One Hundred Ways**	A&M 2387
11/18/89	#19	18	I'll Be Good To You***	Qwest 22697
3/17/90	#30	12	The Secret Garden****	Qwest 19992

182

Debut Date	Peak Pos	Wks Chr	ARTIST/Song Title	Label & Number
6/02/90	#70	5	Tomorrow (A Better You, Better Me)***** . . . . Qwest 19881	

*released as by QUINCY JONES featuring THE BROTHERS JOHNSON
**released as by QUINCY JONES featuring JAMES INGRAM
***released as by QUINCY JONES featuring RAY CHARLES and CHAKA KHAN
****released as by QUINCY JONES/AL B. SURE!/JAMES INGRAM/
       EL DeBARGE/BARRY WHITE
*****released as by QUINCY JONES featuring TEVIN CAMPBELL

RICKIE LEE JONES

4/28/79	#4	19	Chuck E.'s In Love . . . . Warner Brothers 8825	
7/28/79	#44	8	Young Blood . . . . Warner Brothers 49018	
9/26/81	#53	9	A Lucky Guy . . . . Warner Brothers 49816	

TAMIKO JONES

3/15/75	#70	10	Touch Me Baby . . . . Arista 0110	

TOM JONES

4/03/65	#10	14	It's Not Unusual . . . . Parrot 9737	
6/05/65	#55	5	Little Lonely One . . . . Tower 126	
6/12/65	#2	13	What's New Pussycat? . . . . Parrot 9765	
8/28/65	#25	8	With These Hands . . . . Parrot 9787	
12/04/65	#22	11	Thunderball . . . . Parrot 9801	
2/19/66	#72	5	Promise Her Anything . . . . Parrot 9809	
6/25/66	#71	4	Not Responsible . . . . Parrot 40006	
12/24/66	#10	12	Green, Green Grass Of Home . . . . Parrot 40009	
3/11/67	#22	8	Detroit City . . . . Parrot 40012	
5/20/67	#45	7	Funny Familiar Forgotten Feelings . . . . Parrot 40014	
8/12/67	#77	3	Sixteen Tons . . . . Parrot 40016	
9/09/67	#46	7	I'll Never Fall In Love Again . . . . Parrot 40018	
12/30/67	#64	4	I'm Coming Home . . . . Parrot 40024	
3/16/68	#20	17	Delilah . . . . Parrot 40025	
8/17/68	#31	11	Help Yourself . . . . Parrot 40029	
12/14/68	#38	9	A Minute Of Your time . . . . Parrot 40035	
5/24/69	#7	12	Love Me Tonight . . . . Parrot 40038	
7/19/69	#6	16	I'll Never Fall In Love Again . . . . Parrot 40018	
12/27/69	#5	10	Without Love (There Is Nothing) . . . . Parrot 40045	
4/25/70	#10	11	Daughter Of Darkness . . . . Parrot 40048	
8/15/70	#11	10	I (Who Have Nothing) . . . . Parrot 40051	
11/14/70	#23	9	Can't Stop Loving You . . . . Parrot 40056	
1/30/71	#1	16	She's A Lady . . . . Parrot 40058	
5/22/71	#14	9	Puppet Man/ . . . . Parrot 40064	
6/26/71	#40	7	Resurrection Shuffle . . . . Parrot 40064	
10/23/71	#40	7	Till . . . . Parrot 40067	
5/06/72	#60	6	The Young New Mexican Puppeteer . . . . Parrot 40070	
5/05/73	#34	10	Letter To Lucille . . . . Parrot 40074	
12/25/76	#15	19	Say You'll Stay Until Tomorrow . . . . Epic 50308	
11/26/88	#37	12	Kiss* . . . . China 871038	

*released as by THE ART OF NOISE featuring TOM JONES

JONESES

10/12/74	#54	15	Sugar Pie Guy (Part 1) . . . . Mercury 73614	

JONES GIRLS

6/23/79	#32	12	You Gonna Make Me Love Somebody Else . . . . Philadelphia Int. 3680	

JANIS JOPLIN

11/15/69	#39	7	Kozmic Blues . . . . Columbia 45023	
1/30/71	#1	14	Me And Bobby McGee . . . . Columbia 45314	
5/08/71	#20	8	Cry Baby . . . . Columbia 45379	
8/28/71	#58	5	Get It While You Can . . . . Columbia 45433	
7/08/72	#79	4	Down On Me . . . . Columbia 45630	

JEREMY JORDAN

12/19/92	#15	26	The Right Kind Of Love . . . . Giant 18718	
5/15/93	#25	19	Wannagirl . . . . Giant 18548	

SASS JORDAN

5/30/92	#67	9	Make You A Believer . . . . Impact 54347	

JORDAN BROTHERS

11/19/60	#83	5	Things I Didn't Say . . . . Jamie 1169	

Debut Date	Peak Pos	Wks Chr	ARTIST/Song Title	Label & Number
			JORDY	
6/26/93	#49	10	Dur Dur D'etre Bebe! (It's Tough To Be A Baby)	Columbia 74987
			MARGIE JOSEPH	
3/27/71	#66	5	Stop! In The Name Of Love	Volt 4056
7/13/74	#75	7	My Love	Atlantic 3032
12/06/75	#87	2	What's Come Over Me*	Atco 7030
			*released as by MARGIE JOSEPH and BLUE MAGIC	
			JOURNEY	
4/01/78	#52	10	Wheel In The Sky	Columbia 10700
8/26/78	#67	7	Lights	Columbia 10800
3/17/79	#63	11	Just The Same Way	Columbia 10928
7/14/79	#15	23	Lovin', Touchin', Squeezin'	Columbia 11036
12/29/79	#89	5	Too Late	Columbia 11143
3/01/80	#21	16	Any Way You Want It	Columbia 11213
5/24/80	#41	13	Walks Like A Lady	Columbia 11275
8/16/80	#70	8	Good Morning Girl/Stay Awhile	Columbia 11339
2/28/81	#41	13	The Party's Over (Hopelessly In Love)	Columbia 60505
7/18/81	#3	22	Who's Crying Now	Columbia 02241
10/31/81	#8	16	Don't Stop Believin'	Columbia 02567
1/16/82	#1	18	Open Arms	Columbia 02687
5/22/82	#25	14	Still They Ride	Columbia 02883
2/05/83	#9	16	Separate Ways (Worlds Apart)	Columbia 03513
4/16/83	#15	16	Faithfully	Columbia 03840
7/09/83	#23	12	After The Fall	Columbia 04004
10/01/83	#31	16	Send Her My Love	Columbia 04151
1/26/85	#18	14	Only The Young	Geffen 29090
4/12/86	#10	15	Be Good To Yourself	Columbia 05869
6/21/86	#20	14	Suzanne	Columbia 06134
8/30/86	#17	15	Girl Can't Help It	Columbia 06302
12/06/86	#12	20	I'll Be Alright Without You	Columbia 06301
4/25/87	#68	7	Why Can't This Night Go On Forever	Columbia 07043
1/23/93	#71	8	Lights	Columbia 74842
			RODDIE JOY	
3/27/65	#77	4	Come Back Baby	Red Bird 021
			JOY OF COOKING	
4/24/71	#87	4	Brownsville	Capitol 3075
			JUDAS PRIEST	
11/20/82	#78	5	You've Got Another Thing Comin'	Columbia 03168
			JULIE	
1/24/76	#91	4	One Fine Day	Tom Cat 10454
			JUMP 'N THE SADDLE	
12/03/83	#9	15	The Curly Shuffle	Atlantic 89718
			ROB JUNGKLAS	
2/07/87	#81	4	Make It Mean Something	Manhattan 50054
			JUNIOR	
2/27/82	#30	13	Mama Used To Say	Mercury 76132
			BILL JUSTIS	
11/02/57	#1	17	Raunchy	Phillips Intl. 3519
3/01/58	#37	7	College Man	Phillips Intl. 3522
			JUST US	
3/05/66	#41	11	I Can't Grow Peaches On A Cherry	Tree Colpix 803

K

			JOSHUA KADISON	
10/30/93	#26	25	Jessie	SBK 50429
			BERT KAEMPFERT	
11/12/60	#1	18	Wonderland By Night	Decca 31141
2/11/61	#89	6	Cerveza	Decca 30866
4/08/61	#45	6	Tenderly	Decca 31236
8/05/61	#59	9	Now And Forever	Decca 31279
1/27/62	#37	10	Afrikaan Beat	Decca 31350
5/26/62	#76	6	That Happy Feeling	Decca 31388
1/23/65	#9	14	Red Roses For A Blue Lady	Decca 31722
5/01/65	#29	7	Three O'Clock In The Morning	Decca 31778

Debut Date	Peak Pos	Wks Chr	ARTIST/Song Title	Label & Number
6/26/65	#51	12	Moon Over Naples	Decca 31812
1/15/66	#41	9	Bye Bye Blues	Decca 31882
10/01/66	#97	2	I Can't Give You Anything But Love	Decca 32008
			KAJAGOOGOO	
4/23/83	#5	21	Too Shy	EMI America 8161
			KALIN TWINS	
6/14/58	#5	17	When	Decca 30642
10/11/58	#29	12	Forget Me Not	Decca 30745
1/24/59	#54	6	It's Only The Beginning	Decca 30807
			KITTY KALLEN	
5/22/54	#1	19	Little Things Mean A Lot	Decca 29037
8/21/54	#3	8	In The Chapel In The Moonlight	Decca 29130
10/10/59	#25	12	If I Give My Heart To You	Columbia 41473
3/03/60	#100	1	That Old Feeling	Columbia 41546
12/22/62	#13	12	My Coloring Book	RCA 8124
			GUNTER KALLMANN CHORUS	
12/10/66	#59	10	Wish Me A Rainbow	4 Corners 138
			MADLEEN KANE	
12/26/81	#83	7	You Can	Chalet 1225
			KANE GANG	
10/17/87	#39	18	Motortown	Capitol 44062
2/13/88	#70	7	Don't Look Any Further	Capitol 44115
			KANSAS	
12/11/76	#7	25	Carry On My Wayward Son	Kirshner 4267
6/25/77	#85	4	What's On My Mind	Kirshner 4270
11/05/77	#17	15	Point Of Know Return	Kirshner 4273
1/28/78	#3	20	Dust In The Wind	Kirshner 4274
6/03/78	#53	8	Portrait	Kirshner 4276
1/20/79	#64	5	Lonely Wind	Kirshner 4280
6/02/79	#28	12	People Of The South Wind	Kirshner 4284
9/01/79	#51	10	Reason To Be	Kirshner 4285
9/27/80	#39	13	Hold On	Kirshner 4291
12/20/80	#75	8	Got To Rock On	Kirshner 4292
5/08/82	#22	15	Play The Game Tonight	Kirshner 02903
8/21/82	#76	5	Right Away	Kirshner 03084
9/17/83	#74	5	Fight Fire With Fire	CBS Associated 04057
11/01/86	#24	16	All I Wanted	MCA 52958
2/28/87	#88	3	Power	MCA 53027
			KAOMA	
3/10/90	#46	9	Lambada	Epic 73090
			GABRIEL KAPLAN	
1/08/77	#82	7	Up Your Nose	Elektra 45369
			ANTON KARAS	
3/25/50	#1	21	The Third Man Theme	London 536
			KENNY KAREN	
8/25/73	#60	5	That's Why You Remember	Big Tree 16007
			KASENETZ-KATZ SINGING ORCHESTRAL CIRCUS	
7/27/68	#98	1	Down At Tennessee	Buddah 52
10/05/68	#18	12	Quick Joey Small (Run Joey Run)	Buddah 64
1/25/69	#77	2	I'm In Love With You	Buddah 85
			KATFISH	
9/20/75	#57	7	Dear Prudence	Big Tree 16045
			KATRINA and THE WAVES	
3/30/85	#9	19	Walking On Sunshine	Capitol 5466
7/27/85	#31	12	Do You Want Crying	Capitol 5450
10/19/85	#75	6	Que Te Quiero	Capitol 5528
5/03/86	#82	3	Is That It?	Capitol 5566
7/29/89	#17	18	That's The Way	SBK 07303
			JOHN KAY	
4/15/72	#45	9	I'm Movin' On	Dunhill 4309
5/26/73	#67	7	Moonshine	Dunhill 4351
9/08/73	#92	3	Easy Evil	Dunhill 4360
			KAYAK	
4/08/78	#50	13	I Want You To Be Mine	Janus 274

Debut Date	Peak Pos	Wks Chr	**ARTIST**/Song Title	Label & Number
			MARY KAYE TRIO	
4/04/59	#71	7	You Can't Be True Dear	Warner Brothers 5050
			SAMMY KAYE	
3/25/50	#1	18	It Isn't Fair	RCA 3609
6/03/50	#7	5	Wanderin'	RCA 3680
6/24/50	#5	7	Roses	RCA 3754
10/21/50	#1	20	Harbor Lights	Columbia 38963
4/11/64	#31	7	Charade	Decca 31589
			KAY GEES	
8/10/74	#81	8	You've Got To Keep On Bumpin'	Gang 321
			BOB KAYLI	
10/04/58	#99	2	Everyone Was There	Carlton 482
			LAINE KAZAN	
2/18/67	#84	3	Kiss Tomorrow Goodbye	MGM 13657
			KBC BAND	
11/29/86	#79	7	It's Not You, It's Not Me	Arista 9526
			KC and THE SUNSHINE BAND	
6/28/75	#1	18	Get Down Tonight	T.K. 1009
9/13/75	#84	4	Shotgun Shuffle*	T.K. 1010
10/18/75	#1	16	That's The Way (I Like It)	T.K. 1015
3/20/76	#63	4	Queen Of Clubs	T.K. 1005
7/10/76	#1	21	(Shake, Shake, Shake) Shake Your Booty	T.K. 1019
12/18/76	#63	10	I Like To Do It	T.K. 1020
3/05/77	#1	22	I'm Your Boogie Man	T.K. 1022
7/23/77	#2	20	Keep It Comin' Love	T.K. 1023
11/26/77	#80	7	Wrap Your Arms Around Me	T.K. 1022
2/04/78	#33	16	Boogie Shoes	T.K. 1025
5/06/78	#41	11	It's The Same Old Song	T.K. 1028
10/28/78	#83	4	Do You Feel Alright	T.K. 1030
12/16/78	#87	6	Who Do Ya Love	T.K. 1031
6/16/79	#43	9	Do You Wanna Go Party	T.K. 1033
8/25/79	#3	29	Please Don't Go	T.K. 1035
11/17/79	#3	25	Yes I'm Ready**	Casablanca 2227
6/28/80	#70	4	Dancin' In The Streets**	Casablanca 2278
3/19/83	#79	5	Don't Run (Come Back To Me)	Epic 03556
12/24/83	#17	24	Give It Up***	Meca 1001
			*released as by **THE SUNSHINE BAND**	
			released as by **TERI DeSARIO with K.C.	
			***released as by **KC**	
			ERNIE K-DOE	
3/18/61	#1	16	Mother-In-Law	Minit 623
6/17/61	#43	7	Te-Ta-Te-Ta-Ta	Minit 627
			KEEDY	
3/23/91	#14	19	Save Some Love	Arista 2153
			KEITH	
8/27/66	#31	11	Ain't Gonna Lie	Mercury 72596
12/03/66	#7	15	98.6	Mercury 72639
3/11/67	#31	7	Tell Me To My Face	Mercury 72652
6/24/67	#85	2	Daylight Savin' Time	Mercury 72695
			LISA KEITH	
9/25/93	#32	19	Better Than You	Perspective 7430
			JERRY KELLER	
7/04/59	#24	13	Here Comes Summer	Kapp 277
			MURRY KELLUM	
11/09/63	#51	10	Long Tall Texan	M.O.C. 653
			CASEY KELLY	
10/07/72	#65	5	Poor Boy	Elektra 45804
			MONTY KELLY	
3/05/60	#27	9	Summer Set	Carlton 527
			PAUL KELLY	
6/13/70	#54	11	Stealing In the Name Of The Lord	Happy Tiger 541
			R. KELLY & PUBLIC ANNOUNCEMENT	
3/21/92	#54	13	She's Got That Vibe	Jive 42026
7/04/92	#32	11	Honey Love	Jive 42031

Debut Date	Peak Pos	Wks Chr	ARTIST/Song Title	Label & Number
8/29/92	#46	9	Slow Dance (Hey Mr. DJ)	Jive 42092
4/03/93	#36	16	Dedicated	Jive 42115
11/06/93	#19	21	Sex Me*	Jive 42161
			*released as by R. KELLY	
			JOHNNY KEMP	
5/14/88	#13	22	Just Got Paid	Columbia 07744
2/18/89	#31	16	Birthday Suit	Columbia 68569
			TARA KEMP	
1/19/91	#3	25	Hold You Tight	Giant 19458
5/25/91	#9	20	Piece Of My Heart	Giant 19364
			KENDALLS	
10/15/77	#47	16	Heaven's Just A Sin Away	Ovation 1103
			NAT KENDRICK and THE SWANS	
1/23/60	#52	9	(Do The) Mashed Potatoes (Part 1)	Dade 1804
			EDDIE KENDRICKS	
5/15/71	#61	6	It's So Hard For Me To Say Good-Bye	Tamla 54203
11/20/71	#92	4	Can I	Tamla 54210
6/17/72	#83	4	Eddie's Love	Tamla 54218
9/23/72	#50	11	If You Let Me	Tamla 54222
3/03/73	#98	2	Girl You Need A Change Of Mind	Tamla 54230
6/30/73	#91	7	Darling Come Back Home	Tamla 54236
8/18/73	#1	17	Keep On Truckin' (Part 1)	Tamla 54238
12/29/73	#1	16	Boogie Down	Tamla 54243
5/04/74	#20	10	Son Of Sagittarius	Tamla 54247
7/27/74	#38	12	Tell Her Love Has Felt The Need	Tamla 54249
12/07/74	#55	7	One Tear	Tamla 54255
2/08/75	#22	19	Shoeshine Boy	Tamla 54257
7/05/75	#58	8	Get The Cream Off The Top	Tamla 54260
10/18/75	#59	12	Happy	Tamla 54263
2/14/76	#65	11	He's A Friend	Tamla 54266
			KENJOLAIRS	
1/12/63	#99	1	Little White Lies	A&M 704
			JOYCE KENNEDY	
8/18/84	#44	13	The Last Time I Made Love*	A&M 2656
			*released as by JOYCE KENNEDY & JEFFREY OSBORNE	
			MIKE KENNEDY	
3/04/72	#65	7	Louisiana	ABC 11309
			CHRIS KENNER	
6/03/61	#2	17	I Like It Like That (Part 1)	Instant 3229
7/13/63	#81	8	Land Of 1000 Dances	Instant 3252
			G.W. KENNY	
8/25/73	#89	3	Everybody But Me	Buddah 581
			KENNY & CORKY	
12/26/59	#100	1	Nuttin' For Christmas	Big Top 3031
			KENNY G	
4/11/87	#4	23	Songbird	Arista 9588
8/29/87	#20	22	Don't Make Me Wait For Love	Arista 9625
10/22/88	#14	18	Silhouette	Arista 9751
2/04/89	#40	11	We've Saved The Best For Last*	Arista 9785
12/23/89	#50	10	Going Home	Arista 9913
12/26/92	#16	26	Forever In Love	Arista 2482
5/22/93	#26	20	By The Time This Night Is Over**	Arista 2565
12/18/93	#75	13	Sentimental	Arista 2618
			*released as by KENNY G with SMOKEY ROBINSON	
			**released as by KENNY G with PEABO BRYSON	
			AL KENT	
8/05/67	#46	12	You've Got To Pay The Price	Ric-Tic 127
			STAN KENTON	
11/18/50	#6	7	Orange Colored Sky*	Capitol 1184
7/16/60	#43	11	My Love*	Capitol 4393
10/20/62	#31	8	Mama Sang A Song	Capitol 4847
			*released as by NAT KING COLE-STAN KENTON	
			KERMIT	
9/29/79	#43	13	Rainbow Connection	Atlantic 3610

Debut Date	Peak Pos	Wks Chr	ARTIST/Song Title	Label & Number
			NIK KERSHAW	
4/14/84	#47	12	Wouldn't It Be Good	MCA 52371
			TROY KEYES	
1/28/68	#89	4	Love Explosion	ABC 11027
			KEYMEN	
1/24/59	#63	8	Miss You	ABC-Paramount 9991
			CHAKA KHAN	
10/07/78	#19	17	I'm Every Woman	Warner Brothers 8683
5/16/81	#49	10	What 'Cha Gonna Do For Me	Warner Brothers 49692
1/15/83	#80	7	Got To Be There	Warner Brothers 29881
9/08/84	#1	26	I Feel For You	Warner Brothers 29195
1/19/85	#58	8	This Is My Night	Warner Brothers 29097
4/27/85	#68	6	Through The Fire	Warner Brothers 29025
7/06/85	#88	5	Through The Fire	Warner Brothers 29025
12/28/85	#61	8	Own The Night	MCA 52730
7/12/86	#45	12	Love Of A Lifetime	Warner Brothers 28671
11/18/89	#19	18	I'll Be Good To You*	Qwest 22697
5/02/92	#49	11	Love You All My Lifetime	Warner Brothers 18987
1/30/93	#68	8	Feels Like Heaven**	Warner Brothers 18651
			*released as by **QUINCY JONES featuring RAY CHARLES and CHAKA KHAN**	
			released as by **PETER CETERA with CHAKA KHAN	
			KIARA	
3/04/89	#80	4	This Time	Arista 9772
			KID FROST	
8/04/90	#47	10	La Raza	Virgin 98947
4/25/92	#93	4	No Sunshine	Virgin 98583
			KIDS NEXT DOOR	
10/09/65	#96	5	Inky Dinky Spider (The Spider Song)	4 Corners 129
			GREG KIHN BAND	
5/23/81	#18	23	The Breakup Song (They Don't Write 'Em)	Beserkley 47149
5/29/82	#67	6	Happy Man	Beserkley 47463
1/29/83	#5	23	Jeopardy	Beserkley 69847
6/04/83	#59	8	Love Never Fails	Beserkley 69820
2/16/85	#36	13	Lucky*	EMI America 8255
			*released as by **GREG KIHN**	
			THEOLA KILGORE	
4/13/63	#21	14	The Love Of My Man	Serock 2004
8/17/63	#72	9	This Is My Prayer	Serock 2006
			ANDY KIM	
4/13/68	#16	14	How'd We Ever Get This Way	Steed 707
9/07/68	#35	9	Shoot 'Em Up Baby	Steed 710
11/30/68	#45	9	Rainbow Ride	Steed 711
3/29/69	#91	6	Tricia Tell Your Daddy	Steed 715
5/17/69	#6	17	Baby, I Love You	Steed 716
9/20/69	#20	9	So Good Together	Steed 720
1/24/70	#63	4	A Friend In The City	Steed 723
7/25/70	#78	5	It's Your Life	Steed 727
10/31/70	#12	12	Be My Baby	Steed 729
3/20/71	#68	5	I Wish I Were	Steed 731
7/03/71	#94	4	I Been Moved	Steed 734
6/15/74	#1	19	Rock Me Gently	Capitol 3895
10/26/74	#32	9	Fire, Baby I'm On Fire	Capitol 3962
			ADRIAN KIMBERLY	
6/24/61	#44	6	The Graduation Song....Pomp And Circumstance	Calliope 6501
			TOM KIMMEL	
6/20/87	#61	9	That's Freedom	Mercury 888571
			KING	
7/13/85	#49	14	Love & Pride	Epic 04917
			ALBERT KING	
1/20/68	#65	6	Cold Feet	Stax 241
7/22/72	#73	4	I'll Play The Blues	Stax 0137
1/27/73	#96	3	Breaking Up Somebody's Home	Stax 0147
			ANNA KING	
12/28/63	#69	6	If Somebody Told You	Smash 1858

Debut Date	Peak Pos	Wks Chr	ARTIST/Song Title	Label & Number
3/28/64	#63	8	Baby Baby Baby*	Smash 1884
			*released as by ANNA KING-BOBBY BYRD	
			B.B. KING	
6/11/60	#100	1	Got A Right To Love My Baby	Kent 333
7/30/64	#89	2	Partin' Time	Kent 346
3/21/64	#92	3	How Blue Can You Get	ABC-Paramount 10527
5/02/64	#28	10	Rock Me Baby	Kent 393
7/25/64	#95	1	You're Gonna Miss Me/	Kent 396
8/15/64	#96	3	Let Me Love You	Kent 396
10/24/64	#80	6	Beautician Blues	Kent 403
6/12/65	#98	1	Blue Shadows	Kent 426
10/15/66	#45	9	Don't Answer The Door (Part 1)	ABC 10856
4/15/67	#100	1	The Jungle	Kent 462
4/06/68	#54	10	Paying The Cost To Be The Boss	BluesWay 61015
7/20/68	#82	5	I'm Gonna Do What They Do To Me	BluesWay 61018
9/07/68	#86	2	The B.B. Jones/	BluesWay 61019
10/12/68	#84	3	You Put It On Me	BluesWay 61019
5/24/69	#78	8	Why I Sing The Blues	BluesWay 61024
8/02/69	#92	3	I Want You So Bad/	BluesWay 61026
9/06/69	#80	5	Get Off My Back Woman	BluesWay 61026
10/18/69	#74	5	Just A Little Love	BluesWay 61029
12/27/69	#15	12	The Thrill Is Gone	BluesWay 61032
4/11/70	#50	5	So Excited	BluesWay 61035
7/18/70	#42	8	Hummingbird	ABC 11268
10/24/70	#45	8	Chains And Things	ABC 11280
2/20/71	#43	9	Ask Me No Questions	ABC 11290
6/05/71	#65	4	Help The Poor	ABC 11302
9/18/71	#56	6	Ghetto Woman	ABC 11310
10/30/71	#56	11	Ain't Nobody Home	ABC 11316
3/04/72	#63	4	Sweet Sixteen	ABC 11319
4/22/72	#68	7	I Got Some Help I Don't Need	ABC 11321
8/26/72	#62	9	Guess Who	ABC 11330
8/11/73	#38	12	To Know You Is To Love You	ABC 11373
12/15/73	#25	16	I Like To Live The Love	ABC 11406
6/15/74	#95	3	Who Are You	ABC 11433
12/07/74	#79	7	Philadelphia	ABC 12029
			BEN E. KING	
12/24/60	#91	5	First Taste Of Love/	Atco 6185
1/14/61	#9	15	Spanish Harlem	Atco 6185
5/13/61	#3	13	Stand By Me	Atco 6194
8/05/61	#19	10	Amor	Atco 6203
10/28/61	#86	4	Young Boy Blues	Atco 6207
2/10/62	#50	6	Ecstasy	Atco 6215
4/21/62	#11	14	Don't Play That Song (You Lied)	Atco 6222
8/04/62	#88	4	Too Bad	Atco 6231
3/09/63	#82	3	How Can I Forget	Atco 6256
6/29/63	#25	13	I (Who Have Nothing)	Atco 6267
3/21/64	#57	8	That's When It Hurts	Atco 6288
9/26/64	#93	3	It's All Over	Atco 6315
12/12/64	#58	9	Seven Letters	Atco 6328
1/08/66	#87	3	Goodnight My Love	Atco 6390
5/07/66	#54	5	So Much Love	Atco 6413
1/25/75	#5	16	Supernatural Thing (Part 1)	Atlantic 3241
6/14/75	#64	4	Do It In The Name Of Love	Atlantic 3274
10/04/86	#10	22	Stand By Me	Atlantic 89361
			CAROLE KING	
8/25/62	#29	9	It Might As Well Rain Until September	Dimension 2000
5/04/63	#100	1	He's A Bad Boy	Dimension 1009
5/15/71	#1	17	It's Too Late	Ode 66015
8/28/71	#10	10	So Far Away	Ode 66019
1/22/72	#8	11	Sweet Seasons	Ode 66022
11/25/72	#20	10	Been To Canaan	Ode 66031
7/14/73	#24	10	Believe In Humanity/	Ode 66035
7/14/73	#62	5	You Light Up My Life	Ode 66035
10/20/73	#27	10	Corazon	Ode 66039
8/31/74	#1	15	Jazzman	Ode 66101
12/28/74	#16	12	Nightingale	Ode 66106
2/14/76	#27	11	Only Love Is Real	Ode 66119
7/23/77	#25	12	Hard Rock Cafe	Capitol 4455

Debut Date	Peak Pos	Wks Chr	ARTIST/Song Title	Label & Number
			CAROLE KING—*continued*	
5/17/80	#19	17	One Fine Day	Capitol 4864
3/27/82	#47	13	One To One	Atlantic 4026
			CLAUDE KING	
11/18/61	#76	9	The Commancheros	Columbia 42196
5/26/62	#5	17	Wolverton Mountain	Columbia 42352
9/29/62	#45	6	The Burning Of Atlanta	Columbia 42581
			EVELYN "CHAMPAGNE" KING	
5/27/78	#8	24	Shame	RCA 11122
12/30/78	#17	20	I Don't Know If It's Right	RCA 11386
7/25/81	#44	13	I'm In Love*	RCA 12243
8/28/82	#27	17	Love Come Down*	RCA 13273
1/22/83	#36	10	Betcha She Don't Love You*	RCA 13380
			*released as by EVELYN KING	
			FREDDY KING	
3/04/61	#48	12	Hide Away	Federal 12401
			JONATHAN KING	
9/11/65	#12	14	Everyone's Gone To The Moon	Parrot 9774
12/25/65	#75	5	Where The Sun Has Never Shone	Parrot 9804
			PEE WEE KING	
12/15/51	#1	14	Slow Poke	RCA 0489
			SLEEPY KING	
11/04/61	#84	11	Pushin' Your Luck	Joy 257
			SOLOMON KING	
4/06/68	#92	2	She Wears My Ring	Capitol 2114
			KINGBEES	
6/28/80	#79	6	My Mistake	RSO 1032
			KING CURTIS	
2/17/62	#14	17	Soul Twist*	Enjoy 1000
7/21/62	#87	6	Beach Party*	Capitol 4788
4/11/64	#86	6	Soul Serenade	Capitol 5109
9/02/67	#39	9	Memphis Soul Stew	Atco 6511
9/23/67	#34	7	Ode To Billie Joe**	Atco 6516
1/20/68	#84	2	I Was Made To Love Her***	Atco 6547
1/30/71	#60	5	Whole Lotta Love***	Atco 6779
			*released as by KING CURTIS and THE NOBLE KNIGHTS	
			**released as by THE KINGPINS	
			***released as by KING CURTIS and THE KINGPINS	
			KING HARVEST	
10/28/72	#10	20	Dancing In The Moonlight	Perception 515
5/19/73	#87	4	A Little Bit Like Magic	Perception 527
			KING PINS	
8/03/63	#90	3	It Won't Be This Way (Always)	Federal 12484
			KINGS	
8/23/80	#50	22	This Beat Goes On/	Elektra 47052
8/23/80	#50	22	Switchin' To Glide	Elektra 47052
			KINGSMEN (Bill Haley's backup band)	
9/06/58	#56	6	Weekend	East West 115
			KINGSMEN (Portland vocal group)	
11/09/63	#1	17	Louie Louie	Wand 143
3/07/64	#17	13	Money	Wand 150
7/18/64	#49	8	Little Latin Lupe Lu	Wand 157
9/19/64	#33	8	Death Of An Angel	Wand 164
1/09/65	#8	13	The Jolly Green Giant	Wand 172
5/01/65	#45	7	The Climb	Wand 183
8/07/65	#43	9	Annie Fanny	Wand 189
12/11/65	#98	1	(You Got) The Gamma Goochee	Wand 1107
4/02/66	#81	3	Killer Joe	Wand 1115
4/23/66	#65	5	Louie Louie	Wand 143
			KINGSTON TRIO	
9/27/58	#1	22	Tom Dooley	Capitol 4049
1/17/59	#43	7	Raspberries, Strawberries/	Capitol 4114
1/17/59	#80	2	Sally	Capitol 4114
2/21/59	#18	11	The Tijuana Jail	Capitol 4167

Debut Date	Peak Pos	Wks Chr	ARTIST/Song Title	Label & Number
6/13/59	#17	12	M.T.A.	Capitol 4221
9/12/59	#20	12	A Worried Man	Capitol 4271
12/05/59	#61	6	CooCoo-U	Capitol 4303
2/27/60	#73	5	Home From The Hill/	Capitol 4338
2/27/60	#53	10	Matador	Capitol 4338
6/25/60	#63	10	Bad Man's Blunder	Capitol 4379
10/01/60	#80	7	Everglades	Capitol 4441
1/13/62	#22	15	Where Have All The Flowers Gone	Capitol 4671
4/28/62	#82	6	Scotch And Soda	Capitol 4740
11/10/62	#84	3	One More Town	Capitol 4842
2/02/63	#17	11	Greenback Dollar	Capitol 4898
4/13/63	#7	11	Reverend Mr.Black	Capitol 4951
8/03/63	#36	9	Desert Pete	Capitol 5005
11/23/63	#60	5	Ally Ally Oxen Free	Capitol 5078
			KINKS	
10/03/64	#5	15	You Really Got Me	Reprise 0306
1/02/65	#6	12	All Day And All Of The Night	Reprise 0334
3/13/65	#5	12	Tired Of Waiting For You	Reprise 0347
6/12/65	#24	9	Set Me Free	Reprise 0379
8/07/65	#40	7	Who'll Be The Next In Line	Reprise 0366
11/27/65	#9	16	A Well Respected Man	Reprise 0420
4/02/66	#43	5	Till The End Of The Day	Reprise 0454
5/14/66	#59	7	Dedicated Follower Of Fashion	Reprise 0471
8/13/66	#11	10	Sunny Afternoon	Reprise 0497
12/31/66	#72	4	Deadend Street	Reprise 0540
7/01/67	#64	5	Mr. Pleasant	Reprise 0587
1/31/70	#54	8	Victoria	Reprise 0863
8/15/70	#8	16	Lola	Reprise 0930
1/02/71	#39	9	Apeman	Reprise 0979
4/02/77	#69	3	Sleepwalker	Arista 0240
7/15/78	#36	12	A Rock 'N' Roll Fantasy	Arista 0342
5/05/79	#42	10	(Wish I Could Fly Like) Superman	Arista 0409
5/07/83	#11	20	Come Dancing	Arista 1054
8/20/83	#34	11	Don't Forget To Dance	Arista 9075
12/22/84	#50	13	Do It Again	Arista 9309
			KATHY KIRBY	
9/04/65	#91	5	The Way Of Love	Parrot 9775
			JIM KIRK and THE TM SINGERS	
2/16/80	#83	3	Voice Of Freedom	Capitol 4834
			KISS	
5/25/74	#79	5	Kissin' Time	Casablanca 0011
5/17/75	#57	6	Rock And Roll All Nite (studio version)	Casablanca 829
11/08/75	#17	15	Rock And Roll All Nite (live version)	Casablanca 850
3/13/76	#24	13	Shout It Out Loud (studio version)	Casablanca 854
6/19/76	#80	4	Flaming Youth	Casablanca 858
8/28/76	#25	5	Detroit Rock City/	Casablanca 863
9/04/76	#7	21	Beth	Casablanca 863
12/18/76	#19	16	Hard Luck Woman	Casablanca 873
3/12/77	#10	18	Calling Dr. Love	Casablanca 880
7/16/77	#20	11	Christine Sixteen	Casablanca 889
9/24/77	#55	7	Love Gun	Casablanca 895
3/04/78	#46	10	Rocket Ride	Casablanca 915
5/26/79	#8	19	I Was Made For Lovin' You	Casablanca 983
9/01/79	#44	11	Sure Know Something	Casablanca 2205
6/21/80	#56	8	Shandi	Casablanca 2282
12/12/81	#57	9	A World Without Heroes	Casablanca 2343
10/13/84	#53	11	Heaven's On Fire	Mercury 880205
10/19/85	#51	15	Tears Are Falling	Mercury 884141
9/26/87	#79	7	Crazy Crazy Nights	Mercury 888796
12/12/87	#82	7	Reason To Live	Mercury 870022
1/21/89	#93	2	Let's Put The X In Sex	Mercury 872246
12/09/89	#83	8	Hide Your Heart	Mercury 876146
2/03/90	#8	20	Forever	Mercury 876716
6/16/90	#79	5	Rise To It	Mercury 875098
			MAC and KATIE KISSOON	
7/31/71	#18	13	Chirpy Chirpy Cheep Cheep	ABC 11306

Debut Date	Peak Pos	Wks Chr	ARTIST/Song Title	Label & Number
			EARTHA KITT	
9/05/53	#7	5	C'est Si Bon	RCA 5358
1/02/54	#8	3	Santa Baby	RCA 5502
			KIX	
10/07/89	#9	20	Don't Close Your Eyes	Atlantic 88902
			KLAATU	
4/02/77	#91	1	Calling Occupants/	Capitol 4412
4/09/77	#57	5	Sub-Rosa Subway	Capitol 4412
			KLF	
6/29/91	#15	20	3 A.M. Eternal	Arista 2230
1/25/92	#8	19	Justified And Ancient	Arista 2401
5/30/92	#86	4	Last Train To Transcentral	Arista 2382
			KLIQUE	
10/08/83	#54	11	Stop Doggin' Me Around	MCA 52250
			KLOWNS	
12/12/70	#81	2	Lady Love	RCA 0393
			KLYMAXX	
5/11/85	#66	9	Meeting In The Ladies Room	Constellation 52545
9/28/85	#13	27	I Miss You	Constellation 52606
2/15/86	#70	8	The Men All Pause	Constellation 52486
7/05/86	#16	16	Man Size Love	MCA 52841
5/16/87	#26	19	I'd Still Say Yes	Constellation 53028
			K.M.C. KRU	
9/21/91	#65	10	The Devil Came Up To Michigan	Curb 76884
			KNACK	
6/23/79	#1	25	My Sharona	Capitol 4731
9/08/79	#11	16	Good Girls Don't	Capitol 4771
2/09/80	#30	11	Baby Talks Dirty	Capitol 4822
4/05/80	#68	6	You Can't Put A Price On Love	Capitol 4853
10/31/81	#69	7	Pay The Devil	Capitol 5054
			KNICKERBOCKERS	
12/11/65	#24	12	Lies	Challenge 59321
3/26/66	#52	6	One Track Mind	Challenge 59326
			BOB KNIGHT FOUR	
4/29/61	#90	8	(Good Goodbye) So So Long	Laurel 1020
			EARL KNIGHT and GEORGE KELLY	
6/20/59	#87	1	Let It Roll	ABC-Paramount 10023
			FREDERICK KNIGHT	
4/22/72	#20	14	I've Been Lonely For So Long	Stax 0117
9/16/72	#80	2	Trouble	Stax 0139
			GLADYS KNIGHT & THE PIPS	
5/27/61	#13	12	Every Beat Of My Heart*	Vee-Jay 386
12/16/61	#17	15	Letter Full Of Tears	Fury 1054
4/28/62	#82	4	Operator	Fury 1064
5/16/64	#46	11	Giving Up	Maxx 326
7/22/67	#54	7	Everybody Needs Love	Soul 35034
10/21/67	#1	17	I Heard It Through The Grapevine	Soul 35039
2/03/68	#11	10	The End Of Our Road	Soul 35042
6/01/68	#38	8	It Should Have Been Me	Soul 35045
8/31/68	#43	6	I Wish It Would Rain	Soul 35047
3/08/69	#61	4	Didn't You Know	Soul 35057
7/19/69	#27	10	The Nitty Gritty	Soul 35063
10/25/69	#25	13	Friendship Train	Soul 35068
3/21/70	#28	8	You Need Love Like I Do (Don't You)	Soul 35071
11/21/70	#5	16	If I Were Your Woman	Soul 35078
5/22/71	#9	13	I Don't Want To Do Wrong	Soul 35083
12/11/71	#22	10	Make Me The Woman That You Go Home To	Soul 35091
3/25/72	#37	7	Help Me Make It Through The Night	Soul 35094
1/20/73	#1	16	Neither One Of Us (Wants To Be The First To Say Goodbye)	Soul 35098
4/28/73	#15	13	Daddy Could Swear, I Declare	Soul 35105
6/09/73	#23	11	Where Peaceful Waters Flow	Buddah 363
8/18/73	#81	4	All I Need Is Time	Soul 35107
9/01/73	#1	16	Midnight Train To Georgia	Buddah 383
11/24/73	#7	14	I've Got To Use My Imagination	Buddah 393

Debut Date	Peak Pos	Wks Chr	ARTIST/Song Title	Label & Number
2/16/74	#3	15	Best Thing That Ever Happened To Me	Buddah 403
5/11/74	#9	14	On And On	Buddah 423
7/06/74	#76	6	Between Her Goodbye And My Hello	Soul 35111
10/12/74	#11	16	I Feel A Song (In My Heart)	Buddah 433
2/15/75	#33	8	Love Finds Its Own Way	Buddah 453
4/26/75	#10	17	The Way We Were/Try To Remember	Buddah 463
8/23/75	#40	9	Money	Buddah 487
11/01/75	#27	12	Part Time Love	Buddah 513
10/16/76	#56	14	So Sad The Song	Buddah 544
6/25/77	#51	7	Baby Don't Change Your Mind	Buddah 569
6/07/80	#63	10	Landlord	Columbia 11239
5/28/83	#61	10	Save The Overtime (For Me)	Columbia 03761
11/09/85	#1	26	That's What Friends Are For**	Arista 9422
12/26/87	#23	19	Love Overboard	MCA 53210

*released as by THE PIPS
**released as by DIONNE and FRIENDS: ELTON JOHN, GLADYS KNIGHT, STEVIE WONDER and DIONNE WARWICK

HOLLY KNIGHT

9/03/88	#61	10	Heart Don't Fail Me Now	Columbia 07932

JEAN KNIGHT

5/29/71	#2	16	Mr. Big Stuff	Stax 0088
10/16/71	#75	3	You Think You're Hot Stuff	Stax 0105
5/04/85	#64	11	My Toot Toot	Mirage 99643

ROBERT KNIGHT

9/30/67	#11	12	Everlasting Love	Rising Sons 705

SONNY KNIGHT

11/10/56	#20	11	Confidential	Dot 15507
9/26/64	#94	8	If You Want This Love	Aura 403

TERRY KNIGHT and THE PACK

5/07/66	#96	3	Better Man Than I	Lucky Eleven 226
8/27/66	#81	3	A Change On The Way	Lucky Eleven 229
10/15/66	#42	14	I (Who Have Nothing)	Lucky Eleven 230
2/11/67	#82	4	This Precious Time	Lucky eleven 235

KNIGHT BROTHERS

5/29/65	#56	6	Temptation 'Bout To Get Me	Checker 1107

KNIGHTSBRIDGE STRINGS

7/25/59	#44	7	Cry	Top Rank 2006
11/28/59	#98	1	Wheel Of Fortune	Top Rank 2014

FRED KNOBLOCK

7/05/80	#32	14	Why Not Me	Scotti Brothers 600
11/22/80	#64	13	Killin' Time*	Scotti Brothers 609

*released as by FRED KNOBLOCK and SUSAN ANTON

KNOCKOUTS

12/19/59	#35	13	Darling Lorraine	Shad 5013

BUDDY KNOX

2/16/57	#1	18	Party Doll*	Roulette 4002
5/04/57	#25	14	Rock Your Little Baby To Sleep*	Roulette 4009
8/24/57	#16	17	Hula Love*	Roulette 4018
1/11/58	#49	3	Swingin' Daddy*	Roulette 4042
7/12/58	#63	1	C'mon Baby*/	Roulette 4082
7/19/58	#30	15	Somebody Touched Me*	Roulette 4082
4/18/59	#61	5	I Think I'm Gonna Kill Myself	Roulette 4140
11/09/59	#100	1	I Ain't Sharin' Sharon	Roulette 4179
12/10/60	#44	11	Lovey Dovey	Liberty 55290
4/08/61	#95	2	Ling-Ting-Tong	Liberty 55305

*released as by BUDDY KNOX and THE RHYTHM ORCHIDS

MOE KOFFMAN QUARTETTE

1/18/58	#18	12	The Swingin' Shepherd Blues	Jubilee 5311
5/24/58	#44	6	Little Pixie	Jubilee 5324

KOKOMO

2/11/61	#14	15	Asia Minor	Felsted 8612

DIANE KOLBY

9/19/70	#76	4	Holy Man	Columbia 45169

KONGAS

4/29/78	#92	3	Gimme Some Lovin'	Polydor 14461

Debut Date	Peak Pos	Wks Chr	**ARTIST**/Song Title	Label & Number
			JOHN KONGOS	
7/10/71	#64	6	He's Gonna Step On You Again	Elektra 45729
			KON KAN	
12/31/88	#22	19	I Beg Your Pardon	Atlantic 88969
9/09/89	#62	9	Puss N' Boots/These Boots (Are Made For Walkin')	Atlantic 88828
			KOOL & THE GANG	
9/06/69	#76	6	Kool And The Gang	De-Lite 519
1/10/70	#80	3	The Gang's Back Again	De-Lite 523
6/13/70	#88	6	Let The Music Take Your Mind	De-Lite 529
9/05/70	#91	5	Funky Man	De-Lite 534
1/16/71	#94	2	Who's Gonna Take The Weight	De-Lite 538
9/22/73	#44	9	Funky Stuff	De-Lite 557
12/15/73	#8	16	Jungle Boogie	De-Lite 559
4/13/74	#7	17	Hollywood Swinging	De-Lite 561
8/31/74	#39	10	Higher Plane	De-Lite 1562
1/11/75	#52	7	Rhyme Tyme People	De-Lite 1563
4/12/75	#27	16	Spirit Of The Boogie	De-Lite 1567
10/25/75	#45	11	Caribbean Festival	De-Lite 1573
12/11/76	#73	9	Open Sesame (Part 1)	De-Lite 1586
10/13/79	#4	24	Ladies Night	De-Lite 801
1/19/80	#7	20	Too Hot	De-Lite 802
11/01/80	#1	32	Celebration	De-Lite 807
5/23/81	#40	10	Jones Vs. Jones	De-Lite 813
10/10/81	#19	19	Take My Heart	De-Lite 815
2/27/82	#12	21	Get Down On It	De-Lite 818
8/28/82	#30	11	Big Fun	De-Lite 822
10/30/82	#29	17	Let's Go Dancin' (Ooh La, La, La)	De-Lite 824
11/12/83	#3	24	Joanna	De-Lite 829
2/25/84	#15	19	Tonight	De-Lite 830
11/24/84	#11	24	Misled	De-Lite 880431
3/23/85	#10	19	Fresh	De-Lite 880623
7/06/85	#3	25	Cherish	De-Lite 880869
10/26/85	#19	19	Emergency	De-Lite 884199
11/01/86	#14	18	Victory	Mercury 888074
2/14/87	#16	18	Stone Love	Mercury 888292
6/27/87	#65	9	Holiday	Mercury 888712
10/10/87	#86	9	Special Way	Mercury 888867
			KOOL MOE DEE	
5/14/88	#80	8	Wild, Wild West	Jive 1086
			KORGIS	
10/11/80	#23	18	Everybody's Got To Learn Sometime	Elektra 47055
			KORONA	
3/22/82	#47	9	Let Me Be	United Artists 1341
			KRAFTWERK	
3/22/75	#19	9	Autobahn	Vertigo 203
6/03/78	#91	5	Trans-Europe Express	Capitol 4460
			BILLY J. KRAMER with THE DAKOTAS	
4/18/64	#7	16	Little Children/	Imperial 66027
6/06/64	#10	10	Bad To Me	Imperial 66027
7/25/64	#39	6	I'll Keep You Satisfied	Imperial 66048
8/29/64	#29	10	From A Window	Imperial 66051
2/06/65	#97	5	It's Gotta Last Forever	Imperial 66085
6/19/65	#52	8	Trains And Boats And Planes	Imperial 66115
			LENNY KRAVITZ	
2/03/90	#85	4	Let Love Rule	Virgin 99166
6/01/91	#6	22	It Ain't Over Til It's Over	Virgin 98795
10/12/91	#64	10	Stand By My Woman	Virgin 98736
7/17/93	#47	15	Believe	Virgin 12662
			KRIS KROSS	
4/11/92	#1	22	Jump	Ruffhouse 74197
6/13/92	#13	22	Warm It Up	Ruffhouse 74376
10/10/92	#56	10	I Missed The Bus	Ruffhouse 74496
8/14/93	#18	18	Alright*	Ruffhouse 77103

Debut Date	Peak Pos	Wks Chr	ARTIST/Song Title	Label & Number
11/27/93	#83	10	I'm Real . . . . Ruffhouse 77237	
			*released as by KRIS KROSS featuring SUPERCAT	
			KRIS KRISTOFFERSON	
8/21/71	#33	12	Loving Her Was Easier (Than Anything I'll Ever	
			Do Again) . . . . Monument 8525	
3/11/72	#69	5	Josie . . . . Monument 8536	
1/06/73	#86	3	Jesus Was A Capricorn . . . . Monument 8558	
5/05/73	#32	31	Why Me . . . . Monument 8571	
11/10/73	#33	10	A Song I'd Like To Sing* . . . . A&M 1475	
3/30/74	#97	2	Loving Arms* . . . . A&M 1498	
5/28/77	#68	5	Watch Closely Now . . . . Columbia 10525	
			*released as by KRIS KRISTOFFERSON and RITA COOLIDGE	
			KROKUS	
9/22/84	#70	7	Midnight Maniac . . . . Arista 9248	
6/07/86	#66	5	School's Out . . . . Arista 9468	
			K-7	
9/25/93	#15	30	Come Baby Come . . . . Tommy Boy 7572	
			BOB KUBAN and THE IN-MEN	
1/29/66	#15	10	The Cheater . . . . Musicland 20001	
4/30/66	#99	2	The Teaser . . . . Musicland 20006	
7/30/66	#99	1	Drive My Car . . . . Musicland 20007	
			CHARLIE KULIS	
3/15/75	#42	9	Runaway . . . . Playboy 6023	
			K.W.S.	
9/12/92	#6	24	Please Don't Go . . . . Next Plateau 339	
			KYPER	
7/28/90	#16	13	Tic-Tac-Toe . . . . Atlantic 87910	

L

Debut Date	Peak Pos	Wks Chr	ARTIST/Song Title	Label & Number
			LABAN	
11/08/86	#77	4	Love In Siberia . . . . Critique 725	
			PATTI LaBELLE	
9/14/63	#39	15	Down The Aisle (Wedding Song)* . . . . Newton 5777	
1/11/64	#41	7	You'll Never Walk Alone* . . . . Parkway 896	
11/27/65	#83	3	All Or Nothing* . . . . Atlantic 2311	
12/24/66	#94	3	Take Me For A Little While* . . . . Atlantic 2373	
1/11/75	#1	17	Lady Marmalade** . . . . Epic 50048	
5/10/75	#52	7	What Can I Do For You?** . . . . Epic 50097	
1/21/84	#39	12	If Only You Knew . . . . Philadelphia Int. 04248	
3/31/84	#80	5	Love Has Finally Come At Last*** . . . . Beverly Glen 2012	
2/23/85	#19	20	New Attitude . . . . MCA 52517	
6/15/85	#42	13	Stir It Up . . . . MCA 52610	
3/22/86	#1	22	On My Own**** . . . . MCA 52770	
7/19/86	#37	12	Oh, People . . . . MCA 52877	
10/14/89	#85	5	If You Asked Me To . . . . MCA 53358	
11/09/91	#86	4	Feels Like Another One . . . . MCA 54225	
			*released as by PATTI LaBELLE & THE BLUE BELLES	
			**released as by LABELLE	
			***released as by BOBBY WOMACK and PATTI LABELLE	
			****released as by PATTI LaBELLE and MICHAEL McDONALD	
			BILL LaBOUNTY	
5/20/78	#68	10	This Night Won't Last Forever . . . . Warner Brothers 8529	
			L.A. CAR POOL	
8/16/75	#84	2	Like They Say In L.A. . . . . GRC 2064	
			CHERYL LADD	
7/22/78	#44	11	Think It Over . . . . Capitol 4599	
			LADY FLASH	
7/17/76	#27	13	Street Singin' . . . . RSO 852	
			LAFAYETTES	
7/14/62	#78	4	Life's Too Short . . . . RCA 8044	

195

Debut Date	Peak Pos	Wks Chr	ARTIST/Song Title	Label & Number
			DAVID LaFLAMME	
12/11/76	#85	6	White Bird	Amherst 717
			JACK LaFORGE	
2/13/65	#50	1	Goldfinger	Regina 1323
			L.A. GUNS	
4/14/90	#31	20	The Ballad Of Jayne	Vertigo 876984
2/29/92	#67	15	It's Over Now	Polydor 865494
			FRANCIS LAI	
1/23/71	#36	10	Theme From Love Story	Paramount 0064
			LAID BACK	
3/17/84	#22	15	White Horse	Sire 29346
			FRANKIE LAINE	
6/09/51	#2	16	Jezebel	Columbia 39267
6/23/51	#3	8	Rose, Rose I Love You	Columbia 39367
12/08/51	#3	9	Jealousy	Columbia 39585
4/12/52	#10	3	Hambone*	Columbia 39672
8/30/52	#5	11	High Noon	Columbia 39770
3/28/53	#1	17	I Believe	Columbia 39938
4/04/53	#5	6	Tell Me A Story**	Columbia 39945
9/19/53	#7	4	Hey Joe	Columbia 40036
8/20/55	#6	5	Humming Bird	Columbia 40526
12/01/56	#6	20	Moonlight Gambler	Columbia 40780
3/23/57	#19	10	Love Is A Golden Ring	Columbia 40856
5/04/63	#60	7	Don't Make My Baby Blue	Columbia 42767
1/14/67	#52	11	I'll Take Care Of Your Cares	ABC 10891
4/08/67	#41	9	Making Memories	ABC 10924
6/17/67	#46	7	You Wanted Someone To Play With	ABC 10946
8/12/67	#53	6	Laura, What's He Got That I Ain't Got	ABC 10967
9/30/67	#66	5	You, No One But You	ABC 10983
1/06/68	#76	5	To Each His Own	ABC 11032
3/23/68	#96	2	I Found You	ABC 11057
1/25/69	#19	14	You Gave Me A Mountain	ABC 11174
6/21/69	#100	1	Dammit Isn't God's Last Name	ABC 11224
			*released as by JO STAFFORD and FRANKIE LAINE	
			**released as by FRANKIE LAINE with JIMMY BOYD	
			L.A. JETS	
6/19/76	#91	4	Dancin' Thru The Night	RCA 10668
12/18/76	#80	4	Prisoner (Captured By Your Eyes)	RCA 10826
			LAKE	
11/05/77	#88	7	Time Bomb	Columbia 10614
			GREG LAKE	
12/20/75	#92	3	I Believe In Father Christmas	Atlantic 3305
8/27/77	#87	5	C'est La Vie	Atlantic 3405
11/21/81	#38	14	Let Me Love You Once	Chrysalis 2571
			LAKESIDE	
1/31/81	#56	10	Fantastic Voyage	Solar 12129
			BECKY LAMB	
12/23/67	#59	2	Little Becky's Christmas Wish	Warner Brothers 7154
			KEVIN LAMB	
6/17/78	#71	5	On The Wrong Track	Arista 0316
			GEORGE LAMOND	
5/19/90	#30	16	Bad Of The Heart	Columbia 73339
8/25/90	#60	8	Look Into My Eyes	Columbia 73486
12/01/90	#42	15	No Matter What*	Columbia 73603
8/15/92	#62	5	Where Does That Leave Love	Columbia 74425
12/12/92	#62	8	Baby, I Beleive In You	Columbia 74756
			*released as by GEORGE LAMOND with BRENDA K. STARR	
			MAJOR LANCE	
7/13/63	#7	16	Monkey Time	Okeh 7175
10/19/63	#17	10	Hey Little Girl	Okeh 7181
12/28/63	#4	13	Um, Um, Um, Um, Um, Um	Okeh 7187
3/28/64	#21	9	The Matador	Okeh 7191
6/13/64	#84	8	It Ain't No Use/	Okeh 7197
6/20/64	#72	4	Girls	Okeh 7197
8/29/64	#23	10	Rhythm	Okeh 7203

Debut Date	Peak Pos	Wks Chr	ARTIST/Song Title	Label & Number
12/12/64	#54	7	Sometimes I Wonder	Okeh 7209
3/06/65	#49	6	Come See	Okeh 7216
6/05/65	#91	3	Ain't It A Shame	Okeh 7223
8/28/65	#80	2	Too Hot To Hold	Okeh 7726
7/25/70	#79	9	Stay Away From Me	Curtom 1953
			MICKEY LEE LANE	
10/10/64	#38	10	Shaggy Dog	Swan 4183
			ROBIN LANE & THE CHARTBUSTERS	
7/12/80	#96	2	When Things Go Wrong	Warner Brothers 49246
			LANE BROTHERS	
5/10/58	#53	2	Boppin' In A Sack	RCA 7220
			k.d. LANG	
8/08/92	#29	23	Constant Craving	Sire 18942
			MARIO LANZA	
2/10/51	#2	18	Be My Love	RCA 1561
7/14/51	#5	18	The Loveliest Night Of The Year	RCA 3300
11/17/56	#31	4	Because You're Mine	RCA 3914
3/22/58	#32	6	Arrivederci Roma	RCA 7164
			LARKS (North Carolina group)	
3/25/61	#92	1	It's Unbelievable	Sheryl 334
			LARKS (Los Angeles group)	
11/07/64	#6	16	The Jerk	Money 106
			JULIUS LaROSA	
10/10/53	#1	12	Eh Cumpari	Cadence 1232
9/03/55	#10	1	Domani (Tomorrow)	Cadence 1265
10/29/55	#8	4	Suddenly There's A Valley	Cadence 1270
11/03/56	#31	3	Priscilla	RCA 6700
2/02/57	#36	6	Stashu Pandowski	RCA 6802
5/11/57	#57	1	Mama Guitar	RCA 6878
			LARSEN-FEITEN BAND	
8/09/80	#25	16	Who'll Be The Fool Tonight	Warner Brothers 49282
			NICOLETTE LARSON	
11/25/78	#8	18	Lotta Love	Warner Brothers 8664
3/31/79	#41	9	Rhumba Girl	Warner Brothers 8795
12/29/79	#36	14	Let Me Go, Love	Warner Brothers 49130
2/28/81	#85	5	Ooo-Eee	Warner Brothers 49666
7/31/82	#48	13	I Only Want To Be With You	Warner Brothers 29948
			La's	
8/03/91	#47	12	There She Goes	London 869370
			DENISE LaSALLE	
8/21/71	#13	15	Trapped By A Thing Called Love	Westbound 182
1/22/72	#33	11	Now Run And Tell That	Westbound 201
9/30/72	#40	11	Man Sized Job	Westbound 206
5/12/73	#97	2	What It Takes To Get A Good Woman	Westbound 215
2/04/78	#88	5	Love Me Right	ABC 12312
			DAVID LASLEY	
3/13/82	#38	13	If I Had My Wish Tonight	EMI America 8111
			JAMES LAST BAND	
3/29/80	#26	13	The Seduction (Love Theme)	Polydor 2071
			LAST WORD	
10/07/67	#82	4	Can't Stop Loving You	Atco 6498
			LATIMORE	
12/22/73	#92	1	Stormy Monday	Glades 1716
9/28/74	#32	14	Let's Straighten It Out	Glades 1722
1/29/77	#66	9	Somethin' 'Bout 'Cha	Glades 1739
			LaTOUR	
4/20/91	#40	12	People Are Still Having Sex	Smash 879666
			STACY LATTISAW	
8/16/80	#21	24	Let Me Be Your Angel	Cotillion 46001
6/20/81	#23	17	Love On A Two Way Street	Cotillion 46015
10/23/82	#93	4	Attack Of The Name Game	Cotillion 99968
8/13/83	#35	17	Miracles	Cotillion 99855
4/14/84	#79	5	Perfect Combination*	Cotillion 99785

197

Debut Date	Peak Pos	Wks Chr	ARTIST/Song Title	Label & Number
			STACY LATTISAW—*continued*	
10/25/86	#57	13	Nail It To The Wall	Motown 1859
			*released as by STACY LATTISAW & JOHNNY GILL	
			CYNDI LAUPER	
12/17/83	#1	27	Girls Just Want To Have Fun	Portrait 04120
4/14/84	#1	20	Time After Time	Portrait 04432
7/21/84	#3	19	She Bop	Portrait 04516
10/06/84	#8	19	All Through The Night	Portrait 04639
12/22/84	#31	13	Money Changes Everything	Portrait 04737
5/18/85	#14	16	The Goonies 'R' Good Enough	Portrait 04918
8/30/86	#1	21	True Colors	Portrait 06247
11/29/86	#4	20	Change Of Heart	Portrait 06431
3/14/87	#15	14	What's Going On	Portrait 06970
6/06/87	#84	6	Boy Blue	Portrait 07181
7/09/88	#51	10	Hole In My Heart (All The Way To China)	Epic 07940
5/06/89	#5	20	I Drove All Night	Epic 68759
8/05/89	#55	10	My First Night Without You	Epic 68945
			ROD LAUREN	
12/12/59	#24	13	If I Had A Girl	RCA 7645
			LINDA LAURIE	
1/10/59	#46	8	Ambrose (Part Five)	Glory 290
			LaVERNE & SHIRLEY	
11/20/76	#69	5	Sixteen Reasons	Atlantic 3367
			BETTY LAVETT	
1/05/63	#97	1	My Man - He's A Lovin' Man	Atlantic 2160
			LAW	
10/11/75	#92	4	Wake Up	GRC 2072
			EDDIE LAWRENCE	
8/04/56	#33	8	The Old Philosopher	Coral 61671
			JOEY LAWRENCE	
3/13/93	#12	22	Nothin' My Love Can't Fix	Impact 54562
7/24/93	#54	14	Stay Forever	Impact 54653
			STEVE LAWRENCE	
12/29/56	#5	2	The Banana Boat Song	Coral 61761
2/16/57	#1	18	Party Doll	Coral 61792
6/01/57	#38	7	Can't Wait For Summer	Coral 61834
9/21/57	#41	8	Fraulein	Coral 61876
3/15/58	#52	3	Uh-Huh, Oh Yeah	Coral 61950
10/18/58	#100	1	Many A Time	Coral 62025
3/21/59	#72	8	(I Don't Care) Only Love Me	ABC-Paramount 10005
11/28/59	#7	16	Pretty Blue Eyes	ABC-Paramount 10058
3/05/60	#9	15	Footsteps	ABC-Paramount 10085
7/02/60	#82	3	Girls, Girls, Girls	United Artists 233
3/18/61	#11	15	Portrait Of My Love	United Artists 291
7/15/61	#88	2	My Claire De Lune/	United Artists 335
7/15/61	#90	3	In Time	United Artists 335
11/17/62	#1	19	Go Away Little Girl	Columbia 42601
3/09/63	#19	8	Don't Be Afraid Little Darlin'	Columbia 42699
5/18/63	#36	8	Poor Little Rich Girl	Columbia 42795
7/27/63	#28	11	I Want To Stay Here*	Columbia 42815
10/05/63	#27	12	Walking Proud	Columbia 42865
12/21/63	#51	9	I Can't Stop Talking About You*	Columbia 42932
5/23/64	#57	6	Everybody Knows	Columbia 43037
8/22/64	#68	6	Yet...I Know	Columbia 43095
9/23/72	#64	7	We Can Make It Together**	MGM 14383
			*released as by STEVE and EYDIE (Steve Lawrence and Eydie Gorme)	
			**released as by STEVE and EYDIE featuring THE OSMONDS	
			VICKI LAWRENCE	
2/10/73	#1	18	The Night The Lights Went Out In Georgia	Bell 45303
6/09/73	#49	10	He Did With Me	Bell 45362
9/27/75	#70	5	The Other Woman	Private Stock 45036
			RONNIE LAWS	
9/05/81	#47	13	Stay Awake	Liberty 1424

Debut Date	Peak Pos	Wks Chr	**ARTIST**/Song Title	Label & Number
			JOY LAYNE	
2/16/57	#29	5	Your Wild Heart	Mercury 71038
4/06/57	#35	3	After School	Mercury 71080
			LAZY RACER	
7/07/79	#81	5	You Keep Running Away	A&M 2152
			JOE LEAHY ORCHESTRA	
7/20/57	#57	1	By The Bend Of The River	Unique 397
			LEAPY LEE	
10/19/68	#16	12	Little Arrows	Decca 32380
			LEAVES	
5/21/66	#43	9	Hey Joe	Mira 222
			OTIS LEAVILLE	
1/30/65	#88	4	Let Her Love Me	Blue Rock 4002
12/06/69	#71	7	I Love You	Dakar 614
9/26/70	#69	7	Love Uprising	Dakar 620
			LENNY LeBLANC	
6/05/76	#99	2	Sharing The Night Together	Big Tree 16062
6/25/77	#55	7	Something About You*	Big Tree 16092
9/03/77	#56	6	Hound Dog Man (Play It Again)	Big Tree 16062
10/22/77	#11	27	Falling*	Big Tree 16100
6/10/78	#94	3	Midnight Light*	Big Tree 16114
3/28/81	#61	8	Somebody Send My Baby Home	Capitol 4979
			*released as by LeBLANC & CARR	
			LED ZEPPELIN	
4/05/69	#66	4	Good Times Bad Times	Atlantic 2613
11/15/69	#2	16	Whole Lotta Love	Atlantic 2690
11/21/70	#8	13	Immigrant Song	Atlantic 2777
12/18/71	#9	12	Black Dog	Atlantic 2849
3/11/72	#42	8	Rock And Roll	Atlantic 2865
6/09/73	#28	11	Over The Hills And Far Away	Atlantic 2970
10/13/73	#16	16	D'yer Mak'er	Atlantic 2986
4/12/75	#28	9	Trampled Under Foot	Swan Song 70102
12/22/79	#31	14	Fool In The Rain	Swan Song 71003
			BRENDA LEE	
6/15/57	#54	2	Dynamite	Decca 30333
1/09/60	#3	21	Sweet Nothin's	Decca 30967
6/04/60	#11	13	That's All You Gotta Do/	Decca 31093
6/11/60	#1	20	I'm Sorry	Decca 31093
9/24/60	#2	15	I Want To Be Wanted	Decca 31149
12/17/60	#22	4	Rockin' Around The Christmas Tree	Decca 30776
1/07/61	#6	12	Emotions	Decca 31195
4/01/61	#7	12	You Can Depend On Me/	Decca 31231
4/08/61	#100	1	It's Never Too Late	Decca 31231
6/24/61	#4	13	Dum Dum/	Decca 31272
6/24/61	#41	6	Eventually	Decca 31272
9/30/61	#23	10	Anybody But Me/	Decca 31309
10/07/61	#6	15	Fool #1	Decca 31309
12/23/61	#71	3	Rockin' Around The Christmas Tree	Decca 30776
1/13/62	#6	13	Break It To Me Gently/	Decca 31348
1/13/62	#43	4	So Deep	Decca 31348
4/14/62	#6	12	Everybody Loves Me But You/	Decca 31379
4/14/62	#57	4	Here Comes That Feelin'	Decca 31379
7/07/62	#21	10	Heart In Hand/	Decca 31407
7/07/62	#26	8	It Started All Over Again	Decca 31407
9/29/62	#3	15	All Alone Am I/	Decca 31424
9/29/62	#38	5	Save All Your Lovin' For Me	Decca 31424
12/15/62	#89	4	Rockin' Around The Christmas Tree	Decca 30776
1/26/63	#23	9	Your Used To Be/	Decca 31454
2/02/63	#50	5	She'll Never Know	Decca 31454
4/13/63	#10	13	Losing You	Decca 31478
7/06/63	#22	8	My Whole World Is Falling Down/	Decca 31510
7/06/63	#23	9	I Wonder	Decca 31510
9/28/63	#21	9	The Grass Is Greener/	Decca 31539
10/05/63	#94	4	Sweet Impossible You	Decca 31539
12/14/63	#11	12	As Usual	Decca 31570
3/07/64	#18	10	Think	Decca 31599
3/14/64	#97	2	The Waiting Game	Decca 31599

Debut Date	Peak Pos	Wks Chr	ARTIST/Song Title	Label & Number
			BRENDA LEE—continued	
6/06/64	#27	7	Alone With You	Decca 31628
8/08/64	#36	8	When You Loved Me	Decca 31654
10/10/64	#14	11	Is It True	Decca 31690
1/16/65	#34	7	Thanks A Lot/	Decca 31728
1/16/65	#93	2	The Crying Game	Decca 31728
4/03/65	#41	5	Truly Truly True	Decca 31762
5/22/65	#15	14	Too Many Rivers/	Decca 31792
5/22/65	#95	1	No One	Decca 31792
10/09/65	#30	9	Rusty Bells	Decca 31849
6/18/66	#91	1	It Takes One To Know One/	Decca 31970
6/25/66	#86	4	Ain't Gonna Cry No More	Decca 31970
10/08/66	#18	12	Coming On Strong	Decca 32018
1/07/67	#47	8	Ride Ride Ride	Decca 32079
4/01/67	#91	2	Take Me	Decca 32199
4/08/67	#93	1	Born To Be By Your Side	Decca 32119
2/01/69	#34	13	Johnny One Time	Decca 32428
5/24/69	#76	3	You Don't Need Me For Anything Anymore	Decca 32491
5/16/70	#84	5	I Think I Love You Again	Decca 32675
3/24/71	#80	5	Nobody Wins	MCA 40003
			CURTIS LEE	
7/01/61	#6	14	Pretty Little Angel Eyes	Dunes 2007
10/07/61	#42	8	Under The Moon Of Love	Dunes 2008
			DICKEY LEE	
8/18/62	#4	16	Patches	Smash 1758
12/08/62	#8	13	I Saw Linda Yesterday	Smash 1791
3/16/63	#74	5	Don't Wanna Think About Paula	Smash 1808
12/26/64	#100	1	Big Brother	TCF Hall 1924
5/22/65	#11	12	Laurie (Strange Things Happen)	TCF Hall 102
9/18/65	#93	2	The Girl From Peyton Place	TCF Hall 111
11/13/76	#67	11	9,999,999 Tears	RCA 10764
			GARY LEE	
5/16/59	#71	3	Why	Time 1009
			JACKIE LEE	
11/27/65	#13	12	The Duck	Mirwood 5502
2/26/66	#76	5	Your P-E-R-S-O-N-A-L-I-T-Y	Mirwood 5509
			JOHNNY LEE	
7/12/80	#4	22	Lookin' For Love	Full Moon 47004
10/17/81	#61	8	Bet Your Heart On Me	Full Moon 47215
			LAURA LEE	
9/09/67	#55	9	Dirty Man	Chess 2013
11/25/67	#94	1	Wanted: Lover, No Experience Necessary/	Chess 2030
12/30/67	#90	6	Up Tight Good Man	Chess 2030
4/06/68	#80	3	As Long As I Got You	Chess 2041
9/04/71	#20	10	Women's Love Rights	Hot Wax 7105
2/26/72	#43	7	Since I Fell For You	Hot Wax 7201
5/27/72	#51	8	Rip Off	Hot Wax 7204
10/07/72	#84	4	If You Can Beat Me Rockin'	Hot Wax 7207
			MICHELLE LEE	
2/24/68	#60	11	L. David Sloane	Columbia 44413
			PEGGY LEE	
7/05/52	#8	4	Lover	Decca 28215
12/21/57	#52	3	Fever	Capitol 3998
7/12/58	#6	14	Fever	Capitol 3998
11/08/58	#92	2	Sweetheart	Capitol 4071
1/17/59	#62	7	Alright, Okay, You Win/	Capitol 4115
1/17/59	#49	8	My Man	Capitol 4115
5/16/59	#93	3	Hallelujah, I Love Him So	Capitol 4189
4/09/60	#97	1	Heart	Capitol 4349
1/12/63	#71	6	I'm A Woman	Capitol 4888
2/20/65	#86	4	Pass Me By	Capitol 5346
9/27/69	#10	11	Is That All There Is	Capitol 2602
			LEE and PAUL	
3/14/59	#84	3	The Chick	Columbia 41337
			RAYMOND LEFEVRE	
9/13/58	#17	19	The Day The Rains Came	Kapp 231
2/17/68	#36	11	Ame Caline (Soul Coaxing)	4 Corners 147

Debut Date	Peak Pos	Wks Chr	**ARTIST**/Song Title	Label & Number
			LEFT BANKE	
9/10/66	#2	14	Walk Away Renee	Smash 2041
12/31/66	#12	12	Pretty Ballerina	Smash 2074
			LEGACY OF SOUND	
8/14/93	#63	11	Happy*	RCA 62538
			*released as by LEGACY OF SOUND featuring MEJA	
			MICHEL LeGRAND	
1/22/72	#51	10	Brian's Song	Bell 45171
			LEILA K with ROB 'n' RAZ	
2/17/90	#46	10	Got To Get	Arista 9931
			PAUL LEKAKIS	
2/21/87	#48	15	Boom Boom (Let's Go Back To My Room)	ZYX 1266
			BILLY LEMMONS	
3/26/77	#93	2	Six Packs A Day	Ariola America 7661
			LEMONHEADS	
11/27/93	#75	10	Into Your Arms	Atlantic 85294
			LEMON PIPERS	
12/09/67	#1	16	Green Tambourine	Buddah 23
3/09/68	#42	8	Rice Is Nice	Buddah 31
5/11/68	#30	7	Jelly Jungle (Of Orange Marmalade)	Buddah 41
			JOHN LENNON (also PLASTIC ONO BAND)	
7/26/69	#11	9	Give Peace A Chance*	Apple 1809
11/15/69	#32	10	Cold Turkey*	Apple 1813
2/21/70	#3	14	Instant Karma (We All Shine On)	Apple 1818
1/09/71	#19	7	Mother**	Apple 1827
4/03/71	#10	9	Power To The People**	Apple 1830
10/16/71	#2	11	Imagine**	Apple 1840
12/18/71	#36	3	Happy Xmas (War Is Over)***	Apple 1842
6/03/72	#93	1	Woman Is The Nigger Of The World	Apple 1848
11/10/73	#10	12	Mind Games	Apple 1868
9/28/74	#1	13	Whatever Gets You Thru The Night****	Apple 1874
12/28/74	#10	11	#9 Dream	Apple 1878
3/15/75	#20	8	Stand By Me	Apple 1881
11/01/80	#1	21	(Just Like) Starting Over	Geffen 49604
1/17/81	#1	20	Woman	Geffen 49644
3/28/81	#7	18	Watching The Wheels	Geffen 49695
1/21/84	#6	14	Nobody Told Me	Polydor 817254
3/31/84	#57	8	I'm Stepping Out	Polydor 821107
10/15/88	#64	5	Jealous Guy*****	Capitol 44230
			*released as by THE PLASTIC ONO BAND	
			**released as by JOHN LENNON/PLASTIC ONO BAND	
			***released as by JOHN & YOKO with THE HARLEM COMMUNITY CHOIR	
			****released as by JOHN LENNON with THE PLASTIC ONO NUCLEAR BAND	
			*****released as by JOHN LENNON and THE PLASTIC ONO BAND	
			JULIAN LENNON	
10/20/84	#9	19	Valotte	Atlantic 89609
1/19/85	#7	20	Too Late For Goodbyes	Atlantic 89589
4/20/85	#23	14	Say You're Wrong	Atlantic 89567
8/03/85	#65	7	Jesse	Atlantic 89529
3/22/86	#34	13	Stick Around	Atlantic 89437
4/29/89	#72	8	Now You're In Heaven	Atlantic 88925
			LENNON SISTERS (see LAWRENCE WELK)	
			ANNIE LENNOX	
11/05/88	#5	20	Put A Little Love In Your Heart*	A&M 1255
5/30/92	#23	15	Why	Arista 2419
9/12/92	#11	31	Walking On Broken Glass	Arista 2452
1/30/93	#50	16	Little Bird	Arista 2508
			*released as by ANNIE LENNOX & AL GREEN	
			TOMMY LEONETTI	
1/04/64	#99	1	Soul Dance	RCA 8251
1/11/69	#68	8	Kum Ba Yah	Decca 32421

Debut Date	Peak Pos	Wks Chr	ARTIST/Song Title	Label & Number
			LE PAMPLEMOUSSE	
1/14/78	#80	6	Le Spank	AVI 153
			LE ROUX	
7/01/78	#55	13	New Orleans Ladies*	Capitol 4586
2/13/82	#22	13	Nobody Said It Was Easy	RCA 13059
5/22/82	#71	6	The Last Safe Place On Earth	RCA 13224
3/19/83	#80	5	Carrie's Gone	RCA 13456
			*released as by LOUISIANA'S LE ROUX	
			JAMES LeROY	
8/11/73	#94	3	Touch Of Magic	Janus 219
			KETTY LESTER	
2/17/62	#7	17	Love Letters	Era 3068
6/16/62	#50	8	But Not For Me	Era 3080
			LETTERMEN	
8/19/61	#8	16	The Way You Look Tonight	Capitol 4586
11/25/61	#13	14	When I Fall In Love	Capitol 4658
2/17/62	#19	11	Come Back Silly Girl	Capitol 4699
5/12/62	#50	9	How Is Julie?/	Capitol 4746
5/12/62	#85	2	Turn Around Look At Me	Capitol 4746
9/08/62	#97	2	Silly Boy (She Doesn't Love You)	Capitol 4810
10/27/62	#95	3	Again	Capitol 4851
6/26/65	#17	9	Theme From "A Summer Place"	Capitol 5437
9/25/65	#56	7	Secretly	Capitol 5499
12/18/65	#97	2	Sweet September	capitol 5544
6/25/66	#82	3	I Only Have Eyes For You	Capitol 5649
12/16/67	#7	14	Goin' Out Of My Head/Can't Take My Eyes Off You	Capitol 2054
3/23/68	#35	8	Sherry Don't Go	Capitol 2132
11/09/68	#52	9	Put Your Head On My Shoulder	Capitol 2324
6/21/69	#14	19	Hurt So Bad	Capitol 2482
10/11/69	#55	7	Shangri-La	Capitol 2643
12/13/69	#51	9	Traces/Memories (medley)	Capitol 2697
6/06/70	#54	8	She Cried	Capitol 2820
1/23/71	#78	7	Everything Is Good About You	Capitol 3020
10/02/71	#44	10	Love	Capitol 3192
			LEVEL 42	
2/15/86	#8	24	Something About You	Polydor 883362
7/26/86	#78	5	Hot Water	Polydor 885155
4/04/87	#19	19	Lessons In Love	Polydor 883956
8/08/87	#79	5	Running In The Family	Polydor 885957
			LEVERT	
8/15/87	#5	23	Casanova	Atlantic 89217
4/17/93	#80	6	Good 'Ol Days	Atlantic 87379
6/12/93	#82	6	ABC-123	Atlantic 87366
			GERALD LEVERT	
3/28/92	#71	6	Baby Hold On To Me*	Atco East West 98639
			*released as by GERALD LEVERT with EDDIE LEVERT	
			MARCY LEVY	
11/15/80	#63	10	Help Me!*	RSO 1047
			*released as by MARCY LEVY and ROBIN GIBB	
			BARBARA LEWIS	
4/20/63	#4	18	Hello Stranger	Atlantic 2184
8/10/63	#50	7	Straighten Up Your Heart	Atlantic 2200
1/11/64	#88	3	Snap Your Fingers/	Atlantic 2214
1/18/64	#58	12	Puppy Love	Atlantic 2214
5/16/64	#94	1	Spend A Little Time	Atlantic 2227
6/05/65	#10	15	Baby, I'm Yours	Atlantic 2283
9/11/65	#19	12	Make Me Your Baby	Atlantic 2300
7/23/66	#49	9	Make Me Belong To You	Atlantic 2346
11/05/66	#85	4	Baby What Do You Want Me To Do	Atlantic 2361
			BOBBY LEWIS	
5/20/61	#1	20	Tossin' And Turnin'	Beltone 1002
9/02/61	#24	11	One Track Mind	Beltone 1012
12/02/61	#82	3	What A Walk	Beltone 1015
			EPHRAIM LEWIS	
9/19/92	#68	10	Drowning In Your Eyes	Elektra 64710

Debut Date	Peak Pos	Wks Chr	ARTIST/Song Title	Label & Number
			GARY LEWIS and THE PLAYBOYS	
1/09/65	#1	14	This Diamond Ring	Liberty 55756
4/03/65	#3	12	Count Me In	Liberty 55778
7/03/65	#4	11	Save Your Heart For Me	Liberty 55809
9/25/65	#6	11	Everybody Loves A Clown	Liberty 55818
12/04/65	#4	12	She's Just My Style	Liberty 55846
3/05/66	#10	8	Sure Gonna Miss Her	Liberty 55865
5/07/66	#9	9	Green Grass	Liberty 55880
7/30/66	#15	8	My Heart's Symphony	Liberty 55898
10/08/66	#16	8	(You Don't Have To) Paint Me A Picture	Liberty 55914
12/10/66	#20	10	Where Will The Words Come From	Liberty 55933
3/04/67	#31	7	The Loser (With A Broken Heart)	Liberty 55949
5/13/67	#35	7	Girls In Love	Liberty 55971
8/05/67	#31	9	Jill	Liberty 55985
6/15/68	#8	15	Sealed With A Kiss	Liberty 56037
11/02/68	#67	5	Main Street	Liberty 56075
3/29/69	#49	12	Rhythm Of The Rain	Liberty 56093
			HUEY LEWIS and THE NEWS	
2/06/82	#13	17	Do You Believe In Love	Chrysalis 2589
5/22/82	#33	10	Hope You Love Me Like You Say You Do	Chrysalis 2604
8/21/82	#53	7	Workin' For A Livin'	Chrysalis 2630
9/10/83	#10	21	Heart And Soul	Chrysalis 42726
1/21/84	#5	21	I Want A New Drug	Chrysalis 42766
4/21/84	#7	22	The Heart Of Rock & Roll	Chrysalis 42782
7/21/84	#6	18	If This Is It	Chrysalis 42803
10/20/84	#23	15	Walking On A Thin Line	Chrysalis 42825
6/29/85	#1	20	Power Of Love	Chrysalis 42876
8/02/86	#1	20	Stuck With You	Chrysalis 43019
10/18/86	#6	18	Hip To Be Square	Chrysalis 43065
1/17/87	#1	18	Jacob's Ladder	Chrysalis 43097
4/04/87	#10	15	I Know What I Like	Chrysalis 43108
7/18/87	#11	19	Doing It All For My Baby	Chrysalis 43143
7/16/88	#4	16	Perfect World	Chrysalis 43265
10/08/88	#21	16	Small World	Chrysalis 43306
1/21/89	#38	10	Give Me The Keys	Chrysalis 43335
4/27/91	#8	20	Couple Days Off	EMI 50346
7/20/91	#15	17	It Hit Me Like A Hammer	EMI 50364
			JERRY LEWIS	
11/24/56	#9	17	Rock-A-Bye Your Baby With A Dixie Melody	Decca 30124
			JERRY LEE LEWIS	
7/06/57	#5	23	Whole Lotta Shakin' Going On	Sun 267
11/23/57	#2	14	Great Balls Of Fire	Sun 281
3/01/58	#10	9	Breathless	Sun 288
5/31/58	#20	8	High School Confidential	Sun 296
9/13/58	#74	4	Break Up	Sun 303
3/21/59	#81	3	Lovin' Up A Storm	Sun 317
8/01/59	#83	2	Let's Talk About Us	Sun 324
4/08/61	#33	8	What'd I Say	Sun 356
4/04/64	#100	1	I'm On Fire	Smash 1886
6/22/68	#97	1	What's Made Milwaukee Famous	Smash 2164
12/04/71	#63	8	Me And Bobby McGee	Mercury 73248
3/11/72	#56	8	Chantilly Lace	Mercury 73273
3/31/73	#25	12	Drinking Wine Spo-Dee-O'Dee	Mercury 73374
			RAMSEY LEWIS	
10/07/64	#71	6	Something You Got*	Argo 5481
7/31/65	#4	17	The "In" Crowd*	Argo 5506
8/14/65	#12	8	Hang On Sloopy*	Cadet 5522
1/22/66	#29	7	A Hard Day's Night*	Cadet 5525
3/26/66	#60	6	Hi Heel Sneakers (Part 1)*	Cadet 5531
7/16/66	#18	12	Wade In The Water	Cadet 5541
10/08/66	#53	5	Uptight	Cadet 5547
2/18/67	#75	5	One, Two, Three	Cadet 5556
11/18/67	#68	4	Soul Man	Cadet 5583
9/07/68	#92	2	Since You've Been Gone	Cadet 5609
10/18/69	#69	5	Julia	Cadet 5640
7/29/72	#79	5	Slippin' Into Darkness	Columbia 45634
12/28/74	#72	8	Hot Dawgit**	Columbia 10056
3/15/75	#67	7	Sun Goddess**	Columbia 10103

Debut Date	Peak Pos	Wks Chr	ARTIST/Song Title	Label & Number
			RAMSEY LEWIS—*continued*	
1/31/76	#88	2	What's The Name Of This Funk	Columbia 10235
			*released as by THE RAMSEY LEWIS TRIO	
			**released as by RAMSEY LEWIS and EARTH, WIND & FIRE	
			LEWIS & CLARKE EXPEDITION	
8/19/67	#67	6	I Feel Good (I Feel Bad)	Colgems 1006
			ORSA LIA	
3/24/79	#92	4	I Never Said I Love You	Infinity 50004
			LIFEGUARDS	
5/16/59	#99	1	Everybody Ou'ta The Pool	ABC-Paramount 10021
			ENOCH LIGHT & THE LIGHT BRIGADE	
11/08/58	#30	11	I Want To Be Happy Cha Cha	Grand Award 1020
6/06/59	#74	3	With My Eyes Open	Grand Award 1032
			LIGHTER SHADE OF BROWN	
8/03/91	#77	10	Latin Active*	Pump 15168
12/19/92	#56	16	Homies*	Pump 19134
			*released as by LIGHTER SHADE OF BROWN featuring TEARDROP & SHIRO	
			GORDON LIGHTFOOT	
12/26/70	#5	15	If You Could Read My Mind	Reprise 0974
6/19/71	#69	7	Talking In Your Sleep	Reprise 1020
5/20/72	#67	7	Beautiful	Reprise 1088
4/13/74	#1	17	Sundown	Reprise 1194
8/31/74	#13	14	Carefree Highway	Reprise 1309
3/29/75	#32	11	Rainy Day People	Reprise 1328
9/04/76	#1	18	The Wreck Of The Edmund Fitzgerald	Reprise 1369
2/19/77	#78	5	Race Among The Ruins	Reprise 1380
2/11/78	#31	12	The Circle Is Small	Warner Brothers 8518
5/01/82	#77	4	Baby Step Back	Warner Brothers 50012
			LIGHTHOUSE	
9/11/71	#16	13	One Fine Morning	Evolution 1048
12/11/71	#63	7	Take It Slow	Evolution 1052
10/14/72	#37	11	Sunny Days	Evolution 1069
10/13/73	#31	11	Pretty Lady	Polydor 14198
			LIGHTNING SEEDS	
5/26/90	#29	16	Pure	MCA 53816
			LIMAHL	
3/23/85	#22	19	The Never Ending Story	EMI America 8230
7/20/85	#47	11	Only For Love	EMI America 8277
			LIMELITERS	
4/22/61	#91	2	A Dollar Down	RCA 7859
			LIMITED WARRANTY	
7/26/86	#84	5	Victory Line	Atco 99541
			LIMMIE & FAMILY COOKIN'	
11/11/72	#64	10	You Can Do Magic	Avco 4602
			BOB LIND	
1/22/66	#7	12	Elusive Butterfly	World Pacific 77808
4/23/66	#92	2	Remember The Rain/	World Pacific 77822
4/23/66	#71	5	Truly Julie's Blues (I'll Be There)	World Pacific 77822
			KATHY LINDEN	
3/08/58	#14	12	Billy	Felsted 8510
5/31/58	#33	7	You'd Be Surprised	Felsted 8521
4/11/59	#14	14	Goodbye Jimmy, Goodbye	Felsted 8571
8/08/59	#84	4	So Close To My Heart	Felsted 8587
			LINDISFARNE	
9/09/72	#79	5	Lady Eleanor	Elektra 45799
9/30/78	#35	16	Run For Home	Atco 7093
			MARK LINDSAY	
7/12/69	#98	2	First Hymn From Grand Terrace	Columbia 44875
11/29/69	#9	16	Arizona	Columbia 45037
4/04/70	#31	7	Miss America	Columbia 45125
6/13/70	#20	11	Silver Bird	Columbia 45180
9/26/70	#37	10	And The Grass Won't Pay No Mind	Columbia 45229
12/26/70	#59	5	Problem Child	Columbia 45286

Debut Date	Peak Pos	Wks Chr	ARTIST/Song Title	Label & Number
5/29/71	#63	5	Been Too Long On The Road	Columbia 45385
10/02/71	#69	4	Are You Old Enough	Columbia 45462
			LINEAR	
3/03/90	#5	25	Sending All My Love	Atlantic 87961
7/21/90	#72	6	Don't You Come Cryin'	Atlantic 87877
5/16/92	#26	16	T.L.C.	Atlantic 87484
			ART LINKLETTER	
11/01/69	#44	6	We Love You, Call Collect	Capitol 2678
			LIPPS INC.	
3/29/80	#1	23	Funkytown	Casablanca 2233
8/02/80	#69	7	Rock It	Casablanca 2281
			PEGGY LIPTON	
12/27/69	#70	6	Lu	Ode 124
			LIQUID GOLD	
5/12/79	#66	6	My Baby's Baby	Parachute 524
9/24/83	#92	3	What's She Got	Critique 701
			LIQUID SMOKE	
4/11/70	#78	4	I Who Have Nothing	Avco Embassy 4522
			LISA LISA and CULT JAM	
6/08/85	#33	19	I Wonder If I Take You Home*	Columbia 04886
11/30/85	#71	9	Can You Feel The Beat*	Columbia 05669
8/02/86	#9	25	All Cried Out*	Columbia 05844
4/11/87	#1	23	Head To Toe	Columbia 07008
8/01/87	#1	26	Lost In Emotion	Columbia 07267
8/06/88	#85	5	Go For Yours*	Columbia 07982
4/15/89	#31	16	Little Jackie Wants To Be A Star	Columbia 68674
7/06/91	#82	9	Let The Beat Hit 'Em	Columbia 73847
			*released as by LISA LISA and CULT JAM with FULL FORCE	
			LITTLE ANTHONY and THE IMPERIALS	
8/16/58	#7	19	Tears On My Pillow	End 1027
11/22/58	#73	6	So Much	End 1036
2/21/59	#50	8	Wishful Thinking	End 1039
6/06/59	#71	7	A Prayer And A Juke Box	End 1047
12/05/59	#21	17	Shimmy, Shimmy, Ko-Ko-Bop	End 1060
4/16/60	#81	4	My Empty Room	End 1067
8/22/64	#20	12	I'm On The Outside (Looking In)	DCP 1104
11/07/64	#5	14	Goin' Out Of My Head	DCP 1119
2/06/65	#14	10	Hurt So Bad	DCP 1128
6/26/65	#22	10	Take Me Back	DCP 1136
10/02/65	#40	7	I Miss You So	DCP 1149
1/01/66	#75	6	Hurt	DCP 1154
5/07/66	#48	6	Better Use Your Head	Veep 1228
7/12/69	#50	10	Out Of Sight, Out Of Mind	United Artists 50552
11/08/69	#83	3	The Ten Commandments Of Love	United Artists 50598
2/28/70	#98	2	Don't Get Close	United Artists 50625
11/28/70	#65	7	Help Me Find A Way (To Say I Love You)	United Artists 50720
6/22/74	#90	3	I'm Falling In Love With You	Avco 4635
			LITTLE CAESAR	
6/23/90	#78	6	Chain Of Fools	DGC 19693
3/09/91	#75	8	In Your Arms	DGC 19003
			LITTLE CAESAR and THE CONSULS	
8/14/65	#76	5	My Girl Sloopy	Mala 512
			LITTLE CAESAR and THE ROMANS	
5/13/61	#9	13	Those Oldies But Goodies (Remind Me Of You)	Del-Fi 4158
			LITTLE DIPPERS	
1/30/60	#11	13	Forever	University 210
			LITTLE EVA	
6/30/62	#1	18	The Loco-Motion	Dimension 1000
11/03/62	#15	12	Keep Your Hands Off My Baby	Dimension 1003
2/02/63	#21	11	Let's Turkey Trot	Dimension 1006
5/25/63	#21	11	Swinging On A Star*	Dimension 1010
5/25/63	#42	6	Old Smokey Locomotion	Dimension 1011
8/10/63	#91	2	What I Gotta Do	Dimension 1013
			*released as by BIG DEE IRWIN with LITTLE EVA	

Debut Date	Peak Pos	Wks Chr	ARTIST/Song Title	Label & Number
			LITTLE FEAT	
5/06/78	#92	5	Oh Atlanta	Warner Brothers 8566
			LITTLE JO ANN	
6/30/62	#71	7	My Daddy Is President	Kapp 467
			LITTLE JOE & THE THRILLERS	
9/21/57	#32	13	Peanuts	Okeh 7088
			LITTLE JOEY and THE FLIPS	
6/09/62	#30	11	Bongo Stomp	Joy 262
			LITTLE MILTON	
12/26/64	#47	8	Blind Man	Checker 1096
4/03/65	#18	10	We're Gonna Make It	Checker 1105
6/12/65	#42	8	Who's Cheating Who?	Checker 1113
12/08/65	#89	3	Your People	Checker 1128
2/05/66	#84	3	We Got The Winning Hand	Checker 1132
2/08/69	#80	3	Grits Ain't Groceries	Checker 1212
1/03/70	#52	8	If Walls Could Talk	Checker 1226
4/25/70	#82	6	Baby I Love You	Checker 1227
12/12/72	#71	5	That's What Love Will Make You Do	Stax 0111
			LITTLE RICHARD	
5/26/56	#7	4	Long Tall Sally	Specialty 572
8/04/56	#21	9	Rip It Up/	Specialty 579
8/04/56	#32	1	Ready Teddy	Specialty 579
10/20/56	#50	1	Heeby-Jeebies	Specialty 584
3/16/57	#22	11	Lucille	Specialty 598
6/15/57	#27	13	Jenny, Jenny	Specialty 606
9/28/57	#12	13	Keep A Knockin'	Specialty 611
2/15/58	#18	9	Good Golly Miss Molly	Specialty 624
6/14/58	#52	2	Ooh! My Soul	Specialty 633
9/20/58	#58	4	Baby Face	Specialty 645
11/25/61	#91	3	He's Not Just Another Soldier	Mercury 71884
11/13/65	#83	3	I Don't Know What You've Got But It's Got Me (Part 1) . .	Vee-Jay 698
5/30/70	#62	5	Freedom Blues	Reprise 0907
9/26/70	#96	1	Greenwood Mississippi	Reprise 0942
3/08/86	#47	11	Great Gosh A'Mighty!	MCA 52780
			LITTLE RIVER BAND	
9/25/76	#31	15	It's A Long Way There	Harvest 4318
2/05/77	#71	7	I'll Always Call Your Name	Harvest 4380
7/30/77	#14	21	Help Is On Its Way	Harvest 4428
12/17/77	#22	17	Happy Anniversary	Harvest 4524
7/22/78	#3	21	Reminiscing	Harvest 4605
1/13/79	#10	20	Lady	Harvest 4667
7/14/79	#7	20	Lonesome Loser	Capitol 4748
10/20/79	#13	18	Cool Change	Capitol 4789
5/03/80	#62	6	It's Not A Wonder	Capitol 4862
8/22/81	#7	21	Night Owls	Capitol 5033
12/05/81	#13	17	Take It Easy On Me	Capitol 5057
4/03/82	#13	16	Man On Your Mind	Capitol 5061
11/20/82	#8	19	The Other Guy	Capitol 5185
5/07/83	#26	14	We Two	Capitol 5231
7/30/83	#42	10	You're Driving Me Out Of My Mind	Capitol 5256
1/26/85	#49	11	Playing To Win*	Capitol 5411
			*released as by LRB	
			LITTLE SISTER	
2/14/70	#20	13	You're The One (Part 2)	Stone Flower 9000
12/12/70	#22	12	Somebody's Watching You	Stone Flower 9001
			LITTLE STEVEN & THE DISCIPLES OF SOUL	
12/25/82	#76	7	Forever	EMI America 8144
			LITTLE TEXAS	
9/04/93	#78	7	What Might Have Been	Warner Brothers 18516
			LIVERPOOL EXPRESS	
9/25/76	#96	5	You Are My Love	Atco 7058
			JOHN LiVIGNI	
10/25/75	#84	5	Machines	Raintree 2204
			LIVING COLOUR	
3/11/89	#8	21	Cult Of Personality	Epic 68611

Debut Date	Peak Pos	Wks Chr	ARTIST/Song Title	Label & Number
7/01/89	#69	6	Open Letter (To A Landlord)	Epic 68934
8/26/89	#26	21	Glamour Boys	Epic 68548
			LIVING IN A BOX	
6/27/87	#20	15	Living In A Box	Chrysalis 43104
			L.L. COOL J	
8/08/87	#14	13	I Need Love	Def Jam 07350
2/20/88	#43	13	Going Back To Cali	Def Jam 07679
6/24/89	#23	15	I'm That Type Of Guy	Def Jam 68902
10/06/90	#37	10	The Boomin' System	Def Jam 73457
12/08/90	#22	26	Around The Way Girl	Def Jam 73610
5/18/91	#63	10	Mama Said Knock You Out	Def Jam 73706
7/03/93	#50	12	Back Seat (Of My Jeep)	Def Jam 74984
			IAN LLOYD	
10/27/79	#73	5	Slip Away	Scotti Brothers 505
			LOBO	
3/27/71	#8	13	Me And You And A Dog Named Boo	Big Tree 112
6/12/71	#76	3	I'm The Only One/	Big Tree 116
6/19/71	#44	8	She Didn't Do Magic	Big Tree 116
9/11/71	#82	3	California Kid And Reemo	Big Tree 119
6/24/72	#52	10	A Simple Man	Big Tree 141
9/16/72	#1	15	I'd Love You To Want Me	Big Tree 147
12/30/72	#4	12	Don't Expect Me To Be Your Friend	Big Tree 158
4/07/73	#27	10	It Sure Took A Long, Long Time	Big Tree 16001
6/16/73	#20	15	How Can I Tell Her	Big Tree 16004
10/13/73	#50	8	There Ain't No Way	Big Tree 16012
3/30/74	#30	10	Standing At The End Of The Line	Big Tree 15001
7/20/74	#37	8	Rings	Big Tree 15008
3/22/75	#30	10	Don't Tell Me Goodnight	Big Tree 16033
7/28/79	#16	18	Where Were You When I Was Falling In Love	MCA 41065
12/22/79	#93	5	Holdin' On For Dear Love	MCA 41152
			HANK LOCKLIN	
6/04/60	#6	19	Please Help Me, I'm Falling	RCA 7692
			DAVE LOGGINS	
5/11/74	#7	21	Please Come To Boston	Epic 11115
10/26/74	#67	9	Someday	Epic 50035
			KENNY LOGGINS	
7/16/77	#53	13	I Believe In Love	Columbia 10569
7/29/78	#5	22	Whenever I Call You "Friend"	Columbia 10794
12/09/78	#54	8	Easy Driver	Columbia 10866
10/13/79	#8	24	This Is It	Columbia 11109
3/01/80	#42	11	Keep The Fire	Columbia 11215
7/12/80	#4	24	I'm Alright (Theme From "Caddyshack")	Columbia 11317
8/28/82	#15	15	Don't Fight It*	Columbia 03192
11/27/82	#15	16	Heart To Heart	Columbia 03377
3/05/83	#25	16	Welcome To Heartlight	Columbia 03555
1/28/84	#1	25	Footloose	Columbia 04310
6/16/84	#17	13	I'm Free (Heaven Helps The Man)	Columbia 04452
3/23/85	#22	13	Vox Humana	Columbia 04849
5/25/85	#37	17	Forever	Columbia 04931
5/10/86	#4	20	Danger Zone	Columbia 05893
8/16/86	#56	7	Playing With The Boys	Columbia 05902
3/07/87	#10	26	Meet Me Halfway	Columbia 06690
7/09/88	#9	19	Nobody's Fool	Columbia 07971
11/12/88	#76	6	I'm Gonna Miss You	Columbia 08091
1/28/89	#64	5	Tell Her	Columbia 68531
10/19/91	#45	16	Convictions Of The Heart	Columbia 74029
3/07/92	#85	8	The Real Thing	Columbia 74186
			*released as by KENNY LOGGINS with STEVE PERRY	
			LOGGINS and MESSINA	
4/22/72	#83	4	Vahevella	Columbia 45550
6/17/72	#88	3	Nobody But You	Columbia 45617
11/04/72	#5	17	Your Mama Don't Dance	Columbia 45719
3/24/73	#11	13	Thinking Of You	Columbia 45815
10/27/73	#13	12	My Music	Columbia 45952
2/23/74	#41	6	Watching The River Run	Columbia 46010
1/25/75	#62	6	Changes	Columbia 10077
3/29/75	#45	9	Growin'	Columbia 10118

Debut Date	Peak Pos	Wks Chr	**ARTIST**/Song Title	Label & Number
			LOGGINS and MESSINA—*continued*	
9/06/75	#92	2	I Like It Like That	Columbia 10188
11/01/75	#94	2	A Lover's Question	Columbia 10222
			LO-KEY?	
11/21/92	#24	21	I Gotta Thang 4 Ya!	Perspective 0008
			LOLITA	
10/08/60	#7	20	Sailor (Your Home Is The Sea)	Kapp 349
2/18/61	#85	4	Cowboy Jimmy Joe	Kapp 370
			GUY LOMBARDO	
3/25/50	#1	21	Third Man Theme	Decca 24839
			JOE LONDON	
10/24/59	#65	7	It Might Have Been	Liberty 55209
			LAURIE LONDON	
3/15/58	#1	17	He's Got The Whole World (In His Hands)	Capitol 3891
			LONDONBEAT	
2/09/91	#1	24	I've Been Thinking About You	Radioactive 53992
5/11/91	#12	19	A Better Love	Radioactive 54101
			LONDON QUIREBOYS	
9/29/90	#69	8	I Don't Love You Anymore	Capitol 44588
			LONDON SYMPHONY ORCHESTRA	
7/16/77	#18	16	Star Wars	20th Century 2345
1/20/79	#69	5	Theme From Superman (Main Title)	Warner Brothers 8729
			LONE JUSTICE	
5/11/85	#59	8	Ways To Be Wicked	Geffen 29023
8/03/85	#83	4	Sweet, Sweet Baby (I'm Falling)	Geffen 28965
1/17/87	#54	11	Shelter	Geffen 28520
			SHORTY LONG	
2/03/68	#71	6	Night Fo' Last	Soul 35040
6/01/68	#10	9	Here Comes The Judge	Soul 35044
3/15/69	#97	1	I Had A Dream	Soul 35054
9/20/69	#100	1	A Whiter Shade Of Pale	Soul 35064
			CLAUDINE LONGET	
8/31/68	#94	1	Walk In	A&M 967
			LOOKING GLASS	
6/10/72	#1	16	Brandy (You're A Fine Girl)	Epic 10874
11/18/72	#75	3	Golden Rainbow	Epic 10900
2/24/73	#94	2	Rainbow Man	Epic 10953
7/14/73	#31	16	Jimmy Loves Mary-Anne	Epic 11001
			SHELLEY LOONEY	
3/01/80	#98	3	This Is My Country, Thank You Canada	Mercury 76050
			LOOSE ENDS	
7/20/85	#46	11	Hangin' On A String (Contemplating)	MCA 52570
			DENISE LOPEZ	
6/18/85	#40	18	Sayin' Sorry (Don't Make It Right)	Vendetta 7200
11/12/88	#81	5	If You Feel It	Vendetta 7213
12/17/88	#75	7	The Love You Take*	A&M 1264
11/10/90	#84	3	Don't You Wanna Be Mine	A&M 1526
			*released as by DAN HARTMAN and DENISE LOPEZ	
			TRINI LOPEZ	
7/27/63	#3	15	If I Had A Hammer	Reprise 20198
11/16/63	#26	11	Kansas City	Reprise 20236
5/16/64	#51	13	What Have I Got Of My Own	Reprise 0276
8/15/64	#41	9	Michael	Reprise 0300
1/16/65	#22	10	Lemon Tree	Reprise 0336
4/17/65	#81	4	Sad Tomorrows	Reprise 0328
10/16/65	#64	8	Sinner Man	Reprise 0405
4/02/66	#48	7	I'm Comin' Home, Cindy	Reprise 0455
7/02/66	#100	1	La Bamba (Part 1)	Reprise 0480
2/11/67	#93	4	Gonna Get Along Without You Now	Reprise 0547
6/21/75	#76	5	Somethin' 'Bout You Baby I Like	Private Stock 45024
			DENISE LOR	
10/02/54	#1	14	If I Give My Heart To You	Majar 27

Debut Date	Peak Pos	Wks Chr	ARTIST/Song Title	Label & Number
			A'ME LORAIN	
1/27/90	#13	21	Whole Wide World	RCA 9098
6/16/90	#56	9	Follow My Heartbeat	RCA 2620
			JEFF LORBER	
12/13/86	#31	16	Facts Of Love*	Warner Brothers 28588
			*released as by JEFF LORBER featuring KARYN WHITE	
			LORD ROCKINGHAM'S XI	
10/04/58	#97	1	Fried Onions	London 1810
			LORDS OF THE UNDERGROUND	
4/03/93	#70	8	Funky Child	Pendulum 64672
7/17/93	#61	20	Chief Rocka	Pendulum 64631
			LORELEI	
11/18/72	#99	1	S.T.O.P.	Columbia 45629
			TREY LORENZ	
10/10/92	#13	19	Someone To Hold	Epic 74482
			GLORIA LORING & CARL ANDERSON	
7/12/86	#5	21	Friends And Lovers	Carrere 06122
			LOS BRAVOS	
8/13/66	#3	13	Black Is Black	Press 60002
12/03/66	#69	5	Going Nowhere	Press 60003
5/18/68	#34	9	Bring A Little Lovin'	Parrot 3020
			LOS INDIOS TABAJARAS	
9/21/63	#7	16	Maria Elena	RCA 8216
2/29/64	#97	3	Always In My Heart	RCA 8313
			LOS LOBOS	
3/30/85	#79	6	Will The Wolf Survive?	Slash 29093
7/04/87	#1	23	La Bamba	Slash 28336
9/12/87	#24	18	Come On, Let's Go	Slash 28186
			LOS POP TOPS	
10/05/68	#93	3	Oh Lord, Why Lord	Calla 154
			LOST GENERATION	
6/27/70	#39	11	The Sly, Slick, And The Wicked	Brunswick 55436
			JOHN D. LOUDERMILK	
3/09/57	#15	11	Sittin' In The Balcony*	Colonial 430
11/11/61	#28	10	Language Of Love	RCA 7938
4/14/62	#93	4	Thou Shalt Not Steal	RCA 7993
12/01/62	#74	5	Road Hog	RCA 8101
			*released as by JOHNNY DEE	
			LOUIE LOUIE	
5/05/90	#18	16	Sittin' In The Lap Of Luxury	WTG 73266
8/25/90	#61	8	I Wanna Get Back With You	WTG 73472
			LOVE	
4/30/66	#35	9	My Little Red Book	Elektra 45603
8/13/66	#33	9	7 And 7 Is	Elektra 45605
			DARLENE LOVE	
3/30/63	#38	9	(Today I Met) The Boy I'm Gonna Marry	Philles 111
7/20/63	#27	10	Wait Til' My Bobby Gets Home	Philles 114
10/26/63	#69	5	A Fine Fine Boy	Philles 117
			JOHNNY LOVE	
9/27/58	#55	13	Whose Heart Are You Breaking Now	Tee Pee 395
			MARION LOVE	
3/06/71	#97	3	I Believe In Music	A&R 505
			MONIE LOVE	
4/13/91	#55	12	It's A Shame (My Sister)*	Warner Brothers 19515
8/15/92	#93	3	Full Term Love	Giant 18954
			*released as by MONIE LOVE featuring TRUE IMAGE	
			RONNIE LOVE	
1/21/61	#74	4	Chills And Fever	Dot 16144
			LOVE and KISSES	
5/20/78	#44	12	Thank God It's Friday	Casablanca 925
			LOVE and MONEY	
2/25/89	#74	6	Halleluiah Man	Mercury 870596

Debut Date	Peak Pos	Wks Chr	ARTIST/Song Title	Label & Number
			LOVE and ROCKETS	
5/20/89	#4	23	So Alive	RCA 8956
9/30/89	#82	5	No Big Deal	Big Time 9045
			LOVE GENERATION	
7/08/67	#81	4	Groovy Summertime	Imperial 66243
9/07/68	#93	1	Montage From How Sweet It Is	Imperial 66310
			LOVELITES	
1/24/70	#86	4	How Can I Tell My Mom And Dad	Uni 55181
			LOVERBOY	
2/07/81	#33	19	Turn Me Loose	Columbia 11421
6/20/81	#63	8	The Kid Is Hot Tonite	Columbia 02068
11/14/81	#25	20	Working For The Weekend	Columbia 02589
4/10/82	#25	16	When It's Over	Columbia 02814
12/04/82	#71	8	Jump	Columbia 03346
6/11/83	#17	17	Hot Girls In Love	Columbia 03941
9/17/83	#33	13	Queen Of The Broken Hearts	Columbia 04096
8/24/85	#12	21	Lovin' Every Minute Of It	Columbia 05569
11/16/85	#66	11	Dangerous	Columbia 05711
1/18/86	#12	18	This Could Be The Night	Columbia 05765
4/26/86	#65	7	Lead A Double Life	Columbia 05867
8/02/86	#10	16	Heaven In Your Eyes	Columbia 06178
8/29/87	#43	13	Notorious	Columbia 07324
12/02/89	#80	3	Too Hot	Columbia 73066
			LOVER SPEAKS	
9/06/86	#88	3	No More "I Love You's"	A&M 2846
			BETTY LOVETTE	
5/08/65	#90	2	Let Me Down Easy	Calla 102
			EDDIE LOVETTE	
5/17/69	#79	5	Too Experienced	Steady 124
			LOVE UNLIMITED	
3/18/72	#7	16	Walkin' In The Rain With The One I Love	Uni 55319
12/29/73	#87	3	It May Be Winter Outside	20th Century 2062
4/20/74	#87	3	Under The Influence Of Love	20th Century 2082
11/16/74	#29	15	I Belong To You	20th Century 2141
			LOVE UNLIMITED ORCHESTRA	
12/01/73	#1	17	Love's Theme	20th Century 2069
4/27/74	#66	6	Rhapsody In White	20th Century 2090
2/01/75	#28	13	Satin Soul	20th Century 2162
10/02/76	#95	6	My Sweet Summer Suite	20th Century 2301
2/12/77	#78	5	Theme From King Kong (Part 1)	20th Century 2325
			LOVIN' SPOONFUL	
8/28/65	#8	13	Do You Believe In Magic	Kama Sutra 201
11/20/65	#11	13	You Didn't Have To Be So Nice	Kama Sutra 205
2/26/66	#1	12	Daydream	Kama Sutra 208
5/07/66	#4	10	Did You Ever Have To Make Up Your Mind?	Kama Sutra 209
7/09/66	#1	12	Summer In The City	Kama Sutra 211
10/15/66	#9	10	Rain On The Roof	Kama Sutra 216
12/17/66	#10	10	Nashville Cats/	Kama Sutra 219
1/21/67	#97	1	Full Measure	Kama Sutra 219
2/11/67	#15	9	Darling Be Home Soon	Kama Sutra 220
4/29/67	#17	9	Six O'Clock	Kama Sutra 225
10/28/67	#16	6	She Is Still A Mystery	Kama Sutra 239
1/06/68	#40	6	Money	Kama Sutra 241
7/13/68	#59	5	Never Goin' Back	Kama Sutra 250
1/25/69	#82	5	Me About You	Kama Sutra 255
			ANDY FAIRWEATHER LOW	
3/29/75	#83	5	Spider Jivin'	A&M 1649
			BERNIE LOWE	
11/29/58	#57	7	Sing Sing Sing	Cameo 153
			JIM LOWE	
9/15/56	#2	25	The Green Door	Dot 15486
5/04/57	#11	10	Four Walls/	Dot 15569
5/18/57	#33	7	Talkin' To The Blues	Dot 15569
			NICK LOWE	
7/21/79	#12	20	Cruel To Be Kind	Columbia 11018

210

Debut Date	Peak Pos	Wks Chr	ARTIST/Song Title	Label & Number
			L.T.D.	
9/25/76	#22	23	Love Ballad	A&M 1847
9/17/77	#6	24	(Every Time I Turn Around) Back In Love Again	A&M 1974
3/18/78	#81	6	Never Get Enough Of Your Love	A&M 2005
8/26/78	#54	10	Holding On (When Love Is Gone)	A&M 2057
11/15/80	#38	19	Shine On	A&M 2283
			L'TRIMM	
10/01/88	#65	9	Cars With The Boom	Atlantic 89005
			FRANK LUCAS	
5/21/77	#72	5	Good Thing Man	ICA 001
			MATT LUCAS	
5/04/63	#45	9	I'm Movin' On	Smash 1813
			LUKE	
7/28/90	#18	11	Banned In The U.S.A.*	Luke 98915
			*released as by LUKE featuring 2 LIVE CREW	
			ROBIN LUKE	
8/02/58	#6	19	Susie Darlin'	Dot 15781
11/08/58	#97	1	My Girl	Dot 15839
			LULU	
7/25/64	#95	4	Shout*	Parrot 9678
9/02/67	#1	17	To Sir With Love	Epic 10187
12/09/67	#37	8	Best Of Both Worlds	Epic 10260
3/30/68	#44	7	Me, The Peaceful Heart	Epic 10302
8/03/68	#62	7	Morning Dew	Epic 10367
12/13/69	#18	16	Oh Me Oh My (I'm A Fool For You Baby)	Atco 6722
4/18/70	#41	7	Hum A Song (From Your Heart)	Atco 6749
7/04/70	#95	2	After The Feeling Is Gone	Atco 6761
8/01/81	#14	18	I Could Never Miss You (More Than I Do)	Alfa 7006
11/21/81	#42	12	If I Were You	Alfa 7011
			*released as by LULU and THE LUVERS	
			BOB LUMAN	
9/10/60	#5	15	Let's Think About Living	Warner Brothers 5172
5/06/61	#95	3	The Great Showman	Warner Brothers 5204
			LUNAR FUNK	
1/29/72	#56	8	Mr. Penguin (Part 1)	Bell 45172
			VICTOR LUNDBERG	
11/11/67	#6	7	An Open Letter To My Teenage Son	Liberty 55996
			PAT LUNDI	
10/04/75	#91	3	Party Music	Vigor 1723
			LY-DELLS	
8/12/61	#67	7	The Wizard Of Love	Master 251
			ARTHUR LYMAN	
6/13/59	#36	8	Taboo	Hi Fi 550
5/27/61	#6	15	Yellow Bird*	Hi Fi 5024
2/02/63	#49	11	Love For Sale	Hi Fi 5066
			*released as by THE ARTHUR LYMAN GROUP	
			LYME & CYBELLE	
4/09/66	#93	2	Follow Me	White Whale 228
			FRANKIE LYMON and THE TEENAGERS	
3/17/56	#6	12	Why Do Fools Fall In Love*	Gee 1002
8/04/56	#33	3	I Promise To Remember	Gee 1018
10/06/56	#42	6	The ABC's Of Love	Gee 1022
7/20/57	#20	12	Goody Goody	Gee 1039
2/28/59	#81	5	Up Jumped A Rabbit	Roulette 4128
7/30/60	#45	8	Little Bitty Pretty One**	Roulette 4257
			*released as by THE TEENAGERS featuring FRANKIE LYMON	
			**released as by FRANKIE LYMON	
			BARBARA LYNN	
6/16/62	#4	15	You'll Lose A Good Thing	Jamie 1229
9/22/62	#75	7	Second Fiddle Girl	Jamie 1233
2/23/63	#82	5	Don't Be Cruel	Jamie 1244
8/31/63	#75	5	(I Cried At) Laura's Wedding	Jamie 1260

Debut Date	Peak Pos	Wks Chr	ARTIST/Song Title	Label & Number
			BARBARA LYNN—*continued*	
7/04/64	#69	6	Oh! Baby (We Got A Good Thing Goin')	Jamie 1277
8/21/71	#98	1	(Until Then) I'll Suffer	Atlantic 2182
			CHERYL LYNN	
11/25/78	#10	17	Got To Be Real	Columbia 10808
4/21/79	#65	8	Star Love	Columbia 10907
8/08/81	#68	9	Shake It Up Tonight	Columiba 02102
2/11/84	#72	9	Encore	Columbia 04256
			LORETTA LYNN	
2/06/71	#90	6	After The Fire Is Gone*	Decca 32776
3/08/75	#49	7	The Pill	MCA 40358
			*released as by LORETTA LYNN/CONWAY TWITTY	
			VERA LYNN	
7/12/52	#1	16	Auf Wiederseh'n Sweetheart	London 1227
11/29/52	#6	9	Yours	London 1261
6/19/54	#5	6	If You Love Me	London 1412
5/04/57	#40	8	Don't Cry My Love	London 1729
			GLORIA LYNNE	
4/29/61	#78	8	He Needs Me	Everest 19409
1/18/64	#22	13	I Wish You Love	Everest 2036
4/18/64	#98	1	I Should Care	Everest 2042
4/18/64	#95	1	Be Anything (But Be Mine)	Fontana 1890
6/12/65	#65	7	Watermelon Man	Fontana 1511
			LYNYRD SKYNYRD	
7/27/74	#7	17	Sweet Home Alabama	MCA 40258
11/23/74	#25	12	Free Bird (studio version)	MCA 40328
6/07/75	#41	10	Saturday Night Special	MCA 40416
3/27/76	#86	5	Double Trouble	MCA 40532
12/04/76	#32	13	Free Bird (live version)	MCA 40665
11/26/77	#7	22	What's Your Name	MCA 40819
4/08/78	#68	5	You Got That Right	MCA 40888
			JOHNNY LYTLE	
1/15/66	#78	5	The Loop	Tuba 2004

M

			M	
8/11/79	#4	24	Pop Muzik	Sire 49033
			M+M	
7/07/84	#79	6	Black Stations/White Stations	RCA 13824
			HARRY M & THE MARVELS	
10/07/61	#95	2	The "U-T"	ABC-Paramount 10243
			MOMS MABLEY	
6/21/69	#47	6	Abraham, Martin And John	Mercury 72935
			JAMES MacARTHUR	
6/22/63	#90	4	The Ten Commandments Of Love	Scepter 1250
			RALPH MacDONALD	
9/04/84	#54	10	In The Name Of Love*	Polydor 881221
			*released as by RALPH MacDONALD with BILL WITHERS	
			BYRON MacGREGOR	
12/29/73	#1	10	Americans	Westbound 222
			MARY MacGREGOR	
11/13/76	#1	25	Torn Between Two Lovers	Ariola America 7638
5/07/77	#69	6	This Girl (Has Turned Into A Woman)	Ariola America 7662
8/06/77	#93	5	For A While	Ariola America 7667
8/11/79	#44	13	Good Friend	RSO 938
			MACHINE	
4/21/79	#93	4	There But For The Grace Of God Go I	RCA 11456
			LONNIE MACK	
6/01/63	#5	15	Memphis	Fraternity 906
8/24/63	#28	8	Wham!	Fraternity 912
10/23/65	#80	4	Honky Tonk '65	Fraternity 951
			WARNER MACK	
11/23/57	#44	3	Roc-A-Chicka	Decca 30471

Debut Date	Peak Pos	Wks Chr	ARTIST/Song Title	Label & Number
			GISELE MacKENZIE	
7/23/55	#3	11	Hard To Get	X 0137
12/15/56	#49	1	The Star You Wished Upon Last Night	Vik 0233
			GORDON MacRAE	
9/20/58	#31	13	The Secret	Capitol 4033
			MAD COBRA	
10/24/92	#13	23	Flex	Columbia 74373
			JOHNNY MADDOX	
3/05/55	#1	16	The Crazy Otto	Dot 15325
			BETTY MADIGAN	
8/09/58	#27	11	Dance Everyone Dance	Coral 62007
			MAD LADS	
10/23/65	#90	4	Don't Have To Shop Around	Volt 127
3/12/66	#71	6	I Want Someone	Volt 131
7/19/69	#89	4	By The Time I Get To Phoenix	Volt 4016
			MADNESS	
4/30/83	#5	21	Our House	Geffen 29668
8/20/83	#33	11	It Must Be Love	Geffen 29562
			MADONNA	
10/29/83	#12	25	Holiday	Sire 29478
3/10/84	#9	28	Borderline	Sire 29354
8/18/84	#7	22	Lucky Star	Sire 29177
11/17/84	#1	21	Like A Virgin	Sire 29210
2/09/85	#1	19	Material Girl	Sire 29083
3/02/85	#2	21	Crazy For You	Geffen 29051
4/27/85	#7	18	Angel	Sire 29008
8/17/85	#7	16	Dress You Up	Sire 28919
4/12/86	#1	18	Live To Tell	Sire 28717
6/28/86	#1	16	Papa Don't Preach	Sire 28660
10/04/86	#3	18	True Blue	Sire 28591
12/06/86	#1	21	Open Your Heart	Sire 28508
3/21/87	#4	17	La Isla Bonita	Sire 28425
7/11/87	#1	20	Who's That Girl	Sire 28341
9/12/87	#3	21	Causing A Commotion	Sire 28224
3/18/89	#1	19	Like A Prayer	Sire 27539
6/03/89	#1	17	Express Yourself	Sire 22948
8/19/89	#1	16	Cherish	Sire 22883
11/04/89	#15	15	Oh Father	Sire 22723
2/03/90	#8	16	Keep It Together	Sire 19986
4/14/90	#1	21	Vogue	Sire 19863
6/23/90	#8	15	Hanky Panky	Sire 19789
11/17/90	#1	20	Justify My Love	Sire 19485
7/04/92	#1	21	This Used To Be My Playground	Sire 18822
10/17/92	#3	17	Erotica	Maverick 18782
12/12/92	#6	20	Deeper And Deeper	Maverick 18639
2/27/93	#27	12	Bad Girl	Maverick 18650
7/10/93	#21	28	Rain	Maverick 18505
			JOHNNY MAESTRO	
2/25/61	#36	10	Model Girl	Coed 545
5/06/61	#53	9	What A Surprise	Coed 549
8/12/61	#98	1	Mr. Happiness	Coed 552
			MAGAZINE 60	
5/17/86	#68	9	Don Quichotte	Baja 001
			CLEDUS MAGGARD and THE CITIZEN'S BAND	
1/03/76	#20	14	The White Knight	Mercury 73751
			MAGIC LANTERNS	
10/19/68	#17	12	Shame, Shame	Atlantic 2560
1/23/71	#91	4	One Night Stand	Big Tree 109
7/08/72	#90	3	Country Woman	Charisma 100
			MAGISTRATES	
6/01/68	#45	7	Here Comes The Judge	MGM 13946
			MAGNIFICENT MEN	
6/03/67	#98	1	I'm Glad I Could Be So Happy	Capitol 5905
9/09/67	#90	4	Sweet Soul Medley (Part 1)	Capitol 5976

Debut Date	Peak Pos	Wks Chr	ARTIST/Song Title	Label & Number
			GEORGE MAHARIS	
4/21/62	#31	12	Teach Me Tonight/	Epic 9504
5/05/62	#94	2	After The Lights Go Down Low	Epic 9504
7/21/62	#61	8	Love Me As I Love You	Epic 9522
11/10/62	#60	6	Baby Has Gone Bye Bye	Epic 9555
6/22/63	#89	2	Where Can You Go	Epic 9600
9/14/63	#84	5	That's How It Goes	Epic 9613
			MAHOGANY RUSH	
8/03/74	#88	4	A New Rock And Roll	20th Century 2111
			JOHN CULLITON MAHONEY	
9/14/74	#85	2	Ballad Of Evel Knievel	Amherst 701
			MAIN INGREDIENT	
6/27/70	#53	11	You've Been My Inspiration	RCA 0340
10/17/70	#83	3	I'm Better Off Without You	RCA 0382
12/19/70	#41	13	I'm So Proud	RCA 0401
5/08/71	#47	9	Spinning Around	RCA 0456
9/04/71	#74	5	Black Seeds Keep On Growing	RCA 0517
7/08/72	#1	20	Everybody Plays The Fool	RCA 0731
12/23/72	#48	9	You've Got To Take It (If You Want It)	RCA 0856
5/26/73	#78	3	You Can Call Me Rover	RCA 0939
2/09/74	#8	19	Just Don't Want To Be Lonely	RCA 0205
6/15/74	#23	13	Happiness Is Just Around The Bend	RCA 0305
5/17/75	#80	6	Rolling Down A Mountainside	RCA 10224
			MAI TAI	
5/24/86	#84	5	Female Intuition	Critique 722
			MAJORS	
8/04/62	#20	14	A Wonderful Dream	Imperial 5855
11/10/62	#61	6	A Little Bit Now (A Little Bit Later)/	Imperial 5879
11/24/62	#72	8	She's A Troublemaker	Imperial 5879
2/15/64	#93	1	I'll Be There (To Bring You Love)	Impeial 66009
			MIRIAM MAKEBA	
10/07/67	#13	12	Pata Pata	Reprise 0606
1/20/68	#64	4	Malayisha	Reprise 0654
			MITCH MALLOY	
4/25/92	#36	19	Anything At All	RCA 62196
8/15/92	#64	5	Nobody Wins In This War	RCA 62270
			SIW MALMKVIST & UMBERTO MARCATO	
7/25/64	#86	5	Sole Sole Sole	Jubilee 5479
			MALO	
2/26/72	#12	14	Suavecito	Warner Brothers 7559
			RICHARD MALTBY	
11/19/60	#83	4	Theme From The Rat Race	Roulette 4270
			MAMA CASS	
7/06/68	#10	11	Dream A Little Dream Of Me	Dunhill 4145
11/02/68	#74	3	California Earthquake	Dunhill 4166
3/15/69	#59	5	Move In A Little Closer Baby	Dunhill 4184
6/07/69	#35	14	It's Getting Better	Dunhill 4195
10/18/69	#25	9	Make Your Own Kind Of Music*	Dunhill 4214
1/24/70	#30	7	New World Coming*	Dunhill 4225
			*released as by MAMA CASS ELLIOT	
			MAMA'S & PAPA'S	
1/01/66	#4	19	California Dreamin'	Dunhill 4020
4/09/66	#1	11	Monday, Monday	Dunhill 4026
7/02/66	#6	9	I Saw Her Again	Dunhill 4031
10/22/66	#14	7	Look Through My Window	Dunhill 4050
12/03/66	#6	12	Words Of Love/	Dunhill 4057
12/03/66	#86	2	Dancing In The Street	Dunhill 4057
2/25/67	#2	11	Dedicated To The One I Love	Dunhill 4077
4/29/67	#5	10	Creeque Alley	Dunhill 4083
8/26/67	#15	8	Twelve Thirty	Dunhill 4099
10/21/67	#23	7	Glad To Be Unhappy	Dunhill 4107
12/09/67	#36	6	Dancing Bear	Dunhill 4113
6/01/68	#46	7	Safe In My Garden	Dunhill 4125
9/07/68	#59	4	For The Love Of Ivy	Dunhill 4150
11/23/68	#43	5	Do You Wanna Dance	Dunhill 4171

Debut Date	Peak Pos	Wks Chr	ARTIST/Song Title	Label & Number
			MELISSA MANCHESTER	
5/10/75	#7	19	Midnight Blue	Arista 0116
9/20/75	#32	11	Just Too Many People	Arista 0146
2/14/76	#46	8	Just You And I	Arista 0168
5/08/76	#88	4	Better Days	Arista 0183
11/11/78	#10	23	Don't Cry Out Loud	Arista 0373
4/28/79	#87	4	Theme From Ice Castles (Through The Eyes Of Love)	Arista 0405
10/13/79	#44	15	Pretty Girls	Arista 0456
2/23/80	#35	14	Fire In The Morning	Arista 0485
3/07/81	#74	7	Lovers After All*	Arista 0587
5/29/82	#4	25	You Should Hear How She Talks About You	Arista 0676
2/05/83	#40	12	Nice Girls	Arista 1045
4/27/85	#72	5	Mathematics	MCA 52575
			*released as by MELISSA MANCHESTER and PEABO BRYSON	
			HENRY MANCINI	
3/26/60	#20	13	Mr. Lucky	RCA 7705
3/18/61	#87	5	Theme From The Great Imposter	RCA 7830
10/07/61	#5	29	Moon River	RCA 7916
7/07/62	#89	3	Theme From Hatari	RCA 8037
2/02/63	#29	19	Days Of Wine And Roses	RCA 8120
6/15/63	#98	3	Banzai Pipeline	RCA 8184
12/14/63	#43	11	Charade	RCA 8256
4/04/64	#54	9	The Pink Panther Theme	RCA 8286
7/24/65	#89	5	Sweetheart Tree	RCA 8624
5/03/69	#1	14	Love Theme From Romeo & Juliet	RCA 0131
9/27/69	#96	2	Moonlight Sonata	RCA 0212
1/16/71	#11	12	Theme From Love Story	RCA 9927
3/04/72	#95	1	All His Children*	RCA 0624
3/19/77	#73	6	Theme From Charlie's Angels	RCA 10888
1/12/80	#59	8	Ravel's Bolero	Warner Brothers 49139
			*released as by CHARLEY PRIDE with HENRY MANCINI	
			BARBARA MANDRELL	
3/11/78	#93	2	Woman To Woman	ABC/Dot 17736
3/17/79	#27	16	(If Loving You Is Wrong) I Don't Want To Be Right	ABC 12451
7/18/81	#95	3	I Was Country When Country Wasn't Cool	MCA 51107
			MANDRILL	
6/12/71	#98	2	Mandrill	Polydor 14070
7/01/72	#100	1	I Refuse To Smile	Polydor 14127
4/07/73	#47	11	Fencewalk	Polydor 14163
8/18/73	#92	2	Hang Loose	Polydor 14187
			MANFRED MANN	
9/05/64	#1	14	Do Wah Diddy Diddy	Ascot 2157
11/14/64	#15	12	Sha La La	Ascot 2165
2/20/65	#52	6	Come Tomorrow	Ascot 2170
10/16/65	#100	1	If You Gotta Go, Go Now	Ascot 2194
7/02/66	#27	8	Pretty Flamingo	United Artists 50040
8/27/66	#94	3	Just Like A Woman	Mercury 72607
3/02/68	#4	12	Mighty Quinn (Quinn The Eskimo)	Mercury 72770
7/13/68	#64	5	My Name Is Jack	Mercury 72822
3/11/72	#93	2	Living Without You*	Polydor 14113
11/20/76	#1	21	Blinded By The Light*	Warner Brothers 8252
4/23/77	#59	8	Spirit In The Night*	Warner Brothers 8355
6/09/79	#53	8	You Angel You*	Warner Brothers 8850
1/21/84	#26	16	Runner*	Arista 9143
			*released as by MANFRED MANN'S EARTH BAND	
			SILVANNA MANGANO	
5/16/53	#5	9	Anna	MGM 11457
			CHUCK MANGIONE	
7/10/71	#61	6	Hill Where The Lord Hides	Mercury 73208
1/28/78	#6	28	Feels So Good	A&M 2001
1/26/80	#19	16	Give It All You Got	A&M 2211
			MANHATTANS	
1/23/65	#84	6	I Wanna Be (Your Everything)	Carnival 507
12/18/65	#70	7	Follow Your Heart	Carnival 512
4/09/66	#99	1	Baby I Need You	Carnival 514
11/05/66	#100	2	I Bet'cha	Carnival 522
12/02/67	#93	2	I Call It Love	Carnival 533

Debut Date	Peak Pos	Wks Chr	ARTIST/Song Title	Label & Number
			MANHATTANS—*continued*	
6/27/70	#100	1	If My Heart Could Speak	Deluxe 122
10/28/72	#72	3	One Life To Live	Deluxe 139
5/05/73	#29	16	There's No Me Without You	Columbia 45838
9/29/73	#84	3	You'd Better Believe	Columbia 45927
12/28/74	#37	10	Don't Take Your Love From Me	Columbia 10045
5/17/75	#70	6	Hurt	Columbia 10140
4/24/76	#1	27	Kiss And Say Goodbye	Columbia 10310
11/13/76	#71	10	I Kinda Miss You	Columbia 10430
3/18/78	#89	4	Am I Losing You	Columbia 10674
4/26/80	#7	25	Shining Star	Columbia 11222
8/06/83	#76	5	Crazy	Columbia 03939
			MANHATTAN TRANSFER	
8/02/75	#95	3	Clap Your Hands	Atlantic 3277
9/20/75	#24	13	Operator	Atlantic 3292
4/05/80	#35	18	Twilight Zone/Twilight Tone	Atlantic 3649
11/29/80	#82	9	Trickle Trickle	Atlantic 3772
5/23/81	#8	20	Boy From New York City	Atlantic 3816
6/05/82	#90	4	Route 66	Atlantic 4034
9/10/83	#44	13	Spice Of Life	Atlantic 89786
			BARRY MANILOW	
11/16/74	#1	17	Mandy	Bell 45613
3/01/75	#10	14	It's A Miracle	Arista 0108
6/21/75	#7	18	Could It Be Magic	Arista 0126
11/08/75	#1	20	I Write The songs	Arista 0157
3/13/76	#10	17	Tryin' To Get The Feeling Again	Arista 0172
9/18/76	#21	12	This One's For You	Arista 0206
11/27/76	#9	26	Weekend In New England	Arista 0212
5/07/77	#3	20	Looks Like We Made It	Arista 0244
10/01/77	#21	12	Daybreak	Arista 0273
2/04/78	#2	20	Can't Smile Without You	Arista 0305
5/06/78	#17	14	Even Now	Arista 0330
6/10/78	#10	17	Copacabana (At The Copa)	Arista 0339
9/09/78	#7	19	Ready To Take A Chance Again	Arista 0357
12/16/78	#13	14	Somewhere In The Night	Arista 0382
10/13/79	#11	14	Ships	Arista 0464
12/15/79	#24	16	When I Wanted You	Arista 0481
4/12/80	#43	11	I Don't Want To Walk Without You	Arista 0501
11/22/80	#18	16	I Made It Through The Rain	Arista 0566
3/14/81	#47	10	Lonely Together	Arista 0596
10/10/81	#16	16	The Old Songs	Arista 0633
12/19/81	#21	14	Somewhere Down The Road	Arista 0658
3/27/82	#35	11	Let's Hang On	Arista 0675
7/31/82	#50	9	Oh Julie	Arista 0698
11/20/82	#37	15	Memory	Arista 1025
2/26/83	#31	14	Some Kind Of Friend	Arista 1046
11/19/83	#18	15	Read 'Em And Weep	Arista 9101
7/12/86	#69	5	I'm Your Man	RCA 14397
			MANITOBA	
11/21/70	#98	2	Something In You	RCA 9908
			BARRY MANN	
8/05/61	#7	13	Who Put The Bomp	ABC-Paramount 10237
11/18/61	#99	2	Little Miss U.S.A.	ABC-Paramount 10263
7/23/66	#96	3	Angelica	Capitol 5695
6/06/70	#83	3	Feelings	Scepter 12281
8/14/76	#84	5	The Princess And The Punk	Arista 0194
			CARL MANN	
6/13/59	#30	16	Mona Lisa	Phillips Int. 3539
10/17/59	#56	9	Pretend	Phillips Int. 3546
			GLORIA MANN	
1/21/56	#6	7	Teen Age Prayer	Sound 126
			HERBIE MANN	
2/24/68	#83	2	Unchain My Heart	A&M 896
6/14/69	#88	5	Memphis Underground	Atlantic 2621
2/22/75	#22	14	Hijack	Atlantic 3246
1/27/79	#35	15	Superman	Atlantic 3547

Debut Date	Peak Pos	Wks Chr	ARTIST/Song Title	Label & Number
			MANTOVANI	
12/22/51	#7	9	Charmaine	London 1020
6/15/57	#6	23	Around The World	London 1746
11/26/60	#3	6	Main Theme From Exodus (Ari's Theme)	London 1953
11/05/66	#93	2	Games That Lovers Play	London 20015
			MANTRONIX	
3/10/90	#75	5	Got To Have Your Love*	Capitol 44466
			*released as by MANTRONIX featuring WONDRESS	
			TOMMY MARA	
8/30/58	#68	6	Where The Blue Of The Night	Felsted 8532
			MARATHONS	
5/06/61	#21	11	Peanut Butter	Arvee 5027
			MARCELS	
3/11/61	#1	15	Blue Moon	Colpix 186
5/20/61	#80	5	Summertime	Colpix 196
10/21/61	#16	12	Heartaches	Colpix 612
2/03/62	#87	3	My Melancholy Baby	Colpix 624
			LITTLE PEGGY MARCH	
3/16/63	#1	16	I Will Follow Him	RCA 8139
6/01/63	#42	7	I Wish I Were A Princess	RCA 8189
8/31/63	#33	10	Hello Heartache, Goodbye Love	RCA 8221
11/23/63	#70	5	The Impossible Happened	RCA 8267
			BOBBY MARCHAN	
6/25/60	#19	10	There's Something On Your Mind (Part 2)	Fire 1022
			MARCY JOE	
5/20/61	#64	6	Ronnie	Robbee 110
			BENNY MARDONES	
6/07/80	#10	22	Into The Night	Polydor 2091
5/13/89	#30	16	Into The Night '89	Polydor 889368
			ERNIE MARESCA	
3/17/62	#11	17	Shout! Shout! (Knock Yourself Out)	Seville 117
			CHARLIE MARGULIS	
3/08/58	#48	4	Gigi	Carlton 456
			TEENA MARIE	
11/22/80	#44	12	I Need Your Lovin'	Gordy 7189
7/18/81	#49	13	Square Biz	Gordy 7202
12/22/84	#5	24	Lovergirl	Epic 04619
			MARIE & REX	
2/28/59	#92	3	I Can't Sit Down	Carlton 502
			MARILLION	
10/12/85	#78	5	Kayleigh	Capitol 5493
			MARK II	
10/15/60	#50	10	Night Theme	Wye 1001
			MARK IV	
2/28/58	#51	3	(Make With) The Shake	Cosmic 704
1/24/59	#9	13	I Got A Wife	Mercury 71403
4/25/59	#93	2	Move Over Rover	Mercury 71445
9/30/72	#96	2	Honey I Still Love You	Mercury 73319
			MARK-ALMOND	
2/26/72	#94	3	One Way Sunday	Blue Thumb 206
			MARKETTS	
1/13/62	#31	9	Surfer's Stomp	Liberty 55401
4/21/62	#52	12	Balboa Blue	Liberty 55443
12/14/63	#3	14	Out Of Limits	Warner Brothers 5391
2/12/66	#14	7	Batman Theme	Warner Brothers 5696
			MAR-KEYS	
7/01/61	#3	17	Last Night	Satellite 107
10/14/61	#65	5	Morning After	Stax 112
3/05/66	#92	3	Philly Dog	Stax 185
			PIGMEAT MARKHAM	
6/15/68	#23	8	Here Comes The Judge	Chess 2049

217

Debut Date	Peak Pos	Wks Chr	ARTIST/Song Title	Label & Number
			GUY MARKS	
4/06/68	#58	8	Loving You Has Made Me Bananas	ABC 11055
			MARKY MARK & THE FUNKY BUNCH	
7/27/91	#4	27	Good Vibrations*	Interscope 98764
11/02/91	#12	24	Wildside	Interscope 98673
2/22/92	#57	10	I Need Money	Interscope 98614
10/03/92	#40	15	You Gotta Believe	Interscope 98492
			*released as by MARKY MARK & THE FUNKY BUNCH featuring LOLEATTA HOLLOWAY	
			BOB MARLEY & THE WAILERS	
7/03/76	#75	5	Roots, Rock, Reggae	Island 060
			ZIGGY MARLEY and THE MELODY MAKERS	
5/21/88	#43	13	Tomorrow People	Virgin 99347
9/28/91	#89	4	Good Time	Virgin 98735
			MARMALADE	
2/28/70	#7	16	Reflections Of My Life	London 20058
8/01/70	#48	9	Rainbow	London 20059
4/03/76	#55	8	Falling Apart At The Seams	Ariola America 7619
			HANK MARR	
12/28/63	#68	5	The Greasy Spoon	Federal 12508
			M/A/R/R/S	
11/28/87	#15	23	Pump Up The Volume	4th & B'way 7452
			MARSHALL HAIN	
12/09/78	#39	14	Dancing In The City	Harvest 4648
			MARSHALL TUCKER BAND	
11/01/75	#55	11	Fire On The Mountain	Capricorn 0244
3/12/77	#10	22	Heard It In A Love Song	Capricorn 0270
8/20/77	#70	6	Can't You See	Capricorn 0278
7/01/78	#81	3	Dream Lover	Capricorn 0300
6/23/79	#43	10	Last Of The Singing Cowboys	Warner Brothers 8841
			RALPH MARTERIE	
3/14/53	#4	4	Pretend	Mercury 70045
9/18/54	#3	11	Skokiaan	Mercury 70432
4/13/57	#55	1	Tricky	Mercury 71050
4/27/57	#31	8	Shish-Kebab	Mercury 71092
			MARTHA & THE VANDELLAS	
4/13/63	#20	15	Come And Get These Memories	Gordy 7014
7/27/63	#4	16	Heat Wave	Gordy 7022
11/23/63	#14	12	Quicksand	Gordy 7025
2/08/64	#34	7	Live Wire	Gordy 7027
4/11/64	#52	6	In My Lonely Room	Gordy 7031
8/22/64	#4	15	Dancing In The Street	Gordy 7033
12/05/64	#31	8	Wild One	Gordy 7036
2/27/65	#9	11	Nowhere To Run	Gordy 7039
8/21/65	#57	4	You've Been In Love Too Long/	Gordy 7045
12/11/65	#80	6	Love (Makes Me Do Foolish Things)	Gordy 7045
1/29/66	#23	10	My Baby Loves Me	Gordy 7048
6/11/66	#68	3	What Am I Going To Do Without Your Love	Gordy 7053
10/22/66	#11	12	I'm Ready For Love	Gordy 7056
2/25/67	#6	13	Jimmy Mack	Gordy 7058
8/19/67	#27	9	Love Bug Leave My Heart Alone	Gordy 7062
11/18/67	#12	11	Honey Chile*	Gordy 7067
4/20/68	#37	6	I Promise To Wait My Love*	Gordy 7070
8/10/68	#40	7	I Can't Dance To That Music You're Playin'*	Gordy 7075
11/02/68	#86	2	Sweet Darlin'*	Gordy 7080
4/12/69	#57	5	(We've Got) Honey Love*	Gordy 7085
9/20/69	#86	3	Taking My Love (And Leaving Me)*	Gordy 7094
11/21/70	#83	4	I Gotta Let You Go*	Gordy 7103
10/09/71	#44	6	Bless You*	Gordy 7110
2/05/72	#70	8	In And Out Of My Life*	Gordy 7113
			*released as by MARTHA REEVES & THE VANDELLAS	
			MARTIKA	
12/24/88	#17	21	More Than You Know	Columbia 08103
5/20/89	#4	20	Toy Soldiers	Columbia 68747
9/02/89	#26	13	I Feel The Earth Move	Columbia 68996

Debut Date	Peak Pos	Wks Chr	ARTIST/Song Title	Label & Number
8/10/91	#10	20	Love...Thy Will Be Done	Columbia 73853
11/30/91	#74	8	Martika's Kitchen	Columbia 74094
			BOBBI MARTIN	
11/28/64	#18	12	Don't Forget I Still Love You	Coral 62426
3/13/65	#44	9	I Can't Stop Thinking Of You	Coral 62447
6/05/65	#81	5	I Love You So	Coral 62452
2/12/66	#91	3	Don't Take It Out On Me	Coral 62475
3/14/70	#9	14	For The Love Of Him	United Artists 50602
6/27/70	#63	5	Give A Woman Love	United Artists 50687
			DEAN MARTIN	
12/12/53	#2	15	That's Amore	Capitol 2589
12/24/55	#1	14	Memories Are Made Of This	Capitol 3295
3/29/58	#3	22	Return To Me	Capitol 3894
6/28/58	#38	8	Angel Baby	Capitol 3988
8/16/58	#17	17	Volare (Nel Blu Dipinto Di Blu)	Capitol 4028
11/08/58	#94	2	Once Upon A Time	Capitol 4065
1/31/59	#80	3	It Takes So Long	Capitol 4124
7/04/59	#36	14	On An Evening In Roma	Capitol 4222
2/25/61	#98	2	Sparklin' Eyes	Capitol 4518
1/05/63	#93	6	From The Bottom Of My Heart	Reprise 20116
6/27/64	#1	16	Everybody Loves Somebody	Reprise 0281
10/03/64	#8	11	The Door Is Still Open To My Heart	Reprise 0307
12/19/64	#26	8	You're Nobody Till Somebody Loves You/	Reprise 0333
12/19/64	#79	7	You'll Always Be The One I Love	Reprise 0333
2/20/65	#20	8	Send Me The Pillow You Dream On	Reprise 0344
5/22/65	#35	6	(Remember Me) I'm The One Who Loves You	Reprise 0369
8/07/65	#24	9	Houston	Reprise 0393
10/30/65	#11	12	I Will	Reprise 0415
2/12/66	#34	7	Somewhere There's A Someone	Reprise 0443
5/07/66	#40	7	Come Running Back	Reprise 0466
7/23/66	#45	5	A Million And One	Reprise 0500
10/01/66	#52	8	Nobody's Baby Again/	Reprise 0516
10/01/66	#89	4	It Just Happened That Way	Reprise 0516
12/10/66	#55	6	Let The Good Times In	Reprise 0538
4/22/67	#55	6	Lay Some Happiness On Me	Reprise 0571
7/01/67	#30	8	In The Chapel In The Moonlight	Reprise 0601
8/19/67	#48	6	Little Ole Wine Drinker Me	Reprise 0608
12/02/67	#62	7	In The Misty Moonlight	Reprise 0640
3/23/68	#44	6	You've Still Got A Place In My Heart	Reprise 0672
8/10/68	#67	4	April Again	Reprise 0761
10/26/68	#44	7	Not Enough Indians	Reprise 0780
3/01/69	#93	3	Gentle On My Mind	Reprise 0812
8/09/69	#71	5	I Take A Lot Of Pride In What I Am	Reprise 0841
10/11/69	#82	3	One Cup Of Happiness	Reprise 0857
8/15/70	#97	1	My Woman, My Woman, My Wife	Reprise 0934
10/24/70	#99	2	Detroit City	Reprise 0955
			DEREK MARTIN	
7/10/65	#52	10	You Better Go	Roulette 4631
			ERIC MARTIN	
8/24/85	#82	5	Information	Capitol 5502
			GEORGE MARTIN	
7/25/64	#71	3	And I Love Her/	United Artists 745
8/01/64	#57	8	Ringo's Theme (This Boy)	United Artists 745
			MARILYN MARTIN	
10/05/85	#1	24	Separate Lives (Love Theme From White Nights)*	Atlantic 89498
1/18/86	#27	17	Night Moves	Atlantic 89465
			*released as by **PHIL COLLINS and MARILYN MARTIN**	
			MOON MARTIN	
8/18/79	#28	12	Rolene	Capitol 4765
11/03/79	#55	8	No Chance	Capitol 4794
			STEVE MARTIN	
12/03/77	#94	2	Grandmother's Song	Warner Brothers 8503
5/20/78	#18	17	King Tut*	Warner Brothers 8577
			*released as by **STEVE MARTIN and THE TOOT UNCOMMONS**	

219

Debut Date	Peak Pos	Wks Chr	ARTIST/Song Title	Label & Number
			TONY MARTIN	
3/25/50	#7	3	There's No Tomorrow	RCA 3582
8/19/50	#4	16	La Vie En Rose	RCA 3819
8/25/51	#3	18	I Get Ideas	RCA 4141
11/24/51	#8	4	Domino	RCA 4343
5/01/54	#4	9	Here	RCA 5665
			TRADE MARTIN	
10/06/62	#39	10	That Stranger Used To Be My Girl	Coed 570
			VINCE MARTIN (see TARRIERS)	
			MARTIN & WARREN	
3/25/50	#2	6	I Said My Pajamas (And Put On My Prayers)	RCA 3613
			WINK MARTINDALE	
9/12/59	#4	18	Deck Of Cards	Dot 15968
8/12/61	#85	5	Black Land Farmer	Dot 16243
			LAYNG MARTINE	
9/18/71	#63	10	Rub It In	Barnaby 2041
12/25/71	#93	4	Come On Over To My House	Barnaby 2053
			NANCY MARTINEZ	
10/18/86	#37	21	For Tonight	Atlantic 89371
			AL MARTINO	
6/07/52	#1	15	Here In My Heart	BBS 101
5/02/59	#43	10	I Can't Get You Out Of My Heart	20th Century Fox 132
8/15/59	#52	15	Darling I Love You	20th Century Fox 153
3/18/61	#92	3	Little Girl, Little Boy	20th Century Fox 237
4/06/63	#3	16	I Love You Because	Capitol 4930
7/20/63	#19	14	Painted, Tainted Rose	Capitol 5000
10/26/63	#23	11	Living A Lie	Capitol 5060
2/01/64	#11	12	I Love You More And More Every Day	Capitol 5108
5/16/64	#18	9	Tears And Roses	Capitol 5183
8/15/64	#41	9	Always Together/	Capitol 5239
8/22/64	#96	1	Thank You For Loving Me	Capitol 5239
10/31/64	#44	8	We Could	Capitol 5293
1/23/65	#50	6	My Heart Would Know	Capitol 5341
3/27/65	#64	6	Somebody Else Is Taking My Place/	Capitol 5384
3/27/65	#99	1	With All My Heart	Capitol 5384
6/19/65	#79	3	My Cherie	Capitol 5434
10/09/65	#73	7	Forgive Me	Capitol 5506
11/27/65	#16	14	Spanish Eyes	Capitol 5542
3/05/66	#33	9	Think I'll Go Somewhere And Cry Myself To Sleep	Capitol 5598
5/14/66	#61	7	Wiederseh'n	Capitol 5652
7/23/66	#71	6	Just Yesterday	Capitol 5702
10/15/66	#57	8	The Wheel Of Hurt	Capitol 5741
1/28/67	#46	10	Daddy's Little Girl	Capitol 5825
5/27/67	#27	9	Mary In The Morning	Capitol 5904
9/16/67	#47	8	More Than The Eye Can See	Capitol 5989
12/09/67	#81	6	A Voice In The Choir	Capitol 2053
2/10/68	#60	6	Love Is Blue	Capitol 2102
4/27/68	#82	7	Lili Marlene	Capitol 2158
1/04/69	#93	2	I Can't Help It (If I'm Still In Love With You)	Capitol 2355
4/19/69	#62	9	Sausalito	Capitol 2468
11/15/69	#74	10	I Started Loving You Again	Capitol 2674
2/14/70	#57	6	I Can't Help Falling In Love	Capitol 2746
5/06/72	#81	3	Speak Softly Love	Capitol 3313
12/14/74	#21	16	To The Door Of The Sun	Capitol 3987
11/01/75	#41	10	Volare	Capitol 4134
12/03/77	#55	12	The Next Hundred Years	Capitol 4508
			MARVELETTES	
9/16/61	#2	22	Please Mr. Postman	Tamla 54046
1/27/62	#32	10	Twistin' Postman	Tamla 54054
5/05/62	#8	15	Playboy	Tamla 54060
8/04/62	#18	13	Beechwood 4-5789	Tamla 54065
12/01/62	#50	14	Strange I Know	Tamla 54072
3/16/63	#54	9	Locking Up My Heart/	Tamla 54077
5/25/63	#89	4	Forever	Tamla 54077
7/27/63	#89	3	My Daddy Knows Best	Tamla 54082
11/09/63	#43	12	As Long As I Know He's Mine	Tamla 54088
2/22/64	#59	7	He's A Good Guy (Yes He Is)	Tamla 54091

Debut Date	Peak Pos	Wks Chr	ARTIST/Song Title	Label & Number
7/04/64	#54	7	You're My Remedy	Tamla 54097
11/14/64	#21	12	Too Many Fish In The Sea	Tamla 54105
6/05/65	#36	6	I'll Keep Holding On	Tamla 54116
8/14/65	#57	6	Danger Heartbreak Dead Ahead	Tamla 54120
1/01/66	#9	13	Don't Mess With Bill	Tamla 54126
4/23/66	#46	6	You're The One	Tamla 54131
1/28/67	#16	10	The Hunter Gets Captured By The Game	Tamla 54143
4/29/67	#30	9	When You're Young And In Love	Tamla 54150
12/16/67	#10	11	My Baby Must Be A Magician	Tamla 54158
5/25/68	#44	8	Here I Am Baby	Tamla 54166
10/05/68	#58	4	Destination: Anywhere	Tamla 54171
1/25/69	#49	3	I'm Gonna Hold On As Long As I Can	Tamla 54177
11/15/69	#81	2	That's How Heartaches Are Made	Tamla 54186
			MARVELOWS	
5/22/65	#32	8	I Do	ABC-Paramount 10629
			RICHARD MARX	
6/13/87	#5	21	Don't Mean A Thing	Manhattan 50079
9/26/87	#4	23	Should've Known Better	Manhattan 50083
1/23/88	#4	21	Endless Summer Nights	EMI-Manhattan 50113
5/21/88	#3	22	Hold On To The Night	EMI-Manhattan 50106
5/06/89	#1	19	Satisfied	EMI 50189
7/08/89	#1	20	Right Here Waiting	EMI 50219
10/07/89	#2	19	Angelia	EMI 50218
1/20/90	#14	14	Too Late To Say Goodbye	EMI 50234
4/28/90	#12	18	Children Of The Night	EMI 50288
11/02/91	#5	23	Keep Coming Back	Capitol 44753
2/08/92	#6	25	Hazard	Capitol 44796
6/13/92	#21	20	Take This Heart	Capitol 44782
10/10/92	#35	20	Chains Around My Heart	Capitol 44848
			MARY JANE GIRLS	
3/16/85	#5	23	In My House	Gordy 1741
7/20/85	#43	11	Wild And Crazy Love	Gordy 1798
7/12/86	#47	11	Walk Like A Man	Motown 1851
			CAROLYNE MAS	
9/08/79	#72	6	Stillsane	Mercury 76004
			HUGH MASEKELA	
1/06/68	#97	1	Up Up And Away	Uni 55037
6/08/68	#1	13	Grazing In The Grass	Uni 55066
9/28/68	#50	5	Puffin' On Down The Track	Uni 55085
1/18/69	#60	6	Riot	Uni 55102
			MASHMAKHAN	
8/29/70	#30	15	As The Years Go By	Epic 10634
			MASKMAN & THE AGENTS	
2/08/69	#89	6	One Eye Open	Dynamo 125
			BARBARA MASON	
5/15/65	#3	15	Yes, I'm Ready	Arctic 105
8/07/65	#33	8	Sad, Sad Girl	Arctic 108
7/02/66	#99	1	I Need Love	Arctic 120
12/30/67	#48	8	Oh, How It Hurts	Arctic 137
6/24/72	#66	4	Bed And Board	Buddah 296
12/30/72	#18	13	Give Me Your Love	Buddah 331
11/30/74	#34	10	From His Woman To You	Buddah 441
4/19/75	#76	6	Shackin' Up	Buddah 459
			DAVE MASON	
8/01/70	#37	8	Only You Know And I Know	Blue Thumb 114
12/05/70	#95	3	Satin Red And Black Velvet Woman	Blue Thumb 7117
5/14/77	#69	6	So High	Columbia 10509
9/03/77	#15	20	We Just Disagree	Columbia 10575
1/14/78	#49	9	Let It Go, Let It Flow	Columbia 10662
5/27/78	#40	13	Will You Still Love Me Tomorrow	Columbia 10749
7/05/80	#78	5	Save Me	Columbia 11289
			VAUGHAN MASON and CREW	
3/08/80	#96	3	Bounce, Rock, Skate, Roll (Part 1)	Brunswick 55548
			MASQUERADERS	
9/21/68	#75	4	I Ain't Got To Love Nobody Else	Bell 733
2/21/76	#94	7	(Call Me) The Traveling Man	ABC 12157

221

Debut Date	Peak Pos	Wks Chr	ARTIST/Song Title	Label & Number
			WAYNE MASSEY	
10/04/80	#92	3	One Life To Live	Polydor 2112
			MASS PRODUCTION	
8/11/79	#33	14	Firecracker	Cotillion 44254
			TOBIN MATHEWS & CO.	
11/05/60	#27	9	Ruby Duby Du	Chief 7022
			JOHNNY MATHIS	
3/16/57	#12	27	Wonderful! Wonderful!	Columbia 40784
4/27/57	#2	27	It's Not For Me To Say	Columbia 40851
9/07/57	#1	23	Chances Are/	Columbia 40993
9/07/57	#38	10	The Twelfth Of Never	Columbia 40993
11/30/57	#20	11	Wild Is The Wind/	Columbia 41060
12/14/57	#26	7	No Love (But Your Love)	Columbia 41060
1/25/58	#23	9	Come To Me	Columbia 41082
4/26/58	#35	7	All The Time/	Columbia 41152
4/26/58	#20	9	Teacher, Teacher	Columbia 41152
6/21/58	#15	16	A Certain Smile	Columbia 41193
10/04/58	#14	15	Call Me	Columbia 41253
12/27/58	#40	10	Let's Love/	Columbia 41304
12/27/58	#60	7	You Are Beautiful	Columbia 41304
4/04/59	#33	11	Someone/	Columbia 41355
4/11/59	#88	4	Very Much In Love	Columbia 41355
6/13/59	#19	16	Small World	Columbia 41410
10/03/59	#14	17	Misty	Columbia 41483
10/24/59	#67	10	Best Of Everything	Columbia 41491
3/05/60	#24	12	Starbright	Columbia 41583
6/04/60	#50	7	Maria	Columbia 41684
8/20/60	#35	13	My Love For You	Columbia 41764
12/31/60	#83	4	How To Handle A Woman	Columbia 41866
4/22/61	#95	2	You Set My Heart To Music	Columbia 41980
2/24/62	#75	5	Sweet Thursday	Columbia 42261
9/22/62	#8	14	Gina	Columbia 42582
1/26/63	#9	13	What Will My Mary Say	Columbia 42666
5/25/63	#40	9	Every Step Of The Way	Columbia 42799
10/05/63	#50	6	Come Back/	Mercury 72184
10/12/63	#69	4	Your Teenage Dream	Mercury 72184
2/01/64	#55	6	Bye Bye Barbara	Mercury 72229
10/17/64	#64	10	Listen Lonely Girl	Mercury 72339
5/29/65	#98	1	Take The Time	Mercury 72432
8/07/65	#75	6	The Sweetheart Tree	Mercury 72464
6/01/68	#97	2	Venus	Columbia 44517
8/16/69	#100	1	A Time For Us	Columbia 44915
9/08/73	#72	8	I'm Coming Home	Columbia 45908
1/12/74	#64	10	Life Is A Song Worth Singing	Columbia 45975
3/18/78	#2	21	Too Much, Too Little, Too Late*	Columbia 10693
7/15/78	#67	9	You're All I Need To Get By*	Columbia 10772
5/01/82	#48	10	Friends In Love**	Arista 0673
			*released as by JOHNNY MATHIS/DENIECE WILLIAMS	
			**released as by DIONNE WARWICK and JOHNNY MATHIS	
			IAN MATTHEWS	
11/25/78	#10	18	Shake It	Mushroom 7039
3/31/79	#65	5	Give Me An Inch	Mushroom 7040
			SHIRLEY MATTHEWS	
2/01/64	#91	3	Big Town Boy	Atlantic 2210
			MATTHEWS' SOUTHERN COMFORT	
3/06/71	#17	15	Woodstock	Decca 32774
			MATYS BROTHERS	
1/24/59	#63	9	Rummy Polka	Sunnyside 3102
1/19/63	#55	8	Who Stole The Keeshka?	Select 719
			MAUDS	
9/28/68	#55	6	Soul Drippin'	Mercury 72832
			PAUL MAURIAT	
12/30/67	#1	19	Love Is Blue	Philips 40495
5/11/68	#55	6	Love In Every Room	Philips 40530
8/17/68	#88	3	San Francisco	Philips 40550
11/16/68	#86	5	Chitty Chitty Bang Bang	Philips 40574

Debut Date	Peak Pos	Wks Chr	**ARTIST**/Song Title	Label & Number
			CHRISTOPHER MAX	
12/09/89	#67	8	Serious Kind Of Girl	EMI 50229
			ROBERT MAXWELL	
3/21/64	#9	14	Shangri-La	Decca 25622
6/20/64	#51	6	Peg O' My Heart	Decca 25637
			JOHN MAYALL	
9/27/69	#66	5	Don't Waste My Time	Polydor 14004
12/20/69	#95	4	Room To Move	Polydor 14010
			NATHANIEL MAYER and THE FABULOUS TWILIGHTS	
4/07/62	#26	16	Village Of Love	Fortune 449
			CURTIS MAYFIELD	
11/28/70	#24	12	(Don't Worry) If There's A Hell Below We're All Going To Go	Curtom 1955
11/13/71	#52	9	Get Down	Curtom 1966
3/04/72	#81	2	We Got To Have Peace	Curtom 1968
8/19/72	#6	17	Freddie's Dead (Theme From "Superfly")	Curtom 1975
11/11/72	#6	14	Superfly	Curtom 1978
7/28/73	#39	8	Future Shock	Curtom 1987
11/10/73	#94	1	If I Were Only A Child Again	Curtom 1991
1/05/74	#89	4	Can't Say Nothin'	Curtom 1993
6/29/74	#32	11	Kung Fu	Curtom 1999
9/27/75	#58	8	So In Love	Curtom 0105
9/26/81	#88	3	She Don't Let Nobody (But Me)	Boardwalk 122
			MAZE	
5/14/77	#71	8	While I'm Alone	Capitol 4392
6/16/79	#73	5	Feel That You're Feelin'	Capitol 4686
3/30/85	#81	5	Back In Stride	Capitol 5431
			MAC McANALLY	
6/25/77	#58	12	It's A Crazy World	Ariola America 7665
3/05/83	#38	13	Minimum Love	Geffen 29736
			McAULEY SCHENKER GROUP	
2/24/90	#68	7	Anytime	Capitol 44471
			M.C. BRAINS	
7/11/92	#57	6	Brainstorming	Motown 2170
			C.W. McCALL	
7/06/74	#52	5	Old Home Filler-Up An' Keep On-A-Truckin' Cafe	MGM 14738
2/08/75	#73	5	Wolfcreek Pass	MGM 14764
11/22/75	#1	16	Convoy	MGM 14839
3/20/76	#52	8	There Won't Be No Country Music	Polydor 14310
			CASH McCALL	
7/16/66	#86	7	When You Wake Up	Thomas 307
			TOUSSAINT McCALL	
3/25/67	#38	12	Nothing Takes The Place Of You	Ronn 3
7/08/67	#89	3	I'll Do It For You	Ronn 9
			DAVID McCALLUM	
3/05/66	#99	1	Communication	Capitol 5571
			LES McCANN & EDDIE HARRIS	
1/17/70	#96	2	Compared To What	Atlantic 2694
			PETER McCANN	
4/23/77	#9	21	Do You Wanna Make Love	20th Century 2335
			GEORGE McCANNON	
5/09/70	#97	2	Birds Of All Nations	Amos 135
			PAUL McCARTNEY (also WINGS)	
3/06/71	#6	11	Another Day/	Apple 1829
3/06/71	#55	2	Oh Woman Oh Why	Apple 1829
8/14/71	#1	12	Uncle Albert/Admiral Halsey*	Apple 1837
3/11/72	#38	8	Give Ireland Back To The Irish**	Apple 1847
6/17/72	#48	6	Mary Had A Little Lamb**/	Apple 1851
7/22/72	#95	1	Little Woman Love**	Apple 1851
12/16/72	#6	10	Hi Hi Hi**	Apple 1857
4/14/73	#1	16	My Love***	Apple 1861
6/30/73	#1	14	Live And Let Die**	Apple 1863
11/17/73	#5	12	Helen Wheels***	Apple 1869
2/02/74	#5	12	Jet***	Apple 1871

223

Debut Date	Peak Pos	Wks Chr	ARTIST/Song Title	Label & Number
			PAUL McCARTNEY—continued	
4/13/74	#1	16	Band On The Run***	Apple 1873
11/09/74	#4	12	Junior's Farm***/	Apple 1875
1/18/75	#49	6	Sally G***	Apple 1875
5/31/75	#1	14	Listen To What The Man Said**	Capitol 4091
10/04/75	#41	5	Letting Go**	Capitol 4145
11/01/75	#16	9	Venus And Mars Rock Show**	Capitol 4175
4/10/76	#1	21	Silly Love Songs**	Capitol 4256
6/26/76	#1	18	Let 'Em In**	Capitol 4293
2/12/77	#10	15	Maybe I'm Amazed (live version)**	Capitol 4385
6/11/77	#58	7	Seaside Woman****	Epic 50403
11/19/77	#31	11	Girl's School**	Capitol 4504
11/19/77	#31	11	Mull Of Kintyre**	Capitol 4504
3/25/78	#1	18	With A Little Luck**	Capitol 4559
6/17/78	#28	12	I've Had Enough**	Capitol 4594
9/09/78	#42	9	London Town**	Capitol 4625
3/31/79	#4	15	Goodnight Tonight**	Columbia 10939
6/16/79	#20	12	Getting Closer**	Columbia 11020
8/25/79	#36	10	Arrow Through Me**	Columbia 11070
12/29/79	#83	3	Wonderful Christmastime	Columbia 11162
4/26/80	#2	20	Coming Up (Live At Glasgow)***	Columbia 11263
4/10/82	#1	20	Ebony And Ivory*****	Columbia 02860
7/10/82	#6	16	Take It Away	Columbia 03018
10/02/82	#61	7	Tug Of War	Columbia 03235
11/06/82	#3	18	This Girl Is Mine******	Epic 03288
10/15/83	#1	27	Say, Say, Say*******	Columbia 04168
12/24/83	#21	15	So Bad	Columbia 04296
10/13/84	#10	19	No More Lonely Nights	Columbia 04581
11/23/85	#10	22	Spies Like Us	Capitol 5537
8/02/86	#25	13	Press	Capitol 5597
11/22/86	#75	8	Stranglehold	Capitol 5636
5/27/89	#22	15	My Brave Face	Capitol 44367
9/16/89	#90	3	This One	Capitol 44438
2/27/93	#87	5	Hope Of Deliverance	Capitol 44904
			*released as by PAUL & LINDA McCARTNEY	
			**released as by WINGS	
			***released as by PAUL McCARTNEY & WINGS	
			****released as by SUZY and THE RED STRIPES	
			*****released as by PAUL McCARTNEY with STEVIE WONDER	
			******released as by MICHAEL JACKSON/PAUL McCARTNEY	
			*******released as by PAUL McCARTNEY and MICHAEL JACKSON	
			ALTON McCLAIN & DESTINY	
3/24/79	#45	14	It Must Be Love	Polydor 14532
			DELBERT McCLINTON	
12/06/80	#10	18	Giving It Up For Your Love	Capitol 4948
4/11/81	#80	4	Shotgun Rider	Capitol 4984
			BOBBY McCLURE	
2/06/65	#29	12	Don't Mess Up A Good Thing*	Checker 1097
6/12/65	#99	1	You'll Miss Me (When I'm Gone)	Checker 1111
12/24/66	#98	1	Peak Of Love	Checker 1152
			*released as by FONTELLA BASS & BOBBY McCLURE	
			MARILYN McCOO & BILLY DAVIS JR.	
4/17/76	#71	10	I Hope We Get To Love In Time	ABC 12170
10/02/76	#1	24	You Don't Have To Be A Star	ABC 12208
3/12/77	#16	15	Your Love	ABC 12262
8/20/77	#61	8	Look What You've Done To My Heart	ABC 12298
			GAYLE McCORMICK	
7/17/71	#91	4	Gonna Be Alright Now	Dunhill 4281
9/25/71	#43	10	It's A Cryin' Shame	Dunhill 4288
			VAN McCOY	
8/24/74	#89	4	Love Is The Answer	Avco 4639
4/26/75	#1	19	The Hustle*	Avco 4653
10/04/75	#52	8	Change With The Times	Avco 4660

Debut Date	Peak Pos	Wks Chr	ARTIST/Song Title	Label & Number
7/31/76	#85	6	Party	H&L 4670
			*released as by VAN McCOY with THE SOUL CITY SYMPHONY	
			McCOYS	
8/14/65	#1	16	Hang On Sloopy	Bang 506
11/06/65	#9	12	Fever	Bang 511
2/12/66	#50	6	Up And Down	Bang 516
4/23/66	#17	10	Come On Let's Go	Bang 522
7/30/66	#53	6	(You Make Me Feel) So Good	Bang 527
9/24/66	#60	5	Don't Worry Mother	Bang 532
1/07/67	#90	6	I Got To Go Back	Bang 538
5/20/67	#79	4	Beat The Clock	Bang 543
11/02/68	#94	2	Jesse Brady	Mercury 72843
			JIMMY McCRACKLIN	
2/22/58	#26	8	The Walk	Checker 885
11/18/61	#67	8	Just Got To Know	Art-Tone 825
3/20/65	#92	2	Every Night, Every Day	Imperial 66094
10/02/65	#72	10	Think	Imperial 66129
1/22/66	#92	2	My Answer	Imperial 66147
			DARLENE McCRAE	
9/05/59	#92	1	You	Roulette 4173
			GEORGE McCRAE	
5/25/74	#1	17	Rock Your Baby	T.K. 1004
10/19/74	#58	6	I Can't Leave You Alone/	T.K. 1007
1/18/75	#54	9	I Get Lifted	T.K. 1007
5/24/75	#79	4	Look At You	T.K. 1011
1/17/76	#69	5	Honey I	T.K. 1016
			GWEN McCRAE	
5/03/75	#10	17	Rockin' Chair	Cat 1996
			McCRARYS	
8/05/78	#51	9	You	Portrait 70014
			GEORGE McCURN	
3/09/63	#81	5	I'm Just A Country Boy	A&M 705
			DONNA McDANIEL	
6/18/77	#84	4	Save Me	Midsong Intl. 11005
			GENE McDANIELS	
3/18/61	#3	18	A Hundred Pounds Of Clay	Liberty 55308
7/08/61	#24	9	A Tear	Liberty 55344
9/30/61	#9	14	Tower Of Strength	Liberty 55371
1/20/62	#16	11	Chip Chip	Liberty 55405
8/11/62	#32	9	Point Of No Return	Liberty 55480
11/10/62	#38	10	Spanish Lace	Liberty 55510
8/24/63	#72	4	It's A Lonely Town	Liberty 55597
			MICHAEL McDONALD	
8/07/82	#4	24	I Keep Forgettin'	Warner Brothers 29933
11/13/82	#31	16	I Gotta Try	Warner Brothers 29862
12/17/83	#25	18	Ya Mo B There*	Qwest 29394
7/27/85	#31	14	No Lookin' Back	Warner Brothers 28960
3/22/86	#1	22	On My Own**	MCA 52770
6/14/86	#6	21	Sweet Freedom	MCA 52857
6/16/90	#88	5	Take It To Heart	Reprise 19828
			*released as by JAMES INGRAM with MICHAEL McDONALD	
			**released as by PATTI LaBELLE and MICHAEL McDONALD	
			RONNIE McDOWELL	
9/10/77	#14	12	The King Is Gone	Scorpion 135
			BOB McFADDEN and DOR	
8/22/59	#42	8	The Mummy	Brunswick 55140
			McFADDEN & WHITEHEAD	
4/28/79	#12	20	Ain't No Stoppin' Us Now	Philadelphia Int. 3681
			BOBBY McFERRIN	
7/30/88	#1	18	Don't Worry Be Happy	EMI-Manhattan 50146
			MC5	
2/22/69	#65	8	Kick Out The Jams	Elektra 45648

Debut Date	Peak Pos	Wks Chr	ARTIST/Song Title	Label & Number
			PARKER McGEE	
1/15/77	#55	11	I Can't Say No To You	Big Tree 16082
			BOB McGILPIN	
10/07/78	#94	3	When You Feel Love	Butterfly 1211
			MAUREEN McGOVERN	
6/16/73	#3	15	The Morning After	20th Century 2010
10/20/73	#72	5	I Won't Last A Day Without You	20th Century 2051
2/16/74	#96	3	Nice To Be Around	20th Century 2072
9/21/74	#68	10	Give Me A Reason To Be Gone	20th Century 2109
2/01/75	#91	4	We May Never Love Like This Again	20th Century 2158
3/03/79	#69	8	Can You Read My Mind	Warner Brothers 8750
6/30/79	#26	19	Different Worlds	Warner Brothers 8835
			JIMMY McGRIFF	
10/13/62	#34	10	I've Got A Woman (Part 1)	Sue 770
1/12/63	#63	10	All About My Girl	Sue 777
5/16/64	#87	5	Kiko	Sue 10001
			McGUFFEY LANE	
1/31/81	#88	4	Long Time Lovin' You	Atco 7319
			McGUINN, CLARK & HILLMAN	
3/17/79	#33	12	Don't You Write Her Off	Capitol 4693
			McGUINNESS FLINT	
12/26/70	#35	10	When I'm Dead And Gone	Capitol 3014
			BARRY McGUIRE	
8/14/65	#1	13	Eve Of Destruction	Dunhill 4009
11/06/65	#90	3	Child Of Our Times	Dunhill 4014
5/28/66	#85	3	Cloudy Summer Afternoon	Dunhill 4028
			PHYLIS McGUIRE	
12/12/64	#85	3	I Don't Want To Walk Without You	Reprise 0310
			McGUIRE SISTERS	
7/31/54	#5	10	Goodnight Sweetheart, Goodnight	Coral 61187
11/20/54	#9	2	Muskrat Ramble	Coral 61278
2/05/55	#1	14	Sincerely	Coral 61323
7/02/55	#3	11	Something's Gotta Give	Coral 61423
11/12/55	#4	11	He	Coral 61501
8/04/56	#42	3	Weary Blues*	Coral 61670
9/22/56	#33	9	Ev'ry Day Of My Life/	Coral 61703
9/22/56	#36	3	Endless	Coral 61703
12/08/56	#23	8	Goodnight My Love, Pleasant Dreams	Coral 61748
2/16/57	#36	4	Kid Stuff	Coral 61771
12/28/57	#7	18	Sugartime	Coral 61924
5/31/58	#43	6	Ding Dong	Coral 61991
12/27/58	#21	17	May You Always	Coral 62059
5/09/59	#64	8	Summer Dreams/	Coral 62106
5/09/59	#97	2	Peace	Coral 62106
3/11/61	#17	16	Just For Old Time's Sake	Coral 62249
7/22/61	#55	5	Tears On My Pillow	Coral 62276
			*released as by THE McGUIRE SISTERS and LAWRENCE WELK	
			M.C. HAMMER	
4/07/90	#4	22	You Can't Touch This	Capitol 15571
6/30/90	#4	23	Have You Seen Her	Capitol 44573
9/15/90	#3	19	Pray	Capitol 44609
12/22/90	#54	13	Here Comes The Hammer	Capitol 44572
11/02/91	#37	22	2 Legit 2 Quit*	Capitol 44785
12/14/91	#21	19	Addams Groove*	Capitol 44794
2/22/92	#43	17	Do Not Pass Me By*	Capitol 44797
5/30/92	#79	4	This Is The Way We Roll*	Capitol 44786
			*released as by HAMMER	
			PETER McIAN	
3/29/80	#53	10	Solitaire	ARC 11214
			BOB & DOUG McKENZIE	
1/30/82	#14	17	Take Off	Mercury 76134
			SCOTT McKENZIE	
5/27/67	#4	13	San Francisco (Be Sure To Wear Flowers In Your Hair) . . .	Ode 103

Debut Date	Peak Pos	Wks Chr	ARTIST/Song Title	Label & Number
10/21/67	#18	7	Like An Old Time Movie	Ode 105
4/13/68	#95	2	Holy Man	Ode 107
			BRIAN McKNIGHT	
1/30/93	#2	38	Love Is*	Giant 18630
6/26/93	#14	23	One Last Cry	Mercury 862404
			***released as by VANESSA WILLIAMS & BRIAN McKNIGHT**	
			ROD McKUEN	
1/20/62	#70	7	Oliver Twist	Spiral 1407
			TOMMY McLAIN	
7/02/66	#17	11	Sweet Dreams	MSL 197
			DON McLEAN	
11/27/71	#1	20	American Pie (Parts 1 & 2)	United Artists 50856
3/18/72	#11	11	Vincent	United Artists 50887
12/23/72	#19	11	Dreidel	United Artists 51100
3/31/73	#68	5	If We Try	United Artists 206
6/21/75	#94	3	Wonderful Baby	United Artists 614
1/24/81	#6	17	Crying	Millenium 11799
4/11/81	#28	11	Since I Don't Have You	Millenium 11804
10/24/81	#31	16	Castles In The Air	Millenium 11819
			PENNY McLEAN	
1/10/76	#61	8	Lady Bump	Atco 7038
			PHIL McLEAN	
12/09/61	#20	9	Small Sad Sam	Versatile 107
			MC LYTE	
7/24/93	#38	28	Ruffneck	First Priority 98401
			ROBIN McNAMARA	
5/23/70	#7	17	Lay A Little Lovin' On Me	Steed 724
9/26/70	#75	5	Got To Believe In Love	Steed 728
			MC NAS-D & DJ FRED	
9/26/92	#90	2	It's My Cadillac (Got That Bass)	Pandisc 079
			BIG JAY McNEELY	
6/06/59	#41	12	There's Something On Your Mind	Swingin' 614
			KRISTY and JIMMY McNICHOL	
7/29/78	#83	4	He's So Fine	RCA 11271
			SHAMUS M'COOL	
7/04/81	#93	3	American Memories	Perspective 107
			CLYDE McPHATTER	
8/04/56	#29	3	Treasure Of Love	Atlantic 1092
1/12/57	#48	3	Without Love	Atlantic 1117
5/04/57	#46	2	Just To Hold My Hand	Atlantic 1133
7/27/57	#33	9	Long Lonely Nights	Atlantic 1149
10/18/58	#10	21	A Lover's Question	Atlantic 1199
3/28/59	#80	6	Lovey Dovey	Atlantic 2018
4/11/59	#48	7	I Told Myself A Lie	MGM 12780
6/06/59	#31	13	Since You've Been Gone	Atlantic 2028
8/01/59	#79	7	Twice As Nice	MGM 12816
10/17/59	#96	2	You Went Back On Your Word	Atlantic 2038
12/19/59	#60	8	Let's Try Again	MGM 12843
3/19/60	#84	9	Think Me A Kiss	MGM 12877
7/30/60	#23	14	Ta Ta	Mercury 71660
7/29/61	#82	5	I Never Know	Mercury 71841
2/24/62	#7	16	Lover Please	Mercury 71941
6/16/62	#26	8	Little Bitty Pretty One	Mercury 71987
1/11/64	#68	4	Deep In The Heart Of Harlem	Mercury 72220
			CARMEN McRAE	
8/04/56	#13	10	You Don't Know Me	Decca 29949
			MC SERCH	
10/24/92	#67	8	Here It Comes	Def Jam 74414
			CHRISTINE McVIE	
1/28/84	#11	16	Got A Hold On Me	Warner Brothers 29372
4/28/84	#35	11	Love Will Show Us How	Warner Brothers 29313
			SISTER JANET MEAD	
2/16/74	#5	14	The Lord's Prayer	A&M 1491

Debut Date	Peak Pos	Wks Chr	ARTIST/Song Title	Label & Number
			MEATLOAF	
5/22/71	#79	5	What You See Is What You Get*	Rare Earth 5027
12/10/77	#97	1	You Took The Words Right Out Of My Mouth	Epic 50467
3/25/78	#9	25	Two Out Of Three Ain't Bad	Epic 50513
8/12/78	#37	10	Paradise By The Dashboard Light	Epic 50588
11/18/78	#42	12	You Took The Words Right Out Of My Mouth	Epic 50634
9/25/93	#1	29	I'd Do Anything For Love (But I Won't Do That)	MCA 54625
			*released as by STONEY & MEATLOAF	
			MECO	
7/30/77	#1	21	Star Wars Theme/Cantina Band	Millenium 604
12/24/77	#29	13	Theme From Close Encounters	Millenium 608
9/02/78	#34	12	Themes From The Wizard Of Oz	Millenium 620
6/14/80	#24	14	Empire Strikes Back (medley)	RSO 1038
2/13/82	#46	12	Pop Goes The Movies (Part 1)	Arista 0660
7/02/83	#61	12	Ewok Celebration	Arista 9045
			GLENN MEDEIROS	
2/21/87	#18	24	Nothing's Gonna Change My Love For You	Amherst 311
8/27/88	#82	7	Long And Lasting Love (Once In A Lifetime)	Amherst 324
5/19/90	#1	20	She Ain't Worth It*	MCA 79047
8/11/90	#32	14	All I'm Missing Is You**	MCA 53886
11/03/90	#69	5	Me - U = Blue***	MCA 53945
			*released as by GLENN MEDEIROS featuring BOBBY BROWN	
			**released as by GLENN MEDEIROS featuring RAY PARKER JR.	
			***released as by GLENN MEDEIROS featuring THE STYLISTICS	
			BILL MEDLEY	
5/04/68	#76	2	I Can't Make It Alone	MGM 13931
7/20/68	#35	13	Brown Eyed Woman	MGM 13959
11/02/68	#55	5	Peace Brother Peace	MGM 14000
3/28/81	#88	4	Don't Know Much	Liberty 1402
10/09/82	#67	7	Right Here And Now	Planet 13317
9/19/87	#1	23	(I've Had) The Time Of My Life*	RCA 5224
			*released as by BILL MEDLEY and JENNIFER WARNES	
			JOE MEDLIN	
3/14/59	#55	8	I Kneel At Your Throne	Mercury 71415
			MONKEY MEEKS	
12/08/73	#93	3	Take Me To Your Heart	Roxbury 0133
			MEGADETH	
8/15/92	#48	27	Symphony Of Destruction	Capitol 44886
			MEGATRONS	
5/23/59	#60	11	Velvet Waters	Acousticon 101
			RANDY MEISNER	
10/18/80	#27	16	Deep Inside My Heart	Epic 50989
1/24/81	#15	16	Hearts On Fire	Epic 50964
5/30/81	#83	3	Gotta Get Away	Epic 02059
7/31/82	#23	14	Never Been In Love	Epic 03032
			MEL & KIM	
3/07/87	#91	5	Showing Out (Get Fresh At The Weekend)	Atlantic 89329
			MEL and TIM	
10/25/69	#12	11	Backfield In Motion	Bamboo 107
2/07/70	#42	7	Good Guys Only Win In The Movies	Bamboo 109
6/24/72	#18	22	Starting All Over Again	Stax 0127
			MELANIE	
4/18/70	#3	17	Lay Down (Candles In The Rain)*	Buddah 167
8/15/70	#20	8	Peace Will Come (According To Plan)	Buddah 186
12/05/70	#34	6	Ruby Tuesday	Buddah 202
4/24/71	#78	2	The Good Book	Buddah 224
10/23/71	#1	19	Brand New Key	Neighborhood 4201
1/22/72	#21	9	Ring The Living Bell	Neighborhood 4202
1/22/72	#25	9	The Nickel Song	Buddah 268
5/20/72	#79	4	Someday I'll Be A Farmer	Neighborhood 4204
10/07/72	#57	7	Together Alone	Neighborhood 4207
2/10/73	#30	12	Bitter Bad	Neighborhood 4210
11/24/73	#54	10	Will You Love Me Tomorrow	Neighborhood 4213

Debut Date	Peak Pos	Wks Chr	**ARTIST**/Song Title	Label & Number
7/27/74	#70	8	Lover's Cross	Neighborhood 4215
			*released as by MELANIE with THE EDWIN HAWKINS SINGERS	
			JOHN COUGAR MELLENCAMP	
10/06/79	#32	16	I Need A Lover*	Riva 202
2/09/80	#93	3	Small Paradise*	Riva 203
9/27/80	#28	19	This Time*	Riva 205
1/31/81	#15	21	Ain't Even Done With The Night*	Riva 207
4/24/82	#1	29	Hurts So Good*	Riva 209
7/24/82	#1	25	Jack & Diane*	Riva 210
11/06/82	#22	16	Hand To Hold On To*	Riva 211
10/15/83	#8	17	Crumblin' Down	Riva 214
12/10/83	#12	16	Pink Houses	Riva 215
3/17/84	#12	17	Authority Song	Riva 216
8/17/85	#10	16	Lonely Ol' Night	Riva 880984
11/02/85	#6	18	Small Town	Riva 884202
2/01/86	#4	18	R.O.C.K. In The U.S.A.	Riva 884455
4/26/86	#28	11	Rain On The Scarecrow	Riva 884635
6/28/86	#32	14	Rumbleseat	Riva 884856
8/15/87	#10	17	Paper In Fire	Mercury 888763
10/24/87	#18	18	Cherry Bomb	Mercury 888934
2/06/88	#22	16	Check It Out	Mercury 870126
5/14/88	#70	10	Rooty Toot Toot	Mercury 870327
4/29/89	#11	17	Pop Singer	Mercury 874012
7/22/89	#45	10	Jackie Brown	Mercury 874644
10/05/91	#13	20	Get A Leg Up**	Mercury 867890
1/25/92	#13	20	Again Tonight**	Mercury 866414
10/02/93	#40	18	Human Wheels**	Mercury 862704
			*released as by JOHN COUGAR	
			**released as by JOHN MELLENCAMP	
			MELLO-TONES	
5/04/57	#27	7	Rosie Lee	Gee 1037
			MELLOW MAN ACE	
5/19/90	#14	16	Mentirosa	Capitol 44533
			MELODEERS	
12/24/60	#54	2	Rudolph The Red Nosed Reindeer	Studio 9908
			HAROLD MELVIN and THE BLUE NOTES	
6/24/72	#40	11	I Miss You (Part 1)	Philadelphia Int. 3516
9/30/72	#2	15	If You Don't Know Me By Now	Philadelphia Int. 3520
3/10/73	#52	5	Yesterday I Had The Blues	Philadelphia Int. 3525
9/22/73	#9	15	The Love I Lost (Part 1)	Philadelphia Int. 3533
4/13/74	#79	6	Satisfaction Guaranteed	Philadelphia Int. 3543
12/07/74	#67	7	Where Are All My Friends	Philadelphia Int. 3552
3/29/75	#13	15	Bad Luck (Part 1)	Philadelphia Int. 3562
7/05/75	#31	9	Hope That We Can Be Together Soon*	Philadelphia Int, 3569
11/22/75	#15	18	Wake Up Everybody (Part 1)	Philadelphia Int. 3579
4/03/76	#67	8	Tell The World How I Feel About 'Cha Baby	Philadelphia Int. 3588
2/26/77	#73	6	Reaching For The World	ABC 12240
			*released as by SHARON PAIGE and HAROLD MELVIN and THE BLUENOTES	
			MEN AT LARGE	
2/27/93	#37	18	So Alone	East West 98459
			MEN AT WORK	
7/10/82	#1	29	Who Can It Be Now?	Columbia 02888
11/06/82	#1	28	Down Under	Columbia 03303
4/09/83	#5	16	Overkill	Columbia 03795
7/02/83	#12	15	It's A Mistake	Columbia 03959
9/17/83	#26	11	Dr. Heckyll & Mr. Jive	Columbia 04111
5/25/85	#41	10	Everything I Need	Columbia 04929
			SERGIO MENDES & BRASIL '66	
10/01/66	#75	5	Mas Que Nada	A&M 807
12/31/66	#100	2	Constant Rain (Chove Chuva)	A&M 825
5/27/67	#93	3	Night And Day	A&M 853
5/18/68	#5	12	The Look Of Love	A&M 924
8/10/68	#7	12	The Fool On The Hill	A&M 961
11/16/68	#19	10	Scarborough Fair	A&M 986
4/26/69	#59	7	Pretty World	A&M 1049

Debut Date	Peak Pos	Wks Chr	ARTIST/Song Title	Label & Number
			SERGIO MENDES & BRASIL '66—*continued*	
6/28/69	#84	4	(Sittin' On) The Dock Of The Bay	A&M 1073
5/19/73	#99	1	Love Music*	Bell 45335
4/16/83	#3	26	Never Gonna Let You Go**	A&M 2540
8/20/83	#51	8	Rainbow's End**	A&M 2563
4/07/84	#62	7	Olympia**	A&M 2623
5/26/84	#31	20	Alibis**	A&M 2639
			*released as by SERGIO MENDES & BRASIL '77	
			**released as by SERGIO MENDES	
			MENUDO	
5/11/85	#61	9	Hold Me	RCA 14087
			MEN WITHOUT HATS	
6/25/83	#1	26	The Safety Dance	Backstreet 52232
11/19/83	#85	4	I Like	MCA 52293
10/24/87	#27	24	Pop Goes The World	Mercury 888859
4/09/88	#89	3	Moonbeam	Mercury 870153
			FREDDIE MERCURY	
9/29/84	#61	8	Love Kills	Columbia 04606
4/27/85	#70	5	I Was Born To Love You	Columbia 04869
			MERCY	
4/05/69	#2	14	Love (Can Make You Happy)	Sundi 6811
6/28/69	#75	4	Forever	Warner Brothers 7297
			MERMAN & BOLGER	
4/08/50	#5	9	Dearie	Decca 24873
			MERRY-GO-ROUND	
4/01/67	#57	9	Live	A&M 834
9/02/67	#96	2	You're A Very Lovely Woman	A&M 863
			MESA	
2/12/77	#64	10	Sailing Ships	Ariola America 7654
			MESSENGERS	
9/11/71	#42	8	That's The Way A Woman Is	Rare Earth 5032
			METALLICA	
2/25/89	#61	9	One	Elektra 69329
9/14/91	#28	24	Enter Sandman	Elektra 64857
12/28/91	#73	16	The Unforgiven	Elektra 64814
3/01/92	#31	17	Nothing Else Matters	Elektra 64770
7/18/92	#62	12	Wherever I May Roam	Elektra 64741
11/07/92	#82	5	Sad But True	Elektra 64896
			METERS	
2/01/69	#44	9	Sophisticated Cissy	Josie 1001
4/12/69	#33	10	Cissy Strut	Josie 1005
7/19/69	#55	7	Ease Back	Josie 1008
12/13/69	#55	9	Look-Ka Py Py	Josie 1015
3/21/70	#53	10	Chicken Strut	Josie 1018
6/20/70	#84	4	Hand Clapping Song	Josie 1021
9/17/77	#83	7	Be My Lady	Warner Brothers 8434
			METROS	
1/14/67	#97	3	Sweetest One	RCA 8994
			MFSB	
3/02/74	#1	16	TSOP (The Sound Of Philadelphia)*	Philadelphia Int. 3540
6/29/74	#48	6	Love Is The Message*	Philadelphia Int. 3547
6/07/75	#43	9	Sexy	Philadelphia Int. 3567
			*released as by MFSB featuring THE THREE DEGREES	
			MIAMI SOUND MACHINE (see GLORIA ESTEFAN)	
			GEORGE MICHAEL (also WHAM!)	
8/06/83	#50	11	Bad Boys*	Columbia 03932
9/08/84	#1	24	Wake Me Up Before You Go-Go**	Columbia 04552
12/22/84	#1	22	Careless Whisper***	Columbia 04691
3/23/85	#1	19	Everything She Wants**	Columbia 04840
7/27/85	#10	17	Freedom**	Columbia 05409
11/30/85	#3	21	I'm Your Man**	Columbia 05721
4/26/86	#8	16	A Different Corner	Columbia 05888
7/05/86	#10	15	The Edge Of Heaven**	Columbia 06182
10/11/86	#49	8	Where Did Your Heart Go?**	Columbia 06294
2/21/87	#1	21	I Knew You Were Waiting (For Me)****	Arista 9559

Debut Date	Peak Pos	Wks Chr	**ARTIST**/Song Title	Label & Number
6/06/87	#2	22	I Want Your Sex	Columbia 07164
10/24/87	#1	23	Faith	Columbia 07623
1/16/88	#1	19	Father Figure	Columbia 07682
4/16/88	#1	19	One More Try	Columbia 07773
7/09/88	#1	17	Monkey	Columbia 07941
10/08/88	#4	18	Kissing A Fool	Columbia 08050
2/25/89	#4	21	Heaven Help Me*****	Mika 871538
9/01/90	#1	15	Praying For Time	Columbia 73512
10/27/90	#7	19	Freedom	Columbia 73559
1/19/91	#21	15	Waiting For That Day	Columbia 73663
12/07/91	#1	22	Don't Let The Sun Go Down On Me******	Columbia 74086
6/20/92	#10	19	Too Funky	Columbia 74353
5/01/93	#38	1	Somebody To Love*******	Hollywood 64647
5/22/93	#32	10	Somebody To Love*******	Hollywood 64647
7/10/93	#77	11	Killer/Papa Was A Rollin' Stone	Hollywood 64626

*released as by WHAM! U.K.
**released as by WHAM!
***released as by WHAM! featuring GEORGE MICHAEL
****released as by ARETHA FRANKLIN and GEORGE MICHAEL
*****released as by DEON ESTUS with GEORGE MICHAEL
******released as by GEORGE MICHAEL/ELTON JOHN
*******released as by GEORGE MICHAEL and QUEEN

			MICHAEL LEARNS TO ROCK	
8/31/91	#70	8	My Blue Angel	Impact 54160
			LEE MICHAELS	
9/20/69	#90	3	Heighty Hi	A&M 1095
8/07/71	#4	16	Do You Know What I Mean	A&M 1262
11/20/71	#39	9	Can I Get A Witness	A&M 1303
			MICHEL'LE	
12/09/89	#6	23	No More Lies	Ruthless 99149
4/21/90	#26	15	Nicety	Ruthless 98980
			MICKEY and SYLVIA	
1/05/57	#7	17	Love Is Strange	Groove 0175
4/06/57	#39	4	Dearest/	Vik 0267
4/06/57	#41	3	There Oughta Be A Law	Vik 0267
6/14/58	#53	2	Bewildered	Vik 0324
12/24/60	#47	11	What Would I Do	RCA 7811
9/09/61	#97	2	Baby You're So Fine	Willow 23000
			BETTE MIDLER	
12/23/72	#13	14	Do You Want To Dance?	Atlantic 2928
5/05/73	#6	16	Boogie Woogie Bugle Boy	Atlantic 2964
9/29/73	#40	6	Friends	Atlantic 2980
1/19/74	#31	8	In The Mood	Atlantic 3004
5/07/77	#62	9	You're Movin' Out Today	Atlantic 3379
1/28/78	#66	9	Storybook Children (Daybreak)	Atlantic 3431
6/02/79	#46	9	Married Men	Atlantic 3582
1/19/80	#47	10	When A Man Loves A Woman	Atlantic 3643
3/22/80	#1	26	The Rose	Atlantic 3656
11/22/80	#42	14	My Mother's Eyes	Atlantic 3771
9/03/83	#78	4	All I Need To Know	Atlantic 89789
10/22/83	#89	4	Favorite Waste Of Time	Atlantic 89761
2/18/84	#79	4	Beast Of Burden	Atlantic 89712
3/11/89	#1	24	Wind Beneath My Wings	Atlantic 88972
10/06/90	#2	25	From A Distance	Atlantic 87820
1/19/91	#54	13	Night And Day	Atlantic 87825
11/30/91	#70	11	Every Road Leads Back To You	Atlantic 87572
			MIDNIGHT OIL	
4/02/88	#26	20	Beds Are Burning	Columbia 07433
7/30/88	#49	12	The Dead Heart	Columbia 07964
2/17/90	#27	13	Blue Sky Mine	Columbia 73250
			MIDNIGHT STAR	
8/13/83	#51	17	Freak-A-Zoid	Solar 69828
12/10/83	#53	11	Wet My Whistle	Solar 69790
12/01/84	#19	17	Operator	Solar 69684
3/09/85	#81	5	Scientific Love	Solar 69659

231

Debut Date	Peak Pos	Wks Chr	ARTIST/Song Title	Label & Number
			MIDNIGHT STAR—*continued*	
7/12/85	#88	3	Headlines	Solar 69547
10/11/86	#54	14	Midas Touch	Solar 69525
			MIGHTY CLOUDS OF JOY	
3/20/76	#77	5	Mighty High	ABC 12164
			MIGHTY HANNIBAL	
11/05/66	#79	4	Hymn No. 5	Shurfine 021
			MIGHTY POPE	
8/13/77	#83	4	Heaven Is On The Seventh Floor	Private Stock 45157
			MIGHTY SAM	
9/17/66	#98	1	Fannie May	Amy 963
			MIKE + THE MECHANICS	
11/30/85	#5	24	Silent Running	Atlantic 89488
3/22/86	#9	19	All I Need Is A Miracle	Atlantic 89450
6/28/86	#30	15	Taken In	Atlantic 89404
11/12/88	#58	10	Nobody's Perfect	Atlantic 88990
12/31/88	#1	23	The Living Years	Atlantic 88964
4/22/89	#53	10	Seeing Is Believing	Atlantic 88921
3/30/91	#62	9	Word Of Mouth	Atlantic 87714
			BUDDY MILES	
6/13/70	#99	1	Them Changes*	Mercury 73008
7/25/70	#68	6	Down By The River	Mercury 73086
12/12/70	#81	7	We Got To Live Together (Part 1)	Mercury 73159
5/22/71	#62	5	Wholesale Love	Mercury 73205
9/18/71	#82	3	Them Changes	Mercury 73228
9/13/75	#81	5	Rockin' And Rollin' On The Streets Of Hollywood	Casablanca 839
			*released as by **BUDDY MILES & THE FREEDOM EXPRESS**	
			GARRY MILES	
6/25/60	#13	14	Look For A Star	Liberty 55261
			JOHN MILES	
2/07/76	#58	15	Highfly	London 20084
5/29/76	#91	3	Music	London 20086
5/07/77	#64	7	Slowdown	London 20092
			LENNY MILES	
1/21/61	#69	6	Don't Believe Him, Donna	Scepter 1212
			CLINT MILLER	
1/18/58	#49	3	Bertha Lou	ABC-Paramount 9878
			FRANKIE MILLER (from Texas)	
8/12/61	#85	5	Black Land Farmer	Starday 424
			FRANKIE MILLER (from Scotland)	
6/25/77	#69	5	The Doodle Song	Chrysalis 2145
6/19/82	#60	8	To Dream The Dream	Capitol 5131
			JODY MILLER	
4/24/65	#22	8	Queen Of The House	Capitol 5402
6/26/65	#79	6	Silver Threads And Golden Needles	Capitol 5429
9/04/65	#31	7	Home Of The Brave	Capitol 5483
7/03/71	#57	7	He's So Fine	Epic 10734
9/25/71	#83	5	Baby, I'm Yours	Epic 10785
			MITCH MILLER	
9/03/55	#1	15	Yellow Rose Of Texas	Columbia 40540
8/04/56	#9	13	Theme Song From "Song For A Summer Night"	Columbia 40730
11/03/56	#46	1	Song Of The Sparrow	Columbia 40772
1/04/58	#15	13	March From The River Kwai And Colonel Bogey	Columbia 41066
1/10/59	#5	15	The Children's Marching Song	Columbia 41317
7/18/59	#96	2	Join The Cavalry	Columbia 41424
11/07/59	#48	13	Do-Re-Mi	Columbia 41499
11/10/62	#86	1	The Longest Day	Columbia 42585
			MRS. MILLER	
5/07/66	#100	1	Downtown/	Capitol 5640
5/14/66	#100	1	A Lover's Concerto	Capitol 5640
			NED MILLER	
12/15/62	#6	17	From A Jack To A King	Fabor 114
12/26/64	#52	9	Do What You Do Do Well	Fabor 137

Debut Date	Peak Pos	Wks Chr	ARTIST/Song Title	Label & Number
			ROGER MILLER	
12/03/60	#96	1	You Don't Want My Love	RCA 7776
6/06/64	#7	13	Dang Me	Smash 1881
9/12/64	#6	12	Chug-A-Lug	Smash 1926
11/28/64	#34	8	Do-Wacka-Do	Smash 1947
1/30/65	#3	15	King Of The Road	Smash 1965
5/08/65	#9	9	Engine Engine #9	Smash 1983
7/10/65	#30	6	One Dyin' And A Buryin'/	Smash 1994
7/10/65	#88	3	It Happened Just That Way	Smash 1994
9/11/65	#38	6	Kansas City Star	Smash 1998
10/30/65	#8	13	England Swings	Smash 2010
2/12/66	#20	8	Husbands And Wives/	Smash 2024
2/12/66	#92	1	I've Been A Long Time Leavin'	Smash 2024
6/25/66	#43	5	You Can't Roller Skate In A Buffalo Herd	Smash 2043
9/10/66	#45	6	My Uncle Used To Love Me But She Died	Smash 2055
10/29/66	#86	5	Heartbreak Hotel	Smash 2066
3/18/67	#39	10	Walkin' In The Sunshine	Smash 2081
10/14/67	#91	2	The Ballad Of Waterhole #3	Smash 2121
2/24/68	#51	8	Little Green Apples	Smash 2148
11/30/68	#52	8	Vance	Smash 2197
			STEVE MILLER BAND	
11/09/68	#76	3	Living In The U.S.A.	Capitol 2287
8/15/70	#81	3	Going To The Country	Capitol 2878
10/20/73	#1	19	The Joker	Capitol 3732
2/23/74	#40	9	Your Cash Ain't Nothin' But Trash	Capitol 3837
15/18/74	#38	8	Living In The U.S.A.	Capitol 3884
5/08/76	#9	18	Take The Money And Run*	Capitol 4260
8/14/76	#1	24	Rock 'N Me*	Capitol 4323
12/18/76	#3	18	Fly Like An Eagle*	Capitol 4372
4/30/77	#3	18	Jet Airliner	Capitol 4424
8/06/77	#17	14	Jungle Love	Capitol 4466
10/15/77	#13	15	Swingtown	Capitol 4496
10/31/81	#28	14	Heart Like A Wheel	Capitol 5068
2/06/82	#88	3	Circle Of Love	Capitol 5086
5/29/82	#1	28	Abracadabra	Capitol 5126
10/09/82	#53	8	Cool Magic	Capitol 5162
12/11/82	#70	8	Give It Up	Capitol 5194
10/06/84	#53	9	Shangri-La	Capitol 5407
2/16/85	#80	5	Bongo Bongo	Capitol 5442
11/08/86	#79	5	I Want To Make The World Turn Around	Capitol 5646
7/17/93	#52	11	Wide River	Sailor 859194
			*released as by STEVE MILLER	
			MILLIONS LIKE US	
11/07/87	#72	10	Guaranteed For Life	Virgin 99412
			MILLI VANILLI	
12/31/88	#1	26	Girl You Know It's True	Arista 9781
4/29/89	#2	21	Baby Don't Forget My Number	Arista 9832
8/05/89	#1	20	Girl I'm Gonna Miss You	Arista 9870
10/14/89	#1	21	Blame It On The Rain	Arista 9904
12/30/89	#4	17	All Or Nothing	Arista 9923
			FRANK MILLS	
1/22/72	#45	9	Love Me, Love Me Love	Sunflower 118
1/27/79	#2	20	Music Box Dancer	Polydor 14517
10/27/79	#57	11	Peter Piper	Polydor 2002
			GARRY MILLS	
7/09/60	#13	12	Look For A Star	Imperial 5674
			HAYLEY MILLS	
9/09/61	#5	14	Let's Get Together	Vista 385
3/24/62	#31	9	Johnny Jingo	Vista 395
			STEPHANIE MILLS	
8/04/79	#28	13	What Cha Gonna Do With My Lovin'	20th Century 2403
6/14/80	#55	8	Sweet Sensation	20th Century 2449
8/09/80	#8	26	Never Knew Love Like This Before	20th Century 2460
5/09/81	#45	14	Two Hearts*	20th Century 2492
10/13/84	#61	9	The Medicine Song	Casablanca 880180
7/13/85	#76	5	Bit By Bit (Theme From "Fletch")	MCA 52617

Debut Date	Peak Pos	Wks Chr	ARTIST/Song Title	Label & Number
			STEPHANIE MILLS—*continued*	
5/24/86	#88	3	I Learned To Respect The Power Of Love	MCA 52799
			released as by STEPHANIE MILLS featuring TEDDY PENDERGRASS	
			MILLS BROTHERS	
12/09/50	#4	13	Nevertheless	Decca 27253
3/22/52	#10	1	Be My Life's Companion	Decca 27889
10/18/52	#2	18	Glow Worm	Decca 28384
2/06/54	#7	4	The Jones Boy	Decca 28945
6/08/57	#41	5	Queen Of The Senior Prom	Decca 30299
12/06/58	#84	6	Yellow Bird	Dot 15858
2/03/68	#21	13	Cab Driver	Dot 17041
5/11/68	#73	5	My Shy Violet	Dot 17096
11/02/68	#78	4	The Ol' Race Track	Dot 17162
			RONNIE MILSAP	
10/23/65	#94	4	Never Had It So Good	Scepter 12109
9/21/74	#96	2	Please Don't Tell Me How The Story Ends	RCA 0313
4/19/75	#87	4	Too Late To Worry, Too Blue To Cry	RCA 10228
6/25/77	#11	23	It Was Almost Like A Song	RCA 10976
1/21/78	#89	3	What A Difference You've Made In My Life	RCA 11146
7/01/78	#80	4	Only One Love In My Life	RCA 11270
9/22/79	#50	13	Get It Up	RCA 11695
11/29/80	#23	23	Smoky Mountain Rain	RCA 12084
6/27/81	#9	20	(There's) No Gettin' Over Me	RCA 12264
10/24/81	#25	21	I Wouldn't Have Missed It For The World	RCA 12342
5/01/82	#15	15	Any Day Now	RCA 13216
8/21/82	#60	10	He Got You	RCA 13286
3/26/83	#24	17	Stranger In My House	RCA 13470
8/20/83	#67	6	Don't You Know How Much I Love You	RCA 13564
8/04/84	#80	6	She Loves My Car	RCA 13847
			GARNET MIMMS & THE ENCHANTERS	
9/24/63	#4	14	Cry Baby	United Artists 629
11/09/63	#40	10	Baby Don't You Weep/	United Artists 658
11/16/63	#34	11	For Your Precious Love	United Artists 658
2/24/64	#81	5	Tell Me Baby	United Artists 694
5/23/64	#96	3	One Girl/	United Artists 715
7/11/64	#89	8	A Quiet Place	United Artists 715
10/10/64	#73	6	Look Away	United Artists 733
3/26/66	#34	9	I'll Take Good Care Of You*	United Artists 995
			released as by GARNET MIMMS	
			MINA	
5/06/61	#82	4	This World We Love In	Time 1030
			MINDBENDERS	
3/20/65	#1	11	Game Of Love*	Fontana 1509
6/12/65	#52	7	It's Just A Little Bit Too Late*	Fontana 1514
4/02/66	#1	16	A Groovy Kind Of Love	Fontana 1541
8/13/66	#67	6	Ashes To Ashes	Fontana 1555
			released as by WAYNE FONTANA & THE MINDBDENDERS	
			SAL MINEO	
5/18/57	#6	13	Start Movin' (In My Direction)	Epic 9216
9/14/57	#38	4	Lasting Love	Epic 9227
11/02/57	#45	3	Party Time	Epic 9246
2/01/58	#53	3	Little Pigeon	Epic 9260
8/22/59	#66	5	Young As We Are	Epic 9327
			KYLIE MINOGUE	
5/14/88	#31	16	I Should Be So Lucky	Geffen 27922
8/27/88	#4	22	The Loco-Motion	Geffen 27752
12/03/88	#57	9	It's No Secret	Geffen 27651
2/03/90	#83	4	Wouldn't Change A Thing	Geffen 22794
			MINT CONDITION	
2/15/92	#15	23	Breakin' My Heart	Perspective 0004
6/27/92	#77	5	Forever In Your Eyes	Perspective 0009
			MIRACLES (also SMOKEY ROBINSON & THE MIRACLES)	
10/03/59	#62	6	Bad Girl	Chess 1734
12/10/60	#2	18	Shop Around	Tamla 54034
4/08/61	#62	5	Ain't It Baby	Tamla 54036

Debut Date	Peak Pos	Wks Chr	ARTIST/Song Title	Label & Number
10/07/61	#76	10	Everybody's Gotta Pay Some Dues	Tamla 54048
1/13/62	#22	11	What's So Good About Good-By	Tamla 54053
5/12/62	#33	11	I'll Try Something New	Tamla 54059
12/08/62	#6	17	You've Really Got A Hold On Me	Tamla 54073
4/06/63	#43	9	A Love She Can Count On	Tamla 54078
8/17/63	#9	13	Mickey's Monkey	Tamla 54083
11/23/63	#42	10	I Gotta Dance To Keep From Crying	Tamla 54089
3/07/64	#65	6	The Man In You	Tamla 54092
7/04/64	#25	9	I Like It Like That	Tamla 54098
9/19/64	#37	6	That's What Love Is Made Of	Tamla 54102
12/19/64	#62	5	Come On Do The Jerk	Tamla 54109
3/27/65	#16	11	Ooo Baby Baby	Tamla 54113
7/10/65	#16	13	The Tracks Of My Tears	Tamla 54118
10/16/65	#21	10	My Girl Has Gone	Tamla 54123
12/25/65	#10	12	Going To A Go-Go	Tamla 54127
6/18/66	#50	7	Whole Lot Of Shakin' In My Heart	Tamla 54134
11/05/66	#25	10	(Come 'Round Here) I'm The One You Need . . .	Tamla 54140
2/18/67	#45	10	The Love I Saw In You Was Just A Mirage*	Tamla 54145
6/17/67	#19	12	More Love*	Tamla 54152
11/04/67	#3	15	I Second That Emotion*	Tamla 54159
2/24/68	#17	12	If You Can Want*	Tamla 54162
6/01/68	#24	8	Yester Love*	Tamla 54167
8/10/68	#24	9	Special Occasion*	Tamla 54172
1/04/69	#9	13	Baby, Baby Don't Cry*	Tamla 54178
6/14/69	#36	9	Doggone Right*	Tamla 54183
6/28/69	#44	5	Abraham, Martin And John*	Tamla 54184
9/06/69	#53	5	Here I Go Again*	Tamla 54183
12/06/69	#41	8	Point It Out*	Tamla 54189
5/23/70	#52	6	Who's Gonna Take The Blame*	Tamla 54194
10/10/70	#1	16	Tears Of A Clown*	Tamla 54199
3/13/71	#18	12	I Don't Blame You At All*	Tamla 54205
6/26/71	#49	5	Crazy About The La La La*	Tamla 54206
11/13/71	#55	9	Satisfaction*	Tamla 54211
6/03/72	#46	10	We've Come Too Far To End It Now*	Tamla 54220
12/09/72	#64	9	I Can't Stand To See You Cry*	Tamla 54225
8/11/73	#99	1	Don't Let It End	Tamla 54237
8/03/74	#13	17	Do It Baby	Tamla 54248
12/14/74	#63	9	Don't Cha Love It	Tamla 54256
11/08/75	#1	26	Love Machine (Part 1)	Tamla 54262
			*released as by SMOKEY ROBINSON & THE MIRACLES	
			MIRETTES	
2/10/68	#52	8	In The Midnight Hour	Revue 11004
			MISSING PERSONS	
7/03/82	#37	13	Words	Capitol 5127
10/09/82	#40	15	Destination Unknown	Capitol 5161
1/15/83	#62	8	Windows	Capitol 5200
3/12/83	#62	7	Walking In L.A.	Capitol 5212
4/07/84	#78	5	Give	Capitol 5326
			MISTA GRIMM	
10/30/93	#50	20	Indo Smoke	Epic 77256
			MR. BIG (British quintet)	
3/05/77	#64	9	Romeo	Arista 0229
			MR. BIG (American quartet)	
12/14/91	#1	32	To Be With You	Atlantic 87580
4/25/92	#9	20	Just Take My Heart	Atlantic 87509
10/23/93	#25	22	Wild World	Atlantic 87308
			MR. MISTER	
3/24/83	#66	8	Hunters Of The Night	RCA 13741
9/21/85	#1	26	Broken Wings	RCA 14136
12/21/85	#1	22	Kyrie	RCA 14258
3/29/86	#11	17	Is It Love	RCA 14313
8/22/87	#33	12	Something Real (Inside Me/Inside You)	RCA 5273
11/14/87	#88	3	The Border	RCA 5325
			MISTRESS	
12/01/79	#81	4	Mistrusted Love	RSO 1009

Debut Date	Peak Pos	Wks Chr	ARTIST/Song Title	Label & Number
			CHAD MITCHELL TRIO	
1/27/62	#35	9	Lizzie Borden	Kapp 439
5/12/62	#84	4	The John Birch Society	Kapp 457
11/30/63	#46	10	The Marvelous Toy	Mercury 72197
			GUY MITCHELL	
1/06/51	#1	17	My Heart Cries For You/	Columbia 39067
1/27/51	#5	9	The Roving Kind	Columbia 39067
4/07/51	#5	10	Sparrow In The Tree Top	Columbia 39190
6/03/51	#3	15	My Truly, Truly Fair	Columbia 39415
9/22/51	#9	4	Belle, Belle, My Liberty Belle	Columbia 39512
4/26/52	#6	6	Pittsburgh, Pennsylvania	Columbia 39663
10/27/56	#1	23	Singing The Blues	Columbia 40769
1/19/57	#15	10	Knee Deep In The Blues/	Columbia 40820
1/26/57	#38	5	Take Me Back Baby	Columbia 40820
4/06/57	#13	13	Rock-A-Billy	Columbia 40877
6/29/57	#51	2	Sweet Stuff	Columbia 40940
10/10/59	#1	19	Heartaches By The Number	Columbia 41476
			JONI MITCHELL	
7/11/70	#100	1	Big Yellow Taxi (studio version)	Reprise 0906
8/21/71	#92	2	Carey	Reprise 1029
11/11/72	#20	15	You Turn Me On, I'm A Radio	Asylum 11010
12/29/73	#50	8	Raised On Robbery	Asylum 11029
3/02/74	#8	19	Help Me	Asylum 11034
7/20/74	#23	13	Free Man In Paris	Asylum 11041
12/21/74	#25	10	Big Yellow Taxi (live version)	Asylum 45221
2/07/76	#55	6	In France They Kiss On Main Street	Asylum 45296
11/20/82	#73	8	(You're So Square) Baby, I Don't Care	Geffen 29849
			KIM MITCHELL	
6/15/85	#80	5	Go For Soda	Bronze 99652
			WILLIE MITCHELL	
8/22/64	#33	9	20-75	Hi 2075
7/03/65	#91	3	Buster Browne	Hi 2091
5/07/66	#68	4	Bad Eye	Hi 2103
2/17/68	#27	18	Soul Serenade	Hi 2140
7/20/68	#54	6	Prayer Meetin'	Hi 2147
9/28/68	#63	5	Up-Hard	Hi 2151
1/18/69	#95	1	30-60-90	Hi 2154
			ROBERT MITCHUM	
3/03/62	#52	8	Ballad Of Thunder Road	Capitol 3986
			MIXTURES	
3/06/71	#44	10	Pushbike Song	Sire 350
			MOB	
12/26/70	#90	5	I Dig Everything About You	Colossus 130
2/27/71	#87	6	Give It To Me	Colossus 134
			MOBY GRAPE	
7/08/67	#94	2	Hey Grandma	Columbia 44174
7/22/67	#70	2	Omaha	Columbia 44173
			MOCEDADES	
12/29/73	#9	17	Eres Tu (Touch The Wind)	Tara 100
			MODELS	
4/26/86	#33	14	Out Of Mind, Out Of Sight	Geffen 28762
			MODERN ENGLISH	
3/26/83	#68	7	I Melt With You	Sire 29775
6/30/90	#75	7	I Melt With You	TVT 2812
			DOMENICO MODUGNO	
7/26/58	#1	20	Nel Blu Dipinto Di Blue (Volare)	Decca 30677
11/15/58	#24	11	Come Prima	Decca 30777
			MOJO MEN	
11/06/65	#91	3	Dance With Me	Autumn 19
1/28/67	#39	11	Sit Down, I Think I Love You	Reprise 0539
6/10/67	#93	1	Me About You	Reprise 0580
			MOLLY HATCHET	
12/29/79	#45	12	Flirtin' With Disaster	Epic 50822
2/06/82	#89	5	Power Play	Epic 02680

Debut Date	Peak Pos	Wks Chr	ARTIST/Song Title	Label & Number
			MOMENTS	
12/21/68	#60	7	Not On The Outside	Stang 5000
5/10/69	#84	3	Sunday	Stang 5003
8/16/69	#57	5	I Do	Stang 5005
4/18/70	#8	13	Love On A Two-Way Street	Stang 5012
8/15/70	#37	8	If I Didn't Care	Stang 5016
11/21/70	#74	5	All I Have	Stang 5017
4/10/71	#90	2	I Can't Help It	Stang 5020
9/04/71	#97	1	Lucky Me	Stang 5031
10/06/73	#71	5	Gotta Find A Way	Stang 5050
1/05/74	#20	12	Sexy Mama	Stang 5052
6/15/74	#91	3	Sho Nuff Boogie (Part 1)	All Platinum 2350
1/11/75	#85	5	Girls*	Stang 5057
5/31/75	#39	11	Look At Me (I'm In Love)	Stang 5060
4/15/78	#97	2	I Could Have Loved You	Stang 5075
			*released as by **THE MOMENTS & THE WHATNAUTS**	
			STEPHEN MONAHAN	
7/07/67	#78	4	City Of Windows	Kapp 835
			MONARCHS	
3/07/64	#52	11	Look Homeward Angel	Sound Stage 2516
			JULIE MONDAY	
8/13/66	#92	3	Come Share The Good Times With Me	Rainbow 500
			MONDO ROCK	
5/16/87	#73	7	Primitive Love Rites	Columbia 06981
			EDDIE MONEY	
1/28/78	#5	26	Baby Hold On	Columbia 10663
7/01/78	#20	15	Two Tickets To Paradise	Columbia 10765
12/02/78	#67	8	You've Really Got A Hold On Me	Columbia 10842
1/27/79	#25	14	Maybe I'm A Fool	Columbia 10900
5/12/79	#65	6	Can't Keep A Good Man Down	Columbia 10981
8/25/79	#55	9	Get A Move On	Columbia 11064
9/20/80	#91	3	Running Back	Columbia 11325
10/25/80	#86	4	Let's Be Lovers Again	Columbia 11377
6/26/82	#21	16	Think I'm In Love	Columbia 02964
10/16/82	#62	11	Shakin'	Columbia 03252
12/03/83	#59	9	The Big Crash	Columbia 04199
3/10/84	#77	6	Club Michelle	Columbia 04376
8/16/86	#5	24	Take Me Home Tonight	Columbia 06231
12/13/86	#15	20	I Wanna Go Back	Columbia 06569
4/11/87	#25	18	Endless Nights	Columbia 07035
10/01/88	#7	21	Walk On Water	Columbia 08060
1/21/89	#15	15	The Love In Your Eyes	Columbia 68532
4/15/89	#66	9	Let Me In	Columbia 68739
12/02/89	#8	19	Peace In Our Time	Columbia 73047
9/14/91	#52	9	Heaven In The Back Seat	Columbia 73976
12/07/91	#6	30	I'll Get By	Columbia 74109
5/30/92	#47	11	Fall In Love Again	Columbia 74262
			MONITORS	
4/02/66	#99	1	Greetings (This Is Uncle Sam)	V.I.P. 25032
			T.S. MONK	
3/07/81	#94	3	Bon Bon Vie (Gimme The Good Life)	Mirage 3780
			MONKEES	
9/03/66	#1	16	Last Train To Clarksville	Colgems 1001
12/03/66	#1	17	I'm A Believer/	Colgems 1002
12/10/66	#25	8	(I'm Not Your) Steppin' Stone	Colgems 1002
3/25/67	#1	10	A Little Bit Me, A Little Bit You	Colgems 1004
7/22/67	#3	10	Pleasant Valley Sunday	Colgems 1007
7/22/67	#5	10	Words	Colgems 1007
11/11/67	#1	13	Daydream Believer	Colgems 1012
3/09/68	#1	11	Valleri/	Colgems 1019
3/09/68	#47	5	Tapioca Tundra	Colgems 1019
6/15/68	#10	8	D.W. Washburn/	Colgems 1023
6/15/68	#26	6	It's Nice To Be With You	Colgems 1023
10/12/68	#41	5	Porpoise Song	Colgems 1031
2/15/69	#37	8	Tear Drop City	Colgems 5000
5/10/69	#80	2	Someday Man/	Colgems 5004
5/24/69	#57	8	Listen To The Band	Colgems 5004

Debut Date	Peak Pos	Wks Chr	ARTIST/Song Title	Label & Number
			MONKEES—*continued*	
9/27/69	#90	3	Good Clean Fun	Colgems 5005
5/02/70	#94	2	Oh My My	Colgems 5011
7/05/86	#24	14	That Was Then, This Is Now*	Arista 9505
10/25/86	#78	5	Daydream Believer	Arista 9532
			*released as by MICKEY DOLENZ and PETER TORK of THE MONKEES	
			MONOTONES	
3/22/58	#7	15	Book Of Love	Argo 5290
			MATT MONRO	
5/20/61	#38	15	My Kind Of Girl	Warwick 636
10/07/61	#78	6	Why Not Now	Warwick 669
8/25/62	#84	5	Softly As I Leave You	Liberty 55449
11/21/64	#24	11	Walk Away	Liberty 55745
			VAUGHN MONROE	
3/25/50	#8	2	Bamboo	RCA 3627
6/09/51	#4	7	Sound Off	RCA 4113
9/04/54	#3	9	They Were Doin' The Mambo	RCA 5747
8/25/56	#22	10	In The Middle Of The House	RCA 6619
			MONROES	
5/29/82	#50	9	What Do All The People Know	Alfa 7119
			MONTANAS	
2/17/68	#41	9	You've Got To Be Loved	Independence 83
11/16/68	#96	2	Run To Me	Independence 89
			MONTCLAIRS	
7/17/65	#96	1	Happy Feet Time	Sunburst 106
			LOU MONTE	
3/13/54	#9	5	At The Darktown Strutters' Ball	RCA 5611
2/27/57	#50	2	Roman Guitar	RCA 6769
3/08/58	#12	12	Lazy Mary	RCA 7160
6/14/58	#58	4	Eh Marie, Eh Marie/	RCA 7265
7/12/58	#59	5	Sheik Of Araby	RCA 7265
11/24/62	#7	13	Pepino The Italian Mouse	Reprise 20106
3/09/63	#55	4	Pepino's Friend Pasqual	Reprise 20146
			HUGO MONTENEGRO	
3/09/68	#4	18	The Good, The Bad And The Ugly	RCA 9423
7/06/68	#94	3	Hang 'Em High	RCA 9554
			CHRIS MONTEZ	
8/04/62	#6	16	Let's Dance	Monogram 505
12/01/62	#43	9	Some Kinda Fun	Monogram 507
1/08/66	#22	11	Call Me	A&M 780
4/23/66	#19	11	The More I See You	A&M 796
8/13/66	#37	7	There Will Never Be Another You	A&M 810
11/05/66	#34	6	Time After Time	A&M 822
3/11/67	#55	5	Because Of You	A&M 839
8/10/68	#97	2	Love Is Here To Stay	A&M 958
			JOHN MICHAEL MONTGOMERY	
6/12/93	#74	6	I Love The Way You Love Me	Atlantic 87371
			MELBA MONTGOMERY	
3/30/74	#54	11	No Charge	Elektra 45883
			WES MONTGOMERY	
11/25/67	#78	6	Windy	A&M 883
			MOODY BLUES	
2/13/65	#6	16	Go Now!	London 9726
6/05/65	#70	4	From The Bottom Of My Heart	London 9764
2/12/66	#93	5	Stop	London 9810
3/09/68	#93	2	Nights In White Satin	Deram 85023
6/29/68	#26	13	Tuesday Afternoon (Forever Afternoon)	Deram 85028
10/05/68	#41	7	Ride My See-Saw	Deram 85033
5/10/69	#90	4	Never Comes The Day	Deram 85044
5/02/70	#19	11	Question	Threshold 67004
8/07/71	#14	11	The Story In Your Eyes	Threshold 67006
4/22/72	#20	10	Isn't Life Strange	Threshold 67009
8/05/72	#1	18	Nights In White Satin	Deram 85023
1/20/73	#8	13	I'm Just A Singer (In A Rock And Roll Band)	Threshold 67012

Debut Date	Peak Pos	Wks Chr	ARTIST/Song Title	Label & Number
7/29/78	#46	8	Steppin' In A Slide Zone	London 270
11/04/78	#68	7	Driftwood	London 273
6/06/81	#13	16	Gemini Dream	Threshold 601
8/08/81	#15	15	The Voice	Threshold 602
11/07/81	#60	10	Talking Out Of Turn	Threshold 603
9/03/83	#30	10	Sitting At The Wheel	Threshold 604
11/19/83	#72	6	Blue World	Threshold 605
4/26/86	#10	19	Your Wildest Dreams	Polydor 883906
8/23/86	#76	8	The Other Side Of Life	Polydor 885201
6/11/88	#40	13	I Know You're Out There Somewhere	Polydor 887600
			ART MOONEY	
5/28/55	#5	11	Honey-Babe	MGM 11900
1/04/58	#22	4	The River Kwai March And Colonel Bogey	MGM 12590
1/24/59	#95	2	Bye Bye Blackbird	MGM 12744
6/18/60	#80	3	Banjo Boy	MGM 12908
			MOONGLOWS	
10/06/56	#25	8	See Saw	Chess 1629
9/13/58	#39	10	Ten Commandments Of Love*	Chess 1705
			*released as by HARVEY and THE MOONGLOWS	
			BOB MOORE	
8/19/61	#6	16	Mexico	Monument 446
6/01/63	#75	5	Kentucky	Monument 814
			BOBBY MOORE & THE RHYTHM ACES	
4/09/66	#25	15	Searching For My Baby	Checker 1129
			DOROTHY MOORE	
3/06/76	#3	25	Misty Blue	Malaco 1029
8/14/76	#73	5	Funny How Time Slips Away	Malaco 1033
7/23/77	#28	15	I Believe You	Malaco 1042
			JACKIE MOORE	
11/21/70	#11	17	Precious Precious	Atlantic 2681
5/08/71	#91	2	Sometimes It's Got To Rain	Atlantic 2798
3/18/72	#97	3	Darling Baby	Atlantic 2861
6/30/73	#32	15	Sweet Charlie Babe	Atlantic 2956
8/16/75	#81	6	Make Me Feel Like A Woman	Kayvette 5122
			MELBA MOORE	
6/13/70	#87	2	I Got Love	Mercury 73072
12/16/78	#47	13	You Stepped Into My Life	Epic 50600
			TIM MOORE	
4/21/73	#94	1	Fool Like Me	Dunhill 4337
7/27/74	#59	13	Second Avenue	Asylum 45208
2/01/75	#79	4	Charmer	Asylum 45214
7/09/77	#68	9	In The Middle	Asylum 45394
12/10/77	#93	7	Second Avenue	Asylum 45427
			MICHAEL MORALES	
5/06/89	#14	20	Who Do You Give Your Love To?	Wing 887743
8/19/89	#25	17	What I Like About You	Wing 889678
7/13/91	#74	9	I Don't Want To See You	Wing 867396
			DENROY MORGAN	
9/12/81	#87	3	I'll Do Anything For You	Becket 5
			JANE MORGAN	
10/13/56	#22	4	Two Different Worlds*	Kapp 161
8/10/57	#5	22	Fascination	Kapp 191
9/13/58	#17	19	The Day The Rains Came	Kapp 235
8/08/59	#48	8	With Open Arms	Kapp 284
10/24/59	#34	14	Happy Anniversary	Kapp 305
			*released as by ROGER WILLIAMS/JANE MORGAN	
			JAYE P. MORGAN	
1/22/55	#3	11	That's All I Want From You	RCA 5896
10/01/55	#8	6	The Longest Walk	RCA 6182
11/24/56	#24	5	Mutual Admiration Society*	RCA 6708
2/07/59	#69	6	Miss You/	MGM 12752
2/28/59	#67	4	Are You Lonesome Tonight	MGM 12752
5/09/59	#70	3	It Took One Kiss	MGM 12786
9/03/60	#55	7	I Walk The Line	MGM 12924
			*released as by EDDY ARNOLD and JAYE P. MORGAN	

Debut Date	Peak Pos	Wks Chr	ARTIST/Song Title	Label & Number
			MELI'SA MORGAN	
2/01/86	#52	13	Do Me Baby	Capitol 5523
			RUSS MORGAN	
5/06/50	#3	15	Sentimental Me	Decca 24904
			MORGAN BROTHERS	
1/31/59	#44	3	Nola	MGM 12747
			COZY MORLEY	
4/27/57	#45	3	I Love My Girl	ABC-Paramount 9811
			MORMON TABERNACLE CHOIR	
9/12/59	#11	15	Battle Hymn Of The Republic	Columbia 41459
			GIORGIO MORODER	
2/19/72	#34	10	Son Of My Father*	Dunhill 4304
1/20/79	#38	12	Chase	Casablanca 956
7/28/84	#76	5	Reach Out	Columbia 04511
			***released as by GIORGIO**	
			MARLOWE MORRIS QUINTET	
3/17/62	#81	7	Play The Thing	Columbia 42218
			JOHNNY MORRISETTE	
4/21/62	#90	10	Meet Me At The Twistin' Place	Sar 126
			VAN MORRISON	
7/22/67	#8	15	Brown Eyed Girl	Bang 545
3/28/70	#30	7	Come Running	Warner Brothers 7383
11/07/70	#9	12	Domino	Warner Brothers 7434
2/06/71	#23	12	Blue Money	Warner Brothers 7462
10/16/71	#25	10	Wild Night	Warner Brothers 7518
1/01/72	#43	7	Tupelo Honey	Warner Brothers 7543
8/19/72	#73	5	Jackie Wilson Said	Warner Brothers 7616
1/13/73	#89	3	Gypsy	Warner Brothers 7665
11/05/77	#91	5	Moondance	Warner Brothers 8450
8/23/78	#61	8	Wavelength	Warner Brothers 8661
			ELLA MAE MORSE	
4/05/52	#3	10	Blacksmith Blues	Capitol 1922
			MOTELS	
5/01/82	#8	23	Only The Lonely	Capitol 5114
9/04/82	#48	9	Take The L.	Capitol 5149
11/13/82	#64	9	Forever Mine	Capitol 5182
9/03/83	#10	21	Suddenly Last Summer	Capitol 5271
12/03/83	#37	13	Remember The Nights	Capitol 5246
7/20/85	#25	14	Shame	Capitol 5497
10/26/85	#83	5	Shock	Capitol 5529
			WENDY MOTEN	
2/27/93	#52	16	Come In Out Of The Rain	EMI 50417
			MOTHERLODE	
8/02/69	#12	13	When I Die	Buddah 131
11/15/69	#99	2	Memories Of A Broken Promise	Buddah 144
			MOTHER'S FINEST	
9/24/77	#86	6	Baby Love	Epic 50407
			MOTLEY CRUE	
1/28/84	#49	13	Looks That Kill	Elektra 69756
7/13/85	#22	16	Smokin' In The Boys Room	Elektra 69625
10/26/85	#81	5	Home Sweet Home	Elektra 69591
3/08/86	#80	5	Home Sweet Home	Elektra 69591
5/30/87	#14	17	Girls, Girls, Girls	Elektra 69465
12/05/87	#84	5	You're All I Need	Elektra 69429
9/02/89	#5	20	Dr. Feelgood	Elektra 69271
12/02/89	#27	16	Kickstart My Heart	Elektra 69248
2/24/90	#7	18	Without You	Elektra 64985
5/26/90	#15	17	Don't Go Away Mad (Just Go Away)	Elektra 64962
9/01/90	#50	8	Same 'Ol Situation (S.O.S.)	Elektra 64942
11/02/91	#19	21	Home Sweet Home	Elektra 64818
			MOTORS	
5/17/80	#83	4	Love And Loneliness	Virgin 67007

Debut Date	Peak Pos	Wks Chr	ARTIST/Song Title	Label & Number
			MOTT THE HOOPLE	
9/23/72	#34	10	All The Young Dudes	Columbia 45673
4/27/74	#72	9	The Golden Age Of Rock 'N' Roll	Columbia 46035
			MOUNTAIN	
5/09/70	#24	13	Mississippi Queen	Windfall 532
9/12/70	#73	5	For Yasgur's Farm	Windfall 533
4/03/71	#71	5	The Animal Trainer And The Toad	Windfall 534
			MOUTH & MACNEAL	
4/29/72	#5	19	How Do You Do?	Philips 40715
10/07/72	#68	4	Hey, You Love	Philips 40717
			MOVE	
11/04/72	#97	1	Do Ya	United Artists 50928
			MOVEMENT	
8/15/92	#45	10	Jump!	Sunshine 2456
			MOVING PICTURES	
9/18/82	#21	27	What About Me	Network 69952
9/09/89	#67	8	What About Me	Geffen 22859
			ALISON MOYET	
3/16/85	#30	17	Invisible	Columbia 04781
7/27/85	#81	4	Love Resurrection	Columbia 05411
			MICKEY MOZART QUINTET	
5/09/59	#25	13	Little Dipper	Roulette 4148
			MS. ADVENTURES	
9/22/90	#67	6	Undeniable	Atco 98938
			MTUME	
6/11/83	#35	14	Juicy Fruit	Epic 03578
			MARIA MULDAUR	
3/09/74	#4	18	Midnight At The Oasis	Reprise 1183
12/21/74	#24	13	I'm A Woman	Reprise 1319
			MUNGO JERRY	
7/11/70	#2	13	In The Summertime	Janus 125
			JERRY MURAD'S HARMONICATS	
11/21/53	#9	1	The Story Of Three Loves*	Mercury 70202
12/17/60	#30	11	Cherry Pink And Apple Blossom White	Columbia 41816
			*released as by THE HARMONICATS	
			SHIRLEY MURDOCK	
1/24/87	#30	16	As We Lay	Elektra 69518
			MURMAIDS	
11/23/63	#3	15	Popsicles And Icicles	Chattahoochee 628
			MICHAEL MURPHEY	
8/12/72	#49	10	Geronimo's Cadillac	A&M 1368
3/22/75	#2	20	Wildfire	Epic 50084
8/16/75	#23	12	Carolina In The Pines	Epic 50131
1/17/76	#42	8	Renegade	Epic 50184
7/24/82	#23	17	What's Forever For	Liberty 1466
			EDDIE MURPHY	
10/05/85	#2	26	Party All The Time	Columbia 05609
7/29/89	#32	14	Put Your Mouth On Me	Columbia 68897
			PETER MURPHY	
3/31/90	#57	10	Cuts You Up	Beggars Banquet 9140
			WALTER MURPHY	
5/22/76	#1	30	A Fifth Of Beethoven*	Private Stock 45073
11/06/76	#36	14	Flight '76	Private Stock 45123
7/31/82	#32	11	Themes From E.T.	MCA 52099
			*released as by WALTER MURPHY & THE BIG APPLE BAND	
			ANNE MURRAY	
7/18/70	#6	17	Snowbird	Capitol 2738
12/12/70	#83	5	Sing High - Sing Low	Capitol 2988
9/18/71	#79	5	Talk It Over In The Morning	Capitol 3159
10/30/71	#72	3	I Say A Little Prayer/By The Time I Get To Phoenix*	Capitol 3200
12/23/72	#6	20	Danny's Song	Capitol 3481
5/26/73	#37	8	What About Me	Capitol 3600
8/04/73	#96	2	Send A Little Love My Way	Capitol 3648

Debut Date	Peak Pos	Wks Chr	ARTIST/Song Title	Label & Number
			ANNE MURRAY—*continued*	
12/15/73	#10	15	Love Song	Capitol 3776
4/20/74	#8	17	You Won't See Me	Capitol 3867
10/05/74	#93	2	Just One Look	Capitol 3955
12/21/74	#44	7	Day Tripper	Capitol 4000
11/22/75	#94	3	Sunday Sunrise	Capitol 4142
2/28/76	#91	3	The Call	Capitol 4207
3/25/78	#92	2	Walk Right Back	Capitol 4527
7/08/78	#4	25	You Needed Me	Capitol 4574
1/20/79	#11	18	I Just Fall In Love Again	Capitol 4675
5/19/79	#27	13	Shadows In The Moonlight	Capitol 4716
9/22/79	#22	14	Broken Hearted Me	Capitol 4773
12/22/79	#17	16	Daydream Believer	Capitol 4813
3/29/80	#45	11	Lucky Me	Capitol 4848
9/06/80	#53	15	Could I Have This Dance	Capitol 4920
3/28/81	#40	13	Blessed Are The Believers	Capitol 4987
10/03/81	#62	8	It's All I Can Do	Capitol 5023
2/13/82	#45	9	Another Sleepless Night	Capitol 5083
9/24/83	#80	4	A Little Good News	Capitol 5264
			*released as by GLEN CAMPBELL/ANNE MURRAY	
			MICKEY MURRAY	
10/14/67	#49	5	Shout Bamalama	SSS International 715
			MUSIC EXPLOSION	
5/06/67	#2	16	Little Bit O' Soul	Laurie 3380
9/09/67	#69	4	Sunshine Games	Laurie 3400
			MUSIC MACHINE	
11/19/66	#21	11	Talk Talk	Original Sound 61
2/11/67	#79	3	The People In Me	Original Sound 67
5/20/67	#100	1	Double Yellow Line	Original Sound 71
			MUSIC MAKERS	
12/23/67	#87	6	United (Part 1)	Gamble 210
			MUSICAL YOUTH	
12/18/82	#14	19	Pass The Dutchie	MCA 52149
12/31/83	#56	10	She's Trouble	MCA 52312
			MUSIQUE	
10/14/78	#58	10	In The Bush	Prelude 71110
			MUSTANGS	
10/17/64	#98	1	The Dartell Stomp	Providence 401
			ALANNAH MYLES	
12/30/89	#1	25	Black Velvet	Atlantic 88742
5/05/90	#32	15	Love Is	Atlantic 87945
			BILLY MYLES	
11/16/57	#20	10	The Joker (That's What They Call Me)	Ember 1026
			MYSTIC MOODS	
4/28/73	#78	4	Cosmic Sea	Warner Brothers 7686
7/19/75	#84	3	Honey Trippin'	Sound Bird 5002
			MYSTICS	
5/30/59	#22	15	Hushabye	Laurie 3028
10/10/59	#75	7	Don't Take The Stars	Laurie 3038

N

Debut Date	Peak Pos	Wks Chr	ARTIST/Song Title	Label & Number
			NAKED EYES	
3/12/83	#7	23	Always Something There To Remind Me	EMI America 8155
7/16/83	#12	20	Promises, Promises	EMI America 8170
10/29/83	#37	15	When The Lights Go Out	EMI America 8183
8/11/84	#39	11	(What) In The Name Of Love	EMI America 8219
			PHIL NAPOLEAN	
12/10/60	#42	1	Artificial Flowers	Capitol 4485
			NAPOLEON XIV	
7/23/66	#1	7	They're Coming To Take Me Away, Ha-Haaa!	Warner Brothers 5831
			GRAHAM NASH	
5/29/71	#29	13	Chicago	Atlantic 2804
9/04/71	#66	4	Military Madness	Atlantic 2827
5/06/72	#31	8	Immigration Man*	Atlantic 2873

Debut Date	Peak Pos	Wks Chr	ARTIST/Song Title	Label & Number
6/24/72	#52	5	War Song**	Reprise 1099
11/08/75	#44	8	Carry Me*	ABC 12140
7/24/76	#77	5	Out Of The Darkness*	ABC 12199
5/10/86	#85	4	Innocent Eyes	Atlantic 89434
			*released as by GRAHAM NASH & DAVID CROSBY	
			**released as by NEIL YOUNG and GRAHAM NASH	
			JOHNNY NASH	
12/14/57	#30	11	A Very Special Love	ABC-Paramount 9874
9/13/58	#98	1	You're Looking At Me	ABC-Paramount 9942
10/18/58	#49	7	Almost In Your Arms	ABC-Paramount 9960
11/22/58	#46	9	Teen Commandments*	ABC-Paramount 9974
1/10/59	#48	10	Walk With Faith In Your Heart	ABC-Paramount 9989
3/14/59	#48	10	As Time Goes By	ABC-Paramount 9996
3/11/61	#83	2	Some Of Your Lovin'	ABC-Paramount 10181
9/22/62	#91	3	Ol' Man River	Warner Brothers 5301
10/02/65	#92	4	Let's Move & Groove (Together)	JoDa 102
9/21/68	#7	13	Hold Me Tight	JAD 207
12/21/68	#55	5	You Got Soul	JAD 209
11/08/69	#36	12	Cupid	JAD 220
8/26/72	#1	21	I Can See Clearly Now	Epic 10902
2/03/73	#11	15	Stir It Up	Epic 10949
6/16/73	#74	7	My Merry-Go-Round	Epic 11003
3/09/74	#67	8	Loving You	Epic 11070
9/21/74	#90	3	You Can't Go Halfway	Epic 50021
4/24/76	#82	5	Wonderful World	Epic 50219
			*released as by PAUL ANKA/GEORGE HAMILTON IV/JOHNNY NASH	
			NASHVILLE TEENS	
9/05/64	#14	13	Tobacco Road	London 9689
			NATIONAL LAMPOON	
10/21/72	#88	3	Deteriorata	Banana 218
			NATURAL FOUR	
12/22/73	#25	12	Can This Be Real	Curtom 1990
			NATURAL SELECTION	
8/10/91	#2	28	Do Anything	East West 98724
11/30/91	#15	25	Hearts Don't Think (They Feel)	East West 98652
			NATURE'S DIVINE	
11/10/79	#70	6	I Just Can't Control Myself	Infinity 50027
			DAVID NAUGHTON	
3/17/79	#5	28	Makin' It	RSO 916
			NAUGHTY BY NATURE	
10/26/91	#52	16	O.P.P.	Tommy Boy 988
2/06/93	#7	23	Hip Hop Hooray	Tommy Boy 554
7/03/93	#58	13	It's On	Tommy Boy 569
10/23/93	#88	5	Written On Ya Kitten	Tommy Boy 583
			JERRY NAYLOR	
3/21/70	#42	6	But For Love	Columbia 45106
			NAZARETH	
11/22/75	#9	24	Love Hurts	A&M 1671
3/08/80	#74	9	Holiday	A&M 2219
			NAZZ	
1/18/69	#47	10	Hello It's Me	SGC 001
4/12/69	#98	2	Not Wrong Long	SGC 006
1/24/70	#69	4	Hello It's Me	SGC 001
			SAM NEELY	
8/12/72	#31	15	Loving You Just Crossed My Mind	Capitol 3381
1/27/73	#58	7	Rosalie	Capitol 3510
8/31/74	#35	13	You Can Have Her	A&M 1612
1/25/75	#41	7	I Fought The Law	A&M 1651
			NEIGHBORHOOD	
7/04/70	#24	9	Big Yellow Taxi	Big Tree 102
			VINCE NEIL	
6/12/93	#63	5	Sister Of Pain	Warner Brothers 45260
			NELSON	
7/21/90	#1	21	(Can't Live Without Your) Love And Affection	DGC 19689
11/03/90	#8	24	After The Rain	DGC 19667

Debut Date	Peak Pos	Wks Chr	ARTIST/Song Title	Label & Number
			NELSON—*continued*	
3/09/91	#11	21	More Than Ever	DGC 19002
6/22/91	#31	16	Only Time Will Tell	DGC 19014
			KAREN NELSON and BILLY T	
8/13/77	#96	4	Love Me One More Time	Amherst 724
			PHYLLIS NELSON	
2/15/86	#63	10	I Like You	Carrere 05719
			RICKY NELSON	
5/18/57	#12	7	I'm Walking/	Verve 10047
5/25/57	#8	12	A Teenager's Romance	Verve 10047
8/24/57	#23	9	You're My One And Only Love	Verve 10070
10/05/57	#6	16	Be-Bop Baby/	Imperial 5463
10/05/57	#21	8	Have I Told You Lately That I Love You?	Imperial 5463
12/28/57	#3	12	Stood Up/	Imperial 5483
12/28/57	#6	9	Waitin' In School	Imperial 5483
3/29/58	#12	10	Believe What You Say/	Imperial 5503
3/29/58	#20	7	My Bucket's Got A Hole In It	Imperial 5503
6/21/58	#64	2	Poor Little Fool (EP)	Imperial 158
7/05/58	#2	15	Poor Little Fool	Imperial 5528
10/11/58	#15	18	I Got A Feeling/	Imperial 5545
10/18/58	#7	18	Lonesome Town	Imperial 5545
2/28/59	#5	13	Never Be Anyone Else But You/	Imperial 5565
3/07/59	#6	13	It's Late	Imperial 5565
7/04/59	#18	11	Just A Little Too Much/	Imperial 5595
7/04/59	#11	11	Sweeter Than You	Imperial 5595
11/21/59	#21	11	I Wanna Be Loved/	Imperial 5614
11/28/59	#57	10	Mighty Good	Imperial 5614
4/23/60	#11	15	Young Emotions/	Imperial 5663
4/23/60	#70	6	Right By My Side	Imperial 5663
9/03/60	#40	10	I'm Not Afraid/	Imperial 5685
9/03/60	#49	9	Yes Sir, That's My Baby	Imperial 5685
12/24/60	#29	9	You Are The Only One	Imperial 5707
4/22/61	#1	18	Travelin' Man/	Imperial 5741
4/22/61	#9	16	Hello Mary Lou	Imperial 5741
10/07/61	#11	13	A Wonder Like You*/	Imperial 5770
10/07/61	#20	10	Everlovin'*	Imperial 5770
3/03/62	#9	14	Young World*	Imperial 5805
8/11/62	#9	12	Teen Age Idol*	Imperial 5864
12/15/62	#7	13	It's Up To You*/	Imperial 5901
12/22/62	#91	3	I Need You*	Imperial 5901
2/23/63	#51	6	I'm In Love Again*/	Imperial 5910
2/23/63	#53	5	That's All*	Imperial 5910
3/09/63	#58	6	I Got A Woman*/	Decca 31475
3/16/63	#48	6	You Don't Love Me Anymore*	Decca 31475
4/27/63	#86	4	Old Enough To Love*	Imperial 5935
5/18/63	#17	11	String Along*/	Decca 31495
6/29/63	#91	3	Gypsy Woman*	Decca 31495
9/14/63	#12	15	Fools Rush In*	Decca 31533
11/30/63	#65	7	Today's Teardrops*	Imperial 66004
12/28/63	#8	12	For You*	Decca 31574
4/25/64	#19	7	The Very Thought Of You*	Decca 31612
8/22/64	#49	7	There's Nothing I Can Say*	Decca 31656
11/28/64	#83	6	A Happy Guy*	Decca 31703
3/20/65	#94	1	Mean Old World*	Decca 31756
6/25/66	#76	4	You Just Can't Quit*	Decca 31956
10/18/69	#30	16	She Belongs To Me**	Decca 32550
3/07/70	#50	5	Easy To Be Free*	Decca 32635
8/12/72	#3	18	Garden Party**	Decca 32980
2/10/73	#79	4	Palace Guard**	MCA 40001
			*released as by **RICK NELSON**	
			released as by **RICK NELSON & THE STONE CANYON BAND	
			SANDY NELSON	
9/05/59	#4	15	Teen Beat	Original Sound 5
11/04/61	#9	15	Let There Be Drums	Imperial 5775
2/17/62	#57	5	Drums Are My Beat	Imperial 5809
6/02/62	#100	2	Drum Stomp	Imperial 5829
10/13/62	#95	1	And Then There Were Drums	Imperial 5870
9/26/64	#37	9	Teen Beat '65	Imperial 66060

Debut Date	Peak Pos	Wks Chr	ARTIST/Song Title	Label & Number
			WILLIE NELSON	
8/23/75	#25	18	Blue Eyes Crying In The Rain	Columbia 10176
1/17/76	#72	6	Remember Me	Columbia 10275
2/14/76	#37	9	Good Hearted Woman*	RCA 10529
2/11/78	#44	8	Mammas Don't Let Your Babies Grow Up To	
			Be Cowboys*	RCA 11198
6/17/78	#93	4	Georgia On My Mind	Columbia 10704
2/16/80	#67	8	My Heroes Have Always Been Cowboys	Columbia 11186
9/06/80	#22	20	On The Road Again	Columbia 11351
3/13/82	#4	22	Always On My Mind	Columbia 02741
4/03/82	#57	9	Just To Satisfy You*	RCA 13073
8/07/82	#47	12	Let It Be Me	Columbia 03073
3/03/84	#3	22	To All The Girls I've Loved Before**	Columbia 04217
			*released as by WAYLON & WILLIE (Waylon Jennings & Willie Nelson)	
			**released as by JULIO IGLESIAS & WILLIE NELSON	
			NELSON TRIO	
1/16/60	#94	2	All In Good Time	Guyden 203
			NENA	
12/10/83	#1	26	99 Luftballons	Epic 04108
			NEON PHILHARMONIC	
4/12/69	#15	12	Morning Girl	Warner Brothers 7261
			PETER NERO	
10/23/71	#21	13	Theme From "Summer Of '42"	Columbia 45399
			NERVOUS NORVUS	
6/02/56	#35	2	Transfusion	Dot 15470
8/04/56	#37	5	Ape Call	Dot 15485
			MICHAEL NESMITH & THE FIRST NATIONAL BAND	
8/15/70	#17	10	Joanne	RCA 0368
11/21/70	#28	9	Silver Moon	RCA 0399
4/17/71	#73	4	Nevada Fighter	RCA 0453
11/06/71	#95	2	I've Just Begun To Care	RCA 0540
			LOZ NETTO	
6/25/83	#88	4	Fade Away	21 Records 104
			ROBBIE NEVIL	
10/18/86	#3	23	C'est La Vie	Manhattan 50047
2/21/87	#13	15	Dominoes	Manhattan 50053
5/30/87	#15	16	Wot's It To Ya?	Manhattan 50075
11/12/88	#30	16	Back On Holiday	EMI 50152
3/18/89	#54	10	Somebody Like You	EMI 50176
6/29/91	#25	17	Just Like You	EMI 50356
10/12/91	#63	11	For Your Mind	EMI 50367
			AARON NEVILLE	
11/26/66	#3	15	Tell It Like It Is	Parlo 101
4/08/67	#94	1	She Took You For A Ride	Parlo 103
9/30/89	#2	25	Don't Know Much*	Elektra 69261
1/27/90	#11	19	All My Life*	Elektra 64987
5/19/90	#80	5	When Something Is Wrong With My Baby*	Elektra 64968
7/13/91	#11	28	Everybody Plays The Fool	A&M 1563
12/07/91	#66	11	Somewhere, Somebody	A&M 1557
6/12/93	#52	19	Don't Take Away My Heaven	A&M 0240
			*released as by LINDA RONSTADT featuring AARON NEVILLE	
			IVAN NEVILLE	
10/01/88	#27	20	Not Just Another Girl	Polydor 887814
3/04/89	#83	4	Falling Out Of Love	Polydor 871484
			NEWBEATS	
8/08/64	#2	14	Bread And Butter	Hickory 1269
10/24/64	#16	10	Everything's Alright	Hickory 1288
1/23/65	#34	9	Break Away (From That Boy)	Hickory 1290
4/10/65	#71	5	The Birds Are For The Bees	Hickory 1305
10/09/65	#14	12	Run, Baby Run (Back Into My Arms)	Hickory 1332
2/26/66	#62	4	Shake Hands	Hickory 1366
12/13/69	#85	6	Groovin' (Out On Life)	Hickory 1552

Debut Date	Peak Pos	Wks Chr	ARTIST/Song Title	Label & Number
			NEW BIRTH	
10/16/71	#46	8	It's Impossible	RCA 0520
3/17/73	#28	11	I Can Understand It	RCA 0912
2/23/74	#59	7	It's Been A Long Time	RCA 0185
4/27/74	#49	10	Wildflower	RCA 0265
5/10/75	#87	2	Granddaddy (Part 1)	Buddah 464
7/05/75	#31	11	Dream Merchant	Buddah 470
			MICKEY NEWBURY	
11/06/71	#46	11	An American Trilogy	Elektra 45750
7/14/73	#82	5	Sunshine	Elektra 45853
			NEW CHRISTY MINSTRELS	
6/29/63	#14	13	Green, Green	Columbia 42805
10/26/63	#38	7	Saturday Night	Columbia 42887
4/25/64	#20	12	Today	Columbia 43000
5/01/65	#95	1	Chim, Chim, Cheree	Columbia 43215
			NEWCITY ROCKERS	
4/18/87	#66	7	Black Dog	Critique 99451
			NEWCLEUS	
7/07/84	#78	6	Jam On It	Sunnyview 3010
			NEW COLONY SIX	
2/05/66	#71	6	I Confess	Centaur 1201
1/28/67	#55	9	Love You So Much	Sentar 1205
4/15/67	#98	3	You're Gonna Be Mine	Sentar 1206
3/16/68	#22	15	I Will Always Think About You	Mercury 72775
6/22/68	#69	7	Can't You See Me Cry	Mercury 72817
12/28/68	#13	16	Things I'd Like To Say	Mercury 72858
5/03/69	#40	7	I Could Never Lie To You	Mercury 72920
9/13/69	#71	4	I Want You To Know	Mercury 72961
1/17/70	#93	3	Barbara I Love You	Mercury 73004
9/04/71	#63	6	Roll On	Sunlight 1001
			NEWCOMERS	
10/09/71	#100	1	Pin The Tail On The Donkey	Stax 0099
			NEW EDITION	
4/30/83	#47	16	Candy Girl	Streetwise 2208
9/29/84	#2	25	Cool It Now	MCA 52455
12/22/84	#9	18	Mr. Telephone Man	MCA 52484
3/30/85	#41	14	Lost In Love	MCA 52553
11/09/85	#52	14	Count Me Out	MCA 52703
2/22/86	#52	13	A Little Bit Of Love Is All It Takes	MCA 52768
6/14/86	#78	9	With You All The Way	MCA 52829
8/16/86	#37	14	Earth Angel	MCA 52905
7/02/88	#5	20	If It Isn't Love	MCA 53264
2/18/89	#60	8	Can You Stand The Rain	MCA 53464
			NEW ENGLAND	
5/05/79	#40	11	Don't Ever Wanna Lose Ya	Infinity 50013
9/08/79	#75	5	Hello, Hello, Hello	Infinity 50021
			NEW HOPE	
1/03/70	#75	6	Won't Find Better (Than Me)	Jamie 1381
			NEW KIDS ON THE BLOCK	
6/25/88	#12	21	Please Don't Go Girl	Columbia 07700
11/19/88	#4	26	You Got It (The Right Stuff)	Columbia 08092
4/01/89	#5	22	I'll Be Loving You Forever	Columbia 68671
7/22/89	#2	20	Hangin' Tough	Columbia 68960
9/16/89	#4	20	Cover Girl	Columbia 69088
9/23/89	#13	19	Didn't I (Blow Your Mind)	Columbia 68960
11/18/89	#7	15	This One's For The Children	Columbia 73064
5/26/90	#1	18	Step By Step	Columbia 73343
7/21/90	#8	19	Tonight	Columbia 73461
10/06/90	#57	9	Let's Try It Again	Columbia 73443
2/22/92	#24	19	If You Go Away*	Columbia 74225
			*released as by NKOTB	
			ANTHONY NEWLEY	
6/18/60	#53	8	Do You Mind?	London 1918
9/03/60	#71	9	If She Should Come To You	London 1929
11/18/61	#55	9	Pop Goes The Weasel	London 9501

Debut Date	Peak Pos	Wks Chr	ARTIST/Song Title	Label & Number
8/25/62	#73	3	What Kind Of Fool Am I	London 9546
1/25/64	#91	2	Tribute	Acappella 778
			JIMMY NEWMAN	
6/22/57	#24	11	A Fallen Star	Dot 15574
			RANDY NEWMAN	
11/12/77	#1	21	Short People	Warner Brothers 8492
1/15/83	#54	10	The Blues*	Warner Brothers 29803
11/05/88	#52	11	It's Money That Matters	Reprise 27709
			*released as by RANDY NEWMAN and PAUL SIMON	
			TED NEWMAN	
9/14/57	#28	11	Plaything	Rev 3505
			NEW ORDER	
11/07/87	#30	18	True Faith	Qwest 28271
5/14/88	#75	7	Blue Monday 1988	Qwest 27979
4/08/89	#54	12	Round & Round	Qwest 27524
5/15/93	#19	23	Regret	Qwest 18586
			NEW RIDERS OF THE PURPLE SAGE	
10/30/71	#100	1	Louisiana Lady	Columbia 45469
			NEW SEEKERS	
8/29/70	#10	12	Look What They've Done To My Song Ma	Elektra 45699
1/16/71	#53	5	Beautiful People	Elektra 45710
3/27/71	#96	4	Nickel Song	Elektra 45719
11/27/71	#11	12	I'd Like To Teach The World To Sing	Elektra 45762
4/22/72	#86	3	Beg, Steal Or Borrow	Elektra 45780
8/05/72	#93	3	Circles	Elektra 45787
1/20/73	#92	3	Come Softly To Me	Verve 10698
2/17/73	#21	13	Pinball Wizard/See Me, Feel Me	Verve 10709
1/19/74	#99	1	Reach Out I'll Be There/	MGM 14683
1/26/74	#75	5	You Won't Find Another Fool Like Me	MGM 14683
			JUICE NEWTON	
4/08/78	#93	2	It's A Heartache	Capitol 4552
2/21/81	#2	24	Angel Of The Morning	Capitol 4976
5/30/81	#2	28	Queen Of Hearts	Capitol 4997
10/17/81	#7	24	The Sweetest Thing (I've Ever Known)	Capitol 5046
5/08/82	#5	18	Love's Been A Little Bit Hard On Me	Capitol 5120
8/21/82	#9	16	Break It To Me Gently	Capitol 5148
11/27/82	#22	16	Heart Of The Night	Capitol 5192
8/13/83	#29	11	Tell Her No	Capitol 5265
6/02/84	#49	12	A Little Love	RCA 13823
8/11/84	#80	7	Can't Wait All Night	RCA 13863
			WAYNE NEWTON	
4/06/63	#52	8	Heart! (I Hear You Beating)	Capitol 4920
7/20/63	#12	12	Danke Shoen	Capitol 4989
11/02/63	#74	6	Shirl Girl	Capitol 5058
3/06/65	#11	5	Red Roses For A Blue Lady	Capitol 5366
5/22/65	#76	4	I'll Be With You In Apple Blossom Time	Capitol 5419
8/07/65	#86	3	Summer Wind	Capitol 5470
10/23/65	#87	3	Remember When	Capitol 5514
12/25/65	#96	2	Some Sunday Morning	Capitol 5553
10/29/66	#97	1	Games That Lovers Play	Capitol 5754
6/29/68	#58	6	Dreams Of The Everyday Housewife	MGM 13955
12/14/68	#97	1	Husbands And Wives	MGM 14014
4/15/72	#1	22	Daddy Don't You Walk So Fast	Chelsea 0100
9/30/72	#38	7	Can't You Hear The Song?	Chelsea 0105
12/16/72	#45	7	Anthem	Chelsea 0109
11/16/74	#83	3	Lady Lay	Chelsea 3003
6/12/76	#81	4	The Hungry Years	Chelsea 3041
9/08/79	#91	6	You Stepped Into My Life	Aries II 101
1/26/80	#32	14	Years	Aries II 108
7/25/92	#1	31	The Letter	Curb 1008
			OLIVIA NEWTON-JOHN	
6/12/71	#23	15	If Not For You	Uni 55281
10/23/71	#94	1	Banks Of The Ohio	Uni 55304
10/27/73	#4	20	Let Me Be There	MCA 40101
4/06/74	#6	18	If You Love Me (Let Me Know)	MCA 40209
8/17/74	#1	6	I Honestly Love You	MCA 40280
1/25/75	#1	15	Have You Never Been Mellow	MCA 40349

OLIVIA NEWTON-JOHN

247

Debut Date	Peak Pos	Wks Chr	**ARTIST**/Song Title	Label & Number
			OLIVIA NEWTON-JOHN—*continued*	
5/31/75	#1	14	Please Mr. Please	MCA 40418
9/20/75	#15	10	Something Better To Do	MCA 40459
11/29/75	#80	1	He Ain't Heavy...He's My Brother/	MCA 40495
12/06/75	#28	9	Let It Shine	MCA 40495
3/13/76	#30	12	Come On Over	MCA 40525
8/07/76	#47	14	Don't Stop Believin'	MCA 40600
11/13/76	#71	5	Every Face Tells A Story	MCA 40642
1/29/77	#34	14	Sam	MCA 40670
11/12/77	#60	6	I Honestly Love You	MCA 40811
4/01/78	#3	25	You're The One That I Want*	RSO 891
7/08/78	#3	19	Hopelessly Devoted To You	RSO 903
8/05/78	#3	15	Summer Nights*	RSO 906
11/25/78	#4	21	A Little More Love	MCA 40975
4/14/79	#19	12	Deeper Than The Night	MCA 41009
7/28/79	#72	5	Totally Hot	MCA 41074
3/39/80	#13	14	I Can't Help It**	RSO 1026
5/24/80	#1	25	Magic	MCA 41247
8/09/80	#9	20	Xanadu***	MCA 41285
10/18/80	#19	19	Suddenly****	MCA 51007
10/03/81	#1	26	Physical	MCA 51182
2/13/82	#5	16	Make A Move On Me	MCA 52000
6/12/82	#54	9	Landslide	MCA 52069
9/04/82	#2	20	Heart Attack	MCA 52100
1/15/83	#42	9	Tied Up	MCA 52155
11/05/83	#5	21	Twist Of Fate	MCA 52284
2/11/84	#29	12	Livin' In Desperate Times	MCA 52341
10/05/85	#20	17	Soul Kiss	MCA 52686
6/07/86	#81	7	The Best Of Me*****	Atlantic 89420
8/20/88	#79	7	The Rumour	MCA 53294
6/27/92	#68	7	I Need Love	Geffen 19128
			*released as by **JOHN TRAVOLTA** and **OLIVIA NEWTON-JOHN**	
			released as by **ANDY GIBB and **OLIVIA NEWTON-JOHN**	
			***released as by **OLIVIA NEWTON-JOHN/ELECTRIC LIGHT ORCHESTRA**	
			****released as by **OLIVIA NEWTON-JOHN** and **CLIFF RICHARD**	
			*****released as by **DAVID FOSTER** and **OLIVIA NEWTON-JOHN**	
			NEW VAUDEVILLE BAND	
10/29/66	#1	16	Winchester Cathedral	Fontana 1562
2/25/67	#94	2	Peek-A-Boo	Fontana 1573
			NEW YORK CITY	
2/24/73	#12	20	I'm Doin' Fine Now	Chelsea 0113
8/18/73	#78	6	Make Me Twice The Man	Chelsea 0025
1/26/74	#78	7	Quick, Fast, In A Hurry	Chelsea 0150
			NEW YORKERS	
5/27/61	#86	2	Miss Fine	Wall 547
			PAUL NICHOLAS	
8/13/77	#5	26	Heaven On The 7th Floor	RSO 878
7/22/78	#73	5	On The Strip	RSO 887
			STEVIE NICKS	
7/25/81	#4	18	Stop Draggin' My Heart Around*	Modern 7336
10/24/81	#9	21	Leather And Lace**	Modern 7341
2/20/82	#19	13	Edge Of Seventeen	Modern 7401
5/15/82	#31	12	After The Glitter Fades	Modern 7405
6/04/83	#9	21	Stand Back	Modern 99863
9/10/83	#15	15	If Anyone Falls	Modern 99832
12/17/83	#35	13	Nightbird***	Modern 99799
11/16/85	#4	21	Talk To Me	Modern 99582
2/01/86	#43	12	Needles And Pins****	MCA 52772
2/22/86	#13	13	I Can't Wait	Modern 99565
5/17/86	#63	7	Has Anyone Ever Written Anything For You	Modern 99532
5/06/89	#16	19	Rooms On Fire	Modern 99216
9/07/91	#43	12	Sometimes (It's A Bitch)	Modern 98758
			*released as by **STEVIE NICKS** with **TOM PETTY** and **THE HEARTBREAKERS**	
			released as by **STEVIE NICKS with **DON HENLEY**	
			***released as by **STEVIE NICKS** with **SANDY STEWART**	
			****released as by **TOM PETTY** and **THE HEARTBREAKERS** with **STEVIE NICKS**	

Debut Date	Peak Pos	Wks Chr	ARTIST/Song Title	Label & Number
			NIELSEN/PEARSON	
9/27/80	#52	13	If You Should Sail	Capitol 4910
8/08/81	#54	8	The Sun Ain't Gonna Shine Anymore	Capitol 5032
			NIGHT	
6/23/79	#26	16	Hot Summer Nights	Planet 45903
8/18/79	#19	22	If You Remember Me*	Planet 45909
			*released as by CHRIS THOMPSON & NIGHT	
			NIGHTCRAWLERS	
12/24/66	#78	5	Little Black Egg	Kapp 709
			NIGHTCRAWLERS	
10/30/93	#73	4	Push The Feeling On	Great Jones 530620
			MAXINE NIGHTINGALE	
2/14/76	#1	20	Right Back Where We Started From	United Artists 752
7/10/76	#84	5	Gotta Be The One	United Artists 820
5/05/79	#5	29	Lead Me On	Windsong 11530
11/17/79	#91	3	(Bringing Out) The Girl In Me	Windsong 11729
			NIGHT RANGER	
1/22/83	#46	10	Don't Tell Me You Love Me	Boardwalk 171
4/16/83	#62	10	Sing Me Away	Boardwalk 175
12/03/83	#51	12	(You Can Still) Rock In America	MCA 52305
3/17/84	#6	23	Sister Christian	MCA 52350
7/14/84	#18	18	When You Close Your Eyes	MCA 52420
5/25/85	#10	16	Sentimental Street	MCA 52591
8/24/85	#24	14	Four In The Morning	MCA 52661
11/09/85	#27	18	Goodbye	MCA 52729
3/21/87	#60	9	The Secret Of My Success	MCA 53013
10/08/88	#76	5	I Did It For Love	MCA 53364
			NIKKI	
5/05/90	#18	17	Notice Me	Geffen 19946
			NILSSON	
9/02/67	#91	2	You Can't Do That	RCA 9298
8/10/68	#54	6	Everybody's Talkin'	RCA 9544
8/02/69	#7	15	Everybody's Talkin'	RCA 0161
11/01/69	#35	7	I Guess The Lord Must Be In New York City	RCA 0261
3/27/71	#27	14	Me And My Arrow	RCA 0443
12/11/71	#1	19	Without You	RCA 0604
3/18/72	#22	9	Jump Into The Fire	RCA 0673
6/03/72	#12	16	Coconut	RCA 0718
9/16/72	#23	10	Spaceman	RCA 0788
12/09/72	#40	9	Remember (Christmas)	RCA 0855
8/25/73	#64	7	As Time Goes By	RCA 0039
4/06/74	#23	11	Daybreak	RCA 0246
7/27/74	#78	4	Many Rivers To Cross	RCA 10001
			9.9	
8/31/85	#48	12	All Of Me For All Of You	RCA 14082
			1910 FRUITGUM COMPANY	
1/27/68	#2	16	Simon Says	Buddah 24
4/20/68	#45	8	May I Take A Giant Step	Buddah 39
7/13/68	#3	15	1,2,3 Red Light	Buddah 54
10/26/68	#31	9	Goody Goody Gumdrops	Buddah 71
1/25/69	#4	14	Indian Giver	Buddah 91
5/10/69	#31	9	Special Delivery	Buddah 114
8/09/69	#52	9	The Train	Buddah 130
12/20/69	#93	3	When We Get Married	Buddah 146
			95 SOUTH	
6/19/93	#13	20	Whoot, There It Is	Wrap 0150
			NINO & THE EBB TIDES	
8/26/61	#62	8	Juke Box Saturday Night	Madison 166

Debut Date	Peak Pos	Wks Chr	ARTIST/Song Title	Label & Number
			NIRVANA	
11/30/91	#5	29	Smells Like Teen Spirit	DGC 19050
3/07/92	#19	23	Come As You Are	DGC 19120
8/15/92	#48	8	Lithium	DGC 19134
			NITEFLYTE	
10/13/79	#59	10	If You Want It	Ariola 7747
			NITE-LITERS	
7/31/71	#39	13	K-Jee	RCA 0461
2/26/72	#39	8	Afro Strut	RCA 0591
			NITTY GRITTY DIRT BAND (also DIRT BAND)	
4/01/67	#45	9	Buy For Me The Rain	Liberty 55948
10/31/70	#9	23	Mr. Bojangles	Liberty 56197
5/01/71	#38	10	House At Pooh Corner	United Artists 50769
9/18/71	#64	6	Some Of Shelly's Blues	United Artists 50817
4/08/72	#91	3	Jambalaya	United Artists 50890
10/19/74	#77	3	Battle Of New Orleans	United Artists 544
8/02/75	#57	9	All I Have To Do Is Dream	United Artists 655
8/26/78	#76	6	In For The Night*	United Artists 1228
12/01/79	#11	22	An American Dream*	United Artists 1330
6/14/80	#28	15	Make A Little Magic*	United Artists 1356
9/26/81	#65	7	Fire In The Sky*	Liberty 1429
			*released as by THE DIRT BAND	
			JACK NITZSCHE	
8/03/63	#37	9	The Lonely Surfer	Reprise 20202
			DON NIX	
10/30/71	#96	2	Olena	Elektra 45746
			NICK NOBLE	
10/15/55	#10	2	The Bible Tells Me So	Wing 90003
6/29/57	#35	2	A Fallen Star	Mercury 71124
9/28/57	#41	5	Moonlight Swim	Mercury 71169
8/06/60	#85	5	The Tip Of My Fingers	Coral 62213
10/06/62	#85	4	Hello Out There	Liberty 55488
			CLIFF NOBLES & CO.	
6/01/68	#4	12	The Horse	Phil-L.A. Of Soul 313
9/28/68	#94	1	Horse Fever	Phil-L.A. Of Soul 318
2/08/69	#95	3	Switch It On	Phil-L.A. Of Soul 324
			NOCERA	
2/07/87	#88	4	Summertime, Summertime	Sleeping Bag 22
			NOEL	
9/19/87	#64	18	Silent Morning	4th & B'way 7439
4/16/88	#77	5	Like A Child	4th & B'way 7458
			JACKY NOGUEZ	
6/20/59	#18	13	Ciao, Ciao Bambina	Jamie 1127
1/16/60	#51	7	Amapola	Jamie 1148
			NOLAN	
9/25/71	#70	9	I Like What You Give	Lizard 1003
12/18/71	#95	1	Keep On Keeping On*	Lizard 1010
			*released as by N.F. PORTER	
			KENNY NOLAN	
11/13/76	#3	27	I Like Dreamin'	20th Century 2287
4/09/77	#25	19	Love's Grown Deep	20th Century 2331
2/02/80	#56	8	Us And Love (We Go Together)	Casablanca 2234
			JIMMY NORMAN	
5/26/62	#43	13	I Don't Love You No More	Little Star 113
			FREDDIE NORTH	
10/02/71	#30	10	She's All I Got	Mankind 12004
2/19/72	#90	4	You And Me Together	Mankind 12009
			NORTHERN LIGHT	
5/10/75	#77	5	Minnesota	Columbia 10136
			NORTHERN PIKES	
12/21/91	#69	11	She Ain't Pretty	Scotti Brothers 75287
			DOROTHY NORWOOD	
1/19/74	#74	8	There's Got To Be Rain In Your Life	GRC 1011

Debut Date	Peak Pos	Wks Chr	ARTIST/Song Title	Label & Number
			NOTORIOUS	
12/08/90	#73	9	The Swalk	DGC 19698
			ALDO NOVA	
3/20/82	#24	17	Fantasy	Portrait 02799
7/17/82	#69	5	Foolin' Yourself	Portrait 03001
			NOVAS	
1/16/65	#79	5	The Crusher	Parrot 45005
			NRBQ	
1/26/74	#55	6	Get That Gasoline Blues	Kama Sutra 586
			N2DEEP	
2/20/93	#91	3	Toss-Up	Profile 5383
			TED NUGENT	
4/03/76	#84	6	Hey Baby	Epic 50197
11/20/76	#82	5	Dog Eat Dog	Epic 50301
7/23/77	#21	16	Cat Scratch Fever	Epic 50425
4/08/78	#59	5	Yank Me, Crank Me	Epic 50533
			GARY NUMAN	
2/16/80	#4	28	Cars	Atco 7211
6/28/80	#96	2	Are 'Friends' Electric?	Atco 7206
			STU NUNNERY	
11/03/73	#67	7	Sally From Syracuse	Evolution 1084
3/16/74	#86	7	Madelaine	Evolution 1086
			NU SHOOZ	
3/08/86	#3	23	I Can't Wait	Atlantic 89446
7/05/86	#36	21	Point Of No Return	Atlantic 89392
4/16/88	#42	16	Should I Say Yes?	Atlantic 89108
			NU TORNADOS	
11/22/58	#22	11	Philadelphia U.S.A.	Carlton 492
2/14/59	#96	2	Ole 'Mummer's' Strut	Carlton 497
			NUTTY SQUIRRELS	
11/07/59	#3	13	Uh! Oh! (Part 2)	Hanover 4540
			NYLONS	
5/09/87	#15	18	Kiss Him Goodbye	Open Air 0022
9/05/87	#86	5	Happy Together	Open Air 0024
			LAURA NYRO	
12/03/66	#96	3	Wedding Bell Blues	Verve Forecast 5024

O

			OAK	
7/14/79	#55	8	This Is Love	Mercury 74076
5/17/80	#53	14	King Of The Hill*	Mercury 76049
			*released as by RICK PINETTE and OAK	
			OAK RIDGE BOYS	
5/09/81	#1	25	Elvira	MCA 51084
9/26/81	#95	4	Fancy Free	MCA 51169
1/23/82	#13	16	Bobbie Sue	MCA 51231
6/12/82	#77	4	So Fine	MCA 52065
			JOHN O'BANION	
3/21/81	#26	14	Love You Like I Never Loved Before	Elektra 47125
			O'BRYAN	
3/27/82	#66	8	The Gigolo	Capitol 5067
			RIC OCASEK	
2/12/83	#53	8	Something To Grab For	Geffen 29784
9/06/86	#18	19	Emotion In Motion	Geffen 28617
12/13/86	#69	9	True To You	Geffen 28504
			OCEAN	
3/13/71	#2	15	Put Your Hand In The Hand	Kama Sutra 519
6/19/71	#70	4	Deep Enough For Me	Kama Sutra 525
7/31/71	#99	3	We Got A Dream	Kama Sutra 529
9/30/72	#88	3	One More Chance	Kama Sutra 556
			BILLY OCEAN	
4/03/76	#16	13	Love Really Hurts Without You	Ariola 7621

251

Debut Date	Peak Pos	Wks Chr	**ARTIST**/Song Title	Label & Number
			BILLY OCEAN—*continued*	
8/18/84	#2	23	Caribbean Queen	Jive 9199
12/01/84	#4	23	Loverboy	Jive 9284
3/23/85	#4	19	Suddenly	Jive 9323
7/06/85	#24	14	Mystery Lady	Jive 9374
11/30/85	#1	23	When The Going Gets Tough, The Tough Get Going	Jive 9432
4/19/86	#1	21	There'll Be Sad Songs (To Make You Cry)	Jive 9465
7/26/86	#10	17	Love Zone	Jive 9510
10/25/86	#20	17	Love Is Forever	Jive 9540
2/13/88	#1	20	Get Outta My Dreams, Get Into My Car	Jive 9678
5/28/88	#19	18	The Colour Of Love	Jive 9707
10/07/89	#34	16	Licence To Chill	Jive 1283
			CARROLL O'CONNOR and JEAN STAPLETON	
12/25/71	#79	5	Those Were The Days	Atlantic 2847
			SINEAD O'CONNOR	
3/24/90	#1	20	Nothing Compares To U	Ensign 23488
6/23/90	#57	10	The Emperor's New Clothes	Ensign 23528
			ALAN O'DAY	
4/02/77	#1	25	Undercover Angel	Pacific 001
10/08/77	#93	4	Started Out Dancing, Ended Up Making Love	Pacific 002
			ODDS & ENDS	
3/20/71	#83	5	Love Makes The World Go Round	Today 1003
			BROOKS O'DELL	
12/07/63	#70	8	Watch Your Step	Gold 214
			KENNY O'DELL	
11/11/67	#35	8	Beautiful People	Vegas 718
3/09/68	#98	1	Springfield Plane	Vegas 722
			JOE ODOM	
5/24/69	#94	2	It's In Your Power	1-2-3 1710
			ODYSSEY	
11/12/77	#15	20	Native New Yorker	RCA 11129
4/29/78	#80	7	Weekend Lover	RCA 11245
			ESTHER & ABI OFARIM	
3/16/68	#67	7	Cinderella Rockefella	Philips 40526
			OFF BROADWAY	
3/15/80	#54	10	Stay In Time	Atlantic 3647
			LENNY O'HENRY	
4/18/64	#73	8	Across The Street	Atco 6291
			OHIO EXPRESS	
10/07/67	#23	11	Beg, Borrow And Steal	Cameo 483
1/28/68	#80	4	Try It	Cameo 2001
4/27/68	#4	15	Yummy Yummy Yummy	Buddah 38
7/27/68	#25	11	Down At Lulu's	Buddah 56
10/19/68	#8	14	Chewy Chewy	Buddah 70
2/08/69	#83	4	Sweeter Than Sugar	Buddah 92
3/22/69	#26	9	Mercy	Buddah 102
6/14/69	#72	3	Pinch Me (Baby, Convince Me)	Buddah 117
8/30/69	#84	4	Sausalito (Is The Place To Go)	Buddah 129
11/22/69	#61	4	Cowboy Convention	Buddah 147
			OHIO PLAYERS	
12/04/71	#71	10	Pain	Westbound 188
6/24/72	#90	4	Got Pleasure	Westbound 204
2/17/73	#13	18	Funky Worm	Westbound 214
8/04/73	#31	13	Ecstasy	Westbound 216
6/01/74	#51	8	Jive Turkey (Part 1)	Mercury 73480
8/03/74	#11	16	Skin Tight	Mercury 73609
12/14/74	#1	16	Fire	Mercury 73643
4/05/75	#32	9	I Want To Be Free	Mercury 73675
9/06/75	#31	10	Sweet Sticky Thing	Mercury 73713
11/15/75	#3	18	Love Rollercoaster	Mercury 73734
2/28/76	#41	9	Fopp	Mercury 73775
7/10/76	#35	19	Who'd She Coo?	Mercury 73814
8/13/77	#95	4	O-H-I-O	Mercury 73932
			HERB OHTA	
7/06/74	#88	3	Song For Anna	A&M 1905

Debut Date	Peak Pos	Wks Chr	ARTIST/Song Title	Label & Number
			OINGO BOINGO	
8/31/85	#42	13	Weird Science	MCA 52633
12/21/85	#79	9	Just Another Day	MCA 52726
			O'JAYS	
9/21/63	#93	3	Lonely Drifter	Imperial 5976
5/08/65	#52	8	Lipstick Traces (On A Cigarette)	Imperial 66102
8/07/65	#93	3	I've Cried My Last Tear	Imperial 66121
11/18/67	#48	10	I'll Be Sweeter Tomorrow	Bell 691
6/22/68	#73	6	Look Over Your Shoulder	Bell 704
8/23/69	#98	2	One Night Affair	Neptune 12
3/02/70	#58	8	Deeper (In Love With You)	Neptune 22
8/22/70	#97	4	Looky Looky	Neptune 31
7/08/72	#1	17	Back Stabbers	Philadelphia Int. 3517
11/11/72	#43	8	992 Arguments	Philadelphia Int. 3522
1/13/73	#1	15	Love Train	Philadelphia Int. 3524
5/26/73	#30	10	Time To Get Down	Philadelphia Int. 3531
12/29/73	#14	12	Put Your Hands Together	Philadelphia Int. 3535
4/20/74	#7	13	For The Love Of Money	Philadelphia Int. 3544
4/26/75	#33	11	Give The People What They Want	Philadelphia Int. 3565
7/26/75	#56	5	Let Me Make Love To You	Philadelphia Int. 3573
10/25/75	#7	19	I Love Music (Part 1)	Philadelphia Int. 3577
3/06/76	#24	13	Livin' For The Weekend	Philadelphia Int. 3587
9/11/76	#66	11	Message In Our Music	Philadelphia Int. 3601
12/18/76	#79	8	Darlin' Darlin' Baby	Philadelphia Int. 3610
5/06/78	#5	20	Use Ta Be My Girl	Philadelphia Int. 3642
8/12/78	#76	7	Brandy	Philadelphia Int. 3652
12/01/79	#26	15	Forever Mine	Philadelphia Int. 3727
8/23/80	#54	11	Girl, Don't Let It Get You Down	TSOP 4790
			O'KAYSIONS	
8/17/68	#5	14	Girl Watcher	ABC 11094
11/23/68	#47	6	Love Machine	ABC 11153
			DANNY O'KEEFE	
8/26/72	#10	14	Good Time Charlie's Got The Blues	Signpost 70006
			OLA & THE JANGLERS	
5/31/69	#91	3	Let's Dance	GNP Crescendo 423
			MIKE OLDFIELD	
2/23/74	#6	16	Tubular Bells	Virgin 55100
			OLIVER	
5/17/69	#4	13	Good Morning Starshine	Jubilee 5659
8/09/69	#2	15	Jean	Crewe 334
11/15/69	#23	10	Sunday Mornin'	Crewe 337
4/11/70	#84	2	Angelica	Crewe 341
7/18/70	#94	1	I Can Remember	Crewe 346
			JANE OLIVER	
9/03/77	#89	4	Some Enchanted Evening	Columbia 10527
5/20/78	#67	7	He's So Fine	Columbia 10724
			SY OLIVER	
12/20/58	#95	2	In A Little Spanish Town Cha Cha	Jubilee 5349
			OLLIE & JERRY	
6/02/84	#8	18	Breakin'...There's No Stopping Us	Polydor 821708
			NIGEL OLSSON	
3/08/75	#92	4	Only One Woman	Rocket 40337
12/09/78	#17	19	Dancin' Shoes	Bang 740
4/07/79	#33	13	Little Bit Of Soap	Bang 4800
			OLYMPICS	
7/19/58	#11	14	Western Movies	Demon 1508
2/06/60	#57	9	(Baby) Hully Gully	Arvee 562
6/18/60	#20	17	Big Boy Pete	Arvee 595
9/17/60	#33	12	Shimmy Like Kate	Arvee 5006
12/24/60	#25	11	Dance By The Light Of The Moon	Arvee 5020
3/11/61	#71	7	Little Pedro	Arvee 5023
4/20/63	#49	10	The Bounce	Tri Disc 106
7/20/63	#71	4	Dancin' Holiday	Tri Disc 107
5/01/65	#92	2	Good Lovin'	Loma 2013
4/23/66	#80	7	Mine Exclusively	Mirwood 5513
10/08/66	#97	2	Baby, Do The Philly Dog	Mirwood 5523

Debut Date	Peak Pos	Wks Chr	ARTIST/Song Title	Label & Number
			LENORE O'MALLEY	
7/19/80	#56	10	First....Be A Woman	Polydor 2055
			ALEXANDER O'NEAL	
2/15/86	#33	16	Saturday Love*.........................	Tabu 05767
7/18/87	#29	16	Fake	Tabu 07100
11/28/87	#81	7	Criticize	Tabu 07600
1/30/88	#34	14	Never Knew Love*......................	Tabu 07646
3/02/91	#45	14	All True Man	Tabu 73627
			*released as by CHERRELLE with ALEXANDER O'NEAL	
			SHAQUILLE O'NEAL	
7/17/93	#36	15	What's Up Doc? (Can We Rock)*...........	Jive 42164
10/30/93	#32	21	(I Know I Got) Skillz	Jive 42177
			*released as by FU-SCHNICKENS with SHAQUILLE O'NEAL	
			100 PROOF AGED IN SOUL	
8/29/70	#6	16	Somebody's Been Sleeping	Hot Wax 7004
2/27/71	#79	4	One Man's Leftovers	Hot Wax 7009
11/06/71	#83	3	Ninety Day Freeze	Hot Wax 7108
4/01/72	#49	8	Everything Good Is Bad	Hot Wax 7202
			ONE OF THE GIRLS	
7/10/93	#81	5	Do Da What	East West 98419
			ONE TO ONE	
8/23/86	#79	5	Angel In My Pocket	Warner Brothers 28739
			ONE 2 MANY	
4/01/89	#38	14	Downtown	A&M 1272
			ONE 2 ONE	
2/22/92	#56	9	Peace Of Mind (Love Goes On)	A&M 1591
			ONE WAY	
5/29/82	#45	12	Cutie Pie	MCA 52049
			YOKO ONO	
2/28/81	#41	12	Walking On Thin Ice	Geffen 49638
			ONYX	
6/12/93	#5	20	Slam	JMJ 74882
10/23/93	#84	6	Shifftee	Def Jam 77163
			OPUS	
2/01/86	#35	15	Live Is Life	Polydor 883730
			ROY ORBISON	
1/30/60	#70	7	Uptown	Monument 412
6/04/60	#2	20	Only The Lonely (Know How I Feel)	Monument 421
9/24/60	#13	13	Blue Angel	Monument 425
12/17/60	#28	9	I'm Hurtin'	Monument 433
4/22/61	#1	15	Running Scared	Monument 438
8/19/61	#1	16	Crying	Monument 447
8/19/61	#34	16	Candy Man	Monument 447
2/17/62	#9	12	Dream Baby (How Long Must I Dream)	Monument 456
5/26/62	#21	11	The Crowd	Monument 461
9/15/62	#32	13	Workin' For The Man/	Monument 467
10/06/62	#27	12	Leah	Monument 467
2/09/63	#10	14	In Dreams	Monument 806
6/01/63	#23	9	Falling	Monumnet 815
9/07/63	#21	12	Blue Bayou/	Monument 824
9/14/63	#7	14	Mean Woman Blues	Monument 824
12/07/63	#16	8	Pretty Paper	Monument 830
4/11/64	#10	12	It's Over	Monument 837
8/29/64	#1	17	Oh, Pretty Woman*	Monument 851
2/13/65	#20	8	Goodnight	Monument 873
7/10/65	#49	4	(Say) You're My Girl	Monument 891
8/28/65	#18	9	Ride Away	MGM 13386
11/06/65	#36	6	Crawling Back	MGM 13410
11/20/65	#96	2	Let The Good Times Roll	Monument 906
1/22/66	#31	8	Breakin' Up Is Breakin' My Heart	MGM 13446
4/30/66	#40	7	Twinkle Toes	MGM 13498
7/23/66	#62	6	Too Soon To Know	MGM 13549
12/10/66	#70	6	Communication Breakdown	MGM 13634
7/22/67	#45	7	Cry Softly Lonely One	MGM 13764
7/06/68	#99	1	Walk On	MGM 13950
6/16/79	#92	4	Easy Way Out	Asylum 46048
6/21/80	#59	9	That Lovin' You Feelin' Again**	Warner Brothers 49262

Debut Date	Peak Pos	Wks Chr	ARTIST/Song Title	Label & Number
1/21/89	#16	21	You Got It	Virgin 99245
			*released as by ROY ORBISON and THE CANDY MEN	
			**released as by ROY ORBISON & EMMYLOU HARRIS	
			ORCHESTRAL MANOEUVRES IN THE DARK	
9/07/85	#26	19	So In Love	A&M 2746
12/21/85	#71	10	Secret	A&M 2794
3/08/86	#8	19	If You Leave	A&M 2811
9/27/86	#22	18	(Forever) Live And Die	A&M 2872
3/12/88	#17	19	Dreaming	A&M 3002
			ORIGINAL CASTE	
11/01/69	#50	14	One Tin Soldier	T-A 186
			ORIGINAL CASUALS	
2/01/58	#28	12	So Tough	Back Beat 503
			ORIGINALS	
11/08/58	#96	1	Anna	Jackpot 48012
			ORIGINALS	
9/06/69	#16	17	Baby, I'm For Real	Soul 35066
1/31/70	#18	13	The Bells	Soul 35069
12/12/70	#52	12	God Bless Whoever Sent You	Soul 35079
12/11/76	#99	2	Down To Love Town	Soul 35119
			ORIOLES	
9/26/53	#1	8	Crying In The Chapel	Jubilee 5122
10/02/59	#53	10	Crying In The Chapel	Jubilee 5122
			ORION THE HUNTER	
6/16/84	#78	5	So You Ran	Portrait 04483
			TONY ORLANDO (see also DAWN)	
4/08/61	#17	14	Halfway To Paradise	Epic 9441
8/05/61	#17	14	Bless You	Epic 9452
11/25/61	#76	5	Happy Times (Are Here To Stay)	Epic 9476
7/07/79	#55	8	Sweets For My Sweet	Casablanca 991
			ORLEANS	
4/26/75	#53	7	Let There Be Music	Asylum 45243
7/19/75	#5	18	Dance With Me	Asylum 45261
7/24/76	#6	21	Still The One	Asylum 45336
1/22/77	#45	10	Reach	Asylum 45375
3/24/79	#12	15	Love Takes Time	Infinity 50006
8/04/79	#92	3	Don't Throw Our Love Away	Infinity 50017
			ORLONS	
10/28/61	#79	4	I'll Be True	Cameo 198
6/09/62	#2	15	The Wah Watusi	Cameo 218
10/13/62	#6	16	Don't Hang Up	Cameo 231
2/09/63	#3	15	South Street	Cameo 243
6/08/63	#12	12	Not Me	Cameo 257
9/21/63	#20	10	Cross Fire!	Cameo 273
12/14/63	#43	6	Bon-Doo-Wah	Cameo 287
2/01/64	#62	5	Shimmy Shimmy	Cameo 295
5/23/64	#84	3	Rules Of Love	Cameo 319
8/29/64	#75	5	Knock! Knock! (Who's There)	Cameo 332
			OR-N-MORE	
9/07/91	#49	10	Everyotherday*	EMI 50359
			*released as by OR-N-MORE featuring FATHER M.C.	
			ORPHEUS	
3/02/68	#88	6	Can't Find The Time	MGM 13882
5/24/69	#88	5	Brown Arms In Houston	MGM 14022
8/30/69	#72	4	Can't Find The Time	MGM 13882
			BENJAMIN ORR	
11/08/86	#20	20	Stay The Night	Elektra 69506
			ROBERT ELLIS ORRALL	
3/26/83	#35	13	I Couldn't Say No*	RCA 13431
			*released as by ROBERT ELLIS ORRALL with CARLENE CARTER	
			FRANK ORTEGA TRIO	
4/18/59	#38	2	77 Sunset Strip	Jubilee 5365

Debut Date	Peak Pos	Wks Chr	ARTIST/Song Title	Label & Number
			JEFFREY OSBORNE	
6/26/82	#51	11	I Really Don't Need No Light	A&M 2410
10/02/82	#23	20	On The Wings Of Love	A&M 2434
3/12/83	#68	7	Eenie Meenie	A&M 2530
7/23/83	#27	13	Don't You Get So Mad	A&M 2561
10/29/83	#27	19	Stay With Me Tonight	A&M 2591
3/03/84	#47	11	We're Going All The Way	A&M 2618
8/18/84	#44	13	The Last Time I Made Love*	A&M 2656
10/20/84	#41	17	Don't Stop	A&M 2687
1/26/85	#39	13	The Borderlines	A&M 2695
5/24/86	#11	21	You Should Be Mine (The Woo Woo Song)	A&M 2814
7/11/87	#11	15	Love Power**	Arista 9567
8/20/88	#53	13	She's On The Left	A&M 1227
			*released as by JOYCE KENNEDY & JEFFREY OSBORNE	
			**released as by DIONNE WARWICK & JEFFREY OSBORNE	
			OZZY OSBOURNE	
4/26/86	#83	4	Shot In The Dark	CBS Associated 05810
3/04/89	#13	23	Close My Eyes Forever*	RCA 8899
2/08/92	#11	27	Mama, I'm Coming Home	Epic Associated 74093
			*released as by LITA FORD with OZZY OSBORNE	
			SHAD O'SHEA	
2/28/76	#79	5	Colorado Call	Private Stock 45071
			LEE OSKAR	
6/26/76	#77	5	BLT	United Artists 807
			DONNY OSMOND	
3/20/71	#7	18	Sweet And Innocent	MGM 14227
8/07/71	#1	14	Go Away Little Girl	MGM 14285
11/20/71	#9	11	Hey Girl/	MGM 14322
11/20/71	#83	4	I Knew You When	MGM 14322
2/19/72	#3	12	Puppy Love	MGM 14367
6/10/72	#8	10	Too Young	MGM 14407
8/12/72	#16	13	Why	MGM 14424
3/03/73	#5	13	The Twelfth Of Never	MGM 14503
7/14/73	#41	7	Young Love/	MGM 14583
7/28/73	#28	10	A Million To One	MGM 14583
11/17/73	#16	13	Are You Lonesome Tonight/	MGM 14677
12/01/73	#73	3	When I Fall In Love	MGM 14677
2/22/75	#54	5	I Have A Dream	MGM 14781
5/29/76	#44	12	C'mon Marianne	Polydor 14320
10/01/77	#99	1	You've Got Me Dangling On A String	Polydor 14471
3/25/89	#2	23	Soldier Of Love	Capitol 44369
6/17/89	#10	19	Sacred Emotion	Capitol 44379
9/30/89	#72	7	Hold On	Capitol 44423
10/13/90	#25	17	My Love Is A Fire	Capitol 44634
1/19/91	#45	12	Sure Lookin'	Capitol 44670
4/20/91	#79	5	Love Will Survive	Capitol 44707
			DONNY and MARIE OSMOND	
7/06/74	#7	14	I'm Leaving It (All) Up To You	MGM 14735
11/23/74	#6	14	Morning Side Of The Mountain	MGM 14765
6/07/75	#45	7	Make The World Go Away	MGM 14807
12/13/75	#20	22	Deep Purple	MGM 14840
11/20/76	#30	16	Ain't Nothing Like The Real Thing	Polydor 14363
11/19/77	#46	11	(You're My) Soul And Inspiration	Polydor 14439
10/07/78	#53	10	On The Shelf	Polydor 14510
			LITTLE JIMMY OSMOND	
4/22/72	#41	9	Long Haired Lover From Liverpool	MGM 14376
12/30/72	#49	7	Tweedlee Dee	MGM 14468
			MARIE OSMOND	
9/08/73	#6	15	Paper Roses	MGM 14609
3/01/75	#39	8	Who's Sorry Now	MGM 14786
4/16/77	#52	9	This Is The Way That I Feel	Polydor 14385
			OSMONDS	
12/26/70	#1	16	One Bad Apple	MGM 14193
5/15/71	#9	10	Double Lovin'	MGM 14259
9/11/71	#2	14	Yo-Yo	MGM 14295
1/22/72	#3	13	Down By The Lazy River	MGM 14324
6/24/72	#15	9	Hold Her Tight	MGM 14405

Debut Date	Peak Pos	Wks Chr	ARTIST/Song Title	Label & Number
9/23/72	#64	7	We Can Make It Together*	MGM 14383
10/21/72	#19	10	Crazy Horses	MGM 14450
6/09/73	#21	8	Goin' Home	MGM 14562
9/08/73	#19	10	Let Me In	MGM 14617
8/31/74	#8	12	Love Me For A Reason	MGM 14746
7/26/75	#33	10	The Proud One	MGM 14791
9/25/76	#53	10	I Can't Live In A Dream	Polydor 14348
			*released as by STEVE & EYDIE featuring THE OSMONDS	
			GILBERT O'SULLIVAN	
6/17/72	#1	18	Alone Again (Naturally)	MAM 3619
10/21/72	#3	16	Clair	MAM 3626
3/10/73	#22	12	Out Of The Question	MAM 3628
6/23/73	#4	15	Get Down	MAM 3629
10/13/73	#11	10	Ooh Baby	MAM 3633
3/09/74	#34	9	Happiness Is Me And You	MAM 3636
2/01/75	#95	4	You Are You	MAM 3642
			OTHER ONES	
4/18/87	#49	12	We Are What We Are	Virgin 99473
8/08/87	#36	19	Holiday	Virgin 99428
			CLYDE OTIS	
3/25/61	#79	7	Jungle Dreams	Mercury 71776
			JOHNNY OTIS SHOW	
6/07/58	#16	17	Willie And The Hand Jive	Capitol 3966
4/25/59	#75	4	Castin' My Spell	Capitol 4168
			OTIS & CARLA (OTIS REDDING & CARLA THOMAS)	
5/06/67	#19	10	Tramp	Stax 216
8/12/67	#60	9	Knock On Wood	Stax 228
2/17/68	#50	3	Lovey Dovey	Stax 244
			OUTFIELD	
2/15/86	#10	20	Your Love	Columbia 05796
6/07/86	#19	16	All The Love In The World	Columbia 05894
9/20/86	#57	9	Every Time You Cry	Columbia 06295
6/13/87	#33	15	Since You've Been Gone	Columbia 07170
3/25/89	#26	19	The Voices Of Babylon	Columbia 68601
10/27/90	#22	19	For You	MCA 53935
5/23/92	#31	15	Closer To Me	MCA 54378
			OUTLAWS	
9/06/75	#26	10	There Goes Another Love Song	Arista 0150
7/16/77	#78	6	Hurry Sundown	Arista 0258
12/23/78	#94	4	Take It Anyway You Want It	Arista 0378
1/17/81	#36	14	(Ghost) Riders In The Sky	Arista 0582
			OUTSIDERS	
2/26/66	#6	13	Time Won't Let Me	Capitol 5573
5/14/66	#24	9	Girl In Love	Capitol 5646
8/06/66	#13	9	Respectable	Capitol 5701
10/29/66	#40	11	Help Me Girl	Capitol 5759
			OVATIONS	
5/15/65	#54	7	It's Wonderful To Be In Love	Goldwax 113
10/13/73	#73	8	Having A Party	MGM 14623
			OVERLANDERS	
5/23/64	#52	4	Yesterday's Gone	Hickory 1258
			REG OWEN	
12/13/58	#14	15	Manhattan Spiritual	Palette 5005
			OWEN B.	
2/21/70	#81	4	Mississippi Mama	Janus 107
			BUCK OWENS	
8/29/64	#86	4	I Don't Care	Capitol 5240
1/23/65	#31	8	I've Got A Tiger By The Tail	Capitol 5336
5/08/65	#78	4	Before You Go	Capitol 5410
11/20/65	#58	7	Buckaroo	Capitol 5517
2/12/66	#66	6	Waitin' In Your Welfare Line	Capitol 5566
5/21/66	#76	6	Think Of Me	Capitol 5647
4/22/67	#92	1	Sam's Place	Capitol 5865
11/29/69	#97	2	Big In Vegas	Capitol 2646

Debut Date	Peak Pos	Wks Chr	ARTIST/Song Title	Label & Number
			DONNIE OWENS	
9/27/58	#20	15	Need You	Guyden 2001
12/27/58	#89	3	Tomorrow	Guyden 2006
			OXO	
2/19/83	#29	15	Whirly Girl	Geffen 29765
			OZARK MOUNTAIN DAREDEVILS	
4/27/74	#21	12	If You Wanna Get To Heaven	A&M 1515
10/26/74	#88	4	Look Away	A&M 1623
2/08/75	#1	19	Jackie Blue	A&M 1654
1/24/76	#71	5	If I Only Knew	A&M 1772
1/22/77	#55	12	You Know Like I Know	A&M 1888
5/10/80	#83	7	Take You Tonight	Columbia 11247
			OZO	
7/17/76	#72	7	Listen To The Buddha	DJM 1012

P ▬▬▬▬▬▬▬▬

Debut Date	Peak Pos	Wks Chr	ARTIST/Song Title	Label & Number
			PABLO CRUISE	
4/09/77	#3	25	Whatcha Gonna Do?	A&M 1920
9/24/77	#42	8	A Place In The Sun	A&M 1976
1/28/78	#89	5	Never Had A Love	A&M 1999
5/27/78	#5	21	Love Will Find A Way	A&M 2048
9/23/78	#18	16	Don't Want To Live Without It	A&M 2076
1/20/79	#56	7	I Go To Rio	A&M 2112
10/13/79	#21	15	I Want You Tonight	A&M 2195
7/04/81	#17	17	Cool Love	A&M 2349
10/31/81	#86	3	Slip Away	A&M 2373
			PACIFIC GAS & ELECTRIC	
5/23/70	#12	13	Are You Ready?	Columbia 45158
2/26/72	#95	4	Thank God For You Baby	Columbia 45519
			PACKERS	
11/13/65	#29	12	Hole In The Wall	Pure Soul 1107
			PATTI PAGE	
9/30/50	#1	16	All My Love	Mercury 5455
12/16/50	#1	20	The Tennessee Waltz	Mercury 5534
3/17/51	#3	11	Would I Love You (Love You, Love You)	Mercury 5571
3/31/51	#1	17	Mockin' Bird Hill	Mercury 5595
6/30/51	#7	6	Mister And Mississippi	Mercury 5645
10/27/51	#6	9	And So To Sleep Again	Mercury 5706
9/27/52	#1	18	I Went To Your Wedding	Mercury 5899
2/28/53	#1	16	The Doggie In The Window	Mercury 70070
1/02/54	#2	14	Changing Partners	Mercury 70260
4/10/54	#3	13	Cross Over The Bridge	Mercury 70302
8/04/56	#6	15	Allegheny Moon	Mercury 70878
10/20/56	#14	14	Mama From The Train	Mercury 70971
3/02/57	#42	5	The Wall/	Mercury 71059
3/09/57	#25	8	A Poor Man's Roses	Mercury 71059
5/25/57	#8	18	Old Cape Cod	Mercury 71101
10/05/57	#18	14	I'll Remember Today	Mercury 71189
1/25/58	#28	8	Belonging To Someone	Mercury 71247
4/12/58	#38	4	Another Time, Another Place	Mercury 71294
6/21/58	#9	15	Left Right Out Of Your Heart	Mercury 71331
9/27/58	#28	10	Fibbin'	Mercury 71355
1/03/59	#36	11	Trust In Me/	Mercury 71400
1/10/59	#95	2	Under The Sun Valley Moon	Mercury 71400
4/11/59	#77	5	Walls Have Ears	Mercury 71428
6/06/59	#57	7	With My Eyes Wide Open I'm Dreaming	Mercury 71469
10/03/59	#70	8	Goodbye Charlie	Mercury 71510
1/16/60	#74	4	The Sound Of Music	Mercury 71555
6/11/60	#32	12	One Of Us (Will Weep Tonight)	Mercury 71639
10/01/60	#62	9	I Wish I'd Never Been Born	Mercury 71695
1/07/61	#70	6	Don't Read The Letter	Mercury 71745
7/08/61	#70	5	You'll Answer To Me	Mercury 71823
12/16/61	#35	11	Go On Home	Mercury 71906
4/07/62	#26	10	Most People Get Married	Mercury 71950
8/04/62	#60	9	The Boys' Night Out	Mercury 72013
6/08/63	#82	6	Say Wonderful Things	Columbia 42791
5/01/65	#10	13	Hush, Hush, Sweet Charlotte	Columbia 43251

Debut Date	Peak Pos	Wks Chr	ARTIST/Song Title	Label & Number
8/28/65	#91	2	You Can't Be True Dear	Columbia 43345
			TOMMY PAGE	
2/18/89	#31	20	A Shoulder To Cry On	Sire 27645
2/17/90	#1	20	I'll Be Your Everything	Sire 19959
5/12/90	#31	15	When I Dream Of You	Sire 19839
6/01/91	#89	4	Whenever You Close Your Eyes	Sire 19323
			PAGES	
11/17/79	#80	5	I Do Believe In You	Epic 50769
			KEVIN PAIGE	
8/26/89	#17	24	Don't Shut Me Out	Chrysalis 23389
1/27/90	#32	12	Anything I Want	Chrysalis 23444
			SHARON PAIGE and HAROLD MELVIN and THE BLUENOTES	
7/05/75	#31	9	Hope That We Can Be Together Soon	Philadelphia Int. 3569
			PAINTER	
9/22/73	#64	8	West Coast Woman	Elektra 45862
			PAJAMA PARTY	
12/02/89	#88	5	Over And Over	Atlantic 88799
3/17/90	#67	7	Hide And Seek	Atlantic 87973
			MORTY PALITZ ORCHESTRA	
1/24/59	#92	3	Eso Es El Amour	Jubilee 850
			ROBERT PALMER	
7/19/75	#96	3	Sneakin' Sally Through The Alley	Island 006
2/14/76	#88	5	Give Me An Inch Girl	Island 049
11/27/76	#70	8	Man Smart, Woman Smarter	Island 075
3/25/78	#13	21	Every Kinda People	Island 100
7/21/79	#10	18	Bad Case Of Loving You (Doctor, Doctor)	Island 49016
12/15/79	#50	12	Can We Still Be Friends	Island 49137
11/23/85	#79	5	Discipline Of Love (Why Did You Do It)	Island 99597
2/08/86	#1	23	Addicted To Love	Island 99520
6/07/86	#27	13	Hyperactive	Island 99545
8/16/86	#4	23	I Didn't Mean To Turn You On	Island 99537
7/02/88	#2	19	Simply Irresistible	EMI-Manhattan 50133
10/22/88	#19	17	Early In The Morning	EMI-Manhattan 50157
7/22/89	#50	8	Tell Me I'm Not Dreaming	EMI 50206
11/17/90	#29	15	You're Amazing	EMI 50338
2/16/91	#13	18	Mercy Mercy Me (The Ecology)	EMI 50344
			NICOLA PAONE	
1/31/59	#36	8	Blah, Blah, Blah	ABC-Paramount 9993
			PAPERBOY	
12/26/92	#23	29	Ditty	Next Plateau 350012
			PAPER LACE	
4/20/74	#68	6	Billy, Don't Be A Hero	Mercury 73479
6/15/74	#1	17	The Night Chicago Died	Mercury 73492
10/05/74	#41	8	The Black-Eyed Boys	Mercury 73620
			PARADE	
4/22/67	#26	9	Sunshine Girl	A&M 841
			PARADONS	
9/03/60	#17	15	Diamonds And Pearls	Milestone 2003
			BOBBY PARIS	
9/14/68	#82	4	Per-so-nal-ly	Tetragrammaton 1504
			PARIS RED	
3/21/92	#83	5	Good Friend	Epic 74157
			PARIS SISTERS	
5/06/61	#68	6	Be My Boy	Gregmark 2
9/02/61	#7	16	I Love How You Love Me	Gregmark 6
2/03/62	#41	8	He Knows I Love Him Too Much	Gregmark 10
5/19/62	#90	2	Let Me Be The One	Gregmark 12
7/04/64	#94	2	Dream Lover	MGM 13236
			FESS PARKER	
1/19/57	#12	13	Wringle Wrangle	Disneyland 43

Debut Date	Peak Pos	Wks Chr	ARTIST/Song Title	Label & Number
			GRAHAM PARKER and THE RUMOUR	
4/30/77	#77	6	Hold Back The Night*	Mercury 74000
5/04/85	#38	12	Wake Up (Next To You)**	Elektra 69654
			*released as by GRAHAM PARKER and THE RUMOUR	
			**released as by GRAHAM PARKER and THE SHOT	
			LITTLE JUNIOR PARKER	
12/31/60	#87	3	Stand By Me	Duke 330
6/10/61	#93	4	Driving Wheel	Duke 335
3/17/62	#54	8	Annie Get Your Yo-Yo	Duke 345
			RAY PARKER JR. (also RAYDIO)	
12/24/77	#6	25	Jack And Jill*	Arista 0283
4/21/79	#10	25	You Can't Change That*	Arista 0399
3/22/80	#27	19	Two Places At The Same Time**	Arista 0494
3/07/80	#5	24	A Woman Needs Love (Just Like You Do)**	Arista 0592
7/11/81	#27	14	That Old Song**	Arista 0616
3/20/82	#2	21	The Other Woman	Arista 0669
7/24/82	#56	10	Let Me Go	Arista 0695
11/27/82	#28	16	Bad Boy	Arista 1030
11/12/83	#15	19	I Still Can't Get Over Loving You	Arista 9116
6/16/84	#1	21	Ghostbusters	Arista 9212
11/17/84	#19	17	Jamie	Arista 9293
10/05/85	#30	15	Girls Are More Fun	Arista 9352
8/29/87	#63	9	I Don't Think That Man Should Sleep Alone	Geffen 28417
8/11/90	#32	14	All I'm Missing Is You***	MCA 53886
			*released as by RAYDIO	
			**released as by RAY PARKER JR. & RAYDIO	
			***released as by GLENN MEDEIROS featuring RAY PARKER JR.	
			ROBERT PARKER	
4/23/66	#11	13	Barefootin'	Nola 721
			MICHAEL PARKS	
2/28/70	#13	12	Long Lonesome Highway	MGM 14104
			PARLIAMENT	
6/28/75	#86	3	Chocolate City	Casablanca 831
5/15/76	#20	19	Tear The Roof Off The Sucker	Casablanca 856
2/11/78	#15	16	Flash Light	Casablanca 909
			PARLIAMENTS	
6/17/67	#18	16	(I Wanna) Testify	Revilot 207
10/21/67	#62	7	All Your Goodies Are Gone	Revilot 211
			JOHN PARR	
12/22/84	#30	18	Naughty, Naughty	Atlantic 89612
4/13/85	#69	6	Magical	Atlantic 89568
6/29/85	#1	23	St. Elmo's Fire (Man In Motion)	Atlantic 89541
11/23/85	#82	8	Love Grammar	Atlantic 89484
			DEAN PARRISH	
7/16/66	#94	2	Tell Her	Boom 60012
			ALAN PARSONS PROJECT	
7/24/76	#54	12	(The System Of) Doctor Tarr And Professor Fether	20th Century 2297
8/13/77	#27	13	I Wouldn't Want To Be Like You*	Arista 0260
11/26/77	#65	8	Don't Let It Show	Arista 0288
9/29/79	#30	17	Damned If I Do	Arista 0454
12/06/80	#18	20	Games People Play	Arista 0573
4/18/81	#14	22	Time	Arista 0598
7/10/82	#3	23	Eye In The Sky	Arista 0696
12/04/82	#58	11	Psychobabble	Arista 1029
11/19/83	#65	10	You Don't Believe	Arista 9108
3/03/84	#17	17	Don't Answer Me	Arista 9160
5/19/84	#33	13	Prime Time	Arista 9208
2/23/85	#47	11	Let's Talk About Me	Arista 9282
5/04/85	#76	4	Days Are Numbers	Arista 9349
2/15/86	#71	6	Stereotomy	Arista 9433
			*released as by ALAN PARSONS	
			BILL PARSONS (see BOBBY BARE)	
			PARTLAND BROTHERS	
4/25/87	#30	17	Soul City	Manhattan 50065

Debut Date	Peak Pos	Wks Chr	**ARTIST**/Song Title	Label & Number
			PARTNERS IN KRYME	
4/28/90	#12	15	Turtle Power!	SBK 07325
			DOLLY PARTON	
12/22/73	#80	10	Jolene	RCA 0145
8/02/75	#91	3	The Seeker	RCA 10310
10/08/77	#7	24	Here You Come Again	RCA 11123
3/18/78	#24	12	Two Doors Down	RCA 11240
8/19/78	#56	9	Heartbreaker	RCA 11296
12/16/78	#34	13	Baby I'm Burnin'	RCA 11420
6/30/79	#68	6	You're The Only One	RCA 11577
4/05/80	#57	8	Starting Over Again	RCA 11926
12/06/80	#1	25	9 To 5	RCA 12133
4/04/81	#47	9	But You Know I Love You	RCA 12200
7/31/82	#41	15	I Will Always Love You	RCA 13260
8/27/83	#1	29	Islands In The Stream*	RCA 13615
12/10/83	#50	13	Save The Last Dance For Me	RCA 13703
4/17/93	#66	8	Romeo**	Columbia 74876
			***released as by KENNY ROGERS with DOLLY PARTON**	
			****released as by DOLLY PARTON & FRIENDS**	
			PARTRIDGE FAMILY	
9/26/70	#1	19	I Think I Love You	Bell 910
2/06/71	#1	13	Doesn't Somebody Want To Be Wanted	Bell 963
5/08/71	#2	10	I'll Meet You Halfway	Bell 996
8/07/71	#9	12	I Woke Up In Love This Morning	Bell 45130
12/11/71	#13	10	It's One Of Those Nights (Yes Love)	Bell 45160
3/25/72	#31	7	Am I Losing You	Bell 45200
7/01/72	#25	10	Breaking Up Is Hard To Do	Bell 45235
12/09/72	#25	10	Looking Through The Eyes Of Love	Bell 45301
3/31/73	#92	3	Friend And A Lover	Bell 45336
			PARTY	
8/18/90	#68	6	Summer Vacation	Hollywood 64945
2/23/91	#52	15	That's Why	Hollywood 64903
11/09/91	#24	22	In My Dreams	Hollywood 64832
			PASEDENAS	
2/25/89	#42	11	Tribute (Right On)	Columbia 68575
			PASSIONS	
9/05/59	#48	18	Just To Be With You	Audicon 102
3/05/60	#93	2	I Only Want You	Audicon 105
			PASTELS	
3/22/58	#60	1	Been So Long	Argo 5287
			PASTEL SIX	
12/22/62	#22	11	The Cinnamon Cinder	Zen 102
			PAT & MICK	
12/22/90	#69	8	Use It Up And Wear It Out	Charisma 98870
			JOHNNY PATE QUINTET	
1/18/58	#18	12	Swinging Shepherd Blues	Federal 12312
			PATIENCE & PRUDENCE	
8/11/56	#3	20	Tonight You Belong To Me	Liberty 55022
11/24/56	#13	14	Gonna Get Along Without Ya Now	Liberty 55040
			PATSY	
12/24/83	#98	3	"Kid" Santa Claus	Roperry 2255
12/22/84	#92	4	"Kid" Santa Claus	Roperry 2255
12/21/85	#94	4	"Kid" Santa Claus	Roperry 2255
			KELLEE PATTERSON	
12/10/77	#81	9	If It Don't Fit, Don't Force It	Shady Brook 1041
			ROBBIE PATTON	
7/11/81	#26	13	Don't Give It Up	Liberty 1420
3/05/83	#46	15	Smiling Islands	Atlantic 89955
			PATTY & THE EMBLEMS	
6/27/64	#28	9	Mixed Up, Shook-Up, Girl	Herald 590
			BILLY PAUL	
10/21/72	#1	17	Me And Mrs. Jones	Philadelphia Int. 3521
4/14/73	#99	1	Am I Black Enough For You	Philadelphia Int. 3526

Debut Date	Peak Pos	Wks Chr	**ARTIST**/Song Title	Label & Number
			BILLY PAUL—*continued*	
2/02/74	#43	15	Thanks For Saving My Life	Philadelphia Int. 3538
3/20/76	#79	5	Let's Make A Baby	Philadelphia Int. 3584
			HENRY PAUL BAND	
12/12/81	#57	9	Keeping Our Love Alive	Atlantic 3883
			LES PAUL	
9/27/52	#4	8	Meet Mr. Callaghan	Capitol 2193
			LES PAUL & MARY FORD	
3/31/51	#1	17	Mockin' Bird Hill.......................	Capitol 1373
5/05/51	#1	16	How High The Moon	Capitol 1451
9/29/51	#4	10	The World Is Waiting For The Sunrise/	Capitol 1748
11/20/51	#6	5	Whispering	Capitol 1748
2/09/52	#5	8	Tiger Rag	Capitol 1920
2/21/53	#10	1	Bye Bye Blues	Capitol 2316
2/21/53	#8	3	My Baby's Coming Home	Capitol 2265
4/25/53	#10	2	I'm Sitting On Top Of The World	Capitol 2400
7/18/53	#1	22	Vaya Con Dios	Capitol 2486
8/20/55	#6	5	Hummingbird	Capitol 3165
1/12/57	#24	5	Cinco Robles (Five Oaks)	Capitol 3612
8/23/58	#43	9	Put A Ring On My Finger	Columbia 41222
11/15/58	#71	2	Jealous Heart	Columbia 41278
6/03/61	#81	7	Jura (I Swear I Love You)	Columbia 41994
			PAUL & PAULA	
1/05/63	#1	15	Hey Paula	Philips 40084
3/16/63	#7	11	Young Lovers	Philips 40096
6/01/63	#21	8	First Quarrel	Philips 40114
8/17/63	#82	5	Something Old, Something New	Philips 40130
10/12/63	#75	3	First Day Back At School	Philips 40142
			PAULETTE SISTERS	
10/25/58	#87	3	Calla Calla	Aamco 101
			RITA PAVONE	
5/30/64	#35	10	Remember Me	RCA 8365
10/17/64	#97	1	Wait For Me	RCA 8420
			FREDA PAYNE	
5/02/70	#2	19	Band Of Gold	Invictus 9075
9/12/70	#21	11	Deeper & Deeper	Invictus 9080
2/06/71	#36	8	Cherish What Is Dear To You	Invictus 9085
5/29/71	#7	14	Bring The Boys Home	Invictus 9092
9/25/71	#45	9	You Brought The Joy	Invictus 9100
			PC QUEST	
8/17/91	#42	12	After The Summer's Gone	RCA 62051
			PEACHES & HERB	
1/07/67	#39	13	Let's Fall In Love	Date 1523
4/01/67	#12	12	Close Your Eyes	Date 1549
6/24/67	#22	8	For Your Love	Date 1563
9/30/67	#13	10	Love Is Strange	Date 1574
12/16/67	#37	9	Two Little Kids	Date 1586
2/24/68	#51	4	The Ten Commandments Of Love	Date 1592
5/18/68	#25	7	United	Date 1603
10/26/68	#66	5	Let's Make A Promise	Date 1623
2/15/69	#51	8	When He Touches Me	Date 1637
8/09/69	#92	3	Let Me Be The One	Date 1649
7/03/71	#94	1	The Sounds Of Silence	Columbia 45386
12/09/78	#5	21	Shake Your Groove Thing	Polydor 14514
3/17/79	#1	21	Reunited	Polydor 14547
6/30/79	#47	9	We've Got Love	Polydor 14577
2/02/80	#25	18	I Pledge My Love	Polydor 2053
			LESLIE PEARL	
5/22/82	#25	19	If The Love Fits Wear It	RCA 13235
			PEARLETTES	
3/17/62	#95	2	Duchess Of Earl	Vee-Jay 435
			PEARL JAM	
12/25/93	#23	15	Daughter	Epic album cut
			PEBBLES	
2/06/88	#6	21	Girlfriend	MCA 53185

Debut Date	Peak Pos	Wks Chr	**ARTIST**/Song Title	Label & Number
5/07/88	#4	20	Mercedes Boy	MCA 53279
8/18/90	#3	25	Giving You The Benefit	MCA 79079
12/01/90	#27	21	Love Makes Things Happen	MCA 53973
4/27/91	#88	4	Backyard*	MCA 53982
			*released as by PEBBLES with SALT-N-PEPA	
			BOBBY PEDRICK JR.	
11/01/58	#83	4	White Bucks And Saddle Shoes	Big Top 3004
			ANN PEEBLES	
9/19/70	#27	13	Part Time Love	Hi 2178
3/13/71	#84	4	I Pity The Fool	Hi 2186
2/12/72	#83	3	Breaking Up Somebody's Home	Hi 2205
9/15/73	#45	19	I Can't Stand The Rain	Hi 2248
			DAN PEEK	
10/06/79	#95	3	All Things Are Possible	Lamb & Lion 817
			PEELS	
3/12/66	#55	5	Juanita Banana	Karate 522
			NIA PEEPLES	
5/07/88	#45	14	Trouble	Mercury 870154
10/12/91	#8	21	Street Of Dreams	Charisma 98690
2/22/92	#54	9	Kissing The Wind	Charisma 98633
7/11/92	#88	4	Faces Of Love	Charisma 98568
			TEDDY PENDERGRASS	
5/28/77	#43	12	I Don't Love You Anymore	Philadelphia Int. 3622
7/01/78	#19	16	Close The Door	Philadelphia Int. 3648
6/30/79	#50	9	Turn Off The Lights	Philadelphia Int. 3696
8/30/80	#52	10	Can't We Try	Philadelphia Int. 3107
11/29/80	#41	15	Love T.K.O.	Philadelphia Int. 3116
5/09/81	#45	14	Two Hearts*	20th Century 2492
1/16/82	#49	9	You're My Latest, My Greatest Inspiration	Philadelphia Int. 2619
6/16/84	#46	16	Hold Me**	Asylum 69720
6/25/88	#81	5	Joy	Asylum 69401
			*released as by STEPHANIE MILLS featuring TEDDY PENDERGRASS	
			**released as by TEDDY PENDERGRASS with WHITNEY HOUSTON	
			PENGUINS	
2/19/55	#3	9	Earth Angel (Will You Be Mine)	Dootone 348
			CE CE PENISTON	
11/16/91	#7	27	Finally	A&M 1586
2/29/92	#19	23	We Got A Love Thang	A&M 1594
6/20/92	#12	23	Keep On Walkin'	A&M 1598
10/17/92	#90	5	Inside That I Cried	A&M 0059
			MICHAEL PENN	
1/20/90	#14	18	No Myth	RCA 9111
4/28/90	#49	10	This & That	RCA 2512
			PENTAGONS	
3/04/61	#56	10	To Be Loved (Forever)	Donna 1337
			PEOPLE	
3/23/68	#13	18	I Love You	Capitol 2078
			PEOPLE'S CHOICE	
7/31/71	#50	8	I Likes To Do It	Phil-L.A. Of Soul 349
8/09/75	#14	18	Do It Any Way You Wanna	TSOP 4769
1/31/76	#78	6	Nursery Rhymes (Part 1)	TSOP 4773
			PEPPERMINT RAINBOW	
1/04/69	#21	19	Will You Be Staying After Sunday	Decca 32410
6/07/69	#50	11	Don't Wake Me Up In The Morning Michael	Decca 32498
			PEPPERMINT TROLLEY COMPANY	
6/08/68	#45	8	Baby You Come Rollin' Across My Mind	Acta 815
			PEPPERS	
2/16/74	#61	10	Pepper Box	Event 213
			PEPSI and SHIRLIE	
8/22/87	#83	6	Heartache	Polydor 885470
2/20/88	#82	7	All Right Now	Polydor 887277

Debut Date	Peak Pos	Wks Chr	ARTIST/Song Title	Label & Number
			PERCELLS	
3/16/63	#63	7	What Are Boys Made Of	ABC-Paramount 10401
			PERFECT GENTLEMEN	
4/21/90	#9	16	Ooh La La (I Can't Get Over You)	Columbia 73211
			EMILIO PERICOLI	
5/19/62	#6	15	Al Di La'	Warner Brothers 5259
			CARL PERKINS	
4/14/56	#2	12	Blue Suede Shoes	Sun 234
1/25/58	#60	1	Lend Me Your Comb	Sun 287
5/23/59	#86	1	Pointed Toe Shoes	Columbia 41379
			GEORGE PERKINS & THE SILVER STARS	
3/21/70	#52	7	Cryin' In The Streets (Part 1)	Silver Fox 18
			JOE PERKINS	
9/28/63	#77	4	Little Eeefin Annie	Sound Stage 2511
			TONY PERKINS	
9/28/57	#41	5	Moon-Light Swim	RCA 7020
11/30/57	#60	1	When School Starts Again Next Year	RCA 7078
			JEAN JACQUES PERREY	
6/20/70	#94	2	Passport To The Future	Vanguard 35105
			STEVE PERRY	
8/28/82	#15	15	Don't Fight It*	Columbia 03192
4/07/84	#4	20	Oh Sherrie	Columbia 04391
6/30/84	#22	13	She's Mine	Columbia 04496
9/08/84	#38	12	Strung Out	Columbia 04598
11/24/84	#23	18	Foolish Heart	Columbia 04693
			*released as by **KENNY LOGGINS** with **STEVE PERRY**	
			PERSUADERS	
8/14/71	#10	15	Thin Line Between Love & Hate	Atco 6822
12/11/71	#54	10	Love Gonna Pack Up (And Walk Out)	Win Or Lose 220
11/18/72	#92	3	Peace In The Valley Of Love	Win Or Lose 225
6/02/73	#100	1	Bad Bold And Beautiful Girl	Atco 6919
10/20/73	#39	12	Some Guys Have All The Luck	Atco 6943
2/16/74	#64	4	Best Thing That Ever Happened To Me	Atco 6956
			PETER and GORDON	
5/09/64	#1	13	A World Without Love	Capitol 5175
6/27/64	#12	9	Nobody I Know	Capitol 5211
10/03/64	#18	9	I Don't Want To See You Again	Capitol 5272
1/09/65	#6	11	I Go To Pieces	Capitol 5335
4/11/65	#13	11	True Love Ways	Capitol 5406
7/10/65	#25	7	To Know You Is To Love You	Capitol 5461
11/13/65	#96	1	Don't Pity Me	Capitol 5532
2/12/66	#17	11	Woman	Capitol 5579
5/07/66	#61	5	There's No Livin' Without Your Lovin'	Capitol 5650
7/30/66	#92	1	To Show I Love You	Capitol 5684
10/08/66	#5	15	Lady Godiva	Capitol 5740
12/31/66	#13	9	Knight In Rusty Armour	Capitol 5808
3/25/67	#22	6	Sunday For Tea	Capitol 5864
1/20/68	#95	2	Never Ever	Capitol 2071
			PETER, PAUL & MARY	
4/28/62	#54	10	Lemon Tree	Warner Brothers 5274
8/11/62	#13	14	If I Had A Hammer (The Hammer Song)	Warner Brothers 5296
1/05/63	#98	1	Big Boat	Warner Brothers 5325
1/26/63	#94	3	Settle Down	Warner Brothers 5334
3/16/63	#2	15	Puff The Magic Dragon	Warner Brothers 5348
7/06/63	#2	14	Blowin' In The Wind	Warner Brothers 5368
9/21/63	#15	10	Don't Think Twice, It's All Right	Warner Brothers 5385
11/30/63	#38	8	Stewball	Warner Brothers 5399
12/21/63	#79	2	A Soalin'	Warner Brothers 5402
3/07/64	#31	8	Tell It On The Mountain	Warner Brothers 5418
1/23/65	#25	9	For Lovin' Me	Warner Brothers 5496
5/08/65	#83	3	When The Ship Comes In	Warner Brothers 5625
10/09/65	#96	2	Early Morning Rain	Warner Brothers 5659
4/23/66	#77	4	Cruel War	Warner Brothers 5809
8/26/67	#11	10	I Dig Rock And Roll Music	Warner Brothers 7067
11/25/67	#61	6	Too Much Of Nothing	Warner Brothers 7092

Debut Date	Peak Pos	Wks Chr	ARTIST/Song Title	Label & Number
4/19/69	#20	11	Day Is Done	Warner Brothers 7279
10/25/69	#1	17	Leaving On A Jet Plane	Warner Brothers 7340
			BERNADETTE PETERS	
3/29/80	#33	15	Gee Whiz	MCA 41210
8/08/81	#70	7	Dedicated To The One I Love	MCA 51152
			PAUL PETERSEN	
3/10/62	#32	12	She Can't Find Her Keys	Colpix 620
6/23/62	#95	4	Keep Your Love Locked	Colpix 632
9/01/62	#86	6	Lollipops And Roses	Colpix 649
11/10/62	#6	17	My Dad	Colpix 663
3/16/63	#69	6	Amy	Colpix 676
12/14/63	#93	4	Cheer Leader	Colpix 707
			BOBBY PETERSON QUINTET	
10/31/59	#46	8	The Hunch	V-Tone 205
9/10/60	#67	13	Irresistible You*	V-Tone 214
			*released as by BOBBY PETERSON	
			RAY PETERSON	
5/23/59	#19	13	The Wonder Of You	RCA 7513
9/12/59	#88	5	Come And Get It	RCA 7578
11/14/59	#50	10	Goodnight My Love	RCA 7635
6/25/60	#5	14	Tell Laura I Love Her	RCA 7745
12/03/60	#7	15	Corinna, Corinna	Dunes 2002
3/25/61	#93	2	Sweet Little Kathy	Dunes 2004
6/24/61	#27	20	Missing You	Dunes 2006
12/16/61	#65	8	I Could Have Loved You So Well	Dunes 2009
6/08/63	#73	5	Give Us Your Blessing	Dunes 2025
5/02/64	#98	1	The Wonder Of You	RCA 8333
1/16/65	#99	2	Across The Street	MGM 13299
			PETS	
5/24/58	#18	9	Cha-Hua-Hua	Arwin 109
			PET SHOP BOYS	
3/01/86	#1	22	West End Girls	EMI America 8307
5/31/86	#9	16	Opportunities (Let's Make Lots Of Money)	EMI America 8330
8/30/86	#56	9	Love Comes Quickly	EMI America 8338
11/22/86	#79	12	Suburbia	EMI America 8355
9/05/87	#12	23	It's A Sin	EMI America 43027
12/12/87	#1	21	What Have I Done To Deserve This?*	EMI-Manhattan 50107
3/26/88	#7	17	Always On My Mind	EMI-Manhattan 50123
10/08/88	#21	19	Domino Dancing	EMI-Manhattan 50161
1/28/89	#74	5	Left To My Own Devices	EMI-Manhattan 50171
10/27/90	#66	7	So Hard	EMI 50329
5/25/91	#81	5	Where The Streets Have No Name	EMI 50351
			*released as by the PET SHOP BOYS and DUSTY SPRINGFIELD	
			NORMAN PETTY TRIO	
2/23/57	#18	6	Almost Paradise	ABC-Paramount 9787
			TOM PETTY and THE HEARTBREAKERS	
12/03/77	#33	15	Breakdown	Shelter 62008
6/24/78	#53	9	I Need To Know	Shelter 62010
9/23/78	#73	6	Listen To Her Heart	Shelter 62011
11/17/79	#7	18	Don't Do Me Like That	Backstreet 41138
1/26/80	#11	16	Refugee	Backstreet 41169
4/26/80	#64	7	Here Comes My Girl	Backstreet 41227
5/02/81	#14	14	The Waiting	Backstreet 51100
7/25/81	#62	8	A Woman In Love (It's Not Me)	Backstreet 51136
7/25/81	#4	18	Stop Draggin' My Heart Around*	Modern 7336
11/13/82	#16	17	You Got Lucky	Backstreet 52144
2/26/83	#31	10	Change Of Heart	Backstreet 52181
3/16/85	#13	17	Don't Come Around Here No More	MCA 52496
6/08/85	#53	9	Make It Better (Forget About Me)	MCA 52605
8/24/85	#78	5	Rebels	MCA 52658
2/01/86	#43	12	Needles And Pins**	MCA 52772
4/25/87	#29	13	Jammin' Me	MCA 53065
4/29/89	#11	19	I Won't Back Down***	MCA 53369
8/12/89	#22	17	Runnin' Down A Dream***	MCA 53682
11/04/89	#6	22	Free Fallin'***	MCA 53728
2/24/90	#42	10	A Face In The Crowd***	MCA 53781

Debut Date	Peak Pos	Wks Chr	ARTIST/Song Title	Label & Number
			TOM PETTY and THE HEARTBREAKERS—*continued*	
6/22/91	#35	18	Learning To Fly	MCA 54124
11/16/91	#68	11	Into The Great Wide Open	MCA 54131
			*released as by STEVIE NICKS with TOM PETTY and THE HEARTBREAKERS	
			**released as by TOM PETTY and THE HEARTBREAKERS with STEVIE NICKS	
			***released as by TOM PETTY	
			PHARCYDE	
5/22/93	#49	12	Passin' Me By	Atlantic 98434
			JAMES PHELPS	
5/08/65	#48	7	Love Is A 5-Letter Word	Argo 5499
			PHILADELPHIA	
10/15/77	#99	2	School's Back	Warner Brothers 8470
			PHILADELPHIA INTERNATIONAL ALL STARS	
10/08/77	#100	1	Let's Clean Up The Ghetto	Philadelphia Int'l. 3627
			ESTHER PHILLIPS	
11/03/62	#8	14	Release Me*	Lenox 5555
2/09/63	#98	2	Am I That Easy To Forget*/	Lenox 5560
2/16/63	#85	3	I Really Don't Want To Know*	Lenox 5560
5/08/65	#58	8	And I Love Him	Atlantic 2281
5/28/66	#59	4	When A Woman Loves A Man	Atlantic 2335
4/01/72	#86	7	Home Is Where The Hatred Is	Kudu 904
12/23/72	#72	6	I've Never Found A Man	Kudu 910
8/16/75	#21	14	What A Diff'rence A Day Makes	Kudu 925
			*released as by LITTLE ESTHER PHILLIPS	
			JOHN PHILLIPS	
5/09/70	#37	12	Mississippi	Dunhill 4236
			PHIL PHILLIPS with THE TWILIGHTS	
6/27/59	#2	19	Sea Of Love	Mercury 71465
			SHAWN PHILLIPS	
2/10/73	#71	7	Lost Horizon	A&M 1405
			PHILLY DEVOTIONS	
2/15/75	#96	2	I Just Can't Say Goodbye	Columbia 10076
			JIM PHOTOGLO	
4/05/80	#45	12	We Were Meant To Be Lovers*	20th Century 2446
4/11/81	#23	18	Fool In Love With You	20th Century 2487
			*released as by PHOTOGLO	
			BOBBY "BORIS" PICKETT and THE CRYPT-KICKERS	
9/01/62	#1	16	Monster Mash	Garpax 44167
12/08/62	#29	6	Monster's Holiday	Garpax 44171
7/11/70	#72	4	Monster Mash	Parrot 348
5/12/73	#10	18	Monster Mash	Parrot 348
			WILSON PICKETT	
4/20/63	#57	4	If You Need Me	Double-L 713
7/20/63	#31	11	It's Too Late	Double-L 717
7/17/65	#22	12	In The Midnight Hour	Atlantic 2289
11/06/65	#100	1	It's All Over/	Atlantic 2306
11/27/65	#63	4	Don't Fight It	Atlantic 2306
2/12/66	#9	12	634-5789 (Soulsville U.S.A.)	Atlantic 2320
5/28/66	#45	6	Ninety-Nine And A Half (Won't Do)	Atlantic 2334
7/30/66	#9	10	Land Of 1000 Dances	Atlantic 2348
11/19/66	#16	11	Mustang Sally	Atlantic 2365
2/04/67	#40	7	Everybody Needs Somebody To Love	Atlantic 2381
4/01/67	#38	7	I Found A Love (Part 1)	Atlantic 2394
6/03/67	#63	3	You Can't Stand Alone/	Atlantic 2412
6/17/67	#87	2	Soul Dance Number Three	Atlantic 2412
8/05/67	#10	13	Funky Broadway	Atlantic 2430
10/28/67	#17	8	Stag-O-Lee/	Atlantic 2448
12/02/67	#40	9	I'm In Love	Atlantic 2448
2/24/68	#47	3	Jealous Love	Atlantic 2484
4/13/68	#23	10	She's Lookin' Good	Atlantic 2504
6/22/68	#23	8	I'm A Midnight Mover	Atlantic 2528
9/21/68	#40	4	I Found A True Love	Atlantic 2558
11/16/68	#48	6	A Man And A Half	Atlantic 2575
12/21/68	#20	10	Hey Jude	Atlantic 2591
3/22/69	#41	5	Mini-Skirt Minnie	Atlantic 2611

Debut Date	Peak Pos	Wks Chr	ARTIST/Song Title	Label & Number
5/10/69	#50	5	Born To Be Wild	Atlantic 2631
7/05/69	#40	7	Hey Joe	Atlantic 2648
11/29/69	#63	4	You Keep Me Hanging On	Atlantic 2682
3/28/70	#61	4	Cole, Cooke & Redding/	Atlantic 2722
5/02/70	#16	11	Sugar Sugar	Atlantic 2722
8/22/70	#52	4	She Said Yes	Atlantic 2753
9/26/70	#14	13	Engine Number 9	Atlantic 2765
1/16/71	#40	7	Don't Let The Green Grass Fool You	Atlantic 2781
4/24/71	#7	13	Don't Knock My Love (Part 1)	Atlantic 2797
8/21/71	#41	7	Call My Name, I'll Be There	Atlantic 2824
12/25/71	#17	11	Fire And Water	Atlantic 2852
5/20/72	#53	7	Funk Factory	Atlantic 2878
11/11/72	#81	4	Mama Told Me Not To Come	Atlantic 2909
3/17/73	#83	3	Mr. Magic Man	RCA 0898
9/15/73	#58	6	Take A Closer Look At The Woman You're With	RCA 0049
			PICKETTYWITCH	
5/16/70	#40	12	That Same Old Feeling	Janus 118
			PIECES OF EIGHT	
6/17/67	#58	8	Lonely Drifter	A&M 854
			WEBB PIERCE	
8/15/59	#25	11	I Ain't Never	Decca 30923
1/09/60	#60	7	No Love Have I	Decca 31021
			PILOT	
4/05/75	#5	19	Magic	EMI 3992
10/11/75	#75	5	Just A Smile	EMI 4135
2/07/76	#87	6	January	EMI 4202
			PILTDOWN MEN	
9/24/60	#82	2	Brontosaurus Stomp	Capitol 4414
			MIKE PINERA	
1/12/80	#71	5	Goodnight My Love	Spector 00003
			PING PING	
5/13/61	#90	4	Sucu Sucu	Kapp 377
			PINK FLOYD	
5/19/73	#10	15	Money	Harvest 3609
2/23/74	#72	3	Us And Them	Harvest 3832
1/19/80	#1	25	Another Brick In The Wall (Part 2)	Columbia 11187
5/17/80	#77	4	Run Like Hell	Columbia 11265
10/10/87	#83	6	Learning To Fly	Columbia 07363
			PINK LADY	
6/09/79	#49	10	Kiss In The Dark	Elektra 46040
			PIPKINS	
5/16/70	#7	13	Gimme Dat Ding	Capitol 2819
			PIPS (see GLADYS KNIGHT & THE PIPS)	
			GENE PITNEY	
1/14/61	#31	13	(I Wanna) Love My Life Away	Musicor 1002
5/13/61	#88	3	Louisiana Mama	Musicor 1006
8/05/61	#34	11	Every Breath I Take	Musicor 1011
11/18/61	#11	18	Town Without Pity	Musicor 1009
5/05/62	#8	13	(The Man Who Shot) Liberty Valence	Musicor 1020
9/01/62	#5	17	Only Love Can Break A Heart/	Musicor 1022
9/01/62	#67	6	If I Didn't Have A Dime	Musicor 1022
12/15/62	#14	13	Half Heaven - Half Heartache	Musicor 1026
3/16/63	#13	12	Mecca	Musicor 1028
7/13/63	#30	11	True Love Never Runs Smooth	Musicor 1032
10/26/63	#18	11	Twenty Four Hours From Tulsa	Musicor 1034
1/18/64	#50	7	That Girl Belongs To Yesterday	Musicor 1036
5/16/64	#97	2	Yesterday's Hero	Musicor 1038
8/01/64	#15	15	It Hurts To Be In Love	Musicor 1040
10/24/64	#11	12	I'm Gonna Be Strong	Musicor 1045
2/20/65	#26	9	I Must Be Seeing Things	Musicor 1070
3/27/65	#97	2	I've Got Five Dollars And It's Saturday Night*	Musicor 1066
5/08/65	#16	9	Last Chance To Turn Around	Musicor 1093
7/31/65	#23	7	Looking Through The Eyes Of Love	Musicor 1103
11/13/65	#34	9	Princess In Rags	Musicor 1130

Debut Date	Peak Pos	Wks Chr	ARTIST/Song Title	Label & Number
			GENE PITNEY—*continued*	
3/05/66	#87	2	Nessuno Mi Puo' Giudcare	Musicor 1155
4/16/66	#24	9	Backstage	Musicor 1171
10/01/66	#83	2	(In The) Cold Light Of Day	Musicor 1200
12/03/66	#76	8	Just One Smile	Musicor 1219
5/04/68	#16	14	She's A Heartbreaker	Musicor 1306
11/09/68	#92	4	Billy You're My Friend	Musicor 1331
			***released as by GEORGE and GENE (George Jones and Gene Pitney)**	
			PIXIES THREE	
8/17/63	#48	10	Birthday Party	Mercury 72130
1/11/64	#51	9	442 Glenwood Avenue	Mercury 72208
4/18/64	#79	4	Gee	Mercury 72250
			MARY KAY PLACE	
10/23/76	#66	8	Baby Boy	Columbia 10422
			PLANET P	
4/02/83	#51	11	Why Me?	Geffen 29705
			ROBERT PLANT	
9/18/82	#79	5	Burning Down One Side	Swan Song 99979
11/13/82	#90	6	Pledge Pin	Swan Song 99952
8/13/83	#21	16	Big Log	Atlantic 99844
11/26/83	#36	12	In The Mood	Es Paranza 99820
5/18/85	#34	14	Little By Little	Es Paranza 99644
4/23/88	#31	17	Tall Cool One	Es Paranza 99348
3/24/90	#47	10	Hurting Kind (I've Got My Eyes On You)	Es Paranza 98985
			PLASTIC ONO BAND (see JOHN LENNON)	
			EDDIE PLATT	
5/24/58	#18	9	Cha-Hua-Hua	Gone 5031
			PLATTERS	
11/05/55	#3	13	Only You (And You Alone)	Mercury 70633
1/21/56	#1	12	The Great Pretender	Mercury 70753
5/05/56	#3	9	(You've Got) The Magic Touch	Mercury 70819
8/04/56	#1	18	My Prayer	Mercury 70893
9/29/56	#14	13	You'll Never Never Know/	Mercury 70948
9/29/56	#14	12	It Isn't Right	Mercury 70948
12/22/56	#24	11	On My Word Of Honor/	Mercury 71011
12/29/56	#36	6	One In A Million	Mercury 71011
3/16/57	#15	12	I'm Sorry/	Mercury 71032
3/23/57	#31	7	He's Mine	Mercury 71032
6/01/57	#22	9	My Dream	Mercury 71093
9/28/57	#56	1	The Mystery Of You/	Mercury 71184
10/05/57	#41	3	Only Because	Mercury 71184
1/25/58	#38	5	Helpless	Mercury 71246
4/05/58	#1	18	Twilight Time	Mercury 71289
6/14/58	#32	9	You're Making A Mistake	Mercury 71320
9/13/58	#34	12	I Wish/	Mercury 71353
10/04/58	#59	5	It's Raining Outside	Mercury 71353
11/22/58	#1	20	Smoke Gets In Your Eyes	Mercury 71383
3/21/59	#12	14	Enchanted	Mercury 71427
6/20/59	#26	11	Remember When	Mercury 71467
9/05/59	#38	10	Where/	Mercury 71502
9/26/59	#85	3	Wish It Were Me	Mercury 71502
12/12/59	#98	1	My Secret/	Mercury 71538
12/19/59	#83	4	What Does It Matter	Mercury 71538
1/30/60	#7	15	Harbor Lights	Mercury 71563
5/14/60	#38	7	Ebb Tide	Mercury 71624
7/23/60	#27	11	Red Sails In The Sunset	Mercury 71656
10/08/60	#14	13	To Each His Own	Mercury 71697
1/07/61	#35	9	If I Didn't Care	Mercury 71749
4/01/61	#51	6	Trees	Mercury 71791
7/29/61	#32	10	I'll Never Smile Again	Mercury 71847
2/17/62	#88	3	It's Magic	Mercury 71921
4/23/66	#35	13	I Love You 1000 Times	Musicor 1166
11/12/66	#92	2	I'll Be Home	Musicor 1211
2/25/67	#19	13	With This Ring	Musicor 1229
7/01/67	#54	8	Washed Ashore	Musicor 1251
10/21/67	#83	6	Sweet Sweet Lovin'	Musicor 1275

Debut Date	Peak Pos	Wks Chr	ARTIST/Song Title	Label & Number
			PLAYBOYS	
7/12/58	#29	12	Over The Weekend	Cameo 142
			PLAYER	
10/01/77	#1	27	Baby Come Back	RSO 879
3/11/78	#13	16	This Time I'm In It For Love	RSO 890
9/09/78	#30	13	Prisoner Of Your Love	RSO 908
12/30/78	#74	6	Silver Lining	RSO 914
6/14/80	#72	7	It's For You	Casablanca 2265
1/23/82	#52	9	If Looks Could Kill	RCA 13006
			PLAYERS	
9/10/66	#100	1	He'll Be Back	Minit 32001
			PLAYMATES	
1/11/58	#19	9	Jo-Ann	Roulette 4037
3/29/58	#45	3	Let's Be Lovers	Roulette 4056
5/24/58	#23	11	Don't Go Home	Roulette 4072
11/01/58	#4	15	Beep Beep	Roulette 4115
7/11/59	#15	12	What Is Love?	Roulette 4160
10/08/60	#28	13	Wait For Me	Roulette 4276
2/25/61	#47	8	Little Miss Stuck-Up	Roulette 4322
			JACK PLEIS	
11/10/56	#50	1	I'll Always Be In Love With You	Decca 30086
			P.M. DAWN	
10/19/91	#4	22	Set Adrift On Memory Bliss	Gee Street 866094
1/25/92	#14	16	Paper Doll	Gee Street 866375
9/19/92	#3	31	I'd Die Without You	Laface 4034
3/27/93	#1	30	Looking Through Patient Eyes	Gee Street 862024
7/31/93	#51	13	The Ways Of The Wind	Gee Street 862475
			P-NUT GALLERY	
6/05/71	#54	6	Do You Know What Time It Is?	Buddah 239
			POCKETS	
12/31/77	#94	4	Come Go With Me	Columbia 10632
			POCO	
9/19/70	#74	9	You Better Think Twice	Epic 10636
3/20/71	#63	8	C'mon	Epic 10714
11/06/71	#88	3	Just For Me And You	Epic 10804
9/20/75	#45	9	Keep On Tryin'	ABC 12126
7/23/77	#62	11	Indian Summer	ABC 12295
1/13/79	#14	18	Crazy Love	ABC 12439
5/12/79	#19	14	Heart Of The Night	MCA 41023
7/12/80	#45	11	Under The Gun	MCA 41269
10/11/80	#89	5	Midnight Rain	MCA 41326
3/20/82	#95	3	Sea Of Heartbreak	MCA 52001
12/25/82	#44	13	Shoot For The Moon	Atlantic 89919
8/26/89	#18	22	Call It Love	RCA 9038
			POETS	
3/19/66	#38	11	She Blew A Good Thing	Symbol 214
			BUSTER POINDEXTER	
12/19/87	#60	12	Hot Hot Hot	RCA 5357
			POINT BLANK	
4/18/81	#94	5	Let Me Stay With You Tonight	MCA 51083
6/27/81	#58	15	Nicole	MCA 51132
			BONNIE POINTER	
11/18/78	#99	1	Free Me From My Freedom	Motown 1451
6/23/79	#10	23	Heaven Must Have Sent You	Motown 1459
12/22/79	#43	13	I Can't Help Myself	Motown 1478
			POINTER SISTERS	
8/18/73	#10	14	Yes We Can Can	Blue Thumb 229
12/22/73	#69	8	Wang Dang Doodle	Blue Thumb 243
3/23/74	#84	4	Steam Heat	Blue Thumb 248
10/12/74	#19	13	Fairytale	Blue Thumb 254
3/01/75	#72	5	Live Your Life Before You Die	Blue Thumb 262
7/26/75	#17	13	How Long (Betcha' Got A Chick On The Side)	Blue Thumb 265
11/22/75	#51	7	Going Down Slowly	Blue Thumb 268
11/11/78	#2	23	Fire	Planet 45901
3/10/79	#28	11	Happiness	Planet 45902

Debut Date	Peak Pos	Wks Chr	ARTIST/Song Title	Label & Number
			POINTER SISTERS—*continued*	
7/26/80	#3	29	He's So Shy	Planet 47916
11/08/80	#64	11	Could I Be Dreaming	Planet 47920
5/30/81	#2	24	Slow Hand	Planet 47929
1/16/82	#16	17	Should I Do It	Planet 47960
6/26/82	#15	15	American Music	Planet 13254
9/18/82	#33	17	I'm So Excited	Planet 13327
3/26/83	#60	7	If You Wanna Get Back Your Lady	Planet 13430
10/15/83	#49	15	I Need You	Planet 13639
1/28/84	#8	22	Automatic	Planet 13730
4/28/84	#6	25	Jump (For My Love)	Planet 13780
8/04/84	#10	20	I'm So Excited	Planet 13857
11/24/84	#10	22	Neutron Dance	Planet 13951
3/23/85	#41	10	Baby Come And Get It	Planet 14041
7/13/85	#12	17	Dare Me	RCA 14126
11/02/85	#52	11	Freedom	RCA 14224
3/15/86	#82	6	Twist My Arm	RCA 14197
11/01/86	#31	14	Goldmine	RCA 5062
8/08/87	#56	9	Be There	MCA 53120
			POISON	
3/14/87	#15	17	Talk Dirty To Me	Capitol 5686
6/13/87	#55	12	I Want Action	Enigma 44004
9/05/87	#16	24	I Won't Forget You	Enigma 44038
4/23/88	#12	19	Nothin' But A Good Time	Enigma 44145
7/30/88	#15	16	Fallen Angel	Enigma 44191
10/29/88	#1	20	Every Rose Has Its Thorn	Enigma 44203
2/11/89	#11	19	Your Mama Don't Dance	Enigma 44293
7/07/90	#3	18	Unskinny Bop	Enigma 44584
10/06/90	#5	22	Something To Believe In	Enigma 44617
2/02/91	#36	15	Ride The Wind	Enigma 44616
5/18/91	#42	18	Life Goes On	Capitol 44705
2/06/93	#51	12	Stand	Capitol 44905
			POLICE	
2/10/79	#31	15	Roxanne	A&M 2096
11/17/79	#62	10	Message In A Bottle	A&M 2190
10/25/80	#13	22	De Do Do Do, De Da Da Da	A&M 2275
2/07/81	#9	18	Don't Stand So Close To Me	A&M 2301
9/26/81	#6	20	Every Little Thing She Does Is Magic	A&M 2371
1/16/82	#15	15	Spirits In The Material World	A&M 2390
4/10/82	#47	9	Secret Journey	A&M 2408
6/04/83	#1	27	Every Breath You Take	A&M 2542
8/27/83	#5	20	King Of Pain	A&M 2569
11/05/83	#15	14	Synchronicity II	A&M 2571
1/14/84	#11	15	Wrapped Around Your Finger	A&M 2614
10/25/86	#56	8	Don't Stand So Close To Me '86	A&M 2879
			MICHEL POLNAREFF	
2/21/76	#66	7	If You Only Believe (Jesus For Tonite)	Atlantic 3314
			PONDEROSA TWINS + ONE	
9/25/71	#63	5	You Send Me	Horoscope 102
			PONI-TAILS	
2/16/57	#35	3	Your Wild Heart	Point 8
7/19/58	#10	18	Born Too Late	ABC-Paramount 9934
11/29/58	#77	4	Seven Minutes In Heaven	ABC-Paramount 9969
10/03/59	#48	7	I'll Be Seeing You	ABC-Paramount 10047
			IGGY POP	
12/01/90	#35	18	Candy*	Virgin 98900
			***released as by IGGY POP with KATE PIERSON**	
			POPPIES	
2/26/66	#67	7	Lullaby Of Love	Epic 9893
5/28/66	#94	3	He's Ready	Epic 10019
			POPPY FAMILY	
3/14/70	#2	19	Which Way You Goin' Billy?*	London 129
8/01/70	#20	14	That's Where I Went Wrong*	London 139
4/03/71	#90	2	I Was Wondering/	London 148
7/31/71	#50	12	Where Evil Grows	London 148
12/11/71	#80	3	No Good To Cry	London 164

270

Debut Date	Peak Pos	Wks Chr	ARTIST/Song Title	Label & Number
2/12/72	#74	4	Good Friends . . . . London 172	
			*released as by THE POPPY FAMILY featuring SUSAN JACKS	
			POP-TOPS	
10/16/71	#68	6	Mammy Blue . . . . ABC 11311	
			PORNO FOR PYROS	
7/17/93	#58	10	Pets . . . . Warner Brothers 18480	
			NOLAN PORTER	
9/25/71	#70	9	I Like What You Give* . . . . Lizard 1008	
12/18/71	#95	1	Keep On Keeping On** . . . . Lizard 1010	
			*released as by NOLAN	
			**released as by N.F. PORTER	
			GARY PORTNOY	
5/14/83	#93	5	Where Everybody Knows Your Name . . . . Applause 106	
			PORTRAIT	
11/21/92	#10	27	Here We Go Again! . . . . Capitol 44865	
			SANDY POSEY	
7/23/66	#12	15	Born A Woman . . . . MGM 13501	
11/26/66	#13	11	Single Girl . . . . MGM 13612	
3/11/67	#39	7	What A Woman In Love Won't Do . . . . . . MGM 13702	
6/03/67	#17	13	I Take It Back . . . . MGM 13744	
10/14/67	#68	6	Are You Never Coming Home . . . . MGM 13824	
3/02/68	#83	3	Something I'll Remember . . . . MGM 13892	
			POSITIVE K	
12/26/92	#24	25	I Got A Man . . . . Island 864305	
			MIKE POST	
5/24/75	#10	16	The Rockford Files . . . . MGM 14772	
9/27/75	#64	7	Manhattan Spiritual . . . . MGM 14829	
4/02/77	#96	4	Theme From Baa Baa Black Sheep . . . . . Epic 50325	
8/22/81	#15	23	The Theme From Hill Street Blues . . . . Elektra 47186	
2/13/82	#27	17	Theme From Magnum P.I. . . . . Elektra 47400	
			POTLIQUOR	
2/12/72	#64	8	Cheer . . . . Janus 179	
			FRANK POURCEL	
4/04/59	#8	15	Only You . . . . Capitol 4165	
			POUSETTE-DART BAND	
9/01/79	#91	5	For Love . . . . Capitol 4764	
			BOBBY POWELL	
11/13/65	#60	12	C.C. Rider . . . . Whit 714	
			COZY POWELL	
3/23/74	#50	8	Dance With The Devil . . . . Chrysalis 2029	
			JANE POWELL	
9/08/56	#4	15	True Love . . . . Verve 2018	
			JOEY POWERS	
11/09/63	#10	14	Midnight Mary . . . . Amy 892	
			POWER SOURCE	
12/19/87	#73	7	Dear Mr. Jesus . . . . Power Vision 8603	
			POWER STATION	
3/16/85	#6	19	Some Like It Hot . . . . Capitol 5444	
6/08/85	#10	19	Get It On (Bang A Gong) . . . . Capitol 5479	
9/07/85	#32	12	Communication . . . . Capitol 5511	
			POZO-SECO SINGERS	
1/08/66	#44	6	Time . . . . Columbia 43437	
9/17/66	#41	10	I Can Make It With You . . . . Columbia 43784	
12/17/66	#47	9	Look What You've Done . . . . Columbia 43927	
			PEREZ PRADO	
4/16/55	#1	20	Cherry Pink And Apple Blossom White . . . RCA 5965	
6/14/58	#1	25	Patricia . . . . RCA 7245	
10/04/58	#18	12	Guaglione . . . . RCA 7337	
2/28/59	#82	4	Millionaire . . . . RCA 7456	
			ANDY PRATT	
5/26/73	#69	6	Avenging Annie . . . . Columbia 45804	

271

Debut Date	Peak Pos	Wks Chr	**ARTIST**/Song Title	Label & Number
			PRATT & McCLAIN	
4/03/76	#6	16	Happy Days	Reprise 1351
			PRECISIONS	
9/30/67	#71	6	If This Is Love (I'd Rather Be Lonely)	Drew 1003
			PRELUDE	
9/14/74	#17	15	After The Goldrush	Island 002
12/06/75	#66	8	For A Dancer	Pye 71045
			PREMIERS	
6/20/64	#19	9	Farmer John	Warner Brothers 5443
			PRESIDENTS	
10/03/70	#7	15	5-10-15-20 (25-30 Years Of Love)	Sussex 207
1/30/71	#52	7	Triangle Of Love (Hey Diddle Diddle)	Sussex 212
			ELVIS PRESLEY	
4/21/56	#1	11	Heartbreak Hotel	RCA 6420
7/07/56	#4	14	I Want You, I Need You, I Love You	RCA 6540
8/04/56	#1	20	Hound Dog/	RCA 6604
8/11/56	#1	23	Don't Be Cruel	RCA 6604
9/29/56	#42	3	Blue Moon	RCA 6640
10/06/56	#1	21	Love Me Tender	RCA 6643
10/13/56	#50	1	I Don't Care If The Sun Don't Shine (EP)	RCA 965
12/01/56	#10	13	Love Me (EP)	RCA 992
1/26/57	#1	14	Too Much/	RCA 6800
1/26/57	#33	4	Playing For Keeps	RCA 6800
4/06/57	#1	18	All Shook Up	RCA 6870
4/06/57	#32	7	(There'll Be) Peace In The Valley (For Me) (EP)	RCA 4054
6/29/57	#1	16	(Let Me Be Your) Teddy Bear/	RCA 7000
7/06/57	#21	9	Loving You	RCA 7000
10/05/57	#1	20	Jailhouse Rock/	RCA 7035
10/19/57	#56	2	Treat Me Nice	RCA 7035
1/25/58	#1	13	Don't/	RCA 7150
1/25/58	#9	9	I Beg Of You	RCA 7150
4/19/58	#4	14	Wear My Ring Around Your Neck	RCA 7240
6/28/58	#3	15	Hard Headed Woman/	RCA 7280
7/05/58	#54	6	Don't Ask Me Why	RCA 7280
7/26/58	#20	13	King Creole (EP)	RCA 4319
11/08/58	#3	16	One Night/	RCA 7410
11/08/58	#5	14	I Got Stung	RCA 7410
3/28/59	#2	13	(Now And Then There's) A Fool Such As I/	RCA 7506
3/28/59	#6	12	I Need Your Love Tonight	RCA 7506
7/11/59	#2	13	A Big Hunk O' Love/	RCA 7600
7/18/59	#23	11	My Wish Came True	RCA 7600
4/09/60	#1	15	Stuck On You/	RCA 7740
4/09/60	#40	9	Fame And Fortune	RCA 7740
7/23/60	#1	19	It's Now Or Never/	RCA 7777
8/06/60	#84	2	A Mess Of Blues	RCA 7777
11/19/60	#1	16	Are You Lonesome Tonight?/	RCA 7810
11/26/60	#46	5	I Gotta Know	RCA 7810
2/25/61	#1	13	Surrender/	RCA 7850
3/11/61	#82	3	Lonely Man	RCA 7850
4/22/61	#30	7	Flaming Star (EP)	RCA 128
5/20/61	#5	10	I Feel So Bad/	RCA 7880
5/20/61	#42	8	Wild In The Country	RCA 7880
8/26/61	#5	13	Little Sister/	RCA 7908
8/26/61	#21	11	(Marie's The Name) His Latest Flame	RCA 7908
12/09/61	#4	15	Can't Help Falling In Love/	RCA 7968
12/09/61	#28	9	Rock-A-Hula Baby	RCA 7968
3/17/62	#1	14	Good Luck Charm/	RCA 7992
3/17/62	#51	8	Anything That's Part Of You	RCA 7992
5/05/62	#18	12	Follow That Dream (EP)	RCA 4368
8/04/62	#4	12	She's Not You/	RCA 8041
8/04/62	#64	6	Just Tell Her Jim Said Hello	RCA 8041
9/08/62	#31	9	Kid Galahad (EP)	RCA 4371
10/20/62	#1	17	Return To Sender	RCA 8100
2/16/63	#10	10	One Broken Heart For Sale/	RCA 8134
2/23/63	#87	2	They Remind Me Of You	RCA 8134
7/06/63	#3	12	(You're The) Devil In Disguise	RCA 8188
10/12/63	#8	13	Bossa Nova Baby/	RCA 8243
10/19/63	#33	8	Witchcraft	RCA 8243
2/22/64	#10	11	Kissin' Cousins/	RCA 8307

Debut Date	Peak Pos	Wks Chr	**ARTIST**/Song Title	Label & Number
3/07/64	#48	7	It Hurts Me	RCA 8307
5/02/64	#38	7	Kiss Me Quick (EP)	RCA 0639
5/16/64	#13	9	What'd I Say/	RCA 8360
5/16/64	#16	8	Viva Las Vegas	RCA 8360
7/25/64	#16	8	Such A Night	RCA 8400
10/10/64	#13	10	Ain't That Loving You Baby/	RCA 8440
10/17/64	#10	12	Ask Me	RCA 8440
2/27/65	#16	8	Do The Clam	RCA 8500
4/24/65	#4	16	Crying In The Chapel	RCA 0643
6/12/65	#14	10	(Such An) Easy Question/	RCA 8585
6/19/65	#57	4	It Feels So Right	RCA 8585
8/14/65	#71	4	Tickle Me (EP)	RCA 4383
8/28/65	#9	12	I'm Yours/	RCA 8657
8/28/65	#96	1	Long Lonely Highway	RCA 8657
11/13/65	#15	10	Puppet On A String	RCA 0650
1/01/66	#20	9	Tell Me Why/	RCA 8740
1/08/66	#96	1	Blue River	RCA 8740
3/19/66	#19	8	Frankie And Johnny/	RCA 8780
3/26/66	#62	5	Please Don't Stop Loving Me	RCA 8780
6/25/66	#19	8	Love Letters/	RCA 8870
6/25/66	#94	1	Come What May	RCA 8870
10/01/66	#32	8	Spinout/	RCA 8941
10/01/66	#39	8	All That I Am	RCA 8941
1/21/67	#26	10	Indescribably Blue	RCA 9056
5/13/67	#35	7	Long Legged Girl (With The Short Dress On)	RCA 9115
8/26/67	#45	5	There's Always Me	RCA 9287
10/14/67	#35	7	You Don't Know Me/	RCA 9341
10/14/67	#42	7	Big Boss Man	RCA 9341
1/27/68	#39	6	Guitar Man/	RCA 9425
2/03/68	#69	3	Hi-Heel Sneakers	RCA 9425
3/16/68	#26	11	U.S. Male/	RCA 9465
3/16/68	#50	3	Stay Away	RCA 9465
6/15/68	#55	6	Let Yourself Go/	RCA 9547
6/15/68	#63	4	Your Time Hasn't Come Yet, Baby	RCA 9547
9/28/68	#53	6	A Little Less Conversation/	RCA 9610
10/05/68	#91	2	Almost In Love	RCA 9610
11/30/68	#9	14	If I Can Dream	RCA 9670
3/15/69	#24	7	Memories	RCA 9731
5/03/69	#1	13	In The Ghetto	RCA 9741
7/05/69	#25	7	Clean Up Your Own Back Yard	RCA 9747
9/13/69	#1	13	Suspicious Minds	RCA 9764
11/29/69	#6	13	Don't Cry Daddy/	RCA 9768
12/06/69	#68	3	Rubberneckin'	RCA 9768
2/14/70	#10	9	Kentucky Rain	RCA 9791
5/09/70	#10	13	The Wonder Of You/	RCA 9835
5/09/70	#65	2	Mama Liked The Roses	RCA 9835
8/01/70	#18	8	I've Lost You/	RCA 9873
8/01/70	#30	9	The Next Step Is Love	RCA 9873
10/24/70	#10	9	You Don't Have To Say You Love Me	RCA 9916
12/26/70	#13	10	I Really Don't Want To Know/	RCA 9960
12/26/70	#57	3	There Goes My Everything	RCA 9960
3/06/71	#34	7	Where Did They Go, Lord/	RCA 9980
3/13/71	#45	5	Rags To Riches	RCA 9980
5/15/71	#40	6	Life	RCA 9985
7/10/71	#36	8	I'm Leavin'	RCA 9998
10/16/71	#51	4	It's Only Love	RCA 1017
1/22/72	#31	8	Until It's Time For You To Go	RCA 0619
5/06/72	#73	5	An American Trilogy	RCA 0672
8/19/72	#1	16	Burning Love	RCA 0769
11/25/72	#15	14	Separate Ways	RCA 0815
4/14/73	#10	11	Steamroller Blues/	RCA 0910
5/12/73	#79	2	Fool	RCA 0910
9/22/73	#27	9	Raised On Rock	RCA 0088
2/02/74	#30	10	I've Got A Thing About You Baby/	RCA 0196
2/02/74	#63	3	Take Good Care Of Her	RCA 0196
6/01/74	#23	12	If You Talk In Your Sleep	RCA 0280
10/19/74	#22	14	Promised Land	RCA 10074
1/25/75	#17	11	My Boy	RCA 10191
5/10/75	#40	8	T-R-O-U-B-L-E	RCA 10278
11/01/75	#75	5	Bringing It Back	RCA 10401
3/27/76	#31	11	Hurt	RCA 10601

273

Debut Date	Peak Pos	Wks Chr	ARTIST/Song Title	Label & Number
			ELVIS PRESLEY—*continued*	
12/18/76	#39	16	Moody Blue	RCA 10857
6/18/77	#25	21	Way Down	RCA 10998
11/12/77	#31	12	My Way (live)	RCA 11165
1/24/81	#30	14	Guitar Man	RCA 12158
11/20/82	#71	10	The Elvis Medley	RCA 13351
			BILLY PRESTON	
7/26/69	#74	7	That's The Way God Planned It	Apple 1808
2/13/71	#82	4	My Sweet Lord	Apple 1826
2/05/72	#96	2	I Wrote A Simple Song/	A&M 1320
4/22/72	#1	16	Outa-Space	A&M 1320
8/19/72	#96	1	That's The Way God Planned It	Apple 1808
9/09/72	#46	8	Slaughter	A&M 1380
3/03/73	#1	24	Will It Go Round In Circles	A&M 1411
9/15/73	#6	15	Space Race	A&M 1463
12/29/73	#30	10	You're So Unique	A&M 1492
7/13/74	#1	18	Nothing From Nothing	A&M 1544
12/07/74	#22	10	Struttin'	A&M 1644
10/11/75	#81	4	Fancy Lady	A&M 1735
12/29/79	#5	27	With You I'm Born Again*	Motown 1477
6/14/80	#50	12	One More Time For Love*	Tamla 54312
			***released as by BILLY PRESTON & SYREETA**	
			JOHNNY PRESTON	
10/17/59	#1	25	Running Bear	Mercury 71474
3/19/60	#6	16	Cradle Of Love	Mercury 71598
6/25/60	#9	15	Feel So Fine	Mercury 71651
10/15/60	#59	7	Charming Billy	Mercury 71691
1/28/61	#80	6	Leave My Kitten Alone	Mercury 71761
1/06/62	#97	2	Free Me	Mercury 71908
			MIKE PRESTON	
11/08/58	#57	9	A House, A Car And A Wedding Ring	London 1834
			PRETENDERS	
2/23/80	#13	22	Brass In Pocket (I'm Special)	Sire 49181
6/14/80	#76	5	Stop Your Sobbing	Sire 49506
12/18/82	#5	25	Back On The Chain Gang	Sire 29840
12/17/83	#13	18	Middle Of The Road	Sire 29444
3/17/84	#33	14	Show Me	Sire 29317
10/11/86	#11	20	Don't Get Me Wrong	Sire 28630
2/07/87	#75	7	My Baby	Sire 28496
			PRETTY POISON	
10/03/87	#8	24	(Catch Me) I'm Falling	Virgin 99416
4/02/88	#34	14	Nightime	Virgin 99350
			ANDRE PREVIN with DAVID ROSE	
6/06/59	#31	14	Like Young	MGM 12792
			LLOYD PRICE	
3/09/57	#22	12	Just Because	ABC-Paramount 9792
12/20/58	#1	17	Stagger Lee	ABC-Paramount 9972
2/28/59	#19	10	Where Were You (On Our Wedding Day?)	ABC-Paramount 9997
5/02/59	#2	18	Personality	ABC-Paramount 10018
8/08/59	#2	14	I'm Gonna Get Married/	ABC-Paramount 10032
8/08/59	#76	3	Three Little Pigs	ABC-Paramount 10032
10/31/59	#16	14	Come Into My Heart/	ABC-Paramount 10062
11/14/59	#53	8	Wont'cha Come Home	ABC-Paramount 10062
2/06/60	#11	12	Lady Luck	ABC-Paramount 10075
4/23/60	#38	8	No If's - No And's/	ABC-Paramount 10102
4/23/60	#43	7	For Love	ABC-Paramount 10102
6/25/60	#21	13	Question	ABC-Paramount 10123
9/10/60	#76	5	Just Call Me (And I'll Understand)/	ABC-Paramount 10139
9/24/60	#95	2	Who Coulda' Told You (They Lied)	ABC-Paramount 10139
11/19/60	#72	5	(You Better) Know What You're Doin'	ABC-Paramount 10162
1/21/61	#84	3	I'm Gonna Cry	ABC-Paramount 10177
9/28/63	#21	11	Misty	Double-L 722
8/25/73	#95	3	Trying To Slip (Away)	GSF 6904
			RAY PRICE	
4/01/67	#84	4	Danny Boy	Columbia 44042
9/05/70	#13	23	For The Good Times	Columbia 45178
3/13/71	#51	8	I Won't Mention It Again	Columbia 45329

Debut Date	Peak Pos	Wks Chr	ARTIST/Song Title	Label & Number
8/07/71	#63	7	I'd Rather Be Sorry	Columbia 45425
1/20/73	#78	4	She's Got To Be A Saint	Columbia 45724
9/01/73	#75	6	You're The Best Thing That Ever Happened To Me	Columbia 45889
			CHARLEY PRIDE	
8/23/69	#86	4	All I Have To Offer You (Is Me)	RCA 0167
3/21/70	#93	3	Is Anybody Goin' To San Antone	RCA 9806
10/31/70	#81	6	I Can't Believe That You've Stopped Loving Me	RCA 9902
11/27/71	#19	14	Kiss An Angel Good Mornin'	RCA 0550
3/04/72	#95	1	All His Children*	RCA 0624
			*released as by CHARLEY PRIDE with HENRY MANCINI	
			MAXI PRIEST	
10/29/88	#25	19	Wild World	Virgin 99269
7/07/90	#4	28	Close To You	Charisma 98951
12/15/90	#53	13	Just A Little Bit Longer	Charisma 98883
9/21/91	#5	27	Set The Night To Music*	Atlantic 87607
11/23/91	#67	11	Housecall**	Epic 73928
11/07/92	#57	13	Groovin' In The Midnight	Charisma 12617
			*released as by ROBERTA FLACK with MAXI PRIEST	
			**released as by SHABBA RANKS featuring MAXI PRIEST	
			LOUIS PRIMA & KEELY SMITH	
12/30/50	#8	4	Oh Babe!*	Robin Hood 101
11/01/58	#13	14	That Old Black Magic	Capitol 4063
2/21/59	#77	4	I've Got You Under My Skin	Capitol 4140
7/04/59	#50	8	Bei Mir Bist Du Schon	Dot 15956
12/24/60	#2	2	Wonderland By Night*	Dot 16151
			*released as by LOUIS PRIMA	
			PRINCE	
10/21/78	#94	5	Soft And Wet	Warner Brothers 8619
11/24/79	#12	19	I Wanna Be Your Lover	Warner Brothers 49050
10/24/81	#72	12	Controversy	Warner Brothers 49808
11/06/82	#46	16	1999	Warner Brothers 29896
2/26/83	#6	23	Little Red Corvette	Warner Brothers 29746
6/04/83	#14	19	1999	Warner Brothers 29896
9/03/83	#9	21	Delirious	Warner Brothers 29503
12/17/83	#46	13	Let's Pretend We're Married	Warner Brothers 29548
6/02/84	#1	22	When Doves Cry	Warner Brothers 29286
8/04/84	#1	20	Let's Go Crazy*	Warner Brothers 29216
10/06/84	#1	20	Purple Rain*	Warner Brothers 29174
12/15/84	#10	14	I Would Die 4 U*	Warner Brothers 29121
2/09/85	#27	14	Take Me With U*	Warner Brothers 29079
5/18/85	#1	20	Raspberry Beret*	Paisley Park 28972
7/27/85	#7	15	Pop Life*	Paisley Park 28998
10/19/85	#46	10	America*	Paisley Park 28999
2/22/86	#1	19	Kiss*	Paisley Park 28751
5/24/86	#19	12	Mountains*	Paisley Park 28711
7/19/86	#74	9	Anotherloverholenyhead*	Paisley Park 28620
3/07/87	#4	17	Sign 'O' The Times	Paisley Park 28399
5/23/87	#78	7	If I Was Your Girlfriend	Paisley Park 28334
7/25/87	#3	27	U Got The Look	Paisley Park 28289
11/14/87	#10	20	I Could Never Take The Place Of Your Man/	Paisley Park 28288
2/13/88	#69	6	Hot Thing	Paisley Park 28288
4/30/88	#9	15	Alphabet St.	Paisley Park 27900
6/17/89	#1	19	Batdance	Warner Brothers 22924
8/26/89	#15	13	Partyman	Warner Brothers 22814
10/28/89	#33	15	The Arms Of Orion**	Warner Brothers 22757
8/04/90	#1	18	Thieves In The Temple	Paisley Park 19751
10/20/90	#54	9	New Power Generation	Paisley Park 19525
9/28/91	#1	27	Cream***	Paisley Park 19175
12/07/91	#1	28	Diamonds And Pearls***	Paisley Park 19083
3/28/92	#20	18	Money Don't Matter 2 Night***	Paisley Park 19020
8/01/92	#55	5	Sexy MF***	Paisley Park 18817
10/17/92	#20	15	My Name Is Prince***	Paisley Park 18707
11/28/92	#6	28	7***	Paisley Park 18824
3/27/93	#35	15	The Morning Papers***	Paisley Park 18583
9/25/93	#33	10	Pink Cashmere	Paisley Park 18371
			*released as by PRINCE and THE REVOLUTION	
			**released as by PRINCE with SHENNA EASTON	
			***released as by PRINCE and THE N.P.G.	

Debut Date	Peak Pos	Wks Chr	ARTIST/Song Title	Label & Number
			PRINCE BUSTER	
1/21/67	#48	7	Ten Commandments	Philips 40427
			PRINCE MARKIE DEE & SOUL CONVENTION	
5/08/93	#67	10	Typical Reasons (Swing My Way)	Soul Convention 74866
			PRISM	
11/05/77	#100	1	Spaceship Superstar	Ariola America 7672
12/24/77	#56	9	Take Me To The Kaptin	Ariola America 7678
7/22/78	#63	10	Flyin'	Ariola America 7714
2/06/82	#40	11	Don't Let Him Know	Capitol 5082
5/01/82	#73	5	Turn On Your Radio	Capitol 5106
			P.J. PROBY	
8/29/64	#73	6	Hold Me	London 9688
1/30/65	#73	4	Somewhere	Liberty 55757
2/04/67	#33	9	Niki Hoeky	Liberty 55936
			PROCLAIMERS	
6/12/93	#4	24	I'm Gonna Be (500 Miles)	Chrysalis 21668
			PROCOL HARUM	
6/24/67	#5	12	A Whiter Shade Of Pale	Deram 7507
10/21/67	#35	6	Homburg	A&M 885
5/27/72	#18	12	Conquistador	A&M 1347
11/18/72	#86	3	A Whiter Shade Of Pale	A&M 1389
			PRODUCERS	
6/13/81	#63	7	What She Does To Me (The Diana Song)	Portrait 02092
			PROFESSOR MORRISON'S LOLLIPOP	
9/14/68	#70	6	You Got The Love	White Whale 275
			BRIAN PROTHEROE	
4/12/75	#84	4	Pinball	Chrysalis 2104
			JEANNE PRUETT	
5/12/73	#24	12	Satin Sheets	MCA 40015
			ARTHUR PRYSOCK	
7/10/65	#59	10	It's Too Late, Baby Too Late	Old Town 1183
1/06/68	#82	5	A Working Man's Prayer	Verve 10574
9/29/73	#95	4	In The Rain	Old Town 100
12/25/76	#74	11	When Love Is New	Old Town 1000
			PSEUDO ECHO	
4/04/87	#55	8	Living In A Dream	RCA 5125
5/16/87	#12	16	Funky Town	RCA 5217
			PSYCHEDELIC FURS	
3/05/83	#41	13	Love My Way	Columbia 03340
5/12/84	#55	11	The Ghost In You	Columbia 04416
4/12/86	#42	12	Pretty In Pink	A&M 2826
3/14/87	#32	15	Heartbreak Beat	Columbia 06420
			GARY PUCKETT and THE UNION GAP	
11/11/67	#3	18	Woman, Woman*	Columbia 44297
3/02/68	#1	15	Young Girl*	Columbia 44450
6/08/68	#1	13	Lady Willpower	Columbia 44547
9/14/69	#5	12	Over You	Columbia 44644
3/15/69	#12	10	Don't Give In To Him	Columbia 44788
8/16/69	#5	12	This Girl Is A Woman Now	Columbia 44967
2/28/70	#38	6	Let's Give Adam And Eve Another Chance	Columbia 45097
10/17/70	#44	8	I Just Don't Know What To Do With Myself**	Columbia 45249
1/30/71	#50	5	Keep The Customer Satisfied**	Columbia 45303
			*released as by THE UNION GAP featuring GARY PUCKETT	
			**released as by GARY PUCKETT	
			LEROY PULLINS	
6/25/66	#66	5	I'm A Nut	Kapp 758
			PURE PRAIRIE LEAGUE	
3/01/75	#27	13	Amie	RCA 10184
6/14/75	#87	5	Two Lane Highway	RCA 10302
5/10/80	#13	17	Let Me Love You Tonight	Casablanca 2266
8/16/80	#40	14	I'm Almost Ready	Casablanca 2294
12/13/80	#78	7	I Can't Stop The Feelin'	Casablanca 2319
4/18/81	#28	14	Still Right Here In My Heart	Casablanca 2332

Debut Date	Peak Pos	Wks Chr	ARTIST/Song Title	Label & Number
			JAMES & BOBBY PURIFY	
9/24/66	#6	15	I'm Your Puppet	Bell 648
1/28/67	#35	6	Wish You Didn't Have To Go	Bell 660
4/15/67	#27	10	Shake A Tail Feather	Bell 669
7/15/67	#67	4	I Take What I Want	Bell 680
9/09/67	#30	10	Let Love Come Between Us	Bell 685
1/20/68	#62	5	Do Unto Me	Bell 700
4/27/68	#61	6	I Can Remember	Bell 721
12/07/74	#71	6	Do Your Thing	Casablanca 812
			PURPLE REIGN	
11/29/75	#48	7	This Old Man	Private Stock 45052
			BILL PURSELL	
1/26/63	#7	15	Our Winter Love	Columbia 42619
			PYRAMIDS	
1/11/64	#17	13	Penetration	Best 13002
			PYTHON LEE JACKSON	
6/17/72	#75	6	In A Broken Dream	GNP Crescendo 449

Q

			Q	
3/12/77	#20	13	Dancin' Man	Epic 50335
			CHRISTINE QUAITE	
5/16/64	#85	5	Tell Me Mamma	World Artists 1022
			QUAKER CITY BOYS	
12/27/58	#33	8	Teasin'	Swan 4023
3/21/59	#93	6	Everywhere You Go	Swan 4026
			QUARTERFLASH	
10/17/81	#4	24	Harden My Heart	Geffen 49824
2/13/82	#16	14	Find Another Fool	Geffen 50006
5/29/82	#47	9	Right Kind Of Love	Geffen 29994
8/14/82	#57	7	Night Shift	Warner Brothers 29932
6/18/83	#15	16	Take Me To Heart	Geffen 29603
10/01/83	#64	6	Take Another Picture	Geffen 29523
			BILL QUATEMAN	
4/14/73	#99	2	Only Love	Columbia 45792
			MIKE QUATRO	
7/01/72	#74	6	Circus	Evolution 1062
			SUZI QUATRO	
4/27/74	#90	4	Forty Eight Crash	Bell 45401
7/13/74	#63	9	All Shook Up	Bell 45477
1/24/76	#62	6	Can The Can	Big Tree 16053
1/27/79	#6	19	Stumblin' In*	RSO 917
5/26/79	#53	8	If You Can't Give Me Love	RSO 929
9/08/79	#56	8	I've Never Been In Love	RSO 1001
11/24/79	#51	10	She's In Love With You	RSO 1014
1/31/81	#62	8	Lipstick	Dreamland 107
			*released as by SUZI QUATRO and CHRIS NORMAN	
			QUEEN	
2/15/75	#12	17	Killer Queen	Elektra 45226
8/16/75	#89	3	Keep Yourself Alive	Elektra 45268
12/27/75	#6	26	Bohemian Rhapsody	Elektra 45297
5/29/76	#9	18	You're My Best Friend	Elektra 45318
11/20/76	#9	16	Somebody To Love	Elektra 45362
3/19/77	#54	5	Tie Your Mother Down	Elektra 45385
10/22/77	#3	24	We Are The Champions	Elektra 45441
5/06/78	#66	5	It's Late	Elektra 45478
11/11/78	#18	13	Bicycle Race/	Elektra 45541
11/11/78	#18	13	Fat Bottomed Girls	Elektra 45541
2/10/79	#77	4	Don't Stop Me Now	Elektra 46008
12/22/79	#1	23	Crazy Little Thing Called Love	Elektra 46579
6/28/80	#38	11	Play The Game	Elektra 46652
8/16/80	#1	34	Another One Bites The Dust	Elektra 47031
12/19/80	#66	10	Need Your Loving Tonight	Elektra 47086
1/17/81	#39	10	Flash's Theme aka Flash	Elektra 47092
11/07/81	#22	18	Under Pressure*	Elektra 47235

Debut Date	Peak Pos	Wks Chr	ARTIST/Song Title	Label & Number
			QUEEN—*continued*	
5/01/82	#11	15	Body Language	Elektra 47452
7/31/82	#61	6	Calling All Girls	Elektra 69981
2/18/84	#14	15	Radio Ga Ga	Capitol 5317
4/28/84	#53	8	I Want To Break Free	Capitol 5350
8/04/84	#79	5	It's A Hard Life	Capitol 5372
12/07/85	#52	11	One Vision	Capitol 5530
6/21/86	#42	12	A Kind Of Magic	Capitol 5590
5/13/89	#48	13	I Want It All	Capitol 44372
3/28/92	#1	27	Bohemian Rhapsody	Hollywood 64794
8/08/92	#44	10	We Will Rock You/We Are The Champions	Hollywood 64725
5/01/93	#38	1	Somebody To Love**	Hollywood 64647
5/22/93	#32	10	Somebody To Love**	Hollywood 64647
			*released as by QUEEN & DAVID BOWIE	
			**released as by GEORGE MICHAEL and QUEEN	
			QUEEN LATIFAH	
12/04/93	#24	21	U.N.I.T.Y.	Motown 2225
			QUEENSRYCHE	
3/23/91	#15	23	Silent Lucidity	EMI 50345
11/23/91	#73	10	Another Rainy Night (Without You)	EMI 50372
			? & THE MYSTERIANS	
8/27/66	#1	16	96 Tears	Cameo 428
11/26/66	#22	10	I Need Somebody	Cameo 441
3/25/67	#51	7	Can't Get Enough Of You Baby	Cameo 467
6/03/67	#94	2	Girl (You Captivate Me)	Cameo 479
			QUICKSILVER MESSENGER SERVICE	
10/10/70	#71	7	Fresh Air	Capitol 2920
			QUIET RIOT	
9/17/83	#5	25	Cum On Feel The Noize	Pasha 04005
1/14/84	#24	13	Bang Your Head (Metal Health)	Pasha 04267
7/14/84	#49	14	Mama Weer All Crazee Now	Pasha 04505
			QUIN-TONES	
8/23/58	#24	11	Down The Aisle Of Love . . . . , ...	Hunt 321
			EDDIE QUINTEROS	
4/09/60	#76	5	Come Dance With Me	Brent 7009
			QUOTATIONS	
1/13/62	#82	6	Imagination	Verve 10245

R

Debut Date	Peak Pos	Wks Chr	ARTIST/Song Title	Label & Number
			RAAB	
10/23/93	#70	6	Foreplay	Rip-It 1001
			EDDIE RABBITT	
7/31/76	#88	7	Rocky Mountain Music	Elektra 45315
6/17/78	#64	8	You Don't Love Me Anymore	Elektra 45488
1/20/79	#34	13	Every Which Way But Loose	Elektra 45554
6/09/79	#19	18	Suspicions	Elektra 46053
5/17/80	#95	3	Gone Too Far	Elektra 46613
6/21/80	#5	31	Drivin' My Life Away	Elektra 46656
11/08/80	#1	28	I Love A Rainy Night	Elektra 47066
7/25/81	#5	22	Step By Step	Elektra 47174
11/14/81	#15	18	Someone Could Lose A Heart Tonight	Elektra 47239
5/08/82	#65	7	I Don't Know Where To Start	Elektra 47435
10/16/82	#20	26	You And I*	Elektra 69936
4/23/83	#65	8	You Can't Run From Love	Warner Brothers 29712
			*released as by EDDIE RABBITT with CRYSTAL GAYLE	
			RADIANTS	
12/26/64	#38	10	Voice Your Choice	Chess 1904
5/01/65	#91	5	It Ain't No Big Thing	Chess 1925
			RADIOHEAD	
7/10/93	#37	20	Creep	Capitol 44932
			RAELETTES	
4/08/67	#71	6	One Hurt Deserves Another	Tangerine 972
5/09/70	#83	5	I Want To (Do Everything For You)	Tangerine 1006
2/27/71	#80	5	Bad Water	Tangerine 1014
9/04/71	#99	1	Leave My Man Alone	Tangerine 1017

Debut Date	Peak Pos	Wks Chr	ARTIST/Song Title	Label & Number
			RAES	
12/02/78	#66	12	A Little Lovin' (Keeps The Doctor Away)	A&M 2091
			GERRY RAFFERTY	
4/15/78	#1	24	Baker Street	United Artists 1192
8/12/78	#8	17	Right Down The Line	United Artists 1233
11/25/78	#23	15	Home And Dry	United Artists 1266
6/02/79	#22	11	Days Gone Down	United Artists 1298
8/11/79	#23	14	Get It Right Next Time	United Artists 1316
7/19/80	#59	8	The Royal Mile (Sweet Darlin')	United Artists 1366
			RAG DOLLS	
9/05/64	#96	4	Society Girl	Parkway 921
1/16/65	#48	8	Dusty	Mala 493
			RAIDERS (see PAUL REVERE & THE RAIDERS)	
			RAINBOW	
11/10/79	#56	10	Since You Been Gone	Polydor 2014
4/24/82	#39	13	Stone Cold	Mercury 76146
11/19/83	#68	10	Street Of Dreams	Mercury 815660
			RAINDROPS	
4/13/63	#34	10	What A Guy	Jubilee 5444
8/10/63	#15	11	The Kind Of Boy You Can't Forget	Jubilee 5455
11/23/63	#87	8	That Boy John	Jubilee 5466
3/21/64	#58	6	Book Of Love	Jubilee 5469
			MARVIN RAINWATER	
5/25/57	#24	14	Gonna Find Me A Bluebird	MGM 12412
7/04/59	#85	5	Half-Breed	MGM 12803
			RAINY DAZE	
2/25/67	#75	7	That Acapulco Gold	Uni 55002
			BONNIE RAITT	
6/04/77	#52	8	Runaway	Warner Brothers 8382
12/01/79	#80	8	You're Gonna Get What's Coming	Warner Brothers 49116
3/10/90	#45	9	Have A Heart	Capitol 44501
5/19/90	#70	5	Nick Of Time	Capitol 44364
7/13/91	#8	29	Something To Talk About	Capitol 44724
11/09/91	#7	30	I Can't Make You Love Me	Capitol 44729
4/04/92	#23	18	Not The Only One	Capitol 44764
			DON RALKE	
3/07/59	#38	11	77 Sunset Strip	Warner Brothers 5025
6/06/59	#97	2	Zooba	Warner Brothers 5058
			EDDIE RAMBEAU	
5/01/65	#12	10	Concrete And Clay	DynoVoice 204
4/02/66	#100	1	I'm The Sky	DynoVoice 217
10/15/66	#95	1	Clock	DynoVoice 225
			RAMBLERS	
10/22/60	#62	12	Rambling	Addit 1257
8/15/64	#97	2	Father Sebastian	Almont 311
			RAM JAM	
6/04/77	#14	20	Black Betty	Epic 50357
			RAMONES	
7/23/77	#96	6	Sheena Is A Punk Rocker	Sire 746
4/15/78	#91	3	Do You Wanna Dance	Sire 1017
			RAMRODS	
1/07/61	#25	11	(Ghost) Riders In The Sky	Amy 813
			TEDDY RANDAZZO	
7/06/57	#59	1	Next Stop Paradise	Vik 0277
7/05/58	#45	7	Little Serenade	Vik 0330
12/27/58	#100	1	It's Magic	ABC-Paramount 9983
10/03/59	#94	3	Lies	ABC-Paramount 10043
3/12/60	#30	15	The Way Of A Clown	ABC-Paramount 10088
1/26/63	#61	9	Big Wide World	Colpix 662
			ELLIOTT RANDALL	
4/23/77	#91	5	High On Love	Kirshner 4269
			RAN-DELLS	
8/03/63	#13	13	Martian Hop	Chairman 4403

279

Debut Date	Peak Pos	Wks Chr	**ARTIST**/Song Title	Label & Number
			BOOTS RANDOLPH	
2/23/63	#33	10	Yakety Sax	Monument 804
4/25/64	#87	3	Hey, Mr. Sax Man	Monument 835
12/17/66	#91	5	The Shadow Of Your Smile	Monument 976
6/10/67	#91	4	Temptation	Monument 1009
			DON RANDY	
4/03/65	#79	4	Mexican Pearls	Palomar 2203
			RANDY & THE RAINBOWS	
6/15/63	#13	17	Denise	Rust 5059
			SUE RANEY	
5/21/60	#88	2	Biology	Capitol 4360
			BILLY RANKIN	
3/17/84	#59	10	Baby Come Back	A&M 2613
			SHABBA RANKS	
11/23/91	#67	11	Housecall*	Epic 73928
6/27/92	#54	8	Mr. Loverman	Epic 74257
10/31/92	#37	21	Slow And Sexy**	Epic 74741
			*released as by SHABBA RANKS featuring MAXI PRIEST	
			**released as by SHABBA RANKS featuring JOHNNY GILL	
			RARE BIRD	
4/18/70	#82	3	Sympathy	Probe 477
			RARE EARTH	
3/14/70	#2	20	Get Ready	Rare Earth 5012
8/01/70	#5	15	(I Know) I'm Losing You	Rare Earth 5017
12/12/70	#18	11	Born To Wander	Rare Earth 5021
7/24/71	#7	12	I Just Want To Celebrate	Rare Earth 5031
11/20/71	#24	12	Hey Big Brother	Rare Earth 5038
4/15/72	#76	3	What'd I Say	Rare Earth 5043
11/25/72	#83	3	Good Time Sally	Rare Earth 5048
5/06/78	#42	11	Warm Ride	Prodigal 0640
			RASCALS (also YOUNG RASCALS)	
12/11/65	#63	8	I Ain't Gonna Eat Out My Heart Anymore*	Atlantic 2312
3/12/66	#1	14	Good Lovin'*	Atlantic 2321
6/11/66	#23	8	You Better Run*	Atlantic 2338
10/01/66	#54	5	Come On Up*	Atlantic 2353
1/28/67	#17	12	I've Been Lonely Too Long*	Atlantic 2377
4/22/67	#1	14	Groovin'*	Atlantic 2401
7/08/67	#8	10	A Girl Like You*	Atlantic 2424
9/09/67	#2	12	How Can I Be Sure*	Atlantic 2438
12/09/67	#15	8	It's Wonderful*	Atlantic 2463
4/06/68	#3	13	A Beautiful Morning	Atlantic 2493
7/20/68	#1	14	People Got To Be Free	Atlantic 2537
11/30/68	#12	8	A Ray Of Hope	Atlantic 2584
2/08/69	#17	7	Heaven	Atlantic 2599
5/17/69	#13	9	See	Atlantic 2634
8/30/69	#12	9	Carry Me Back	Atlantic 2664
12/27/69	#29	8	Hold On	Atlantic 2695
7/18/70	#42	7	Glory Glory	Atlantic 2743
7/03/71	#74	5	Love Me	Columbia 45400
			*released as by THE YOUNG RASCALS	
			RASPBERRIES	
4/29/72	#90	3	Don't Want To Say Goodbye	Capitol 3280
7/08/72	#4	18	Go All The Way	Capitol 3348
11/11/72	#10	13	I Wanna Be With You	Capitol 3473
3/17/73	#18	17	Let's Pretend	Capitol 3546
8/18/73	#37	9	Tonight	Capitol 3610
11/24/73	#75	3	I'm A Rocker	Capitol 3765
9/14/74	#24	11	Overnight Sensation (Hit Record)	Capitol 3946
			RATIONALS	
10/15/66	#80	4	Respect	Cameo 437
3/02/68	#91	3	I Need You	Capitol 2124
			RATT	
6/16/84	#16	19	Round And Round	Atlantic 89693
7/06/85	#44	13	Lay It Down	Atlantic 89546
2/21/87	#53	11	Dance	Atlantic 89354
12/17/88	#67	7	Way Cool Jr.	Atlantic 88985

Debut Date	Peak Pos	Wks Chr	ARTIST/Song Title	Label & Number
			RATTLES	
6/20/70	#95	3	The Witch	Probe 480
			GENYA RAVAN	
8/12/78	#90	3	Back In My Arms Again	20th Century 2374
			RAVEN-SYMONE	
8/21/93	#73	7	That's What Little Girls Are Made Of	MCA 54625
			LOU RAWLS	
9/03/66	#16	15	Love Is A Hurtin' Thing	Capitol 5709
11/26/66	#47	7	You Can Bring Me All Your Heartaches	Capitol 5790
2/11/67	#91	3	Trouble Down Here Below	Capitol 5824
3/25/67	#31	11	Dead End Street	Capitol 5869
7/01/67	#42	6	Show Business	Capitol 5941
12/23/67	#78	2	Little Drummer Boy	Capitol 2026
6/01/68	#94	3	You're Good For Me	Capitol 2172
7/19/69	#23	13	Your Good Thing (Is About To End)	Capitol 2550
11/15/69	#93	3	I Can't Make It Alone	Capitol 2668
8/15/70	#100	1	Bring It On Home	Capitol 2856
8/28/71	#27	18	A Natural Man	MGM 14262
2/19/72	#93	2	His Song Shall Be Sung	MGM 14349
5/29/76	#4	25	You'll Never Find Another Love Like Mine	Philadelphia Int. 3592
10/30/76	#76	4	Groovy People	Philadelphia Int. 3604
8/06/77	#87	3	See You When I Get There	Philadelphia Int. 3623
1/21/78	#20	17	Lady Love	Philadelphia Int. 3634
7/14/79	#92	4	Let Me Be Good To You	Philadelphia Int. 3684
3/26/83	#54	9	Wind Beneath My Wings	Epic 03758
			DIANE RAY	
8/10/63	#33	8	Please Don't Talk To The Lifeguard	Mercury 72117
			DON RAY	
9/16/78	#49	9	Got To Have Loving	Polydor 14489
			JAMES RAY	
11/18/61	#18	15	If You Gotta Make A Fool Of Somebody	Caprice 110
4/07/62	#55	10	Itty Bitty Pieces	Captice 114
			JOHNNIE RAY	
12/29/51	#1	20	Cry/	Okeh 6840
1/12/52	#2	14	The Little White Cloud That Cried	Okeh 6840
2/23/52	#5	9	Please Mr. Sun/	Columbia 39636
3/22/52	#9	3	Brokenhearted	Columbia 39636
6/21/52	#4	14	Walkin' My Baby Back Home	Columbia 39750
9/08/56	#3	25	Just Walking In The Rain	Columbia 40729
1/12/57	#10	12	You Don't Owe Me A Thing/	Columbia 40803
1/12/57	#42	4	Look Homeward Angel	Columbia 40803
4/20/57	#24	10	Yes Tonight, Josephine	Columbia 40893
7/06/57	#31	8	Build Your Love	Columbia 40942
9/13/58	#87	2	Up Until Now	Columbia 41213
9/19/59	#76	6	I'll Never Fall In Love Again	Columbia 41438
			RICARDO RAY	
10/12/68	#99	1	Nitty Gritty	Alegre 4024
			MARGIE RAYBURN	
10/12/57	#16	15	I'm Available	Liberty 55102
			RAYDIO (see RAY PARKER JR.)	
			SUSAN RAYE	
5/08/71	#92	3	L.A. International Airport	Capitol 3035
			RAY, GOODMAN & BROWN	
1/26/80	#7	20	Special Lady	Polydor 2033
5/10/80	#79	3	Inside Of You	Polydor 2074
8/23/80	#55	10	My Prayer	Polydor 2116
			RAYS	
10/12/57	#3	17	Silhouettes	Cameo 117
7/29/61	#55	12	Magic Moon	XYZ 607
			RAZOR'S EDGE	
7/16/66	#72	7	Let's Call It A Day Girl	Pow! 101
			RAZZY	
5/25/74	#49	7	I Hate Hate	MGM 14728

Debut Date	Peak Pos	Wks Chr	ARTIST/Song Title	Label & Number
			CHRIS REA	
7/01/78	#10	16	Fool (If You Think It's Over)	United Artists 1198
11/11/78	#77	4	Whatever Happened to Benny Santini?	United Artists 1252
3/31/79	#44	9	Diamonds	United Artists 1285
4/03/82	#75	5	Loving You	Columbia 02727
9/05/87	#84	4	Let's Dance	Motown 1900
3/25/89	#65	8	Working On It	Geffen 27535
			JOHN DAWSON READ	
9/20/75	#80	5	A Friend Of Mine Is Going Blind	Chrysalis 2105
			READY FOR THE WORLD	
8/03/85	#3	24	Oh Shiela	MCA 52636
12/14/85	#29	18	Digital Display	MCA 52734
11/29/86	#16	20	Love You Down	MCA 52947
			REAL LIFE	
11/26/83	#22	19	Send Me An Angel	Curb 52287
3/24/84	#46	13	Catch Me I'm Falling	Curb 52362
5/13/89	#20	18	Send Me An Angel '89	Curb 10531
			REAL THING	
7/24/76	#78	6	You To Me Are Everything	United Artists 833
			REBEL PEBBLES	
4/20/91	#48	14	Dream Lover	I.R.S. 13821
			REBELS	
1/05/63	#8	17	Wild Weekend	Swan 4125
5/04/63	#88	4	Rockin' Crickets*	Swan 4140
			***released as by THE ROCKIN' REBELS**	
			RECORDS	
9/15/79	#76	7	Starry Eyes	Virgin 67000
			REDBONE	
12/12/70	#72	6	Maggie	Epic 10670
7/17/71	#60	9	Maggie	Epic 10670
11/27/71	#19	14	The Witch Queen Of New Orleans	Epic 10749
1/05/74	#5	22	Come And Get Your Love	Epic 11035
8/31/74	#76	5	Suzie Girl	Epic 50015
			LEON REDBONE	
4/25/81	#92	4	Seduced	Emerald City 7326
			GENE REDDING	
3/16/74	#22	22	This Heart	Haven 7000
			OTIS REDDING	
5/04/63	#84	7	These Arms Of Mine	Volt 103
11/30/63	#47	13	Pain In My Heart	Volt 112
4/11/64	#83	3	Come To Me	Volt 116
10/10/64	#53	9	Chained And Bound	Volt 121
1/30/65	#94	2	That's How Strong My Love Is/	Volt 124
2/13/65	#55	9	Mr. Pitiful	Volt 124
5/15/65	#15	11	I've Been Loving You Too Long	Volt 126
9/04/65	#38	12	Respect	Volt 128
12/11/65	#65	5	Just One More Day	Volt 130
3/05/66	#30	9	Satisfaction	Volt 132
6/04/66	#49	7	My Lover's Prayer	Volt 136
9/24/66	#38	9	Fa-Fa-Fa-Fa-Fa (Sad Song)	Volt 138
12/03/66	#20	11	Try A Little Tenderness	Volt 141
4/15/67	#65	2	I Love You More Than Words Can Say	Volt 146
5/06/67	#19	10	Tramp*	Stax 216
5/20/67	#49	5	Shake	Volt 149
7/22/67	#41	5	Glory Of Love	Volt 152
8/12/67	#60	9	Knock On Wood*	Stax 228
1/27/68	#3	16	(Sittin' On) The Dock Of The Bay	Volt 157
2/17/68	#50	3	Lovey Dovey*	Stax 244
4/27/68	#24	7	The Happy Song (Dum-Dum)	Volt 163
7/06/68	#37	5	Amen/	Atco 6592
7/27/68	#100	2	Hard To Handle	Atco 6592
9/21/68	#37	7	I've Got Dreams To Remember	Atco 6612
11/30/68	#22	8	Papa's Got A Brand New Bag	Atco 6636
2/15/69	#38	7	A Lover's Question	Atco 6654
5/17/69	#53	4	Love Man	Atco 6677
8/02/69	#66	5	Free Me	Atco 6700

Debut Date	Peak Pos	Wks Chr	ARTIST/Song Title	Label & Number
4/04/70	#75	2	Demonstration . . . . Atco 6742	

*released as by OTIS & CARLA (Otis Redding & Carla Thomas)

REDDINGS

Debut Date	Peak Pos	Wks Chr	ARTIST/Song Title	Label & Number
1/24/81	#95	2	Remote Control . . . . Believe In A Dream 5600	
6/19/82	#57	8	(Sittin' On) The Dock Of The Bay . . . . Believe In A Dream 02836	

HELEN REDDY

Debut Date	Peak Pos	Wks Chr	ARTIST/Song Title	Label & Number
3/06/71	#19	17	I Don't Know How To Love Him . . . . Capitol 3027	
7/24/71	#38	11	Crazy Love . . . . Capitol 3138	
12/11/71	#56	7	No Sad Songs . . . . Capitol 3231	
7/15/72	#1	22	I Am Woman . . . . Capitol 3350	
2/10/73	#14	14	Peaceful . . . . Capitol 3527	
6/23/73	#1	19	Delta Dawn . . . . Capitol 3645	
10/27/73	#1	15	Leave Me Alone (Ruby Red Dress) . . . . Capitol 3768	
3/09/74	#10	12	Keep On Singing . . . . Capitol 3845	
6/08/74	#10	18	You And Me Against The World . . . . Capitol 3897	
10/19/74	#1	15	Angie Baby . . . . Capitol 3972	
2/01/75	#23	10	Emotion . . . . Capitol 4021	
6/28/75	#34	7	Bluebird . . . . Capitol 4108	
8/09/75	#5	16	Ain't No Way To Treat A Lady . . . . Capitol 4128	
11/29/75	#20	15	Somewhere In The Night . . . . Capitol 4192	
8/07/76	#41	8	I Can't Hear You No More/ . . . . Capitol 4312	
8/14/76	#75	3	Music Is My Life . . . . Capitol 4312	
4/30/77	#16	22	You're My World . . . . Capitol 4418	
10/22/77	#75	4	The Happy Girls . . . . Capitol 4487	
7/22/78	#87	3	Ready Or Not . . . . Capitol 4582	
5/19/79	#59	7	Make Love To Me . . . . Capitol 4712	
5/23/81	#95	4	I Can't Say Goodbye To You . . . . MCA 51106	

REDEYE

Debut Date	Peak Pos	Wks Chr	ARTIST/Song Title	Label & Number
11/14/70	#22	14	Games . . . . Pentagram 204	
4/10/71	#77	7	Red Eye Blues . . . . Pentagram 206	

RED FLAG

Debut Date	Peak Pos	Wks Chr	ARTIST/Song Title	Label & Number
3/18/89	#83	4	Russian Radio . . . . Enigma 75519	

RED HOT CHILI PEPPERS

Debut Date	Peak Pos	Wks Chr	ARTIST/Song Title	Label & Number
5/09/92	#1	27	Under The Bridge . . . . Warner Brothers 18978	
9/04/93	#15	25	Soul To Squeeze . . . . Warner Brothers 18401	

EIVETS REDNOW (Stevie Wonder spelled backwards)

Debut Date	Peak Pos	Wks Chr	ARTIST/Song Title	Label & Number
9/14/68	#73	6	Alfie . . . . Gordy 7076	

RED RIDER

Debut Date	Peak Pos	Wks Chr	ARTIST/Song Title	Label & Number
4/05/80	#65	7	White Hot . . . . Capitol 4845	
6/23/84	#74	8	Young Thing, Wild Dreams (Rock Me) . . . . Capitol 5335	

RED RIVER DAVE

Debut Date	Peak Pos	Wks Chr	ARTIST/Song Title	Label & Number
7/16/60	#82	5	There's A Star Spangled Banner Waving Somewhere #2 . . Savoy 3020	

RED ROCKERS

Debut Date	Peak Pos	Wks Chr	ARTIST/Song Title	Label & Number
6/18/83	#60	9	China . . . . Columbia 03786	

MICHAEL REDWAY

Debut Date	Peak Pos	Wks Chr	ARTIST/Song Title	Label & Number
1/27/73	#77	4	Good Morning . . . . Philips 40720	

RED WING

Debut Date	Peak Pos	Wks Chr	ARTIST/Song Title	Label & Number
4/24/71	#83	2	California Blues . . . . Fantasy 657	

DAN REED NETWORK

Debut Date	Peak Pos	Wks Chr	ARTIST/Song Title	Label & Number
3/19/88	#51	10	Ritual . . . . Mercury 870183	

JERRY REED

Debut Date	Peak Pos	Wks Chr	ARTIST/Song Title	Label & Number
7/28/62	#89	1	Goodnight Irene . . . . Columbia 42417	
11/28/70	#8	20	Amos Moses . . . . RCA 9904	
4/24/71	#9	14	When You're Hot, You're Hot . . . . RCA 9976	
8/28/71	#53	7	Ko-Ko Joe . . . . RCA 1011	
1/08/72	#72	5	Another Puff . . . . RCA 0613	
7/29/72	#82	5	Alabama Wild Man . . . . RCA 0738	
6/30/73	#52	9	Lord, Mr. Ford . . . . RCA 0960	
2/09/74	#93	4	The Crude Oil Blues . . . . RCA 0024	
7/24/82	#67	6	She Got The Goldmine (I Got The Shaft) . . . . RCA 13268	

JIMMY REED

Debut Date	Peak Pos	Wks Chr	ARTIST/Song Title	Label & Number
1/30/60	#41	12	Baby, What You Want Me To Do . . . . Vee-Jay 333	
6/11/60	#73	3	Found Love . . . . Vee-Jay 347	
10/01/60	#79	6	Hush Hush . . . . Vee-Jay 357	

Debut Date	Peak Pos	Wks Chr	**ARTIST**/Song Title	Label & Number
			JIMMY REED—*continued*	
2/04/61	#77	4	Close Together	Vee-Jay 373
6/10/61	#83	3	Big Boss Man	Vee-Jay 380
9/16/61	#63	7	Bright Lights Big City	Vee-Jay 398
2/03/62	#97	2	Aw Shucks, Hush Your Mouth	Vee-Jay 425
6/30/62	#100	1	Good Lover	Vee-Jay 449
4/20/63	#52	9	Shame, Shame, Shame	Vee-Jay 509
			LOU REED	
2/17/73	#17	13	Walk On The Wild Side	RCA 0887
			VIVIAN REED	
7/06/88	#93	3	Yours Until Tomorrow	Epic 10319
			DELLA REESE	
8/10/57	#15	17	And That Reminds Me	Jubilee 5292
9/19/59	#1	19	Don't You Know	RCA 7591
12/12/59	#15	12	Not One Minute More	RCA 7644
3/19/60	#31	8	Someday (You'll Want Me To Want You)	RCA 7706
6/04/60	#82	3	Everyday	RCA 7750
8/27/60	#56	9	And Now	RCA 7784
1/21/61	#80	7	The Most Beautiful Words	RCA 7833
7/10/65	#81	4	After Loving You	ABC-Paramount 10691
			DEL REEVES	
5/29/65	#99	1	Girl On The Billboard	United Artists 824
			JIM REEVES	
5/04/57	#11	14	Four Walls	RCA 6874
7/19/58	#53	11	Blue Boy	RCA 7266
1/02/60	#2	24	He'll Have To Go	RCA 7643
7/02/60	#44	8	I'm Gettin' Better/	RCA 7756
7/09/60	#96	1	I Know One	RCA 7756
11/12/60	#29	10	Am I Losing You/	RCA 7800
11/12/60	#59	8	I Missed Me	RCA 7800
4/01/61	#63	4	The Blizzard	RCA 7855
7/22/61	#91	4	What Would You Do	RCA 7905
5/12/62	#78	5	Adios Amigo	RCA 8019
8/29/64	#96	1	I Guess I'm Crazy	RCA 8383
3/27/65	#100	2	This Is It	RCA 8508
8/07/65	#62	7	Is It Really Over?	RCA 8625
1/01/66	#58	8	Snow Flake	RCA 8719
4/09/66	#55	10	Distant Drums	RCA 8789
9/03/66	#64	5	Blue Side Of Lonesome	RCA 8902
			MARTHA REEVES	
3/09/74	#71	8	Power Of Love	MCA 40194
			REFLECTIONS (Detroit group)	
3/28/64	#9	15	(Just Like) Romeo & Juliet	Golden World 9
7/11/64	#83	2	Like Columbus Did	Golden World 12
1/02/65	#80	6	Shabby Little Hut	Golden World 19
3/06/65	#55	6	Poor Man's Son	Golden World 20
			REFLECTIONS (New York group)	
7/19/75	#90	3	Three Steps From True Love	Capitol 4078
			RE-FLEX	
12/03/83	#23	22	The Politics Of Dancing	Capitol 5301
5/12/84	#85	5	Hurt	Capitol 5348
			REGENTS	
5/13/61	#13	11	Barbara Ann	Gee 1065
7/15/61	#32	8	Runaround	Gee 1071
			REGINA	
6/21/86	#10	21	Baby Love	Atlantic 89417
			CLARENCE REID	
7/26/69	#36	10	Nobody But You Babe	Alston 4574
11/01/69	#97	1	I'm Gonna Tear You A New Heart	Alston 4578
7/27/74	#91	2	Funky Party	Alston 4621
			JOHN REID	
5/17/75	#91	2	It Hurts A Little Even Now	Arista 0114
			MIKE REILLY	
4/10/71	#98	2	1927 Kansas City	Paramount 0053

Debut Date	Peak Pos	Wks Chr	**ARTIST**/Song Title	Label & Number
			JOE REISMAN	
8/05/61	#89	4	The Guns Of Navarone	Landa 674
			R.E.M.	
7/07/84	#82	6	So. Central Rain (I'm Sorry)	I.R.S. 9927
10/11/86	#88	3	Fall On Me	I.R.S. 52883
9/19/87	#10	22	The One I Love	I.R.S. 53171
1/30/88	#84	4	It's The End Of The World As We Know It	I.R.S. 53220
1/21/89	#6	21	Stand	Warner Brothers 27688
6/17/89	#80	6	Pop Song 89	Warner Brothers 27640
3/30/91	#6	25	Losing My Religion	Warner Brothers 19392
7/27/91	#8	21	Shiny Happy People	Warner Brothers 19242
11/02/91	#75	8	Radio Song	Warner Brothers 19246
11/07/92	#23	16	Drive	Warner Brothers 18729
2/13/93	#17	17	Man On The Moon	Warner Brothers 18642
9/25/93	#18	25	Everybody Hurts	Warner Brothers 40992
			REMBRANDTS	
2/09/91	#14	24	Just The Way It Is Baby	Atco 98874
5/25/91	#54	11	Someone	Atco 98786
9/28/91	#84	6	Save Me	Atco 98799
10/10/92	#48	15	Johnny Have You Seen Her?	Atco East West 98504
			DIANE RENAY	
1/25/64	#6	13	Navy Blue	20th Century Fox 456
4/11/64	#28	8	Kiss Me Sailor	20th Century Fox 477
11/28/64	#95	2	Watch Out Sally	MGM 13296
			RENE GOOGIE COMBO	
3/15/58	#60	1	Wiggle-Tail	Class 221
3/05/66	#98	1	Smokey Joe's La La	Class 1517
			HENRI RENE ORCHESTRA	
7/28/51	#7	6	I'm In Love Again	RCA 4148
6/12/54	#4	4	The Happy Wanderer	RCA 5715
			RENE and ANGELA	
10/05/85	#54	11	I'll Be Good	Mercury 884009
6/21/86	#78	4	You Don't Have To Cry	Mercury 884587
			RENE and RAY	
5/19/62	#75	7	Queen Of My Heart	Donna 1360
			RENE & RENE	
6/13/64	#38	13	Angelito	Columbia 43045
11/09/68	#15	14	Lo Mucho Que Te Quiero	White Whale 287
			MIKE RENO and ANN WILSON	
5/12/84	#7	19	Almost Paradise...Love Theme From "Footloose"	Columbia 04418
			REO SPEEDWAGON	
6/04/77	#97	2	Ridin' The Storm Out	Epic 50367
7/22/78	#70	7	Time For Me To Fly	Epic 50582
11/24/79	#91	4	Only The Strong Survive	Epic 50790
5/24/80	#72	6	Time For Me To Fly	Epic 50858
11/29/80	#1	28	Keep On Loving You	Epic 50953
3/21/81	#4	20	Take It On The Run	Epic 01054
6/13/81	#26	13	Don't Let Him Go	Epic 02127
8/08/81	#28	13	In Your Letter	Epic 02457
6/12/82	#10	15	Keep The Fire Burnin'	Epic 02967
8/28/82	#28	12	Sweet Time	Epic 03175
10/27/84	#28	15	I Do'wanna Know	Epic 04659
1/19/85	#1	21	Can't Fight This Feeling	Epic 04713
3/30/85	#24	15	One Lonely Night	Epic 04848
7/13/85	#34	12	Live Every Moment	Epic 05412
1/31/87	#23	15	That Ain't Love	Epic 06656
5/09/87	#66	8	Variety Tonight	Epic 07055
7/18/87	#18	27	In My Dreams	Epic 07255
6/25/88	#23	18	Here With Me	Epic 07901
10/06/90	#62	8	Love Is A Rock	Epic 73540
			REPARATA and THE DELRONS	
1/16/65	#44	8	Whenever A Teenager Cries	World Artists 1036
4/17/65	#64	6	Tommy	World Artists 1051
7/12/75	#92	4	Shoes*	Polydor 14271
			*released as by REPARATA	

285

Debut Date	Peak Pos	Wks Chr	ARTIST/Song Title	Label & Number
			REPLACEMENTS	
4/15/89	#57	10	I'll Be You	Sire 22992
			JOHNNY RESTIVO	
8/22/59	#54	6	The Shape I'm In	RCA 7559
			RESTLESS HEART	
4/11/87	#41	18	I'll Still Be Loving You	RCA 5065
11/21/92	#9	24	When She Cries	RCA 62412
4/10/93	#40	14	Tell Me What You Dream	RCA 62468
			REUNION	
9/07/74	#7	14	Life Is A Rock (But The Radio Rolled Me)	RCA 10056
			REVELS	
10/31/59	#35	10	Midnight Stroll	Norgolde 103
			PAUL REVERE and THE RAIDERS (also RAIDERS)	
3/18/61	#38	9	Like, Long Hair	Gardena 116
9/04/65	#58	10	Steppin' Out	Columbia 43375
12/11/65	#11	14	Just Like Me	Columbia 43461
3/19/66	#4	14	Kicks	Columbia 43556
6/25/66	#6	10	Hungry	Columbia 43678
10/01/66	#20	8	The Great Airplane Strike	Columbia 43810
12/03/66	#4	12	Good Thing	Columbia 43907
2/18/67	#22	9	Ups And Downs	Columbia 44018
4/29/67	#5	10	Him Or Me - What's It Gonna Be?	Columbia 44094
8/19/67	#17	10	I Had A Dream	Columbia 44227
11/18/67	#35	6	Peace Of Mind	Columbia 44335
2/17/68	#19	8	Too Much Talk	Columbia 44444
6/22/68	#27	8	Don't Take It So Hard	Columbia 44553
10/19/68	#47	4	Cinderella Sunshine	Columbia 44655
2/08/69	#18	12	Mr. Sun, Mr. Moon	Columbia 44744
5/10/69	#20	11	Let Me	Columbia 44854
8/30/69	#25	9	We Gotta All Get Together	Columbia 44970
2/14/70	#73	4	Just Seventeen*	Columbia 45082
5/02/70	#92	1	Gone Movin' On*	Columbia 45150
5/01/71	#1	20	Indian Reservation*	Columbia 45332
9/18/71	#23	9	Birds Of A Feather*	Columbia 45453
1/22/72	#28	7	Country Wine*	Columbia 45535
5/13/72	#43	9	Powder Blue Mercedes Queen*	Columbia 45601
10/14/72	#89	3	Song Seller*	Columbia 45688
1/13/73	#61	6	Love Music*	Columbia 45759
			***released as by THE RAIDERS**	
			ANN REYNOLDS	
4/20/57	#38	1	Wind In The Willow	Kapp 179
			BURT REYNOLDS	
10/25/80	#87	5	Let's Do Something Cheap And Superficial	MCA 51004
			DEBBIE REYNOLDS	
3/10/51	#5	10	Aba Daba Honeymoon*	MGM 30282
7/06/57	#1	25	Tammy	Coral 61851
12/14/57	#30	7	A Very Special Love	Coral 61897
1/23/60	#19	15	Am I That Easy To Forget	Dot 15985
5/07/60	#64	6	City Lights	Dot 16071
12/17/60	#70	1	Satisfied (Part 2)	Dot 16151
			***released as by CARLETON CARPENTER & DEBBIE REYNOLDS**	
			JODY REYNOLDS	
5/03/58	#10	16	Endless Sleep	Demon 1507
			LAWRENCE REYNOLDS	
9/27/69	#31	9	Jesus Is A Soul Man	Warner Brothers 7322
			RHINOCEROS	
3/22/69	#55	6	Apricot Brandy	Elektra 45647
			EMITT RHODES	
12/26/70	#38	11	Fresh As A Daisy	Dunhill 4267
			RHYTHM HERITAGE	
11/15/75	#1	25	Theme From S.W.A.T.	ABC 12135
4/17/76	#16	14	Baretta's Theme ("Keep Your Eye On The Sparrow")	ABC 12177
3/19/77	#95	3	Theme From Rocky (Gonna Fly Now)	ABC 12243

Debut Date	Peak Pos	Wks Chr	ARTIST/Song Title	Label & Number
			RIBBONS	
1/26/63	#87	4	Ain't Gonna Kiss Ya	Marsh 202
			CHARLIE RICH	
3/26/60	#27	18	Lonely Weekends	Phillips Int. 3552
8/28/65	#18	11	Mohair Sam	Smash 1993
3/21/70	#72	4	July 12, 1939	Epic 10585
5/12/73	#17	17	Behind Closed doors	Epic 10950
9/29/73	#1	22	The Most Beautiful Girl	Epic 11040
2/02/74	#22	11	There Won't Be Anymore	RCA 0195
2/16/74	#8	13	A Very Special Love Song	Epic 11091
5/04/74	#59	9	I Don't See Me In Your Eyes Anymore	RCA 0260
8/03/74	#29	10	I Love My Friend	Epic 20006
10/05/74	#90	5	She Called Me Baby	RCA 10062
2/01/75	#49	7	My Elusive Dreams	Epic 50064
5/31/75	#22	12	Every Time You Touch Me (I Get High)	Epic 50103
9/20/75	#90	2	All Over Me	Epic 50142
1/17/76	#82	6	Since I Fell For You	Epic 50182
5/08/76	#78	4	America The Beautiful	Epic 50222
9/17/77	#94	2	Rollin' With The Flow	Epic 50392
			CLIFF RICHARD	
9/12/59	#38	13	Living Doll*	ABC-Paramount 10042
8/10/63	#76	7	Lucky Lips	Epic 9597
12/21/63	#24	12	It's All In The Game	Epic 9633
5/02/64	#90	2	I'm The Lonely One	Epic 9670
4/10/65	#98	1	The Minute You're Gone	Epic 9757
6/26/76	#5	24	Devil Woman	Rocket 40574
6/11/77	#87	4	Don't Turn The Light Out	Rocket 40724
10/20/79	#6	21	We Don't Talk Anymore	EMI America 8025
2/23/80	#39	12	Carrie	EMI America 8035
9/13/80	#9	20	Dreaming	EMI America 8057
10/18/80	#19	19	Suddenly**	MCA 51007
12/13/80	#15	18	A Little In Love	EMI America 8068
4/25/81	#36	11	Give A Little Bit More	EMI America 8076
10/10/81	#70	6	Wired For Sound	EMI America 8095
1/16/82	#22	15	Daddy's Home	EMI America 8103
10/02/82	#69	9	The Only Way Out	EMI America 8135
10/22/83	#78	6	Never Say Die (Give Me A Little Bit More)	EMI America 8180
			*released as by CLIFF RICHARD and THE DRIFTERS	
			**released as by OLIVIA NEWTON-JOHN and CLIFF RICHARD	
			RICHARD and THE YOUNG LIONS	
9/17/66	#70	6	Open Up Your Door	Philips 40381
			TURLEY RICHARDS	
3/14/70	#76	7	Love Minus Zero - No Limit	Warner Brothers 7376
1/26/80	#71	8	You Might Need Somebody	Atlantic 3645
			LIONEL RICHIE	
7/04/81	#1	29	Endless Love*	Motown 1519
10/09/82	#1	22	Truly	Motown 1644
1/15/83	#2	22	You Are	Motown 1657
4/09/83	#9	16	My Love	Motown 1677
9/17/83	#1	27	All Night Long	Motown 1698
11/26/83	#9	19	Running With The Night	Motown 1710
3/03/84	#1	24	Hello	Motown 1722
6/23/84	#3	20	Stuck On You	Motown 1746
10/06/84	#15	18	Penny Lover	Motown 1762
11/09/85	#1	24	Say You Say Me	Motown 1819
7/19/86	#4	17	Dancing On The Ceiling	Motown 1843
10/04/86	#10	20	Love Will Conquer All	Motown 1866
12/06/86	#9	20	Ballerina Girl/	Motown 1873
1/24/87	#86	3	Deep River Woman**	Motown 1973
3/28/87	#24	15	Se La	Motown 1883
5/16/92	#20	15	Do It To Me	Motown 2160
			*released as by DIANA ROSS & LIONEL RICHIE	
			**released as by LIONEL RICHIE with ALABAMA	
			RICK and THE KEENS	
7/15/61	#77	8	Peanuts	Smash 1705
			JIMMY RICKS	
3/21/59	#82	5	Secret Love	Felsted 8560

287

Debut Date	Peak Pos	Wks Chr	ARTIST/Song Title	Label & Number
			NELSON RIDDLE	
2/04/56	#1	15	Lisbon Antigua	Capitol 3287
8/04/56	#27	4	Theme From "The Proud Ones"	Capitol 3472
6/16/62	#40	11	Route 66 Theme	Capitol 4741
11/05/83	#38	14	What's New*	Asylum 69780
			***released as by LINDA RONSTADT & THE NELSON RIDDLE ORCHESTRA**	
			ANDREW RIDGELY	
5/05/90	#68	8	Shake	Columbia 73337
			RIFF	
3/23/91	#38	17	My Heart Is Failing Me	SBK 07342
5/23/92	#87	3	White Men Can't Jump	SBK 07384
			RIGHTEOUS BROTHERS	
5/11/63	#47	7	Little Latin Lupe Lu	Moonglow 215
9/07/63	#66	7	My Babe	Moonglow 223
12/19/64	#1	15	You've Lost That Lovin' Feelin'	Philles 124
4/10/65	#10	10	Just Once In My Life	Philles 127
5/22/65	#93	2	You Can Have Her	Moonglow 239
7/03/65	#94	2	Justine	Moonglow 242
7/10/65	#5	14	Unchained Melody/	Philles 129
7/17/65	#43	6	Hung On You	Philles 129
11/27/65	#4	10	Ebb Tide	Philles 130
2/12/66	#90	3	Georgia On My Mind	Moonglow 244
3/12/66	#1	12	(You're My) Soul And Inspiration	Verve 10383
6/04/66	#15	8	He	Verve 10406
8/06/66	#30	7	Go Ahead And Cry	Verve 10430
10/01/66	#87	2	The White Cliffs Of Dover	Philles 132
10/29/66	#51	6	On This Side Of Goodbye	Verve 10449
4/22/67	#51	6	Melancholy Music Man	Verve 10507
10/14/67	#93	1	Stranded In The Middle Of No Place/	Verve 10551
10/14/67	#99	1	Been So Nice	Verve 10551
5/18/74	#4	16	Rock And Roll Heaven	Haven 7002
9/07/74	#27	9	Give It To The People	Haven 7004
11/09/74	#32	10	Dream On	Haven 7006
8/25/90	#9	17	Unchained Melody	Verve 871882
			RIGHT SAID FRED	
12/21/91	#4	30	I'm Too Sexy	Charisma 98671
4/25/92	#60	9	Don't Talk Just Kiss	Charisma 98595
			BILLY LEE RILEY	
10/07/72	#99	2	I Got A Thing About You Baby	Entrance 7508
			CHERYL "PEPSI" RILEY	
10/29/88	#36	16	Thanks For My Child	Columbia 07996
			JEANNIE C. RILEY	
8/24/68	#1	13	Harper Valley P.T.A.	Plantation 3
11/30/68	#45	7	The Girl Most Likely	Plantation 7
3/22/69	#81	6	There Never Was A Time	Plantation 16
3/27/71	#61	6	Oh Singer	Plantation 72
7/24/71	#51	6	Good Enough To Be Your Wife	Plantation 75
			RINGS	
2/21/81	#82	7	Let Me Go	MCA 51069
			RINKY DINKS	
2/21/59	#75	4	Catch A Little Moonbeam	Capitol 4146
			RINKY-DINKS (Bobby Darin)	
7/26/58	#25	10	Early In The Morning	Atco 6121
			AUGIE RIOS	
12/20/58	#36	5	Donde Esta Santa Claus?	Metro 20010
			MIGUEL RIOS	
6/06/70	#9	10	A Song Of Joy	A&M 1193
			WALDO DE LOS RIOS	
5/22/71	#57	11	Mozart Symphony No. 40 In G Minor	United Artists 50772
			RIP CHORDS	
3/30/63	#61	9	Here I Stand	Columbia 42687
8/24/63	#83	4	Gone	Columbia 42812
12/14/63	#4	15	Hey Little Cobra	Columbia 42921
5/02/64	#29	8	Three Window Coupe	Columbia 43035

Debut Date	Peak Pos	Wks Chr	ARTIST/Song Title	Label & Number
			MINNIE RIPERTON	
1/25/75	#1	16	Lovin' You	Epic 50057
8/02/75	#72	4	Inside My Love	Epic 50128
			RIPPLE	
11/10/73	#59	5	I Don't Know What It Is, But It Sure Is Funky	GRC 1004
2/09/74	#94	5	Willie Pass The Water	GRC 1013
			RODNEY ALLEN RIPPY	
10/13/73	#75	4	Take Life A Little Easier	Bell 45403
			RITCHIE FAMILY	
8/16/75	#10	13	Brazil	20th Century 2218
12/13/75	#81	6	I Want To Dance With You	20th Century 2252
9/04/76	#18	20	The Best Disco In Town	Marlin 3306
			LEE RITENOUR	
4/18/81	#17	19	Is It You	Elektra 47124
12/11/82	#81	6	Cross My Heart	Elektra 69892
			TEX RITTER	
7/08/61	#28	12	I Dreamed Of A Hill-Billy Heaven	Capitol 4567
			HECTOR RIVERA	
12/31/66	#98	5	At The Party	Barry 1010
			JOHNNY RIVERS	
6/06/64	#2	13	Memphis	Imperial 66032
8/15/64	#11	9	Maybelline	Imperial 66056
10/31/64	#10	12	Mountain Of Love	Imperial 66075
2/13/65	#37	7	Midnight Special/	Imperial 66087
2/13/65	#82	2	Cupid	Imperial 66087
5/29/65	#7	12	Seventh Son	Imperial 66112
10/02/65	#34	8	Where Have All The Flowers Gone	Imperial 66133
12/11/65	#49	8	Under Your Spell Again	Imperial 66144
3/12/66	#4	11	Secret Agent Man	Imperial 66159
6/11/66	#18	8	(I Washed My Hands In) Muddy Water	Imperial 66175
9/17/66	#1	15	Poor Side Of Town	Imperial 66205
2/04/67	#6	11	Baby I Need Your Lovin'	Imperial 66227
6/03/67	#10	10	The Tracks Of My Tears	Imperial 66244
11/18/67	#10	12	Summer Rain	Imperial 66267
3/30/68	#25	9	Look To Your Soul	Imperial 66286
11/09/68	#42	6	Right Relations	Imperial 66335
3/01/69	#42	5	These Are Not My People	Imperial 66360
7/05/69	#30	8	Muddy River	Imperial 66386
10/25/69	#69	3	One Woman	Imperial 66418
5/02/70	#38	8	Into The Mystic	Imperial 66448
8/22/70	#71	5	Fire And Rain	Imperial 66453
5/01/71	#74	7	Sea Cruise	United Artists 50778
9/04/71	#71	5	Think His Name	United Artists 50822
10/14/72	#5	18	Rockin' Pneumonia - Boogie Woogie Flu	United Artists 50960
3/10/73	#27	10	Blue Suede Shoes	United Artists 198
7/12/75	#30	9	Help Me Rhonda	Epic 50121
6/25/77	#6	26	Swayin' To The Music (Slow Dancin')	Big Tree 16094
12/17/77	#34	13	Curious Mind (Um, Um, Um, Um, Um, Um)	Big Tree 16106
			RIVIERAS (Indiana group)	
1/18/64	#6	13	California Sun	Riviera 1401
4/25/64	#84	4	Little Donna	Riviera 1402
			RIVIERAS (New Jersey group)	
9/06/58	#67	5	Count Every Star	Coed 503
2/21/59	#56	9	Moonlight Serenade	Coed 508
			RIVINGTONS	
8/04/62	#35	10	Papa-Oom-Mow-Mow	Liberty 55427
4/06/63	#43	8	The Bird's The Word	Liberty 55553
			ROACHFORD	
4/22/89	#30	16	Cuddly Toy (Feel For Me)	Epic 68549
			ROAD	
2/01/69	#88	3	She's Not There	Kama Sutra 256
			ROAD APPLES	
10/04/75	#48	16	Let's Live Together	Polydor 14285
			ROB BASE & D.J. E-Z ROCK	
9/03/88	#64	12	It Takes Two	Profile 5186

Debut Date	Peak Pos	Wks Chr	**ARTIST**/Song Title	Label & Number
			MARTY ROBBINS	
10/27/56	#36	1	Singing The Blues	Columbia 21545
4/13/57	#3	18	A White Sport Coat (And A Pink Carnation)	Columbia 40864
9/14/57	#60	1	Please Don't Blame Me	Columbia 40969
11/16/57	#32	9	The Story Of My Life	Columbia 41013
4/19/58	#51	2	Stairway Of Love	Columbia 41143
8/16/58	#56	8	She Was Only Seventeen	Columbia 41208
2/14/59	#42	10	The Hanging Tree	Columbia 41325
6/27/59	#77	3	Cap And Gown	Columbia 41408
11/21/59	#2	20	El Paso	Columbia 41511
3/09/60	#26	10	Big Iron	Columbia 41589
7/02/60	#47	10	Is There Any Chance	Columbia 41686
10/29/60	#35	13	Ballad Of The Alamo	Columbia 41809
1/21/61	#3	17	Don't Worry	Columbia 41922
6/03/61	#45	6	Jimmy Martinez/	Columbia 42008
6/03/61	#100	1	Ghost Train	Columbia 42008
9/09/61	#85	8	It's Your World	Columbia 42065
12/30/61	#84	4	I Told The Brook	Columbia 42246
5/05/62	#88	4	Love Can't Wait	Columbia 42375
7/28/62	#16	13	Devil Woman	Columbia 42486
11/17/62	#26	10	Ruby Ann	Columbia 42614
12/14/63	#100	1	Begging To You	Columbia 42890
2/15/64	#76	5	Girl From Spanish Town	Columbia 42968
11/30/68	#90	2	I Walk Alone	Columbia 44633
3/07/70	#38	8	My Woman My Woman, My Wife	Columbia 45091
			ROCKIE ROBBINS	
7/19/80	#88	2	You And Me	A&M 2231
			SYLVIA ROBBINS	
5/07/60	#85	5	Frankie And Johnny	Jubilee 5386
			ROBERT & JOHNNY	
3/22/58	#58	2	We Belong Together	Old Town 1047
			AUSTIN ROBERTS	
9/09/72	#10	18	Something's Wrong With Me	Chelsea 0101
1/27/73	#39	8	Keep On Singing	Chelsea 0110
7/19/75	#11	16	Rocky	Private Stock 45020
			DERRIK ROBERTS	
12/18/65	#77	2	There Won't Be Any Snow (Christmas In The Jungle)	Roulette 4656
			JOHN ROBERTS	
11/18/67	#79	8	Sockin' 1-2-3-4	Duke 425
			KANE ROBERTS	
4/27/91	#33	17	Does Anybody Really Fall In Love Anymore?	DGC 19009
			DON ROBERTSON	
6/16/56	#8	3	The Happy Whistler	Capitol 3391
			ROBEY	
3/02/85	#75	5	One Night In Bangkok	Silver Blue 04774
			IVO ROBIC	
8/15/59	#12	14	Morgen	Laurie 3033
1/09/60	#50	9	The Happy Muleteer	Laurie 3045
			ROBIN S.	
5/01/93	#4	30	Show Me Love	Big Beat 10118
9/04/93	#54	15	Love For Love	Big Beat 98382
			JIMMY ROBINS	
1/14/67	#80	3	I Can't Please You	Jerhart 207
			ALVIN ROBINSON	
5/23/64	#46	9	Something You Got	Tiger 104
			FLOYD ROBINSON	
8/01/59	#17	13	Makin' Love	RCA 7529
			FREDDY ROBINSON	
8/01/79	#45	8	Black Fox	World Pacific 88155
			J.P. ROBINSON	
11/01/69	#96	2	You Got Your Thing On A String	Alston 4577
			ROSCOE ROBINSON	
7/09/66	#54	12	That's Enough	Wand 1125

Debut Date	Peak Pos	Wks Chr	ARTIST/Song Title	Label & Number
			SMOKEY ROBINSON (see also MIRACLES)	
7/21/73	#60	9	Sweet Harmony	Tamla 54233
11/24/73	#36	16	Baby Come Close	Tamla 54239
5/18/74	#69	8	It's Her Turn To Live	Tamla 54246
9/07/74	#70	9	Virgin Man	Tamla 54250
12/28/74	#60	7	I Am I Am	Tamla 54251
4/26/75	#38	11	Baby That's Backatcha	Tamla 54258
8/16/75	#50	14	The Agony And The Ecstasy	Tamla 54261
1/17/76	#77	7	Quiet Storm	Tamla 54265
3/12/77	#66	6	There Will Come A Day	Tamla 54279
7/01/78	#90	4	Daylight And Darkness	Tamla 54293
1/20/79	#65	6	Pops, We Love You*	Motown 1455
10/20/79	#1	26	Cruisin'	Tamla 54306
3/15/80	#37	13	Let Me Be The Clock	Tamla 54311
2/21/81	#2	24	Being With You	Tamla 54321
6/20/81	#66	5	You Are Forever	Tamla 54327
1/16/82	#29	15	Tell Me Tomorrow (Part 1)	Tamla 1601
4/24/82	#70	5	Old Fashioned Love	Tamla 1615
7/02/83	#49	12	Blame It On Love**	Tamla 1684
12/10/83	#45	12	Ebony Eyes***	Gordy 1714
4/04/87	#7	22	Just To See Her	Motown 1877
7/18/87	#11	20	One Heartbeat	Motown 1897
11/28/87	#80	7	What's Too Much	Motown 1911
2/04/89	#40	11	We've Saved The Best For Last****	Arista 9785
10/26/91	#84	8	Double Good Everything	SBK 07370
			*released as by DIANA ROSS, MARVIN GAYE, SMOKEY ROBINSON & STEVIE WONDER	
			**released as by SMOKEY ROBINSON and BARBARA MITCHELL	
			***released as by RICK JAMES featuring SMOKEY ROBINSON	
			****released as by KENNY G with SMOKEY ROBINSON	
			STAN ROBINSON	
3/14/59	#75	7	Boom-A-Dip-Dip	Monument 402
			VICKI SUE ROBINSON	
5/08/76	#15	24	Turn The Beat Around	RCA 10562
10/16/76	#97	4	Daylight	RCA 10775
			ROCHELL and THE CANDLES	
2/25/61	#27	11	Once Upon A Time	Swingin' 623
			ROCK and HYDE	
5/02/87	#63	9	Dirty Water	Capitol 5691
			ROCK AND ROLL DOUBLE BUBBLE TRADING CARD CO. OF PHILADELPHIA 19141	
1/25/69	#64	4	Bubble Gum Music	Buddah 78
			ROCK-A-TEENS	
9/26/59	#18	13	Woo-Hoo	Roulette 4192
			ROCKETS	
4/21/79	#56	10	Can't Sleep	RSO 926
7/07/79	#39	12	Oh Well	RSO 935
2/23/80	#76	4	Desire	RSO 1022
			ROCK FLOWERS	
12/11/71	#78	6	Number Wonderful	Wheel 0032
			DAVID ROCKINGHAM TRIO	
11/09/63	#80	7	Dawn	Josie 913
			ROCKIN' R'S	
3/21/59	#83	6	The Beat	Tempus 7541
			ROCKPILE	
11/29/80	#75	10	Teacher Teacher	Columbia 11388
			ROCKWELL	
1/28/84	#2	22	Somebody's Watching Me	Motown 1702
5/12/84	#30	15	Obscene Phone Caller	Motown 1731
			ROCKY FELLERS	
3/09/63	#16	15	Killer Joe	Scepter 1246
6/22/63	#62	5	Like The Big Guys Do	Scepter 1254

Debut Date	Peak Pos	Wks Chr	**ARTIST**/Song Title	Label & Number
			EILEEN RODGERS	
9/08/56	#24	11	Miracle Of Love	Columbia 40708
3/02/57	#42	5	The Wall	Columbia 40850
9/13/58	#45	13	Treasure Of Your Love	Columbia 41214
			JIMMIE RODGERS	
8/03/57	#1	21	Honeycomb	Roulette 4015
11/09/57	#5	16	Kisses Sweeter Than Wine	Roulette 4031
2/08/58	#13	11	Oh-Oh, I'm Falling In Love Again/	Roulette 4045
2/08/58	#49	1	The Long Hot Summer	Roulette 4045
5/03/58	#4	18	Secretly/	Roulette 4070
5/03/58	#31	8	Make Me A Miracle	Roulette 4070
8/02/58	#14	14	Are You Really Mine	Roulette 4090
11/15/58	#11	14	Bimbombey	Roulette 4116
2/21/59	#30	10	Because You're Young/	Roulette 4129
2/21/59	#39	12	I'm Never Gonna Tell	Roulette 4129
5/30/59	#38	10	Ring-A-Ling-A-Lario	Roulette 4158
9/19/59	#34	10	Tucumcari	Roulette 4191
1/16/60	#27	10	T.L.C. Tender Love And Care	Roulette 4218
4/30/60	#55	8	Just A Closer Walk With Thee	Roulette 4234
7/23/60	#50	12	The Wreck Of The "John B"	Roulette 4260
8/25/62	#50	12	No One Will Ever Know	Dot 16378
11/24/62	#62	8	Rainbow At Midnight	Dot 16407
9/19/63	#70	5	Two-Ten, Six-Eighteen	Dot 16527
5/23/64	#61	11	The World I Used To Know	Dot 16595
5/14/66	#55	8	It's Over	Dot 16861
9/09/67	#30	10	Child Of Clay	A&M 871
11/26/68	#90	4	Today	A&M 976
			JOHNNY RODRIGUEZ	
10/13/73	#75	5	Ridin' My Thumb To Mexico	Mercury 73416
			RODWAY	
12/18/82	#78	6	Don't Stop Trying	Millennium 13111
			TOMMY ROE	
7/21/62	#2	16	Sheila	ABC-Paramount 10329
10/13/62	#34	7	Susie Darlin'	ABC-Paramount 10362
5/04/63	#96	4	The Folk Singer	ABC-Paramount 10423
10/05/63	#5	16	Everybody	ABC-Paramount 10478
1/18/64	#27	8	Come On	ABC-Paramount 10515
4/25/64	#61	6	Carol	ABC-Paramount 10543
5/28/66	#8	16	Sweet Pea	ABC-Paramount 10762
9/24/66	#6	12	Hooray For Hazel	ABC 10852
12/24/66	#22	11	It's Now Winters Day	ABC 10888
3/11/67	#91	3	Sing Along With Me	ABC 10908
6/24/67	#90	2	Little Miss Sunshine	ABC 10945
2/24/68	#85	2	Dottie I Like It	ABC 11039
1/18/69	#1	17	Dizzy	ABC 11164
4/26/69	#14	8	Heather Honey	ABC 11211
7/12/69	#40	11	Jack And Jill	ABC 11229
11/15/69	#5	14	Jam Up Jelly Tight	ABC 11247
2/21/70	#32	8	Stir It Up And Serve It	ABC 11258
6/20/70	#30	9	Pearl	ABC 11266
9/05/70	#35	7	We Can Make Music	ABC 11273
8/14/71	#19	14	Stagger Lee	ABC 11307
4/07/73	#67	8	Working Class Hero	MGM South 7013
			ROGER	
10/24/81	#75	12	I Heard It Through The Grapevine	Warner Brothers 49786
11/21/87	#6	21	I Want To Be Your Man	Reprise 28229
6/25/88	#57	13	Boom! There She Was*	Warner Brothers 27976
8/21/93	#55	24	Mega Medley**	Reprise 18420
11/06/93	#29	22	Slow And Easy**	Reprise 18315
			*released as by **SCRITTI POLITTI** featuring **ROGER**	
			released as by **ZAPP & ROGER	
			DANN ROGERS	
12/15/79	#51	11	Looks Like Love Again	IA 500
			JULIE ROGERS	
11/14/64	#9	13	The Wedding	Mercury 72332
2/06/65	#69	6	Like A Child	Mercury 72380

Debut Date	Peak Pos	Wks Chr	ARTIST/Song Title	Label & Number
			KENNY ROGERS	
4/26/58	#51	3	That Crazy Feeling	Carlton 454
4/02/77	#6	18	Lucille	United Artists 929
8/06/77	#28	11	Daytime Friends	United Artists 1027
12/17/77	#60	9	Sweet Music Man	United Artists 1095
6/03/78	#38	12	Love Or Something Like It	United Artists 1210
11/18/78	#13	22	The Gambler	United Artists 1250
4/21/79	#7	20	She Believes In Me	United Artists 1273
9/08/79	#7	19	You Decorated My Life	United Artists 1315
11/17/79	#1	21	Coward Of The County	United Artists 1327
3/29/80	#4	18	Don't Fall In Love With A Dreamer*	United Artists 1345
6/14/80	#17	16	Love The World Away	United Artists 1359
10/04/80	#1	26	Lady	Liberty 1380
3/28/81	#15	21	What Are We Doin' In Love**	Liberty 1404
6/13/81	#5	17	I Don't Need You	Liberty 1415
9/05/81	#14	13	Share Your Love With Me	Liberty 1430
11/21/81	#68	8	Blaze Of Glory	Liberty 1441
12/26/81	#12	18	Through The Years	Liberty 1444
7/03/82	#12	17	Love Will Turn You Around	Liberty 1471
10/09/82	#44	15	A Love Song	Liberty 1485
1/29/83	#10	19	We've Got Tonight***	Liberty 1492
4/30/83	#37	12	All My Life	Liberty 1495
8/27/83	#1	29	Islands In The Stream****	RCA 13615
1/14/84	#30	13	This Woman	RCA 13710
9/15/84	#21	18	What About Me?*****	RCA 13899

*released as by **KENNY ROGERS with KIM CARNES**
released as by **DOTTIE WEST with KENNY ROGERS
***released as by **KENNY ROGERS and SHEENA EASTON**
****released as by **KENNY ROGERS with DOLLY PARTON**
*****released as by **KENNY ROGERS with KIM CARNES and JAMES INGRAM**

Debut Date	Peak Pos	Wks Chr	ARTIST/Song Title	Label & Number
			KENNY ROGERS and THE FIRST EDITION	
2/03/68	#5	12	Just Dropped In (To See What Condition My Condition Was In)*	Reprise 0655
1/11/69	#15	12	But You Know I Love You*	Reprise 0799
6/07/69	#7	14	Ruby, Don't Take Your Love To Town	Reprise 0829
9/27/69	#14	12	Ruben James	Reprise 0854
2/07/70	#5	17	Something's Burning	Reprise 0888
7/04/70	#17	12	Tell It All Brother	Reprise 0923
10/10/70	#21	10	Heed The Call	Reprise 0953
3/20/71	#48	8	Someone Who Cares	Reprise 0999

*released as by **THE FIRST EDITION**

Debut Date	Peak Pos	Wks Chr	ARTIST/Song Title	Label & Number
			LEE ROGERS	
12/05/64	#87	8	I Want You To Have Everything	D-Town 1035
			ROY ROGERS	
12/21/74	#61	7	Hoppy, Gene And Me	20th Century 2154
			TIMMIE "OH YEAH!" ROGERS	
10/12/57	#30	7	Back To School Again	Cameo 116
			DANA ROLLIN	
11/05/66	#94	3	Winchester Cathedral	Tower 283
			ROLLING STONES	
5/09/64	#44	11	Not Fade Away	London 9657
7/04/64	#27	11	Tell Me (You're Coming Back)	London 9682
7/25/64	#25	10	It's All Over Now	London 9687
10/17/64	#6	13	Time Is On My Side	London 9708
1/09/65	#16	11	Heart Of Stone	London 9725
3/27/65	#10	11	The Last Time	London 9741
6/12/65	#1	14	(I Can't Get No) Satisfaction	London 9766
10/09/65	#1	12	Get Off My Cloud	London 9792
12/25/65	#3	8	As Tears Go By	London 9808
2/26/66	#1	10	19th Nervous Breakdown	London 9823
5/14/66	#1	11	Paint It, Black	London 901
7/09/66	#4	9	Mothers Little Helper/	London 902
7/09/66	#46	7	Lady Jane	London 902
10/08/66	#4	7	Have You Seen Your Mother, Baby, Standing In The Shadow?	London 903
1/21/67	#1	13	Ruby Tuesday/	London 904
1/21/67	#28	8	Let's Spend The Night Together	London 904

Debut Date	Peak Pos	Wks Chr	ARTIST/Song Title	Label & Number
			ROLLING STONES—continued	
9/09/67	#6	9	Dandelion/	London 905
9/09/67	#54	6	We Love You	London 905
12/30/67	#10	8	She's A Rainbow	London 906
6/08/68	#1	12	Jumpin' Jack Flash	London 908
9/07/68	#30	6	Street Fighting Man	London 909
7/19/69	#1	16	Honky Tonk Women	London 910
4/24/71	#2	12	Brown Sugar	Rolling Stones 19100
6/19/71	#18	8	Wild Horses	Rolling Stones 19101
4/22/72	#10	11	Tumbling Dice	Rolling Stones 19103
7/08/72	#14	10	Happy/	Rolling Stones 19104
7/22/72	#77	2	All Down The Line	Rolling Stones 19104
4/21/73	#34	10	You Can't Always Get What You Want	London 910
9/08/73	#1	14	Angie	Rolling Stones 19105
1/12/74	#10	8	Doo Doo Doo Doo Doo (Heartbreaker)	Rolling Stones 19109
8/10/74	#18	9	It's Only Rock 'N Roll (But I Like It)	Rolling Stones 19301
11/09/74	#15	10	Ain't Too Proud To Beg	Rolling Stones 19302
6/07/75	#37	8	I Don't Know Why	Abkco 4701
8/16/75	#65	5	Out Of Time	Abkco 4702
4/24/76	#9	14	Fool To Cry/	Rolling Stones 19304
6/19/76	#60	11	Hot Stuff	Rolling Stones 19304
5/27/78	#1	23	Miss You	Rolling Stones 19307
9/09/78	#7	15	Beast Of Burden	Rolling Stones 19309
12/16/78	#27	11	Shattered	Rolling Stones 19310
7/05/80	#3	21	Emotional Rescue	Rolling Stones 20001
9/27/80	#21	17	She's So Cold	Rolling Stones 21001
8/22/81	#4	24	Start Me Up	Rolling Stones 21003
12/05/81	#14	15	Waiting On A Friend	Rolling Stones 21004
3/20/82	#32	11	Hang Fire	Rolling Stones 21300
6/12/82	#20	12	Going To A Go Go	Rolling Stones 21301
11/12/83	#12	15	Undercover Of The Night	Rolling Stones 99813
2/04/84	#52	9	She Was Hot	Rolling Stones 99788
3/15/86	#5	15	Harlem Shuffle	Rolling Stones 05802
5/17/86	#30	12	One Hit (To The Body)	Rolling Stones 05906
9/02/89	#3	20	Mixed Emotions	Rolling Stones 69008
11/04/89	#18	15	Rock And A Hard Place	Rolling Stones 73057
2/10/90	#53	8	Almost Hear You Sigh	Rolling Stones 73093
3/09/91	#49	10	Highwire	Rolling Stones 73742
			DICK ROMAN	
8/04/62	#75	6	Theme From A Summer Place	Harmon 1004
			ROMAN HOLLIDAY	
6/18/83	#57	12	Stand By	Jive 9036
10/01/83	#66	7	Don't Try To Stop It	Jive 9092
			ROMANTICS	
2/16/80	#53	8	What I Like About You	Nemperor 7527
10/08/83	#4	29	Talking In Your Sleep	Nemperor 04135
2/25/84	#39	13	One In A Million	Nemperor 04373
8/31/85	#64	8	Test Of Time	Nemperor 05587
			ROME & PARIS	
6/18/66	#95	2	Because Of You	Roulette 4681
			ROMEOS	
4/15/67	#82	5	Precious Memories	Mark II 101
			ROMEO'S DAUGHTER	
10/15/88	#68	7	Don't Break My Heart	Jive 1140
2/25/89	#72	4	I Cry Myself To Sleep At Night	Jive 1176
			ROMEO VOID	
9/01/84	#30	14	A Girl In Trouble (Is A Temporary Thing)	Columbia 04534
			RONALD and RUBY	
3/08/58	#2	12	Lollipop	RCA 7174
			RONDELS	
7/29/61	#68	8	Back Beat No. 1	Amy 825
			RON-DELS	
7/03/65	#91	2	If You Really Want Me To, I'll Go	Smash 1986
			DON RONDO	
10/13/56	#12	16	Two Different Worlds	Jubilee 5256
6/29/57	#6	16	White Silver Sands	Jubilee 5288

Debut Date	Peak Pos	Wks Chr	**ARTIST**/Song Title	Label & Number
10/05/57	#58	4	There's Only You	Jubilee 5297
8/09/58	#74	4	City Lights/	Jubilee 5334
8/16/58	#74	5	As Long As I Have You	Jubilee 5334
			RONETTES	
8/31/63	#1	14	Be My Baby	Philles 116
12/21/63	#24	9	Baby, I Love You	Philles 118
4/11/64	#48	8	(The Best Part Of) Breakin' Up	Philles 120
6/27/64	#36	8	Do I Love You?	Philles 121
10/31/64	#20	11	Walking In The Rain	Philles 123
2/13/65	#67	4	Born To Be Together*	Philles 126
5/29/65	#92	2	Is This What I Get For Loving You?*	Philles 128
4/05/69	#92	3	You Came, You Saw, You Conquered	A&M 1040
			*released as by **THE RONETTES featuring VERONICA**	
			RONNIE & ROBYN	
7/23/66	#100	1	Cradle Of Love	HBR 489
			RONNIE and THE HI-LITES	
3/31/62	#18	13	I Wish That We Were Married	Joy 260
			RONNY & THE DAYTONAS	
8/01/64	#5	14	G.T.O.	Mala 481
11/14/64	#74	3	California Bound	Mala 490
12/26/64	#61	6	Bucket "T"	Mala 492
12/11/65	#41	9	Sandy	Mala 513
9/10/66	#76	4	Dianne, Dianne	RCA 8896
			LINDA RONSTADT	
11/04/67	#12	19	Different Drum*	Capitol 2004
3/28/70	#98	2	Will You Love Me Tomorrow	Capitol 2767
10/08/70	#26	10	Long Long Time	Capitol 2846
1/16/71	#74	2	The Long Way Around/	Capitol 3021
1/30/71	#99	1	(She's A) Very Lovely Woman	Capitol 3021
12/08/73	#45	9	Love Has No Pride	Asylum 11026
5/04/74	#89	4	Silver Threads And Golden Needles	Asylum 11032
12/07/74	#1	15	You're No Good	Capitol 3990
4/12/75	#1	16	When Will I Be Loved/	Capitol 4050
8/02/75	#80	3	It Doesn't Matter Anymore	Capitol 4050
9/06/75	#70	3	Love Is A Rose/	Asylum 45282
9/27/75	#4	12	Heat Wave	Asylum 45282
12/20/75	#25	14	Tracks Of My Tears	Asylum 45295
8/21/76	#11	16	That'll Be The Day	Asylum 45340
12/04/76	#65	10	Someone To Lay Down Beside Me	Asylum 45361
9/10/77	#2	24	Blue Bayou	Asylum 45431
10/08/77	#9	18	It's So Easy	Asylum 45438
1/28/78	#26	10	Poor Poor Pitiful Me	Asylum 45462
4/22/78	#40	9	Tumbling Dice	Asylum 45479
8/19/78	#11	16	Back In The U.S.A.	Asylum 45519
11/11/78	#7	16	Ooh Baby Baby	Asylum 45546
2/17/79	#46	8	Just One Look	Asylum 46011
2/02/80	#6	16	How Do I Make You	Asylum 46602
4/05/80	#9	16	Hurt So Bad	Asylum 46624
6/28/80	#27	13	I Can't Let Go	Asylum 46654
10/02/82	#20	12	Get Closer	Asylum 69948
12/11/82	#30	15	I Knew You When	Asylum 69853
5/14/83	#66	6	Easy For You To Say	Asylum 69838
11/05/83	#38	14	What's New**	Asylum 69780
12/20/86	#4	23	Somewhere Out There***	MCA 52973
9/30/89	#2	25	Don't Know Much****	Elektra 69261
1/27/90	#11	19	All My Life****	Elektra 64987
5/19/90	#80	5	When Something Is Wrong With My Baby****	Elektra 64968
			*released as by **THE STONE PONEYS featuring LINDA RONSTADT**	
			released as by **LINDA RONSTADT & THE NELSON RIDDLE ORCHESTRA	
			***released as by **LINDA RONSTADT and JAMES INGRAM**	
			****released as by **LINDA RONSTADT featuring AARON NEVILLE**	
			ROOFTOP SINGERS	
12/29/62	#1	16	Walk Right In	Vanguard 35017
3/30/63	#20	10	Tom Cat	Vanguard 35019
7/13/63	#48	7	Mama Don't Allow	Vanguard 35020

Debut Date	Peak Pos	Wks Chr	ARTIST/Song Title	Label & Number
			ROOMMATES	
4/15/61	#44	10	Glory Of Love	Valmor 008
9/23/61	#83	5	Band Of Gold	Valmor 010
			ROOSTERS	
4/27/68	#98	2	Love Machine	Philips 40504
			EDMUNDO ROS	
1/04/58	#15	5	Colonel Bogey	London 1779
12/13/58	#46	11	I Talk To The Trees	London 1831
			ANDY ROSE	
9/20/58	#28	7	Just Young	Aamco 100
			DAVID ROSE	
3/02/57	#33	10	Calypso Melody	MGM 12430
2/01/58	#18	6	Swinging Shepherd Blues	MGM 12608
5/12/62	#1	18	The Stripper	MGM 13064
			ROSE COLORED GLASS	
4/17/71	#53	12	Can't Find The Time	Bang 584
10/30/71	#97	1	If It's Alright With You	Bang 588
			ROSE GARDEN	
10/28/67	#15	15	Next Plane To London	Atco 6510
			JIMMY ROSELLI	
7/01/67	#90	9	There Must Be A Way	United Artists 50179
			ROSE ROYCE	
11/06/76	#1	20	Car Wash	MCA 40615
3/05/77	#10	16	I Wanna Get Next To You	MCA 40662
5/14/77	#64	8	I'm Going Down	MCA 40721
10/08/77	#67	7	Do Your Dance (Part 1)	Whitfield 8440
12/03/77	#48	10	Ooh Boy	Whitfield 8491
11/18/78	#28	16	Love Don't Live Here Anymore	Whitfield 8712
			ROSIE and THE ORIGINALS	
12/10/60	#6	14	Angel Baby	Highland 1011
3/04/61	#48	7	Lonely Blue Nights	Brunswick 55205
			CHARLIE ROSS	
1/11/75	#61	7	Thanks For The Smiles	Big Tree 16025
2/21/76	#44	9	Without Your Love (Mr. Jordan)	Big Tree 16056
			DIANA ROSS	
4/18/70	#10	9	Reach Out And Touch (Somebody's Hand)	Motown 1165
8/08/70	#1	12	Ain't No Mountain High Enough	Motown 1169
12/26/70	#8	11	Remember Me	Motown 1176
5/01/71	#19	8	Reach Out I'll Be There	Motown 1184
8/21/71	#47	6	Surrender	Motown 1188
10/30/71	#71	5	I'm Still Waiting	Motown 1192
1/06/73	#30	12	Good Morning Heartache	Motown 1211
6/02/73	#1	19	Touch Me In The Morning	Motown 1239
9/29/73	#14	11	You're A Special Part Of Me*	Motown 1280
12/29/73	#9	13	Last Time I Saw Him	Motown 1278
2/16/74	#20	14	My Mistake (Was To Love You)*	Motown 1269
4/27/74	#53	8	Sleepin'	Motown 1295
7/20/74	#38	7	Don't Knock My Love*	Motown 1296
3/08/75	#84	5	Sorry Doesn't Always Make It Right	Motown 1335
11/01/75	#1	16	Theme From Mahogany	Motown 1377
3/20/76	#60	4	I Thought It Took A Little Time	Motown 1387
4/10/76	#1	17	Love Hangover	Motown 1392
7/31/76	#34	16	One Love In My Lifetime	Motown 1398
10/29/77	#32	15	Gettin' Ready For Love	Motown 1427
3/04/78	#75	7	Your Love Is So Good For Me	Motown 1436
5/06/78	#69	7	You Got It	Motown 1442
9/02/78	#36	14	Ease On Down The Road**	MCA 40947
1/20/79	#65	6	Pops, We Love You***	Motown 1455
7/07/79	#21	19	The Boss	Motown 1462
7/12/80	#1	28	Upside Down	Motown 1494
9/13/80	#6	22	I'm Coming Out	Motown 1491
10/25/80	#18	21	It's My Turn	Motown 1496
7/04/81	#1	29	Endless Love****	Motown 1519
10/17/81	#7	18	Why Do Fools Fall In Love	RCA 12349
1/16/82	#7	15	Mirror, Mirror	RCA 13021
4/10/82	#41	9	Work That Body	RCA 13201

Debut Date	Peak Pos	Wks Chr	ARTIST/Song Title	Label & Number
10/02/82	#7	18	Muscles	RCA 13348
2/05/83	#35	11	So Close	RCA 13424
6/25/83	#30	12	Pieces Of Ice	RCA 13549
7/07/84	#12	18	All Of You*****	Columbia 04507
9/01/84	#22	16	Swept Away	RCA 13864
12/01/84	#13	29	Missing You	RCA 13966
9/21/85	#80	5	Eaten Alive	RCA 14181
5/03/86	#77	6	Chain Reaction	RCA 14244

*released as by DIANA ROSS & MARVIN GAYE
**released as by DIANA ROSS/MICHAEL JACKSON
***released as by DIANA ROSS, MARVIN GAYE, SMOKEY ROBINSON & STEVIE WONDER
****released as by DIANA ROSS & LIONEL RICHIE
*****released as by JULIO IGLESIAS & DIANA ROSS

GENE ROSS
| 5/03/58 | #47 | 2 | Endless Sleep | Herald 517 |

JACK ROSS
| 1/06/62 | #53 | 8 | Happy Jose | Dot 16302 |
| 3/24/62 | #35 | 7 | Cinderella | Dot 16333 |

JACKIE ROSS
7/25/64	#11	12	Selfish One	Chess 1903
11/07/64	#98	2	I've Got The Skill	Chess 1913
2/06/65	#73	3	Jerk And Twine	Chess 1920

SPENCER ROSS
| 1/02/60 | #15 | 14 | Tracy's Theme | Columbia 41532 |

ROSSINGTON COLLINS BAND
| 7/26/80 | #58 | 8 | Don't Misunderstand Me | MCA 41284 |

NINI ROSSO
| 10/30/65 | #84 | 6 | Il Silenzio | Columbia 43363 |

NINO ROTA
| 5/06/72 | #84 | 5 | Love Theme From "The Godfather" | Paramount 0152 |

ROTARY CONNECTION
| 12/13/69 | #80 | 3 | Want You To Know | Cadet Concept 7018 |

DAVID LEE ROTH
1/19/85	#3	16	California Girls	Warner Brothers 29102
3/23/85	#20	17	Just A Gigolo/I Ain't Got Nobody	Warner Brothers 29040
7/05/86	#27	14	Yankee Rose	Warner Brothers 28656
9/27/86	#69	7	Goin' Crazy!	Warner Brothers 28584
11/29/86	#86	7	That's Life	Warner Brothers 28511
1/16/88	#8	17	Just Like Paradise	Warner Brothers 28119
4/23/88	#74	6	Stand Up	Warner Brothers 28108

ROUGH TRADE
| 12/18/82 | #75 | 7 | All Touch | Boardwalk 167 |

ROUND ROBIN
| 5/23/64 | #68 | 10 | Kick That Little Foot Sally Ann | Domain 1404 |

DEMIS ROUSSOS
| 5/27/78 | #79 | 8 | That Once In A Lifetime | Mercury 73992 |

ROUTERS
| 10/20/62 | #27 | 16 | Let's Go (Pony) | Warner Brothers 5283 |
| 4/27/63 | #45 | 10 | Sting Ray | Warner Brothers 5349 |

ROVER BOYS
| 6/30/56 | #6 | 3 | Graduation Day | ABC-Paramount 9700 |
| 9/01/56 | #43 | 4 | From A School Ring To A Wedding Ring | ABC-Paramount 9732 |

ROVERS (see IRISH ROVERS)

ROWANS
| 10/09/76 | #69 | 7 | If Only I Could | Elektra 45347 |

JOHN ROWLES
| 1/16/71 | #78 | 5 | Cheryl Moana Marie | Kapp 2102 |

ROXANNE
| 3/19/88 | #73 | 8 | Play That Funky Music | Scotti Brothers 07724 |

Debut Date	Peak Pos	Wks Chr	ARTIST/Song Title	Label & Number
			ROXETTE	
2/11/89	#2	23	The Look	EMI 50190
5/27/89	#14	18	Dressed For Success	EMI 50204
8/26/89	#1	23	Listen To Your Heart	EMI 50223
12/16/89	#1	21	Dangerous	EMI 50233
4/07/90	#2	24	It Must Have Been Love	EMI 50283
3/02/91	#1	24	Joyride	EMI 50342
6/15/91	#3	21	Fading Like A Flower	EMI 50355
10/26/91	#14	23	Spending My Time	EMI 50366
2/22/92	#32	16	Church Of Your Heart	EMI 50380
10/17/92	#53	9	How Do You Do!	EMI 50410
6/26/93	#88	3	Almost Unreal	Capitol 44942
			ROXY MUSIC	
12/20/75	#24	16	Love Is The Drug	Atco 7042
4/21/79	#51	11	Dance Away	Atco 7100
8/09/80	#90	4	Over You	Atco 7301
			BILLY JOE ROYAL	
7/03/65	#6	13	Down In The Boondocks	Columbia 43305
9/18/65	#14	11	I Knew You When	Columbia 43390
12/04/65	#35	8	I've Got To Be Somebody	Columbia 43465
5/28/66	#100	1	Heart's Desire	Columbia 43622
8/27/66	#97	4	Campfire Girls	Columbia 43740
10/07/67	#55	8	Hush	Columbia 44277
9/27/69	#15	15	Cherry Hill Park	Columbia 44902
2/27/71	#88	4	Tulsa	Columbia 45289
5/27/78	#60	4	Under The Boardwalk	Private Stock 45192
6/06/81	#96	3	You Really Got A Hold On Me	Kat Family 2074
			ROYALETTES	
7/24/65	#37	10	It's Gonna Take A Miracle	MGM 13366
10/23/65	#78	7	I Want To Meet Him	MGM 13405
			ROYAL GUARDSMEN	
12/10/66	#2	13	Snoopy Vs. The Red Baron	Laurie 3366
2/25/67	#15	8	Return Of The Red Baron	Laurie 3379
6/24/67	#76	4	Airplane Song (My Airplane)	Laurie 3391
12/09/67	#10	4	Snoopy's Christmas	Laurie 3416
2/24/68	#82	3	I Say Love	Laurie 3428
11/09/68	#33	12	Baby Let's Wait	Laurie 3461
			ROYAL PHILHARMONIC ORCHESTRA	
10/31/81	#10	22	Hooked On Classics	RCA 12304
			ROYAL SCOTS DRAGOON GUARDS	
5/13/72	#10	10	Amazing Grace	RCA 0709
			ROYAL TEENS	
1/25/58	#3	12	Short Shorts	ABC-Paramount 9882
5/28/58	#59	3	Big Name Button	ABC-Paramount 9918
10/03/59	#24	16	Believe Me	Capitol 4261
			ROYALTONES	
10/04/58	#31	18	Poor Boy	Jubilee 5338
12/24/60	#49	9	Flamingo Express	Goldisc 3011
4/25/64	#92	3	Our Faded Love	Mala 473
5/01/65	#90	2	Poor Boy	MGM 13327
			ROZALLA	
8/01/92	#39	20	Everybody's Free (To Feel Good)	Epic 74388
			RTZ	
8/17/91	#39	11	Face The Music	Giant 19273
1/18/92	#5	23	Until Your Love Comes Back Around	Giant 19051
6/13/92	#50	10	All You've Got	Giant 19112
			RUBETTES	
7/20/74	#30	10	Sugar Baby Love	Polydor 15089
			RUBICON	
2/18/78	#31	12	I'm Gonna Take Care Of Everything	20th Century 2362
			RUBINOOS	
2/26/77	#46	14	I Think We're Alone Now	Beserkley 5741
			RUBY and THE ROMANTICS	
2/02/63	#1	15	Our Day Will Come	Kapp 501
5/11/63	#20	12	My Summer Love	Kapp 525

Debut Date	Peak Pos	Wks Chr	ARTIST/Song Title	Label & Number
8/10/63	#34	9	Hey There Lonely Boy	Kapp 544
10/19/63	#40	9	Young Wings Can Fly	Kapp 557
3/07/64	#49	8	Our Everlasting Love	Kapp 578
7/11/64	#86	7	Baby Come Home	Kapp 601
10/10/64	#58	7	When You're Young And In Love	Kapp 615
2/13/65	#82	4	Does He Really Care For Me	Kapp 646
			RUDE BOYS	
4/13/91	#35	17	Written All Over Your Face	Atlantic 87805
			DAVID RUFFIN	
2/08/69	#9	10	My Whole World Ended (The Moment You Left Me)	Motown 1140
7/12/69	#54	3	I've Lost Everything I've Ever Loved	Motown 1149
12/06/69	#59	6	I'm So Glad I Fell For You	Motown 1158
10/24/70	#57	6	Stand By Me*	Soul 35076
11/15/75	#8	16	Walk Away From Love	Motown 1376
3/20/76	#69	7	Heavy Love	Motown 1388
6/26/76	#70	6	Everything's Coming Up Love	Motown 1393
			*released as by DAVID & JIMMY RUFFIN	
			JIMMY RUFFIN	
8/20/66	#9	17	What Becomes Of The Broken Hearted	Soul 35022
12/10/66	#17	9	I've Passed This Way Before	Soul 35027
3/18/67	#42	7	Gonna Give Her All The Love I Got	Soul 35032
7/22/67	#55	5	Don't You Miss Me A Little Bit Baby	Soul 35035
3/16/68	#70	3	I'll Say Forever My Love	Soul 35043
10/24/70	#57	6	Stand By Me*	Soul 35076
2/20/71	#90	2	Maria (You Were The Only One)	Soul 35077
3/01/80	#14	16	Hold On To My Love	RSO 1021
			*released as by DAVID & JIMMY RUFFIN	
			RUFUS featuring CHAKA KHAN	
4/28/73	#90	3	Slip N' Slide	ABC 11356
6/22/74	#1	16	Tell Me Something Good*	ABC 11427
10/12/74	#10	15	You Got The Love	ABC 12032
2/08/75	#6	13	Once You Get Started	ABC 12066
5/24/75	#44	7	Please Pardon Me	ABC 12099
12/27/75	#5	23	Sweet Thing	ABC 12149
4/24/76	#37	7	Dance Wit Me	ABC 12179
2/05/77	#30	14	At Midnight (My Love Will Lift You Up)	ABC 12239
4/30/77	#39	12	Hollywood	ABC 12269
4/22/78	#45	8	Stay**	ABC 12349
11/17/79	#22	17	Do You Love What You Feel***	MCA 41131
10/01/83	#23	20	Ain't Nobody**	Warner Brothers 29555
			*released as by RUFUS	
			**released as by RUFUS and CHAKA KHAN	
			***released as by RUFUS and CHAKA	
			RUFUS & CARLA (see RUFUS THOMAS or CARLA THOMAS)	
			RUGBYS	
8/16/69	#22	12	You, I	Amazon 1
			RUMBLERS	
2/23/63	#85	3	Boss	Dot 16421
			TODD RUNDGREN	
11/07/70	#21	17	We Gotta Get You A Woman*	Ampex 31001
5/01/71	#87	4	Be Nice To Me*	Bearsville 31002
4/01/72	#11	14	I Saw The Light	Bearsville 0003
9/29/73	#2	19	Hello It's Me	Bearsville 0009
3/23/74	#46	8	A Dream Goes On Forever	Bearsville 0020
1/18/75	#94	2	Wolfman Jack	Bearsville 0301
4/12/75	#84	5	Real Man	Bearsville 0304
6/05/76	#47	9	Good Vibrations	Bearsville 0309
6/03/78	#38	13	Can We Still Be Friends	Bearsville 0324
4/30/83	#73	7	Bang The Drum All Day	Bearsville 29686
			*released as by RUNT	
			RUN-D.M.C.	
7/26/86	#9	19	Walk This Way	Profile 5112
10/25/86	#35	17	You Be Illin'	Profile 5119
2/28/87	#77	9	It's Tricky	Profile 5131
8/06/88	#91	3	Mary, Mary	Profile 5211
3/27/93	#30	17	Down With The King	Profile 5391

Debut Date	Peak Pos	Wks Chr	ARTIST/Song Title	Label & Number
			RUNT (see TODD RUNDGREN)	
			RUPAUL	
2/20/93	#50	16	Supermodel (You Better Work)	Tommy Boy 542
			RUSH	
10/29/77	#79	8	Closer To The Heart	Mercury 73958
2/23/80	#60	9	Spirit Of The Radio	Mercury 76044
3/14/81	#66	8	Limelight	Mercury 76095
6/27/81	#47	11	Tom Sawyer	Mercury 76109
12/05/81	#73	7	Closer To The Heart	Mercury 76124
9/18/82	#35	13	New World Man	Mercury 76179
11/16/85	#45	13	The Big Money	Mercury 884191
			JENNIFER RUSH	
2/15/86	#64	11	The Power Of Love	Epic 05754
5/16/87	#38	14	Flames Of Paradise*	Epic 07119
			*released as by JENNIFER RUSH with ELTON JOHN	
			MERRILEE RUSH and THE TURNABOUTS	
5/04/68	#3	15	Angel Of The Morning	Bell 705
8/24/68	#40	7	That Kind Of Woman	Bell 738
11/23/68	#87	4	Reach Out*	AGP 107
6/04/77	#78	6	Save Me	United Artists 993
			*released as by MERILEE RUSH	
			PATRICE RUSHEN	
1/26/80	#52	9	Haven't You Heard	Elektra 46551
1/24/81	#96	3	Look Up	Elektra 47067
5/08/82	#22	16	Forget Me Nots	Elektra 47427
7/07/84	#80	4	Feels So Real (Won't Let Go)	Elektra 69742
			LONNIE RUSS	
12/15/62	#66	8	My Wife Can't Cook	4J 501
			BOBBY RUSSELL	
10/05/68	#41	10	1432 Franklin Pike Circle Hero	Elf 90020
7/10/71	#34	15	Saturday Morning Confusion	United Artists 50788
			BRENDA RUSSELL	
8/11/79	#26	18	So Good, So Right	Horizon 123
2/13/88	#9	25	Piano In The Dark	A&M 3003
			LEON RUSSELL	
6/20/70	#91	2	Roll Away The Stone	Shelter 7301
8/19/72	#10	13	Tight Rope	Shelter 7325
12/09/72	#94	1	Slipping Into Christmas	Shelter 7328
9/15/73	#87	3	Queen Of The Roller Derby	Shelter 7337
10/13/73	#66	3	Roll In My Sweet Baby's Arms*	Shelter 7336
5/04/74	#96	3	If I Were A Carpenter	Shelter 40210
7/26/75	#8	20	Lady Blue	Shelter 40378
12/27/75	#56	7	Back To The Island	Shelter 40483
6/26/76	#62	11	Rainbow In Your Eyes**	Paradise 8208
			*released as by HANK WILSON	
			**released as by LEON & MARY RUSSELL	
			CHARLIE RUSSO	
3/23/63	#82	6	Preacherman	Diamond 131
			BARRY RYAN	
12/21/68	#50	6	Eloise	MGM 14010
			CHARLIE RYAN and THE TIMBERLINE RIDERS	
8/13/60	#25	11	Hot Rod Lincoln	4 Star 1733
			BOBBY RYDELL	
8/01/59	#16	12	Kissin' Time	Cameo 167
10/24/59	#4	17	We Got Love/	Cameo 169
10/24/59	#68	4	I Dig Girls	Cameo 169
1/30/60	#3	16	Wild One/	Cameo 171
1/30/60	#43	12	Little Bitty Girl	Cameo 171
4/30/60	#6	14	Swingin' School/	Cameo 175
4/30/60	#17	10	Ding-A-Ling	Cameo 175
7/30/60	#4	15	Volare	Cameo 179
11/05/60	#12	14	Sway	Cameo 182
1/28/61	#13	11	Good Time Baby/	Cameo 186
1/28/61	#87	2	Cherie	Cameo 186
4/29/61	#21	10	That Old Black Magic	Cameo 190

Debut Date	Peak Pos	Wks Chr	ARTIST/Song Title	Label & Number
7/08/61	#17	8	The Fish	Cameo 192
10/21/61	#22	10	I Wanna Thank You/	Cameo 201
10/21/61	#81	5	Door To Paradise	Cameo 201
12/16/61	#38	4	Jingle Bell Rock*	Cameo 205
2/10/62	#17	12	I've Got Bonnie/	Cameo 209
2/10/62	#66	3	Lose Her	Cameo 209
4/28/62	#76	3	Teach Me How To Twist*	Cameo 214
5/26/62	#19	13	I'll Never Dance Again	Cameo 217
10/06/62	#13	13	The Cha-Cha-Cha	Cameo 228
12/15/62	#59	4	Jingle Bell Rock*	Cameo 205
2/09/63	#24	9	Butterfly Baby	Cameo 242
5/11/63	#26	9	Wildwood Days	Cameo 252
8/17/63	#92	2	Woodpecker Song	Cameo 265
9/28/63	#92	3	Let's Make Love Tonight	Cameo 272
11/16/63	#5	16	Forget Him	Cameo 280
3/21/64	#57	7	Make Me Forget	Cameo 309

released as by BOBBY RYDELL/CHUBBY CHECKER

JOHN & ANNE RYDER

| 9/20/69 | #56 | 10 | I Still Believe In Tomorrow | Decca 32506 |

MITCH RYDER and THE DETROIT WHEELS

12/18/65	#17	11	Jenny Take A Ride!	New Voice 806
3/12/66	#16	9	Little Latin Lupe Lu	New Voice 808
6/04/66	#72	3	Break Out	New Voice 811
10/08/66	#4	16	Devil With A Blue Dress On & Good Golly Miss Molly	New Voice 817
2/04/67	#4	12	Sock It To Me Baby!	New Voice 820
4/29/67	#26	7	Too Many Fish In The Sea & Three Little Fishes	New Voice 822
7/01/67	#39	6	Joy*	New Voice 824
9/09/67	#22	7	What Now My Love*	DynoVoice 901
10/28/67	#71	4	You Are My Sunshine*	New Voice 826
1/27/68	#63	6	(You've Got) Personality & Chantilly Lace*	DynoVoice 905
9/06/69	#92	2	Sugar Bee*	Dot 17290

released as by MITCH RYDER

JOHN WESLEY RYLES I

| 1/18/69 | #97 | 1 | Kay | Columbia 44682 |

JIMMY RYSER

| 7/28/90 | #66 | 5 | Same Old Look | Arista 2039 |

RYTHM SYNDICATE

6/01/91	#3	21	P.A.S.S.I.O.N.	Impact 54046
9/07/91	#11	21	Hey Donna	Impact 54208
12/28/91	#58	11	Blinded By Love	Impact 54275
9/19/92	#66	8	I Wanna Make Love To You	Impact 54458

S

SAD CAFE

| 2/03/79 | #81 | 6 | Run Home Girl | A&M 2111 |

SADE

3/02/85	#6	21	Smooth Operator	Portrait 04807
6/22/85	#52	10	Your Love Is King	Portrait 05408
11/30/85	#8	23	The Sweetest Taboo	Portrait 05713
3/29/86	#23	14	Never As Good As The First Time	Portrait 05846
5/14/88	#20	17	Paradise	Epic 07904
11/14/92	#21	24	No Ordinary Love	Epic 74734
3/20/93	#44	13	Kiss Of Life	Epic 74848

SSgt. BARRY SADLER

| 1/29/66 | #1 | 15 | The Ballad Of The Green Berets | RCA 8739 |
| 4/23/66 | #18 | 8 | The "A" Team | RCA 8804 |

SAFARIS

| 6/18/60 | #7 | 17 | Image Of A Girl | Eldo 101 |

SA-FIRE

10/22/88	#66	8	Boy, I've Been Told	Cutting 870514
2/11/89	#11	25	Thinking Of You	Cutting 872502
7/01/89	#82	5	Gonna Make It	Cutting 874278
12/23/89	#49	11	I Will Survive	Mercury 876369
3/09/91	#83	6	Made Up My Mind	Mercury 878874

Debut Date	Peak Pos	Wks Chr	ARTIST/Song Title	Label & Number
			SAGA	
12/04/82	#35	16	On The Loose	Portrait 03359
4/02/83	#51	10	Wind Him Up	Portrait 03791
			CAROLE BAYER SAGER	
9/17/77	#57	12	You're Moving Out Today	Elektra 45422
5/16/81	#34	13	Stronger Than Before	Boardwalk 02054
9/05/81	#76	5	Easy To Love Again	Boardwalk 118
			SAGITTARIUS	
6/24/67	#79	6	My World Fell Down	Columbia 44163
7/12/69	#84	5	In My Room	Together 105
			SAIGON KICK	
9/12/92	#11	26	Love Is On The Way	Third Stone 98530
			SAILCAT	
6/24/72	#19	14	Motorcycle Mama	Elektra 45782
			OLIVER SAIN	
2/28/76	#78	5	She's A Disco Queen	Abet 9463
			BUFFY SAINTE-MARIE	
12/04/71	#89	2	I'm Gonna Be A Country Girl Again	Vanguard 35143
3/25/72	#40	9	Mister Can't You See	Vanguard 35151
			ST. PAUL	
7/21/90	#50	7	Stranger To Love	Atlantic 87899
			CRISPIAN ST. PETERS	
6/18/66	#4	12	The Pied Piper	Jamie 1320
9/24/66	#70	4	Changes	Jamie 1324
6/24/67	#71	7	You Were On My Mind	Jamie 1310
			KIRBY ST. ROMAIN	
6/15/63	#52	7	Summer's Comin'	Inette 103
			SAINT TROPEZ	
4/28/79	#70	7	One More Minute	Butterfly 41080
			KYU SAKAMOTO	
5/04/63	#1	16	Sukiyaki	Capitol 4945
8/17/63	#51	6	China Nights	Capitol 5016
			SOUPY SALES	
4/03/65	#49	8	The Mouse	ABC-Paramount 10646
			SALSOUL ORCHESTRA	
9/27/75	#90	3	Salsoul Hustle	Salsoul 2002
1/31/76	#40	12	Tangerine	Salsoul 2004
10/16/76	#77	5	Nice 'N' Naasty	Salsoul 2011
			SALT-N-PEPA	
11/28/87	#22	23	Push It	Next Plateau 315
3/17/90	#26	18	Expression	Next Plateau 50101
4/27/91	#88	4	Backyard*	MCA 53982
5/04/91	#85	5	Do You Want Me	Next Plateau 50137
9/21/91	#22	22	Let's Talk About Sex	Next Plateau 333
2/15/92	#60	19	You Showed Me	Next Plateau 50165
10/23/93	#5	31	Shoop	Next Plateau 857314
			*released as by PEBBLES with SALT-N-PEPA	
			SALVAGE	
3/06/71	#64	8	Hot Pants	Odax 420
			SAM & BILL	
9/18/65	#87	5	For Your Love	JoDa 100
			SAM & DAVE	
1/08/66	#80	4	You Don't Know Like I Know	Stax 180
4/23/66	#16	13	Hold On, I'm Comin'	Stax 189
10/08/66	#81	2	Said I Wasn't Gonna Tell Nobody	Stax 198
12/10/66	#65	8	You Got Me Hummin'	Stax 204
2/11/67	#49	11	When Something Is Wrong With My Baby	Stax 210
6/24/67	#47	6	Soothe Me	Stax 218
9/09/67	#1	15	Soul Man	Stax 231
1/27/68	#8	13	I Thank You	Stax 242
5/25/68	#40	6	You Don't Know What You Mean To Me	Atlantic 2517
8/03/68	#57	5	Can't You Find Another Way	Atlantic 2540
11/02/68	#91	2	Everybody Got To Believe In Somebody	Atlantic 2568

Debut Date	Peak Pos	Wks Chr	**ARTIST**/Song Title	Label & Number
12/21/68	#43	9	Soul Sister, Brown Sugar	Atlantic 2590
3/22/69	#96	2	Born Again	Atlantic 2608
11/08/69	#98	1	Ooh Ooh Ooh	Atlantic 2668
11/06/71	#96	3	Don't Pull Your Love	Atlantic 2839
			RICHIE SAMBORA	
9/21/91	#53	11	Ballad Of Youth	Mercury 868790
3/07/92	#65	14	One Light Burning	Mercury 866292
			SAM THE SHAM and THE PHARAOHS	
4/03/65	#2	18	Wooly Bully	MGM 13322
7/31/65	#28	6	Ju Ju Hand	MGM 13364
10/02/65	#28	10	Ring Dang Doo	MGM 13397
2/05/66	#70	5	Red Hot	MGM 13452
6/18/66	#1	14	Lil' Red Riding Hood	MGM 13506
10/01/66	#20	8	The Hair On My Chinny Chin Chin	MGM 13581
12/24/66	#31	7	How Do You Catch A Girl	MGM 13649
3/18/67	#50	8	Oh That's Good, No That's Bad	MGM 13713
6/17/67	#74	6	Black Sheep	MGM 13747
			DAVID SANBORN	
9/05/92	#50	11	Bang Bang	Elektra 64735
			SANDPEBBLES	
8/26/67	#86	4	Forget It	Calla 134
12/02/67	#36	12	Love Power	Calla 141
			SANDPIPERS	
7/23/66	#7	13	Guantanamera	A&M 806
10/22/66	#35	8	Louie Louie	A&M 819
12/27/69	#13	18	Come Saturday Morning	A&M 1134
9/05/70	#94	2	Santo Domingo	A&M 1208
			EVIE SANDS	
8/23/69	#45	9	Any Way That You Want Me	A&M 1090
3/29/75	#63	9	You Brought The Woman Out Of Me	Haven 7010
8/09/75	#44	10	I Love Makin' Love To You	Haven 7013
			JODIE SANDS	
5/25/57	#19	14	With All My Heart	Chancellor 1003
9/27/58	#97	1	Someday (You'll Want Me To Want You)	Chancellor 1023
			TOMMY SANDS	
2/23/57	#2	13	Teen-Age Crush	Capitol 3639
4/13/57	#31	7	Ring-A-Ding-A-Ding/	Capitol 3690
4/20/57	#25	5	My Love Song	Capitol 3690
5/18/57	#24	8	Goin' Steady	Capitol 3723
2/08/58	#52	3	Sing Boy Sing	Capitol 3867
10/04/58	#89	2	Blue Ribbon Baby	Capitol 4036
1/10/59	#76	4	The Worrying Kind	Capitol 4082
9/26/59	#48	8	I'll Be Seeing You	Capitol 4259
9/03/60	#79	4	The Old Oaken Bucket	Capitol 4405
			SANFORD/TOWNSEND BAND	
6/25/77	#9	18	Smoke From A Distant Fire	Warner Brothers 8370
			SAMANTHA SANG	
11/12/77	#1	28	Emotion	Private Stock 45178
5/06/78	#66	8	You Keep Me Dancing	Private Stock 45188
			SAN REMO GOLDEN STRINGS	
9/11/65	#42	8	Hungry For Love	Ric Tic 104
11/20/65	#90	3	I'm Satisfied	Ric Tic 108
			BILLY SANS	
1/19/74	#97	4	Bicycle Morning	Atco 6945
			SANTA ESMERALDA	
11/05/77	#14	19	Don't Let Me Be Misunderstood	Casablanca 902
			MONGO SANTAMARIA	
3/09/63	#9	13	Watermelon Man	Battle 45909
2/15/69	#50	6	Cloud Nine	Columbia 44740
6/28/69	#99	1	25 Miles	Columbia 44886
			SANTANA	
10/25/69	#37	7	Jingo	Columbia 45010
1/31/70	#7	12	Evil Ways	Columbia 45069
11/07/70	#4	14	Black Magic Woman	Columbia 45270

Debut Date	Peak Pos	Wks Chr	**ARTIST**/Song Title	Label & Number
			SANTANA—*continued*	
2/20/71	#10	9	Oye Como Va	Columbia 45330
10/09/71	#10	11	Everybody's Everything	Columbia 45472
2/05/72	#17	10	No One To Depend On	Columbia 45552
9/09/72	#67	5	Evil Ways*	Columbia 45666
10/01/77	#20	16	She's Not There	Columbia 10616
12/23/78	#33	14	Stormy	Columbia 10873
4/14/79	#68	6	One Chain	Columbia 10938
11/24/79	#33	12	You Know That I Love You	Columbia 11144
4/11/81	#15	21	Winning	Columbia 01050
8/01/81	#60	9	The Sensitive Kind	Columbia 02178
8/14/82	#9	16	Hold On	Columbia 03160
11/27/82	#69	7	Nowhere To Run	Columbia 03376
2/23/85	#40	12	Say It Again	Columbia 04758
			***released as by CARLOS SANTANA & BUDDY MILES**	
			SANTO & JOHNNY	
7/18/59	#2	18	Sleep Walk	Canadian American 103
11/21/59	#22	13	Tear Drop	Canadian American 107
3/12/60	#39	8	Caravan . . . . :	Canadian American 111
10/01/60	#83	5	Love Lost	Canadian American 118
12/10/60	#39	6	Twistin' Bells	Canadian American 120
4/01/61	#84	6	Hop Scotch	Canadian American 124
1/25/64	#67	6	I'll Remember (In The Still Of The Night)	Canadian American 164
			LARRY SANTOS	
2/21/76	#57	9	We Can't Hide It Anymore	Casablanca 844
			SAPPHIRES	
7/13/63	#100	3	Where Is Johnny Now	Swan 4143
1/18/64	#23	12	Who Do You Love	Swan 4162
4/24/65	#96	1	Gotta Have Your Love	ABC-Paramount 10639
			SARAYA	
8/05/89	#57	7	Love Has Taken Its Toll	Polydor 889292
11/11/89	#75	10	Back To The Bullet	Polydor 889976
12/30/89	#82	6	Timeless Love	SBK 07316
			FRANKIE SARDO	
12/06/58	#68	6	Fake Out	ABC-Paramount 9963
			SAVERIO SARIDIS	
1/27/62	#79	7	Our Love Is The Sweetest Thing	Warner Brothers 5243
			PETER SARSTEDT	
3/22/69	#61	8	Where Do You Go To (My Lovely)	World Pacific 77911
			BILLY SATELLITE	
8/25/84	#77	5	Satisfy Me	Capitol 5356
12/01/84	#72	8	I Wanna Go Back	Capitol 54099
			LONNIE SATIN	
7/23/60	#98	2	I'll Fly Away	Warner Brothers 5158
			SATISFACTIONS	
6/27/70	#93	3	This Bitter Earth	Lionel 3201
			SAVAGE GRACE	
7/18/70	#92	2	Come On Down	Reprise 6399
			TELLY SAVALAS	
11/23/74	#89	4	If	MCA 40301
			RONNIE SAVOY	
1/21/61	#100	1	And The Heavens Cried	MGM 12950
			SAVOY BROWN	
11/22/69	#42	8	I'm Tired	Parrot 40042
11/13/71	#92	1	Tell Mama	Parrot 40066
10/10/81	#73	8	Run To Me	Town House 1055
			RAY SAWYER	
10/30/76	#68	7	(One More Year Of) Daddy's Little Girl	Capitol 4344
			LEO SAYER	
2/22/75	#6	15	Long Tall Glasses (I Can Dance)	Warner Brothers 8043
10/16/76	#1	23	You Make Me Feel Like Dancing	Warner Brothers 8283
2/26/77	#1	21	When I Need You	Warner Brothers 8332
7/09/77	#9	14	How Much Love	Warner Brothers 8319
10/01/77	#35	8	Thunder In My Heart	Warner Brothers 8465

Debut Date	Peak Pos	Wks Chr	ARTIST/Song Title	Label & Number
12/10/77	#51	12	Easy To Love	Warner Brothers 8502
9/23/78	#43	10	Raining In My Heart	Warner Brothers 8682
9/27/80	#3	24	More Than I Can Say	Warner Brothers 49565
1/24/81	#23	13	Living In A Fantasy	Warner Brothers 49657
			SCAFFOLD	
2/03/68	#65	6	Thank U Very Much	Bell 701
			BOZ SCAGGS	
4/17/71	#44	6	We Were Always Sweethearts	Columbia 45353
4/10/76	#43	9	It's Over	Columbia 10319
7/03/76	#1	23	Lowdown	Columbia 10367
11/27/76	#59	10	What Can I Say	Columbia 10440
3/12/77	#6	16	Lido Shuffle	Columbia 10491
10/15/77	#58	8	Hard Times	Columbia 10606
2/04/78	#65	7	Hollywood	Columbia 10679
3/29/80	#12	15	Breakdown Dead Ahead	Columbia 11241
6/14/80	#21	16	Jo Jo	Columbia 11281
8/23/80	#13	21	Look What You've Done To Me	Columbia 11349
11/29/80	#18	17	Miss Sun	Columbia 11406
4/30/88	#38	13	Heart Of Mine	Columbia 07780
			HARVEY SCALES & THE SEVEN SOUNDS	
10/28/67	#96	1	Get Down	Magic Touch 2007
			SCANDAL	
11/13/82	#60	15	Goodbye To You	Columbia 03234
4/02/83	#38	16	Love's Got A Hold On You	Columbia 03615
6/30/84	#5	21	The Warrior*	Columbia 04424
10/20/84	#39	13	Hands Tied*	Columbia 04650
1/26/85	#40	13	Beat Of A Heart*	Columbia 04750
			***released as by SCANDAL featuring PATTY SMYTH**	
			JOEY SCARBURY	
1/16/71	#87	4	Mixed Up Guy	Lionel 3208
5/16/81	#1	23	Theme From "Greatest American Hero"	Elektra 47174
10/10/81	#63	8	When She Dances	Elektra 47201
			SCARLETT & BLACK	
1/30/88	#23	18	You Don't Know	Virgin 99405
			PAUL SCHAFFER	
8/19/89	#77	5	When The Radio Is On	Capitol 44413
			LALO SCHIFRIN	
1/13/68	#39	12	Mission-Impossible	Dot 17059
			PETER SCHILLING	
10/01/83	#10	22	Major Tom (Coming Home)	Elektra 69811
4/01/89	#53	12	The Different Story (World Of Lust And Crime)	Elektra 69307
			TIMOTHY B. SCHMIT	
10/02/82	#64	11	So Much In Love	Full Moon 69939
9/19/87	#29	19	Boy's Night Out	MCA 53137
			FRED SCHNEIDER	
6/29/91	#81	6	Monster	Reprise 19262
			JOHN SCHNEIDER	
5/30/81	#32	17	It's Now Or Never	Scotti Brothers 02105
10/03/81	#76	5	Still	Scotti Brothers 02489
5/15/82	#69	7	Dreamin'	Scotti Brothers 02889
			SCHOOLBOYS	
2/23/57	#50	1	Shirley	Okeh 7076
			SCHOOL OF FISH	
3/07/92	#34	20	3 Strange Days	Capitol 15675
			EDDIE SCHWARTZ	
12/12/81	#32	14	All Our Tomorrows	Atco 7342
			SCORPIONS	
6/12/82	#75	6	No One Like You	Mercury 76153
3/31/84	#20	18	Rock You Like A Hurricane	Mercury 818440
7/14/84	#69	8	Still Loving You	Mercury 880082
6/11/88	#90	5	Rhythm Of Love	Mercury 870323
6/01/91	#6	25	Wind Of Change	Mercury 868180
11/09/91	#30	25	Send Me An Angel	Mercury 868956

Debut Date	Peak Pos	Wks Chr	ARTIST/Song Title	Label & Number
			BILLY SCOTT	
12/28/57	#53	3	You're The Greatest	Cameo 121
			BOBBY SCOTT	
2/25/56	#10	1	Chain Gang	ABC-Paramount 9658
			FREDDIE SCOTT	
7/20/63	#10	13	Hey, Girl	Colpix 692
11/09/63	#55	6	I Got A Woman	Colpix 709
4/18/64	#94	2	Where Does Love Go	Colpix 724
12/17/66	#29	12	Are You Lonely For Me	Shout 207
4/01/67	#68	4	Cry To Me	Shout 211
5/20/67	#74	4	Am I Grooving You	Shout 212
11/18/67	#93	2	He Ain't Giving You None	Shout 220
			JACK SCOTT	
5/24/58	#35	7	Leroy/	Carlton 462
6/14/58	#7	20	My True Love	Carlton 462
10/04/58	#29	9	With Your Love	Carlton 483
12/13/58	#10	16	Goodbye Baby/	Carlton 493
12/13/58	#96	1	Save My Soul	Carlton 493
3/21/59	#82	2	Bella/	Carlton 504
3/28/59	#69	7	I Never Felt Like This	Carlton 504
6/27/59	#25	12	The Way I Walk	Carlton 514
10/10/59	#54	6	There Comes A Time	Carlton 519
1/20/60	#5	17	What In The World's Come Over You	Top Rank 2028
4/23/60	#4	16	Burning Bridges/	Top Rank 2041
4/23/60	#55	8	Oh, Little One	Top Rank 2041
7/30/60	#28	10	It Only Happened Yesterday/	Top Rank 2055
7/30/60	#52	5	Cool Water	Top Rank 2055
10/15/60	#49	7	Patsy	Top Rank 2075
12/31/60	#74	4	Is There Something On Your Mind	Top Rank 2093
5/13/61	#55	7	A Little Feeling	Capitol 4554
11/04/61	#67	6	Steps 1 And 2	Capitol 4637
			LINDA SCOTT	
3/11/61	#6	16	I've Told Every Little Star	Canadian American 123
7/01/61	#10	14	Don't Bet Money Honey/	Canadian American 127
7/08/61	#45	11	Starlight, Starbright	Canadian American 127
11/04/61	#11	14	I Don't Know Why/	Canadian American 129
11/11/61	#72	8	It's All Because	Canadian American 129
2/10/62	#78	6	Bermuda	Canadian American 134
2/10/62	#55	8	Yessiree	Congress 101
4/21/62	#47	6	Count Every Star	Canadian American 133
6/16/62	#47	10	Never In A Million Years	Congress 103
9/29/62	#72	6	I Left My Heart In The Balcony	Congress 106
			MARILYN SCOTT	
12/24/77	#88	7	God Only Knows	Big Tree 16105
			NEIL SCOTT	
6/24/61	#52	8	Bobby	Portrait 102
			PEGGY SCOTT & JO JO BENSON	
5/25/68	#22	13	Lover's Holiday	SSS International 736
10/12/68	#27	11	Pickin' Wild Mountain Berries	SSS International 748
1/25/69	#41	7	Soul Shake	SSS International 761
4/26/69	#73	4	I Want To Love You Baby	SSS International 769
			SCOTT BROTHERS	
2/27/60	#88	9	Stolen Angel	Ribbon 6905
			SCRITTI POLITTI	
9/14/85	#10	23	Perfect Way	Warner Brothers 28949
2/22/86	#89	3	Wood Beez (Pray Like Aretha Franklin)	Warner Brothers 28811
6/25/88	#57	13	Boom! There She Was*	Warner Brothers 27976
			*released as by SCRITTI POLITTI featuring ROGER	
			JOHNNY SEA	
6/11/66	#27	5	Day For Decision	Warner Brothers 5820
			SEAL	
6/22/91	#6	21	Crazy	Sire 19298
3/14/92	#50	16	Killer	Sire 19119
			SEA LEVEL	
6/18/77	#100	1	Shake A Leg	Capricorn 0272
3/04/78	#53	11	That's Your Secret	Capricorn 0287

Debut Date	Peak Pos	Wks Chr	ARTIST/Song Title	Label & Number
			DAN SEALS	
8/09/80	#74	6	Late At Night*	Atlantic 3674
2/01/86	#48	12	Bop	EMI America 8289
			*released as by ENGLAND DAN SEALS	
			SEALS & CROFTS	
9/23/72	#6	15	Summer Breeze	Warner Brothers 7606
1/27/73	#15	12	Hummingbird	Warner Brothers 7671
5/19/73	#8	16	Diamond Girl	Warner Brothers 7708
9/22/73	#18	11	We May Never Pass This Way (Again)	Warner Brothers 7740
2/23/74	#65	8	Unborn Child	Warner Brothers 7771
5/18/74	#50	7	King Of Nothing	Warner Brothers 7810
3/22/75	#35	17	I'll Play For You	Warner Brothers 8075
9/13/75	#97	2	Castles In The Sand	Warner Brothers 8130
4/10/76	#7	27	Get Closer	Warner Brothers 8190
11/20/76	#88	3	Baby, I'll Give It To You	Warner Brothers 8277
9/03/77	#25	16	My Fair Share	Warner Brothers 8405
4/08/78	#20	18	You're The Love	Warner Brothers 8551
			SEARCHERS	
2/29/64	#12	12	Needles And Pins	Kapp 577
4/18/64	#65	6	Ain't That Just Like Me	Kapp 584
4/25/64	#45	8	Sugar And Spice	Liberty 55689
5/30/64	#13	11	Don't Throw Your Love Away	Kapp 593
8/15/64	#36	8	Some Day We're Gonna Love Again	Kapp 609
10/10/64	#29	8	When You Walk Into The Room	Kapp 618
11/28/64	#2	16	Love Potion Number Nine	Kapp 27
1/30/65	#28	7	What Have They Done To The Rain	Kapp 644
3/20/65	#18	8	Bumble Bee	Kapp 49
4/10/65	#42	6	Goodbye My Lover, Goodbye	Kapp 658
7/31/65	#88	4	He's Got No Love	Kapp 686
1/22/66	#57	8	Take Me For What I'm Worth	Kapp 729
11/12/66	#60	6	Have You Ever Loved Somebody	Kapp 783
8/14/71	#79	5	Desdemona	RCA 0484
			SEATRAIN	
4/10/71	#53	11	13 Questions	Capitol 3067
			JOHN SEBASTIAN	
12/14/68	#62	6	She's A Lady	Kama Sutra 254
3/27/76	#1	18	Welcome Back Kotter	Reprise 1349
			JON SECADA	
4/04/92	#6	43	Just Another Day	SBK 07383
10/03/92	#12	33	Do You Believe In Us	SBK 50408
2/06/93	#23	23	Angel	SBK 50406
7/03/93	#27	21	I'm Free	SBK 50434
			SECRETS	
11/16/63	#28	10	The Boy Next Door	Philips 40146
			NEIL SEDAKA	
12/06/58	#22	14	The Diary	RCA 7408
3/07/59	#40	8	I Go Ape	RCA 7473
6/27/59	#89	2	Crying My Heart Out For You	RCA 7530
10/03/59	#5	21	Oh! Carol	RCA 7595
3/26/60	#6	15	Stairway To Heaven	RCA 7709
8/06/60	#19	16	You Mean Everything To Me/	RCA 7781
8/20/60	#31	14	Run Samson Run	RCA 7781
12/24/60	#4	15	Calendar Girl	RCA 7829
4/29/61	#9	12	Little Devil	RCA 7874
8/26/61	#44	5	Sweet Little You	RCA 7922
11/18/61	#9	13	Happy Birthday, Sweet Sixteen	RCA 7957
4/07/62	#47	7	King Of Clowns	RCA 8007
6/30/62	#1	15	Breaking Up Is Hard To Do	RCA 8046
10/06/62	#10	11	Next Door To An Angel	RCA 8086
2/02/63	#23	9	Alice In Wonderland	RCA 8137
4/27/63	#35	9	Let's Go Steady Again	RCA 8169
8/03/63	#69	5	The Dreamer	RCA 8209
11/16/63	#49	9	Bad Girl	RCA 8254
7/18/64	#92	4	Sunny	RCA 8382
9/04/65	#84	4	The World Through A Tear	RCA 8637
2/05/66	#84	3	The Answer To My Prayer	RCA 8737
10/19/74	#1	20	Laughter In The Rain	Rocket 40313
3/22/75	#28	10	The Immigrant	Rocket 40370

Debut Date	Peak Pos	Wks Chr	ARTIST/Song Title	Label & Number
			NEIL SEDAKA—*continued*	
7/05/75	#30	10	That's When The Music Takes Me	Rocket 40426
9/13/75	#1	14	Bad Blood	Rocket 40460
12/13/75	#7	14	Breaking Up Is Hard To Do	Rocket 40500
4/10/76	#17	13	Love In The Shadows	Rocket 40543
6/19/76	#53	9	Steppin' Out	Rocket 40582
9/18/76	#55	10	You Gotta Make Your Own Sunshine	Rocket 40614
6/11/77	#50	7	Amarillo	Elektra 45406
3/29/80	#21	21	Should've Never Let You Go*	Elektra 46615
			*released as by NEIL SEDAKA and DARA SEDAKA	
			SEDUCTION	
8/12/89	#24	18	(You're My One And Only) True Love	Vendetta 1433
11/18/89	#1	22	Two To Make It Right	Vendetta 1464
3/03/90	#12	17	Heartbeat	Vendetta 1473
6/09/90	#11	22	Could This Be Love	A&M 1509
10/13/90	#76	5	Breakdown	A&M 1503
			SEEDS	
11/26/66	#40	17	Pushin' Too Hard	GNP Crescendo 372
4/15/67	#55	10	Can't Seem To Make You Mine	GNP Crescendo 354
7/29/67	#86	3	A Thousand Shadows	GNP Crescendo 394
			PETE SEEGER	
1/18/64	#72	6	Little Boxes	Columbia 42940
			SEEKERS	
3/27/65	#4	13	I'll Never Find Another You	Capitol 5383
6/05/65	#21	8	A World Of Our Own	Capitol 5430
11/20/65	#100	1	The Carnival Is Over	Capitol 5531
12/10/66	#1	16	Georgy Girl	Capitol 5756
2/18/67	#41	8	Morningtown Ride	Capitol 5787
9/16/67	#96	1	On The Other Side	Capitol 5974
			JEANNIE SEELY	
6/04/66	#88	3	Don't Touch Me	Monument 933
			BOB SEGER	
9/09/67	#70	7	Heavy Music (Part 1)*	Cameo 494
6/08/68	#90	3	2 + 2 = ?	Capitol 2143
11/16/68	#22	15	Ramblin' Gamblin' Man**	Capitol 2297
4/18/70	#72	5	Lucifer**	Capitol 2748
11/20/71	#97	2	Lookin' Back	Capitol 3187
7/15/72	#91	2	If I Were A Carpenter	Palladium 1079
8/03/74	#82	4	Get Out Of Denver	Palladium 1205
8/09/75	#45	10	Katmandu	Capitol 4116
6/19/76	#77	4	Nutbush City Limits	Capitol 4269
12/04/76	#6	21	Night Moves	Capitol 4369
4/23/77	#19	13	Mainstreet	Capitol 4422
7/09/77	#40	10	Rock And Roll Never Forgets	Capitol 4449
5/13/78	#4	19	Still The Same***	Capitol 4581
8/12/78	#13	13	Hollywood Nights***	Capitol 4618
10/28/78	#11	18	We've Got Tonight***	Capitol 4653
4/07/79	#34	11	Old Time Rock & Roll***	Capitol 4702
2/23/80	#6	17	Fire Lake	Capitol 4836
5/03/80	#8	18	Against The Wind	Capitol 4863
7/26/80	#20	17	You'll Accomp'ny Me	Capitol 4904
11/08/80	#55	11	The Horizontal Bop	Capitol 4951
9/12/81	#8	15	Tryin' To Live My Life Without You	Capitol 5042
12/19/81	#54	9	Feel Like A Number***	Capitol 5077
12/18/82	#5	19	Shame On The Moon***	Capitol 5187
3/12/83	#9	15	Even Now***	Capitol 5213
5/28/83	#28	10	Roll Me Away***	Capitol 5235
9/17/83	#38	13	Old Time Rock & Roll***	Capitol 5276
11/10/84	#20	16	Understanding***	Capitol 5413
3/15/86	#17	14	American Storm***	Capitol 5532
5/24/86	#15	14	Like A Rock***	Capitol 5592
8/16/86	#62	10	It's You***	Capitol 5623
11/15/86	#60	10	Miami***	Capitol 5658
5/23/87	#1	20	Shakedown	MCA 53094
8/24/91	#25	14	The Real Love***	Capitol 44743
			*released as by BOB SEGER & THE LAST HEARD	
			**released as by THE BOB SEGER SYSTEM	
			***released as by BOB SEGER & THE SILVER BULLET BAND	

Debut Date	Peak Pos	Wks Chr	**ARTIST**/Song Title	Label & Number
			SEIKO and DONNIE WAHLBERG	
6/23/90	#70	8	The Right Combination	Columbia 73417
			RONNIE SELF	
3/08/58	#60	1	Bop-A-Lena	Columbia 41101
			MARILYN SELLARS	
8/31/74	#67	7	One Day At A Time	Mega 1205
			MICHAEL SEMBELLO	
6/04/83	#3	25	Maniac	Casablanca 812516
10/01/83	#37	10	Automatic Man	Warner Brothers 29485
			SENATOR BOBBY	
1/07/67	#14	7	Wild Thing	Parkway 127
			SENOR WENCES	
3/21/59	#86	4	'S All Right	Joy 228
			SENSATIONS	
9/02/61	#83	7	Music, Music, Music	Argo 5391
1/06/62	#3	18	Let Me In	Argo 5405
5/12/62	#85	4	That's My Desire	Argo 5412
			SERENDIPITY SINGERS	
2/29/64	#5	15	Don't Let The Rain Come Down (Crooked Little Man)	Philips 40175
5/23/64	#28	7	Beans In My Ears	Philips 40198
8/01/64	#96	2	Down Where The Winds Blow	Philips 40215
			TAJA SEVELLE	
9/12/87	#52	9	Love Is Contagious	Paisley Park 28257
			707	
10/11/80	#77	6	I Could Be Good For You	Casablanca 2280
7/03/82	#59	7	Mega Force	Boardwalk 146
			DAVID SEVILLE (see also CHIPMUNKS)	
12/08/56	#34	6	Armen's Theme	Liberty 55041
4/12/58	#1	17	Witch Doctor	Liberty 55132
6/21/58	#61	9	The Bird On My Head	Liberty 55140
9/20/58	#93	1	Little Brass Band	Liberty 55153
5/23/59	#95	2	Judy	Liberty 55193
			SEVILLES	
1/11/61	#88	4	Charlena	J.C. 116
			CHARLIE SEXTON	
12/21/85	#27	21	Beat's So Lonely	MCA 52715
			PHIL SEYMOUR	
1/17/81	#29	17	Precious To Me	Boardwalk 5703
			SHACK	
3/06/71	#81	2	Too Many Lovers	Volt 4051
			SHACKLEFORDS	
5/18/63	#71	4	A Stranger In Your Town	Mercury 72112
			SHADES OF BLUE	
4/30/66	#13	12	Oh How Happy	Impact 1007
8/06/66	#74	4	Lonely Summer	Impact 1014
10/15/66	#96	1	Happiness	Impact 1015
			SHADOWS OF KNIGHT	
3/19/66	#7	11	Gloria	Dunwich 116
6/04/66	#47	6	Oh Yeah	Dunwich 122
9/03/66	#100	1	Bad Little Woman	Dunwich 128
10/19/68	#39	9	Shake	Team 520
			BOBBY SHAFTO	
6/20/64	#86	4	She's My Girl	Rust 5082
			SHAGGY	
10/09/93	#62	7	Oh Carolina	Virgin 12672
			SHAI	
10/24/92	#2	31	If I Ever Fall In Love	Gasoline Alley 54518
1/30/93	#11	28	Comforter	Gasoline Alley 54596
6/12/93	#13	27	Baby I'm Yours	Gasoline Alley 54574
12/18/93	#26	13	Yours	Gasoline Alley 54770

Debut Date	Peak Pos	Wks Chr	ARTIST/Song Title	Label & Number
			SHAKESPEAR'S SISTER	
7/11/92	#4	20	Stay	London 869730
12/05/92	#53	12	I Don't Care	London 869946
			SHALAMAR	
4/16/77	#61	11	Uptown Festival (Part 1)	Soul Train 10885
1/20/79	#82	5	Take That To The Bank	Solar 11379
12/15/79	#10	23	The Second Time Around	Solar 11709
2/14/81	#93	3	Full Of Fire	Solar 12152
4/25/81	#61	11	Make That Move	Solar 12192
4/10/82	#31	14	A Night To Remember	Solar 48005
7/02/83	#16	22	Dead Giveaway	Solar 69819
3/10/84	#18	20	Dancing In The Sheets	Columbia 04372
11/17/84	#71	10	Amnesia	Solar 69682
			SHAMEN	
12/21/91	#34	21	Move Any Mountain	Epic 74044
			SHANA	
3/31/90	#83	5	You Can't Get Away	Vision 4515
			SHA NA NA	
5/08/71	#94	3	Only One Song	Kama Sutra 522
8/14/71	#97	2	Top Forty (Of The Lord)	Kama Sutra 528
4/26/75	#46	8	(Just Like) Romeo And Juliet	Kama Sutra 602
			SHANGO	
3/01/69	#59	8	Day After Day (It's Slippin' Away)	A&M 1014
7/25/70	#90	2	Some Things A Man's Gotta Do	Dunhill 4242
			SHANGRI-LAS	
8/22/64	#5	11	Remember (Walkin' In The Sand)	Red Bird 008
10/10/64	#1	14	Leader Of The Pack	Red Bird 014
12/26/64	#15	10	Give Him A Great Big Kiss	Red Bird 018
4/10/65	#75	4	Out In The Streets	Red Bird 025
5/29/65	#33	7	Give Us Your Blessings	Red Bird 030
11/06/65	#7	10	I Can Never Go Home Anymore	Red Bird 043
1/29/66	#35	7	Long Live Our Love	Red Bird 048
4/09/66	#60	5	He Cried	Red Bird 053
7/02/66	#78	3	Past, Present And Future	Ree Bird 068
			SHANICE	
12/07/91	#2	27	I Love Your Smile	Motown 2093
5/23/92	#37	11	Silent Prayer	Motown 2165
10/31/92	#3	28	Saving Forever For You	Giant 18719
7/24/93	#55	11	It's For You	Motown 2207
			BUD SHANK	
1/22/66	#86	3	Michelle	World Pacific 77814
			SHANNON (real name MARTY WILDE)	
7/05/69	#42	9	Abergavenny	Heritage 814
			SHANNON (full name SHANNON GREENE)	
11/19/83	#8	25	Let The Music Play	Mirage 99810
3/31/84	#40	5	Give Me Tonight	Mirage 99775
4/06/85	#50	11	Do You Wanna Get Away	Mirage 99655
			DEL SHANNON	
3/18/61	#1	16	Runaway	Big Top 3067
6/17/61	#2	13	Hats Off To Larry	Big Top 3075
9/16/61	#38	10	So Long Baby	Big Top 3083
11/25/61	#47	10	Hey! Little Girl	Big Top 3091
8/25/62	#76	8	The Swiss Maid	Big Top 3117
12/22/62	#11	15	Little Town Flirt	Big Top 3131
4/20/63	#55	7	Two Kinds Of Teardrops	Big Top 3143
7/06/63	#67	4	From Me To You	Big Top 3152
11/09/63	#68	5	Sue's Gotta Be Mine	Berlee 501
7/04/64	#19	11	Handy Man	Amy 905
9/19/64	#45	6	Do You Want To Dance	Amy 911
11/21/64	#8	15	Keep Searchin' (We'll Follow The Sun)	Amy 915
2/27/65	#33	6	Stranger In Town	Amy 919
5/22/65	#83	3	Break Up	Amy 925
4/23/66	#93	2	The Big Hurt	Liberty 55866
9/17/66	#99	2	Under My Thumb	Liberty 55904
12/05/81	#33	14	Sea Of Love	Network 47951

Debut Date	Peak Pos	Wks Chr	ARTIST/Song Title	Label & Number
			PAT SHANNON	
1/24/70	#92	2	Back To Dreamin' Again	Uni 55191
			FEARGAL SHARKEY	
3/29/86	#81	5	A Good Heart	A&M 2804
			DEE DEE SHARP	
3/03/62	#1	20	Mashed Potato Time	Cameo 212
6/16/62	#9	12	Gravy (For My Mashed Potatoes)	Cameo 219
10/20/62	#9	14	Ride!	Cameo 230
2/23/63	#12	13	Do The Bird	Cameo 244
6/29/63	#49	7	Rock Me In The Cradle Of Love	Cameo 260
9/28/63	#29	10	Wild!	Cameo 274
2/08/64	#89	2	Where Did I Go Wrong	Cameo 296
11/13/65	#68	6	I Really Love You	Cameo 375
2/26/66	#96	1	It's A Funny Situation	Cameo 382
			MIKE SHARPE	
2/04/67	#64	5	Spooky	Liberty 55922
			RAY SHARPE	
7/18/59	#42	11	Linda Lu	Jamie 1128
			SHARPEES	
1/22/66	#90	3	Tired Of Being Lonely	One-derful! 4839
			BOB SHARPLES	
9/22/56	#42	7	Sandie's Shawl	London 1661
			GEORGIE SHAW	
3/06/54	#7	4	Till We Two Are One	Decca 28937
			MARLENA SHAW	
3/11/67	#66	6	Mercy, Mercy, Mercy	Cadet 5557
9/09/67	#97	2	Waiting For Charlie To Come Home	Cadet 5571
5/28/77	#76	5	Go Away Little Boy	Columbia 10542
			SANDIE SHAW	
11/28/64	#49	7	(There's) Always Something There To Remind Me	Reprise 0320
3/13/65	#35	7	Girl Don't Come	Reprise 0342
6/26/65	#88	2	Long Live Love	Reprise 0375
			TIMMY SHAW	
1/18/63	#41	8	Gonna Send You Back To Georgia	Wand 146
			TOMMY SHAW	
9/29/84	#30	12	Girls With Guns	A&M 2676
12/15/84	#57	10	Lonely School	A&M 2696
10/19/85	#84	5	Remo's Theme (What If)	A&M 2773
2/20/88	#78	7	Ever Since The World Began	Atlantic 89138
			JULES SHEAR	
4/13/85	#62	6	Steady	EMI America 8259
			SHEEP	
1/29/66	#53	6	Hide & Seek	Boom 60000
			SHEILA	
12/05/81	#61	10	Little Darlin'	Carrere 02564
			SHEILA E.	
6/23/84	#9	24	The Glamorous Life	Warner Brothers 29285
10/27/84	#30	16	The Belle Of St. Mark	Warner Brothers 29180
11/16/85	#13	24	A Love Bizarre	Paisley Park 28890
2/07/87	#83	6	Hold Me	Paisley Park 28580
			PETER SHELLEY	
11/30/74	#82	6	Gee Baby	Bell 45614
			SHELLS	
12/17/60	#23	11	Baby Oh Baby	Johnson 104
			ANNE SHELTON	
10/13/56	#22	4	Lay Down Your Arms	Columbia 40759
			SHEP and THE LIMELITES	
4/08/61	#3	15	Daddy's Home	Hull 740
7/22/61	#59	4	Ready For Your Love	Hull 742
10/14/61	#51	10	Three Steps From The Altar	Hull 747
2/10/62	#65	11	Our Anniversary	Hull 748

Debut Date	Peak Pos	Wks Chr	ARTIST/Song Title	Label & Number
			SHEPHERD SISTERS	
9/21/57	#22	14	Alone (Why Must I Be Alone)	Lance 125
3/02/63	#76	9	Don't Mention My Name	Atlantic 2176
			T.G. SHEPPARD	
2/01/75	#64	8	Devil In The Bottle	Melodyland 6002
5/31/75	#94	3	Tryin' To Beat The Morning Home	Melodyland 6006
3/28/81	#35	14	I Loved 'Em Every One	Warner Brothers 49690
2/13/82	#67	6	Only One You	Warner Brothers 49858
4/03/82	#45	12	Finally	Warner Brothers 50041
2/25/84	#62	8	Make My Day*	Warner Brothers 29343
			*released as by T.G. SHEPPARD with CLINT EASTWOOD	
			SHEPSTONE & DIBBONS	
9/15/73	#68	6	Shady Lady	Buddah 379
			SHERBS	
8/28/76	#73	7	Howzat*	MCA 40610
3/14/81	#89	5	I Have The Skill	Atco 7325
			*released as by SHERBET	
			SHERIFF	
4/23/83	#61	11	When I'm With You	Capitol 5199
11/19/88	#1	21	When I'm With You	Capitol 44302
			ALLAN SHERMAN	
7/27/63	#1	11	Hello Muddah, Hello Fadduh!	Warner Brothers 5378
12/28/63	#93	1	The Twelve Gifts Of Christmas	Warner Brothers 5406
8/08/64	#65	4	Hello Muddah, Hello Fadduh - 1964	Warner Brothers 5449
3/27/65	#25	8	Crazy Downtown	Warner Brothers 5614
			BOBBY SHERMAN	
8/16/69	#1	14	Little Woman	Metromedia 121
11/15/69	#11	13	La La La (If I Had You)	Metromedia 150
2/07/70	#7	14	Easy Come, Easy Go	Metromedia 177
5/16/70	#23	9	Hey, Mister Sun	Metromedia 188
7/25/70	#3	15	Julie, Do You Love Me	Metromedia 194
12/26/70	#70	1	Goin' Home	Metromedia 204
2/06/71	#10	11	Cried Like A Baby	Metromedia 206
5/01/71	#22	7	The Drum	Metromedia 217
8/14/71	#45	6	Waiting At The Bus Stop	Metromedia 222
10/09/71	#38	6	Jennifer	Metromedia 227
2/12/72	#53	5	Together Again	Metromedia 240
			JOE SHERMAN	
10/12/63	#88	3	Toys In The Attic	World Artists 1008
			SHERRYS	
10/06/62	#40	8	Pop Pop Pop-Pie	Guyden 2068
			HOLLY SHERWOOD	
10/02/71	#91	1	Day By Day	Carousel 1038
			SHIELDS	
8/09/58	#11	19	You Cheated	Dot 15805
			BILLY SHIELDS	
4/26/69	#89	2	I Was A Boy When You Needed A Man	Harbour 304
			SHIRELLES	
3/22/58	#24	10	I Met Him On A Sunday (Ronde-Ronde)	Decca 30588
5/16/59	#67	10	Dedicated To The One I Love	Scepter 1203
9/10/60	#20	15	Tonight's The Night	Scepter 1208
12/03/60	#1	18	Will You Love Me Tomorrow	Scepter 1211
2/04/61	#3	15	Dedicated To The One I Love	Scepter 1203
4/22/61	#4	13	Mama Said	Scepter 1217
7/01/61	#22	11	A Thing Of The Past/	Scepter 1220
7/01/61	#30	10	What A Sweet Thing That Was	Scepter 1220
9/30/61	#26	9	Big John	Scepter 1223
12/16/61	#8	15	Baby It's You	Scepter 1227
3/17/62	#1	16	Soldier Boy	Scepter 1228
6/16/62	#30	11	Welcome Home Baby	Scepter 1234
9/08/62	#43	7	Stop The Music	Scepter 1237
12/01/62	#17	12	Everybody Loves A Lover	Scepter 1243
3/30/63	#6	13	Foolish Little Girl	Scepter 1248
6/15/63	#29	10	Don't Say Goodnight And Mean Goodbye	Scepter 1255
9/07/63	#56	5	What Does A Girl Do/	Scepter 1259
9/14/63	#93	1	Don't Let It Happen To Us	Scepter 1259

Debut Date	Peak Pos	Wks Chr	ARTIST/Song Title	Label & Number
11/02/63	#90	3	31 Flavors . . . . Scepter 1260	
1/04/64	#44	6	Tonight You're Gonna Fall In Love With Me . . . . Scepter 1264	
3/14/64	#59	5	Sha-La-La . . . . Scepter 1267	
8/01/64	#79	5	Thank You Baby . . . . Scepter 1278	
1/02/65	#95	2	Are You Still My Baby . . . . Scepter 1292	
2/04/67	#87	3	Don't Go Home . . . . Scepter 12185	
			DON SHIRLEY TRIO	
7/29/61	#44	10	Water Boy . . . . Cadence 1392	
			SHIRLEY AND COMPANY	
1/18/75	#8	14	Shame, Shame, Shame . . . . Vibration 532	
			SHIRLEY & LEE	
8/25/56	#24	15	Let The Good Times Roll . . . . Aladdin 3325	
12/01/56	#40	4	I Feel Good . . . . Aladdin 3338	
7/09/60	#90	8	I've Been Loved Before . . . . Warwick 535	
9/17/60	#87	4	Let The Good Times Roll . . . . Warwick 581	
			SHIRLEY & SQUIRRELY	
6/26/76	#85	5	Hey Shirley (This Is Squirrely) . . . . GRT 054	
			MICHELLE SHOCKED	
12/17/88	#70	7	Anchorage . . . . Mercury 870611	
			SHOCKING BLUE	
12/06/69	#1	16	Venus . . . . Colossus 108	
3/07/70	#30	8	Mighty Joe . . . . Colossus 111	
6/13/70	#75	3	Long And Lonesome Road . . . . Colossus 116	
1/30/71	#93	2	Never Marry A Railroad Man . . . . Colossus 123	
			SHOES	
11/03/79	#74	5	Too Late . . . . Elektra 46557	
			TROY SHONDELL	
9/09/61	#5	16	This Time . . . . Liberty 55353	
1/20/62	#87	2	Tears From An Angel/ . . . . Liberty 55398	
1/20/62	#100	1	Island In The Sky . . . . Liberty 55398	
			SHOOTING STAR	
3/29/80	#83	6	You've Got What I Need . . . . Virgin 67005	
3/27/82	#80	5	Hollywood . . . . Epic/Virgin 02755	
			DINAH SHORE	
3/10/51	#7	5	A Penny A Kiss . . . . RCA 4019	
8/04/51	#3	12	Sweet Violets . . . . RCA 4174	
8/04/56	#47	1	I Could Have Danced All Night . . . . RCA 6469	
3/09/57	#39	5	Chantez-Chantez . . . . RCA 6792	
10/11/58	#41	10	Scene Of The Crime . . . . RCA 7349	
			MICKEY SHORR and THE CUTUPS	
6/16/62	#85	4	Dr. Ben Basey . . . . Tuba 8001	
			GLENN SHORROCK	
10/08/83	#79	5	Don't Girls Get Lonely . . . . Capitol 5267	
			SHOT IN THE DARK	
4/11/81	#91	5	Playing With Lightning . . . . RSO 1061	
			SHOWMEN	
11/25/61	#58	10	It Will Stand . . . . Minit 632	
			SHOW STOPPERS	
6/08/68	#89	3	Ain't Nothin' But A House Party . . . . Heritage 800	
			SIDE EFFECT	
6/04/77	#98	2	Keep That Same Old Feeling . . . . Fantasy 792	
			SIDEKICKS	
7/30/66	#45	11	Suspicions . . . . RCA 8864	
			BUNNY SIGLER	
7/01/67	#21	10	Let The Good Times Roll & Feel So Good . . . . Parkway 153	
10/07/67	#72	6	Lovey Dovey (You're So Fine) . . . . Parkway 6000	
3/11/78	#55	8	Let Me Party With You (Part 1) . . . . Gold Mind 4008	
			SILENCERS (Pittsburgh group)	
7/26/80	#88	3	Shiver And Shake . . . . Precision 9800	
			SILENCERS (Scottish group)	
9/05/87	#87	4	Painted Moon . . . . RCA 5220	

313

Debut Date	Peak Pos	Wks Chr	ARTIST/Song Title	Label & Number
			SILHOUETTES	
1/18/58	#1	13	Get A Job	Ember 1029
			SILK	
2/13/93	#85	7	Happy Days	Keia 64701
2/27/93	#2	35	Freak Me	Keia 64654
6/26/93	#18	22	Girl U For Me	Keia 64643
			SILKIE	
10/09/65	#14	12	You've Got To Hide Your Love Away	Fontana 1525
			SILVER	
6/26/76	#16	22	Wham Bam Shang-A-Lang	Arista 0189
			SILVER CONDOR	
7/25/81	#35	14	You Could Take My Heart Away	Columbia 02268
			SILVER CONVENTION	
4/19/75	#88	5	Save Me	Midland Int'l. 10212
10/04/75	#1	18	Fly, Robin, Fly	Midland Int'l. 10339
3/20/76	#1	23	Get Up And Boogie (That's Right)	Midland Int'l. 10571
8/21/76	#78	4	No, No, Joe	Midland Int'l. 10723
			SILVER HAWK	
5/22/71	#94	2	Awaiting On You All	Westbound 172
			DOOLEY SILVERSPOON	
3/08/75	#82	4	Bump Me Baby (Part 1)	Cotton 636
			SILVETTI	
3/05/77	#97	4	Spring Rain	Salsoul 2014
			HARRY SIMEONE CHORALE	
12/27/58	#10	8	The Little Drummer Boy	20th Century Fox 121
12/05/59	#26	7	The Little Drummer Boy	20th Century Fox 121
12/24/60	#47	3	The Little Drummer Boy	20th Century Fox 121
12/23/61	#66	3	The Little Drummer Boy	20th Century Fox 121
12/15/62	#38	4	The Little Drummer Boy	20th Century Fox 121
12/28/63	#96	1	The Little Drummer Boy	20th Century Fox 429
			GENE SIMMONS	
12/02/78	#51	9	Radioactive	Casablanca 951
			JUMPIN GENE SIMMONS	
7/04/64	#11	17	Haunted House	Hi 2076
11/14/64	#83	4	The Dodo	Hi 2080
			PATRICK SIMMONS	
3/19/83	#32	14	So Wrong	Elektra 69839
			CARLY SIMON	
4/24/71	#9	16	That's The Way I've Always Heard It Should Be	Elektra 45724
12/04/71	#10	14	Anticipation	Elektra 45759
3/25/72	#61	7	Legend In Your Own Time	Elektra 45774
12/02/72	#1	17	You're So Vain	Elektra 45824
3/24/73	#10	11	The Right Thing To Do	Elektra 45843
2/02/74	#3	14	Mockingbird*	Elektra 45880
5/04/74	#7	12	Haven't Got Time For The Pain	Elektra 45887
5/10/75	#25	9	Attitude Dancing	Elektra 45246
7/26/75	#76	3	Waterfall	Elektra 45263
10/18/75	#90	2	More And More	Elektra 45278
6/12/76	#49	10	It Keeps You Runnin'	Elektra 45323
7/23/77	#2	25	Nobody Does It Better	Elektra 45413
4/15/78	#9	19	You Belong To Me	Elektra 45477
8/19/78	#48	8	Devoted To You*	Elektra 45506
12/09/78	#86	7	Tranquillo	Elektra 45544
6/09/79	#52	7	Vengeance	Elektra 46051
8/02/80	#9	26	Jesse	Warner Brothers 49518
7/10/82	#73	7	Why	Mirage 4051
6/29/85	#63	7	Tired Of Being Blonde	Epic 05419
11/08/86	#30	16	Coming Around Again	Arista 9525
5/16/87	#70	9	Give Me All Night	Arista 9587
1/30/88	#68	7	All I Want Is You	Arista 9653
3/11/89	#51	8	Let The River Run	Arista 9793
			*released as by CARLY SIMON and JAMES TAYLOR	
			JOE SIMON	
10/17/64	#76	3	My Adorable One	Vee-Jay 609
7/02/66	#76	5	Teenager's Prayer	Sound Stage 2564

314

Debut Date	Peak Pos	Wks Chr	ARTIST/Song Title	Label & Number
1/21/67	#87	3	My Special Prayer	Sound Stage 2577
10/07/67	#82	5	Nine Pound Steel	Sound Stage 2589
1/13/68	#56	6	No Sad Songs	Sound Stage 2602
4/06/68	#42	15	(You Keep Me) Hangin' On	Sound Stage 2608
10/05/68	#75	3	A Message From Maria	Sound Stage 2617
12/21/68	#94	1	Looking Back	Sound Stage 2622
3/15/69	#13	12	The Chokin' Kind	Sound Stage 2628
6/21/69	#55	5	Baby, Don't Be Looking In My Mind	Sound Stage 2634
10/25/69	#90	2	It's Hard To Get Along	Sound Stage 2641
12/27/69	#40	9	Moon Walk (Part 1)	Sound Stage 2651
4/18/70	#58	6	Farther On Down The Road	Sound Stage 2656
7/25/70	#74	6	Yours Love	Sound Stage 2664
10/24/70	#92	1	That's The Way I Want Our Love	Sound Stage 2667
12/12/70	#30	13	Your Time To Cry	Spring 108
4/24/71	#65	7	Help Me Make It Through The Night	Spring 113
7/03/71	#63	7	You're The One For Me	Spring 115
9/11/71	#87	4	All My Hard Times	Spring 118
11/13/71	#8	15	Drowning In The Sea Of Love	Spring 120
3/25/72	#49	7	Pool Of Bad Luck	Spring 124
7/01/72	#10	15	Power Of Love	Spring 128
10/07/72	#62	7	Misty Blue	Sound Stage 1508
11/04/72	#74	3	I Found My Dad/	Spring 130
12/02/72	#69	5	Trouble In My Home	Spring 130
2/24/73	#29	11	Step By Step	Spring 133
7/21/73	#14	14	Theme From Cleopatra Jones	Spring 138
11/03/73	#42	9	River	Spring 141
4/05/75	#9	15	Get Down, Get Down (Get On The Floor)	Spring 156
8/30/75	#60	4	Music In My Bones	Spring 159
1/17/76	#63	6	I Need You, You Need Me	Spring 163
			PAUL SIMON	
2/05/72	#4	14	Mother And Child Reunion	Columbia 45547
4/01/72	#7	11	Me And Julio Down By The Schoolyard	Columbia 45585
7/08/72	#58	5	Duncan	Columbia 45638
5/19/73	#2	13	Kodachrome	Columbia 45859
7/28/73	#1	15	Loves Me Like A Rock*	Columbia 45907
12/01/73	#27	10	American Tune	Columbia 45900
5/04/74	#97	3	The Sounds Of Silence	Columbia 46038
8/09/75	#20	11	Gone At Last**	Columbia 10197
12/13/75	#1	20	50 Ways To Leave Your Lover	Columbia 10270
5/01/76	#45	7	Still Crazy After All These Years	Columbia 10332
10/15/77	#6	20	Slip Slidin' Away	Columbia 10630
1/21/78	#15	12	(What A) Wonderful World***	Columbia 10676
8/09/80	#9	17	Late In The Evening	Warner Brothers 49511
10/25/80	#52	12	One-Trick Pony	Warner Brothers 49601
1/15/83	#54	10	The Blues****	Warner Brothers 29803
11/05/83	#48	11	Allergies	Warner Brothers 29453
8/09/86	#44	14	You Can Call Me Al	Warner Brothers 28667
11/29/86	#69	8	Graceland	Warner Brothers 28522
3/14/87	#84	3	The Boy In The Bubble	Warner Brothers 28460
3/28/87	#26	14	You Can Call Me Al	Warner Brothers 28667
12/15/90	#78	8	Obvious Child	Warner Brothers 19549
			*released as by PAUL SIMON with THE DIXIE HUMMINGBIRDS	
			**released as by PAUL SIMON/PHOEBE SNOW with THE JESSY DIXON SINGERS	
			***released as by ART GARFUNKEL with JAMES TAYLOR & PAUL SIMON	
			****released as by RANDY NEWMAN and PAUL SIMON	
			SIMON & GARFUNKEL	
12/21/57	#51	6	Hey, Schoolgirl*	Big 613
11/20/65	#1	15	The Sounds Of Silence	Columbia 43396
2/12/66	#5	11	Homeward Bound	Columbia 43511
4/30/66	#4	12	I Am A Rock	Columbia 43617
8/06/66	#15	8	The Dangling Conversation	Columbia 43728
11/05/66	#17	9	A Hazy Shade Of Winter	Columbia 43873
3/11/67	#15	11	At The Zoo	Columbia 44046
7/29/67	#15	8	Fakin' It	Columbia 44232
3/02/68	#19	12	Scarborough Fair	Columbia 44465
4/27/68	#1	14	Mrs. Robinson	Columbia 44511
4/05/69	#4	10	The Boxer	Columbia 44785

Debut Date	Peak Pos	Wks Chr	ARTIST/Song Title	Label & Number
			SIMON & GARFUNKEL—*continued*	
1/31/70	#1	14	Bridge Over Troubled Water	Columbia 45079
4/11/70	#1	12	Cecilia	Columbia 45133
9/05/70	#11	11	El Condor Pasa	Columbia 45237
9/02/72	#72	5	For Emily, Whenever I May Find Her	Columbia 45663
10/18/75	#7	13	My Little Town	Columbia 10230
4/03/82	#30	12	Wake Up Little Susie	Warner Brothers 50053
			***released as by TOM & JERRY**	
			NINA SIMONE	
8/01/59	#15	15	I Loves You, Porgy	Bethlehem 11021
1/14/61	#94	2	Trouble In Mind	Colpix 175
1/10/70	#90	3	To Be Young, Gifted And Black	RCA 0269
			SIMON F.	
10/10/87	#83	4	American Dream	Reprise 28237
			SIMPLE MINDS	
2/23/85	#1	22	Don't You (Forget About Me)	A&M 2703
10/19/85	#3	23	Alive & Kicking	A&M 2783
1/25/86	#10	16	Sanctify Yourself	A&M 2810
4/05/86	#28	14	All The Things She Said	A&M 2828
5/11/91	#43	15	See The Lights	A&M 1553
			SIMPLY RED	
4/12/86	#4	22	Holding Back The Years	Elektra 69564
7/19/86	#27	16	Money$ Too Tight (To Mention)	Elektra 69528
3/07/87	#35	15	The Right Thing	Elektra 69487
2/18/89	#49	9	It's Only Love	Elektra 69317
5/06/89	#2	24	If You Don't Know Me By Now	Elektra 69297
9/21/91	#20	19	Something Got Me Started	East West 98711
12/21/91	#32	23	Stars	East West 98636
			VALERIE SIMPSON	
12/16/72	#58	9	Silly Wasn't I	Tamla 54224
			SIMPSONS	
12/08/90	#22	6	Do The Bart Man	Geffen album cut
3/09/91	#66	9	Deep Deep Trouble*	Geffen 19007
			***released as by THE SIMPSONS featuring BART & HOMER**	
			KYM SIMS	
12/07/91	#73	8	Too Blind To See It	Atco 96255
			SIMS TWINS	
11/04/61	#56	12	Soothe Me	Sar 117
			FRANK SINATRA	
3/27/54	#2	18	Young At Heart	Capitol 2703
6/18/55	#2	15	Learnin' The Blues	Capitol 3102
12/17/55	#4	7	Love And Marriage	Capitol 3260
8/11/56	#48	2	You're Sensational	Capitol 3469
10/20/56	#8	17	Hey! Jealous Lover	Capitol 3552
1/19/57	#20	9	Can I Steal A Little Love/	Capitol 3608
2/09/57	#43	1	Your Love For Me	Capitol 3608
4/27/57	#54	2	Crazy Love/	Capitol 3703
4/27/57	#51	2	So Long, My Love	Capitol 3703
7/06/57	#50	4	You're Cheatin' Yourself	Capitol 3744
10/05/57	#7	21	All The Way/	Capitol 3793
10/05/57	#45	5	Chicago	Capitol 3793
1/18/58	#13	13	Witchcraft/	Capitol 3859
1/18/58	#48	5	Tell Her You Love Her	Capitol 3859
7/26/58	#74	2	Same Old Song And Dance	Capitol 4003
10/25/58	#29	12	Mr. Success	Capitol 4070
1/03/59	#100	1	To Love And Be Loved	Capitol 4103
3/07/59	#49	9	French Foreign Legion	Capitol 4155
6/13/59	#22	18	High Hopes	Capitol 4214
10/17/59	#27	13	Talk To Me	Capitol 4284
5/28/60	#61	5	River Stay Away From My Door	Capitol 4376
8/13/60	#55	9	Nice 'N' Easy	Capitol 4408
11/19/60	#32	9	Ol' MacDonald	Capitol 4466
2/25/61	#55	10	The Second Time Around	Reprise 20001
7/08/61	#58	6	Granada	Reprise 20010
10/14/61	#62	6	I'll Be Seeing You	Reprise 20023
12/23/61	#26	9	Pocketful Of Miracles	Reprise 20040
3/31/62	#81	4	Everybody's Twistin'	Reprise 20063

Debut Date	Peak Pos	Wks Chr	ARTIST/Song Title	Label & Number
12/08/62	#79	5	Me And My Shadow*	Reprise 20128
4/13/63	#62	8	Call Me Irresponsible	Reprise 20151
6/15/63	#92	3	Come Blow Your Horn	Reprise 20184
9/19/64	#38	10	Softly, As I Leave You	Reprise 0301
12/26/64	#32	10	Somewhere In Your Heart	Reprise 0332
3/13/65	#54	5	Anytime At All	Reprise 0350
5/29/65	#87	2	Tell Her (You Love Her Every Day)	Reprise 0373
6/26/65	#58	5	Forget Domani	Reprise 0380
12/18/65	#33	8	It Was A Very Good Year	Reprise 0429
5/07/66	#1	15	Strangers In The Night	Reprise 0470
9/03/66	#26	8	Summer Wind	Reprise 0509
11/12/66	#5	13	That's Life	Reprise 0531
3/18/67	#1	14	Somethin' Stupid**	Reprise 0561
8/05/67	#22	8	The World We Knew (Over And Over)	Reprise 0610
10/28/67	#41	5	This Town	Reprise 0631
4/06/68	#63	7	I Can't Believe I'm Losing You	Reprise 0677
8/24/68	#60	5	My Way Of Life/	Reprise 0764
9/21/68	#41	9	Cycles	Reprise 0764
12/28/68	#51	7	Rain In My Heart	Reprise 0798
3/22/69	#29	10	My Way	Reprise 0817
9/06/69	#61	6	Love's Been Good To Me	Reprise 0852
11/22/69	#96	1	Goin' Out Of My Head	Reprise 0865
11/17/73	#61	6	Let Me Try Again	Reprise 1181
4/26/75	#93	2	Anytime (I'll Be There)	Reprise 1327
8/02/75	#52	7	I Believe I'm Gonna Love You	Reprise 1335
1/15/77	#92	3	I Love My Wife	Reprise 1383
5/03/80	#35	15	Theme From New York, New York	Reprise 49233

*released as by FRANK SINATRA and SAMMY DAVIS JR.
**released as by NANCY SINATRA & FRANK SINATRA

NANCY SINATRA

Debut Date	Peak Pos	Wks Chr	ARTIST/Song Title	Label & Number
10/16/65	#95	2	So Long Babe	Reprise 0407
1/29/66	#1	13	These Boots Are Made For Walkin'	Reprise 0432
4/16/66	#13	8	How Does That Grab You Darlin'?	Reprise 0461
7/09/66	#52	6	Friday's Child	Reprise 0491
9/24/66	#67	5	In Our Time	Reprise 0514
11/12/66	#4	14	Sugar Town	Reprise 0527
4/01/67	#23	7	Love Eyes	Reprise 0559
3/18/67	#1	14	Somethin' Stupid*	Reprise 0561
6/24/67	#13	10	Jackson**/	Reprise 0595
6/24/67	#97	1	You Only Live Twice	Reprise 0595
9/23/67	#19	7	Lightning's Girl	Reprise 0620
10/21/67	#40	6	Lady Bird**	Reprise 0629
1/06/68	#37	9	Some Velvet Morning**	Reprise 0651
3/23/68	#51	5	100 Years	Reprise 0670
7/20/68	#53	5	Happy	Reprise 0756
11/30/68	#96	2	Goodtime Girl	Reprise 0789
3/08/69	#99	1	God Knows I Love You	Reprise 0813
9/13/69	#96	1	Drummer Man	Reprise 0851

*released as by NANCY SINATRA & FRANK SINATRA
**released as by NANCY SINATRA & LEE HAZLEWOOD

GORDON SINCLAIR

Debut Date	Peak Pos	Wks Chr	ARTIST/Song Title	Label & Number
1/12/74	#36	7	The Americans (A Canadian's Opinion)	Avco 4628

SINGING BELLES

3/19/60	#53	11	Someone Loves You, Joe	Madison 126

SINGING DOGS

1/01/72	#72	1	Jingle Bells	RCA 1020

SINGING NUN

11/02/63	#1	16	Dominique	Philips 40152
2/01/64	#96	2	Tous Les Chemins	Philips 40165

SIOUXSIE and THE BANSHEES

10/29/88	#60	12	Peek-A-Boo	Geffen 27760
8/24/91	#34	15	Kiss Them For Me	Geffen 19031

SIR CHAUNCEY

5/07/60	#70	5	Beautiful Obsession	Warner Brothers 5150

SIR DOUGLAS QUINTET

4/10/65	#24	11	She's About A Mover	Tribe 8308
1/22/66	#42	13	The Rains Came	Tribe 8314

Debut Date	Peak Pos	Wks Chr	ARTIST/Song Title	Label & Number
			SIR DOUGLAS QUINTET—*continued*	
1/18/69	#14	14	Mendocino	Smash 2191
7/26/69	#78	4	Dynamite Woman	Smash 2233
			SIR MIX-A-LOT	
12/24/88	#86	6	Posse On Broadway	Nastymix 75555
4/18/92	#1	36	Baby Got Back	Def American 18947
			SISTER SLEDGE	
2/03/79	#8	20	He's The Greatest Dancer	Cotillion 44245
4/28/79	#2	17	We Are Family	Cotillion 44251
1/19/80	#87	5	Got To Love Somebody	Cotillion 45007
1/30/82	#29	15	My Guy	Cotillion 47000
6/22/85	#79	7	Frankie	Atlantic 89547
			SIX TEENS	
9/08/56	#35	3	A Casual Look	Flip 315
			PETER SKELLERN	
11/11/72	#59	9	You're A Lady	London 20075
1/31/76	#90	2	Hard Times	Private Stock 45054
			RED SKELTON	
3/15/69	#51	6	The Pledge Of Allegiance	Columbia 44798
			SKID ROW	
7/15/89	#5	20	18 And Life	Atlantic 88883
11/25/89	#7	20	I Remember You	Atlantic 88886
			SKIP & FLIP	
6/20/59	#12	17	It Was I	Brent 7002
11/07/59	#82	5	Fancy Nancy	Brent 7005
3/26/60	#11	16	Cherry Pie	Brent 7010
			SKIPWORTH & TURNER	
7/20/85	#80	5	Thinking About Your Love	4th & B'Way 414
			SKYLARK	
2/24/73	#9	17	Wildflower	Capitol 3511
9/08/73	#85	4	I'll Have To Go Away	Capitol 3661
			SKYLINERS	
2/14/59	#7	18	Since I Don't Have You	Calico 103
5/30/59	#31	12	This I Swear	Calico 106
9/26/59	#43	11	It Happened Today	Calico 109
2/06/60	#98	2	How Much	Calico 114
5/07/60	#24	14	Pennies From Heaven	Calico 117
7/10/65	#88	4	The Loser	Jubilee 5506
4/29/78	#96	2	Oh How Happy	RCA 11243
			SKYY	
1/16/82	#27	13	Call Me	Salsoul 2152
1/27/90	#51	10	Real Love	Atlantic 88816
			SLADE	
9/23/72	#80	4	Take Me Back Home	Polydor 15046
11/25/72	#60	7	Mama Weer All Crazee Now	Polydor 15053
3/03/73	#62	7	Gudbuy T' Jane	Polydor 15060
6/02/73	#91	2	Cum On Feel The Noize	Polydor 15069
4/07/84	#20	19	Run Runaway	CBS Associated 04398
7/07/84	#37	13	My Oh My	CBS Associated 04528
			SLADES	
8/09/58	#61	3	You Cheated	Domino 500
			FELIX SLATKIN	
10/08/60	#38	10	Theme From The Sundowners	Liberty 55282
			SLAUGHTER	
5/12/90	#24	15	Up All Night	Chrysalis 23486
8/25/90	#18	17	Fly To The Angels	Chrysalis 23527
12/15/90	#51	16	Spend My Life	Chrysalis 23605
8/29/92	#64	8	Real Love	Chrysalis 50401
			SLAVE	
6/11/77	#27	18	Slide	Cotillion 44218
12/27/80	#94	6	Watching You	Cotillion 46006
			FRANK SLAY	
12/02/61	#43	10	Flying Circle	Swan 4085

Debut Date	Peak Pos	Wks Chr	ARTIST/Song Title	Label & Number
			PERCY SLEDGE	
4/09/66	#1	13	When A Man Loves A Woman	Atlantic 2326
7/16/66	#16	11	Warm And Tender Love	Atlantic 2342
10/22/66	#14	12	It Tears Me Up	Atlantic 2358
2/18/67	#95	3	Baby, Help Me	Atlantic 2383
4/15/67	#53	5	Out Of Left Field	Atlantic 2396
6/17/67	#45	7	Love Me Tender	Atlatnic 2414
8/26/67	#54	4	Just Out Of Reach	Atlantic 2434
11/18/67	#70	10	Cover Me	Atlantic 2453
3/09/68	#13	15	Take Time To Know Her	Atlantic 2490
8/03/68	#90	4	Sudden Stop	Atlantic 2539
10/19/68	#72	2	You're All Around Me	Atlantic 2563
4/12/69	#77	4	Any Day Now	Atlantic 2616
11/02/74	#59	9	I'll Be Your Everything	Capricorn 0209
			SLIK	
5/01/76	#98	2	Forever & Ever	Arista 0179
			P.F. SLOAN	
9/11/65	#74	5	The Sins Of A Family	Dunhill 4007
			SLY & THE FAMILY STONE	
2/17/68	#8	15	Dance To The Music	Epic 10256
7/06/68	#65	4	Life/	Epic 10353
8/17/68	#90	3	M'Lady	Epic 10353
12/07/68	#1	17	Everyday People	Epic 10407
4/12/69	#23	7	Stand!/	Epic 10450
6/07/69	#67	4	I Want To Take You Higher	Epic 10450
8/02/69	#6	16	Hot Fun In The Summertime	Epic 10497
12/27/69	#1	15	Thank You (Falettinme Be Mice Elf Agin)/	Epic 10555
12/27/69	#40	9	Everybody Is A Star	Epic 10555
6/06/70	#40	6	I Want To Take You Higher	Epic 10450
10/30/71	#1	15	Family Affair	Epic 10805
2/05/72	#11	10	Runnin' Away	Epic 10829
4/15/72	#25	9	Smilin'	Epic 10850
6/23/73	#15	15	If You Want Me To Stay	Epic 11017
12/01/73	#65	3	Frisky	Epic 11060
6/29/74	#39	11	Time For Livin'	Epic 11140
10/26/74	#90	5	Loose Booty	Epic 50033
8/23/75	#58	8	I Get High On You*	Epic 50135
12/06/86	#56	10	Crazay**	A&M 2878
			*released as by SLY STONE	
			**released as by JESSE JOHNSON featuring SLY STONE	
			SLY FOX	
1/18/86	#9	22	Let's Go All The Way	Capitol 5463
			MILLIE SMALL	
5/16/64	#4	13	My Boy Lollipop	Smash 1893
8/01/64	#33	7	Sweet William	Smash 1920
			SMALL FACES	
11/11/67	#13	19	Itchycoo Park	Immediate 501
3/16/68	#73	6	Tin Soldier	Immediate 5003
			SMART E's	
10/17/92	#54	16	Sesame's Treet	Pyrotech 10083
			SMITH	
9/06/69	#4	16	Baby It's You	Dunhill 4206
2/14/70	#26	8	Take A Look Around	Dunhill 4228
5/16/70	#50	7	What Am I Gonna Do	Dunhill 4238
			BETTY SMITH GROUP	
5/24/58	#51	7	Bewitched	London 1787
			BRO SMITH	
4/24/76	#58	8	Bigfoot	Big Tree 16061
			CAL SMITH	
4/07/73	#87	3	The Lord Knows I'm Drinking	Decca 33040
			CARL SMITH	
7/04/59	#45	9	Ten Thousand Drums	Columbia 41417
			CONNIE SMITH	
10/10/64	#96	3	Once A Day	RCA 8416

Debut Date	Peak Pos	Wks Chr	ARTIST/Song Title	Label & Number
			FRANKIE SMITH	
5/30/81	#29	19	Double Dutch Bus	WMOT 5356
			HUEY "PIANO" SMITH and THE CLOWNS	
3/15/58	#12	11	Don't You Just Know It	Ace 545
2/17/62	#46	9	Pop-Eye*	Ace 649
			*released as by HUEY SMITH	
			HURRICANE SMITH	
11/18/72	#1	17	Oh Babe, What Would You Say?	Capitol 3383
3/17/73	#44	8	Who Was It?	Capitol 3455
			JERRY SMITH	
5/03/69	#72	7	Truck Stop	ABC 11162
8/09/69	#95	1	Sweet 'N' Sassy	ABC 11230
6/27/70	#98	2	Drivin' Home	Decca 32679
			JIMMY SMITH	
5/19/62	#15	13	Walk On The Wild Side (Part 1)	Verve 10255
9/22/62	#91	3	Ol' Man River	Verve 10262
3/23/63	#97	4	Back At The Chicken Shack (Part 1)	Blue Note 1877
5/25/63	#77	3	Hobo Flats (Part 1)	Verve 10283
8/29/64	#89	7	The Cat	Verve 10330
10/16/65	#96	3	The Organ Grinder's Swing*	Verve 10363
3/19/66	#45	9	Got My Mojo Working	Verve 10393
8/06/66	#93	1	I'm Your Hoochie Coochie Man (Part 1)	Verve 10426
			*released as by JIMMY SMITH with KENNY BURRELL and GRADY TATE	
			MARVIN SMITH	
10/01/66	#79	4	Time Stopped	Brunswick 55299
			MICHAEL W. SMITH	
5/04/91	#3	23	Place In This World	Reunion 19019
8/31/91	#49	13	For You	Reunion 19103
9/12/92	#24	24	I Will Be Here For You	Reunion 19139
3/20/93	#64	12	Somebody Love Me	Reunion 62465
			O.C. SMITH	
3/02/68	#47	13	The Son Of Hickory Holler's Tramp	Columbia 44425
8/24/68	#3	16	Little Green Apples	Columbia 44616
12/07/68	#47	7	Isn't It Lonely Together	Columbia 44705
2/08/69	#64	4	Honey	Columbia 44751
5/17/69	#54	5	Friend, Lover, Woman, Wife	Columbia 44859
8/23/69	#33	9	Daddy's Little Man	Columbia 44948
11/22/69	#93	4	Me And You	Columbia 45038
5/23/70	#72	8	Primrose Lane	Columbia 45160
9/05/70	#72	6	Baby I Need Your Loving	Columbia 45206
10/19/74	#90	4	La La Peace Song	Columbia 10031
			PATTI SMITH GROUP	
4/08/78	#10	18	Because The Night	Arista 0318
			RAY SMITH	
1/02/60	#25	15	Rockin' Little Angel	Judd 1016
5/21/60	#93	3	Put Your Arms Around Me Honey	Judd 1017
8/20/60	#99	2	One Wonderful Love	Judd 1019
			REX SMITH	
4/21/79	#7	16	You Take My Breath Away	Columbia 10908
6/27/81	#34	13	Everlasting Love*	Columbia 02169
			*released as by REX SMITH/RACHEL SWEET	
			ROGER SMITH	
6/13/59	#59	7	Beach Time	Warner Brothers 5068
			SAMMI SMITH	
1/23/71	#9	15	Help Me Make It Through The Night	Mega 0015
2/05/72	#92	2	Kentucky	Mega 0056
9/16/72	#77	4	I've Got To Have You	Mega 0079
			SOMETHIN' SMITH & THE REDHEADS	
8/13/56	#10	1	It's A Sin To Tell A Lie	Epic 9093
9/13/58	#100	1	I Don't Want To Set The World On Fire	Epic 9280
			VERDELLE SMITH	
2/12/66	#63	6	In My Room	Capitol 5567
6/25/66	#65	11	Tar And Cement	Capitol 5632

Debut Date	Peak Pos	Wks Chr	ARTIST/Song Title	Label & Number
			WHISTLING JACK SMITH	
4/22/67	#14	10	I Was Kaiser Bill's Batman	Deram 85005
			SMITHEREENS	
12/23/89	#45	15	A Girl Like You	Enigma 44480
5/12/90	#87	4	Blues Before And After	Enigma 44516
2/01/92	#8	23	Too Much Passion	Capitol 44784
			SMOKE RING	
2/08/69	#58	5	No Not Much	Buddah 77
			SMOKIE	
12/04/76	#18	19	Living Next Door To Alice	RSO 860
9/24/77	#93	4	Needles And Pins	RSO 881
			PATTY SMYTH	
6/30/84	#5	21	The Warrior*	Columbia 04424
10/20/84	#39	13	Hands Tied*	Columbia 04650
1/26/85	#40	13	Beat Of A Heart*	Columbia 04750
2/28/87	#57	11	Never Enough	Columbia 06643
8/08/92	#2	34	Sometimes Love Just Ain't Enough	MCA 54403
1/16/93	#32	15	No Mistakes	MCA 54554
			*released as by SCANDAL featuring PATTY SMYTH	
			SNAP	
5/19/90	#2	25	The Power	Arista 2013
9/15/90	#41	10	Oops Up	Arista 2060
8/22/92	#5	42	Rhythm Is A Dancer	Arista 2437
			SNEAKER	
11/14/81	#37	15	More Than Just The Two Of Us	Handshake 02557
2/27/82	#69	6	Don't Let Me In	Handshake 02714
			SNIFF 'n THE TEARS	
7/21/79	#15	17	Driver's Seat	Atlantic 3604
			SNOOP DOGGY DOGG	
12/18/93	#8	16	What's My Name?	Death Row 98340
			SNOW	
1/16/93	#1	26	Informer	East West 98471
5/22/93	#17	20	Girl, I've Been Hurt	East West 98438
			HANK SNOW	
10/13/62	#80	6	I've Been Everywhere	RCA 8072
			PHOEBE SNOW	
1/11/75	#5	16	Poetry Man	Shelter 40353
5/24/75	#81	3	Harpo's Blues	Shelter 40400
8/09/75	#20	11	Gone At Last*	Columbia 10197
3/07/81	#80	7	Games	Mirage 3800
5/09/81	#75	6	Mercy, Mercy, Mercy	Mirage 3818
			*released as by PAUL SIMON/PHOEBE SNOW with THE JESSY DIXON SINGERS	
			BILL SNYDER	
5/06/50	#1	19	Bewitched	Tower 1473
			SO	
2/27/88	#48	11	Are You Sure	EMI-Manhattan 50109
			ERROL SOBER	
3/17/79	#90	3	Heart To Heart	Number 1 215
			SOCIAL DISTORTION	
5/30/92	#92	3	Bad Luck	Epic 74229
			GINO SOCCIO	
4/14/79	#59	7	Dancer	Warner Brothers 8757
			SOFT CELL	
1/30/82	#7	36	Tainted Love	Sire 49855
			SOHO	
9/15/90	#15	18	Hippy Chick	Atco 98908
			BELOUIS SOME	
8/10/85	#68	6	Some People	Capitol 5492
			JIMMY SOMERVILLE	
4/14/90	#81	4	You Make Me Feel (Mighty Real)	London 886973

Debut Date	Peak Pos	Wks Chr	ARTIST/Song Title	Label & Number
			BERT SOMMER	
7/25/70	#59	7	We're All Playing In The Same Band	Eleuthera 470
12/12/70	#93	2	Battle Of New Orleans	Eleuthera 472
			JOANIE SOMMERS	
7/16/60	#56	9	One Boy	Warner Brothers 5157
6/02/62	#11	14	Johnny Get Angry	Warner Brothers 5275
			SONNY	
8/21/65	#11	9	Laugh At Me	Atco 6369
11/27/65	#65	3	The Revolution Kind	Atco 6386
			SONNY & CHER	
7/17/65	#1	13	I Got You Babe	Atco 6359
8/28/65	#10	12	Baby Don't Go	Reprise 0309
8/28/65	#31	7	Just You	Atco 6345
10/09/65	#23	6	But You're Mine	Atco 6381
1/29/66	#18	8	What Now My Love	Atco 6395
6/04/66	#51	6	Have I Stayed Too Long	Atco 6420
10/01/66	#17	7	Little Man	Atco 6440
12/03/66	#98	1	Living For You	Atco 6449
1/14/67	#7	12	The Beat Goes On	Atco 6461
4/29/67	#64	8	A Beautiful Story	Atco 6480
6/10/67	#78	2	Plastic Man	Atco 6486
8/12/67	#60	6	Little Things	Atco 6507
12/16/67	#68	6	Good Combination	Atco 6541
10/16/71	#6	15	All I Ever Need Is You	Kapp 2151
2/19/72	#6	15	A Cowboys Work Is Never Done	Kapp 2163
7/08/72	#30	9	When You Say Love	Kapp 2176
3/17/73	#60	5	Mama Was A Rock And Roll Singer Papa Used To Write All Her Songs	MCA 40026
			SONOMA	
11/03/73	#83	5	Love For You	Dunhill 4365
			SONS OF CHAMPLIN	
6/19/76	#59	9	Hold On	Ariola America 7627
1/29/77	#71	5	Here Is Where Your Love Belongs	Ariola America 7653
6/18/77	#89	4	Saved By The Grace Of Your Love	Ariola America 7664
			SOPWITH "CAMEL"	
12/10/66	#25	12	Hello Hello	Kama Sutra 217
3/18/67	#86	5	Postcard From Jamaica	Kama Sutra 224
			S.O.S. BAND	
5/31/80	#1	24	Take Your Time (Do It Right) (Part 1)	Tabu 5522
8/27/83	#42	14	Just Be Good To Me	Tabu 03955
12/17/83	#67	8	Tell Me If You Still Care	Tabu 04160
8/25/84	#76	7	Just The Way You Like It	Tabu 04523
5/17/86	#48	11	The Finest	Tabu 05848
			DAVID SOUL	
1/29/77	#1	19	Don't Give Up On Us	Private Stock 45129
4/30/77	#55	10	Going In With My Eyes Open	Private Stock 45150
10/01/77	#53	9	Silver Lady	Private Stock 45163
			JIMMY SOUL	
3/31/62	#17	15	Twistin' Matilda	S.P.Q.R. 3300
3/23/63	#1	16	If You Wanna Be Happy	S.P.Q.R. 3305
7/13/63	#92	4	Treat 'Em Tough	S.P.Q.R. 3310
			SOUL ASYLUM	
6/19/93	#4	33	Runaway Train	Columbia 74966
			SOUL BROTHERS SIX	
7/29/67	#95	2	Some Kind Of Wonderful	Atlantic 2406
			SOUL CHILDREN	
10/25/69	#63	3	The Sweeter He Is (Part 1)	Stax 0050
3/25/72	#22	10	Hearsay	Stax 0119
7/22/72	#73	6	Don't Take My Kindness For Weakness	Stax 0132
3/02/74	#52	11	I'll Be The Other Woman	Stax 0182
			SOULFUL STRINGS	
2/10/68	#74	5	Burning Spear	Cadet 5576
			SOUL RUNNERS	
1/28/67	#99	2	Grits 'N Cornbread	MoSoul 101

Debut Date	Peak Pos	Wks Chr	**ARTIST**/Song Title	Label & Number
			SOULSISTER	
9/23/89	#44	16	The Way To Your Heart	EMI 50217
			SOUL SISTERS	
2/22/64	#42	11	I Can't Stand It	Sue 799
			SOULS OF MISCHIEF	
11/27/93	#73	10	93 'Til Infinity	Jive 42157
			SOUL SURVIVORS	
9/09/67	#7	14	Expressway To Your Heart	Crimson 1010
12/23/67	#41	8	Explosion In Your Soul	Crimson 1012
4/27/68	#88	3	Impossible Mission	Crimson 1016
			S.O.U.L. SYSTEM	
12/05/92	#31	15	It's Gonna Be A Lovely Day	Arista 2486
			SOUL II SOUL	
7/08/89	#8	20	Keep On Movin'	Virgin 99205
10/07/89	#3	23	Back To Life (However Do You Want Me)	Virgin 99171
4/21/90	#54	8	Get A Life	Virgin 98981
7/07/90	#81	5	A Dreams A Dream	Virgin 98955
			SOUL TRAIN GANG	
11/22/75	#74	6	Soul Train "75"	Soul Train 10400
			SOUND FACTORY	
1/16/93	#53	9	Understand This Groove	RCA 62473
			SOUNDS OF SUNSHINE	
5/29/71	#40	12	Love Means (You Never Have To Say You're Sorry)	Ranwood 896
			SOUNDS ORCHESTRAL	
3/20/65	#9	13	Cast Your Fate To The Wind	Parkway 942
7/24/65	#81	5	Canadian Sunset	Parkway 958
			SOUP DRAGONS	
11/24/90	#75	4	I'm Free	Big Life 877568
8/08/92	#28	20	Divine Thing	Big Life 865764
12/19/92	#70	9	Pleasure	Big Life 867416
			JOE SOUTH	
1/08/68	#94	1	Birds Of A Feather	Capitol 2060
12/28/68	#10	13	Games People Play	Capitol 2248
8/30/69	#47	8	Don't It Make You Want To Go Home*	Capitol 2592
12/20/69	#12	13	Walk A Mile In My Shoes*	Capitol 2704
3/14/70	#48	7	Children	Capitol 2755
11/27/71	#93	3	Fool Me	Capitol 3204
			*released as by JOE SOUTH and THE BELIEVERS	
			SOUTHCOTE	
3/09/74	#91	3	She	Buddah 399
			J.D. SOUTHER	
9/15/79	#7	21	You're Only Lonely	Columbia 11079
3/14/81	#8	13	Her Town Too*	Columbia 60514
			*released as by JAMES TAYLOR and J.D. SOUTHER	
			SOUTHER, HILLMAN, FURAY BAND	
8/24/74	#24	10	Fallin' In Love	Asylum 45201
12/07/74	#80	6	Safe At Home	Asylum 45217
			SOUTH SHORE COMMISSION	
7/12/75	#79	5	Free Man	Wand 11287
3/20/76	#98	2	Train Called Freedom	Wand 11294
			SOUTHSIDE JOHNNY & THE ASBURY JUKES	
9/29/79	#92	3	I'm So Anxious	Mercury 76007
8/02/80	#92	2	On The Beach	Mercury 76014
8/09/86	#82	6	Walk Away Renee*	Atlantic 89394
			*released as by SOUTHSIDE JOHNNY & THE JUKES	
			SOUTH SIDE MOVEMENT	
2/24/73	#54	8	I Been Watchin' You	Wand 11251
			SOUTHWEST F.O.B.	
9/21/68	#63	7	Smell Of Incense	Hip 8002
			RED SOVINE	
1/29/66	#95	2	Giddyup Go	Starday 737
7/03/76	#40	13	Teddy Bear	Starday 142

Debut Date	Peak Pos	Wks Chr	ARTIST/Song Title	Label & Number
			SPACE	
4/28/79	#67	7	My Love Is Music	Casablanca 974
			SPACEMEN	
10/24/59	#36	14	The Clouds	Alton 254
			SPAGHETTI HEAD	
5/10/75	#90	4	Big Noise From Winnetka	Private Stock 45014
			SPANDAU BALLET	
7/30/83	#4	25	True	Chrysalis 42720
11/19/83	#29	15	Gold	Chrysalis 42743
4/07/84	#80	4	Communication	Chrysalis 42770
7/28/84	#32	13	Only When You Leave	Chrysalis 42792
			SPANKY and OUR GANG	
5/13/67	#9	10	Sunday Will Never Be The Same	Mercury 72679
8/19/67	#22	8	Making Every Minute Count	Mercury 72714
10/14/67	#18	12	Lazy Day	Mercury 72732
1/13/68	#19	8	Sunday Mornin'	Mercury 72765
4/20/68	#13	12	Like To Get To Know You	Mercury 72795
8/10/68	#27	7	Give A Damn	Mercury 72831
11/23/68	#67	5	Yesterday's Rain	Mercury 72871
6/07/69	#100	1	And She's Mine	Mercury 72926
			SPARKS	
11/04/72	#92	4	Wonder Girl	Bearsville 0006
5/29/82	#77	6	I Predict	Atlantic 4030
4/09/83	#44	15	Cool Places*	Atlantic 89866
			*released as by SPARKS and JANE WIEDLIN	
			RANDY SPARKS	
3/29/58	#57	3	Walkin' The Low Road	Verve 10116
			BILLIE JO SPEARS	
5/03/69	#97	3	Mr. Walker, It's All Over	Capitol 2436
5/03/75	#69	7	Blanket On The Ground	United Artists 584
			SPECIAL DELIVERY	
6/05/76	#96	3	The Lonely One*	Mainstream 5581
			*released as by SPECIAL DELIVERY featuring TERRY HUFF	
			RONNIE SPECTOR	
5/08/71	#65	4	Try Some, Buy Some	Apple 1832
			SPELLBINDERS	
12/04/65	#84	3	For You	Columbia 43384
			SPELLBOUND	
8/05/78	#89	3	Rumor At The Honky Tonk	EMI America 8002
			BENNY SPELLMAN	
6/02/62	#89	3	Lipstick Traces (On A Cigarette)	Minit 644
			JUDSON SPENCE	
10/15/88	#30	16	Yeah, Yeah, Yeah	Atlantic 88999
			TRACIE SPENCER	
10/08/88	#38	15	Symptoms Of True Love	Capitol 44140
2/18/89	#82	4	Imagine	Capitol 44268
12/22/90	#4	26	This House	Capitol 44652
6/01/91	#73	7	This Time Make It Funky	Capitol 44699
			STEVE SPERRY	
7/02/77	#91	3	Flame	Mercury 73905
			SPIDER	
4/19/80	#37	10	New Romance (It's A Mystery)	Dreamland 100
5/30/81	#50	10	It Didn't Take Long	Dreamland 111
			SPIN DOCTORS	
2/06/93	#3	27	Two Princes	Epic Assoc. 74804
10/30/93	#73	12	Jimmy Olsen's Blues	Epic 74929
			SPINNERS	
7/08/61	#39	7	That's What Girls Are Made For	Tri-Phi 1001
7/03/65	#44	8	I'll Always Love You	Motown 1078
5/28/66	#67	3	Truly Yours	Motown 1093
7/18/70	#15	16	It's A Shame	V.I.P. 25057
1/16/71	#75	4	We'll Have It Made	V.I.P. 25060
8/12/72	#89	3	How Could I Let You Get Away/	Atlantic 2904

324

Debut Date	Peak Pos	Wks Chr	ARTIST/Song Title	Label & Number
9/02/72	#1	16	I'll Be Around	Atlantic 2904
12/30/72	#1	16	Could It Be I'm Falling In Love	Atlantic 2927
4/21/73	#8	14	One Of A Kind (Love Affair)	Atlantic 2962
4/28/73	#76	4	Together We Can Make Such Sweet Music	Motown 1235
8/18/73	#24	6	Ghetto Child	Atlantic 2973
1/19/74	#15	13	Mighty Love (Part 1)	Atlantic 3006
5/11/74	#20	10	I'm Coming Home	Atlantic 3027
7/20/74	#1	16	Then Came You*	Atlantic 3202
9/21/74	#24	11	Love Don't Love Nobody (Part 1)	Atlantic 3206
3/01/75	#33	8	Living A Little, Laughing A Little	Atlantic 3252
5/03/75	#45	7	Sadie	Atlantic 3268
8/02/75	#2	19	They Just Can't Stop It The (Games People Play)	Atlantic 3284
12/20/75	#35	11	Love Or Leave	Atlantic 3309
7/24/76	#76	5	Wake Up Susan	Atlantic 3341
9/11/76	#3	25	The Rubberband Man	Atlantic 3355
4/09/77	#83	4	You're Throwing A Good Love Away	Atlantic 3382
8/05/78	#73	5	If You Wanna Do A Dance	Atlantic 3493
12/15/79	#3	26	Working My Way Back To You/Forgive Me, Girl	Atlantic 3637
5/17/80	#5	18	Cupid/I've Loved You For A Long Time	Atlantic 3664
2/21/81	#62	8	Yesterday Once More/Nothing Remains The Same	Atlantic 3798
12/04/82	#60	10	Funny How Time Slips Away	Atlantic 89922

*released as by DIONNE WARWICKE and THE SPINNERS

SPIRAL STARECASE

Debut Date	Peak Pos	Wks Chr	ARTIST/Song Title	Label & Number
3/29/69	#7	14	More Today Than Yesterday	Columbia 44741
8/23/69	#42	9	No One For Me To Turn To	Columbia 44924
1/03/70	#75	6	She's Ready	Columbia 45048

SPIRIT

6/01/68	#92	1	Mechanical World	Ode 108
1/25/69	#25	11	I Got A Line On You	Ode 115
2/14/70	#69	5	1984	Ode 128
9/19/70	#98	2	Animal Zoo	Epic 10648
7/21/73	#85	5	Mr. Skin	Epic 10701

SPLINTER

12/21/74	#69	6	Costafine Town	Dark Horse 10002

SPLIT ENZ

8/23/80	#50	12	I Got You	A&M 2252
6/12/82	#81	4	Six Months In A Leaky Boat	A&M 2411

SPOKESMEN

9/18/65	#22	7	Dawn Of Correction	Decca 31844

SPORTS

10/13/79	#70	7	Who Listens To The Radio	Arista 0468

DUSTY SPRINGFIELD

1/18/64	#14	12	I Only Want To Be With You	Philips 40162
4/04/64	#42	7	Stay Awhile	Philips 40180
6/20/64	#4	14	Wishin' And Hopin'	Philips 40207
9/26/64	#31	8	All Cried Out	Philips 40229
12/26/64	#90	3	Live It Up/	Philips 40245
12/26/64	#92	3	Guess Who	Philips 40245
3/13/65	#84	3	Losing You	Philips 40270
5/14/66	#3	15	You Don't Have To Say You Love Me	Philips 40371
9/10/66	#21	9	All I See Is You	Philips 40396
3/25/67	#29	7	I'll Try Anything	Philips 40439
7/01/67	#60	5	Give Me Time/	Philips 40465
9/16/67	#29	11	The Look Of Love	Philips 40465
11/18/67	#57	6	What's It Gonna Be	Philips 40498
11/23/68	#12	13	Son-Of-A Preacher Man	Atlantic 2580
3/01/69	#52	5	Don't Forget About Me	Atlantic 2606
4/26/69	#87	1	I Don't Want To Hear It Anymore/	Atlantic 2623
5/03/69	#22	8	The Windmills Of Your Mind	Atlantic 2623
7/05/69	#71	5	Willie & Laura Mae Jones	Atlantic 2647
11/15/69	#22	11	A Brand New Me	Atlantic 2685
2/21/70	#60	5	Silly Silly Fool	Atlantic 2705
3/17/73	#93	3	Who Gets Your Love	Dunhill 4341
12/12/87	#1	21	What Have I Done To Deserve This?*	EMI-Manhattan 50107

*released as by THE PET SHOP BOYS and DUSTY SPRINGFIELD

Debut Date	Peak Pos	Wks Chr	**ARTIST**/Song Title	Label & Number
			RICK SPRINGFIELD	
7/29/72	#15	14	Speak To The Sky	Capitol 3340
11/25/72	#76	4	What Would The Children Think	Capitol 3466
7/06/74	#64	6	American Girls	Columbia 46057
8/21/76	#47	10	Take A Hand	Chelsea 3051
3/28/81	#1	31	Jessie's Girl	RCA 12201
8/22/81	#9	21	I've Done Everything For You	RCA 12166
12/05/81	#27	17	Love Is Alright Tonight	RCA 13008
3/06/82	#2	21	Don't Talk To Strangers	RCA 13070
6/05/82	#19	12	What Kind Of Fool Am I	RCA 13245
9/11/82	#34	11	I Get Excited	RCA 13303
4/16/83	#10	18	Affair Of The Heart	RCA 13497
7/09/83	#23	17	Human Touch	RCA 13576
10/15/83	#31	16	Souls	RCA 13650
3/10/84	#3	17	Love Somebody	RCA 13738
5/26/84	#30	13	Don't Walk Away	RCA 13813
8/18/84	#30	13	Bop 'Til You Drop	RCA 13861
11/17/84	#26	15	Bruce	Mercury 880405
11/17/84	#66	10	Taxi Dancing*	RCA 13861
4/06/85	#26	13	Celebrate Youth	RCA 14047
6/08/85	#24	17	State Of The Heart	RCA 14120
2/06/88	#28	14	Rock Of Life	RCA 6853
			*released as by RICK SPRINGFIELD & RANDY CRAWFORD	
			SPRINGFIELDS	
7/28/62	#23	13	Silver Threads And Golden Needles	Philips 40038
11/17/62	#96	2	Dear Hearts And Gentle People	Philips 40072
5/04/63	#95	2	Island Of Dreams	Philips 40099
			BRUCE SPRINGSTEEN	
9/13/75	#17	12	Born To Run	Columbia 10209
1/10/76	#63	6	Tenth Avenue Freeze Out	Columbia 10274
6/24/78	#53	8	Prove It All Night	Columbia 10763
9/02/78	#52	6	Badlands	Columbia 10801
11/08/80	#6	19	Hungry Heart	Columbia 11391
2/07/81	#20	14	Fade Away	Columbia 11431
5/26/84	#1	22	Dancing In The Dark	Columbia 04463
8/11/84	#10	19	Cover Me	Columbia 04561
11/10/84	#8	19	Born In The U.S.A.	Columbia 04680
2/16/85	#8	20	I'm On Fire	Columbia 04772
6/01/85	#9	18	Glory Days	Columbia 04924
9/07/85	#9	14	I'm Goin' Down	Columbia 05603
12/07/85	#7	18	My Hometown	Columbia 05728
11/22/86	#9	13	War*	Columbia 06432
1/31/87	#45	9	Fire*	Columbia 06657
10/03/87	#4	19	Brilliant Disguise	Columbia 07595
12/05/87	#12	19	Tunnel Of Love	Columbia 07663
2/27/88	#17	16	One Step Up	Columbia 07726
3/21/92	#13	17	Human Touch	Columbia 74273
6/27/92	#62	7	57 Channels (And Nothin' On)	Columbia 74354
			*released as by BRUCE SPRINGSTEEN & THE E STREET BAND	
			SPRINGWELL	
9/18/71	#60	6	It's For You	Parrot 359
			SPYRO GYRA	
7/08/78	#95	2	Shaker Song	Amherst 730
6/02/79	#27	17	Morning Dance	Infinity 50011
4/12/80	#77	6	Catching The Sun	MCA 41180
1/31/81	#93	4	Cafe Amore	MCA 51035
			SPYS	
8/14/82	#72	5	Don't Run My Life	EMI America 8124
			SQUEEZE	
7/25/81	#50	11	Tempted	A&M 2345
9/19/87	#17	20	Hourglass	A&M 2967
12/19/87	#38	13	853-5937	A&M 2994
			BILLY SQUIRE	
5/16/81	#17	21	The Stroke	Capitol 5005
9/12/81	#41	14	In The Dark	Capitol 5040
11/21/81	#43	14	My Kinda Lover	Capitol 5037
7/31/82	#61	7	Emotions In Motion	Capitol 5135

Debut Date	Peak Pos	Wks Chr	**ARTIST**/Song Title	Label & Number
10/02/82	#31	19	Everybody Wants You	Capitol 5163
2/12/83	#89	4	She's A Runner	Capitol 5202
7/07/84	#10	16	Rock Me Tonight	Capitol 5370
10/20/84	#80	6	All Night Long	Capitol 5422
12/15/84	#69	7	Eye On You	Capitol 5416
9/27/86	#65	7	Love Is The Hero	Capitol 5619
7/22/89	#83	4	Don't Say You Love Me	Capitol 44420
			STACEY Q	
7/19/86	#7	22	Two Of Hearts	Atlantic 89381
12/20/86	#45	18	We Connect	Atlantic 89331
2/27/88	#75	7	Don't Make A Fool Of Yourself	Atlantic 89135
			JIM STAFFORD	
5/12/73	#31	12	Swamp Witch	MGM 14496
11/03/73	#3	22	Spiders & Snakes	MGM 14648
4/13/74	#10	12	My Girl Bill	MGM 14718
7/06/74	#5	13	Wildwood Weed	MGM 14737
12/21/74	#35	9	Your Bulldog Drinks Champagne	MGM 14775
8/30/75	#62	7	I Got Stoned And I Missed It	MGM 14819
4/17/76	#86	4	Jasper	Polydor 14309
			JO STAFFORD	
8/19/50	#4	9	Play A Simple Melody	Capitol 1039
12/29/51	#5	8	Shrimp Boats	Columbia 39581
4/12/52	#10	3	Hambone*	Columbia 39672
9/06/52	#1	17	You Belong To Me	Columbia 39811
9/20/52	#6	14	Jambalaya	Columbia 39838
12/27/52	#4	8	Keep It A Secret	Columbia 39891
3/20/54	#1	9	Make Love To Me!	Columbia 40143
10/29/55	#8	4	Suddenly There's A Valley	Columbia 40559
11/24/56	#33	6	On London Bridge	Columbia 40782
3/30/57	#33	9	Wind In The Willow	Columbia 40832
			*released as by JO STAFFORD and FRANKIE LAINE	
			TERRY STAFFORD	
2/29/64	#3	15	Suspicion	Crusader 101
5/23/64	#22	8	I'll Touch A Star	Crusader 105
			STAGE DOLLS	
8/12/89	#61	8	Love Cries	Chrysalis 23366
			STALLION	
3/12/77	#42	11	Old Fashioned Boy (You're The One)	Casablanca 877
			FRANK STALLONE	
7/30/83	#10	17	Far From Over	RSO 815023
5/19/84	#87	4	Darlin'	Polydor 821382
			STAMPEDERS	
7/31/71	#7	14	Sweet City Woman	Bell 45120
12/04/71	#60	6	Devil You	Bell 45154
2/14/76	#41	9	Hit The Road Jack	Quality 501
			JOE STAMPLEY	
1/13/73	#33	10	Soul Song	Dot 17442
			STANDELLS	
4/30/66	#8	15	Dirty Water	Tower 185
8/20/66	#59	6	Sometimes Good Guys Don't Wear White	Tower 257
10/29/66	#68	6	Why Pick On Me	Tower 282
12/02/67	#96	2	Can't Help But Love You	Tower 348
			MICHAEL STANLEY BAND	
11/15/80	#27	18	He Can't Love You	EMI America 8063
3/28/81	#75	5	Lover	EMI America 8064
8/08/81	#55	8	Falling In Love Again	EMI America 8090
10/01/83	#46	12	My Town	EMI America 8178
			PAUL STANLEY	
11/04/78	#41	12	Hold Me, Touch Me	Casablanca 940
			LISA STANSFIELD	
2/03/90	#3	22	All Around The World	Arista 9928
5/26/90	#17	17	You Can't Deny It	Arista 2024
8/18/90	#18	18	This Is The Right Time	Arista 2049
11/09/91	#20	19	Change	Arista 2362
3/28/92	#47	11	All Woman	Arista 2398

Debut Date	Peak Pos	Wks Chr	ARTIST/Song Title	Label & Number
			MAVIS STAPLES	
9/19/70	#92	2	I Have Learned To Do Without You	Volt 4044
10/07/72	#85	3	Endlessly	Volt 4086
			STAPLE SINGERS	
9/09/67	#74	4	For What It's Worth	Epic 10220
2/20/71	#24	10	Heavy Makes You Happy	Stax 0083
7/17/71	#85	2	You've Got To Earn It	Stax 0093
10/02/71	#10	17	Respect Yourself	Stax 0104
4/01/72	#1	14	I'll Take You There	Stax 0125
7/22/72	#36	9	This World	Stax 0137
3/10/73	#35	9	Oh La De Da	Stax 0156
6/16/73	#71	5	Be What You Are	Stax 0164
11/03/73	#9	13	If You're Ready (Come Go With Me)	Stax 0179
2/23/74	#23	11	Touch A Hand, Make A Friend	Stax 0196
7/13/74	#58	9	City In The Sky	Stax 0215
12/14/74	#70	6	Main Man	Stax 0227
10/18/75	#1	16	Let's Do It Again	Curtom 0109
2/21/76	#57	7	New Orleans	Curtom 0113
			CYRIL STAPLETON	
8/11/56	#36	12	The Italian Theme	London 1672
8/31/57	#43	4	Forgotten Dreams	London 1754
1/10/59	#5	15	The Children's Marching Song	London 1851
			STARBUCK	
4/17/76	#3	23	Moonlight Feels Right	Private Stock 45039
8/28/76	#40	13	I Got To Know	Private Stock 45104
11/27/76	#48	12	Lucky Man	Private Stock 45125
4/09/77	#48	10	Everybody Be Dancin'	Private Stock 45144
9/23/78	#45	10	Searching For A Thrill	United Artists 1245
			BUDDY STARCHER	
4/02/66	#40	8	History Repeats Itself	Boone 1038
			STARGARD	
1/14/78	#24	16	Theme Song From "Which Way Is Up"	MCA 40825
			STARK & McBRIEN	
1/25/75	#69	6	Isn't It Lonely Together	RCA 10109
			STARLAND VOCAL BAND	
5/01/76	#1	24	Afternoon Delight	Windsong 10588
1/01/77	#89	5	Hail! Hail! Rock And Roll!	Windsong 10855
3/08/80	#79	3	Loving You With My Eyes	Windsong 11899
			STARLETS (see BLUE-BELLES)	
			STARPOINT	
9/28/85	#26	22	Object Of My Desire	Elektra 69621
3/22/86	#55	10	Restless	Elektra 69561
			BRENDA K. STARR	
4/02/88	#14	22	I Still Believe	MCA 53288
8/06/88	#27	14	What You See Is What You Get	MCA 53367
12/01/90	#42	15	No Matter What*	Columbia 73603
			***released as by GEORGE LAMOND with BRENDA K. STARR**	
			EDWIN STARR	
7/24/65	#27	11	Agent Double-O-Soul	Ric-Tic 103
11/20/65	#81	3	Back Street	Ric-Tic 107
2/26/66	#48	8	Stop Her On Sight (S.O.S)	Ric-Tic 109
5/07/66	#86	2	Headline News	Ric-Tic 114
4/20/68	#86	2	I Am The Man For You Baby	Gordy 7071
2/22/69	#6	13	Twenty-Five Miles	Gordy 7083
6/14/69	#41	5	I'm Just A Struggling Man	Gordy 7087
8/30/69	#93	1	Oh How Happy*	Gordy 7090
7/11/70	#1	15	War	Gordy 7101
12/12/70	#24	8	Stop The War Now	Gordy 7104
4/24/71	#54	5	Funky Music Sho Nuff Turns Me On	Gordy 7107
7/07/73	#74	5	There You Go	Soul 35103
2/03/79	#64	7	Contact	20th Century 2396
			***released as by BLINKY & EDWIN STARR**	
			KAY STARR	
6/10/50	#4	12	Hoop-Dee-Doo	Capitol 980
9/02/50	#8	11	Bonaparte's Retreat	Capitol 936
10/21/50	#3	11	I'll Never Be Free*	Capitol 1124

Debut Date	Peak Pos	Wks Chr	ARTIST/Song Title	Label & Number
12/30/50	#8	4	Oh Babe!	Capitol 1278
3/08/52	#1	19	Wheel Of Fortune	Capitol 1964
2/28/53	#6	8	Side By Side	Capitol 2334
7/25/53	#9	2	Allez-Vous-En/	Capitol 2464
8/01/53	#7	4	Half A Photograph	Capitol 2464
6/05/54	#8	2	The Man Upstairs/	Capitol 2769
6/19/54	#5	9	If You Love Me	Capitol 2769
1/28/56	#1	12	Rock And Roll Waltz	RCA 6359
4/13/57	#36	6	Jamie Boy/	RCA 6864
4/13/57	#52	3	A Little Loneliness	RCA 6864
8/10/57	#16	8	My Heart Reminds Me	RCA 6981
5/10/58	#56	5	Stroll Me	RCA 7218
4/08/61	#57	8	Foolin' Around	Capitol 4542
7/08/61	#91	2	I'll Never Be Free	Capitol 4583
			*released as by KAY STARR with TENNESSEE ERNIE FORD	
			KENNY STARR	
12/13/75	#84	5	The Blind Man In The Bleachers	MCA 40474
			LUCILLE STARR	
5/23/64	#53	7	The French Song	Almo 204
			RANDY STARR	
4/06/57	#33	11	After School	Dale 100
			RINGO STARR	
11/07/70	#69	5	Beaucoups Of Blues	Apple 2969
4/24/71	#1	13	It Don't Come Easy	Apple 1831
3/25/72	#10	11	Back Off Boogaloo	Apple 1849
10/06/73	#1	14	Photograph	Apple 1865
12/08/73	#1	15	You're Sixteen	Apple 1870
3/02/74	#6	13	Oh My My	Apple 1872
11/16/74	#6	12	Only You	Apple 1876
2/08/75	#1	14	No No Song	Apple 1880
6/14/75	#29	7	It's All Down To Goodnight Vienna	Apple 1882
10/02/76	#26	11	A Dose Of Rock 'N' Roll	Atlantic 3361
12/18/76	#62	12	Hey Baby	Atlantic 3371
11/07/81	#37	12	Wrack My Brain	Boardwalk 130
			STARSHIP (see JEFFERSON STARSHIP)	
			STARS ON 45	
4/11/81	#1	24	Stars On 45	Radio 3810
7/11/81	#63	10	Stars On 45 II	Radio 3830
9/19/81	#60	7	More Stars On 45	Radio 3863
3/27/82	#40	11	Stars On 45 III	Radio 4019
			STAR TREK II	
7/31/82	#95	3	Theme From Star Trek II	Atlantic 4057
			STAR WARS INTERGALACTIC DROID CHOIR & CHORALE	
12/20/80	#81	5	What Can You Get A Wookie For Christmas	RSO 1058
			STARZ	
11/27/76	#98	4	(She's Just A) Fallen Angel	Capitol 4343
3/19/77	#27	13	Cherry Baby	Capitol 4399
6/18/77	#53	9	Sing It, Shout It	Capitol 4434
3/18/78	#96	2	(Any Way That You Want It) I'll Be There	Capitol 4546
10/21/78	#73	6	So Young, So Bad	Capitol 4637
			STATLER BROTHERS	
11/20/65	#8	12	Flowers On The Wall	Columbia 43315
1/23/71	#73	7	Bed Of Rose's	Mercury 73141
10/11/75	#96	3	I'll Go To My Grave Loving You	Mercury 73687
			CANDI STATON	
6/21/69	#43	7	I'd Rather Be An Old Man's Sweetheart	Fame 1456
1/24/70	#73	4	I'm Just A Prisoner	Fame 1460
4/25/70	#44	11	Sweet Feeling	Fame 1466
9/05/70	#21	13	Stand By Your Man	Fame 1472
12/26/70	#48	10	He Called Me Baby	Fame 1476
5/15/71	#63	4	Mr. And Mrs. Untrue	Fame 1478
6/10/72	#36	12	In The Ghetto	Fame 91000
11/11/72	#70	6	Lovin' You, Lovin' Me	Fame 91005
2/10/73	#63	8	Do It In The Name Of Love	Fame 91009
12/14/74	#42	9	As Long As He Takes Care Of Home	Warner Brothers 8038
5/22/76	#25	20	Young Hearts Run Free	Warner Brothers 8181

Debut Date	Peak Pos	Wks Chr	ARTIST/Song Title	Label & Number
			STATUES	
8/13/60	#80	7	Blue Velvet	Liberty 55245
			STATUS QUO	
5/11/68	#11	18	Pictures Of Matchstick Men	Cadet Concept 7001
9/14/68	#54	7	Ice In The Sun	Cadet Concept 7006
			STEALERS WHEEL	
3/10/73	#3	16	Stuck In The Middle With You	A&M 1416
7/07/73	#33	9	Everyone's Agreed That Everything Will Turn Out Fine . .	A&M 1450
12/22/73	#20	16	Star	A&M 1483
			STEAM	
10/18/69	#3	15	Na Na Hey Hey Kiss Him Goodbye	Fontana 1667
1/24/70	#38	6	I've Gotta Make You Love Me	Mercury 73020
			STEEL BREEZE	
8/28/82	#19	20	You Don't Want Me Anymore	RCA 13283
1/15/83	#34	12	Dreamin' Is Easy	RCA 13427
			MAUREEN STEELE	
5/11/85	#76	5	Save The Night For Me	Motown 1787
			STEELERS	
11/08/69	#55	7	Get It From The Bottom	Date 1642
			STEELHEART	
5/04/91	#33	21	I'll Never Let You Go	MCA 53801
9/07/91	#62	11	She's Gone (Lady)	MCA 54167
			STEELY DAN	
11/25/72	#7	16	Do It Again	ABC 11338
3/17/73	#7	13	Reeling In The Years	ABC 11352
8/04/73	#30	8	Show Biz Kids	ABC 11382
10/27/73	#56	9	My Old School	ABC 11396
5/04/74	#3	18	Rikki Don't Lose That Number	ABC 11439
9/28/74	#59	7	Pretzel Logic	ABC 12033
5/24/75	#31	8	Black Friday	ABC 12101
8/30/75	#90	4	Bad Sneakers	ABC 12128
10/09/76	#71	6	The Fez	ABC 12222
11/26/77	#8	20	Peg	ABC 12320
4/01/78	#17	15	Deacon Blues	ABC 12355
6/03/78	#24	13	FM (No Static At All)	MCA 40894
8/26/78	#21	13	Josie	ABC 12404
11/29/80	#10	19	Hey Nineteen	MCA 51036
3/14/81	#23	10	Time Out Of Mind	MCA 51082
			STEFAN	
10/21/72	#96	3	Holy Cow	Stax 0145
			LOU STEIN	
2/23/57	#16	10	Almost Paradise	RKO Unique 385
6/21/58	#31	6	Got A Match?	Mercury 71328
			JIM STEINMAN	
5/30/81	#29	17	Rock And Roll Dreams Come Through	Epic 02111
			VAN STEPHENSON	
4/21/84	#22	19	Modern Day Delilah	MCA 52376
8/04/84	#44	11	What The Big Girls Do	MCA 52437
			STEPPENWOLF	
7/13/68	#2	13	Born To Be Wild	Dunhill 4138
10/12/68	#2	15	Magic Carpet Ride	Dunhill 4161
3/01/69	#8	11	Rock Me	Dunhill 4182
5/10/69	#35	5	It's Never Too Late	Dunhill 4192
8/16/69	#16	9	Move Over	Dunhill 4205
12/27/69	#23	9	Monster	Dunhill 4221
4/04/70	#21	7	Hey Lawdy Mama	Dunhill 4234
8/15/70	#42	7	Screaming Night Hog	Dunhill 4248
11/07/70	#45	7	Who Needs Ya	Dunhill 4261
3/06/71	#51	7	Snow Blind Friend	Dunhill 4269
7/17/71	#31	7	Ride With Me	Dunhill 4283
11/13/71	#61	4	For Ladies Only	Dunhill 4292
8/31/74	#20	11	Straight Shootin' Woman	Mums 6031
			STEREO MC's	
4/03/93	#15	25	Connected	Gee Street 864744
7/10/93	#56	16	Step It Up	Gee Street 862308

Debut Date	Peak Pos	Wks Chr	ARTIST/Song Title	Label & Number
			STEREOS	
10/07/61	#25	8	I Really Love You	Cub 9095
			STEVE and EYDIE (see STEVE LAWRENCE and EYDIE GORME)	
			CAT STEVENS	
3/25/67	#92	2	Matthew And Son	Deram 7505
2/13/71	#18	12	Wild World	A&M 1231
6/19/71	#26	11	Moon Shadow	A&M 1265
9/25/71	#4	13	Peace Train	A&M 1291
1/29/72	#98	1	Where Are You	Deram 85079
3/25/72	#11	14	Morning Has Broken	A&M 1335
11/11/72	#21	11	Sitting	A&M 1396
7/07/73	#25	11	The Hurt	A&M 1418
3/16/74	#10	16	Oh Very Young	A&M 1503
8/03/74	#9	13	Another Saturday Night	A&M 1602
11/30/74	#29	11	Ready	A&M 1645
7/12/75	#45	9	Two Fine People	A&M 1700
2/07/76	#50	6	Banapple Gas	A&M 1785
6/18/77	#38	11	(Remember The Days Of The) Old Schoolyard	A&M 1948
11/19/77	#68	8	Was Dog A Doughnut	A&M 1971
			CONNIE STEVENS	
4/25/59	#3	13	Kookie, Kookie (Lend Me Your Comb)*	Warner Brothers 5047
2/20/60	#5	21	Sixteen Reasons	Warner Brothers 5137
7/16/60	#86	5	Too Young To Go Steady	Warner Brothers 5159
5/12/62	#57	8	Why'd You Wanna Make Me Cry	Warner Brothers 5265
8/11/62	#61	7	Mr. Songwriter	Warner Brothers 5289
4/24/65	#55	6	Now That You've Gone	Warner Brothers 5610
			***released as by EDWARD BYRNES and CONNIE STEVENS**	
			DODIE STEVENS	
2/28/59	#3	17	Pink Shoe Laces	Crystalette 724
5/23/59	#75	2	Five Pennies/	Crystalette 728
5/30/59	#87	3	Yes-Sir-ee	Crystalette 728
8/13/60	#61	7	No	Dot 16103
1/07/61	#68	5	Yes, I'm Lonesome Tonight	Dot 16167
			GERALDINE STEVENS	
9/06/69	#89	2	Billy I've Got To Take My Love To Town World	Pacific 77927
			RAY STEVENS	
8/19/61	#38	8	Jeremiah Peabody's Poly Unsaturated Quick Dissolving Fast Acting Pleasant Tasting Green And Purple Pills . . .	Mercury 71843
6/23/62	#2	13	Ahab, The Arab	Mercury 71966
10/20/62	#97	3	Further More	Mercury 72039
12/15/62	#37	4	Santa Claus Is Watching You	Mercury 72058
3/23/63	#83	5	Funny Man	Mercury 72098
6/15/63	#19	9	Harry The Hairy Ape	Mercury 72125
10/05/63	#74	5	Speed Ball	Mercury 72189
7/09/66	#96	1	Freddy Feelgood	Monument 946
3/30/68	#44	12	Unwind	Monumnet 1048
8/03/68	#15	8	Mr. Businessman	Monument 1083
11/09/68	#88	2	The Great Escape	Monument 1099
4/05/69	#7	12	Gitarzan	Monument 1131
6/28/69	#24	9	Along Came Jones	Monument 1150
10/04/69	#76	4	Sunday Mornin' Comin' Down	Monument 1163
3/28/70	#1	15	Everything Is Beautiful	Barnaby 2011
7/18/70	#38	7	America, Communicate With Me	Barnaby 2016
10/31/70	#79	5	Sunset Strip	Barnaby 2021
12/19/70	#43	11	Bridget The Midget	Barnaby 2024
5/01/71	#66	4	A Mama And A Papa	Barnaby 2029
8/28/71	#74	3	All My Trials	Barnaby 2039
4/13/74	#1	15	The Streak	Barnaby 600
7/29/74	#55	7	Moonlight Special	Barnaby 604
11/30/74	#83	4	Everybody Needs A Rainbow	Barnaby 610
4/12/75	#16	17	Misty	Barnaby 614
9/20/75	#63	7	Indian Love Call	Barnaby 616
1/24/76	#87	3	Young Love	Barnaby 618
12/25/76	#37	12	In The Mood*	Warner Brothers 8301
3/24/79	#34	9	I Need Your Help Barry Manilow	Warner Brothers 8785
3/15/80	#95	3	Shriner's Convention	RCA 11911
			***released as by THE HENHOUSE FIVE PLUS TOO**	

Debut Date	Peak Pos	Wks Chr	ARTIST/Song Title	Label & Number
			SHAKIN' STEVENS	
4/21/84	#73	8	I Cry Just A Little Bit	Epic 04338
			TERRI STEVENS	
11/08/58	#69	7	All Alone	Felsted 8538
8/22/59	#79	3	Adonis	Felsted 8586
			B.W. STEVENSON	
5/19/73	#77	6	Shambala	RCA 0952
7/28/73	#7	15	My Maria	RCA 0030
11/17/73	#36	10	The River Of Love	RCA 0171
4/02/77	#76	6	Down To The Station	Warner Brothers 8343
			STEVIE B	
4/16/88	#78	6	Dreamin' Of Love	LMR 74001
7/16/88	#59	16	Spring Love (Come Back To Me)	LMR 74002
3/04/89	#44	14	I Wanna Be The One	LMR 74003
10/21/89	#67	9	Girl I Am Searching For You	LMR 74005
2/10/90	#30	14	Love Me For Life	LMR 84006
7/07/90	#15	18	Love And Emotion	LMR 2645
10/06/90	#1	25	Because I Love You (The Postman Song)	LMR 2724
2/02/91	#15	20	I'll Be By Your Side	LMR 2758
			AL STEWART	
12/11/76	#4	21	Year Of The Cat	Janus 266
4/23/77	#39	9	On The Border	Janus 267
9/30/78	#9	17	Time Passages	Arista 0362
1/27/79	#27	10	Song On The Radio	Arista 0389
8/23/80	#24	15	Midnight Rocks	Arista 0552
			AMII STEWART	
1/27/79	#1	22	Knock On Wood	Ariola 7736
6/23/79	#72	5	Light My Fire	Ariola 7753
8/30/80	#62	10	My Guy/My Girl*	Handshake 5300
			*released as by AMII STEWART & JOHNNY BRISTOL	
			ANDY STEWART	
4/15/61	#79	7	A Scottish Soldier	Warwick 627
			BARON STEWART	
9/06/75	#97	3	We Been Singin' Songs	United Artists 686
			BILLY STEWART	
7/21/62	#50	9	Reap What You Sow	Chess 1820
9/28/63	#79	6	Strange Feeling	Chess 1868
3/13/65	#24	12	I Do Love You	Chess 1922
6/26/65	#21	8	Sitting In The Park	Chess 1932
9/25/65	#80	3	How Nice It Is	Chess 1941
12/18/65	#81	3	Mountain Of Love	Chess 1948
1/08/66	#82	2	Because I Love You	Chess 1948
7/16/66	#8	11	Summertime	Chess 1966
10/15/66	#37	7	Secret Love	Chess 1978
2/11/67	#71	5	Every Day I Have The Blues	Chess 1991
1/13/68	#77	4	Cross My Heart	Chess 2002
			DAVE STEWART and BARBARA GASKIN	
12/05/81	#85	9	It's My Party	Platinum 4
			DAVID A. STEWART	
5/18/91	#9	20	Lily Was Here*	Arista 2187
			*released as by DAVID A. STEWART introducing CANDY DULFER	
			JERMAINE STEWART	
2/02/85	#37	14	The Word Is Out	Arista 9256
5/24/86	#9	21	We Don't Have To Take Our Clothes Off	Arista 9424
9/20/86	#46	10	Jody	Arista 9476
3/19/88	#33	12	Say It Again	Arista 9636
			JOHN STEWART	
8/30/69	#65	5	Armstrong	Capitol 2605
5/19/79	#6	20	Gold	RSO 931
8/25/79	#33	12	Midnight Wind	RSO 1000
12/08/79	#40	13	Lost Her In The Sun	RSO 1016
			ROD STEWART	
7/24/71	#80	7	Reason To Believe/	Mercury 73224
8/14/71	#1	18	Maggie May	Mercury 73224

Debut Date	Peak Pos	Wks Chr	ARTIST/Song Title	Label & Number
11/20/71	#22	9	(I Know) I'm Losing You*	Mercury 73244
2/05/72	#38	8	Handbags And Gladrags	Mercury 73031
8/19/72	#14	11	You Wear It Well	Mercury 73330
11/18/72	#39	8	Angel	Mercury 73344
8/04/73	#35	9	Twisting The Night Away	Mercury 73412
10/13/73	#56	5	Oh! No Not My Baby	Mercury 73426
10/18/75	#49	7	Sailing	Warner Brothers 8146
1/17/76	#72	4	This Old Heart Of Mine	Warner Brothers 8170
10/09/76	#1	22	Tonight's The Night (Gonna Be Alright)	Warner Brothers 8262
2/12/77	#17	13	The First Cut Is The Deepest	Warner Brothers 8321
6/11/77	#38	9	The Killing Of Georgie (Part 1 & 2)	Warner Brothers 8396
10/22/77	#3	23	You're In My Heart (The Final Acclaim)	Warner Brothers 8475
2/11/78	#25	11	Hot Legs	Warner Brothers 8535
4/29/78	#19	14	I Was Only Joking	Warner Brothers 8568
12/23/78	#1	22	Do Ya Think I'm Sexy?	Warner Brothers 8724
4/28/79	#14	11	Ain't Love A Bitch	Warner Brothers 8810
12/22/79	#47	10	I Don't Want To Talk About It	Warner Brothers 49138
11/22/80	#4	18	Passion	Warner Brothers 49617
3/21/81	#79	4	Somebody Special	Warner Brothers 49686
10/17/81	#5	20	Young Turks	Warner Brothers 49843
1/23/82	#15	14	Tonight I'm Yours (Don't Hurt Me)	Warner Brothers 49886
4/24/82	#56	7	How Long	Warner Brothers 50051
5/28/83	#18	16	Baby Jane	Warner Brothers 29608
8/27/83	#37	12	What Am I Gonna Do	Warner Brothers 29564
5/26/84	#8	21	Infatuation	Warner Brothers 29256
8/25/84	#16	16	Some Guys Have All The Luck	Warner Brothers 29215
12/15/84	#77	6	All Right Now	Warner Brothers 29122
6/15/85	#44	12	People Get Ready**	Epic 05416
5/31/86	#7	18	Love Touch (Theme From Legal Eagles)	Warner Brothers 28668
8/30/86	#46	9	Another Heartache	Warner Brothers 28631
11/22/86	#80	8	Every Beat Of My Heart	Warner Brothers 28625
7/11/87	#72	7	Twistin' The Night Away	Geffen 28303
5/07/88	#15	18	Lost In You	Warner Brothers 27927
8/06/88	#17	19	Forever Young	Warner Brothers 27796
12/03/88	#4	28	My Heart Can't Tell You No	Warner Brothers 27729
5/06/89	#11	22	Crazy About Her	Warner Brothers 27657
11/25/89	#1	20	Downtown Train	Warner Brothers 22685
3/24/90	#10	19	This Old Heart Of Mine***	Warner Brothers 19983
3/16/91	#1	26	Rhythm Of My Heart	Warner Brothers 19366
7/06/91	#9	20	The Motown Song	Warner Brothers 19322
10/19/91	#9	23	Broken Arrow	Warner Brothers 19274
5/08/92	#2	25	Have I Told You Lately	Warner Brothers 18511
9/04/93	#10	22	Reason To Believe	Warner Brothers 18427
12/18/93	#1	24	All For Love****	A&M 0476

*released as by ROD STEWART with FACES
**released as by JEFF BECK and ROD STEWART
***released as by ROD STEWART with RONALD ISLEY
****released as by BRYAN ADAMS/ROD STEWART/STING

SANDY STEWART

12/22/62	#13	12	My Coloring Book	Colpix 669

CURTIS STIGERS

9/07/91	#9	26	I Wonder Why	Arista 2331
2/01/92	#50	12	You're All That Matters To Me	Arista 2391
6/27/92	#80	5	Sleeping With The Lights On	Arista 2430

STEPHEN STILLS

12/05/70	#16	11	Love The One You're With	Atlantic 2778
3/06/71	#31	6	Sit Yourself Down	Atlantic 2790
6/12/71	#38	8	Change Partners	Atlantic 2806
8/14/71	#31	10	Marianne	Atlantic 2820
5/13/72	#49	6	It Doesn't Matter	Atlantic 2876
5/05/73	#62	6	Isn't It About Time*	Atlantic 2959
8/02/75	#76	4	Turn Back The Pages	Columbia 10179
8/25/84	#63	8	Stranger	Atlantic 89633
10/13/84	#77	5	Can't Let Go**	Atlantic 89611

*released as by STEPHEN STILLS & MANASSAS
**released as by STEPHEN STILLS featuring MICHAEL FINNIGAN

STILLWATER

11/05/77	#43	17	Mind Bender	Capricorn 0280

Debut Date	Peak Pos	Wks Chr	ARTIST/Song Title	Label & Number
			STING	
6/08/85	#2	20	If You Love Somebody Set Them Free	A&M 2738
8/24/85	#10	17	Fortress Around Your Heart	A&M 2767
11/09/85	#20	16	Love Is The Seventh Wave	A&M 2787
1/18/86	#16	16	Russians	A&M 2799
10/10/87	#7	19	We'll Be Together	A&M 2983
1/16/88	#20	17	Be Still My Beating Heart	A&M 2992
4/16/88	#80	4	Englishman In New York	A&M 1200
1/19/91	#5	20	All This Time	A&M 1541
5/04/91	#87	4	Why Should I Cry For You	A&M 1560
2/27/93	#5	21	If I Ever Lose My Faith In You	A&M 0111
5/29/93	#16	26	Fields Of Gold	A&M 0258
10/09/93	#43	20	Nothing 'Bout Me	A&M 0350
12/18/93	#1	24	All For Love*	A&M 0476
			*released as by BRYAN ADAMS/ROD STEWART/STING	
			GARY STITES	
4/11/59	#29	13	Lonely For You	Carlton 508
8/01/59	#70	5	A Girl Like You/	Carlton 516
8/08/59	#86	1	Hey Little Girl	Carlton 516
11/07/59	#78	8	Starry Eyed	Carlton 521
3/05/60	#80	6	Lawdy Miss Clawdy	Carlton 525
			SIMON STOKES	
12/27/69	#87	4	Voodoo Woman*	Elektra 45670
6/22/74	#64	10	Captain Howdy	Casablanca 0007
			*released as by SIMON STOKES & THE NIGHTHAWKS	
			MORRIS STOLOFF	
5/19/56	#1	18	Moonglow And Theme From "Picnic"	Decca 29888
			STOMPERS	
3/17/62	#97	2	Quarter To Four Stomp	Landa 684
			J.C. STONE	
10/05/74	#92	3	Carrie's Gone	Private Stock 45002
			STONEBOLT	
7/29/78	#30	16	I Will Still Love You	Parachute 512
2/24/79	#91	3	Love Struck	Parachute 522
			KIRBY STONE FOUR	
6/28/58	#31	7	Baubles, Bangles And Beads	Columbia 41183
6/18/60	#91	3	Kids	Columbia 41668
			STONE PONEYS	
11/04/67	#12	19	Different Drum*	Capitol 2004
			*released as by THE STONE PONEYS featuring LINDA RONSTADT	
			STONE TEMPLE PILOTS	
6/26/93	#81	3	Plush	Atlantic album cut
			STONEY & MEATLOAF	
5/22/71	#79	5	What You See Is What You Get	Rare Earth 5027
			PAUL STOOKEY	
7/31/71	#21	13	Wedding Song (There Is Love)	Warner Brothers 7511
			STOREY SISTERS	
2/22/58	#44	6	Bad Motorcycle	Cameo 126
			STORIES	
6/10/72	#26	10	I'm Coming Home	Kama Sutra 545
6/09/73	#1	19	Brother Louie	Kama Sutra 577
10/20/73	#21	9	Mammy Blue	Kama Sutra 584
3/02/74	#69	9	If It Feels Good, Do It*	Kama Sutra 588
8/17/74	#98	3	Another Love	Kama Sutra 594
			*released as by IAN LLOYD & THE STORIES	
			BILLY STORM	
4/25/59	#24	12	I've Come Of Age	Columbia 41356
			GALE STORM	
12/03/55	#2	10	I Hear You Knocking	Dot 15412
1/21/56	#6	7	Teen Age Prayer	Dot 15436
6/09/56	#2	8	Ivory Tower	Dot 15458
9/22/56	#50	1	Now Is The Hour/	Dot 15492

Debut Date	Peak Pos	Wks Chr	ARTIST/Song Title	Label & Number
9/29/56	#46	3	A Heart Without A Sweetheart	Dot 15492
4/20/57	#5	18	Dark Moon	Dot 15558
			STORM	
9/18/71	#89	2	Bend Me, Shape Me	Sunflower 113
			STORM	
10/26/91	#18	29	I've Got A Lot To Learn About Love	Interscope 98726
3/07/92	#82	10	Show Me The Way	Interscope 98616
			WARREN STORM	
9/20/58	#96	1	Prisoner's Song	Nasco 6015
			BILLY STRANGE	
8/22/64	#62	9	The James Bond Theme	GNP Crescendo 320
2/13/65	#50	1	Goldfinger	GNP Crescendo 334
			STRANGELOVES	
6/19/65	#12	11	I Want Candy	Bang 501
9/11/65	#42	11	Cara-Lin	Bang 508
1/15/66	#21	9	Night Time	Bang 514
12/14/68	#83	4	Honey Do	Sire 4102
			MARCIA STRASSMAN	
5/27/67	#95	3	Flower Children	Uni 55006
			STRAWBERRY ALARM CLOCK	
9/23/67	#1	16	Incense And Peppermints	Uni 55018
12/30/67	#14	11	Tomorrow	Uni 55046
3/16/68	#56	5	Sit With Guru	Uni 55055
8/10/68	#54	6	Barefoot In Baltimore	Uni 55076
11/30/68	#98	2	Sea Shell	Uni 55093
5/24/69	#85	2	Good Morning Starshine	Uni 55125
			STRAY CATS	
9/18/82	#11	24	Rock This Town	EMI America 8132
12/25/82	#3	19	Stray Cat Strut	EMI America 8122
8/06/83	#4	19	(She's) Sexy + 17	EMI America 8168
10/29/83	#37	14	I Won't Stand In Your Way	EMI America 8185
2/11/84	#84	4	Look At That Cadillac	EMI America 8194
			STREEK	
10/10/81	#54	9	One More Night	Columbia 02529
			JANEY STREET	
10/06/84	#74	5	Say Hello To Ronnie	Arista 9265
			STREET PEOPLE	
12/13/69	#36	14	Jennifer Tomkins	Musicor 1365
			BARBRA STREISAND	
4/11/64	#5	19	People	Columbia 42965
9/26/64	#47	7	Funny Girl	Columbia 43127
3/27/65	#72	9	Why Did I Choose You	Columbia 43248
10/02/65	#51	10	He Touched Me	Columbia 43403
12/18/65	#36	7	Second Hand Rose	Columbia 43469
2/12/66	#96	2	Where Am I Going	Columbia 43518
5/07/66	#79	2	Sam, You Made The Pants Too Long	Columbia 43612
10/01/66	#66	8	Free Again	Columbia 43808
3/16/68	#74	4	Our Corner Of The Night	Columbia 44474
10/17/70	#7	20	Stoney End	Columbia 45236
3/20/71	#48	6	Time And Love	Columbia 45341
5/15/71	#69	3	Flim Flam Man	Columbia 45384
7/24/71	#40	7	Where You Lead	Columbia 45414
10/23/71	#88	3	Mother	Columbia 45471
6/24/72	#41	9	Sweet Inspiration/Where You Lead	Columbia 45626
12/09/72	#65	8	Didn't We	Columbia 45739
12/01/73	#1	19	The Way We Were	Columbia 45944
3/30/74	#60	6	All In Love Is Fair	Columbia 46024
1/04/75	#83	3	Guava Jelly	Columbia 10075
12/11/76	#1	25	Love Theme From "A Star Is Born" (Evergreen)	Columbia 10450
5/21/77	#5	17	My Heart Belongs To Me	Columbia 10555
6/10/78	#33	13	Songbird	Columbia 10756
7/29/78	#35	11	Love Theme From "Eyes Of Laura Mars" (Prisoner) . . .	Columbia 10777
10/28/78	#1	18	You Don't Bring Me Flowers*	Columbia 10840
6/16/79	#3	19	The Main Event/Fight	Columbia 11008
10/20/79	#1	17	No More Tears (Enough Is Enough)**	Columbia 11125
1/26/80	#50	9	Kiss Me In The Rain	Columbia 11179

Debut Date	Peak Pos	Wks Chr	ARTIST/Song Title	Label & Number
			BARBRA STREISAND—*continued*	
9/06/80	#1	24	Woman In Love	Columbia 11364
11/01/80	#8	22	Guilty***	Columbia 11390
1/31/81	#10	16	What Kind Of Fool***	Columbia 11430
5/23/81	#48	11	Promises	Columbia 02065
11/14/81	#9	16	Comin' In And Out Of Your Life	Columbia 02621
2/20/82	#48	11	Memory	Columbia 02717
10/22/83	#26	15	The Way He Makes Me Feel	Columbia 04177
9/22/84	#37	13	Left In The Dark	Columbia 04605
12/15/84	#42	11	Make No Mistake, He's Mine****	Columbia 04695
3/09/85	#79	5	Emotion	Columbia 04707
12/07/85	#50	14	Somewhere (From "West Side Story")	Columbia 05680
10/22/88	#26	14	Till I Loved You*****	Columbia 08062
			*released as by BARBRA & NEIL (Barbra Streisand & Neil Diamond)	
			**released as by BARBRA STREISAND/DONNA SUMMER	
			***released as by BARBRA STREISAND & BARRY GIBB	
			****released as by BARBRA STREISAND with KIM CARNES	
			*****released as by BARBRA STREISAND and DON JOHNSON	
			STRING-A-LONGS	
1/07/61	#4	17	Wheels	Warwick 603
4/01/61	#44	7	Brass Buttons	Warwick 625
6/17/61	#54	10	Should I	Warwick 654
			BARRETT STRONG	
1/30/60	#14	18	Money (That's What I Want)	Anna 1111
			NOLAN STRONG	
11/03/62	#82	2	Mind Over Matter	Fortune 546
			JUD STRUNK	
2/10/73	#10	16	Daisy A Day	MGM 14463
9/28/74	#74	3	My Country	Capitol 3960
7/12/75	#55	6	The Biggest Parakeets In Town	Melodyland 6015
			STRYPER	
11/14/87	#25	18	Honestly	Enigma 75009
7/30/88	#72	9	Always There For You	Enigma 75019
			CHAD STUART & JILL	
4/16/66	#99	1	The Cruel War	Columbia 43467
			STYLE COUNCIL	
4/21/84	#31	16	My Ever Changing Moods	Geffen 29359
			STYLISTICS	
1/16/71	#66	5	You're A Big Girl Now	Avco Embassy 4555
6/05/71	#34	15	Stop, Look, Listen (To Your Heart)	Avco Embassy 4572
10/30/71	#9	17	You Are Everything	Avco 4581
2/19/72	#3	15	Betcha By Golly, Wow	Avco 4591
5/27/72	#18	11	People Make The World Go Round	Avco 4595
10/14/72	#9	14	I'm Stone In Love With You	Avco 4603
2/10/73	#10	12	Break Up To Make Up	Avco 4611
5/12/73	#16	10	You'll Never Get To Heaven (If You Break My Heart) . . .	Avco 4618
10/13/73	#20	14	Rockin' Roll Baby	Avco 4625
3/16/74	#1	19	You Make Me Feel Brand New	Avco 4634
7/20/74	#14	12	Let's Put It All Together	Avco 4640
10/19/74	#31	12	Heavy Fallin' Out	Avco 4647
1/25/75	#58	6	Star On A TV Show	Avco 4649
4/26/75	#67	5	Thank You Baby	Avco 4652
7/05/75	#54	9	Can't Give You Anything (But My Love)	Avco 4656
1/03/76	#85	5	Funky Weekend	Avco 4661
2/28/76	#81	5	You Are Beautiful	Avco 4664
11/03/90	#69	5	Me - U = Blue*	MCA 53945
			*released as by GLENN MEDEIROS featuring THE STLYISTICS	
			STYX	
12/14/74	#6	17	Lady	Wooden Nickel 10102
5/10/75	#81	4	You Need Love	Wooden Nickel 10272
2/14/76	#30	13	Lorelei	A&M 1786
11/06/76	#57	10	Mademoiselle	A&M 1877
9/10/77	#9	27	Come Sail Away	A&M 1977
2/11/78	#23	15	Fooling Yourself (The Angry Young Man)	A&M 2007

Debut Date	Peak Pos	Wks Chr	ARTIST/Song Title	Label & Number
9/09/78	#21	13	Blue Collar Man (Long Nights)	A&M 2087
12/30/78	#41	12	Sing For The Day/	A&M 2110
3/17/79	#18	18	Renegade	A&M 2110
10/06/79	#1	20	Babe	A&M 2188
12/15/79	#19	15	Why Me	A&M 2206
3/29/80	#74	5	Borrowed Time	A&M 2228
1/24/81	#5	18	The Best Of Times	A&M 2300
3/21/81	#8	18	Too Much Time On My Hands	A&M 2323
7/11/81	#54	9	Nothing Ever Goes As Planned	A&M 2348
2/12/83	#1	20	Mr. Roboto	A&M 2525
4/30/83	#14	17	Don't Let It End	A&M 2543
8/20/83	#60	7	High Time	A&M 2568
5/05/84	#44	10	Music Time	A&M 2625
10/27/90	#74	6	Love Is A Ritual	A&M 1525
12/15/90	#6	26	Show Me The Way	A&M 1536
4/06/91	#19	22	Love At First Sight	A&M 1548
			SUAVE	
3/19/88	#29	17	My Girl	Capitol 44124
			SUGAR BEARS	
3/11/72	#38	11	You Are The One	Big Tree 122
			SUGARHILL GANG	
11/03/79	#36	15	Rapper's Delight	Sugar Hill 542
2/14/81	#94	3	8th Wonder	Sugar Hill 553
2/13/82	#60	8	Apache	Sugar Hill 774
			SUGARLOAF	
8/08/70	#5	18	Green-Eyed Lady	Liberty 56183
2/27/71	#40	9	Tongue In Cheek	Liberty 56218
7/03/71	#89	3	Mother Nature's Wine	United Artists 50784
12/28/74	#12	17	Don't Call Us, We'll Call You*	Claridge 402
			*released as by SUGARLOAF/JERRY CORBETTA	
			DONNA SUMMER	
11/08/75	#3	21	Love To Love You Baby	Oasis 401
5/01/76	#63	5	Could It Be Magic	Oasis 405
1/08/77	#47	12	Winter Melody	Casablanca 874
8/06/77	#4	21	I Feel Love	Casablanca 884
12/10/77	#26	13	I Love You	Casablanca 907
3/11/78	#72	4	Rumour Has It	Casablanca 916
5/13/78	#4	22	Last Dance	Casablanca 926
9/09/78	#1	22	MacArthur Park	Casablanca 939
1/13/79	#4	16	Heaven Knows*	Casablanca 959
4/21/79	#1	21	Hot Stuff	Casablanca 978
5/26/79	#1	21	Bad Girls	Casablanca 988
8/25/79	#3	21	Dim All The Lights	Casablanca 2201
10/20/79	#1	17	No More Tears (Enough Is Enough)**	Columbia 11125
1/19/80	#4	16	On The Radio	Casablanca 2236
9/13/80	#48	13	Walk Away	Casablanca 2300
9/20/80	#2	21	The Wanderer	Geffen 49563
12/06/80	#49	12	Cold Love	Geffen 49634
3/21/81	#38	12	Who Do You Think You're Foolin'	Geffen 49664
6/26/82	#11	19	Love Is In Control (Finger On The Trigger)	Geffen 29982
10/02/82	#46	11	State Of Independence	Geffen 29895
12/18/82	#28	18	The Woman In Me	Geffen 29805
5/28/83	#3	26	She Works Hard For The Money	Mercury 812370
9/03/83	#40	11	Unconditional Love	Mercury 814088
1/21/84	#77	7	Love Has A Mind Of Its Own***	Mercury 814922
8/11/84	#24	15	There Goes My Baby	Geffen 29291
11/10/84	#80	6	Supernatural Love	Geffen 29142
8/29/87	#56	10	Dinner With Gershwin	Geffen 28418
4/29/89	#6	20	This Time I Know It's For Real	Atlantic 88899
			*released as by DONNA SUMMER with BROOKLYN DREAMS	
			**released as by BARBRA STREISAND/DONNA SUMMER	
			***released as by DONNA SUMMER with MATTHEW WARD	
			HENRY LEE SUMMER	
2/13/88	#26	18	I Wish I Had A Girl	CBS Associated 07720
5/28/88	#57	10	Darlin' Danielle Don't	CBS Associated 07909
5/20/89	#19	22	Hey Baby	CBS Associated 68891
8/17/91	#42	12	Till Somebody Loves You	CBS Associated 73893

Debut Date	Peak Pos	Wks Chr	ARTIST/Song Title	Label & Number
			SUMMER WINE	
2/24/73	#100	1	Why Do Fools Fall In Love	Sire 701
			SUNDOWN COMPANY	
5/08/76	#86	6	Norma Jean Wants To Be A Movie Star	Polydor 14312
			SUNNY & THE SUNGLOWS	
9/07/63	#9	13	Talk To Me	Tear Drop 3014
11/23/63	#58	7	Rags To Riches*	Tear Drop 3022
4/24/65	#54	7	Peanuts (La Cacahuata)**	Sunglow 107
			*released as by SUNNY & THE SUNLINERS	
			**released as by THE SUNGLOWS	
			SUNRAYS	
8/07/65	#45	13	I Live For The Sun	Tower 148
1/15/66	#44	9	Andrea	Tower 191
4/16/66	#96	3	Still	Tower 224
			SUNSCREAM	
3/13/93	#26	16	Love U More	Columbia 74769
			SUNSHINE COMPANY	
7/22/67	#31	10	Happy	Imperial 66247
10/21/67	#45	7	Back On The Street Again	Imperial 66260
2/03/68	#57	6	Look, Here Comes The Sun	Imperial 66280
			SUPERBS	
10/03/60	#84	3	Baby Baby All The Time	Dore 715
			SUPERTRAMP	
4/19/75	#53	7	Bloody Well Right	A&M 1660
5/14/77	#12	21	Give A Little Bit	A&M 1938
4/07/79	#4	19	The Logical Song	A&M 2128
7/07/79	#16	16	Goodbye Stranger	A&M 2162
10/13/79	#15	17	Take The Long Way Home	A&M 2193
9/20/80	#15	17	Dreamer	A&M 2269
12/13/80	#69	7	Breakfast In America	A&M 2292
10/30/82	#7	18	It's Raining Again	A&M 2502
1/29/83	#23	12	My Kind Of Lady	A&M 2517
5/25/85	#31	13	Cannonball	A&M 2731
			SUPREMES	
12/01/62	#82	13	Let Me Go The Right Way	Motown 1034
8/10/63	#75	4	A Breath Taking Guy	Motown 1044
12/07/63	#20	10	When The Lovelight Starts Shining Through His Eyes . . .	Motown 1051
2/29/64	#86	4	Run, Run, Run	Motown 1054
7/11/64	#1	15	Where Did Our Love Go	Motown 1060
10/03/64	#1	14	Baby Love	Motown 1066
11/14/64	#1	15	Come See About Me	Motown 1068
2/20/65	#1	13	Stop! In The Name Of Love	Motown 1074
5/01/65	#1	11	Back In My Arms Again	Motown 1075
7/31/65	#8	10	Nothing But Heartaches	Motown 1080
10/23/65	#1	12	I Hear A Symphony	Motown 1083
1/15/66	#5	11	My World Is Empty Without You	Motown 1089
4/23/66	#9	10	Love Is Like An Itching In My Heart	Motown 1094
8/13/66	#1	12	You Can't Hurry Love	Motown 1097
10/29/66	#1	12	You Keep Me Hangin' On	Motown 1101
1/28/67	#1	10	Love Is Here And Now You're Gone	Motown 1103
4/08/67	#1	11	The Happening	Motown 1107
8/05/67	#2	13	Reflections*	Motown 1111
11/11/67	#10	9	In And Out Of Love*	Motown 1116
3/16/68	#13	10	Forever Came Today*	Motown 1122
6/08/68	#22	7	Some Things You Never Get Used To*	Motown 1126
10/19/68	#1	15	Love Child*	Motown 1135
12/07/68	#1	11	I'm Gonna Make You Love Me**	Motown 1137
1/25/69	#8	8	I'm Livin' In Shame*	Motown 1139
3/15/69	#21	7	I'll Try Something New**	Motown 1142
4/12/69	#21	7	The Composer*	Motown 1146
5/24/69	#27	7	No Matter What Sign You Are*/	Motown 1148
7/26/69	#89	4	The Young Folks*	Motown 1148
9/13/69	#39	5	The Weight**	Motown 1153
11/01/69	#1	16	Someday We'll Be Together*	Motown 1156
3/07/70	#9	11	Up The Ladder To The Roof	Motown 1162
7/11/70	#14	11	Everybody's Got The Right To Love	Motown 1167
10/31/70	#5	15	Stoned Love	Motown 1172

338

Debut Date	Peak Pos	Wks Chr	ARTIST/Song Title	Label & Number
11/21/70	#15	11	River Deep - Mountain High***	Motown 1173
5/01/71	#10	10	Nathan Jones	Motown 1182
6/05/71	#51	4	You Gotta Have Love In Your Heart	Motown 1181
10/02/71	#53	4	Touch	Motown 1190
1/08/72	#16	13	Floy Joy	Motown 1195
4/29/72	#37	9	Automatically Sunshine	Motown 1200
8/05/72	#70	6	Your Wonderful Sweet Sweet Love	Motown 1206
11/04/72	#100	1	I Guess I'll Lose The Man	Motown 1213
6/16/73	#92	3	Bad Weather	Motown 1225

*released as by DIANA ROSS and THE SUPREMES
**released as by DIANA ROSS and THE SUPREMES & THE TEMPTATIONS
***released as by THE SUPREMES & FOUR TOPS

SURFACE

5/23/87	#23	17	Happy	Columbia 06611
4/15/89	#59	11	Closer Than Friends	Columbia 08537
7/08/89	#5	22	Shower Me With Your Love	Columbia 68746
11/11/89	#85	5	You Are My Everything	Columbia 69016
11/10/90	#1	25	The First Time	Columbia 73502
5/18/91	#32	17	Never Gonna Let You Down	Columbia 73643

SURFARIS

6/08/63	#5	17	Wipe Out/	Dot 16479
9/07/63	#61	7	Surfer Joe	Dot 16479
9/21/63	#52	9	Point Panic	Decca 31538
8/06/66	#9	14	Wipe Out	Dot 144

SURVIVOR

10/17/81	#48	13	Poor Man's Son	Scotti Brothers 02560
2/20/82	#65	6	Summer Nights	Scotti Brothers 02700
6/05/82	#1	25	Eye Of The Tiger	Scotti Brothers 02912
9/25/82	#39	16	American Heartbeat	Scotti Brothers 03213
10/22/83	#78	6	Caught In The Game	Scotti Brothers 04074
6/16/84	#67	7	The Moment Of Truth	Casablanca 880053
9/22/84	#14	21	I Can't Hold Back	Scotti Brothers 04603
1/26/85	#19	16	High On You	Scotti Brothers 04685
4/20/85	#12	21	The Search Is Over	Scotti Brothers 04871
8/17/85	#52	9	First Night	Scotti Brothers 05579
11/02/85	#2	25	Burning Heart	Scotti Brothers 05563
10/25/86	#11	20	Is This Love	Scotti Brothers 06381
2/14/87	#52	12	How Much Love	Scotti Brothers 06705
5/09/87	#81	5	Man Against The World	Scotti Brothers 07070
10/15/88	#53	9	Didn't Know It Was Love	Scotti Brothers 08067
1/21/89	#67	8	Across The Miles	Scotti Brothers 68526

SUTHERLAND BROTHERS & QUIVER

8/11/73	#20	12	(I Don't Want To Love You But) You Got Me Anyway . . .	Island 1217
4/10/76	#71	6	Arms Of Mary	Columbia 10284
1/08/77	#97	4	Secrets	Columbia 10460

GLENN SUTTON

12/30/78	#60	6	The Football Card	Mercury 55052

SUZY and THE RED STRIPES

6/11/77	#58	7	Seaside Woman	Epic 50403

SWAMPSEEDS

4/20/68	#100	1	Can I Carry Your Balloon	Epic 10281

BILLY SWAN

9/28/74	#1	18	I Can Help	Monument 8621
3/22/75	#63	3	I'm Her Fool	Monument 8641
9/27/75	#67	11	Everything's The Same	Monument 8661
5/22/76	#74	5	Number One	Monument 8697

BETTYE SWANN

5/27/67	#20	13	Make Me Yours	Money 126
9/16/67	#85	3	Fall In Love With Me	Money 129
3/22/69	#40	7	Don't Touch Me	Capitol 2382
6/21/69	#100	1	Angel Of The Morning	Capitol 2515
6/10/72	#65	6	Victim Of A Foolish Heart	Atlantic 2869
1/20/73	#44	9	Today I Started Loving You Again	Atlantic 2921

PATRICK SWAYZE

12/19/87	#2	21	She's Like The Wind	RCA 5363

Debut Date	Peak Pos	Wks Chr	ARTIST/Song Title	Label & Number
			KEITH SWEAT	
1/23/88	#6	20	I Want Her	Vintertainment 69431
5/07/88	#78	7	Something Just Ain't Right	Vintertainment 69411
7/23/88	#55	11	Make It Last Forever*	Vintertainment 69386
1/27/90	#65	8	All Nite**	Vintertainment 69260
6/02/90	#12	20	Make You Sweat	Vintertainment 64961
12/01/90	#18	20	I'll Give All My Love To You	Vintertainment 64915
6/15/91	#81	7	Your Love	Vintertainment 98801
12/21/91	#16	23	Keep It Comin'	Elektra 64812
			*released as by KEITH SWEAT with JACCI McGHEE	
			**released as by ENTOUCH featuring KEITH SWEAT	
			SWEATHOG	
11/13/71	#28	11	Hallelujah	Columbia 45492
			SWEDEN HEAVEN AND HELL SOUNDTRACK*	
8/30/69	#44	7	Mah-Na-Mah-Na	Ariel 500
			*actually no artist is listed on the record label, just the composer,	
			Pierre Umiliani, and the movie listed above	
			SWEENEY TODD	
8/28/76	#93	2	Roxy Roller	London 240
			SWEET	
9/25/71	#85	3	Co-Co	Bell 45126
1/20/73	#3	20	Little Willy	Bell 45251
6/16/73	#43	9	Blockbuster	Bell 45361
6/21/75	#9	21	Ballroom Blitz	Capitol 4055
11/15/75	#5	15	Fox On The Run	Capitol 4157
2/14/76	#10	15	Action	Capitol 4220
9/10/77	#90	3	Funk It Up	Capitol 4454
2/25/78	#8	24	Love Is Like Oxygen	Capitol 4549
8/12/78	#88	5	California Nights	Capitol 4610
			SWEET DREAMS	
9/14/74	#69	5	Honey Honey	ABC 12008
			SWEET INSPIRATIONS	
3/09/68	#20	13	Sweet Inspiration	Atlantic 2476
7/06/68	#95	1	To Love Somebody	Atlantic 2529
			SWEET SENSATION (group from Manchester, England)	
1/18/75	#17	13	Sad Sweet Dreamer	Pye 71002
			SWEET SENSATION (group from New York City)	
1/31/87	#82	8	Hooked On You	Next Plateau 308
4/09/88	#57	13	Take It While It's Hot	Atco 99352
2/11/89	#17	21	Sincerely Yours	Atco 99246
6/10/89	#28	20	Hooked On You	Atco 99210
3/17/90	#12	19	Love Child	Atco 98983
6/09/90	#1	23	If Wishes Came True	Atco 98953
10/20/90	#61	9	Each And Every Time	Atco 98906
			SWINGING BLUE JEANS	
3/07/64	#23	10	Hippy Hippy Shake	Imperial 66021
5/09/64	#58	7	Good Golly Miss Molly	Imperial 66030
			SWINGIN' MEDALLIONS	
4/30/66	#18	14	Double Shot (Of My Baby's Love)	Smash 2033
9/03/66	#68	4	She Drives Me Out Of My Mind	Smash 2050
4/15/67	#95	2	I Found A Rainbow	Smash 2084
			SWING OUT SISTER	
8/22/87	#5	25	Breakout	Mercury 888016
12/26/87	#53	16	Twilight World	Mercury 888484
9/05/92	#32	20	Am I The Same Girl	Fontana 864170
			SWITCH	
10/07/78	#46	14	There'll Never Be	Gordy 7159
7/14/79	#81	8	Best Beat In Town	Gordy 7168
12/08/79	#86	10	I Call Your Name	Gordy 7175
			SWV	
2/13/93	#6	33	I'm So Into You	RCA 62451
5/01/93	#1	27	Weak	RCA 62521
7/24/93	#2	31	Right Here (Human Nature)/Downtown	RCA 62614

Debut Date	Peak Pos	Wks Chr	ARTIST/Song Title	Label & Number
			SYBIL	
10/14/89	#21	19	Don't Make Me Over	Next Plateau 325
2/03/90	#68	6	Walk On By	Next Plateau 327
			SYLVERS	
1/27/73	#57	10	Wish That I Could Talk To You	Pride 1019
8/25/73	#93	1	Stay Away From Me	Pride 1029
1/31/76	#1	24	Boogie Fever	Capitol 4179
7/10/76	#74	5	Cotton Candy	Capitol 4255
10/30/76	#4	21	Hot Line	Capitol 4336
4/16/77	#13	20	High School Dance	Capitol 4405
10/29/77	#92	6	Any Way You Want Me	Capitol 4493
			FOSTER SYLVERS	
5/26/73	#14	13	Misdemeanor	MGM 14580
10/03/73	#93	4	Hey Little Girl	MGM 14630
			SYLVESTER	
8/26/78	#30	18	Dance (Disco Heat)	Fantasy 827
12/30/78	#53	11	You Make Me Feel (Mighty Real)	Fantasy 846
4/21/79	#88	4	I (Who Have Nothing)	Fantasy 855
			SYLVIA (Sylvia Robinson, r&b singer)	
3/31/73	#2	16	Pillow Talk	Vibration 521
7/21/73	#74	4	Didn't I	Vibration 524
6/15/74	#91	3	Sho Nuff Boogie (Part 1)*	All Platinum 2350
			*released as by SYLVIA & THE MOMENTS	
			SYLVIA (Sylvia Allen, c&w singer)	
8/21/82	#9	26	Nobody	RCA 13223
			SYLVIA SYMS	
8/04/56	#47	1	I Could Have Danced All Night	Decca 29903
			SYNCH	
3/11/89	#16	23	Where Are You Now?*	WTG 68625
			*released as by JIMMY HARNEN with SYNCH	
			SYNDICATE OF SOUND	
5/28/66	#8	12	Little Girl	Bell 640
8/27/66	#69	7	Rumors	Bell 646
4/11/70	#82	2	Brown Paper Bag	Buddah 156
			SYSTEM	
3/05/83	#56	9	You Are In My System	Mirage 99937
4/11/87	#10	23	Don't Disturb This Groove	Atlantic 89320
7/16/88	#85	3	Coming To America (Part 1)	Atco 99320

T

Debut Date	Peak Pos	Wks Chr	ARTIST/Song Title	Label & Number
			TACO	
6/25/83	#1	25	Puttin' On The Ritz	RCA 13574
			TAG TEAM	
6/12/93	#2	49	Whomp! (There It Is)	Life 79001
			TALKING HEADS	
11/04/78	#31	19	Take Me To The River	Sire 1032
8/06/83	#10	23	Burning Down The House	Sire 29565
12/03/83	#71	9	This Must Be The Place (Naive Melody)	Sire 29451
9/28/85	#48	16	And She Was	Sire 28917
4/12/86	#82	6	Once In A Lifetime	Sire 29163
8/30/86	#25	22	Wild Wild Life	Sire 28629
			TALK TALK	
11/06/82	#88	3	Talk Talk	EMI America 8136
3/24/84	#33	19	It's My Life	EMI America 8195
2/08/86	#88	3	Life's What You Make It	EMI America 8303
			TA MARA & THE SEEN	
10/26/85	#25	20	Everybody Dance	A&M 2768
			RUSS TAMBLYN	
1/10/59	#86	5	Tom Thumb's Tune	Metro 20012
			TAMI SHOW	
8/03/91	#34	16	The Truth	RCA 2694
2/01/92	#78	6	Did He Do It To You	RCA 62171

Debut Date	Peak Pos	Wks Chr	ARTIST/Song Title	Label & Number
			TAMS	
10/13/62	#61	7	Untie Me	Arlen 11
12/28/63	#9	13	What Kind Of Fool (Do You Think I Am)	ABC-Paramount 10502
3/28/64	#74	5	You Lied To Your Daddy/	ABC-Paramount 10533
3/28/64	#81	5	It's All Right (You're Just In Love)	ABC-Paramount 10533
7/18/64	#41	10	Hey Girl Don't Bother Me	ABC-Paramount 10573
6/08/68	#63	7	Be Young, Be Foolish, Be Happy	ABC 11066
			NORMA TANEGA	
2/26/66	#25	10	Walkin' My Cat Named Dog	New Voice 807
			TANGIER	
9/02/89	#72	6	On The Line	Atco 99208
			GARY TANNER	
5/27/78	#74	4	Over The Rainbow	20th Century 2373
			MARC TANNER BAND	
3/10/79	#52	7	Elena	Elektra 46003
			TARNEY/SPENCER BAND	
7/24/76	#71	5	I'm Your Rock 'N' Roll Man	Private Stock 45088
7/15/78	#89	5	It's Really You	A&M 2049
5/19/79	#66	7	No Time To Lose	A&M 2124
9/19/81	#74	5	No Time To Lose	A&M 2366
			TARRIERS	
10/06/56	#9	19	Cindy, Oh Cindy*	Glory 247
12/15/56	#2	18	The Banana Boat Song	Glory 249
			*released as by VINCE MARTIN with THE TARRIERS	
			TASSELS	
5/30/59	#47	13	To A Soldier Boy	Madison 117
			TASTE OF HONEY	
6/24/78	#1	25	Boogie Oogie Oogie	Capitol 4565
3/07/81	#4	25	Sukiyaki	Capitol 4953
3/13/82	#42	10	I'll Try Something New	Capitol 5099
			HOWARD TATE	
8/06/66	#57	8	Ain't Nobody Home	Verve 10420
12/24/66	#63	8	Look At Granny Run, Run	Verve 10464
1/27/68	#80	5	Stop	Verve 10573
			TOMMY TATE	
6/03/72	#68	8	School Of Life	KoKo 2112
12/09/72	#93	3	More Power To You	KoKo 2114
			TAVARES	
9/29/73	#34	9	Check It Out	Capitol 3674
2/09/74	#94	4	That's The Sound That Lonely Makes	Capitol 3794
6/08/74	#66	7	Too Late	Capitol 3882
10/19/74	#66	9	She's Gone	Capitol 3957
4/12/75	#23	11	Remember What I Told You To Forget	Capitol 4010
7/26/75	#10	18	It Only Takes A Minute Girl	Capitol 4111
12/13/75	#56	6	Free Ride	Capitol 4184
6/05/76	#10	24	Heaven Must Be Missing An Angel	Capitol 4270
10/30/76	#40	15	Don't Take Away The Music	Capitol 4348
3/19/77	#16	18	Whodunit	Capitol 4398
2/18/78	#39	15	More Than A Woman	Capitol 4500
1/26/80	#64	6	Bad Times	Capitol 4811
9/25/82	#28	19	A Penny For Your Thoughts	RCA 13292
			ANDY TAYLOR	
5/31/86	#16	16	Take It Easy	Atlantic 89414
10/18/86	#58	7	When The Rain Comes Down	MCA 52946
			AUSTIN TAYLOR	
12/03/60	#100	1	Push Push	Laurie 3067
			B.E. TAYLOR GROUP	
1/28/84	#70	7	Vitamin L	MCA 52311
5/11/85	#80	4	Reggae Rock 'n Roll	Epic 04862
			BOBBY TAYLOR & THE VANCOUVERS	
4/06/68	#44	11	Does Your Mama Know About Me	Gordy 7069
7/20/68	#87	5	I Am Your Man	Gordy 7073
12/14/68	#67	5	Malinda	Gordy 7079

Debut Date	Peak Pos	Wks Chr	ARTIST/Song Title	Label & Number
			DEBBIE TAYLOR	
5/03/69	#86	4	Never Gonna Let Him Know	GWP 501
			FELICE TAYLOR	
1/14/67	#77	6	It May Be Winter Outside	Mustang 3024
			GLORIA TAYLOR	
10/25/69	#38	11	You Got To Pay The Price	Silver Fox 14
			JAMES TAYLOR	
9/12/70	#4	15	Fire And Rain	Warner Brothers 7423
11/14/70	#72	5	Carolina In My Mind	Apple 1805
2/06/71	#25	8	Country Road	Warner Brothers 7460
5/29/71	#1	16	You've Got A Friend	Warner Brothers 7498
10/02/71	#16	7	Long Ago And Far Away	Warner Brothers 7521
11/25/72	#15	10	Don't Let Me Be Lonely Tonight	Warner Brothers 7655
2/24/73	#53	5	One Man Parade	Warner Brothers 7682
2/02/74	#3	14	Mockingbird*	Elektra 45880
6/28/75	#7	13	How Sweet It Is (To Be Loved By You)	Warner Brothers 8109
10/11/75	#38	7	Mexico	Warner Brothers 8137
7/21/76	#49	15	Shower The People	Warner Brothers 8222
6/11/77	#2	19	Handy Man	Columbia 10557
10/01/77	#12	16	Your Smiling Face	Columbia 10602
1/21/78	#15	12	(What A) Wonderful World**	Columbia 10676
3/04/78	#70	3	Honey Don't Leave L.A.	Columbia 10689
8/19/78	#48	8	Devoted To You*	Elektra 45506
6/02/79	#32	12	Up On The Roof	Columbia 11005
3/14/81	#8	13	Her Town Too***	Columbia 60514
6/13/81	#82	5	Hard Times	Columbia 02093
11/09/85	#62	12	Everyday	Columbia 05681
			***released as by CARLY SIMON and JAMES TAYLOR**	
			****released as by ART GARFUNKEL with JAMES TAYLOR & PAUL SIMON**	
			*****released as by JAMES TAYLOR and J.D. SOUTHER**	
			JOHN TAYLOR	
3/08/86	#25	13	I Do What I Do	Capitol 5551
			JOHNNIE TAYLOR	
12/02/67	#98	1	Somebody's Sleeping In My Bed	Stax 235
10/19/68	#6	14	Who's Making Love	Stax 0009
1/11/69	#26	10	Take Care Of Your Homework	Stax 0023
5/10/69	#36	8	Testify (I Wonna)	Stax 0033
8/09/69	#54	7	I Could Never Be President	Stax 0046
1/30/70	#32	7	Love Bones	Stax 0055
5/23/70	#23	12	Steal Away	Stax 0068
10/03/70	#30	10	I Am Somebody (Part 2)	Stax 0078
1/16/71	#27	9	Jody's Got Your Girl And Gone	Stax 0085
5/22/71	#67	4	I Don't Wanna Lose You	Stax 0089
9/11/71	#57	5	Hijackin' Love	Stax 0096
1/29/72	#70	4	Standing In For Jody	Stax 0114
4/01/72	#63	7	Doing My Own Thing	Stax 0122
9/09/72	#70	6	Stop Doggin' Me	Stax 0142
6/23/73	#5	15	I Believe In You (You Believe In Me)	Stax 0161
10/06/73	#18	11	Cheaper To Keep Her	Stax 0176
2/02/74	#49	8	We're Getting Careless With Our Love	Stax 0193
6/08/74	#62	8	I've Been Born Again	Stax 0208
2/14/76	#1	19	Disco Lady	Columbia 10281
6/19/76	#73	6	Somebody's Gettin' It	Columbia 10334
3/05/77	#65	7	Love Is Better In The A.M. (Part 1)	Columbia 10478
			KATE TAYLOR	
9/10/77	#74	5	It's In His Kiss (The Shoop Shoop Song)	Columbia 10596
			KO KO TAYLOR	
4/09/66	#36	10	Wang Dang Doodle	Checker 1135
			LITTLE JOHNNY TAYLOR	
8/24/63	#19	14	Part Time Love	Galaxy 722
1/11/64	#90	3	Since I Found A New Love	Galaxy 725
12/18/71	#66	6	Everybody Knows About My Good Thing	Ronn 55
			LIVINGSTON TAYLOR	
10/21/78	#28	15	I Will Be In Love With You	Epic 50604
3/31/79	#72	4	I'll Come Running	Epic 50667
8/02/80	#48	11	First Time Love	Epic 50894

Debut Date	Peak Pos	Wks Chr	ARTIST/Song Title	Label & Number
			R. DEAN TAYLOR	
8/29/70	#1	15	Indiana Wants Me	Rare Earth 5013
2/06/71	#63	5	Ain't It A Sad Thing	Rare Earth 5023
4/10/71	#48	6	Gotta See Jane	Rare Earth 5026
8/07/71	#92	2	Candy Apple Red	Rare Earth 5030
4/08/72	#90	3	Taos New Mexico	Rare Earth 5041
			SAM "THE MAN" TAYLOR	
2/08/58	#35	4	Big Guitar	MGM 12613
			TED TAYLOR	
7/30/60	#81	6	I Need You	Top Rank 2048
12/03/60	#95	3	Look Out	Top Rank 2076
12/11/65	#94	4	Stay Away From My Baby	Okeh 7231
			T-BONES	
12/04/65	#3	14	No Matter What Shape (Your Stomach's In)	Liberty 55836
3/19/66	#64	6	Sippin' 'N Chippin'	Liberty 55867
			BRAM TCHAIKOVSKY	
7/07/79	#40	9	Girl Of My Dreams	Polydor 14575
			T-CONNECTION	
5/07/77	#80	6	Do What You Wanna Do	Dash 5032
			TEARS FOR FEARS	
8/13/83	#74	7	Change	Mercury 812677
3/16/85	#1	25	Everybody Wants To Rule The World	Mercury 880659
6/15/85	#1	19	Shout	Mercury 880294
9/14/85	#3	22	Head Over Heels	Mercury 880899
4/12/86	#25	14	Mothers Talk	Mercury 884638
9/02/89	#1	23	Sowing The Seeds Of Love	Fontana 874710
12/09/89	#32	14	Woman In Chains	Fontana 876248
3/03/90	#62	7	Advice For The Young At Heart	Fontana 876894
7/10/93	#26	33	Break It Down Again	Mercury 862330
			TECHNIQUES	
11/23/57	#43	8	Hey! Little Girl	Roulette 4030
			TECHNOTRONIC	
10/28/89	#1	23	Pump Up The Jam*	SBK 07311
2/03/90	#9	19	Get Up! (Before The Night Is Over)	SBK 07315
9/12/90	#12	15	Move This	SBK 50400
			*released as by TECHNOTRONIC featuring FELLY	
			TEDDY & THE PANDAS	
9/10/66	#99	2	We Can't Go On This Way	Musicor 1190
			TEDDY & THE TWILIGHTS	
5/12/62	#64	10	Woman Is A Man's Best Friend	Swan 4102
			TEDDY BEARS	
10/11/58	#1	19	To Know Him, Is To Love Him	Dore 503
1/31/59	#53	6	Oh Why/	Imperial 5562
1/31/59	#96	1	I Don't Need You Anymore	Imperial 5562
4/25/59	#96	1	If You Only Knew	Imperial 5581
			WILLIE TEE	
3/06/65	#88	2	Teasin' You	Atlantic 2273
			TEEGARDEN & VAN WINKLE	
9/12/70	#14	11	God, Love And Rock & Roll	Westbound 170
1/02/71	#91	2	Everything Is Going To Be Alright	Westbound 171
			TEENAGERS (see FRANKIE LYMON & THE TEENAGERS)	
			TEE SET	
1/17/70	#6	13	Ma Belle Amie	Colossus 107
5/02/70	#58	6	If You Do Believe In Love	Colossus 114
			NINO TEMPO & APRIL STEVENS	
7/07/62	#86	5	Sweet And Lovely	Atco 6224
9/21/63	#1	15	Deep Purple	Atco 6273
12/21/63	#11	9	Whispering	Atco 6281
2/22/64	#30	6	Stardust	Atco 6286
5/09/64	#86	3	Tea For Two	Atco 6294
9/10/66	#29	7	All Strung Out	White Whale 236
6/23/73	#91	3	Put It Where You Want It	A&M 1443
9/08/73	#40	10	Sister James*	A&M 1461
			*released as by NINO TEMPO and 5TH AVE. SAX	

Debut Date	Peak Pos	Wks Chr	ARTIST/Song Title	Label & Number
			TEMPOS	
6/07/58	#60	3	Prettiest Girl In School	Kapp 199
7/04/59	#22	14	See You In September	Climax 102
			TEMPREES	
8/26/72	#75	4	Dedicated To The One I Love	We Produce 1808
			TEMPTATIONS (New York group)	
4/09/60	#38	11	Barbara	Goldisc 3001
			TEMPTATIONS (Detroit group)	
2/22/64	#10	13	The Way You Do The Things You Do	Gordy 7028
5/23/64	#85	3	The Girl's Alright With Me/	Gordy 7032
5/30/64	#32	9	I'll Be In Trouble	Gordy 7032
9/12/64	#27	7	Girl (Why You Wanna Make Me Blue)	Gordy 7035
1/09/65	#2	15	My Girl	Gordy 7038
4/10/65	#19	8	It's Growing	Gordy 7040
7/24/65	#18	11	Since I Lost My Baby	Gordy 7043
10/23/65	#18	9	My Baby/	Gordy 7047
12/04/65	#78	2	Don't Look Back	Gordy 7047
2/26/66	#29	8	Get Ready	Gordy 7049
5/21/66	#10	15	Ain't Too Proud To Beg	Gordy 7054
8/20/66	#5	11	Beauty Is Only Skin Deep	Gordy 7055
11/19/66	#11	11	(I Know) I'm Losing You	Gordy 7057
4/29/67	#8	11	All I Need	Gordy 7061
7/29/67	#7	11	You're My Everything	Gordy 7063
10/14/67	#11	8	(Loneliness Made Me Realize) It's You That I Need . . .	Gordy 7065
1/06/68	#2	14	I Wish It Would Rain/	Gordy 7068
3/30/68	#93	1	I Truly, Truly Believe	Gordy 7068
5/04/68	#10	11	I Could Never Love Another (After Loving You)	Gordy 7072
7/27/68	#23	9	Please Return Your Love To Me	Gordy 7074
11/16/68	#8	13	Cloud Nine	Gordy 7081
12/07/68	#1	11	I'm Gonna Make You Love Me*	Motown 1137
2/15/69	#8	10	Run Away Child, Running Wild	Gordy 7084
3/15/69	#21	7	I'll Try Something New*	Motown 1142
5/17/69	#20	9	Don't Let The Joneses Get You Down	Gordy 7086
8/16/69	#3	16	I Can't Get Next To You	Gordy 7093
9/13/69	#39	5	The Weight*	Motown 1153
1/17/70	#4	12	Psychedelic Shack	Gordy 7096
5/23/70	#1	14	Ball Of Confusion (That's What The World Is Today)	Gordy 7099
10/03/70	#30	6	Ungena Za Ulimwengu (Unite The World)/	Gordy 7102
10/31/70	#88	2	Hum Along And Dance	Gordy 7102
1/30/71	#1	16	Just My Imagination (Running Away With Me)	Gordy 7105
7/17/71	#40	7	It's Summer	Gordy 7109
11/06/71	#13	10	Superstar (Remember How You Got Where You Are)	Gordy 7111
2/19/72	#28	10	Take A Look Around	Gordy 7115
7/01/72	#82	2	Mother Nature	Gordy 7119
10/14/72	#1	14	Papa Was A Rollin' Stone	Gordy 7121
2/17/73	#9	13	Masterpiece	Gordy 7126
6/02/73	#33	9	The Plastic Man	Gordy 7129
8/18/73	#27	9	Hey Girl (I Like Your Style)	Gordy 7131
12/15/73	#27	9	Let Your Hair Down	Gordy 7133
3/09/74	#45	9	Heavenly	Gordy 7135
6/15/74	#56	7	You've Got My Soul On Fire	Gordy 7136
12/14/74	#44	10	Happy People	Gordy 7138
3/29/75	#28	13	Shakey Ground	Gordy 7142
7/05/75	#41	11	Glasshouse	Gordy 7144
2/07/76	#53	7	Keep Holding On	Gordy 7146
5/10/80	#57	7	Power	Gordy 7183
9/26/81	#75	4	Aiming At Your Heart	Gordy 7208
5/08/82	#67	6	Standing On The Top (Part 1)**	Gordy 1616
4/14/84	#67	6	Sail Away	Gordy 1720
12/22/84	#48	13	Treat Her Like A Lady	Gordy 1765
10/11/86	#56	8	Lady Soul	Gordy 1856
			*released as by **DIANA ROSS** and **THE SUPREMES & THE TEMPTATIONS**	
			released as by **THE TEMPTATIONS featuring **RICK JAMES**	
			10cc	
9/08/73	#43	10	Rubber Bullets	UK 49015
7/13/74	#84	6	The Wall Street Shuffle	UK 49023
5/10/75	#3	18	I'm Not In Love	Mercury 73678
12/06/75	#63	5	Art For Art's Sake	Mercury 73725

Debut Date	Peak Pos	Wks Chr	**ARTIST**/Song Title	Label & Number
			10cc—*continued*	
3/27/76	#88	6	I'm Mandy Fly Me	Mercury 73779
1/01/77	#4	23	The Things We Do For Love	Mercury 73875
5/28/77	#72	6	People In Love	Mercury 73917
8/13/77	#75	8	Good Morning Judge	Mercury 73943
9/30/78	#46	10	Dreadlock Holiday	Polydor 14511
1/20/79	#73	4	For You And I	Polydor 14528
			TENDER SLIM	
1/02/60	#94	5	Teenage Hayride	Grey Cliff 723
			10,000 MANIACS	
5/21/88	#84	6	Like The Weather	Elektra 69418
6/24/89	#83	4	Trouble Me	Elektra 69298
12/05/92	#68	9	These Are Days	Elektra 64700
3/20/93	#55	12	Candy Everybody Wants	Elektra 64665
11/27/93	#9	28	Because The Night	Elektra 64595
			TEN WHEEL DRIVE	
8/01/70	#74	6	Morning Much Better*	Polydor 14037
			*released as by **TEN WHEEL DRIVE with GENYA RAVAN**	
			TEN YEARS AFTER	
5/09/70	#73	4	Love Like A Man	Deram 7529
9/11/71	#28	12	I'd Love To Change The World	Columbia 45457
1/15/72	#73	5	Baby Won't You Let Me Rock 'N Roll You	Columbia 45530
			ROBERT TEPPER	
1/25/86	#25	15	No Easy Way Out	Scotti Brothers 05750
5/03/86	#80	3	Don't Walk Away	Scotti Brothers 05879
			TAMMI TERRELL	
1/15/66	#86	4	I Can't Believe You Love Me	Motown 1086
6/04/66	#97	2	Come On And See Me	Motown 1095
5/20/67	#22	12	Ain't No Mountain High Enough*	Tamla 54149
9/16/67	#6	12	Your Precious Love*	Tamla 54156
12/02/67	#18	12	If I Could Build My Whole World Around You*/	Tamla 54161
3/09/68	#70	3	If This World Were Mine*	Tamla 54161
4/13/68	#9	12	Ain't Nothing Like The Real Thing*	Tamla 54163
7/27/68	#7	11	You're All I Need To Get By*	Tamla 54169
10/05/68	#25	8	Keep On Lovin' Me Honey*	Tamla 54173
1/11/69	#83	4	This Old Heart Of Mine	Motown 1138
2/01/69	#45	6	Good Lovin' Ain't Easy To Come By*	Tamla 54179
11/22/69	#47	8	What You Gave Me*	Tamla 54187
4/18/70	#63	5	California Soul*	Tamla 54192
			*released as by **MARVIN GAYE & TAMMI TERRELL**	
			TONY TERRY	
7/02/88	#88	4	Forever Yours	Epic 07900
9/28/91	#29	20	With You	Epic 73713
2/15/92	#90	4	Everlasting Love	Epic 74119
			TESLA	
5/09/87	#80	5	Little Suzi	Geffen 28353
10/21/89	#9	24	Love Song	Geffen 22856
3/17/90	#56	10	The Way It Is	Geffen 19948
12/22/90	#11	27	Signs	Geffen 19653
4/25/92	#77	9	What You Give	Geffen 19117
			JOE TEX	
12/19/64	#6	12	Hold What You've Got	Dial 4001
2/27/65	#53	6	You Better Get It/	Dial 4003
3/20/65	#76	3	You Got What It Takes	Dial 4003
4/10/65	#59	7	A Woman Can Change A Man	Dial 4006
7/03/65	#90	2	One Monkey Don't Stop No Show	Dial 4011
8/21/65	#18	13	I Want To (Do Everything For You)	Dial 4016
12/04/65	#20	10	A Sweet Woman Like You	Dial 4022
3/05/66	#41	8	The Love You Save	Dial 4026
5/14/66	#53	6	S.Y.S.L.J.F.M.	Dial 4028
7/16/66	#55	7	I Believe I'm Gonna Make It	Dial 4033
10/08/66	#57	5	I've Got To Do A Little Bit Better	Dial 4045
12/10/66	#29	9	Papa Was Too	Dial 4051
2/25/67	#43	10	Show Me	Dial 4055
6/03/67	#51	7	Woman Like That, Yeah	Dial 4059
8/05/67	#59	4	A Woman's Hands	Dial 4061
10/28/67	#9	16	Skinny Legs And All	Dial 4063

Debut Date	Peak Pos	Wks Chr	ARTIST/Song Title	Label & Number
2/03/68	#26	8	Men Are Gettin' Scarce	Dial 4069
5/18/68	#45	6	I'll Never Do You Wrong	Dial 4076
8/10/68	#56	6	Keep The One You Got	Dial 4083
10/12/68	#66	3	You Need Me, Baby	Dial 4086
1/18/69	#86	3	That's Your Baby	Dial 4089
4/12/69	#39	7	Buying A Book	Dial 4090
7/05/69	#56	6	That's The Way	Dial 4093
11/29/69	#95	2	I Can't See You No More	Dial 4095
2/28/70	#95	2	You're Right, Ray Charles	Dial 4096
10/02/71	#98	1	Give The Baby Anything	Dial 1008
1/29/72	#3	19	I Gotcha	Dial 1010
5/20/72	#35	9	You Said A Bad Word	Dial 1012
3/26/77	#15	17	Ain't Gonna Bump No More (With No Big Fat Woman)	Epic 50313
			TEXANS	
3/11/61	#84	5	Green Grass Of Texas	Infinity 001
			TEXAS	
9/16/89	#84	4	I Don't Want A Lover	Mercury 872350
			THEE MIDNIGHTERS	
2/27/65	#57	3	Land Of A Thousand Dances (Part 1)	Chattahoochee 666
			THEE PROPHETS	
3/08/69	#39	9	Playgirl	Kapp 962
			THEM	
4/17/65	#95	2	Baby Please Don't Go/	Parrot 9727
5/01/65	#88	3	Gloria	Parrot 9727
5/22/65	#18	11	Here Comes The Night	Parrot 9749
10/30/65	#29	8	Mystic Eyes	Parrot 9796
			THINK	
12/11/71	#29	8	Once You Understand	Laurie 3583
3/02/74	#53	8	Once You Understand	Big Tree 15000
			THIN LIZZY	
5/15/76	#10	17	The Boys Are Back In Town	Mercury 73786
10/01/77	#92	5	Dancing In The Moonlight	Mercury 73945
			THIRD BASS	
7/27/91	#61	12	Pop Goes The Weasel	Def Jam 73728
			THIRD BOOTH	
6/22/68	#88	5	I Need Love	Independence 86
			THIRD RAIL	
7/29/67	#54	11	Run, Run, Run	Epic 10191
3/09/68	#84	3	It's Time To Say Goodbye	Epic 10285
			THIRD WORLD	
2/03/79	#41	10	Now That We Found Love	Island 8663
			THIRTEENTH FLOOR ELEVATORS	
8/27/66	#50	6	You're Gonna Miss Me	Int'l. Artists 107
			38 SPECIAL	
1/26/80	#50	10	Rockin' Into The Night	A&M 2205
3/07/81	#32	15	Hold On Loosely	A&M 2316
6/06/81	#58	9	Fantasy Girl	A&M 2330
5/01/82	#9	17	Caught Up In You	A&M 2412
8/14/82	#34	12	You Keep Runnin' Away	A&M 2431
11/12/83	#23	16	If I'd Been The One	A&M 2594
2/04/84	#31	13	Back Where You Belong	A&M 2615
9/29/84	#26	13	Teacher Teacher	Capitol 5405
5/03/86	#18	16	Like No Other Night	A&M 2831
7/19/86	#47	12	Somebody Like You	A&M 2854
7/25/87	#49	12	Back To Paradise	A&M 2955
10/29/88	#57	9	Rock & Roll Strategy	A&M 1246
2/04/89	#7	23	Second Chance	A&M 1273
7/01/89	#50	9	Comin' Down Tonight	A&M 1424
7/20/91	#37	15	The Sound Of Your Voice	Charisma 98773
			B.J. THOMAS	
2/19/66	#9	14	I'm So Lonesome I Could Cry*	Scepter 12129
5/14/66	#15	8	Mama	Scepter 12139
6/18/66	#33	12	Billy And Sue*	Hickory 1395
7/23/66	#83	4	Bring Back The Time	Scepter 12154
9/24/66	#99	3	Tomorrow Never Comes	Scepter 12165

Debut Date	Peak Pos	Wks Chr	ARTIST/Song Title	Label & Number
			B.J. THOMAS—continued	
6/10/67	#99	3	I Can't Help It (If I'm Still In Love With You)	Scepter 12194
6/08/68	#31	14	The Eyes Of A New York Woman	Scepter 12219
10/26/68	#5	19	Hooked On A Feeling	Scepter 12230
3/22/69	#28	8	It's Only Love	Scepter 12244
7/05/69	#90	3	Pass The Apple Eve	Scepter 12255
10/25/69	#1	22	Raindrops Keep Falling On My Head	Scepter 12265
3/28/70	#21	7	Everybody's Out Of Town	Scepter 12277
6/20/70	#11	13	I Just Can't Help Believing	Scepter 12283
11/28/70	#30	10	Most Of All	Scepter 12299
2/20/71	#14	12	No Love At All	Scepter 12307
6/26/71	#39	10	Mighty Clouds Of Joy	Scepter 12320
10/30/71	#57	7	Long Ago Tomorrow	Scepter 12335
2/05/72	#12	12	Rock And Roll Lullaby	Scepter 12344
7/08/72	#85	4	That's What Friends Are For	Scepter 12354
9/16/72	#86	2	Happier Than The Morning Sun	Scepter 12364
2/01/75	#1	18	(Hey Won't You Play) Another Somebody Done Somebody Wrong Song	ABC 12054
9/20/75	#62	7	Help Me Make It (To My Rockin' Chair)	ABC 12121
7/09/77	#13	19	Don't Worry Baby	MCA 40735
11/26/77	#92	4	Still The Lovin' Is Fun	MCA 40812
1/21/78	#44	9	Everybody Loves A Rain Song	MCA 40854
			*released as by B.J. THOMAS and THE TRIUMPHS	
			BUDDY THOMAS	
7/08/61	#95	3	Have A Drink On Me	Todd 1063
			CARLA THOMAS	
1/21/61	#9	15	Gee Whiz (Look At His Eyes)	Atlantic 2086
5/13/61	#63	7	A Love Of My Own	Atlantic 2101
10/13/62	#51	8	I'll Bring It On Home To You	Atlantic 2163
6/13/64	#90	2	That's Really Some Good*	Stax 151
8/01/64	#53	10	I've Got No Time To Lose	Atlantic 2238
11/28/64	#82	6	A Woman's Love	Atlantic 2258
7/10/65	#98	1	Stop! Look What You're Doing	Stax 172
5/14/66	#80	2	Let Me Be Good To You	Stax 188
8/20/66	#16	17	B-A-B-Y	Stax 195
1/14/67	#80	4	Something Good	Stax 207
5/06/67	#19	10	Tramp**	Stax 216
6/24/67	#70	4	I'll Always Have Faith In You	Stax 222
8/12/67	#60	9	Knock On Wood**	Stax 228
12/23/67	#74	4	Pick Up The Pieces	Stax 239
2/17/68	#50	3	Lovey Dovey	Stax 244
4/27/68	#99	1	A Dime A Dozen	Stax 251
2/22/69	#58	8	I Like What You're Doing (To Me)	Stax 0024
			*released as by RUFUS & CARLA	
			**released as by OTIS & CARLA (Otis Redding & Carla Thomas)	
			GENE THOMAS	
9/09/61	#62	7	Sometime	United Artists 338
12/21/63	#83	5	Baby's Gone	United Artists 640
			IAN THOMAS	
10/20/73	#27	13	Painted Ladies	Janus 224
			IRMA THOMAS	
3/28/64	#17	13	Wish Someone Would Care	Imperial 66013
6/27/64	#60	8	Anyone Who Knows What Love Is	Imperial 66041
10/24/64	#96	3	Times Have Changed	Imperial 66069
1/02/65	#85	4	He's My Guy	Imperial 66080
			JAMO THOMAS & HIS PARTY BROTHERS ORCHESTRA	
3/26/66	#94	1	I Spy (For The FBI)	Thomas 303
			JON THOMAS	
6/18/60	#27	12	Heartbreak (It's Hurtin' Me)	ABC-Paramount 10122
			MICKEY THOMAS	
2/04/89	#73	5	Sing	Columbia 68558
			NOLAN THOMAS	
1/19/85	#58	10	Yo' Little Brother	Mirage 99697

Debut Date	Peak Pos	Wks Chr	ARTIST/Song Title	Label & Number
			RUFUS THOMAS	
2/23/63	#95	2	The Dog	Stax 130
10/12/63	#10	15	Walking The Dog	Stax 140
2/01/64	#37	8	Can Your Monkey Do The Dog	Stax 144
6/13/64	#90	2	That's Really Some Good*	Stax 151
10/03/64	#72	7	Jump Back	Stax 157
1/31/70	#50	11	Do The Funky Chicken	Stax 0059
7/04/70	#72	3	Sixty Minute Man	Stax 0071
12/12/70	#20	15	(Do The) Push And Pull (Part 1)	Stax 0079
8/07/71	#31	11	The Breakdown (Part 1)	Stax 0098
12/18/71	#61	10	Do The Funky Penguin (Part 1)	Stax 0112
			*released as by RUFUS & CARLA	
			TIMMY THOMAS	
11/25/72	#2	16	Why Can't We Live Together	Glades 1703
4/07/73	#86	5	People Are Changin'	Glades 1709
			CHRIS THOMPSON (see NIGHT)	
			ROBBIN THOMPSON BAND	
10/25/80	#78	6	Brite Eyes	Ovation 1157
			SUE THOMPSON	
9/02/61	#5	16	Sad Movies (Make Me Cry)	Hickory 1153
12/16/61	#4	15	Norman	Hickory 1159
3/17/62	#37	9	Two Of A Kind	Hickory 1166
6/09/62	#31	13	Have A Good Time	Hickory 1174
9/29/62	#22	11	James (Hold The Ladder Steady)	Hickory 1183
1/19/63	#77	5	Willie Can	Hickory 1196
11/26/65	#18	14	Paper Tiger	Hickory 1284
			THOMPSON TWINS	
1/22/83	#31	15	Lies	Arista 1024
4/30/83	#48	10	Love On Your Side	Arista 1056
2/11/84	#3	23	Hold Me Now	Arista 9164
5/26/84	#10	18	Doctor! Doctor!	Arista 9209
8/25/84	#43	10	You Take Me Up	Arista 9244
11/10/84	#71	6	The Gap	Arista 9290
9/21/85	#9	20	Lay Your Hands On Me	Arista 9396
1/18/86	#9	17	King For A Day	Arista 9450
7/26/86	#47	12	Nothing In Common	Arista 9511
3/28/87	#28	14	Get That Love	Arista 9577
9/23/89	#24	17	Sugar Daddy	Warner Brothers 22819
			ALI THOMSON	
6/14/80	#15	18	Take A Little Rhythm	A&M 2243
9/06/80	#39	14	Live Every Minute	A&M 2260
			GEORGE THOROGOOD & THE DESTROYERS	
3/31/79	#71	5	Who Do You Love	Rounder 4519
6/22/85	#61	8	Willie And The Hand Jive	EMI America 8270
			BILLY THORPE	
7/21/79	#50	11	Children Of The Sun	Capricorn 0321
			THREE DEGREES	
2/27/65	#69	6	Gee Baby (I'm Sorry)	Swan 4197
1/08/66	#97	2	Look In My Eyes	Swan 4235
6/13/70	#24	12	Maybe	Roulette 7079
9/12/70	#43	7	I Do Take You	Roulette 7088
1/16/71	#57	5	You're The One	Roulette 7091
7/15/72	#96	2	I Wanna Be Your Baby	Roulette 7125
3/02/74	#1	16	TSOP (The Sound Of Philadelphia)*	Philadelphia Int. 3540
6/29/74	#48	6	Love Is The Message*	Philadelphia Int. 3547
9/28/74	#1	18	When Will I See You Again	Philadelphia Int. 3550
			*released as by MFSB featuring THE THREE DEGREES	
			THREE DOG NIGHT	
11/23/68	#80	8	Nobody	Dunhill 4168
2/15/69	#22	10	Try A Little Tenderness	Dunhill 4177
4/26/69	#2	18	One	Dunhill 4191
8/02/69	#3	14	Easy To Be Hard	Dunhill 4203
10/18/69	#8	15	Eli's Coming	Dunhill 4215
2/21/70	#12	9	Celebrate	Dunhill 4229
5/23/70	#1	14	Mama Told Me (Not To Come)	Dunhill 4239
8/29/70	#9	12	Out In The Country	Dunhill 4250

Debut Date	Peak Pos	Wks Chr	ARTIST/Song Title	Label & Number
			THREE DOG NIGHT—*continued*	
11/14/70	#13	12	One Man Band	Dunhill 4262
3/06/71	#1	18	Joy To The World	Dunhill 4272
7/03/71	#8	13	Liar	Dunhill 4282
11/06/71	#4	13	An Old Fashioned Love Song	Dunhill 4294
12/25/71	#5	11	Never Been To Spain	Dunhill 4299
3/25/72	#10	9	The Family Of Man	Dunhill 4306
7/29/72	#1	14	Black & White	Dunhill 4317
11/11/72	#18	11	Pieces Of April	Dunhill 4331
5/19/73	#1	15	Shambala	Dunhill 4352
11/03/73	#12	9	Let Me Serenade You	Dunhill 4370
3/16/74	#1	13	The Show Must Go On	Dunhill 4382
7/06/74	#18	10	Sure As I'm Sittin' Here	Dunhill 15001
9/21/74	#26	13	Play Something Sweet (Brickyard Blues)	Dunhill 15013
7/05/75	#29	10	Til The World Ends	ABC 12114
			3 FRIENDS	
7/22/61	#79	4	Dedicated (To The Songs I Love)	Imperial 5763
			THREE GRACES	
8/29/59	#100	2	Billy Boy's Tune	Golden Crest 528
			3 MAN ISLAND	
4/02/88	#90	4	Jack The Lad	Chrysalis 43231
			THUNDER	
6/08/91	#67	10	Dirty Love	Geffen 19026
			JOHNNY THUNDER	
12/22/62	#9	12	Loop De Loop	Diamond 129
12/04/65	#70	5	Everybody Do The Sloopy	Diamond 192
3/12/66	#90	2	My Prayer	Diamond 196
3/18/67	#96	2	Make Love To Me*	Diamond 218
			*released as by JOHNNY THUNDER & RUBY WINTERS	
			THUNDERCLAP NEWMAN	
8/16/69	#45	10	Something In The Air	Track 2656
			BILLY THUNDERKLOUD & THE CHIEFTONES	
7/12/75	#97	2	What Time Of Day	20th Century 2181
			WUF TICKET	
2/19/83	#94	4	Ya Mama	Prelude 644
			TIDAL WAVES	
5/28/66	#76	6	Farmer John	HBR 482
			TIERRA	
11/08/80	#23	22	Together	Boardwalk 5702
4/04/81	#74	5	Memories	Boardwalk 70073
10/24/81	#64	9	La La Means I Love You	Boardwalk 129
			TIFFANY	
8/29/87	#1	26	I Think We're Alone Now	MCA 53167
11/28/87	#1	23	Could've Been	MCA 53231
2/27/88	#13	14	I Saw Him Standing There	MCA 53285
6/11/88	#55	10	Feelings Of Forever	MCA 53325
11/05/88	#8	23	All This Time	MCA 53371
2/25/89	#45	10	Radio Romance	MCA 53623
			BERTHA TILLMAN	
5/05/62	#67	8	Oh My Angel	Brent 7029
			JOHNNY TILLOTSON	
8/29/59	#49	7	True True Happiness	Cadence 1365
1/16/60	#31	14	Why Do I Love You So	Cadence 1372
4/09/60	#61	8	Earth Angel/	Cadence 1377
4/09/60	#73	7	Pledging My Love	Cadence 1377
10/18/60	#2	16	Poetry In Motion	Cadence 1384
8/19/61	#12	11	Without You	Cadence 1404
11/25/61	#46	15	Dreamy Eyes	Cadence 1409
5/05/62	#5	17	It Keeps Right On A-Hurtin'	Cadence 1418
8/11/62	#14	9	Send Me The Pillow You Dream On	Cadence 1424
10/27/62	#29	10	I Can't Help It (If I'm Still In Love With You)/	Cadence 1432
12/08/62	#94	1	I'm So Lonesome I Could Cry	Cadence 1432
3/02/63	#23	10	Out Of My Mind	Cadence 1434
8/10/63	#18	10	You Can Never Stop Me Loving You	Cadence 1437
10/26/63	#62	6	Funny How Time Slips Away	Cadence 1441

Debut Date	Peak Pos	Wks Chr	ARTIST/Song Title	Label & Number
11/09/63	#7	14	Talk Back Trembling Lips	MGM 13181
2/15/64	#38	7	Worried Guy	MGM 13193
5/02/64	#44	8	I Rise, I Fall	MGM 13232
7/18/64	#45	10	Worry	MGM 13255
10/31/64	#29	12	She Understands Me	MGM 13284
2/13/65	#53	6	Angel	MGM 13316
5/15/65	#67	7	Then I'll Count Again	MGM 13344
8/21/65	#32	9	Heartaches By The Number	MGM 13376
11/20/65	#54	5	Our World	MGM 13408
2/25/67	#91	3	Tommy Jones	MGM 13684
6/21/69	#98	2	Tears On My Pillow	Amos 117
			'TIL TUESDAY	
4/13/85	#8	22	Voices Carry	Epic 04795
8/24/85	#62	7	Looking Over My Shoulder	Epic 04935
11/30/85	#88	3	Love In A Vacuum	Epic 05673
9/20/86	#28	17	What About Love	Epic 06289
1/17/87	#74	10	Coming Up Close	Epic 06571
			TIMBUK 3	
10/25/86	#21	18	The Future's So Bright I Gotta Wear Shades	I.R.S. 52940
			TIME	
11/10/84	#21	20	Jungle Love	Warner Brothers 29181
2/23/85	#37	13	The Bird	Warner Brothers 29094
6/30/90	#5	17	Jerk Out	Paisley Park 19750
			TIMELORDS	
12/24/88	#78	6	Doctorin' The Tardis	TVT 4025
			TIMES TWO	
3/12/88	#24	19	Strange But True	Reprise 27998
			TIMEX SOCIAL CLUB	
6/14/86	#8	20	Rumors	Jay 001
			TIMMY T.	
12/29/90	#1	26	One More Try	Quality 15114
6/08/91	#86	3	Over And Over	Quality 15111
9/14/91	#85	4	Too Young To Love You	Quality 15116
			TIN TIN	
4/03/71	#16	11	Toast And Marmalade For Tea	Atco 6794
9/04/71	#67	5	Is That The Way	Atco 6821
			BABS TINO	
8/18/62	#97	4	Forgive Me	Kapp 472
			TINY TIM	
5/25/68	#19	8	Tip-Toe Thru' The Tulips With Me	Reprise 0679
9/07/68	#98	1	Bring Back Those Rockabye Baby Days	Reprise 0760
2/01/69	#76	4	Great Balls Of Fire	Reprise 0802
			TITIYO	
6/08/91	#63	12	My Body Says Yes	Arista 2224
			CAL TJADER	
5/15/65	#87	5	Soul Sauce (Guacha Guaro)	Verve 10345
			TKA	
7/19/86	#85	3	One Way Love	Tommy Boy 866
8/18/90	#70	8	I Won't Give Up On You	Tommy Boy 19730
12/08/90	#69	7	Crash (Have Some Fun)*	Tommy Boy 19527
			*released as by TKA with MICHELLE VISAGE	
			TLC	
4/18/92	#11	16	Ain't 2 Proud To Beg	Laface 4008
6/13/92	#2	33	Baby-Baby-Baby	Laface 4028
9/12/92	#7	33	What About Your Friends	Laface 4025
2/13/93	#29	13	Hat 2 Da Back	Laface 4043
7/10/93	#33	16	Get It Up	Laface 77059
			T.M.G.	
3/03/79	#94	3	Lazy Eyes	Atco 7096
			TOAD THE WET SPROCKET	
6/13/92	#10	27	All I Want	Columbia 74355
11/21/92	#14	24	Walk On The Ocean	Columbia 74706

351

Debut Date	Peak Pos	Wks Chr	**ARTIST**/Song Title	Label & Number
			TOBY BEAU	
5/27/68	#10	19	My Angel Baby	RCA 11250
8/04/79	#62	10	Then You Can Tell Me Goodbye	RCA 11670
			ART and DOTTY TODD	
4/12/58	#7	15	Chanson d'Amour (Song Of Love)	Era 1064
			DICK TODD	
3/25/50	#4	10	Daddy's Little Girl	Rainbow 80080
			NICK TODD	
9/14/57	#28	11	Plaything	Dot 15643
			TOKENS	
3/18/61	#15	13	Tonight I Fell In Love	Warwick 615
11/18/61	#1	15	The Lion Sleeps Tonight	RCA 7954
2/10/62	#53	6	B'wa Nina (Pretty Girl)	RCA 7991
7/07/62	#91	3	La Bomba	RCA 8052
8/10/63	#67	6	Hear The Bells	RCA 8210
5/03/64	#92	3	Swing	B.T. Puppy 500
8/15/64	#44	8	He's In Town	B.T. Puppy 502
3/12/66	#40	8	I Hear Trumpets Blow	B.T. Puppy 518
4/15/67	#25	10	Portrait Of My Love	Warner Brothers 5900
7/29/67	#91	2	It's A Happening World	Warner Brothers 7056
3/09/68	#97	1	Till	Warner Brothers 7169
12/06/69	#59	9	She Let's Her Hair Down	Buddah 151
3/07/70	#71	4	Don't Worry Baby	Buddah 159
			ISRAEL TOLBERT	
11/14/70	#58	6	Big Leg Woman	Warren 106
			TOM and JERRIO	
4/17/65	#43	10	Boo-Ga-Loo	ABC-Paramount 10638
			TOM & JERRY (see SIMON & GARFUNKEL)	
			TOMMY TUTONE	
5/17/80	#53	8	Angel Say No	Columbia 11278
1/23/82	#5	27	867-5309/Jenny	Columbia 02646
			GARY TOMS EMPIRE	
6/28/75	#35	14	7-6-5-4-3-2-1 (Blow Your Whistle)	P.I.P. 6504
12/06/75	#93	3	Drive My Car	P.I.P. 6509
			TOM TOM CLUB	
1/30/82	#38	16	Genius Of Love	Sire 49882
			TONE LOC	
12/03/88	#3	20	Wild Thing	Delicious Vinyl 102
3/04/89	#2	20	Funky Cold Medina	Delicious Vinyl 104
			OSCAR TONEY JR.	
5/27/67	#28	10	For Your Precious Love	Bell 672
8/12/67	#80	4	Turn On Your Love Light	Bell 681
10/21/67	#86	2	You Can Lead Your Woman To The Altar	Bell 688
1/20/68	#96	3	Without Love (There Is Nothing)	Bell 699
			TONY and JOE	
7/12/58	#46	6	The Freeze	Era 1075
			TONY! TONI! TONE!	
5/28/88	#48	12	Little Walter	Wing 887385
6/09/90	#47	10	The Blues	Wing 873994
9/08/90	#8	24	Feels Good	Wing 877436
12/29/90	#45	14	It Never Rains (In Southern California)	Wing 879068
6/19/93	#6	31	If I Had No Loot	Wing 859056
10/02/93	#6	25	Anniversary	Wing 859566
			TOO SHORT	
11/24/90	#44	14	The Ghetto	Jive 1414
10/30/93	#78	7	I'm A Player	Jive 45152
			MEL TORME	
11/17/62	#49	9	Comin' Home Baby	Atlantic 2165
			TORNADOES (American group)	
10/27/62	#71	6	Bustin' Surfboards	Aertaun 100
			TORNADOES (British group)	
10/27/62	#1	18	Telstar	London 9561

Debut Date	Peak Pos	Wks Chr	**ARTIST**/Song Title	Label & Number
2/09/63	#72	6	Ridin' The Wind	London 9581
3/09/63	#93	1	Globetrottin'	London 9579
			MITCHELL TOROK	
4/06/57	#14	11	Pledge Of Love	Decca 30230
8/01/59	#30	12	Caribbean	Guyden 2018
10/24/59	#77	5	Mexican Joe	Guyden 2028
5/07/60	#59	11	Pink Chiffon	Guyden 2034
			TORONTO	
8/07/82	#72	6	Your Daddy Don't Know	Network 69986
			GEORGE TORRENCE & THE NATURALS	
3/02/68	#99	1	(Mama Come Quick And Bring Your) Lickin' Stick	Shout 224
			PETER TOSH	
6/25/83	#86	7	Johnny B. Goode	EMI America 8159
			TOTAL COELO	
3/26/83	#65	10	I Eat Cannibals	Chrysalis 42669
			TOTO	
10/07/78	#5	24	Hold The Line	Columbia 10830
2/10/79	#46	8	I'll Supply The Love	Columbia 10898
4/28/79	#44	10	Georgy Porgy	Columbia 10944
12/22/79	#17	18	99	Columbia 11173
4/17/82	#2	24	Rosanna	Columbia 02811
8/07/82	#19	13	Make Believe	Columbia 03143
10/30/82	#3	26	Africa	Columbia 03335
3/12/83	#14	16	I Won't Hold You Back	Columbia 03597
7/23/83	#87	4	Waiting For Your Love	Columbia 03981
10/27/84	#26	15	Stranger In Town	Columbia 04672
2/02/85	#64	7	Holyanna	Columbia 04752
8/30/86	#12	23	I'll Be Over You	Columbia 06280
12/27/86	#38	12	Without Your Love	Columbia 06570
2/20/88	#28	16	Pamela	Columbia 07715
			TOUCH	
7/26/80	#77	7	(Call Me) When The Spirit Moves You	Atco 7222
1/31/81	#86	7	Don't You Know What Love Is	Atco 7311
			TOWER OF POWER	
7/08/72	#22	13	You're Still A Young Man	Warner Brothers 7612
10/21/72	#67	4	Down To The Nightclub	Warner Brothers 7635
5/19/73	#19	14	So Very Hard To Go	Warner Brothers 7687
9/15/73	#62	5	This Time It's For Real	Warner Brothers 7733
5/11/74	#93	5	Time Will Tell	Warner Brothers 7796
7/27/74	#59	9	Don't Change Horses (In The Middle Of A Stream)	Warner Brothers 7828
			CAROL LYNN TOWNES	
7/28/84	#78	6	99 1/2	Polydor 881008
			LIDELL TOWNSELL & M.T.F.	
8/22/92	#94	1	Get With U	Mercury 864080
			ED TOWNSEND	
4/05/58	#14	16	For Your Love	Capitol 3926
9/27/58	#79	5	When I Grow Too Old To Dream	Capitol 4048
			PETE TOWNSHEND	
6/14/80	#11	18	Let My Love Open The Door	Atco 7217
10/11/80	#89	5	A Little Is Enough	Atco 7312
11/15/80	#99	1	Rough Boys	Atco 7318
11/09/85	#31	17	Face The Face	Atco 99590
			TOY DOLLS	
1/05/63	#80	3	Little Tin Soldier	Era 3093
			TOYS	
9/11/65	#1	14	A Lover's Concerto	DynoVoice 209
12/11/65	#22	10	Attack	DynoVoice 214
9/10/66	#92	2	Baby Toys	DynoVoice 222
7/06/68	#93	2	Sealed With A Kiss	Musicor 1319
			T'PAU	
5/02/87	#4	25	Heart And Soul	Virgin 99466
6/15/91	#82	6	Only A Heartbeat	Charisma 98787
			TRADEWINDS (New Jersey group)	
7/11/59	#64	8	Furry Murray	RCA 7553

353

Debut Date	Peak Pos	Wks Chr	ARTIST/Song Title	Label & Number
			TRADEWINDS (New York City group)	
2/13/65	#38	8	New York's A Lonely Town	Red Bird 020
9/10/66	#56	9	Mind Excursion	Kama Sutra 212
			TRAFFIC	
8/12/67	#70	5	Paper Sun*	United Artists 50195
9/05/70	#73	5	Empty Pages	United Artists 50692
10/23/71	#56	6	Gimme Some Lovin' (Part 1)	United Artists 50841
			*released as by TRAFFIC featuring STEVIE WINWOOD	
			TRAITS	
11/19/66	#91	3	Harlem Shuffle	Scepter 12169
			TRAMMPS	
6/17/72	#55	14	Zing Went The Strings Of My Heart	Buddah 306
1/10/76	#44	11	Hold Back The Night	Buddah 507
3/27/76	#44	18	That's Where The Happy People Go	Atlantic 3306
4/09/77	#70	6	Disco Inferno	Atlantic 3389
2/11/78	#8	21	Disco Inferno	Atlantic 3389
			TRANSVISION VAMP	
10/01/88	#82	4	Tell That Girl To Shut Up	Uni 50001
			TRANS-X	
5/17/86	#77	8	Living On Video	Atco 99534
			TRASHMEN	
12/07/63	#4	13	Surfin' Bird	Garrett 4002
2/15/64	#31	13	Bird Dance Beat	Garrett 4003
			TRAVELING WILBURYS	
10/22/88	#39	15	Handle With Care	Wilbury 27732
2/04/89	#71	5	End Of The Line	Wilbury 27637
			MARY TRAVERS	
6/26/71	#70	6	Follow Me	Warner Brothers 7481
			PAT TRAVERS BAND	
9/01/79	#65	7	Boom Boom (Out Go The Lights)	Polydor 2003
5/10/80	#56	8	Is This Love	Polydor 2080
			McKINLEY TRAVIS	
7/25/70	#97	2	Baby, Is There Something On Your Mind	Pride 2
			TRAVIS & BOB	
3/21/59	#11	13	Tell Him No	Sandy 1017
7/04/59	#95	2	Little Bitty Johnny	Sandy 1019
			JOEY TRAVOLTA	
6/03/78	#59	8	I Don't Wanna Go	Millennium 615
			JOHN TRAVOLTA	
5/08/76	#5	22	Let Her In	Midland Int'l. 10623
10/09/76	#62	9	Whenever I'm Away From You	Midland Int'l. 10780
2/19/77	#28	11	All Strung Out On You	Midland Int'l. 10907
4/01/78	#3	25	You're The One That I Want*	RSO 891
8/05/78	#3	15	Summer Nights*	RSO 906
9/30/78	#45	9	Greased Lightnin'	RSO 909
			*released as by JOHN TRAVOLTA and OLIVIA NEWTON-JOHN	
			TREE SWINGERS	
9/03/60	#59	6	Kookie Little Paradise	Guyden 2036
			TREMELOES	
8/15/64	#64	7	Somcone, Someone*	Monument 846
4/08/67	#11	11	Here Comes My Baby	Epic 10139
6/24/67	#9	14	Silence Is Golden	Epic 10184
9/30/67	#44	7	Even The Bad Times Are Good	Epic 10233
2/24/68	#40	8	Suddenly You Love Me	Epic 10293
			*released as by BRIAN POOLE and THE TREMELOES	
			RALPH TRESVANT	
11/10/90	#3	25	Sensitivity	MCA 53932
3/02/91	#36	14	Stone Cold Gentleman	MCA 54043
7/25/92	#49	10	Money Can't Buy You Love	Perspective 0011
			T. REX	
1/09/71	#60	7	Ride A White Swan	Blue Thumb 7121
5/01/71	#54	7	Hot Love	Reprise 1006

Debut Date	Peak Pos	Wks Chr	ARTIST/Song Title	Label & Number
12/18/71	#12	17	Bang A Gong (Get It On)	Reprise 1032
4/15/72	#64	5	Telegram Sam	Reprise 1078
			TRIBE CALLED QUEST	
11/27/93	#54	17	Award Tour	Jive 42187
			TRIPLETS	
3/16/91	#9	20	You Don't Have To Go Home Tonight	Mercury 878864
6/29/91	#76	5	Sunrise	Mercury 868414
			TRIUMPH	
6/16/79	#42	15	Hold On	RCA 11569
11/10/79	#77	6	Lay It On The Line	RCA 11690
5/24/80	#99	2	I Can Survive	RCA 11945
10/03/81	#46	15	Magic Power	RCA 12298
8/30/86	#38	15	Somebody's Out There	MCA 52898
			TRIXTER	
12/15/90	#67	11	Give It To Me Good	Mechanic/MCA 53863
3/23/91	#74	8	One In A Million	Mechanic/MCA 54044
6/22/91	#77	8	Surrender	Mechanic/MCA 54105
			KATHY TROCCOLI	
2/22/92	#6	24	Everything Changes	Reunion 19118
7/18/92	#65	8	You've Got A Way	Reunion 19126
			TROGGS	
6/18/66	#1	13	Wild Thing	Fontana 1548
8/06/66	#41	9	With A Girl Like You	Fontana 1552
10/15/66	#38	5	I Can't Control Myself	Fontana 1557
2/17/68	#12	17	Love Is All Around	Fontana 1607
7/20/68	#93	3	You Can Cry If You Want To	Fontana 1622
			TROIANO	
6/23/79	#93	3	We All Need Love	Capitol 4709
			TROOP	
6/27/92	#57	6	Whatever It Takes (To Make You Stay)	Atlantic 87475
10/03/92	#58	11	Sweet November	Atlantic 87445
			TROOPER	
8/12/78	#71	7	Raise A Little Hell	MCA 40924
			ROBIN TROWER	
12/18/76	#81	5	Caledonia	Chrysalis 2122
			DORIS TROY	
6/15/63	#9	14	Just One Look	Atlantic 2188
			ERIC TROYER	
7/19/80	#97	2	Mirage	Chrysalis 2445
			TRUCE	
8/15/92	#90	2	Mother Tone	Voodoo Music 127077
			ANDREA TRUE CONNECTION	
3/20/76	#3	26	More, More, More (Part 1)	Buddah 515
9/11/76	#87	3	Party Line	Buddah 538
2/26/77	#86	5	N.Y., You Got Me Dancing	Buddah 564
2/04/78	#99	2	What's Your Name, What's Your Number	Buddah 582
			TRUMPETEERS	
4/25/59	#59	10	String Of Trumpets	Splash 800
			TRUTH	
5/09/87	#59	10	Weapons Of Love	I.R.S. 53084
			T.S.U. TORNADOES	
1/25/69	#80	2	Getting The Corners	Atlantic 2579
			TUBES	
6/26/76	#68	5	Don't Touch Me There	A&M 1826
6/20/81	#35	13	Don't Want To Wait Anymore	Capitol 5007
4/09/83	#8	21	She's A Beauty	Capitol 5217
7/23/83	#57	8	Tip Of My Tongue	Capitol 5258
10/01/83	#77	5	The Monkey Time	Capitol 5254
			LOUISE TUCKER	
6/18/83	#48	13	Midnight Blue	Arista 9022

Debut Date	Peak Pos	Wks Chr	**ARTIST**/Song Title	Label & Number
			TANYA TUCKER	
6/16/73	#94	2	What's Your Mama's Name	Columbia 45799
9/15/73	#94	2	Blood Red And Goin' Down	Columbia 45892
3/09/74	#54	8	Would You Lay With Me	Columbia 45991
8/10/74	#91	4	The Man That Turned My Mama On	Columbia 46047
5/03/75	#35	9	Lizzie And The Rainman	MCA 40402
1/13/79	#90	4	Not Fade Away	MCA 40976
			TOMMY TUCKER	
2/08/64	#10	13	Hi-Heel Sneakers	Checker 1067
			TUFANO & GIAMMARESE	
4/21/73	#70	7	Music Is Everywhere	Ode 66033
			TUNE ROCKERS	
8/30/58	#40	9	The Green Mosquito	United Artists 139
			TUNE WEAVERS	
9/07/57	#7	16	Happy, Happy Birthday Baby	Checker 872
			CILE TURNER	
12/12/59	#84	5	The Golden Rule	Colonial 7004
			IKE & TINA TURNER	
8/27/60	#19	16	A Fool In Love	Sue 730
12/10/60	#49	7	I Idolize You	Sue 735
3/11/61	#83	4	I'm Jealous	Sue 740
7/29/61	#21	17	It's Gonna Work Out Fine	Sue 749
11/25/61	#23	13	Poor Fool	Sue 753
3/31/62	#55	6	Tra La La La La	Sue 757
5/03/69	#91	2	I've Been Loving You Too Long	Blue Thumb 101
1/10/70	#74	5	Bold Soul Sister	Blue Thumb 104
2/21/70	#52	6	Come Together*	Minit 32087
6/06/70	#42	15	I Want To Take You Higher*	Liberty 56177
11/28/70	#91	4	Workin' Together	Liberty 56207
1/30/71	#5	13	Proud Mary	Liberty 56216
5/15/71	#37	7	Ooh Poo Pah Doo	United Artists 50782
11/06/71	#80	5	I'm Yours	United Artists 50837
2/19/72	#70	4	Up In Heah	United Artists 50881
8/25/73	#26	16	Nutbush City Limits	United Artists 298
11/09/74	#67	10	Sexy Ida (Part 1)	United Artists 528
6/14/75	#70	4	Baby Get It On	United Artists 598
			***released as by IKE & TINA TURNER & THE IKETTES**	
			JESSE LEE TURNER	
1/03/59	#18	11	The Little Space Girl	Carlton 496
			JOE TURNER	
1/30/60	#86	2	Honey Hush	Atlantic 2044
			SAMMY TURNER	
6/27/59	#4	16	Lavendar-Blue	Big Top 3016
10/24/59	#17	14	Always	Big Top 3029
2/20/60	#34	10	Paradise	Big Top 3032
			SPYDER TURNER	
12/10/66	#11	12	Stand By Me	MGM 13617
4/01/67	#100	1	I Can't Make It Anymore	MGM 13692
			TINA TURNER	
1/21/84	#24	19	Let's Stay Together	Capitol 5322
5/26/84	#1	27	What's Love Got To Do With It	Capitol 5354
9/15/84	#7	22	Better Be Good To Me	Capitol 5387
1/19/85	#8	19	Private Dancer	Capitol 5433
4/20/85	#38	11	Show Some Respect	Capitol 5461
7/06/85	#3	21	We Don't Need Another Hero	Capitol 5491
10/05/85	#16	17	One Of The Living	Capitol 5518
11/23/85	#14	17	It's Only Love*	A&M 2791
8/30/86	#1	21	Typical Male	Capitol 5615
11/22/86	#29	12	Two People	Capitol 5644
2/07/87	#21	15	What You Get Is What You See	Capitol 5668
5/09/87	#78	5	Break Every Rule	Capitol 44003
9/02/89	#12	21	The Best	Capitol 44442
12/02/89	#40	11	Steamy Windows	Capitol 44473
10/26/91	#77	8	Love Thing	Capitol 44778
5/29/93	#9	29	I Don't Wanna Fight	Virgin 12652

Debut Date	Peak Pos	Wks Chr	ARTIST/Song Title	Label & Number
10/30/93	#83	4	Why Must We Wait Until Tonight	Virgin 12683
			*released as by BRYAN ADAMS/TINA TURNER	
			TITUS TURNER	
11/21/59	#77	7	We Told You Not To Marry	Glover 201
1/21/61	#65	6	Sound-Off	Jamie 1174
			TURTLES	
7/31/65	#8	13	It Ain't Me Babe	White Whale 222
10/30/65	#26	8	Let Me Be	White Whale 224
1/29/66	#17	12	You Baby	White Whale 227
6/18/66	#95	3	Grim Reaper Of Love	White Whale 231
11/05/66	#97	3	Can I Get To Know You Better	White Whale 238
2/11/67	#1	16	Happy Together	White Whale 244
5/20/67	#2	10	She'd Rather Be With Me	White Whale 249
8/12/67	#12	11	You Know What I Mean	White Whale 254
11/04/67	#15	12	She's My Girl	White Whale 260
3/02/68	#32	7	Sound Asleep	White Whale 264
6/15/68	#40	5	The Story Of Rock And Roll	White Whale 273
9/21/68	#5	11	Elenore	White Whale 276
12/28/68	#4	13	You Showed Me	White Whale 292
6/07/69	#52	6	You Don't Have To Walk In The Rain	White Whale 308
9/27/69	#61	4	Love In The City	White Whale 326
11/22/69	#67	6	Lady-O	White Whale 334
			TUXEDO JUNCTION	
5/06/78	#62	12	Chattanooga Choo Choo	Butterfly 1205
			TWENNYNINE	
1/26/80	#70	4	Peanut Butter*	Elektra 46552
			*released as by TWENNYNINE featuring LENNY WHITE	
			TWICE AS MUCH	
6/25/66	#98	3	Sittin' On A Fence	MGM 13530
			TWILIGHT 22	
2/04/84	#97	2	Electric Kingdom	Vanguard 35241
			DWIGHT TWILLEY BAND	
5/17/75	#23	14	I'm On Fire	Shelter 40380
2/18/84	#16	17	Girls	EMI America 8196
5/19/84	#77	5	Little Bit Of Love	EMI America 8206
			TWINS	
1/08/60	#89	2	Heart Of Gold	Lancer 106
			TWISTED SISTER	
7/28/84	#18	16	We're Not Gonna Take It	Atlantic 89641
10/20/84	#77	6	I Wanna Rock	Atlantic 89617
11/30/85	#51	12	Leader Of The Pack	Atlantic 89478
			CONWAY TWITTY	
5/04/57	#57	1	I Need Your Lovin'	Mercury 71086
9/13/58	#1	21	It's Only Make Believe	MGM 12677
1/31/59	#30	10	The Story Of My Love	MGM 12748
5/02/59	#98	1	When I'm With You/	MGM 12785
5/09/59	#80	4	Hey Little Lucy	MGM 12785
8/01/59	#30	9	Mona Lisa	MGM 12804
9/26/59	#7	18	Danny Boy	MGM 12826
1/02/60	#8	14	Lonely Blue Boy	MGM 12857
4/02/60	#19	11	What Am I Living For	MGM 12886
6/25/60	#33	10	Is A Blue Bird Blue	MGM 12911
10/08/60	#94	1	What A Dream	MGM 12918
10/29/60	#48	7	Whole Lot Of Shakin' Going On	MGM 12962
12/31/60	#31	10	C'est Si Bon (It's So Good)	MGM 12969
4/15/61	#72	5	The Next Kiss (Is The Last Goodbye)	MGM 12998
6/27/70	#82	7	Hello Darlin'	Decca 32661
11/21/70	#90	2	Fifteen Years Ago	Decca 32742
2/06/71	#90	6	After The Fire Is Gone*	Decca 32776
8/18/73	#18	12	You've Never Been This Far Before	MCA 40094
8/14/74	#81	5	As Soon As I Hang Up The Phone	MCA 40251
2/15/75	#48	10	Linda On My Mind	MCA 40339
6/28/75	#75	4	Touch The Hand (Of The Man)/	MCA 40407
12/13/75	#51	8	Don't Cry Joni	MCA 40407
			*released as by LORETTA LYNN/CONWAY TWITTY	

Debut Date	Peak Pos	Wks Chr	ARTIST/Song Title	Label & Number
			II D EXTREME	
6/12/93	#45	20	Cry No More	MCA 54650
			2 IN A ROOM	
10/06/90	#17	21	Wiggle It	Charisma 98887
			2 LIVE CREW	
10/07/89	#48	16	Me So Horny	Skyywalker 130
7/28/90	#18	11	Banned In The U.S.A.*	Luke 98915
			released as by LUKE featuring 2 LIVE CREW	
			2 NU	
12/15/90	#50	14	This Is Ponderous	Atlantic 87771
			2 OF CLUBS	
12/24/66	#75	9	Walk Tall	Fraternity 975
			2 PAC	
7/10/93	#9	33	I Get Around	Interscope 98372
11/06/93	#13	24	Keep Ya Head Up	Interscope 98345
			2 UNLIMITED	
8/01/92	#35	11	Twilight Zone	Radikal 15486
9/26/92	#68	7	Get Ready For This	Radikal 15490
			TYCOON	
3/10/79	#21	15	Such A Woman	Arista 0398
			BONNIE TYLER	
3/25/78	#3	26	It's A Heartache	RCA 11249
7/16/83	#1	30	Total Eclipse Of The Heart	Columbia 03906
12/03/83	#53	9	Take Me Back	Columbia 04246
2/25/84	#35	16	Holding Out For A Hero	Columbia 04370
8/25/84	#81	6	Here She Comes	Columbia 04548
7/12/86	#82	4	Loving You's A Dirty Job But Somebody's Gotta Do It . . .	Columbia 06151
			TYMES	
6/01/63	#2	16	So Much In Love	Parkway 871
8/17/63	#10	11	Wonderful! Wonderful!	Parkway 884
12/07/63	#14	11	Somewhere	Parkway 891
3/07/64	#69	5	To Each His Own	Parkway 908
11/07/64	#88	6	Here She Comes	Parkway 924
11/16/68	#58	8	People	Columbia 44630
8/10/74	#16	13	You Little Trustmaker	RCA 10022
1/04/75	#100	1	Ms. Grace	RCA 10128

U

Debut Date	Peak Pos	Wks Chr	ARTIST/Song Title	Label & Number
			UB40	
2/04/84	#36	16	Red Red Wine	A&M 2600
8/03/85	#32	14	I Got You Babe	A&M 2758
8/13/88	#1	19	Red Red Wine	A&M 1244
9/29/90	#4	24	The Way You Do The Things You Do	Virgin 98978
3/30/91	#8	27	Here I Am (Come And Take Me)	Virgin 99141
5/22/93	#1	36	Can't Help Falling In Love	Virgin 12653
10/30/93	#40	21	Higher Ground	Virgin 12687
			UFO	
8/27/77	#94	2	Too Hot To Handle	Chrysalis 2157
			UGLY KID JOE	
3/14/92	#6	28	Everything About You	Stardog 866632
2/20/93	#9	22	Cat's In The Cradle	Stardog 864888
			U-KREW	
2/03/90	#56	8	If U Were Mine	Enigma 75051
6/16/90	#64	7	Let Me Be Your Lover	Enigma 75069
			TRACY ULLMAN	
2/25/84	#10	20	They Don't Know	MCA 52347
6/23/84	#81	5	Break-A-Way	MCA 52385
			ULTRAVOX	
3/26/83	#58	10	Reap The Wild Wind	Chrysalis 42682
			UNCHAINED MYNDS	
4/26/69	#96	5	We Can't Go On This Way	Buddah 111
			UNCLE DOG	
3/17/73	#95	2	River Road	MCA 40005

Debut Date	Peak Pos	Wks Chr	**ARTIST**/Song Title	Label & Number
			UNDERGROUND SUNSHINE	
7/12/69	#19	12	Birthday	Intrepid 75002
			UNDERWORLD	
4/30/88	#79	6	Underneath The Radar	Sire 27968
9/02/89	#66	8	Stand Up	Sire 22852
			UNDISPUTED TRUTH	
6/26/71	#1	18	Smiling Faces Sometimes	Gordy 7108
12/11/71	#71	6	You Make Your Own Heaven And Hell Right Here On Earth	Gordy 7112
3/18/72	#96	1	What Is It	Gordy 7114
6/17/72	#93	1	Papa Was A Rolling Stone	Gordy 7117
5/04/74	#74	5	Help Yourself	Gordy 7134
2/05/77	#56	10	You + Me = Love	Whitfield 8306
			UNIFICS	
9/28/68	#20	9	Court Of Love	Kapp 935
12/14/68	#52	9	Beginning Of My End	Kapp 957
3/29/69	#92	4	It's A Groovy World	Kapp 985
			UNION GAP (see GARY PUCKETT & THE UNION GAP)	
			UNIQUES	
3/06/65	#62	7	Not Too Long Ago	Paula 219
4/30/66	#98	2	All These Things	Paula 238
6/11/66	#82	6	All These Things	Paula 238
10/29/66	#100	1	Run And Hide	Paula 245
			UNIT FOUR PLUS TWO	
4/24/65	#12	11	Concrete And Clay	London 9751
			UNIVERSAL ROBOT BAND	
4/09/77	#87	5	Dance And Shake Your Tambourine	Red Greg 207
			UNKNOWNS	
9/24/66	#87	5	Melody For An Unknown Girl	Parrot 307
			U.N.V.	
6/19/93	#34	19	Something's Goin' On	Maverick 18564
			UPBEATS	
7/19/58	#66	3	Just Like In The Movies	Swan 4010
			PHILIP UPCHURCH COMBO	
6/17/61	#19	11	You Can't Sit Down (Part 2)	Boyd 3398
			URBAN DANCE SQUAD	
12/22/90	#36	17	Deeper Shade Of Soul	Arista 2026
			MIDGE URE	
3/18/89	#90	3	Dear God	Chrysalis 43319
			URGENT	
8/24/85	#81	5	Running Back	Manhattan 50005
			URIAH HEEP	
7/22/72	#32	11	Easy Livin	Mercury 73307
1/20/73	#91	3	Sweet Lorraine	Mercury 73349
10/06/73	#62	8	Stealin'	Warner Brothers 7738
			U.S.A. FOR AFRICA	
3/23/85	#1	19	We Are The World	Columbia 04839
			U.S. 1	
11/22/75	#90	3	Bye Bye Baby	Private Stock 45045
			US3	
12/18/93	#7	28	Cantaloop (Flip Fantasia)	Blue Note 15892
			UTAH SAINTS	
11/28/92	#92	2	Something Good	London 869842
			UTOPIA	
2/16/80	#29	14	Set Me Free	Bearsville 49180
5/31/80	#80	4	The Very Last Time	Bearsville 49247
			U2	
4/02/83	#50	12	New Year's Day	Island 99915
1/21/84	#80	5	I Will Follow	Island 99789
10/27/84	#34	17	Pride (In The Name Of Love)	Island 99704
3/21/87	#1	21	With Or Without You	Island 99469
6/13/87	#1	19	I Still Haven't Found What I'm Looking For	Island 99430

Debut Date	Peak Pos	Wks Chr	ARTIST/Song Title	Label & Number
			U2—continued	
9/12/87	#16	15	Where The Streets Have No Name	Island 99408
12/05/87	#58	11	In God's Country	Island 99385
10/01/88	#2	21	Desire	Island 99250
12/17/88	#14	16	Angel Of Harlem	Island 99254
4/01/89	#74	6	When Love Comes To Town	Island 99225
7/08/89	#64	7	All I Want Is You	Island 99199
11/23/91	#3	27	Mysterious Ways	Island 866189
3/14/92	#3	24	One	Island 866533
7/04/92	#21	20	Even Better Than The Real Thing	Island 866977
11/14/92	#31	17	Who's Gonna Ride Your Wild Horses	Island 864521
12/25/93	#57	13	Stay (Faraway, So Close!)	Island 858076

V

Debut Date	Peak Pos	Wks Chr	ARTIST/Song Title	Label & Number
			VACELS	
7/17/65	#60	6	You're My Baby	Kama Sutra 200
			JERRY VALE	
8/04/56	#13	17	You Don't Know Me	Columbia 40710
11/23/57	#29	9	Pretend You Don't See Her	Columbia 41010
10/18/58	#80	8	Go Chase A Moonbeam	Columbia 41238
12/12/64	#29	12	Have You Looked Into Your Heart	Columbia 43181
2/27/65	#35	7	For Mama	Columbia 43232
5/15/65	#65	5	Tears Keep On Falling	Columbia 43252
8/07/65	#92	2	Where Were You When I Needed You	Columbia 43337
4/15/67	#95	1	Time Alone Will Tell	Columbia 44087
			RITCHIE VALENS	
9/27/58	#51	12	Come On Let's Go	Del-Fi 4106
11/29/58	#2	22	Donna/	Del-Fi 4110
12/20/58	#49	12	La Bamba	Del-Fi 4110
4/04/59	#43	8	That's My Little Susie	Del-Fi 4114
8/01/59	#93	1	Little Girl	Del-Fi 4117
			CATERINA VALENTE	
5/28/55	#8	4	The Breeze And I	Decca 29467
5/30/59	#83	5	La Strada Del' Amore	RCA 7525
			JOHN VALENTI	
8/14/76	#43	16	Anything You Want	Ariola America 7625
			DANNY VALENTINO	
5/07/60	#65	9	Biology	MGM 12881
			MARK VALENTINO	
11/03/62	#30	11	The Push And Kick	Swan 4121
			VALENTINOS	
9/01/62	#63	6	Looking For A Love	Sar 132
6/27/64	#63	7	It's All Over Now	Sar 152
			DANA VALERY	
6/19/76	#95	3	Will You Love Me Tomorrow	Phantom 10566
			JOE VALINO	
10/27/56	#15	16	Garden Of Eden	Vik 0226
			VALJEAN	
5/12/62	#32	11	Theme From Ben Casey	Carlton 573
9/01/62	#100	1	Till There Was You	Carlton 576
			JIM VALLEY	
8/12/67	#99	2	Try, Try, Try	Dunhill 4096
			FRANKIE VALLI	
1/15/66	#40	7	(You're Gonna) Hurt Yourself	Smash 2015
4/30/66	#93	2	You're Ready Now	Smash 2037
11/05/66	#77	6	Proud One	Philips 40407
5/13/67	#1	17	Can't Take My Eyes Off You	Philips 40446
8/26/67	#21	8	I Make A Fool Of Myself	Philips 40484
12/23/67	#17	10	To Give (The Reason I Live)	Philips 40510
6/07/69	#28	8	The Girl I'll Never Know	Philips 40622
11/09/74	#1	24	My Eyes Adored You	Private Stock 45003
5/10/75	#7	17	Swearin' To God	Private Stock 45021
10/18/75	#14	13	Our Day Will Come	Private Stock 45043
4/03/76	#49	8	Fallen Angel	Private Stock 45074
8/07/76	#74	3	We're All Alone	Private Stock 45098

Debut Date	Peak Pos	Wks Chr	**ARTIST**/Song Title	Label & Number
10/16/76	#90	4	Boomerang	Private Stock 45109
5/27/78	#1	23	Grease	RSO 897
			JUNE VALLI	
8/29/53	#1	12	Crying In The Chapel	RCA 5368
7/05/54	#4	9	I Understand Just How You Feel	RCA 5740
4/20/57	#57	1	Strictly Sentimental	RCA 6852
11/29/58	#19	13	The Wedding	Mercury 71382
3/14/59	#94	2	The Answer To A Maiden's Prayer	Mercury 71422
3/26/60	#24	11	Apple Green	Mercury 71588
			BOBBY VAN	
9/06/58	#71	5	You'll Always Be My Sweetheart	ABC-Paramount 9940
			VANDENBERG	
12/25/82	#47	13	Burning Heart	Atco 99947
			LUTHER VANDROSS	
10/03/81	#27	19	Never Too Much	Epic 02409
11/20/82	#91	5	Bad Boy/Having A Party	Epic 03205
10/08/83	#36	15	How Many Times Can We Say Goodbye*	Arista 9073
3/23/85	#35	16	'Til My Baby Comes Home	Epic 04760
8/23/86	#51	9	Give Me The Reason	Epic 06129
11/15/86	#15	21	Stop To Love	Epic 06523
3/21/87	#46	13	There's Nothing Better Than Love	Epic 06978
10/08/88	#46	12	Any Love	Epic 08047
2/04/89	#34	13	She Won't Talk To Me	Epic 08513
1/20/90	#7	23	Here And Now	Epic 73029
4/27/91	#6	22	Power Of Love/Love Power	Epic 73778
8/03/91	#19	29	Don't Want To Be A Fool	Epic 73879
12/28/91	#64	10	The Rush	Epic 74049
6/06/92	#9	22	The Best Things In Life Are Free	Perspective 0010
5/29/93	#33	14	Little Miracles (Happen Every Day)	Epic 74945
9/25/93	#73	5	Heaven Knows	Epic 74996
			*released as by **DIONNE WARWICK** and **LUTHER VANDROSS**	
			LEROY VAN DYKE	
12/08/56	#22	10	The Auctioneer	Dot 15503
10/28/61	#3	18	Walk On By	Mercury 71834
3/03/62	#33	9	If A Woman Answers (Hang Up The Phone)	Mercury 71926
			VAN DYKES	
3/19/66	#97	2	No Man Is An Island	Mala 520
7/09/66	#100	1	I've Got To Go On Without You	Mala 530
			VANGELIS	
12/12/81	#1	31	Chariots Of Fire -- Titles	Polydor 2189
			VAN HALEN	
1/21/78	#44	11	You Really Got Me	Warner Brothers 8515
4/28/79	#22	16	Dance The Night Away	Warner Brothers 8823
9/01/79	#80	5	Beautiful Girls	Warner Brothers 49035
5/24/80	#69	7	And The Cradle Will Rock	Warner Brothers 49501
2/13/82	#10	15	(Oh) Pretty Woman	Warner Brothers 50003
5/22/82	#39	11	Dancing In The Street	Warner Brothers 29986
1/14/84	#1	23	Jump	Warner Brothers 29384
4/14/84	#17	16	I'll Wait	Warner Brothers 29307
6/23/84	#13	17	Panama	Warner Brothers 29250
10/27/84	#64	12	Hot For Teacher	Warner Brothers 29199
3/15/86	#1	19	Why Can't This Be Love	Warner Brothers 28740
5/24/86	#24	12	Dreams	Warner Brothers 28702
8/09/86	#18	16	Love Walks In	Warner Brothers 28626
11/22/86	#83	8	Best Of Both Worlds	Warner Brothers 28505
5/21/88	#47	10	Black And Blue	Warner Brothers 27891
7/02/88	#8	18	When It's Love	Warner Brothers 27827
10/01/88	#14	21	Finish What Ya Started	Warner Brothers 27746
2/04/89	#35	12	Feels So Good	Warner Brothers 27565
10/05/91	#15	24	Top Of The World	Warner Brothers 19151
2/01/92	#27	22	Right Now	Warner Brothers 19059
			VANILLA FUDGE	
7/01/67	#87	4	You Keep Me Hangin' On	Atco 6495
2/03/68	#92	2	Where Is My Mind	Atco 6554
7/20/68	#7	11	You Keep Me Hangin' On	Atco 6590
10/12/68	#46	4	Take Me For A Little While	Atco 6616
12/07/68	#72	3	Season Of The Witch (Part 1)	Atco 6632

361

Debut Date	Peak Pos	Wks Chr	**ARTIST**/Song Title	Label & Number
			VANILLA FUDGE—*continued*	
2/22/69	#74	4	Shotgun	Atco 6655
5/24/69	#81	2	Some Velvet Morning	Atco 6679
			VANILLA ICE	
9/08/90	#1	22	Ice Ice Baby	SBK 07335
12/08/90	#5	22	Play That Funky Music	SBK 07339
3/02/91	#63	9	I Love You	SBK 07346
10/05/91	#67	9	Cool As Ice (Everybody Get Loose)	SBK 07369
			VANITY	
9/08/84	#70	7	Pretty Mess	Motown 1752
4/26/86	#77	4	Under The Influence	Motown 1833
			VANITY FARE	
11/08/69	#10	16	Early In The Morning	Page One 21027
3/21/70	#4	21	Hitchin' A Ride	Page One 21029
8/15/70	#61	6	(I Remember) Summer Morning	Page One 21033
			VANITY KILLS	
5/18/91	#85	4	Give Me Your Heart	Hollywood 64898
			TEDDY VANN	
2/27/60	#59	9	Cindy	Triple-X 101
6/17/61	#95	2	The Lonely Crowd	Columbia 41996
			GINO VANNELLI	
9/07/74	#27	13	People Gotta Move	A&M 1614
9/04/76	#57	11	Love Of My Life	A&M 1861
9/09/78	#2	21	I Just Wanna Stop	A&M 2072
3/03/79	#79	3	Wheels Of Life	A&M 2114
3/21/81	#9	19	Living Inside Myself	Arista 0588
6/27/81	#43	11	Nightwalker	Arista 0613
5/11/85	#46	13	Black Cars	HME 04889
10/05/85	#53	15	Hurts To Be In Love	CBS Associated 05586
5/09/87	#55	12	Wild Horses	CBS Associated 06699
			RANDY VANWARMER	
3/17/79	#5	21	Just When I Needed You Most	Bearsville 0334
7/26/80	#89	4	Whatever You Decide	Bearsville 49258
6/20/81	#54	9	Suzi	Bearsville 49752
			VAPORS	
9/13/80	#31	23	Turning Japanese	United Artists 1364
			MARIANNE VASEL & ERICH STORZ	
4/12/58	#40	7	The Little Train	Mercury 71286
			FRANKIE VAUGHAN	
5/31/58	#42	6	Judy	Epic 9273
			SARAH VAUGHAN	
1/15/55	#7	5	Make Yourself Comfortable	Mercury 70469
3/12/55	#5	11	How Important Can It Be?	Mercury 70534
5/14/55	#5	8	Whatever Lola Wants	Mercury 70595
12/29/56	#15	1	The Banana Boat Song	Mercury 71020
7/06/57	#36	11	Passing Strangers	Mercury 71122
9/21/57	#47	3	Please Mr. Brown	Mercury 71157
6/06/59	#98	1	Separate Ways	Mercury 71433
7/18/59	#6	17	Broken-Hearted Melody/	Mercury 71477
7/18/59	#79	5	Misty	Mercury 71477
10/31/59	#32	11	Smooth Operator	Mercury 71519
1/30/60	#53	9	Eternally/	Mercury 71562
2/06/60	#65	5	You're My Baby	Mercury 71562
5/07/60	#83	3	Our Waltz	Mercury 71610
11/05/60	#100	1	Serenata	Roulette 4285
4/02/66	#73	6	A Lover's Concerto	Mercury 72543
			VAUGHAN BROTHERS	
10/20/90	#50	7	Tick Tock	Epic Assoc. 73576
			BILLY VAUGHN	
1/15/55	#1	19	Melody Of Love	Dot 15247
10/29/55	#5	8	The Shifting Whispering Sands	Dot 15409
8/25/56	#16	10	When The White Lilacs Bloom Again	Dot 15491
3/16/57	#41	4	The Ship That Never Sailed	Dot 15546
11/16/57	#25	1	Raunchy	Dot 15661
12/07/57	#4	21	Sail Along Silvery Moon	Dot 15661

Debut Date	Peak Pos	Wks Chr	ARTIST/Song Title	Label & Number
3/29/58	#30	7	Tumbling Tumbleweeds	Dot 15710
8/09/58	#27	14	La Paloma	Dot 15795
10/18/58	#36	11	Cimarron (Roll On)	Dot 15836
12/27/58	#33	10	Blue Hawaii	Dot 15879
2/21/59	#51	6	Hawaiian War Chant/	Dot 15900
2/21/59	#52	6	Trade Winds	Dot 15900
4/25/59	#74	5	Your Cheatin' Heart/	Dot 15936
5/02/59	#100	1	Lights Out	Dot 15936
7/25/59	#94	1	All Night Long/	Dot 15960
7/25/59	#82	3	Blues Stay Away From Me	Dot 15960
11/14/59	#96	4	(It's No) Sin	Dot 15993
4/30/60	#98	2	Beg Your Pardon	Dot 16064
7/09/60	#13	12	Look For A Star	Dot 16106
10/08/60	#38	10	The Sundowners	Dot 16133
3/11/61	#100	1	Orange Blossom Special	Dot 16174
6/03/61	#60	8	Blue Tomorrow	Dot 16220
9/16/61	#55	7	Berlin Melody/	Dot 16262
9/30/61	#55	9	Come September	Dot 16262
7/14/62	#11	14	A Swingin' Safari	Dot 16374
4/03/65	#79	4	Mexican Pearls	Dot 16706
1/15/66	#61	4	Michelle	Dot 16809

BILLY VAUGHN SINGERS

Debut Date	Peak Pos	Wks Chr	ARTIST/Song Title	Label & Number
2/18/67	#82	2	Sweet Maria	Dot 16985

BOBBY VEE

Debut Date	Peak Pos	Wks Chr	ARTIST/Song Title	Label & Number
6/04/60	#91	3	One Last Kiss	Liberty 55251
8/20/60	#4	18	Devil Or Angel	Liberty 55270
12/10/60	#6	14	Rubber Ball	Liberty 55287
2/04/61	#32	10	Stayin' In/	Liberty 55296
3/04/61	#48	6	More Than I Can Say	Liberty 55296
5/13/61	#43	8	How Many Tears/	Liberty 55325
5/13/61	#97	2	Baby Face	Liberty 55325
8/12/61	#1	15	Take Good Care Of My Baby	Liberty 55354
11/18/61	#4	14	Run To Him/	Liberty 55388
11/25/61	#89	6	Walkin' With My Angel	Liberty 55388
2/24/62	#18	10	Please Don't Ask About Barbara/	Liberty 55419
2/24/62	#90	3	I Can't Say Goodbye	Liberty 55419
5/19/62	#20	11	Sharing You	Liberty 55451
9/01/62	#32	8	Punish Her	Liberty 55479
12/01/62	#4	16	The Night Has A Thousand Eyes	Liberty 55521
3/30/63	#15	10	Charms	Liberty 55530
6/15/63	#36	8	Be True To Yourself/	Liberty 55581
6/29/63	#100	1	A Letter From Betty	Liberty 55581
10/26/63	#53	7	Yesterday And You (Armen's Theme)	Liberty 55636
2/01/64	#90	1	Stranger In Your Arms	Liberty 55654
5/22/64	#54	8	I'll Make You Mine*	Liberty 55670
6/20/64	#81	4	Hickory, Dick And Doc	Liberty 55700
12/05/64	#80	4	Pretend You Don't See Her/	Liberty 55751
12/05/64	#89	6	(There'll Come A Day When) Ev'ry Little Bit Hurts	Liberty 55751
5/08/65	#84	3	Keep On Trying	Liberty 55790
7/09/66	#67	5	Look At Me Girl**	Liberty 55877
7/08/67	#3	18	Come Back When You Grow Up**	Liberty 55964
11/11/67	#27	8	Beautiful People**	Liberty 56009
2/17/68	#38	5	Maybe Just Today**	Liberty 56014
4/13/68	#17	11	My Girl/Hey Girl	Liberty 56033
8/17/68	#65	4	Do What You Gotta Do	Liberty 56057
12/28/68	#92	2	Someone To Love	Liberty 56080
7/26/69	#97	3	Let's Call It A Day Girl	Liberty 56124
11/07/70	#94	1	Sweet Sweetheart	Liberty 56208

*released as by BOBBY VEE with THE ELIGIBLES
**released as by BOBBY VEE and THE STRANGERS

SUZANNE VEGA

Debut Date	Peak Pos	Wks Chr	ARTIST/Song Title	Label & Number
6/06/87	#4	20	Luka	A&M 2937
10/06/90	#4	24	Tom's Diner*	A&M 1529

*released as by D.N.A. featuring SUZANNE VEGA

VELAIRES

Debut Date	Peak Pos	Wks Chr	ARTIST/Song Title	Label & Number
9/02/61	#86	5	Roll Over Beethoven	Jamie 1198

VELS

Debut Date	Peak Pos	Wks Chr	ARTIST/Song Title	Label & Number
2/23/85	#71	6	Look My Way	Mercury 880547

Debut Date	Peak Pos	Wks Chr	ARTIST/Song Title	Label & Number
			VELVELETTES	
10/24/64	#49	8	Needle In A Haystack	V.I.P. 25007
2/06/65	#71	4	He Was Really Sayin' Somethin'	V.I.P. 25013
6/12/65	#95	1	Lonely Lonely Girl	V.I.P. 25017
10/22/66	#71	4	These Things Will Keep Me Loving You	Soul 35025
			JIMMY VELVET	
12/21/63	#75	5	We Belong Together	ABC-Paramount 10488
5/15/65	#89	5	It's Almost Tomorrow	Philips 40285
			VELVETS	
4/01/61	#94	4	That Lucky Old Sun	Monument 435
6/03/61	#18	11	Tonight (Could Be The Night)	Monument 441
10/21/61	#83	3	Laugh	Monument 448
			VENTURES	
7/23/60	#3	18	Walk--Don't Run	Dolton 25
11/12/60	#18	13	Perfidia	Dolton 28
2/04/61	#50	8	Ram-Bunk-Shush	Dolton 32
5/06/61	#81	4	Lullabye Of The Leaves	Dolton 41
8/19/61	#76	6	(Theme From) Silver City	Dolton 44
11/04/61	#90	3	Blue Moon	Dolton 47
8/11/62	#100	1	Lolita Ya Ya	Dolton 60
2/09/63	#94	2	The 2,000 Pound Bee (Part 2)	Dolton 67
7/18/64	#9	12	Walk--Don't Run '64	Dolton 96
10/31/64	#48	7	Slaughter On Tenth Avenue	Dolton 300
2/20/65	#96	2	Diamond Head	Dolton 303
3/05/66	#74	5	Secret Agent Man	Dolton 316
6/04/66	#81	4	Blue Star	Dolton 320
3/15/69	#6	12	Hawaii Five-O	Liberty 56068
6/21/69	#63	6	Theme From "A Summer Place"	Liberty 56115
			VIK VENUS	
6/14/69	#23	10	Moonflight	Buddah 118
			BILLY VERA	
12/02/67	#58	8	Storybook Children*	Atlantic 2445
2/17/68	#49	6	Country Girl - City Man*	Atlantic 2480
6/15/68	#25	9	With Pen In Hand	Atlantic 2526
4/25/81	#42	12	I Can Take Care Of Myself**	Alfa 7002
9/05/81	#77	4	At This Moment**	Alfa 7005
11/15/86	#1	22	At This Moment**	Rhino 74403
			***released as by BILLY VERA & JUDY CLAY**	
			****released as by BILLY & THE BEATERS**	
			LARRY VERNE	
9/03/60	#3	14	Mr. Custer	Era 3024
12/17/60	#74	5	Mr. Livingston	Era 3034
			VESTA	
9/16/89	#58	10	Congratulations	A&M 1407
			VIBRATIONS	
2/04/61	#29	11	The Watusi	Checker 969
3/28/64	#29	11	My Girl Sloopy	Atlantic 2221
10/23/65	#74	5	Misty	Okeh 7230
4/13/68	#88	6	Love In Them There Hills	Okeh 7311
			VICTORIANS	
7/13/63	#84	3	What Makes Little Girls Cry	Liberty 55574
			MARIA VIDAL	
9/15/84	#43	12	Body Rock	EMI America 8233
			VIDELS	
4/16/60	#66	13	Mr. Lonely	JDS 5004
			VIDEOS	
9/13/58	#90	1	Trickle Trickle	Climax 102
			VIGRASS & OSBORNE	
6/10/72	#45	7	Men Of Learning	Uni 55330
			VILLAGE PEOPLE	
6/24/78	#28	17	Macho Man	Casablanca 922
10/21/78	#3	28	Y.M.C.A.	Casablanca 945
3/17/79	#3	17	In The Navy	Casablanca 973
5/26/79	#48	8	Go West	Casablanca 984
11/10/79	#72	6	Ready For The 80's	Casablanca 2220

Debut Date	Peak Pos	Wks Chr	ARTIST/Song Title	Label & Number
			VILLAGE SOUL CHOIR	
2/14/70	#63	8	The Cat Walk	Abbott 2010
			VILLAGE STOMPERS	
9/28/63	#2	15	Washington Square	Epic 9617
4/25/64	#67	5	From Russia With Love	Epic 9674
12/19/64	#96	2	Fiddler On The Roof	Epic 9740
			GENE VINCENT and HIS BLUE CAPS	
8/04/56	#5	10	Be-Bop-A-Lula	Capitol 3450
9/22/56	#50	2	Race With The Devil	Capitol 3530
8/17/57	#12	17	Lotta Lovin'	Capitol 3763
11/23/57	#36	8	Dance To The Bop	Capitol 3839
			BOBBY VINTON	
6/02/62	#1	17	Roses Are Red (My Love)	Epic 9509
8/18/62	#39	8	I Love You The Way You Are	Diamond 121
8/25/62	#18	11	Rain Rain Go Away	Epic 9532
11/24/62	#33	11	Let's Kiss And Make Up/	Epic 9561
11/24/62	#37	11	Trouble Is My Middle Name	Epic 9561
3/16/63	#20	9	Over The Mountain (Across The Sea)	Epic 9577
5/18/63	#3	14	Blue On Blue	Epic 9593
8/17/63	#1	15	Blue Velvet	Epic 9614
11/30/63	#1	14	There! I've Said It Again	Epic 9638
2/22/64	#8	11	My Heart Belongs To Only You	Epic 9662
5/23/64	#11	9	Tell Me Why	Epic 9687
8/08/64	#14	9	Clinging Vine	Epic 9705
10/31/64	#2	16	Mr. Lonely	Epic 9730
3/06/65	#14	8	Long Lonely Nights	Epic 9768
5/08/65	#20	8	L-O-N-E-L-Y	Epic 9791
7/03/65	#69	5	Theme From "Harlow" (Lonely Girl)	Epic 9814
9/11/65	#34	7	What Color (Is A Man)	Epic 9846
11/27/65	#21	10	Satin Pillows/	Epic 9869
12/18/65	#82	3	Careless	Epic 9869
2/12/66	#43	7	Tears	Epic 9894
4/23/66	#32	7	Dum-De-Da	Epic 10014
7/23/66	#76	5	Petticoat White (Summer Sky Blue)	Epic 10048
11/12/66	#8	13	Coming Home Soldier	Epic 10090
3/11/67	#54	5	For He's A Jolly Good Fellow	Epic 10136
5/20/67	#90	3	Red Roses For Mom	Epic 10168
9/23/67	#5	14	Please Love Me Forever	Epic 10228
12/30/67	#14	9	Just As Much As Ever	Epic 10266
3/30/68	#26	8	Take Good Care Of My Baby	Epic 10305
7/13/68	#17	8	Halfway To Paradise	Epic 10350
10/26/68	#4	15	I Love How You Love Me	Epic 10397
3/29/69	#22	8	To Know You Is To Love You	Epic 10461
6/07/69	#24	9	The Days Of Sand And Shovels	Epic 10485
1/31/70	#34	9	My Elusive Dreams	Epic 10576
7/04/70	#58	6	No Arms Can Ever Hold You	Epic 10629
9/26/70	#90	3	Why Don't They Understand	Epic 10651
1/29/72	#18	16	Every Day Of My Life	Epic 10822
6/03/72	#14	15	Sealed With A Kiss	Epic 10861
1/06/73	#71	6	But I Do	Epic 10936
9/21/74	#2	16	My Melody Of Love	ABC 12022
3/01/75	#87	1	Dick And Jane/	ABC 12056
3/08/75	#45	9	Beer Barrel Polka	ABC 12056
5/31/75	#70	7	Wooden Heart	ABC 12100
9/27/75	#78	3	Midnight Show	ABC 12131
1/19/80	#78	4	Make Believe It's Your First Time	Tapestry 002
4/04/81	#96	4	Let Me Love You Goodbye	Tapestry 006
3/13/82	#93	4	She Will Survive (Poland)	Tapestry 008
			VIRTUES	
3/07/59	#5	16	Guitar Boogie Shuffle	Hunt 324
			VISCOUNTS	
12/12/59	#28	17	Harlem Nocturne	Madison 123
7/30/60	#52	6	Night Train	Madison 133
12/17/60	#81	6	Wabash Blues	Madison 140
11/13/65	#59	11	Harlem Nocturne	Amy 940
			VITAMIN Z	
6/22/85	#70	8	Burning Flame	Geffen 29039

Debut Date	Peak Pos	Wks Chr	**ARTIST**/Song Title	Label & Number
			VITO & THE SALUTATIONS	
10/12/63	#51	9	Unchained Melody	Herald 583
			VIXEN	
9/17/88	#33	18	Edge Of A Broken Heart	EMI-Manhattan 50141
1/28/89	#25	17	Cryin'	EMI-Manhattan 50167
8/11/90	#41	13	How Much Love	EMI 50302
11/03/90	#71	5	Love Is A Killer	EMI 50332
			VOGUES	
9/11/65	#7	13	You're The One	Co & Ce 229
12/04/65	#3	12	Five O'Clock World	Co & Ce 232
2/19/66	#20	11	Magic Town	Co & Ce 234
6/11/66	#36	8	The Land Of Milk And Honey	Co & Ce 238
9/24/66	#50	8	Please Mr. Sun	Co & Ce 240
6/22/68	#4	13	Turn Around, Look At Me	Reprise 0686
9/07/68	#6	10	My Special Angel	Reprise 0766
11/16/68	#16	8	Till	Reprise 0788
1/25/69	#33	6	Woman Helping Man/	Reprise 0803
3/01/69	#48	7	No Not Much	Reprise 0803
4/12/69	#30	7	Earth Angel (Will You Be Mine)	Reprise 0820
6/21/69	#42	5	Moments To Remember	Reprise 0831
8/16/69	#84	3	Green Fields	Reprise 0844
			VOICE OF THE BEEHIVE	
10/19/91	#73	14	Monsters And Angels	London 869428
			VOICES	
9/12/92	#68	7	Yeah, Yeah, Yeah	Zoo 14051
			VOICES OF AMERICA	
4/12/86	#78	9	Hands Across America	EMI America 8319
			VOICES THAT CARE	
3/16/91	#24	18	Voices That Care	Giant 19350
			VOLUMES	
4/14/62	#20	15	I Love You	Chex 1002
			VONNAIR SISTERS	
3/03/62	#87	4	Goodbye To Toyland	Vista 390
			VONTASTICS	
9/24/66	#98	2	Day Tripper	St. Lawrence 1014
			ROGER VOUDOURIS	
3/17/79	#22	18	Get Used To It	Warner Brothers 8762
			VOXPOPPERS	
3/15/58	#17	12	Wishing For Your Love	Mercury 71282
			VOYAGE	
2/17/79	#92	4	Souvenirs	Marlin 3330

W

Debut Date	Peak Pos	Wks Chr	**ARTIST**/Song Title	Label & Number
			WACKERS	
11/25/72	#79	4	Day And Night	Elektra 45816
			ADAM WADE	
1/09/60	#45	9	Tell Her For Me	Coed 520
3/12/60	#43	10	Ruby	Coed 526
6/11/60	#54	10	I Can't Help It	Coed 530
12/10/60	#79	6	Gloria's Theme	Coed 541
3/04/61	#10	16	Take Good Care Of Her	Coed 546
5/27/61	#10	11	The Writing On The Wall	Coed 550
7/29/61	#19	9	As If I Didn't Know	Coed 553
9/30/61	#57	7	Tonight I Won't Be There	Coed 556
11/25/61	#73	5	Overview Of Paradise	Coed 560
1/27/62	#91	2	It's So Good To Have You Back	Coed 565
12/29/62	#95	2	There'll Be No Teardrops Tonight	Epic 9557
			WADSWORTH MANSION	
12/05/70	#5	16	Sweet Mary	Sussex 209
4/24/71	#99	2	Michigan Harry Slaughter	Sussex 215
			JACK WAGNER	
10/20/84	#2	23	All I Need	Qwest 29238
5/25/85	#81	6	Lady Of My Heart	Qwest 29085

Debut Date	Peak Pos	Wks Chr	ARTIST/Song Title	Label & Number
10/26/85	#53	14	Too Young	Qwest 28931
4/25/87	#65	9	Weatherman Says	Qwest 28387
			PORTER WAGONER	
2/01/69	#97	3	The Carroll County Accident	RCA 9651
			WAIKIKIS	
11/21/64	#34	10	Hawaii Tattoo	Kapp 30
3/27/65	#93	3	Hawaii Honeymoon	Kapp 52
			WAILERS	
5/16/59	#45	10	Tall Cool One	Golden Crest 518
3/28/64	#50	12	Tall Cool One	Golden Crest 518
			LOUDON WAINWRIGHT III	
1/20/73	#12	16	Dead Skunk	Columbia 45726
			JOHN WAITE	
6/30/84	#1	24	Missing You	EMI America 8212
10/20/84	#37	14	Tears	EMI America 8238
2/02/85	#58	9	Restless Heart	EMI America 8252
3/02/85	#54	10	Change	Chrysalis 42606
8/10/85	#24	14	Every Step Of The Way	EMI America 8282
11/02/85	#81	4	Welcome To Paradise	EMI America 8278
6/21/86	#64	7	If Anybody Had A Heart	EMI America 8315
6/20/87	#52	11	These Times Are Hard For Lovers	EMI America 43018
9/26/87	#79	6	Don't Lose Any Sleep	EMI America 43040
			WAITRESSES	
5/08/82	#74	5	I Know What Boys Like	Polydor 2196
			JOHNNY WAKELIN & THE KINSHASA BAND	
3/15/75	#22	23	Black Superman - "Muhammad Ali"	Pye 71012
			JIMMY WAKELY	
4/14/51	#7	8	Beautiful Brown Eyes	Capitol 1393
			NARADA MICHAEL WALDEN	
4/07/79	#52	9	I Don't Want Nobody Else (To Dance With You)	Atlantic 3541
2/16/80	#77	5	I Shoulda Loved Ya	Atlantic 3631
			WENDY WALDMAN	
8/12/78	#89	6	Long Hot Summer Nights	Warner Brothers 8617
			CHRIS WALKER	
3/07/92	#21	21	Take Time	Pendulum 64813
			CLAY WALKER	
11/06/93	#75	7	What's It To You	Giant 18450
			DAVID T. WALKER	
5/20/72	#66	7	Hot Fun In The Summertime	Ode 66025
			GLORIA WALKER	
10/26/68	#57	6	Talking About My Baby	Flaming Arrow 35
			JERRY JEFF WALKER	
7/06/68	#52	7	Mr. Bojangles	Atco 6594
7/14/73	#78	5	L.A. Freeway	MCA 40054
			JR. WALKER & THE ALL STARS	
2/20/65	#4	14	Shotgun	Soul 35008
6/05/65	#35	6	Do The Boomerang	Soul 35012
7/31/65	#33	10	Shake And Fingerpop/	Soul 35013
10/09/65	#37	10	Cleo's Back	Soul 35013
1/22/66	#62	3	Cleo's Mood	Soul 35017
4/16/66	#21	11	(I'm A) Road Runner	Soul 35015
7/30/66	#21	11	How Sweet It Is (To Be Loved By You)	Soul 35024
11/19/66	#32	6	Money (That's What I Want) (Part 1)	Soul 35026
2/04/67	#35	10	Pucker Up Buttercup	Soul 35030
7/15/67	#47	7	Shoot Your Shot	Soul 35036
11/25/67	#27	11	Come See About Me	Soul 35041
8/10/68	#28	9	Hip City (Part 2)	Soul 35048
1/18/69	#63	4	Home Cookin'	Soul 35055
5/17/69	#5	16	What Does It Take (To Win Your Love)	Soul 35062
10/25/69	#27	13	These Eyes	Soul 35067
2/21/70	#14	9	Gotta Hold On To This Feeling	Soul 35070
7/11/70	#25	8	Do You See My Love (For You Growing)	Soul 35073
12/26/70	#67	4	Holly Holy	Soul 35081
8/07/71	#44	8	Take Me Girl, I'm Ready	Soul 35084

Debut Date	Peak Pos	Wks Chr	ARTIST/Song Title	Label & Number
			JR. WALKER & THE ALL STARS—*continued*	
12/04/71	#91	5	Way Back Home	Soul 35090
4/01/72	#50	10	Walk In The Night	Soul 35095
			WALKER BROTHERS	
10/09/65	#23	11	Make It Easy On Yourself	Smash 2009
1/29/66	#68	5	My Ship Is Comin' In	Smash 2016
4/09/66	#14	5	The Sun Ain't Gonna Shine (Anymore)	Smash 2032
			JERRY WALLACE	
7/19/58	#19	18	How The Time Flies	Challenge 59013
8/15/59	#5	22	Primrose Lane*	Challenge 59047
12/26/59	#41	10	Little Coco Palm	Challenge 59060
5/14/60	#91	2	You're Singing Our Love Song	Challenge 59072
8/20/60	#97	1	Swingin' Down The Lane	Challenge 59082
12/17/60	#20	14	There She Goes	Challenge 59098
4/22/61	#90	3	Life's A Holiday	Challenge 9107
11/10/62	#20	15	Shutters And Boards	Challenge 9171
7/18/64	#19	13	In The Misty Moonlight	Challenge 59246
7/18/64	#83	4	It's A Cotton Candy World	Mercury 72292
4/22/72	#74	7	To Get To You	Decca 32914
7/22/72	#39	13	If You Leave Me Tonight I'll Cry	Decca 32989
			*released as by JERRY WALLACE with THE JEWELS	
			WALLACE BROTHERS	
6/27/64	#95	2	Precious Words	Sims 174
9/05/64	#95	2	Lover's Prayer	Sims 189
			WALL OF VOODOO	
3/19/83	#50	10	Mexican Radio	I.R.S. 9912
			JAMES WALSH GYPSY BAND (see GYPSY)	
			JOE WALSH	
8/04/73	#13	16	Rocky Mountain Way	Dunhill 4361
12/29/73	#77	6	Meadows	Dunhill 4373
2/15/75	#64	5	Turn To Stone	Dunhill 15026
6/03/78	#6	19	Life's Been Good	Asylum 45493
5/17/80	#18	17	All Night Long	Full Moon 46639
5/23/81	#35	13	A Life Of Illusion	Asylum 47144
6/18/83	#61	8	Space Age Whiz Kids	Full Moon 29611
			STEVE WALSH	
5/17/80	#98	2	Every Step Of The Way	Kirshner 4288
			TRAVIS WAMMACK	
10/17/64	#69	12	Scratchy	ARA 204
3/26/66	#88	2	Louie Louie	Atlantic 2322
7/29/72	#65	10	Whatever Turns You On	Fame 91001
12/30/72	#59	11	How Can I Tell You	Fame 91008
7/05/75	#50	7	(Shu-Doo-Pa-Poo-Poop) Love Being Your Fool	Capricorn 0239
10/25/75	#99	1	Easy Evil	Capricorn 0242
			WANDERERS	
4/22/61	#64	7	For Your Love	Cub 9089
8/18/62	#77	6	There Is No Greater Love	MGM 13082
			WALTER WANDERLY	
8/27/66	#30	9	Summer Samba (So Nice)	Verve 10421
			WANG CHUNG	
2/11/84	#48	11	Don't Let Go	Geffen 29377
4/28/84	#17	21	Dance Hall Days	Geffen 29310
10/12/85	#38	18	To Live And Die In L.A.	Geffen 28891
10/04/86	#1	22	Everybody Have Fun Tonight	Geffen 28562
1/24/87	#10	17	Let's Go	Geffen 28531
6/06/87	#36	13	Hypnotize Me	Geffen 28359
5/27/89	#57	11	Praying To A New God	Geffen 22969
			WANTED	
4/08/67	#78	3	In The Midnight Hour	A&M 844
			WAR	
5/30/70	#1	19	Spill The Wine*	MGM 14118
12/19/70	#37	7	They Can't Take Away Our Music*	MGM 14196
4/17/71	#71	4	Lonely Feelin'	United Artists 50746
8/07/71	#28	10	All Day Music	United Artists 50815
12/25/71	#12	25	Slippin' Into Darkness	United Artists 50867

Debut Date	Peak Pos	Wks Chr	**ARTIST**/Song Title	Label & Number
11/25/72	#9	15	The World Is A Ghetto	United Artists 50975
3/10/73	#2	13	The Cisco Kid	United Artists 163
7/14/73	#7	14	Gypsy Man	United Artists 281
11/10/73	#12	15	Me And Baby Brother	United Artists 350
6/01/74	#35	10	Ballero	United Artists 432
5/03/75	#5	21	Why Can't We Be Friends?	United Artists 629
9/13/75	#5	15	Low Rider	United Artists 706
7/10/76	#15	17	Summer	United Artists 834
7/30/77	#62	7	L.A. Sunshine	Blue Note 1009
12/31/77	#46	10	Galaxy	MCA 40820
4/28/79	#94	3	Good, Good Feelin'	MCA 40995
7/10/82	#94	3	Outlaw	RCA 13238
			*released as by ERIC BURDON & WAR	
			ANITA WARD	
5/19/79	#1	20	Ring My Bell	Juana 3422
			BILLY WARD and HIS DOMINOES	
8/04/56	#24	13	St. Therese Of The Roses	Decca 29933
6/22/57	#13	16	Star Dust	Liberty 55071
9/14/57	#28	9	Deep Purple	Liberty 55099
5/17/58	#46	1	Jennie Lee	Liberty 55136
			DALE WARD	
1/04/64	#29	10	Letter From Sherry	Dot 16520
			JACKY WARD	
3/04/78	#77	8	A Lover's Question	Mercury 55018
			ROBIN WARD	
10/26/63	#15	13	Wonderful Summer	Dot 16530
			JENNIFER WARNES	
2/05/77	#5	19	Right Time Of The Night	Arista 0223
7/23/77	#62	11	I'm Dreaming	Arista 0252
7/07/79	#21	22	I Know A Heartache When I See One	Arista 0430
12/29/79	#74	4	Don't Make Me Over	Arista 0455
3/29/80	#59	8	When The Feeling Comes Around	Arista 0497
12/12/81	#59	12	Could It Be Love	Arista 0611
8/28/82	#1	25	Up Where We Belong*	Island 99996
9/19/87	#1	23	(I've Had) The Time Of My Life**	RCA 5224
			*released as by JOE COCKER and JENNIFER WARNES	
			**released as by BILL MEDLEY and JENNIFER WARNES	
			WARRANT	
4/29/89	#32	18	Down Boys	Columbia 68606
7/29/89	#2	23	Heaven	Columbia 68985
11/11/89	#86	4	Big Talk	Columbia 73035
12/16/89	#16	20	Sometimes She Cries	Columbia 73300
9/08/90	#12	16	Cherry Pie	Columbia 73510
11/24/90	#11	23	I Saw Red	Columbia 73597
4/20/91	#76	6	Uncle Tom's Cabin	Columbia 73644
7/06/91	#84	6	Blind Faith	Columbia 73598
3/28/92	#70	9	We Will Rock You	Columbia 74207
			DEE DEE WARWICK	
11/09/63	#79	3	You're No Good	Jubilee 5459
7/24/65	#94	3	We're Doing Fine	Blue Rock 4027
8/06/66	#55	10	I Want To Be With You	Mercury 72584
11/26/66	#92	3	I'm Gonna Make You Love Me	Mercury 72638
4/29/67	#100	1	When Love Slips Away	Mercury 72667
2/08/69	#81	10	Foolish Fool	Mercury 72880
5/16/70	#53	6	She Didn't Know	Atco 6754
6/26/71	#78	5	Suspicious Minds	Atco 6810
			DIONNE WARWICK	
11/24/62	#17	15	Don't Make Me Over	Scepter 1239
3/30/63	#92	3	This Empty Place	Scepter 1247
12/21/63	#8	13	Anyone Who Had A Heart	Scepter 1262
4/18/64	#6	15	Walk On By	Scepter 1274
8/08/64	#28	10	You'll Never Get To Heaven (If You Break My Heart)/ . . .	Scepter 1282
8/08/64	#50	5	A House Is Not A Home	Scepter 1282
10/24/64	#21	9	Reach Out For Me	Scepter 1285
3/27/65	#75	4	You Can Have Him	Scepter 1294
7/10/65	#71	5	Here I Am	Scepter 12104
10/16/65	#84	4	Looking With My Eyes	Scepter 12111

Debut Date	Peak Pos	Wks Chr	ARTIST/Song Title	Label & Number
			DIONNE WARWICK—*continued*	
12/11/65	#36	11	Are You There (With Another Girl)	Scepter 12122
4/02/66	#9	12	Message To Michael	Scepter 12133
7/02/66	#31	8	Trains And Boats And Planes	Scepter 12153
10/01/66	#24	9	I Just Don't Know What To Do With Myself	Scepter 12167
12/24/66	#44	6	Another Night	Scepter 12181
3/18/67	#95	2	The Beginning Of Loneliness/	Scepter 12187
4/01/67	#15	18	Alfie	Scepter 12187
8/05/67	#40	6	The Windows Of The World	Scepter 12196
10/21/67	#5	13	I Say A Little Prayer/	Scepter 12203
1/20/68	#3	14	(Theme From) Valley Of The Dolls	Scepter 12203
4/13/68	#10	12	Do You Know The Way To San Jose	Scepter 12216
6/08/68	#80	4	Let Me Be Lonely	Scepter 12216
8/24/68	#22	8	Who Is Gonna Love Me/	Scepter 12226
8/24/68	#86	2	(There's) Always Something There To Remind Me	Scepter 12226
11/02/68	#15	10	Promises, Promises	Scepter 12231
2/01/69	#9	10	This Girl's In Love With You	Scepter 12241
5/10/69	#37	7	The April Fools	Scepter 12249
7/26/69	#44	7	Odds And Ends	Scepter 12256
9/20/69	#14	11	You've Lost That Lovin' Feeling	Scepter 12262
12/27/69	#6	11	I'll Never Fall In Love Again	Scepter 12273
4/18/70	#26	7	Let Me Go To Him	Scepter 12276
7/11/70	#31	7	Paper Mache	Scepter 12285
10/03/70	#25	9	Make It Easy On Yourself	Scepter 12294
12/05/70	#45	8	The Green Grass Starts To Grow	Scepter 12300
3/20/71	#62	4	Who Gets The Guy	Scepter 12309
3/04/72	#71	3	If We Only Have Love	Warner Brothers 7560
7/20/74	#1	16	Then Came You*	Atlantic 3202
12/27/75	#75	7	Once You Hit The Road	Warner Brothers 8154
6/23/79	#5	26	I'll Never Love This Way Again	Arista 0419
11/17/79	#11	20	Deja Vu	Arista 0459
4/05/80	#79	3	After You	Arista 0498
7/26/80	#28	17	No Night So Long	Arista 0527
11/29/80	#77	8	Easy Love	Arista 0572
6/20/81	#70	5	Some Changes Are For The Good	Arista 0602
5/01/82	#48	10	Friends In Love**	Arista 0673
10/09/82	#15	20	Heartbreaker	Arista 1015
2/26/83	#32	12	Take The Short Way Home	Arista 1040
10/08/83	#36	15	How Many Times Can We Say Goodbye***	Arista 9073
11/09/85	#1	26	That's What Friends Are For****	Arista 9422
3/15/86	#74	6	Whisper In The Dark	Arista 9460
7/11/87	#11	15	Love Power*****	Arista 9567
11/07/87	#84	6	Reservations For Two******	Arista 9638
			*released as by DIONNE WARWICKE and THE SPINNERS	
			**released as by DIONNE WARWICK and JOHNNY MATHIS	
			***released as by DIONNE WARWICK and LUTHER VANDROSS	
			****released as by DIONNE and FRIENDS: DIONNE WARWICK, ELTON JOHN,	
			GLADYS KNIGHT and STEVIE WONDER	
			*****released as by DIONNE WARWICK & JEFFREY OSBORNE	
			******released as by DIONNE & KASHIF	
			MARTHA WASH	
3/20/93	#91	3	Give It To You	RCA 62433
			BABY WASHINGTON	
5/13/61	#69	8	Nobody Cares (About Me)*	Neptune 122
9/22/62	#96	2	Handful Of Memories	Sue 762
3/30/63	#57	11	That's How Heartaches Are Made	Sue 783
7/27/63	#86	7	Leave Me Alone	Sue 790
9/26/64	#100	1	The Clock	Sue 104
11/21/64	#93	3	It'll Never Be Over For Me	Sue 114
7/31/65	#56	8	Only Those In Love	Sue 129
			*released as by JEANETTE BABY WASHINGTON	
			DINAH WASHINGTON	
8/16/58	#74	1	Never Again	Mercury 71317
5/09/59	#4	24	What A Diff'rence A Day Makes	Mercury 71435
10/03/59	#2	15	Unforgettable	Mercury 71508
1/30/60	#2	16	Baby (You've Got What It Takes)*	Mercury 71565

Debut Date	Peak Pos	Wks Chr	ARTIST/Song Title	Label & Number
3/19/60	#47	9	It Could Happen To You	Mercury 71560
5/21/60	#5	14	A Rockin' Good Way (To Mess Around And Fall In Love)*	Mercury 71629
6/18/60	#23	16	This Bitter Earth	Mercury 71635
10/08/60	#18	12	Love Walked In	Mercury 71696
12/24/60	#51	6	We Have Love/	Mercury 71744
12/31/60	#92	2	Looking Back	Mercury 71744
3/04/61	#75	5	Early Every Morning	Mercury 71778
5/13/61	#70	6	Our Love Is Here To Stay	Mercury 71812
10/14/61	#19	14	September In The Rain	Mercury 71876
2/03/62	#56	7	Tears And Laughter	Mercury 71922
4/28/62	#92	2	Dream	Mercury 71958
5/19/62	#38	13	Where Are You	Roulette 4424

*released as by DINAH WASHINGTON & BROOK BENTON

ELLA WASHINGTON
| 1/25/69 | #92 | 1 | He Called Me Baby . . . . | Sound Stage 2621 |

GROVER WASHINGTON JR.
| 5/03/75 | #77 | 7 | Mister Magic . . . . | Kudu 924 |
| 2/07/81 | #4 | 24 | Just The Two Of Us . . . . | Elektra 47103 |

JUSTINE WASHINGTON
| 3/07/64 | #86 | 3 | Who's Going To Take Care Of Me . . . . | Sue 797 |

KEITH WASHINGTON
| 6/08/91 | #58 | 14 | Kissing You . . . . | Qwest 19414 |

WAS (NOT WAS)
10/08/88	#28	18	Spy In The House Of Love	Chrysalis 43266
1/28/89	#7	18	Walk The Dinosaur	Chrysalis 43331
4/29/89	#72	8	Anything Can Happen	Chrysalis 43365

WATERFRONT
| 4/08/89 | #10 | 20 | Cry . . . . | Polydor 871110 |
| 8/12/89 | #58 | 7 | Nature Of Love . . . . | Polydor 871414 |

CRYSTAL WATERS
| 5/25/91 | #30 | 19 | Gypsy Woman (She's Homeless) . . . . | Mercury 868284 |

JODY WATLEY
3/07/87	#2	23	Looking For A New Love	MCA 52956
6/20/87	#66	8	Still A Thrill	MCA 53081
10/10/87	#5	21	Don't You Want Me	MCA 53162
2/06/88	#9	20	Some Kind Of Lover	MCA 53235
4/30/88	#66	12	Most Of All	MCA 53258
3/18/89	#1	22	Real Love	MCA 53484
6/24/89	#8	23	Friends	MCA 53660
10/21/89	#36	13	Everything	MCA 53714
3/24/90	#54	6	Precious Love	MCA 53790
12/28/91	#68	10	I Want You	MCA 54137
3/14/92	#15	22	I'm The One You Need	MCA 54276

JOHNNY "GUITAR" WATSON
| 7/02/77 | #42 | 12 | A Real Mother For Ya . . . . | DJM 1024 |

WATTS 103rd STREET RHYTHM BAND (see CHARLES WRIGHT)

WA WA NEE
| 9/12/87 | #35 | 15 | Sugar Free . . . . | Epic 07283 |

WAX
| 3/22/86 | #42 | 13 | Right Between The Eyes . . . . | RCA 14306 |

THOMAS WAYNE with THE DeLONS
| 2/07/59 | #7 | 15 | Tragedy . . . . | Fernwood 109 |
| 5/23/59 | #85 | 3 | Eternally . . . . | Fernwood 111 |

WEATHER GIRLS
| 1/29/83 | #46 | 11 | It's Raining Men . . . . | Columbia 03354 |

JIM WEATHERLY
12/23/72	#90	4	Loving You Is Just An Old Habit	RCA 0822
8/24/74	#16	15	The Need To Be	Buddah 420
1/25/75	#77	4	I'll Still Love You	Buddah 444

WEAVERS
| 4/28/51 | #2 | 17 | On Top Of Old Smokey . . . . | Decca 27515 |

PAULA WEBB
| 2/01/75 | #76 | 4 | Please Mr. President . . . . | Westbound 5001 |

Debut Date	Peak Pos	Wks Chr	ARTIST/Song Title	Label & Number
			WEBBS	
12/09/67	#89	4	This Thing Called Love	Pop Side 4593
			JOAN WEBER	
12/25/54	#1	9	Let Me Go Lover	Columbia 40366
			WEDNESDAY	
11/17/73	#45	18	Last Kiss	Sussex 507
5/11/74	#73	5	Teen Angel	Sussex 515
			WE FIVE	
7/31/65	#2	16	You Were On My Mind	A&M 770
11/13/65	#31	7	Let's Get Together	A&M 784
6/04/66	#99	2	There Stands The Door	A&M 800
			BOB WEIR	
3/25/78	#63	6	Bombs Away	Arista 0315
			FRANK WEIR ORCHESTRA	
6/12/54	#4	11	Happy Wanderer	London 1448
			ERIC WEISSBERG & STEVE MANDELL	
1/06/73	#1	15	Dueling Banjos	Warner Brothers 7659
			BOB WELCH	
10/08/77	#4	19	Sentimental Lady	Capitol 4479
1/28/78	#12	17	Ebony Eyes	Capitol 4543
6/03/78	#49	10	Hot Love, Cold World	Capitol 4588
2/10/79	#17	15	Precious Love	Capitol 4685
5/26/79	#76	5	Church	Capitol 4719
			LENNY WELCH	
3/12/60	#42	12	You Don't Know Me	Cadence 1373
10/26/63	#4	17	Since I Fell For You	Cadence 1439
3/28/64	#27	9	Ebb Tide	Cadence 1422
6/05/65	#55	9	Darling Take Me Back	Kapp 662
8/28/65	#48	7	Two Different Worlds	Kapp 689
11/06/65	#94	4	Run To My Lovin' Arms	Kapp 712
2/26/66	#85	5	Rags To Riches	Kapp 740
1/03/70	#32	11	Breaking Up Is Hard To Do	Comm. United 3004
8/19/72	#95	4	A Sunday Kind Of Love	Atco 6894
			LAWRENCE WELK	
8/25/56	#18	3	When The White Lilacs Bloom Again/	Coral 61701
10/06/56	#3	11	Tonight You Belong To Me*	Coral 61701
1/12/57	#29	1	Cinco Robles (Five Oaks)	Coral 61765
12/24/60	#1	17	Calcutta	Dot 16161
4/01/61	#28	8	Theme From My Three Sons	Dot 16198
9/16/61	#69	4	Riders In The Sky	Dot 16237
11/25/61	#94	3	A-One A-Two A-Cha Cha Cha	Dot 16285
4/14/62	#87	4	Runaway	Dot 16336
7/18/62	#84	5	Baby Elephant Walk	Dot 16364
12/15/62	#79	5	Zero-Zero	Dot 16420
7/06/63	#100	1	Scarlett O'Hara	Dot 16488
4/17/65	#88	3	Apples And Bananas	Dot 16697
4/15/67	#94	1	The Beat Goes On	Dot 17001
			***released as by LAWRENCE WELK with THE LENNON SISTERS**	
			MARY WELLS	
1/21/61	#41	16	Bye Bye Baby	Motown 1003
7/08/61	#83	7	I Don't Want To Take A Chance	Motown 1011
3/17/62	#4	20	The One Who Really Loves You	Motown 1024
8/11/62	#9	13	You Beat Me To The Punch	Motown 1032
12/01/62	#10	14	Two Lovers	Motown 1035
2/23/63	#27	10	Laughing Boy	Motown 1039
5/11/63	#48	9	Your Old Standby	Motown 1042
9/21/63	#22	12	You Lost The Sweetest Boy/	Motown 1048
11/30/63	#47	15	What's Easy For Two Is So Hard For One	Motown 1048
4/04/64	#1	16	My Guy	Motown 1056
5/02/64	#27	9	Once Upon A Time*/	Motown 1057
5/09/64	#25	12	What's The Matter With You Baby*	Motown 1057
10/31/64	#42	8	Ain't It The Truth	20th Century Fox 544
1/09/65	#41	6	Use Your Head	20th Century Fox 555
3/13/65	#53	6	Never Never Leave Me	20th Century Fox 570
6/12/65	#82	4	He's A Lover	20th Century Fox 590

Debut Date	Peak Pos	Wks Chr	**ARTIST**/Song Title	Label & Number
9/18/65	#99	1	Me Without You	20th Century Fox 606
1/22/66	#91	3	Can't You See (You're Losing Me)/	Atco 6392
2/12/66	#45	8	Dear Lover	Atco 6392
7/02/66	#93	2	Such A Sweet Thing	Atco 6423
5/11/68	#79	7	The Doctor	Jubilee 5621
1/24/70	#80	3	Dig The Way I Feel	Jubilee 5684
			*released as by MARVIN GAYE & MARY WELLS	
			WENDY and LISA	
9/19/87	#54	10	Waterfall	Columbia 07243
			MAX WERNER	
5/16/81	#76	5	Rain In May	Radio 3821
			FRED WESLEY & THE JB'S (see JB'S)	
			DOTTIE WEST	
1/13/73	#90	5	If It's All Right With You	RCA 0828
9/15/73	#45	10	Country Sunshine	RCA 0072
3/15/80	#78	4	A Lesson In Leavin'	United Artists 1339
3/28/81	#15	21	What Are We Doin' In Love*	Liberty 1404
			*released as by DOTTIE WEST with KENNY ROGERS	
			WEST COAST RAP ALL-STARS	
6/30/90	#40	14	We're All In The Same Gang	Warner Brothers 19819
			KIM WESTON	
7/06/63	#65	11	Love Me All The Way	Tamla 54076
10/24/64	#73	4	What Good Am I Without You*/	Tamla 54104
10/24/64	#98	1	I Want You 'Round*	Tamla 54104
9/25/65	#48	10	Take Me In Your Arms (Rock Me A Little While)	Gordy 7046
3/19/66	#53	7	Helpless	Gordy 7050
1/21/67	#43	11	It Takes Two*	Tamla 54141
4/29/67	#79	3	I Got What You Need	MGM 13720
			*released as by MARVIN GAYE & KIM WESTON	
			WEST STREET MOB	
10/24/81	#94	4	Let's Dance (Make Your Body Move)	Sugar Hill 559
			WET WET WET	
5/28/88	#58	10	Wishing I Was Lucky	Uni 50000
			WET WILLIE	
5/25/74	#16	17	Keep On Smilin'	Capricorn 0043
10/19/74	#62	6	Country Side Of Life	Capricorn 0212
3/01/75	#65	6	Leona	Capricorn 0224
5/29/76	#84	2	Everything That 'Cha Do	Capricorn 0254
12/03/77	#26	15	Street Corner Serenade	Epic 50478
4/01/78	#45	8	Make You Feel Love Again	Epic 50528
5/26/79	#29	14	Weekend	Epic 50714
			WHAM! (see GEORGE MICHAEL)	
			WHAT IS THIS	
8/24/85	#69	6	I'll Be Around	MCA 52593
			WHATNAUTS	
5/08/71	#64	5	I'll Erase Away Your Pain	Stang 5023
5/05/73	#96	3	Instigating (Trouble Making) Fool	GSF 6987
1/11/75	#85	5	Girls*	Stang 5057
			*released as by THE MOMENTS & THE WHATNAUTS	
			BILLY ED WHEELER	
12/26/64	#53	9	Ode To The Little Brown Shack Out Back	Kapp 617
			CARON WHEELER	
10/06/90	#45	12	Livin' In The Light	EMI 50286
			WHEELS	
1/23/60	#79	6	Clap Your Hands (Part 1)	Folly 800
			WHEN IN ROME	
9/10/88	#15	24	The Promise	Virgin 99323
1/28/89	#66	8	Heaven Knows	Virgin 99253
			NANCY WHISKEY	
5/18/57	#18	5	Freight Train	Chic 1008
			WHISPERS	
10/10/70	#62	6	Seems Like I Gotta Do Wrong	Soul Clock 1004
6/12/71	#100	1	Your Love Is So Doggone Good	Janus 150

373

Debut Date	Peak Pos	Wks Chr	ARTIST/Song Title	Label & Number
			WHISPERS—*continued*	
2/02/74	#92	4	Mother For My Children	Janus 231
8/13/77	#90	3	Make It With You	Soul Train 10996
2/02/80	#19	17	And The Beat Goes On	Solar 11894
4/19/80	#38	11	Lady	Solar 11928
3/21/81	#25	15	It's A Love Thing	Solar 12154
6/06/87	#10	23	Rock Steady	Solar 70006
8/11/90	#51	8	Innocent	Capitol 44593
			WHISTLE	
6/10/89	#82	6	Right Next To Me	Select 2005
4/14/90	#36	15	Always And Forever	Select 2014
			IAN WHITCOMB	
2/20/65	#87	4	This Sporting Life	Tower 120
5/15/65	#10	14	You Turn Me On (Turn On Song)*	Tower 134
8/28/65	#47	6	N-E-R-V-O-U-S!	Tower 155
			*released as by IAN WHITCOMB and BLUESVILLE	
			BARRY WHITE	
4/07/73	#4	15	I'm Gonna Love You Just A Little More Baby	20th Century 2018
8/11/73	#38	9	I've Got So Much To Give	20th Century 2042
11/03/73	#9	16	Never, Never Gonna Give You Up	20th Century 2058
2/16/74	#23	10	Honey Please, Can't Ya See	20th Century 2077
7/27/74	#1	14	Can't Get Enough Of Your Love, Babe	20th Century 2120
11/02/74	#1	15	You're The First, The Last, My Everything	20th Century 2133
3/08/75	#8	11	What Am I Gonna Do Without You	20th Century 2177
5/24/75	#32	8	I'll Do For You Anything You Want Me To	20th Century 2208
12/20/75	#31	11	Let The Music Play	20th Century 2265
9/03/77	#7	17	It's Ecstasy When You Lay Down Next To Me	20th Century 2350
2/18/78	#95	1	Playing Your Game, Baby	20th Century 2361
4/22/78	#32	11	Oh What A Night For Dancing	20th Century 2365
11/11/78	#47	11	Your Sweetness Is My Weakness	20th Century 2380
3/17/90	#30	12	The Secret Garden*	Qwest 19992
			*released as by QUINCY JONES/AL B. SURE!/JAMES INGRAM/EL DeBARGE/ BARRY WHITE	
			KARYN WHITE	
12/13/86	#31	16	Facts Of Love*	Warner Brothers 28588
10/22/88	#5	24	The Way You Love Me	Warner Brothers 27773
2/04/89	#8	19	Superwoman	Warner Brothers 27783
5/27/89	#7	24	Secret Rendezvous	Warner Brothers 27863
8/17/91	#1	28	Romantic	Warner Brothers 19319
11/30/91	#3	27	The Way I Feel About You	Warner Brothers 19088
			*released as by JEFF LORBER featuring KARYN WHITE	
			MAURICE WHITE	
9/14/85	#48	12	Stand By Me	Columbia 05571
			TONY JOE WHITE	
7/05/69	#9	10	Polk Salad Annie	Monument 1104
10/18/69	#42	7	Roosevelt And Ira Lee	Monument 1169
7/18/70	#99	3	Save Your Sugar For Me	Monument 1206
7/05/80	#75	5	I Get Off On It	Casablanca 2279
			WHITE LION	
2/27/88	#10	21	Wait	Atlantic 89126
7/09/88	#60	12	Tell Me	Atlantic 89051
11/19/88	#4	21	When The Children Cry	Atlantic 89015
7/01/89	#71	7	Little Fighter	Atlantic 88874
9/30/89	#66	11	Radar Love	Atlantic 88836
			WHITE PLAINS	
4/11/70	#10	16	My Baby Loves Lovin'	Deram 85058
9/12/70	#63	5	Lovin' You Baby	Deram 85066
			WHITESNAKE	
8/02/80	#62	9	Fool For Your Loving	Mirage 3672
7/04/87	#1	30	Here I Go Again	Geffen 28339
10/24/87	#2	22	Is This Love	Geffen 28233
2/20/88	#61	10	Give Me All Your Love	Geffen 28103
11/04/89	#31	15	Fool For Your Loving	Geffen 22715
1/20/90	#26	14	The Deeper The Love	Geffen 19951
6/09/90	#81	6	Now You're Gone	Geffen 19976

Debut Date	Peak Pos	Wks Chr	ARTIST/Song Title	Label & Number
			MARGARET WHITING	
10/01/66	#50	12	The Wheel Of Hurt	London 101
5/27/67	#94	4	Only Love Can Break A Heart	London 108
11/04/67	#98	2	I Almost Called Your Name	London 115
			MARVA WHITNEY	
5/31/69	#83	4	It's My Thing (You Can't Tell Me Who To Sock It To) . . .	King 6229
			ROGER WHITTAKER	
3/29/75	#17	16	The Last Farewell	RCA 50030
			WHO	
2/20/65	#57	10	I Can't Explain	Decca 31725
12/18/65	#99	2	My Generation	Decca 31877
8/13/66	#85	2	The Kids Are Alright	Decca 31988
4/08/67	#13	12	Happy Jack	Decca 32114
7/01/67	#60	6	Pictures Of Lily	Decca 32156
10/07/67	#8	13	I Can See For Miles	Decca 32206
3/02/68	#38	10	Call Me Lightning	Decca 32288
8/10/68	#10	11	Magic Bus	Decca 32362
4/05/69	#15	11	Pinball Wizard	Decca 32465
7/12/69	#30	9	I'm Free	Decca 32519
4/11/70	#30	8	The Seeker	Decca 32670
7/04/70	#14	11	Summertime Blues	Decca 32708
9/26/70	#8	13	See Me, Feel Me	Decca 32729
7/10/71	#9	14	Won't Get Fooled Again	Decca 32846
10/30/71	#24	12	Behind Blue Eyes	Decca 32888
7/15/72	#28	11	Join Together	Decca 32983
12/09/72	#33	8	The Relay	Track 33041
11/17/73	#54	7	Love, Reign O'er Me	Track 40152
1/26/74	#82	3	The Real Me	Track 40182
11/23/74	#64	4	Postcard	MCA 40330
11/15/75	#11	20	Squeeze Box	MCA 40475
8/26/78	#9	16	Who Are You	MCA 40948
7/07/79	#66	6	Long Live Rock	MCA 41053
9/29/79	#53	7	5:15	Polydor 2022
3/21/81	#15	15	You Better You Bet	Warner Brothers 49698
6/27/81	#77	4	Don't Let Go The Coat	Warner Brothers 49743
9/04/82	#31	13	Athena	Warner Brothers 29905
12/25/82	#77	7	Eminence Front	Warner Brothers 29814
			JANE WIEDLIN	
4/09/83	#44	15	Cool Places*	Atlantic 89866
10/05/85	#74	7	Blue Kiss	I.R.S. 52674
5/07/88	#10	21	Rush Hour	EMI-Manhattan 50118
8/27/88	#56	8	Inside A Dream	EMI-Manhattan 50145
			*released as by SPARKS and JANE WIEDLIN	
			STEVE WIGHTMAN	
5/15/76	#90	3	You Know The Feelin'	Farr 003
			HARLOW WILCOX and THE OAKIES	
9/27/69	#25	14	Groovy Grubworm	Plantation 28
			JACK WILD	
6/06/70	#94	2	Some Beautiful	Capitol 2742
			WILD BLUE	
5/24/86	#75	5	Fire With Fire	Chrysalis 42985
			WILD-CATS	
1/17/59	#65	7	Gazachstahagen	United Artists 154
			WILD CHERRY	
6/12/76	#1	25	Play That Funky Music	Epic 50225
1/08/77	#57	9	Baby Don't You Know	Epic 50306
8/27/77	#69	6	Hold On	Epic 50401
3/11/78	#74	5	I Love My Music	Epic 50500
			EUGENE WILDE	
12/28/85	#88	6	Don't Say No Tonight	Philly World 99608
			KIM WILDE	
5/22/82	#20	20	Kids In America	EMI America 8110
1/26/85	#63	8	Go For It	MCA 52513
3/28/87	#2	22	You Keep Me Hangin' On	MCA 53024
7/18/87	#56	8	Say You Really Want Me	MCA 53130
9/10/88	#41	12	You Came	MCA 53370

375

Debut Date	Peak Pos	Wks Chr	ARTIST/Song Title	Label & Number
			MARTY WILDE	
2/06/60	#53	9	Bad Boy	Epic 9356
			MATTHEW WILDER	
9/17/83	#2	32	Break My Stride	Private I 04113
2/18/84	#40	12	The Kid's American	Private I 04363
9/22/84	#46	10	Bouncin' Off The Walls	Private I 04617
			WILDFIRE	
6/18/77	#43	8	Here Comes Summer	Casablanca 885
			WILDWEEDS	
5/13/67	#85	6	No Good To Cry	Cadet 5561
			WILL-O-BEES	
1/20/68	#90	5	It's Not Easy	Date 1583
			ANDRE WILLIAMS	
2/05/66	#99	1	Rib Tip's (Part 1)	Alvin 103
8/05/67	#97	1	Pearl Time	Sport 105
			ANDY WILLIAMS	
8/11/56	#2	18	Canadian Sunset	Cadence 1297
12/01/56	#35	10	Baby Doll	Cadence 1303
2/16/57	#3	17	Butterfly	Cadence 1308
5/25/57	#10	14	I Like Your Kind Of Love	Cadence 1323
9/14/57	#20	9	Lips Of Wine	Cadence 1336
2/08/58	#7	15	Are You Sincere	Cadence 1340
9/13/58	#33	10	Promise Me, Love	Cadence 1351
12/27/58	#6	21	The Hawaiian Wedding Song/	Cadence 1358
12/27/58	#86	2	House Of Bamboo	Cadence 1358
9/12/59	#7	15	Lonely Street	Cadence 1370
12/19/59	#9	12	The Village Of St. Bernadette	Cadence 1374
3/19/60	#58	7	Wake Me When It's Over	Cadence 1378
6/18/60	#53	8	Do You Mind	Cadence 1381
12/03/60	#51	9	You Don't Want My Love	Cadence 1389
4/29/61	#25	12	The Bilbao Song	Cadence 1398
10/28/61	#78	6	Danny Boy/	Columbia 42199
11/04/61	#73	4	Fly By Night	Columbia 42199
7/07/62	#10	6	Stranger On The Shore	Columbia 42451
9/08/62	#50	12	Don't You Believe It	Columbia 42523
12/01/62	#97	6	Twilight Time	Cadence 1433
2/23/63	#1	17	Can't Get Used To Losing You/	Columbia 42674
3/23/63	#29	12	Days Of Wine And Roses	Columbia 42674
6/22/63	#17	12	Hopeless	Columbia 42784
12/21/63	#81	2	White Christmas	Columbia 42894
1/04/64	#13	12	A Fool Never Learns	Columbia 42950
4/11/64	#27	10	Wrong For Each Other	Columbia 43015
9/12/64	#40	7	On The Street Where You Live/	Columbia 43128
11/07/64	#100	1	Almost There	Columbia 43128
11/28/64	#15	12	Dear Heart	Columbia 43180
4/03/65	#34	8	And Roses And Roses	Columbia 43257
9/04/65	#35	8	Ain't It True	Columbia 43358
11/27/65	#97	3	Quiet Nights Of Quiet Stars	Columbia 43456
9/03/66	#72	5	In The Arms Of Love	Columbia 43737
4/01/67	#50	7	Music To Watch Girls By	Columbia 44065
7/22/67	#100	1	More And More	Columbia 44202
6/15/68	#82	3	Sweet Memories	Columbia 44527
11/02/68	#48	12	Battle Hymn Of The Republic	Columbia 44650
4/05/69	#26	11	Happy Heart	Columbia 44818
11/08/69	#91	1	A Woman's Way	Columbia 45003
2/28/70	#85	3	Can't Help Falling In Love	Columbia 45094
7/18/70	#92	1	One Day Of Your Life	Columbia 45175
2/06/71	#10	14	(Where Do I Begin) Love Story	Columbia 45317
8/21/71	#95	3	A Song For You	Columbia 45434
4/08/72	#24	10	Love Theme From "The Godfather"	Columbia 45579
6/29/74	#73	4	What's Your Name*	Barnaby 601
1/24/76	#85	4	Tell It Like It Is	Columbia 10263
			*released as by ANDY & DAVID WILLIAMS	
			ANSON WILLIAMS	
3/19/77	#84	5	Deeply	Chelsea 3061

Debut Date	Peak Pos	Wks Chr	ARTIST/Song Title	Label & Number
			BILLY WILLIAMS	
8/25/51	#7	4	Shanghai	MGM 10998
6/15/57	#2	17	I'm Gonna Sit Right Down And Write Myself A Letter . . .	Coral 61830
10/12/57	#51	2	Got A Date With An Angel	Coral 61886
7/05/58	#60	6	I'll Get By (As Long As I Have You)	Coral 61999
1/31/59	#27	12	Nola	Coral 62069
5/02/59	#86	2	Goodnight Irene	Coral 62101
			CHRISTOPHER WILLIAMS	
9/09/89	#56	18	Talk To Myself	Geffen 22936
5/22/93	#65	6	Every Little Thing U Do	Uptown 54603
			DANNY WILLIAMS	
3/07/64	#10	14	White On White	United Artists 685
6/20/64	#82	4	A Little Toy Balloon	United Artists 729
			DENIECE WILLIAMS	
11/20/76	#21	25	Free	Columbia 10429
2/04/78	#91	3	Baby, Baby, My Love's All For You	Columbia 10648
3/18/78	#2	21	Too Much, Too Little, Too Late*	Columbia 10693
7/15/78	#67	9	You're All I Need To Get By*	Columbia 10772
8/15/81	#55	10	Silly	ARC/Columbia 02406
4/03/82	#16	19	It's Gonna Take A Miracle	ARC/Columbia 02812
4/07/84	#1	22	Let's Hear It For The Boy	Columbia 04417
8/18/84	#79	4	Next Love	Columbia 04537
9/24/88	#56	10	I Can't Wait	Columbia 08014
			*released as by **JOHNNY MATHIS/DENIECE WILLIAMS**	
			DIANA WILLIAMS	
9/25/76	#84	7	Teddy Bear's Last Ride	Capitol 4317
			DON WILLIAMS	
5/21/77	#99	2	Some Broken Hearts Never Mend	ABC/Dot 17683
11/25/78	#96	3	Tulsa Time	ABC 12425
9/20/80	#25	22	I Believe In You	MCA 41304
			FREEDOM WILLIAMS	
6/12/93	#72	4	Voice Of Freedom	Columbia 77061
			GEOFFREY WILLIAMS	
3/28/92	#81	8	It's Not A Love Thing	Giant 19029
			HANK WILLIAMS JR.	
1/25/64	#67	9	Long Gone Lonesome Blues	MGM 13208
10/31/64	#81	8	Endless Sleep	MGM 13278
			JOHN WILLIAMS (see also **LONDON SYMPHONY ORCHESTRA**)	
8/16/75	#25	10	Main Title (Theme From "Jaws")	MCA 40439
12/24/77	#13	15	Theme From "Close Encounters Of The Third Kind"	Arista 0300
			JOHNNY WILLIAMS	
1/13/73	#80	4	Slow Motion (Part 1)	Philadelphia Int. 3518
			LARRY WILLIAMS	
6/29/57	#12	15	Short Fat Fannie	Specialty 608
10/26/57	#60	2	You Bug Me, Baby/	Specialty 615
11/09/57	#17	14	Bony Moronie	Specialty 615
3/11/67	#81	5	Mercy, Mercy, Mercy*	Okeh 7274
			*released as by **LARRY WILLIAMS/JOHNNY WATSON**	
			MARION WILLIAMS	
2/27/71	#93	1	Standing Here Wondering Which Way To Go	Atlantic 2788
			MASON WILLIAMS	
6/29/68	#1	12	Classical Gas	Warner Brothers 7190
10/12/68	#79	3	Baroque-A-Nova	Warner Brothers 7235
5/03/69	#96	1	Greensleeves	Warner Brothers 7272
			MAURICE WILLIAMS & THE ZODIACS	
9/17/60	#4	20	Stay	Herald 552
2/04/61	#94	3	I Remember	Herald 556
			MIKE WILLIAMS	
7/02/66	#59	5	Lonely Soldier	Atlantic 2339
			OTIS WILLIAMS and HIS CHARMS	
5/19/56	#2	11	Ivory Tower	DeLuxe 6093

Debut Date	Peak Pos	Wks Chr	ARTIST/Song Title	Label & Number
			PAUL WILLIAMS	
2/12/72	#51	10	Waking Up Alone	A&M 1325
12/08/73	#69	7	Inspiration	A&M 1479
			ROGER WILLIAMS	
10/08/55	#1	15	Autumn Leaves	Kapp 116
9/01/56	#34	2	Tumbling Tumbleweeds	Kapp 156
10/13/56	#22	4	Two Different Worlds*	Kapp 161
2/23/57	#16	13	Almost Paradise	Kapp 175
10/26/57	#24	12	Till	Kapp 197
3/01/58	#32	9	Arrivederci, Roma	Kapp 210
6/07/58	#31	11	Young And Warm And Wonderful	Kapp 224
8/23/58	#12	16	Near You	Kapp 233
11/15/58	#25	11	The World Outside	Kapp 246
5/28/60	#62	6	La Montana (If She Should Come To You)	Kapp 331
9/24/60	#72	7	Temptation	Kapp 347
12/02/61	#40	10	Maria	Kapp 437
3/10/62	#89	4	Amor	Kapp 447
4/17/65	#97	2	Try To Remember	Kapp 48
8/07/65	#97	3	Summer Wind**	Kapp 55
6/11/66	#90	2	Lara's Theme From "Dr. Zhivago"	Kapp 738
8/27/66	#7	22	Born Free	Kapp 767
1/28/67	#65	6	Sunrise, Sunset	Kapp 801
5/06/67	#63	5	Love Me Forever	Kapp 821
11/25/67	#100	1	More Than A Whistle	Kapp 843
7/20/68	#52	6	The Impossible Dream	Kapp 907
6/07/69	#99	2	Galveston	Kapp 2007
			*released as by ROGER WILLIAMS/JANE MORGAN	
			**released as by ROGER WILLIAMS with THE HARRY SIMEONE CHORALE	
			TERRY WILLIAMS	
12/16/72	#98	2	Melanie Makes Me Smile	Verve 10686
			VANESSA WILLIAMS	
7/23/88	#59	10	The Right Stuff	Wing 887386
1/28/89	#10	18	Dreamin'	Wing 871078
6/10/89	#82	4	Darlin' I	Wing 871936
8/17/91	#27	24	Running Back To You	Wing 867518
2/08/92	#1	31	Save The Best For Last	Wing 865136
5/30/92	#28	18	Just For Tonight	Wing 865888
10/03/92	#43	16	Work To Do	Wing 863540
1/30/93	#2	38	Love Is*	Giant 18630
			*released as by VANESSA WILLIAMS & BRIAN McKNIGHT	
			WILLIAMS BROTHERS	
2/01/92	#29	19	Can't Cry Hard Enough	Warner Brothers 19326
			WILLIES	
10/22/66	#94	4	The Willy	Co & Ce 239
			BRUCE WILLIS	
1/17/87	#9	16	Respect Yourself	Motown 1876
4/18/87	#82	4	Young Blood	Motown 1886
6/20/87	#76	7	Under The Boardwalk	Motown 1896
			CHUCK WILLIS	
5/18/57	#32	13	C.C. Rider	Atlantic 1130
5/24/58	#9	13	What Am I Living For	Atlantic 1179
9/13/58	#75	3	My Life	Atlantic 1192
			WILL TO POWER	
7/04/87	#59	13	Dreamin'	Epic 07199
6/18/88	#56	12	Say It's Gonna Rain	Epic 07908
9/10/88	#1	25	Baby I Love Your Way/Freebird Medley	Epic 08034
2/11/89	#66	6	Fading Away	Epic 68543
11/17/90	#7	21	I'm Not In Love	Epic 73636
			WILMER and THE DUKES	
6/22/68	#78	9	Give Me One More Chance	Aphrodisiac 260
			AL WILSON	
9/09/67	#99	2	Who Could Be Lovin' You	Soul City 759
1/20/68	#95	4	Do What You Gotta Do	Soul City 761
7/27/68	#32	15	The Snake	Soul City 767
12/28/68	#68	6	Poor Side Of Town	Soul City 771

Debut Date	Peak Pos	Wks Chr	ARTIST/Song Title	Label & Number
8/23/69	#58	6	Lodi	Soul City 775
10/06/73	#1	22	Show And Tell	Rocky Road 30073
3/02/74	#48	9	Touch And Go	Rocky Road 30076
10/19/74	#46	8	La La Peace song	Rocky road 30200
1/11/75	#61	8	I Won't Last A Day Without You/Let Me Be The One	Rocky Road 30202
3/27/76	#41	10	I've Got A Feeling	Playboy 6062
			ANN WILSON	
5/12/84	#7	19	Almot Paradise...Love Theme From "Footloose"*	Columbia 04418
11/29/86	#52	13	The Best Man In The World	Capitol 5654
12/24/88	#11	18	Surrender To Me**	Capitol 44288
			*released as by MIKE RENO and ANN WILSON	
			**released as by ANN WILSON and ROBIN ZANDER	
			BRIAN WILSON	
3/26/66	#38	7	Caroline, No	Capitol 5610
			CARL WILSON	
5/21/83	#72	6	What You Do To Me	Caribou 03590
			HANK WILSON (see LEON RUSSELL)	
			J. FRANK WILSON and THE CAVALIERS	
8/29/64	#1	17	Last Kiss	Josie 923
1/30/65	#99	2	Six Boys	Josie 929
12/01/73	#74	9	Last Kiss	Virgo 506
			JACKIE WILSON	
9/28/57	#35	10	Reet Petite	Brunswick 55024
4/05/58	#37	10	To Be Loved	Brunswick 55052
9/13/58	#76	4	We Have Love	Brunswick 55086
11/22/58	#6	20	Lonely Teardrops	Brunswick 55105
3/21/59	#13	13	That's Why (I Love You So)	Brunswick 55121
6/20/59	#20	11	I'll Be Satisfied	Brunswick 55136
9/12/59	#35	8	You Better Know It	Brunswick 55149
11/14/59	#33	14	Talk That Talk	Brunswick 55165
3/12/60	#3	20	Night	Brunswick 55166
4/16/60	#17	15	Doggin' Around	Brunswick 55166
7/09/60	#8	15	(You Were Made For) All My Love/	Brunswick 55167
7/09/60	#12	15	A Woman, A Lover, A Friend	Brunswick 55167
10/15/60	#10	14	Alone At Last/	Brunswick 55170
10/29/60	#23	12	Am I The Man	Brunswick 55170
1/07/61	#15	10	My Empty Arms/	Brunswick 55201
1/14/61	#40	9	The Tear Of The Year	Brunswick 55201
3/18/61	#23	9	Please Tell Me Why/	Brunswick 55208
3/18/61	#48	5	Your One And Only Love	Brunswick 55208
6/17/61	#30	8	I'm Comin' On Back To You	Brunswick 55216
8/19/61	#51	8	Years From Now/	Brunswick 55219
8/26/61	#78	5	You Don't Know What It Means	Brunswick 55219
10/21/61	#48	6	My Heart Belongs To Only You/	Brunswick 55220
10/28/61	#52	6	The Way I Am	Brunswick 55220
1/13/62	#24	11	The Greatest Hurt/	Brunswick 55221
1/13/62	#81	3	There'll Be No Next Time	Brunswick 55221
3/31/62	#95	2	There's Nothing Like Love	Brunswick 55224
4/21/62	#62	6	Hearts	Brunswick 55225
6/23/62	#71	8	I Just Can't Help It	Brunswick 55229
9/29/62	#98	3	Baby That's All	Brunswick 55233
3/02/63	#4	14	Baby Workout	Brunswick 55239
5/25/63	#36	7	Shake A Hand*	Brunswick 55243
7/13/63	#40	8	Shake! Shake! Shake!	Brunswick 55246
9/28/63	#80	3	Baby Get It (And Don't Quit It)	Brunswick 55250
6/19/65	#54	12	No Pity (In The Naked City)	Brunswick 55280
10/16/65	#71	4	I Believe I'll Love On	Brunswick 55283
1/22/66	#94	2	Think Twice**	Brunswick 55287
10/08/66	#19	14	Whispers (Gettin' Louder)	Brunswick 55300
3/04/67	#96	3	I Don't Want To Lose You	Brunswick 55309
5/13/67	#78	3	I've Lost You	Brunswick 55321
8/05/67	#6	14	(Your Love Keeps Lifting Me) Higher And Higher	Brunswick 55336
11/25/67	#36	6	Since You Showed Me How To Be Happy	Brunswick 55354
2/17/68	#60	6	For Your Precious Love***	Brunswick 55365
4/20/68	#80	5	Chain Gang***	Brunswick 55373
7/13/68	#45	10	I Get The Sweetest Feeling	Brunswick 55381
11/02/68	#65	4	For Once In My Life	Brunswick 55392
3/15/69	#79	3	I Still Love You	Brunswick 55402

Debut Date	Peak Pos	Wks Chr	ARTIST/Song Title	Label & Number
			JACKIE WILSON—*continued*	
9/13/69	#93	3	Helpless	Brunswick 55418
5/16/70	#95	4	Let This Be A Letter (To My Baby)	Brunswick 55435
12/26/70	#64	6	This Love Is Real	Brunswick 55443
11/20/71	#75	5	Love Is Funny That Way	Brunswick 55461
			*released as by JACKIE WILSON and LINDA HOPKINS	
			**released as by JACKIE WILSON and LAVERN BAKER	
			***released as by JACKIE WILSON and COUNT BASIE	
			MERI WILSON	
6/04/77	#25	14	Telephone Man	GRT 127
			NANCY WILSON	
8/03/63	#77	5	Tell Me The Truth	Capitol 4991
6/20/64	#12	14	(You Don't Know) How Glad I Am	Capitol 5198
9/26/64	#62	5	I Wanna Be With You	Capitol 5254
2/06/65	#97	2	Don't Come Running Back	Capitol 5340
5/18/68	#41	14	Face It Girl, It's Over	Capitol 2136
10/05/68	#65	6	Peace Of Mind	Capitol 2283
12/20/69	#82	3	Can't Take My Eyes Off You	Capitol 2644
			SHANICE WILSON	
11/07/87	#51	12	(Baby Tell Me) Can You Dance	A&M 2939
			WILSON PHILLIPS	
3/24/90	#1	24	Hold On	SBK 07322
6/30/90	#2	23	Release Me	SBK 07327
10/13/90	#3	23	Impulsive	SBK 07337
2/09/91	#3	22	You're In Love	SBK 07346
6/01/91	#11	18	The Dream Is Still Alive	SBK 07356
5/09/92	#15	18	You Won't See Me Cry	SBK 07385
8/15/92	#25	13	Give It Up	SBK 53098
			WILTON PLACE STREET BAND	
1/22/77	#19	17	Disco Lucy (I Love Lucy Theme)	Island 078
			JESSE WINCHESTER	
8/06/77	#82	4	Nothing But A Breeze	Bearsville 0318
4/18/81	#33	13	Say What	Bearsville 49711
			WIND	
9/06/69	#18	10	Make Believe	Life 200
			KAI WINDING	
7/06/63	#8	14	More	Verve 10295
			WING & A PRAYER FIFE & DRUM CORPS	
11/15/75	#26	20	Baby Face	Wing & A Prayer 103
			WINGER	
12/24/88	#85	5	Madeline	Atlantic 89041
2/25/89	#30	18	Seventeen	Atlantic 88958
6/03/89	#18	22	Headed For A Heartbreak	Atlantic 88922
9/30/89	#91	3	Hungry	Atlantic 88859
7/28/90	#28	14	Can't Get Enough	Atlantic 87884
10/13/90	#14	23	Miles Away	Atlantic 87820
2/09/91	#35	14	Easy Come Easy Go	Atlantic 87773
			PETE WINGFIELD	
8/30/75	#14	18	Eighteen With A Bullet	Island 026
			WINGS (see PAUL McCARTNEY)	
			WINKLY & NUTLEY	
11/05/60	#80	3	Report To The Nation	MK 101
			WINSTONS	
5/24/69	#8	13	Color Him Father	Metromedia 117
9/13/69	#44	6	Love Of The Common People	Metromedia 142
			EDGAR WINTER GROUP	
12/25/71	#58	9	Keep Playin' That Rock 'N' Roll*	Epic 10788
5/13/72	#89	3	I Can't Turn You Loose*	Epic 10855
3/17/73	#1	16	Frankenstein	Epic 10967
8/04/73	#10	15	Free Ride	Epic 11024
12/08/73	#39	8	Hangin' Around	Epic 11069
7/20/74	#53	8	River's Risin'**	Epic 11143
10/05/74	#88	5	Easy Street	Epic 50034

Debut Date	Peak Pos	Wks Chr	ARTIST/Song Title	Label & Number
			*released as by EDGAR WINTER'S WHITE TRASH	
			**released as by EDGAR WINTER	
			HUGO WINTERHALTER	
6/24/50	#8	14	Count Every Star	RCA 3697
8/07/54	#2	11	The Little Shoemaker	RCA 5769
8/04/56	#2	19	Canadian Sunset*	RCA 6537
			*released as by HUGO WINTERHALTER/EDDIE HEYWOOD	
			RUBY WINTERS	
2/08/69	#90	5	I Don't Want To Cry	Diamond 255
9/27/69	#95	1	Always David	Diamond 265
1/10/70	#69	4	Guess Who	Diamond 269
11/23/74	#95	3	Love Me Now	Polydor 14249
			STEVE WINWOOD	
8/12/67	#70	5	Paper Sun*	United Artists 50195
2/07/81	#10	19	While You See A Chance	Island 49656
5/16/81	#64	7	Arc Of A Diver	Island 49726
7/31/82	#44	11	Still In The Game	Island 29940
11/06/82	#76	6	Valerie	Island 29879
6/14/86	#1	22	Higher Love	Island 28710
9/27/86	#21	17	Freedom Overspill	Island 28595
2/07/87	#7	22	The Finer Things	Island 28498
5/30/87	#13	20	Back In The High Life Again	Island 28472
10/10/87	#9	21	Valerie	Island 28231
2/13/88	#59	10	Talking Back To The Night	Island 28122
6/11/88	#1	20	Roll With It	Virgin 99326
8/20/88	#5	18	Don't You Know What The Night Can Do?	Virgin 99290
11/26/88	#9	18	Holding On	Virgin 99261
3/18/89	#55	9	Hearts On Fire	Virgin 99234
11/03/90	#16	18	One And Only Man	Virgin 98892
			*released as by TRAFFIC featuring STEVIE WINWOOD	
			BILL WITHERS	
7/03/71	#4	18	Ain't No Sunshine	Sussex 219
10/30/71	#31	8	Grandma's Hands	Sussex 227
4/29/72	#1	18	Lean On Me	Sussex 235
8/19/72	#5	13	Use Me	Sussex 241
12/02/72	#42	8	Let Us Love	Sussex 247
2/03/73	#26	10	Kissing My Love	Sussex 250
4/13/74	#43	10	The Same Love That Made Me Laugh	Sussex 513
12/13/75	#67	11	Make Love To Your Mind	Columbia 10255
11/19/77	#23	15	Lovely Day	Columbia 10627
9/04/84	#54	10	In The Name Of Love*	Polydor 881221
			*released as by RALPH MacDONALD with BILL WITHERS	
			JIMMY WITHERSPOON	
2/13/65	#72	5	You're Next	Prestige 341
			CHARLES WOLCOTT	
11/05/60	#27	9	Ruby Duby Du From "Key Witness"	MGM 12944
			WOLF	
12/25/82	#80	6	Papa Was A Rolling Stone	Constellation 69849
			PETER WOLF	
7/14/84	#13	16	Lights Out	EMI America 8208
10/13/84	#40	10	I Need You Tonight	EMI America 8241
4/27/85	#67	6	Oo-Ee-Diddley-Bop!	EMI America 8254
2/28/87	#14	15	Come As You Are	EMI America 8350
5/23/87	#79	6	Can't Get Started	EMI America 43012
3/03/90	#59	8	99 Worlds	MCA 53726
			BOBBY WOMACK	
8/31/68	#80	6	Fly Me To The Moon	Minit 32048
12/07/68	#54	8	California Dreamin'	Minit 32055
12/20/69	#80	2	How I Miss You Baby	Minit 32081
4/11/70	#90	3	More Than I Can Stand	Minit 32093
11/20/71	#22	13	That's The Way I Feel About Cha*	United Artists 50847
4/22/72	#32	12	Woman's Gotta Have It	United Artists 50902
8/26/72	#42	9	Sweet Caroline*/	United Artists 50946
12/09/72	#25	12	Hairy Hippie*	United Artists 50988
3/17/73	#49	7	Across 110th Street*	United Artists 196
6/09/73	#30	15	Nobody Wants You When You're Down And Out	United Artists 255
2/09/74	#8	15	Lookin' For A Love	United Artists 375

Debut Date	Peak Pos	Wks Chr	ARTIST/Song Title	Label & Number
			BOBBY WOMACK—*continued*	
6/22/74	#53	10	You're Welcome, Stop On By	United Artists 439
4/19/75	#74	6	Check It Out	United Artists 621
3/27/76	#88	4	Daylight	United Artists 763
2/13/82	#90	6	If You Think You're Lonely Now	Beverly Glen 2000
3/31/84	#80	5	Love Has Finally Come At Last**	Beverly Glen 2012
			*released as by BOBBY WOMACK with PEACE	
			**released as by BOBBY WOMACK and PATTI LaBELLE	
			WOMBLES	
8/03/74	#59	7	Wombling Summer Party	Columbia 10013
			WOMENFOLK	
5/02/64	#96	3	Little Boxes	RCA 8301
			STEVIE WONDER	
6/22/63	#1	16	Fingertips (Part 2)*	Tamla 54080
10/05/63	#34	6	Workout Stevie, Workout*	Tamla 54086
3/14/64	#52	7	Castles In The Sand*	Tamla 54090
6/13/64	#32	8	Hey Harmonica Man	Tamla 54096
9/04/65	#54	6	High Heel Sneakers	Tamla 54119
12/11/65	#3	16	Uptight (Everything's Alright)	Tamla 54124
4/16/66	#20	7	Nothing's Too Good For My Baby/	Tamla 54130
7/02/66	#94	1	With A Child's Heart	Tamla 54130
7/16/66	#11	11	Blowin' In The Wind	Tamla 54136
11/12/66	#10	11	A Place In The Sun	Tamla 54139
3/04/67	#41	6	Travlin' Man/	Tamla 54147
4/22/67	#92	2	Hey Love	Tamla 54147
6/03/67	#2	16	I Was Made To Love Her	Tamla 54151
9/30/67	#10	9	I'm Wondering	Tamla 54157
4/06/68	#7	12	Shoo-Be-Doo-Be-Doo-Da-Day	Tamla 54165
7/13/68	#28	8	You Met Your Match	Tamla 54168
9/14/68	#73	6	Alfie**	Gordy 7076
11/02/68	#1	13	For Once In My Life	Tamla 54174
2/22/69	#41	4	I Don't Know Why/	Tamla 54180
5/31/69	#3	15	My Cherie Amour	Tamla 54180
10/18/69	#9	14	Yester-Me, Yester-You, Yesterday	Tamla 54188
1/31/70	#22	8	Never Had A Dream Come True	Tamla 54191
6/20/70	#1	14	Signed, Sealed, Delivered I'm Yours	Tamla 54196
10/17/70	#9	11	Heaven Help Us All	Tamla 54200
3/13/71	#9	12	We Can Work It Out	Tamla 54202
8/07/71	#9	14	If You Really Love Me	Tamla 54208
5/20/72	#32	11	Superwoman (Where Were You When I Needed You)	Tamla 54216
9/02/72	#76	5	Keep On Running	Tamla 54223
11/11/72	#1	16	Superstition	Tamla 54226
3/17/73	#1	14	You Are The Sunshine Of My Life	Tamla 54232
8/18/73	#1	13	Higher Ground	Tamla 54235
11/10/73	#6	15	Living For The City	Tamla 54242
3/30/74	#10	12	Don't You Worry 'Bout A Thing	Tamla 54245
8/10/74	#1	15	You Haven't Done Nothin	Tamla 54252
11/09/74	#1	17	Boogie On Reggae Woman	Tamla 54254
12/04/76	#1	19	I Wish	Tamla 54274
4/02/77	#1	16	Sir Duke	Tamla 54281
8/27/77	#36	9	Another Star	Tamla 54286
11/12/77	#69	10	As	Tamla 54291
1/20/79	#65	6	Pops, We Love You***	Motown 1455
11/03/79	#5	16	Send One Your Love	Tamla 54303
3/08/80	#55	6	Outside My Window	Tamla 54308
9/27/80	#1	24	Master Blaster (Jammin')	Tamla 54317
12/13/80	#13	21	I Ain't Gonna Stand For It	Tamla 54320
4/25/81	#88	3	Lately	Tamla 54323
1/16/82	#1	19	That Girl	Tamla 1602
4/10/82	#1	20	Ebony And Ivory****	Columbia 02860
5/29/82	#14	14	Do I Do	Tamla 1612
9/18/82	#57	9	Ribbon In The Sky	Tamla 1612
10/30/82	#48	13	Used To Be*****	Motown 1650
8/18/84	#1	24	I Just Called To Say I Love You	Motown 1745
12/01/84	#16	17	Love Light In Flight	Motown 1769
9/07/85	#1	21	Part-Time Lover	Tamla 1808
11/09/85	#1	26	That's What Friends Are For******	Arista 9422
11/23/85	#12	19	Go Home	Tamla 1817
2/22/86	#29	13	Overjoyed	Tamla 1832
6/14/86	#83	4	Land Of La La	Tamla 1846

Debut Date	Peak Pos	Wks Chr	ARTIST/Song Title	Label & Number
10/17/87	#32	15	Skeletons	Motown 1907
2/06/88	#87	5	You Will Know	Motown 1919
5/07/88	#84	5	Get It*******	Motown 1930
5/14/88	#82	7	My Love********	Columbia 07781
7/13/91	#83	6	Gotta Have You	Motown 2081
			*released as by LITTLE STEVIE WONDER	
			**released as by EIVETS REDNOW	
			***released as by DIANA ROSS, MARVIN GAYE, SMOKEY ROBINSON & STEVIE WONDER	
			****released as by PAUL McCARTNEY with STEVIE WONDER	
			*****released as by CHARLENE & STEVIE WONDER	
			******released as by DIONNE and FRIENDS: DIONNE WARWICK, ELTON JOHN, GLADYS KNIGHT and STEVIE WONDER	
			*******released as by STEVIE WONDER & MICHAEL JACKSON	
			********released as by JULIO IGLESIAS featuring STEVIE WONDER	
			WONDER WHO? (see FOUR SEASONS)	
			BOBBY WOOD	
6/27/64	#57	12	If I'm A Fool For Loving You	Joy 285
12/09/67	#96	2	Break My Mind	MGM 13797
			BRENTON WOOD	
4/29/67	#43	11	Oogum Boogum Song	Double Shot 111
8/19/67	#7	13	Gimme Little Sign	Double Shot 116
11/18/67	#55	10	Baby You Got It	Double Shot 121
			DEL WOOD	
10/27/51	#3	12	Down Yonder	Tempo 775
			LAUREN WOOD	
9/22/79	#31	13	Please Don't Leave	Warner Brothers 49043
			STEVIE WOODS	
10/10/81	#35	17	Steal The Night	Cotillion 46016
2/20/82	#65	7	Just Can't Win 'Em All	Cotillion 46030
5/15/82	#94	3	Fly Away	Cotillion 47006
			SHEB WOOLEY	
5/31/58	#1	14	The Purple People Eater	MGM 12651
12/27/58	#93	1	Santa And The Purple People Eater	MGM 12733
6/13/59	#54	5	Sweet Chile	MGM 12781
12/30/61	#47	12	That's My Pa	MGM 13046
12/01/62	#71	6	Don't Go Near The Eskimos*	MGM 13104
3/23/63	#100	1	Hello Walls #2*	MGM 13122
8/03/63	#93	2	Still #2*	MGM 13157
10/08/66	#51	6	Almost Persuaded #2*	MGM 13590
10/19/68	#86	5	Harper Valley P.T.A. (Later That Same Day)*	MGM 13997
			*released as by BEN COLDER	
			WOOLIES	
2/25/67	#82	5	Who Do You Love	Dunhill 4052
			WORLD OF OZ	
11/09/68	#94	3	King Croesus	Deram 85034
			WORLD PARTY	
3/07/87	#34	13	Ship Of Fools (Save Me From Tomorrow)	Chrysalis 43052
			MARION WORTH	
12/29/62	#47	9	Shake Me I Rattle (Squeeze Me I Cry)	Columbia 42640
			LINK WRAY & HIS RAY MEN	
4/26/58	#18	12	Rumble	Cadence 1347
2/07/59	#34	10	Raw-Hide	Epic 9300
5/25/63	#58	11	Jack The Ripper	Swan 4137
			WRECKX-N-EFFECT	
10/31/92	#2	29	Rump Shaker	MCA 54388
2/27/93	#79	6	Knock-N-Boots	MCA 54582
			BETTY WRIGHT	
8/03/68	#43	9	Girls Can't Do What The Guys Do	Alston 4569
7/24/71	#84	7	I Love The Way You Love Me	Alston 4594

BETTY WRIGHT

Debut Date	Peak Pos	Wks Chr	ARTIST/Song Title	Label & Number
			BETTY WRIGHT—*continued*	
11/20/71	#4	15	Clean Up Woman	Alston 4601
4/15/72	#98	2	If You Love Me Like You Say You Love Me	Alston 4609
9/30/72	#41	9	Baby Sitter	Alston 4614
3/31/73	#83	7	It's Hard To Stop	Alston 4617
10/13/73	#84	4	Let Me Be Your Lovemaker	Alston 4619
6/29/74	#48	9	Secretary	Alston 4622
4/12/75	#73	4	Where Is The Love	Alston 3713
3/18/78	#8	24	Dance With Me*	Drive 6269
9/08/79	#91	2	You Should Do It*	Drive 6272
			*released as by **PETER BROWN with BETTY WRIGHT**	
			CHARLES WRIGHT and THE WATTS 103RD STREET RHYTHM BAND	
9/09/67	#78	5	Spreadin' Honey*	Keymen 108
2/15/69	#14	14	Do Your Thing*	Warner Brothers 7250
6/28/69	#62	8	Till You Get Enough*	Warner Brothers 7298
3/28/70	#16	20	Love Land	Warner Brothers 7365
8/15/70	#17	14	Express Yourself	Warner Brothers 7417
1/02/71	#61	4	Solution For Pollution	Warner Brothers 7451
4/10/71	#56	8	Your Love (Means Everything To Me)	Warner Brothers 7475
7/24/71	#81	3	Nobody	Warner Brothers 7504
			*released as by **THE WATTS 103rd STREET RHYTHM BAND**	
			DALE WRIGHT	
1/25/58	#50	6	She's Neat*	Fraternity 792
			*released as by **DALE WRIGHT with THE ROCK-ITS**	
			GARY WRIGHT	
1/10/76	#1	21	Dream Weaver	Warner Brothers 8167
4/17/76	#3	23	Love Is Alive	Warner Brothers 8143
9/25/76	#97	3	Made To Love You	Warner Brothers 8250
3/05/77	#53	6	Phantom Writer	Warner Brothers 8331
7/04/81	#19	17	Really Wanna Know You	Warner Brothers 49769
			O.V. WRIGHT	
7/31/65	#74	7	You're Gonna Make Me Cry	Back Beat 548
4/15/67	#60	8	Eight Men And Four Women	Back Beat 580
11/21/70	#61	7	Ace Of Spades	Back Beat 615
			RUEBEN WRIGHT	
6/04/66	#92	1	I'm Walking Out On You	Capitol 5588
			WU-TANG CLAN	
10/30/93	#72	14	Method Man	Loud 62544
			BILL WYMAN	
12/09/67	#62	6	In Another Land	London 907
			TAMMY WYNETTE	
7/22/67	#96	3	My Elusive Dreams*	Epic 10194
6/29/68	#96	2	D-I-V-O-R-C-E	Epic 10315
11/23/68	#23	14	Stand By Your Man	Epic 10398
4/19/69	#77	4	Singing My Song	Epic 10462
9/20/69	#85	3	The Ways To Love A Man	Epic 10512
4/24/76	#91	3	'Til I Can Make It On My Own	Epic 50196
			*released as by **DAVID HOUSTON and TAMMY WYNETTE**	
			WYNONNA (Wynonna Judd)	
10/31/92	#85	6	No One Else On Earth	Curb 54449
7/03/93	#45	12	A Bad Goodbye*	RCA 62503
7/17/93	#72	7	Tell Me Why	Curb 54606
			*released as by **CLINT BLACK with WYNONNA**	

X

			XSCAPE	
10/02/93	#1	29	Just Kickin' It	So So Def 77119
			XTC	
4/29/89	#67	8	The Mayor Of Simpleton	Geffen 27552
			XYMOX	
3/10/90	#81	4	Imagination	Wing 873000

Debut Date	Peak Pos	Wks Chr	ARTIST/Song Title	Label & Number
			Y	
			Y&T	
7/13/85	#51	11	Summertime Girls	A&M 2748
			"WEIRD AL" YANKOVIC	
4/30/83	#58	9	Ricky	Rock 'n' Roll 03849
7/30/83	#78	4	I Love Rocky Road	Rock 'n' Roll 03998
3/10/84	#4	14	Eat It	Rock 'n' Roll 04374
5/05/84	#63	6	King Of Suede	Rock 'n' Roll 04451
6/22/85	#41	10	Like A Surgeon	Rock 'n' Roll 04937
5/28/88	#89	4	Fat	Rock 'n' Roll 07769
5/02/92	#22	17	Smells Like Nirvana	Scotti Brothers 75314
			ZALMAN YANOVSKY	
10/07/67	#63	4	As Long As You're Here	Buddah 12
			GLENN YARBROUGH	
3/27/65	#13	12	Baby The Rain Must Fall	RCA 8498
7/10/65	#66	7	It's Gonna Be Fine	RCA 8619
			YARBROUGH & PEOPLES	
1/31/81	#17	20	Don't Stop The Music	Mercury 76085
4/21/84	#45	11	Don't Waste Your Time	Total Experience 2400
6/28/86	#82	4	I Wouldn't Lie	Total Experience 2437
			YARDBIRDS	
5/08/65	#6	12	For Your Love	Epic 9790
7/31/65	#12	12	Heart Full Of Soul	Epic 9823
10/30/65	#25	9	I'm A Man	Epic 9857
3/12/66	#10	13	Shapes Of Things	Epic 10006
6/25/66	#12	12	Over Under Sideways Down	Epic 10035
11/26/66	#34	8	Happenings Ten Years Time Ago	Epic 10094
4/15/67	#48	8	Little Games	Epic 10156
8/12/67	#52	4	Ha Ha Said The Clown	Epic 10204
11/04/67	#71	5	Ten Little Indians	Epic 10248
			YAZ	
3/12/83	#69	6	Only You	Sire 29844
			TRISHA YEARWOOD	
12/04/93	#88	12	The Song Remembers When	MCA 54734
			YELLO	
8/15/87	#49	11	Oh Yeah	Mercury 884930
			YELLOW BALLOON	
4/08/67	#47	9	Yellow Balloon	Canterbury 508
7/08/67	#88	3	Good Feelin' Time	Canterbury 513
			YELLOW MAGIC ORCHESTRA	
2/09/80	#87	6	Computer Game "Theme From Circus"	Horizon 127
			YES	
10/02/71	#29	12	Your Move	Atlantic 2819
2/05/72	#10	14	Roundabout	Atlantic 2854
8/05/72	#44	7	America	Atlantic 2899
11/04/72	#32	8	And You And I (Part 1)	Atlantic 2920
11/05/83	#1	26	Owner Of A Lonely Heart	Atco 99817
3/03/84	#24	15	Leave It	Atco 99787
6/30/84	#62	8	It Can Happen	Atco 99745
10/03/87	#36	17	Love Will Find A Way	Atco 99449
12/26/87	#49	12	Rhythm Of Love	Atco 99419
5/18/91	#64	8	Lift Me Up	Arista 2218
			YIPES!!	
8/02/80	#71	5	Darlin'	Millenium 11791
			DWIGHT YOAKAM	
12/18/93	#79	10	Fast As You	Reprise 19341
			YONAH	
9/01/79	#97	3	After The First One	Free Flight 11696
			RUSTY YORK	
7/25/59	#64	4	Sugaree	Chess 1730
			DENNIS YOST	
3/29/75	#88	3	My First Day Without Her	MGM 14785

Debut Date	Peak Pos	Wks Chr	ARTIST/Song Title	Label & Number
			YOU KNOW WHO GROUP	
12/05/64	#46	8	Roses Are Red My Love	4 Corners 113
			BARRY YOUNG	
10/30/65	#21	12	One Has My Name (The Other Has My Heart)	Dot 16756
			FARON YOUNG	
4/15/61	#10	16	Hello Walls	Capitol 4533
9/30/61	#99	4	Backtrack	Capitol 4616
2/16/63	#92	4	The Yellow Bandana	Mercury 72085
			GEORGIE YOUNG and THE ROCKIN' BOCS	
10/04/58	#62	6	Nine More Miles	Cameo 150
			JOHN PAUL YOUNG	
12/20/75	#44	9	Yesterday's Hero	Ariola America 7607
7/15/78	#13	19	Love Is In The Air	Scotti Brothers 402
12/09/78	#68	8	Lost In Your Love	Scotti Brothers 405
			KAREN YOUNG	
9/30/78	#90	5	Hot Shot	West End 1211
			KATHY YOUNG with THE INNOCENTS	
10/29/60	#4	18	A Thousand Stars	Indigo 108
2/18/61	#30	11	Happy Birthday Blues	Indigo 115
			NEIL YOUNG	
6/20/70	#56	8	Cinnamon Girl*	Reprise 0911
10/31/70	#20	10	Only Love Can Break Your Heart	Reprise 0958
4/17/71	#93	1	When You Dance I Can Really Love	Reprise 0992
1/29/72	#1	15	Heart Of Gold	Reprise 1065
4/29/72	#26	8	Old Man	Reprise 1084
6/24/72	#52	5	War Song**	Reprise 1099
7/13/74	#54	8	Walk On	Reprise 1209
2/10/79	#69	6	Four Strong Winds	Reprise 1396
10/27/79	#94	3	Rust Never Sleeps (Hey Hey, My My)*	Reprise 49031
12/19/81	#77	7	Southern Pacific*	Reprise 49870
1/29/83	#76	6	Little Thing Called Love	Geffen 29887
			***released as by NEIL YOUNG & CRAZY HORSE**	
			****released as by NEIL YOUNG and GRAHAM NASH**	
			PAUL YOUNG	
10/15/83	#76	5	Wherever I Lay My Hat (That's My Home)	Columbia 04071
2/04/84	#29	17	Come Back And Stay	Columbia 04313
5/19/84	#50	11	Love Of The Common People	Columbia 04453
5/11/85	#1	24	Everytime You Go Away	Columbia 04867
9/07/85	#10	19	I'm Gonna Tear Your Playhouse Down	Columbia 05577
11/23/85	#47	12	Everything Must Change	Columbia 05712
11/15/86	#59	11	Some People	Columbia 06423
7/21/90	#6	22	Oh Girl	Columbia 73377
1/25/92	#8	22	What Becomes Of The Broken Hearted	MCA 54331
			VICTOR YOUNG	
8/19/50	#4	9	La Vie En Rose	Decca 24816
8/28/54	#3	9	The High And The Mighty	Decca 29203
5/25/57	#6	26	(Main Theme) Around The World	Decca 30262
			YOUNG & RESTLESS	
5/12/90	#56	8	"B" Girls	Pandisc 056
			YOUNG BLACK TEENAGERS	
5/01/93	#66	12	Tap The Bottle	Soul 54535
			SYDNEY YOUNGBLOOD	
9/01/90	#42	11	I'd Rather Go Blind	Arista 2055
			YOUNGBLOODS	
12/24/66	#48	9	Grizzly Bear	RCA 9015
9/09/67	#80	5	Get Together	RCA 9264
6/28/69	#4	18	Get Together	RCA 9752
11/15/69	#97	2	Sunlight	RCA 0270
5/09/70	#87	2	Darkness, Darkness	RCA 0342
			YOUNG HEARTS	
11/09/68	#83	3	I've Got Love For My Baby	Minit 32049
			YOUNG-HOLT UNLIMITED	
12/17/66	#53	8	Wack Wack*	Brunswick 55305
11/16/68	#4	13	Soulful Strut	Brunswick 55391

Debut Date	Peak Pos	Wks Chr	**ARTIST**/Song Title	Label & Number
2/22/69	#67	4	Who's Making Love	Brunswick 55400
7/26/69	#95	2	Straight Ahead	Brunswick 55417
			*released as by THE YOUNG HOLT TRIO	
			YOUNG MC	
9/23/89	#9	18	Bust A Move	Delicious Vinyl 105
12/02/89	#36	14	Principal's Office	Delicious Vinyl 99137
3/10/90	#55	9	I Come Off	Delicious Vinyl 98993
12/29/90	#83	8	Pick Up The Pace	Delicious Vinyl 6644
8/17/91	#66	9	That's The Way It Goes	Capitol 44740
			YOUNG RASCALS (see RASCALS)	
			YOUNG SISTERS	
9/29/62	#93	2	Casanova Brown	Twirl 2001
			YO-YO	
8/21/93	#74	6	The Bonnie And Clyde Theme	East West 98394
			TIMI YURO	
7/22/61	#4	14	Hurt	Liberty 55343
11/11/61	#39	7	Smile	Liberty 55375
2/10/62	#91	3	Let Me Call You Sweetheart	Liberty 55410
7/14/62	#15	12	What's A Matter Baby	Liberty 55469
12/01/62	#46	9	The Love Of A Boy	Liberty 55519
7/13/63	#23	12	Make The World Go Away	Liberty 55587
10/19/63	#71	6	Gotta Travel On	Liberty 55634
9/05/64	#92	2	If	Mercury 72316
			YUTAKA	
7/18/81	#82	3	Love Light	Alfa 7004
			YVONNE	
2/03/90	#89	4	There's A Party Going On	Cutting 228

Z

Debut Date	Peak Pos	Wks Chr	**ARTIST**/Song Title	Label & Number
			FLORIAN ZABACH	
8/25/56	#16	10	When The White Lilacs Bloom Again	Mercury 70936
			HELMUT ZACHARIAS and HIS MAGIC VIOLINS	
8/25/56	#16	13	When The White Lilacs Bloom Again	Decca 30039
1/24/59	#98	1	The Tipsy Piano	Decca 30795
			JOHN ZACHERLE	
3/15/58	#16	7	Dinner With Drac (Part 1)	Cameo 130
			PIA ZADORA	
4/10/82	#79	4	I'm In Love Again	Elektra 47428
2/12/83	#79	4	The Clapping Song	Elektra 69889
2/16/85	#48	10	When The Rain Begins To Fall*	Curb 52521
			*released as by JERMAINE JACKSON/PIA ZADORA	
			MICHAEL ZAGER BAND	
2/25/78	#25	16	Let's All Chant	Private Stock 45184
			ZAGER & EVANS	
6/14/69	#1	14	In The Year 2525 (Exordium & Terminus)	RCA 0174
10/11/69	#71	2	Mr. Turnkey	RCA 0246
12/27/69	#100	1	Listen To The People	RCA 0299
			ZAPP	
10/18/80	#88	6	More Bounce To The Ounce (Part 1)	Warner Brothers 49534
8/07/82	#68	7	Dance Floor (Part 1)	Warner Brothers 29961
8/21/93	#55	24	Mega Medley*	Reprise 18420
11/06/93	#29	22	Slow And Easy*	Reprise 18315
			*released as by ZAPP & ROGER	
			FRANK ZAPPA	
10/19/74	#62	6	Don't Eat The Yellow Snow	DiscReet 1312
4/14/79	#45	10	Dancin' Fool	Zappa 10
6/14/80	#98	3	I Don't Wanna Get Drafted	Zappa 1001
7/17/82	#44	18	Valley Girl*	Barking Pumpkin 03069
			*released as by FRANK ZAPPA/MOON UNIT ZAPPA	
			LENA ZAVARONI	
8/03/74	#81	4	Ma! (He's Making Eyes At Me)	Stax 0206
			DANNY ZELLA and HIS ZELL ROCKS	
11/15/58	#83	5	Wicked Ruby	Fox 10057

Debut Date	Peak Pos	Wks Chr	**ARTIST**/Song Title	Label & Number
			ZEBRA	
7/23/83	#70	6	Who's Behind The Door	Atlantic 89821
			SI ZENTNER	
11/11/61	#29	10	Up A Lazy River	Liberty 55374
			WARREN ZEVON	
3/25/78	#15	13	Werewolves Of London	Asylum 45472
3/15/80	#57	8	A Certain Girl	Asylum 46610
			ZHANE	
9/04/93	#5	31	Hey Mr. D.J.	Flavor Unit 77121
			PAT ZILL	
4/29/61	#96	4	Pick Me Up On Your Way Down	Indigo 119
			ZOMBIES	
10/03/64	#1	17	She's Not There	Parrot 9695
1/16/65	#6	11	Tell Her No	Parrot 9723
4/10/65	#48	5	She's Coming Home	Parrot 9747
7/03/65	#92	3	I Want You Back Again	Parrot 9769
2/08/69	#1	14	Time Of The Season	Date 1628
5/17/69	#77	3	Imagine The Swan	Date 1644
			ZWOL	
10/07/78	#81	6	New York City	EMI 8005
1/27/79	#95	3	Call Out My Name	EMI 8009
			ZZ TOP	
5/27/72	#81	5	Francene	London 179
4/13/74	#24	16	La Grange	London 203
7/19/75	#12	10	Tush	London 220
9/04/76	#46	14	It's Only Love	London 241
3/05/77	#74	5	Arrested For Driving While Blind	London 251
5/21/77	#82	4	Enjoy And Get It On	London 252
1/26/80	#43	10	I Thank You	Warner Brothers 49163
7/05/80	#90	3	Cheap Sunglasses	Warner Brothers 49220
9/26/81	#76	4	Leila	Warner Brothers 49782
4/02/83	#43	14	Gimme All Your Lovin'	Warner Brothers 29693
8/27/83	#83	4	Sharp Dressed Man	Warner Brothers 29576
5/19/84	#11	20	Legs	Warner Brothers 29272
10/19/85	#9	18	Sleeping Bag	Warner Brothers 28884
1/18/86	#22	15	Stages	Warner Brothers 28810
3/29/86	#22	14	Rough Boy	Warner Brothers 28733
7/26/86	#34	13	Velcro Fly	Warner Brothers 28650
5/19/90	#42	12	Double Back	Warner Brothers 19812
4/11/92	#49	16	Viva Las Vegas	Warner Brothers 18979

Song Title Index

A

"A" Team . . . . SSgt. Barry Sadler
Aba Daba Honeymoon . . . .
. . . . . . Carleton Carpenter & Debbie Reynolds
Abacab . . . . Genesis
Abadabadango . . . . Kim Carnes
ABC . . . . Jackson Five
ABC's Of Love . . . .
. . . . Frankie Lymon And The Teenagers
ABC-123 . . . . Levert
Abergavenny . . . . Shannon
Abigail Beecher . . . . Freddy Cannon
Abilene . . . . George Hamilton IV
About This Thing Called Love . . . . Fabian
Above The Stars . . . . Mr. Acker Bilk
Abra-Ca-Dabra . . . .
. . . . . DeFranco Family Featuring Tony DeFranco
Abracadabra . . . . Steve Miller Band
Abraham, Martin And John . . . . Dion
Abraham, Martin And John . . . . Miracles
Abraham, Martin And John . . . . . . Moms Mabley
Absolute Beginners . . . . David Bowie
Absolutely Right . . . . . Five Man Electrical Band
Ace Of Spades . . . . O.V. Wright
Achy Breaky Heart . . . . Billy Ray Cyrus
Across 110th Street . . . . Bobby Womack
Across The Miles . . . . Survivor
Across The River . . . Bruce Hornsby And The Range
Across The Street . . . . Lenny O'Henry
Across The Street . . . . Ray Peterson
Act Naturally . . . . Beatles
Action . . . . Freddy Cannon
Action . . . . Sweet
Action Speaks Louder Than Words . . . .
. . . . Chocolate Milk
Add Some Music To Your Day . . . . Beach Boys
Addams Groove . . . . Hammer
Addicted To Love . . . . Robert Palmer
Adios Amigo . . . . Jim Reeves
Adonis . . . . Terri Dean
Adonis . . . . Terri Stevens
Adrienne . . . . Tommy James
Adult Education . . . . . . Daryl Hall & John Oates
Advice For The Young At Heart . . . . Tears For Fears
Affair Of The Heart . . . . Rick Springfield
Affair To Remember (Our Love Affair) . . . .
. . . . Vic Damone
Africa . . . . Toto
African Waltz . . . . Cannonball Adderly
African Waltz . . . . Johnny Dankworth
Afrikaan Beat . . . . Bert Kaempfert
Afro Strut . . . . Nite-Liters
After All . . . . Al Jarreau
After All . . . . Cher And Peter Cetera
After All This Time . . . . Merry Clayton
After Loving You . . . . Della Reese
After Midnight . . . . Eric Clapton
After Midnight . . . . J.J. Cale
After Midnight . . . . Maggie Bell
After School . . . . Joy Layne
After School . . . . Randy Starr
After The Fall . . . . Journey
After The Feeling Is Gone . . . . . Five Flights Up
After The Feeling Is Gone . . . . Lulu
After The Fire . . . . Roger Daltry
After The Fire Is Gone . . . .
. . . . Loretta Lynn/Conway Twitty
After The First One . . . . Yonah
After The Glitter Fades . . . . Stevie Nicks

After The Goldrush . . . . Prelude
After The Lights Go Down Low . . . . . . Al Hibbler
After The Lights Go Down Low . . . George Maharis
After The Love Has Gone . . . . Earth, Wind & Fire
After The Lovin' . . . . Engelbert Humperdinck
After The Rain . . . . Nelson
After The Summer's Gone . . . . PC Quest
After You . . . . Dionne Warwick
Afternoon Delight . . . . Starland Vocal Band
Again . . . . Janet Jackson
Again . . . . Lettermen
Again Tonight . . . . John Mellencamp
Against All Odds . . . . Phil Collins
Against The Wind . . . . Bob Seger
Age For Love . . . . Jimmy Charles
Agent Double-O-Soul . . . . Edwin Starr
Agony And The Ecstasy . . . . . Smokey Robinson
Ah! Leah! . . . . Donnie Iris
Ahab, The Arab . . . . Ray Stevens
Ai No Corrida . . . . Quincy Jones
Aiming At Your Heart . . . . Temptations
Ain't 2 Proud To Beg . . . . TLC
Ain't Doing Too Bad (Part 1) . . . . Bobby Bland
Ain't Even Done With The Night . . . .
. . . . John Mellencamp
Ain't Gonna Be That Way . . . . . Marv Johnson
Ain't Gonna Bump No More (With No
  Big Fat Woman) . . . . Joe Tex
Ain't Gonna Cry No More . . . . Brenda Lee
Ain't Gonna Eat Out My Heart Anymore . . . . Angel
Ain't Gonna Hurt Nobody . . . . Brick
Ain't Gonna Kiss Ya . . . . Ribbons
Ain't Gonna Lie . . . . Keith
Ain't Gonna Rest (Till I Get You) . . . . Five Stairsteps
Ain't Gonna Tell Nobody . . . .
. . . . Jimmy Gilmer And The Fireballs
Ain't Got No Home . . . . Band
Ain't Got No Home . . . . Clarence Henry
Ain't Got Time . . . . Impressions
Ain't It A Sad Thing . . . . R. Dean Taylor
Ain't It A Shame . . . . Major Lance
Ain't It Baby . . . . Miracles
Ain't It Funky Now (Part 1) . . . . . . James Brown
Ain't It The Truth . . . . Mary Wells
Ain't It True . . . . Andy Williams
Ain't Love A Bitch . . . . Rod Stewart
Ain't No Love In The Heart Of The City . . . . . .
. . . . Bobby Bland
Ain't No Mountain High Enough . . . . . Diana Ross
Ain't No Mountain High Enough . . . .
. . . . Marvin Gaye & Tammi Terrell
Ain't No Stoppin' Us Now . . . .
. . . . McFadden & Whitehead
Ain't No Sunshine . . . . Bill Withers
Ain't No Way . . . . Aretha Franklin
Ain't No Way To Treat A Lady . . . . . Helen Reddy
Ain't No Woman (Like The One
  I've Got) . . . . Four Tops
Ain't Nobody . . . . Rufus And Chaka Khan
Ain't Nobody Home . . . . B.B. King
Ain't Nobody Home . . . . Howard Tate
Ain't Nobody Like You . . . . Miki Howard
Ain't Nothin' But A House Party . . . Show Stoppers
(Ain't Nothin' But A) Houseparty . . . J. Geils Band
Ain't Nothin' Goin' On But The Rent . . . .
. . . . Gwen Guthrie
Ain't Nothing Gonna Keep Me From You . . . .
. . . . Teri DeSario

389

Ain't Nothing Like The Real Thing . . . .
. . . . Aretha Franklin
Ain't Nothing Like The Real Thing . . . .
. . . . Donny And Marie Osmond
Ain't Nothing Like The Real Thing . . . .
. . . . Marvin Gaye & Tammi Terrell
Ain't Nothing You Can Do . . . . Bobby Bland
Ain't She Sweet . . . . Beatles
Ain't So Easy . . . . David & David
Ain't That A Groove (Part 1) . . . . James Brown
Ain't That A Shame . . . . Cheap Trick
Ain't That A Shame . . . . Fats Domino
Ain't That A Shame . . . . Four Seasons
Ain't That A Shame . . . . Pat Boone
Ain't That Just Like A Woman . . . . . . Fats Domino
Ain't That Just Like Me . . . . Searchers
Ain't That Love . . . . Harry Belafonte
Ain't That Lovin' You . . . . Luther Ingram
Ain't That Loving You . . . . Bobby Bland
Ain't That Loving You . . . . Isaac Hayes
Ain't That Loving You Baby . . . .
. . . . Betty Everett & Jerry Butler
Ain't That Loving You Baby . . . . Elvis Presley
Ain't That Peculiar . . . . Diamond Reo
Ain't That Peculiar . . . . Fanny
Ain't That Peculiar . . . . Marvin Gaye
Ain't Too Proud To Beg . . . . Rolling Stones
Ain't Too Proud To Beg . . . . Temptations
Ain't Understanding Mellow . . . .
. . . . Jerry Butler And Brenda Lee Eager
Ain't Wastin' Time No More . . . .
. . . . Allman Brothers Band
Air Disaster . . . . Albert Hammond
Air That I Breathe . . . . Hollies
Airplane Song (My Airplane) . . . . Royal Guardsmen
Airport Love Theme (Gwen And Vern) . . . .
. . . . Vincent Bell
Ajax Airlines . . . . Hudson And Landry
Ajax Liquor Store . . . . Hudson And Landry
Al Di La . . . . Connie Francis
Al Di La' . . . . Emilio Pericoli
Al-Di-La . . . . Ray Charles Singers
Alabam . . . . Cowboy Copas
Alabam . . . . Pat Boone
Alabama Getaway . . . . Grateful Dead
Alabama Wild Man . . . . Jerry Reed
Aladdin . . . . Bobby Curtola
Albatross . . . . Fleetwood Mac
Albert Flasher . . . . Guess Who
Alfie . . . . Cher
Alfie . . . . Dionne Warwick
Alfie . . . . Eivets Rednow (Stevie Wonder)
Alibis . . . . Sergio Mendes
Alice Everyday . . . . Book Of Love
Alice In Wonderland . . . . Neil Sedaka
Alice Long (You're Still My Favorite Girlfriend) . . .
. . . . Tommy Boyce & Bobby Hart
Alien . . . . Atlanta Rhythm Section
Alimony . . . . Frankie Ford
Alison . . . . Elvis Costello
Alive . . . . Bee Gees
Alive & Kicking . . . . Simple Minds
Alive Again . . . . Chicago
All . . . . James Darren
All About My Girl . . . . Jimmy McGriff
All About Soul . . . . Billy Joel
All Alone . . . . Terri Stevens
All Alone Am I . . . . Brenda Lee
All Along The Watchtower . . . .
. . . . Jimi Hendrix Experience
All American Boy . . . . Bobby Bare
All Around The World . . . . Lisa Stansfield
All By Myself . . . . Eric Carmen
All Cried Out . . . . Dusty Springfield

All Cried Out . . . . Lisa Lisa And Cult Jam
All Day And All Of The Night . . . . Kinks
All Day Music . . . . War
All Down The Line . . . . Rolling Stones
All Fall Down . . . . Five Star
All Fired Up . . . . Pat Benatar
All For Love . . . . Bryan Adams/Rod Stewart/Sting
All 4 Love . . . . Color Me Badd
All Grown Up . . . . Crystals
All His Children . . . .
. . . . Charley Pride With Henry Mancini
All I Could Do Was Cry . . . . Etta James
All I Ever Need Is You . . . . Sonny & Cher
All I Have . . . . Moments
All I Have To Do Is Dream . . . .
. . . . Andy Gibb And Victoria Principal
All I Have To Do Is Dream . . . .
. . . . Bobbie Gentry & Glen Campbell
All I Have To Do Is Dream . . . . . . Everly Brothers
All I Have To Do Is Dream . . . Nitty Gritty Dirt Band
All I Have To Do Is Dream . . . Richard Chamberlain
All I Have To Offer You (Is Me) . . . . Charley Pride
All I Know . . . . Art Garfunkel
All I Need . . . . Jack Wagner
All I Need . . . . Temptations
All I Need Is A Miracle . . . Mike + The Mechanics
All I Need Is Time . . . . . Gladys Knight & The Pips
All I Need Is You . . . . Blue Train
All I Need To Know . . . . Bette Midler
All I Really Want To Do . . . . Byrds
All I Really Want To Do . . . . Cher
All I See Is You . . . . Dusty Springfield
All I See Is Your Face . . . . Dan Hill
All I Wanna Do . . . . Doucette
All I Wanna Do Is Make Love To You . . . . . Heart
All I Want . . . . Howard Jones
All I Want . . . . Toad The Wet Sprocket
All I Want Is You . . . . Carly Simon
All I Want Is You U2
All I Wanted . . . . Kansas
All I'm Missing Is You . . . .
. . . . . Glenn Medeiros Featuring Ray Parker Jr.
All In Good Time . . . . Nelson Trio
All In Love Is Fair . . . . Barbra Streisand
All In My Mind . . . . Maxine Brown
All My Hard Times . . . . Joe Simon
All My Life . . . . Kenny Rogers
All My Life . . . .
. . . . . Linda Ronstadt Featuring Aaron Neville
All My Love . . . . Patti Page
All My Loving . . . . Beatles
All My Trials . . . . Ray Stevens
All Night Long . . . . Billy Squire
All Night Long . . . . Billy Vaughn
All Night Long . . . . Joe Walsh
All Night Long . . . . Lionel Richie
All Night Thing . . . . Invisible Man's Band
All Nite . . . . . Entouch Featuring Keith Sweat
(All Of A Sudden) My Heart Sings . . . . . Mel Carter
(All Of A Sudden) My Heart Sings . . . . . Paul Anka
All Of Everything . . . . Frankie Avalon
All Of Me For All Of You 9.9
All Of My Life . . . . Lesley Gore
All Of My Love . . . . Bobby Caldwell
All Of You . . . . Julio Iglesias & Diana Ross
All Or Nothing . . . . Milli Vanilli
All Or Nothing . . Patti LaBelle And The Blue Belles
All Our Tomorrows . . . . Eddie Schwartz
All Out Of Love . . . . Air Supply
All Over Again . . . . Johnny Cash
All Over Me . . . . Charlie Rich
All Over The World . . . . . Electric Light Orchestra
All Over The World . . . . Nat King Cole
All Right . . . . Christopher Cross

390

All Right Now . . . . Free
All Right Now . . . . Pepsi And Shirlie
All Right Now . . . . Rod Stewart
All She Wants . . . . Firehouse
All She Wants Is . . . . Duran Duran
All She Wants To Do Is Dance . . . . . Don Henley
All Shook Up . . . . Billy Joel
All Shook Up . . . . Elvis Presley
All Shook Up . . . . Suzi Quatro
All Strung Out . . . . . . Nino Tempo & April Stevens
All Strung Out On You . . . . John Travolta
All That Glitters Isn't Gold . . . . Cover Girls
All That I Am . . . . Elvis Presley
All That She Wants . . . . Ace Of Base
All The King's Horses . . . . Aretha Franklin
All The Kings Horses . . . . Firm
All The Love I've Got . . . . Marv Johnson
All The Love In The World . . . . Outfield
All The Man I Need . . . . Whitney Houston
All The Things She Said . . . . Simple Minds
All The Time . . . . Johnny Mathis
All The Time In The World . . . . Dr. Hook
All The Waiting Is Not In Vain . . . . . Tyrone Davis
All The Way . . . . Brick
All The Way . . . . Calloway
All The Way . . . . Frank Sinatra
All The Way Down . . . . Etta James
All The Way Lover . . . . Millie Jackson
All The Young Dudes . . . . . Mott The Hoople
All These Things . . . . Uniques
All Things Are Possible . . . . Dan Peek
All This I Should Have Known . . . . Breathe
All This Love . . . . DeBarge
All This Time . . . . Sting
All This Time . . . . Tiffany
All Those Lies . . . . Glenn Frey
All Those Years Ago . . . . George Harrison
All Through The Night . . . . Cyndi Lauper
All Time High . . . . Rita Coolidge
All Together Now . . . . Farm
All Touch . . . . Rough Trade
All True Man . . . . Alexander O'Neal
All Woman . . . . Lisa Stansfield
All You Get From Love Is A Love Song . . Carpenters
All You Need Is Love . . . . Beatles
All You Zombies . . . . Hooters
All You've Got . . . . RTZ
All Your Goodies Are Gone . . . . Parliaments
All's Quiet On West 23rd . . . . Julie Budd
Allegheny Moon . . . . Patti Page
Allentown . . . . Billy Joel
Allergies . . . . Paul Simon
Alley Cat . . . . Bent Fabric
Alley-Oop . . . . Dante And The Evergreens
Alley-Oop . . . . Hollywood Argyles
Allez-Vous-En . . . . Kay Starr
Alligator Boogaloo . . . . Lou Donaldson
Allnighter . . . . Glenn Frey
Ally Ally Oxen Free . . . . Kingston Trio
Almost Grown . . . . Chuck Berry
Almost Hear You Sigh . . . . Rolling Stones
Almost In Love . . . . Elvis Presley
Almost In Your Arms . . . . Johnny Nash
Almost Like Being In Love . . . . . Michael Johnson
Almost Over You . . . . Sheena Easton
Almost Paradise . . . . Lou Stein
Almost Paradise . . . . Norman Petty Trio
Almost Paradise . . . . Roger Williams
Almost Paradise...Love Theme From "Footloose" . .
 . . . . Mike Reno And Ann Wilson
Almost Persuaded . . . . David Houston
Almost Persuaded . . . . Etta James
Almost Persuaded #2 . . . . Sheb Wooley
Almost Saturday Night . . . . Dave Edmunds

Almost Saturday Night . . . . John Fogerty
Almost Summer . . . . Celebration
Almost Unreal . . . . Roxette
Almost There . . . . Andy Williams
Alone . . . . Four Seasons
Alone . . . . Heart
Alone Again . . . . Dokken
Alone Again (Naturally) . . . . . . Gilbert O'Sullivan
Alone At Last . . . . Jackie Wilson
Alone (Why Must I Be Alone) . . . . Shepherd Sisters
Alone With You . . . . Brenda Lee
Alone With You . . . . Tevin Campbell
Along Came Jones . . . . Coasters
Along Came Jones . . . . Ray Stevens
Along Comes A Woman . . . . Chicago
Along Comes Mary . . . . Association
Along Comes Mary . . . . Baja Marimba Band
Alphabet St. . . . . Prince
Already Gone . . . . Eagles
Alright . . . . Janet Jackson
Alright . . . . Kris Kross
Alright, Okay, You Win . . . . Peggy Lee
Also Sprach Zarathustra (2001) . . . . . . Deodato
Alvin For President . . . . Chipmunks
Alvin Stone . . . . Fantastic Four
Alvin Twist . . . . Chipmunks
Alvin's Boo-Ga-Loo . . . . Alvin Cash
Alvin's Harmonica . . . . Chipmunks
Alvin's Orchestra . . . . Chipmunks
Always . . . . Atlantic Starr
Always . . . . Firefall
Always . . . . Luther Ingram
Always . . . . Sammy Turner
Always And Forever . . . . Heatwave
Always And Forever . . . . Whistle
Always David . . . . Ruby Winters
Always In My Heart . . . . . Los Indios Tabajaras
Always On My Mind . . . . Pet Shop Boys
Always On My Mind . . . . Willie Nelson
Always Something There To Remind Me . . . .
 . . . . Naked Eyes
Always Something There To Remind Me . . . .
 . . . . R.B. Greaves
Always The Last To Know . . . . del Amitri
Always There For You . . . . Stryper
Always Together . . . . Al Martino
Always Together . . . . Dells
Always Tomorrow . . . . Gloria Estefan
Always With You . . . . Everly Brothers
Am I Black Enough For You . . . . Billy Paul
Am I Blue . . . . Cher
Am I Grooving You . . . . Freddie Scott
Am I Losing You . . . . Jim Reeves
Am I Losing You . . . . Manhattans
Am I Losing You . . . . Partridge Family
Am I That Easy To Forget . . . . Debbie Reynolds
Am I That Easy To Forget . . . .
 . . . . Engelbert Humperdinck
Am I That Easy To Forget . . . . . . Esther Phillips
Am I The Man . . . . Jackie Wilson
Am I The Same Girl . . . . Barbara Acklin
Am I The Same Girl . . . . Swing Out Sister
Amanda . . . . Boston
Amanda . . . . Waylon Jennings
Amapola . . . . Jacky Noguez
Amarillo . . . . Neil Sedaka
Amazing . . . . Aerosmith
Amazing Grace . . . . Amazing Rhythm Aces
Amazing Grace . . . . Judy Collins
Amazing Grace . . . . . Royal Scots Dragoon Guards
Amber Cascades . . . . America
Ambrose (Part Five) . . . . Linda Laurie
Ame Caline (Soul Coaxing) . . . . . Raymond Lefevre
Amen . . . . Impressions

391

Amen . . . . Otis Redding
America . . . . Neil Diamond
America . . . . Prince And The Revolution
America . . . . Yes
America, Communicate With Me . . . . Ray Stevens
America Is My Home (Part 1) . . . . . . James Brown
America The Beautiful . . . . Charlie Rich
American Boys . . . . Petula Clark
American City Suite . . . . Cashman & West
American Dream . . . . Crosby, Stills, Nash & Young
American Dream . . . . Dirt Band
American Dream . . . . Simon F.
American Girls . . . . Rick Springfield
American Heartbeat . . . . Survivor
American Memories . . . . Shamus M'Cool
American Music . . . . Pointer Sisters
American Pie (Parts 1 & 2) . . . . Don McLean
American Storm . . . .
. . . . Bob Seger & The Silver Bullet Band
American Trilogy . . . . Elvis Presley
American Trilogy . . . . Mickey Newbury
American Tune . . . . Paul Simon
American Woman . . . . Guess Who
Americans . . . . Byron MacGregor
Americans (A Canadian's Opinion) . . . .
. . . . Gordon Sinclair
America/Standing/Because I Love You . . . .
. . . . Five Stairsteps
Amerikan Music . . . . Steve Alaimo
Amie . . . . Pure Prairie League
Amnesia . . . . Shalamar
Among My Souvenirs . . . . Connie Francis
Amor . . . . Ben E. King
Amor . . . . Roger Williams
Amos Moses . . . . Jerry Reed
Amy . . . . Paul Petersen
Anaheim, Azusa & Cucamonga Sewing
  Circle, Book Review And Timing
  Association . . . . Jan & Dean
Anastasia . . . . Pat Boone
Anchorage . . . . Michelle Shocked
And Get Away . . . . Esquires
And I Love Her . . . . Beatles
And I Love Her . . . . George Martin
And I Love Him . . . . Esther Phillips
And I Love You So . . . . Bobby Goldsboro
And I Love You So . . . . Perry Como
And I'm Telling You I'm Not Going . . . .
. . . . Jennifer Holliday
And Love Goes On . . . . Earth, Wind & Fire
And My Heart Sang (Tra La La) . . . .
. . . . Brenda & The Tabulations
And Now . . . . Della Reese
And Roses And Roses . . . . Andy Williams
And She Was . . . . Talking Heads
And She's Mine . . . . . . Spanky And Our Gang
And So It Goes . . . . Billy Joel
And So To Sleep Again . . . . Patti Page
And Suddenly . . . . Cherry People
And That Reminds Me . . . . Della Reese
And That Reminds Me . . . . Four Seasons
And The Beat Goes On . . . . Whispers
And The Cradle Will Rock . . . . Van Halen
And The Grass Won't Pay No Mind . . Mark Lindsay
And The Heavens Cried . . . . Ronnie Savoy
And The Night Stood Still . . . . Dion
And Then There Were Drums . . . . . . Sandy Nelson
And We Danced . . . . Hooters
And When I Die . . . . Blood, Sweat & Tears
And You And I (Part 1) . . . . Yes
Andrea . . . . Sunrays
Angel . . . . Aerosmith
Angel . . . . Aretha Franklin
Angel . . . . Atlanta Rhythm Section

Angel . . . . Johnny Tillotson
Angel . . . . Jon Secada
Angel . . . . Madonna
Angel . . . . Rod Stewart
Angel Baby . . . . Angelica
Angel Baby . . . . Dean Martin
Angel Baby . . . . Dusk
Angel Baby . . . . . . Rosie And The Originals
Angel Eyes . . . . Abba
Angel Eyes . . . . Jeff Healey Band
Angel Face . . . . James Darren
Angel In Blue . . . . J. Geils Band
Angel In My Pocket . . . . One To One
Angel In Your Arms . . . . Hot
Angel Of Harlem U2
Angel Of The Morning . . . . Bettye Swann
Angel Of The Morning . . . . Juice Newton
Angel Of The Morning . . . .
. . . . Merrilee Rush And The Turnabouts
Angel On My Shoulder . . . . Shelby Flint
Angel Say No . . . . Tommy Tutone
Angel Smile . . . . Nat King Cole
Angel Song . . . . Great White
Angela Jones . . . . Johnny Ferguson
Angelia . . . . Richard Marx
Angelica . . . . Barry Mann
Angelica . . . . Oliver
Angeline . . . . Allman Brothers Band
Angelito . . . . Rene & Rene
Angels Listened In . . . . Crests
Angie . . . . Rolling Stones
Angie Baby . . . . Helen Reddy
Animal . . . . Def Leppard
Animal House . . . . Stephen Bishop
Animal Instinct . . . . Commodores
Animal Trainer And The Toad . . . . Mountain
Animal Zoo . . . . Spirit
Anna . . . . Jorgen Ingmann
Anna . . . . Originals
Anna . . . . Silvanna Mangano
Anna (Go To Him) . . . . Arthur Alexander
Annabella . . . . . Hamilton, Joe Frank & Reynolds
Annabelle . . . . Daniel Boone
Annie Fanny . . . . Kingsmen
Annie Get Your Yo-Yo . . . . . . Little Junior Parker
Annie's Song . . . . John Denver
Anniversary . . . . Tony! Toni! Tone!
Anniversary Of Love . . . . Caslons
Ann-Marie . . . . Belmonts
Another Brick In The Wall (Part 2) . . . . . Pink Floyd
Another Cup Of Coffee . . . . Brook Benton
Another Day . . . . Paul McCartney
Another Day, Another Heartache . . . Fifth Dimension
Another Day In Paradise . . . . Phil Collins
Another Heartache . . . . Rod Stewart
Another Like My Lover . . . . Jasmine Guy
Another Love . . . . Stories
Another Lover . . . . Giant Steps
Another Minute . . . . Cause & Effect
Another Night . . . . Aretha Franklin
Another Night . . . . Dionne Warwick
Another One Bites The Dust . . . . Queen
Another Page . . . . Connie Francis
Another Park, Another Sunday . . . Doobie Brothers
Another Part Of Me . . . . Michael Jackson
Another Puff . . . . Jerry Reed
Another Rainy Day In New York City . . . . Chicago
Another Rainy Night (Without You) . . . Queensryche
Another Sad Love Song . . . . Toni Braxton
Another Saturday Night . . . . Cat Stevens
Another Saturday Night . . . . Sam Cooke
Another Sleepless Night . . . . Anne Murray
Another Sleepless Night . . . . Jimmy Clanton
Another Star . . . . Stevie Wonder

392

393

At Midnight (My Love Will Lift You Up) . . . . Rufus Featuring Chaka Khan
At My Front Door . . . . Dee Clark
At My Front Door . . . . El Dorados
At My Front Door (Crazy Little Mama) . . . Pat Boone
At Seventeen . . . . Janis Ian
At The Club . . . . Drifters
At The Club . . . . Ray Charles
At The Darktown Strutters' Ball . . . . . . Lou Monte
At The Hop . . . . Danny & The Juniors
At The Party . . . . Hector Rivera
At The Scene . . . . Dave Clark Five
At The Top Of The Stairs . . . . Formations
At The Zoo . . . . Simon & Garfunkel
At This Moment . . . . Billy & The Beaters
Athena . . . . Who
Atlanta Lady . . . . Marty Balin
Atlantis . . . . Donovan
Atomic . . . . Blondie
Attack . . . . Toys
Attack Of The Name Game . . . . . . Stacy Lattisaw
Attitude Dancing . . . . Carly Simon
Aubrey . . . . Bread
Auctioneer . . . . Leroy Van Dyke
Auf Wiederseh'n Sweetheart . . . . . . Vera Lynn
Aunt Dora's Love Soul Shack . . . . . Arthur Conley
Authority Song . . . . . . John Cougar Mellencamp
Autobahn . . . . Kraftwerk
Autograph . . . . John Denver
Automatic . . . . Pointer Sisters
Automatic Man . . . . Michael Sembello
Automatically Sunshine . . . . Supremes
Autumn Leaves . . . . Roger Williams
Autumn Of My Life . . . . Bobby Goldsboro
Avenging Annie . . . . Andy Pratt
Avenging Annie . . . . Roger Daltry
Aw Shucks, Hush Your Mouth . . . . . Jimmy Reed
Awaiting On You All . . . . Silver Hawk
Award Tour . . . . Tribe Called Quest
Axel F . . . . Harold Faltermeyer

B

"B" Girls . . . . Young & Restless
B'wa Nina (Pretty Girl) . . . . Tokens
Babe . . . . Styx
B-A-B-Y . . . . Carla Thomas
Baby Baby . . . . Amy Grant
Baby Baby . . . . Eighth Wonder
Baby Baby All The Time . . . . Superbs
Baby Baby Baby . . . . Anna King/Bobby Byrd
Baby, Baby, Baby . . . . Sam Cooke
Baby, Baby Don't Cry . . . . Miracles
Baby, Baby I Love You . . . . Terry Cashman
Baby, Baby, My Love's All For You . . . . Deniece Williams
Baby Be Mine . . . . Jelly Beans
Baby Blue . . . . Badfinger
Baby Blue . . . . Echoes
Baby Boy . . . . Mary Kay Place
Baby Can I Hold You . . . . Tracy Chapman
Baby Come And Get It . . . . Pointer Sisters
Baby Come Back . . . . Billy Rankin
Baby, Come Back . . . . Equals
Baby Come Back . . . . Player
Baby Come Close . . . . Smokey Robinson
Baby Come Home . . . . . Ruby And The Romantics
Baby Come On Home . . . . Solomon Burke
Baby, Come To Me . . . . Patti Austin With James Ingram
Baby Come To Me . . . . Regina Belle
Baby, Do The Philly Dog . . . . Olympics
Baby Doll . . . . Andy Williams
Baby, Don't Be Looking In My Mind . . . . Joe Simon

Baby Don't Change Your Mind . . . . Gladys Knight & The Pips
Baby Don't Forget My Number . . . . . Milli Vanilli
Baby Don't Get Hooked On Me . . . . . . Mac Davis
Baby Don't Go . . . . Karla Bonoff
Baby Don't Go . . . . Sonny & Cher
Baby, Don't You Cry . . . . Ray Charles
Baby Don't You Do It . . . . Marvin Gaye
Baby Don't You Know . . . . Wild Cherry
Baby Don't You Weep . . . . Garnet Mimms & The Enchanters
Baby Elephant Walk . . . . Lawrence Welk
Baby Face . . . . Bobby Darin
Baby Face . . . . Bobby Vee
Baby Face . . . . Little Richard
Baby Face . . . . Wing & A Prayer Fife & Drum Corps
Baby Fat . . . . Robert Byrne
Baby Get It (And Don't Quit It) . . . . . Jackie Wilson
Baby Get It On . . . . Ike & Tina Turner
Baby Got Back . . . . Sir Mix-A-Lot
Baby Grand . . . . . . Billy Joel Featuring Ray Charles
Baby, Hang Up The Phone . . . . Carl Graves
Baby Has Gone Bye Bye . . . . . . George Maharis
Baby, Help Me . . . . Percy Sledge
Baby Hold On . . . . Eddie Money
Baby Hold On . . . . Grass Roots
Baby Hold On To Me . . . . Gerald Levert With Eddie Levert
(Baby) Hully Gully . . . . Olympics
Baby, I Beleive In You . . . . George Lamond
Baby I Do Love You . . . . Galens
Baby I Lied . . . . Deborah Allen
Baby, I Love You . . . . Andy Kim
Baby I Love You . . . . Aretha Franklin
Baby I Love You . . . . Little Milton
Baby, I Love You . . . . Ronettes
Baby, I Love Your Way . . . . . . Peter Frampton
Baby I Love Your Way/Freebird Medley . . . . Will To Power
Baby I Need You . . . . Manhattans
Baby, I Need Your Lovin' . . . . Eric Carmen
Baby I Need Your Lovin' . . . . Johnny Rivers
Baby I Need Your Loving . . . . Four Tops
Baby I Need Your Loving . . . . O.C. Smith
Baby I Want You . . . . Funky Communications Committee
Baby, I'll Give It To You . . . . Seals & Crofts
Baby I'm A Want You . . . . Bread
Baby, I'm Burnin' . . . . Dolly Parton
Baby, I'm For Real . . . . Originals
Baby I'm For Real/Natural High . . . . . . After 7
Baby I'm Lonely . . . . Intruders
Baby, I'm Yours . . . . Barbara Lewis
Baby, I'm Yours . . . . Jody Miller
Baby I'm Yours . . . . Shai
Baby I've Been Missing You . . . . . Independents
Baby, Is There Something On Your Mind . . . . McKinley Travis
Baby, It's Tonight . . . . Jude Cole
Baby It's You . . . . Shirelles
Baby It's You . . . . Smith
Baby Jane . . . . Rod Stewart
Baby Let Me Kiss You . . . . King Floyd
Baby Let Me Take You (In My Arms) . . . . Detroit Emeralds
Baby Let's Wait . . . . Royal Guardsmen
Baby Love . . . . Mother's Finest
Baby Love . . . . Regina
Baby Love . . . . Supremes
Baby Make It Soon . . . . Flying Machine
Baby Make Your Own Sweet Music . . . . Jay And The Techniques
Baby Makes Her Blue Jeans Talk . . . . . . Dr. Hook
Baby, Now That I've Found You . . . . . Foundations

Ballad Of The Green Berets . . . . SSgt. Barry Sadler	Be Anything (But Be Mine) . . . . . . Connie Francis
Ballad Of Thunder Road . . . . Robert Mitchum	Be Anything (But Be Mine) . . . . Gloria Lynne
Ballad Of Two Brothers . . . . Autry Inman	Be Careful Of Stones That You Throw . . . . . Dion
Ballad Of Waterhole #3 . . . . Roger Miller	Be Good To My Baby . . . . Luther Ingram
Ballad Of You & Me & Pooneil . . Jefferson Airplane	Be Good To Yourself . . . . Journey
Ballad Of Youth . . . . Richie Sambora	Be Mad Little Girl . . . . Bobby Darin
Ballerina . . . . Nat King Cole	Be Mine Tonight . . . . Neil Diamond
Ballerina Girl . . . . Lionel Richie	Be My Baby . . . . Andy Kim
Ballero . . . . War	Be My Baby . . . . Cissy Houston
Ballroom Blitz . . . . Sweet	Be My Baby . . . . Dick And Deedee
Bamboo . . . . Vaughn Monroe	Be My Baby . . . . Ronettes
Banana Boat (Day-O) . . . . . . Harry Belafonte	Be My Boy . . . . Paris Sisters
Banana Boat (Day-O) . . . . Stan Freberg	Be My Girl . . . . Dramatics
Banana Boat Song . . . . Fontane Sisters	Be My Girl . . . . Four-Evers
Banana Boat Song . . . . Sarah Vaughan	Be My Guest . . . . Fats Domino
Banana Boat Song . . . . Steve Lawrence	Be My Lady . . . . Jefferson Starship
Banana Boat Song . . . . Tarriers	Be My Lady . . . . Meters
Banapple Gas . . . . Cat Stevens	Be My Life's Companion . . . . Mills Brothers
Band Of Gold . . . . Don Cherry	Be My Love . . . . Mario Lanza
Band Of Gold . . . . Freda Payne	Be My Lover . . . . Alice Cooper
Band Of Gold . . . . Mel Carter	Be Near Me . . . . ABC
Band Of Gold . . . . Roommates	Be Nice To Me . . . . Runt
Band On The Run . . . . . . Paul McCartney & Wings	Be Still My Beating Heart . . . . Sting
Banda . . . . Herb Alpert & The Tijuana Brass	Be Thankful For What You Got . . William DeVaughn
Bandit Of My Dreams . . . . Eddie Hodges	Be There . . . . Pointer Sisters
Bang A Gong (Get It On) . . . . T. Rex	Be True To Your School . . . . Beach Boys
Bang Bang . . . . Danger Danger	Be True To Yourself . . . . Bobby Vee
Bang Bang . . . . David Sanborn	Be What You Are . . . . Staple Singers
Bang Bang . . . . Joe Cuba Sextet	Be With You . . . . Bangles
Bang Bang (My Baby Shot Me Down) . . . . . . Cher	Be Young, Be Foolish, Be Happy . . . . Tams
Bang The Drum All Day . . . . Todd Rundgren	Be Your Man . . . . Jesse Johnson
Bang Your Head (Metal Health) . . . . . . Quiet Riot	Beach Baby . . . . First Class
Bangla-Desh . . . . George Harrison	Beach Boys Medley . . . . Beach Boys
Bang-Shang-A-Lang . . . . Archies	Beach Girl . . . . Pat Boone
Banjo Boy . . . . Art Mooney	Beach Party . . . . King Curtis
Banjo Boy . . . . Dorothy Collins	Beach Time . . . . Roger Smith
Banjo Boy . . . . Jan And Kjeld	Beachcomber . . . . Bobby Darin
Banks Of The Ohio . . . . Olivia Newton-John	Beans In My Ears . . . . Serendipity Singers
Banned In Boston . . . . Merv Griffin	Beast Of Burden . . . . Bette Midler
Banned In The U.S.A. . . . Luke Featuring 2 Live Crew	Beast Of Burden . . . . Rolling Stones
Banzai Pipeline . . . . Henry Mancini	Beat . . . . Rockin' R's
Barbara . . . . Temptations	Beat Goes On . . . . Lawrence Welk
Barbara Ann . . . . Beach Boys	Beat Goes On . . . . Sonny & Cher
Barbara Ann . . . . Regents	Beat It . . . . Michael Jackson
Barbara I Love You . . . . New Colony Six	Beat Me Daddy Eight To The Bar . . . .
Barefoot In Baltimore . . . . . Strawberry Alarm Clock	. . Commander Cody And His Lost Planet Airmen
Barefootin' . . . . Robert Parker	Beat Of A Heart . . . . Scandal Featuring Patty Smyth
Baretta's Theme ("Keep Your Eye On	Beat Patrol . . . . Starship
The Sparrow") . . . . Rhythm Heritage	Beat The Clock . . . . McCoys
Baroque-A-Nova . . . . Mason Williams	Beat's So Lonely . . . . Charlie Sexton
Barracuda . . . . Alvin Cash	Beatin Up In Love Again . . . . Doves
Barracuda . . . . Heart	Beatnik Fly . . . . Johnny And The Hurricanes
Basketball . . . . Kurtis Blow	Beats There A Heart So True . . . . . . Perry Como
Basketball Jones . . . . Cheech & Chong	Beaucoups Of Blues . . . . Ringo Starr
Batdance . . . . Prince	Beautician Blues . . . . B.B. King
Batman . . . . Jan & Dean	Beautiful . . . . Gordon Lightfoot
Batman & His Grandmother . . . . . Dickie Goodman	Beautiful Brown Eyes . . . . Jimmy Wakely
Batman Theme . . . . Marketts	Beautiful Brown Eyes . . . . Rosemary Clooney
Batman Theme . . . . Neal Hefti	Beautiful Girl . . . . Inxs
Battle . . . . Duane Eddy	Beautiful Girls . . . . Van Halen
Battle Hymn Of Lt. Calley	Beautiful Morning . . . . Young Rascals
. . . . C Company Featuring Terry Nelson	Beautiful Obsession . . . . Sir Chauncey
Battle Hymn Of The Republic . . . . Andy Williams	Beautiful People . . . . Bobby Vee
Battle Hymn Of The Republic	Beautiful People . . . . Kenny O'Dell
. . . . Mormon Tabernacle Choir	Beautiful People . . . . New Seekers
Battle Of Kookamonga . . . . . . Homer And Jethro	Beautiful Story . . . . Sonny & Cher
Battle Of New Orleans . . . . Bert Sommer	Beautiful Sunday . . . . Daniel Boone
Battle Of New Orleans . . . . Johnny Horton	Beauty And The Beast . . . .
Battle Of New Orleans . . . . Nitty Gritty Dirt Band	. . . . Celine Dion And Peabo Bryson
Baubles, Bangles And Beads . . . . Kirby Stone Four	Beauty Is Only Skin Deep . . . . Temptations
B.B. Jones . . . . B.B. King	Be-Bop Baby . . . . Ricky Nelson
B.B.D. (I Thought It Was Me)? . . . . Bell Biv DeVoe	Be-Bop-A-Lula . . . . Everly Brothers
Be . . . . Neil Diamond	Be-Bop-A-Lula . . . Gene Vincent And His Blue Caps
Be Anything . . . . Eddy Howard Orchestra	Because . . . . Dave Clark Five

Big Draft . . . . Four Preps	Bitch Is Back . . . . Elton John
Big Fun . . . . Kool & The Gang	Bite Your Lip . . . . Elton John
Big Girls Don't Cry . . . . Four Seasons	Bits And Pieces . . . . Dave Clark Five
Big Guitar . . . . Owen Bradley Quintet	Bitter Bad . . . . Melanie
Big Guitar . . . . Sam "The Man" Taylor	Bitter Tears . . . . Inxs
Big Gun . . . . AC/DC	Black & White . . . . Three Dog Night
Big Hunk O' Love . . . . Elvis Presley	Black And Blue . . . . Van Halen
Big Hurt . . . . Del Shannon	Black Berries (Part 1) . . . . Isley Brothers
Big Hurt . . . . Miss Toni Fisher	Black Betty . . . . Ram Jam
Big In Japan . . . . Alphaville	Black Byrd . . . . Donald Byrd
Big In Vegas . . . . Buck Owens	Black Cars . . . . Gino Vannelli
Big Iron . . . . Marty Robbins	Black Cat . . . . Janet Jackson
Big John . . . . Shirelles	Black Cloud . . . . Chubby Checker
Big Leg Woman . . . . Israel Tolbert	Black Dog . . . . Led Zeppelin
Big Log . . . . Robert Plant	Black Dog . . . . Newcity Rockers
Big Love . . . . Fleetwood Mac	Black Fox . . . . Freddy Robinson
Big Love . . . . Joe Henderson	Black Friday . . . . Steely Dan
Big Man . . . . Four Preps	Black Hands White Cotton . . . . Caboose
Big Man In Town . . . . Four Seasons	Black Is Black . . . . Los Bravos
Big Mistake . . . . Peter Cetera	Black Kisses (Never Make You Blue) . . . .
Big Money . . . . Rush	. . . . . . Curtie And The Boombox
Big Name Button . . . . Royal Teens	Black Knight . . . . Lowell Fulsom
Big Noise From Winnetka . . . . . . Spaghetti Head	Black Land Farmer . . . . Frankie Miller
Big River . . . . Buddy Brennan Quartet	Black Land Farmer . . . . Wink Martindale
Big Shot . . . . Billy Joel	Black Lassie . . . . Cheech & Chong
Big Talk . . . . Warrant	Black Magic Woman . . . . Santana
Big Time . . . . Peter Gabriel	Black Night . . . . Deep Purple
Big Time Operator . . . . Keith Hampshire	Black Or White . . . . Michael Jackson
Big Town Boy . . . . Shirley Matthews	Black Pearl . . . .
Big Wide World . . . . Teddy Randazzo	. . . . . . Sonny Charles And The Checkmates Ltd.
Big Yellow Taxi . . . . Neighborhood	Black Seeds Keep On Growing . . . . Main Ingredient
Big Yellow Taxi (live version) . . . . . Joni Mitchell	Black Sheep . . . . . Sam The Sham And The Pharaohs
Big Yellow Taxi (studio version) . . . . . Joni Mitchell	Black Slacks . . . . Joe Bennett And The Sparkletones
Bigfoot . . . . Bro Smith	Black Stations/White Stations . . . . M+M
Biggest Parakeets In Town . . . . Jud Strunk	Black Superman - "Muhammad Ali" . . . .
Biggest Part Of Me . . . . Ambrosia	. . . . . . Johnny Wakelin & The Kinshasa Band
Biggest Sin . . . . Connie Francis	Black Velvet . . . . Alannah Myles
Bikini . . . . Bikinis	Black Water . . . . Doobie Brothers
Bilbao Song . . . . Andy Williams	Black-Eyed Blues . . . . Joe Cocker
Billie Jean . . . . Michael Jackson	Black-Eyed Boys . . . . Paper Lace
Billion Dollar Babies . . . . Alice Cooper	Blackjack . . . . Rupert Holmes
Billy . . . . Kathy Linden	Blacksmith Blues . . . . Ella Mae Morse
Billy And Sue . . . . B.J. Thomas	Blah, Blah, Blah . . . . Nicola Paone
Billy Boy's Tune . . . . Three Graces	Blame It On Love . . . .
Billy, Don't Be A Hero	. . . . . . Smokey Robinson And Barbara Mitchell
. . . . . . Bo Donaldson And The Heywoods	Blame It On The Boogie . . . . Jacksons
Billy, Don't Be A Hero . . . . Paper Lace	Blame It On The Boogie . . . . Mick Jackson
Billy Goat . . . . Bill Haley And His Comets	Blame It On The Bossa Nova . . . . . . Eydie Gorme
Billy I've Got To Take My Love To	Blame It On The Rain . . . . Milli Vanilli
Town World . . . . Geraldine Stevens	Blanket On The Ground . . . . Billie Jo Spears
Billy You're My Friend . . . . Gene Pitney	Blaze Of Glory . . . . Jon Bon Jovi
Bimbombey . . . . Jimmie Rodgers	Blaze Of Glory . . . . Kenny Rogers
Biology . . . . Danny Valentino	Bless Our Love . . . . Gene Chandler
Biology . . . . Sue Raney	Bless You . . . . Martha & The Vandellas
Biplane Evermore . . . . Irish Rovers	Bless You . . . . Tony Orlando
Bird . . . . Time	Blessed Are The Believers . . . . Anne Murray
Bird Dance Beat . . . . Trashmen	Blessed Is The Rain . . . . Brooklyn Bridge
Bird Dog . . . . Everly Brothers	Blind Faith . . . . Warrant
Bird Has Flown . . . . Deep Purple	Blind Man . . . . Bobby Bland
Bird Man . . . . Highwaymen	Blind Man . . . . Little Milton
Bird On My Head . . . . David Seville	Blind Man In The Bleachers . . . . . . Kenny Starr
Bird's The Word . . . . Rivingtons	Blinded By Love . . . . Rythm Syndicate
Birdland . . . . Chubby Checker	Blinded By The Light . . Manfred Mann's Earth Band
Birds And The Bees . . . . Jewel Akens	Blistered . . . . Johnny Cash
Birds Are For The Bees . . . . Newbeats	Blizzard . . . . Jim Reeves
Birds Of A Feather . . . . Joe South	Bloat On . . . . Cheech & Chong
Birds Of A Feather . . . . Raiders	Blob . . . . Five Blobs
Birds Of All Nations . . . . George McCannon	Blockbuster . . . . Sweet
Birmingham Blues . . . . . . Charlie Daniels Band	Blood Is Thicker Than Water . . . William DeVaughn
Birthday . . . . Underground Sunshine	Blood Red And Goin' Down . . . . . . Tanya Tucker
Birthday Party . . . . Pixies Three	Bloody Well Right . . . . Supertramp
Birthday Suit . . . . Johnny Kemp	Blossom Fell . . . . Nat King Cole
Biscuit's In The House . . . . Biscuit	Blow Away . . . . George Harrison
Bit By Bit (Theme From "Fletch") . . Stephanie Mills	Blowin' In The Wind . . . . Peter, Paul & Mary

Blowin' In The Wind	Stevie Wonder	Bombs Away	Bob Weir
Blowing Away	Fifth Dimension	Bon Bon Vie (Gimme The Good Life)	T.S. Monk
Blowing Kisses In The Wind	Paula Abdul	Bon Voyage	Janice Harper
BLT	Lee Oskar	Bonanza	Al Caiola
Blue Angel	Roy Orbison	Bonaparte's Retreat	Billy Grammer
Blue Autumn	Bobby Goldsboro	Bonaparte's Retreat	Kay Starr
Blue Bayou	Linda Ronstadt	Bon-Doo-Wah	Orlons
Blue Bayou	Roy Orbison	Bongo Bongo	Steve Miller Band
Blue Blue Day	Don Gibson	Bongo Bongo Bongo	Preston Epps
Blue Boy	Jim Reeves	Bongo Rock	Incredible Bongo Band
Blue Collar	Bachman-Turner Overdrive	Bongo Rock	Preston Epps
Blue Collar Man (Long Nights)	Styx	Bongo Stomp	Little Joey And The Flips
Blue Eyes	Elton John	Bonnie And Clyde Theme	Yo-Yo
Blue Eyes Crying In The Rain	Willie Nelson	Bonnie Came Back	Duane Eddy
Blue Guitar	Justin Hayward & John Lodge	Bony Moronie	Appalachians
Blue Guitar	Richard Chamberlain	Bony Moronie	Cheeks
Blue Hawaii	Billy Vaughn	Bony Moronie	Larry Williams
Blue Jean	David Bowie	Boo, Boo, Don't 'Cha Be Blue	Tommy James
Blue Kiss	Jane Wiedlin	Boo Boo Stick Beat	Chet Atkins
Blue Light	David Gilmour	Boo-Ga-Loo	Tom And Jerrio
Blue Monday	Fats Domino	Boogaloo Down Broadway	Fantastic Johnny C
Blue Monday 1988	New Order	Boogaloo Party	Flamingos
Blue Money	Van Morrison	Boogie Bands And One Night Stands	Kathy Dalton
Blue Moon	Elvis Presley	Boogie Bear	Boyd Bennett And His Rockets
Blue Moon	Jimmy Bowen With The Rhythm Orchids	Boogie Child	Bee Gees
Blue Moon	Marcels	Boogie Down	Jarreau
Blue Moon	Ventures	Boogie Down	Eddie Kendricks
Blue Morning, Blue Day	Foreigner	Boogie Fever	Sylvers
Blue On Blue	Bobby Vinton	Boogie Nights	Heatwave
Blue Ribbon Baby	Tommy Sands	Boogie On Reggae Woman	Stevie Wonder
Blue River	Elvis Presley	Boogie Oogie Oogie	Taste Of Honey
Blue Shadows	B.B. King	Boogie Shoes	KC And The Sunshine Band
Blue Side	Crystal Gayle	Boogie Wonderland	Earth, Wind & Fire With The Emotions
Blue Side Of Lonesome	Jim Reeves	Boogie Woogie Bugle Boy	Bette Midler
Blue Sky	Joan Baez	Boogie Woogie Dancin' Shoes	Claudja Barry
Blue Sky Mine	Midnight Oil	Boogie Woogie Man	Paul Davis
Blue Star	Ventures	Book Of Love	Monotones
Blue Suede Shoes	Carl Perkins	Book Of Love	Raindrops
Blue Suede Shoes	Johnny Rivers	Boom-A-Dip-Dip	Stan Robinson
Blue Tango	Bill Black's Combo	Boom Boom	Animals
Blue Tango	Leroy Anderson	Boom Boom	John Lee Hooker
Blue Tomorrow	Billy Vaughn	Boom Boom (Let's Go Back To My Room)	Paul Lekakis
Blue Velvet	Bobby Vinton	Boom Boom (Out Go The Lights)	Pat Travers Band
Blue Velvet	Statues	Boom! Shake The Room	D.J. Jazzy Jeff & The Fresh Prince
Blue Water Line	Brothers Four	Boom! There She Was	Scritti Politti Featuring Roger
Blue Winter	Connie Francis	Boomerang	Frankie Valli
Blue World	Moody Blues	Boomin' System	L.L. Cool J
Blue's Theme	Davie Allan And The Arrows	Boot-Leg	Booker T & The MG's
Blueberry Hill	Fats Domino	Booty Butt	Ray Charles
Bluebird	Buffalo Springfield	Bootzilla	Bootsy's Rubber Band
Bluebird	Helen Reddy	Bop	Dan Seals
Bluebird, The Buzzard & The Oriole	Bobby Day	Bop 'Til You Drop	Rick Springfield
Bluebirds Over The Mountain	Beach Boys	Bop-A-Lena	Ronnie Self
Bluebirds Over The Mountain	Echoes	Boppin' In A Sack	Lane Brothers
Bluebirds Over The Mountain	Ersel Hickey	Border	America
Bluer Than Blue	Michael Johnson	Border	Mr. Mister
Blues	Randy Newman And Paul Simon	Border Song	Elton John
Blues	Tony! Toni! Tone!	Border Song (Holy Moses)	Aretha Franklin
Blues Before And After	Smithereens	Borderline	Madonna
Blues (Stay Away From Me)	Ace Cannon	Borderlines	Jeffrey Osborne
Blues Stay Away From Me	Billy Vaughn	Born A Woman	Sandy Posey
Boats Against The Current	Eric Carmen	Born Again	Sam & Dave
Bobbie Sue	Oak Ridge Boys	Born Free	Hesitations
Bobby	Neil Scott	Born Free	Roger Williams
Bobby Sox To Stockings	Frankie Avalon	Born In East L.A.	Cheech & Chong
Bobby's Girl	Marcie Blane	Born In The U.S.A.	Bruce Springsteen
Body	Jacksons	Born To Be Alive	Patrick Hernandez
Body Language	Queen	Born To Be By Your Side	Brenda Lee
Body Rock	Maria Vidal	Born To Be My Baby	Bon Jovi
Body Talk	Deele	Born To Be Together	Ronettes
Bohemian Rhapsody	Queen		
Bold Soul Sister	Ike & Tina Turner		
Boll Weevil Song	Brook Benton		

399

Born To Be Wild . . . . Steppenwolf	Break Your Promise . . . . Delfonics
Born To Be Mad . . . . Wilson Pickett	Breakadawn . . . . De La Soul
Born To Be With You . . . . Chordettes	Breakaway . . . . Art Garfunkel
Born To Lose . . . . Ray Charles	Breakaway . . . . Big Pig
Born To Run . . . . Bruce Springsteen	Breakaway . . . . Millie Jackson
Born To Wander . . . . Rare Earth	Break-A-Way . . . . Tracy Ullman
Born Too Late . . . . Poni-Tails	Breakdance . . . . Irene Cara
Born Under A Bad Sign . . . . William Bell	Breakdown . . . . Seduction
Borrowed Time . . . . Styx	Breakdown . . . . . Tom Petty And The Heartbreakers
Boss . . . . Diana Ross	Breakdown Dead Ahead . . . . Boz Scaggs
Boss . . . . Rumblers	Breakdown (Part 1) . . . . Rufus Thomas
Boss Guitar . . . . Duane Eddy	Breakfast In America . . . . Supertramp
Bossa Nova Baby . . . . Elvis Presley	Breakin' Away . . . . Al Jarreau
Bossa Nova U.S.A. . . . . Dave Brubeck Quartet	Breakin' In A Brand New Broken Heart . . . .
Botch-A-Me . . . . Rosemary Clooney	. . . . Connie Francis
Both Sides Now . . . . Judy Collins	Breakin' My Heart . . . . Mint Condition
Both Sides Of The Story . . . . Phil Collins	Breakin' Up Is Breakin' My Heart . . . . Roy Orbison
Bottle Of Wine . . . . Fireballs	Breakin'...There's No Stopping Us . . . Ollie & Jerry
Boulevard . . . . Jackson Browne	Breaking Away . . . . Balance
Bounce . . . . Olympics	Breaking Down The Walls Of Heartache . . . .
Bounce Back . . . . Alisha	. . . . Bandwagon
Bounce, Rock, Skate, Roll (Part 1)	Breaking Up Is Hard On You . . . .
. . . . Vaughan Mason And Crew	. . . . American Comedy Network
Bouncin' Off The Walls . . . . Matthew Wilder	Breaking Up Is Hard To Do . . . . Happenings
Bowling Green . . . . Everly Brothers	Breaking Up Is Hard To Do . . . .
Boxer . . . . Simon & Garfunkel	. . . . Jivin' Gene And The Jokers
Boy Blue . . . . Cyndi Lauper	Breaking Up Is Hard To Do . . . . Lenny Welch
Boy From New York City . . . . Ad Libs	Breaking Up Is Hard To Do . . . . Neil Sedaka
Boy From New York City . . . . Manhattan Transfer	Breaking Up Is Hard To Do . . . . . Partridge Family
Boy, I've Been Told . . . . Sa-Fire	Breaking Up Somebody's Home . . . . . Albert King
Boy In The Box . . . . Corey Hart	Breaking Up Somebody's Home . . . . . Ann Peebles
Boy In The Bubble . . . . Paul Simon	Breaking Us In Two . . . . Joe Jackson
Boy Named Sue . . . . Johnny Cash	Breakout . . . . Swing Out Sister
Boy Next Door . . . . Secrets	Breaks (Part 1) . . . . Kurtis Blow
Boy Without A Girl . . . . Frankie Avalon	Breakup Song (They Don't Write 'Em) . . . .
Boy's Night Out . . . . Timothy B. Schmit	. . . . Greg Kihn Band
Boys . . . . Beatles	Breath Taking Guy . . . . Supremes
Boys Are Back In Town . . . . Thin Lizzy	Breathe Again . . . . Toni Braxton
Boys Do Cry . . . . Joe Bennett And The Sparkletones	Breathless . . . . Jerry Lee Lewis
Boys Do Fall In Love . . . . Robin Gibb	Breeze And I . . . . Caterina Valente
Boys Of Summer (After The Boys Of	Brenda . . . . Cupids
Summer Have Gone) . . . . Don Henley	Brian's Song . . . . Michel LeGrand
Boys' Night Out . . . . Patti Page	Brick House . . . . Commodores
Bra . . . . Cymande	Bridge Of Love . . . . Joe Dowell
Brainstorming . . . . M.C. Brains	Bridge Over Troubled Water . . . . . . Aretha Franklin
Brand New Heartache . . . . Everly Brothers	Bridge Over Troubled Water . . . . . . Linda Clifford
Brand New Key . . . . Melanie	Bridge Over Troubled Water . . . . Simon & Garfunkel
Brand New Love Affair . . . . Chicago	Bridget The Midget . . . . Ray Stevens
Brand New Love Affair . . . . Jigsaw	Brigade Of Broken Hearts . . . . Paul Evans
Brand New Lover . . . . Dead Or Alive	Bright Lights Big City . . . . Jimmy Reed
Brand New Me . . . . Aretha Franklin	Bright Lights, Big City . . . . Sonny James
Brand New Me . . . . Dusty Springfield	Brighton Hill . . . . Jackie DeShannon
Brandy . . . . O'Jays	Brilliant Disguise . . . . Bruce Springsteen
Brandy . . . . Scott English	Bring A Little Lovin' . . . . Los Bravos
Brandy (You're A Fine Girl) . . . . . Looking Glass	Bring A Little Sunshine . . . . Vic Dana
Brass Buttons . . . . String-A-Longs	Bring Back The Time . . . . B.J. Thomas
Brass In Pocket (I'm Special) . . . . . . Pretenders	Bring Back Those Rockabye Baby Days . . . Tiny Tim
Brass Monkey . . . . Beastie Boys	Bring Back Your Heart . . . . Dell-Vikings
Brazil . . . . Ritchie Family	Bring Down The Moon . . . . Boy Meets Girl
Bread And Butter . . . . Newbeats	Bring It On Home . . . . Lou Rawls
Break Away . . . . Beach Boys	Bring It On Home To Me . . . . Animals
Break Away (From That Boy) . . . . Newbeats	Bring It On Home To Me . . . . Eddie Floyd
Break Every Rule . . . . Tina Turner	Bring It On Home To Me . . . . Sam Cooke
Break It Down Again . . . . Tears For Fears	Bring It Up . . . . James Brown
Break It To Me Gently . . . . Brenda Lee	Bring The Boys Home . . . . Freda Payne
Break It To Me Gently . . . . Juice Newton	Bringin' On The Heartbreak . . . . Def Leppard
Break It To Them Gently . . . . . Burton Cummings	Bringing It Back . . . . Elvis Presley
Break It Up . . . . Foreigner	(Bringing Out) The Girl In Me . . Maxine Nightingale
Break My Mind . . . . Bobby Wood	Brink Of Disaster . . . . Lesley Gore
Break My Stride . . . . Matthew Wilder	Bristol Stomp . . . . Dovells
Break Out . . . Mitch Ryder And The Detroit Wheels	Bristol Twistin' Annie . . . . Dovells
Break Up . . . . Del Shannon	Brite Eyes . . . . Robbin Thompson Band
Break Up . . . . Jerry Lee Lewis	Broadway . . . . Freddy Cannon
Break Up To Make Up . . . . Stylistics	Broken . . . . Guess Who

Broken Arrow	Rod Stewart	But I Do	Clarence Henry
Broken Heart	Fiestas	But It's Alright	J.J. Jackson
Broken Hearted Me	Anne Murray	But Not For Me	Ketty Lester
Broken Land	Adventures	But On The Other Hand Baby	Ray Charles
Broken Promise	Four Coins	But You Know I Love You	Dolly Parton
Broken Wings	Mr. Mister	But You Know I Love You	First Edition
Brokenhearted	Johnnie Ray	But You're Mine	Sonny & Cher
Broken-Hearted Melody	Sarah Vaughan	Butter Boy	Fanny
Brontosaurus Stomp	Piltdown Men	Butterfly	Andy Williams
Brooklyn	Cody Jameson	Butterfly	Charlie Gracie
Brooklyn Girls	Robbie Dupree	Butterfly	Danyel Gerard
Brooklyn Roads	Neil Diamond	Butterfly Baby	Bobby Rydell
Broomstick Cowboy	Bobby Goldsboro	Buy For Me The Rain	Nitty Gritty Dirt Band
Brother Don't You Walk Away	Hooters	Buying A Book	Joe Tex
Brother Louie	Stories	Buzz Buzz A Diddle It	Freddy Cannon
Brother Love's Travelling Salvation Show		Buzz-Buzz-Buzz	Hollywood Flames
	Neil Diamond	Buzzy Brown	Tim Davis
Brother Rapp (Parts 1 & 2)	James Brown	By The Bend Of The River	Joe Leahy Orchestra
Brother's Gonna Work It Out	Willie Hutch	By The Light Of The Silvery Moon	
Brown Arms In Houston	Orpheus		Jimmy Bowen With The Rhythm Orchids
Brown Eyed Girl	El Chicano	By The Time I Get To Phoenix	Glen Campbell
Brown Eyed Girl	Van Morrison	By The Time I Get To Phoenix	Isaac Hayes
Brown Eyed Woman	Bill Medley	By The Time I Get To Phoenix	Mad Lads
Brown Paper Bag	Syndicate Of Sound	By The Time This Night Is Over	
Brown Sugar	Rolling Stones		Kenny G With Peabo Bryson
Brownsville	Joy Of Cooking	Bye Bye Baby	Mary Wells
Bruce	Rick Springfield	Bye Bye Baby	U.S. 1
Bubble Gum Music		Bye, Bye, Baby (Baby Goodbye)	Four Seasons
Rock And Roll Double Bubble Trading Card		Bye Bye Baby, Goodbye	Teresa Brewer
Co. Of Philadelphia 19141		Bye Bye Barbara	Johnny Mathis
Buchanan And Goodman On Trial		Bye Bye Blackbird	Art Mooney
	Buchanan And Goodman	Bye Bye Blues	Bert Kaempfert
Buckaroo	Buck Owens	Bye Bye Blues	Les Paul & Mary Ford
Bucket "T"	Ronny & The Daytonas	Bye Bye Johnny	Chuck Berry
Buddy X	Neneh Cherry	Bye Bye Love	Everly Brothers
Buffalo Soldier	Flamingos		
Buffalo Stance	Neneh Cherry		

C

Build Me Up Buttercup	Foundations	C'est La Vie	Greg Lake
Build Your Love	Johnnie Ray	C'est La Vie	Robbie Nevil
Bulldog	Fireballs	C'est Si Bon	Eartha Kitt
Bumble Bee	Lavern Baker	C'est Si Bon	Johnny Desmond
Bumble Bee	Searchers	C'est Si Bon (It's So Good)	Conway Twitty
Bumble Boogie	B. Bumble & The Stingers	C'mon	Poco
Bump Me Baby (Part 1)	Dooley Silverspoon	C'mon And Get My Love	D-Mob
Bungle In The Jungle	Jethro Tull	C'mon And Swim	Bobby Freeman
Bunny Hop	Applejacks	C'mon Baby	Buddy Knox
Burn Rubber	Gap Band	C'mon Everybody	Eddie Cochran
Burnin' For You	Blue Oyster Cult	C'mon Marianne	Donny Osmond
Burnin' Sky	Bad Company	C'mon Marianne	Four Seasons
Burnin' Thing	Mac Davis	Ca, C'est L'Amour	Tony Bennett
Burning Bridges	Jack Scott	Ca Plane Pour Moi	Plastic Bertrand
Burning Bridges	Mike Curb Congregation	Cab Driver	Mills Brothers
Burning Down One Side	Robert Plant	Cabaret	Herb Alpert & The Tijuana Brass
Burning Down The House	Talking Heads	Cafe Amore	Spyro Gyra
Burning Flame	Vitamin Z	Cajun Queen	Jimmy Dean
Burning Heart	Survivor	Calcutta	Lawrence Welk
Burning Heart	Vandenberg	Caledonia	Robin Trower
Burning Like A Flame	Dokken	Calendar Girl	Neil Sedaka
Burning Love	Elvis Presley	Calico	Tommy James
Burning Of Atlanta	Claude King	California	Debby Boone
Burning Spear	Soulful Strings	California Blues	Red Wing
Bus Stop	Hollies	California Bound	Ronny & The Daytonas
Bus Stop Song (A Paper Of Pins)	Four Lads	California Dreamin'	America
Bushel And A Peck	Perry Como	California Dreamin'	Beach Boys
Bust A Move	Young MC	California Dreamin'	Bobby Womack
Bust Out	Busters	California Dreamin'	Mama's & Papa's
Busted	Ray Charles	California Earthquake	Mama Cass
Buster Browne	Willie Mitchell	California Girl	Eddie Floyd
Bustin' Loose (Part 1)		California Girls	Beach Boys
	Chuck Brown & The Soul Searchers	California Girls	David Lee Roth
Bustin' Out	Rick James	California Here I Come	Sophie B. Hawkins
Bustin' Surfboards	Tornadoes	California Kid And Reemo	Lobo
But For Love	Jerry Naylor	California Nights	Lesley Gore
But I Do	Bobby Vinton	California Nights	Sweet

Candy . . . . Cameo
Candy . . . . Iggy Pop
Candy And Cake . . . . Mindy Carson
Candy Apple Red . . . . R. Dean Taylor
Candy Everybody Wants . . . . 10,000 Maniacs
Candy Girl . . . . Four Seasons
Candy Girl . . . . New Edition
Candy Man . . . . Roy Orbison
Candy Man . . . . Sammy Davis Jr.
Candy Sweet . . . . Pat Boone
Candy To Me . . . . Eddie Holland
Candy's Going Bad . . . . Golden Earring
Canned Ham . . . . Norman Greenbaum
Cannonball . . . . Duane Eddy
Cannonball . . . . Supertramp
Cantaloop (Flip Fantasia) Us3
Cap And gown . . . . Marty Robbins
Captain Howdy . . . . Simon Stokes
Captain Of Her Heart . . . . Double
Capture The Moment . . . . . . Jay & The Americans
Capture Your Heart . . . . Blue
Car Wash . . . . Rose Royce
Cara Mia . . . . Jay & The Americans
Cara-Lin . . . . Strangeloves
Caramba . . . . Champs
Caravan . . . . Santo & Johnny
Caravan II . . . . Cozy Cole
Caravan Of Love . . . . Isley, Jasper, Isley
Carefree Highway . . . . Gordon Lightfoot
Carefree Wanderer . . . . Bobby Bare
Careful Man . . . . John Edwards
Careless . . . . Bobby Vinton
Careless Love . . . . Ray Charles
Careless Whisper . . . .
. . . . Wham! Featuring George Michael
Carey . . . . Joni Mitchell
Caribbean . . . . Mitchell Torok
Caribbean Festival . . . . Kool & The Gang
Caribbean Queen . . . . Billy Ocean
Carmen . . . . Herb Alpert & The Tijuana Brass
Carnival Is Over . . . . Seekers
Carol . . . . Chuck Berry
Carol . . . . Tommy Roe
Carolina In My Mind . . . . Crystal Mansion
Carolina In My Mind . . . . James Taylor
Carolina In The Pines . . . . Michael Murphey
Caroline . . . . Concrete Blonde
Caroline, No . . . . Brian Wilson
Carolyn . . . . Merle Haggard
Carpet Man . . . . Fifth Dimension
Carribean Blue . . . . Enya
Carrie . . . . Cliff Richard
Carrie . . . . Europe
Carrie's Gone . . . . J.C. Stone
Carrie's Gone . . . . Le Roux
Carrie-Anne . . . . Hollies
Carroll County Accident . . . . Porter Wagoner
Carry Me . . . . . . David Crosby/Graham Nash
Carry Me Back . . . . Rascals
Carry Me, Carrie . . . . Dr. Hook
Carry On My Wayward Son . . . . Kansas
Cars . . . . Gary Numan
Cars With The Boom . . . . L'Trimm
Casanova . . . . Levert
Casanova Brown . . . . Young Sisters
Casino Royale . . . . Herb Alpert & The Tijuana Brass
Casonova (Your Playing Days Are Over) . . . .
. . . . Ruby Andrews
Cast Your Fate To The Wind . . . . . . Shelby Flint
Cast Your Fate To The Wind . . . Sounds Orchestral
Cast Your Fate To The Wind . . . Vince Guaraldi Trio
Castin' My Spell . . . . Johnny Otis Show
Castles In The Air . . . . Don McLean
Castles In The Sand . . . . Seals & Crofts

Castles In The Sand . . . . . . Little Stevie Wonder
Casual Look . . . . Six Teens
Cat . . . . Jimmy Smith
Cat In The Window . . . . Petula Clark
Cat Nip . . . . Dave "Baby" Cortez
Cat People (Putting Out Fire) . . . . . David Bowie
Cat Scratch Fever . . . . Ted Nugent
Cat Walk . . . . Village Soul Choir
Cat's Eye In The Window . . . . Tommy James
Cat's In The Cradle . . . . Harry Chapin
Cat's In The Cradle . . . . Ugly Kid Joe
Catch A Falling Star . . . . Perry Como
Catch A Little Moonbeam . . . . Doc Burch
Catch A Little Moonbeam . . . . Rinky Dinks
(Catch Me) I'm Falling . . . . Pretty Poison
Catch Me I'm Falling . . . . Real Life
Catch My Fall . . . . Billy Idol
Catch The Wind . . . . Donovan
Catch Us If You Can . . . . Dave Clark Five
Catching The Sun . . . . Spyro Gyra
Caterina . . . . Perry Como
Catfish . . . . Four Tops
Cathy's Clown . . . . Everly Brothers
Caught In A Dream . . . . Alice Cooper
Caught In The Game . . . . Survivor
Caught Up In The Rapture . . . . Anita Baker
Caught Up In You . . . . 38 Special
Causing A Commotion . . . . Madonna
C.B. Savage . . . . Rod Hart
C.C. Rider . . . . Bobby Powell
C.C. Rider . . . . Chuck Willis
Ce Soir . . . . Golden Earring
Cecilia . . . . Simon & Garfunkel
Celebrate . . . . Three Dog Night
Celebrate Youth . . . . Rick Springfield
Celebration . . . . Kool & The Gang
Celebration . . . . Tommy James
Celia Of The Seals . . . . Donovan
Centerfield . . . . John Fogerty
Centerfold . . . . J. Geils Band
Centipede . . . . Rebbie Jackson
Century's End . . . . Donald Fagen
Certain Girl . . . . Warren Zevon
Certain Smile . . . . Johnny Mathis
Cervesa . . . . . . Boots Brown And His Blockbusters
Cerveza . . . . Bert Kaempfert
Ch Ch Cherie . . . . Johnny Average Band
Cha-Cha-Cha . . . . Bobby Rydell
Cha-Hua-Hua . . . . Eddie Platt
Cha-Hua-Hua . . . . Hugo & Luigi
Cha-Hua-Hua . . . . Pets
Chain Gang . . . . Bobby Scott
Chain Gang . . . . . Jackie Wilson And Count Basie
Chain Gang . . . . Sam Cooke
Chain Gang Medley . . . . Jim Croce
Chain Of Fools . . . . Aretha Franklin
Chain Of Fools . . . . Little Caesar
Chain Reaction . . . . Diana Ross
Chained . . . . Marvin Gaye
Chained And Bound . . . . Otis Redding
Chains . . . . Cookies
Chains And Things . . . . B.B. King
Chains Around My Heart . . . . Richard Marx
Chains Of Love . . . . Bobby Bland
Chains Of Love . . . . Erasure
Chains Of Love . . . . Pat Boone
Chairman Of The Board . . . Chairmen Of The Board
Chameleon . . . . Herbie Hancock
Champagne Jam . . . . . Atlanta Rhythm Section
Chance For Heaven . . . . Christopher Cross
Chances Are . . . . Johnny Mathis
Change . . . . John Waite
Change . . . . Lisa Stansfield
Change . . . . Tears For Fears

403

405

407

Danny Boy	Sil Austin	Days Of Wine And Roses	Henry Mancini
Danny's Song	Anne Murray	Daytime Friends	Kenny Rogers
Dare Me	Pointer Sisters	Daytime Night-Time	Keith Hampshire
Dare To Fall In Love	Brent Bourgeois	Dazz	Brick
Dark End Of The Street	James Carr	Dazzy Duks	Duice
Dark Horse	George Harrison	De Do Do Do, De Da Da Da	Police
Dark Lady	Cher	Deacon Blues	Steely Dan
Dark Moon	Bonnie Guitar	Dead Beat Club	B-52's
Dark Moon	Gale Storm	Dead End Street	Lou Rawls
Darkest Street In Town	Jimmy Clanton	Dead Giveaway	Shalamar
Darkness, Darkness	Youngbloods	Dead Heart	Midnight Oil
Darlin'	Beach Boys	Dead Man's Curve	Jan & Dean
Darlin'	Frank Stallone	Dead Skunk	Loudon Wainwright III
Darlin'	Paul Davis	Deadend Street	Kinks
Darlin'	Yipes!!	Dear Abby	Hearts
Darlin' Danielle Don't	Henry Lee Summer	Dear Ann	George Baker Selection
Darlin' Darlin' Baby	O'Jays	Dear Eloise	Hollies
Darlin' I	Vanessa Williams	Dear God	Midge Ure
Darling Baby	Elgins	Dear Heart	Andy Williams
Darling Baby	Jackie Moore	Dear Heart	Jack Jones
Darling Be Home Soon	Association	Dear Hearts And Gentle People	Springfields
Darling Be Home Soon	Lovin' Spoonful	Dear Ivan	Jimmy Dean
Darling Come Back Home	Eddie Kendricks	Dear John	Pat Boone
Darling I Love You	Al Martino	Dear Lady Twist	Gary U.S. Bonds
Darling It's Wonderful	Dale & Grace	Dear Lonely Hearts	Nat King Cole
Darling Je Vous Aime Beaucoup	Nat King Cole	Dear Lover	Mary Wells
Darling Lorraine	Knockouts	Dear Mr. Jesus	Power Source
Darling Take Me Back	Lenny Welch	Dear Mrs. Applebee	Flip Cartridge
Dartell Stomp	Mustangs	Dear One	Larry Finnegan
Daughter	Blenders	Dear Prudence	Five Stairsteps
Daughter	Pearl Jam	Dear Prudence	Katfish
Daughter Of Darkness	Tom Jones	Dearer Than Life	Brook Benton
Dawn	David Rockingham Trio	Dearest	Mickey And Sylvia
Dawn (Go Away)	Four Seasons	Dearie	Merman & Bolger
Dawn Of Correction	Spokesmen	Death Of An Angel	Kingsmen
Day After Day	Badfinger	December, 1963 (Oh, What A Night)	Four Seasons
Day After Day (It's Slippin' Away)	Shango	Deck Of Cards	Wink Martindale
Day And Night	Wackers	Declaration	Fifth Dimension
Day By Day	Godspell	Dede Dinah	Frankie Avalon
Day By Day	Holly Sherwood	Dedicated	R. Kelly & Public Announcement
Day By Day	Hooters	Dedicated Follower Of Fashion	Kinks
Day By Day (Every Minute Of The Hour)		Dedicated To The One I Love	Bernadette Peters
	Continental 4	Dedicated To The One I Love	Mama's & Papa's
Day Dreaming	Aretha Franklin	Dedicated To The One I Love	Shirelles
Day For Decision	Johnny Sea	Dedicated To The One I Love	Temprees
Day I Found Myself	Honeycone	Dedicated (To The Songs I Love)	3 Friends
Day In The Life Of A Fool	Jack Jones	Dedication	Bay City Rollers
Day Is Done	Brooklyn Bridge	Dedication Song	Freddy Cannon
Day Is Done	Peter, Paul & Mary	Deep Blue Sea	Jimmy Dean
Day That Curly Billy Shot Down Crazy		Deep Deep Trouble	Simpsons
Sam McGee	Hollies	Deep Enough For Me	Ocean
Day The Rains Came	Jane Morgan	Deep In The Heart Of Harlem	Clyde McPhatter
Day The Rains Came	Raymond Lefevre	Deep In The Heart Of Harlem	Walter Jackson
Day Tripper	Anne Murray	Deep In The Heart Of Texas	Duane Eddy
Day Tripper	Beatles	Deep Inside My Heart	Randy Meisner
Day Tripper	Vontastics	Deep Purple	Billy Ward And His Dominoes
Daybreak	Barry Manilow	Deep Purple	Donny And Marie Osmond
Daybreak	Nilsson	Deep Purple	Nino Tempo & April Stevens
Daybreaker	Electric Light Orchestra	Deep River Woman	Lionel Richie With Alabama
Daydream	David Cassidy	Deeper	Boss
Daydream	Lovin' Spoonful	Deeper & Deeper	Freda Payne
Daydream Believer	Anne Murray	Deeper And Deeper	Madonna
Daydream Believer	Monkees	Deeper (In Love With You)	O'Jays
Daydreams	Johnny Crawford	Deeper Shade Of Soul	Urban Dance Squad
Day-In Day-Out	David Bowie	Deeper Than The Night	Olivia Newton-John
Daylight	Bobby Womack	Deeper The Love	Whitesnake
Daylight	Vicki Sue Robinson	Deeply	Anson Williams
Daylight And Darkness	Smokey Robinson	Deja Vu	Dionne Warwick
Daylight Savin' Time	Keith	Deleware	Perry Como
Days Are Numbers	Alan Parsons Project	Delia Gone	Pat Boone
Days Gone Down	Gerry Rafferty	Delicado	Percy Faith
Days Like These	Asia	Delicate	Terence Trent D'arby
Days Of Sand And Shovels	Bobby Vinton	Delicious	Jim Backus And Friend
Days Of Wine And Roses	Andy Williams	Delilah	Tom Jones

Delirious . . . . Prince
Delta Dawn . . . . Helen Reddy
Delta Lady . . . . Joe Cocker
Delta Queen . . . . Don Fardon
Demonstration . . . . Otis Redding
Denise . . . . Randy & The Rainbows
Department Of Youth . . . . Alice Cooper
Dependin' On You . . . . . . Doobie Brothers
Der Kommissar . . . . After The Fire
Der Kommissar . . . . Falco
Desafinado . . . . Stan Getz/Charlie Byrd
Desdemona . . . . Searchers
Desert Moon . . . . Dennis DeYoung
Desert Pete . . . . Kingston Trio
Desiderata . . . . Les Crane
Desire . . . . Andy Gibb
Desire . . . . Rockets
Desire U2
Desire Me . . . . Sam Cooke
Desiree . . . . Neil Diamond
Desperate But Not Serious . . . . Adam Ant
Destination Unknown . . . . . . Missing Persons
Destination: Anywhere . . . . Marvelettes
Destiny . . . . Jose Feliciano
Deteriorata . . . . National Lampoon
Detroit City . . . . Bobby Bare
Detroit City . . . . Dean Martin
Detroit City . . . . Solomon Burke
Detroit City . . . . Tom Jones
Detroit Rock City . . . . Kiss
Devil Came Up To Michigan . . . . K.M.C. Kru
Devil In The Bottle . . . . T.G. Sheppard
Devil Inside . . . . Inxs
Devil Made Me Do It . . . . Golden Earring
Devil Or Angel . . . . Bobby Vee
Devil Or Angel . . . . Hollywood Flames
Devil Went Down To Georgia . . Charlie Daniels Band
Devil With A Blue Dress On & Good
  Golly Miss Molly . . . .
  . . . . Mitch Ryder And The Detroit Wheels
Devil Woman . . . . Cliff Richard
Devil Woman . . . . Marty Robbins
Devil You . . . . Stampeders
Devil's Gun . . . . C.J. & Co.
Devoted To You . . . . Carly Simon And James Taylor
Devoted To You . . . . Everly Brothers
Devotion . . . . Earth, Wind & Fire
Devotion . . . . Janice Harper
Dial My Heart . . . . Boys
Dialogue (Parts 1 & 2) . . . . Chicago
Diamond Girl . . . . Seals & Crofts
Diamond Head . . . . Ventures
Diamonds . . . . Chris Rea
Diamonds . . . . Herb Alpert
Diamonds And Pearls . . . . Paradons
Diamonds And Pearls . . . . Prince And The N. P. G.
Diamonds And Rust . . . . Joan Baez
Diamonds Are Forever . . . . . . Shirley Bassey
Diana . . . . Paul Anka
Diane . . . . Bachelors
Diane . . . . Joe Harnell
Dianne, Dianne . . . . Ronny & The Daytonas
Diary . . . . Bread
Diary . . . . Neil Sedaka
Dick And Jane . . . . Bobby Vinton
Did He Do It To You . . . . Tami Show
Did It In A Minute . . . . Daryl Hall & John Oates
Did You Boogie (With Your Baby) . . . .
  . . . . . . Flash Cadillac & The Continental Kids
Did You Ever Have To Make Up Your Mind?
  . . . . Lovin' Spoonful
Did You Ever See A Dream Walking . . . Fats Domino
Did You See Her Eyes . . . . Illusion
Diddle-De-Dum . . . . Belmonts

Didn't I . . . . Sylvia
Didn't I (Blow Your Mind) . . . .
  . . . . New Kids On The Block
Didn't I (Blow Your Mind This Time) . . . Delfonics
Didn't It Look So Easy . . . . . Five Stairsteps
Didn't Know It Was Love . . . . Survivor
Didn't We . . . . Barbra Streisand
Didn't We . . . . Richard Harris
Didn't We Almost Have It All . . . . Whitney Houston
Didn't You Know . . . . . Gladys Knight & The Pips
Different Corner . . . . George Michael
Different Drum . . . .
  . . . . . . Stone Poneys Featuring Linda Ronstadt
Different Story (World Of Lust And Crime) . . . . . .
  . . . . Peter Schilling
Different Strokes . . . . Syl Johnson
Different Worlds . . . . Maureen McGovern
Dig The Gold . . . . Joyce Cobb
Dig The Way I Feel . . . . Mary Wells
Digging In The Dirt . . . . Peter Gabriel
Digging Your Scene . . . . Blow Monkees
Digital Display . . . . Ready For The World
Dim All The Lights . . . . Donna Summer
Dime A Dozen . . . . Carla Thomas
Ding Dong . . . . McGuire Sisters
Ding Dong; Ding Dong . . . . . George Harrison
Ding Dong! The Witch Is Dead . . . . . Fifth Estate
Ding-A-Ling . . . . Bobby Rydell
Dinner With Drac (Part 1) . . . . . . John Zacherle
Dinner With Gershwin . . . . . . Donna Summer
Dirty Cash (Money Talks) . . Adventures Of Stevie V
Dirty Deeds . . . . . . Joan Jett & The Blackhearts
Dirty Diana . . . . Michael Jackson
Dirty Laundry . . . . Don Henley
Dirty Love . . . . Thunder
Dirty Man . . . . Laura Lee
Dirty Water . . . . Inmates
Dirty Water . . . . Rock And Hyde
Dirty Water . . . . Standells
Dirty White Boy . . . . Foreigner
Dis-Advantages Of You . . . . . . Brass Ring
Disappear . . . . Inxs
Discipline Of Love (Why Did You Do It) . . . .
  . . . . Robert Palmer
Disco Duck (Part 1) . . . . Rick Dees
Disco Inferno . . . . Trammps
Disco Lady . . . . Johnnie Taylor
Disco Lucy (I Love Lucy Theme) . . . .
  . . . . Wilton Place Street Band
Disco Nights (Rock-Freak) . . . . GQ
Disco Queen . . . . Hot Chocolate
Dis-Gorilla (Part 1) . . . . Rick Dees
Distant Drums . . . . Jim Reeves
Distant Drums . . . . Vic Dana
Distant Lover . . . . Marvin Gaye
Distant Shores . . . . Chad & Jeremy
Ditty . . . . Paperboy
Divided Hearts . . . . Kim Carnes
Divine Thing . . . . Soup Dragons
D-I-V-O-R-C-E . . . . Tammy Wynette
Dizzy . . . . Tommy Roe
Do Anything . . . . Natural Selection
Do Anything You Wanna . . . . . . Harold Betters
Do Da What . . . . One Of The Girls
Do I Do . . . . Stevie Wonder
Do I Have To Say The Words . . . . Bryan Adams
Do I Love You . . . . Donna Fargo
Do I Love You . . . . Paul Anka
Do I Love You? . . . . Ronettes
Do I Make Myself Clear . . . .
  . . . . Etta James & Sugar Pie DeSanto
Do It . . . . Neil Diamond
Do It -- Rat Now . . . . Bill Black's Combo
Do It ('Til You're Satisfied) . . . . . . B.T. Express

410

Dominique . . . . Singing Nun
Domino . . . . Tony Martin
Domino . . . . Van Morrison
Domino Dancing . . . . Pet Shop Boys
Dominoes . . . . Robbie Nevil
Don Quichotte . . . . Magazine 60
Don't . . . . Elvis Presley
Don't Answer Me . . . . Alan Parsons Project
Don't Answer The Door (Part 1) . . . . . . B.B. King
Don't Ask Me To Be Friends . . . . Everly Brothers
Don't Ask Me Why . . . . Billy Joel
Don't Ask Me Why . . . . Elvis Presley
Don't Ask Me Why . . . . Eurythmics
Don't Ask My Neighbors . . . . Emotions
Don't Be A Dropout . . . . James Brown
Don't Be Afraid Little Darlin' . . . . Steve Lawrence
Don't Be Afraid Of The Dark . . . . Robert Cray Band
Don't Be Angry . . . . Crew-Cuts
Don't Be Angry . . . . Nappy Brown
Don't Be Cruel . . . . Barbara Lynn
Don't Be Cruel . . . . Bill Black's Combo
Don't Be Cruel . . . . Bobby Brown
Don't Be Cruel . . . . Cheap Trick
Don't Be Cruel . . . . Elvis Presley
Don't Believe Him, Donna . . . . Lenny Miles
Don't Bet Money Honey . . . . Linda Scott
Don't Blame Me . . . . Everly Brothers
Don't Blame The Children . . . . . . Sammy Davis Jr.
Don't Break My Heart . . . . . . Romeo's Daughter
Don't Break The Heart That Loves You . . . .
. . . . Connie Francis
Don't Bring Me Down . . . . Animals
Don't Bring Me Down . . . Electric Light Orchestra
Don't Call Us, We'll Call You . . . .
. . . . Sugarloaf/Jerry Corbetta
Don't Cha Love It . . . . Miracles
Don't Change Horses (In The Middle
Of A Stream) . . . . Tower Of Power
Don't Change On Me . . . . Ray Charles
Don't Change Your Love . . . . Five Stairsteps
Don't Close Your Eyes . . . . Kix
Don't Come Around Here No More . . . .
. . . . Tom Petty And The Heartbreakers
Don't Come Knockin' . . . . Fats Domino
Don't Come Running Back . . . . . . Nancy Wilson
Don't Cost You Nothing . . . . . Ashford & Simpson
Don't Cross The River . . . . America
Don't Cry . . . . Asia
Don't Cry . . . . Guns N' Roses
Don't Cry Baby . . . . Etta James
Don't Cry Daddy . . . . Elvis Presley
Don't Cry For Me Argentina . . . . Festival
Don't Cry Joni . . . . Conway Twitty
Don't Cry My Love . . . . Impressions
Don't Cry My Love . . . . Vera Lynn
Don't Cry No More . . . . Bobby Bland
Don't Cry Out Loud . . . . Melissa Manchester
Don't Deceive Me . . . . Ruth Brown
Don't Destroy Me . . . . . . Billy "Crash" Craddock
Don't Disturb This Groove . . . . System
Don't Do It . . . . Band
Don't Do It . . . . Mickey Dolenz
Don't Do Me Like That . . . .
. . . . Tom Petty And The Heartbreakers
Don't Dream It's Over . . . . Crowded House
Don't Eat The Yellow Snow . . . . . . Frank Zappa
Don't Ever Be Lonely (A Poor Little Fool
Like Me) . . . . . . Cornelius Brothers & Sister Rose
Don't Ever Leave Me . . . . Connie Francis
Don't Ever Leave Me . . . . Paul Anka
Don't Ever Wanna Lose Ya . . . . . . New England
Don't Expect Me To Be Your Friend . . . . Lobo
Don't Fall In Love With A Dreamer . . . .
. . . . Kenny Rogers With Kim Carnes

(Don't Fear) The Reaper . . . . . . Blue Oyster Cult
Don't Fence Me In . . . . Tommy Edwards
Don't Fight It . . . . Kenny Loggins With Steve Perry
Don't Fight It . . . . Wilson Pickett
Don't Forbid Me . . . . Pat Boone
Don't Forget About Me . . . . American Breed
Don't Forget About Me . . . . . . Dusty Springfield
Don't Forget I Still Love You . . . . . . Bobbi Martin
Don't Forget Me (When I'm Gone) . . . . Glass Tiger
Don't Forget To Dance . . . . Kinks
Don't Forget To Remember . . . . Bee Gees
Don't Get Around Much Anymore . . . . . . Belmonts
Don't Get Around Much Anymore . . . . . Tab Hunter
Don't Get Close . . Little Anthony And The Imperials
Don't Get Me Wrong . . . . Pretenders
Don't Girls Get Lonely . . . . Glenn Shorrock
Don't Give In To Him . . . .
. . . . Gary Puckett And The Union Gap
Don't Give It Up . . . . Robbie Patton
Don't Give Up . . . . Peter Gabriel/Kate Bush
Don't Give Up . . . . Petula Clark
Don't Give Up On Us . . . . David Soul
Don't Go Away Mad (Just Go Away) . . . Motley Crue
Don't Go Breaking My Heart . . . .
. . . . Elton John And Kiki Dee
Don't Go Home . . . . Playmates
Don't Go Home . . . . Shirelles
Don't Go Near The Eskimos . . . . . . Sheb Wooley
Don't Go Near The Indians . . . . Rex Allen
Don't Go Out Into The Rain . . . . Herman's Hermits
Don't Go To Strangers . . . . Etta Jones
Don't Hang Up . . . . Orlons
Don't Have To Shop Around . . . . Mad Lads
Don't Hide Your Love . . . . Cher
Don't Hold Back . . . . Chanson
Don't Hold Back Your Love . . . .
. . . . Daryl Hall & John Oates
Don't It Make My Brown Eyes Blue . . Crystal Gayle
Don't It Make You Wanna Go Home . . Brook Benton
Don't It Make You Want To Go Home . . . Joe South
Don't Just Stand There . . . . Patty Duke
Don't Knock My Love . . Diana Ross & Marvin Gaye
Don't Knock My Love (Part 1) . . . . . Wilson Pickett
Don't Know Much . . . . Bill Medley
Don't Know Much . . . .
. . . . Linda Ronstadt Featuring Aaron Neville
Don't Know What You Got (Till It's Gone) . . . . . .
. . . . Cinderella
Don't Leave Me In The Morning . . . . Odia Coates
Don't Leave Me Starvin' For Your Love
(Part 1) . . . . Holland-Dozier
Don't Leave Me This Way . . . . Communards
Don't Leave Me This Way . . . . . Thelma Houston
Don't Let Go . . . .
. . Commander Cody And His Lost Planet Airmen
Don't Let Go . . . . Isaac Hayes
Don't Let Go . . . . Roy Hamilton
Don't Let Go . . . . Wang Chung
Don't Let Go The Coat . . . . Who
Don't Let Her Be Your Baby . . . . Contours
Don't Let Him Go . . . . REO Speedwagon
Don't Let Him Know . . . . Prism
Don't Let Him Take Your Love From Me . . . .
. . . . Four Tops
Don't Let It End . . . . Miracles
Don't Let It End . . . . Styx
Don't Let It Get You Down . . . . Crusaders
Don't Let It Happen To Us . . . . Shirelles
Don't Let It Show . . . . Alan Parsons Project
Don't Let Love Hang You Up . . . . . . Jerry Butler
Don't Let Me Be Lonely Tonight . . . . James Taylor
Don't Let Me Be Misunderstood . . . . . . Animals
Don't Let Me Be Misunderstood . . Santa Esmeralda
Don't Let Me Cross Over . . . . Carl Butler

412

Don't You Care . . . . Buckinghams
Don't You Come Cryin' . . . . Linear
Don't You (Forget About Me) . . . . . Simple Minds
Don't You Get So Mad . . . . Jeffrey Osborne
Don't You Just Know It . . . . Fendermen
Don't You Just Know It . . . .
. . . . Huey "Piano" Smith And The Clowns
Don't You Know . . . . Della Reese
Don't You Know How Much I Love You . . . .
. . . . Ronnie Milsap
Don't You Know I Love You . . . . . . Fats Domino
Don't You Know What Love Is . . . . Touch
Don't You Know What The Night Can Do? . . . . . .
. . . . Steve Winwood
Don't You Love Me . . . . 49er's
Don't You Miss Me A Little Bit Baby . . Jimmy Ruffin
Don't You Wanna Be Mine . . . . Denise Lopez
Don't You Want Me . . . . Human League
Don't You Want Me . . . . Jody Watley
Don't You Worry . . Don Gardner And Dee Dee Ford
Don't You Worry 'Bout A Thing . . . . Stevie Wonder
Don't You Write Her Off . . . .
. . . . McGuinn, Clark & Hillman
Donde Esta Santa Claus? . . . . Augie Rios
Done Too Soon . . . . Neil Diamond
Donna . . . . Ritchie Valens
Donna The Prima Donna . . . . Dion
Donnie . . . . Bermudas
Doo Doo Doo Doo Doo (Heartbreaker) . . . .
. . . . Rolling Stones
Doodle Song . . . . Frankie Miller
Door Is Open . . . . Tommy Hunt
Door Is Still Open To My Heart . . . . Dean Martin
Door To Paradise . . . . Bobby Rydell
Door To Your Heart . . . . Dramatics
Doraville . . . . Atlanta Rhythm Section
Do-Re-Mi . . . . Anita Bryant
Do-Re-Mi . . . . Lee Dorsey
Do-Re-Mi . . . . Mitch Miller
Dose Of Rock 'N' Roll . . . . Ringo Starr
Dottie . . . . Danny & The Juniors
Dottie I Like It . . . . Tommy Roe
Double Back . . . . ZZ Top
Double Barrel . . . . Dave And Ansil Collins
Double Dutch Bus . . . . Frankie Smith
Double Good Everything . . . . . Smokey Robinson
Double Lovin' . . . . Osmonds
Double Shot (Of My Baby's Love) . . . .
. . . . Swingin' Medallions
Double Trouble . . . . Lynyrd Skynyrd
Double Vision . . . . Foreigner
Double Yellow Line . . . . Music Machine
Double-O-Seven . . . . Detergents
Do-Wacka-Do . . . . Roger Miller
Down And Out In New York City . . . . James Brown
Down At Lulu's . . . . Ohio Express
(Down At) Papa Joe's . . . . Dixiebelles
Down At Tennessee . . . .
. . . . . Kasenetz-Katz Singing Orchestral Circus
Down Boys . . . . Warrant
Down By The Lazy River . . . . Osmonds
Down By The River . . . . . . Albert Hammond
Down By The River . . . . Buddy Miles
Down By The Station . . . . Four Preps
Down In The Alley . . . . Ronnie Hawkins
Down In The Boondocks . . . . Billy Joe Royal
Down In The Valley . . . . Solomon Burke
Down On Love . . . . Foreigner
Down On Me . . . .
. . . . . . Big Brother And The Holding Company
Down On Me . . . . Janis Joplin
Down On My Knees . . . . Heartbeats
Down On The Corner . . . .
. . . . Creedence Clearwater Revival

Down The Aisle Of Love . . . . Quin-Tones
Down The Aisle (Wedding Song) . . . .
. . . . Patti LaBelle And The Blue Belles
Down The Hall . . . . Four Seasons
Down The Road . . . . Bachman-Turner Overdrive
Down To Love Town . . . . Originals
Down To The Line . . . . Bachman-Turner Overdrive
Down To The Nightclub . . . . Tower Of Power
Down To The Station . . . . B.W. Stevenson
Down Under . . . . Men At Work
Down Where The Winds Blow . . Serendipity Singers
Down With The King . . . . Run-D.M.C.
Down Yonder . . . . Champ Butler
Down Yonder . . . . Del Wood
Down Yonder . . . . . Johnny And The Hurricanes
Downeaster "Alexa" . . . . Billy Joel
Downtown . . . . Mrs. Miller
Downtown . . . . One 2 Many
Downtown . . . . Petula Clark
Downtown Life . . . . Daryl Hall & John Oates
Downtown Train . . . . Rod Stewart
Dr. Ben Basey . . . . . Mickey Shorr And The Cutups
Dr. Feelgood . . . . Motley Crue
Dr. Heckyll & Mr. Jive . . . . Men At Work
Dr. Jon (The Medicine Man) . . . .
. . . . Jon & Robin And The In Crowd
Drag City . . . . Jan & Dean
Drag My Bad Name Down . . . . 4 Of Us
Draggin' The Line . . . . Tommy James
Dragnet . . . . Ray Anthony
Draw Of The Cards . . . . Kim Carnes
Draw The Line . . . . Aerosmith
Dre Day . . . . Dr. Dre
Dreadlock Holiday 10cc
Dream . . . . Betty Johnson
Dream . . . . Dinah Washington
Dream . . . . Etta James
Dream A Little Dream Of Me . . . . . . Mama Cass
Dream Baby (How Long Must I Dream) . . . .
. . . . Glen Campbell
Dream Baby (How Long Must I Dream) . . . .
. . . . Roy Orbison
Dream Goes On Forever . . . . Todd Rundgren
Dream (Hold On To Your Dream) . . . . . Irene Cara
Dream Is Still Alive . . . . Wilson Phillips
Dream Lover . . . . Bobby Darin
Dream Lover . . . . Mariah Carey
Dream Lover . . . . Marshall Tucker Band
Dream Lover . . . . Paris Sisters
Dream Lover . . . . Rebel Pebbles
Dream Me A Home . . . . Mac Davis
Dream Merchant . . . . New Birth
Dream Never Dies . . . . Cooper Brothers
Dream On . . . . Aerosmith
Dream On . . . . Righteous Brothers
Dream On Little Dreamer . . . . Perry Como
Dream Police . . . . Cheap Trick
Dream Weaver . . . . Gary Wright
Dreamboat Annie . . . . Heart
Dreamer . . . . Association
Dreamer . . . . Neil Sedaka
Dreamer . . . . Supertramp
Dreamin' . . . . John Schneider
Dreamin' . . . . Johnny Burnette
Dreamin' . . . . Vanessa Williams
Dreamin' . . . . Will To Power
Dreamin' Is Easy . . . . Steel Breeze
Dreamin' Of Love . . . . Stevie B
Dreaming . . . . Blondie
Dreaming . . . . Cliff Richard
Dreaming . . Orchestral Manoeuvres In The Dark
Dreaming A Dream . . . . . Crown Heights Affair
Dreams . . . . Fleetwood Mac
Dreams . . . . Gabrielle

E

415

Eight Men And Four Women . . . . O.V. Wright	Endless Sleep . . . . Jody Reynolds
Eight Miles High . . . . Byrds	Endless Summer Nights . . . . Richard Marx
867-5309/Jenny . . . . Tommy Tutone	Endlessly . . . . Brook Benton
Eighteen . . . . Alice Cooper	Endlessly . . . . Mavis Staples
18 And Life . . . . Skid Row	Endlessly . . . . Sonny James
Eighteen With A Bullet . . . . Pete Wingfield	Energy Crisis '74 . . . . Dickie Goodman
8th Wonder . . . . Sugarhill Gang	Energy Crisis '79 . . . . Dickie Goodman
18 Yellow Roses . . . . Bobby Darin	Engine Engine #9 . . . . Roger Miller
81 . . . . Candy And The Kisses	Engine Number 9 . . . . Wilson Pickett
El Bimbo . . . . Bimbo Jet	England Swings . . . . Roger Miller
El Condor Pasa . . . . Simon & Garfunkel	Englishman In New York . . . . Sting
El Paso . . . . Marty Robbins	Enjoy And Get It On . . . . ZZ Top
El Pito . . . . Joe Cuba Sextet	Enjoy The Silence . . . . Depeche Mode
El Rancho Rock . . . . Champs	Enjoy Yourself . . . . Jacksons
El Watusi . . . . Ray Barretto	Enough Is Enough . . . . April Wine
Eleanor Rigby . . . . Aretha Franklin	Enter Sandman . . . . Metallica
Eleanor Rigby . . . . Beatles	Entertainer . . . . Billy Joel
Eleanor Rigby . . . . Ray Charles	Entertainer . . . . Marvin Hamlisch
Elected . . . . Alice Cooper	Entertainer . . . . Tony Clarke
Election Day . . . . Arcadia	Epic . . . . Faith No More
Electric Avenue . . . . Eddy Grant	Epistle To Dippy . . . . Donovan
Electric Blue . . . . Icehouse	Eres Tu (Touch The Wind) . . . . Mocedades
Electric Boogie . . . . Marcia Griffiths	Erotica . . . . Madonna
Electric Kingdom . . . . Twilight 22	Escalator Of Life . . . . Robert Hazard
Electric Stories . . . . Four Seasons	Escapade . . . . Janet Jackson
Electric Youth . . . . Debbie Gibson	Escape (The Pina Colada Song) . . . . Rupert Holmes
Electricland . . . . Bad Company	Escape-Ism (Part 1) . . . . James Brown
Electronic Magnetism . . . . . . Solomon Burke	Eso Beso (That Kiss!) . . . . Paul Anka
Elena . . . . Marc Tanner Band	Eso Es El Amour . . . . Morty Palitz Orchestra
Elenore . . . . Turtles	Eternal Flame . . . . Bangles
Eli's Coming . . . . Three Dog Night	Eternally . . . . Chantels
Eloise . . . . Barry Ryan	Eternally . . . . Sarah Vaughan
Elusive Butterfly . . . . Bob Lind	Eternally . . . . . Thomas Wayne With The DeLons
Elvira . . . . Dallas Frazier	Eternity . . . . Vikki Carr
Elvira . . . . Oak Ridge Boys	Europa And The Pirate Twins . . . . . Thomas Dolby
Elvis Medley . . . . Elvis Presley	Ev'ry Day Of My Life . . . . McGuire Sisters
Emergency . . . . Kool & The Gang	Eve Of Destruction . . . . Barry McGuire
Eminence Front . . . . Who	Even A Fool Can See . . . . Peter Cetera
Emma . . . . Hot Chocolate	Even Better Than The Real Thing U2
Emmaretta . . . . Deep Purple	Even It Up . . . . Heart
Emotion . . . . Barbra Streisand	Even Now . . . . Barry Manilow
Emotion . . . . Helen Reddy	Even Now . . . . Bob Seger & The Silver Bullet Band
Emotion . . . . Samantha Sang	Even Now . . . . Eddie Fisher
Emotion In Motion . . . . Ric Ocasek	Even The Bad Times Are Good . . . . . . Tremeloes
Emotional Rescue . . . . Rolling Stones	Even The Nights Are Better . . . . Air Supply
Emotions . . . . Brenda Lee	Evening Rain . . . . Earl Grant
Emotions . . . . Mariah Carey	Eventually . . . . Brenda Lee
Emotions In Motion . . . . Billy Squire	Ever Since The World Began . . . . . Tommy Shaw
Emperor's New Clothes . . . . . . Sinead O'Connor	Everglades . . . . Kingston Trio
Empire Strikes Back (medley) . . . . Meco	Everlasting Love . . . . Andy Gibb
Empty Arms . . . . Ivory Joe Hunter	Everlasting Love . . . . Carl Carlton
Empty Arms . . . . Teresa Brewer	Everlasting Love . . . . Howard Jones
Empty Beach . . . . Tricia Leigh Fisher	Everlasting Love . . . . . Rex Smith/Rachel Sweet
Empty Garden (Hey Hey Johnnie) . . . . Elton John	Everlasting Love . . . . Robert Knight
Empty Pages . . . . Traffic	Everlasting Love . . . . Tony Terry
Enamorado . . . . Keith Colley	Everlovin' . . . . Rick Nelson
Enchanted . . . . Platters	Every 1's A Winner . . . . Hot Chocolate
Enchanted Island . . . . Four Lads	Every Beat Of My Heart . . . Crown Heights Affair
Enchanted Sea . . . . Islanders	Every Beat Of My Heart . . . . Pips
Enchanted Sea . . . . Martin Denny	Every Beat Of My Heart . . . . Rod Stewart
Encore . . . . Cheryl Lynn	Every Breath I Take . . . . Gene Pitney
End . . . . Earl Grant	Every Breath You Take . . . . Police
End Is Not In Sight . . . . . Amazing Rhythm Aces	Every Day I Have The Blues . . . . . Billy Stewart
End Of Our Road . . . . Gladys Knight & The Pips	Every Day I Have To Cry . . . . Steve Alaimo
End Of Our Road . . . . Marvin Gaye	Every Day I Have To Cry Some . . . Arthur Alexander
End Of The Innocence . . . . Don Henley	Every Day Of My Life . . . . Bobby Vinton
End Of The Line . . . . Traveling Wilburys	Every Face Tells A Story . . . . . Olivia Newton-John
End Of The Road . . . . Boyz II Men	Every Heartbeat . . . . Amy Grant
End Of The World . . . . Skeeter Davis	Every Home Should Have One . . . . . . Patti Austin
Endless . . . . McGuire Sisters	Every Kinda People . . . . Robert Palmer
Endless Love . . . . . . Diana Ross & Lionel Richie	Every Little Bit Hurts . . . . Brenda Holloway
Endless Nights . . . . Eddie Money	Every Little Kiss . . . Bruce Hornsby And The Range
Endless Sleep . . . . Gene Ross	Every Little Step . . . . Bobby Brown
Endless Sleep . . . . Hank Williams Jr.	Every Little Teardrop . . . . Gallagher And Lyle

416

Every Little Thing She Does Is Magic . . . . . . Police	Everybody's Had The Blues . . . . . . Merle Haggard
Every Little Thing U Do . . . . Christopher Williams	Everybody's Out Of Town . . . . B.J. Thomas
Every Little Thing You Do . . Dion And The Belmonts	Everybody's Somebody's Fool . . . . Connie Francis
Every Man Ought To Have A Woman . . William Bell	Everybody's Talkin' . . . . Nilsson
Every Night . . . . Paul Anka	Everybody's Twistin' . . . . Frank Sinatra
Every Night, Every Day . . . . . Jimmy McCracklin	Everyday . . . . Buddy Holly
Every Night (I Pray) . . . . Chantels	Everyday . . . . Della Reese
Every Road Leads Back To You . . . . . Bette Midler	Everyday . . . . James Taylor
Every Rose Has Its Thorn . . . . Poison	Everyday . . . . John Denver
Every Step Of The Way . . . . John Waite	Everyday I Write The Book . . . . . . Elvis Costello
Every Step Of The Way . . . . . . Johnny Mathis	Everyday People . . . . . Joan Jett & The Blackhearts
Every Step Of The Way . . . . Steve Walsh	Everyday People . . . . . Sly & The Family Stone
Every Time I Think Of You . . . . Babys	Everyday With You Girl . . . . Classics IV
(Every Time I Turn Around) Back In Love	Everyday Without You . . . .
Again . . . . L.T.D.	. . . . Hamilton, Joe Frank & Reynolds
Every Time You Cry . . . . Outfield	Everyone Was There . . . . Bob Kayli
Every Time You Touch Me (I Get High)	Everyone's Agreed That Everything Will
. . . . Charlie Rich	Turn Out Fine . . . . Stealers Wheel
Every Which Way But Loose . . . . . . Eddie Rabbitt	Everyone's Gone To The Moon . . . . Jonathan King
Every Woman In The World . . . . . . Air Supply	Everyotherday . . Or-N-More Featuring Father M.C.
Everybody . . . . Tommy Roe	Everything . . . . Jody Watley
Everybody Be Dancin' . . . . Starbuck	Everything A Man Could Ever Need . . Glen Campbell
Everybody But Me . . . . G.W. Kenny	Everything About You . . . . Ugly Kid Joe
Everybody Dance . . . . Chic	Everything Changes . . . . Kathy Troccoli
Everybody Dance . . . . . . Ta Mara & The Seen	Everything Counts . . . . Depeche Mode
Everybody Do The Sloopy . . . . . Johnny Thunder	Everything Good Is Bad . . . . 100 Proof Aged In Soul
Everybody Everybody . . . . Black Box	Everything I Do Gohn Be Funky . . . . Lee Dorsey
Everybody Go Home . . . . Eydie Gorme	(Everything I Do) I Do It For You . . . . Bryan Adams
Everybody Got To Believe In Somebody	Everything I Need . . . . Men At Work
. . . . Sam & Dave	Everything I Own . . . . Bread
Everybody Have Fun Tonight . . . . . . Wang Chung	Everything In My Heart . . . . Corey Hart
Everybody Hurts . . . . R.E.M.	Everything Is Beautiful . . . . Ray Stevens
Everybody Is A Star . . . . . Sly & The Family Stone	Everything Is Going To Be Alright . . . .
Everybody Knows . . . . Dave Clark Five	. . . . Teegarden & Van Winkle
Everybody Knows . . . . Steve Lawrence	Everything Is Good About You . . . . . . Lettermen
Everybody Knows About My Good Thing	Everything Must Change . . . . Paul Young
. . . . Little Johnny Taylor	Everything She Wants . . . . . . George Michael
Everybody Knows (I Still Love You)	Everything That 'Cha Do . . . . Wet Willie
. . . . Dave Clark Five	Everything That Touches You . . . . . . Association
Everybody Knows Matilda . . . . Duke Baxter	Everything Works If You Let It . . . . . Cheap Trick
Everybody Likes To Cha Cha Cha . . . . Sam Cooke	Everything You Do (You're Sexing Me) . . . .
Everybody Loves A Clown	. . . . Fiona With Kip Winger
. . . . . . Gary Lewis And The Playboys	Everything Your Heart Desires . . . .
Everybody Loves A Love Song . . . . . . Mac Davis	. . . . Daryl Hall & John Oates
Everybody Loves A Lover . . . . Doris Day	Everything's Alright . . . . Newbeats
Everybody Loves A Lover . . . . Shirelles	Everything's Alright . . . . Yvonne Elliman
Everybody Loves A Nut . . . . Johnny Cash	Everything's Been Changed . . . . . Fifth Dimension
Everybody Loves A Rain Song . . . . . B.J. Thomas	Everything's Coming Up Love . . . . . David Ruffin
Everybody Loves A Winner . . . . . . William Bell	Everything's Gonna Be Alright . . . . . Father M.C.
Everybody Loves Me But You . . . . . . Brenda Lee	Everything's The Same . . . . Billy Swan
Everybody Loves Somebody . . . . . . Dean Martin	Everything's Tuesday . . . . Chairmen Of The Board
Everybody Monkey . . . . Freddy Cannon	Everytime . . . . . . Joey Dee & The Starliters
Everybody Needs A Rainbow . . . . . . Ray Stevens	Everytime You Go Away . . . . Paul Young
Everybody Needs Love . . Gladys Knight & The Pips	Everywhere . . . . Fleetwood Mac
Everybody Needs Love . . . . . . Stephen Bishop	Everywhere You Go . . . . Quaker City Boys
Everybody Needs Somebody To Love	Evil . . . . Earth, Wind & Fire
. . . . Solomon Burke	Evil Boll-Weevil . . . . Grand Canyon
Everybody Needs Somebody To Love	Evil Ways . . . . Carlos Santana & Buddy Miles
. . . . Wilson Pickett	Evil Ways . . . . Santana
Everybody Ou'ta The Pool . . . . Lifeguards	Evil Woman . . . . Electric Light Orchestra
Everybody Ought To Be In Love . . . . . Paul Anka	Evil Woman Don't Play Your Games With Me . . Crow
Everybody Plays The Fool . . . . . Aaron Neville	Evol-Not Love . . . . Five Americans
Everybody Plays The Fool . . . . . Main Ingredient	Ewok Celebration . . . . Meco
(Everybody Wanna Get Rich) Rite Away . . . Dr. John	Exclusively Yours . . . . Carl Dobkins Jr.
Everybody Wants To Find A Bluebird	Exodus . . . . Eddie Harris
. . . . Randy Edelman	Exodus . . . . Ferrante & Teicher
Everybody Wants To Rule The World	Exodus Song (This Land Is Mine) . . . . Pat Boone
. . . . Tears For Fears	Expecting To Fly . . . . . . Buffalo Springfield
Everybody Wants You . . . . Billy Squire	Explosion In Your Soul . . . . Soul Survivors
Everybody's Everything . . . . Santana	Express . . . . B.T. Express
Everybody's Free (To Feel Good) . . . . . Rozalla	Express Yourself . . . . Charles Wright And
Everybody's Got The Right To Love . . . . Supremes	. . . . . . The Watts 103rd Street Rhythm Band
Everybody's Got To Learn Sometime . . . . Korgis	Express Yourself . . . . Madonna
Everybody's Gotta Pay Some Dues . . . . Miracles	Expression . . . . Salt-N-Pepa

417

Expressway To Your Heart	Soul Survivors	Fantastic Voyage	Lakeside
Eye In The Sky	Alan Parsons Project	Fantasy	Aldo Nova
Eye Of The Tiger	Survivor	Fantasy	Earth, Wind & Fire
Eye On You	Billy Squire	Fantasy Girl	38 Special
Eye To Eye	Go West	Far Far Away	Don Gibson
Eyes Of A New York Woman	B.J. Thomas	Far From Over	Frank Stallone
Eyes Of God	Four Lads	Farewell Andromeda	John Denver
Eyes Of Silver	Doobie Brothers	Farewell My Summer Love	Michael Jackson
Eyes Without A Face	Billy Idol	Farmer John	Premiers
		Farmer John	Tidal Waves

F

Fabulous	Charlie Gracie	Farther On Down The Road	Joe Simon
Face In The Crowd		Fascinated	Company B
Tom Petty And The Heartbreakers		Fascination	Dick Jacobs
Face It Girl, It's Over	Nancy Wilson	Fascination	Jane Morgan
Face The Face	Pete Townshend	Fascination Street	Cure
Face The Music	RTZ	Fashion	David Bowie
Faces Of Love	Nia Peeples	Fast As You	Dwight Yoakam
Facts Of Love	Jeff Lorber Featuring Karyn White	Fast Car	Tracy Chapman
Fade Away	Bruce Springsteen	Fat	"Weird Al" Yankovic
Fade Away	Loz Netto	Fat Bottomed Girls	Queen
Fading Away	Will To Power	Father Figure	George Michael
Fading Like A Flower	Roxette	Father Sebastian	Ramblers
Fa-Fa-Fa-Fa-Fa (Sad Song)	Otis Redding	Favorite Waste Of Time	Bette Midler
Fair Game	Crosby, Stills & Nash	Feel Alright	Cargoe
Fairweather Friend	Johnny Gill	Feel It	Sam Cooke
Fairytale	Pointer Sisters	Feel It Again	Honeymoon Suite
Faith	George Michael	Feel Like A Number	
Faithful	Go West		Bob Seger & The Silver Bullet Band
Faithful And True	Z.Z. Hill	Feel Like Makin' Love	Bad Company
Faithfully	Journey	Feel Like Makin' Love	Roberta Flack
Fake	Alexander O'Neal	Feel So Bad	Ray Charles
Fake Friends	Joan Jett & The Blackhearts	Feel So Fine	Johnny Preston
Fake Out	Frankie Sardo	Feel That You're Feelin'	Maze
Fakin' It	Simon & Garfunkel	Feel The Groove	Cartouche
Fall In Love Again	Eddie Money	Feel The Heat	Jean Beauvoir
Fall In Love With Me	Bettye Swann	Feel The Need	Leif Garrett
Fall In Love With Me	Earth, Wind & Fire	Feel The Need In Me	Detroit Emeralds
Fall On Me	R.E.M.	Feelin' Alright	Grand Funk Railroad
Fallen Angel	Frankie Valli	Feelin' Satisfied	Boston
Fallen Angel	Poison	Feelin' So Good (S.k.o.o.b.y-D.o.o)	Archies
Fallen Star	Ferlin Husky	Feelin' Stronger Every Day	Chicago
Fallen Star	Hilltoppers	Feeling Alright	Joe Cocker
Fallen Star	Jimmy Newman	Feeling Is Right	Clarence Carter
Fallen Star	Nick Noble	Feelings	Barry Mann
Fallin'	Connie Francis	Feelings	Morris Albert
Fallin' In Love	Hamilton, Joe Frank & Reynolds	Feelings Of Forever	Tiffany
Fallin' In Love	Souther, Hillman, Furay Band	Feels Good	Tony! Toni! Tone!
Falling	Lenny LeBlanc	Feels Like Another One	Patti LaBelle
Falling	Roy Orbison	Feels Like Heaven	Peter Cetera With Chaka Khan
Falling Apart At The Seams	Marmalade	Feels Like The First Time	Foreigner
Falling In Love	Balance	Feels So Good	Chuck Mangione
Falling In Love	Fat Boys	Feels So Good	Van Halen
Falling In Love Again	Michael Stanley Band	Feels So Real (Won't Let Go)	Patrice Rushen
Falling In Love (Uh-Oh)	Miami Sound Machine	Feels So Right	Alabama
Falling Out Of Love	Ivan Neville	Feet Start Walkin'	Doris Duke
Falling To Pieces	Faith No More	Felicidad	Sally Field
Fame	David Bowie	Feliz Navidad	Jose Feliciano
Fame	Irene Cara	Fell For You	Dramatics
Fame And Fortune	Elvis Presley	Fell In Love On Monday	Fats Domino
Family Affair	Sly & The Family Stone	Female Intuition	Mai Tai
Family Man	Daryl Hall & John Oates	Fencewalk	Mandrill
Family Of Man	Three Dog Night	Fernando	Abba
Fanatic	Felony	Ferris Wheel	Everly Brothers
Fancy	Bobbie Gentry	Ferry Across The Mersey	
Fancy Dancer	Commodores		Gerry And The Pacemakers
Fancy Free	Oak Ridge Boys	Fever	Pete Bennett
Fancy Lady	Billy Preston	Fever	Rita Coolidge
Fancy Nancy	Skip & Flip	Fever	Peggy Lee
Fancy Pants	Al Hirt	Fever	Little Willie John
Fannie Mae	Buster Brown	Fever	McCoys
Fannie May	Mighty Sam	Fez	Steely Dan
Fanny	Gino Cunico	Ffun	Con Funk Shun
Fanny (Be Tender With My Love)	Bee Gees	Fibbin'	Patti Page
		Fiddle Around	Jan & Dean

418

Title	Artist
Fiddler On The Roof	Village Stompers
Fields Of Fire	Big Country
Fields Of Gold	Sting
Fields Of Gray	Bruce Hornsby And The Range
Fife Piper	Dynatones
Fifteen Years Ago	Conway Twitty
5 D (Fifth Dimension)	Byrds
Fifth Of Beethoven	Walter Murphy
50 Ways To Leave Your Lover	Paul Simon
57 Channels (And Nothin' On)	Bruce Springsteen
59th Street Bridge Song	Harpers Bizarre
Fight Fire With Fire	Kansas
Fight The Power (Part 1)	Isley Brothers
Fightin' Side Of Me	Merle Haggard
Final Countdown	Europe
Finally	Ce Ce Peniston
Finally	T.G. Sheppard
Finally Got Myself Together	Impressions
Find A Way	Amy Grant
Find Another Fool	Quarterflash
Find Another Girl	Jerry Butler
Find Your Way Back	Jefferson Starship
Finder's Keepers	Chairmen Of The Board
Fine Fine Boy	Darlene Love
Fine Fine Day	Tony Carey
Finer Things	Steve Winwood
Finest	S.O.S. Band
Finger Poppin' Time	Hank Ballard And The Midnighters
Fingertips (Part 2)	Little Stevie Wonder
Finish What Ya Started	Van Halen
Fins	Jimmy Buffett
Fire	Bruce Springsteen & The E Street Band
Fire	Crazy World Of Arthur Brown
Fire	Five By Five
Fire	Ohio Players
Fire	Pointer Sisters
Fire & Rain	R.B. Greaves
Fire And Ice	Pat Benatar
Fire And Rain	James Taylor
Fire And Rain	Johnny Rivers
Fire And Water	Wilson Pickett
Fire, Baby I'm On Fire	Andy Kim
Fire In The Morning	Melissa Manchester
Fire In The Sky	Dirt Band
Fire Lake	Bob Seger
Fire On The Mountain	Marshall Tucker Band
Fire Sign	Cory
Fire With Fire	Wild Blue
Fire Woman	Cult
Firecracker	Mass Production
Fireflies	Fleetwood Mac
Firefly	Tony Bennett
First Anniversary	Cathy Carr
First Born	Tennessee Ernie Ford
First Cut Is The Deepest	Keith Hampshire
First Cut Is The Deepest	Rod Stewart
First Date, First Kiss, First Love	Sonny James
First Day Back At School	Paul & Paula
First Day Of Summer	Tony Carey
First Hymn From Grand Terrace	Mark Lindsay
First I Look At The Purse	Contours
First Love, First Tears	Duane Eddy
First Name Initial	Annette
First Night	Survivor
First Night Of The Full Moon	Jack Jones
First Of May	Bee Gees
First Quarrel	Paul & Paula
First Taste Of Love	Ben E. King
First Time	Surface
First Time Ever I Saw Your Face	Roberta Flack
First Time Love	Livingston Taylor
First....Be A Woman	Lenore O'Malley
Fish	Bobby Rydell
Fish Ain't Bitin'	Lamont Dozier
Fishnet	Morris Day
Five Card Stud	Lorne Greene
Five Feet High And Rising	Johnny Cash
5:15	Who
Five Hundred Miles	Heaven Bound
500 Miles Away From Home	Bobby Bare
Five O'Clock World	Vogues
Five Pennies	Dodie Stevens
5.7.0.5.	City Boy
5-10-15-20 (25-30 Years Of Love)	Presidents
Flame	Cheap Trick
Flame	Steve Sperry
Flames Of Paradise	Jennifer Rush With Elton John
Flamethrower	J. Geils Band
Flaming Star (EP)	Elvis Presley
Flaming Youth	Kiss
Flamingo	Herb Alpert & The Tijuana Brass
Flamingo Express	Royaltones
Flamingo l'Amore	Gaylords
Flash Light	Parliament
Flash's Theme aka Flash	Queen
Flashback	Fifth Dimension
Flashdance....What A Feeling	Irene Cara
Flesh And Blood	Johnny Cash
Flesh For Fantasy	Billy Idol
Flex	Mad Cobra
Flight '76	Walter Murphy
Flim Flam Man	Barbra Streisand
Flirtin' With Disaster	Molly Hatchet
Float On	Floaters
Floor	Johnny Gill
Flower Children	Marcia Strassman
Flower Of Love	Crests
Flowers On The Wall	Statler Brothers
Floy Joy	Supremes
Fly	Chubby Checker
Fly At Night	Chilliwack
Fly Away	Blackfoot
Fly Away	John Denver
Fly Away	Peter Allen
Fly Away	Stevie Woods
Fly By Night	Andy Williams
Fly High Michelle	Enuff Z'nuff
Fly Like An Eagle	Steve Miller
Fly Little White Dove Fly	Bells
Fly Me To The Moon	Bobby Womack
Fly Me To The Moon	Tony Bennett
Fly Me To The Moon Bossa Nova	Joe Harnell
Fly, Robin, Fly	Silver Convention
Fly To The Angels	Slaughter
Fly With Me	Avant-Garde
Flyin'	Prism
Flyin' High	Blackbyrds
Flying Circle	Frank Slay
Flying High	Commodores
Flying Saucer (Parts 1 & 2)	Buchanan And Goodman
Flying Saucer The 2nd	Buchanan And Goodman
FM (No Static At All)	Steely Dan
Foggy Mountain Breakdown	Flatt & Scruggs
Folk Singer	Tommy Roe
Follow Me	Four Esquires
Follow Me	Lyme & Cybelle
Follow Me	Mary Travers
Follow My Heartbeat	A'me Lorain
Follow That Dream (EP)	Elvis Presley
Follow The Boys	Connie Francis
Follow You	Glen Burtnick
Follow You Follow Me	Genesis
Follow Your Daughter Home	Guess Who
Follow Your Heart	Manhattans
Folsom Prison Blues	Johnny Cash
Fonz Song	Heyettes

419

Funky Music Sho Nuff Turns Me On   . . . Edwin Starr
Funky Nassau (Part 1) . . . . . . Beginning Of The End
Funky Party . . . . Clarence Reid
Funky President (People It's Bad) . . . . James Brown
Funky Street . . . . Arthur Conley
Funky Stuff . . . . Kool & The Gang
Funky Town . . . . Pseudo Echo
Funky Walk (Part 1) . . . . . . Dyke And The Blazers
Funky Way . . . . Calvin Arnold
Funky Weekend . . . . Stylistics
Funky Worm . . . . Ohio Players
Funkytown . . . . Lipps Inc.
Funniest Thing . . . . Classics IV
Funny . . . . Joe Hinton
Funny . . . . Maxine Brown
Funny Face . . . . Donna Fargo
Funny Familiar Forgotten Feelings . . . . Tom Jones
Funny Feeling . . . . Delfonics
Funny Girl . . . . Barbra Streisand
Funny How Love Can Be . . . . First Class
Funny How Time Slips Away . . . . . Dorothy Moore
Funny How Time Slips Away . . . . . Jimmy Elledge
Funny How Time Slips Away . . . . Johnny Tillotson
Funny How Time Slips Away . . . . Spinners
Funny Little Butterflies . . . . Patty Duke
Funny Man . . . . Ray Stevens
Funny Way Of Laughin' . . . . Burl Ives
Furry Murray . . . . Tradewinds
Further More . . . . Ray Stevens
Future Shock . . . . Curtis Mayfield
Future Shock . . . . Hello People
Future's So Bright I Gotta Wear Shades . . . Timbuk 3

G

Galaxy . . . . War
Galileo . . . . Indigo Girls
Gallant Men . . . . Senator Everett McKinley Dirksen
Galveston . . . . Glen Campbell
Galveston . . . . Roger Williams
Gambler . . . . Kenny Rogers
Gambler's Guitar . . . . Rusty Draper
Game Is Over . . . . Brown Sugar
Game Of Love . . Wayne Fontana & The Mindbenders
Games . . . . Chuckii Booker
Games . . . . Phoebe Snow
Games . . . . Redeye
Games People Play . . . . Alan Parsons Project
Games People Play . . . . Joe South
Games That Lovers Play . . . . . . Eddie Fisher
Games That Lovers Play . . . . Mantovani
Games That Lovers Play . . . . Wayne Newton
Games Without Frontiers . . . . . . Peter Gabriel
Gang's Back Again . . . . . Kool & The Gang
Gangsta . . . . Bell Biv DeVoe
Gangsta Bitch . . . . Apache
Gangsta Lean . . . . DRS
Gap . . . . Thompson Twins
Garden In The Rain . . . . Vic Dana
Garden Of Eden . . . . Joe Valino
Garden Party . . . .
. . . . . . Rick Nelson & The Stone Canyon Band
Gas Lamps And Clay . . . . Blues Image
Gazachstahagen . . . . Wild-Cats
Gee . . . . George Hamilton IV
Gee . . . . Pixies Three
Gee Baby . . . . Joe & Ann
Gee Baby . . . . Peter Shelley
Gee Baby (I'm Sorry) . . . . Three Degrees
Gee, But I'm Lonesome . . . . Ron Holden
Gee, But It's Lonely . . . . Pat Boone
Gee Whiz . . . . Bernadette Peters
Gee Whiz . . . . Bobby Day
Gee Whiz . . . . Innocents
Gee Whiz (Look At His Eyes) . . . . . . Carla Thomas

Gemini Dream . . . . Moody Blues
General Hospi-Tale . . . . Afternoon Delights
Genius Of Love . . . . Tom Tom Club
Gentle . . . . Dino
Gentle On My Mind . . . . Aretha Franklin
Gentle On My Mind . . . . Dean Martin
Gentle On My Mind . . . . Glen Campbell
George Jackson . . . . Bob Dylan
Georgia On My Mind . . . . Michael Bolton
Georgia On My Mind . . . . Ray Charles
Georgia On My Mind . . . . . . Righteous Brothers
Georgia On My Mind . . . . Willie Nelson
Georgia Pines . . . . Candymen
Georgia Porcupine . . . . George Fischoff
Georgia Rhythm . . . . . . Atlanta Rhythm Section
Georgia Rose . . . . Tony Bennett
Georgia Took Her Back . . . . R.B. Greaves
Georgie Porgie . . . . Jewel Akens
Georgy Girl . . . . Seekers
Georgy Porgy . . . . Toto
Geronimo's Cadillac . . . . Michael Murphey
Get A Job . . . . Silhouettes
Get A Leg Up . . . . John Mellencamp
Get A Life . . . . Soul II Soul
Get A Move On . . . . Eddie Money
Get Away . . . . Bobby Brown
Get Away . . . . Georgie Fame
Get Back . . . . Beatles
Get Closer . . . . Linda Ronstadt
Get Closer . . . . Seals & Crofts
Get Dancin' . . . . . Disco Tex & The Sex-O-Lettes
Get Down . . . . Curtis Mayfield
Get Down . . . . Gene Chandler
Get Down . . . . Gilbert O'Sullivan
Get Down . . . . Harvey Scales & The Seven Sounds
Get Down, Get Down (Get On The Floor) . . . .
. . . . Joe Simon
Get Down On It . . . . Kool & The Gang
Get Down People . . . . Fabulous Counts
Get Down Tonight . . . . KC And The Sunshine Band
Get Here . . . . Oleta Adams
Get Into Something . . . . Isley Brothers
Get It . . . . . . Stevie Wonder & Michael Jackson
Get It From The Bottom . . . . Steelers
Get It On . . . . Chase
Get It On (Bang A Gong) . . . . Power Station
Get It Right . . . . Aretha Franklin
Get It Right Next Time . . . . Gerry Rafferty
Get It Together . . . . Jackson Five
Get It Together (Part 1) . . . . James Brown
Get It Up . . . . Ronnie Milsap
Get It Up . . . . TLC
Get It While You Can . . . . Janis Joplin
Get Me To The World On Time . . . . Electric Prunes
Get Off . . . . Foxy
Get Off My Back Woman . . . . B.B. King
Get Off My Cloud . . . . Rolling Stones
Get On The Good Foot (Part 1) . . . . James Brown
Get On Up . . . . Esquires
Get On Your Feet . . . . Gloria Estefan
Get Out Now . . . . Tommy James
Get Out Of Denver . . . . Bob Seger
Get Out Of My Life, Woman . . . . . . Lee Dorsey
Get Outta My Dreams, Get Into My Car . . . .
. . . . Billy Ocean
Get Ready . . . . Rare Earth
Get Ready . . . . Temptations
Get Ready For This . . . . 2 Unlimited
Get Rhythm . . . . Johnny Cash
Get That Gasoline Blues . . . . NRBQ
Get That Love . . . . Thompson Twins
Get The Cream Off The Top . . . . . Eddie Kendricks
Get The Funk Out Ma Face . . . . Brothers Johnson
Get Together . . . . Youngbloods

422

Get Up And Boogie (That's Right) . . Silver Convention
Get Up And Get Down . . . . Dramatics
Get Up And Go . . . . Go Go's
Get Up! (Before The Night Is Over) . . . Technotronic
Get Up, Get Into It, Get Involved . . . . James Brown
Get Up I Feel Like Being A Sex Machine . . . .
. . . . James Brown
Get Up Offa That Thing . . . . James Brown
Get Used To It . . . . Roger Voudouris
Get With U . . . . Lidell Townsell & M.T.F.
Getaway . . . . Earth, Wind & Fire
Getcha Back . . . . Beach Boys
Gettin' Ready For Love . . . . Diana Ross
Gettin' Together . . . . Tommy James
Getting Away With It . . . . Electronic
Getting Closer . . . . Wings
Getting Mighty Crowded . . . . Betty Everett
Getting The Corners . . . . T.S.U. Tornadoes
Getto Jam . . . . Domino
Ghetto . . . . Too Short
Ghetto (Part 1) . . . . Donny Hathaway
Ghetto Child . . . . Spinners
Ghetto Woman . . . . B.B. King
Ghost Dancer . . . . Addrisi Brothers
Ghost In You . . . . Psychedelic Furs
Ghost Riders In The Sky . . . . Baja Marimba Band
(Ghost) Riders In The Sky . . . . Outlaws
(Ghost) Riders In The Sky . . . . Ramrods
Ghost Town . . . . Cheap Trick
Ghost Town . . . . Don Cherry
Ghost Train . . . . Marty Robbins
Ghostbusters . . . . Ray Parker Jr.
Giddyup Go . . . . Red Sovine
Gidget . . . . James Darren
Gigi . . . . Billy Eckstine
Gigi . . . . Charlie Margulis
Gigi . . . . Vic Damone
Gigolo . . . . O'Bryan
Gimme All Your Lovin' . . . . ZZ Top
Gimme Dat Ding . . . . Pipkins
Gimme Gimme Good Lovin' . . . . . . Crazy Elephant
Gimme Little Sign . . . . Brenton Wood
Gimme Shelter . . . . Grand Funk Railroad
Gimme Shelter . . . . Merry Clayton
Gimme Some Lovin' . . . . Blues Brothers
Gimme Some Lovin' . . . . Kongas
Gimme Some Lovin' . . . . . Spencer Davis Group
Gimme Some Lovin' (Part 1) . . . . Traffic
Gimme Some More . . . . JB's
Gimme Your Money Please . . . .
. . . . Bachman-Turner Overdrive
Gina . . . . Johnny Mathis
Ginger Bread . . . . Frankie Avalon
Ginnie Bell . . . . Paul Dino
Ginny Come Lately . . . . Brian Hyland
Girl Can't Help It . . . . Journey
Girl Come Running . . . . Four Seasons
Girl Don't Care . . . . Gene Chandler
Girl Don't Come . . . . Sandie Shaw
Girl, Don't Let It Get You Down . . . . O'Jays
Girl From Ipanema . . . . Stan Getz/Astrud Gilberto
Girl From Peyton Place . . . . Dickey Lee
Girl From Spanish Town . . . . Marty Robbins
Girl Has To Know . . . . G-Clefs
Girl I Am Searching For You . . . . Stevie B
Girl I Need You . . . . Artistics
Girl I Used To Know . . . . Brother Beyond
Girl I'll Never Know . . . . Frankie Valli
Girl I'm Gonna Miss You . . . . Milli Vanilli
Girl, I've Been Hurt . . . . Snow
Girl In Love . . . . Outsiders
Girl In Trouble (Is A Temporary Thing) . . . .
. . . . Romeo Void
Girl Like You . . . . Gary Stites

Girl Like You . . . . Young Rascals
Girl Like You . . . . Smithereens
Girl Most Likely . . . . Jeannie C. Riley
Girl Of My Best Friend . . . . Ral Donner
Girl Of My Dreams . . . . Bram Tchaikovsky
Girl On A Swing . . . . . Gerry And The Pacemakers
Girl On Page 44 . . . . Four Lads
Girl On The Billboard . . . . Del Reeves
Girl That Stood Beside Me . . . . Bobby Darin
Girl U For Me . . . . Silk
Girl Watcher . . . . O'Kaysions
Girl Who Loved Me When . . . . Glass Bottle
Girl (Why You Wanna Make Me Blue) . . Temptations
Girl With The Golden Braids . . . . . . Perry Como
Girl With The Hungry Eyes . . . . Jefferson Starship
Girl (You Captivate Me) . . . . . . ? & The Mysterians
Girl You Know It's True . . . . Milli Vanilli
Girl You Need A Change Of Mind . . . .
. . . . Eddie Kendricks
Girl, You'll Be A Woman Soon . . . . . Neil Diamond
Girl You're Too Young . . . . Archie Bell & The Drells
Girl's A Devil . . . . Dukays
Girl's Alright With Me . . . . Temptations
Girl's School . . . . Wings
Girl's Song . . . . Fifth Dimension
Girlfriend . . . . Bobby Brown
Girlfriend . . . . Pebbles
Girls . . . . Dwight Twilley Band
Girls . . . . Major Lance
Girls . . . . Moments & Whatnauts
Girls Ain't Nothing But Trouble . . . .
. . . . D.J. Jazzy Jeff & The Fresh Prince
Girls Are More Fun . . . . Ray Parker Jr.
Girls Are Out To Get You . . . . Fascinations
Girls Can Get It . . . . Dr. Hook
Girls Can't Do What The Guys Do . . . . Betty Wright
Girls, Girls, Girls . . . . Coasters
Girls, Girls, Girls . . . . Motley Crue
Girls, Girls, Girls . . . . Steve Lawrence
(Girls, Girls, Girls) Made To Love . . . Eddie Hodges
Girls Grow Up Faster Than Boys . . . . . . Cookies
Girls In Love . . . . . . Gary Lewis And The Playboys
Girls It Ain't Easy . . . . Honeycone
Girls Just Want To Have Fun . . . . . Cyndi Lauper
Girls Nite Out . . . . Tyler Collins
Girls Talk . . . . Dave Edmunds
Girls Will Be Girls, Boys Will Be Boys . . . .
. . . . Isley Brothers
Girls With Guns . . . . Tommy Shaw
Gitarzan . . . . Ray Stevens
Give . . . . Missing Persons
Give A Damn . . . . Spanky And Our Gang
Give A Little Bit . . . . Supertramp
Give A Little Bit More . . . . Cliff Richard
Give A Little More . . . . Robert John
Give A Woman Love . . . . Bobbi Martin
Give All Your Love To Me . . . .
. . . . Gerry And The Pacemakers
Give Everybody Some . . . . Bar-Kays
Give Him A Great Big Kiss . . . . Shangri-Las
Give Ireland Back To The Irish . . . . Wings
Give It All You Got . . . . Chuck Mangione
Give It Away . . . . Chi-Lites
Give It To Me . . . . J. Geils Band
Give It To Me . . . . Mob
Give It To Me Baby . . . . Rick James
Give It To Me Good . . . . Trixter
Give It To The People . . . . Righteous Brothers
Give It To You . . . . Martha Wash
Give It Up . . . . KC
Give It Up . . . . Steve Miller Band
Give It Up . . . . Wilson Phillips
Give It Up Or Turn It A Loose . . . . . James Brown
Give It Up, Turn It Loose . . . . En Vogue

423

Give It Up (Turn It Loose) . . . . Tyrone Davis
Give It What You Got . . . . B.T. Express
Give Me A Reason To Be Gone
. . . . Maureen McGovern
Give Me All Night . . . . Carly Simon
Give Me All Your Love . . . . Whitesnake
Give Me An Inch . . . . Ian Matthews
Give Me An Inch Girl . . . . Robert Palmer
Give Me Just A Little More Time . . . .
. . . . Chairmen Of The Board
Give Me Love (Give Me Peace On Earth) . . . . . .
. . . . George Harrison
Give Me One More Chance . . Wilmer And The Dukes
Give Me The Keys . . . . Huey Lewis And The News
Give Me The Night . . . . George Benson
Give Me The Reason . . . . Luther Vandross
Give Me Time . . . . Dusty Springfield
Give Me Tonight . . . . Shannon
Give Me Your Heart . . . . Vanity Kills
Give Me Your Love . . . . Barbara Mason
Give Me Your Love . . . . Nat King Cole
Give Peace A Chance . . . . Plastic Ono Band
Give The Baby Anything . . . . Joe Tex
Give The People What They Want . . . . . . O'Jays
Give To Live . . . . Sammy Hagar
Give U My Heart . . Babyface Featuring Toni Braxton
Give Up Your Guns . . . . Buoys
Give Us This Day . . . . Joni James
Give Us Your Blessing . . . . Ray Peterson
Give Us Your Blessings . . . . Shangri-Las
Give Your Baby A Standing Ovation . . . . . . Dells
Givin' It All Up . . . . J. Geils Band
Giving Him Something He Can Feel . . . . En Vogue
Giving It All Away . . . . Roger Daltry
Giving It Up For Your Love . . . Delbert McClinton
Giving Up . . . . Donny Hathaway
Giving Up . . . . Gladys Knight & The Pips
Giving Up On Love . . . . Jerry Butler
Giving Up On Love . . . . Rick Astley
Giving You The Benefit . . . . Pebbles
Giving You The Best That I Got . . . . . Anita Baker
Glad All Over . . . . Dave Clark Five
Glad She's A Woman . . . . . . Bobby Goldsboro
Glad To Be Unhappy . . . . Mama's & Papa's
Glamorous Life . . . . Sheila E.
Glamour Boy . . . . Guess Who
Glamour Boys . . . . Living Colour
Glasshouse . . . . Temptations
Glendora . . . . Perry Como
Globe . . . . Big Audio Dynamite II
Globetrottin' . . . . Tornadoes
Gloria . . . . Enchantment
Gloria . . . . Laura Branigan
Gloria . . . . Shadows Of Knight
Gloria . . . . Them
Gloria's Theme . . . . Adam Wade
Glory Bound . . . . Grass Roots
Glory Days . . . . Bruce Springsteen
Glory, Glory . . . . Byrds
Glory Glory . . . . Rascals
Glory Of Love . . . . Dells
Glory Of Love . . . . Don Gardner And Dee Dee Ford
Glory Of Love . . . . Otis Redding
Glory Of Love . . . . Peter Cetera
Glory Of Love . . . . Roommates
Glow Worm . . . . Mills Brothers
Go . . . . Asia
Go Ahead And Cry . . . . . . Righteous Brothers
Go All The Way . . . . Raspberries
Go Away From My World . . . . . Marianne Faithfull
Go Away Little Boy . . . . . . Marlena Shaw
Go Away Little Girl . . . . Donny Osmond
Go Away Little Girl . . . . Happenings
Go Away Little Girl . . . . Steve Lawrence

Go Back . . . . Crabby Appleton
Go Chase A Moonbeam . . . . Jerry Vale
Go Down Gamblin' . . . . . . Blood, Sweat & Tears
Go For It . . . . Kim Wilde
Go For It! (Heart And Fire) . . . .
. . . . Joey B. Ellis & Tynetta Hare
Go For Soda . . . . Kim Mitchell
Go For Yours . . . . Lisa Lisa And Cult Jam
Go Home . . . . Stevie Wonder
Go Insane . . . . Lindsey Buckingham
Go, Jimmy, Go . . . . Jimmy Clanton
Go Now! . . . . Moody Blues
Go On Fool . . . . Marion Black
Go On Home . . . . Patti Page
Go West . . . . Village People
Go Where You Wanna Go . . . . . . Fifth Dimension
Go With Me . . . . Gene & Debbe
Go Your Own Way . . . . Fleetwood Mac
God Bless . . . . Arthur Conley
God Bless America . . . . Connie Francis
God Bless Our Love . . . . Ballads
God Bless Our Love . . . . Charles Brimmer
God Bless Whoever Sent You . . . . Originals
God, Country And My Baby . . . . . Johnny Burnette
God Knows I Love You . . . . Nancy Sinatra
God, Love And Rock & Roll . . . .
. . . . Teegarden & Van Winkle
God Only Knows . . . . Beach Boys
God Only Knows . . . . Marilyn Scott
Go-Go Girl . . . . Lee Dorsey
Goin' Away . . . . Fireballs
Goin' Back . . . . Byrds
Goin' Crazy! . . . . David Lee Roth
Goin' Down . . . . Gregg Guidry
Goin' Down (On The Road To L.A.) . . . .
. . . . Terry Black And Laurel Ward
Goin' Down Slow . . . . Bobby Bland
Goin' Home . . . . Bobby Sherman
Goin' Home . . . . Osmonds
Goin' Out Of My Head . . . . Frank Sinatra
Goin' Out Of My Head . . . .
. . . . Little Anthony And The Imperials
Goin' Out Of My Head/Can't Take My Eyes
Off You . . . . Lettermen
Goin' Places . . . . Jacksons
Goin' Steady . . . . Tommy Sands
Goin' To The Bank . . . . Commodores
Going Back To Cali . . . . L.L. Cool J
Going Back To Louisiana . . . . Bruce Channel
Going Down Slowly . . . . Pointer Sisters
Going Going Gone . . . . Brook Benton
Going Home . . . . Kenny G
Going In Circles . . . . . . Friends Of Distinction
Going In With My Eyes Open . . . . David Soul
Going Nowhere . . . . Los Bravos
Going Out With The Tide . . . .
. . . . Jivin' Gene And The Jokers
Going Through The Motions . . . . . . After Shock
Going Through The Motions . . . Hot Chocolate
Going To A Go Go . . . . Rolling Stones
Going To A Go-Go . . . . Miracles
Going To The Country . . . . Steve Miller Band
Going Up The Country . . . . Canned Heat
Gold . . . . John Stewart
Gold . . . . Spandau Ballet
Golden Age Of Rock 'N' Roll . . . . Mott The Hoople
Golden Rainbow . . . . Looking Glass
Golden Rule . . . . Cile Turner
Golden Years . . . . David Bowie
Goldfinger . . . . Billy Strange
Goldfinger . . . . Jack LaForge
Goldfinger . . . . John Barry
Goldfinger . . . . Shirley Bassey
Goldmine . . . . Pointer Sisters

Goodnight Tonight	Wings	Gravy Waltz	Steve Allen
Goodtime Girl	Nancy Sinatra	Grazing In The Grass	Friends Of Distinction
Goody Goody	Frankie Lymon And The Teenagers	Grazing In The Grass	Hugh Masekela
Goody Goody Gumdrops	1910 Fruitgum Company	Grease	Frankie Valli
Goody Two Shoes	Adam Ant	Greased Lightnin'	John Travolta
Goofus	Carpenters	Greasy Heart	Jefferson Airplane
Goonies 'R' Good Enough	Cyndi Lauper	Greasy Spoon	Hank Marr
Got A Date With An Angel	Billy Williams	Great Airplane Strike	Paul Revere And The Raiders
Got A Girl	Four Preps	Great Balls Of Fire	Jerry Lee Lewis
Got A Hold On Me	Christine McVie	Great Balls Of Fire	Tiny Tim
Got A Love For You	Jomanda	Great Commandment	Camouflage
Got A Match	Daddy-O's	Great Escape	Ray Stevens
Got A Match?	Frank Gallop	Great Gosh A'Mighty!	Little Richard
Got A Match?	Lou Stein	Great Imposter	Fleetwoods
Got A New Love	Good Question	Great Pretender	Platters
Got A Right To Love My Baby	B.B. King	Great Showman	Bob Luman
Got It Made	Crosby, Stills, Nash & Young	Greatest Hurt	Jackie Wilson
Got My Mind Set On You	George Harrison	Greatest Love	Dorsey Burnette
Got My Mojo Working	Jimmy Smith	Greatest Love Of All	George Benson
Got Pleasure	Ohio Players	Greatest Love Of All	Whitney Houston
Got The Feeling	Fabian	Green Chritma	Stan Freberg
Got To Be Real	Cheryl Lynn	Green Door	Jim Lowe
Got To Be There	Chaka Khan	Green Fields	Vogues
Got To Be There	Michael Jackson	Green Grass	Gary Lewis And The Playboys
Got To Believe In Love	Robin McNamara	Green Grass Of Texas	Texans
Got To Get	Leila K With Rob 'n' Raz	Green Grass Starts To Grow	Dionne Warwick
Got To Get You Into My Life	Beatles	Green, Green	New Christy Minstrels
Got To Get You Into My Life	Blood, Sweat & Tears	Green, Green Grass Of Home	Tom Jones
Got To Get You Into My Life	Earth, Wind & Fire	Green Leaves Of Summer	Brothers Four
Got To Get You Off My Mind	Solomon Burke	Green Leaves Of Summer	Kenny Ball
Got To Give In To Love	Bonnie Boyer	Green Light	American Breed
Got To Give It Up (Part 1)	Marvin Gaye	Green Mosquito	Tune Rockers
Got To Have Loving	Don Ray	Green Onions	Booker T & The MG's
Got To Have You Back	Isley Brothers	Green Onions	Dick Hyman
Got To Have Your Love	Mantronix	Green River	Creedence Clearwater Revival
Got To Have Your Lovin'	King Floyd	Green Tambourine	Lemon Pipers
Got To Love Somebody	Sister Sledge	Greenback Dollar	Kingston Trio
Got To Rock On	Kansas	Greenberg, Glickstein, Charles, David	
Got To See If I Can't Get Mommy (To		Smith & Jones	Cryan' Shames
Come Back Home)	Jerry Butler	Green-Eyed Lady	Sugarloaf
Got To Tell Me Something	Ana	Greenfields	Brothers Four
Got What You Need	Fantastic Johnny C	Greensleeves	Beverly Sisters
Got You On My Mind	Cookie And His Cupcakes	Greensleeves	Mason Williams
Gotta Be Funky	Monk Higgins	Greenwood Mississippi	Little Richard
Gotta Be The One	Maxine Nightingale	Greetings (This Is Uncle Sam)	Monitors
Gotta Find A Way	Moments	Gretchen	Diamonds
Gotta Get Away	Randy Meisner	Grim Reaper Of Love	Turtles
Gotta Get Back To You	Tommy James	Grits 'N Cornbread	Soul Runners
Gotta Get To Know You	Bobby Bland	Grits Ain't Groceries	Little Milton
Gotta Have Love	Steve Alaimo	Grizzly Bear	Youngbloods
Gotta Have More Love	Climax Blues Band	Groove Is In The Heart	Deee-Lite
Gotta Have Rain	Eydie Gorme	Groove Line	Heatwave
Gotta Have You	Stevie Wonder	Groove Me	King Floyd
Gotta Have Your Love	Sapphires	Grooviest Girl In The World	Fun And Games
Gotta Hold On To This Feeling		Groovin'	Booker T & The MG's
	Jr. Walker & The All Stars	Groovin'	Young Rascals
Gotta New Girl	Bobby Day	Groovin' In The Midnight	Maxi Priest
Gotta See Jane	R. Dean Taylor	Groovin' (Out On Life)	Newbeats
Gotta Serve Somebody	Bob Dylan	Groovin' With Mr. Bloe	Cool Heat
Gotta Travel On	Billy Grammer	Groovy	Joe Dodo & The Groovers
Gotta Travel On	Timi Yuro	Groovy Baby	Billy Abbott And The Jewels
Graceland	Paul Simon	Groovy Grubworm	Harlow Wilcox And The Oakies
Graduation Day	Arbors	Groovy Kind Of Love	Mindbenders
Graduation Day	Four Freshmen	Groovy Kind Of Love	Phil Collins
Graduation Day	Rover Boys	Groovy People	Lou Rawls
Graduation Song....Pomp And Circumstance		Groovy Situation	Gene Chandler
	Adrian Kimberly	Groovy Summertime	Love Generation
Graduation's Here	Fleetwoods	Groovy Train	Farm
Granada	Frank Sinatra	Grover Henson Feels Forgotten	Bill Cosby
Granddaddy (Part 1)	New Birth	Grow Some Funk Of Your Own	Elton John
Grandma's Hands	Bill Withers	Growin'	Loggins And Messina
Grandmother's Song	Steve Martin	Growin' Up	Dan Hill
Grass Is Greener	Brenda Lee	G.T.O.	Ronny & The Daytonas
Gravy (For My Mashed Potatoes)	Dee Dee Sharp	Guaglione	Perez Prado

H

Happy Weekend . . . . Dave "Baby" Cortez	Haven't You Heard . . . . Patrice Rushen
Happy Whistler . . . . Don Robertson	Havin' Fun . . . . Dion
Happy Xmas (War Is Over) . . . . . John & Yoko	Having A Party . . . . Ovations
. . . . With The Harlem Community Choir	Having A Party . . . . Sam Cooke
Happy-Go-Lucky Me . . . . Paul Evans	Hawaii Five-O . . . . Ventures
Harbor Lights . . . . Platters	Hawaii Honeymoon . . . . Waikikis
Harbor Lights . . . . Sammy Kaye	Hawaii Tattoo . . . . Martin Denny
Hard Day's Night . . . . Beatles	Hawaii Tattoo . . . . Waikikis
Hard Day's Night . . . . Ramsey Lewis Trio	Hawaiian War Chant . . . . Billy Vaughn
Hard Habit To Break . . . . Chicago	Hawaiian Wedding Song . . . . . . Andy Williams
Hard Headed Woman . . . . Elvis Presley	Hazard . . . . Richard Marx
Hard Hearted Hannah . . . . Ray Charles	Hazy Shade Of Winter . . . . Bangles
Hard Luck Woman . . . . Kiss	Hazy Shade Of Winter . . . . . . Simon & Garfunkel
Hard Rock Cafe . . . . Carole King	He . . . . Al Hibbler
Hard Times . . . . Boz Scaggs	He . . . . McGuire Sisters
Hard Times . . . . James Taylor	He . . . . Righteous Brothers
Hard Times . . . . Peter Skellern	He Ain't Giving You None . . . . Freddie Scott
Hard Times For Lovers . . . . . . Jennifer Holliday	He Ain't Heavy, He's My Brother . . . . . . Hollies
Hard Times For Lovers . . . . Judy Collins	He Ain't Heavy...He's My Brother . . . Neil Diamond
Hard To Get . . . . Gisele MacKenzie	He Ain't Heavy...He's My Brother
Hard To Handle . . . . Black Crowes	. . . . Olivia Newton-John
Hard To Handle . . . . Otis Redding	He Called Me Baby . . . . Candi Staton
Hard To Say . . . . Dan Fogelberg	He Called Me Baby . . . . Ella Washington
Hard To Say I'm Sorry . . . . Chicago	He Can't Love You . . . . Michael Stanley Band
Hard Work . . . . John Handy	He Could Be The One . . . . Josie Cotton
Harden My Heart . . . . Quarterflash	He Cried . . . . Shangri-Las
Harder I Try . . . . Free Movement	He Did Me Wrong . . . . Patti Dahlstrom
Hardest Part . . . . Blondie	He Did With Me . . . . Vicki Lawrence
Harem Dance . . . . Armenian Jazz Sextet	He Don't Love You (Like I Love You) . . . . . Dawn
Harlan County . . . . Jim Ford	He Gives Me Love . . . . Lesley Gore
Harlem . . . . Fifth Dimension	He Got You . . . . Ronnie Milsap
Harlem Nocturne . . . . Viscounts	He Knows I Love Him Too Much . . . . Paris Sisters
Harlem Shuffle . . . . Bob & Earl	He Made A Woman Out Of Me . . . . Bobbie Gentry
Harlem Shuffle . . . . Rolling Stones	He Needs Me . . . . Gloria Lynne
Harlem Shuffle . . . . Traits	He Says The Same Things To Me . . . . Skeeter Davis
Harper Valley P.T.A. . . . . . . Jeannie C. Riley	He Thinks I Still Care . . . . Connie Francis
Harper Valley P.T.A. (Later That Same Day)	He Touched Me . . . . Barbra Streisand
. . . . Sheb Wooley	He Was Really Sayin' Somethin' . . . . . Velvelettes
Harpo's Blues . . . . Phoebe Snow	He Will Break Your Heart . . . . Jerry Butler
Harry The Hairy Ape . . . . Ray Stevens	He Won't Ask Me . . . . Cilla Black
Harry Truman . . . . Chicago	He'd Rather Have The Rain . . . . . Heaven Bound
Harvest For The World . . . . . Isley Brothers	He'll Be Back . . . . Players
Has Anyone Ever Written Anything For You	He'll Have To Go . . . . Jim Reeves
. . . . Stevie Nicks	He'll Have To Go . . . . Solomon Burke
Hat 2 Da Back . . . . TLC	He'll Have To Stay . . . . Jeanne Black
Hats Off To Larry . . . . Del Shannon	He'll Never Love You (Like I Do) . . Freddie Jackson
Haunted House . . . . Jumpin Gene Simmons	He's A Bad Boy . . . . Carole King
Have A Drink On Me . . . . Buddy Thomas	He's A Friend . . . . Eddie Kendricks
Have A Good Time . . . . Sue Thompson	He's A Good Guy (Yes He Is) . . . . . Marvelettes
Have A Heart . . . . Bonnie Raitt	He's A Liar . . . . Bee Gees
Have I Stayed Too Long . . . . . Sonny & Cher	He's A Lover . . . . Mary Wells
Have I The Right? . . . . Honeycombs	He's A Rebel . . . . Crystals
Have I Told You Lately . . . . Rod Stewart	He's Gone . . . . Bee Gees
Have I Told You Lately That I Love You?	He's Gonna Step On You Again . . . . . John Kongos
. . . . Ricky Nelson	He's Got No Love . . . . Searchers
Have Mercy Baby . . . . Bobbettes	He's Got The Power . . . . Exciters
Have You Ever Been Lonely . . . . Caravelles	He's Got The Whole World (In His Hands) . . . . .
Have You Ever Loved Somebody . . Freddie Jackson	. . . . Laurie London
Have You Ever Loved Somebody . . . . . Searchers	He's In Town . . . . Tokens
Have You Ever Needed Someone So Bad	He's Mine . . . . Alice Wonder Land
. . . . Def Leppard	He's Mine . . . . Platters
Have You Ever Seen The Rain	(He's My) Dreamboat . . . . Connie Francis
. . . . Creedence Clearwater Revival	He's My Girl . . . . David Hallyday
Have You Heard . . . . Duprees	He's My Guy . . . . Irma Thomas
Have You Heard . . . . Joni James	He's Not Just Another Soldier . . . . . Little Richard
Have You Looked Into Your Heart . . . Jerry Vale	(He's) Raining In My Sunshine . . . . .
Have You Never Been Mellow . . Olivia Newton-John	. . . . Jay & The Americans
Have You Seen Her . . . . Chi-Lites	He's Ready . . . . Poppies
Have You Seen Her . . . . M.C. Hammer	He's So Fine . . . . Chiffons
Have You Seen Her Face . . . . Byrds	He's So Fine . . . . Jane Oliver
Have You Seen Your Mother, Baby, Standing	He's So Fine . . . . Jody Miller
In The Shadow? . . . . Rolling Stones	He's So Fine . . . . . Kristy And Jimmy McNichol
Haven't Got Time For The Pain . . . . . Carly Simon	He's So Shy . . . . Pointer Sisters
Haven't Stopped Dancing Yet . . . . Gonzales	He's Sure The Boy I Love . . . . Crystals

Hello Fool . . . . Ralph Emery
Hello Goodbye . . . . Beatles
Hello Heartache, Goodbye Love . . . .
. . . . Little Peggy March
Hello Hello . . . . Sopwith "Camel"
Hello, Hello, Hello . . . . New England
Hello Hurray . . . . Alice Cooper
Hello, I Love You . . . . Doors
Hello It's Me . . . . Nazz
Hello It's Me . . . . Todd Rundgren
Hello Jim . . . . Paul Anka
Hello Mary Lou . . . . Ricky Nelson
Hello Muddah, Hello Fadduh! . . . . . Allan Sherman
Hello Muddah, Hello Fadduh - 1964 . . . .
. . . . Allan Sherman
Hello Old Friend . . . . Eric Clapton
Hello Out There . . . . Carl Belew
Hello Out There . . . . Nick Noble
Hello Pretty Girl . . . . Ronnie Dove
Hello Stranger . . . . Barbara Lewis
Hello Stranger . . . . Yvonne Elliman
Hello Walls #2 . . . . Sheb Wooley
Hello Walls . . . . Faron Young
Hello Young Lovers . . . . Paul Anka
Helluva . . . . Brotherhood Creed
Help . . . . Beatles
Help Is On Its Way . . . . Little River Band
Help Me . . . . Joni Mitchell
Help Me! . . . . . . Marcy Levy And Robin Gibb
Help Me Find A Way (To Say I Love You) . . . . . .
. . . . . . Little Anthony And The Imperials
Help Me Girl . . . . Animals
Help Me Girl . . . . Outsiders
Help Me Make It Through The Night . . . .
. . . . Gladys Knight & The Pips
Help Me Make It Through The Night . . . . Joe Simon
Help Me Make It Through The Night . . Sammi Smith
Help Me Make It (To My Rockin' Chair) . . . .
. . . . B.J. Thomas
Help Me Rhonda . . . . Beach Boys
Help Me Rhonda . . . . Johnny Rivers
Help The Poor . . . . B.B. King
Help Wanted . . . . Hudson Brothers
Help Yourself . . . . Tom Jones
Help Yourself . . . . Undisputed Truth
Helpless . . . . Jackie Wilson
Helpless . . . . Kim Weston
Helpless . . . . Platters
Henrietta . . . . . Jimmy Dee And The Offbeats
Her Royal Majesty . . . . James Darren
Her Town Too . . . . James Taylor And J.D. Souther
Here . . . . Tony Martin
Here And Now . . . . Luther Vandross
Here Come Da Judge . . . . Buena Vistas
Here Come Those Tears Again . . . . Jackson Browne
Here Comes Heaven . . . . Eddy Arnold
Here Comes My Baby . . . . Tremeloes
Here Comes My Girl . . . .
. . . . Tom Petty And The Heartbreakers
Here Comes Summer . . . . Jerry Keller
Here Comes Summer . . . . Wildfire
Here Comes That Feelin' . . . . Brenda Lee
Here Comes That Rainy Day Feeling Again . . . . . .
. . . . Fortunes
Here Comes The Boy . . . . Tracey Dey
Here Comes The Hammer . . . . . . M.C. Hammer
Here Comes The Judge . . . . Magistrates
Here Comes The Judge . . . . . . Pigmeat Markham
Here Comes The Judge . . . . Shorty Long
Here Comes The Night . . . . Beach Boys
Here Comes The Night . . . . Nick Gilder
Here Comes The Night . . . . Them
Here Comes The Rain . . . . Eurythmics
Here Comes The Rain, Baby . . . . Eddy Arnold

Here Comes The Sun . . . . Richie Havens
Here I Am . . . . Dionne Warwick
Here I Am Baby . . . . Marvelettes
Here I Am (Come And Take Me) . . . . . . Al Green
Here I Am (Come And Take Me) UB40
Here I Am (Just When I Thought I Was
Over You) . . . . Air Supply
Here I Go Again . . . . Miracles
Here I Go Again . . . . Whitesnake
Here I Stand . . . . Rip Chords
Here I Stand . . . . Wade Flemons
Here In My Heart . . . . Al Martino
Here Is Where Your Love Belongs . . . .
. . . . Sons Of Champlin
Here It Comes . . . . MC Serch
Here It Comes Again . . . . Fortunes
Here She Comes . . . . Bonnie Tyler
Here She Comes . . . . Tymes
Here, There And Everywhere . . . . Emmylou Harris
Here, There And Everywhere . . . . . . Fourmost
Here To Love You . . . . Doobie Brothers
Here We Are . . . . Gloria Estefan
Here We Go . . . . C + C Music Factory
Here We Go Again! . . . . Portrait
Here We Go Again . . . . Ray Charles
Here With Me . . . . REO Speedwagon
Here You Come Again . . . . Dolly Parton
Here's To You . . . . Hamilton Camp
Hernando's Hideaway . . . . Archie Bleyer
Hero . . . . David Crosby & Phil Collins
Hero . . . . Mariah Carey
Heroes . . . . Commodores
Heroes And Villains . . . . Beach Boys
Hey! Baby . . . . Bruce Channel
Hey Baby . . . . Henry Lee Summer
Hey! Baby . . . . Jose Feliciano
Hey Baby . . . . Ringo Starr
Hey Baby . . . . Ted Nugent
Hey Baby (They're Playing Our Song) . . . .
. . . . Buckinghams
Hey Big Brother . . . . Rare Earth
Hey, Bobba Needle . . . . Chubby Checker
Hey Deanie . . . . Shaun Cassidy
Hey Donna . . . . Rythm Syndicate
Hey, E.T. . . . . Dickie Goodman
Hey Girl . . . . Donny Osmond
Hey, Girl . . . . Freddie Scott
Hey Girl Don't Bother Me . . . . Tams
Hey Girl (I Like Your Style) . . . . . Temptations
Hey Grandma . . . . Moby Grape
Hey Harmonica Man . . . . Stevie Wonder
Hey Hey Bunny . . . . John Fred & His Playboy Band
Hey! Jealous Lover . . . . Frank Sinatra
Hey Jealousy . . . . Gin Blossoms
Hey Jean, Hey Dean . . . . Dean And Jean
Hey Joe . . . . Cher
Hey Joe . . . . Frankie Laine
Hey Joe . . . . Leaves
Hey Joe . . . . Wilson Pickett
Hey Jude . . . . Beatles
Hey Jude . . . . Wilson Pickett
Hey Ladies . . . . Beastie Boys
Hey Lawdy Mama . . . . Steppenwolf
Hey, Leroy, Your Mama's Callin' You . . . .
. . . . Jimmy Castor
Hey, Let's Twist . . . . . Joey Dee & The Starliters
Hey Little Cobra . . . . Rip Chords
Hey Little Girl . . . . Dee Clark
Hey! Little Girl . . . . Del Shannon
Hey Little Girl . . . . Foster Sylvers
Hey Little Girl . . . . Gary Stites
Hey Little Girl . . . . Major Lance
Hey! Little Girl . . . . Techniques
Hey Little Lucy . . . . Conway Twitty

430

431

Hold The Line . . . . Toto	Honeythief . . . . Hipsway
Hold What You've Got . . . . Joe Tex	Honky Cat . . . . Elton John
Hold You Tight . . . . Tara Kemp	Honky Tonk '65 . . . . Lonnie Mack
Hold Your Head Up . . . . Argent	Honky Tonk (Part 1) . . . . James Brown
Holdin' On . . . . Tane Cain	Honky Tonk (Parts 1 & 2) . . . . . Bill Doggett
Holdin' On For Dear Love . . . . Lobo	Honky Tonk Women . . . . . . Rolling Stones
Holdin' On To Yesterday . . . . Ambrosia	Honolulu Lulu . . . . Jan & Dean
Holding Back The Years . . . . Simply Red	Hoochi Coochi Coo
Holding My Heart . . . . Bang	. . . . Hank Ballard And The Midnighters
Holding On . . . . Steve Winwood	Hook And Sling (Part 1) . . . . Eddie Bo
Holding On (When Love Is Gone) . . . . . . L.T.D.	Hooka Tooka . . . . Chubby Checker
Holding Out For A Hero . . . . Bonnie Tyler	Hooked On A Feeling . . . . B.J. Thomas
Hole Hearted . . . . Extreme	Hooked On A Feeling . . . . Blue Swede
Hole In My Heart (All The Way To China)	Hooked On Classics . . Royal Philharmonic Orchestra
. . . . Cyndi Lauper	Hooked On Swing . . . . Larry Elgart And
Hole In My Pocket . . . . Barry Goldberg	. . . . His Manhattan Swing Orchestra
Hole In The Wall . . . . Packers	Hooked On You . . . . Bread
Holiday . . . . Bee Gees	Hooked On You . . . . Sweet Sensation
Holiday . . . . Kool & The Gang	Hoopa Hoola . . . . Betty Johnson
Holiday . . . . Madonna	Hoop-De-Doo . . . . Perry Como
Holiday . . . . Nazareth	Hoop-Dee-Doo . . . . Kay Starr
Holiday . . . . Other Ones	Hooray For Hazel . . . . Tommy Roe
Holiday For Clowns . . . . Brian Hyland	Hooray For The Salvation Army Band . . . Bill Cosby
Holly Go Softly . . . . Cornerstone	Hootenanny . . . . Glencoves
Holly Holy . . . . . Jr. Walker & The All Stars	Hop Scotch . . . . Santo & Johnny
Holly Holy . . . . Neil Diamond	Hope Of Deliverance . . . . Paul McCartney
Hollywood . . . . Boz Scaggs	Hope That We Can Be Together Soon . . Sharon Paige
Hollywood . . . . Connie Francis	. . . . And Harold Melvin And The Bluenotes
Hollywood . . . . Rufus Featuring Chaka Khan	Hope You Love Me Like You Say You Do . . . .
Hollywood . . . . Shooting Star	. . . . Huey Lewis And The News
Hollywood Hot . . . . Eleventh Hour	Hopeless . . . . Andy Williams
Hollywood Nights	Hopelessly . . . . Rick Astley
. . . . Bob Seger & The Silver Bullet Band	Hopelessly Devoted To You . . . Olivia Newton-John
Hollywood Swinging . . . . . Kool & The Gang	Hoppy, Gene And Me . . . . Roy Rogers
Holy Cow . . . . Lee Dorsey	Horizontal Bop . . . . Bob Seger
Holy Cow . . . . Stefan	Horse . . . . Cliff Nobles & Co.
Holy Man . . . . Diane Kolby	Horse Fever . . . . Cliff Nobles & Co.
Holy Man . . . . Scott McKenzie	Horse With No Name . . . . America
Holyanna . . . . Toto	Hot 'N' Nasty . . . . Humble Pie
Homburg . . . . Procol Harum	Hot Blooded . . . . Foreigner
Home And Dry . . . . Gerry Rafferty	Hot Child In The City . . . . Nick Gilder
Home Cookin' . . . . . Jr. Walker & The All Stars	Hot Dawgit . . . .
Home From The Hill . . . . Kingston Trio	. . . . . . Ramsey Lewis And Earth, Wind & Fire
Home Is Where The Hatred Is . . . Esther Phillips	Hot Diggity (Dog Ziggity Boom) . . . Perry Como
Home Of The Brave . . . . Bonnie And The Treasures	Hot For Teacher . . . . Van Halen
Home Of The Brave . . . . Jody Miller	Hot Fun In The Summertime . . . . David T. Walker
Home Sweet Home . . . . Motley Crue	Hot Fun In The Summertime . . . . . Dayton
Home Tonight . . . . Aerosmith	Hot Fun In The Summertime . . . .
Homecoming . . . . Hagood Hardy	. . . . Sly & The Family Stone
Homely Girl . . . . Chi-Lites	Hot Girls In Love . . . . Loverboy
Homeward Bound . . . . . . Simon & Garfunkel	Hot Hot Hot . . . . Buster Poindexter
Homies . . . . . . Lighter Shade Of Brown	Hot Hot Hot!!! . . . . Cure
Honest I Do . . . . Innocents	Hot In The City . . . . Billy Idol
Honestly . . . . Stryper	Hot Legs . . . . Rod Stewart
Honestly And Truly . . . . Tommy Edwards	Hot Line . . . . Sylvers
Honesty . . . . Billy Joel	Hot Love . . . . T. Rex
Honey . . . . Bobby Goldsboro	Hot Love, Cold World . . . . Bob Welch
Honey . . . . O.C. Smith	Hot Number . . . . Foxy
Honey Child . . . . Bad Company	Hot Pants . . . . Salvage
Honey Chile . . . . . Martha & The Vandellas	Hot Pants - I'm Coming, I'm Coming,
Honey Come Back . . . . Glen Campbell	I'm Coming Brown . . . . Bobby Byrd
Honey Do . . . . Strangeloves	Hot Pants (She Got To Use What She Got,
Honey Don't Leave L.A. . . . . . . James Taylor	To Get What She Wants) (Part 1) . . . James Brown
Honey, Honey . . . . Abba	Hot Pastrami . . . . Dartells
Honey, Honey . . . . David Hudson	Hot Pastrami With Mashed Potatoes (Part 1) . . . . . .
Honey Honey . . . . Sweet Dreams	. . . . Joey Dee & The Starliters
Honey Hush . . . . Joe Turner	Hot Pepper . . . . Floyd Cramer
Honey I . . . . George McCrae	Hot Rod Hearts . . . . Robbie Dupree
Honey I Still Love You . . . . Mark IV	Hot Rod Lincoln . . . .
Honey Love . . . R. Kelly & Public Announcement	. . . . Charlie Ryan And The Timberline Riders
Honey Please, Can't Ya See . . . . . . Barry White	Hot Rod Lincoln . . . .
Honey Trippin' . . . . Mystic Moods	. . Commander Cody And His Lost Planet Airmen
Honey-Babe . . . . Art Mooney	Hot Rod Lincoln . . . . Johnny Bond
Honeycomb . . . . Jimmie Rodgers	Hot Shot . . . . Buena Vistas

433

I Don't Care If The Sun Don't Shine (EP) . . . .
. . . . Elvis Presley
(I Don't Care) Only Love Me . . . . Steve Lawrence
I Don't Have The Heart . . . . James Ingram
I Don't Know . . . . Ruth Brown
I Don't Know Anybody else . . . . Black Box
I Don't Know How To Love Him . . . . Helen Reddy
I Don't Know How To Love Him . . Yvonne Elliman
I Don't Know If It's Right . . . .
. . . . Evelyn "Champagne" King
I Don't Know What It Is . . . . Bluenotes
I Don't Know What It Is, But It Sure
Is Funky . . . . Ripple
I Don't Know What You've Got But
It's Got Me (Part 1) . . . . Little Richard
I Don't Know Where To Start . . . . . Eddie Rabbitt
I Don't Know Why . . . . Linda Scott
I Don't Know Why . . . . Rolling Stones
I Don't Know Why . . . . Stevie Wonder
I Don't Like Mondays . . . . Boomtown Rats
I Don't Like To Sleep Alone . . . .
. . . . Paul Anka With Odia Coates
I Don't Love You Anymore . . . . London Quireboys
I Don't Love You Anymore . . . . Teddy Pendergrass
I Don't Love You No More . . . . . . Jimmy Norman
I Don't Mind . . . . James Brown
I Don't Mind At All . . . . Bourgeois Tagg
I Don't Need No Doctor . . . . Humble Pie
I Don't Need You . . . . Kenny Rogers
I Don't Need You . . . . Rupert Holmes
I Don't Need You Anymore . . . . . . Teddy Bears
I Don't See Me In Your Eyes Anymore . . Charlie Rich
I Don't Think That Man Should Sleep Alone . . . . .
. . . . Ray Parker Jr.
I Don't Wanna Be A Loser . . . . Lesley Gore
I Don't Wanna Cry . . . . Mariah Carey
I Don't Wanna Cry . . . . Ronnie Dyson
I Don't Wanna Dance . . . . Eddy Grant
I Don't Wanna Fight . . . . Tina Turner
I Don't Wanna Get Drafted . . . . Frank Zappa
I Don't Wanna Go . . . . Joey Travolta
I Don't Wanna Go On With You Like That . . . . .
. . . . Elton John
I Don't Wanna Live Without Your Love . . . . Chicago
I Don't Wanna Lose You . . Daryl Hall & John Oates
I Don't Wanna Lose You . . . . Johnnie Taylor
I Don't Wanna Lose You Baby . . . . . Chad & Jeremy
I Don't Wanna Lose Your Love . . . . Emotions
I Don't Want A Lover . . . . Texas
I Don't Want Nobody Else (To Dance
With You) . . . . Narada Michael Walden
I Don't Want Nobody To Give Me Nothing (Open Up
The Door, I'll Get It Myself) . . . . . . James Brown
I Don't Want To Be A Hero . . . . Johnny Hates Jazz
I Don't Want To Be Hurt Anymore . . . Nat King Cole
I Don't Want To Cry . . . . Chuck Jackson
I Don't Want To Cry . . . . Ruby Winters
I Don't Want To Do Wrong . . . .
. . . . Gladys Knight & The Pips
I Don't Want To Hear It Anymore . . . .
. . . . Dusty Springfield
I Don't Want To Know Your Name . . . Glen Campbell
I Don't Want To Live Without You . . . . Foreigner
I Don't Want To Lose You . . . . . . Jackie Wilson
(I Don't Want To Love You But) You
Got Me Anyway . . Sutherland Brothers & Quiver
I Don't Want To Make Sweet Music . . . . . Delfonics
I Don't Want To See Tomorrow . . . . Nat King Cole
I Don't Want To See You . . . . . Michael Morales
I Don't Want To See You Again . . Peter And Gordon
I Don't Want To Set The World On Fire . . . .
. . . . Somethin' Smith & The Redheads
I Don't Want To Spoil The Party . . . . Beatles
I Don't Want To Take A Chance . . . . . . Mary Wells

I Don't Want To Talk About It . . . . . . Rod Stewart
I Don't Want To Walk Without You . . Barry Manilow
I Don't Want To Walk Without You . . . .
. . . . Phylis McGuire
I Don't Want Your Love . . . . Duran Duran
I Dreamed . . . . Betty Johnson
I Dreamed Last Night . . . .
. . . . Justin Hayward & John Lodge
I Dreamed Of A Hill-Billy Heaven . . . . . Tex Ritter
I Drove All Night . . . . Cyndi Lauper
I Eat Cannibals . . . . Total Coelo
I Fall To Pieces . . . . Patsy Cline
I Feel A Song (In My Heart) . . . .
. . . . Gladys Knight & The Pips
I Feel Fine . . . . Beatles
I Feel For You . . . . Chaka Khan
I Feel For You . . . . Depeche Mode
I Feel Free . . . . Belinda Carlisle
I Feel Good . . . . Shirley & Lee
I Feel Good (I Feel Bad) . . . .
. . . . Lewis & Clarke Expedition
I Feel Like A Bullet (In The Gun Of
Robert Ford) . . . . Elton John
I Feel Love . . . . Donna Summer
I Feel Sanctified . . . . Commodores
I Feel So Bad . . . . Elvis Presley
I Feel The Earth Move . . . . Martika
I Feel The Magic . . . . Belinda Carlisle
I Fooled You This Time . . . . Gene Chandler
I Forgot To Be Your Lover . . . . William Bell
I Fought The Law . . . . Bobby Fuller Four
I Fought The Law . . . . Sam Neely
I Found A Girl . . . . Jan & Dean
I Found A Love . . . . Falcons
I Found A Love Oh What A Love . . . . Jo Ann & Troy
I Found A Love (Part 1) . . . . Wilson Pickett
I Found A Rainbow . . . . Swingin' Medallions
I Found A True Love . . . . Wilson Pickett
I Found My Dad . . . . Joe Simon
I Found Somebody . . . . Glenn Frey
I Found Someone . . . . Cher
I Found Someone . . . . Laura Branigan
I Found Sunshine . . . . Chi-Lites
I Found You . . . . Frankie Laine
I Get Around . . . . 2 Pac
I Get Around . . . . Beach Boys
I Get Excited . . . . Rick Springfield
I Get High On You . . . . Sly Stone
I Get Ideas . . . . Tony Martin
I Get Lifted . . . . George McCrae
I Get Off On It . . . . Tony Joe White
I Get So Lonely . . . . Four Knights
I Get The Sweetest Feeling . . . . . . Jackie Wilson
I Get Weak . . . . Belinda Carlisle
I Go Ape . . . . Neil Sedaka
I Go Crazy . . . . Paul Davis
I Go To Extremes . . . . Billy Joel
I Go To Pieces . . . . . Cotton, Lloyd And Christian
I Go To Pieces . . . . Peter And Gordon
I Go To Rio . . . . Pablo Cruise
I Got A Bag Of My Own . . . . James Brown
I Got A Feeling . . . . Ricky Nelson
I Got A Line On You . . . . Spirit
I Got A Man . . . . Positive K
I Got A Name . . . . Jim Croce
I Got A Thing About You Baby . . . . Billy Lee Riley
I Got A Thing, You Got A Thing,
Everybody's Got A Thing . . . . Funkadelic
I Got A Wife . . . . Mark IV
I Got A Woman . . . . Freddie Scott
I Got A Woman . . . . Ray Charles
I Got A Woman . . . . Rick Nelson
I Got Ants In My Pants (Part 1) . . . . . James Brown
I Got Love . . . . Melba Moore

436

438

440

441

I'll Take Care Of You . . . . Bobby Bland
I'll Take Care Of Your Cares . . . . . . Frankie Laine
I'll Take Good Care Of You . . . . . Garnet Mimms
I'll Take You Home . . . . Corsairs
I'll Take You Home . . . . Drifters
I'll Take You There . . . . Staple Singers
I'll Take You Where The Music's Playing . . Drifters
I'll Touch A Star . . . . Terry Stafford
I'll Try Anything . . . . Dusty Springfield
I'll Try Something New . . . . Miracles
I'll Try Something New . . . Supremes & Temptations
I'll Try Something New . . . . Taste Of Honey
I'll Tumble 4 Ya . . . . Culture Club
I'll Turn To Stone . . . . Four Tops
I'll Wait . . . . Van Halen
I'll Wait For You . . . . Frankie Avalon
I'll Walk Alone . . . . Don Cornell
I'm A Believer . . . . Giant
I'm A Believer . . . . Monkees
I'm A Believer . . . . Neil Diamond
I'm A Better Man . . . . . . Engelbert Humperdinck
I'm A Drifter . . . . Bobby Goldsboro
I'm A Fool . . . . Dino, Desi & Billy
I'm A Fool To Care . . . . Joe Barry
I'm A Fool To Care . . . . Ray Charles
I'm A Greedy Man (Part 1) . . . . James Brown
I'm A Happy Man . . . . Jive Five
I'm A Hog For You . . . . Coasters
I'm A Man . . . . Chicago
I'm A Man . . . . Fabian
I'm A Man . . . . Spencer Davis Group
I'm A Man . . . . Yardbirds
I'm A Midnight Mover . . . . Wilson Pickett
I'm A Nut . . . . Leroy Pullins
I'm A Player . . . . Too Short
I'm A Ramblin' Man . . . . Waylon Jennings
(I'm A) Road Runner . . . Jr. Walker & The All Stars
I'm A Rocker . . . . Raspberries
I'm A Stranger Here . . . . . Five Man Electrical Band
I'm A Telling You . . . . Jerry Butler
I'm A Train . . . . Albert Hammond
I'm A Witness . . . . Tommy Hunt
I'm A Woman . . . . Maria Muldaur
I'm A Woman . . . . Peggy Lee
(I'm A) Yo Yo Man . . . . Rick Cunha
I'm Afraid To Go Home . . . . Brian Hyland
I'm Alive . . . . Electric Light Orchestra
I'm Alive . . . . Gamma
I'm Alive . . . . Hollies
I'm Alive . . . . Neil Diamond
I'm Almost Ready . . . . Pure Prairie League
I'm Alright (Theme From
   "Caddyshack") . . . . Kenny Loggins
I'm Available . . . . Margie Rayburn
I'm Better Off Without You . . . . . Main Ingredient
I'm Blue (The Gong Gong Song) . . . . Ikettes
I'm Comin' Home . . . . Dave Edmunds
I'm Comin' Home . . . . Tommy James
I'm Comin' Home, Cindy . . . . Trini Lopez
I'm Comin' On Back To You . . . . . . Jackie Wilson
I'm Coming Home . . . . Johnny Mathis
I'm Coming Home . . . . Marv Johnson
I'm Coming Home . . . . Spinners
I'm Coming Home . . . . Stories
I'm Coming Home . . . . Tom Jones
I'm Coming Out . . . . Diana Ross
I'm Confessin' . . . . Terri Dean
I'm Confessin' (That I Love You) . . . . . Frank Ifield
I'm Crying . . . . Animals
I'm Doin' Fine Now . . . . New York City
I'm Dreaming . . . . Jennifer Warnes
I'm Drowning My Sorrows . . . . . . Teresa Brewer
I'm Easy . . . . Keith Carradine
I'm Every Woman . . . . Chaka Khan

I'm Every Woman . . . . Whitney Houston
I'm Falling In Love With You . . . .
   . . . . Little Anthony And The Imperials
I'm Free . . . . Al Hibbler
I'm Free . . . . Jon Secada
I'm Free . . . . Soup Dragons
I'm Free . . . . Who
I'm Free (Heaven Helps The Man) . . Kenny Loggins
I'm Gettin' Better . . . . Jim Reeves
I'm Girl Scoutin' . . . . Intruders
I'm Glad I Could Be So Happy . . . Magnificent Men
I'm Goin' Down . . . . Bruce Springsteen
I'm Going Back To School . . . . Dee Clark
I'm Going Down . . . . Rose Royce
I'm Gonna Be (500 Miles) . . . . Proclaimers
I'm Gonna Be A Country Girl
   Again . . . . Buffy Sainte-Marie
I'm Gonna Be A Wheel Some Day . . . . Fats Domino
I'm Gonna Be Strong . . . . Gene Pitney
I'm Gonna Be Warm This Winter . . . Connie Francis
I'm Gonna Change Him . . . . Cathy Carr
I'm Gonna Cry . . . . Lloyd Price
I'm Gonna Do What They Do To Me . . . . B.B. King
I'm Gonna Get Married . . . . Lloyd Price
I'm Gonna Get You . . . . Bizarre Inc.
I'm Gonna Hire A Wino To Decorate
   Our Home . . . . David Frizzell
I'm Gonna Hold On As Long As I Can . . Marvelettes
I'm Gonna Knock On Your Door . . . . Eddie Hodges
I'm Gonna Love You . . . . Intrigues
I'm Gonna Love You Just A Little More
   Baby . . . . Barry White
I'm Gonna Love You Too . . . . Buddy Holly
I'm Gonna Love You Too . . . . Hullaballoos
I'm Gonna Make You Love Me . . . Dee Dee Warwick
I'm Gonna Make You Love Me . . . Madeline Bell
I'm Gonna Make You Love
   Me . . . . Supremes & Temptations
I'm Gonna Make You Mine . . . . . . Lou Christie
I'm Gonna Miss You . . . . Artistics
I'm Gonna Miss You . . . . Kenny Loggins
I'm Gonna Sit Right Down . . . . Fabian
I'm Gonna Sit Right Down And
   Write Myself A Letter . . . . . Billy Williams
I'm Gonna Take Care Of Everything . . . . Rubicon
I'm Gonna Tear You A New Heart . . . Clarence Reid
I'm Gonna Tear Your Playhouse Down . . Paul Young
I'm Happy Just To Dance With You . . . . . Beatles
I'm Happy That Love Has Found You . . . Jimmy Hall
I'm Henry VIII I Am . . . . Herman's Hermits
I'm Her Fool . . . . Billy Swan
I'm Here To Get My Baby Out Of
   Jail . . . . Everly Brothers
I'm Hurtin' . . . . Roy Orbison
I'm In A Different World . . . . Four Tops
I'm In A Philly Mood . . . . Daryl Hall
I'm In Love . . . . Aretha Franklin
I'm In Love . . . . Evelyn "Champagne" King
I'm In Love . . . . Wilson Pickett
I'm In Love Again . . . . Fats Domino
I'm In Love Again . . . . Henri Rene Orchestra
I'm In Love Again . . . . Pia Zadora
I'm In Love Again . . . . Rick Nelson
I'm In Love With You . . . .
   . . . . . Kasenetz-Katz Singing Orchestral Circus
I'm In Luv . . . . Joe
I'm In The Mood For Love . . . . Chimes
I'm In You . . . . Peter Frampton
I'm Indestructable . . . . Jack Jones
I'm Into Somethin' Good . . . . Earl-Jean
I'm Into Something Good . . . . . Herman's Hermits
I'm Jealous . . . . Ike & Tina Turner
I'm Just A Country Boy . . . . George McCurn
(I'm Just A) Fool For You . . . . . . Gene Chandler

442

In My Dreams . . . . REO Speedwagon
In My Father's Footsteps . . . . Terry Jacks
In My House . . . . Mary Jane Girls
In My Little Corner Of The World . . . . Anita Bryant
In My Lonely Room . . . . . . Martha & The Vandellas
In My Room . . . . Beach Boys
In My Room . . . . Sagittarius
In My Room . . . . Verdelle Smith
In Need Of A Friend . . . . Cowsills
In Neon . . . . Elton John
In Our Time . . . . Nancy Sinatra
In Real Life . . . . Chuck Jackson
In Some Time . . . . Ronnie Dove
In The Air Tonight . . . . Phil Collins
In The Arms Of Love . . . . Andy Williams
In The Bad Bad Old Days . . . . Foundations
In The Basement (Part 1) . . . .
. . . . Etta James & Sugar Pie DeSanto
In The Bottle . . . . Brother To Brother
In The Bush . . . . Musique
In The Chapel In The Moonlight . . . . Dean Martin
In The Chapel In The Moonlight . . . . Kitty Kallen
In The Closet . . . . Michael Jackson
(In The) Cold Light Of Day . . . . Gene Pitney
In The Dark . . . . Billy Squire
In The Ghetto . . . . Candi Staton
In The Ghetto . . . . Elvis Presley
In The Heat Of The Night . . . . Ray Charles
In The Middle . . . . Tim Moore
In The Middle Of A Heartache . . . . . Wanda Jackson
In The Middle Of An Island . . . . . . Tony Bennett
In The Middle Of The House . . . . . . Rusty Draper
In The Middle Of The House . . . . Vaughn Monroe
In The Midnight Hour . . . . Cross Country
In The Midnight Hour . . . . Mirettes
In The Midnight Hour . . . . Wanted
In The Midnight Hour . . . . Wilson Pickett
In The Misty Moonlight . . . . Dean Martin
In The Misty Moonlight . . . . Jerry Wallace
In The Mood . . . . Bette Midler
In The Mood . . . . Ernie Fields
In The Mood . . . .
. . . . . . Henhouse Five Plus Too (Ray Stevens)
In The Mood . . . . Robert Plant
In The Name Of Love . . . .
. . . . Ralph MacDonald With Bill Withers
In The Navy . . . . Village People
In The Quiet Morning . . . . Joan Baez
In The Rain . . . . Arthur Prysock
In The Rain . . . . Dramatics
In The Shape Of A Heart . . . . . . Jackson Browne
In The Still Of The Night . . . . Boyz II Men
In The Still Of The Night . . . Dion And The Belmonts
In The Still Of The Night . . . . Paul Anka
In The Still Of The Nite . . . . Five Satins
In The Stone . . . . Earth, Wind & Fire
In The Summer Of His Years . . . . Connie Francis
In The Summertime . . . . Mungo Jerry
In The Time Of Our Lives . . . . . . Iron Butterfly
In The Winter . . . . Janis Ian
In The Year 2525 (Exordium & Terminus) . . . .
. . . . Zager & Evans
In Thee . . . . Blue Oyster Cult
In These Arms . . . . Bon Jovi
In Time . . . . Engelbert Humperdinck
In Time . . . . Steve Lawrence
In Too Deep . . . . Genesis
In Your Arms . . . . Little Caesar
In Your Eyes . . . . Peter Gabriel
In Your Letter . . . . REO Speedwagon
In Your Room . . . . Bangles
In Your Soul . . . . Corey Hart
In-A-Gadda-Da-Vida . . . . Iron Butterfly
Incense And Peppermints . . . Strawberry Alarm Clock

Indescribably Blue . . . . Elvis Presley
Indestructable . . . . Four Tops
Indian Giver . . . . 1910 Fruitgum Company
Indian Lady . . . . Lou Christie
Indian Lake . . . . Cowsills
Indian Love Call . . . . Ray Stevens
Indian Reservation . . . . Don Fardon
Indian Reservation . . . . Raiders
Indian Summer . . . . Audience
Indian Summer . . . . Poco
Indiana Wants Me . . . . R. Dean Taylor
Indo Smoke . . . . Mista Grimm
Infatuation . . . . Rod Stewart
Information . . . . Eric Martin
Informer . . . . Snow
Inky Dinky Spider (The Spider Song) . . . .
. . . . Kids Next Door
Inner City Blues . . . . Marvin Gaye
Innocent . . . . Whispers
Innocent Child . . . . Colorhaus
Innocent Eyes . . . . Graham Nash
Innocent Man . . . . Billy Joel
Insane In The Brain . . . . Cypress Hill
Insanity Comes Quietly To The
   Structured Mind . . . . Janis Ian
Inseparable . . . . Natalie Cole
Inside A Dream . . . . Jane Wiedlin
Inside Love (So Personal) . . . . . . George Benson
Inside My Love . . . . Minnie Riperton
Inside Of You . . . . Ray, Goodman & Brown
Inside Outside . . . . Cover Girls
Inside That I Cried . . . . Ce Ce Peniston
Inside-Looking Out . . . . Animals
Inspiration . . . . Paul Williams
Instant Karma (We All Shine On) . . . . John Lennon
Instant Replay . . . . Dan Hartman
Instigating (Trouble Making) Fool . . . . Whatnauts
Into The Great Wide Open . . . .
. . . . Tom Petty And The Heartbreakers
Into The Mystic . . . . Johnny Rivers
Into The Night . . . . Benny Mardones
Into The Night '89 . . . . Benny Mardones
Into You . . . . Giant Steps
Into Your Arms . . . . Lemonheads
Invincible (Theme From The Legend
   Of Billie Jean) . . . . Pat Benatar
Invisible . . . . Alison Moyet
Invisible Hands . . . . Kim Carnes
Invisible Tears . . . . . Ray Conniff And The Singers
Invisible Touch . . . . Genesis
Invitation To Dance . . . . Kim Carnes
I.O.U. . . . . Jimmy Dean
I.O.U. . . . . Lee Greenwood
Iron Man . . . . Black Sabbath
Irresistable You . . . . Bobby Darin
Irresistable You . . . . Bobby Peterson
Is A Blue Bird Blue . . . . Conway Twitty
Is Anybody Goin' To San Antone . . . . Charley Pride
Is It Love . . . . J.J. Fad
Is It Love . . . . Mr. Mister
Is It Love That We're Missin' . . . .
. . . Quincy Jones Featuring The Brothers Johnson
Is It Really Over? . . . . Jim Reeves
Is It Something You've Got . . . . . . Tyrone Davis
Is It True . . . . Brenda Lee
Is It You . . . . Lee Ritenour
Is She Really Going Out With Him? . . . Joe Jackson
Is That All There Is . . . . Peggy Lee
Is That It? . . . . Katrina And The Waves
Is That The Way . . . . Tin Tin
Is There Any Chance . . . . Marty Robbins
Is There Something I Should Know . . . . Duran Duran
Is There Something On Your Mind . . . . . Jack Scott
Is This Love . . . . Pat Travers Band

448

Keep Your Love Locked	Paul Petersen	Kiss Me Goodbye	Petula Clark
Keep Yourself Alive	Queen	Kiss Me In The Rain	Barbra Streisand
Keeper Of The Castle	Four Tops	Kiss Me Quick (EP)	Elvis Presley
Keeping Our Love Alive	Henry Paul Band	Kiss Me Sailor	Diane Renay
Keeping The Faith	Billy Joel	Kiss Of Fire	Georgia Gibbs
Kentucky	Bob Moore	Kiss Of Life	Sade
Kentucky	Sammi Smith	Kiss On My List	Daryl Hall & John Oates
Kentucky Rain	Elvis Presley	Kiss The Bride	Elton John
Kentucky Woman	Deep Purple	Kiss The Dirt	Inxs
Kentucky Woman	Neil Diamond	Kiss Them For Me	Siouxsie And The Banshees
Kewpie Doll	Perry Como	Kiss This Thing Goodbye	del Amitri
Key Largo	Bertie Higgins	Kiss Tomorrow Goodbye	Laine Kazan
Kick It Out	Heart	Kiss You All Over	Exile
Kick Out The Jams	MC5	Kiss You (When It's Dangerous)	Eight Seconds
Kick That Little Foot Sally Ann	Round Robin	Kisses On The Wind	Neneh Cherry
Kick The Wall	Jimmy Davis & Junction	Kisses Sweeter Than Wine	Jimmie Rodgers
Kickin' It	After 7	Kissin' And Twistin'	Fabian
Kicks	Paul Revere And The Raiders	Kissin' Cousins	Elvis Presley
Kickstart My Heart	Motley Crue	Kissin' Game	Dion
Kid Galahad (EP)	Elvis Presley	Kissin' On The Phone	Paul Anka
Kid Is Hot Tonite	Loverboy	Kissin' Time	Bobby Rydell
"Kid" Santa Claus	Patsy	Kissin' Time	Kiss
Kid Stuff	McGuire Sisters	Kissing A Fool	George Michael
Kid's American	Matthew Wilder	Kissing My Love	Bill Withers
Kiddio	Brook Benton	Kissing The Wind	Nia Peeples
Kids	Kirby Stone Four	Kissing Tree	Billy Grammer
Kids Are Alright	Who	Kissing You	Keith Washington
Kids In America	Kim Wilde	Kitty Doyle	Dino, Desi & Billy
Kiko	Jimmy McGriff	K-Jee	Nite-Liters
Killer	Seal	Knee Deep In The Blues	Guy Mitchell
Killer Cut	Charlie	Knight In Rusty Armour	Peter And Gordon
Killer Joe	Kingsmen	Knock Knock (Who's There)	Mary Hopkin
Killer Joe	Quincy Jones	Knock! Knock! (Who's There)	Orlons
Killer Joe	Rocky Fellers	Knock On Wood	Amii Stewart
Killer Queen	Queen	Knock On Wood	Eddie Floyd
Killer/Papa Was A Rollin' Stone	George Michael	Knock On Wood	Otis & Carla
Killin' Time	Fred Knoblock	Knock Three Times	Dawn
Killing Me Softly	Al B. Sure!	Knocked Out	Paula Abdul
Killing Me Softly With His Song	Roberta Flack	Knockin' Boots	Candyman
Killing Of Georgie (Part 1 & 2)	Rod Stewart	Knockin' Da Boots	H-Town
Kind Of A Drag	Buckinghams	Knockin' On Heaven's Door	Bob Dylan
Kind Of Boy You Can't Forget	Raindrops	Knocking At Your Back Door	Deep Purple
Kind Of Magic	Queen	Knock-N-Boots	Wreckx-N-Effect
King Creole (EP)	Elvis Presley	Knowing Me, Knowing You	Abba
King Croesus	World Of Oz	Knucklehead	Bar-Kays
King For A Day	Thompson Twins	Ko Ko Mo (I Love You So)	Crew-Cuts
King Heroin	James Brown	Ko Ko Mo (I Love You So)	Perry Como
King Is Gone	Ronnie McDowell	Kodachrome	Paul Simon
King Kong (Parts 1 & 2)	Jimmy Castor	Ko-Ko Joe	Jerry Reed
King Midas In Reverse	Hollies	Kokomo	Beach Boys
King Of Clowns	Neil Sedaka	Kommotion	Duane Eddy
King Of Love	Fabian	Kong	Dickie Goodman
King Of Nothing	Seals & Crofts	Kookie, Kookie (Lend Me Your Comb)	
King Of Pain	Police		Edward Byrnes And Connie Stevens
King Of Rock 'N' Roll	Cashman & West	Kookie Little Paradise	Jo Ann Campbell
King Of Suede	"Weird Al" Yankovic	Kookie Little Paradise	Tree Swingers
King Of The Hill	Oak	Kookie's Mad Pad	Edward Byrnes
King Of The Road	Roger Miller	Kool And The Gang	Kool & The Gang
King Of Wishful Thinking	Go West	Kozmic Blues	Janis Joplin
King Tut	Steve Martin	Kum Ba Yah	Tommy Leonetti
Kings And Queens	Aerosmith	Kung Fu	Curtis Mayfield
Kings Of The Party	Brownsville Station	Kung Fu Fighting	Carl Douglas
Kiss	Art Of Noise Featuring Tom Jones	Kyrie	Mr. Mister
Kiss	Prince And The Revolution		
Kiss An Angel Good Mornin'	Charley Pride		
Kiss And Say Goodbye	Manhattans	L. David Sloane	Michelle Lee
Kiss And Tell	Breakfast Club	La Bamba	Carlos Brothers
Kiss And Tell	Bryan Ferry	La Bamba	Los Lobos
Kiss And Tell	Isley, Jasper, Isley	La Bamba	Ritchie Valens
Kiss Away	Ronnie Dove	La Bamba (Part 1)	Trini Lopez
Kiss Her Now	Ed Ames	La Bomba	Tokens
Kiss Him Goodbye	Nylons	La Dee Dah	Billy & Lillie
Kiss In The Dark	Pink Lady	L.A. Freeway	Jerry Jeff Walker
Kiss Me Deadly	Lita Ford	L.A. Goodbye	Ides Of March

L

453

Life . . . . Sly & The Family Stone
Life Ain't Easy . . . . Dr. Hook
Life And Breath . . . . Climax
Life And Death In G & A . . . . Abaco Dream
Life Goes On . . . . Poison
Life In A Northern Town . . . . Dream Academy
Life In One Day . . . . Howard Jones
Life In The Fast Lane . . . . Eagles
Life Is A Carnival . . . . Band
Life Is A Highway . . . . Tom Cochran
Life Is A Rock (But The Radio
  Rolled Me) . . . . Reunion
Life Is A Song Worth Singing . . . . Johnny Mathis
Life Is But A Dream . . . . Earls
Life Of Illusion . . . . Joe Walsh
Life's A Holiday . . . . Jerry Wallace
Life's Been Good . . . . Joe Walsh
Life's Too Short . . . . Lafayettes
Life's What You Make It . . . . Talk Talk
Lifetime Of Loneliness . . . . . Jackie DeShannon
Lift Me Up . . . . Howard Jones
Lift Me Up . . . . Yes
Light My Fire . . . . Amii Stewart
Light My Fire . . . . Doors
Light My Fire . . . . Jose Feliciano
Light My Fire . . . . Rhetta Hughes
Light Of Day . . . . . . Joan Jett & The Blackhearts
Light Sings . . . . Fifth Dimension
Light The Sky . . . . Jefferson Starship
Lightnin' Strikes . . . . Lou Christie
Lightning's Girl . . . . Nancy Sinatra
Lights . . . . Journey
Lights Out . . . . Billy Vaughn
Lights Out . . . . Peter Wolf
(Lights Went Out In) Massachusetts . . . . Bee Gees
Like A Baby . . . . Len Barry
Like A Child . . . . Julie Rogers
Like A Child . . . . Noel
Like A Prayer . . . . Madonna
Like A Rock . . . Bob Seger & The Silver Bullet Band
Like A Rolling Stone . . . . Bob Dylan
Like A Rolling Stone . . . .
  . . . . Phil Flowers And The Flowershop
Like A Sad Song . . . . John Denver
Like A Sunday In Salem (The Amos
  & Andy Song) . . . . Gene Cotton
Like A Sunday Morning . . . . Lana Cantrell
Like A Surgeon . . . . "Weird Al" Yankovic
Like A Virgin . . . . Madonna
Like An Old Time Movie . . . . . . Scott McKenzie
Like An Open Door . . . . Fuzz
Like Columbus Did . . . . Reflections
Like Flames . . . . Berlin
Like I Love You . . . . Edward Byrnes
Like, Long Hair . . . . . Paul Revere And The Raiders
Like No Other Night . . . . 38 Special
Like Strangers . . . . Everly Brothers
Like The Big Guys Do . . . . Rocky Fellers
Like The Weather . . . . 10,000 Maniacs
Like They Say In L.A. . . . . L.A. Car Pool
Like To Get To Know You . . Spanky And Our Gang
Like To Get To Know You Well . . . Howard Jones
Like Young . . . . . . Andre Previn With David Rose
Lil' Red Riding Hood . . . .
  . . . . . . Sam The Sham And The Pharaohs
Lili Marlene . . . . Al Martino
Lily Was Here . . . .
  . . . . David A. Stewart Introducing Candy Dulfer
Limbo Rock . . . . Champs
Limbo Rock . . . . Chubby Checker
Limelight . . . . Mr. Acker Bilk
Limelight . . . . Rush
Linda . . . . Jan & Dean
Linda Lu . . . . Ray Sharpe

Linda On My Mind . . . . Conway Twitty
Linger . . . . Cranberries
Ling-Ting-Tong . . . . Buddy Knox
Lion Sleeps Tonight . . . . Robert John
Lion Sleeps Tonight . . . . Tokens
Lip Sync . . . . Len Barry
Lips Of Wine . . . . Andy Williams
Lipstick . . . . Suzi Quatro
Lipstick On Your Collar . . . . . . Connie Francis
Lipstick Traces (On A Cigarette) . . . Benny Spellman
Lipstick Traces (On A Cigarette) . . . . . O'Jays
Lisa . . . . Ferrante & Teicher
Lisa . . . . Jeanne Black
Lisa, Listen To Me . . . . Blood, Sweat & Tears
Lisbon Antigua . . . . Nelson Riddle
Listen Here . . . . Eddie Harris
Listen Like Thieves . . . . Inxs
Listen Lonely Girl . . . . Johnny Mathis
Listen People . . . . Herman's Hermits
Listen To Her Heart . . . .
  . . . . . . Tom Petty And The Heartbreakers
Listen To The Band . . . . Monkees
Listen To The Buddha . . . . Ozo
Listen To The Music . . . . Doobie Brothers
Listen To The People . . . . Zager & Evans
Listen To What The Man Said . . . . Wings
Listen To Your Heart . . . . Roxette
Lithium . . . . Nirvana
Little Altar Boy . . . . Vic Dana
Little Arrows . . . . Leapy Lee
Little Band Of Gold . . . . James Gilreath
Little Becky's Christmas Wish . . . . Becky Lamb
Little Bell . . . . Dixie Cups
Little Bird . . . . Annie Lennox
Little Bit Like Magic . . . . King Harvest
Little Bit Me, A Little Bit You . . . . . Monkees
Little Bit More . . . . Dr. Hook
Little Bit Now . . . . Dave Clark Five
Little Bit Now (A Little Bit Later) . . . . . . Majors
Little Bit O' Soul . . . . Music Explosion
Little Bit Of Heaven . . . . Ronnie Dove
Little Bit Of Love . . . . Corey Hart
Little Bit Of Love . . . . Dwight Twilley Band
Little Bit Of Love Is All It Takes . . . . . New Edition
Little Bit Of Soap . . . . Exciters
Little Bit Of Soap . . . . Jarmels
Little Bit Of Soap . . . . Nigel Olsson
Little Bit Of Soap . . . . Paul Davis
Little Bit Of Soul . . . . Bullet
Little Bitty Girl . . . . Bobby Rydell
Little Bitty Johnny . . . . Travis & Bob
Little Bitty Pretty One . . . . Bobby Day
Little Bitty Pretty One . . . . . . Clyde McPhatter
Little Bitty Pretty One . . . . Frankie Lymon
Little Bitty Pretty One . . . . Jackson Five
Little Bitty Pretty One . . . . Thurston Harris
Little Bitty Tear . . . . Burl Ives
Little Black Book . . . . Jimmy Dean
Little Black Egg . . . . Nightcrawlers
Little Blonde Girl . . . . Don French
Little Blue Man . . . . Betty Johnson
Little Boxes . . . . Pete Seeger
Little Boxes . . . . Womenfolk
Little Boy . . . . Crystals
Little Boy . . . . Tony Bennett
Little Boy (In Grown Up Clothes) . . . Four Seasons
Little Boy Sad . . . . Johnny Burnette
Little Brass Band . . . . David Seville
Little By Little . . . . Nappy Brown
Little By Little . . . . Robert Plant
Little Children . . . Billy J. Kramer With The Dakotas
Little Coco Palm . . . . Jerry Wallace
Little Darlin' . . . . Diamonds
Little Darlin' . . . . Sheila

Little Darling (I Need You) . . . . . . Doobie Brothers	Little Star . . . . Elegants
Little Darling, I Need You . . . . Marvin Gaye	Little Susie . . . . Ray Bryant Combo
Little Deuce Coupe . . . . Beach Boys	Little Suzi . . . . Tesla
Little Devil . . . . Neil Sedaka	Little Thing Called Love . . . . Neil Young
Little Diane . . . . Dion	Little Things . . . . Bobby Goldsboro
Little Dipper . . . . Mickey Mozart Quintet	Little Things . . . . Sonny & Cher
Little Donna . . . . Rivieras	Little Things Mean A Lot . . . . Joni James
Little Drummer Boy . . . . . Harry Simeone Chorale	Little Things Mean A Lot . . . . Kitty Kallen
Little Drummer Boy . . . . Johnny Cash	Little Tin Soldier . . . . Toy Dolls
Little Drummer Boy . . . . Lou Rawls	Little Too Late . . . . Pat Benatar
Little Eeefin Annie . . . . Joe Perkins	Little Too Much . . . . Clarence Henry
Little Egypt . . . . Coasters	Little Town Flirt . . . . Del Shannon
Little Feeling . . . . Jack Scott	Little Toy Balloon . . . . Danny Williams
Little Fighter . . . . White Lion	Little Train . . . . . . Marianne Vasel & Erich Storz
Little Games . . . . Yardbirds	Little Walter . . . . Tony! Toni! Tone!
Little Girl . . . . Ritchie Valens	Little White Cloud That Cried . . . . . . Johnnie Ray
Little Girl . . . . Syndicate Of Sound	Little White Lies . . . . Betty Johnson
Little Girl Gone . . . . Donna Fargo	Little White Lies . . . . Kenjolairs
Little Girl I Once Knew . . . . Beach Boys	Little Willy . . . . Sweet
Little Girl, Little Boy . . . . Al Martino	Little Woman . . . . Bobby Sherman
Little Good News . . . . Anne Murray	Little Woman Love . . . . Wings
Little Green Apples . . . . O.C. Smith	Little You . . . . . . Freddie And The Dreamers
Little Green Apples . . . . Roger Miller	Live . . . . Merry-Go-Round
Little Green Bag . . . . . . George Baker Selection	Live And Learn . . . . Joe Public
Little Honda . . . . Hondells	Live And Let Die . . . . Guns N' Roses
Little In Love . . . . Cliff Richard	Live And Let Die . . . . Wings
Little Is Enough . . . . Pete Townshend	Live Every Minute . . . . Ali Thomson
Little Jackie Wants To Be A Star	Live Every Moment . . . . REO Speedwagon
. . . . Lisa Lisa And Cult Jam	Live For Loving You . . . . Gloria Estefan
Little Jeannie . . . . Elton John	Live Is Life . . . . Opus
Little Lady . . . . Duke Jupiter	Live It Up . . . . Dusty Springfield
Little Latin Lupe Lu . . . . Kingsmen	Live It Up . . . . Gardner Cole
Little Latin Lupe Lu	Live It Up (Part 1) . . . . Isley Brothers
. . . . Mitch Ryder And The Detroit Wheels	Live My Life . . . . Boy George
Little Latin Lupe Lu . . . . Righteous Brothers	Live To Tell . . . . Madonna
Little Less Conversation . . . . Elvis Presley	Live Wire . . . . Martha & The Vandellas
Little Liar . . . . Joan Jett & The Blackhearts	Live Your Life Before You Die . . . . Pointer Sisters
Little Lies . . . . Fleetwood Mac	Livin' Above Your Head . . . . Jay & The Americans
Little Loneliness . . . . Kay Starr	Livin' Ain't Livin' . . . . Firefall
Little Lonely One . . . . Tom Jones	Livin' For The Weekend . . . . O'Jays
Little Love . . . . Juice Newton	Livin' For You . . . . Al Green
Little Lovin' (Keeps The Doctor Away) . . . . Raes	Livin' In Desperate Times . . . Olivia Newton-John
Little Man . . . . Sonny & Cher	Livin' In The Life . . . . Isley Brothers
Little Marie . . . . Chuck Berry	Livin' In The Light . . . . Caron Wheeler
Little Miracles (Happen Every Day) . . Luther Vandross	Livin' It Up (Friday Night) . . . . . . Bell & James
Little Miss Sad . . . . Five Emprees	Livin' On A Prayer . . . . Bon Jovi
Little Miss Stuck-Up . . . . Playmates	Livin' On The Edge . . . . Aerosmith
Little Miss Sunshine . . . . Tommy Roe	Livin' Thing . . . . Electric Light Orchestra
Little Miss U.S.A. . . . . Barry Mann	Living A Lie . . . . Al Martino
Little More Love . . . . . . Olivia Newton-John	Living A Little, Laughing A Little . . . . . Spinners
Little Old Lady (From Pasadena) . . . . Jan & Dean	Living Doll . . . . . Cliff Richard And The Drifters
Little Ole Man (Uptight - Everything's	Living Doll . . . . David Hill
Alright) . . . . Bill Cosby	Living Eyes . . . . Bee Gees
Little Ole Wine Drinker Me . . . . . . Dean Martin	Living For The City . . . . Ray Charles
Little One . . . . Chicago	Living For The City . . . . Stevie Wonder
Little Pearly . . . . Click-Clacks	Living For You . . . . Sonny & Cher
Little Pedro . . . . Olympics	Living In A Box . . . . Living In A Box
Little Pigeon . . . . Sal Mineo	Living In A Dream . . . . Pseudo Echo
Little Pixie . . . . . . Moe Koffman Quartette	Living In A Fantasy . . . . Leo Sayer
Little Queen . . . . Heart	Living In A House Divided . . . . Cher
Little Queenie . . . . Chuck Berry	Living In America . . . . James Brown
Little Rain Must Fall . . . . Epic Splendor	Living In Oblivion . . . . Anything Box
Little Red Corvette . . . . Prince	Living In Sin . . . . Bon Jovi
Little Red Rented Rowboat . . . . . . Joe Dowell	Living In The Past . . . . Jethro Tull
Little Red Riding Hood . . . . Big Bopper	Living In The U.S.A. . . . . . Steve Miller Band
Little Red Rooster . . . . Sam Cooke	Living Inside Myself . . . . Gino Vannelli
Little Respect . . . . Erasure	Living It Down . . . . Freddy Fender
Little Saint Nick . . . . Beach Boys	Living Next Door To Alice . . . . Smokie
Little Serenade . . . . Ames Brothers	Living On The Edge . . . . Jim Capaldi
Little Serenade . . . . Teddy Randazzo	Living On Video . . . . Trans-X
Little Shoemaker . . . . Gaylords	Living Together, Growing Together . . Fifth Dimension
Little Shoemaker . . . . Hugo Winterhalter	Living Without You . . . Manfred Mann's Earth Band
Little Sister . . . . Elvis Presley	Living Years . . . . Mike + The Mechanics
Little Space Girl . . . . Jesse Lee Turner	Livingston Saturday Night . . . . Jimmy Buffett

457

Lizzie And The Rainman . . . . Tanya Tucker
Lizzie Borden . . . . Chad Mitchell Trio
Lo Mucho Que Te Quiero . . . . Rene & Rene
Load Out . . . . Jackson Browne
Locking Up My Heart . . . . Marvelettes
Loco-Motion . . . . Grand Funk
Loco-Motion . . . . Kylie Minogue
Loco-Motion . . . . Little Eva
Locomotive Breath . . . . Jethro Tull
Loddy Lo . . . . Chubby Checker
Lodi . . . . Al Wilson
Lodi . . . . Creedence Clearwater Revival
Logical Song . . . . Supertramp
Lola . . . . Kinks
Lolita Ya Ya . . . . Ventures
Lollipop . . . . Chordettes
Lollipop . . . . Ronald And Ruby
Lollipop (I Like You) . . . . Intruders
Lollipops And Roses . . . . Jack Jones
Lollipops And Roses . . . . Paul Petersen
London Town . . . . Wings
Lone Ranger . . . . Oscar Brown Jr.
Loneliest Man On The Moon . . . . . . David Castle
Loneliest Night . . . . Dale & Grace
(Loneliness Made Me Realize) It's
  You That I Need . . . . Temptations
L-O-N-E-L-Y . . . . Bobby Vinton
Lonely Again . . . . Eddy Arnold
Lonely Blue Boy . . . . Conway Twitty
Lonely Blue Nights . . . . . Rosie And The Originals
Lonely Boy . . . . Andrew Gold
Lonely Boy . . . . Paul Anka
Lonely Boy, Lonely Guitar . . . . . . Duane Eddy
Lonely Bull . . . . . Herb Alpert & The Tijuana Brass
Lonely Crowd . . . . Teddy Vann
Lonely Days . . . . Bee Gees
Lonely Drifter . . . . O'Jays
Lonely Drifter . . . . Pieces Of Eight
Lonely Eyes . . . . Robert John
Lonely Feelin' . . . . War
Lonely For You . . . . Gary Stites
Lonely Guitar . . . . Annette
Lonely In Love . . . . Giuffria
Lonely Is The Night . . . . Air Supply
Lonely Island . . . . Sam Cooke
Lonely Little Robin . . . . Browns
Lonely Lonely Girl . . . . Velvelettes
Lonely Man . . . . Chi-Lites
Lonely Man . . . . Elvis Presley
Lonely Night (Angel Face) . . . . . Captain & Tennille
Lonely Nights . . . . Bryan Adams
Lonely Ol' Night . . . . . . John Cougar Mellencamp
Lonely One . . . . Duane Eddy
Lonely One . . . . Special Delivery
Lonely People . . . . America
Lonely Saturday Night . . . . Don French
Lonely School . . . . Tommy Shaw
Lonely School Year . . . . Hudson Brothers
Lonely Soldier . . . . Jerry Butler
Lonely Soldier . . . . Mike Williams
Lonely Street . . . . Andy Williams
Lonely Street . . . . Clarence Henry
Lonely Summer . . . . Shades Of Blue
Lonely Surfer . . . . Jack Nitzsche
Lonely Teardrops . . . . Brian Hyland
Lonely Teardrops . . . . Jackie Wilson
Lonely Teardrops . . . . Narvel Felts
Lonely Teenager . . . . Dion
Lonely Together . . . . Barry Manilow
Lonely Weekends . . . . Charlie Rich
Lonely Wind . . . . Kansas
Lonely Winds . . . . Drifters
Lonesome Loser . . . . Little River Band
Lonesome Mary . . . . Chilliwack

Lonesome Number One . . . . Don Gibson
Lonesome Road . . . . Wonder Who?
Lonesome Town . . . . Ricky Nelson
Long Ago And Far Away . . . . James Taylor
Long Ago Tomorrow . . . . B.J. Thomas
Long And Lasting Love (Once In A
  Lifetime) . . . . Glenn Medeiros
Long And Lonesome Road . . . . Shocking Blue
Long And Winding Road . . . . Beatles
Long As I Can See The Light . . . .
  . . . . Creedence Clearwater Revival
Long As The Rose Is Red . . . . . . Florraine Darlin
Long Cool Woman (In A Black Dress) . . . . . Hollies
Long Dark Road . . . . Hollies
Long Gone Lonesome Blues . . . . . Hank Williams Jr.
Long Green . . . . Fireballs
Long Haired Country Boy . . . . Charlie Daniels Band
Long Haired Lover From Liverpool . . . .
  . . . . Little Jimmy Osmond
Long Hot Summer . . . . Jimmie Rodgers
Long Hot Summer Nights . . . . . Wendy Waldman
Long Legged Girl (With The Short
  Dress On) . . . . Elvis Presley
Long Line Rider . . . . Bobby Darin
Long Live Love . . . . Sandie Shaw
Long Live Our Love . . . . Shangri-Las
Long Live Rock . . . . Who
Long Lonely Highway . . . . Elvis Presley
Long Lonely Nights . . . . Bobby Vinton
Long Lonely Nights . . . . Clyde McPhatter
Long Lonely Nights . . . . Dells
Long, Lonely Nights . . . . Four Seasons
Long Lonely Nights . . . Lee Andrews And The Hearts
Long Lonesome Highway . . . . Michael Parks
Long Long Time . . . . Linda Ronstadt
Long, Long Way From Home . . . . Foreigner
Long Promised Road . . . . Beach Boys
Long Run . . . . Eagles
Long Tall Glasses (I Can Dance) . . . . . Leo Sayer
Long Tall Sally . . . . Little Richard
Long Tall Texan . . . . Murry Kellum
Long Time . . . . Boston
Long Time Lovin' You . . . . McGuffey Lane
Long Train Runnin' . . . . Doobie Brothers
Long Way Around . . . . Linda Ronstadt
Long Way Home . . . . Neil Diamond
Longer . . . . Dan Fogelberg
Longest Day . . . . Mitch Miller
Longest Time . . . . Billy Joel
Longest Walk . . . . Jaye P. Morgan
Longfellow Serenade . . . . Neil Diamond
Look . . . . Roxette
Look At Granny Run, Run . . . . Howard Tate
Look At Me Girl . . . . Bobby Vee
Look At Me (I'm In Love) . . . . Moments
Look At Mine . . . . Petula Clark
Look At That Cadillac . . . . Stray Cats
Look At You . . . . George McCrae
Look Away . . . . Big Country
Look Away . . . . Chicago
Look Away . . . . . Garnet Mimms & The Enchanters
Look Away . . . . . Ozark Mountain Daredevils
Look For A Star . . . . Billy Vaughn
Look For A Star . . . . Deane Hawley
Look For A Star . . . . Garry Miles
Look For A Star . . . . Garry Mills
Look For A Star . . . . Nicky Como
Look, Here Comes The Sun . . . . Sunshine Company
Look Homeward Angel . . . . Johnnie Ray
Look Homeward Angel . . . . Monarchs
Look In My Eyes . . . . Chantels
Look In My Eyes . . . . Three Degrees
Look In My Eyes Pretty Woman . . . . Dawn
Look Into My Eyes . . . . George Lamond

Love Hangover . . . . Fifth Dimension
Love Has A Mind Of Its Own . . . .
. . . . Donna Summer With Matthew Ward
Love Has Finally Come At Last . . . .
. . . . Bobby Womack And Patti LaBelle
Love Has No Pride . . . . Linda Ronstadt
Love Has Taken Its Toll . . . . Saraya
Love Heals . . . . Colours
Love Her Madly . . . . Doors
Love Hurts . . . . Jim Capaldi
Love Hurts . . . . Nazareth
Love I Lost (Part 1) . . . .
. . . . Harold Melvin And The Blue Notes
Love I Saw In You Was Just A Mirage . . . . Miracles
Love In 'C' Minor (Part 1) . . . . Cerrone
Love In A Vacuum . . . . 'Til Tuesday
Love In An Elevator . . . . Aerosmith
Love In Every Room . . . . Paul Mauriat
Love In Siberia . . . . Laban
Love In Store . . . . Fleetwood Mac
Love In The City . . . . Turtles
Love In The First Degree . . . . Alabama
Love In The First Degree . . . . Bananarama
Love In The Shadows . . . . Neil Sedaka
Love In Them There Hills . . . . Vibrations
Love In Your Eyes . . . . Eddie Money
Love Is . . . . Alannah Myles
Love Is . . . . Vanessa Williams & Brian McKnight
Love Is A 5-Letter Word . . . . James Phelps
Love Is A Battlefield . . . . Pat Benatar
Love Is A Golden Ring . . . . Frankie Laine
Love Is A Hurtin' Thing . . . . Lou Rawls
Love Is A Killer . . . . Vixen
Love Is A Many Splendored Thing . . . . . . Four Aces
Love Is A Ritual . . . . Styx
Love Is A Rock . . . . REO Speedwagon
Love Is A Rose . . . . Linda Ronstadt
Love Is A Stranger . . . . Eurythmics
Love Is A Wonderful Thing . . . . . . Michael Bolton
Love Is Alive . . . . Gary Wright
Love Is All . . . . . . Engelbert Humperdinck
Love Is All Around . . . . Troggs
Love Is All I Have To Give . . . . . Checkmates Ltd.
Love Is All We Need . . . . Mel Carter
Love Is All We Need . . . . Tommy Edwards
Love Is All We Need . . . . Vic Dana
Love Is Alright Tonight . . . . . Rick Springfield
Love Is Better In The A.M. (Part 1) . . Johnnie Taylor
Love Is Blue . . . . Al Martino
Love Is Blue . . . . Paul Mauriat
Love Is Contagious . . . . Taja Sevelle
Love Is For The Best In Us . . . . Gypsy
Love Is Forever . . . . Billy Ocean
Love Is Funny That Way . . . . Jackie Wilson
Love Is Gonna Come At Last . . . . Badfinger
Love Is Here And Now You're Gone . . . . Supremes
Love Is Here To Stay . . . . Chris Montez
Love Is In Control (Finger On The
    Trigger) . . . . Donna Summer
Love Is In The Air . . . . John Paul Young
Love Is Just A Four-Letter Word . . . . . . Joan Baez
Love Is Life . . . . Earth, Wind & Fire
(Love Is Like) A Baseball Game . . . . . . Intruders
Love Is Like A Rock . . . . Donnie Iris
Love Is Like An Itching In My Heart . . . Supremes
Love Is Like Oxygen . . . . Sweet
Love Is Me, Love Is You . . . . . . Connie Francis
Love Is On The Way . . . . Saigon Kick
Love Is Strange . . . . Buddy Holly
Love Is Strange . . . . Everly Brothers
Love Is Strange . . . . Mickey And Sylvia
Love Is Strange . . . . Peaches & Herb
Love Is The Answer . . . .
. . . . England Dan & John Ford Coley

Love Is The Answer . . . . Van McCoy
Love Is The Drug . . . . Roxy Music
Love Is The Hero . . . . Billy Squire
Love Is The Message . . . .
. . . . MFSB Featuring The Three Degrees
Love Is The Seventh Wave . . . . Sting
(Love Is) Thicker Than Water . . . . Andy Gibb
Love Is What You Make It . . . . Grass Roots
Love Jones . . . . Brighter Side Of Darkness
Love Kills . . . . Freddie Mercury
Love Land . . . . Charles Wright And The
. . . . Watts 103rd Street Rhythm Band
Love Letters . . . . Elvis Presley
Love Letters . . . . Ketty Lester
Love Letters In The Sand . . . . Pat Boone
Love Light . . . . Yutaka
Love Light In Flight . . . . Stevie Wonder
Love Like A Man . . . . Ten Years After
Love Look Away . . . . Tony Bennett
Love Lost . . . . Santo & Johnny
L-O-V-E (Love) . . . . Al Green
Love, Love, Love . . . . Clovers
Love, Love, Love . . . . Donny Hathaway
Love Machine . . . . O'Kaysions
Love Machine . . . . Roosters
Love Machine (Part 1) . . . . Miracles
Love Makes A Fool Of You . . . Bobby Fuller Four
Love Makes A Woman . . . . Barbara Acklin
Love (Makes Me Do Foolish Things) . . . .
. . . . Martha & The Vandellas
Love (Makes The World Go 'Round) . . . . Paul Anka
Love Makes The World Go 'Round . . . Perry Como
Love Makes The World Go Round . . . Deon Jackson
Love Makes The World Go Round . . . Kiki Dee
Love Makes The World Go Round . . . Odds & Ends
Love Makes Things Happen . . . . Pebbles
Love Man . . . . Otis Redding
Love Me . . . . Bobby Hebb
Love Me (EP) . . . . Elvis Presley
Love Me . . . . Rascals
Love Me . . . . Yvonne Elliman
Love Me Again . . . . John Hall Band
Love Me Again . . . . Rita Coolidge
Love Me All The Way . . . . Kim Weston
Love Me All Up . . . . Stacy Earl
Love Me As I Love You . . . . . . George Maharis
Love Me Do . . . . Beatles
Love Me For A Reason . . . . Osmonds
Love Me For Life . . . . Stevie B
Love Me Forever . . . . Eydie Gorme
Love Me Forever . . . . Four Esquires
Love Me Forever . . . . Roger Williams
Love Me In A Special Way . . . . DeBarge
Love Me, Love Me Love . . . . Frank Mills
(Love Me) Love The Life I Lead . . . . . Fantastics
Love Me Now . . . . Brook Benton
Love Me Now . . . . Ruby Winters
Love Me One More Time . Karen Nelson And Billy T
Love Me Right . . . . Denise LaSalle
Love Me Tender . . . . Elvis Presley
Love Me Tender . . . . Percy Sledge
Love Me Tender . . . . Richard Chamberlain
Love Me To Pieces . . . . Jill Corey
Love Me Tomorrow . . . . Chicago
Love Me Tonight . . . . Blackjack
Love Me Tonight . . . . Head East
Love Me Tonight . . . . Tom Jones
Love Me Two Times . . . . Doors
Love Me Warm And Tender . . . . . . Paul Anka
Love Me With All Your Heart . . . . Bachelors
Love Me With All Your Heart . . Ray Charles Singers
Love Means (You Never Have To Say
    You're Sorry) . . . . Sounds Of Sunshine
Love Minus Zero - No Limit . . . . . Turley Richards

Loverboy	Billy Ocean	Lullabye Of The Leaves	Ventures
Lovergirl	Teena Marie	Lumberjack	Brook Benton
Lovers After All		Lyin' Eyes	Eagles
Melissa Manchester And Peabo Bryson		Lyin' To Myself	David Cassidy
Lovers By Night, Strangers By Day	Fleetwoods	Lying	Peter Frampton
Lovers Never Say Goodbye	Flamingos		
Lovers Who Wander	Dion		

Loves Me Like A Rock	Paul Simon	M'Lady	Sly & The Family Stone
Lovesick Blues	Frank Ifield	Ma Belle Amie	Tee Set
Lovesick Blues	Sonny James	Ma! (He's Making Eyes At Me)	Lena Zavaroni
Love...Thy Will Be Done	Martika	Ma Ma Ma Marie	Gaylords
Lovey Dovey	Buddy Knox	MacArthur Park	Donna Summer
Lovey Dovey	Clyde McPhatter	MacArthur Park	Richard Harris
Lovey Dovey	Otis & Carla	MacArthur Park	Waylon Jennings
Lovey Dovey (You're So Fine)	Bunny Sigler	MacArthur Park (Part 2)	Four Tops
Lovin' Every Minute Of It	Loverboy	Machine Gun	Commodores
Lovin' Place	Gale Garnett	Machinery	Sheena Easton
Lovin' Season	Gene & Debbe	Machines	John Livigni
Lovin' Sound	Ian & Sylvia	Macho Man	Village People
Lovin' The Night Away	Dillman Band	Mack The Knife	Bobby Darin
Lovin' Things	Grass Roots	Mack The Knife	Ella Fitzgerald
Lovin' Touch	Mark Dinning	Mad About You	Belinda Carlisle
Lovin', Touchin', Squeezin'	Journey	Made To Love You	Gary Wright
Lovin' Up A Storm	Jerry Lee Lewis	Made Up My Mind	Sa-Fire
Lovin' You	Bobby Darin	Madelaine	Stu Nunnery
Lovin' You	Minnie Riperton	Madeline	Winger
Lovin' You Baby	White Plains	Mademoiselle	Styx
Lovin' You, Lovin' Me	Candi Staton	Madison	Al Brown's Tunetoppers
Loving Arms	Dobie Gray	Madison Time (Part 1)	Ray Bryant Combo
Loving Arms	Kris Kristofferson And Rita Coolidge	Madrid	Nat King Cole
Loving Her Was Easier (Than Anything		Maggie	Redbone
I'll Ever Do Again)	Kris Kristofferson	Maggie May	Rod Stewart
Loving Power	Impressions	Magic	Cars
Loving You	Chris Rea	Magic	Olivia Newton-John
Loving You	Elvis Presley	Magic	Pilot
Loving You	Johnny Nash	Magic Bus	Who
Loving You Has Made Me Bananas	Guy Marks	Magic Carpet Ride	Bardeux
Loving You Is Just An Old Habit	Jim Weatherly	Magic Carpet Ride	Steppenwolf
Loving You Is Sweeter Than Ever	Four Tops	Magic Man	Heart
Loving You Just Crossed My Mind	Sam Neely	Magic Moments	Perry Como
Loving You More Every Day	Etta James	Magic Moon	Rays
Loving You With My Eyes	Starland Vocal Band	Magic Power	Triumph
Loving You's A Dirty Job But		Magic Town	Vogues
Somebody's Gotta Do It	Bonnie Tyler	Magic Woman Touch	Hollies
Low Rider	War	Magical	John Parr
Lowdown	Boz Scaggs	Magical Mystery Tour	Ambrosia
Lowdown	Chicago	Magnet And Steel	Walter Egan
Lowdown Popcorn	James Brown	Magnetic	Earth, Wind & Fire
Lu	Peggy Lipton	Magnificent Seven	Al Caiola
Lucifer	Bob Seger	Mah-Na-Mah-Na	
Lucille	Everly Brothers	Sweden Heaven And Hell Soundtrack	
Lucille	Kenny Rogers	Main Event/Fight	Barbra Streisand
Lucille	Little Richard	Main Man	Staple Singers
Luckenbach, Texas	Waylon Jennings	Main Street	Gary Lewis And The Playboys
Lucky	Greg Kihn Band	(Main Theme) Around The World	Victor Young
Lucky Devil	Carl Dobkins Jr.	Main Theme From Exodus (Ari's	
Lucky Guy	Rickie Lee Jones	Theme)	Mantovani
Lucky In Love	Mick Jagger	Main Title (Theme From "Jaws")	John Williams
Lucky Ladybug	Billy & Lillie	Mainstreet	Bob Seger
Lucky Lips	Cliff Richard	Mairzy Doats	Innocence
Lucky Lips	Ruth Brown	Majestic	Dion
Lucky Man	Emerson, Lake & Palmer	Major Tom (Coming Home)	Peter Schilling
Lucky Man	Starbuck	Make A Little Magic	Dirt Band
Lucky Me	Anne Murray	Make A Move On Me	Olivia Newton-John
Lucky Me	Moments	Make Believe	Toto
Lucky One	Laura Branigan	Make Believe	Wind
Lucky Star	Madonna	Make Believe It's Your First Time	Bobby Vinton
Lucretia Mac Evil	Blood, Sweat & Tears	Make It Better (Forget About Me)	
Lucy In The Sky With Diamonds	Elton John	Tom Petty And The Heartbreakers	
Luka	Suzanne Vega	Make It Easy On Yourself	Dionne Warwick
Lullaby	Cure	Make It Easy On Yourself	Jerry Butler
Lullaby Of Love	Frank Gari	Make It Easy On Yourself	Walker Brothers
Lullaby Of Love	Poppies	Make It Funky (Part 1)	James Brown
Lullabye	Chevrons	Make It Happen	Mariah Carey

Marching Along To The Blues . . . . . . Perry Como	Maybe Tomorrow . . . . Badfinger
Marching Saints . . . . Harry Belafonte	Maybe Tomorrow . . . . Jackson Five
Marching Thru Madrid	Maybe You'll Be There . . . . Billy & The Essentials
. . . . Herb Alpert & The Tijuana Brass	Maybellene . . . . Chuck Berry
Margaritaville . . . . Jimmy Buffett	Maybelline . . . . Johnny Rivers
Margie . . . . Fats Domino	Mayor Of Simpleton . . . . XTC
Margo . . . . Browns	Me - U = Blue . . . .
Maria . . . . Johnny Mathis	. . . . . Glenn Medeiros Featuring The Stylistics
Maria . . . . Roger Williams	Me About You . . . . Lovin' Spoonful
Maria Elena . . . . Los Indios Tabajaras	Me About You . . . . Mojo Men
Maria (You Were The Only One) . . . . . Jimmy Ruffin	Me And Baby Brother . . . . War
Marianne . . . . Hilltoppers	Me And Bobby McGee . . . . Janis Joplin
Marianne . . . . Stephen Stills	Me And Bobby McGee . . . . Jerry Lee Lewis
Marianne . . . . . Terry Gilkyson And The Easy Riders	Me And Julio Down By The
Marie . . . . Bachelors	Schoolyard . . . . Paul Simon
Marie . . . . Four Tunes	Me And Mrs. Jones . . . . Billy Paul
(Marie's The Name) His Latest Flame	Me And Mrs. Jones . . . . Dramatics
. . . . Elvis Presley	Me And My Arrow . . . . Nilsson
Marina . . . . Rocco Granata	Me And My Shadow . . . .
Marina . . . . Willy Alberti	. . . . Frank Sinatra And Sammy Davis Jr.
Marlena . . . . Four Seasons	Me And You . . . . O.C. Smith
Marley Purt Drive . . . . Jose Feliciano	Me And You And A Dog Named Boo . . . . . . Lobo
Marrakesh Express . . . . . Crosby, Stills & Nash	Me Japanese Boy I Love You . . . . Bobby Goldsboro
Married Man . . . . Richard Burton	Me, Myself And I . . . . De La Soul
Married Men . . . . Bette Midler	Me So Horny . . . . 2 Live Crew
Marta . . . . Bachelors	Me, The Peaceful Heart . . . . Lulu
Martha . . . . Gabriel	Me (Without You) . . . . Andy Gibb
Martian Boogie . . . . Brownsville Station	Me Without You . . . . Mary Wells
Martian Hop . . . . Ran-Dells	Meadows . . . . Joe Walsh
Martika's Kitchen . . . . Martika	Mean Mistreater . . . . . Grand Funk Railroad
Martinique . . . . Martin Denny	Mean Old World . . . . Rick Nelson
Marvelous Toy . . . . Chad Mitchell Trio	Mean Woman Blues . . . . Roy Orbison
Mary Ann Regrets . . . . Burl Ives	Mecca . . . . Gene Pitney
Mary Ann Thomas . . . . Bobby Freeman	Mechanical World . . . . Spirit
Mary Don't You Weep . . . . . . Stonewall Jackson	Medicine Man (Part 1) . . . . . . Buchanan Brothers
Mary Had A Little Lamb . . . . Wings	Medicine Song . . . . Stephanie Mills
Mary Hartman, Mary Hartman . . . Deadly Nightshade	Meditation . . . . Charlie Byrd
Mary In The Morning . . . . Al Martino	Meditation . . . . Pat Boone
Mary Jane . . . . Rick James	Meet El Presidente . . . . Duran Duran
Mary Lou . . . . Ronnie Hawkins	Meet Me At The Twistin' Place . . Johnny Morrisette
Mary, Mary . . . . Run-D.M.C.	Meet Me Halfway . . . . Kenny Loggins
Mary's Boy Child . . . . Harry Belafonte	Meet Mr. Callaghan . . . . Les Paul
Mary's Little Lamb . . . . James Darren	Meeting In The Ladies Room . . . . Klymaxx
Mary's Prayer . . . . Danny Wilson	Meeting Over Yonder . . . . Impressions
Mas Que Nada . . . . . . Sergio Mendes & Brasil '66	Mega Force 707
Mashed Potato Time . . . . Dee Dee Sharp	Mega Medley . . . . Zapp & Roger
Masquerade . . . . Berlin	Melancholy Music Man . . . . Righteous Brothers
Master Blaster (Jammin') . . . . Stevie Wonder	Melanie Makes Me Smile . . . . . Terry Williams
Master Jack . . . . Four Jacks And A Jill	Melanie Makes Me Smile . . . . . . Tony Burrows
Master Of Eyes . . . . Aretha Franklin	Mellow Yellow . . . . Donovan
Masterpiece . . . . Atlantic Starr	Melodie D'Amour . . . . Ames Brothers
Masterpiece . . . . Temptations	Melody For An Unknown Girl . . . . . . Unknowns
Matador . . . . Johnny Cash	Melody Of Love . . . . Billy Vaughn
Matador . . . . Kingston Trio	Melody Of Love . . . . David Carroll
Matador . . . . Major Lance	Melody Of Love . . . . Four Aces
Matchbox . . . . Beatles	Melt In Your Mouth . . . . Candyman
Material Girl . . . . Madonna	Melting Pot . . . . Blue Mink
Mathematics . . . . Melissa Manchester	Melting Pot . . . . Booker T & The MG's
Matter Of Trust . . . . Billy Joel	Memories . . . . Elvis Presley
Matthew And Son . . . . Cat Stevens	Memories . . . . Tierra
May I . . . . Bill Deal & The Rhondels	Memories Are Made Of This . . . . . . Dean Martin
May I Take A Giant Step . . 1910 Fruitgum Company	Memories Are Made Of This . . . . Drifters
May The Bird Of Paradise Fly Up	Memories Of A Broken Promise . . . . Motherlode
Your Nose . . . . . . "Little" Jimmy Dickens	Memories Of Days Gone By . . . . Five Satins
May You Always . . . . McGuire Sisters	Memories Of Maria . . . . Jerry Byrd
Maybe . . . . Chantels	Memory . . . . Barbra Streisand
Maybe . . . . Perry Como	Memory . . . . Barry Manilow
Maybe . . . . Three Degrees	Memory Lane . . . . Hippies
Maybe Baby . . . . Crickets	Memphis . . . . Donnie Brooks
Maybe I Know . . . . Lesley Gore	Memphis . . . . Johnny Rivers
Maybe I'm A Fool . . . . Eddie Money	Memphis . . . . Lonnie Mack
Maybe I'm Amazed (live version) . . . . . . Wings	Memphis At Sunrise . . . . Bar-Kays
Maybe Just Today . . . . Bobby Vee	Memphis Soul Stew . . . . King Curtis
Maybe The Rain Will Fall . . . . Cascades	Memphis Tennessee . . . . Chuck Berry

464

Memphis Underground . . . . Herbie Mann	Midnight Light . . . . Lenny LeBlanc
Men All Pause . . . . Klymaxx	Midnight Love Affair . . . . Carol Douglas
Men Are Gettin' Scarce . . . . Joe Tex	Midnight Love Affair . . . . Dawn
Men Are Getting Scarce . . . Chairmen Of The Board	Midnight Man . . . . James Gang
Men In My Little Girl's Life . . . . . Mike Douglas	Midnight Maniac . . . . Krokus
Men Of Learning . . . . Vigrass & Osborne	Midnight Mary . . . . Joey Powers
Mendelssohn's 4th (Second	Midnight Oil . . . . Charlie Blackwell
Movement) . . . . Apollo 100	Midnight Rain . . . . Poco
Mendocino . . . . Sir Douglas Quintet	Midnight Rendezvous . . . . Babys
Mentirosa . . . . Mellow Man Ace	Midnight Rider . . . . Gregg Allman
Mercedes Boy . . . . Pebbles	Midnight Rider . . . . Joe Cocker
Mercy . . . . Ohio Express	Midnight Rocks . . . . Al Stewart
Mercy, Mercy . . . . Don Covay	Midnight Show . . . . Bobby Vinton
Mercy Mercy Me (The Ecology) . . . . Marvin Gaye	Midnight Show . . . . Ron Dante
Mercy Mercy Me (The Ecology) . . . . Robert Palmer	Midnight Sky . . . . Isley Brothers
Mercy, Mercy, Mercy . . . . Buckinghams	Midnight Special . . . . Johnny Rivers
Mercy, Mercy, Mercy . . . . . . Cannonball Adderly	Midnight Stroll . . . . Revels
Mercy, Mercy, Mercy	Midnight Sun . . . . Five Whispers
. . . . Larry Williams/Johnny Watson	Midnight Train To Georgia . . . .
Mercy, Mercy, Mercy . . . . Marlena Shaw	. . . . Gladys Knight & The Pips
Mercy, Mercy, Mercy . . . . Phoebe Snow	Midnight Wind . . . . John Stewart
Merry Christmas Baby . . . . Chuck Berry	Midnite Special . . . . Paul Evans
Merry Christmas Darling . . . . Carpenters	Might Just Take Your Life . . . . Deep Purple
Merry-Go-Round . . . . Marv Johnson	Mighty Clouds Of Joy . . . . B.J. Thomas
Mess Of Blues . . . . Elvis Presley	Mighty Good . . . . Ricky Nelson
Message . . . . Cymande	Mighty High . . . . Mighty Clouds Of Joy
Message . . . Grand Master Flash & The Furious Five	Mighty Joe . . . . Shocking Blue
Message From Maria . . . . Joe Simon	Mighty Love (Part 1) . . . . Spinners
Message In A Bottle . . . . Police	Mighty Mighty . . . . Earth, Wind & Fire
Message In Our Music . . . . O'Jays	Mighty Quinn (Quinn The Eskimo) . . Manfred Mann
Message To Michael . . . . Dionne Warwick	Miles Away . . . . Fotomaker
Method Man . . . . Wu-Tang Clan	Miles Away . . . . Winger
Method Of Modern Love . . Daryl Hall & John Oates	Military Madness . . . . Graham Nash
Metro . . . . Berlin	Miller's Cave . . . . Bobby Bare
Mexican Hat Rock . . . . Applejacks	Million And One . . . . Dean Martin
Mexican Joe . . . . Mitchell Torok	Million And One . . . . Vic Dana
Mexican Pearls . . . . Billy Vaughn	Million To One . . . . Brian Hyland
Mexican Pearls . . . . Don Randy	Million To One . . . . Donny Osmond
Mexican Radio . . . . Wall Of Voodoo	Million To One . . . . Five Stairsteps
Mexican Shuffle . . . Herb Alpert & The Tijuana Brass	Million To One . . . . Jimmy Charles
Mexico . . . . Bob Moore	Millionaire . . . . Dr. Hook
Mexico . . . . James Taylor	Millionaire . . . . Perez Prado
Mi Casa, Su Casa . . . . Perry Como	Milord . . . . Bobby Darin
Miami . . . . . Bob Seger & The Siver Bullet Band	Mind Bender . . . . Stillwater
Miami . . . . Eugene Church	Mind, Body And Soul . . . . Flaming Ember
"Miami Vice" Theme . . . . Jan Hammer	Mind Excursion . . . . Tradewinds
Michael . . . . C.O.D.'S	Mind Games . . . . John Lennon
Michael . . . . Highwaymen	Mind Over Matter . . . . Nolan Strong
Michael . . . . Trini Lopez	Mine Exclusively . . . . Olympics
Michelle . . . . Billy Vaughn	Minimum Love . . . . Mac McAnally
Michelle . . . . Bud Shank	Mini-Skirt Minnie . . . . Wilson Pickett
Michelle . . . . David & Jonathan	Minnesota . . . . Northern Light
Michigan Harry Slaughter . . . . Wadsworth Mansion	Minotaur . . . . Dick Hyman
Mickey . . . . Toni Basil	Minute By Minute . . . . Doobie Brothers
Mickey's Monkey . . . . Miracles	Minute Of Your time . . . . Tom Jones
Midas Touch . . . . Midnight Star	Minute You're Gone . . . . Cliff Richard
Middle Of The Road . . . . Pretenders	Minute You're Gone . . . . Sonny James
Midlife Crisis . . . . Faith No More	Mio Amore . . . . Flamingos
Midnight . . . . Classics IV	Miracle . . . . Frankie Avalon
Midnight . . . . Johnny Gibson	Miracle . . . . Jon Bon Jovi
Midnight . . . . Paul Anka	Miracle . . . . Whitney Houston
Midnight At The Oasis . . . . Maria Muldaur	Miracle Of Love . . . . Eileen Rodgers
Midnight Blue . . . . Lou Gramm	Miracle Of Love . . . . Ginny Gibson
Midnight Blue . . . . Louise Tucker	Miracles . . . . Jefferson Starship
Midnight Blue . . . . Melissa Manchester	Miracles . . . . Stacy Lattisaw
Midnight Confessions . . . . Grass Roots	Mirage . . . . Eric Troyer
Midnight Cowboy . . . . Ferrante & Teicher	Mirage . . . . . . Tommy James And The Shondells
Midnight Flower . . . . Four Tops	Mirror Man . . . . Human League
Midnight Flyer . . . . Nat King Cole	Mirror, Mirror . . . . Diana Ross
Midnight In Moskow . . . . Kenny Ball	Misdemeanor . . . . Foster Sylvers
Midnight Lace . . . . David Carroll	Misery . . . . Dynamics
Midnight Lace . . . . Ray Ellis	Misfit . . . . Curiosity Killed The Cat
Midnight Lace (Part 1)	Misfits . . . . Don Costa
. . . . Ray Conniff And The Singers	Misled . . . . Kool & The Gang

Miss America . . . . Mark Lindsay	Money Changes Everything . . . . Cyndi Lauper
Miss Fine . . . . New Yorkers	Money Don't Matter 2 Night . . . .
Miss Me Blind . . . . Culture Club	. . . . Prince And The N. P. G.
Miss Sun . . . . Boz Scaggs	Money For Nothing . . . . Dire Straits
Miss You . . . . Jaye P. Morgan	Money Honey . . . . Bay City Rollers
Miss You . . . . Keymen	Money, Money, Money . . . . Abba
Miss You . . . . Rolling Stones	Money Runner . . . . Quincy Jones
Miss You In A Heartbeat . . . . Def Leppard	Money Talks . . . . AC/DC
Miss You Like Crazy . . . . Natalie Cole	Money (That's What I Want) . . . . . Barrett Strong
Miss You Much . . . . Janet Jackson	Money (That's What I Want) (Part 1) . . . .
Missed Opportunity . . . . . Daryl Hall & John Oates	. . . . Jr. Walker & The All Stars
Missing You . . . . Dan Fogelberg	Money Won't Change You (Part 1) . . . James Brown
Missing You . . . . Diana Ross	Money$ Too Tight (To Mention) . . . . Simply Red
Missing You . . . . John Waite	Mongoose . . . . Elephant's Memory
Missing You . . . . Luther Ingram	Monkey . . . . George Michael
Missing You . . . . Ray Peterson	Monkey Shine . . . . Bill Black's Combo
Missing You Now . . . . Michael Bolton	Monkey Time . . . . Major Lance
Mission Bell . . . . Donnie Brooks	Monkey Time . . . . Tubes
Missionary Man . . . . Eurythmics	Monster . . . . Fred Schneider
Mission-Impossible . . . . Lalo Schifrin	Monster . . . . Steppenwolf
Mississippi . . . . John Phillips	Monster Mash . . . .
Mississippi Mama . . . . Owen B.	. . . Bobby "Boris" Pickett And The Crypt-Kickers
Mississippi Queen . . . . Mountain	Monster's Holiday . . . .
Missunderstanding . . . . Al B. Sure!	. . . Bobby "Boris" Pickett And The Crypt-Kickers
Mistake No. 3 . . . . Culture Club	Monsters And Angels . . . . . Voice Of The Beehive
Mistaken Identity . . . . Kim Carnes	Montage From How Sweet It Is . . . Love Generation
Mister And Mississippi . . . . Patti Page	Montego Bay . . . . Amazulu
Mister Can't You See . . . . . . Buffy Sainte-Marie	Montego Bay . . . . Bobby Bloom
Mister Fire Eyes . . . . Bonnie Guitar	Monterey . . . . Animals
Mister Magic . . . . Grover Washington Jr.	Mony Mony . . . . . Tommy James And The Shondells
Mister Sandman . . . . Emmylou Harris	Mony Mony (live version) . . . . Billy Idol
Mistrusted Love . . . . Mistress	Mony Mony (studio version) . . . . Billy Idol
Misty . . . . Johnny Mathis	Moody Blue . . . . Elvis Presley
Misty . . . . Lloyd Price	Moody River . . . . Pat Boone
Misty . . . . Ray Stevens	Moody Woman . . . . Jerry Butler
Misty . . . . Richard "Groove" Holmes	Moon Over Naples . . . . Bert Kaempfert
Misty . . . . Sarah Vaughan	Moon River . . . . Henry Mancini
Misty . . . . Vibrations	Moon River . . . . Jerry Butler
Misty Blue . . . . Dorothy Moore	Moon Shadow . . . . Cat Stevens
Misty Blue . . . . Eddy Arnold	Moon Talk . . . . Perry Como
Misty Blue . . . . Joe Simon	Moon Walk (Part 1) . . . . Joe Simon
Misunderstanding . . . . Genesis	Moonbeam . . . . Men Without Hats
Mixed Emotions . . . . Rolling Stones	Moondance . . . . Van Morrison
Mixed Up Guy . . . . Joey Scarbury	Moonflight . . . . Vik Venus
Mixed Up, Shook-Up, Girl . . . Patty & The Emblems	Moonglow And Theme From "Picnic" . . . .
Mockin' Bird Hill . . . . Les Paul & Mary Ford	. . . . George Cates
Mockin' Bird Hill . . . . Patti Page	Moonglow And Theme From
Mocking Bird . . . . Four Lads	"Picnic" . . . . Morris Stoloff
Mockingbird . . . . Aretha Franklin	Moonlight And Roses . . . . Vic Dana
Mockingbird . . . . . Carly Simon And James Taylor	Moonlight Bay . . . . Drifters
Mockingbird . . . . Inez Foxx	Moonlight Feels Right . . . . Starbuck
Model Girl . . . . Johnny Maestro	Moonlight Gambler . . . . Frankie Laine
Modern Day Delilah . . . . . . Van Stephenson	Moonlight Love . . . . Perry Como
Modern Girl . . . . Sheena Easton	Moonlight On Water . . . . Laura Branigan
Modern Love . . . . David Bowie	Moonlight Serenade . . . . Rivieras
Modern Woman . . . . Billy Joel	Moonlight Sonata . . . . Henry Mancini
Mohair Sam . . . . Charlie Rich	Moonlight Special . . . . Ray Stevens
Mojo Workout . . . . Larry Bright	Moonlight Swim . . . . Nick Noble
Molly . . . . Bobby Goldsboro	Moon-Light Swim . . . . Tony Perkins
Moment Of Truth . . . . Survivor	Moonlighting . . . . Al Jarreau
Moments . . . . Jennell Hawkins	Moonshine . . . . John Kay
Moments To Remember . . . . Four Lads	More . . . . Kai Winding
Moments To Remember . . . . Vogues	More . . . . Perry Como
Mona Lisa . . . . Carl Mann	More . . . . Vic Dana
Mona Lisa . . . . Conway Twitty	More And More . . . . Andy Williams
Mona Lisa . . . . Nat King Cole	More And More . . . . . . Captain Hollywood Project
Monday, Monday . . . . Mama's & Papa's	More And More . . . . Carly Simon
Money . . . . Flying Lizards	More And More Of Your Amor . . . Nat King Cole
Money . . . . Gladys Knight & The Pips	More Bounce To The Ounce (Part 1) . . . . Zapp
Money . . . . Kingsmen	More I See You . . . . Chris Montez
Money . . . . Lovin' Spoonful	More Love . . . . Kim Carnes
Money . . . . Pink Floyd	More Love . . . . Miracles
Money Back Guarantee . . . Five Man Electrical Band	More Money For You And Me . . . . Four Preps
Money Can't Buy You Love . . . . . . Ralph Tresvant	

Ms. Grace . . . . Tymes	My Boyfriend's Back . . . . Angels
M.T.A. . . . . Kingston Trio	My Brave Face . . . . Paul McCartney
Muddy Mississippi Line . . . . . . Bobby Goldsboro	My Bucket's Got A Hole In It . . . . . . Ricky Nelson
Muddy River . . . . Johnny Rivers	My Buddy Seat . . . . Hondells
Mule . . . . James Boys	My Cherie . . . . Al Martino
Mule Skinner Blues . . . . Fendermen	My Cherie Amour . . . . Stevie Wonder
Mule Skinner Blues . . . . Rusty Draper	My Claire De Lune . . . . Steve Lawrence
Mull Of Kintyre . . . . Wings	My Coloring Book . . . . Kitty Kallen
Multiplication . . . . Bobby Darin	My Coloring Book . . . . Sandy Stewart
Mummy . . . . Bob McFadden And Dor	My Country . . . . Jud Strunk
Murphy's Law . . . . Cher	My Crew . . . . Rita Coolidge
Muscles . . . . Diana Ross	My Cup Runneth Over . . . . Ed Ames
Museum . . . . Herman's Hermits	My Dad . . . . Paul Petersen
Music . . . . John Miles	My Daddy Is President . . . . Little Jo Ann
Music Box Dancer . . . . Frank Mills	My Daddy Knows Best . . . . Marvelettes
Music Eyes . . . . Heartsfield	My Dearest Darling . . . . Etta James
Music, Harmony And Rhythm . . . Brooklyn Dreams	My Deceiving Heart . . . . Impressions
Music In My Bones . . . . Joe Simon	My Ding-A-Ling . . . . Chuck Berry
Music Is Everywhere . . . . . . Tufano & Giammarese	My Dream . . . . Platters
Music Is Love . . . . David Crosby	My Elusive Dreams . . . . Bobby Vinton
Music Is My Life . . . . Helen Reddy	My Elusive Dreams . . . . Charlie Rich
Music, Music, Music . . . . Happenings	My Elusive Dreams
Music, Music, Music . . . . Sensations	. . . . David Houston And Tammy Wynette
Music! Music! Music! . . . . Teresa Brewer	My Empty Arms . . . . Jackie Wilson
Music Never Stopped . . . . Grateful Dead	My Empty Room
Music Time . . . . Styx	. . . . Little Anthony And The Imperials
Music To Watch Girls By . . . . Andy Williams	My Ever Changing Moods . . . . . . Style Council
Music To Watch Girls By . . . Bob Crewe Generation	My Eyes Adored You . . . . Frankie Valli
Muskrat . . . . Everly Brothers	My Fair Share . . . . Seals & Crofts
Muskrat Love . . . . America	My Faith, My Hope, My Love . . . . . . Don Cornell
Muskrat Love . . . . Captain & Tennille	My Favorite Things
Muskrat Ramble . . . . Freddy Cannon	. . . . Herb Alpert & The Tijuana Brass
Muskrat Ramble . . . . McGuire Sisters	My First Day Without Her . . . . Dennis Yost
Must Be Love . . . . James Gang	My First Night Without You . . . . . . Cyndi Lauper
Must Have Been Crazy . . . . Chicago	My Foolish Heart . . . . Billy Eckstine
Must Of Got Lost . . . . J. Geils Band	My Foolish Heart . . . . Demensions
Must To Avoid . . . . Herman's Hermits	My Foolish Heart . . . . Gordon Jenkins Orchestra
Mustang Sally . . . . Wilson Pickett	My Generation . . . . Who
Mutual Admiration Society	My Girl . . . . Donnie Iris
. . . . Eddy Arnold And Jaye P. Morgan	My Girl . . . . Eddie Floyd
Mutual Admiration Society . . . . . . Teresa Brewer	My Girl . . . . Robin Luke
Mutual Surrender (What A	My Girl . . . . Suave
Wonderful World) . . . . Bourgeois Tagg	My Girl . . . . Temptations
My Adorable One . . . . Joe Simon	My Girl Bill . . . . Jim Stafford
My Angel Baby . . . . Toby Beau	My Girl (Gone, Gone, Gone) . . . . Chilliwack
My Answer . . . . Jimmy McCracklin	My Girl Has Gone . . . . Miracles
My Babe . . . . Righteous Brothers	My Girl Josephine . . . . Fats Domino
My Babe . . . . Ronnie Dove	My Girl Josephine . . . . Jerry Jaye
My Baby . . . . Pretenders	My Girl Sloopy . . . . . Little Caesar And The Consuls
My Baby . . . . Temptations	My Girl Sloopy . . . . Vibrations
My Baby Don't Dig Me . . . . Ray Charles	My Girl/Hey Girl . . . . Bobby Vee
(My Baby Don't Love Me) No More	My Guy . . . . Mary Wells
. . . . DeJohn Sisters	My Guy . . . . Petula Clark
My Baby Loves Lovin' . . . . White Plains	My Guy . . . . Sister Sledge
My Baby Loves Me . . . . . Martha & The Vandellas	My Guy/My Girl . . . Amii Stewart & Johnny Bristol
My Baby Must Be A Magician . . . . . . Marvelettes	My Happiness . . . . Connie Francis
My Baby's Baby . . . . Liquid Gold	My Heart Belongs To Me . . . . . . Barbra Streisand
My Baby's Coming Home . . . Les Paul & Mary Ford	My Heart Belongs To Only You . . . . . Bobby Vinton
My Back Pages . . . . Byrds	My Heart Belongs To Only You . . . . Jackie Wilson
My Backscratcher . . . . Frank Frost	My Heart Belongs To You . . . . Russ Irwin
My Balloon's Going Up . . . Archie Bell & The Drells	My Heart Can't Tell You No . . . . . . Rod Stewart
My Best Friend . . . . Jefferson Airplane	My Heart Cries For You . . . . . . Connie Francis
My Best Friend's Girl . . . . Cars	My Heart Cries For You . . . . Guy Mitchell
My Best Friend's Wife . . . . Paul Anka	My Heart Cries For You . . . . Ray Charles
My Block . . . . Four Pennies	My Heart Has A Mind Of Its Own . . Connie Francis
My Blue Angel . . . . . . Michael Learns To Rock	My Heart Is An Open Book . . . . . Carl Dobkins Jr.
My Blue Heaven . . . . Bobby Day	My Heart Is Bleeding . . . . Fats Domino
My Blue Heaven . . . . Duane Eddy	My Heart Is Failing Me . . . . Riff
My Body Says Yes . . . . Titiyo	My Heart Reminds Me . . . . Kay Starr
My Bonnie . . . . Beatles	My Heart Skips A Beat . . . . Cover Girls
My Boomerang Won't Come Back . . . Charlie Drake	My Heart Would Know . . . . Al Martino
My Boy . . . . Elvis Presley	My Heart's Symphony . . . .
My Boy . . . . Richard Harris	. . . . Gary Lewis And The Playboys
My Boy Lollipop . . . . Millie Small	

N

469

Natural High . . . . Bloodstone
Natural Man . . . . Lou Rawls
Natural Woman (You Make Me
  Feel Like) . . . . Aretha Franklin
Naturally Stoned . . . . Avant-Garde
Nature Boy . . . . Bobby Darin
Nature Of Love . . . . Waterfront
Naughty Girls (Need Love Too) . . . . Samantha Fox
Naughty Lady Of Shady Lane . . . . . Ames Brothers
Naughty, Naughty . . . . John Parr
Navy Blue . . . . Diane Renay
Neanderthal Man . . . . Hotlegs
Near You . . . . Roger Williams
Nearer To You . . . . Betty Harris
Nee Nee Na Na Na Na Nu Nu
  . . . . Dicky Doo And The Don'ts
Need A Little Taste Of Love . . . . . Doobie Brothers
Need To Be . . . . Jim Weatherly
Need To Belong . . . . Jerry Butler
Need You . . . . Donnie Owens
Need You Tonight . . . . Inxs
Need Your Love . . . . Bobby Freeman
Need Your Loving Tonight . . . . Queen
Needle In A Haystack . . . . Velvelettes
Needles And Pins . . . . Jackie DeShannon
Needles And Pins . . . . Searchers
Needles And Pins . . . . Smokie
Needles And Pins . . Tom Petty And The Heartbreakers
  . . . . With Stevie Nicks
Neighbor, Neighbor . . . . Jimmy Hughes
Neither One Of Us (Wants To Be The First
  To Say Goodbye) . . . . Gladys Knight & The Pips
Nel Blu Dipinto Di Blue (Volare) . . . .
  . . . . Domenico Modugno
Neon Nites . . . . Atlanta Rhythm Section
Neon Rainbow . . . . Box Tops
N-E-R-V-O-U-S! . . . . Ian Whitcomb
Nessuno Mi Puo' Giudcare . . . . . . Gene Pitney
Neutron Dance . . . . Pointer Sisters
Nevada Fighter
  . . . . Michael Nesmith & The First National Band
Never . . . . Earls
Never . . . . Heart
Never 2 Much Of U . . . . Dino
Never A Time . . . . Genesis
Never Again . . . . Dinah Washington
Never As Good As The First Time . . . . Sade
Never Be Afraid . . . . Bing Crosby
Never Be Anyone Else But You . . . . Ricky Nelson
Never Be The Same . . . . Christopher Cross
Never Been Any Reason . . . . Head East
Never Been In Love . . . . Randy Meisner
Never Been To Spain . . . . Three Dog Night
Never Before . . . . Connie Francis
Never Can Say Goodbye . . . . Communards
Never Can Say Goodbye . . . . Gloria Gaynor
Never Can Say Goodbye . . . . Isaac Hayes
Never Can Say Goodbye . . . . Jackson Five
Never Comes The Day . . . . Moody Blues
Never Ending Song Of Love . . . . Delaney & Bonnie
Never Ending Story . . . . Limahl
Never Enough . . . . Cure
Never Enough . . . . Patty Smyth
Never Ever . . . . Peter And Gordon
Never Get Enough Of Your Love . . . . L.T.D.
Never Give Up . . . . Sammy Hagar
Never Give Up On A Good Thing . . . George Benson
Never Give You Up . . . . Jerry Butler
Never Goin' Back . . . . Lovin' Spoonful
Never Gonna Fall In Love Again . . . . Eric Carmen
Never Gonna Give You Up . . . . Rick Astley
Never Gonna Let Him Know . . . . . Debbie Taylor
Never Gonna Let You Down . . . . Surface
Never Gonna Let You Go . . Sergio Mendes & Brasil '66

Never Had A Dream Come True . . . . . Stevie Wonder
Never Had A Lot To Lose . . . . Cheap Trick
Never Had A Love . . . . Pablo Cruise
Never Had It So Good . . . . Ronnie Milsap
Never Have To Say Goodbye Again . . . .
  . . . . Deardorff & Joseph
Never In A Million Years . . . . Linda Scott
Never Keeping Secrets . . . . Babyface
Never Knew Love Like This . . . .
  . . . . Cherrelle With Alexander O'Neal
Never Knew Love Like This Before . . Stephanie Mills
Never Let Her Go . . . . David Gates
Never Let Her Slip Away . . . . Andrew Gold
Never Let Me Down . . . . David Bowie
Never Let Me Down Again . . . . . . Depeche Mode
Never Let You Go . . . . Bloodstone
Never Marry A Railroad Man . . . . Shocking Blue
Never My Love . . . . Addrisi Brothers
Never My Love . . . . Association
Never My Love . . . . Blue Swede
Never My Love . . . . Fifth Dimension
Never, Never . . . . Jive Five
Never, Never Gonna Give You Up . . . . Barry White
Never Never Leave Me . . . . Mary Wells
Never, Never, Never . . . . Shirley Bassey
Never On Sunday . . . . Chordettes
Never On Sunday . . . . Don Costa
Never Say Die (Give Me A Little Bit
  More) . . . . Cliff Richard
Never Should've Let You Go . . . . Hi-Five
Never Surrender . . . . Corey Hart
Never Tear Us Apart . . . . Inxs
Never Thought (That I Could Love) . . . . Dan Hill
Never Too Much . . . . Luther Vandross
Nevertheless . . . . Mills Brothers
Nevertheless . . . . Ralph Flanagan Orchestra
New Attitude . . . . Patti LaBelle
New Breed . . . . James Brown
New Day For You . . . . Basia
(New) Frankie And Johnny
  . . . . Greenwood County Singers
New Frontier . . . . Donald Fagen
New Girl In School . . . . Jan & Dean
New Girl Now . . . . Honeymoon Suite
(New In) The Ways Of Love . . . . . Tommy Edwards
New Kid In Town . . . . Eagles
New Mexican Rose . . . . Four Seasons
New Moon On Sunday . . . . Duran Duran
New Orleans . . . . Eddie Hodges
New Orleans . . . . Gary U.S. Bonds
New Orleans . . . . Neil Diamond
New Orleans . . . . Staple Singers
New Orleans Ladies . . . . Louisiana's Le Roux
New Power Generation . . . . Prince
New Rock And Roll . . . . Mahogany Rush
New Romance (It's A Mystery) . . . . Spider
New Sensation . . . . Inxs
New Song . . . . Howard Jones
New Thing . . . . Enuff Z'nuff
New World Coming . . . . Mama Cass Elliot
New World Man . . . . Rush
New Year's Day U2
New York City . . . . Zwol
New York Groove . . . . Ace Frehley
New York Mining Disaster 1941
  (Have You Seen My Wife, Mr. Jones) . . . Bee Gees
New York Minute . . . . Don Henley
New York's A Lonely Town . . . . . . Tradewinds
Newsy Neighbors . . . . First Choice
Next Door To An Angel . . . . Neil Sedaka
Next Door To The Blues . . . . Etta James
Next Hundred Years . . . . Al Martino
Next Kiss (Is The Last Goodbye) . . . Conway Twitty

470

No One Like You . . . . Scorpions
No One To Cry To . . . . Ray Charles
No One To Depend On . . . . Santana
No One Will Ever Know . . . . Jimmie Rodgers
No Ordinary Love . . . . Sade
No Other Arms, No Other Lips . . . . . . Chordettes
No Other Arms, No Other Lips . . . . . . Four Aces
No Other Love . . . . Perry Como
No Particular Place To Go . . . . Chuck Berry
No Pity (In The Naked City) . . . . Jackie Wilson
No Promises . . . . Icehouse
No Rain . . . . Blind Melon
No Reply At All . . . . Genesis
No Sad Songs . . . . Helen Reddy
No Sad Songs . . . . Joe Simon
No Son Of Mine . . . . Genesis
No Substitute For Love . . . . Roy Hamilton
No Sugar Tonight . . . . Guess Who
No Sunshine . . . . Kid Frost
No Tell Lover . . . . Chicago
No Time . . . . Guess Who
No Time For Talk . . . . Christopher Cross
No Time Like The Right Time . . . . . Blues Project
No Time To Lose . . . . Tarney/Spencer Band
No Way Out . . . . Jefferson Starship
No Wheels . . . . Chordettes
Nobody . . . . Charles Wright And
. . . . The Watts 103rd Street Rhythm Band
Nobody . . . . Doobie Brothers
Nobody . . . . Doucette
Nobody . . . . Sylvia
Nobody . . . . Three Dog Night
Nobody But Me . . . . Human Beinz
Nobody But You . . . . Dee Clark
Nobody But You . . . . Loggins And Messina
Nobody But You Babe . . . . Clarence Reid
Nobody Cares (About Me) . . . . . Baby Washington
Nobody Does It Better . . . . Carly Simon
Nobody I Know . . . . Peter And Gordon
Nobody Knows What's Goin' On . . . . . . Chiffons
Nobody Loves Me Like You . . . . Flamingos
Nobody Said It Was Easy . . . . Le Roux
Nobody Told Me . . . . John Lennon
Nobody Wants You When You're
    Down And Out . . . . Bobby Womack
Nobody Wins . . . . Brenda Lee
Nobody Wins . . . . Elton John
Nobody Wins In This War . . . . Mitch Malloy
Nobody's Baby Again . . . . Dean Martin
Nobody's Fool . . . . Cinderella
Nobody's Fool . . . . Kenny Loggins
Nobody's Perfect . . . . . . Mike + The Mechanics
Nola . . . . Billy Williams
Nola . . . . Morgan Brothers
Non Dimenticar (Don't Forget) . . . . Nat King Cole
Norma Jean Wants To Be A Movie
Star . . . . Sundown Company
Norman . . . . Sue Thompson
North To Alaska . . . . Johnny Horton
Not Enough Indians . . . . Dean Martin
Not Enough Love In The World . . . . . Don Henley
Not Enough Time . . . . Inxs
Not Fade Away . . . . Eric Hine
Not Fade Away . . . . Rolling Stones
Not Fade Away . . . . Tanya Tucker
Not Just Another Girl . . . . Ivan Neville
(Not Just) Knee Deep (Part 1) . . . . . . Funkadelic
Not Me . . . . Orlons
Not On The Outside . . . . Moments
Not One Minute More . . . . Della Reese
Not Responsible . . . . Tom Jones
Not The Lovin' Kind . . . . Dino, Desi & Billy
Not The Only One . . . . Bonnie Raitt
Not Too Long Ago . . . . Uniques

Not Too Young To Get Married . . . .
. . . . Bob B. Soxx And The Blue Jeans
Not Wrong Long . . . . Nazz
Nothin (That Compares 2 U) . . . . Jacksons
Nothin' At All . . . . Heart
Nothin' But A Good Time . . . . Poison
Nothin' Heavy . . . . David Bellamy
Nothin' My Love Can't Fix . . . . . . Joey Lawrence
Nothing 'Bout Me . . . . Sting
Nothing Broken But My Heart . . . . . Celine Dion
Nothing But A Breeze . . . . Jesse Winchester
Nothing But A Heartache . . . . Flirtations
Nothing But Heartaches . . . . Supremes
Nothing Can Change This Love . . . . Sam Cooke
Nothing Can Stop Me . . . . Gene Chandler
Nothing Can Take The Place Of You . . Brook Benton
Nothing Compares To U . . . . Sinead O'Connor
Nothing Else Matters . . . . Metallica
Nothing Ever Goes As Planned . . . . Styx
Nothing From Nothing . . . . Billy Preston
Nothing Goes Up (Without Coming
    Down) . . . . Nat King Cole
Nothing In Common . . . . Thompson Twins
Nothing In The World . . . . Nat King Cole
Nothing Succeeds Like Success . . . .
    . . . . Bill Deal & The Rhondels
Nothing Takes The Place Of You . . Toussaint McCall
Nothing To Hide . . . . Tommy James
Nothing's Gonna Change My Love
    For You . . . . Glenn Medeiros
Nothing's Gonna Stop Me Now . . . . Samantha Fox
Nothing's Gonna Stop Us Now . . . . Starship
Nothing's Too Good For My Baby . . . Stevie Wonder
Notice Me . . . . Nikki
Notorious . . . . Duran Duran
Notorious . . . . Loverboy
November Rain . . . . Guns N' Roses
Now! . . . . Lena Horne
Now And For Always . . . . . . George Hamilton IV
Now And Forever . . . . Bert Kaempfert
(Now And Then There's) A Fool
    Such As I . . . . Elvis Presley
Now I Know . . . . Jack Jones
Now Is The Hour . . . . Gale Storm
Now Or Never . . . . Axe
Now Run And Tell That . . . . Denise LaSalle
Now That We Found Love . . . Heavy D. & The Boyz
Now That We Found Love . . . . Third World
Now That You've Gone . . . . Connie Stevens
Now You're Gone . . . . Whitesnake
Now You're In Heaven . . . . Julian Lennon
Nowhere Man . . . . Beatles
Nowhere To Run . . . . . . Martha & The Vandellas
Nowhere To Run . . . . Santana
Number One . . . . Billy Swan
Number One Man . . . . Bruce Channel
#9 Dream . . . . John Lennon
Number Wonderful . . . . Rock Flowers
Nursery Rhymes (Part 1) . . . . People's Choice
Nut Rocker . . . . B. Bumble & The Stingers
Nutbush City Limits . . . . Bob Seger
Nutbush City Limits . . . . Ike & Tina Turner
Nuthin' But A "G" Thang . . . . Dr. Dre
Nutrocker . . . . Emerson, Lake & Palmer
Nuttin' For Christmas . . . . Kenny & Corky
N.Y., You Got Me Dancing . . . .
    . . . . Andrea True Connection

O

O Dio Mio . . . . Annette
O' Falling Star . . . . Four Knights
Object Of My Desire . . . . Starpoint
Ob-La-Di, Ob-La-Da . . . . Arthur Conley
Ob-La-Di, Ob-La-Da . . . . Beatles

472

476

477

478

Promised Land . . . . Chuck Berry	Put Your Hand In The Hand . . . . Ocean
Promised Land . . . . Elvis Presley	Put Your Hands Together . . . . O'Jays
Promises . . . . Barbra Streisand	Put Your Head On My Shoulder . . . . . Leif Garrett
Promises . . . . Basia	Put Your Head On My Shoulder . . . . Lettermen
Promises . . . . Eric Clapton	Put Your Head On My Shoulder . . . . . . Paul Anka
Promises In The Dark . . . . Pat Benatar	Put Your Mind At Ease . . . . . . Every Mothers' Son
Promises, Promises . . . . Dionne Warwick	Put Your Mouth On Me . . . . Eddie Murphy
Promises, Promises . . . . Naked Eyes	Put Yourself In My Place . . . . Elgins
Prophecy Of Daniel And John The	Puttin' On The Ritz . . . . Taco
Divine (Six-Six-Six) . . . . Cowsills	Puzzle Song . . . . Shirley Ellis
Proud . . . . Joe Chemay Band	P.Y.T. (Pretty Young Thing) . . . . . Michael Jackson
Proud . . . . Johnny Crawford	
Proud Mary . . . . Checkmates Ltd.	

Proud Mary . . . . . Creedence Clearwater Revival	Quality Time . . . . Hi-Five
Proud Mary . . . . Ike & Tina Turner	Quarter To Four Stomp . . . . Stompers
Proud Mary . . . . Solomon Burke	Quarter To Three . . . . Gary U.S. Bonds
Proud One . . . . Frankie Valli	Que Sera, Sera . . . . High Keys
Proud One . . . . Osmonds	Que Sera Sera . . . . Mary Hopkin
Prove It All Night . . . . Bruce Springsteen	Que Te Quiero . . . . Katrina And The Waves
Prove Your Love . . . . Taylor Dayne	Queen Of Clubs . . . . . KC And The Sunshine Band
P.S. I Love You . . . . Beatles	Queen Of Hearts . . . . Juice Newton
P.S. I Love You . . . . Hilltoppers	Queen Of My Heart . . . . Rene And Ray
Psychedelic Shack . . . . Temptations	Queen Of My Soul . . . . . . Average White Band
Psycho . . . . Bobby Hendricks	Queen Of The Broken Hearts . . . . . . Loverboy
Psychobabble . . . . Alan Parsons Project	Queen Of The Hop . . . . Bobby Darin
Psychotic Reaction . . . . Count Five	Queen Of The House . . . . Jody Miller
P.T. 109 . . . . Jimmy Dean	Queen Of The Roller Derby . . . . . Leon Russell
Pucker Up Buttercup . . . Jr. Walker & The All Stars	Queen Of The Senior Prom . . . . . Mills Brothers
Puddin N' Tain . . . . Alley Cats	Quentin's Theme . . Charles Randolph Grean Sounde
Puff The Magic Dragon . . . Peter, Paul & Mary	Question . . . . Lloyd Price
Puffin' On Down The Track . . . Hugh Masekela	Question . . . . Moody Blues
Pull Up To The Bumper . . . . Grace Jones	Question Of Temperature . . . . . Balloon Farm
Pump Up The Jam . . . . Technotronic Featuring Felly	Questions . . . . Bang
Pump Up The Volume . . . . M/A/R/R/S	Questions 67 & 68 . . . . Chicago
Punish Her . . . . Bobby Vee	Questions And Answers . . . . In Crowd
Puppet Man . . . . Fifth Dimension	Quick, Fast, In A Hurry . . . . . . New York City
Puppet Man . . . . Tom Jones	Quick Joey Small (Run Joey Run)
Puppet On A String . . . . Elvis Presley	. . . . Kasenetz-Katz Singing Orchestral Circus
Puppet Song . . . . Frankie Avalon	Quicksand . . . . Martha & The Vandellas
Puppy Love . . . . Barbara Lewis	Quiet Nights Of Quiet Stars . . . . . Andy Williams
Puppy Love . . . . Donny Osmond	Quiet Place . . . . . Garnet Mimms & The Enchanters
Puppy Love . . . . Paul Anka	Quiet Storm . . . . Smokey Robinson
Pure . . . . Lightning Seeds	Quiet Three . . . . Duane Eddy
Purple Haze . . . . Dion	Quiet Village . . . . Martin Denny
Purple Haze . . . . Jimi Hendrix Experience	Quite A Party . . . . Fireballs
Purple People Eater . . . . Sheb Wooley	Race Among The Ruins . . . . . Gordon Lightfoot
Purple Rain . . . . . Prince And The Revolution	Race Is On . . . . Jack Jones
Push And Kick . . . . Mark Valentino	Race With The Devil
Push It . . . . Salt-N-Pepa	. . . . Gene Vincent And His Blue Caps
Push Push . . . . Austin Taylor	

Push The Feeling On . . . . Nightcrawlers	Radar Love . . . . Golden Earring
Pushbike Song . . . . Mixtures	Radar Love . . . . White Lion
Pushin' Too Hard . . . . Seeds	Radio Ga Ga . . . . Queen
Pushin' Your Luck . . . . Sleepy King	Radio Romance . . . . Tiffany
Pushover . . . . Etta James	Radio Song . . . . R.E.M.
Puss N' Boots/These Boots (Are	Radioactive . . . . Firm
Made For Walkin') . . . . Kon Kan	Radioactive . . . . Gene Simmons
Pussy Cat . . . . Ames Brothers	Rag Doll . . . . Aerosmith
Put A Light In The Window . . . . Four Lads	Rag Doll . . . . Four Seasons
Put A Little Love Away . . . . Emotions	Rag Doll . . . . Sammy Johns
Put A Little Love In Your Heart	Rag Mama Rag . . . . Band
. . . . Annie Lennox & Al Green	Rag Mop . . . . Ames Brothers
Put A Little Love In Your Heart . . Jackie DeShannon	Rags To Riches . . . . Elvis Presley
Put A Ring On My Finger . . . . Les Paul & Mary Ford	Rags To Riches . . . . Lenny Welch
Put Away Your Love . . . . Alessi	Rags To Riches . . . . . Sunny & The Sunliners
Put It In A Magazine . . . . Sonny Charles	Rags To Riches . . . . Tony Bennett
Put It Where You Want It . . . . Crusaders	Ragtime Cowboy Joe . . . . Chipmunks
Put It Where You Want It	Rain . . . . Beatles
. . . . Nino Tempo & April Stevens	Rain . . . . Jose Feliciano
Put On Your Shoes And Walk . . . . . Clarence Carter	Rain . . . . Madonna
Put Out The Light . . . . Joe Cocker	Rain . . . . Oran "Juice" Jones
Put This Love To The Test . . . . Jon Astley	Rain Dance . . . . Guess Who
Put Your Arms Around Me Honey . . . . Fats Domino	Rain Forest . . . . Paul Hardcastle
Put Your Arms Around Me Honey . . . . . Ray Smith	

Right Time Of The Night . . . . Jennifer Warnes
Riki Tiki Tavi . . . . Donovan
Rikki Don't Lose That Number . . . . Steely Dan
Ring Dang Doo . . Sam The Sham And The Pharaohs
Ring My Bell . . . . Anita Ward
Ring My Bell . . . D.J. Jazzy Jeff & The Fresh Prince
Ring Of Fire . . . . Duane Eddy
Ring Of Fire . . . . Johnny Cash
Ring The Living Bell . . . . Melanie
Ring-A-Ding-A-Ding . . . . Tommy Sands
Ring-A-Ling-A-Lario . . . . Jimmie Rodgers
Ringo . . . . Lorne Greene
Ringo . . . . Reuben Howell
Ringo's Theme (This Boy) . . . . . . George Martin
Rings . . . . Cymarron
Rings . . . . Lobo
Rinky Dink . . . . Dave "Baby" Cortez
Rio . . . . Duran Duran
Riot . . . . Hugh Masekela
Rip It Up . . . . Bill Haley And His Comets
Rip It Up . . . . Little Richard
Rip Off . . . . Laura Lee
Rip Van Winkle . . . . Devotions
Rise . . . . Herb Alpert
Rise To It . . . . Kiss
Ritual . . . . Dan Reed Network
River . . . . Joe Simon
River Deep - Mountain High . . . .
. . . . Supremes & Four Tops
River Deep-Mountain High . . . . . . Deep Purple
River Is Wide . . . . Forum
River Is Wide . . . . Grass Roots
River Of Dreams . . . . Billy Joel
River Of Love . . . . B.W. Stevenson
River Road . . . . Uncle Dog
River Stay Away From My Door . . . . Frank Sinatra
River's Risin' . . . . Edgar Winter
Rivers Of Babylon . . . . Boney M
Road Hog . . . . John D. Loudermilk
Road House Blues . . . . Doors
Road Runner . . . . Bo Diddley
Road Runner . . . . Gants
Roam . . . . B-52's
Robbin' The Cradle . . . . Tony Bellus
Roberta . . . . Barry And The Tamerlanes
Roberta . . . . Bones
Roc-A-Chicka . . . . Warner Mack
Rock And A Hard Place . . . . Rolling Stones
Rock And Roll . . . . Led Zeppelin
Rock And Roll All Nite (live version) . . . . . . Kiss
Rock And Roll All Nite (studio version) . . . . . Kiss
Rock And Roll Dancin' . . . . . Beckmeier Brothers
Rock And Roll Dreams Come
Through . . . . Jim Steinman
Rock And Roll Girls . . . . John Fogerty
Rock And Roll Heaven . . . . . Righteous Brothers
Rock And Roll, Hoochie Koo . . . . . Rick Derringer
Rock And Roll Is Here To Stay . . . .
. . . . Danny & The Juniors
Rock And Roll Love Letter . . . . . Bay City Rollers
Rock And Roll Lullaby . . . . B.J. Thomas
Rock And Roll Music . . . . Beach Boys
Rock & Roll Music . . . . Chuck Berry
Rock And Roll Never Forgets . . . . Bob Seger
Rock And Roll (Part 2) . . . . Gary Glitter
Rock & Roll Runaway . . . . Ace
Rock And Roll Star . . . . Champagne
Rock & Roll Strategy . . . . 38 Special
Rock And Roll Waltz . . . . Kay Starr
Rock Brigade . . . . Def Leppard
R.O.C.K. In The U.S.A. . . . . John Cougar Mellencamp
Rock Island Line . . . .
. . . . . . Lonnie Donegan And His Skiffle Group
Rock It . . . . Lipps Inc.

Rock Lobster . . . . B-52's
Rock Love . . . . Fontane Sisters
Rock Me . . . . Great White
Rock Me . . . . Steppenwolf
Rock Me Amadeus . . . . Falco
Rock Me Baby . . . . B.B. King
Rock Me Baby . . . . David Cassidy
Rock Me Gently . . . . Andy Kim
Rock Me In The Cradle Of Love . . . Dee Dee Sharp
Rock Me On The Water . . . . Jackson Browne
Rock Me Tonight . . . . Billy Squire
Rock Me Tonight (For Old Times
Sake) . . . . Freddie Jackson
Rock 'N Me . . . . Steve Miller
Rock 'N' Roll . . . . . . Detroit Featuring Mitch Ryder
Rock 'N' Roll Fantasy . . . . Bad Company
Rock 'N' Roll Fantasy . . . . Kinks
Rock 'N' Roll (I Gave You The Best
Years Of My Life) . . . . Terry Jacks
Rock 'N Roll (I Gave You The Best
Years Of My Life) . . . . Kevin Johnson
Rock N' Roll (I Gave You The Best
Years Of My Life) . . . . Mac Davis
Rock 'N' Roll Is King . . . . Electric Light Orchestra
Rock 'N Roll Soul . . . . . Grand Funk Railroad
Rock 'N' Roll To The Rescue . . . . . . Beach Boys
Rock 'N' Roll Woman . . . . . . Buffalo Springfield
Rock Of Ages . . . . Def Leppard
Rock Of Life . . . . Rick Springfield
Rock On . . . . David Essex
Rock On . . . . Michael Damian
Rock Steady . . . . Aretha Franklin
Rock Steady . . . . Whispers
Rock The Boat . . . . Hues Corporation
Rock The Casbah . . . . Clash
Rock The Night . . . . Europe
Rock This Town . . . . Stray Cats
Rock Wit'cha . . . . Bobby Brown
Rock With You . . . . Michael Jackson
Rock You Like A Hurricane . . . . Scorpions
Rock Your Baby . . . . George McCrae
Rock Your Little Baby To Sleep . . . . . Buddy Knox
Rock-A-Billy . . . . Guy Mitchell
Rock-A-Bye Your Baby With A Dixie
Melody . . . . Aretha Franklin
Rock-A-Bye Your Baby With A Dixie
Melody . . . . Jerry Lewis
Rocka-Conga . . . . Applejacks
Rock-A-Hula Baby . . . . Elvis Presley
Rock-A-Lott . . . . Aretha Franklin
Rocket . . . . Def Leppard
Rocket 2 U . . . . Jets
Rocket Man . . . . Elton John
Rocket Ride . . . . Kiss
Rockford Files . . . . Mike Post
Rock-In Robin . . . . Bobby Day
Rockin' All Over The World . . . . . John Fogerty
Rockin' And Rollin' On The Streets Of
Hollywood . . . . Buddy Miles
Rockin' Around The Christmas Tree . . . Brenda Lee
Rockin' At Midnight . . . . Honeydrippers
Rockin' Bicycle . . . . Fats Domino
Rockin' Chair . . . . Gwen McCrae
Rockin' Crickets . . . . Hot Toddy's
Rockin' Crickets . . . . Rebels
Rockin' Good Way (To Mess Around And Fall
In Love) . . . . Dinah Washington & Brook Benton
Rockin' Goose . . . . Johnny And The Hurricanes
Rockin' In The Jungle . . . . Eternals
Rockin' In The Same Old Boat . . . . Bobby Bland
Rockin' Into The Night . . . . 38 Special
Rockin' Lady . . . . Penny Candy
Rockin' Little Angel . . . . Ray Smith

Rockin' Pneumonia Boogie Woogie
Flu . . . . Johnny Rivers
Rockin' Robin . . . . Michael Jackson
Rockin' Roll Baby . . . . Stylistics
Rockin' Shoes . . . . Ames Brothers
Rockin' Soul . . . . Hues Corporation
Rockit . . . . Herbie Hancock
Rocky . . . . Austin Roberts
Rocky Mountain High . . . . John Denver
Rocky Mountain Music . . . . Eddie Rabbitt
Rocky Mountain Way . . . . Joe Walsh
Rocky Raccoon . . . . Richie Havens
Roland The Roadie And Gertrude
The Groupie . . . . Dr. Hook
Rolene . . . . Moon Martin
Roll Away The Stone . . . . Leon Russell
Roll In My Sweet Baby's Arms . . . .
. . . . Hank Wilson (Leon Russell)
Roll Me Away . . Bob Seger & The Silver Bullet Band
Roll On . . . . New Colony Six
Roll On Down The Highway . . . .
. . . . Bachman-Turner Overdrive
Roll Over Beethoven . . . . Beatles
Roll Over Beethoven . . . . . Electric Light Orchestra
Roll Over Beethoven . . . . Velaires
Roll With It . . . . Steve Winwood
Roller . . . . April Wine
Roller Coaster . . . . Blood, Sweat & Tears
Rollin' With The Flow . . . . Charlie Rich
Rolling Down A Mountainside . . . . Main Ingredient
Roly Poly . . . . Joey Dee & The Starliters
Roman Guitar . . . . Lou Monte
Romancing The Stone . . . . Eddy Grant
Romantic . . . . Karyn White
Romeo . . . . Dino
Romeo . . . . Dolly Parton & Friends
Romeo . . . . Mr. Big
Romeo And Juliet . . . . Stacy Earl
Romeo's Tune . . . . Steve Forbert
Roni . . . . Bobby Brown
Ronnie . . . . Four Seasons
Ronnie . . . . Marcy Joe
Ronnie, Call Me When You Get A
Chance . . . . Shelley Fabares
Room At The Top . . . . Adam Ant
Room Full Of Roses . . . . Mickey Gilley
Room To Move . . . . Animotion
Room To Move . . . . John Mayall
Rooms On Fire . . . . Stevie Nicks
Roosevelt And Ira Lee . . . . Tony Joe White
"Roots" Medley . . . . Quincy Jones
Roots, Rock, Reggae . . . Bob Marley & The Wailers
Rooty Toot Toot . . . . . John Cougar Mellencamp
Rosalie . . . . Sam Neely
Rosanna . . . . Caprees
Rosanna . . . . Classics IV
Rosanna . . . . Toto
Rose . . . . Bette Midler
Rose And A Baby Ruth . . . . . George Hamilton IV
Rose Garden . . . . Dobie Gray
Rose Garden . . . . Lynn Anderson
Rose, Rose I Love You . . . . Frankie Laine
Roses . . . . Sammy Kaye
Roses And Rainbows . . . . Danny Hutton
Roses Are Red (My Love) . . . . Bobby Vinton
Roses Are Red My Love . . . You Know Who Group
Roses Of Rio . . . . Four Aces
Rosie . . . . Chubby Checker
Rosie Lee . . . . Mello-Tones
Rotation . . . . Herb Alpert
Rough Boy . . . . ZZ Top
Rough Boys . . . . Pete Townshend
Round & Round . . . . New Order
Round And Round . . . . Perry Como

Round And Round . . . . Ratt
Round And Round . . . . Tevin Campbell
Round Every Corner . . . . Petula Clark
Roundabout . . . . Connie Francis
Roundabout . . . . Yes
Route 101 . . . . Herb Alpert
Route 66 . . . . Manhattan Transfer
Route 66 Theme . . . . Nelson Riddle
Route 66/Behind The Wheel . . . . . . Depeche Mode
Roving Kind . . . . Guy Mitchell
Roxanne . . . . Police
Roxy Roller . . . . Sweeney Todd
Royal Mile (Sweet Darlin') . . . . . . Gerry Rafferty
Rub It In . . . . Billy "Crash" Craddock
Rub It In . . . . Layng Martine
Rub You The Right Way . . . . Johnny Gill
Rubber Ball . . . . Bobby Vee
Rubber Biscuit . . . . Blues Brothers
Rubber Bullets 10cc
Rubber Duckie . . . . Ernie
Rubberband Man . . . . Spinners
Ruben James . . Kenny Rogers And The First Edition
Ruberneckin' . . . . Elvis Presley
Ruby . . . . Adam Wade
Ruby . . . . Ray Charles
Ruby . . . . Richard Hayman Orchestra
Ruby Ann . . . . Marty Robbins
Ruby Baby . . . . Billy "Crash" Craddock
Ruby Baby . . . . Dion
Ruby, Don't Take Your Love To Town . . . .
. . . . Kenny Rogers And The First Edition
Ruby Duby Du . . . . Tobin Mathews & Co.
Ruby Duby Du From "Key Witness" . . . .
. . . . Charles Wolcott
Ruby Tuesday . . . . Melanie
Ruby Tuesday . . . . Rolling Stones
Rudolph The Red Nosed Reindeer . . . . Chipmunks
Rudolph The Red Nosed Reindeer . . . . Melodeers
Rudolph The Red-Nosed Reindeer . . . . Paul Anka
Rudy's Rock . . . . . Bill Haley And His Comets
Ruffneck . . . . MC Lyte
Rules Of Love . . . . Orlons
Rumble . . . . Link Wray & His Ray Men
Rumbleseat . . . . John Cougar Mellencamp
Rummy Polka . . . . Matys Brothers
Rumor At The Honky Tonk . . . . Spellbound
Rumors . . . . Johnny Crawford
Rumors . . . . Syndicate Of Sound
Rumors . . . . Timex Social Club
Rumour . . . . Olivia Newton-John
Rumour Has It . . . . Donna Summer
Rump Shaker . . . . Wreckx-N-Effect
Run And Hide . . . . Uniques
Run Away Child, Running Wild . . . . . Temptations
Run, Baby Run (Back Into My Arms) . . . Newbeats
Run For Home . . . . Lindisfarne
Run For The Roses . . . . Dan Fogelberg
Run Home Girl . . . . Sad Cafe
Run Joey Run . . . . David Geddes
Run Like Hell . . . . Pink Floyd
Run Red Run . . . . Coasters
Run, Run, Look And See . . . . Brian Hyland
Run, Run, Run . . . . Gestures
Run Run Run . . . . Jo Jo Gunne
Run, Run, Run . . . . Supremes
Run, Run, Run . . . . Third Rail
Run Runaway . . . . Slade
Run Sally Run . . . . Cuff Links
Run Samson Run . . . . Neil Sedaka
Run Through The Jungle . . . .
. . . . Creedence Clearwater Revival
Run To Him . . . . Bobby Vee
Run To Me . . . . Bee Gees
Run To Me . . . . Montanas

S

485

Satisfied (Part 2) . . . . Cashmeres	Say Man . . . . Bo Diddley
Satisfied (Part 2) . . . . Debbie Reynolds	Say Man, Back Again . . . . Bo Diddley
Satisfied With You . . . . Dave Clark Five	Say Maybe . . . . Neil Diamond
Satisfy Me . . . . Billy Satellite	Say, Say, Say
Saturday In The Park . . . . Chicago	. . . . Paul McCartney And Michael Jackson
Saturday Love . . . Cherrelle With Alexander O'Neal	Say Something Funny . . . . Patty Duke
Saturday Morning Confusion . . . . . Bobby Russell	Say What . . . . Jesse Winchester
Saturday Night . . . . Bay City Rollers	Say Wonderful Things . . . . Patti Page
Saturday Night . . . . Herman Brood	Say Wonderful Things . . . . Ronnie Carroll
Saturday Night . . . . New Christy Minstrels	Say You . . . . Ronnie Dove
Saturday Night At The Movies . . . . Drifters	Say You Love Me . . . . Fleetwood Mac
Saturday Night Special . . . . Lynyrd Skynyrd	Say You Love Me . . . . Impressions
Saturday Night, Sunday Morning . . Thelma Houston	Say You Really Want Me . . . . Kim Wilde
Saturday Night's Alright For Fighting . . . Elton John	Say You Say Me . . . . Lionel Richie
Saturday Nite . . . . Earth, Wind & Fire	Say You Will . . . . Foreigner
Saturday's Father . . . . Four Seasons	Say You'll Be Mine . . . . Christopher Cross
Saturday's Sunshine . . . . Burt Bacharach	Say You'll Stay Until Tomorrow . . . . . Tom Jones
Sausalito . . . . Al Martino	Say You're Mine Again . . . . Perry Como
Sausalito (Is The Place To Go) . . . . . Ohio Express	(Say) You're My Girl . . . . Roy Orbison
Sausalito Summernight . . . . Diesel	Say You're Wrong . . . . Julian Lennon
Savannah Nights . . . . Tom Johnston	Sayin' Sorry (Don't Make It Right) . . . Denise Lopez
Save A Prayer . . . . Duran Duran	Sayonara . . . . Eddie Fisher
Save All Your Lovin' For Me . . . . Brenda Lee	Scarborough Fair . . . . . Sergio Mendes & Brasil '66
Save It For A Rainy Day . . . . Stephen Bishop	Scarborough Fair . . . . . . Simon & Garfunkel
Save It For Me . . . . Four Seasons	Scarlet Ribbons (For Her Hair) . . . . Browns
Save Me . . . . Dave Mason	Scarlett O'Hara . . . . . Bobby Gregg And His Friends
Save Me . . . . Donna McDaniel	Scarlett O'Hara . . . . Lawrence Welk
Save Me . . . . Fleetwood Mac	Scavenger . . . . Dick Dale And The Del-Tones
Save Me . . . . Lisa Fischer	Scene Of The Crime . . . . Dinah Shore
Save Me . . . . . Merrilee Rush And The Turnabouts	School Boy Crush . . . . . . Average White Band
Save Me . . . . Rembrandts	School Day . . . . Chuck Berry
Save Me . . . . Silver Convention	School Is In . . . . Gary U.S. Bonds
Save My Soul . . . . Jack Scott	School Is Out . . . . Gary U.S. Bonds
Save Some Love . . . . Keedy	School Of Life . . . . Tommy Tate
Save The Best For Last . . . . Vanessa Williams	School's Back . . . . Philadelphia
Save The Country . . . . Fifth Dimension	School's Out . . . . Alice Cooper
Save The Country . . . . Thelma Houston	School's Out . . . . Krokus
Save The Last Dance For Me	Scientific Love . . . . Midnight Star
. . . . . DeFranco Family Featuring Tony DeFranco	Scorpio . . . . Dennis Coffey And
Save The Last Dance For Me . . . . Dolly Parton	. . . . The Detroit Guitar Band
Save The Last Dance For Me . . . . Drifters	Scotch And Soda . . . . Kingston Trio
Save The Night For Me . . . . Maureen Steele	Scotch On The Rocks . . . Band Of The Black Watch
Save The Overtime (For Me)	Scottish Soldier . . . . Andy Stewart
. . . . Gladys Knight & The Pips	Scratch . . . . Crusaders
Save Up All Your Tears . . . . Cher	Scratch My Back . . . . Clarence Carter
Save Your Heart For Me	Scratchy . . . . Travis Wammack
. . . . Gary Lewis And The Playboys	Screaming Night Hog . . . . Steppenwolf
Save Your Kisses For Me . . . . . Brotherhood Of Man	Screams Of Passion . . . . Family
Save Your Love . . . . Great White	Se La . . . . Lionel Richie
Save Your Sugar For Me . . . . Tony Joe White	Sea Cruise . . . . Frankie Ford
Saved . . . . Lavern Baker	Sea Cruise . . . . Johnny Rivers
Saved By The Grace Of Your Love	Sea Of Heartbreak . . . . Don Gibson
. . . . Sons Of Champlin	Sea Of Heartbreak . . . . Poco
Saved By Zero . . . . Fixx	Sea Of Love . . . . Del Shannon
Savin' Myself . . . . Eria Fachin	Sea Of Love . . . . Honeydrippers
Saving All My Love For You . . . . Whitney Houston	Sea Of Love . . . . . . Phil Phillips With The Twilights
Saving Forever For You . . . . Shanice	Sea Shell . . . . Strawberry Alarm Clock
Saw A New Morning . . . . Bee Gees	Seal Our Fate . . . . Gloria Estefan
Sax Fifth Avenue . . . . Johnny Beecher	Sealed With A Kiss . . . . Bobby Vinton
Say A Prayer . . . . Breathe	Sealed With A Kiss . . . . Brian Hyland
Say Goodbye To Hollywood . . . . Billy Joel	Sealed With A Kiss . . . Gary Lewis And The Playboys
Say Goodbye To Little Jo . . . . Steve Forbert	Sealed With A Kiss . . . . Toys
Say, Has Anybody Seen My Sweet	Search Is Over . . . . Survivor
Gypsy Rose . . . . Dawn	Searchin' . . . . Ace Cannon
Say Hello To Ronnie . . . . Janey Street	Searchin' . . . . Coasters
Say I Am (What I Am)	Searching . . . . Jack Eubanks
. . . . Tommy James And The Shondells	Searching For A Thrill . . . . Starbuck
Say It Again . . . . Jermaine Stewart	Searching For My Baby . . . .
Say It Again . . . . Santana	. . . . Bobby Moore & The Rhythm Aces
Say It Isn't So . . . . . . Daryl Hall & John Oates	Seaside Woman . . . . . . Suzy And The Red Stripes
Say It Loud - I'm Black And I'm	Season Of The Witch (Part 1) . . . . . . Vanilla Fudge
Proud . . . . James Brown	Seasons . . . . Charles Fox
Say It, Say It . . . . E.G. Daily	Seasons Change . . . . Expose
Say It's Gonna Rain . . . . Will To Power	Seasons In The Sun . . . . Terry Jacks

Sgt. Pepper's Lonely Hearts Club Band/With
A Little Help From My Friends . . . . . . Beatles
Sha La Boom Boom . . . . Bobby Bloom
Sha La La . . . . Manfred Mann
Shabby Little Hut . . . . Reflections
Shackin' Up . . . . Barbara Mason
Shaddup Your Face . . . . Joe Dolce
Shades Of Green . . . . Flaming Ember
Shadow Dancing . . . . Andy Gibb
Shadow Of Your Love . . . . Five Stairsteps
Shadow Of Your Smile . . . . . . Boots Randolph
Shadows . . . . Five Satins
Shadows In The Moonlight . . . . . Anne Murray
Shadows Of The Night . . . . Pat Benatar
Shadrack . . . . Brook Benton
Shady Lady . . . . Shepstone & Dibbons
Shag (Is Totally Cool) . . . . Billy Graves
Shaggy Dog . . . . Mickey Lee Lane
Shake . . . . Andrew Ridgely
Shake . . . . British Walkers
Shake . . . . Otis Redding
Shake . . . . Sam Cooke
Shake . . . . Shadows Of Knight
Shake A Hand . . . Jackie Wilson And Linda Hopkins
Shake A Hand . . . . Lavern Baker
Shake A Hand . . . . Ruth Brown
Shake A Leg . . . . Sea Level
Shake A Poo Poo
. . Chet "Poison" Ivey And His Fabulous Avengers
Shake A Tail Feather . . . . Five Du-Tones
Shake A Tail Feather . . . . . James & Bobby Purify
Shake And Dance With Me . . . . Con Funk Shun
Shake And Fingerpop . . Jr. Walker & The All Stars
Shake For The Sheik . . . . Escape Club
Shake Hands . . . . Newbeats
Shake It . . . . Ian Matthews
Shake It Up . . . . Cars
Shake It Up Tonight . . . . Cheryl Lynn
Shake It Well . . . . Dramatics
Shake Me I Rattle (Squeeze Me I Cry) . . . .
. . . . Marion Worth
Shake Me, Wake Me (When It's Over) . . . Four Tops
Shake, Rattle And Roll . . . . Arthur Conley
Shake, Rattle And Roll . . Bill Haley And His Comets
Shake! Shake! Shake! . . . . Jackie Wilson
(Shake, Shake, Shake) Shake Your Booty . . . .
. . . . KC And The Sunshine Band
Shake Sherry . . . . Contours
Shake You Down . . . . Gregory Abbott
Shake Your Body (Down To The Ground) . . Jacksons
Shake Your Groove Thing . . . . . . Peaches & Herb
Shake Your Hips . . . . Slim Harpo
Shake Your Love . . . . Debbie Gibson
Shake Your Rump To The Funk . . . . . Bar-Kays
Shakedown . . . . Bob Seger
Shakedown Cruise . . . . Jay Ferguson
Shaker Song . . . . Spyro Gyra
Shakey Ground . . . . Temptations
Shakin' . . . . Eddie Money
Shakin' All Over . . . . Guess Who
Sha-La-La . . . . Shirelles
Sha-La-La (Make Me Happy) . . . . . . Al Green
Shambala . . . . B.W. Stevenson
Shambala . . . . Three Dog Night
Shame . . . . Evelyn "Champagne" King
Shame . . . . Motels
Shame On Me . . . . Bobby Bare
Shame On Me . . . . Chuck Jackson
Shame On The Moon . . . .
. . . . . . Bob Seger & The Silver Bullet Band
Shame, Shame . . . . Magic Lanterns
Shame, Shame, Shame . . . . Jimmy Reed
Shame, Shame, Shame . . . . Shirley And Company
Shamrocks And Shenanigans . . . . . House Of Pain

Shandi . . . . Kiss
Shanghai . . . . Billy Williams
Shanghai . . . . Doris Day
Shanghai Breezes . . . . John Denver
Shangri-La . . . . Four Coins
Shangri-La . . . . Lettermen
Shangri-La . . . . Robert Maxwell
Shangri-La . . . . Steve Miller Band
Shangri-La . . . . Vic Dana
Shannon . . . . Henry Gross
Shape I'm In . . . . Johnny Restivo
Shape Of Things To Come . . . .
. . . . Max Frost And The Troopers
Shapes Of Things . . . . Yardbirds
Share The Land . . . . Guess Who
Share Your Love With Me . . . . Aretha Franklin
Share Your Love With Me . . . . . Bobby Bland
Share Your Love With Me . . . . . Kenny Rogers
Sharing The Night Together . . . Arthur Alexander
Sharing The Night Together . . . . . . Dr. Hook
Sharing The Night Together . . . . Lenny LeBlanc
Sharing You . . . . Bobby Vee
Sharing You . . . . Mitty Collier
Sharp Dressed Man . . . . ZZ Top
Shattered . . . . Rolling Stones
Shattered Dreams . . . . . . Johnny Hates Jazz
Shattered Glass . . . . Laura Branigan
Shaving Cream . . . . Benny Bell
Shazam! . . . . Duane Eddy
Sh-Boom . . . . Chords
Sh-Boom . . . . Crew-Cuts
She . . . . Southcote
She . . . . . Tommy James And The Shondells
She Ain't Lovin' You . . . . . . Distant Cousins
She Ain't Pretty . . . . Northern Pikes
She Ain't Worth It . . . .
. . . . . Glenn Medeiros Featuring Bobby Brown
She Believes In Me . . . . Kenny Rogers
She Belongs To Me . . . .
. . . . Rick Nelson & The Stone Canyon Band
She Blew A Good Thing . . . . Poets
She Blinded Me With Science . . . . Thomas Dolby
She Bop . . . . Cyndi Lauper
She Called Me Baby . . . . Charlie Rich
She Came In Through The Bathroom
Window . . . . Joe Cocker
She Can't Find Her Keys . . . . . . Paul Petersen
She Comes To Me . . . . Chicago Loop
She Cried . . . . Jay & The Americans
She Cried . . . . Lettermen
She Did It . . . . Eric Carmen
She Did It . . . . Michael Damian
She Didn't Do Magic . . . . Lobo
She Didn't Know . . . . Dee Dee Warwick
She Don't Know Me . . . . Bon Jovi
She Don't Let Nobody (But Me) . . . Curtis Mayfield
She Don't Look Back . . . . Dan Fogelberg
She Drives Me Crazy . . . . Fine Young Cannibals
She Drives Me Out Of My Mind . . . .
. . . . Swingin' Medallions
She Got The Goldmine (I Got The
Shaft) . . . . Jerry Reed
She Is Still A Mystery . . . . . . Lovin' Spoonful
She Let's Her Hair Down . . . . Tokens
She Looks A Lot Like You . . . . Clocks
She Loves My Car . . . . Ronnie Milsap
She Loves To Be In Love . . . . Charlie
She Loves You . . . . Beatles
She Said Yes . . . . Wilson Pickett
She Say (Oom Dooby Doom) . . . . . . Diamonds
She Shot A Hole In My Soul . . . . Clifford Curry
She Talks To Angels . . . . Black Crowes
She Took You For A Ride . . . . . . Aaron Neville
She Understands Me . . . . Johnny Tillotson

488

489

Smells Like Teen Spirit . . . . Nirvana	So Long Dearie . . . . Louis Armstrong
Smile . . . . Betty Everett & Jerry Butler	So Long Dixie . . . . Blood, Sweat & Tears
Smile . . . . Ferrante & Teicher	So Long Marianne . . . . Brian Hyland
Smile . . . . Nat King Cole	So Long, My Love . . . . Frank Sinatra
Smile . . . . Sunny Gale	So Many Men, So Little Time . . . . . . Miguel Brown
Smile . . . . Timi Yuro	So Many People . . . . Chase
Smile . . . . Tony Bennett	So Many Ways . . . . Brook Benton
Smile A Little Smile For Me . . . . . Flying Machine	So Much . . . . Little Anthony And The Imperials
Smile Has Left Your Eyes . . . . Asia	So Much In Love . . . . Timothy B. Schmit
Smilin' . . . . Sly & The Family Stone	So Much In Love . . . . Tymes
Smiling Faces Sometimes . . . . . . Undisputed Truth	So Much Love . . . . Ben E. King
Smiling Islands . . . . Robbie Patton	So Much Love . . . . Faith, Hope & Charity
Smoke From A Distant Fire . . Sanford/Townsend Band	So Much Love . . . . Steve Alaimo
Smoke Gets In Your Eyes . . . . Blue Haze	So Rare . . . . Jimmy Dorsey
Smoke Gets In Your Eyes . . . . Platters	So Sad The Song . . . . . Gladys Knight & The Pips
Smoke On The Water . . . . Deep Purple	So Sad (To Watch Good Love Go Bad) . . . .
Smoke! Smoke! Smoke! (That Cigarette)	. . . . Everly Brothers
. . . Commander Cody And His Lost Planet Airmen	So This Is Love . . . . Castells
Smokey Joe's La La . . . . Rene Googie Combo	So Tough . . . . Original Casuals
Smokie (Part 2) . . . . Bill Black's Combo	So Very Hard To Go . . . . Tower Of Power
Smokin' In The Boys Room . . . Brownsville Station	So What . . . . Bill Black's Combo
Smokin' In The Boys Room . . . . . . Motley Crue	So What'cha Want . . . . Beastie Boys
Smoking Gun . . . . Robert Cray Band	So Wrong . . . . Patrick Simmons
Smoky Mountain Rain . . . . Ronnie Milsap	So Wrong . . . . Patsy Cline
Smoky Places . . . . Corsairs	So You Are A Star . . . . Hudson Brothers
Smooth Criminal . . . . Michael Jackson	So You Ran . . . . Orion The Hunter
Smooth Operator . . . . Sade	So You Want To Be A Rock 'N' Roll Star . . . .
Smooth Operator . . . . Sarah Vaughan	. . . . Byrds
Smuggler's Blues . . . . Glenn Frey	So You Win Again . . . . Hot Chocolate
Snake . . . . Al Wilson	So Young, So Bad . . . . Starz
Snap Out . . . . Interpretations	Soalin' . . . . Peter, Paul & Mary
Snap Your Fingers . . . . Barbara Lewis	Society Girl . . . . Rag Dolls
Snap Your Fingers . . . . Joe Henderson	Society's Child . . . . Janis Ian
Snatching It Back . . . . Clarence Carter	Sock It To Me Baby! . . . .
Sneakin' Sally Through The Alley . . . Robert Palmer	. . . . . . Mitch Ryder And The Detroit Wheels
Sneakin' Up Behind You . . . . . Brecker Brothers	Sockin' 1-2-3-4 . . . . John Roberts
Sneaky Snake . . . . Tom T. Hall	Soft And Wet . . . . Prince
Snoopy Vs. The Red Baron . . . . Royal Guardsmen	Soft Sands . . . . Chordettes
Snoopy's Christmas . . . . Royal Guardsmen	Soft Summer Breeze . . . . Eddie Heywood
Snow Blind Friend . . . . Steppenwolf	Softly, As I Leave You . . . . Frank Sinatra
Snow Flake . . . . Jim Reeves	Softly As I Leave You . . . . Matt Monro
Snowbird . . . . Anne Murray	Softly Whispering I Love You . . . .
So Alive . . . . Love And Rockets	. . . . English Congregation
So Alone . . . . Men At Large	Sold Me Down The River . . . . Alarm
So Bad . . . . Paul McCartney	Soldier Boy . . . . Shirelles
So Close . . . . Brook Benton	Soldier Of Love . . . . Donny Osmond
So Close . . . . . . Daryl Hall & John Oates	Sole Sole Sole . . Siw Malmkvist & Umberto Marcato
So Close . . . . Diana Ross	Soledad . . . . . Eric Burdon & Jimmy Witherspoon
So Close . . . . Dina Carroll	Solid . . . . Ashford & Simpson
So Close . . . . Jake Holmes	Solitaire . . . . Carpenters
So Close To My Heart . . . . Kathy Linden	Solitaire . . . . Embers
So Deep . . . . Brenda Lee	Solitaire . . . . Laura Branigan
So Emotional . . . . Whitney Houston	Solitaire . . . . Peter McIan
So Excited . . . . B.B. King	Solitary Man . . . . Neil Diamond
So Far Away . . . . Carole King	So-Long . . . . Fats Domino
So Far Away . . . . Dire Straits	Solsbury Hill . . . . Peter Gabriel
So Far Away . . . . Hank Jacobs	Solution For Pollution . . . . . . Charles Wright And
So Far So Good . . . . Sheena Easton	. . . . The Watts 103rd Street Rhythm Band
So Fine . . . . Fiestas	Some Beautiful . . . . Jack Wild
So Fine . . . . Oak Ridge Boys	Some Broken Hearts Never Mend . . . . Don Williams
So Good, So Right . . . . Brenda Russell	Some Changes Are For The Good . . Dionne Warwick
So Good Together . . . . Andy Kim	Some Come Running . . . . Jim Capaldi
So Hard . . . . Pet Shop Boys	Some Day We're Gonna Love Again . . . . Searchers
So Hard Livin' Without You . . . . . . Airwaves	Some Days Are Diamonds . . . . . . John Denver
So High . . . . Dave Mason	Some Enchanted Evening . . . . Jane Oliver
So High, So Low . . . . Lavern Baker	Some Enchanted Evening . . Jay & The Americans
So I Can Love You . . . . Emotions	Some Guys Have All The Luck . . . . . Persuaders
So In Love . . . . Curtis Mayfield	Some Guys Have All The Luck . . . . . Rod Stewart
So In Love . . . . Orchestral Manoeuvres In The Dark	Some Kind A-Earthquake . . . . Duane Eddy
So Into You . . . . Atlanta Rhythm Section	Some Kind Of Friend . . . . Barry Manilow
So Long . . . . Firefall	Some Kind Of Lover . . . . Jody Watley
So Long . . . . Gordon Jenkins Orchestra	Some Kind Of Wonderful . . . . Drifters
So Long Babe . . . . Nancy Sinatra	Some Kind Of Wonderful . . . . Grand Funk
So Long Baby . . . . Del Shannon	Some Kind Of Wonderful . . . . . . Soul Brothers Six

493

Song	Artist
Somewhere In Your Heart	Frank Sinatra
Somewhere My Love	Ray Conniff And The Singers
Somewhere Out There	Linda Ronstadt And James Ingram
Somewhere, Somebody	Aaron Neville
Somewhere There's A Someone	Dean Martin
Son Of A Lovin' Man	Buchanan Brothers
Son Of A Travelin' Man	Ed Ames
Son Of Hickory Holler's Tramp	O.C. Smith
Son Of My Father	Chicory
Son Of My Father	Giorgio
Son Of Rebel Rouser	Duane Eddy
Son Of Sagittarius	Eddie Kendricks
Son Of Shaft	Bar-Kays
Song For Anna	Herb Ohta
Song For You	Andy Williams
Song For You	Ray Charles
Song From MASH	Al DeLory
Song From Moulin Rouge	Percy Faith
Song I'd Like To Sing	Kris Kristofferson And Rita Coolidge
Song Of Joy	Miguel Rios
Song Of Raintree County	Nat King Cole
Song Of The Nairobi Trio	Fortune Tellers
Song Of The Sparrow	Mitch Miller
Song On The Radio	Al Stewart
Song Remembers When	Trisha Yearwood
Song Seller	Raiders
Song Sung Blue	Neil Diamond
Songbird	Barbra Streisand
Songbird	Kenny G
Songman	Cashman & West
Son-In-Law	Blossoms
Son-In-Law	Louise Brown
Son-Of-A Preacher Man	Dusty Springfield
Soolaimon (African Trilogy II)	Neil Diamond
Soon	Four Seasons
Sooner Or Later	Grass Roots
Sooner Or Later	Impressions
Soothe Me	Sam & Dave
Soothe Me	Sims Twins
Sophisticated Cissy	Meters
Sophisticated Lady (She's A Different Lady)	Natalie Cole
Sorrow	David Bowie
Sorry Doesn't Always Make It Right	Diana Ross
Sorry (I Ran All The Way Home)	Impalas
Sorry Seems To Be The Hardest Word	Elton John
Sorry Suzanne	Hollies
SOS	Abba
S.O.S.	Christine Cooper
Soul City	Partland Brothers
Soul Dance	Tommy Leonetti
Soul Dance Number Three	Wilson Pickett
Soul Deep	Box Tops
Soul Drippin'	Mauds
Soul Experience	Iron Butterfly
Soul Finger	Bar-Kays
Soul Heaven	Dixie Drifter
Soul Hootenany	Gene Chandler
Soul Inspiration	Anita Baker
Soul Kiss	Olivia Newton-John
Soul Limbo	Booker T & The MG's
Soul Makossa	Afrique
Soul Makossa	Manu Dibango
Soul Man	Blues Brothers
Soul Man	Ramsey Lewis
Soul Man	Sam & Dave
Soul Power (Part 1)	James Brown
Soul Pride (Part 1)	James Brown
Soul Provider	Michael Bolton
Soul Sauce (Guacha Guaro)	Cal Tjader
Soul Serenade	King Curtis
Soul Serenade	Willie Mitchell
Soul Shake	Delaney & Bonnie
Soul Shake	Peggy Scott & Jo Jo Benson
Soul Sister, Brown Sugar	Sam & Dave
Soul Song	Joe Stampley
Soul Time	Shirley Ellis
Soul To Squeeze	Red Hot Chili Peppers
Soul Train	Classics IV
Soul Train "75"	Soul Train Gang
Soul Twist	King Curtis
Soulful Strut	Young-Holt Unlimited
Souls	Rick Springfield
Soulsville	Isaac Hayes
Sound And Vision	David Bowie
Sound Asleep	Turtles
Sound Of Love	Five Americans
Sound Of Music	Patti Page
Sound Of Your Voice	38 Special
Sound Off	Vaughn Monroe
Sound-Off	Titus Turner
Sounds Of Silence	Paul Simon
Sounds Of Silence	Peaches & Herb
Sounds Of Silence	Simon & Garfunkel
Sour Suite	Guess Who
South Central Rain (I'm Sorry)	R.E.M.
South Street	Orlons
South's Gonna Do It Again	Charlie Daniels Band
Southern Cross	Crosby, Stills & Nash
Southern Love	Ronnie Hawkins
Southern Nights	Glen Campbell
Southern Pacific	Neil Young & Crazy Horse
Southtown U.S.A.	Dixiebelles
Souvenirs	Voyage
Sowing The Seeds Of Love	Tears For Fears
Space Age Love Song	Flock Of Seagulls
Space Age Whiz Kids	Joe Walsh
Space Oddity	David Bowie
Space Race	Billy Preston
Spaceman	Nilsson
Spaceship Superstar	Prism
Spanish Eddie	Laura Branigan
Spanish Eyes	Al Martino
Spanish Flea	Herb Alpert & The Tijuana Brass
Spanish Harlem	Aretha Franklin
Spanish Harlem	Ben E. King
Spanish Hustle	Fatback Band
Spanish Lace	Gene McDaniels
Spanish Nights And You	Connie Francis
Spanish Wine	Lou Christie
Sparkle And Shine	Clique
Sparklin' Eyes	Dean Martin
Sparrow In The Tree Top	Guy Mitchell
Speak Her Name	Walter Jackson
Speak Softly Love	Al Martino
Speak To The Sky	Rick Springfield
Special Delivery	1910 Fruitgum Company
Special Lady	Ray, Goodman & Brown
Special Memory	Jerry Butler
Special Occasion	Miracles
Special Someone	Heywoods
Special Way	Kool & The Gang
Speed	Alpha Team
Speed Ball	Ray Stevens
Speedy Gonzales	Pat Boone
Spend A Little Time	Barbara Lewis
Spend My Life	Slaughter
Spending My Time	Roxette
Spice Of Life	Manhattan Transfer
Spider Jivin'	Andy Fairweather Low
Spiders & Snakes	Jim Stafford
Spies Like Us	Paul McCartney
Spill The Wine	Eric Burdon And War
Spill The Wine	Isley Brothers
Spin That Wheel	Hi Tek 3
Spinning Around	Main Ingredient

494

495

Stealer . . . . Free
Stealin' . . . . Uriah Heep
Stealing In the Name Of The Lord . . . . . Paul Kelly
Stealing Love . . . . Emotions
Stealing Moments . . . . Glass House
Steam . . . . Peter Gabriel
Steam Heat . . . . Pointer Sisters
Steamroller Blues . . . . Elvis Presley
Steamy Windows . . . . Tina Turner
Steel Bars . . . . Michael Bolton
Steel Guitar And A Glass Of Wine . . . . Paul Anka
Steel Guitar Rag . . . . Dynatones
Steel Men . . . . Jimmy Dean
Step By Step . . . . Crests
Step By Step . . . . Eddie Rabbitt
Step By Step . . . . Joe Simon
Step By Step . . . . Kiki Dee
Step By Step . . . . . . New Kids On The Block
Step Inside Love . . . . Cilla Black
Step Into Christmas . . . . Elton John
Step It Up . . . . Stereo MC's
Step On . . . . Happy Mondays
Step Out Of Your Mind . . . . . American Breed
Steppin' In A Slide Zone . . . . . . Moody Blues
Steppin' Out . . . . Joe Jackson
Steppin' Out . . . . Neil Sedaka
Steppin' Out . . . . . . Paul Revere And The Raiders
Steppin' Out (Gonna Boogie Tonight) . . . . . . Dawn
Steps 1 And 2 . . . . Jack Scott
Stereotomy . . . . Alan Parsons Project
Stewball . . . . Peter, Paul & Mary
Stick Around . . . . Julian Lennon
Stick Shift . . . . Duals
Stick Up . . . . Honeycone
Stick With Me Baby . . . . Everly Brothers
Sticks And Stones . . . . Ray Charles
Sticky Sticky . . . . Bobby Harris
Still . . . . Bill Anderson
Still . . . . Commodores
Still . . . . John Schneider
Still . . . . Sunrays
Still #2 . . . . Sheb Wooley
Still A Thrill . . . . Jody Watley
Still As The Night . . . . Sanford Clark
Still Crazy After All These Years . . . . Paul Simon
Still In Saigon . . . . Charlie Daniels Band
Still In The Game . . . . Steve Winwood
Still Loving You . . . . Scorpions
Still Right Here In My Heart . . . Pure Prairie League
Still The Lovin' Is Fun . . . . B.J. Thomas
Still The One . . . . Orleans
Still The Same . . . .
. . . . Bob Seger & The Silver Bullet Band
Still They Ride . . . . Journey
Still Water (Love) . . . . Four Tops
Still Waters Run Deep . . . . Brook Benton
Stillsane . . . . Carolyne Mas
Sting Ray . . . . Routers
Stir It Up . . . . Johnny Nash
Stir It Up . . . . Patti LaBelle
Stir It Up And Serve It . . . . Tommy Roe
Stolen Angel . . . . Scott Brothers
Stomp! . . . . Brothers Johnson
Stone Blue . . . . Foghat
Stone Cold . . . . Rainbow
Stone Cold Gentleman . . . . Ralph Tresvant
Stone Cold Sober . . . . Crawler
Stone Love . . . . Kool & The Gang
Stone Of Years . . . . . Emerson, Lake & Palmer
Stoned Cowboy . . . . Fantasy
Stoned Love . . . . Supremes
Stoned Out Of My Head . . . . Chi-Lites
Stoned Soul Picnic . . . . Fifth Dimension
Stoned To The Bone (Part 1) . . . . . . James Brown

Stones . . . . Neil Diamond
Stoney End . . . . Barbra Streisand
Stood Up . . . . Ricky Nelson
Stop . . . . Howard Tate
Stop . . . . Moody Blues
Stop . . . . Sam Brown
S.T.O.P. . . . . Lorelei
Stop And Smell The Roses . . . . Mac Davis
Stop And Think It Over . . . . Dale & Grace
Stop! And Think It Over . . . . Perry Como
Stop Doggin' Me . . . . Johnnie Taylor
Stop Doggin' Me Around . . . . Klique
Stop Draggin' My Heart Around . . Stevie Nicks With
. . . . Tom Petty And The Heartbreakers
Stop! Get A Ticket . . . . . Clefs Of Lavender Hill
Stop Her On Sight (S.O.S) . . . . Edwin Starr
Stop In The Name Of Love . . . . Hollies
Stop! In The Name Of Love . . . . . Margie Joseph
Stop! In The Name Of Love . . . . . . Supremes
Stop, Look, Listen (To Your Heart) . . . . . Stylistics
Stop! Look What You're Doing . . . Carla Thomas
Stop Stop Stop . . . . Hollies
Stop The Music . . . . Shirelles
Stop The War Now . . . . Edwin Starr
Stop The Wedding . . . . Etta James
Stop The World . . . . Extreme
Stop The World And Let Me Off . . . Flaming Ember
Stop This Game . . . . Cheap Trick
Stop To Love . . . . Luther Vandross
Stop To Start . . . . Blue Magic
Stop, Wait & Listen . . . . Circus
Stop Your Sobbing . . . . Pretenders
Stories? . . . . Chakachas
Stormy . . . . Classics IV
Stormy . . . . Santana
Stormy Monday . . . . Latimore
Stormy Monday Blues . . . . Bobby Bland
Story In Your Eyes . . . . Moody Blues
Story Of My Life . . . . Marty Robbins
Story Of My Love . . . . Conway Twitty
Story Of My Love . . . . Paul Anka
Story Of Rock And Roll . . . . Turtles
Story Of Three Loves . . . Jerry Murad's Harmonicats
(Story Of) Woman, Love, And A Man . . Tony Clarke
Story Untold . . . . Emotions
Storybook Children . . . . . Billy Vera & Judy Clay
Storybook Children (Daybreak) . . . . . Bette Midler
Straight Ahead . . . . Young-Holt Unlimited
Straight From The Heart . . . . Allman Brothers Band
Straight From The Heart . . . . . . Bryan Adams
Straight From The Heart . . . . . Coyote Sisters
Straight Life . . . . Bobby Goldsboro
Straight On . . . . Heart
Straight Shootin' Woman . . . . Steppenwolf
Straight To Your Heart . . . . . . Bad English
Straight Up . . . . Paula Abdul
Straighten Up Your Heart . . . . . Barbara Lewis
Stranded . . . . Heart
Stranded In The Jungle . . . . Cadets
Stranded In The Jungle . . . . Jayhawks
Stranded In The Middle Of No Place . . . . . .
. . . . Righteous Brothers
Strange . . . . Jellyroll
Strange Are The Ways Of Love . . . . . Gogi Grant
Strange But True . . . . Times Two
Strange Days . . . . School Of Fish
Strange Feeling . . . . Billy Stewart
Strange I Know . . . . Marvelettes
Strange Magic . . . . . Electric Light Orchestra
Strange Way . . . . Firefall
Strangelove . . . . Depeche Mode
Stranger . . . . Jefferson Starship
Stranger . . . . Stephen Stills
Stranger In My Home Town . . . . Foghat

497

498

T

Take It Back . . . . J. Geils Band	Taking It All Too Hard . . . . Genesis
Take It Easy . . . . Andy Taylor	Taking My Love (And Leaving Me) . . . .
Take It Easy . . . . Eagles	. . . . Martha & The Vandellas
Take It Easy On Me . . . . Little River Band	Talk About It . . . . Boom Crash Opera
Take It Like A Man . . . . Bachman-Turner Overdrive	Talk About Love . . . . Adam Faith
Take It Off Him And Put It On Me . . Clarence Carter	Talk Back Trembling Lips . . . . . . Johnny Tillotson
Take It Off The Top . . . . Dixie Dregs	Talk Dirty To Me . . . . Poison
Take It On The Run . . . . REO Speedwagon	Talk It Over . . . . Grayson Hugh
Take It Slow . . . . Lighthouse	Talk It Over In The Morning . . . . Anne Murray
Take It To Heart . . . . Michael McDonald	Talk Talk . . . . Music Machine
Take It To The Limit . . . . Eagles	Talk Talk . . . . Talk Talk
Take It While It's Hot . . . . Sweet Sensation	Talk That Talk . . . . Jackie Wilson
Take Life A Little Easier . . . . . Rodney Allen Rippy	Talk To Me . . . . Anita Baker
Take Me . . . . Brenda Lee	Talk To Me . . . . Chico DeBarge
Take Me . . . . Grand Funk Railroad	Talk To Me . . . . Fiona
Take Me . . . . Solomon Burke	Talk To Me . . . . Frank Sinatra
Take Me Back . . . . Bonnie Tyler	Talk To Me . . . . Stevie Nicks
Take Me Back . . . Little Anthony And The Imperials	Talk To Me . . . . Sunny & The Sunglows
Take Me Back Baby . . . . Guy Mitchell	Talk To Me Baby . . . . Annette
Take Me Back Home . . . . Slade	Talk To Me, Talk To Me . . . . . . Little Willie John
Take Me Back To Chicago . . . . Chicago	Talk To Myself . . . . Christopher Williams
Take Me Down . . . . Alabama	Talkin' Bout A Revolution . . . . . . Tracy Chapman
Take Me For A Little While	Talkin' To The Blues . . . . Jim Lowe
. . . . Patti LaBelle And The Blue Belles	Talking About My Baby . . . . Gloria Walker
Take Me For A Little While . . . . . . Vanilla Fudge	Talking About My Baby . . . . Impressions
Take Me For What I'm Worth . . . . . . Searchers	Talking Back To The Night . . . . . . Steve Winwood
Take Me Girl, I'm Ready	Talking In Your Sleep . . . . Crystal Gayle
. . . . Jr. Walker & The All Stars	Talking In Your Sleep . . . . Gordon Lightfoot
Take Me Home . . . . Balcones Fault	Talking In Your Sleep . . . . Romantics
Take Me Home . . . . Cher	Talking Loud And Saying Nothing . . . James Brown
Take Me Home . . . . Phil Collins	Talking Out Of Turn . . . . Moody Blues
Take Me Home, Country Roads . . . . John Denver	Tall Cool One . . . . Robert Plant
Take Me Home Tonight . . . . Eddie Money	Tall Cool One . . . . Wailers
Take Me In Your Arms . . . . . Isley Brothers	Tall Paul . . . . Annette
Take Me In Your Arms (Rock Me) . . Doobie Brothers	Tallahassee Lassie . . . . Freddy Cannon
Take Me In Your Arms (Rock Me A	Tamiami . . . . Bill Haley And His Comets
Little While) . . . . Kim Weston	Tammy . . . . Ames Brothers
Take Me Now . . . . David Gates	Tammy . . . . Debbie Reynolds
Take Me To Heart . . . . Quarterflash	Tammy . . . . . . Richard Hayman Orchestra
Take Me To The Kaptin . . . . Prism	Tangerine . . . . Salsoul Orchestra
Take Me To The Next Phase . . . . . Isley Brothers	Tangled Up In Blue . . . . Bob Dylan
Take Me To The River . . . . Syl Johnson	Taos New Mexico . . . . R. Dean Taylor
Take Me To The River . . . . . . Talking Heads	Tap The Bottle . . . . . Young Black Teenagers
Take Me To Your Heart . . . . . . Monkey Meeks	Tapioca Tundra . . . . Monkees
Take Me With U . . . . . Prince And The Revolution	Tar And Cement . . . . Verdelle Smith
Take Me With You . . . . Honeycone	Tarkio Road . . . . Brewer & Shipley
Take My Breath Away . . . . Berlin	Tarzan Boy . . . . Baltimora
Take My Heart . . . . Kool & The Gang	Taste Of Honey . . . Herb Alpert & The Tijuana Brass
Take No Prisoners (In The Game Of	Taste Of Honey . . . . Martin Denny
Love) . . . . Peabo Bryson	Taste Of Honey . . . . Tony Bennett
Take Off . . . . Bob & Doug McKenzie	Tasty Love . . . . Freddie Jackson
Take On Me . . . . A-Ha	Taurus . . . . Dennis Coffey And
Take Some Time Out For Love . . . . . Isley Brothers	. . . . The Detroit Guitar Band
Take That To The Bank . . . . Shalamar	Taxi . . . . Harry Chapin
Take The L. . . . . Motels	Taxi Dancing . . Rick Springfield & Bobby Crawford
Take The Long Way Home . . . . . . Supertramp	Tea For Two . . . . Nino Tempo & April Stevens
Take The Money And Run . . . . . . Steve Miller	Tea For Two Cha Cha Cha . . . .
Take The Short Way Home . . . . . Dionne Warwick	. . . . Tommy Dorsey Orchestra
Take The Time . . . . Johnny Mathis	. . . . Starring Warren Covington
Take These Chains From My Heart . . . Ray Charles	Teach Me How To Twist . . . .
Take This Heart . . . . Richard Marx	. . . . Chubby Checker/Bobby Rydell
Take This Heart Of Mine . . . . Marvin Gaye	Teach Me Tonight . . . . Al Jarreau
Take Time . . . . Chris Walker	Teach Me Tonight . . . . DeCastro Sisters
Take Time To Know Her . . . . . . Percy Sledge	Teach Me Tonight . . . . George Maharis
Take You Tonight . . . Ozark Mountain Daredevils	Teach Me Tonight Cha Cha . . . . DeCastro Sisters
Take Your Love And Shove It . . . . Cane's Cousins	Teach Your Children . . Crosby, Stills, Nash & Young
Take Your Time (Do It Right) (Part 1) . . S.O.S. Band	Teacher . . . . Falcons
Taken In . . . . Mike + The Mechanics	Teacher Teacher . . . . 38 Special
Taker . . . . Waylon Jennings	Teacher, Teacher . . . . Johnny Mathis
Takes Two To Tango . . . . Pearl Bailey	Teacher Teacher . . . . Rockpile
Takin' Care Of Business	Teacher's Pet . . . . Doris Day
. . . . Bachman-Turner Overdrive	Tear . . . . Gene McDaniels
Takin' It Back . . . . Breathless	Tear After Tear . . . . Blue-Belles
Takin' It To The Streets . . . . . . Doobie Brothers	Tear Drop . . . . Santo & Johnny

Tear Drop City . . . . Monkees	Tell Him . . . . Patti Drew
Tear Drops . . . . Lee Andrews And The Hearts	Tell Him I'm Not Home . . . . Chuck Jackson
Tear Fell . . . . Ray Charles	Tell Him No . . . . Travis & Bob
Tear Fell . . . . Teresa Brewer	Tell It All Brother
Tear Of The Year . . . . Jackie Wilson	. . . . Kenny Rogers And The First Edition
Tear The Roof Off The Sucker . . . . . . Parliament	Tell It Like It Is . . . . Aaron Neville
Teardrops . . . . George Harrison	Tell It Like It Is . . . . Andy Williams
Teardrops In My Heart . . . . Joe Barry	Tell It Like It Is . . . . Heart
Teardrops In My Heart . . . . Teresa Brewer	Tell It On The Mountain . . . . . Peter, Paul & Mary
Teardrops Will Fall . . . . Dicky Doo And The Don'ts	Tell It To My Heart . . . . Taylor Dayne
Tears . . . . Bobby Vinton	Tell It To The Rain . . . . Four Seasons
Tears . . . . John Waite	Tell Laura I Love Her . . . . Johnny T. Angel
Tears And Laughter . . . . Dinah Washington	Tell Laura I Love Her . . . . Ray Peterson
Tears And Roses . . . . Al Martino	Tell Mama . . . . Etta James
Tears Are Falling . . . . Kiss	Tell Mama . . . . Savoy Brown
Tears From An Angel . . . . Troy Shondell	Tell Me . . . . Dick And Deedee
Tears From My Heart . . . . Thurston Harris	Tell Me . . . . White Lion
Tears In Heaven . . . . Eric Clapton	Tell Me A Lie . . . . Sami Jo
Tears Keep On Falling . . . . Jerry Vale	Tell Me A Story . . . Frankie Laine With Jimmy Boyd
Tears Of A Clown . . . . Miracles	Tell Me Baby . . . . Garnet Mimms & The Enchanters
Tears On My Pillow . . . . Johnny Tillotson	Tell Me I'm Not Dreaming . . . . Robert Palmer
Tears On My Pillow	Tell Me If You Still Care . . . . S.O.S. Band
. . . . Little Anthony And The Imperials	Tell Me Mamma . . . . Christine Quaite
Tears On My Pillow . . . . McGuire Sisters	Tell Me Something . . . . . . Indecent Obsession
Tears Run Rings . . . . Marc Almond	Tell Me Something Good . . . . Rufus
Teaser . . . . Bob Kuban And The In-Men	Tell Me That You Love Me . . . . . . Fats Domino
Teasin' . . . . Quaker City Boys	Tell Me The Truth . . . . Nancy Wilson
Teasin' You . . . . Willie Tee	Tell Me This Is A Dream . . . . Delfonics
Teddy . . . . Connie Francis	Tell Me To My Face . . . . Keith
Teddy Bear . . . . G-Wiz	Tell Me Tomorrow (Part 1) . . . Smokey Robinson
Teddy Bear . . . . Red Sovine	Tell Me What You Dream . . . . . Restless Heart
Teddy Bear Song . . . . Barbara Fairchild	Tell Me What You Want Me To Do . . Tevin Campbell
Teddy Bear's Last Ride . . . . Diana Williams	Tell Me Why . . . . Belmonts
Teen Age Idol . . . . Rick Nelson	Tell Me Why . . . . Bobby Vinton
Teen Age Prayer . . . . Gale Storm	Tell Me Why . . . . Elvis Presley
Teen Age Prayer . . . . Gloria Mann	Tell Me Why . . . . Expose
Teen Angel . . . . Mark Dinning	Tell Me Why . . . . Four Aces
Teen Angel . . . . Wednesday	Tell Me Why . . . . Wynonna
Teen Beat . . . . Sandy Nelson	Tell Me (You're Coming Back) . . . . Rolling Stones
Teen Beat '65 . . . . Sandy Nelson	Tell Me You're Mine . . . . Gaylords
Teen Commandments	Tell Someone You Love Them . . . Dino, Desi & Billy
. . . . Paul Anka/George Hamilton IV/Johnny Nash	Tell That Girl To Shut Up . . . . . Transvision Vamp
Teen Queen Of The Week . . . . . Freddy Cannon	Tell The Truth . . . . Jude Cole
Teenage Cleopatra . . . . Tracey Dey	Tell The Truth . . . . Ray Charles
Teen-Age Crush . . . . Tommy Sands	Tell The World How I Feel About 'Cha Baby . . . .
Teenage Hayride . . . . Tender Slim	. . . . Harold Melvin And The Blue Notes
Teenage Heaven . . . . Johnny Cymbal	Telling Lies . . . . Fats Domino
Teenage Lament '74 . . . . Alice Cooper	Telstar . . . . Tornadoes
Teenage Love Affair . . . . Rick Derringer	Temma Harbour . . . . Mary Hopkin
Teenage Sonata . . . . Sam Cooke	Temple Of Love . . . . Harriet
Teenage Vows Of Love . . . . Dreamers	Temptation . . . . Boots Randolph
Teenager In Love . . . . . Dion And The Belmonts	Temptation . . . . Corina
Teenager's Mother . . . Bill Haley And His Comets	Temptation . . . . Everly Brothers
Teenager's Prayer . . . . Joe Simon	Temptation . . . . Roger Williams
Teenager's Romance . . . . Ricky Nelson	Temptation 'Bout To Get Me . . . Knight Brothers
Teensville . . . . Chet Atkins	Temptation Eyes . . . . Grass Roots
Telefone (Long Distance Love Affair)	Tempted . . . . Squeeze
. . . . Sheena Easton	Ten Commandments . . . . Prince Buster
Telegram Sam . . . . T. Rex	Ten Commandments Of Love . . . . James MacArthur
Telephone Line . . . . . . Electric Light Orchestra	Ten Commandments Of Love
Telephone Man . . . . Meri Wilson	. . . . Little Anthony And The Imperials
Tell 'Em Willie Boy's A'Comin' . . . . Tommy James	Ten Commandments Of Love
Tell All The People . . . . Doors	. . . . Harvey And The Moonglows
Tell Her . . . . Dean Parrish	Ten Commandments Of Love . . . Peaches & Herb
Tell Her . . . . Kenny Loggins	10 Little Bottles . . . . Johnny Bond
Tell Her About It . . . . Billy Joel	Ten Little Indians . . . . Beach Boys
Tell Her For Me . . . . Adam Wade	Ten Little Indians . . . . Yardbirds
Tell Her Love Has Felt The Need . . Eddie Kendricks	Ten Lonely Guys . . . . Pat Boone
Tell Her No . . . . Juice Newton	10-9-8 . . . . Face To Face
Tell Her No . . . . Zombies	Ten Thousand Drums . . . . Carl Smith
Tell Her She's Lovely . . . . El Chicano	Ten To Eight . . . . David Castle
Tell Her You Love Her . . . . Frank Sinatra	Tender Is The Night . . . . Jackson Browne
Tell Her (You Love Her Every Day) . . . Frank Sinatra	Tender Love . . . . Force M.D.'s
Tell Him . . . . Exciters	Tender Lover . . . . Babyface

501

502

503

There's A Chance We Can Make It . . . Blues Magoos
There's A Girl . . . . Jan & Dean
There's A Goldmine In The Sky . . . . Pat Boone
There's A Kind Of Hush . . . . . . Herman's Hermits
There's A Kind Of Hush (All Over The
    World) . . . . Carpenters
There's A Moon Out Tonight . . . . Capris
There's A Party Going On . . . . Yvonne
There's A Star Spangled Banner Waving
    Somewhere #2 . . . . Red River Dave
There's Always Me . . . . Elvis Presley
(There's) Always Something There To
    Remind Me . . . . Dionne Warwick
(There's) Always Something There To
    Remind Me . . . . Lou Johnson
(There's) Always Something There To
    Remind Me . . . . Sandie Shaw
There's Gonna Be A Showdown . . . .
    . . . . Archie Bell & The Drells
There's Got To Be A Word! . . . . Innocence
There's Got To Be Rain In Your Life . . . .
    . . . . Dorothy Norwood
There's No Easy Way Out . . . . James Ingram
There's No Fool Like A Young Fool . . . . Tab Hunter
(There's) No Gettin' Over Me . . . . . Ronnie Milsap
There's No Livin' Without Your Lovin' . . . .
    . . . . Peter And Gordon
There's No Me Without You . . . . Manhattans
There's No Other Like My Baby . . . . Crystals
There's No Other Way . . . . Blur
There's No Tomorrow . . . . Tony Martin
There's Nothing Better Than Love . . Luther Vandross
There's Nothing I Can Say . . . . Rick Nelson
There's Nothing Like Love . . . . . . Jackie Wilson
There's Only One Of You . . . . Four Lads
There's Only You . . . . Don Rondo
There's Something On Your Mind . . . . . Baby Ray
There's Something On Your Mind . . . .
    . . . . Big Jay McNeely
There's Something On Your Mind (Part 2) . . . . . .
    . . . . Bobby Marchan
There's The Girl . . . . Heart
These Are Days . . . . 10,000 Maniacs
These Are Not My People . . . . . . Johnny Rivers
(These Are) The Young Years . . . . . . Floyd Cramer
These Arms Of Mine . . . . Otis Redding
These Boots Are Made For Walkin' . . Nancy Sinatra
These Dreams . . . . Heart
These Eyes . . . . Guess Who
These Eyes . . . . Jr. Walker & The All Stars
These Foolish Things . . . . James Brown
These Hands (Small But Mighty) . . . . Bobby Bland
These Things Will Keep Me Loving You . . Velvelettes
These Times Are Hard For Lovers . . . . . John Waite
They Can't Take Away Our Music . . . .
    . . . . Eric Burdon And War
They Don't Know . . . . Tracy Ullman
They Don't Make Love Like They Used
    To . . . . Eddy Arnold
They Just Can't Stop It The (Games
    People Play) . . . . Spinners
(They Long To Be) Close To You . . . . . Carpenters
(They Long To Be) Close To You . . . .
    . . . . . Jerry Butler And Brenda Lee Eager
They Remind Me Of You . . . . Elvis Presley
They Were Doin' The Mambo . . . . Vaughn Monroe
They're Coming To Take Me Away, Ha-Haaa! . . . .
    . . . . Napoleon XIV
Thieves In The Temple . . . . Prince
Thin Line Between Love & Hate . . . . . Persuaders
Thing . . . . Phil Harris
Thing Of The Past . . . . Shirelles
Things . . . . Bobby Darin
Things Can Only Get Better . . . . . Howard Jones

Things I Didn't Say . . . . Jordan Brothers
Things I Should Have Said . . . . Grass Roots
Things I'd Like To Say . . . . New Colony Six
Things In This House . . . . Bobby Darin
Things That I Used To Do . . . . . James Brown
Things That Make You Go Hmmmm... . . . .
    . . . . C + C Music Factory
Things We Did Last Summer . . . Shelley Fabares
Things We Do For Love 10cc
Think . . . . Aretha Franklin
Think . . . . Brenda Lee
Think . . . . Information Society
Think . . . . James Brown
Think . . . . Jimmy McCracklin
Think (About It) . . . . Lyn Collins
Think About Me . . . . Fleetwood Mac
Think His Name . . . . Johnny Rivers
Think I'll Go Somewhere And Cry Myself
    To Sleep . . . . Al Martino
Think I'm In Love . . . . Eddie Money
Think It Over . . . . Crickets
Think It Over . . . . Cheryl Ladd
Think It Over . . . . Delfonics
Think Me A Kiss . . . . Clyde McPhatter
Think Of Laura . . . . Christopher Cross
Think Of Me . . . . Buck Owens
Think Of Me . . . . Maxine Brown
Think Of The Good Times . . . . Jay & The Americans
Think Twice . . . . Brook Benton
Think Twice . . . . Jackie Wilson And Lavern Baker
Thinkin' Back . . . . Color Me Badd
Thinking About Your Love . . . Skipworth & Turner
Thinking Of You . . . . Don Cherry
Thinking Of You . . . . Earth, Wind & Fire
Thinking Of You . . . . Eddie Fisher
Thinking Of You . . . . Loggins And Messina
Thinking Of You . . . . Paul Davis
Thinking Of You . . . . Sa-Fire
Third Man Theme . . . . Anton Karas
Third Man Theme . . . . Guy Lombardo
3rd Man Theme . . . Herb Alpert & The Tijuana Brass
Third Rate Romance . . . . . Amazing Rhythm Aces
Third Time Lucky . . . . Foghat
13 Questions . . . . Seatrain
30-60-90 . . . . Willie Mitchell
31 Flavors . . . . Shirelles
This & That . . . . Michael Penn
This Beat Goes On . . . . Kings
This Bitter Earth . . . . Dinah Washington
This Bitter Earth . . . . Satisfactions
This Can't Be True . . . . Eddie Holman
This Could Be The Night . . . . Loverboy
This Could Be The One . . . . Bad Company
This Could Be The Right One . . . . . . April Wine
This Diamond Ring . . . .
    . . . . Gary Lewis And The Playboys
This Door Swings Both Ways . . . . Herman's Hermits
This Empty Place . . . . Dionne Warwick
This Friendly World . . . . Fabian
This Girl (Has Turned Into A Woman) . . . .
    . . . . Mary MacGregor
This Girl Is A Woman Now . . . .
    . . . . . . Gary Puckett And The Union Gap
This Girl Is Mine . . Michael Jackson/Paul McCartney
This Girl's In Love With You . . . . Dionne Warwick
This Golden Ring . . . . Fortunes
This Guy's In Love With You . . . . . Herb Alpert
This Heart . . . . Gene Redding
This House . . . . Tracie Spencer
This I Swear . . . . Skyliners
This I Swear . . . . Tyrone Davis
This Is All I Ask . . . . Burl Ives
This Is All I Ask . . . . Tony Bennett
This Is It . . . . Jay & The Americans

Tightrope Ride . . . . Doors	Tin Man . . . . America
Tijuana Jail . . . . Kingston Trio	Tin Soldier . . . . Small Faces
Tijuana Taxi . . . . . Herb Alpert & The Tijuana Brass	Tina Marie . . . . Perry Como
'Til . . . . Angels	Tiny Bubbles . . . . Don Ho And The Aliis
'Til I Can Make It On My Own . . . Tammy Wynette	Tiny Dancer . . . . Elton John
('Til) I Kissed You . . . . Everly Brothers	Tiny Tim . . . . Lavern Baker
'Til It's Time To Say Goodbye . . . . . Jonathan Cain	Tip Of My Fingers . . . . Eddy Arnold
'Til My Baby Comes Home . . . . . Luther Vandross	Tip Of My Fingers . . . . Nick Noble
Til The World Ends . . . . Three Dog Night	Tip Of My Tongue . . . . Tubes
Till . . . . Percy Faith	Tip On In . . . . Slim Harpo
Till . . . . Roger Williams	Tippy Toeing . . . . Harden Trio
Till . . . . Tokens	Tips Of My Fingers . . . . Roy Clark
Till . . . . Tom Jones	Tipsy Piano . . . .
Till . . . . Vogues	. . . . . . Helmut Zacharias And His Magic Violins
Till Death Do Us Part . . . . Bob Braun	Tip-Toe Thru' The Tulips With Me . . . . . Tiny Tim
Till I Loved You	Tired Of Being Alone . . . . Al Green
. . . . Barbra Streisand And Don Johnson	Tired Of Being Blonde . . . . Carly Simon
Till I Waltz Again With You . . . . . . Teresa Brewer	Tired Of Being Lonely . . . . Sharpees
Till Somebody Loves You . . . . Henry Lee Summer	Tired Of Toein' The Line . . . . . . Rocky Burnette
Till The End Of The Day . . . . Kinks	Tired Of Waiting For You . . . . Kinks
Till Then . . . . Classics	Tit For Tat (Ain't No Taking Back) . . . James Brown
Till Then . . . . Hilltoppers	T.L.C. . . . . Linear
Till There Was You . . . . Anita Bryant	T.L.C. Tender Love And Care . . . . . Jimmie Rodgers
Till There Was You . . . . Valjean	To A Sleeping Beauty . . . . Jimmy Dean
Till We Two Are One . . . . Georgie Shaw	To A Soldier Boy . . . . Tassels
Till You Get Enough . . . . . Charles Wright And The	To All The Girls I've Loved Before . . . .
. . . . Watts 103rd Street Rhythm Band	. . . . Julio Iglesias & Willie Nelson
Time . . . . Alan Parsons Project	To Be A Lover . . . . Billy Idol
Time . . . . Pozo-Seco Singers	To Be A Lover . . . . Gene Chandler
Time After Time . . . . Chris Montez	To Be Loved . . . . Jackie Wilson
Time After Time . . . . Cyndi Lauper	To Be Loved (Forever) . . . . Pentagons
Time After Time . . . . Frankie Ford	To Be With You . . . . Mr. Big
Time Alone Will Tell . . . . Jerry Vale	To Be Young, Gifted And Black . . . . . Nina Simone
Time Alone With You . . . . Bad English	To Dream The Dream . . . . Frankie Miller
Time And Chance . . . . Color Me Badd	To Each His Own . . . . Faith, Hope & Charity
Time And Love . . . . Barbra Streisand	To Each His Own . . . . Frankie Laine
Time And The River . . . . Nat King Cole	To Each His Own . . . . Platters
Time And Tide . . . . Basia	To Each His Own . . . . Tymes
Time Bomb . . . . Lake	To Get To You . . . . Jerry Wallace
Time (Clock Of The Heart) . . . . Culture Club	To Give (The Reason I Live) . . . . . Frankie Valli
Time For Letting Go . . . . Jude Cole	To Know Him, Is To Love Him . . . . Teddy Bears
Time For Livin' . . . . Association	To Know Someone Deeply Is To Love
Time For Livin' . . . . Sly & The Family Stone	Someone Softly . . . . . . Terence Trent D'Arby
Time For Me To Fly . . . . . . REO Speedwagon	To Know You Is To Love You . . . . B.B. King
Time For Us . . . . Johnny Mathis	To Know You Is To Love You . . . . Bobby Vinton
Time Has Come Today . . . . . . Chambers Brothers	To Know You Is To Love You . . . Peter And Gordon
Time In A Bottle . . . . Jim Croce	To Live And Die In L.A. . . . . Wang Chung
Time Is On My Side . . . . Rolling Stones	To Love And Be Loved . . . . Frank Sinatra
Time Is Tight . . . . Booker T & The MG's	To Love Somebody . . . . Bee Gees
Time Is Time . . . . Andy Gibb	To Love Somebody . . . . Michael Bolton
Time, Love And Tenderness . . . . . Michael Bolton	To Love Somebody . . . . Sweet Inspirations
Time Machine . . . . Dante And The Evergreens	To Show I Love You . . . . Peter And Gordon
Time Machine . . . . Grand Funk Railroad	To Sir With Love . . . . Lulu
Time Marches On . . . . Roy Hamilton	To Susan On The West Coast Waiting . . . Donovan
Time Of The Season . . . . Zombies	To The Aisle . . . . Five Satins
Time Out Of Mind . . . . Steely Dan	To The Aisle . . . . Roy Hamilton
Time Passages . . . . Al Stewart	To The Door Of The Sun . . . . Al Martino
Time Seller . . . . Spencer Davis Group	To The Ends Of The Earth . . . . . . Nat King Cole
Time Stopped . . . . Marvin Smith	To The Other Man . . . . Luther Ingram
Time Time . . . . Ed Ames	To The Other Woman . . . . Doris Duke
Time To Get Down . . . . O'Jays	To Think You've Chosen Me . . . .
Time To Get It Together . . . . . . Country Coalition	. . . . Eddy Howard Orchestra
Time To Kill . . . . Band	To Wait For Love . . . . Herb Alpert
Time To Love - A Time To Cry . . . . . Lou Johnson	Toast And Marmalade For Tea . . . . Tin Tin
Time Waits For No One . . . . . Friends Of Distinction	Toast To The Fool . . . . Dramatics
Time Was . . . . Canned Heat	Tobacco Road . . . . Nashville Teens
Time Was . . . . Flamingos	Today . . . . Jimmie Rodgers
Time Will Reveal . . . . DeBarge	Today . . . . New Christy Minstrels
Time Will Tell . . . . Tower Of Power	(Today I Met) The Boy I'm Gonna Marry
Time Won't Let Me . . . . Outsiders	. . . . Darlene Love
Timeless Love . . . . Saraya	Today I Sing The Blues . . . . Aretha Franklin
Times Have Changed . . . . Irma Thomas	Today I Started Loving You Again . . . Bettye Swann
Times Of Your Life . . . . Paul Anka	Today Is The Day . . . . Bar-Kays
Timothy . . . . Buoys	Today's Teardrops . . . . Rick Nelson

506

507

Touch Of Magic . . . . James Leroy	Tribute To A King . . . . William Bell
Touch Of You . . . . Brenda & The Tabulations	Tricia Tell Your Daddy . . . . Andy Kim
Touch The Hand (Of The Man) . . . . . Conway Twitty	Trick Of The Night . . . . Bananarama
Touchables . . . . Dickie Goodman	Trickle Trickle . . . . Manhattan Transfer
Touchables In Brooklyn . . . . Dickie Goodman	Trickle Trickle . . . . Videos
Tough All Over	Tricky . . . . Ralph Marterie
. . . . . John Cafferty And The Beaver Brown Band	Tried To Love . . . . Peter Frampton
Tough World . . . . Donnie Iris	Troglodyte (Cave Man) . . . . Jimmy Castor
Tous Les Chemins . . . . Singing Nun	T-R-O-U-B-L-E . . . . Elvis Presley
Tower Of Strength . . . . Gene McDaniels	Trouble . . . . Frederick Knight
Town Without Pity . . . . Gene Pitney	Trouble . . . . Lindsey Buckingham
Toy Soldier . . . . Four Seasons	Trouble . . . . Nia Peeples
Toy Soldiers . . . . Martika	Trouble Down Here Below . . . . Lou Rawls
Toyland . . . . Alan Bown	Trouble In Mind . . . . Nina Simone
Toys In The Attic . . . . Joe Sherman	Trouble In My Home . . . . Joe Simon
Tra La La . . . . Georgia Gibbs	Trouble In Paradise . . . . Jarreau
Tra La La La La . . . . Ike & Tina Turner	Trouble In Paradise . . . . Crests
Tra La La La Suzy . . . . Dean And Jean	Trouble Is My Middle Name . . . . . Bobby Vinton
Traces . . . . Classics IV	Trouble Maker . . . . Lee Hazlewood
Traces/Memories (medley) . . . . Lettermen	Trouble Man . . . . Marvin Gaye
Tracks Of My Tears . . . . Johnny Rivers	Trouble Me . . . . 10,000 Maniacs
Tracks Of My Tears . . . . Linda Ronstadt	Truck Stop . . . . Jerry Smith
Tracks Of My Tears . . . . Miracles	Truckin' . . . . Grateful Dead
Tracy . . . . Cuff Links	True . . . . Spandau Ballet
Tracy's Theme . . . . Spencer Ross	True Blue . . . . Madonna
Trade Winds . . . . Aki Aleong	True Blue Love . . . . Lou Gramm
Trade Winds . . . . Billy Vaughn	True Colors . . . . Cyndi Lauper
Tragedy . . . . Argent	True Companion . . . . Marc Cohn
Tragedy . . . . Bee Gees	True Faith . . . . New Order
Tragedy . . . . Brian Hyland	True Grit . . . . Glen Campbell
Tragedy . . . . Fleetwoods	True Love . . . . Bing Crosby And George Kelly
Tragedy . . . . John Hunter	True Love . . . . Glenn Frey
Tragedy . . . . Thomas Wayne With The Delons	True Love . . . . Jane Powell
Train . . . . 1910 Fruitgum Company	True Love . . . . Elton John And Kiki Dee
Train Called Freedom . . . . South Shore Commission	True Love Goes On And On . . . . Burl Ives
Train In Vain (Stand By Me) . . . . Clash	True Love Never Runs Smooth . . . . . Gene Pitney
Train Of Glory . . . . Jonathan Edwards	True Love Ways . . . . Mickey Gilley
Train Of Love . . . . Annette	True Love Ways . . . . Peter And Gordon
Train Of Thought . . . . Cher	True To You . . . . Ric Ocasek
Train, Train . . . . Blackfoot	True True Happiness . . . . Johnny Tillotson
Trains And Boats And Planes	Truly . . . . Lionel Richie
. . . . Billy J. Kramer With The Dakotas	Truly Julie's Blues (I'll Be There) . . . . . Bob Lind
Trains And Boats And Planes . . . . Dionne Warwick	Truly Truly True . . . . Brenda Lee
Tramp . . . . Lowell Fulsom	Truly Yours . . . . Spinners
Tramp . . . . Otis & Carla	Trumpet Cha Cha . . . . Danny Davis
Trampled Under Foot . . . . Led Zeppelin	Trust In Me . . . . Etta James
Tranquillo . . . . Carly Simon	Trust In Me . . . . Patti Page
Trans-Europe Express . . . . Kraftwerk	Trust Me . . . . Cindy Bullens
Transfusion . . . . Nervous Norvus	Truth . . . . Tami Show
Transistor Sister . . . . Freddy Cannon	Try A Little Kindness . . . . Glen Campbell
Trapped By A Thing Called Love . . . Denise Lasalle	Try A Little Tenderness . . . . Commitments
Travelin' Band . . . . . Creedence Clearwater Revival	Try A Little Tenderness . . . . Otis Redding
Travelin' Man . . . . Ricky Nelson	Try A Little Tenderness . . . . . . Three Dog Night
Travelin' Prayer . . . . Billy Joel	Try Again . . . . Champaign
Travelin' Shoes . . . . Elvin Bishop	Try It . . . . Ohio Express
Traveling Boy . . . . Art Garfunkel	Try It Baby . . . . Marvin Gaye
Travlin' Man . . . . Stevie Wonder	Try Me . . . . James Brown
Treasure Of Love . . . . Clyde McPhatter	Try Me . . . . Jimmy Hughes
Treasure Of Your Love . . . . Eileen Rodgers	Try Some, Buy Some . . . . Ronnie Spector
Treat 'Em Tough . . . . Jimmy Soul	Try The Impossible . . . Lee Andrews And The Hearts
Treat Her Like A Lady	Try To Remember . . . . Ed Ames
. . . . Cornelius Brothers & Sister Rose	Try To Remember . . . . Roger Williams
Treat Her Like A Lady . . . . Temptations	Try Too Hard . . . . Dave Clark Five
Treat Her Right . . . . Roy Head	Try (Try To Fall In Love) . . . . Cooker
Treat Me Like A Good Piece Of Candy . . . . Dusk	Try, Try, Try . . . . Jim Valley
Treat Me Nice . . . . Elvis Presley	Tryin' To Beat The Morning Home . . . T.G. Sheppard
Treat Me Right . . . . Pat Benatar	Tryin' To Get The Feeling Again . . . Barry Manilow
Treat My Baby Good . . . . Bobby Darin	Tryin' To Live My Life Without You . . . . Bob Seger
Trees . . . . Platters	Tryin' To Love Two . . . . William Bell
Tres Chic . . . . Gilmore, Geoff & The Sheiks	Tryin' To Stay Alive . . . . Asylum Choir
Triangle . . . . Janie Grant	Trying . . . . Hilltoppers
Triangle Of Love (Hey Diddle Diddle) . . . Presidents	Trying To Hold On To My Woman . . Lamont Dozier
Tribute . . . . Anthony Newley	Trying To Live My Life Without You . . . . . Otis Clay
Tribute (Right On) . . . . Pasedenas	Trying To Make A Fool Out Of Me . . . . . Delfonics

508

Typical Reasons (Swing My Way) . . . .
. . . . Prince Markie Dee & Soul Convention
Tzena, Tzena, Tzena . . . . Gordon Jenkins Orchestra

U

U Got The Look . . . . Prince
Uh! Oh! (Part 2) . . . . Nutty Squirrels
Uhh . . . . Dyke And The Blazers
Uhh Ahh . . . . Boyz II Men
Uh-Huh, Oh Yeah . . . . Steve Lawrence
Uh-Huh--mm . . . . Sonny James
Um, Um, Um, Um, Um, Um . . . . . . Major Lance
Unbelievable . . . . EMF
Unborn Child . . . . Seals & Crofts
Unchain My Heart . . . . Herbie Mann
Unchain My Heart . . . . Ray Charles
Unchained Melody . . . . Al Hibbler
Unchained Melody . . . . Blackwells
Unchained Melody . . . . Les Baxter
Unchained Melody . . . . Righteous Brothers
Unchained Melody . . . . Roy Hamilton
Unchained Melody . . . . . . Vito & The Salutations
Uncle Albert/Admiral Halsey . . . .
. . . . Paul & Linda McCartney
Uncle John's Band . . . . Grateful Dead
Uncle Tom's Cabin . . . . Warrant
Unconditional Love . . . . Donna Summer
Undecided . . . . Ames Brothers
Undeniable . . . . Ms. Adventures
Under My Thumb . . . . Del Shannon
Under My Wheels . . . . Alice Cooper
Under Pressure . . . . Queen & David Bowie
Under The Boardwalk . . . . Billy Joe Royal
Under The Boardwalk . . . . Bruce Willis
Under The Boardwalk . . . . Drifters
Under The Bridge . . . . Red Hot Chili Peppers
Under The Covers . . . . Janis Ian
Under The Gun . . . . Poco
Under The Influence . . . . Vanity
Under The Influence Of Love . . . . Love Unlimited
Under The Milky Way . . . . Church
Under The Moon Of Love . . . . Curtis Lee
Under The Sun Valley Moon . . . . Patti Page
Under Your Spell Again . . . . Johnny Rivers
Undercover Angel . . . . Alan O'Day
Undercover Of The Night . . . . . . Rolling Stones
Underneath The Radar . . . . Underworld
Understand This Groove . . . . Sound Factory
Understand Your Man . . . . Johnny Cash
Understanding . . . .
. . . . Bob Seger & The Silver Bullet Band
Underwater . . . . Frogmen
Undun . . . . Guess Who
Uneasy Rider . . . . Charlie Daniels
Unforgettable . . . . Dinah Washington
Unforgettable . . . . Natalie Cole
Unforgiven . . . . Metallica
Ungena Za Ulimwengu (Unite The World) . . . .
. . . . Temptations
Unicorn . . . . Irish Rovers
Union Man . . . . Cate Brothers
Union Of The Snake . . . . Duran Duran
United . . . . Intruders
United . . . . Peaches & Herb
United (Part 1) . . . . Music Makers
United Together . . . . Aretha Franklin
United We Stand . . . . Brotherhood Of Man
U.N.I.T.Y. . . . . Queen Latifah
Universal Soldier . . . . Donovan
Universal Soldier . . . . Glen Campbell
Unknown Soldier . . . . Doors
Unless You Care . . . . Terry Black
Unloved . . . . Walter Egan

Unskinny Bop . . . . Poison
Unsquare Dance . . . . Dave Brubeck Quartet
Untie Me . . . . Tams
Until It's Time For You To Go . . . . Elvis Presley
Until It's Time For You To Go . . . . . Neil Diamond
Until Now . . . . Bobby Arvon
(Until Then) I'll Suffer . . . . Barbara Lynn
Until You Come Back To Me . . . . Aretha Franklin
Until Your Love Comes Back Around . . . . . RTZ
Unwind . . . . Ray Stevens
Up A Lazy River . . . . Si Zentner
Up Above My Head . . . . Al Hirt
Up All Night . . . . Slaughter
Up And Down . . . . McCoys
Up Around The Bend . . . .
. . . . Creedence Clearwater Revival
Up In A Puff Of Smoke . . . . Polly Brown
Up In Heah . . . . Ike & Tina Turner
Up Jumped A Rabbit . . . .
. . . . Frankie Lymon And The Teenagers
Up On Cripple Creek . . . . Band
Up On The Roof . . . . Cryan' Shames
Up On The Roof . . . . Drifters
Up On The Roof . . . . James Taylor
Up The Ladder To The Roof . . . . . . Supremes
Up Tight Good Man . . . . Laura Lee
Up Until Now . . . . Johnnie Ray
Up Up And Away . . . . Hugh Masekela
Up Where We Belong . . . .
. . . . Joe Cocker And Jennifer Warnes
Up Your Nose . . . . Gabriel Kaplan
Up-Hard . . . . Willie Mitchell
Ups And Downs . . . . Paul Revere And The Raiders
Upsetter . . . . Grand Funk Railroad
Upside Down . . . . Diana Ross
Uptight . . . . Ramsey Lewis
Uptight (Everything's Alright) . . . . Stevie Wonder
Uptown . . . . Crystals
Uptown . . . . Roy Orbison
Uptown Festival (Part 1) . . . . Shalamar
Uptown Girl . . . . Billy Joel
Up-Up And Away . . . . Fifth Dimension
Urge . . . . Freddy Cannon
Urgent . . . . Foreigner
Us And Love (We Go Together) . . . . Kenny Nolan
Us And Them . . . . Pink Floyd
U.S. Male . . . . Elvis Presley
Use It Up And Wear It Out . . . . Pat & Mick
Use Me . . . . Bill Withers
Use Ta Be My Girl . . . . O'Jays
Use Your Head . . . . Mary Wells
Used To Be . . . . Charlene & Stevie Wonder
"U-T" . . . . Harry M & The Marvels
Utopia . . . . Frank Gari

V

Vacation . . . . Connie Francis
Vacation . . . . Go Go's
Vado Via . . . . Drupi
Vahevella . . . . Loggins And Messina
Valentine Love . . . . Norman Connors
Valerie . . . . Cymarron
Valerie . . . . Steve Winwood
Valleri . . . . Monkees
Valley Girl . . . . . . Frank Zappa/Moon Unit Zappa
Valley Of Tears . . . . Fats Domino
Valley Road . . . . . . Bruce Hornsby And The Range
Valley To Pray . . . . Arlo Guthrie
Valotte . . . . Julian Lennon
Vance . . . . Roger Miller
Vanilla Olay . . . . Jackie DeShannon
Vanity Kills . . . . ABC
Vaquero . . . . Fireballs

510

Variety Tonight . . . . REO Speedwagon	Voulez-Vous . . . . Abba
Vaya Con Dios . . . . Dawn	Vox Humana . . . . Kenny Loggins
Vaya Con Dios . . . . Drifters	Voyeur . . . . Kim Carnes
Vaya Con Dios . . . . Freddy Fender	
Vaya Con Dios . . . . Les Paul & Mary Ford	**W**
Vehicle . . . . Ides Of March	Wabash Blues . . . . Viscounts
Velcro Fly . . . . ZZ Top	Wack Wack . . . . Young Holt Trio
Velvet Waters . . . . Megatrons	Wade In The Water . . . .
Vengeance . . . . Carly Simon	. . . . Herb Alpert & The Tijuana Brass
Venice Blue . . . . Bobby Darin	Wade In The Water . . . . Ramsey Lewis
Ventura Highway . . . . America	Wah Watusi . . . . Orlons
Venus . . . . Bananarama	Wait . . . . White Lion
Venus . . . . Frankie Avalon	Wait A Minute . . . . Coasters
Venus . . . . Johnny Mathis	Wait And See . . . . Fats Domino
Venus . . . . Shocking Blue	Wait For Me . . . . Daryl Hall & John Oates
Venus And Mars Rock Show . . . . Wings	Wait For Me . . . . Playmates
Venus In Blue Jeans . . . . Jimmy Clanton	Wait For Me . . . . Rita Pavone
Veronica . . . . Elvis Costello	Wait For You . . . . Bonham
Very Last Time . . . . Utopia	Wait On Love . . . . Michael Bolton
Very Much In Love . . . . Johnny Mathis	Wait Til' My Bobby Gets Home . . . . Darlene Love
Very Precious Love . . . . Ames Brothers	Waitin' In School . . . . Ricky Nelson
Very Special . . . . Big Daddy Kane	Waitin' In Your Welfare Line . . . . . . Buck Owens
Very Special Love . . . . Debbie Reynolds	Waiting . . . . Tom Petty And The Heartbreakers
Very Special Love . . . . Johnny Nash	Waiting At The Bus Stop . . . . Bobby Sherman
Very Special Love Song . . . . Charlie Rich	Waiting For A Girl Like You . . . . . . Foreigner
Very Thought Of You . . . . Rick Nelson	Waiting For A Star To Fall . . . . Boy Meets Girl
Vibeology . . . . Paula Abdul	Waiting For Charlie To Come Home . . Marlena Shaw
Victim Of A Foolish Heart . . . . . . Bettye Swann	Waiting For Love . . . . Alias
Victim Of Love . . . . Elton John	Waiting For That Day . . . . George Michael
Victims Of Love . . . . Bryan Adams	Waiting For Your Love . . . . Toto
Victoria . . . . Kinks	Waiting Game . . . . Brenda Lee
Victory . . . . Kool & The Gang	Waiting Game . . . . Harry Belafonte
Victory Line . . . . Limited Warranty	Waiting On A Friend . . . . . . Rolling Stones
Video Killed The Radio Star . . . . Buggles	Wake Me, Shake Me . . . . Coasters
Vienna Calling . . . . Falco	Wake Me Up Before You Go-Go . . . George Michael
View To A Kill . . . . Duran Duran	Wake Me When It's Over . . . . . . Andy Williams
Village Of Love	Wake The Town And Tell The People . . . . Les Baxter
. . . . Nathaniel Mayer And The Fabulous Twilights	Wake The Town And Tell The People . . . .
Village Of St. Bernadette . . . . Andy Williams	. . . . Mindy Carson
Vincent . . . . Don McLean	Wake Up . . . . Law
Violence Of Summer (Love's Taking Over)	Wake Up And Love Me . . . . April
. . . . Duran Duran	Wake Up Everybody (Part 1) . . . .
Virgin Man . . . . Smokey Robinson	. . . . Harold Melvin And The Blue Notes
Virginia (Touch Me Like You Do) . . . Bill Amesbury	Wake Up Little Susie . . . . Everly Brothers
Vision Of Love . . . . Mariah Carey	Wake Up Little Susie . . . . . . Simon & Garfunkel
Visitors . . . . Abba	Wake Up My Love . . . . George Harrison
Vitamin L . . . . B.E. Taylor Group	Wake Up (Next To You) . . . .
Viva Las Vegas . . . . Elvis Presley	. . . . Graham Parker And The Shot
Viva Las Vegas . . . . ZZ Top	Wake Up Susan . . . . Spinners
Viva Tirado (Part 1) . . . . El Chicano	Wake Up, Wake Up . . . . Grass Roots
Vogue . . . . Madonna	Waking Up Alone . . . . Paul Williams
Voice . . . . Moody Blues	Walk . . . . Inmates
Voice In My Heart . . . . Eydie Gorme	Walk . . . . Jimmy McCracklin
Voice In The Choir . . . . Al Martino	Walk A Mile In My Shoes . . . . Joe South
Voice Of America's Sons	Walk Away . . . . Donna Summer
. . . . . John Cafferty And The Beaver Brown Band	Walk Away . . . . James Gang
Voice Of Freedom . . . . Freedom Williams	Walk Away . . . . Matt Monro
Voice Of Freedom . . . Jim Kirk And The TM Singers	Walk Away From Love . . . . David Ruffin
Voice On The Radio . . . . Conductor	Walk Away Renee . . . . Four Tops
Voice Your Choice . . . . Radiants	Walk Away Renee . . . . Left Banke
Voices . . . . Cheap Trick	Walk Away Renee . . Southside Johnny & The Jukes
Voices . . . . Fontane Sisters	Walk Easy My Son . . . . Jerry Butler
Voices Carry . . . . 'Til Tuesday	Walk In . . . . Claudine Longet
Voices Of Babylon . . . . Outfield	Walk In The Black Forest . . . . . Horst Jankowski
Voices That Care . . . . Voices That Care	Walk In The Night . . . . . Jr. Walker & The All Stars
Volare . . . . Ace Cannon	Walk Like A Man . . . . Four Seasons
Volare . . . . Al Martino	Walk Like A Man . . . . Grand Funk
Volare . . . . Bobby Rydell	Walk Like A Man . . . . Mary Jane Girls
Volare (Nel Blu Dipinto Di Blu) . . . . Dean Martin	Walk Like An Egyptian . . . . Bangles
Volcano . . . . Jimmy Buffett	Walk Of Life . . . . Dire Straits
Volunteers . . . . Jefferson Airplane	Walk On . . . . Neil Young
Voodoo Woman . . . . Bobby Goldsboro	Walk On . . . . Roy Orbison
Voodoo Woman . . . . Simon Stokes	Walk On By . . . . Dionne Warwick

511

515

When Joanna Loved Me . . . . Tony Bennett
When Julie Comes Around . . . . Cuff Links
When Liking Turns To Loving . . . . . . Ronnie Dove
When Love Comes To Town U2
When Love Has Gone Away . . . . Richard Cocciante
When Love Is New . . . . Arthur Prysock
When Love Slips Away . . . . Dee Dee Warwick
When My Dreamboat Comes Home . . . Fats Domino
When My Little Girl Is Smiling . . . . Drifters
When Rock And Roll Came To Trinidad . . . .
. . . . Nat King Cole
When School Starts Again Next Year . . Tony Perkins
When She Cries . . . . Restless Heart
When She Dances . . . . Joey Scarbury
When She Was My Girl . . . . Four Tops
When Smokey Sings . . . . ABC
When Something Is Wrong With My Baby . . . . . .
. . . . . . Linda Ronstadt Featuring Aaron Neville
When Something Is Wrong With My Baby . . . . . .
. . . . Sam & Dave
When The Boy In Your Arms (Is The Boy
In Your Heart) . . . . Connie Francis
When The Boys Talk About The Girls . . . Valerie Carr
When The Children Cry . . . . White Lion
When The Feeling Comes Around . . Jennifer Warnes
When The Going Gets Tough, The Tough
Get Going . . . . Billy Ocean
When The Heart Rules The Mind . . . . GTR
When The Lights Go Out . . . . Naked Eyes
When The Lovelight Starts Shining Through
His Eyes . . . . Supremes
When The Morning Comes . . . . Hoyt Axton
When The Night Comes . . . . Joe Cocker
When The Party Is Over . . . . Robert John
When The Radio Is On . . . . Paul Schaffer
When The Rain Begins To Fall . . . .
. . . . Jermaine Jackson/Pia Zadora
When The Rain Comes Down . . . . . . Andy Taylor
When The Saints Go Marching In . . . . Fats Domino
When The Ship Comes In . . . . . Peter, Paul & Mary
When The Ship Hits The Sand . . . .
. . . . "Little" Jimmy Dickens
When The Snow Is On The Roses . . . . . Ed Ames
When The Swallows Come Back To
Capistrano . . . . Pat Boone
When The White Lilacs Bloom Again . . . .
. . . . Billy Vaughn
When The White Lilacs Bloom Again . . . .
. . . . Florian Zabach
When The White Lilacs Bloom Again . . . .
. . . . . Helmut Zacharias And His Magic Violins
When The White Lilacs Bloom Again . . . .
. . . . Lawrence Welk
When The White Lilacs Bloom Again . . . .
. . . . Leroy Holmes
When There's No You . . . . . Engelbert Humperdinck
When Things Go Wrong . . . .
. . . . Robin Lane & The Chartbusters
When We Get Married . . . 1910 Fruitgum Company
When We Get Married . . . . Dreamlovers
When We Get Married . . . . Intruders
When We Kiss . . . . Bardeux
When We Was Fab . . . . George Harrison
When Will I Be Loved . . . . Everly Brothers
When Will I Be Loved . . . . Linda Ronstadt
When Will I See You Again . . . . Three Degrees
When You And I Were Young Maggie . . Bing Crosby
When You Close Your Eyes . . . . Night Ranger
When You Dance . . . . Jay & The Americans
When You Dance I Can Really Love . . . . Neil Young
When You Feel Love . . . . Bob McGilpin
When You Get Right Down To It . . . . . . Delfonics
When You Get Right Down To It . . . . Ronnie Dyson
When You Loved Me . . . . Brenda Lee

When You Say Love . . . . Sonny & Cher
When You Wake Up . . . . Cash McCall
When You Walk In The Room . . . . Jackie DeShannon
When You Walk In The Room . . . . Paul Carrack
When You Walk Into The Room . . . . . . Searchers
When You Wish Upon A Star . . . .
. . . . Dion And The Belmonts
When You're Gone . . . . . Brenda & The Tabulations
When You're Hot, You're Hot . . . . Jerry Reed
When You're In Love With A Beautiful
Woman . . . . Dr. Hook
When You're Smiling . . . . Bobby Freeman
When You're Young And In Love . . . . . Marvelettes
When You're Young And In Love . . . .
. . . . Ruby And The Romantics
When Your Heart Is Weak . . . . Cock Robin
Whenever A Teenager Cries . . . .
. . . . Reparata And The Delrons
Whenever He Holds You . . . . Bobby Goldsboro
Whenever I Call You "Friend" . . . . Kenny Loggins
Whenever I'm Away From You . . . . . John Travolta
Whenever She Holds You . . . . Patty Duke
Whenever You Close Your Eyes . . . . . Tommy Page
Where . . . . Platters
Where Am I Going . . . . Barbra Streisand
Where Are All My Friends . . . .
. . . . Harold Melvin And The Blue Notes
Where Are We Going . . . . Bobby Bloom
Where Are You . . . . Cat Stevens
Where Are You . . . . Dinah Washington
Where Are You . . . . Duprees
Where Are You . . . . Frankie Avalon
Where Are You Going . . . . Jerry Butler
Where Are You Going To My Love . . . .
. . . . Brotherhood Of Man
Where Are You Now? . . . . Synch
Where Can You Go . . . . George Maharis
Where Did All The Good Times Go . . . . Classics IV
Where Did I Go Wrong . . . . Dee Dee Sharp
Where Did Our Love Go . . . . Donnie Elbert
Where Did Our Love go . . . . J. Geils Band
Where Did Our Love Go . . . . Supremes
Where Did They Go, Lord . . . . Elvis Presley
Where Did Your Heart Go? . . . . . . George Michael
Where Do Broken Hearts Go . . . . . Whitney Houston
(Where Do I Begin) Love Story . . . . Andy Williams
Where Do I Go/Be-In/Hare Krishna . . . Happenings
Where Do The Children Go . . . . Hooters
Where Do You Go . . . . Cher
Where Do You Go To (My Lovely) . . . Peter Sarstedt
Where Does Love Go . . . . Freddie Scott
Where Does My Heart Beat Now . . . . . Celine Dion
Where Does That Leave Love . . . . . George Lamond
Where Does The Lovin' Go . . . . David Gates
Where Everybody Knows Your Name . . Gary Portnoy
Where Evil Grows . . . . Poppy Family
Where Have All The Flowers Gone . . . Johnny Rivers
Where Have All The Flowers Gone . . . Kingston Trio
Where Have You Been (All My Life) . . . .
. . . . Arthur Alexander
Where Have You Been All My Life . . . . . Fotomaker
Where I Fell In Love . . . . Capris
Where Is Johnny Now . . . . Sapphires
Where Is My Mind . . . . Vanilla Fudge
Where Is The Love . . . . Betty Wright
Where Is The Love . . . .
. . . . Roberta Flack & Donny Hathaway
Where Is The Party . . . . Helena Ferguson
Where Love Has Gone . . . . Jack Jones
Where Or When . . . . Dion And The Belmonts
Where Peaceful Waters Flow . . . .
. . . . Gladys Knight & The Pips
Where The Blue Of The Night . . . . . Tommy Mara
Where The Boys Are . . . . Connie Francis

Where The Streets Have No Name . . . Pet Shop Boys
Where The Streets Have No Name U2
Where The Sun Has Never Shone . . . Jonathan King
Where There's Smoke There's Fire . . . Grass Roots
Where Were You (On Our Wedding Day)? . . . . .
. . . . Lloyd Price
Where Were You When I Needed You . . . Grass Roots
Where Were You When I Needed You . . . . Jerry Vale
Where Were You When I Was Falling In Love . . . .
. . . . Lobo
Where Will The Words Come From . . . .
. . . . Gary Lewis And The Playboys
Where Will Your Heart Take You . . . . . Buckeye
Where You Goin' Now . . . . Damn Yankees
Where You Lead . . . . Barbra Streisand
Where's The Playground Susie . . . . . Glen Campbell
Where's Your Angel? . . . . Lani Hall
Wherever I Lay My Hat (That's My Home) . . . . . .
. . . . Paul Young
Wherever I May Roam . . . . Metallica
Wherever Would I Be . . . . Cheap Trick
Which Way You Goin' Billy? . . . . . . Poppy Family
While I'm Alone . . . . Maze
While You See A Chance . . . . Steve Winwood
While You're Out Looking For Sugar . . . Honeycone
Whip Appeal . . . . Babyface
Whip It . . . . Devo
Whip It On Me . . . . Jesse Hill
Whipped Cream . . . Herb Alpert & The Tijuana Brass
Whirly Girl . . . . Oxo
Whiskey On Sunday . . . . Irish Rovers
Whisper In The Dark . . . . Dionne Warwick
Whisper To A Scream (Birds Fly) . . Icicle Works
Whispering . . . . Les Paul & Mary Ford
Whispering . . . . Nino Tempo & April Stevens
Whispering Bells . . . . Dell-Vikings
Whispering/Cherchez La Femme/Se Si Bon . . . . .
. . . . . Dr. Buzzard's Original "Savannah" Band
Whispers . . . . Corina
Whispers (Gettin' Louder) . . . . Jackie Wilson
Whistler . . . . Jethro Tull
Whistling Organ . . . . Dave "Baby" Cortez
White Bird . . . . David Laflamme
White Bucks And Saddle Shoes . . Bobby Pedrick Jr.
White Christmas . . . . Andy Williams
White Christmas . . . . Bing Crosby
White Cliffs Of Dover . . . . . . Righteous Brothers
White Horse . . . . Laid Back
White Hot . . . . Red Rider
White Houses . . . . Animals
White Knight . . . .
. . . . . . Cledus Maggard And The Citizen's Band
White Lies . . . . Grin
White Lies, Blue Eyes . . . . Bullet
White Lightning . . . . George Jones
White Men Can't Jump . . . . Riff
White On White . . . . Danny Williams
White Rabbit . . . . Jefferson Airplane
White Room . . . . Cream
White Rose Of Athens . . . . David Carroll
White Silver Sands . . . . . . Bill Black's Combo
White Silver Sands . . . . Dave Gardner
White Silver Sands . . . . Don Rondo
White Sport Coat (And A Pink Carnation) . . . . . .
. . . . Marty Robbins
White Wedding . . . . Billy Idol
Whiter Shade Of Pale . . . . Hesitations
Whiter Shade Of Pale . . . . Procol Harum
Whiter Shade Of Pale . . . . R.B. Greaves
Whiter Shade Of Pale . . . . Shorty Long
Who Am I . . . . Petula Clark
Who Are You . . . . B.B. King
Who Are You . . . . Who
Who Are You Gonna Love . . . . Ray Charles

Who Can I Turn To . . . . Tony Bennett
Who Can It Be Now? . . . . Men At Work
Who Cares . . . . Don Gibson
Who Cares . . . . Fats Domino
Who Could Be Lovin' You . . . . Al Wilson
Who Coulda' Told You (They Lied) . . . . Lloyd Price
Who Do Ya Love . . . . . KC And The Sunshine Band
Who Do You Give Your Love To? . . Michael Morales
Who Do You Love . . . .
. . . . . . George Thorogood & The Destroyers
Who Do You Love . . . . Sapphires
Who Do You Love . . . . Woolies
Who Do You Think You Are . . . .
. . . . Bo Donaldson And The Heywoods
Who Do You Think You're Foolin' . . Donna Summer
Who Else But You . . . . Frankie Avalon
Who Found Who . . . . Jellybean/Elisa Fiorillo
Who Gets The Guy . . . . Dionne Warwick
Who Gets Your Love . . . . Dusty Springfield
Who Is Gonna Love Me . . . . . Dionne Warwick
Who Is He And What Is He To You . . . .
. . . . Creative Source
Who Is It . . . . Michael Jackson
Who Listens To The Radio . . . . Sports
Who Loves You . . . . Four Seasons
Who Loves You Better . . . . Isley Brothers
Who Needs Ya . . . . Steppenwolf
Who Needs You . . . . Four Lads
Who Put The Bomp . . . . Barry Mann
Who Said I Would . . . . Phil Collins
Who Says . . . . Device
Who Shot J.R.? . . . . Gary Burbank
Who Shot Sam . . . . George Jones
Who Stole The Keeshka? . . . . . . Matys Brothers
Who Was It? . . . . Hurricane Smith
Who Wears These Shoes? . . . . Elton John
Who Were You Thinkin' Of . . . . . . Doolittle Band
Who Will Answer . . . . Ed Ames
Who Will You Run To . . . . Heart
Who'd She Coo? . . . . Ohio Players
Who'll Be The Fool Tonight . . . Larsen-Feiten Band
Who'll Be The Next In Line . . . . Kinks
Who'll Stop The Rain . . . .
. . . . Creedence Clearwater Revival
Who's Behind The Door . . . . Zebra
Who's Cheating Who? . . . . Little Milton
Who's Crying Now . . . . Journey
Who's Going To Take Care Of Me . . . .
. . . . Justine Washington
Who's Gonna Ride Your Wild Horses U2
Who's Gonna Take The Blame . . . . Miracles
Who's Gonna Take The Weight . . . Kool & The Gang
Who's Holding Donna Now . . . . DeBarge
Who's In The Strawberry Patch With Sally . . . . Dawn
Who's Johnny . . . . El DeBarge
Who's Loving You . . . . . Brenda & The Tabulations
Who's Making Love . . . . Blues Brothers
Who's Making Love . . . . Johnnie Taylor
Who's Making Love . . . . Young-Holt Unlimited
Who's Sorry Now . . . . Connie Francis
Who's Sorry Now . . . . Marie Osmond
Who's That Girl . . . . Madonna
Who's That Girl . . . . Eurythmics
Who's That Knocking . . . . Genies
Who's Your Baby? . . . . Archies
Who's Zoomin' Who . . . . Aretha Franklin
Whodunit . . . . Tavares
Who-Dun-It? . . . . Monk Higgins
Whoever Finds This, I Love You . . . . . Mac Davis
Whole Lot Of Shakin' Going On . . . Conway Twitty
Whole Lot Of Shakin' In My Heart . . . . Miracles
Whole Lotta Love . . . . C.C.S.
Whole Lotta Love . . . . King Curtis
Whole Lotta Love . . . . Led Zeppelin

517

518

Wonderful Summer . . . . Robin Ward	World Through A Tear . . . . Neil Sedaka
Wonderful Time Up There . . . . Pat Boone	World We Knew (Over And Over) . . . Frank Sinatra
Wonderful Tonight . . . . Eric Clapton	World Where You Live . . . . Crowded House
Wonderful! Wonderful! . . . . Johnny Mathis	World Without Heroes . . . . Kiss
Wonderful! Wonderful! . . . . Tymes	World Without Love . . . . Peter And Gordon
Wonderful World . . . . . . Herman's Hermits	Worried Guy . . . . Johnny Tillotson
Wonderful World . . . . Johnny Nash	Worried Life Blues . . . . Ray Charles
Wonderful World . . . . Sam Cooke	Worried Man . . . . Kingston Trio
Wonderful World, Beautiful People . . . . Jimmy Cliff	Worried Mind . . . . Ray Anthony
Wondering Where The Lions Are . . Bruce Cockburn	Worry . . . . Johnny Tillotson
Wonderland . . . . Commodores	Worrying Kind . . . . Tommy Sands
Wonderland By Night . . . . Anita Bryant	Worse Comes To Worst . . . . Billy Joel
Wonderland By Night . . . . Bert Kaempfert	Worst That Could Happen . . . . . Brooklyn Bridge
Wonderland By Night . . . Louis Prima & Keely Smith	Wot's It To Ya? . . . . Robbie Nevil
Wont'cha Come Home . . . . Lloyd Price	Would I Lie To You? . . . . Charles & Eddie
Wood Beez (Pray Like Aretha Franklin)	Would I Lie To You? . . . . Eurythmics
. . . . Scritti Politti	Would I Love You (Love You, Love You) . . Patti Page
Woodchopper's Ball	Would It Make Any Difference To You . . Etta James
. . . . Hutch Davie And His Honky Tonkers	Would You Lay With Me . . . . Tanya Tucker
Wooden Heart . . . . Bobby Vinton	Wouldn't Change A Thing . . . . . Kylie Minogue
Wooden Heart . . . . Joe Dowell	Wouldn't It Be Good . . . . Nik Kershaw
Woodpecker Song . . . . Bobby Rydell	Wouldn't It Be Nice . . . . Beach Boys
Woodstock . . . . Assembled Multitude	Wow Wow Wee (He's The Boy For Me) . . . . Angels
Woodstock . . . . Crosby, Stills, Nash & Young	Wrack My Brain . . . . Ringo Starr
Woodstock . . . . . . Matthews' Southern Comfort	Wrap Her Up . . . . Elton John
Woo-Hoo . . . . Rock-A-Teens	Wrap It Up . . . . Fabulous Thunderbirds
Wooly Bully . . . . Sam The Sham And The Pharaohs	Wrap My Body Tight . . . . Johnny Gill
Word In Spanish . . . . Elton John	Wrap Your Arms Around Me . . . .
Word Is Out . . . . Jermaine Stewart	. . . . KC And The Sunshine Band
Word Of Mouth . . . . . Mike + The Mechanics	Wrapped Around Your Finger . . . . Police
Word Up . . . . Cameo	Wrapped Up In Your Warm And Tender Love . . . . .
Words . . . . Bee Gees	. . . . Tyrone Davis
Words . . . . Donny Gerrard	Wreck Of The Edmund Fitzgerald . . . .
Words . . . . F.R. David	. . . . Gordon Lightfoot
Words . . . . Missing Persons	Wreck Of The "John B" . . . . Jimmie Rodgers
Words . . . . Monkees	Wringle, Wrangle . . . . Bill Hayes
Words . . . . Pat Boone	Wringle Wrangle . . . . Fess Parker
Words Get In The Way . . . . Miami Sound Machine	Writing On The Wall . . . . Adam Wade
Words Of Love . . . . Diamonds	Written All Over Your Face . . . . . . Rude Boys
Words Of Love . . . . Mama's & Papa's	Written On The Wind . . . . Four Aces
Work Song . . . . . Herb Alpert & The Tijuana Brass	Written On Ya Kitten . . . . . Naughty By Nature
Work That Body . . . . Diana Ross	Wrong For Each Other . . . . . . Andy Williams
Work To Do . . . . Isley Brothers	Wun'erful Wun'erful! (Parts 1 & 2) . . . Stan Freberg
Work To Do . . . . Vanessa Williams	Wynken, Blynken And Nod . . . Doobie Brothers
Work, Work, Work . . . . Lee Dorsey	
Workin' At The Car Wash Blues . . . . . . Jim Croce	████████████ **X** ████████████
Workin' For A Livin' . . . Huey Lewis And The News	Xanadu . . . .
Workin' For The Man . . . . Roy Orbison	. . . Olivia Newton-John/Electric Light Orchestra
Workin' On A Groovy Thing . . . . . Fifth Dimension	
Workin' Together . . . . Ike & Tina Turner	████████████ **Y** ████████████
Working Class Hero . . . . Tommy Roe	Ya Mama . . . . Wuf Ticket
Working For The Weekend . . . . Loverboy	Ya Ya . . . . Lee Dorsey
Working In The Coal Mine . . . . Devo	Yah Mo B There . . . .
Working In The Coal Mine . . . . Lee Dorsey	. . . . James Ingram With Michael McDonald
Working Man's Prayer . . . . Arthur Prysock	Yakety Axe . . . . Chet Atkins
Working My Way Back To You . . . . . Four Seasons	Yakety Sax . . . . Boots Randolph
Working My Way Back To You/Forgive	Yakety Yak . . . . Coasters
Me, Girl . . . . Spinners	Yank Me, Crank Me . . . . Ted Nugent
Working On A Groovy Thing . . . . . . Patti Drew	Yankee Lady . . . . Brewer & Shipley
Working On It . . . . Chris Rea	Yankee Rose . . . . David Lee Roth
Workout Stevie, Workout . . . . . Little Stevie Wonder	Yard Went On Forever . . . . Richard Harris
World I Used To Know . . . . Jimmie Rodgers	Yeah, Yeah, Yeah . . . . Judson Spence
World In My Eyes . . . . Depeche Mode	Yeah, Yeah, Yeah . . . . Voices
World Is A Ghetto . . . . War	Year Ago Tonight . . . . Crests
World Is Waiting For The Sunrise	Year Of The Cat . . . . Al Stewart
. . . . Les Paul & Mary Ford	Year That Clayton Delaney Died . . . . Tom T. Hall
World Of Fantasy . . . . Five Stairsteps	Yearning For Your Love . . . . Gap Band
World Of Lonely People . . . . Anita Bryant	Years . . . . Wayne Newton
World Of Our Own . . . . Seekers	Years From Now . . . . Dr. Hook
World Outside . . . . Four Aces	Years From Now . . . . Jackie Wilson
World Outside . . . . Four Coins	Yeh, Yeh . . . . Georgie Fame
World Outside . . . . Roger Williams	Yellow Balloon . . . . Yellow Balloon
World (Part 1) . . . . James Brown	Yellow Bandana . . . . Faron Young
World Shut Your Mouth . . . . Julian Cope	Yellow Bird . . . . Arthur Lyman

520

You Can Lead Your Woman To The Altar . . . .
. . . . Oscar Toney Jr.
You Can Never Stop Me Loving You . . . .
. . . . Johnny Tillotson
You Can Run . . . . Jerry Butler
(You Can Still) Rock In America . . . . . Night Ranger
You Can't Always Get What You Want . . . .
. . . . Rolling Stones
You Can't Be A Beacon (If Your Light
  Don't Shine) . . . . Donna Fargo
You Can't Be True Dear . . . . Mary Kaye Trio
You Can't Be True Dear . . . . Patti Page
You Can't Change That . . . . Raydio
You Can't Dance . . England Dan & John Ford Coley
You Can't Deny It . . . . Lisa Stansfield
You Can't Do It Right . . . . Deep Purple
You Can't Do That . . . . Beatles
You Can't Do That . . . . Nilsson
You Can't Get Away . . . . Shana
You Can't Get To Heaven On Roller Skates . . . . .
. . . . Betty Johnson
You Can't Get What You Want . . . . . . Joe Jackson
You Can't Go Halfway . . . . Johnny Nash
You Can't Hurry Love . . . . Phil Collins
You Can't Hurry Love . . . . Supremes
You Can't Hurt Me No More . . . . . Gene Chandler
You Can't Judge A Book By It's Cover . . Bo Diddley
(You Can't Let The Boy Overpower) The
  Man In You . . . . Chuck Jackson
You Can't Put A Price On Love . . . . Knack
You Can't Roller Skate In A Buffalo Herd . . . . . .
. . . . Roger Miller
You Can't Run From Love . . . . Eddie Rabbitt
You Can't Sit Down . . . . Dovells
You Can't Sit Down (Part 2) . . . .
. . . . Philip Upchurch Combo
You Can't Stand Alone . . . . Wilson Pickett
You Can't Take It Away . . . . Fred Hughes
You Can't Touch This . . . . M.C. Hammer
You Can't Turn Me Off . . . . High Inergy
You Cheated . . . . Dell-Vikings
You Cheated . . . . Shields
You Cheated . . . . Slades
You Could Have Been A Lady . . . . April Wine
You Could Have Been With Me . . . . Sheena Easton
You Could Take My Heart Away . . . . Silver Condor
You Decorated My Life . . . . Kenny Rogers
You Didn't Have To Be So Nice . . . Lovin' Spoonful
You Don't Believe . . . . Alan Parsons Project
You Don't Bring Me Flowers . . . .
. . . . Barbra Streisand & Neil Diamond
You Don't Have To Be A Baby To Cry . . . Caravelles
You Don't Have To Be A Star . . . .
. . . . Marilyn McCoo & Billy Davis Jr.
You Don't Have To Cry . . . . Rene And Angela
You Don't Have To Go Home Tonight . . . . . Triplets
(You Don't Have To) Paint Me A Picture . . . . . .
. . . . Gary Lewis And The Playboys
You Don't Have To Say You Love Me . . . .
. . . . Dusty Springfield
You Don't Have To Say You Love Me . . . .
. . . . Elvis Presley
You Don't Have To Say You Love Me . . . Four Sonics
You Don't Have To Walk In The Rain . . . . . Turtles
You Don't Know . . . . Scarlett & Black
(You Don't Know) How Glad I Am . . Nancy Wilson
You Don't Know Like I Know . . . . . Sam & Dave
You Don't Know Me . . . . Carmen McRae
You Don't Know Me . . . . Elvis Presley
You Don't Know Me . . . . Jerry Vale
You Don't Know Me . . . . Lenny Welch
You Don't Know Me . . . . Mickey Gilley
You Don't Know Me . . . . Ray Charles
You Don't Know What It Means . . . . . Jackie Wilson

You Don't Know What Love Is . . . . . . Susan Jacks
You Don't Know What You Mean To Me . . . .
. . . . Sam & Dave
You Don't Know What You've Got (Until
  You Lose It) . . . . Ral Donner
You Don't Love Me Anymore . . . . . Eddie Rabbitt
You Don't Love Me Anymore . . . . . . Rick Nelson
You Don't Mess Around With Jim . . . . Jim Croce
You Don't Need Me For Anything Anymore . . . . . .
. . . . Brenda Lee
You Don't Owe Me . . . . Blue Ridge Rangers
You Don't Owe Me A Thing . . . . Johnnie Ray
You Don't Own Me . . . . Lesley Gore
You Don't Want Me Anymore . . . . . . Steel Breeze
You Don't Want My Love . . . . . . Andy Williams
You Don't Want My Love . . . . Roger Miller
You Dropped A Bomb On Me . . . . . . Gap Band
You Excite Me . . . . Frankie Avalon
You Gave Me A Mountain . . . . . . Frankie Laine
You Gave Me Something . . . . Fantastic Four
You Give Good Love To Me . . . . Whitney Houston
You Give Love A Bad Name . . . . Bon Jovi
You Gonna Make Me Love Somebody Else . . . . . .
. . . . Jones Girls
You Got It . . . . Diana Ross
You Got It . . . . Roy Orbison
You Got It All . . . . Jets
You Got It (The Right Stuff) . . . .
. . . . New Kids On The Block
You Got Lucky . . . Tom Petty And The Heartbreakers
You Got Me Hummin' . . . . Cold Blood
You Got Me Hummin' . . . . Sam & Dave
You Got Soul . . . . Johnny Nash
You Got Style . . . . . Jon & Robin And The In Crowd
You Got That Right . . . . Lynyrd Skynyrd
(You Got) The Gamma Goochee . . . . Kingsmen
You Got The Love . . . Professor Morrison's Lollipop
You Got The Love . . . Rufus Featuring Chaka Khan
You Got The Power . . . . Esquires
You Got To Be The One . . . . Chi-Lites
You Got To Me . . . . Neil Diamond
You Got To Pay The Price . . . . Gloria Taylor
You Got What It Takes . . . . Dave Clark Five
You Got What It Takes . . . . Joe Tex
You Got What It Takes . . . . Marv Johnson
You Got Your Thing On A String . . . J.P. Robinson
You Got Yours And I'll Get Mine . . . . . Delfonics
You Gotta Believe . . . .
. . . . Marky Mark & The Funky Bunch
(You Gotta) Fight For Your Right (To Party!) . . . .
. . . . Beastie Boys
You Gotta Have Love In Your Heart . . . .
. . . . Supremes & Four Tops
You Gotta Have Rain . . . . Max Bygraves
You Gotta Love Someone . . . . Elton John
You Gotta Make Your Own Sunshine . . . Neil Sedaka
You Have Placed A Chill In My Heart . . Eurythmics
You Haven't Done Nothin . . . . Stevie Wonder
You, I . . . . Rugbys
You Just Can't Quit . . . . Rick Nelson
You Just Can't Win . . . Gene Chandler & Jerry Butler
You Keep Me Dancing . . . . Samantha Sang
(You Keep Me) Hangin' On . . . . Joe Simon
You Keep Me Hangin' On . . . . Kim Wilde
You Keep Me Hangin' On . . . . Supremes
You Keep Me Hangin' On . . . . Vanilla Fudge
You Keep Me Hanging On . . . . Wilson Pickett
You Keep Me Holding On . . . . Tyrone Davis
You Keep Runnin' Away . . . . 38 Special
You Keep Running Away . . . . Four Tops
You Keep Running Away . . . . Lazy Racer
You Keep Tightening Up On Me . . . . . . Box Tops
You Know How It Is With A Woman . . . . Jefferson
You Know I Love You...Don't You? . . Howard Jones

You've Got A Friend . . . . Roberta Flack & Donny Hathaway
You've Got A Way . . . . Kathy Troccoli
You've Got Another Thing Comin' . . . . Judas Priest
You've Got Another Thing Coming . . . . Hotel
(You've Got Me) Dangling On A String . . . . Chairmen Of The Board
You've Got Me Dangling On A String . . . . Donny Osmond
You've Got Me Hummin' . . . . Hassles
You've Got Me Runnin' . . . . Gene Cotton
You've Got My Mind Messed Up . . . . . James Carr
You've Got My Soul On Fire . . . . . . Temptations
(You've Got) Personality & Chantilly Lace . . . . Mitch Ryder
(You've Got) The Magic Touch . . . . Platters
You've Got The Power . . . . James Brown
You've Got To Be Loved . . . . Montanas
You've Got To Crawl (Before You Walk) . . . 8th Day
You've Got To Earn It . . . . Staple Singers
You've Got To Hide Your Love Away . . . . . Silkie
You've Got To Keep On Bumpin' . . . . . . Kay Gees
(You've Got To) Move Two Mountains . . . . Marv Johnson
You've Got To Pay The Price . . . . Al Kent
You've Got To Take It (If You Want It) . . . . Main Ingredient
You've Got What I Need . . . . Shooting Star
You've Got Your Troubles . . . . Fortunes
You've Lost That Lovin' Feelin' . . . . Righteous Brothers
You've Lost That Lovin' Feelin' . . . . Roberta Flack & Donny Hathaway
You've Lost That Lovin' Feeling . . . . Daryl Hall & John Oates
You've Lost That Lovin' Feeling . . . Dionne Warwick
You've Made Me So Very Happy . . . . Blood, Sweat & Tears
You've Made Me So Very Happy . . Brenda Holloway
You've Never Been This Far Before . . . . Conway Twitty
You've Really Got A Hold On Me . . Eddie Money
You've Really Got A Hold On Me . . . . Miracles
You've Still Got A Place In My Heart . . Dean Martin
Young Americans . . . . David Bowie
Young And In Love . . . . Chris Crosby
Young And In Love . . . . Dick And Deedee
Young And Warm And Wonderful . . . Roger Williams
Young And Warm And Wonderful . . . . Tony Bennett
Young As We Are . . . . Sal Mineo
Young At Heart . . . . Frank Sinatra
Young Birds Fly . . . . Cryan' Shames
Young Blood . . . . Bad Company
Young Blood . . . . Bruce Willis
Young Blood . . . . Coasters
Young Blood . . . . Rickie Lee Jones
Young Boy . . . . Barbara Greene
Young Boy Blues . . . . Ben E. King
Young Dove's Calling . . . . Couplings
Young Emotions . . . . Ricky Nelson
Young Folks . . . . Supremes
Young Girl . . . . . Union Gap Featuring Gary Puckett
Young Girl . . . . Noel Harrison
Young Hearts Run Free . . . . Candi Staton
Young Ideas . . . . Chico Holiday
Young In Years . . . . Diamonds
Young Love . . . . Air Supply
Young Love . . . . Donny Osmond
Young Love . . . . Janet Jackson
Young Love . . . . Lesley Gore
Young Love . . . . Ray Stevens
Young Love . . . . Sonny James
Young Love . . . . Tab Hunter
Young Lovers . . . . Paul & Paula

Young New Mexican Puppeteer . . . . . . Tom Jones
Young Thing, Wild Dreams (Rock Me) . . . Red Rider
Young Turks . . . . Rod Stewart
Young Wings Can Fly . . . Ruby And The Romantics
Young World . . . . Rick Nelson
Younger Girl . . . . Critters
Younger Girl . . . . Hondells
Your Baby Never Looked Good In Blue . . . . Expose
Your Baby's Gone Surfin' . . . . Duane Eddy
Your Bulldog Drinks Champagne . . . . . Jim Stafford
Your Cash Ain't Nothin' But Trash . . . . Steve Miller Band
Your Cheatin' Heart . . . . Billy Vaughn
Your Cheatin' Heart . . . . George Hamilton IV
Your Cheatin' Heart . . . . Joni James
Your Cheatin' Heart . . . . Ray Charles
Your Daddy Don't Know . . . . Toronto
Your Friends . . . . Dee Clark
Your Good Thing (Is About To End) . . . Lou Rawls
Your Good Thing (Is About to End) . . . . Mable John
Your Graduation Means Goodbye . . . . . Cardigans
Your Husband - My Wife . . . . . Brooklyn Bridge
Your Imagination . . . . . . Daryl Hall & John Oates
Your Last Goodbye . . . . Floyd Cramer
Your Love . . . . Graham Central Station
Your Love . . . . Keith Sweat
Your Love . . . . . Marilyn McCoo & Billy Davis Jr.
Your Love . . . . Outfield
Your Love . . . . Paul Anka
Your Love For Me . . . . Frank Sinatra
(Your Love Has Lifted Me) Higher And Higher . . . . Rita Coolidge
Your Love Is Driving Me Crazy . . . . . Sammy Hagar
Your Love Is King . . . . Sade
Your Love Is So Doggone Good . . . . . . Whispers
Your Love Is So Good For Me . . . . . Diana Ross
(Your Love Keeps Lifting Me) Higher And Higher . . . . Jackie Wilson
Your Love (Means Everything To Me) . . . . Charles Wright . . . . And The Watts 103rd Street Rhythm Band
Your Ma Said You Cried In Your Sleep Last Night . . . . Kenny Dino
Your Mama Don't Dance . . . . Loggins And Messina
Your Mama Don't Dance . . . . Poison
Your Move . . . . Yes
Your Nose Is Gonna Grow . . . . . Johnny Crawford
Your Old Standby . . . . Mary Wells
Your One And Only Love . . . . . . Jackie Wilson
Your Other Love . . . . Connie Francis
Your Other Love . . . . Flamingos
Your Own Back Yard . . . . Dion
Your Own Special Way . . . . Genesis
Your People . . . . Little Milton
Your P-E-R-S-O-N-A-L-I-T-Y . . . . . Jackie Lee
Your Precious Love . . . . Linda Jones
Your Precious Love . . Marvin Gaye & Tammi Terrell
Your Side Of The Bed . . . . Mac Davis
Your Smiling Face . . . . James Taylor
Your Song . . . . Elton John
Your Sweetness Is My Weakness . . . . Barry White
Your Teenage Dream . . . . Johnny Mathis
Your Time Hasn't Come Yet, Baby . . . Elvis Presley
Your Time To Cry . . . . Joe Simon
Your Unchanging Love . . . . Marvin Gaye
Your Used To Be . . . . Brenda Lee
Your Wild Heart . . . . Joy Layne
Your Wild Heart . . . . Poni-Tails
Your Wildest Dreams . . . . Moody Blues
Your Wonderful Sweet Sweet Love . . . . Supremes
Yours . . . . Shai
Yours . . . . Vera Lynn
Yours Love . . . . Joe Simon
Yours Until Tomorrow . . . . Vivian Reed

525

T